T0189262

Lecture Notes in Computer Science 13489

More information about this series at https://link.springer.com/bookseries/558

Ulrike Sattler · Aidan Hogan · Maria Keet ·
Valentina Presutti · João Paulo A. Almeida ·
Hideaki Takeda · Pierre Monnin ·
Giuseppe Pirrò · Claudia d'Amato (Eds.)

The Semantic Web – ISWC 2022

21st International Semantic Web Conference
Virtual Event, October 23–27, 2022
Proceedings

 Springer

Editors
Ulrike Sattler (iD)
University of Manchester
Manchester, UK

Aidan Hogan (iD)
University of Chile
Santiago, Chile

Maria Keet (iD)
University of Cape Town
Cape Town, South Africa

Valentina Presutti (iD)
University of Bologna
Bologna, Italy

João Paulo A. Almeida (iD)
Universidade Federal do Espírito Santo
Vitória, Brazil

Hideaki Takeda (iD)
National Institute of Informatics
Tokyo, Japan

Pierre Monnin (iD)
Orange
Belfort, France

Giuseppe Pirrò (iD)
Sapienza University of Rome
Rome, Italy

Claudia d'Amato (iD)
University of Bari
Bari, Italy

ISSN 0302-9743   ISSN 1611-3349 (electronic)
Lecture Notes in Computer Science
ISBN 978-3-031-19432-0   ISBN 978-3-031-19433-7 (eBook)
https://doi.org/10.1007/978-3-031-19433-7

Preface

The International Semantic Web Conference (ISWC) has established itself down through the years as the premier international forum for the Semantic Web and Knowledge Graph community, discussing and presenting the latest advances in fundamental research, innovative technology, and applications concerning semantics, data, and the Web. ISWC brings together researchers, practitioners, and industry specialists to discuss, advance, and shape the future of semantic technologies.

It is my honor to introduce the proceedings of ISWC 2022 and to be the general chair for the 21st edition of this conference. It has also been a rewarding experience working with the team of chairs and organizers that all together played a key role in driving the conference and leading it to success. My gratitude and acknowledgment also go to the Senior Program Committee (SPC), to the 475 Program Committee (PC) members, and the 66 additional reviewers who produced over 1,139 peer reviews, thus making it possible for ISWC 2022 to keep the excellent reputation as a premier scientific conference.

The original plan for ISWC 2022 was to run it as a hybrid event in Hangzhou, China, thus providing the research community the opportunity to meet in person again (after two virtual conference editions), while taking into account possible COVID-19 restrictions, traveling issues due to limited funds, visa problems, and so forth. Unfortunately, due to the increasing COVID-19 restrictions in China, which also prevented travel within China, we had to switch ISWC 2022 to a fully virtual event.

The conference runs for five days, offering a rich program spanning different tracks (Research, Resources, In-Use, and Industry Tracks), Workshops and Tutorials, Posters, Demos, and Lightning Talks, a Doctoral Consortium, Challenges, and Panels. In collaboration with the Semantic Web Science Association (SWSA), this year we also agreed on a new policy regarding submissions with plagiarized content: authors of such submissions will be banned from submitting to ISWC for two years.

ISWC 2022 received 335 submissions, authored by 1,363 distinct authors from 35 different countries, with China, Germany, the USA, France, and Italy featuring prominently in the submissions list. The final program was the result of a very rigorous and constructive review process, supported also by detailed guidelines for reviewers that were set up and made publicly available for this conference edition. The review process for papers submitted to the Research, Resources, and In-Use Tracks also encompassed the new Objection and Response phase (that replaced the Rebuttal phase usually adopted), aiming at reducing workload on authors and reviewers, while providing an opportunity for author feedback in two exceptional cases: a) highlighting clear factual errors in reviews regarding the content of the submission and b) responding to explicit questions from reviewers. ISWC 2022 further emphasized reproducibility, being a key aspect of scientific research. For this purpose a detailed policy for supplemental materials and reproducibility was made publicly available. It required authors to add a statement, at the end of the submission, covering all of the resources necessary to reproduce or verify the results presented in the paper. These resources may include datasets, queries, code, proofs of results, configuration details, hyperparameters, etc., depending on the contributions of the paper. The statement is aimed at facilitating the independent reproducibility or verification of the results presented, pointing to where supplemental material can be found. Reviewers were asked to evaluate the statement in terms of its ability to ensure reproducibility of the paper results as well as availability (also for the foreseeable future) of resources. Additionally, to facilitate reproducibility and give peer reviewers a characterization of a submission by juxtaposing it with related approaches, authors were encouraged to optionally accompany their submission with a comparison in the Open Research Knowledge Graph (ORKG)[1].

These proceedings collect together accepted papers from the ISWC 2022 Research, Resources, and In-Use Tracks, while accepted papers in the Industry Track, Poster and Demos Track, Doctoral Consortium, and the various accepted workshops and Semantic Web challenges have been published as CEUR Workshop Proceedings[2].

The Research Track this year was chaired by Aidan Hogan and Uli Sattler. The track solicits submissions on novel research contributions that further advance the Semantic Web, and received a total of 156 full paper submissions. As in previous years, we received submissions with a range of contributions which can be classified in the following four categories. Firstly, papers on classic reasoning and query answering over ontologies of various shapes (e.g., RDF(S)/OWL, SHACL, SPARQL, and variations or extensions of these), as well as non-standard tasks like repair, explanation, and database mappings. Following the trend of past years, we also received a number of papers on embeddings of ontologies/knowledge graphs, in particular various forms of graph neural networks, and their usage in a range of applications, including zero/few shot learning, image/object classification, and various NLP tasks. Another category of papers focuses on specific knowledge graph tasks like link or type prediction and entity alignment. Finally, we received a small number of surveys of the state of affairs, e.g. on LOD availability and structural patterns in ontologies. Instrumental to shaping the final program were the 214 Program Committee members who provided reviews, and the 27 Senior Program Committee members who helped oversee the reviewing process and drafted meta-reviews. A total of 46 external reviewers, solicited by PC members, contributed valuable additional reviews to the process. Following the precedent of previous editions of ISWC, the Research Track was double blind. All papers received three to four reviews. Ultimately, 30/156 papers were accepted, giving an acceptance rate of 19.2%, which is comparable with recent years of the ISWC Research Track.

The Resources Track, chaired by Maria Keet and Valentina Presutti, promoted the sharing of resources that support, enable, or utilize Semantic Web research, and in particular datasets, ontologies, software, and benchmarks. This track received 60 papers for review. Each paper was subject to a rigorous single-blind review process involving at least three reviewers, and on average four, and discussions among reviewers as well as

---

[1] https://orkg.org/.

[2] http://ceur-ws.org/.

an Objections and Response phase. The main review criteria focus on impact (novelty of the resource), reusability, the design and technical quality, and availability. Eventually, 11 papers were accepted. The Resources Track was aided by seven SPC and 54 PC members, and nine additional reviewers.

The In-Use Track this year was chaired by João Paulo A. Almeida and Hideaki Takeda. This track provides a forum to explore the benefits and challenges of applying Semantic Web and Knowledge Graph technologies in concrete, practical use cases, in contexts ranging from industry to government and society. In total, seven full papers were accepted for the In-Use Track, selected out of 23 full papers sent for peer review (30.43% acceptance rate). All submissions were thoroughly reviewed in a single-blind process by three Program Committee members. Submissions were assessed in terms of novelty (of the proposed use case or solution), uptake by the target user group, and demonstrated or potential impact, as well as overall soundness and quality. An Objection and Response phase was also implemented this year in line with the other tracks of the conference. Overall, 41 PC members and two additional reviewers participated in a rigorous review process.

These proceedings also include abstracts of the talks given by three excellent keynote speakers, Markus Krötzsch, Francesca Rossi, and Ilaria Capua, that ISWC 2022 was delighted to host. Markus Krötzsch, prominent member of the Semantic Web and Knowledge Graph community, gave the talk on "Data, Ontologies, Rules, and the Return of the Blank Node", presenting his view on how the unification of data and ontology may present an opportunity to the Semantic Web, and how recent results in rule-based reasoning may provide a basis for overcoming related challenges. Francesca Rossi, leading academic and industrial researcher in Artificial Intelligence (AI), gave the talk titled "AI Ethics in the Semantic Web", presenting the main issues around AI ethics, some of the proposed solutions, and the relevance of some AI ethics issues to the Semantic Web. Ilaria Capua, virologist widely recognized internationally and pioneering genetic data sharing to improve pandemic preparedness, gave the talk on "Circular Health", presenting her view of health as a circular model and illustrating how this circular approach could be data driven and implemented by using the Sustainable Development Goals roadmap.

The Industry Track, this year chaired by Anna Lisa Gentile and Petar Ristoski, covers all aspects of innovative commercial or industrial-strength Semantic Technologies and Knowledge Graphs in order to showcase the state of adoption. This track received 15 papers for review, of which eight were accepted (53.3% acceptance rate) following a single-blind review process. The 18 members of the Program Committee assessed each submission in terms of qualitative and quantitative business value, as well as the innovative aspects, impact, and lessons learned of applying Knowledge Graph and Semantic Technologies in the application domain.

The Workshop and Tutorial Track was chaired by Marta Sabou and Raghava Mutharaju. In total, 11 workshops were part of the conference program covering research topics related to ontology engineering (ontology design patterns and ontology matching), data management topics (data evolution and preservation as well as storing, querying, and managing data at Web scale), interaction with users and synergies with other technology fields, in particular deep learning. A number of workshops also focused on applications of Semantic Web technologies such as Wikidata, knowledge graph summarization, linked open science, managing legal documents and managing musical heritage with knowledge graphs. Three workshops (on legal document management, knowledge graphs summarization and musical heritage knowledge graphs) were offered for the first time, bringing new topics in addition to the topics investigated by the other established workshops. Six tutorials offered conference attendees the opportunity to further expand their knowledge on core technical topics such as reasoning, schema discovery, and knowledge-aware zero-shot learning or on topics related to exciting application domains such as autonomous driving and managing earth observation data.

The Semantic Web Challenges Track, chaired by Catia Pesquita and Daniele Dell'Aglio, proposed five challenges to help create and consolidate communities that foster research by developing solutions. Each challenge offered common environments to compare and contrast systems in various settings and tasks. The topics covered include federated query answering, neuro-symbolic reasoning, question answering, knowledge graph construction from language models, and tabular data to knowledge graph matching. Three challenges were re-editions of events proposed in the past (Semantic Answer Type, Entity, and Relation Linking Task; Semantic Reasoning Evaluation Challenge; and Semantic Web Challenge on Tabular Data to Knowledge Graph Matching) continuing their activity of driving and consolidating research trends within the Semantic Web. Two new challenges (Bio2RDF and Kibio federated query in Life Science Challenge and Knowledge Base Construction from Pre-trained Language Models) were introduced as part of the program, with a high potential to follow the successful path of the others and get a stable presence in future ISWC editions.

The Posters, Demos and Lightning Talks Track was chaired by Anastasia Dimou and Armin Haller. This track complements the paper tracks of the conference by offering an opportunity to present late-breaking research results, on-going projects, and speculative or innovative work in progress. Specifically, the Posters, Demos and Lightning Talks Track encourages presenters and participants to submit papers which have the potential to spark discussions about the work, forming an input for the future work of the presenters while offering participants an effective way to broaden their knowledge of emerging research trends and to network with other researchers. This track received 52 papers for review, of which 26 were accepted (50% acceptance rate). Among the accepted papers, 12 were poster papers and 14 were demo papers. The 55 members of the Program Committee were involved in a single-blind review process and assessed each submission based on relevance to the Semantic Web, originality, potential significance, topicality, and clarity.

Another important tradition of ISWC is the Doctoral Consortium (DC) which gives PhD students the opportunity to present their research ideas and initial results and to receive constructive feedback from senior members of the community. This year's DC was chaired by Oshani Seneviratne and Olaf Hartig, and received 10 submissions. Each submission was reviewed by four members of a Program Committee that consisted of 22 members in total. Based on the reviews, that were managed in agreement with a single-blind review process, six submissions were accepted to be published in the DC proceedings and the students of these submissions were invited to present their ideas and work during the DC sessions of the conference, where they received further feedback from senior conference attendees. The DC also hosted a career-advising session, consisting of senior researchers providing career advice with an open Q&A session.

The conference program also included two panel discussions with invited panelists from industry and academia. The first panel was led and moderated by Pascal Hitzler. It was on the topic "Is the deep learning hype good or bad for the Semantic Web?", following the observation that deep learning methods are currently having significant impact on Semantic Web research, perhaps sometimes even leading to a neglect of important topics because they cannot be tackled readily with deep learning approaches. The second panel was led and moderated by Steffen Staab. This panel asked academic and industrial researchers the question "Knowledge Graphs for The Physical World—What is Missing?". Indeed, applications like smart homes, autonomous driving, robotics, or digital twins may benefit from explicit knowledge about the physical world and for this purpose must integrate a wealth of data sources; however, the academic progress appears to be slow, while existing standards seem not to fully meet industry needs.

Any conference cannot be run properly without the precious support of sponsors. As such I would like to express my gratitude to Matteo Palmonari, Guilin Qi, and Francois Scharffe for the great efforts they made to engage sponsors and promote the conference. At the same time my thanks go to all sponsors (listed below and on the conference website) that believed in ISWC 2022 and gave it very important financial support that allowed also the provision of grants to students and researchers who could not have otherwise registered for the conference. In this regard I would also like to mention ORKG which contributed with some additional student grants. A special thank goes to the Diamond and Platinum sponsors, and to Springer for additionally supporting the conference awards.

I would like to thank Pierre Monnin and Giuseppe Pirrò for their very diligent work in setting up the ISWC 2022 proceedings and also for making possible the capturing and publicly sharing of the conference data in a reusable and open format.

ISWC 2022 news and updates have been constantly spread within the Semantic Web and Knowledge Graph community and beyond. This has been possible thanks to the incessant commitment of Neha Keshan, publicity and job fair chair, and Wen Zhang, Web presence chair.

The uncertainty that ISWC 2022 had to face and that successive change of the conference format impacted particularly the local organization team that nevertheless worked diligently to ensure the best conference setting. I am grateful to the local chair, Huajun Chen, and to Wen Zhang and the rest of the team for the careful management of all conference activities.

Finally, my special thanks go once more to the whole organizing committee, that is the family of all chairs that shared with me this complicated but wonderful journey to finally delivering the ISWC 2022 conference, and to the Semantic Web Science Association (SWSA) for the valuable support to this year's conference and for the constant and continuous presence in ISWC's 21 year history.

Claudia d'Amato, ISWC 2022 General Chair, on behalf of all the editors.

September 2022   Ulrike Sattler
                                                             Aidan Hogan
                                                             Maria Keet
                                                         Valentina Presutti
                                                      João Paulo A. Almeida
                                                          Hideaki Takeda
                                                           Pierre Monnin
                                                          Giuseppe Pirrò
                                                         Claudia d'Amato

Organization

Organizing Committee

General Chair

Claudia d'Amato   University of Bari, Italy

Local Chair

Huajun Chen   Zhejiang University, China

Research Track Chairs

Aidan Hogan   Universidad de Chile, Chile
Uli Sattler   University of Manchester, UK

Resources Track Chairs

Maria Keet   University of Cape Town, South Africa
Valentina Presutti   University of Bologna, Italy

In-Use Track Chairs

Hideaki Takeda   National Institute of Informatics, Japan
João Paulo A. Almeida   Federal University of Espírito Santo, Brazil

Workshops and Tutorials Chairs

Marta Sabou   TU Wien, Austria
Raghava Mutharaju   Indraprastha Institute of Information Technology
     Delhi, India

Industry Track Chairs

Annalisa Gentile   IBM Research, San Jose, USA
Petar Ristoski   eBay, San Jose, USA

Doctoral Consortium Chairs

Oshani Seneviratne   Rensselaer Polytechnic Institute, USA
Olaf Hartig   Linköping University, Sweden

Posters, Demos, and Lightning Talks Chairs

Anastasia Dimou	Katholieke Universiteit Leuven, Belgium
Armin Haller	Australian National University, Australia

Semantic Web Challenge Chairs

Daniele Dell'Aglio	Aalborg University, Denmark
Catia Pesquita	University of Lisbon, Portugal

Panel Chairs

Pascal Hitzler	Kansas State University, USA
Steffen Staab	University of Stuttgart, Germany

Sponsor Chairs

Guilin Qi	Southeast University, China
Francois Scharffe	University of Montpellier, France
Matteo Palmonari	University of Milano-Bicocca, Italy

Proceedings and Metadata Chairs

Giuseppe Pirrò	Sapienza University of Rome, Italy
Pierre Monnin	Orange, France

Web Presence and Publicity Chairs

Wen Zhang	Zhejiang University, China
Neha Keshan	Rensselaer Polytechnic Institute, USA

Research Track Senior Program Committee

Maribel Acosta	Ruhr University Bochum, Germany
Gong Cheng	Nanjing University, China
Michael Cochez	Vrije Universiteit Amsterdam, The Netherlands
Mauro Dragoni	FBK-ICT Irst, Italy
Daniel Garijo	Universidad Politécnica de Madrid, Spain
Birte Glimm	University of Ulm, Germany
Peter Haase	metaphacts, Germany
Olaf Hartig	Linköping University, Sweden
Laura Hollink	Centrum Wiskunde & Informatica, The Netherlands
Katja Hose	Aalborg University, Denmark

Wei Hu   Nanjing University, China
Ken Kaneiwa   The University of Electro-Communications, Japan
Sabrina Kirrane   Vienna University of Economics and Business,
                                Austria
Markus Luczak-Roesch   Victoria University of Wellington, New Zealand
Maria Vanina Martinez   Universidad Nacional del Sur, Argentina
Gabriela Montoya   Aalborg University, Denmark
Boris Motik   University of Oxford, UK
Magdalena Ortiz   Vienna University of Technology, Austria
Francesco Osborne   The Open University, UK
Jeff Z. Pan   University of Edinburgh, UK
Catia Pesquita   Universidade de Lisboa, Portugal
Guilin Qi   Southeast University, China
Elena Simperl   King's College London, UK
Hala Skaf-Molli   LS2N, University of Nantes, France
Valentina Tamma   University of Liverpool, UK
Domagoj Vrgoc   Pontificia Universidad Católica de Chile, Chile
Yizheng Zhao   Nanjing University, China

Research Track Program Committee

Shqiponja Ahmetaj   TU Wien, Austria
Mehwish Alam   FIZ Karlsruhe - Leibniz Institute for Information
                                Infrastructure and Karlsruhe Institute of
                                Technology, Germany
Mirza Mohtashim Alam   Institut für Angewandte Informatik, Germany
Panos Alexopoulos   Textkernel B.V., The Netherlands
José Luis Ambite   University of Southern California, USA
Renzo Angles   Universidad de Talca, Chile
Julián Arenas-Guerrero   Universidad Politécnica de Madrid, Spain
Luigi Asprino   University of Bologna, Italy
Amr Azzam   Vienna University of Economics and Business,
                                Austria
Carlos Badenes-Olmedo   Universidad Politécnica de Madrid, Spain
Pierpaolo Basile   Dipartimento di Informatica - University of Bari,
                                Italy
Russa Biswas   Karlsruhe Institute of Technology and FIZ
                                Karlsruhe, Germany
Christian Bizer   University of Mannheim, Germany
Peter Bloem   Vrije Universiteit Amsterdam, The Netherlands
Carlos Bobed   University of Zaragoza, Spain
Alexander Borgida   Rutgers University, USA
Paolo Bouquet   University of Trento, Italy

Zied Bouraoui   CRIL - CNRS and Université d'Artois, France
Janez Brank   Jožef Stefan Institute, Slovenia
Anna Breit   Semantic Web Company, Austria
Carlos Buil Aranda   Universidad Técnica Federico Santa María, Chile
Jean-Paul Calbimonte   HES-SO University of Applied Sciences and Arts
                               Western Switzerland, Switzerland
Pablo Calleja   Universidad Politécnica de Madrid, Spain
Giovanni Casini   ISTI-CNR, Italy
Victor Charpenay   Mines Saint-Etienne, France
Vinay Chaudhri   JPMorgan Chase & Co., USA
David Chaves-Fraga   Universidad Politécnica de Madrid, Spain
Jiaoyan Chen   University of Oxford, UK
Sijin Cheng   Linköping University, Sweden
Cuong Xuan Chu   Max Planck Institute for Informatics, Germany
Philipp Cimiano   Bielefeld University, Germany
Pieter Colpaert   Ghent University, Belgium
Oscar Corcho   Universidad Politécnica de Madrid, Spain
Julien Corman   Free University of Bozen-Bolzano, Italy
Philippe Cudre-Mauroux   University of Fribourg, Switzerland
Victor de Boer   Vrije Universiteit Amsterdam, The Netherlands
Daniele Dell'Aglio   Aalborg University, Denmark
Elena Demidova   University of Bonn, Germany
Stefan Dietze   GESIS - Leibniz Institute for the Social Sciences,
                               Germany
Anastasia Dimou   KU Leuven, Belgium
Dejing Dou   University of Oregon, USA
Jianfeng Du   Guangdong University of Foreign Studies, China
Shusaku Egami   National Institute of Advanced Industrial Science
                               and Technology, Japan
Fajar J. Ekaputra   TU Wien, Austria
Paola Espinoza   BASF, Spain
Lorena Etcheverry   Universidad de la República, Uruguay
David Eyers   University of Otago, New Zealand
Alessandro Faraotti   IBM, Italy
Michael Färber   Karlsruhe Institute of Technology, Germany
Daniel Faria   Universidade de Lisboa, Portugal
Javier D. Fernández   F. Hoffmann-La Roche AG, Switzerland
Alba Fernández-Izquierdo   Universidad Politécnica de Madrid, Spain
Sebastián Ferrada   Linköping University, Sweden
Erwin Filtz   Siemens AG Österreich, Austria
Valeria Fionda   University of Calabria, Italy
Achille Fokoue   IBM, USA

Naoki Fukuta	Shizuoka University, Japan
Mohamed Gad-Elrab	Bosch Center for Artificial Intelligence, Germany
Luis Galárraga	Inria, France
Fabien Gandon	Inria, Université Côte d'Azur, France
Andrés García-Silva	Expert.ai, Spain
Yuxia Geng	Zhejiang University, China
Pouya Ghiasnezhad Omran	Australian National University, Australia
Shrestha Ghosh	Max Planck Institute for Informatics, Germany
Martin Giese	University of Oslo, Norway
Jose Manuel Gomez-Perez	expert.ai, Spain
Jorge Gracia	University of Zaragoza, Spain
Alasdair Gray	Heriot-Watt University, UK
Paul Groth	University of Amsterdam, The Netherlands
Kalpa Gunaratna	Samsung Research, USA
Claudio Gutierrez	Universidad de Chile, Chile
Mohad-Saïd Hacid	Université Lyon 1, France
Tom Hanika	University of Kassel, Germany
Andreas Harth	University of Erlangen-Nuremberg and Fraunhofer IIS-SCS, Germany
Mounira Harzallah	LS2N, University of Nantes, France
Oktie Hassanzadeh	IBM, USA
Lars Heling	Robert Bosch GmbH, Germany
Ryohei Hisano	University of Tokyo, Japan
Vinh Thinh Ho	Max Planck Institute for Informatics, Germany
Rinke Hoekstra	University of Amsterdam, The Netherlands
Jiacheng Huang	Nanjing University, China
Luis-Daniel Ibáñez-Gonzalez	University of Southampton, UK
Ryutaro Ichise	Tokyo Institute of Technology, Japan
Ana Iglesias-Molina	Universidad Politécnica de Madrid, Spain
Prateek Jain	LivePerson Inc., USA
Ernesto Jimenez-Ruiz	City, University of London, UK
Tobias Käfer	Karlsruhe Institute of Technology, Germany
Lucie-Aimée Kaffee	University of Copenhagen, Denmark
Jan-Christoph Kalo	Vrije Universiteit Amsterdam, The Netherlands
Maulik R. Kamdar	Elsevier Inc., The Netherlands
Mayank Kejriwal	University of Southern California, USA
Ilkcan Keles	Aalborg University and TomTom, Denmark
Ankesh Khandelwal	Amazon, USA
Craig Knoblock	University of Southern California, USA
Stasinos Konstantopoulos	NCSR Demokritos, Greece
Roman Kontchakov	Birkbeck, University of London, UK
Adila A. Krisnadhi	Universitas Indonesia, Indonesia

Markus Krötzsch	TU Dresden, Germany
Benno Kruit	Vrije Universiteit Amsterdam, The Netherlands
Jose Emilio Labra Gayo	Universidad de Oviedo, Spain
André Lamurias	Aalborg University, Denmark
Danh Le Phuoc	TU Berlin, Germany
Maxime Lefrançois	Mines Saint-Etienne, France
Maurizio Lenzerini	Sapienza University of Rome, Italy
Yuan-Fang Li	Monash University, Australia
Matteo Lissandrini	Aalborg University, Denmark
Wenqiang Liu	Tencent Inc, China
Essam Mansour	Concordia University, Canada
Albert Meroño-Peñuela	King's College London, UK
Daniel Miranker	University of Texas at Austin, USA
Ralf Möller	University of Luebeck, Germany
Pascal Molli	LS2N, University of Nantes, France
Deshendran Moodley	University of Cape Town, South Africa
Varish Mulwad	GE Research, USA
Summaya Mumtaz	University of Oslo, Norway
Raghava Mutharaju	IIIT-Delhi, India
Hubert Naacke	LIP6, Sorbonne Université, France
Shinichi Nagano	Toshiba Corporation, Japan
María Navas-Loro	Universidad Politécnica de Madrid, Spain
Axel-Cyrille Ngonga Ngomo	Paderborn University, Germany
Tuan-Phong Nguyen	Max Planck Institute for Informatics, Germany
Vinh Nguyen	National Library of Medicine, USA
Andriy Nikolov	AstraZeneca, UK
Kwabena Nuamah	University of Edinburgh, UK
Werner Nutt	Free University of Bozen-Bolzano, Italy
Fabrizio Orlandi	Trinity College Dublin, Ireland
Ana Ozaki	University of Bergen, Norway
Julian Padget	University of Bath, UK
Ankur Padia	Philips Research North America, USA
Matteo Palmonari	University of Milano-Bicocca, Italy
Peter Patel-Schneider	Xerox PARC, USA
Terry Payne	University of Liverpool, UK
Rafael Peñaloza	University of Milano-Bicocca, Italy
Bernardo Pereira Nunes	Australian National University, Australia
Romana Pernisch	Vrije Universiteit Amsterdam, The Netherlands
Alina Petrova	University of Oxford, UK
Patrick Philipp	Karlsruhe Institute of Technology, Germany
Francesco Piccialli	University of Naples Federico II, Italy
Giuseppe Pirrò	Sapienza University of Rome, Italy

Alessandro Piscopo	BBC, UK
Axel Polleres	Vienna University of Economics and Business, Austria
María Poveda-Villalón	Universidad Politécnica de Madrid, Spain
Ehsan Qasemi	University of Southern California, USA
Yuzhong Qu	Nanjing University, China
Alexandre Rademaker	IBM Research and EMAp/FGV, Brazil
David Ratcliffe	Microsoft, Australia
Achim Rettinger	Trier University, Germany
Martin Rezk	Google, USA
Mariano Rico	Universidad Politécnica de Madrid, Spain
Giuseppe Rizzo	LINKS Foundation, Italy
Edelweis Rohrer	Universidad de la República, Uruguay
Oscar Romero	Universitat Politècnica de Catalunya, Spain
Miguel Romero Orth	Universidad de Adolfo Ibañez, Chile
Henry Rosales-Méndez	University of Chile, Chile
Marco Rospocher	Università degli Studi di Verona, Italy
Jose Rozanec	Jožef Stefan Institute, Slovenia
Sebastian Rudolph	TU Dresden, Germany
Anisa Rula	University of Brescia, Italy
Harald Sack	FIZ Karlsruhe – Leibniz Institute for Information Infrastructure and Karlsruhe Institute of Technology, Germany
Tomer Sagi	Aalborg University, Denmark
Angelo Antonio Salatino	The Open University, UK
Muhammad Saleem	University of Leizpig, Germany
Kai-Uwe Sattler	TU Ilmenau, Germany
Marco Luca Sbodio	IBM Research, Ireland
Konstantin Schekotihin	Alpen-Adria Universität Klagenfurt, Austria
Ralf Schenkel	Trier University, Germany
Juan F. Sequeda	data.world, USA
Cogan Shimizu	Wright State University, USA
Kuldeep Singh	Cerence GmbH and Zerotha Research, Germany
Sneha Singhania	Max Planck Institute for Informatics, Germany
Kavitha Srinivas	IBM, USA
Nadine Steinmetz	TU Ilmenau, Germany
Armando Stellato	Tor Vergata University of Rome, Italy
Lise Stork	Vrije Universiteit Amsterdam, The Netherlands
Gerd Stumme	University of Kassel, Germany
Zequn Sun	Nanjing University, China
Pedro Szekely	University of Southern California, USA
Ruben Taelman	Ghent University, Belgium

David Tena Cucala	University of Oxford, UK
Andreas Thalhammer	F. Hoffmann-La Roche AG, Switzerland
Krishnaprasad Thirunarayan	Wright State University, USA
Steffen Thoma	FZI Research Center for Information Technology, Germany
Ilaria Tiddi	Vrije Universiteit Amsterdam, The Netherlands
Riccardo Tommasini	LIRIS, INSA de Lyon, France
Trung-Kien Tran	Bosch Center for Artificial Intelligence, Germany
Takanori Ugai	Fujitsu Ltd., Japan
Jacopo Urbani	Vrije Universiteit Amsterdam, The Netherlands
Guillermo Vega-Gorgojo	Universidad de Valladolid, Spain
Ruben Verborgh	Ghent University, Belgium
Serena Villata	I3S, CNRS, France
Hai Wan	Sun Yat-sen University, China
Haofen Wang	Tongji University, China
Kewen Wang	Griffith University, Australia
Meng Wang	Southeast University, China
Peng Wang	Southeast University, China
Ruijie Wang	University of Zurich, Switzerland
Xiaxia Wang	Nanjing University, China
Xin Wang	Tianjin University, China
Yisong Wang	Guizhou University, China
Zhe Wang	Griffith University, Australia
Tobias Weller	University of Mannheim, Germany
Simon Werner	Trier University, Germany
Xander Wilcke	Vrije Universiteit Amsterdam, The Netherlands
Honghan Wu	University College London, UK
Adam Wyner	Swansea University, Wales
Josiane Xavier Parreira	Siemens AG Österreich, Austria
Guohui Xiao	Free University of Bozen-Bolzano, Italy
Yanghua Xiao	Fudan University, China
Ikuya Yamada	Studio Ousia Inc., Japan
Fadi Zaraket	American University of Beirut, Lebanon
Xiaowang Zhang	Tianjin University, China
Yuanzhe Zhang	Institute of Automation, Chinese Academy of Sciences, China
Lu Zhou	TigerGraph, Inc., USA
Antoine Zimmermann	Mines Saint-Étienne, France

Research Track Additional Reviewers

Sara Abdollahi	Dörthe Arndt
Tobias Backes	Inès Blin
Lorenzo Bongiovanni	Christoph Braun
Alexander Brinkmann	Yiyi Chen
Federico D'Asaro	Rajjat Dadwal
Jacopo de Berardinis	Hang Dong
Nicolas Ferranti	Susmita Gangopadhyay
Manas Gaur	Zhou Gui
Fatma-Zohra Hannou	Tobias Hille
Johannes Hirth	Jacqueline Höllig
Xiang Huang	Kai Kugler
Victor Lacerda	Xingjian Li
Fandel Lin	Stephan Linzbach
Jin Liu	Sebastian Monka
Ralph Peeters	Cosimo Persia
Maximilian Pflueger	Nicholas Popovic
Stefan Schestakov	Sebastian Schmid
Basel Shbita	Sarah Binta Alam Shoilee
Lucia Siciliani	Shirly Stephen
Maximilian Stubbemann	Zequn Sun
Antonis Troumpoukis	Roderick van der Weerdt
Minhong Wang	Yaqing Wang
Xiao Zhang	Tianzhe Zhao

Resources Track Senior Program Committee

Albert Meroño-Peñuela	King's College London, UK
Dimitar Dimitrov	GESIS, Germany
Harald Sack	FIZ Karlsruhe – Leibniz Institute for Information Infrastructure and Karlsruhe Institute of Technology, Germany
Agnieszka Lawrynowicz	Poznan University of Technology, Poland
Vojtěch Svátek	Prague University of Economics and Business, Czech Republic
Matteo Palmonari	University of Milano-Bicocca, Italy
Philipp Cimiano	Bielefeld University, Germany

Resources Track Program Committee

Debanjali Biswas	University of Bonn, Germany
Germán Alejandro Braun	Universidad Nacional del Comahue, Argentina

Sasha Bruns   FIZ Karlsruhe – Leibniz Institute for Information
                                  Infrastructure, Germany
Elena Cabrio   I3S, Université Côte d'Azur, CNRS, Inria, France
Valentina Anita Carriero   University of Bologna, Italy
Francesco Corcoglioniti   Free University of Bozen-Bolzano, Italy
Olivier Curé   LIGM, Université Paris-Est, France
Enrico Daga   The Open University, UK
Jérôme David   Inria, France
Maria Del Mar Roldan-Garcia   Universidad de Malaga, Spain
Anastasia Dimou   KU Leuven, Belgium
Michel Dumontier   Maastricht University, The Netherlands
Pablo Fillottrani   Universidad Nacional del Sur, Argentina
Tudor Groza   The Garvan Institute of Medical Research,
                                  Australia
Christophe Guéret   Accenture Labs, Ireland
Peter Haase   metaphacts, Germany
Fabian Hoppe   FIZ Karlsruhe and Karlsruhe Institute of
                                  Technology, Germany
Antoine Isaac   Europeana and VU Amsterdam, The Netherlands
Yavuz Selim Kartal   GESIS – Leibniz Institute for Social Sciences,
                                  Germany
Zubeida Khan   Council for Scientific and Industrial Research,
                                  South Africa
Tomas Kliegr   Prague University of Economics and Business,
                                  Czech Republic
Jakub Klimek   Charles University, Czech Republic
Adila A. Krisnadhi   Universitas Indonesia, Indonesia
Christoph Lange   Fraunhofer FIT and RWTH Aachen University,
                                  Germany
Paea Le Pendu   University of California, Riverside, USA
Allyson Lister   University of Oxford, UK
Maria Maleshkova   University of Siegen, Germany
Zola Mahlaza   University of Pretoria, South Africa
Lionel Médini   Université Claude Bernard Lyon 1, France
Pascal Molli   University of Nantes, France
Alessandro Mosca   Free University of Bozen-Bolzano, Italy
Andrea Giovanni Nuzzolese   University of Bologna, Italy
Heiko Paulheim   University of Mannheim, Germany
Rafael Peñaloza   University of Milano-Bicocca, Italy
Alina Petrova   University of Oxford, UK
Giuseppe Pirrò   Sapienza University of Rome, Italy
María Poveda-Villalón   Universidad Politécnica de Madrid, Spain
Mariano Rodríguez Muro   Google, USA

Sebastian Schellhammer   GESIS – Leibniz Institute for the Social Sciences,
                                  Germany
Stefan Schlobach   Vrije Universiteit Amsterdam, The Netherlands
Patricia Serrano Alvarado   University of Nantes, France
Cogan Shimizu   Kansas State University, USA
Blerina Spahiu   Università degli Studi di Milano-Bicocca, Italy
Kavitha Srinivas   IBM, USA
Mari Carmen Suárez-Figueroa   Universidad Politécnica de Madrid, Spain
Ruben Taelman   Ghent University, Belgium
Mary Ann Tan   FIZ Karlsruhe, Germany
Tabea Tietz   FIZ Karlsruhe, Germany
Mahsa Vafaie   Karlsruhe Institute of Technology, Germany
Maria Esther Vidal   TIB Hannover, Germany
Joerg Waitelonis   Yovisto GmbH, Germany
Guohui Xiao   Free University of Bozen-Bolzano, Italy
Ondrej Zamazal   Prague University of Economics and Business,
                                  Czech Republic
Ziqi Zhang   University of Sheffield, UK

Resources Track Additional Reviewers

Mark Adamik   Felix Bensman
Pierre-Antoine Champin   Susmita Gangopadhyay
Florian Grensing   Fatma-Zohra Hannou
Hande McGinty   Ebrahim Norouzi
Jennifer Daniel Onwuchekwa   Ondřej Zamazal

In-Use Track Program Committee

Farahnaz Akrami   University of Texas at Arlington, USA
Renzo Angles   Universidad de Talca, Chile
Ghislain A. Atemezing   Mondeca, France
Payam Barnaghi   Imperial College London, UK
Martin Bauer   NEC Laboratories Europe, Germany
Maria Bermudez-Edo   University of Granada, Spain
Stefan Bischof   Siemens AG Österreich, Austria
Carlos Buil Aranda   Universidad Técnica Federico Santa María, Chile
Oscar Corcho   Universidad Politécnica de Madrid, Spain
Christophe Debruyne   Université de Liège, Belgium
Djellel Difallah   New York University, USA
Ying Ding   University of Texas at Austin, USA
Bernadette F. Lóscio   Federal University of Pernambuco, Brazil

Daniel Garijo	Universidad Politécnica de Madrid, Spain
Jose Manuel Gomez-Perez	expert.ai, Spain
Damien Graux	Inria, France
Daniel Gruhl	IBM Almaden Research Center, USA
Peter Haase	metaphacts, Germany
Nicolas Heist	University of Mannheim, Germany
Tobias Käfer	Karlsruhe Institute of Technology, Germany
Tomi Kauppinen	Aalto University, Finland
Takahiro Kawamura	National Agriculture and Food Research Organization, Japan
Mayank Kejriwal	University of Southern California, USA
Craig Knoblock	University of Southern California, USA
Maxime Lefrançois	Mines Saint-Etienne, France
Vanessa Lopez	IBM, Ireland
Michael Luggen	University of Fribourg, Switzerland
Beatrice Markhoff	Université François Rabelais Tours, France
Andriy Nikolov	AstraZeneca, UK
Alexander O'Connor	Autodesk, Inc, USA
Fabrizio Orlandi	Trinity College Dublin, Ireland
Francesco Osborne	The Open University, UK
Artem Revenko	Semantic Web Company GmbH, Austria
Mariano Rico	Universidad Politécnica de Madrid, Spain
Dumitru Roman	SINTEF, Norway
Dezhao Song	Thomson Reuters, USA
Vítor E. Silva Souza	Federal University of Espírito Santo, Brazil
Xuezhi Wang	Google, USA
Josiane Xavier Parreira	Siemens AG Österreich, Austria
Matthäus Zloch	GESIS - Leibniz Institute for the Social Sciences, Germany
Sergio J. Rodríguez	Australian National University, Australia

In-Use Track Additional Reviewers

Binh Vu
Minh Tran Pham

Sponsors

Below we report the list of sponsors that fall in the Silver Plus, Gold, Platinum, and Diamond categories and that joined before the completion of the proceedings, i.e., September 6, 2022. For the final list of sponsors in every category please visit https://iswc2022.sem anticweb.org/index.php/sponsors/.

Diamond Sponsors

https://www.chinascope.com/

https://www.elsevier.com/

Platinum Sponsors

https://research.ibm.com/

Gold Sponsors

https://metaphacts.com/

https://www.memect.cn/

https://www.oracle.com/

Silver Plus Sponsors

https://link.springer.com/conference/semweb

Abstracts of Invited Talks

Circular Health

Ilaria Capua

One Health Center of Excellence, University of Florida,
Gainesville, Florida, USA
icapua@ufl.edu

Pandemics are unique and transformational events as they shake lives by exposing the vulnerability of Homo sapiens to previously unknown pathogens, which become widespread as most human beings on the planet will become infected. But Covid-19 has done much more than this. It has exposed us to another type of vulnerability – the **vulnerability of the systems we operate in**. It has also opened our eyes to the harsh reality that we live in a closed system, in which we are entirely **interconnected and interdependent with other creatures on planet earth**. This awareness has paved the way to acknowledge that as a society we should embrace the One Health [1] approach which recognizes the links between the health of humans, animals, and the environment.

Covid 19 has also shown us that such a major health crisis has multiple drivers and ramifications that include social [2], economic [3], and digital [4] drivers that have caused the pandemic to unravel in the way it did. In addition Covid 19 is the **most measured event** in history and oceans of big data have been generated during this event.

Since the turn of the millennium we have been experiencing several other challenges which concern our closed system and affect our health, for instance the climate [5] and food [6] crises. For example, we are aware of the devastating effect of rising temperatures on the health of our oceans, on the loss of biodiversity and on the migration of humans and animals. We are also well aware that the planet's demographics will require more food to feed a world population expected to reach 9.7bn by 2050 [7] and at the same time we have committed to diminishing greenhouse gas emissions to reduce pollution and $CO2$ footprint.

Following the conceptual blueprint of Circular Economy [8] and Circular Agriculture [9], this could be the right time to expand our approach to health to a circular model which encompasses the intricate and novel links between human health and the health of this closed system. This circular approach would be data driven and could be implemented by using the Sustainable Development Goals (SDGs) roadmap as an accelerator of convergence for health. All the 17 goals have ties to the health of humans, animals, plants, and the environment, and it would seem reasonable to prioritize certain activities and capitalize on existing guidelines and commitments.

The novelty of the Circular Health approach is to use post-Covid-19 renewed health priorities to promote the convergence of health-related issues which can be achieved within the Sustainable Development Goals framework. In this way it will be possible to advance urgent health priorities within an existing framework which aims at sustainability and at advancing health as an essential resource within a closed system, which needs to be regenerated and addressed in its complexity.

References

1. Tripartite and UNEP support OHHLEP's definition of "One Health". https://www.who.int/news/item/01-12-2021-tripartite-and-unep-support-ohhlep-s-definition-of-one-health
2. Gooch A., Colombo F.: Addressing the hidden pandemic: The impact of the COVID-19 crisis on mental health. https://www.oecd-forum.org/posts/addressing-the-hidden-pandemic-the-impact-of-the-covid-19-crisis-on-mental-health-f02d8e3e-6252-4f4e-91f5-476ad2c9a027
3. Yeyati, E.L., Filippini, F.: Social and economic impact of COVID-19 (2021). https://www.brookings.edu/research/social-and-economic-impact-of-covid-19/
4. Pierri, F., Perry, B.L., DeVerna, M.R., et al.: Online misinformation is linked to early COVID-19 vaccination hesitancy and refusal. Sci. Rep. **12**, 5966 (2022). https://doi.org/10.1038/s41598-022-10070-w
5. Salas R.N.: Health as the Central Driver for Action on Climate Change. https://www.oecd-forum.org/posts/health-as-the-central-driver-for-action-on-climate-change
6. Qu Dongyu (FAO) on conflict and food security - Security Council, 9036th meeting. https://media.un.org/en/asset/k1n/k1nzd5fca3
7. Growing at a slower pace, world population is expected to reach 9.7 billion in 2050 and could peak at nearly 11 billion around 2100. https://www.un.org/development/desa/en/news/population/world-population-prospects-2019.html
8. What is a circular economy? https://ellenmacarthurfoundation.org/topics/circular-economy-introduction/overview
9. Circular agriculture: a new perspective for Dutch agriculture. https://www.wur.nl/en/show/circular-agriculture-a-new-perspective-for-dutch-agriculture-1.htm

Data, Ontologies, Rules, and the Return of the Blank Node

Markus Krötzsch

Knowledge-Based Systems Group, TU Dresden, Germany
`markus.kroetzsch@tu-dresden.de`

Abstract. The Semantic Web has long been characterised by the parallel development of machine-readable data and ontological models. Inspired by very different backgrounds – Web data exchange and mathematical logic – the two worlds have sometimes be perceived as complementary, even conflicting. But the general trend towards knowledge graphs made such discussions irrelevant, and modern knowledge models, such as Wikidata, often combine instance and schema data side by side. In my invited talk, I will explain how this unification of data and ontology may present an opportunity to the Semantic Web, and discuss how recent results in rule-based reasoning may provide a basis for overcoming related challenges. This involves some interesting insights about the expressive power that is conferred by extending rules with value invention – the ability to create fresh blank nodes. Besides the theoretical effects of this addition, we can also demonstrate concrete practical uses of this expressive power.

Ontologies have come a long way. In the past two decades of Semantic Web research, the community has re-invented itself several times. The first golden era of "ontology" saw the heydays of upper-level ontologies, design methodologies, and the birth and rise of the first OWL standard. Remarkable accomplishments of engineering and applied logic kept pushing what was possible. Meanwhile, "data" prepared for its comeback, with Linked Data, the first DBpedia releases, and of course SPARQL drawing our attention and resonating with the newly discovered appeal of *Big Data* (a marketing term both decried and revered by the data management community). New hybrids of data and ontology emerged, from *ontology-based data access* to the renewed data-centred modeling approaches of RDF constraint languages (eventually resulting in the unequal siblings ShaCL and ShEx). The new era of *knowledge graphs* finally saw the breakthrough of Semantic Web concepts: Google turned from mere document retrieval to question answering, the majority of Web pages now carry machine-readable annotations in shared vocabularies, and tens of thousands of Wikipedia editors construct a structured world model in Wikidata.

And where did this leave ontology? Considering today's large knowledge graphs with little or no OWL usage, we might wonder whether we lost it along the way. Indeed, this would seem to fit the zeitgeist. With the celebrated successes of machine learning, it seems that end-to-end AI has replaced our once-treasured *shared Conceptualization*. Only a short-sighted observer, however, could mistake this for a sign that (linked) data has finally triumphed over (formal) ontology. Unfazed by the animosities of the past, we see that any such AI-induced *end of ontology* would also be the *end of semantic data*: in a world where any string of symbols is "machine-readable", the Semantic Web endeavour looses its meaning and relevance. Fortunately, such worries are unfounded, as data-driven AI longs for meaning and seeks (but so far fails to find) a method for *explaining* itself – for establishing a shared understanding with its human users.

Did we then falsely abandon ontology in favour of mere data? I do not think so. Instead, what we see in practice rather seems to be a marriage of data and ontology. Syntactically, this is no news to us, with OWL relying on an RDF syntax from its very beginnings. However, conceptually, we have often drawn clear boundaries between ontology (*schema*) and data (*instances*), where the former must adhere to strict formal standards and total consistency, while the latter is entitled to noise and incoherence. In modern knowledge graphs, such as Wikidata, both worlds are one [14]. Indeed, when we see a Wikidata statement like "elephant – has part(s) – elephant's trunk" it is hard not to read this "triple" as a mereological description of all instances of the class elephant. At the same time, such statements can be subject to all the complications associated with other data, from noise to context-dependent validity.

We are not well prepared for this messy new world. Where we used to have W3C-standardised ontology languages and specialised tools to deal with them, we now have noisy fusions of schema and instance data, sometimes with new user-invented expressive features that further blur the line between data and ontology (as in the Wikidata statement "universe – has part(s) of the class – astronomical object"). In the wild, we therefore find makeshift queries and ad-hoc tools where our Semantic Web forebears had planned for a neatly constructed layer cake. The challenge for staying relevant therefore is to combine the flexibility and robustness of custom scripts with the declarativity and reliability of an ontological reasoner.

One possible answer to this call is to turn to *rules*. Statements with an "if-then" structure have a natural place in both computation and logic, and many species of rule languages can be found within this fertile middle ground. The simplest (in syntax and semantics) is *Datalog* [1], where rules merely "materialise" query results by adding inferred relations between existing objects. Recursion adds power to this simple idea. It is easy to see the appeal of this approach: rules are simple "instructions" for data completion and transformation; they are fully declarative (implementation-independent); they are well-suited for handling complex relationships in knowledge graphs.

And rules can capture ontologies. This was known for a long time for some ontologies that could directly be rewritten as rules, most prominently the OWL RL profile [13]. The original idea was to turn ontologies into sets of rules, rather than allowing us to interpret part of the data as ontological information, which is then processed by rules. However, we can also define a set of (Datalog) rules that "implements" a complete OWL RL reasoner for input ontologies given as plain data (e.g., as RDF encoding of the OWL statements). A similar feat can be accomplished for the OWL EL profile although this ontology language cannot be rewritten in Datalog [10]. These approaches show that rules have the potential of capturing ontological semantics while at the same time being user-definable and therefore able to adapt to new forms and features in ways that a classical OWL reasoner could not.

However, this approach soon meets its limits, as can be seen by applying a small amount of complexity theory. Datalog can be evaluated in polynomial time with respect to the size of the input data, so if the input data is our ontological knowledge, we can only solve polynomial ontology reasoning tasks. But beyond lightweight profiles like RL and EL, ontological reasoning is not known for its low computational complexity: OWL 2 DL makes it to a frightening N2ExpTime-completeness. It might seem that rules, after all, can only do simple manipulations but are no use for such heavy lifting.

This is indeed true for Datalog, but it turns out that small extensions suffice to overcome all limits and capture a much larger class of computations. All we need to do is to allow rules to infer the existence of new objects. This so-called *value invention* leads us to *existential rules*. As recently discovered, even the known (and implemented) decidable fragments of this language are powerful enough to express *every* decidable computation that only relies on positive information (since we have no negation here) [2]. A huge leap from Datalog's polynomial time.

Interestingly, the "invented values" that are at the heart of this leap in expressive power are, in Semantic Web terms, nothing but *blank nodes* – the least appreciated type of RDF term, which has long been "considered harmful" in data publishing. This critique in publishing still holds up, but at the same time, blank nodes reveal their virtues when modelling computation. Indeed, the ability to build new structures from such elements is an important ingredient to the expressive power of existential rules. The other important ingredient, as it turns out, is the ability to re-use such blank nodes once they were created. It is this facility that allows even highly complicated computations to come to an end, instead of creating new values forever. The interplay between recursive rule application and the possible re-use of blank nodes is complex and issues such as termination [5], minimisation [9, 11], and negation [6] are studied in current research.

As often, the encodings used to demonstrate such high expressive powers in theory papers [2] are not practical, yet they assure us that existential rules could be used to express even the most complicated ontological inference procedures over a knowledge graph. More applied works have shown that one can really solve some very hard (non-polynomial) tasks in this way [4, 8]. Moreover, even beyond its computational benefits, value invention provides us with a crucial facility for adding new *auxiliary* elements to knowledge graphs, which can be required, e.g., to encode contextual information (such as temporal validity) in RDF graphs [7, 12]. In spite of the long history of existential rules in data exchange research (where they are known as *tuple-generating dependencies*), this capability of rules to perform complex data transformations is hardly explored in knowledge graphs yet. For example, a set of a few dozen existential rules suffices to convert the RDF encoding of an OWL EL ontology into a set of normalised ontology axioms that share common sub-expressions.[3]

All of this has already been implemented, e.g., using the existential rule engine VLog [3]. Nevertheless, the vision of replacing our reliable (but largely decommissioned) tooling of ontological reasoning by a more flexible, rule-based inference mechanism is still far from being realised. Prime challenges remain usability (for designing rule-based computations), scalability to knowledge graph sizes, and the ability of handling noise

---

[3] *Practical Uses of Existential Rules in Knowledge Representation*: tutorial at ECAI 2022; instructions and examples at https://iccl.inf.tu-dresden.de/web/Rules_Tutorial_2020/en.

and context-dependent inferences. In addition, the new ecosystem will need explanation and debugging services, and approaches for adding in other modes of computation that are relevant on knowledge graphs (e.g., based on graph embeddings, network analysis, or graph neural networks). The Semantic Web community will be needed to help invent and analyse the necessary tools and methods, but also to provide their expertise on building good knowledge models that ensure interoperability (of machines) and shared understanding (among humans).

Acknowledgements. The research reported here was partly supported by DFG in project 389792660 (TRR 248, Center for Perspicuous Systems[4]), by the BMBF under project ScaDS.AI[5], by BMBF and DAAD in project 57616814 (SECAI: School of Embedded and Composite AI[6]), and by the Center for Advancing Electronics Dresden[7] (cfaed).

References

1. Abiteboul, S., Hull, R., Vianu, V.: Foundations of Databases. Addison Wesley (1994)
2. Bourgaux, C., Carral, D., Krötzsch, M., Rudolph, S., Thomazo, M.: Capturing homomorphism-closed decidable queries with existential rules. In: Bienvenu, M., Lakemeyer, G., Erdem, E. (eds.) Proceedings of the 18th International Conference on Principles of Knowledge Representation and Reasoning (KR 2021), pp. 141–150 (2021)
3. Carral, D., Dragoste, I., González, L., Jacobs, C., Krötzsch, M., Urbani, J.: VLog: a rule engine for knowledge graphs. In: ISWC 2019. LNCS, vol. 11779, pp. 19–35. Springer, Cham (2019). https://doi.org/10.1007/978-3-030-30796-7_2
4. Carral, D., Dragoste, I., Krötzsch, M., Lewe, C.: Chasing sets: how to use existential rules for expressive reasoning. In: Proceedings of the 28th International Joint Conference on Artificial Intelligence (IJCAI 2019), pp. 1624–1631 (2019). ijcai.org
5. Carral, D., Larroque, L., Mugnier, M., Thomazo, M.: Normalisations of existential rules: Not so innocuous! In: Proceedings of the 19th International Conference on Principles of Knowledge Representation and Reasoning (KR 2022) (2022)
6. Ellmauthaler, S., Krötzsch, M., Mennicke, S.: Answering queries with negation over existential rules. In: Proceedings of the 36th AAAI Conf. on Artificial Intelligence, AAAI 2022, pp. 5626–5633. AAAI Press (2022)
7. Erxleben, F., Günther, M., Krötzsch, M., Mendez, J., Vrandečić, D.: Introducing wikidata to the linked data web. In: ISWC 2014. LNCS, vol. 8796, pp. 50–65. Springer, Cham. https://doi.org/10.1007/978-3-319-11964-9_4
8. Gaggl, S.A., Hanisch, P., Krötzsch, M.: Simulating sets in answer set programming. In: Proceedings of the 31st International Joint Conference on Artificial Intelligence (IJCAI 2022), pp. 2634–2640 (2022)
9. Hogan, A.: Canonical forms for isomorphic and equivalent RDF graphs: algorithms for leaning and labelling blank nodes. ACM Trans. Web **11**(4), 22:1–22:62 (2017)

---

[4] https://www.perspicuous-computing.science/.

[5] https://www.scads.de.

[6] https://secai.org.

[7] https://cfaed.tu-dresden.de.

10. Krötzsch, M.: Efficient rule-based inferencing for OWL EL. In: Proceedings of the 22nd International Joint Conference on Artificial Intelligence (IJCAI 2011), pp. 2668–2673. AAAI Press/IJCAI (2011)
11. Krötzsch, M.: Computing cores for existential rules with the standard chase and ASP. In: Calvanese, D., Erdem, E., Thielscher, M. (eds.) Proceedings 17th International Conference on Principles of Knowledge Representation and Reasoning (KR 2020), pp. 603–613. IJCAI (2020)
12. Krötzsch, M., Thost, V.: Ontologies for knowledge graphs: breaking the rules. In: ISWC 2016. LNCS, vol. 9981, pp. 376–392 (2016). Springer, Cham. https://doi.org/10.1007/978-3-319-46523-4_23
13. Motik, B., Cuenca Grau, B., Horrocks, I., Wu, Z., Fokoue, A., Lutz, C. (eds.) OWL 2 Web Ontology Language: Profiles. W3C Recommendation, 27 October 2009. http://www.w3.org/TR/owl2-profiles/
14. Vrandečić, D., Krötzsch, M.: Wikidata: A free collaborative knowledgebase. Commun. ACM **57**(10) (2014)

AI Ethics in the Semantic Web

Francesca Rossi

IBM Research, Yorktown Heights, NY, USA
Francesca.Rossi2@ibm.com

Abstract. AI is going to bring huge benefits in terms of scientific progress, human wellbeing, economic value, and the possibility of finding solutions to major social and environmental problems. Supported by AI, we will be able to make more grounded decisions and to focus on the main values and goals of a decision process rather than on routine and repetitive tasks. However, such a powerful technology also raises some concerns, related for example to the black-box nature of some AI approaches, the possible discriminatory decisions that AI algorithms may recommend, and the accountability and responsibility when an AI system is involved in an undesirable outcome. Also, since many successful AI techniques rely on huge amounts of data, it is important to know how data are handled by AI systems and by those who produce them. These concerns are among the obstacles that hold AI back or that cause worry for current AI users, adopters, and policy makers. Without answers to these questions, many will not trust AI, and therefore will not fully adopt it nor get its positive impact. In this talk I will present the main issues around AI ethics, some of the proposed technical and non-technical solutions, as well as practical actions and regulations being defined for AI development, deployment, and use. I will also highlight the relevance of some AI ethics issues to the Semantic Web.

Contents

Resources Track

In-Use Track

Research Track

Introducing Semantic Information for Numerical Attribute Prediction over Knowledge Graphs

Bingcong Xue[1], Yanzeng Li[1,2], and Lei Zou[1,2(✉)]

[1] Peking University, Beijing, China
{xuebingcong,zoulei}@pku.edu.cn, liyanzeng@stu.pku.edu.cn
[2] Beijing Institute for General Artificial Intelligence (BIGAI), Beijing, China

Abstract. Knowledge graph (KG) completion has been long studied on link prediction task to infer missing relations, while literals are paid less attention due to the non-discrete and rich-semantic challenges. Numerical attributes such as height, age and birthday are different from other literals that they can be calculated and estimated, thus have huge potential to be predicted and play important roles in a series of tasks. However, only a few researches have made preliminary attempts to predict numerical attributes on KGs with the help of the structural information or the development of embedding techniques. In this paper, we re-examine the numerical attribute prediction task over KGs, and introduce several novel methods to explore and utilize the rich semantic knowledge of language models (LMs) for this task. An effective combination strategy is also proposed to take full advantage of both structural and semantic information. Extensive experiments are conducted to show the great effectiveness of both the semantic methods and the combination strategy.

Keywords: Numerical attribute prediction · Knowledge graph completion · Language model · Ensemble learning

1 Introduction

Knowledge graphs (KGs) store structural data typically in the form of (subject, predicate, object) triples, and have become the backbone of various AI applications such as information retrieval, question answering and recommender systems. Some well known encyclopedia KGs include DBpedia [21], Yago [29] and Wikidata [43], devoting to covering as much factual knowledge as possible. As incompleteness is inherent in all KGs and largely restricts the effectiveness, knowledge graph completion is becoming a topic of extensive research, among which link prediction is the most concerned task and knowledge graph embedding (KGE) methods play an important role.

The core idea behind KGE techniques is to map nodes and edges of KGs into a low dimensional space. The learned representation can then be used to find missing links between entities in link prediction as well as other reasoning tasks.

U. Sattler et al. (Eds.): ISWC 2022, LNCS 13489, pp. 3–21, 2022.
https://doi.org/10.1007/978-3-031-19433-7_1

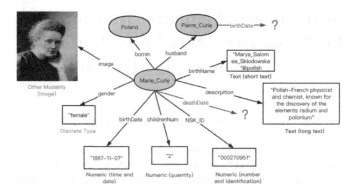

Fig. 1. A small part of a KG, where circles stand for entities and rectangles are literals. The colored text is to describe the different types of literals and the red ones are missing. (Color figure online)

According to the different mapping functions, they are roughly classified into tensor decomposition models, geometric models, and deep learning models [35]. Embedding-based methods have shown great potential in efficiently mining and analyzing on large-scale graphs, and are becoming the mainstream for knowledge graph completion task.

However, relationships among entities are not the only elements in KGs and knowledge graph completion should not be confined to just relations. For instance, various types of literal attributes also exist with rich semantics, and face the same incomplete issue. An example is depicted in Fig. 1, where an entity has not only relations with other entities, but also literal attributes in the form of text, numeric, image, etc., and all of them may be missing. In this paper, we focus on the prediction of numerical attributes over knowledge graphs, which we believe is valuable and potential but challenging as well. The motivations and intuitions are elaborated below.

1.1 Motivation

In this subsection we want to clarify our motivation by answering two questions: (1) why it is necessary to predict missing numerical attributes, and (2) why it is potential to do such a task.

1.1.1 Why do we want to predict numerical attributes? The importance of numerical attribute prediction lies in at least three aspects. Firstly, numerical attributes are widespread in KGs [39] to enrich entity characteristics from different perspectives, especially in cases of product graphs [5] and Internet of Things [12]. Like relational triplets to be completed in link prediction task, the prediction of numerical attributes itself is part of knowledge graph completion and quality management [51]. Secondly, though embedding methods have shown great potential in many reasoning tasks, traditional KGE techniques consider only relational edges and largely suffer from the sparsity problem. Introducing various literals is a powerful way to alleviate sparsity [13] and many recent researches [11,20,39,48] have shown the effectiveness to incorporate numerical attributes into the process of embedding learning. But the same incomplete problem of numerical attributes will limit the application [19]. Last but not least, numerical values can serve as the prediction targets in a chunk of standard machine learning tasks to distinguish the performance of relation representation [39], as well as language models [2,36] recently.

   1.1.2 Why can numerical attributes be predicted? Different from other literals, numerical value shows the uniqueness in its ability to be compared and calculated. It is usually meaningless to approximate attribute values like an actor's name or portrait, though [32] did some attempt to decode multimodal objects with auxiliary reference inputs. But numerical attributes can be estimated even if they are not explicitly mentioned [8]. The prediction can be derived from two sources: one is the relational structure and correlation of the graph, e.g., two entities with *spouse* relation tend to have similar ages, and the other is various language models that hopefully capture and store numerical and common sense in the large-scale pre-training processes. It is our basic foothold that both the explicit structural and the implicit semantic information can produce a marked effect and experiments in Sect. 4 have demonstrated this hypothesis.

1.2   Challenges and Opportunities

Numerical attributes are much more difficult to be predicted compared with relations. Unlike the in-KG entities that are within a limited set, the values of numerical attributes are typically non-discrete, leading to the fact that if we try to encode the values into vectors for the inference, we are very likely to face a serious sparsity problem. As [39] says, the literal attributes seem to cast KGs out of its comfort zone of a bounded space. Besides, rich semantics and dependencies are hidden in the literal values that we cannot treat them as simple relational triples. And the numerical characteristics require extra calculation and comparison capabilities. If we just reduce the literals into identifiers as entity nodes, most of the information will be lost [46].

   But at the same time, there are many opportunities. On the one hand, the continuous development of knowledge graph embedding techniques has shown impressive capacity for different reasoning tasks. And on the other hand, pre-trained language models (PLMs) are proved to have the potential to serve as alternative knowledge bases [31,33]. And efforts on numerical reasoning in the field of natural language processing [41,52] further enhance their ability to capture and store numerical and common sense knowledge. Both the structural information behind KGs and the implicit knowledge in PLMs are promising to play a role and the integration of these two kinds of resources is in the ascendant.

1.3 Contributions

In this paper, we re-examine the less-explored numerical attribute prediction task over knowledge graphs and introduce semantic information for it. The main contributions are summarized as follows:

- We provide several novel strategies to capture the implicit knowledge behind pre-trained language models for numerical attribute prediction over KGs. To the best of our knowledge, we are the first to do such a transfer from text to graph. Compared to traditional structural methods, this line of techniques are able to capture the semantics behind literals and keep stable in zero-shot scenes, which can serve as a powerful supplement.
- After an in-depth analysis on the applicability of graph- and semantic-based methods, we design an effective combination strategy to make full use of both structural and semantic information, where base models are automatically selected for different prediction targets to achieve the best performance.
- Based on rich experimental results, we demonstrate the great effectiveness of both the semantic methods and the combination strategy. Extensive ablation studies are also conducted to show the impact of different components.

2 Preliminaries

2.1 Problem Formalization

In this subsection, we formalize the numerical attribute prediction task over KGs by first defining several key terms.

Definition 1. Knowledge Graph, denoted as $G = (E, P, L)$, is a collection of structured facts typically in the form of *(subject, predicate, object)* triples $\subseteq E \times P \times (E \bigcup L)$, where E is a set of entities, P a set of predicates and L a set of literals. A fact whose object $\in E$ is called a **relational fact**, and the corresponding predicate is called a **relation**, while a fact with a literal object is called an **attributive fact** whose predicate is known as an **attribute**.

Definition 2. Types of Literals are first presented in [13]. Like those depicted in Fig. 1, they generally fall under four kinds: (1) **text literals** of *short text* like names and labels, and *long text* such as comments and descriptions, all of which may be expressed in multiple languages; (2) **numeric literals** that are encoded as integers, float and so on, e.g., height and date; (3) **discrete types** like occupation and class, which can also be regarded as entities in some KGs, and (4) **other modalities** including images, videos and etc.

Definition 3. Numerical Attributes are a specific type of attributes whose objects are numeric literals, or in other words, numbers. They can enrich entity features in terms of quantity (like height and population), time (like birthday) and identification (like phone number and zip code).

Problem Definition. The task of numerical attribute prediction over KGs is first explored in [39] and formalized in [19]. Compared with link prediction that is to complete a missing entity for a given relation and a corresponding entity, numerical attribute prediction aims to predict the numeric value of a given entity and a given attribute. The non-discrete numerical values make it intuitively more suitable to be regarded as a regression rather than a classification problem. The task is under the context of knowledge graphs, i.e., a KG composed of a set of relational and attributive facts is given. To avoid the interference of various types of literals, the attributive facts here are limited to numerical ones. And nominal attributes [40] like the identifications are filtered out as it is typically meaningless to predict such numeric identifiers but only brings noise.

More formally, given a group of relational facts and numerical attributive facts, the task is to predict the missing numerical attribute values for a batch of entities, where the attributes are appointed and limited to non-nominal ones.

2.2   Existing Graph-Based Methods

Three preliminary jobs [1,19,39] have been done to predict numerical attributes over KGs and they are all based solely on graph structures. We summarize these graph-based methods below.

GLOBAL and **LOCAL** are two natural baselines formalized in [19]. For each type of attribute, GLOBAL predicts the missing values by the average (or median) of all the known ones, for example, all missing values of *population* will be predicted equally as the average (or median) of all the known *population* values in a given KG. And similarly, LOCAL considers the average (or median) of the same known attributes in only the neighbor nodes, and thus could get different predictions for different entities.

MRAP [1] is based on the hypothesis that a numerical attribute of entity e_a can be estimated according to e_a's other attributes as well as the attributes of e_a's surrounding entities. For instance, the *birth year* of a man seems to have some correlations with his *death year* as well as his wife's *birth year*. The correlations are modeled as regression weights iteratively estimated from the known structures, which can also be seen as a message passing scheme.

The prediction of non-discrete attributes can also be regarded as a standard regression task, where regression classifiers are trained for each attribute with some input features of the entities. The learned representations of KGE models can play a role here, and we use **KGE-reg** to stand for such a method with the learned entity embeddings serving as the features, similar to those proposed in [19,39]. The details of different KGE features are talked in Sect. 4.

3   Our Methods

3.1   Limitations of Existing Methods

Existing graph-based methods mainly depend on the interaction of the relational structures of the graph, as well as the correlations among attributes.

They ignore the semantics behind numerical values and are usually incapable of handling unseen and isolated entities. GLOBAL treats all entities equally and generally cannot obtain valuable results; LOCAL distinguishes entities based on the neighborhood structures but the simple aggregation strategy is likely to be disturbed by irrelevant noise. MRAP considers the complex interactions among various attributes and relations, which is prone to sparsity and skewness when there is a surge in the predicates number. And the message passing scheme is unfriendly to isolated entities. KGE-reg benefits from the development of various KGE methods. However, these embedding techniques are quite sensitive to the large hyper-parameter space and training strategies [4]. Though some works have published their training results, they are not always available and retraining is needed for new datasets. Also, we cannot expect to obtain good prediction results for those unseen entities during the training processes. And intuitively, not all attributes can be inferred solely from the graph structures, like the *population* of a country, which demands for some common sense and memory.

3.2   Semantic-Based Methods

We believe different types of language models, such as Bert [9], have captured and stored rich knowledge during the large-scale pre-training processes, which have been demonstrated in various natural language processing tasks. We propose semantic-based methods here to introduce the implicit semantic information of PLMs to predict missing attributes. And to better use them for our scene, we should solve two main problems: (1) how to apply them to the context of graphs, and (2) how to fully extract and utilize the implicit semantic knowledge, especially about the numerics.

Transfer for Graphs. For the first problem, we use a simple but general way to transform KG triples into meaningful texts. For a relational fact (s, p, o) in a knowledge graph, the relation predicate is converted to a natural language segment by published paraphrase dictionaries [50] or by simple heuristic rules (e.g., the predicate *happenedOnDate* is split to *happened on date*). Entities are changed from their identifications to names, and sometimes to descriptions for more semantics. Similar way runs on attributive facts, except that literal values are reserved as what they are.

Two Paradigms. For the second problem, we propose two different paradigms. The first one refers to one of the classical pre-training tasks called masked language modeling, also known as a fill-mask task. That is to say, we can change an attributive triple to be predicted into a sentence as mentioned above, leaving the missing numerical value as a masked token, which is then input to a pre-trained language model to predict a masked word. The output word is restricted to the numerical vocabulary of the model here. It actually degenerates the non-discrete numerical prediction task into a classification problem on finite digital

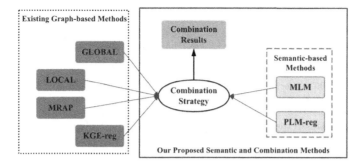

Fig. 2. Methods used in this work. The left four are based on graphs, and the right two on semantics, all of which can serve as the input to get the combination results.

tokens, and the models have no idea with the numbers, but to be tested on the implicit memory and classification abilities. And to enhance the performance of the models on specific domain tasks, fine-tuning and prompt [23] are two helpful learning techniques. The former injects domain knowledge into the model parameters, and the latter into the probe missions, which are exactly the input sentences in our task. The term **MLM** is used throughout this paper to refer to such a prediction method like cloze test, and MLM-tuning and MLM-prompt are for the two enhancement technologies respectively.

The second paradigm similar to KGE-reg, which we call **PLM-reg**, also trains attribute-specific regression classifiers for different attributes. And the difference lies in the input features, which are obtained with the help of the encoding abilities of pre-trained language models for rich semantics. We have attempted to input entity names and descriptions into PLMs and received different results, see the experimental parts for more details.

Semantic-based methods are hopeful to obtain valuable results for any input entity. And with the rapid and continuous development of language models, the ability to capture numerical semantics and predict missing values of such methods can keep growing. But all the results tend to be influenced by the paraphrasing patterns and we actually don't know exactly what the PLMs really know. Morever, MLM is limited to a fixed vocabulary and PLM-reg needs some extra resources like entity names and descriptions.

3.3   Combination Strategy

Both the graph- and semantic-based methods have some strengths and weaknesses. And a combination procedure is capable to achieve better results, where both the explicit structural and the implicit semantic knowledge are working.

As depicted in Fig. 2, we now have four graph-based methods and two semantic-based methods, which can be regarded as different base learners in the idea of ensemble learning [10]. Different models may be good at different numerical attributes, and when we put them together, the advantages of various methods can be brought into full play. We propose three combination strategies **Mean**, **Median** and **Best** respectively. In the Mean and Median strategies,

Table 1. Statistics of the datasets.

	# Ent	# Rel	# Rel_fact	# Attr	# Attr_fact	# Train	# Valid	# Test
FB15K	14,951	1,345	592,213	116	29,395	23,516	2,939	2,940
YAGO15K	15,404	32	122,886	7	23,532[a]	18,825	2,353	2,354

[a] There are 48,406 numerical facts at https://github.com/mniepert/mmkb for YAGO15K, and 23,532 are the actually left ones after removing duplicates.

Table 2. Quantities of the focused attributes following [1,19]. The upper block includes numerical attributes about time and the lower one contains all others. A dash (-) indicates that the corresponding attribute is not in the dataset.

	FB15K			YAGO15K		
	# Train	# Valid	# Test	# Train	# Valid	# Test
date_of_birth	3,528	425	475	6,555	826	837
date_of_death	988	117	115	1,490	163	169
film_release	1,479	204	184	-	-	-
organization_founded	988	126	123	-	-	-
location_founded	737	103	83	-	-	-
date_created	-	-	-	5,244	693	651
date_destroyed	-	-	-	425	55	58
date_happened	-	-	-	311	41	36
latitude	2,545	317	349	2,401	279	309
longitude	2,614	292	302	2,399	296	294
area	1,741	204	221	-	-	-
population	1,532	199	199	-	-	-
height	2,309	305	257	-	-	-
weight	182	20	24	-	-	-

the combination results are obtained as the mean and median predictions of all base models. As for the Best strategy, each attribute will choose the prediction results of the best model for it, which is measured based on the validation results. These are all model-level combination strategies, and we leave more fine-grained schemes in the future work.

4 Experiments

4.1 Experimental Setup

Datasets. We use two benchmark datasets: FB15K and YAGO15K, where the relational and numerical triples are all from MMKG [24]. We randomly divide the numerical facts into an 80/10/10 split of train/valid/test and the statistics are shown in Table 1. We follow [1,19] to focus on 11 and 7 major attributes of FB15K and YAGO15K respectively and the quantities are listed in Table 2.

Metrics. We adopt three evaluation metrics widely used in similar tasks to assess the performance: MAE (Mean Absolute Error), RMSE (Root Mean Square Error) and R^2 (R Squared), which are defined as follows:

$$MAE(y, \hat{y}) = \frac{1}{n} \sum_{i=1}^{n} |y_i - \hat{y}_i| \tag{1}$$

$$RMSE(y, \hat{y}) = \sqrt{\frac{1}{n} \sum_{i=1}^{n} (y_i - \hat{y}_i)^2} \tag{2}$$

$$R^2(y, \hat{y}) = 1 - \frac{\sum_{i=1}^{n} (y_i - \hat{y}_i)^2}{\sum_{i=1}^{n} (y_i - \overline{y})^2} \tag{3}$$

where n is the sample size, y_i the ground truth of the i-th sample, $\hat{y}_i$ the predicated one and $\overline{y}$ the mean of all y values. The metrics are calculated on each type of attribute, and when evaluated on the whole, we introduce the calculation thought of micro- and macro- from the F1 metric, where the former gives the same weight to each sample and the latter to each category. MAE and RMSE reflect the deviation degree from the predictions to the true values, where smaller scores mean better. R^2 represents the proportion of variance that has been explained by the independent variables in the model and is a measure of how well unseen samples are likely to be predicted. The best possible score for R^2 is 1.0 and negative values imply the model fits much worse.

Implementation Details. As shown in Fig. 2, the methods to be compared generally fall under three headings: graph-based, semantic-based, and combination ways. For all the methods, the performances are evaluated on the test set and the validation set is used for hyper-parameters and model selection. The implementations of GLOBAL, LOCAL and MRAP methods refer to MRAP[1]. For both KGE-reg and PLM-reg, we choose three classical regression models, namely linear, ridge and lasso, from scikit-learn [28], with the complexity parameter α among [0.1, 1.0, 10.0]. We use the published KGE embeddings from LibKGE [4] and PLM models from Transformers [47], where TransE[2] and bert-base-uncased[3] are the default respectively and more other models are experimented in Sect. 4.3. The fine-tuning parameters of MLM-tuning are set by reference to [2], with a batch-size of 32 for 10 epochs and two learning rates $\{3e^{-5}, 1e^{-2}\}$, and we found empirically that more epochs would not bring further improvement. Besides, the name and description texts of FB15K entities are from DKRL [49], and the lack resources for YAGO15K are supplemented by aligning to FB15K entities according to the published sameAs links[4]. Experiments are all conducted on a

---

[1] https://github.com/bayrameda/MrAP.
[2] http://web.informatik.uni-mannheim.de/pi1/iclr2020-models/fb15k-237-transe.pt.
[3] https://huggingface.co/bert-base-uncased.
[4] https://github.com/nle-ml/mmkb/blob/master/YAGO15K/.

Linux machine with two NVIDIA Tesla P100 GPUs. We make all our datasets and implementations publicly available[5].

Table 3. Main results of different methods. For each dataset, the three blocks top to bottom contain graph-based, semantic-based and combination methods respectively. Best results in each block are underlined and the best ones of all methods are in boldface. Text in parentheses behind *PLM-reg* indicates the type of inputs to PLMs.

	Methods	micro-			macro-		
		MAE ↓	RMSE ↓	R^2 ↑	MAE ↓	RMSE ↓	R^2 ↑
FB15K[a]	GLOBAL	35.7281	85.5691	−0.0031	46.8625	114.6660	−0.0061
	LOCAL	21.8207	90.9444	0.3755	37.5387	138.3979	0.1270
	MRAP	17.5514	81.9242	−6.9458	30.9281	118.6432	−5.9687
	KGE-reg	28.2156	70.6051	0.4492	41.4302	99.8194	0.3773
	MLM	312.6412	698.1551	−772.3746	265.0596	625.1898	−502.4600
	MLM-tuning	32.1816	78.7322	−0.3053	35.4254	94.1896	−0.1929
	PLM-reg (name)	28.6963	73.3825	0.2947	40.9169	101.8967	0.2481
	PLM-reg (desc)	22.5595	55.8076	0.6072	33.3209	80.5485	0.5647
	Combination_Mean	19.8698	54.3243	0.3508	29.4875	78.9829	0.3188
	Combination_Median	16.0400	**51.4285**	**0.6591**	26.1637	**76.7629**	**0.5729**
	Combination_Best	**12.7935**	53.0444	0.6267	**21.3944**	78.9087	0.5717
YAGO15K	GLOBAL	49.5822	102.8896	−0.0045	49.0409	100.5088	−0.0157
	LOCAL	56.4510	123.1791	0.1312	47.9265	104.5093	0.1999
	MRAP	31.5875	86.7825	0.4539	33.1130	89.2587	0.0045
	KGE-reg	36.9135	87.7188	0.3423	37.6362	86.6269	0.3398
	MLM	187.0013	496.7505	−749.3612	217.3499	563.1464	−821.1300
	MLM-tuning	36.8188	93.1231	0.0596	34.2217	80.9421	0.1579
	PLM-reg (name)	37.9548	89.5944	0.2997	37.2637	88.0866	0.3060
	PLM-reg (desc)	32.4495	81.3838	0.4894	33.1313	80.0946	0.4755
	Combination_Mean	28.8185	**76.3485**	**0.5699**	28.4325	**68.3501**	0.6087
	Combination_Median	26.2166	79.9005	0.5445	25.2935	75.1677	0.5937
	Combination_Best	**25.2432**	82.8491	0.5218	**21.1966**	69.3299	**0.6584**

[a] Experiments show that the results of two attributes, *area* and *population*, vary largely with others. To have a better overview here, we omit these two attributes in the micro- and macro- metrics. And the detailed results can be found in Sect. 4.4.

4.2 Main Results

Table 3 reports the results of different methods for the two datasets, from which we can get the following observations. Firstly, for graph-based methods, MRAP and KGE-reg generally outperform GLOBAL and LOCAL in almost all metrics, showing the learning processes for both the interaction weights and the graph embeddings have capture valuable information for numerical attribute prediction. MRAP performs quite good on the MAE metrics, but when it comes to RMSE and R^2, it often loses to KGE-reg.

---

[5] https://github.com/xbc0112/NumericalPrediction.

Secondly, we can observe that, PLM-reg with entity descriptions consistently achieves the best results on both datasets and all metrics in semantic-based methods. And it also has comparable or better performances with the optimal results of graph-based methods, demonstrating the huge potential of language models for this task. The advantages will be more prominent in zero-shot scenes, since the PLMs can output stable results for any input, while other means are vulnerable to unseen or isolated entities. It is not surprising that the pure MLM performs much worse than all other methods, where it makes use of nothing but the memory of the model to classify on a limited numeric vocabulary, having no idea with the numbers as well as the input dataset. But we also find that when we just fine-tune the PLMs with the known attributes, the performances are significantly improved to be comparable with KGE-reg, which again proves that the PLMs are quite helpful and appropriate ways to extract the implicit knowledge matter much. Morever, in the implementation of PLM-reg, using descriptions brings a further performance improvement compared with the entity names, which conforms to the basic cognition that PLMs are good at capturing information from contextual texts and longer descriptions function better.

Table 4. Ablation results on KGE models for KGE-reg.

	Link Prediction			FB15K		YAGO15K	
	MRR↑	Hits@1↑	Hits@10↑	micro-MAE↓	macro-MAE↓	micro-MAE↓	macro-MAE↓
Random	-	-	-	36.3266	48.4124	49.6527	49.6824
TransE	0.313	0.221	0.497	28.2156	41.4302	36.9135	**37.6362**
RESCAL	**0.356**	**0.263**	**0.541**	28.4982	41.7494	38.7561	41.5883
ComplEx	0.348	0.253	0.536	26.4450	37.9365	38.5046	39.2547
RotatE	0.333	0.240	0.522	**25.5822**	**36.7313**	**36.3934**	37.7898

Finally, the experimental results fully reflect the great advantages of the combination methods. The combinations are conducted by excluding the three austere baselines (GLOBAL, LOCAL and MLM) and the Best selection strategy is measured on the MAE metrics. From Table 3 we can see that all of the three combination strategies greatly improve the performances on all metrics, and the Best strategy is generally the top performer, with the MAE a 20+% and a 30+% improvement on micro- and macro- metrics respectively. And similarly, if we choose the best model according to the RMSE or R^2, we could get further improvements on these metrics as well.

In general, the main results have demonstrated that the semantic-based methods are quite promising to predict numerical attributes over KGs and effective combination strategies making use of both structural and semantic knowledge can significantly improve the performances, which confirm our original motivation and the efficacy of our methods.

4.3   Ablation Study

In this subsection we conduct several ablation studies to explore the impact that the different variants of each module have on the performances, including KGE models, language models, fine-tuning parameters and description texts.

Ablation on KGE Models. Four popular KGE techniques in link prediction are chosen here for KGE-reg, namely, TransE [3], RESCAL [27], ComplEx [42] and RotatE [38]. We use the published models for FB15K from LibKGE and YAGO15K entities are mapped by the SameAs links. The official link prediction results from LibKGE as well as our KGE-reg results for two datasets are listed in Table 4, where we use Random to represent the method with random embeddings. From Table 4 we can see that the results of link prediction and numerical attribute prediction vary among different models and datasets. Though RESCAL performs best on link prediction, its performance on our task is off. At the same time, TransE and RotatE have some satisfactory results on numerical attribute predication but they are inconsistent on the two datasets. This indicates that KGE models may also lose some useful information when just focusing on certain tasks and capabilities, and numeric prediction can serve as an additional assessment, as we have talked in Sect. 1.1.1.

Table 5. Ablation results on language models for MLM.

		b-base	b-large	r-base	r-large	x-base	x-large	numBert
FB15K	micro-MAE↓	312.64	**106.87**	593.10	730.29	889.76	320.48	1,158.64
	macro-MAE↓	265.06	**101.81**	853.13	802.97	947.71	416.67	968.25
YAGO15K	micro-MAE↓	187.00	**180.26**	820.10	1,048.00	1,387.61	688.65	1,069.85
	macro-MAE↓	217.35	**134.10**	896.16	1,035.58	1,321.77	473.88	944.27

Table 6. Ablation results on fine-tuning parameters for MLM-tuning.

	FB15K		YAGO15K	
	micro-MAE↓	macro-MAE↓	micro-MAE↓	macro-MAE↓
No tuning	312.6412	265.0596	187.0013	217.3499
lr=3e−5	**32.1816**	**35.4254**	**36.8188**	**34.2217**
lr=1e−2	1,008.2838	1,081.8034	1,454.5918	1,408.1344

Table 7. Ablation results on multilingual description texts for PLM-reg. (E, F, G are English, French and German for short.)

	E	F	G	E+F	E+G	F+G	E+F+G
micro-MAE↓	22.4099	25.5759	26.0673	22.4126	**21.7161**	24.5054	22.1151
macro-MAE↓	33.5482	35.8706	37.5044	32.9257	**32.2438**	35.4397	32.6784

Ablation on Language Models. We explore the MLM results with various pre-trained language models here, including bert-base/large-uncased [9], roberta-base/large [25], xlm-roberta-base/large [7], and numBert [52]. As shown in Table 5, bert-large-uncased performs best on the two datasets, but the results are still far from satisfactory. And other carefully decorated variants of Bert even produce much worse results, which again illustrates that a pure MLM is not suitable for this task at all.

Ablation on Fine-Tuning Parameters. The impact of fine-tuning parameters (specifically learning rate here) is shown in Table 6. We can see that fine-tuning pre-trained language models with appropriate parameters will significantly improve the numerical prediction results, but on the contrary, poor configurations may bring negative effects. This reveals an inherent defect of PLM-tuning that the parameters can be difficult to choose.

Table 8. Fine-grained MAE results of five methods and the chosen model according to the Best strategy on FB15K. The numbers in bold indicate the best among all methods.

	MRAP	KGE-reg	MLM-tuning	PLM-reg(name)	PLM-reg(desc)	Best Model
date_of_birth	**13.7524**	27.0335	17.8177	28.0877	25.0356	MRAP
date_of_death	**14.1559**	67.0116	22.8152	59.8208	46.8587	MRAP
film_release	5.5087	5.0874	14.3519	11.8329	**4.9622**	PLM-reg (desc)
organization_founded	73.7679	55.7411	**39.5332**	46.5200	46.9082	PLM-reg (desc)
location_founded	152.4245	172.2755	**100.1074**	172.2287	144.9887	MLM-tuning
latitude	**2.2707**	9.7633	5.9728	8.8821	5.6201	MRAP
longitude	**4.8890**	25.1610	106.7638	29.9472	16.2546	MRAP
area	3.01e+6	2.37e+6	**5.77e+5**	1.80e+6	1.54e+6	MLM-tuning
population	1.05e+7	2.22e+7	**4.43e+6**	8.52e+6	1.57e+7	MLM-tuning
height	0.4836	0.1916	**0.1263**	0.1967	0.1881	MLM-tuning
weight	11.1000	10.6064	11.3400	10.7358	**9.0717**	PLM-reg (desc)

Ablation on Description Texts. Gesese et al. [14] have explored the benefits of multilingual descriptions for link prediction, and here we use their trilingual datasets as well as the combinations for PLM-reg (desc) on FB15K. The results are listed in Table 7, by which we can generally conclude that combining multilingual descriptions as the input for PLM-reg is promising to improve the performance but the improvement is not quite significant.

4.4 Case Study

We now start a fine-grained analysis on the performances of the methods over different attributes. The MAE results on FB15K of the five models used in the combination method are listed in Table 8, where the last column is the chosen model of the Best strategy. We can observe that the chosen model for each attribute except *organization_founded* exactly has the best performance among the methods, showing the effectiveness of the selection strategy. By looking into the bold numbers and the best models, it appears that only three methods, i.e., MRAP, MLM-tuning, and PLM-reg (desc), are actually dominant in some attributes and play a role in the combination process, where only the first one is graph-based and the others are semantic-based. This can serve as additional evidence to demonstrate the potential of the semantic methods from the fine-grained aspect.

And a more interesting finding comes when we analyze the relations associated with each attribute. We find that the attributes benefit most from the graph-based methods, such as *latitude* and *longitude*, typically have strong relations making the value derivation from the graph structures possible. A practical example is that many entities with *latitude* often have the relation *isLocatedIn* with other entities that they typically have similar *latitude* values. While other attributes, like the *height* of a person, intuitively have little to do with the graph structures, but are probably contained in the common sense knowledge behind the language models, as people's heights are actually in a small range. This observation partly explains why both structural and semantic information can play a role in the numerical attribute prediction task. And on the other hand, it inspires that we may obtain useful rules from the performance differences of the two paradigms. For instance, we may get an inference rule that *if A is located in B, then A's latitude is similar to B* here. Rule discovery is an important research problem and we will explore it further in the future.

5   Related Work

Numerical Attributes on Knowledge Graphs. Up to now, three works in total have paid attention to predicting numerical attributes over KGs. Tay et al. [39] use the learned embeddings of relational representation approaches as features to train attribute-specific regression models. It is the first to treat non-discrete numeric values as a prediction target and evaluate the performance of different models by the task of attribute value prediction. They also design a novel multi-task neural network to jointly learn from relational and numerical attribute information and experiments show that these two kinds of information are complementary to each other. The work [19] formalizes the numerical attribute prediction problem with the Global and Local baselines, and leverages knowledge graph embedding vectors in a linear regression model to get a better performance. And recently MRAP [1], a multi-relational attribute propagation algorithm in the message passing scheme, is proposed to impute missing numerical values by the learned regression model depending on the graph structure and known attributes. These works are pioneers for numerical attribute prediction over KGs and are regarded as baselines in our experiments. However, all of them focus only on the graph structures and ignore rich semantic information under numeric attributes or external resources like PLMs, and thus have a poor performance, especially in cases of unseen and isolated entities.

Another research line concerns the use of numerical attributes for representation learning [11,20,48]. For example, LiteralE [20] extends existing latent feature models with learnable parameters to incorporate numeric literals into entity embeddings, and gets performance gains in several link prediction benchmarks. These works show the utility of numerical attributes for KGE techniques, which facilitate one of our motivations to predict missing numerics.

Numerical Reasoning in Text Context. Several research topics about numerical prediction and reasoning are thriving in the field of natural language processing in recent days. One line parallel with our task is to predict missing numbers in the context of text. An early work [16] adopts Word2vec embeddings [26] of entity names as input features to regression models for number prediction. Recent empirical investigations [2,37] devote to explore the effectiveness of different combinations of various encoders and regression models. Masked numeral predication task is also used to evaluate language models' ability to capture and memorize numerical knowledge [36,52]. These methods can not be directly applied to numerical prediction over KGs and some effective ways are needed to realize the transfer, which is one of our contributions.

Some probing work has noticed the limitations of existing pre-trained language models on numerical reasoning [34,44] and then several attempts follow to inject such skills into the models by different pre-training or fine-tuning patterns, such as numBert [52], genBert [15] and numGPT [17], which can be regarded as substitutions of the basic Bert model and hopeful to further improve the performance of our method.

PLM and KG. As two major sources of knowledge playing significant roles in a series of AI applications, pre-trained language models and knowledge graphs are recently considered to be complementary to each other and can sometimes work together. On the one hand, pre-trained language models have shown potential to serve as substitute for explicit knowledge bases [31,33] or improve the performance of knowledge representation [53]. And on the other hand, some work [6,30] tries to integrate structured knowledge of KGs into current language models for better interpretability. Combining both explicit and implicit knowledge also shows advantages in tasks like recommender systems [22] and graph completion [18,45]. We are the first to explore such intergation on numerical attribute prediction and experimental results demonstrate the effectiveness of our combination strategy.

6   Conclusion and Future Work

In this paper, we focus on the prediction of numerical attributes over knowledge graphs and devote to introducing semantic information for it. Several novel semantic methods as well as effective combination strategies are proposed, and extensive experiments have shown that both the explicit structural knowledge and the implicit semantic information can help the prediction and an effective combination is of great potential.

Several interesting directions are left for the future. First, we plan to take a deep look at the paraphrase method when converting KG triples into texts, and attempt other paradigms for the use of PLMs, such as prompt. Second, fine-grained combination strategies and the value of numerical attributes on other tasks can be further explored. Last but not least, rule discovery by the compare between PLM and KG seems quite promising.

Supplemental Material Statement: Source code, datasets and results are all available at https://github.com/xbc0112/NumericalPrediction.

Acknowledgments. This work was supported by NSFC under grant 61932001, U20A20174.

References

1. Bayram, E., García-Durán, A., West, R.: Node attribute completion in knowledge graphs with multi-relational propagation. In: ICASSP 2021–2021 IEEE International Conference on Acoustics, Speech and Signal Processing (ICASSP), pp. 3590–3594. IEEE (2021)
2. Berg-Kirkpatrick, T., Spokoyny, D.: An empirical investigation of contextualized number prediction. In: Proceedings of the 2020 Conference on Empirical Methods in Natural Language Processing (EMNLP), pp. 4754–4764 (2020)
3. Bordes, A., Usunier, N., Garcia-Duran, A., Weston, J., Yakhnenko, O.: Translating embeddings for modeling multi-relational data. In: Advances in Neural Information Processing Systems, vol. 26 (2013)
4. Broscheit, S., Ruffinelli, D., Kochsiek, A., Betz, P., Gemulla, R.: LibKGE - A knowledge graph embedding library for reproducible research. In: Proceedings of the 2020 Conference on Empirical Methods in Natural Language Processing: System Demonstrations, pp. 165–174 (2020). https://www.aclweb.org/anthology/2020.emnlp-demos.22
5. Cheng, K., Li, X., Xu, Y.E., Dong, X.L., Sun, Y.: Pge: Robust product graph embedding learning for error detection. arXiv preprint arXiv:2202.09747 (2022)
6. Colon-Hernandez, P., Havasi, C., Alonso, J., Huggins, M., Breazeal, C.: Combining pre-trained language models and structured knowledge. arXiv preprint arXiv:2101.12294 (2021)
7. Conneau, A., et al.: Unsupervised cross-lingual representation learning at scale. arXiv preprint arXiv:1911.02116 (2019)
8. Davidov, D., Rappoport, A.: Extraction and approximation of numerical attributes from the web. In: Proceedings of the 48th Annual Meeting of the Association for Computational Linguistics, pp. 1308–1317 (2010)
9. Devlin, J., Chang, M.W., Lee, K., Toutanova, K.: Bert: Pre-training of deep bidirectional transformers for language understanding. arXiv preprint arXiv:1810.04805 (2018)
10. Dong, X., Yu, Z., Cao, W., Shi, Y., Ma, Q.: A survey on ensemble learning. Front. Comput. Sci. **14**(2), 241–258 (2019). https://doi.org/10.1007/s11704-019-8208-z
11. García-Durán, A., Niepert, M.: KBLRN: End-to-end learning of knowledge base representations with latent, relational, and numerical features. arXiv preprint arXiv:1709.04676 (2017)

12. Gesese, G.A.: Leveraging literals for knowledge graph embeddings. In: Proceedings of the Doctoral Consortium at ISWC 2021, co-located with 20th International Semantic Web Conference (ISWC 2021), Ed.: V. Tamma. p. 9 (2021)
13. Gesese, G.A., Biswas, R., Alam, M., Sack, H.: A survey on knowledge graph embeddings with literals: which model links better literal-ly? Semantic Web **12**(4), 617–647 (2021)
14. Gesese, G.A., Hoppe, F., Alam, M., Sack, H.: Leveraging multilingual descriptions for link prediction: Initial experiments. In: ISWC (Demos/Industry) (2020)
15. Geva, M., Gupta, A., Berant, J.: Injecting numerical reasoning skills into language models. arXiv preprint arXiv:2004.04487 (2020)
16. Gupta, A., Boleda, G., Baroni, M., Padó, S.: Distributional vectors encode referential attributes. In: Proceedings of the 2015 Conference on Empirical Methods in Natural Language Processing, pp. 12–21 (2015)
17. Jin, Z., et al.: NumGPT: Improving numeracy ability of generative pre-trained models. arXiv preprint arXiv:2109.03137 (2021)
18. Kim, B., Hong, T., Ko, Y., Seo, J.: Multi-task learning for knowledge graph completion with pre-trained language models. In: Proceedings of the 28th International Conference on Computational Linguistics, pp. 1737–1743 (2020)
19. Kotnis, B., García-Durán, A.: Learning numerical attributes in knowledge bases. In: Automated Knowledge Base Construction (AKBC) (2018)
20. Kristiadi, A., Khan, M.A., Lukovnikov, D., Lehmann, J., Fischer, A.: Incorporating literals into knowledge graph embeddings. In: Ghidni, C. (ed.) ISWC 2019. LNCS, vol. 11778, pp. 347–363. Springer, Cham (2019). https://doi.org/10.1007/978-3-030-30793-6_20
21. Lehmann, J., et al.: Dbpedia-a large-scale, multilingual knowledge base extracted from wikipedia. Semantic web **6**(2), 167–195 (2015)
22. Lian, J., Zhou, X., Zhang, F., Chen, Z., Xie, X., Sun, G.: xDeepFM: Combining explicit and implicit feature interactions for recommender systems. In: Proceedings of the 24th ACM SIGKDD international conference on knowledge discovery & data mining, pp. 1754–1763 (2018)
23. Liu, P., Yuan, W., Fu, J., Jiang, Z., Hayashi, H., Neubig, G.: Pre-train, prompt, and predict: A systematic survey of prompting methods in natural language processing. arXiv preprint arXiv:2107.13586 (2021)
24. Liu, Y., Li, H., Garcia-Duran, A., Niepert, M., Onoro-Rubio, D., Rosenblum, D.S.: MMKG: multi-modal knowledge graphs. In: Hitzler, P., Fernández, M., Janowicz, K., Zaveri, A., Gray, A.J.G., Lopez, V., Haller, A., Hammar, K. (eds.) ESWC 2019. LNCS, vol. 11503, pp. 459–474. Springer, Cham (2019). https://doi.org/10.1007/978-3-030-21348-0_30
25. Liu, Y., et al.: Roberta: A robustly optimized bert pretraining approach. arXiv preprint arXiv:1907.11692 (2019)
26. Mikolov, T., Chen, K., Corrado, G., Dean, J.: Efficient estimation of word representations in vector space. arXiv preprint arXiv:1301.3781 (2013)
27. Nickel, M., Tresp, V., Kriegel, H.P.: A three-way model for collective learning on multi-relational data. In: Icml (2011)
28. Pedregosa, F., et al.: Scikit-learn: machine learning in Python. J. Mach. Learn. Res. **12**, 2825–2830 (2011)
29. Pellissier Tanon, T., Weikum, G., Suchanek, F.: YAGO 4: a reason-able knowledge base. In: Harth, A., Kirrane, S., Ngonga Ngomo, A.-C., Paulheim, H., Rula, A., Gentile, A.L., Haase, P., Cochez, M. (eds.) ESWC 2020. LNCS, vol. 12123, pp. 583–596. Springer, Cham (2020). https://doi.org/10.1007/978-3-030-49461-2_34

30. Peters, M.E., Neumann, M., Logan IV, R.L., Schwartz, R., Joshi, V., Singh, S., Smith, N.A.: Knowledge enhanced contextual word representations. arXiv preprint arXiv:1909.04164 (2019)
31. Petroni, F., Rocktäschel, T., Lewis, P., Bakhtin, A., Wu, Y., Miller, A.H., Riedel, S.: Language models as knowledge bases? arXiv preprint arXiv:1909.01066 (2019)
32. Pezeshkpour, P., Chen, L., Singh, S.: Embedding multimodal relational data for knowledge base completion. arXiv preprint arXiv:1809.01341 (2018)
33. Roberts, A., Raffel, C., Shazeer, N.: How much knowledge can you pack into the parameters of a language model? arXiv preprint arXiv:2002.08910 (2020)
34. Rogers, A., Kovaleva, O., Rumshisky, A.: A primer in BERTology: What we know about how BERT works. Trans. Assoc. Comput. Linguist. **8**, 842–866 (2020)
35. Rossi, A., Barbosa, D., Firmani, D., Matinata, A., Merialdo, P.: Knowledge graph embedding for link prediction: a comparative analysis. ACM Trans. Knowl. Discovery Data (TKDD) **15**(2), 1–49 (2021)
36. Sakamoto, T., Aizawa, A.: Predicting numerals in natural language text using a language model considering the quantitative aspects of numerals. In: Proceedings of Deep Learning Inside Out (DeeLIO): The 2nd Workshop on Knowledge Extraction and Integration for Deep Learning Architectures, pp. 140–150 (2021)
37. Spithourakis, G.P., Riedel, S.: Numeracy for language models: Evaluating and improving their ability to predict numbers. arXiv preprint arXiv:1805.08154 (2018)
38. Sun, Z., Deng, Z.H., Nie, J.Y., Tang, J.: Rotate: Knowledge graph embedding by relational rotation in complex space. arXiv preprint arXiv:1902.10197 (2019)
39. Tay, Y., Tuan, L.A., Phan, M.C., Hui, S.C.: Multi-task neural network for non-discrete attribute prediction in knowledge graphs. In: Proceedings of the 2017 ACM on Conference on Information and Knowledge Management, pp. 1029–1038 (2017)
40. Thawani, A., Pujara, J., Ilievski, F.: Numeracy enhances the literacy of language models. In: Proceedings of the 2021 Conference on Empirical Methods in Natural Language Processing, pp. 6960–6967 (2021)
41. Thawani, A., Pujara, J., Szekely, P.A., Ilievski, F.: Representing numbers in nlp: a survey and a vision. arXiv preprint arXiv:2103.13136 (2021)
42. Trouillon, T., Welbl, J., Riedel, S., Gaussier, É., Bouchard, G.: Complex embeddings for simple link prediction. In: International conference on machine learning, pp. 2071–2080. PMLR (2016)
43. Vrandečić, D., Krötzsch, M.: Wikidata: a free collaborative knowledgebase. Commun. ACM **57**(10), 78–85 (2014)
44. Wallace, E., Wang, Y., Li, S., Singh, S., Gardner, M.: Do nlp models know numbers? probing numeracy in embeddings. arXiv preprint arXiv:1909.07940 (2019)
45. Wang, L., Zhao, W., Wei, Z., Liu, J.: SimKGC: Simple contrastive knowledge graph completion with pre-trained language models. arXiv preprint arXiv:2203.02167 (2022)
46. Wilcke, X., Bloem, P., de Boer, V., van't Veer, R.: End-to-end learning on multimodal knowledge graphs (2021)
47. Wolf, T., et al.: Transformers: State-of-the-art natural language processing. In: Proceedings of the 2020 conference on empirical methods in natural language processing: system demonstrations, pp. 38–45 (2020)
48. Wu, Y., Wang, Z.: Knowledge graph embedding with numeric attributes of entities. In: Proceedings of The Third Workshop on Representation Learning for NLP, pp. 132–136 (2018)
49. Xie, R., Liu, Z., Jia, J., Luan, H., Sun, M.: Representation learning of knowledge graphs with entity descriptions. In: Proceedings of the AAAI Conference on Artificial Intelligence, vol. 30 (2016)

50. Xue, B., Hu, S., Zou, L., Cheng, J.: The value of paraphrase for knowledge base predicates. In: Proceedings of the AAAI Conference on Artificial Intelligence, vol. 34, pp. 9346–9353 (2020)
51. Xue, B., Zou, L.: Knowledge graph quality management: a comprehensive survey. In: IEEE Transactions on Knowledge and Data Engineering (2022)
52. Zhang, X., Ramachandran, D., Tenney, I., Elazar, Y., Roth, D.: Do language embeddings capture scales? arXiv preprint arXiv:2010.05345 (2020)
53. Zhang, Z., Liu, X., Zhang, Y., Su, Q., Sun, X., He, B.: Pretrain-KGE: learning knowledge representation from pretrained language models. In: Findings of the Association for Computational Linguistics: EMNLP 2020, pp. 259–266 (2020)

Faithful Embeddings for $\mathcal{EL}^{++}$ Knowledge Bases

Bo Xiong[1(✉)], Nico Potyka[2], Trung-Kien Tran[3], Mojtaba Nayyeri[1],
and Steffen Staab[1,4]

[1] University of Stuttgart, Stuttgart, Germany
{bo.xiong,mojtaba.nayyeri,steffen.staab}@ipvs.uni-stuttgart.de
[2] Imperial College London, London, UK
n.potyka@imperial.ac.uk
[3] Bosch Center for Artificial Intelligence, Renningen, Germany
trungkien.tran@de.bosch.com
[4] University of Southampton, Southampton, UK

Abstract. Recently, increasing efforts are put into learning continual representations for symbolic knowledge bases (KBs). However, these approaches either only embed the data-level knowledge (ABox) or suffer from inherent limitations when dealing with concept-level knowledge (TBox), i.e., they cannot faithfully model the logical structure present in the KBs. We present BoxEL, a geometric KB embedding approach that allows for better capturing the logical structure (i.e., ABox and TBox axioms) in the description logic $\mathcal{EL}^{++}$. BoxEL models concepts in a KB as axis-parallel *boxes* that are suitable for modeling concept intersection, entities as points inside boxes, and relations between concepts/entities as *affine transformations*. We show theoretical guarantees (*soundness*) of BoxEL for preserving logical structure. Namely, the learned model of BoxEL embedding with loss 0 is a (logical) model of the KB. Experimental results on (plausible) subsumption reasonings and a real-world application–protein-protein prediction show that BoxEL outperforms traditional knowledge graph embedding methods as well as state-of-the-art $\mathcal{EL}^{++}$ embedding approaches.

Keywords: Ontologies · Knowledge graph embeddings · Semantic web

1 Introduction

Knowledge bases (KBs) provide a *conceptualization* of objects and their relationships, which are of great importance in many applications like biomedical and intelligent systems [5,25]. KBs are often expressed using description logics (DLs) [3], a family of languages allowing for expressing domain knowledge via logical statements (a.k.a axioms). These logical statements are divided into two parts: 1) an ABox consisting of *assertions* over instances, i.e., factual statements like isFatherOf(John, Peter); 2) a TBox consisting of logical statements constraining concepts, e.g., Parent ⊑ Person.

Supplementary Information The online version contains supplementary material available at https://doi.org/10.1007/978-3-031-19433-7_2.

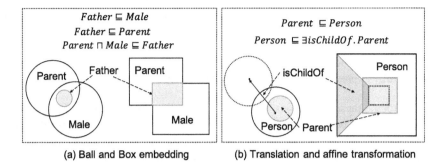

(a) Ball and Box embedding   (b) Translation and affine transformation

Fig. 1. Two counterexamples of ball embedding and its relational transformation. (a) Ball embedding cannot express concept equivalence Parent⊓Male ≡ Father with intersection operator. (b) The *translation* cannot model relation (e.g. isChildOf) between Person and Parent when they should have different volumes. These two issues can be solved by *box* embedding and modelling relation as *affine transformation* among boxes, respectively.

KBs not only provide clear semantics in the application domains but also enable (classic) reasoners [13,30] to perform logical inference, i.e., making implicit knowledge explicit. Existing reasoners are highly optimized and scalable but they are limited to only computing classical logical entailment but not designed to perform inductive (analogical) reasoning and cannot handle noisy data. Embedding based methods, which map the objects in the KBs into a low dimensional vector space while keeping the similarity, have been proposed to complement the classical reasoners and shown remarkable empirical performances on performing (non-classical) analogical reasonings.

Most KB embeddings methods [33] focus on embedding data-level knowledge in ABoxes, a.k.a., knowledge graph embeddings (KGEs). However, KGEs cannot preserve concept-level knowledge expressed in TBoxes. Recently, embedding methods for KBs expressed in DLs have been explored. Prominent examples include $\mathcal{EL}^{++}$ [15] that supports conjunction and full existential quantification, and $\mathcal{ALC}$ [23] that further supports logical negation. We focus on $\mathcal{EL}^{++}$, an underlying formalism of the OWL2 EL profile of the Web Ontology Language [10], which has been used in expressing various biomedical ontologies [5,25]. For embedding $\mathcal{EL}^{++}$ KBs, several approaches such as Onto2Vec [28] and OPA2Vec [29] have been proposed. These approaches require annotation data and do not model logical structure explicitly. Geometric representations, in which the objects are associated with geometric objects such as balls [15] and convex cones [23], provide a high expressiveness on embedding logical properties. For $\mathcal{EL}^{++}$ KBs, ELEm [15] represents concepts as open n-balls and relations as simple translations. Although effective, ELEm suffers from several major limitations:

- Balls are not closed under intersection and cannot faithfully represent concept intersections. For example, the intersection of two concepts Parent ⊓ Male, that is supposed to represent Father, is not a ball (see Fig. 1 (a)). Therefore, the concept equivalence Parent ⊓ Male ≡ Father cannot be captured in the embedding space.
- The relational embedding with simple *translation* causes issues for embedding concepts with varying sizes. For example, Fig. 1 (b) illustrates the embeddings of the axiom ∃isChildOf.Person ⊑ Parent assuming the existence of another axiom

Parent $\sqsubseteq$ Person. In this case, it is impossible to *translate* the larger concept Person into the smaller one Parent,[1] as it does not allow for scaling the size.
- ELEm does not distinguish between entities in ABox and concepts in TBox, but rather regards ABox axioms as special cases of TBox axioms. This simplification cannot fully express the logical structure, e.g., an entity must have minimal volume.

To overcome these limitations, we consider modeling concepts in the KB as *boxes* (i.e., axis-aligned hyperrectangles), encoding entities as points inside the boxes that they should belong to, and the relations as the *affine transformation* between boxes and/or points. Figure 1 (a) shows that the box embedding has closed form of intersection and the *affine transformation* (Fig. 1 (b)) can naturally capture the cases that are not possible in ELEm. In this way, we present BoxEL for embedding $\mathcal{EL}^{++}$ KBs, in which the interpretation functions of $\mathcal{EL}^{++}$ theories in the KB can be represented by the geometric transformations between boxes/points. We formulate BoxEL as an optimization task by designing and minimizing various loss terms defined for each logical statement in the KB. We show theoretical guarantee (*soundness*) of BoxEL in the sense that if the loss of BoxEL embedding is 0, then the trained model is a (logical) model of the KB. Experiments on (plausible) subsumption reasoning over three ontologies and predicting protein-protein interactions show that BoxEL outperforms previous approaches.

2   Related Work

Knowledge graph embeddings (KGEs) have been developed for different tasks. Early works, which focus on link prediction, embed both entities and relations as vectors in a vector space to model the relationships between entities [4,7,31]. Prominent examples include *additive* (or *translational*) family [4,18,34] and *multiplicative* (or *bilinear*) family [19,22,35]. Such techniques only embed the data-level part of KBs and work relatively well for the link prediction tasks. However, KGEs demonstrate limitations when being used to learn the representation of background knowledge such as ontologies of logical rules [9,23], as well as complex logical query [26,27].

Inspired by the theory of conceptual spaces [8], several methods have been proposed to embed concepts as convex regions in vector spaces [11], including balls [15] and convex cones [23]. Such conceptual/geometric methods nicely model the set-theoretic semantics that can be used to capture logical rules of knowledge graphs [1], transitive closure in graphs [32] and logical query for multi-hop question answering [26].

Among embeddings for complex concept descriptions, boxes have some conceptual advantages, but they have not been exploited for representing ontologies yet. BoxE [1] does embed some logical rules but mostly focus on embedding the relational patterns in ABoxes. In contrast, our approach BoxEL focuses on $\mathcal{EL}^{++}$ that has a larger TBox and provides soundness guarantees. BoxEL is closely related to ELEm [15], but instead of using ball embedding and translation, we consider box embedding and affine transformation that have various inherent advantages as discussed before. Another difference of

---

[1] Under the *translation* setting, the embeddings will simply become Parent $\equiv$ Person, which is obviously not what we want as we can express Parent $\not\equiv$ Person with $\mathcal{EL}^{++}$ by propositions like Children $\sqcap$ Parent $\sqsubseteq \bot$, Children $\sqsubseteq$ Person and Children(a).

our method is that we use a different encoding that distinguishes between entities and concepts. Furthermore, we take advantage of the volume of boxes for disjointedness representation, resulting in a more natural encoding of the disjointedness of concepts, i.e., two concepts are disjoint iff their intersection has zero volume.

3 Description Logic $\mathcal{EL}^{++}$

We consider the DL $\mathcal{EL}^{++}$ that underlies multiple biomedical KBs like GALEN [25] and the Gene Ontology [5]. Formally, the syntax of $\mathcal{EL}^{++}$ is built up from a set N_I of *individual names*, N_C of *concept names* and N_R of *role names* (also called *relations*) using the constructors shown in Table 1, where N_I, N_C and N_R are pairwise disjoint.

Table 1. Syntax and semantic of $\mathcal{EL}^{++}$ (role inclusions and concrete domains are omitted).

	Name	Syntax	Semantics
Constructors	Top concept	$\top$	$\Delta^{\mathcal{I}}$
	Bottom concept	$\bot$	$\emptyset$
	Nominal	$\{a\}$	$\{a^{\mathcal{I}}\}$
	Conjunction	$C \sqcap D$	$C^{\mathcal{I}} \cap D^{\mathcal{I}}$
	Existential restriction	$\exists r.C$	$\{x \in \Delta^{\mathcal{I}} \mid \exists y \in \Delta^{\mathcal{I}}$ $(x,y) \in r^{\mathcal{I}} \wedge y \in C^{\mathcal{I}}\}$
ABox	Concept assertion	$C(a)$	$a^{\mathcal{I}} \in C^{\mathcal{I}}$
	Role assertion	$r(a,b)$	$(a^{\mathcal{I}}, b^{\mathcal{I}}) \in r^{\mathcal{I}}$
TBox	Concept inclusion	$C \sqsubseteq D$	$C^{\mathcal{I}} \subseteq D^{\mathcal{I}}$

The semantics of $\mathcal{EL}^{++}$ is defined by *interpretations* $\mathcal{I} = (\Delta^{\mathcal{I}}, \cdot^{\mathcal{I}})$, where the domain $\Delta^{\mathcal{I}}$ is a non-empty set and $\cdot^{\mathcal{I}}$ is a mapping that associates every individual with an element in $\Delta^{\mathcal{I}}$, every concept name with a subset of $\Delta^{\mathcal{I}}$, and every relation name with a relation over $\Delta^{\mathcal{I}} \times \Delta^{\mathcal{I}}$. An *interpretation* is satisfied if it satisfies the corresponding semantic conditions. The syntax and the corresponding semantics (i.e., interpretation of concept expressions) of $\mathcal{EL}^{++}$ are summarized in Table 1.

An $\mathcal{EL}^{++}$ KB $(\mathcal{A}, \mathcal{T})$ consists of an ABox $\mathcal{A}$ and a TBox $\mathcal{T}$. The *ABox* is a set of *concept assertions* $(C(a))$ and *role assertions* $(r(a,b))$, where C is a concept, r is a relation, and a, b are individuals. The TBox is a set of *concept inclusions* of the form $C \sqsubseteq D$. Intuitively, the ABox contains instance-level information (e.g. Person(John)), isFatherOf(John, Peter)), while the TBox contains information about concepts (e.g. Parent $\sqsubseteq$ Person). Every $\mathcal{EL}^{++}$ KB can be transformed such that every TBox statement has the form $C_1 \sqsubseteq D, C_1 \sqcap C_2 \sqsubseteq D, C_1 \sqsubseteq \exists r.C_2, \exists r.C_1 \sqsubseteq D$, where C_1, C_2, D can be the top concept, concept names or nominals and D can also be the bottom concept [2]. The normalized KB can be computed in linear time by introducing new concept names for complex concept expressions and is a conservative extension of the original KB, i.e., every model of the normalized KB is a model of the original KB and every model of the original KB can be extended to be a model of the normalized KB [2].

4 BoxEL for Embedding $\mathcal{EL}^{++}$ Knowledge Bases

In this section, we first present the geometric construction process of $\mathcal{EL}^{++}$ with box embedding and affine transformation, followed by a discussion of the geometric interpretation. Afterward, we describe the BoxEL embedding by introducing proper loss function for each ABox and TBox axiom. Finally, an optimization method is described for the training of BoxEL.

4.1 Geometric Construction

We consider a KB $(\mathcal{A}, \mathcal{T})$ consisting of an ABox $\mathcal{A}$ and a TBox $\mathcal{T}$ where $\mathcal{T}$ has been normalized as explained before. Our goal is to associate entities (or individuals) with points and concepts with boxes in $\mathbb{R}^n$ such that the axioms in the KB are respected.

To this end, we consider two functions m_w, M_w parameterized by a parameter vector w that has to be learned. Conceptually, we consider points as boxes of volume 0. This will be helpful later to encode the meaning of axioms for points and boxes in a uniform way. Intuitively, $m_w : N_I \cup N_C \to \mathbb{R}^n$ maps individual and concept names to the lower left corner and $M_w : N_I \cup N_C \to \mathbb{R}^n$ maps them to the upper right corner of the box that represents them. For individuals $a \in N_I$, we have $m_w(a) = M_w(a)$, so that it is sufficient to store only one of them. The *box associated with C* is defined as

$$\text{Box}_w(C) = \{x \in \mathbb{R}^n \mid m_w(C) \le x \le M_w(C)\}, \tag{1}$$

where the inequality is defined component-wise.

Note that boxes are closed under intersection, which allows us to compute the volume of the intersection of boxes. The lower corner of the box $\text{Box}_w(C) \cap \text{Box}_w(D)$ is $\max(m_w(C), m_w(D))$ and the upper corner is $\min(M_w(C), M_w(D))$, where minimum and maximum are taken component-wise. The volume of boxes can be used to encode axioms in a very concise way. However, as we will describe later, one problem is that points have volume 0. This does not allow distinguishing empty boxes from points. To show that our encoding correctly captures the logical meaning of axioms, we will consider a *modified volume* that assigns a non-zero volume to points and some empty boxes. The (modified) volume of a box is defined as

$$\text{MVol}(\text{Box}_w(C)) = \prod_{i=1}^{n} \max(0, M_w(C)_i - m_w(C)_i + \epsilon), \tag{2}$$

where $\epsilon > 0$ is a small constant. A point now has volume ϵ^n. Some empty boxes can actually have arbitrarily large modified volume. For example the 2D-box with lower corner $(0,0)$ and upper corner $(-\frac{\epsilon}{2}, N)$ has volume $\frac{\epsilon \cdot N}{2}$. While this is not meaningful geometrically, it does not cause any problems for our encoding because we only want to ensure that boxes with zero volume are empty (and not points). In practice, we will use *softplus volume* as approximation (see Sect. 4.5).

We associate every role name $r \in N_r$ with an affine transformation denoted by $T_w^r(x) = D_w^r x + b_w^r$, where D_w^r is an $(n \times n)$ diagonal matrix with non-negative entries and $b_w^r \in \mathbb{R}^n$ is a vector. In a special case where all diagonal entries of D_w^r are -1, $T_w^r(x)$ captures translations. Note that relations have been represented by translation vectors analogous to TransE in [15]. However, this necessarily means that the concept associated with the range of a role has the same size as its domain. This does not seem very intuitive, in particular, for N-to-one relationships like *has_nationality* or *lives_in* that map many objects to the same object. Note that $T_w^r(\text{Box}_w(C)) = \{T_w^r(x) \mid x \in \text{Box}_w(C)\}$ is the box with lower corner $T_w^r(m_w(C))$ and upper corner $T_w^r(M_w(C))$. To show this, note that $m_w(C) < M_w(C)$ implies $D_w^r m_w(C) \le D_w^r M_w(C)$ because D_w^r is a diagonal matrix with non-negative entries. Hence, $T_w^r(m_w(C)) = D_w^r m_w(C) + b_w^r \le D_w^r M_w(C) + b_w^r = T_w^r(M_w(C))$. For $m_w(C) \ge M_w(C)$, both $\text{Box}_w(C)$ and $T_w^r(\text{Box}_w(C))$ are empty.

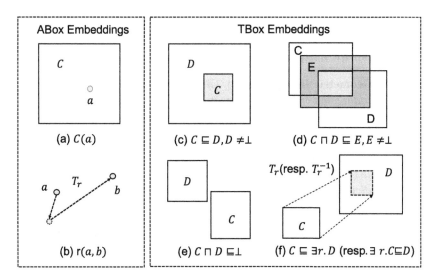

Fig. 2. The geometric interpretation of logical statements in ABox (*left*) and TBox (*right*) expressed by DL $\mathcal{EL}^{++}$ with BoxEL embeddings. The concepts are represented by *boxes*, entities are represented by *points* and relations are represented by *affine transformations*. T_r and T_r^{-1} denote the transformation function of relation r and its inverse function, respectively.

Overall, we have the following parameters:

- for every individual name $a \in N_I$, we have n parameters for the vector $m_w(a)$ (since $m_w(a) = M_w(A)$, we have to store only one of m_w and M_w),
- for every concept name $C \in N_C$, we have $2n$ parameters for the vectors $m_w(C)$ and $M_w(C)$,
- for every role name $r \in N_r$, we have $2n$ parameters. n parameters for the diagonal elements of D_w^r and n parameters for the components of b_w^r.

As we explained informally before, w summarizes all parameters. The overall number of parameters in w is $n \cdot (|N_I| + 2 \cdot |N_C| + 2 \cdot |N_r|)$.

4.2 Geometric Interpretation

The next step is to encode the axioms in our KB. However, we do not want to do this in an arbitrary fashion, but, ideally, in a way that gives us some analytical guarantees. [15] made an interesting first step by showing that their encoding is *sound*. In order to understand soundness, it is important to know that the parameters of the embedding are learnt by minimizing a loss function that contains a loss term for every axiom. Soundness then means that if the loss function yields 0, then the KB is satisfiable. Recall that satisfiability means that there is an interpretation that satisfies all axioms in the KB. Ideally, we should be able to construct such an interpretation directly from our embedding. This is indeed what the authors in [15] did. The idea is that points in the vector space make up the domain of the interpretation, the points that lie in regions associated with concepts correspond to the interpretation of this concept and the interpretation of roles correspond to translations between points like in TransE. In our context, geometric interpretation can be defined as follows.

Definition 1 (Geometric Interpretation). *Given a parameter vector w representing an $\mathcal{EL}^{++}$ embedding, the corresponding geometric interpretation $\mathcal{I}_w = (\Delta^{\mathcal{I}_w}, \cdot^{\mathcal{I}_w})$ is defined as follows:*

1. *$\Delta^{\mathcal{I}_w} = \mathbb{R}^n$,*
2. *for every concept name $C \in N_C$, $C^{\mathcal{I}_w} = \mathrm{Box}_w(C)$,*
3. *for every role $r \in N_R$, $r^{\mathcal{I}_w} = \{(x, y) \in \Delta^{\mathcal{I}_w} \times \Delta^{\mathcal{I}_w} \mid T_w^r(x) = y\}$,*
4. *for every individual name $a \in N_I$, $a^{\mathcal{I}_w} = m_w(a)$.*

We will now encode the axioms by designing one loss term for every axiom in a normalized $\mathcal{EL}^{++}$ KB, such that the axiom is satisfied by the geometric interpretation when the loss is 0. All proofs of propositions are attached in the supplementary material.

4.3   ABox Embedding

ABox contains concept assertions and role assertions. We introduce the following two loss terms that respect the geometric interpretations.

Concept Assertion. Geometrically, a concept assertion $C(a)$ asserts that the point $m_w(a)$ is inside the box $\mathrm{Box}_w(C)$ (see Fig. 2 (a)). This can be expressed by demanding $m_w(C) \leq m_w(a) \leq M_w(C)$ for every component. The loss $\mathcal{L}_{C(a)}(w)$ is defined by

$$\mathcal{L}_{C(a)}(w) = \sum_{i=1}^{n} \|\max(0, m_w(a)_i - M_w(C)_i)\|_2 + \sum_{i=1}^{n} \|\max(0, m_w(C)_i - m_w(a)_i)\|_2.$$

Role Assertion. Geometrically, a role assertion $r(a, b)$ means that the point $m_w(a)$ should be mapped to $m_w(b)$ by the transformation T_w^r (see Fig. 2 (b)). That is, we should have $T_w^r(m_w(a)) = m_w(b)$. We define a loss term

$$\mathcal{L}_{r(a,b)}(w) = \|T_w^r(m_w(a)) - m_w(b)\|_2. \tag{3}$$

It is clear from the definition that when the loss terms are 0, the axioms are satisfied in their geometric interpretation.

Proposition 1. *We have*

1. *If $\mathcal{L}_{C(a)}(w) = 0$, then $\mathcal{I}_w \models C(a)$,*
2. *If $\mathcal{L}_{r(a,b)}(w) = 0$, then $\mathcal{I}_w \models r(a, b)$.*

4.4   TBox Embedding

For the TBox, we define loss terms for the four cases in the normalized KB. Before doing so, we define an auxiliary function that will be used inside these loss terms.

Definition 2 (Disjoint measurement). *Given two boxes B_1, B_2, the disjoint measurement can be defined by the (modified) volumes of B_1 and the intersection box $B_1 \cap B_2$,*

$$\text{Disjoint}(B_1, B_2) = 1 - \frac{\text{MVol}(B_1 \cap B_2)}{\text{MVol}(B_1)}. \tag{4}$$

We have the following guarantees.

Lemma 1. *1.* $0 \leq \text{Disjoint}(B_1, B_2) \leq 1$,
2. $\text{Disjoint}(B_1, B_2) = 0$ *implies* $B_1 \subseteq B_2$,
3. $\text{Disjoint}(B_1, B_2) = 1$ *implies* $B_1 \cap B_2 = \emptyset$.

NF1: Atomic Subsumption. An axiom of the form $C \sqsubseteq D$ geometrically means that $\text{Box}_w(C) \subseteq \text{Box}_w(D)$ (see Fig. 2 (c)). If $D \neq \bot$, we consider the loss term

$$\mathcal{L}_{C \sqsubseteq D}(w) = \text{Disjoint}(\text{Box}_w(C), \text{Box}_w(D)). \tag{5}$$

For the case $D = \bot$ where C is not a nominal, e.g., $C \sqsubseteq \bot$, we define the loss term

$$\mathcal{L}_{C \sqsubseteq \bot}(w) = \max(0, M_w(C)_0 - m_w(C)_0 + \epsilon). \tag{6}$$

If C is a nominal, the axiom is inconsistent and our model can just return an error.

Proposition 2. *If $\mathcal{L}_{C \sqsubseteq D}(w) = 0$, then $\mathcal{I}_w \models C \sqsubseteq D$, where we exclude the inconsistent case $C = \{a\}, D = \bot$.*

NF2: Conjunct Subsumption. An axiom of the form $C \sqcap D \sqsubseteq E$ means that $\text{Box}(C) \cap \text{Box}(D) \subseteq \text{Box}(E)$ (see Fig. 2 (d)). Since $\text{Box}(C) \cap \text{Box}(D)$ is a box again, we can use the same idea as for NF1. For the case $E \neq \bot$, we define the loss term as

$$\mathcal{L}_{C \sqcap D \sqsubseteq E}(w) = \text{Disjoint}(\text{Box}_w(C) \cap \text{Box}_w(D), \text{Box}_w(E)). \tag{7}$$

For $E = \bot$, the axiom states that C and D must be disjoint. The disjointedness can be interpreted as the volume of the intersection of the associated boxes being 0 (see Fig. 2 (e)). However, just using the volume as a loss term may not work well because a minimization algorithm may minimize the volume of the boxes instead of the volume of their intersections. Therefore, we normalize the loss term by dividing by the volume of the boxes. Given by

$$\mathcal{L}_{C \sqcap D \sqsubseteq \bot}(w) = \frac{\text{MVol}(\text{Box}_w(C) \cap \text{Box}_w(D))}{\text{MVol}(\text{Box}_w(C)) + \text{MVol}(\text{Box}_w(D))}. \tag{8}$$

Proposition 3. *If $\mathcal{L}_{C \sqcap D \sqsubseteq E}(w) = 0$, then $\mathcal{I}_w \models C \sqcap D \sqsubseteq E$, where we exclude the inconsistent case $a \sqcap a \sqsubseteq \bot$ (that is, $C = D = \{a\}, E = \bot$).*

NF3: Right Existential. Next, we consider axioms of the form $C \sqsubseteq \exists r.D$. Note that $\exists r.D$ describes those entities that are in relation r with an entity from D. Geometrically, those are points that are mapped to points in $\text{Box}_w(D)$ by the affine transformation corresponding to r. $C \sqsubseteq \exists r.D$ then means that every point in $\text{Box}_w(C)$ must be mapped to a point in $\text{Box}_w(D)$, that is the mapping of $\text{Box}_w(C)$ is contained in $\text{Box}_w(D)$ (see Fig. 2 (f)). Therefore, the encoding comes again down to encoding a subset relationship as before. The only difference to the first normal form is that $\text{Box}_w(C)$ must be mapped by the affine transformation T_w^r. These considerations lead to the following loss term

$$\mathcal{L}_{C \sqsubseteq \exists r.D}(w) = \text{Disjoint}(T_w^r(\text{Box}_w(C)), \text{Box}_w(D)). \tag{9}$$

Proposition 4. *If* $\mathcal{L}_{C \sqsubseteq \exists r.D}(w) = 0$, *then* $\mathcal{I}_w \models C \sqsubseteq \exists r.D$.

NF4: Left Existential. Axioms of the form $\exists r.C \sqsubseteq D$ can be treated symmetrically to the previous case (see Fig. 2 (f)). We only consider the case $D \neq \bot$ and define the loss

$$\mathcal{L}_{\exists r.C \sqsubseteq D}(w) = \text{Disjoint}(T_w^{-r}(\text{Box}_w(C)), \text{Box}_w(D)), \tag{10}$$

where T_w^{-r} is the inverse function of T_w^r that is defined by $T_w^{-r}(x) = D_w^{-r} x - D_w^{-r} b_w^r$, where D_w^{-r} is obtained from D_w^r by replacing all diagonal elements with their reciprocal. Strictly speaking, the inverse only exists if all diagonal entries of D_w^r are non-zero. However, we assume that the entries that occur in a loss term of the form $\mathcal{L}_{\exists r.C \sqsubseteq D}(w)$ remain non-zero in practice when we learn them iteratively.

Proposition 5. *If* $\mathcal{L}_{\exists r.C \sqsubseteq D}(w) = 0$, *then* $\mathcal{I}_w \models \exists r.C \sqsubseteq D$.

4.5   Optimization

Softplus Approximation. For optimization, while the computation of the volume of boxes is straightforward, using a precise *hard volume* is known to cause problems when learning the parameters using gradient descent algorithms, e.g. there is no training signal (gradient flow) when box embeddings that should overlap but become disjoint [6,17,24]. To mitigate the problem, we approximate the volume of boxes by the *softplus volume* [24] due to its simplicity.

$$\text{SVol}(\text{Box}_w(C)) = \prod_{i=1}^{n} \text{Softplus}_t(M_w(C)_i - m_w(C)_i) \tag{11}$$

where t is a temperature parameter. The softplus function is defined as $\text{softplus}_t(x) = t \log(1 + e^{x/t})$, which can be regarded as a smoothed version of the ReLu function ($\max\{0, x\}$) used for calculating the volume of *hard boxes*. In practice, the *softplus volume* is used to replace the *modified volume* in Eq. (2) as it empirically resolves the same issue that point has zero volume.

Regularization. We add a regularization term in Eq. (12) to all non-empty boxes to encourage that the boxes lie in the unit box $[0, 1]^n$.

$$\lambda = \sum_{i=1}^{n} \max(0, M_w(C)_i - 1 + \epsilon) + \max(0, -m_w(C)_i - \epsilon) \tag{12}$$

In practice, this also avoids numerical stability issues. For example, to minimize a loss term, a box that should have a fixed volume could become very *slim*, i.e. some side lengths be extremely large while others become extremely small.

Negative Sampling. In principle, the embeddings can be optimized without negatives. However, we empirically find that the embeddings will be highly overlapped without negative sampling. e.g. for role assertion $r(a, b)$, a and b will simply become the same point. We generate negative samples for the role assertion $r(a, b)$ by randomly replacing one of the head or tail entity. Finally, we sum up all the loss terms, and learn the embeddings by minimizing the loss with Adam optimizer [14].

5   Empirical Evaluation

5.1   A Proof-of-Concept Example

We begin by first validating the model in modeling a toy ontology–family domain [15], which is described by the following axioms:[2]

Male ⊑ Person	Female ⊑ Person
Father ⊑ Male	Mother ⊑ Female
Father ⊑ Parent	Mother ⊑ Parent
Female ⊓ Male ⊑ ⊥	Female ⊓ Parent ⊑ Mother
Male ⊓ Parent ⊑ Father	∃hasChild.Person ⊑ Parent
Parent ⊑ Person	Parent ⊑ ∃ hasChild.Person
Father(Alex)	Father(Bob)
Mother(Marie)	Mother(Alice)

We set the dimension to 2 to visualize the embeddings. Figure 3 shows that the generated embeddings accurately encode all of the axioms. In particular, the embeddings of **Father** and **Mother** align well with the conjunction **Parent ⊓ Male** and **Parent ⊓ Female**, respectively, which is impossible to be achieved by ELEm.

5.2   Subsumption Reasoning

We evaluate the effectiveness of BoxEL on (plausible) subsumption reasoning (also known as ontology completion). The problem is to predict whether a concept is subsumed by another one. For each subsumption pair $C \sqsubseteq D$, the scoring function can be defined by

$$P(C \sqsubseteq D) = \frac{\mathrm{MVol}(\mathrm{Box}(C) \cap \mathrm{Box}(D))}{\mathrm{MVol}(\mathrm{Box}(C))}. \quad (13)$$

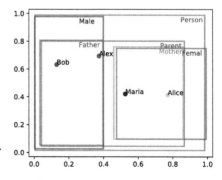

Fig. 3. BoxEL embeddings in the family domain.

Note that such subsumption relations are not necessary to be (logically) entailed by the input KB, e.g., a subsumption relation can be plausibly inferred by $P(C \sqsubseteq D) =$

---

[2] Compared with the example given in [15], we add additional concept assertion statements that distinguish entities and concepts:.

Table 2. Summary of classes, relations and axioms in different ontologies. NF_i represents the ith normal form.

Ontology	GO	GALEN	ANATOMY
Classes	45895	24353	106363
Relations	9	1010	157
NF1	85480	28890	122142
NF2	12131	13595	2121
NF3	20324	28118	152289
NF4	12129	13597	2143
Disjoint	30	0	184

Table 3. The accuracies (for which the prediction is true if and only if the subclass box is exactly inside the superclass box) achieved by the embeddings of different approaches in terms of geometric interpretation of the classes in various ontologies.

	ELEm	EmEL^{++}	BoxEL
GO	0.250	0.415	**0.489**
GALEN	0.480	0.345	**0.788**
ANATOMY	0.069	0.215	**0.453**

Table 4. The ranking based measures of embedding models for sumbsumtion reasoning on the testing set. ∗ denotes the results from [20].

Dataset	Metric	TransE∗	TransH∗	DistMult∗	ELEm	EmEL^{++}	**BoxEL**
GO	Hits@10	0.00	0.00	0.00	0.09	0.10	0.03
	Hits@100	0.00	0.00	0.00	0.16	0.22	0.08
	AUC	0.53	0.44	0.50	0.70	0.76	0.81
	Mean Rank	-	-	-	13719	11050	8980
GALEN	Hits@10	0.00	0.00	0.00	0.07	0.10	0.02
	Hits@100	0.00	0.00	0.00	0.14	0.17	0.03
	AUC	0.54	0.48	0.51	0.64	0.65	0.85
	Mean Rank	-	-	-	8321	8407	3584
ANATOMY	Hits@10	0.00	0.00	0.00	0.18	0.18	0.03
	Hits@100	0.01	0.00	0.00	0.38	0.40	0.04
	AUC	0.53	0.44	0.49	0.73	0.76	0.91
	Mean Rank	-	-	-	28564	24421	10266

0.9, allowing for non-classical plausible reasoning. While the subsumption reasoning does not need negatives, we add an additional regularization term for non-subsumption axiom. In particular, for each atomic subsumption axiom $C \sqsubseteq D$, we generate a non-subsumption axiom $C \not\sqsubseteq D'$ or $C' \not\sqsubseteq D$ by randomly replacing one of the concepts C and D. Note that this does not produce regular negative samples as the generated concepts pair does not have to be disjoint. Thus, the loss term for non-subsumption axiom cannot be simply defined by $\mathcal{L}_{C \not\sqsubseteq D'} = 1 - \mathcal{L}_{C \sqsubseteq D'}$. Instead, we define the loss term as $\mathcal{L}_{C \not\sqsubseteq D'} = \phi(1 - \mathcal{L}_{C \sqsubseteq D'})$ by multiplying a small positive constant ϕ that encourages splitting the non-subsumption concepts while does not encourage them to be disjoint. If $\phi = 1$, the loss would encourage the non-subsumption concepts to be disjoint. We empirically show that $\phi = 1$ produces worse performance as we do not want non-subsumption concepts to be disjoint.

Datasets. We use three biomedical ontologies as our benchmark. 1) **Gene Ontology (GO)** [12] integrates the representation of genes and their functions across all species. 2) **GALEN** [25] is a clinical ontology. 3) **Anatomy** [21] is a ontology that represents linkages of different phenotypes to genes. Table 2 summarizes the statistical information of these datasets. The subclass relations are split into training set (70%), validation set (20%) and testing set (10%), respectively.

Evaluation Protocol. Two strategies can be used to measure the effectiveness of the embeddings. 1) Ranking based measures rank the probability of C subsumed by all concepts. We evaluate and report four ranking based measures. Hits@10, Hits@100 describe the fraction of true cases that appear in the first 10 and 100 test cases of the sorted rank list, respectively. Mean rank computes the arithmetic mean over all individual ranks (i.e. $MR = \frac{1}{|\mathcal{I}|} \sum_{rank \in \mathcal{I}} rank$, where $rank$ is the individual rank), while AUC computes the area under the ROC curve. 2) Accuracy based measure is a stricter criterion, for which the prediction is true if and only if the subclass box is exactly inside the superclass box (even not allowing the subclass box slightly outside the superclass box). We use this measure as it evaluates the performance of embeddings on retaining the underlying characteristics of ontology in vector space. We only compare ELEm and EmEL^{++} as KGE baselines fail in this setting (KGEs cannot preserve the ontology).

Implementation Details. The ontology is normalized into standard normal forms, which comprise a set of axioms that can be used as the *positive samples*. Similar to previous works [15], we perform normalization using the OWL APIs and the APIs offered by the jCel reasoner [18]. The hyperparameter for negative sampling is set to $\phi = 0.05$. For ELEm and EmEL^{++}, the embedding size is searched from $n = [50, 100, 200]$ and margin parameter is searched from $\gamma = [-0.1, 0, 0.1]$. Since box embedding has double the number of parameters of ELEm and EmEL^{++}, we search the embedding size from $n = [25, 50, 100]$ for BoxEL. We summarize the best performing hyperparameters in our supplemental material. All experiments are evaluated with 10 random seeds and the mean results are reported for numerical comparisons.

Baselines. We compare the state-of-the-art $\mathcal{EL}^{++}$ embeddings (ELEm) [15], the first geometric embeddings of $\mathcal{EL}^{++}$, as well as the extension EmEL^{++} [20] that additionally considers the role inclusion and role chain embedding, as our major baselines. For comparison with classical methods, we also include the reported results of three classical KGEs in [20], including TransE [4], TransH [34] and DistMult [35].

Results. Table 4 summarizes the ranking based measures of embedding models. We first observe that both ELEm and EmEL^{++} perform much better than the three standard KGEs (TransE, TransH, and DistMult) on all three datasets, especially on hits@k for which KGEs fail, showcasing the limitation of KGEs and the benefits of geometric embeddings on encoding logic structures. EmEL^{++} performs slightly better than ELEm on all three datasets. Overall, our model BoxEL outperforms ELEm and EmEL^{++}. In particular, we find that for Mean Rank and AUC, our model achieves significant performance gains on all three datasets. Note that Mean Rank and AUC have theoretical advantages over hits@k because hits@k is sensitive to any model performance changes while Mean Rank and AUC reflect the average performance, demonstrating that BoxEL achieves better average performance. Table 4 shows the accuracies of different embeddings in terms of the geometric interpretation of the classes in various ontologies. It clearly demonstrates that BoxEL outperforms ELEm and EmEL^{++} by a large margin, showcasing that BoxEL preserves the underlying ontology characteristics in vector space better than ELEm and EmEL^{++} that use ball embeddings.

Table 5. Prediction performance on protein-protein interaction (yeast).

Method	Raw hits@10	Filtered hits@10	Raw hits@100	Filtered hits@100	Raw mean Rank	Filtered mean rank	Raw AUC	Filtered AUC
TransE	0.06	0.13	0.32	0.40	1125	1075	0.82	0.83
BoxE	0.08	0.14	0.36	0.43	633	620	0.85	0.85
SimResnik	**0.09**	0.17	0.38	0.48	758	707	0.86	0.87
SimLin	0.08	0.15	0.33	0.41	875	825	0.8	0.85
ELEm	0.08	0.17	0.44	0.62	451	394	0.92	0.93
EmEL^{++}	0.08	0.16	0.45	0.63	451	397	0.90	0.91
Onto2Vec	0.08	0.15	0.35	0.48	641	588	0.79	0.80
OPA2Vec	0.06	0.13	0.39	0.58	523	467	0.87	0.88
BoxEL	**0.09**	**0.20**	**0.52**	**0.73**	**423**	**379**	**0.93**	**0.94**

Table 6. Prediction performance on protein-protein interaction (human).

Method	Raw hits@10	Filtered hits@10	Raw hits@100	Filtered hits@100	Raw mean rank	Filtered mean rank	Raw AUC	Filtered AUC
TransE	0.05	**0.11**	0.24	0.29	3960	3891	0.78	0.79
BoxE	0.05	0.10	0.26	0.32	2121	2091	0.87	0.87
SimResnik	0.05	0.09	0.25	0.30	1934	1864	0.88	0.89
SimLin	0.04	0.08	0.20	0.23	2288	2219	0.86	0.87
ELEm	0.01	0.02	0.22	0.26	1680	1638	0.90	0.90
EmEL^{++}	0.01	0.03	0.23	0.26	1671	1638	0.90	0.91
Onto2Vec	0.05	0.08	0.24	0.31	2435	2391	0.77	0.77
OPA2Vec	0.03	0.07	0.23	0.26	1810	1768	0.86	0.88
BoxEL (Ours)	**0.07**	0.10	**0.42**	**0.63**	**1574**	**1530**	**0.93**	**0.93**

5.3 Protein-Protein Interactions

Dataset. We use a biomedical knowledge graph built by [15] from Gene Ontology (TBox) and STRING database (ABox) to conduct this task. Gene Ontology contains information about the functions of proteins, while STRING database consists of the protein-protein interactions. We use the protein-protein interaction data of yeast and human organisms, respectively. For each pair of proteins (P_1, P_2) that exists in STRING, we add a role assertion interacts$(P1, P2)$. If protein P is associated with the function F, we add a membership axiom $\{P\} \sqsubseteq \exists \mathsf{hasFunction}.F$, the membership assertion can be regarded as a special case of NF3, in which P is a point (i.e. zero-volume box). The interaction pairs of proteins are split into training (80%), testing (10%) and validation (10%) sets. To perform prediction for each protein pair (P_1, P_2), we predict whether the role assertion $\mathsf{interacts}(P_1, P_2)$ hold. This can be measured by Eq. (14).

$$P(\mathsf{interacts}(P_1, P_2)) = \left\| T_w^{\mathsf{interacts}}(m_w(P_1)) - m_w(P_2) \right\|_2. \qquad (14)$$

where $T_w^{\mathsf{interacts}}$ is the affine transformation function for relation $\mathsf{interacts}$. For each positive interaction pair $\mathsf{interacts}(P_1, P_2)$, we generate a corrupted negative sample by randomly replacing one of the head and tail proteins.

Baselines. We consider ELEm [15] and EmEL^{++} [20] as our two major baselines as they have been shown outperforming the traditional KGEs. We also report the result of Onto2Vec [28] that treats logical axioms as a text corpus and OPA2Vec [29] that combines logical axioms with annotation properties. Besides, we report the results of two semantic similarity measures: Resnik's similarity and Lin's similarity in [15]. For KGEs, we compare TransE [4]) and BoxE [1]. We report the hits@10, hits@100, mean rank and AUC (area under the ROC curve) as explained before for numerical comparison. Both raw ranking measures and filtered ranking measures that ignore the triples that are already known to be true in the training stage are reported. Baseline results are taken from the standard benchmark developed by [16].[3]

Table 7. The performance of BoxEL with affine transformation (AffineBoxEL) and BoxEL with translation (TransBoxEL) on yeast protein-protein interaction.

Method	EmEL		TransBoxEL		AffineBoxEL	
	Raw	Filtered	Raw	Filtered	Raw	Filtered
Hits@10	0.08	0.17	0.04	0.18	**0.09**	**0.20**
Hits@100	0.44	0.62	0.54	0.68	**0.52**	**0.73**
Mean rank	451	394	445	390	**423**	**379**
AUC	0.92	0.93	**0.93**	0.93	**0.93**	**0.94**

Table 8. The performance of BoxEL with point entity embedding and box entity embedding on yeast protein-protein interaction dataset.

Method	EmEL		BoxEL (boxes)		BoxEL (points)	
	Raw	Filtered	Raw	Filtered	Raw	Filtered
Hits@10	0.08	0.17	**0.09**	0.19	**0.09**	**0.20**
Hits@100	0.44	0.62	0.48	0.68	**0.52**	**0.73**
Mean rank	451	394	450	388	**423**	**379**
AUC	0.92	0.93	0.92	0.93	**0.93**	**0.94**

Overall Results. Table 5 and Table 6 summarize the performance of protein-protein prediction in yeast and human organisms, respectively. We first observe that similarity based methods (SimResnik and SimLin) roughly outperform TransE, showcasing the limitation of classical knowledge graph embeddings. BoxE roughly outperforms TransE as it does encode some logical properties. The geometric methods ELEm and EmEL^{++} fail on the hits@10 measures and does not show significant performance gains on the hits@100 measures in human dataset. However, ELEm and EmEL^{++} outperform TransE, BoxE and similarity based methods on Mean Rank and AUC by a

---

[3] https://github.com/bio-ontology-research-group/machine-learning-with-ontologies.

large margin, especially for the Mean Rank, showcasing the expressiveness of geometric embeddings. Onto2Vec and OPA2Vec achieve relatively better results than TransE and similarity based methods, but cannot compete ELEm and EmEL^{++}. We conjecture that this is due to the fact that they mostly consider annotation information but cannot encode the logical structure explicitly. Our method, BoxEL consistently outperforms all methods in hits@100, Mean Rank and AUC in both datasets, except the competitive results of hits@10, showcasing the better expressiveness of BoxEL.

5.4   Ablation Studies

Transformation vs Translation. To study the contributions of using boxes for modeling concepts and using affine transformation for modeling relations, we conduct an ablation study by comparing relation embeddings with affine transformation (AffineBoxEL) and translation (TransBoxEL). The only difference of TransBox to the AffineBox is that TransBox does not associate a scaling factor for each relation. Table 7 clearly shows that TransBoxEL outperforms EmEL^{++}, showcasing the benefits of box modeling compared with ball modeling. While AffineBoxEL further improves TransBoxEL, demonstrating the advantages of affine transformation. Hence, we could conclude that both of our proposed entity and relation embedding components boost the performance.

Entities as Points vs Boxes. As mentioned before, distinguishing entities and concepts by identifying entities as points has better theoretical properties. Here, we study how this distinction influences the performance. For this purpose, we eliminate the ABox axioms by replacing each individual with a singleton class and rewriting relation assertions $r(a, b)$ and concept assertions $C(a)$ as $\{a\} \sqsubseteq \exists r.\{b\}$ and $\{a\} \sqsubseteq C$, respectively. In this case, we only have TBox embeddings and the entities are embedded as regular boxes. Table 8 shows that for hits@k, there is marginal significant improvement of point entity embedding over boxes entity embedding, however, point entity embedding consistently outperforms box entity embedding on Mean Rank and AUC, showcasing the benefits of distinguishing entities and concepts.

6   Conclusion

This paper proposes BoxEL, a geometric KB embedding method that explicitly models the logical structure expressed by the theories of $\mathcal{EL}^{++}$. Different from the standard KGEs that simply ignore the analytical guarantees, BoxEL provides *soundness* guarantee for the underlying logical structure by incorporating background knowledge into machine learning tasks, offering a more reliable and logic-preserved fashion for KB reasoning. The empirical results further demonstrate that BoxEL outperforms previous KGEs and $\mathcal{EL}^{++}$ embedding approaches on subsumption reasoning over three ontologies and predicting protein-protein interactions in a real-world biomedical KB.

Supplemental Material Statement: Source code and datasets are available for reproducing the results.[4] Full proofs of propositions and lemmas are available in a long version of the paper.[5]

Acknowledgments. The authors thank the International Max Planck Research School for Intelligent Systems (IMPRS-IS) for supporting Bo Xiong. This project has received funding from the European Union's Horizon 2020 research and innovation programme under the Marie Skłodowska-Curie grant agreement No: 860801. Nico Potyka was partially funded by DFG projects Evowipe/COFFEE.

References

1. Abboud, R., Ceylan, İ.İ., Lukasiewicz, T., Salvatori, T.: Boxe: A box embedding model for knowledge base completion. In: NeurIPS (2020)
2. Baader, F., Brandt, S., Lutz, C.: Pushing the el envelope. In: IJCAI. vol. 5, pp. 364–369 (2005)
3. Baader, F., Calvanese, D., McGuinness, D., Patel-Schneider, P., Nardi, D., et al.: The description logic handbook: Theory, implementation and applications. Cambridge University Press (2003)
4. Bordes, A., Usunier, N., García-Durán, A., Weston, J., Yakhnenko, O.: Translating embeddings for modeling multi-relational data. In: NIPS. pp. 2787–2795 (2013)
5. Consortium, G.O.: Gene ontology consortium: going forward. Nucleic acids research **43**(D1), D1049–D1056 (2015)
6. Dasgupta, S.S., Boratko, M., Zhang, D., Vilnis, L., Li, X., McCallum, A.: Improving local identifiability in probabilistic box embeddings. In: NeurIPS (2020)
7. Dettmers, T., Minervini, P., Stenetorp, P., Riedel, S.: Convolutional 2d knowledge graph embeddings. In: AAAI, pp. 1811–1818. AAAI Press (2018)
8. Gärdenfors, P.: Conceptual spaces - the geometry of thought. MIT Press (2000)
9. Garg, D., Ikbal, S., Srivastava, S.K., Vishwakarma, H., Karanam, H.P., Subramaniam, L.V.: Quantum embedding of knowledge for reasoning. In: NeurIPS, pp. 5595–5605 (2019)
10. Graua, B.C., Horrocksa, I., Motika, B., Parsiab, B., Patel-Schneiderc, P., Sattlerb, U.: Web semantics: science, services and agents on the world wide web. Web Semantics: Sci. Serv. Agents World Wide Web **6**, 309–322 (2008)
11. Gutiérrez-Basulto, V., Schockaert, S.: From knowledge graph embedding to ontology embedding? an analysis of the compatibility between vector space representations and rules. In: KR, pp. 379–388. AAAI Press (2018)
12. Harris, M., et al.: The gene ontology (go) database and informatics resource nucleic acids research, 32. D258–D261 (2004)
13. Kazakov, Y., Krötzsch, M., Simancik, F.: The incredible ELK - from polynomial procedures to efficient reasoning with el ontologies. J. Autom. Reason. **53**(1), 1–61 (2014)
14. Kingma, D.P., Ba, J.: Adam: A method for stochastic optimization. In: ICLR (Poster) (2015)
15. Kulmanov, M., Liu-Wei, W., Yan, Y., Hoehndorf, R.: EL embeddings: Geometric construction of models for the description logic EL++. In: IJCAI, pp. 6103–6109. ijcai.org (2019)
16. Kulmanov, M., Smaili, F.Z., Gao, X., Hoehndorf, R.: Semantic similarity and machine learning with ontologies. Briefings Bioinform. **22**(4) (2021)

---

[4] https://github.com/Box-EL/BoxEL.
[5] https://arxiv.org/abs/2201.09919.

17. Li, X., Vilnis, L., Zhang, D., Boratko, M., McCallum, A.: Smoothing the geometry of probabilistic box embeddings. In: ICLR. OpenReview.net (2019)

18. Lin, Y., Liu, Z., Sun, M., Liu, Y., Zhu, X.: Learning entity and relation embeddings for knowledge graph completion. In: AAAI, pp. 2181–2187. AAAI Press (2015)

19. Liu, H., Wu, Y., Yang, Y.: Analogical inference for multi-relational embeddings. In: ICML. Proceedings of Machine Learning Research, vol. 70, pp. 2168–2178. PMLR (2017)

20. Mondal, S., Bhatia, S., Mutharaju, R.: Emel++: Embeddings for EL++ description logic. In: AAAI Spring Symposium: Combining Machine Learning with Knowledge Engineering. CEUR Workshop Proceedings, vol. 2846. CEUR-WS.org (2021)

21. Mungall, C.J., Torniai, C., Gkoutos, G.V., Lewis, S.E., Haendel, M.A.: Uberon, an integrative multi-species anatomy ontology. Genome Biol. **13**(1), 1–20 (2012)

22. Nickel, M., Tresp, V., Kriegel, H.: A three-way model for collective learning on multi-relational data. In: ICML, pp. 809–816. Omnipress (2011)

23. Özçep, Ö.L., Leemhuis, M., Wolter, D.: Cone semantics for logics with negation. In: IJCAI, pp. 1820–1826. ijcai.org (2020)

24. Patel, D., Dasgupta, S.S., Boratko, M., Li, X., Vilnis, L., McCallum, A.: Representing joint hierarchies with box embeddings. In: Automated Knowledge Base Construction (2020). https://openreview.net/forum?id=J246NSqR_l

25. Rector, A.L., Rogers, J.E., Pole, P.: The galen high level ontology. In: Medical Informatics Europe'96, pp. 174–178. IOS Press (1996)

26. Ren, H., Hu, W., Leskovec, J.: Query2box: Reasoning over knowledge graphs in vector space using box embeddings. In: ICLR, OpenReview.net (2020)

27. Ren, H., Leskovec, J.: Beta embeddings for multi-hop logical reasoning in knowledge graphs. In: Neurips (2020)

28. Smaili, F.Z., Gao, X., Hoehndorf, R.: Onto2Vec: joint vector-based representation of biological entities and their ontology-based annotations. Bioinformatics **34**(13), i52–i60 (2018)

29. Smaili, F.Z., Gao, X., Hoehndorf, R.: Opa2vec: combining formal and informal content of biomedical ontologies to improve similarity-based prediction. Bioinformatics **35**(12), 2133–2140 (2019)

30. Steigmiller, A., Liebig, T., Glimm, B.: Konclude: system description. J. Web Semant. **27–28**, 78–85 (2014)

31. Trouillon, T., Welbl, J., Riedel, S., Gaussier, É., Bouchard, G.: Complex embeddings for simple link prediction. In: ICML. JMLR Workshop and Conference Proceedings, vol. 48, pp. 2071–2080. JMLR.org (2016)

32. Vilnis, L., Li, X., Murty, S., McCallum, A.: Probabilistic embedding of knowledge graphs with box lattice measures. In: ACL (1), pp. 263–272. Association for Computational Linguistics (2018)

33. Wang, Q., Mao, Z., Wang, B., Guo, L.: Knowledge graph embedding: a survey of approaches and applications. IEEE Trans. Knowl. Data Eng. **29**(12), 2724–2743 (2017)

34. Wang, Z., Zhang, J., Feng, J., Chen, Z.: Knowledge graph embedding by translating on hyperplanes. In: AAAI, pp. 1112–1119. AAAI Press (2014)

35. Yang, B., Yih, W., He, X., Gao, J., Deng, L.: Embedding entities and relations for learning and inference in knowledge bases. In: ICLR (Poster) (2015)

Enhancing Document-Level Relation Extraction by Entity Knowledge Injection

Xinyi Wang[1], Zitao Wang[1], Weijian Sun[3], and Wei Hu[1,2(✉)] ⓘ

[1] State Key Laboratory for Novel Software Technology, Nanjing University,
Nanjing, China
xywang.nju@gmail.com, ztwang.nju@gmail.com, whu@nju.edu.cn
[2] National Institute of Healthcare Data Science, Nanjing University, Nanjing, China
[3] Huawei Technologies Co., Ltd., Shanghai, China
sunweijian@huawei.com

Abstract. Document-level relation extraction (RE) aims to identify the relations between entities throughout an entire document. It needs complex reasoning skills to synthesize various knowledge such as coreferences and commonsense. Large-scale knowledge graphs (KGs) contain a wealth of real-world facts, and can provide valuable knowledge to document-level RE. In this paper, we propose an entity knowledge injection framework to enhance current document-level RE models. Specifically, we introduce coreference distillation to inject coreference knowledge, endowing an RE model with the more general capability of coreference reasoning. We also employ representation reconciliation to inject factual knowledge and aggregate KG representations and document representations into a unified space. The experiments on two benchmark datasets validate the generalization of our entity knowledge injection framework and the consistent improvement to several document-level RE models.

Keywords: Relation extraction · Knowledge injection · Knowledge graph

1 Introduction

Relation extraction (RE) aims to recognize the semantic relations between entities in texts, which is beneficial to a variety of AI applications such as language understanding and knowledge graph (KG) construction. Early methods [5,34,36] mainly cope with sentence-level RE, which detects the relations in a single sentence. However, a large number of relations span across multiple sentences [32], which calls for document-level RE in recent years. Compared with sentence-level RE, document-level RE is more challenging. It needs the RE models to conduct complex reasoning, e.g., coreference reasoning, factual reasoning and logical reasoning, throughout an entire document.

Figure 1 shows a real example. A document-level RE model is asked to find the relations between three named entities *IBM Research Brazil*, *São Paulo* and

National Natural Science Foundation of China (No. 61872172).

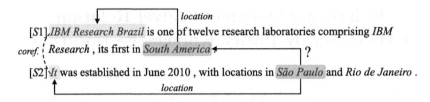

Fig. 1. An example of document-level RE excerpted from [32]

South America. From *S1*, *IBM Research Brazil* is located in *South America* may be first recognized by the model. Then, with the help of coreference knowledge that connects the pronoun *It* in *S2* to *IBM Research Brazil* in *S1*, the model can recognize that *IBM Research Brazil* is located in *São Paulo*. Since the model may not know the exact types of entities, only with the aid of extra knowledge in KGs like *São Paulo* is a city and *South America* is a continent, then it can confidently determine that the relation between them is *continent* rather than others. The entire reasoning process demands the document-level RE model to synthesize various knowledge and have powerful reasoning capabilities.

Recent years have witnessed that large-scale KGs, e.g., Wikidata [26] and DBpedia [1], become a valuable asset in information extraction [2,4,12,19–21,25]. A KG contains a collection of real-world facts, in which a fact is structured in the form of a triple (*entity, property, value*). *Property* can be either an *attribute* or a *relation*, and *value* can be either a *literal* for attribute triple or an *entity* for relation triple. Particularly for the RE task, the works in [2,8,21,25] exploit one or very few attribute and relation triples (e.g., *rdfs:label*) in KGs to enhance their models. Furthermore, they overlook the heterogeneity between KG representations and document representations, and aggregate them in a simple way like vector concatenation.

In this paper, we propose a novel entity knowledge injection framework to enhance existing document-level RE models. Specifically, we introduce a general *knowledge injection layer* between the encoding layer and the prediction layer of popular RE models. Based on it, we focus on injecting various entity knowledge from KGs into the document-level RE models. We tackle two key challenges:

First, *how to inject coreference knowledge into document-level RE models?* Coreference resolution plays a vital role in RE. However, the coreferences derived from coreference resolution tools and aliases in KGs may contain errors. If we directly import them into an RE model as strong guidance information, such as the edges in a document graph [15], it is likely to bring a downside effect. Therefore, we present *coreference distillation* to distill knowledge from the coreferences and inject it into an RE model, so that the model can ultimately acquire generalized coreference knowledge.

Second, *how to inject factual knowledge into document-level RE models?* KG contains a wealth of facts related to entities, which we want to exploit for RE. However, the representations of entities in a KG and the text representations of a document are learned in two different spaces, which demand to be reconciled together. We present *representation reconciliation* to fuse KG representations and document representations into a unified space, endowing the RE model with the factual knowledge of entities.

In summary, our main contributions in this paper are twofold:

- We define a general knowledge injection framework KIRE and design various knowledge injection tasks for document-level RE, such as coreference distillation for coreference knowledge and representation reconciliation for factual knowledge. These knowledge injection and RE tasks are optimized together by multi-task learning. (Sections 3 and 4)
- We perform the experiments on two benchmark datasets DocRED [32] and DWIE [33] for document-level RE. The result comparison between seven RE models and the models after knowledge injection validates the generalization and stable improvement of our framework. (Section 5)

2 Related Work

Document-Level RE. Document-level RE has attracted vast attention in the past few years. A considerable number of studies have been conducted, which can be generally divided into graph-based models [11,13,15,24,27,31,35] as well as sequence-based models [7,18,28,30,38]. Graph-based models build document graphs to capture the semantic information in a document, and design various neural networks to carry out inference on the built document graphs. DISCREX [15] models words in a document as nodes and intra/inter-sentential dependencies as edges. Following this idea, Peng et al. [13] make use of graph LSTM while BRAN [24] employs Transformer to encode document graphs. Recently, LSR [11], GAIN [35] and GLRE [27] define more sophisticated document graphs to reserve more dependency information in a document.

Sequence-based models adopt neural encoders like BERT to implicitly capture dependencies in a document, instead of explicitly building document graphs. Wang et al. [28] use BERT to encode a document and design a two-step pipeline, which predicts whether a relation exists between two entities first, and then predicts the specific relation types. HIN [18] also makes use of BERT but design a hierarchical model that integrates the inference information from the entity, sentence and document levels. Huang et al. [7] extract three types of paths which indicate how the head and tail entities can be possibly related in the context, and predict the relations based on the extracted evidence sentences. ATLOP [38] proposes localized context pooling to transfer attentions from pre-trained language models and adaptive thresholding to resolve the multi-label and multi-entity problem. SSAN [30] modifies the attention mechanism in BERT to model the coreference and co-occurrence structures between entities, to better capture the semantic information in the context.

In this paper, our focus is injecting knowledge into these document-level RE models. Our entity knowledge injection framework KIRE is applicable to various models as long as they fall into our framework formulation.

Knowledge Injection. A few works have studied how to inject external knowledge such as a KG into the RE task for performance improvement. RESIDE [21] uses entity types and aliases while $BERT_{EM+TM}$ [4] only uses entity types. They both consider very limited features of entities. RECON [2] proposes separate models to encode attribute triples and relation triples in a KG and obtain corresponding attribute context embeddings and relation context embeddings, which are combined into sentence embeddings. KB-both [25] utilizes entity representations learned from either hyperlinked text documents (Wikipedia) or a KG (Wikidata) to raise the information extraction performance including document-level RE. Different from all above, we integrate more types of knowledge including coreferences, attributes and relations symbiotically with more effective knowledge injection methods to address the document-level RE task.

Additionally, a few studies [10,29,37] explicitly exploit incorporating knowledge from various sources such as encyclopedia knowledge, commonsense knowledge and linguistic knowledge into pre-trained language models with different injection strategies to improve the performance of language models in downstream tasks. However, the goal of these studies is orthogonal to this paper.

3   Framework Formulation

According to [18,32,38], we formulate the document-level RE task as a *multiple binary classification* problem. Given a document annotated with entities and their corresponding textual mentions, the task aims to predict the relations for each entity pair in the document, where a relation is either a predefined type (e.g., *country*) or *N/A* for no relation. Note that there may be more than one relation for an entity pair.

A basic neural network model [32] for document-level RE contains an encoding layer and a prediction layer. The encoding layer encodes an input document to obtain the context-sensitive representations of tokens (words) in it, and the prediction layer generates entity representations and predicts relations using the entity representations. In this paper, we add a *knowledge injection layer* between the encoding layer and the prediction layer, and many document-level RE models such as [27,32,38] can be used as the basic model.

We regard a KG as the knowledge source for injection. A KG is defined as a 7-tuple $\mathcal{G} = (U, R, A, V, X, Y, C)$, where U, R, A and V denote the sets of entities, relations, attributes and literal values, respectively. $X \subseteq U \times R \times U$ denotes the set of relation triples, $Y \subseteq U \times A \times V$ denotes the set of attribute triples, and C denotes the set of coreference triples derived from $\mathcal{G}$. By the alias information (e.g., *skos:altLabel*) in $\mathcal{G}$, any two aliases of an entity can constitute one coreference triple (m_s, m_t, p_{cr}), where m_s, m_t are two alias mentions and p_{cr} is the coreference probability. We employ off-the-shelf coreference resolution models to find more coreference knowledge for pronouns (e.g., *it* and *he*), possessives (e.g., *herself*), noun phrases (e.g., *this work*), etc., in the document. p_{cr} is set to the resolution confidence. Due to the main scope of this paper, we follow [10,37] and reuse entity linking tools to link the entities in the document to those in the KG.

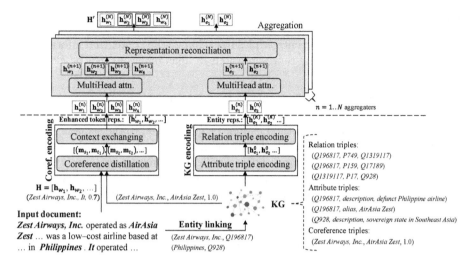

Fig. 2. Architecture of the knowledge injection layer

Framework. Given a document $\mathcal{D} = \{w_1, \ldots, w_J\}$, where w_j denotes the jth token in $\mathcal{D}$, and a KG $\mathcal{G}$, the framework of document-level RE with entity knowledge injection is

$$\mathbf{H} = [\mathbf{h}_{w_1}, \ldots, \mathbf{h}_{w_J}] = \text{Encode}(\mathcal{D}),$$
$$\mathbf{H}' = \text{KnowledgeInject}(\mathcal{D}, \mathbf{H}, \mathcal{G}), \tag{1}$$
$$\mathbf{z} = \text{Predict}(\mathbf{H}'),$$

where $\mathbf{h}_{w_j}$ denotes the hidden representation of w_j, and $\mathbf{z}$ denotes the prediction probability distribution of relations.   □

4   Knowledge Injection

The architecture of the proposed knowledge injection framework KIRE is depicted in Fig. 2, which accepts the document $\mathcal{D}$, the hidden representation $\mathbf{H}$ of $\mathcal{D}$ and the relevant KG $\mathcal{G}$ as input. It injects the entity knowledge from the coreference triples, attribute triples and relation triples into an RE model, and outputs the final hidden representation $\mathbf{H}'$.

Specifically, we inject the coreference triples into the basic document-level RE model with coreference distillation and context exchanging. Apart from this, the attribute triples are semantically encoded with AutoEncoder [16], and the encoded results are then reused to initialize the representations of relation triples. We use a relational graph attention network (R-GAT) [3] to encode the relation triples and generate the KG representations of entities. Finally, the KG representations of entities and the token representations that have been enhanced by coreference knowledge are aggregated by representation reconciliation. Details are described in the following subsections.

4.1 Coreference Encoding

This module leverages coreference triples to exchange the contextual information between aliases, and thus the representations of alias mentions can be closer.

Coreference Distillation. A simple method is to model the coreference triples as a new type of edges in the document graph and reuse graph-based models [11,13,24]. However, such a method cannot be generalized to the sequence-based models since they do not construct document graphs. Furthermore, the accuracy of existing coreference resolution tools is still far from perfect, even they are trained on large corpora. To alleviate error accumulation, it is inappropriate to directly add the edges as strong guidance information in the RE models.

Knowledge distillation [6,19], as a model compression technique and a solution to integrate external knowledge into a target model, has been used in a wide range of NLP tasks. In this paper, we leverage the idea of knowledge distillation and propose coreference distillation to inject coreference triples into the RE models. Our main idea is to leverage a pre-trained coreference resolution model which has been trained on a large coreference dataset as the *teacher* model, and then force the *student* model (i.e., the RE model) to generate a prediction probability distribution that approximates the teacher model on the coreference triples. Finally, the student model learns the coreference knowledge and generalization ability in the teacher model. Formally, for a coreference triple (m_s, m_t, p_{cr}), its coreference probability generated by the teacher model is defined as

$$P_{\text{tea}}(m_s, m_t) = p_{cr}. \tag{2}$$

The student model generates the coreference probability with a multi-layer perceptron (MLP):

$$P_{\text{stu}}(m_s, m_t) = \text{MLP}\Big([\mathbf{m}_s; \mathbf{m}_t; \mathbf{\Delta}(\psi(m_s, m_t))]\Big), \tag{3}$$

where $\mathbf{m}_s$ and $\mathbf{m}_t$ denote the hidden representations of alias mentions m_s and m_t, respectively, which are calculated by averaging the hidden representations of tokens in m_s and m_t, that is, $\mathbf{m}_s = \text{avg}_{w_j \in m_s}(\mathbf{h}_{w_j}), \mathbf{m}_t = \text{avg}_{w_j \in m_t}(\mathbf{h}_{w_j})$. ";" is the concatenation operation, and $\psi(m_s, m_t)$ denotes the shortest distance between m_s, m_t in the document. We divide the distance into $\{1, 2, \ldots, 2^{\beta}\}$ bins, and associate each bin with a trainable distance vector. $\mathbf{\Delta}(\cdot)$ associates each ψ to the distance vector of relevant bin. Empirically, aliases with different distances should have different impacts on each other. Therefore, we propose trainable distance vectors to model and utilize such difference.

We enforce the student model to learn from the teacher model using the following coreference loss:

$$\mathcal{L}_{cr} = \sum_{(m_s, m_t) \in C} \text{KL}\big(P_{\text{tea}}(m_s, m_t) \parallel P_{\text{stu}}(m_s, m_t)\big), \tag{4}$$

where $\text{KL}(\cdot)$ is the Kullback-Leibler divergence.

Context Exchanging. Based on the learned coreference knowledge, we further enable each alias mention to interact with its most similar counterpart, so as to exchange the semantic information between them. Specifically, given an alias mention m_s, we update its hidden representation through $\mathbf{m}_s = \mathbf{m}_s + \mathbf{m}_{t^*}$, where $t^* = \arg\max_t \{P_{\text{stu}}(m_s, m_t) \mid (m_s, m_t) \in C\}$. In this way, the representations of the pronouns in particular can be enriched via their referents.

Finally, we obtain the token representations enhanced by coreference knowledge through the representations of alias mentions (if exists):

$$\mathbf{h}'_{w_j} = \begin{cases} \mathbf{m}_s, & \text{if } w_j \in m_s \\ \mathbf{h}_{w_j}, & \text{otherwise} \end{cases}. \tag{5}$$

In coreference encoding, the MLP contains $d_{\text{MLP}}(2d_{\text{token}} + d_{\text{dist}}) + 2d_{\text{token}}$ parameters, where $d_{\text{MLP}}, d_{\text{token}}, d_{\text{dist}}$ are the dimensions of MLP hidden layers, token representations and trainable distance vectors, respectively.

4.2 Knowledge Graph Encoding

This module aims to encode the attribute triples and the relation triples to generate the KG representations of entities.

Attribute Triple Encoding. A KG defines a set of common attributes, e.g., *rdfs:label* and *schema:description*, to describe its entities. We encode the attribute triples in the KG and generate the attribute representations for corresponding entities. For each attribute triple of an entity, we concatenate the attribute name a and attribute value v into a token sequence $q = [a; v] = (w_1, \ldots, w_M)$. In order to cope with the out-of-vocabulary problem, we define a lookup function to convert each token to a token embedding:

$$\text{LP}(w_j) = \begin{cases} \text{WordEmb}(w_j), & \text{if } w_j \text{ has word emb.} \\ \text{CharEmb}(w_j), & \text{otherwise} \end{cases}, \tag{6}$$

where $\text{WordEmb}(\cdot)$ returns the word embedding in GloVe, and $\text{CharEmb}(\cdot)$ offers the average of character embeddings pre-trained with Skip-gram. Our method can work with other word or character embeddings easily.

Next, we leverage AutoEncoder to encode a sequence of token embeddings into an attribute triple embedding in an unsupervised way:

$$\mathbf{q} = \text{AutoEncoder}\Big([\text{LP}(w_1); \ldots; \text{LP}(w_M)]\Big), \tag{7}$$

where AutoEncoder is pre-trained on the attribute triples. We conduct self-supervised training, and both encoder and decoder of AutoEncoder use BiLSTM. AutoEncoder has good capacity for feature extraction and compression. In our model, the input of AutoEncoder is a concatenation vector of an entity and its attributes. The reconstruction loss of AutoEncoder can help extract a better compressed feature representation while preserving the attribute knowledge.

Finally, we stack all attribute triple embeddings of an entity into a one-dimensional CNN to obtain the attribute representation of the entity:

$$\mathbf{h}_{e_i}^0 = \text{MaxPooling}(\text{CNN}_{1D}(\|_j \mathbf{q}_j)), \tag{8}$$

where $\|$ denotes the stack operation, and $\mathbf{h}_{e_i}^0$ is the attribute representation of entity e_i, which would be used as the input representation for relation triple encoding below. Here, we choose CNN since the convolutional layer is a good feature extractor to learn high-level representations from value embeddings while reducing the dimension of output representations. Furthermore, we use the 1D convolution kernel as its invariance to the order of attribute embeddings.

Relation Triple Encoding. The relation triples present in the form of an entity-relation graph structure, and the topology and relation types are the key to encode such knowledge. Based on the attribute representations of entities, we employ a R-GAT [3] with K layers to convolute the entity-relation graph. R-GAT incorporates relation types using different embeddings and calculates attention scores on all adjacent nodes based on entity embeddings and relation embeddings. Specifically, the node forward-pass update for the $(k+1)^{\text{th}}$ layer is

$$\mathbf{e}_{ij}^{(k,b)} = \mathbf{W}_{\text{out}}^{(k,b)^T} \left[\mathbf{W}_{\text{in}}^{(k,b)} \mathbf{h}_i^{(k)}; \mathbf{W}_{\text{in}}^{(k,b)} \mathbf{h}_j^{(k)}; \mathbf{M}(r_{ij}) \right],$$

$$\alpha_{ij}^{(k,b)} = \frac{\exp\left(\text{LeakyReLU}(\mathbf{e}_{ij}^{(k,b)})\right)}{\sum_{l \in U_i} \exp\left(\text{LeakyReLU}(\mathbf{e}_{il}^{(k,b)})\right)}, \tag{9}$$

$$\mathbf{h}_i^{(k+1)} = \frac{1}{B} \sum_{b=1}^{B} \sigma\left(\sum_{l \in U_i} \alpha_{il}^{(k,b)} \mathbf{W}_{\text{in}}^{(k,b)} \mathbf{h}_l^{(k)} \right),$$

where $\mathbf{W}_{\text{in}}^{(k,b)}$ and $\mathbf{W}_{\text{out}}^{(k,b)}$ denote two trainable parameters of the bth attention head $(1 \le b \le B)$ at the kth layer. $\mathbf{h}_i^{(k)}$ and $\mathbf{h}_j^{(k)}$ are the node representations of entities e_i and e_j at the kth layer, respectively. $\mathbf{M}$ is a trainable mapping matrix corresponding to the relation types in the KG. r_{ij} is the relation type between e_i and e_j. LeakyReLU$(\cdot)$ and $\sigma(\cdot)$ are the activation functions. U_i is the neighbor set of e_i. In this way, the entity representations are updated via their all adjacent entity embeddings and relation embeddings at the previous layer.

We refer to the representations of entities after graph convolution as the *KG representations* of entities, which encode the knowledge in both attribute triples and relation triples. We simply denote the KG representation of entity e_i by $\mathbf{h}_{e_i}$.

In the KG encoding, the attribute encoding has $d_{\text{Auto}} N_{\max} N_{\text{kernel}}(d_{\text{kernel}}^2 + 1)$ parameters, where d_{Auto} is the output dimension of AutoEncoder, $N_{\max}$ is the maximum number of attributes that an entity has, N_{kernel} is the number of kernels, and d_{kernel} is the kernel size of CNN. The R-GAT network in the relation triple encoding contains $2(N_{\text{layer}} - 1)N_{\text{head}} d_{\text{RGAT}}^2 + d_{\text{RGAT}} d_{\text{ent}}$ parameters, where N_{layer} is the number of layers in R-GAT, N_{head} is the number of attention heads at each layer of R-GAT, d_{RGAT} is the hidden dimension of R-GAT hidden layers, and d_{ent} is the dimension of entity representations.

4.3 Representation Reconciliation

The token representations and the KG representations of entities capture different knowledge in independent semantic spaces. Following ERNIE [37] and K-BERT [10], we employ a representation reconciliation module to exchange the knowledge from entities in the KG with their linked tokens in the document.

The representation reconciliation module consists of N-stacked aggregators. For the nth $(1 \leq n \leq N)$ aggregator, given the token representations $\{\mathbf{h}_{w_1}^{n-1}, \ldots, \mathbf{h}_{w_J}^{n-1}\}$ and the KG representations of entities $\{\mathbf{h}_{e_1}^{n-1}, \ldots, \mathbf{h}_{e_I}^{n-1}\}$ from the preceding aggregator, the fusion phase is formulated as

$$\tilde{\mathbf{h}} = \begin{cases} \sigma(\tilde{\mathbf{W}}_w^{(n)} \tilde{\mathbf{h}}_{w_j}^{(n)} + \tilde{\mathbf{W}}_e^{(n)} \tilde{\mathbf{h}}_{e_i}^{(n)} + \tilde{\mathbf{b}}^{(n)}), & \text{if } w_j, e_i \text{ align} \\ \sigma(\tilde{\mathbf{W}}_w^{(n)} \tilde{\mathbf{h}}_{w_j}^{(n)} + \tilde{\mathbf{b}}^{(n)}), & \text{otherwise} \end{cases}, \tag{10}$$

where $\tilde{\mathbf{h}}_{w_j}^{(n)}, \tilde{\mathbf{h}}_{e_i}^{(n)}$ are the token representation and KG representation after the multi-head self-attention [22], respectively. $\tilde{\mathbf{W}}_w^{(n)}, \tilde{\mathbf{W}}_e^{(n)}, \tilde{\mathbf{b}}^{(n)}$ are three trainable parameters. The information in the two semantic spaces is mutually integrated.

Then, the reconstruction phase leverages $\tilde{\mathbf{h}}$ to refine the output representations of each token and entity in the aligned token-entity pairs:

$$\begin{aligned} \mathbf{h}_{w_j}^{(n)} &= \sigma(\mathbf{W}_w^{(n)} \tilde{\mathbf{h}} + \mathbf{b}_w^{(n)}), \\ \mathbf{h}_{e_i}^{(n)} &= \sigma(\mathbf{W}_e^{(n)} \tilde{\mathbf{h}} + \mathbf{b}_e^{(n)}). \end{aligned} \tag{11}$$

Here, the aligned token representations and entity representations are updated and enhanced by the integrated information. Note that the representations of entities without aligned tokens would not be updated.

Finally, we obtain the token representation sequence $\{\mathbf{h}_{w_1}^N, \ldots, \mathbf{h}_{w_J}^N\}$ from the last aggregator, which would constitute $\mathbf{H}'$ and be fed to the prediction layer.

To supervise the above process, we employ a token-entity alignment task. For each aligned token-entity pair (w_j, e_i), we predict the aligned KG entity e_i based on the token w_j. We only ask the model to predict entities within a given entity candidate set. By default, all linked entities in the document form the candidate set. For the token sequence $\{w_1, \ldots, w_J\}$ and the corresponding candidate entities $\{e_1, \ldots, e_I\}$, the token-entity alignment loss is

$$\mathcal{L}_{kg} = \sum_{j=1}^{J} \sum_{i=1}^{I} f_{j,i}^* * P(e_i \mid w_j), \tag{12}$$

where $f_{j,i}^* \in \{0, 1\}$ is the true alignment label between w_j and e_i, and $P(e_i \mid w_j) = \dfrac{\exp\left(\text{Linear}(\mathbf{h}_{w_j}^{(N)}) \cdot \mathbf{h}_{e_i}\right)}{\sum_{l=1}^{I} \exp\left(\text{Linear}(\mathbf{h}_{w_j}^{(N)}) \cdot \mathbf{h}_{e_l}\right)}$ returns the probability that e_i can be predicted by w_j.

We optimize the RE loss, coreference loss and token-entity alignment loss with multi-task learning. The final loss is

$$\mathcal{L} = \alpha_1 \cdot \mathcal{L}_{re} + \alpha_2 \cdot \mathcal{L}_{cr} + \alpha_3 \cdot \mathcal{L}_{kg}, \tag{13}$$

where α_1, α_2 and α_3 are the weight hyperparameters.

Table 1. Dataset statistics. Inst. denotes relation instances excluding N/A relation.

Datasets		#Doc	#Rel	#Inst	#N/A Inst
DocRED	Training set	3,053	96	38,269	1,163,035
	Validation set	1,000	96	12,332	385,263
	Test set	1,000	96	12,842	379,316
DWIE	Training set	544	66	13,524	492,057
	Validation set	137	66	3,488	121,750
	Test set	96	66	2,453	78,995

In the representation reconciliation, for each aggregator, the multi-head self-attention networks contain $4d_{\text{token}}^2 + 4d_{\text{ent}}^2$ parameters, the fusion phase contains $d_{\text{out}}(N_{\text{token}} + N_{\text{align}}) + N_{\text{token}}$ parameters, and the reconstruction phase contains $2N_{\text{align}}(d_{\text{out}} + 1)$ parameters, where d_{out} is the output dimension of multi-head self-attention networks, N_{token} is the number of tokens, and N_{align} is the number of aligned token-entity pairs. Therefore, the parameters of representation reconciliation are $N_{\text{agg}}\big[4d_{\text{token}}^2 + 4d_{\text{ent}}^2 + d_{\text{out}}(N_{\text{token}} + N_{\text{align}}) + N_{\text{token}} + 2N_{\text{align}}(d_{\text{out}} + 1)\big]$, where N_{agg} is the number of aggregators.

Model Complexity. The total parameter number of KIRE is $d_{\text{MLP}}(2d_{\text{token}} + d_{\text{dist}}) + 2d_{\text{token}} + d_{\text{Auto}}N_{\text{max}}(d_{\text{kernel}}^2 + 1) + 2(N_{\text{layer}} - 1)N_{\text{head}}d_{\text{RGAT}}^2 + d_{\text{RGAT}}d_{\text{ent}} + N_{\text{agg}}\big[4d_{\text{token}}^2 + 4d_{\text{ent}}^2 + d_{\text{out}}(N_{\text{token}} + N_{\text{align}}) + N_{\text{token}} + 2N_{\text{align}}(d_{\text{out}} + 1)\big]$.

5   Experiments and Results

We develop KIRE with PyTorch 1.7.1, and test on an X86 server with two Xeon Gold 5117 CPUs, 250 GB memory, two Titan RTX GPUs and Ubuntu 18.04.

5.1   Experiment Setup

Datasets. We select two benchmark datasets in our experiments: (1) DocRED [32] is a crowdsourced dataset for document-level RE. The relation labels in its test set are not public. (2) DWIE [33] is a new dataset for document-level multi-task information extraction. We use the data relevant to RE only. Since DWIE does not have the validation set, we randomly split its training set into 80% for training and 20% for validation. Table 1 lists the statistical data.

Knowledge Graph. We select Wikidata (2020–12–01) as our KG due to its coverage and popularity [2,21]. The numbers of its relation and attribute triples are 506,809,195 and 729,798,070, respectively. To prevent the test leakage, we filter out all the relation triples with entity pairs to be labeled in the test sets.

Evaluation Metrics. We measure F1-score (F1) and Ignore F1-score (Ign F1) in our experiments. We repeat five times using the same hyperparameters but different random seeds, and report the means and standard deviations.

Implementation Details. To achieve good generalization, we do not carry out excessive feature engineering on Wikidata. Numerical attributes are regarded as texts, and their semantics are captured by the word embeddings [14]. We employ NeuralCoref 4.0 as our coreference resolution tool and also use the annotations provided in DocRED and DWIE. We use a two-stage method for training, which first trains a basic RE model and then fine-tunes this model to train the knowledge injection layer. The training procedure is optimized with Adam. Moreover, to compare fairly, the basic RE model and its corresponding KIRE adopt the same hyperparameter values. We set the batch size to 4 and the learning rate to 0.0005. We use three R-GAT layers and two aggregators. Moreover, $\alpha_1, \alpha_2, \alpha_3$ are 1, 0.01 and 0.01, respectively. The dimension of hidden layers in MLP is 256, the dimensions of GloVe and Skip-gram are 100, and the dimension of hidden layers in AutoEncoder is 50. See the source code for more details.

Table 2. Comparison of result improvement on baseline models

Models	DocRED				DWIE			
	Validation set		Test set		Validation set		Test set	
	Ign F1	F1	Ign F1	F1	Ign F1	F1	Ign F1	F1
CNN	$43.91_{\pm 0.02}$	$45.99_{\pm 0.05}$	$42.61_{\pm 0.06}$	$44.80_{\pm 0.08}$	$38.21_{\pm 0.04}$	$49.09_{\pm 0.06}$	$40.06_{\pm 0.08}$	$51.21_{\pm 0.13}$
+ KIRE	$\mathbf{46.18}_{\pm 0.04}$	$\mathbf{48.21}_{\pm 0.06}$	$\mathbf{45.24}_{\pm 0.05}$	$\mathbf{47.27}_{\pm 0.08}$	$\mathbf{39.68}_{\pm 0.05}$	$\mathbf{50.49}_{\pm 0.09}$	$\mathbf{42.09}_{\pm 0.04}$	$\mathbf{53.16}_{\pm 0.08}$
+ RESIDE	$45.03_{\pm 0.06}$	$47.12_{\pm 0.08}$	$43.79_{\pm 0.05}$	$45.96_{\pm 0.09}$	$39.24_{\pm 0.04}$	$50.13_{\pm 0.07}$	$41.31_{\pm 0.06}$	$52.47_{\pm 0.11}$
+ RECON	$45.57_{\pm 0.04}$	$47.64_{\pm 0.07}$	$44.53_{\pm 0.07}$	$46.68_{\pm 0.10}$	$39.42_{\pm 0.03}$	$50.34_{\pm 0.06}$	$41.73_{\pm 0.07}$	$52.74_{\pm 0.09}$
+ KB-graph	$45.49_{\pm 0.03}$	$47.58_{\pm 0.08}$	$44.46_{\pm 0.06}$	$46.61_{\pm 0.09}$	$39.34_{\pm 0.06}$	$50.26_{\pm 0.09}$	$41.65_{\pm 0.08}$	$52.63_{\pm 0.12}$
LSTM	$48.49_{\pm 0.05}$	$50.41_{\pm 0.07}$	$47.41_{\pm 0.04}$	$49.47_{\pm 0.10}$	$52.79_{\pm 0.03}$	$63.61_{\pm 0.08}$	$54.87_{\pm 0.07}$	$65.17_{\pm 0.14}$
+ KIRE	$\mathbf{50.41}_{\pm 0.03}$	$\mathbf{52.49}_{\pm 0.06}$	$\mathbf{49.55}_{\pm 0.06}$	$\mathbf{51.72}_{\pm 0.09}$	$\mathbf{54.11}_{\pm 0.04}$	$\mathbf{64.86}_{\pm 0.08}$	$\mathbf{56.74}_{\pm 0.05}$	$\mathbf{66.91}_{\pm 0.07}$
+ RESIDE	$49.58_{\pm 0.04}$	$51.49_{\pm 0.08}$	$48.52_{\pm 0.06}$	$50.51_{\pm 0.09}$	$53.87_{\pm 0.02}$	$64.56_{\pm 0.06}$	$55.96_{\pm 0.06}$	$66.29_{\pm 0.12}$
+ RECON	$50.03_{\pm 0.03}$	$51.98_{\pm 0.08}$	$49.07_{\pm 0.07}$	$51.12_{\pm 0.12}$	$53.98_{\pm 0.03}$	$64.69_{\pm 0.07}$	$56.35_{\pm 0.04}$	$66.51_{\pm 0.08}$
+ KB-graph	$49.94_{\pm 0.04}$	$51.89_{\pm 0.07}$	$48.98_{\pm 0.05}$	$51.04_{\pm 0.09}$	$53.91_{\pm 0.05}$	$64.61_{\pm 0.08}$	$56.27_{\pm 0.06}$	$66.43_{\pm 0.09}$
BiLSTM	$48.51_{\pm 0.04}$	$50.54_{\pm 0.08}$	$47.58_{\pm 0.05}$	$49.66_{\pm 0.11}$	$53.95_{\pm 0.05}$	$63.96_{\pm 0.07}$	$54.91_{\pm 0.09}$	$65.39_{\pm 0.11}$
+ KIRE	$\mathbf{50.46}_{\pm 0.02}$	$\mathbf{52.65}_{\pm 0.05}$	$\mathbf{49.69}_{\pm 0.04}$	$\mathbf{51.98}_{\pm 0.07}$	$\mathbf{55.86}_{\pm 0.05}$	$\mathbf{65.77}_{\pm 0.09}$	$\mathbf{56.88}_{\pm 0.05}$	$\mathbf{67.02}_{\pm 0.08}$
+ RESIDE	$49.64_{\pm 0.03}$	$51.59_{\pm 0.06}$	$48.62_{\pm 0.04}$	$50.71_{\pm 0.10}$	$55.04_{\pm 0.06}$	$65.01_{\pm 0.09}$	$56.16_{\pm 0.05}$	$66.47_{\pm 0.12}$
+ RECON	$49.97_{\pm 0.04}$	$52.06_{\pm 0.07}$	$49.14_{\pm 0.06}$	$51.32_{\pm 0.09}$	$55.42_{\pm 0.04}$	$65.38_{\pm 0.08}$	$56.51_{\pm 0.06}$	$66.63_{\pm 0.09}$
+ KB-graph	$49.89_{\pm 0.03}$	$51.98_{\pm 0.07}$	$49.05_{\pm 0.05}$	$51.26_{\pm 0.08}$	$55.35_{\pm 0.03}$	$65.31_{\pm 0.09}$	$56.42_{\pm 0.07}$	$66.55_{\pm 0.11}$
Context-aware	$49.79_{\pm 0.03}$	$51.84_{\pm 0.04}$	$48.73_{\pm 0.07}$	$50.91_{\pm 0.12}$	$54.68_{\pm 0.04}$	$64.29_{\pm 0.06}$	$56.53_{\pm 0.07}$	$65.91_{\pm 0.09}$
+ KIRE	$\mathbf{51.07}_{\pm 0.03}$	$\mathbf{53.25}_{\pm 0.07}$	$\mathbf{50.43}_{\pm 0.05}$	$\mathbf{52.75}_{\pm 0.10}$	$\mathbf{56.58}_{\pm 0.03}$	$\mathbf{65.62}_{\pm 0.07}$	$\mathbf{58.41}_{\pm 0.04}$	$\mathbf{67.37}_{\pm 0.08}$
+ RESIDE	$50.43_{\pm 0.04}$	$52.59_{\pm 0.07}$	$49.58_{\pm 0.05}$	$51.86_{\pm 0.09}$	$55.74_{\pm 0.03}$	$65.11_{\pm 0.07}$	$57.64_{\pm 0.05}$	$66.78_{\pm 0.08}$
+ RECON	$50.78_{\pm 0.03}$	$52.89_{\pm 0.06}$	$49.97_{\pm 0.04}$	$52.27_{\pm 0.08}$	$56.12_{\pm 0.05}$	$65.48_{\pm 0.08}$	$58.02_{\pm 0.06}$	$66.94_{\pm 0.10}$
+ KB-graph	$50.69_{\pm 0.05}$	$52.81_{\pm 0.07}$	$49.88_{\pm 0.06}$	$52.19_{\pm 0.11}$	$56.03_{\pm 0.04}$	$65.39_{\pm 0.09}$	$57.94_{\pm 0.05}$	$66.89_{\pm 0.11}$

5.2   Main Results

Improvement on Baseline Models. To validate the effectiveness and versatility of KIRE, we pick four baseline models in [32]. The first three models directly employ CNN, LSTM and BiLSTM to encode documents, while the fourth model is called context-aware, which leverages the attention mechanism with BiLSTM. These four models are native to the DocRED dataset and widely chosen as the competitors in many RE studies [7,11,18,27,28,30,35,38].

Table 2 depicts the result improvement, and we observe that: (1) KIRE consistently improves the performance of all baselines on DocRED and DWIE, which demonstrates the good generalization of KIRE. Small standard deviations also tells the good stability of KIRE. (2) KIRE obtains a significant improvement of Ign F1/F1 up to 2.63/2.47 on DocRED and 2.03/1.95 on DWIE, respectively. This is mainly because the ways that the baseline models encode a document are too simple to capture some part of important contextual information in the document. External knowledge from KIRE makes up for this part, and therefore effectively improves the model performance. (3) CNN performs poorly, because the text order is important for RE while CNN cannot process such order well.

Table 3. Result improvement on state-of-the-art models

Models	DocRED				DWIE			
	Validation set		Test set		Validation set		Test set	
	Ign F1	F1	Ign F1	F1	Ign F1	F1	Ign F1	F1
ATLOP	$59.25_{\pm 0.03}$	$61.14_{\pm 0.07}$	$58.32_{\pm 0.05}$	$60.44_{\pm 0.08}$	$69.12_{\pm 0.04}$	$76.32_{\pm 0.09}$	$73.85_{\pm 0.08}$	$80.38_{\pm 0.12}$
+ KIRE	$\mathbf{59.58}_{\pm 0.04}$	$\mathbf{61.45}_{\pm 0.09}$	$\mathbf{59.35}_{\pm 0.06}$	$\mathbf{61.39}_{\pm 0.11}$	$\mathbf{69.75}_{\pm 0.05}$	$\mathbf{76.75}_{\pm 0.08}$	$\mathbf{74.43}_{\pm 0.07}$	$\mathbf{80.73}_{\pm 0.15}$
SSAN	$56.68_{\pm 0.03}$	$58.95_{\pm 0.04}$	$56.06_{\pm 0.05}$	$58.41_{\pm 0.06}$	$51.80_{\pm 0.05}$	$62.87_{\pm 0.10}$	$57.49_{\pm 0.09}$	$67.77_{\pm 0.12}$
+ KIRE	$57.29_{\pm 0.05}$	$59.31_{\pm 0.06}$	$56.31_{\pm 0.06}$	$58.65_{\pm 0.08}$	$52.67_{\pm 0.06}$	$63.64_{\pm 0.10}$	$60.57_{\pm 0.09}$	$69.58_{\pm 0.12}$
GLRE	$56.57_{\pm 0.06}$	$58.43_{\pm 0.09}$	$55.40_{\pm 0.07}$	$57.40_{\pm 0.13}$	$63.11_{\pm 0.03}$	$71.21_{\pm 0.06}$	$62.95_{\pm 0.05}$	$72.24_{\pm 0.09}$
+ KIRE	$57.31_{\pm 0.05}$	$59.45_{\pm 0.10}$	$56.54_{\pm 0.09}$	$58.49_{\pm 0.14}$	$65.17_{\pm 0.05}$	$71.68_{\pm 0.09}$	$64.32_{\pm 0.06}$	$73.35_{\pm 0.11}$

Comparison with Existing Knowledge Injection Models. We choose three recent models: RESIDE [21], RECON [2] and KB-graph [25], which inject extra knowledge into RE models. Specifically, we use KB-graph instead of the full version KB-both since it selects Wikipedia as another knowledge source, which is unfair to other models. To compare fairly, we only adopt the knowledge injection modules of the above models to enhance the token representations in the documents, and the representations are used by the baseline RE models to predict the relation labels.

Table 2 presents the comparison results, and we obtain several findings: (1) KIRE is consistently superior to RESIDE, RECON and KB-graph with an improvement of Ign F1/F1 up to 0.71/0.66 on DocRED and 0.39/0.43 on DWIE, respectively. Given that the test sets contain (ten) thousand relation instances, we think that the improvement makes sense. For example, on the validation set of DocRED, KIRE can correctly predict an average of 478 more instances than the second best method RECON. Such improvement brought by KIRE attributes to that KIRE absorbs more knowledge like coreferences and fuses the knowledge better. (2) The improvement brought by RESIDE is the lowest since it only injects limited knowledge like entity types and relation aliases. RECON and KB-graph explore more knowledge from the KG, but they still ignore the coreference knowledge. Besides, the methods that they employ to integrate knowledge are representation average or concatenation, which may lose part of semantic information in the injected knowledge.

Improvement on State-of-the-Art Models. We employ two sequence-based models, ATLOP [38] and SSAN [30], as well as a graph-based model, GLRE [27], due to their good performance and open source. Enhancing these models is very challenging, since they have already explored various information in the documents and achieved state-of-the-art results. Due to the limit of GPU RAM, we use the BERT-base versions of ATLOP, SSAN and GLRE and re-run them according to the hyperparameters reported in their papers and source code.

The result improvement is shown in Table 3, and we have several findings: (1) For the two sequence-based models, KIRE obtains an improvement of Ign F1/F1 up to 1.03/0.95 on DocRED and 3.08/1.81 on DWIE, respectively. This mainly attributes to the fact that the extra knowledge injected by KIRE can effectively help the models identify and capture more interactions between entity pairs especially across sentences. (2) For the graph-based model, KIRE obtains an improvement of Ign F1/F1 up to 1.14/1.09 on DocRED and 1.37/1.11, respectively. This is largely due to the fact that the extra knowledge injected by KIRE can enrich the representations of mention nodes and entity nodes in the document graphs for more accurate reasoning between entity pairs especially of longer distance. (3) This also verifies that our knowledge injection framework can be generalized to a broad range of document-level RE models.

5.3 Detailed Analysis

Ablation Study. We conduct an ablation study on the four baseline models. For "w/o distill", we disable the coreference distillation module and directly use the original coreferences as the injected knowledge. For "w/o attr.", we initialize the relation triple representations by max pooling the word embeddings of entity labels. For "w/o rel.", we directly adopt the attribute representations of entities as KG representations. For "w/o KG", we disable the whole KG encoding module. Additionally, we replace KIRE with three simple variants for knowledge injection. For "w/rep. avg", we average the hidden representations of alias mentions, and the token representations are averaged with KG representations of entities. For "w/rep. concat", we concatenate the representations of alias mentions, and the KG representations of entities are concatenated after the aligned token representations. For "w/MLP", we leverage two MLP layers to fuse the representations of alias mentions and the KG representations of entities with the aligned token representations, respectively.

From Fig. 3, we can see that: (1) Ign F1/F1-scores reduce when we disable any modules, showing their contributions. (2) The changes caused by removing one type of knowledge are not obvious, mainly due to the crossovers among the three types of knowledge in the information space. (3) The results decline if we disable the coreference distillation, due to the coreference errors in the injected knowledge. (4) If we remove the KG encoding, the results drop drastically, as the baseline models cannot generate extra relation and attribute knowledge. (5) Compared to the three variants, the larger increase brought by KIRE validates the effectiveness of coreference distillation and representation reconciliation.

Influence of Mention Number. We measure the effectiveness of KIRE w.r.t. average mention number for each entity pair. For DocRED, we evaluate it on the validation set. The results are shown in Table 4. We observe that KIRE gains higher performance for the entity pairs with more mentions, in particular when the average mention number > 3. This is because KIRE injects knowledge into the RE models by updating the token representations of entity mentions, which has a greater impact on the entities with more mentions.

Comparison with Alternative Graph Encoders. We compare R-GAT with GCN [9], GAT [23] and R-GCN [17]. We remove the coreference encoding and attribute triple encoding to eliminate their interference. From Fig. 4, the performance of R-GCN and R-GAT is better than GCN and GAT, as they can capture the relation information in the entity-relation graphs. The results of

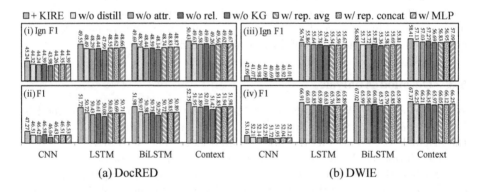

(a) DocRED   (b) DWIE

Fig. 3. Results of ablation study

Table 4. Results w.r.t. average mention number

Models	DocRED						DWIE					
	1		(1,3]		> 3		1		(1,3]		> 3	
	Ign F1	F1	Ign F1	F1	Ign F1	F1	Ign F1	F1	Ign F1	F1	Ign F1	F1
CNN	42.24	44.27	44.42	46.45	45.38	47.35	39.35	50.44	40.81	51.96	41.94	53.05
+KIRE	↑1.64	↑1.75	↑2.71	↑2.89	↑3.21	↑3.43	↑1.52	↑1.49	↑2.35	↑2.32	↑2.95	↑2.98
LSTM	47.39	49.35	48.59	50.53	50.09	52.08	54.14	64.41	55.97	66.14	57.21	67.55
+KIRE	↑1.76	↑1.87	↑2.65	↑2.82	↑3.37	↑3.51	↑1.31	↑1.26	↑1.87	↑1.89	↑2.35	↑2.29
BiLSTM	47.35	49.32	48.61	50.54	50.21	52.28	54.07	64.61	56.01	66.25	57.30	67.79
+KIRE	↑1.83	↑1.95	↑2.73	↑2.91	↑3.31	↑3.43	↑1.49	↑1.12	↑1.91	↑1.86	↑2.34	↑2.16
Context-aware	48.33	50.19	49.63	51.64	51.10	53.34	55.98	65.16	58.02	67.01	58.72	68.41
+KIRE	↑1.43	↑1.56	↑2.35	↑2.47	↑2.87	↑2.98	↑1.35	↑0.91	↑1.92	↑1.57	↑2.32	↑1.95

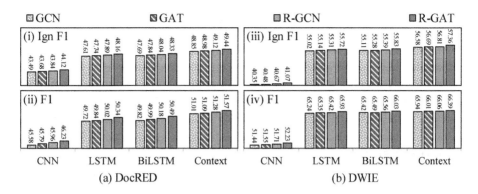

Fig. 4. Result comparison of graph encoders

GAT are greater than GCN, as GAT can selectively aggregate the neighboring information by self-attention. Similarly, R-GAT slightly outperforms R-GCN.

Case Study. We depict two successful cases and a failed case in Table 5. We still use CNN, LSTM, BiLSTM and Context-aware as baselines.

Table 5. Case study. *Target entities* and *related entities* are colored.

[S1]	*The Waterloo Moraine* ... was created as a moraine in the *Regional Municipality of Waterloo*, in Ontario, Canada.
[S2]	*It* covers ... and some parts of the townships of Wellesley and *North Dumfries*.
Case 1	Gold: *P131* Baseline models: *N/A* +KIRE: *P131*
[S1]	The news that British's Prince Harry is engaged to his partner *Meghan Markle* has attracted widespread attention from England, *America* and around the world.
[S10]	*Markle*'s parents *Thomas Markle* and Doria Ragland said in a statement: ...
Case 2	Gold: *citizen_of* Baseline models: *N/A* +KIRE: *citizen_of*
[S1]	*Robert Kingsbury Huntington* ... was a naval aircrewman and member of Torpedo Squadron 8 (or VT-8).
[S2]	*He* was radioman/gunner to *Ensign George Gay*'s TBD Devastator aircraft ...
[S4]	Born in Los Angeles ... *he* was enlisted in *the United States Navy* 21 Apr. 1941.
Case 3	Gold: *P241* Baseline models: *N/A* +KIRE: *N/A*

- **Case 1.** To identify the relation between *North Dumfries* in *S*2 and *Regional Municipality of Waterloo* in *S*1, we use the extra knowledge (*Regional Municipality of Waterloo, instance of, regional municipality of Ontario*) and the coreference of *It* and *The Waterloo Moraine* from NeuralCoref to correctly infer the relation *P131 (located in the administrative territorial entity)*.
- **Case 2.** With the aid of the extra knowledge (*Meghan Markle, country of citizenship, United States of America*) and the coreference of *Meghan Markle* and *Markle* from NeuralCoref, we successfully detect the relation *citizen_of* between *Thomas Markle* in *S*10 and *America* in *S*1.

– **Case 3.** To recognize the relation between *Ensign George Gay* in *S2* and *the United States Navy* in *S4*, we require a bridge entity *Robert Kingsbury Huntington*. Through the coreference of *Robert* and *He* from NeuralCoref, we identify that *Robert* and *George* are comrades. Then from *S4*, we find out that *Robert* is enlisted in *the US Navy*. According to this reasoning chain, we can see that the relation between *George* and *the US Navy* is *P241 (military branch)*. KIRE fails to run such complex reasoning involving three sentences.

6 Conclusion

In this paper, we propose KIRE, an entity knowledge injection framework for enhancing document-level RE. Coreference knowledge is injected by coreference distillation, while factual knowledge is injected and fused with document representations via representation reconciliation. Our experiments validate the generalization and the stable performance increase of KIRE to various RE models. For future work, we plan to exploit other knowledge injection frameworks and integrate more knowledge sources.

Supplemental Material Statement: Source code for KIRE is available from Github at https://github.com/nju-websoft/KIRE. Datasets are available from [32,33].

References

1. Auer, S., Bizer, C., Kobilarov, G., Lehmann, J., Cyganiak, R., Ives, Z.: DBpedia: a nucleus for a web of open data. In: Aberer, K. (ed.) ASWC/ISWC -2007. LNCS, vol. 4825, pp. 722–735. Springer, Heidelberg (2007). https://doi.org/10.1007/978-3-540-76298-0_52
2. Bastos, A., Nadgeri, A., Singh, K., Mulang, I.O., Shekarpour, S., Hoffart, J., Kaul, M.: RECON: Relation extraction using knowledge graph context in a graph neural network. In: WWW, pp. 1673–1685. ACM, Online (2021)
3. Busbridge, D., Sherburn, D., Cavallo, P., Hammerla, N.Y.: Relational graph attention networks. CoRR abs/1904.05811 (2019)
4. Fernàndez-Cañellas, D., et al.: Enhancing online knowledge graph population with semantic knowledge. In: Pan, J.Z. (ed.) ISWC 2020. LNCS, vol. 12506, pp. 183–200. Springer, Cham (2020). https://doi.org/10.1007/978-3-030-62419-4_11
5. Heist, N., Paulheim, H.: Language-agnostic relation extraction from wikipedia abstracts. In: d'Amato, C. (ed.) ISWC 2017. LNCS, vol. 10587, pp. 383–399. Springer, Cham (2017). https://doi.org/10.1007/978-3-319-68288-4_23
6. Hinton, G., Vinyals, O., Dean, J.: Distilling the knowledge in a neural network. CoRR abs/1503.02531 (2015)
7. Huang, Q., Zhu, S., Feng, Y., Ye, Y., Lai, Y., Zhao, D.: Three sentences are all you need: Local path enhanced document relation extraction. In: ACL, pp. 998–1004. ACL, Online (2021)
8. Ji, G., Liu, K., He, S., Zhao, J.: Distant supervision for relation extraction with sentence-level attention and entity descriptions. In: AAAI, pp. 3060–3066. AAAI Press, San Francisco, CA, USA (2017)
9. Kipf, T.N., Welling, M.: Semi-supervised classification with graph convolutional networks. In: ICLR, OpenReview.net, Toulon, France (2017)

10. Liu, W., Zhou, P., Zhao, Z., Wang, Z., Ju, Q., Deng, H., Wang, P.: K-BERT: Enabling language representation with knowledge graph. In: AAAI, pp. 2901–2908. AAAI Press, New York, NY, USA (2020)
11. Nan, G., Guo, Z., Sekulic, I., Lu, W.: Reasoning with latent structure refinement for document-level relation extraction. In: ACL, pp. 1546–1557. ACL, Online (2020)
12. Pan, J.Z., Zhang, M., Singh, K., Harmelen, F., Gu, J., Zhang, Z.: Entity enabled relation linking. In: Ghidini, C. (ed.) ISWC 2019. LNCS, vol. 11778, pp. 523–538. Springer, Cham (2019). https://doi.org/10.1007/978-3-030-30793-6_30
13. Peng, N., Poon, H., Quirk, C., Toutanova, K., Yih, W.t.:Cross-sentence N-ary relation extraction with graph LSTMs.Trans. Assoc. Comput. Linguist. **5**, 101–115 (2017)
14. Pennington, J., Socher, R., Manning, C.D.: GloVe: Global vectors for word representation. In: EMNLP, pp. 1532–1543. ACL, Doha, Qatar (2014)
15. Quirk, C., Poon, H.: Distant supervision for relation extraction beyond the sentence boundary. In: EACL, pp. 1171–1182. ACL, Valencia, Spain (2017)
16. Rumelhart, D.E., Hinton, G.E., Williams, R.J.: Learning representations by back-propagating errors. Nature **323**, 533–536 (1986)
17. Schlichtkrull, M., Kipf, T.N., Bloem, P., van den Berg, R., Titov, I., Welling, M.: Modeling relational data with graph convolutional networks. In: Gangemi, A. (ed.) ESWC 2018. LNCS, vol. 10843, pp. 593–607. Springer, Cham (2018). https://doi.org/10.1007/978-3-319-93417-4_38
18. Tang, H., et al.: HIN: hierarchical inference network for document-level relation extraction. In: Lauw, H.W., Wong, R.C.-W., Ntoulas, A., Lim, E.-P., Ng, S.-K., Pan, S.J. (eds.) PAKDD 2020. LNCS (LNAI), vol. 12084, pp. 197–209. Springer, Cham (2020). https://doi.org/10.1007/978-3-030-47426-3_16
19. Tong, M., Xu, B., Wang, S., Cao, Y., Hou, L., Li, J., Xie, J.: Improving event detection via open-domain trigger knowledge. In: ACL, pp. 5887–5897. ACL, Online (2020)
20. Türker, R., Zhang, L., Alam, M., Sack, H.: Weakly supervised short text categorization using world knowledge. In: Pan, J.Z. (ed.) ISWC 2020. LNCS, vol. 12506, pp. 584–600. Springer, Cham (2020). https://doi.org/10.1007/978-3-030-62419-4_33
21. Vashishth, S., Joshi, R., Prayaga, S.S., Bhattacharyya, C., Talukdar, P.P.: RESIDE: improving distantly-supervised neural relation extraction using side information. In: EMNLP, pp. 1257–1266. ACL, Brussels, Belgium (2018)
22. Vaswani, A., Shazeer, N., Parmar, N., Uszkoreit, J., Jones, L., Gomez, A.N., Kaiser, Ł., Polosukhin, I.: Attention is all you need. In: NIPS, pp. 5998–6008. Curran Associates Inc, Long Beach, CA, USA (2017)
23. Veličković, P., Cucurull, G., Casanova, A., Romero, A., Lio, P., Bengio, Y.: Graph attention networks. In: ICLR, OpenReview.net, Vancouver, BC, Canada (2018)
24. Verga, P., Strubell, E., McCallum, A.: Simultaneously self-attending to all mentions for full-abstract biological relation extraction. In: NAACL, pp. 872–884. ACL, New Orleans, LA, USA (2018)
25. Verlinden, S., Zaporojets, K., Deleu, J., Demeester, T., Develder, C.: Injecting knowledge base information into end-to-end joint entity and relation extraction and coreference resolution. In: Findings of ACL, pp. 1952–1957. ACL, Online (2021)
26. Vrandečić, D., Krötzsch, M.: Wikidata: a free collaborative knowledgebase. CACM **57**(10), 78–85 (2014)
27. Wang, D., Hu, W., Cao, E., Sun, W.: Global-to-local neural networks for document-level relation extraction. In: EMNLP, pp. 3711–3721. ACL, Online (2020)
28. Wang, H., Focke, C., Sylvester, R., Mishra, N., Wang, W.: Fine-tune Bert for DocRED with two-step process. CoRR abs/1909.11898 (2019)

29. Wei, X., Wang, S., Zhang, D., Bhatia, P., Arnold, A.O.: Knowledge enhanced pre-trained language models: A comprehensive survey. CoRR abs/2110.08455 (2021)
30. Xu, B., Wang, Q., Lyu, Y., Zhu, Y., Mao, Z.: Entity structure within and through-out: Modeling mention dependencies for document-level relation extraction. In: AAAI, pp. 14149–14157. AAAI Press, Online (2021)
31. Xu, W., Chen, K., Zhao, T.: Document-level relation extraction with reconstruc-tion. In: AAAI, pp. 14167–14175. AAAI Press, Online (2021)
32. Yao, Y., et al.: DocRED: A large-scale document-level relation extraction dataset. In: ACL, pp. 764–777. ACL, Florence, Italy (2019)
33. Zaporojets, K., Deleu, J., Develder, C., Demeester, T.: DWIE: an entity-centric dataset for multi-task document-level information extraction. IPM **58**(4), 102563 (2021)
34. Zeng, D., Liu, K., Lai, S., Zhou, G., Zhao, J.: Relation classification via convo-lutional deep neural network. In: COLING, pp. 2335–2344. ACL, Dublin, Ireland (2014)
35. Zeng, S., Xu, R., Chang, B., Li, L.: Double graph based reasoning for document-level relation extraction. In: EMNLP, pp. 1630–1640. ACL, Online (2020)
36. Zhang, Y., Qi, P., Manning, C.D.: Graph convolution over pruned dependency trees improves relation extraction. In: EMNLP, pp. 2205–2215. ACL, Brussels, Belgium (2018)
37. Zhang, Z., Han, X., Liu, Z., Jiang, X., Sun, M., Liu, Q.: ERNIE: Enhanced language representation with informative entities. In: ACL, pp. 1441–1451. ACL, Florence, Italy (2019)
38. Zhou, W., Huang, K., Ma, T., Huang, J.: Document-level relation extraction with adaptive thresholding and localized context pooling. In: AAAI, pp. 14612–14620. AAAI Press, Online (2021)

Hashing the Hypertrie: Space- and Time-Efficient Indexing for SPARQL in Tensors

Alexander Bigerl[1]([✉]) [ID], Lixi Conrads[1] [ID], Charlotte Behning[2] [ID],
Muhammad Saleem[3] [ID], and Axel-Cyrille Ngonga Ngomo[1] [ID]

[1] DICE Group, Department of Computer Science, Paderborn University, Paderborn, Germany
{alexander.bigerl,axel.ngonga}@upb.de
[2] Department of Medical Biometry, Informatics and Epidemiology, University Hospital Bonn, Bonn, Germany
behning@imbie.uni-bonn.de
[3] CS Department, Leipzig University, Leipzig, Germany
saleem@informatik.uni-leipzig.de
https://dice-research.org/, https://www.imbie.uni-bonn.de/,
https://www.mathcs.uni-leipzig.de/ifi

Abstract. Time-efficient solutions for querying RDF knowledge graphs depend on indexing structures with low response times to answer SPARQL queries rapidly. Hypertries—an indexing structure we recently developed for tensor-based triple stores—have achieved significant runtime improvements over several mainstream storage solutions for RDF knowledge graphs. However, the space footprint of this novel data structure is still often larger than that of many mainstream solutions. In this work, we detail means to reduce the memory footprint of hypertries and thereby further speed up query processing in hypertrie-based RDF storage solutions. Our approach relies on three strategies: (1) the elimination of duplicate nodes via hashing, (2) the compression of non-branching paths, and (3) the storage of single-entry leaf nodes in their parent nodes. We evaluate these strategies by comparing them with baseline hypertries as well as popular triple stores such as Virtuoso, Fuseki, GraphDB, Blazegraph and gStore. We rely on four datasets/benchmark generators in our evaluation: SWDF, DBpedia, WatDiv, and WikiData. Our results suggest that our modifications significantly reduce the memory footprint of hypertries by up to 70% while leading to a relative improvement of up to 39% with respect to average Queries per Second and up to 740% with respect to Query Mixes per Hour.

1 Introduction

The hypertrie [6], a monolithic indexing data structure based on tries, is designed to support the efficient evaluation of basic graph patterns (BGPs) in SPARQL. While the access order for the positions of the tuples in tries is fixed, a hypertrie allows to iterate or resolve tuple positions in arbitrary order. In previous work [6] we showed that hypertries of depth 3 are both time- and memory-efficient when combined with a worst-case optimal join (WCOJ) based on the Einstein summation algorithm. With the benchmarking of our implementation, dubbed TENTRIS, we also showed that hypertries

© The Author(s) 2022
U. Sattler et al. (Eds.): ISWC 2022, LNCS 13489, pp. 57–73, 2022.
https://doi.org/10.1007/978-3-031-19433-7_4

outperform mainstream triple stores significantly on both synthetic and real-world benchmarks when combined with WCOJs. We analyzed the space requirements of hypertries on four RDF datasets: Semantic Web Dog Food (SWDF), DBpedia 2015-10, WatDiv, and Wikidata (see Sect. 5 for details on the datasets) revealing the following limitations of the current implementation: (1) The hypertries contain a high proportion of duplicate nodes, i.e. between 72% (SWDF) and 84% (WatDiv) (see baseline vs. hash identifiers in Fig. 1)

Two main conclusions can be derived from this analysis. First, the duplicate nodes lead to an unnecessarily high memory footprint. The addition of deduplication to hypertries could hence yield an improved data structure with lower memory requirements. Second, the high number of single-entry nodes might lead to both unnecessary memory consumption and suboptimal query runtimes. A modification of the data structure to accommodate single-entry nodes effectively has the potential to improve both memory footprint and query runtimes.

1. **Hash-Based identifiers (h):** We modify the hypertrie to use hashes of nodes as primary keys. Hence, we store nodes with the same entries exactly once, thus eliminating duplicates.
2. **Single-Entry node (s):** Single-entry nodes store the sub-hypertries of which they are the root node directly, thus saving space and eventually eliminating child nodes.
3. **In-Place storage (i):** Boolean-valued single-entry nodes are eliminated completely.

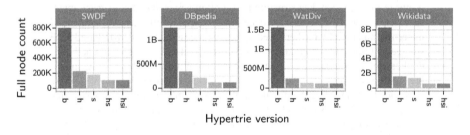

Fig. 1. Full node counts of different hypertrie versions on four datasets. The hypertrie versions are identified by their features: baseline (b), single-entry node (s), hash identifiers (h), and in-place storage of height-1 single-entry nodes (i).

The number of full nodes required by our optimizations is shown in Fig. 1. By applying all three techniques, the number of stored nodes is reduced by 82–90% (SWDF, WatDiv), and the memory consumption is reduced by 58–70% (SWDF, WatDiv), while the number of queries answered per second increases by up to four orders of magnitude on single queries.

The rest of this paper is structured as follows. First, we discuss related work in Sect. 2. In Sect. 3, we specify notations and conventions, introduce relevant concepts and describe the baseline hypertrie. We present our optimizations of the hypertrie in Sect. 4 and evaluate our optimized hypertries in Sect. 5. Finally, we conclude in Sect. 6.

2   Related Work

Many query engines for RDF graphs have been proposed in recent years [1,3,6,9–11,16,17,20,22]. Different engines deploy different mixes of indices and have different query execution approaches partly dependent on their indices. A common approach among SPARQL engines is to build multiple full indices in different collation orders such as Fuseki [10], Virtuoso [9], Blazegraph [20], and GraphDB [17]. Some systems build additional partial indices on aggregates such as RDF-3X [16], or cache data for frequent joins such as gStore [22] for star joins. Building more indexes provides more flexibility in reordering joins to support faster query execution, while fewer indexes accelerate updates and require less memory.

When it comes to worst-case optimal joins (WCOJs) [5], classical indexing reaches its limits as indices for all collation orders are required. A system that takes this approach is Fuseki-LTJ [11], which implements the WCOJ algorithm Leapfrog TrieJoin (LTJ) [21] within a Fuseki triple store with indices in all collation orders. Recent works also propose optimized data structures that provide more concise indices with support for WCOJs. Qdags [15] provide support for WCOJs based on an extension of quad trees. Redundancy in the quad tree is reduced by implementing it as a directed acyclic graph (DAG) and reusing equivalent subtrees. A Circle [3] stores Burrows-Wheeler-transformed ID triples in bent wavelet trees along with an additional index to encode the triples of an RDF graph. Both Qdag and Circle are succinct data structures that must be built at once and do not support updates. In their evaluation of Circle, Arroyuelo et al. showed that Qdag and Circle are very space efficient, and that Fuseki-LTJ and Circle answer queries faster than state-of-the-art triple stores such as Virtuoso and Blazegraph with respect to average and median response times. The Qdag performed considerably worse in the query benchmarks than all other systems tested.

The idea for single-entry node and in-place storage is based on path compression, a common technique to reduce the number of nodes required to encode a tree by storing non-branching paths in a single node. It was first introduced by Morrison in PATRICIA trees [14]. Using hashing for deduplication, like in the proposed hypertrie context for hypertrie nodes (see Sect. 4.1 for details) is inspired by previous works on pervasive computing [13]. The hypertrie that we strive to optimize in this paper is, like the Qdag, internally represented as a DAG. As with the Qdag, the DAG nature of the hypertrie reduces the space requirement from factorial to exponential by the tuple length. The reduction is accomplished by eliminating duplicates among equal subtrees.

3   Background

In this section, we briefly introduce the notation and conventions used in the rest of this paper. In particular, we give a brief overview of relevant aspects of RDF, SPARQL, and tensors. We also provide an overview of the formal specification of hypertries. More details can be found in [6].

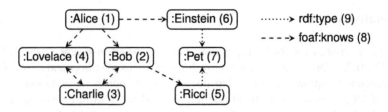

Fig. 2. Example RDF graph. Integer indices for RDF resources are provided in parentheses behind the string identifier.

3.1 Notation and Conventions

The conventions in this paragraph stem from [6]. Let $\mathbb{N}$ be the set of the natural numbers including 0. We use $\mathbb{I}_n := \{i \in \mathbb{N} \mid 1 \leq i \leq n\}$ as a shorthand for the set of natural numbers from 1 to n. The domain of a function f is denoted $\mathrm{dom}\,(f)$ while $\mathrm{cod}\,(f)$ stands for the target (also called codomain) of f. A function which maps x_1 to y_1 and x_2 to y_2 is denoted by $[x_1 \rightarrow y_1, x_2 \rightarrow y_2]$. Sequences with a fixed order are delimited by angle brackets, e.g., $l = \langle a, b, c \rangle$. Their elements are accessible via subscript, e.g., $l_1 = a$. The number of times an element e is contained in any bag or sequence C is denoted by $count\,(e, C)$; for example, $count\,(a, \langle a, a, b, c \rangle) = 2$. We denote the Cartesian product of S with itself i times with $S^i = \underbrace{S \times S \times \ldots S}_{i}$. We use the term *word* to describe a processor word, e.g. a 64-bit data chunk when using the x86-64 instruction set.

3.2 RDF and SPARQL

An RDF statement is a triple $\langle s, p, o \rangle$ and represents an edge $s \xrightarrow{p} o$ in an RDF graph g. s, p and o are called RDF resources. An RDF graph can be regarded as a set of RDF statements. The set of all resources of a graph g is given by $r(g)$. An example of an RDF graph is given in Fig. 2. The graph contains, among others, the RDF statement $\langle$:Alice, foaf:knows, :Bob$\rangle$.

A triple pattern (TP) Q is a triple that has variables or RDF resources as entries, e.g., $\langle$?x, foaf:knows, ?y$\rangle$. Matching a triple pattern Q with a statement t results in a set of zero or one solution mappings. If Q and t have exactly the same resources in the same positions, then matching Q to t results in a solution mapping which maps the variables of Q to the terms of t in the same positions. For example, imagine $Q = \langle$?x, foaf:knows, ?y$\rangle$ and $t = \langle$:Alice, foaf:knows, :Bob$\rangle$. Then $Q(t) = \{[$?x $\rightarrow$:Alice, ?x $\rightarrow$:Bob$]\}$. Otherwise, the set of solutions is empty, i.e., $Q(t) = \emptyset$. The result of matching a triple pattern Q against an RDF graph g is

$$Q(g) = \bigcup_{t \in g} Q(t), \tag{1}$$

i.e., the union of the matches of all triples t in g with Q. A list of triple patterns is called a basic graph pattern (BGP). The result of applying a BGP to an RDF graph g is the natural join of the solutions of its triple patterns.

Similar to previous works [4,6,16], we only consider the subset of SPARQL where a query is considered to consist of a BGP, a projection and a modifier (i.e., DISTINCT) that specifies whether the evaluation of Q follows bag or set semantics.

3.3 Tensors and RDF

Similar to [6], we use tensors that can be represented as finite multi-dimensional arrays. We consider a tensor of rank-n as an n-dimensional array $\mathbf{K}_1 \times \cdots \times \mathbf{K}_n \to \mathbb{N}$ with $\mathbf{K}_1 = \cdots = \mathbf{K}_n \subset \mathbb{N}$. Tuples from the tensor's co-domain $\mathbf{k} \in \mathbf{K}$ are called keys. The entries $\mathbf{k}_1, \ldots, \mathbf{k}_n$ of a key $\mathbf{k}$ are dubbed key parts. The array notation $T[\mathbf{k}] = v$ is used to express that T stores for key $\mathbf{k}$ value v.

The representation of g as a tensor, dubbed RDF tensor or adjacency tensor T, is a rank-3 tensor over $\mathbb{N}$ which encodes g. Let $id : r(g) \to \mathbb{I}_{|r(g)|+1}$ be an index function. The function maps each term of g—of which there are $|r(g)|$—to a fixed value in $\mathbb{I}_{|r(g)|}$. All unbound variables in solution mappings are mapped to $|r(g)| + 1$. For all statements $\langle s, p, o \rangle \in g$, the value of $T[id(s), id(p), id(o)]$ is 1. All other values of T are 0. For example, $T[5, 9, 7] = 1$ for the example graph shown in Fig. 2, while $T[5, 9, 6] = 0$.

Matching a triple pattern Q against a graph g is equivalent to slicing the tensor representation of g with a slice key $\mathbf{s}(Q)$ corresponding to Q. The length of $\mathbf{s}(Q)$ is equal to the order of the tensor to which it is applied. Said slice key has a key part or a place holder, denoted ":" (no quotes), in every position. Slicing g with $\mathbf{s}(Q)$ results in a lower-order tensor that retains only entries where the key parts of the slice key match with the key parts of the tensor entries. For example, the slice key for the TP $Q = \langle ?x, \text{foaf:knows}, ?y \rangle$ executed against the example graph in Fig. 2 is $\langle :, 8, : \rangle$. Applying the TP Q to g is homomorphic to applying the slice key $\mathbf{s}(t)$ to the tensor representation of g.

To define a tensor representation for sets or bags of solutions, we first define an arbitrary but fixed ordering function *order* for variables (e.g., any alphanumeric ordering). A tensor representation T' of a set or bag of solutions is a tensor of rank equal to the number of projection variables in the query. The index for accessing entries of T' corresponds to *order*. For example, given the TP $Q = \langle ?x, \text{foaf:knows}, ?y \rangle$ with the projection variables $?x$ and $?y$, T' would be a matrix with $?x$ as the first dimension and $?y$ as the second dimension. After applying Q to the graph in Fig. 2, we would get a tensor T' with $T'[2, 5] = 1$ and $T'[5, 2] = 0$.

The Einstein summation [8,18] is an operation with variable arity. With this operation, the natural joins between the TPs of a BGP and variable projection can be combined into a single expression that takes the tensor representations of the TPs as input.

The execution of a SPARQL query on an RDF graph g is mapped to operations on tensors as follows. For each triple pattern, the RDF tensor T is sliced with the corresponding slice key. The slices are used as operands to an Einstein summation. Each slice is subscripted with the variables of the corresponding triple pattern. The result is subscripted with the projected variables. A ring with *addition* and *multiplication* is used to evaluate the Einstein summations. For example, evaluating the query with the BGP $\langle\langle ?x, \text{foaf:knows}, ?y \rangle, \langle ?y, \text{rdf:type}, :\text{Pet} \rangle\rangle$ and a projection to $?x$ on the RDF graph g from Fig. 2 is equivalent to calculating $\sum_x T[:, 8, :]_{x,y} \cdot T[:, 9, 7]_y$, where T is the RDF graph of g.

3.4 Hypertrie

A hypertrie is a tensor data structure that maps strings of fixed length d over an alphabet A to some value space V [6]. It is implemented as a directed acyclic graph to store tensors sparsely by storing only non-zero entries. Formally, [6, p.62] defines a hypertrie as follows:

Definition 1 (Hypertrie). *Let $H(d, A, E)$ with $d \geq 0$ be the set of all hypertries with depth d, alphabet A, and values E. If A and E are clear from the context, we use $H(d)$. We set $H(0) = E$ per definition. A hypertrie $h \in H(1)$ has an associated partial function $c_1^{(h)} : A \nrightarrow E$ that specifies outgoing edges by mapping edge labels to children. For $h' \in H(n), n > 1$, partial functions $c_p^{(h')} : A \nrightarrow H(d-1), p \in \mathbb{I}_n$ are defined. Function $c_p^{(h')}$ specifies the edges for resolving the part equivalent to depth p in a trie by mapping edge labels to children. For a hypertrie h, $z(h)$ is the size of the set or mapping it encodes.*

An example of a hypertrie encoding the RDF tensor of the graph in Fig. 2 is given in Fig. 3 with the baseline hypertrie.

To retrieve the value for a tensor key, we start at the root node. If the current node is from $H(0)$, it is the value and we are done. Otherwise, we select a key part from the key at an arbitrary position p. If c_p maps the selected key part, we descend to mapped sub-hypertrie, remove the selected key part from the key and repeat the retrieval recursively on the sub-hypertrie with the shortened key. Otherwise, the value is 0.

Hypertries are designed to satisfy four conditions: (R1) memory efficiency, (R2) efficient slicing, (R3) slicing in any order of dimensions, and (R4) efficient iteration through slices. [6] Furthermore, note that every hypertrie is uniquely identified by the set of tuples it encodes.

Implementation. We refer to the original implementation of the hypertrie [6] as baseline implementation. The baseline hypertrie is implemented in C++. The lifetime of hyper-trie nodes is managed by reference-counting memory pointers which free the memory of a node when it is no longer referenced. For nodes with height $d > 1$, the edge mappings $c_{p \in \mathbb{I}_d}$ are stored in one hash table each. A node h' that is accessible from the root hypertrie h via different paths with equal slices is stored only once. Its parent nodes store a reference to the same physical instance of h'. For example, the slices $h[3, :, :][:, 4]$ and $h[:, :, 4][3, :]$ of a depth-3 hypertrie result in the same node. Nodes of depth $d = 1$ store the leaf edges in a hash set.

Hypertries were introduced as a tensor data structure for the tensor-based triple store TENTRIS. [6] In the following, we briefly describe the implementation of TEN-TRIS, which is later used to evaluate the improvements to the hypertrie presented in this paper. Consider an RDF graph g. A depth-3 Boolean-valued hypertrie is used by TENTRIS to store RDF triples encoded as integer triples. Therefore, the RDF resources $r(g)$ are stored as heap-allocated strings. The integer identifier of a resource is its mem-ory address. We write $id(e)$ to denote the identifier of a resource e. id is implemented using a hash table while its inverse id^{-1} is applied by resolving the ID as memory address. Solutions of triple patterns are represented by pointers to sub-hypertrie nodes.

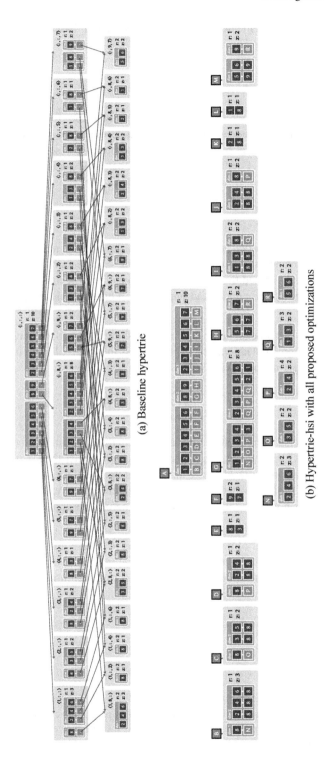

(a) Baseline hypertrie

(b) Hypertrie-hsi with all proposed optimizations

Fig. 3. Both hypertries encode the RDF graph from Fig. 2. RDF resources are encoded by their ID (see also Fig. 2).

Joins and projection are implemented with Einstein summation based on a worst-case optimal join algorithm.

4 Approach

In this section, we introduce three optimizations to the hypertrie. First, we eliminate duplicate nodes by identifying nodes with a hash. In a second step, we further reduce the memory footprint of hypertries by devising a more compact representation for nodes that encode only a single entry. Finally, we eliminate the separate storage of single-entry leaf nodes completely.

4.1 Hash-Based Identifiers

Our analysis of Fig. 1 suggests that equal sub-hypertries are often stored multiple times. To eliminate this redundancy, we first introduce a hashing scheme for hypertries that can be updated incrementally. Based thereupon, we introduce the *hypertrie context*, which keeps track of existing hypertrie nodes and implements a hash-based deduplication.

Hashing Hypertries. Let j be an order-dependent hashing scheme[1] for integer tuples. We define the hash i of a Boolean-valued hypertrie h as the result of applying j to the entries of h and aggregating them with XOR:

$$i(h) := \bigoplus_{\mathbf{k} \in \mathrm{dom}(h)} j(\mathbf{k}) \tag{2}$$

Since XOR is self-inverse, commutative, and associative, the hash can be incrementally updated by $i(h) \oplus j(\mathbf{k})$ when a key $\mathbf{k}$ is added or removed. Rather than rehashing and combining all entries again in $\mathcal{O}(z(h))$, the incremental update of the hash can be done in constant time. The hashing scheme can easily be extended to hypertries that store non-Boolean values by appending the value to the key before j is applied.

Hypertrie Context. The goal of a hypertrie context is to ensure that hypertrie nodes are stored only once, regardless of how often they are referenced. We now describe the design requirements for hypertrie contexts, provide a formal definition, and conclude with implementation considerations.

---

[1] In our implementation, we use the hash functions from https://github.com/martinus/robin-hood-hashing since preliminary experiments showed that they performed well and had no collisions on the datasets from Sect. 5.

In their baseline implementation, hypertrie nodes are retrievable by their path from the root of the hypertrie only. Information pertaining to the location of a node in memory is only available within its parent nodes. Consequently, only nodes with equivalent paths, i.e., with equal slice keys, are deduplicated in the baseline implementation. Equal hypertries with different slice keys are stored independently of each other. Hypertrie contexts eliminate these possible redundancies by storing hypertrie nodes by their hash and tracking how often nodes are referenced. The parent nodes are modified to reference their child nodes using hashes instead of memory pointers. Identifying hypertrie nodes by their hashes ensures that there are no duplicates.

A hypertrie can be *contained* or *primarily contained* in a hypertrie context hc. All nodes managed by a hypertrie context are *contained* therein. A hypertrie is said to be *primarily contained* in a hypertrie context hc iff it was stored explicitly in said context. For example, the root node of a hypertrie used for storing a given graph is commonly *primarily contained* in a hypertrie context. If a hypertrie h is *primarily contained* in a hypertrie context hc, then all sub-hypertries of h are *contained* in hc.

Adding a new primarily contained hypertrie or changing an existing hypertrie may alter the set of hypertries contained in a hypertrie context. To efficiently decide whether a node is still needed after a change, the hypertrie context tracks how often each node is referred to. Nodes that are no longer referenced after a change are removed. In *hypertrie contexts*, hypertries are considered to reference their sub-hypertries by hash.[2]

Formally, we define a *hypertrie context* as follows:

Definition 2 (Hypertrie Context). *Let A be an alphabet, E a set of values, and $d \in \mathbb{N}$ the maximal depth of the hypertries that are to be stored.*

We denote the set of hypertries $\bigcup_{t \leq d} H(t, A, E)$ as Λ_0. Λ_0 without empty hypertries $\{h \in \Lambda_0 \mid z(h) \neq 0\}$ is denoted Λ.

A hypertrie context C for hypertries from Λ_0 is defined by a triple (P, m, r) where

- *P is a bag of elements from Λ_0,*
- *$m : \mathbb{Z} \nrightarrow \Lambda$ maps hashes to non-empty hypertries which are P or are sub-hypertries of one of P's elements, and*
- *$r : \Lambda \to \mathbb{N} \cup 0$ assigns a reference count to non-empty hypertries.*

We define two relations between hypertrie context and hypertries:

- *Hypertries $p \in P$ are primarily contained in C, denoted as $p \overline{\in} C$.*
- *Hypertries $h \in \mathrm{cod}(m)$ are contained in C, denoted as $h \in C$.*

For a hypertrie $h \in \Lambda$, $r(h)$ is calculated from sum of the count of h in P and the number of references to h from hypertrie $h' \in C$:

$$r(h) := count(h, P) + \sum_{\substack{h' \in C \\ p \in \mathbb{I}_d}} count(h, \mathrm{cod}(c_p^{(h')})).$$

(3)

---

[2] The outgoing edges $c_p^{(h)}$ in Definition 1 are considered to map hashes of hypertries instead of hypertries.

4.2 Single-Entry Node

Central properties of a hypertrie are that slicing in any dimension can be carried out efficiently (see R2 and R3 in Sect. 3.4) and that non-zero slices can be iterated efficiently (see R4 in Sect. 3.4). In the implementation of hypertrie node described so far (in the following: full node), this is achieved by maintaining one hash table of non-zero slices for each dimension. The main observation behind this optimization is that R2–R4 also hold for a hypertrie node that represents only a single entry if the hypertrie node stores only the entry itself. We dub such a node *single-entry node* (SEN). A similar technique is used in radix trees [12] to store non-branching paths in a condensed fashion.

For slicing, it is sufficient to match the slice key against the single entry of the node. Thus, the result may have zero or one non-zero entry (see R2, R3). There is exactly one non-zero slice in each dimension. Iteration of the non-zero slices is now trivial (see R4).

SEN are—when applicable—always more memory efficient than full nodes.[3] Compared to a full node h, an SEN eliminates memory overhead in three ways. (1) It does not maintain hash tables $c_p^{(h)}$ for edges to child nodes. (2) Child nodes do not need to be stored, unless they are also needed by other nodes. (3) The node size $z(h)$ does not need to be stored explicitly since it is always 1.

Formally, we define an SEN as follows:

Definition 3 (Single-Entry Hypertrie). *Let H, d, A and E be given as in Definition 1. Further, consider* $h \in H(d)$, *which stores for key* $\langle \mathbf{k}_1, \ldots, \mathbf{k}_n \rangle$, *the value v. If h encodes exactly one entry* $(z(h) = 1)$, *h is defined as* $\langle \langle \mathbf{k}_1, \ldots, \mathbf{k}_n \rangle, v \rangle$ *and is called a single-entry node (SEN). Children mapping functions* $c_p^{(h)}$ *are not defined for h.*

SEN can be used without limitations in a hypertrie context.

4.3 In-Place Storage

Our third optimization is to store certain nodes exactly where a reference to them would be stored otherwise. While the aforementioned optimizations can be used for hypertries with all value types (e.g., Boolean, integer, float), the optimization in this section is only applicable to Boolean-valued hypertries.

The payload of a binary-valued (note that our tensors only contain 0 s and 1 s) height-1 SEN is a single key part (1 word). It takes the same amount of memory as the hash that identifies the hypertrie (1 word) and which is stored in its parent nodes' children mappings to reference it. Therefore, the payload of a height-1 SEN fits into the place of its reference.

We use this property to reduce the total storage required: The payload of child height-1 SENs—their key part—is stored in place of their reference in the children mappings of their parent nodes. To encode if a hash or a key part is stored, a bit in the

---

[3] Consider a hypertrie h with a single entry $z(h) = 1$ and depth $d \geq 1$. A hash table that maps a key part requires more memory than just a single key part. Hence, the d child mapping hash tables of a full hypertrie node encoding h require more memory than the d key parts of the entry stored in an SEN encoding h. Consequently, an SEN node is always more memory efficient than a full node.

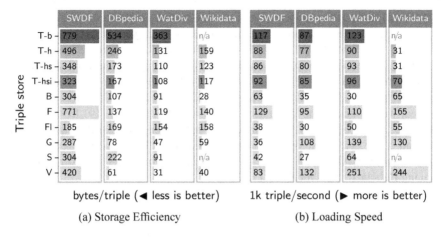

	SWDF	DBpedia	WatDiv	Wikidata	SWDF	DBpedia	WatDiv	Wikidata
T-b	779	534	363	n/a	117	87	123	n/a
T-h	496	246	131	159	88	77	90	31
T-hs	348	173	110	123	86	80	93	31
T-hsi	323	167	108	117	92	85	96	70
B	304	107	91	28	63	35	30	65
F	771	137	119	140	129	95	110	165
Fl	185	169	154	158	38	30	50	55
G	287	78	47	59	36	108	139	130
S	304	222	91	n/a	42	27	64	n/a
V	420	61	31	40	83	132	251	244

bytes/triple (◄ less is better)   1k triple/second (► more is better)

(a) Storage Efficiency   (b) Loading Speed

Fig. 4. Storage efficiency and loading speed of TENTRIS, with different hypertrie versions, and of other triple stores on four datasets. If loading a dataset with a triple store failed, the plot says n/a. The triple stores are TENTRIS (T-*) where * indicates the hypertrie version (see Fig. 1), Blazegraph (B), Fuseki (F), Fuseki-LTJ (Fl), GraphDB (G), gStore (S), and Virtuoso (V).

same fixed position of both key part and hash is reserved and used as a type tagging bit, e.g., the most significant bit. As in-place stored height-1 SEN are not heap-allocated, reference counting is not necessary. The memory is released properly when the hash table is destructed.

4.4 Example

An exemplary comparison of a baseline hypertrie and a hypertrie context containing one primary hypertrie with all three proposed optimizations is given in Fig. 3.

5 Evaluation

We implemented our optimizations within the TENTRIS framework. The goal of our evaluation was twofold: first, we assessed the index sizes and index generation times with four datasets of up to 5.5 B triples. In a second experiment, we evaluated the query performance of the triple stores in a stress test. Throughout our evaluation, we compared the original version of TENTRIS, dubbed TENTRIS-b, our extension of TENTRIS with hash identifiers (h) and single entry nodes (s), dubbed TENTRIS-hs, TENTRIS-hs extended with the in-place storage (i) optimization, dubbed TENTRIS-hsi, and the six popular triple stores, i.e., Blazegraph 2.1.6 Release Candidate, Fuseki 4.4.0, Fuseki-LTJ—a Fuseki that uses a worst-case optimal join algorithm—[4], GraphDB 9.5.1, gStore 0.8[5], and Virtuoso 7.2.6.1. We chose popular triple stores which provide a standard

---

[4] Fuseki-LTJ is based on Apache Jena Fuseki 3.9.0.

[5] We used the modified version from [6] that fixes the SPARQL endpoint and sets a query timeout.

HTTP SPARQL interface, support at least the same subset of SPARQL as TENTRIS and are freely available for benchmarking. We did not include Qdag or Ring because they do not provide a SPARQL HTTP endpoint and do not support projections. We used the datasets Semantic Web Dog Food (SWDF) (372 K triples), the English DBpedia version 2015-10 (681 M triples) and WatDiv [2] (1 B triples) and their respective query lists from [6]. We added Wikidata trusty from 2020-11-11 (5.5 B triples) as another large real-world dataset and generated queries with FEASIBLE [19] from Wikidata query logs. As in [6], FEASIBLE was configured to generate SELECT queries with BGPs and DISTINCT as an optional solution modifier. All experiments were executed on a server with an AMD EPYC 7742, 1 TB RAM and two 3 TB NVMe SSDs in RAID 0 running Debian 10 and OpenJDK 11.0.14.

5.1 Index Size and Loading Time

Storage requirements for indices and index building speeds are reported in Fig. 4. The index sizes of the TENTRIS versions were measured with cgmemtime's[6]"Recursive and acc. high-water RSS+CACHE". For all other triple stores, the total size of the index files after loading was used. cgmemtime's "Child wall" was used to measure the time for loading the datasets.

Two triple stores were not able to load the Wikidata dataset: gStore failed due to a limit on the number of usable RDF Resources and TENTRIS-b ran out of memory.

For all datasets, each additional hypertrie optimization improves the storage efficiency of TENTRIS further: Compared to TENTRIS-b, the optimizations h, hs and hsi take 36–64%, 55–68% and 58–70% less memory respectively. This comes at the cost of decreased index build throughput for TENTRIS-h and TENTRIS-hs by 11–36% and for TENTRIS-his by 2–28%. For the Wikidata dataset, the index sizes of TENTRIS-h, TEN-TRIS-hs and TENTRIS-hsi are reduced by at least 21%, 39% and 42%[7], respectively. Compared to TENTRIS-h, the single entry nodes (s) in TENTRIS-hs save 16–30% with almost no effect on the index building speed. The in-place storage of single-entry leaf nodes (i) in TENTRIS-hsi saves memory, (another 1–7%) compared to TENTRIS-hs, and speeds up the index building (2–57%) on all datasets. For the small to medium-sized datasets SWDF, DBpedia, and WatDiv, the index building is slightly faster by 2–7%; for the large dataset, Wikidata, the margin is considerably larger with 56% improvement.

The index sizes of all TENTRIS versions scale similarly to other triple stores. The TENTRIS-hsi indices are similar in size to the indices produced by other triple stores. Compared to the smallest index for each dataset, TENTRIS-hsi uses 1.14 to 4.24 times more space. The loading time of TENTRIS-hsi is close to the mean of the non-TENTRIS triple stores.

---

[6] https://github.com/gsauthof/cgmemtime.

[7] In comparison to 1TB RAM because TENTRIS-b ran out memory during loading.

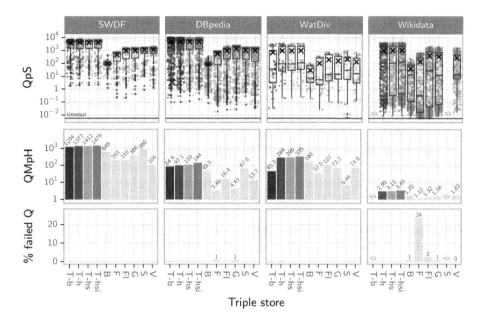

Fig. 5. Performance metrics of query stress tests on four benchmarks for TENTRIS, with different hypertrie versions, and for other triple stores. For triple store abbreviations see Fig. 4. First row shows Boxplots and scatterplots for Queries per Second (QpS). Only successful query executions are considered and aggregated by mean into a single scatter. The boxes indicate the first quartile, median, and third quartile with 1.5 times the interquartile range wiskers. Black dots mark outliers and crosses the means. Second row shows shows Query Mixes per Hour (QMpH). Failed queries are rated with the timeout duration of **180 s**. The third row shows the percentage of queries that failed. If no number is provided, no queries failed. If experiments were not executed for a combination of triple store and benchmark, the plot says n/a.

5.2 Querying Stress Test

Our evaluation setup for query stress tests was similar to that used in [6]. The results are shown in Fig. 5. The experiments were executed using the benchmark execution framework IGUANA v3.2.1 [7]. For each benchmark, the query mix was executed 30 times on each triple store and the timeout for a single query execution was set to 3 min. We report the performance using Queries per Second (QpS), Query Mixes per Hour (QMpH) and the proportion of failed queries. For QpS, only query executions that were successful and finished before the timeout are considered. The reported QpS value of a query on a dataset and triple store is the mean of the single measurements. Failed queries are penalized with the timeout duration for QMpH. We chose to report both QMpH and QpS to get a more fine-grained view of the performance. While QpS is more robust against outliers, QMpH can be strongly influenced by long-running and failed queries.

The baseline version of TENTRIS, TENTRIS-b, already performs better than all non-TENTRIS triple stores w.r.t. QpS and QMpH on the SWDF and DBpedia benchmarks but not on the WatDiv benchmark. Here, gStore and Blazegraph outperform TENTRIS-b by a factor of 1.6 and 3.5 with respect to QMpH. TENTRIS-h, TENTRIS-hs and TENTRIS-hsi all outperform TENTRIS-b and all other triple stores on all datasets with respect to average QpS (avgQpS) and QMpH. For the small real-world dataset SWDF, all TENTRIS versions answered queries with similar avgQpS ranging from 3935 (TENTRIS-b) to 4088 (TENTRIS-hsi, +4%). The same holds true for the larger real-world dataset DBpedia, with avgQpS ranging from 4753 (TENTRIS-b) to 4825 (TENTRIS-hsi, +1.5%). With respect to QMpH, the optimized TENTRIS versions clearly outperform TENTRIS-b by 11%(TENTRIS-h), 14% (TENTRIS-hs) and 20% (TENTRIS-hsi) on the SWDF dataset, and even by 15%, 31% and 71% on the DBpedia dataset. On the synthetic dataset WatDiv, the optimized TENTRIS versions show notable speedups on both metrics, avgQpS and QMpH. AvgQpS is increased from 698 by TENTRIS-h to 946 (+35%), by TENTRIS-hs, to 931 (+33%), by TENTRIS-hs and to 972 (+39%) by TENTRIS-hsi. QMpH is 5.2, 6.6 and 7.4 times higher with TENTRIS-h, TENTRIS-hs and TENTRIS-hsi, respectively, than with TENTRIS-b.

On Wikidata, measurements are available only for the TENTRIS versions h, hs and hsi due to TENTRIS-b not being able to load the dataset. TENTRIS-hsi is again slightly faster than TENTRIS-hs, with 1009 (hs) and 1021 (+1%, hsi) avgQpS, and 3.13 (hs) and 3.45 (+9%, hsi) QMpH. TENTRIS-h is with 989 avgQpS and 2.99 QMpH slightly slower than the more optimized versions.

When compared to the fastest non-TENTRIS triple store on each metric and dataset, TENTRIS-hsi is 3–3.7 times faster with respect to avgQpS and 1.7–2.1 times faster with respect to QMpH. None of the TENTRIS versions had failed queries during execution. On the DBpedia dataset, Fuseki and gStore failed on about 1% of the queries. On the Wikidata dataset, all non-TENTRIS triples stores that succeeded to load the dataset failed on some queries.

5.3   Discussion

The evaluation shows that applying all three optimizations (hsi) is in all aspects superior to applying only the first two optimizations (h, hs). Thus, we will consider only TENTRIS-hsi in the following. The proposed optimizations of the hypertrie improve the storage efficiency by 70% and the query performance with respect to avgQpS by large margins of up to four orders of magnitude. These improvements come at the cost of slightly longer index building times of at most 28%. The optimization of the storage efficiency is clearly attributable to the reduced number of nodes, as shown in Fig. 1. For the improved query performance, definite attribution is difficult. We worked out two main factors we believe are reasonable to assume as the cause: First, information that was stored in a node and its subnodes in the baseline version is in the optimized version more often stored in a single node. This way, the optimizations single-entry node (s) and in-place storage (i) cause fewer CPU cache misses and fewer resolves of memory addresses, resulting in faster execution. Second, key parts are not necessarily stored in a hash table anymore. Whenever a key part is read from a single-entry node (s) or in-place stored node (i), the optimized version saves one hash table lookup compared to the baseline version. On the other side, additional hash table lookups are required to retrieve nodes by their hash identifiers during query evaluation. We minimize this overhead by handling nodes by their memory address during evaluation after they were looked up by their hash first. The memory overhead for storing these handles is negligible as typically only a few are required at the same time.

For triple stores, there is always a trade-off between storage efficiency, index build time, and query performance. In particular, less compressed indices can typically be built faster. Building multiple indices takes longer but multiple indices allow for more optimized query plans. The baseline hypertrie clearly attributed significant weight to good query performance, with average index building time and above average storage requirement. The optimized hypertrie trades a slightly little worse index building time for better query performance and much-improved storage efficiency. The result is a triple store with superior query performance, average storage requirement, and still average index building time. Given the predominantly positive changes in trade-offs, we consider the proposed optimizations a substantial improvement.

6   Conclusion and Outlook

We presented a memory-optimized version of the hypertrie data structure. The three optimizations of hypertries that we developed and evaluated improved both the memory footprint and query performance of hypertries. A clear but small trade-off of our approaches is the slightly longer index building time they require.

The new storage scheme for hypertrie opens up several new avenues for future improvements. The persistence of optimized hypertrie nodes is easier to achieve due to the switch from memory pointers to hashes. Furthermore, the hash identifiable hypertrie nodes provide the building bricks to distribute a hypertrie over multiple nodes in a network. For TENTRIS, the introduction of the hypertrie context opens up the possibility to store the hypertries of multiple RDF graphs in a single context and thereby automatically deduplicate common sub-hypertries. Especially for similar graphs, this optimization has the potential to improve storage efficiency substantially.

Supplementary Material Statement: Source code for our system; a script to recreate the full experimental setup, including all datasets, queries, triple stores, configurations and scripts to run the experiments; and the raw data and scripts for generating the images are available from: https://tentris.dice-research.org/iswc2022.

Acknowledgments. The authors would like to thank Lukas Kerkemeier for his work on the implementation. This work has been supported by the German Federal Ministry for Economic Affairs and Climate Action (BMWK) within the project RAKI under the grant no 01MD19012B, by the German Federal Ministry of Education and Research (BMBF) within the EuroStars project E!114681 3DFed under the grant no 01QE2114B and by the European Union's Horizon 2020 research and innovation programme under the Marie Skłodowska-Curie grant agreement No 860801.

References

1. Ali, W., Saleem, M., Yao, B., Hogan, A., Ngomo, A.C.N.: A survey of rdf stores & sparql engines for querying knowledge graphs (2021)
2. Aluç, G., Hartig, O., Özsu, M.T., Daudjee, K.: Diversified stress testing of RDF data management systems. In: Mika, P., et al. (eds.) ISWC 2014. LNCS, vol. 8796, pp. 197–212. Springer, Cham (2014). https://doi.org/10.1007/978-3-319-11964-9_13
3. Arroyuelo, D., Hogan, A., Navarro, G., Reutter, J.L., Rojas-Ledesma, J., Soto, A.: Worst-case optimal graph joins in almost no space, pp. 102–114. Association for Computing Machinery, New York (2021). https://doi.org/10.1145/3448016.3457256
4. Atre, M., Chaoji, V., Zaki, M.J., Hendler, J.A.: Matrix "bit" loaded: a scalable lightweight join query processor for RDF data. In: Proceedings of the 19th International Conference on World Wide Web, WWW 2010, pp. 41–50. Association for Computing Machinery, New York (2010). https://doi.org/10.1145/1772690.1772696
5. Atserias, A., Grohe, M., Marx, D.: Size bounds and query plans for relational joins. In: 49th Annual IEEE Symposium on Foundations of Computer Science, FOCS 2008, Philadelphia, PA, USA, 25–28 October 2008, pp. 739–748. IEEE Computer Society (2008). https://doi.org/10.1109/FOCS.2008.43
6. Bigerl, A., Conrads, F., Behning, C., Sherif, M.A., Saleem, M., Ngonga Ngomo, A.-C.: Tentris – a tensor-based triple store. In: Pan, J.Z., et al. (eds.) ISWC 2020. LNCS, vol. 12506, pp. 56–73. Springer, Cham (2020). https://doi.org/10.1007/978-3-030-62419-4_4
7. Conrads, F., Lehmann, J., Saleem, M., Morsey, M., Ngonga Ngomo, A.-C.: IGUANA: a generic framework for benchmarking the read-write performance of triple stores. In: d'Amato, C., et al. (eds.) ISWC 2017. LNCS, vol. 10588, pp. 48–65. Springer, Cham (2017). https://doi.org/10.1007/978-3-319-68204-4_5
8. Einstein, A.: Die Grundlage der allgemeinen Relativitätstheorie. Annalen der Physik **354**, 769–822 (1916). https://doi.org/10.1002/andp.19163540702
9. Erling, O.: Virtuoso, a hybrid RDBMS/graph column store. http://vos.openlinksw.com/owiki/wiki/VOS/VOSArticleVirtuosoAHybridRDBMSGraphColumnStore. Accessed 17 Mar 2018
10. Foundation, A.S.: Apache jena documentation - TDB architecture (2019). https://jena.apache.org/documentation/tdb/architecture. Accessed 25 Apr 2019
11. Hogan, A., Riveros, C., Rojas, C., Soto, A.: A worst-case optimal join algorithm for SPARQL. In: Ghidini, C., et al. (eds.) ISWC 2019. LNCS, vol. 11778, pp. 258–275. Springer, Cham (2019). https://doi.org/10.1007/978-3-030-30793-6_15
12. Leis, V., Kemper, A., Neumann, T.: The adaptive radix tree: artful indexing for main-memory databases. In: 2013 IEEE 29th International Conference on Data Engineering (ICDE), pp. 38–49 (2013). https://doi.org/10.1109/ICDE.2013.6544812
13. Malhotra, J., Bakal, J.: A survey and comparative study of data deduplication techniques. In: 2015 International Conference on Pervasive Computing (ICPC), pp. 1–5 (2015). https://doi.org/10.1109/PERVASIVE.2015.7087116
14. Morrison, D.R.: Patricia-practical algorithm to retrieve information coded in alphanumeric. J. ACM **15**(4), 514–534 (1968). https://doi.org/10.1145/321479.321481
15. Navarro, G., Reutter, J.L., Rojas-Ledesma, J.: Optimal joins using compact data structures. In: 23rd International Conference on Database Theory, ICDT 2020, March 30-April 2, 2020, Copenhagen, Denmark. LIPIcs, vol. 155, pp. 21:1–21:21. Schloss Dagstuhl - Leibniz-Zentrum für Informatik (2020). https://doi.org/10.4230/LIPIcs.ICDT.2020.21, https://doi.org/10.4230/LIPIcs.ICDT.2020.21
16. Neumann, T., Weikum, G.: Rdf-3x: a risc-style engine for RDF. In: Proceedings VLDB Endowment, vol. 1, no. 1, pp. 647–659 (2008). https://doi.org/10.14778/1453856.1453927

17. Ontotext USA, I.: Storage - GraphDB free 8.9 documentation. http://graphdb.ontotext.com/documentation/free/storage.html#storage-literal-index. Accessed 16 Apr 2019
18. Ricci, M., Levi-Civita, T.: Méthodes de calcul différentiel absolu et leurs applications. Mathematische Annalen **54**(1–2), 125–201 (1900)
19. Saleem, M., Mehmood, Q., Ngonga Ngomo, A.-C.: FEASIBLE: a feature-based SPARQL benchmark generation framework. In: Arenas, M., et al. (eds.) ISWC 2015. LNCS, vol. 9366, pp. 52–69. Springer, Cham (2015). https://doi.org/10.1007/978-3-319-25007-6_4
20. SYSTAP, LLC: Bigdata Database Architecture - Blazegraph (2013). https://blazegraph.com/docs/bigdata_architecture_whitepaper.pdf. Accessed 29 Nov 2019
21. Veldhuizen, T.L.: Triejoin: a simple, worst-case optimal join algorithm. In: Proceedings of 17th International Conference on Database Theory (ICDT), Athens, Greece, 24–28 March 2014, pp. 96–106. OpenProceedings.org (2014). https://doi.org/10.5441/002/icdt.2014.13
22. Zou, L., Özsu, M.T., Chen, L., Shen, X., Huang, R., Zhao, D.: Gstore: a graph-based sparql query engine. VLDB J. **23**(4), 565–590 (2014). https://doi.org/10.1007/s00778-013-0337-7

Towards Neural Network Interpretability Using Commonsense Knowledge Graphs

Youmna Ismaeil[1,2]([✉]), Daria Stepanova[1], Trung-Kien Tran[1],
Piyapat Saranrittichai[1], Csaba Domokos[1], and Hendrik Blockeel[2]

[1] Bosch Center for Artificial Intelligence, Renningen, Germany
{youmna.ismaeil,daria.stepanova,trung-kien.tran,piyapat.saranrittichai,
csaba.domokos}@de.bosch.com
[2] KU Leuven, Leuven, Belgium
{youmna.ismaeil,hendrik.blockeel}@kuleuven.be

Abstract. Convolutional neural networks (CNNs) classify images by learning intermediate representations of the input throughout many layers. In recent work, latent representations of CNNs have been aligned with semantic concepts. However, for generating such alignments, the majority of existing methods predominantly rely on large amounts of labeled data, which is hard to acquire in practice. In this work, we address this limitation by presenting a framework for mapping hidden units from CNNs to semantic attributes of classes extracted from external commonsense knowledge repositories. We empirically demonstrate the effectiveness of our framework on copy-paste adversarial image classification and generalized zero-shot learning tasks.

Keywords: Interpretability · Image classification · Knowledge graphs

1 Introduction

Convolutional neural networks (CNNs) are well-known for their capacity to learn different powerful representations of the input in their successive layers. It is also well-known that they process images in a way that is not always intuitive to humans [11]. The lack of interpretability of CNNs is clearly undesirable, especially in safety-critical applications such as medical diagnosis or autonomous driving. This has led to an increased interest in methods that make the behavior of a trained CNN more interpretable by trying to assign human-understandable concepts (*e.g.*, face) to the neurons in the intermediate layers, often without explicit supervision [2, 6, 16, 18, 23, 29].

An important class of methods [2, 16, 25] proposes to align neurons with class attributes by using images in which segments are labeled. More specifically, one tries to find out which neurons are activated by particular image segments and, in that manner, associate these neurons with the label of the segment. For instance, if, over multiple images, a particular neuron tends to be active for the image segments labeled with *table*, one could argue that this neuron recognizes tables,

© The Author(s), under exclusive license to Springer Nature Switzerland AG 2022
U. Sattler et al. (Eds.): ISWC 2022, LNCS 13489, pp. 74–90, 2022.
https://doi.org/10.1007/978-3-031-19433-7_5

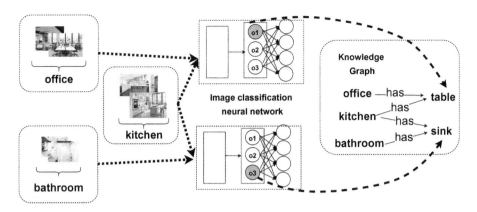

Fig. 1. The goal of our work is to assign meaning to neurons using semantic properties of classes from a knowledge graph.

and neurons in later layers essentially use this high-level information to decide whether the image shows, *e.g.*, an office. However, an important limitation of such methods is that during training they require fine-grained semantic labels of the images that are often not readily available and can be expensive to construct.

In this paper, we provide an alternative. Instead of using semantically labeled images, we assume that external knowledge extracted from a knowledge graph (KG) is available that contains symbolic descriptions of objects. Extensive KGs of this kind exist. For example, ConceptNet [26] or WebChild [27] store semantic (including visual) information about concepts (*e.g.*, *offices contain tables*, *kitchens contain ovens*, *etc.*) acquired using crowd sourcing or information extraction from the Web. We develop methods that exploit such KGs by linking the class label of images to typical visible attributes of this class, and then trying to correlate neuron activation with these attributes. For example, if a particular neuron tends to be active for pictures of offices and kitchens, but not for pictures of bathrooms, and the KG states that offices and kitchens tend to contain tables while bathrooms do not, then this may be an indication that the neuron reflects the presence of a table (see Fig. 1).

We demonstrate experimentally that the methods we propose successfully interpret neurons to the extent that they enable zero-shot learning of new classes with comparable performance to existing methods, but with the advantage of interpreting neurons in human-understandable terms. In the zero-shot learning setting, a model is expected to classify images from classes it has never encountered during training. Earlier works in this direction that likewise make use of external knowledge about classes [17, 20] propose to exploit such knowledge during training. While natural, these methods typically assume that prior to training, the knowledge of both seen and unseen classes is available. This implies that whenever the source of knowledge (e.g., KG) is updated with information about new unseen classes, training needs to be done completely from scratch, which might be undesirable. Removing knowledge about unseen classes during

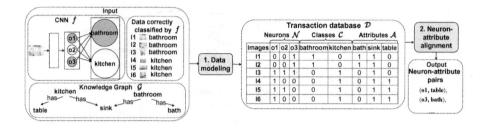

Fig. 2. Workflow of the proposed framework.

training makes the respective methods less effective (see Sect. 5). In contrast, our approach is advantageous in that we require the knowledge about unseen classes to be present in the KG only at the inference phase.

Our main contributions are summarized as follows:

- We propose a framework for mapping neurons in a fully connected layer of a CNN to attributes of classes from an external knowledge graph.
- On the task of copy-paste adversarial classification [16], we show that KGs indeed contain important semantic attributes of classes, which are helpful for CNNs.
- We experimentally demonstrate the usefulness of our framework for zero-shot learning and show how it can be effectively exploited for retrieving class predictions using reasoning over multiple networks.

2   Preliminaries

Image Classification CNN. Assuming a set of object classes $\mathcal{C}$, for a given (RGB) image $I: \Omega \to \mathbb{R}^3$, where Ω denotes the pixel space, we consider a function $f: (\Omega \to \mathbb{R}^3) \to \mathcal{C}$ for a parameter vector w. The function f, providing image classification, is defined as an L-layer *convolutional neural network* (CNN), namely $f(I) = \arg\max_{k \in \mathcal{C}} (\text{softmax}(f_L \circ \cdots \circ f_2 \circ f_1(I))_k)$, where f_l defines the lth layer of the network.

Knowledge Graphs. We will assume a *knowledge graph* (KG) encoding relations between object classes and attributes. Let $\mathcal{V}$ and $\mathcal{P}$ denote a set of entities (*a.k.a.* constants) and so-called predicates, respectively. A KG $\mathcal{G} \subseteq \mathcal{V} \times \mathcal{P} \times \mathcal{V}$ represents collections of factual information encoded by triplets $\langle subject, predicate, object \rangle$. More formally, $\mathcal{G} = \{\langle s, p, o \rangle \mid s, o \in \mathcal{V} \text{ and } p \in \mathcal{P}\}^1$. In this work, we focus on *commonsense KGs* (CSKG), that is, KGs that describe visual and physical properties of object classes (*e.g.*, $\langle bathroom, has, bath \rangle$, $\langle kitchen, has, table \rangle$). Examples of such knowledge graphs include, e.g., Concept-Net [26] or WebChild [27].

---

¹ Alternatively, a KG $\mathcal{G} = (\mathcal{V}, \{\mathcal{E}_p \subseteq \mathcal{V} \times \mathcal{V}\}_{p \in \mathcal{P}})$ can be viewed as a directed super-graph (*i.e.* a composition of directed graphs $\mathcal{G}_p = (\mathcal{V}, \mathcal{E}_p), \forall p \in \mathcal{P}$, where the edges are labeled by the predicates p.

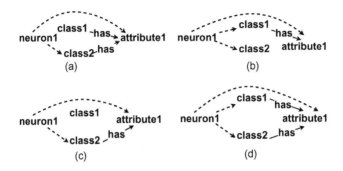

Fig. 3. Illustration of neuron-attribute alignments, where dashed lines show correlations between items in $\mathcal{D}$. (a), (b) present invalid alignments; (c), (d) reflect desirable alignments.

Association Rules. Association rules are widely used in the context of data mining. We will use association rules to model relations between neurons and attributes. First, we define a *transaction database* $\mathcal{D} = \{(i, \mathcal{X}) \mid i \in \mathcal{U} \text{ and } \mathcal{X} \subseteq \mathcal{I}\}$, where $\mathcal{I}$ stands for a set of items, and $\mathcal{U}$ is a set of IDs. A *transaction* $(i, \mathcal{X})$ has a (unique) ID i and $\mathcal{X} \subseteq \mathcal{I}$ denoting an itemset. Furthermore, we introduce the *support* of an itemset $\mathcal{X}$ in a given transaction database $\mathcal{D}$, which is the frequency of transactions in $\mathcal{D}$ containing the itemset $\mathcal{X}$:

$$\mathrm{supp}(\mathcal{X}) = |\{(i, \mathcal{X}') \in \mathcal{D} \mid \mathcal{X} \subseteq \mathcal{X}'\}| \ / \ |\mathcal{D}| \ .$$

We consider bi-directional *association rules*, which are expressions of the form $\mathcal{X} \Leftrightarrow \mathcal{Y}$, where $\mathcal{X}, \mathcal{Y} \subseteq \mathcal{I}$. Association rules can be ranked relying on certain *interestingness metrics* [1]. In this work, we focus on Jaccard index (*a.k.a.* intersection over union), which for a given association rule $\mathcal{X} \Leftrightarrow \mathcal{Y}$ computes the ratio of co-occurrences to all occurrences of $\mathcal{X}$ and $\mathcal{Y}$ in the transaction dataset:[2]

$$J(\mathcal{X} \Leftrightarrow \mathcal{Y}) = \frac{\mathrm{supp}(\mathcal{X} \cup \mathcal{Y})}{\mathrm{supp}(\mathcal{X}) + \mathrm{supp}(\mathcal{Y}) - \mathrm{supp}(\mathcal{X} \cup \mathcal{Y})} \ . \tag{1}$$

3 Generating Neuron-Attribute Alignments

Our goal is to interpret neurons' behavior[3] in human-interpretable terms. In this paper, we consider image classification as an application. In contrast to existing methods [2,16], we aim at developing a framework that can be qualitatively and quantitatively evaluated and that is not limited by the availability of semantically labeled data.

---

[2] We also write $J(\mathcal{X}, \mathcal{Y})$ for conciseness.
[3] A neuron can also be understood as an element of the vector of activation output for a given layer.

We propose to interpret neurons' behavior in terms of the semantic properties (*a.k.a.* attributes, encoded by a set $\mathcal{A}$) from pre-constructed KGs, which store human knowledge about classes from $\mathcal{C}$. To this end, we aim at answering the following key questions:

Q1. Do the extracted alignments comply with the behavior of the CNN from which they were extracted?
Q2. Do networks learn in terms of attributes defined by the knowledge graph?
Q3. Beyond explainability, how can we utilize the extracted explanations?

Framework Overview. First, we present our framework, depicted in Fig. 2, for aligning individual neurons with high-level attributes from a KG.

Let us consider a neural network f trained for image classification on a labeled image dataset $\mathcal{T} = \{(I, c) \mid I : \Omega \to \mathbb{R}^3 \text{ and } c \in \mathcal{C}\}$. Moreover, assume we are given a knowledge graph $\mathcal{G} = \{\langle c, p, a \rangle \mid c \in \mathcal{C} \text{ and } a \in \mathcal{A}\}$ storing semantic properties (*a.k.a.* attributes) $\mathcal{A}$ of classes from $\mathcal{C}$, where the predicate p reflects a visual property, e.g., $hasColor, hasShape, hasPart$. While any kind of relation can be used in this context, we select those that likely provide visual attributes because naturally they are more effective $\ulcorner$ vision tasks than other relations such as $capableOf, isA$, etc.

We aim at aligning the neurons with the nodes $a \in \mathcal{A}$ from the KG $\mathcal{G}$. While, in principle, any set of neurons can be interpreted by our framework, we propose to specifically focus on the neurons from fully-connected layers, since these are known to reflect high-level abstract visual features [22]. Therefore, we consider a layer $f_l : \mathbb{R}^m \to \mathbb{R}^n$, $x \mapsto \sigma(Wx + b)$, where m and n stand for the fan-in and fan-out, respectively, for the given layer indexed by l and $\sigma : \mathbb{R}^n \to \mathbb{R}^n$ is an activation function. For $f_l(x) = \begin{bmatrix} o_1 \, o_2 \, \ldots \, o_n \end{bmatrix}^\top$, we will use the notation $o_1, o_2, \ldots, o_n$ for the individual neurons.

In the first step of our framework, we model the input data as a transaction database (Sect. 3.1). We then compute the neuron-attribute alignments using data mining-based methods (Sect. 3.2). The output of our framework is a set of neuron-attribute pairs ρ of the form (o, a), where o is an individual neuron of f, and $a \in \mathcal{A}$ is an entity in $\mathcal{G}$ corresponding to an attribute of a class in $\mathcal{C}$. In Sect. 4 and Sect. 5, we empirically provide answers to **Q1–Q3**.

3.1   Data Modeling

Suppose we are given a dataset $\mathcal{S} = \{(I, c) \mid f(I) = c\} \subseteq \mathcal{T}$ of images that are correctly classified by f. Given the neural network f, and the set $\mathcal{N} = \{o_1, \ldots, o_n\}$ of individual neurons from the target layer f_l we proceed with constructing the transaction dataset $\mathcal{D}$ with items $\mathcal{I} = \mathcal{C} \cup \mathcal{N} \cup \mathcal{A}$. For every $(I, c) \in \mathcal{S}$, $\mathcal{D}$ stores a transaction $(i, \mathcal{X}_i)$, where i is the unique ID of the image I, and $\mathcal{X}_i \subseteq \{c\} \cup \mathcal{N} \cup \mathcal{A}$. For $a \in \mathcal{A}$, we have that $a \in \mathcal{X}_i$ iff $\langle c, p, a \rangle \in \mathcal{G}$, that is, the class of the image c and all of its attributes from the KG are in $\mathcal{X}_i$.

Intuitively, for every neuron $o \in \mathcal{N}$, it holds that $o \in \mathcal{X}_i$ iff o has high value before softmax when I is passed through f. To detect neurons from $\mathcal{N}$ with high value, the continuous values of the neurons are simply thresholded to a binary value $v_o \in \{0, 1\}$. This can be done *a priori* (*e.g.*, for post-ReLU activations) or by dynamically thresholding above neuron-specific percentile [16,24]. This way, for each image $I_i \in \mathcal{S}$ we identify a set of neurons from $\mathcal{N}$ with high activation value for the given image, and collect them into $\mathcal{X}_i$.

3.2 Neuron-Attribute Alignment

We then rely on the constructed transaction data $\mathcal{D}$ to compute the alignments between neurons and attributes, *i.e.*, items in $\mathcal{N}$ and those in $\mathcal{A}$, respectively. We propose methods for computing such alignments that we describe next.

Direct Method. Intuitively, a neuron o is *correlated* with an attribute a if the following two conditions hold: 1) it is highly probable that the attribute a is visually present in an image given that the neuron o is active for it; 2) it is highly probable that the neuron o is active, given that the attribute a is visually present in the image. Note that we cannot straightly compute the respective probabilities since the images are not explicitly labeled with the attributes. Therefore, instead, we estimate such probabilities by relying on the assumption that an attribute a is likely visible in an image I belonging to the class c if $\langle c, p, a \rangle \in \mathcal{G}$.

The first method that we propose (referred to as *direct*) is to *directly* construct the target alignments by identifying correlated pairs (o, a), where $o \in \mathcal{N}$, and $a \in \mathcal{A}$, such that $J(o, a) \geq \theta$ for a predefined threshold θ. The computed pairs are collected into the set ρ.

Example 1. Given $\mathcal{D}$ from Fig. 2 and $\theta = 0.7$, we have $J(o_1, sink) = 4/6$, $J(o_1, table) = 3/4$ and $J(o_3, bath) = 2/3$, $J(o_3, sink) = 3/6$. Thus, we obtain only $(o_1, table)$ as the resulting alignment.

Constrained Method. While natural, the main drawback of the above *direct* method is that it only considers correlated pairs of neurons and attributes but ignores the knowledge about classes, like both bathrooms and kitchens have sinks, while offices and bedrooms do not. This information is important, especially when the dataset is unbalanced, to ensure that all meaningful alignments are computed.

Example 2. Reconsider Example 1. Looking closer at $\mathcal{D}$, one can observe that o_1 is highly correlated with the class *kitchen*, as it is active for all images of this class. Similarly, o_3 is highly correlated with the class *bathroom*. Since *bath* is the attribute which is relevant only for the class *bathroom* but not for *kitchen*, it would be expected that $(o_3, bath)$ is also included in the resulting set of alignments along with $(o_1, table)$. Decreasing the threshold θ to a lower value (e.g., 0.65) would resolve this, but would also lead to $(o_1, sink)$ being in the result, which is counter-intuitive, since *sink* is an attribute which is relevant both for *bathroom* and *kitchen*, but *o1* is active only for images of the latter class.

Intuitively, an alignment is deemed meaningless if it fits into the cases (a) or (b) depicted in Fig. 3 (more formally defined via constrains below). An alignment in Fig. 3 (a) is undesirable, because we consider the neuron's activity as a sign of the existence or absence of the attribute in the input image. Consequently, if a neuron is active frequently for images of only one particular class, it might be a sign that this neuron is triggered by some attribute that only belongs to this class but not shared with other classes. Similarly, following Fig. 3 (b), if a neuron is active frequently for images of a set of classes, then it might be an indication that it is triggered by attributes that are shared among these classes.

For example, if o is aligned with the sink, then we expect o with high probability to be active for images of classes that typically contain sink (e.g., bathrooms and kitchens), but not those that do not have sink (e.g., bedrooms and offices). To alleviate the threshold's rigidity in the *direct* method, we establish formal constraints that allow us to filter out those and only those alignments that become completely meaningless when the class information is taken into account. The respective constraints are presented below:

(1) if $|\{c_i \in \mathcal{C} \mid \langle c_i, p, a \rangle \in \mathcal{G}\}| \geq 2$, and $|\{c_j \in \mathcal{C} \mid \langle c_j, p, a \rangle \in \mathcal{G}$ and $J(o, c_j) \geq \beta\}| < 2$, then (o, a) is an *invalid* alignment (see Fig. 3 (a)).

(2) if $\langle c_i, p, a \rangle \in \mathcal{G}$, for all $c_j \in \mathcal{C} \setminus \{c_i\}$, $\langle c_j, p, a \rangle \notin \mathcal{G}$ and $|\{c_j \in \mathcal{C} \setminus \{c_i\} \mid J(o, c_j) \geq \beta\}| \geq k - 1$, then (o, a) is an *invalid* alignment, where $2 \leq k \leq |\mathcal{C}|$ is a parameter (see Fig. 3 (b) for $k = 2$).

Intuitively, the first constraint (1) states that if at least two classes have an attribute a, but only less than two out of them are correlated with the neuron o, then the alignment (o, a) is invalid. The second constraint (2) reflects that if a is relevant for a single class only, and the number of other classes correlated with o is larger than k, then (o, a) is invalid.

In the *constrained-k* method, after computing the alignments relying on the Jaccard similarity for a given threshold θ, we post-process the results by removing alignments that violate the above constraints. The *constrained-k* method is illustrated by the following example.

Example 3. We have $\langle c_i, has, sink \rangle \in \mathcal{G}$ for $c_i \in \{kitchen, bathroom\}$ in Example 1, i.e., *sink* is an attribute that is relevant for at least two classes. Moreover, for $\beta = \theta$, we have $J(o_1, kitchen) > \beta$, but $J(o_1, bathroom) < \beta$, namely, the neuron o_1 is only frequently active for images of kitchen, but rarely for those of bathroom. Hence, based on the constraint (1), we remove $(o_1, sink)$ from the list of alignments computed by the *direct* method. Analogously, $(o_3, sink)$ is removed.

4   Evaluation and Applications

We now discuss various strategies for evaluating the computed neuron-attribute alignments as well possible applications, where they can be useful.

Copy-Paste Adversarial Examples. Adversarial images are images that are intentionally perturbed to confuse and deceive visual models. Changes to the image can be made in different ways, one of which is by copying patches from images of one class and pasting them into images of another class. Images with this type of perturbation are known as copy-paste adversarial images (as defined in [3]). Our hypothesis is that, if the network learns in terms of the attributes used in our work for interpreting neurons, then copying an image patch of an attribute relevant only for single class and pasting it into an image from another class should result in confusing the CNN to predict the class of the given image as the one to which the patch belongs. An example of a copy-paste adversarial image can be obtained by copying the image patch representing the bed from a bedroom image and pasting it into a bathroom image. Intuitively, if passing the bathroom image with a bed through a CNN trained on images of bathrooms and bedrooms results in confusing the network to classify the input image as a bedroom, then one can confirm that the network learns in terms of the attributes associated with the classes. We exploit the copy-paste adversarial images to in Sect. 5 to address **(Q1)** and **Q2**.

Towards addressing **(Q3)**, next we propose applications, in which the computed neuron-attribute alignments could be useful.

Zero-Shot Learning. The first application concerns zero-shot learning, *i.e.*, a popular task in image classification, in which images of new (*i.e.*, unseen) classes that do not exist in the training set need to be classified. For that, we develop an image classifier from the obtained neuron-attribute alignments. More specifically, given an image I of an unseen class, the trained network f, the pre-computed neuron-attribute pairs $\rho = \{(o, a) \mid o \in \mathcal{N}, a \in \mathcal{A}\}$, as well as the KG $\mathcal{G}$ storing the semantic information about the (un)seen classes, our goal is to derive the most likely class to which the target image I belongs. First, we pass I through f, and collect the set of activated neurons among $o \in \mathcal{N}$. We then exploit the neuron-attribute pairs ρ to retrieve the list of attributes, with which the active neurons are aligned, *i.e.*, $\mathcal{A}_I = \{a \in \mathcal{A} \mid (o, a) \in \rho$ and o is active by I in $f\}$. Finally, relying on $\mathcal{G}$, the classes $c \in \mathcal{C}$ are ranked based on the following scoring function:

$$\text{Score}(c) = \sum_{a \in \mathcal{A}_I} w_a \ / \ |\{a : \langle c, p, a \rangle \in \mathcal{G}\}| \tag{2}$$

where w_a is the ratio of neurons activated by the given image that are aligned with the attribute a to the total number of neurons activated by the image. The more active neurons are aligned with an attribute a, the more certain we are that a exists in the image and subsequently the greater is w_a. The candidate classes are ranked based on the formula from Eq. 2 and the top-ranked class is selected as the final prediction. Intuitively, the proposed technique referred to as *attribute-based classifier* allows one to reduce the image classification task to reasoning over the KG. The *attribute-based classifier* acts as an evaluator of the extracted alignments; if it gives high classification accuracy, then the extracted alignments reflect what the network learns.

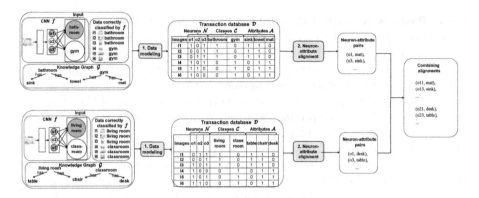

Fig. 4. The figure illustrates how to combine knowledge acquired by two networks. The aggregate alignments are later employed to reason about images from unseen classes.

Reasoning over Multiple Networks. The described *attribute-based classifier* can also be exploited in the setting, where multiple neural networks trained on non-intersecting sets of classes are used to solve tasks that are outside their initial scope (i.e., classify images into classes unseen by either of the networks). The systematic way of combining knowledge extracted from multiple networks is beneficial, as it allows one to avoid massive retraining on a larger number of classes while preserving high accuracy of predictions.

The procedure for attribute-based zero-shot classification can be naturally extended to handle several networks. First, we collect activated neurons for a given image from a number of networks, and then use the neuron-attribute alignments pre-computed for each network separately to detect attributes in the image. Finally, we merge the acquired knowledge using KG to make a decision regarding the most likely class of the image exactly in the same way as described above.

Example 4. Consider two convolutional neural networks f_1 and f_2 trained on the classes $C_1 = \{livingRoom, classroom\}$ and $C_2 = \{gym, bathroom\}$, respectively. Assume that the classes from C_1 have the following attributes $A_1 = \{table, chair, desk\}$, while those from C_2 contain the set of attributes $A_2 = \{mat, sink, towel\}$. Combining the knowledge acquired by the two networks would allow us to classify images into a new class, e.g., *kitchen*, which contains the set of attributes $A_3 = \{table, sink\}$ that were seen separately by the respective networks (see Fig. 4).

5   Experiments

We evaluate the proposed method for aligning neurons of a network with attributes of classes from a knowledge graph by empirically analyzing **(Q1)**-**(Q3)** from Sect. 3.

5.1   Experimental Setup

Datasets. We consider the popular *MITScenes* [19] and *AwA2* [28] datasets, and use *ConceptNet* [26] knowledge graph as a knowledge source.

MITScenes: We have selected images from the MIT scene dataset [19] belonging to classes whose visual properties are well covered in ConceptNet, which resulted in 10,475 images labelled with 15 classes. We use 3,840 images from 10 classes for *training*. For testing the performance on seen classes, we have 2,320 images belonging to the same 10 classes. For testing on the unseen classes, we have 4,675 images from the remaining 5 classes. On average, for each class, we get 645 images.

AwA2: We also consider a subset of the *AwA2* [28] dataset, in which the semantic information about image classes is well covered in the KG. We get 17,746 images spread across 20 classes. For training, we have 7,842 images from 15 classes. For testing on seen classes, we have 5,229 images belonging to the same 15 classes. For testing on unseen classes, we have 4,675 images from the remaining 5 classes.

ConceptNet KG: The *AwA2* and *MITScenes* datasets come with attributes already; however, their coverage is rather low (7.2 attributes per class at most). Our goal is to demonstrate the usefulness of commonsense KGs as sources for acquiring further class knowledge. For that, we have extracted attributes from a popular commonsense KG, ConceptNet [26]. For *MITScenes*, we collect the attributes connected to the classes via the inverse of *atLocation* relation (e.g., ⟨*table, atLocation, kitchen*⟩). In total, we get 1,680 attributes which on average amounts to 112 attributes per class. For *AwA2*, we use the predicate *has* to get 3,352 attributes, which yields 167 attributes per class on average.

CNN Training. We adopt ResNet50 [12] pre-trained on ImageNet [7] as the backbone, which in some experiments is fine-tuned on the considered datasets, while in others trained from scratch as described separately in each subsection. We replaced the fully connected layer before the last one in ResNet50 with a fully connected layer that has 2,048 neurons, which we aim at aligning with the attributes from ConceptNet.

Baselines. We compare our direct (*dir*) and constrained (*con*) methods (with fine-tuned parameters θ and β) for the attribute-based classification against the state-of-the-art methods that likewise make use of KGs (but do not map neurons to the KG entities), namely Dense Graph Propagation method (*DGP*) [14], Attentive Zero-Shot Learning method (*AZSL-D*) [10], and *ZSL-KG* [17]. *AZYL-D* and *ZSL-KG* rely on *DGP*, which is a framework that proposes a dense connection scheme of a knowledge graph to optimize the knowledge propagation between distant nodes in shallow networks such as graph convolution networks.

We run the methods proposed in [10] and [17], ensuring that no semantic information about unseen classes in the KG is used during training.

Fig. 5. Copy-paste adversarial examples: *art studio* with an *island* attribute relevant only for *kitchen* (left) and *office* with a *rug* relevant to classes *bedroom* and *office*.

Table 1. Class samples of adversarial copy-paste examples.

Original class	Inserted attribute	Resulting class
Dining room	Wall with doors	Corridor
Classroom	Shower	Bathroom
Office	Bed	Bedroom
Kitchen	Furniture	Office
Living room	Painting	Art Studio

Evaluation Metrics. We use the standard *hit@1* metric, which reflects the percentage of test images for which the method returned the correct class prediction in the top-1.

5.2   Copy-Paste Adversarial Examples

To answer **(Q1)-(Q2)**, following [16] we first generate the copy-paste adversarial examples using the *MITScenes* dataset, which comes with labeled semantic segments, as follows. Out of all labels, we select those (set $\mathcal{A}$) which are present in ConceptNet. Then, for each class $c \in \mathcal{C}$, we construct the set $\mathcal{A}_c = \{a \mid \langle c, p, a \rangle \in \mathcal{A} \text{ and } \forall c' \in \mathcal{C}, \langle c', p, a \rangle \notin \mathcal{G}\}$. For every pair of images I, I' from the test set belonging to different classes c and c' respectively, we insert the visualization of a randomly selected attribute $a \in \mathcal{A}_{c'}$ from the image I' into the image I, and label it with c'. For example, given an image I of an art studio and I' of a kitchen, as a copy-paste adversarial example, we generate an image I with the kitchen island from I' inserted into I (see Fig. 5 for illustration). The resulting image is labeled as a kitchen. The attributes to be inserted for every class are chosen randomly while making sure that they exist visually in at least one image (see Table 1 for class and attribute examples).

Table 2. Results for copy-paste adversarial classification on the *MITScenes* dataset. The alignment score is the percentage of images on which the attribute-based classifier (i.e., *con-all, con-2*) made the same prediction as *ResNet50*.

Method	hit@1(%)	Alignment(%)
ResNet50	78.2	–
con-all	**82.3**	96.14
con-2	82.1	96.64

This way, we obtain 2,320 adversarial copy-paste examples. We then analyze whether the considered CNN ResNet50 and our attribute-based classifier described in Sect. 4 misclassify the adversarial images relying on the inserted attribute. For instance, in the above example, we expect the network to misclassify the art studio as a kitchen. To perform such an evaluation, we pass every copy-paste adversarial example through the network and compute the *hit@1* score.

The results are presented in Table 2. High misclassification and alignment scores demonstrate that the KG attributes that distinguish classes from each other are indeed important for classification [5].

We have also repeated the same experiment on examples, constructed by inserting attributes relevant for multiple classes into the image (e.g., inserting a kitchen door into the art studio). We observe that in this case, the misclassification score in *hit@1* drops to around 2% for *ResNet50*. This witnesses that not all parts of an image are equally important for the network to make decisions, but only those that are distinguishing a given class from others based on the KG.

5.3 Zero-Shot Learning Task

To answer **(Q1)** and **(Q3)**, we compare the introduced methods for attribute-based classification to the baselines *AZSL-D* [10], *ZSL-KG* [20], and *DGP* [14] with respect to their performance on the zero-shot learning task.

For this task, we trained *ResNet50* on 10 classes of the *MITScene* dataset. We then used the trained network to compute the neuron-attribute alignment pairs for the classes from the training set. The other 5 classes are used for testing.

Since the knowledge graph stores the semantic information about both seen and unseen classes, we effectively exploit this knowledge along with the neuron-attribute alignments computed by our methods to classify the images from the unseen classes as described in Sect. 4. Importantly, the attributes of unseen classes are only used at the inference phase, but not during training.

Table 3 presents the results for the zero-shot learning tasks for *MITScenes* and *AwA2* datasets, respectively. Importantly, we report the performance both when using the attributes based on the semantic labels that accompany the datasets, as well as those from the ConceptNet KG.[4] For the *MITScenes* dataset,

---

[4] We also experimented with the WebChild [27] KG, but the results for ConceptNet are more promising.

Table 3. Zero-shot learning results on *MITScenes* and *AwA2*.

	Attribute source	Method	Unseen hit@1	Seen hit@1
MITScenes		AZSL-D	8.26	8.33
	–	DGP	19.87	9.73
	–	ZSL-KG	9.31	11.14
	Labels	*direct*	20.0	9.4
		con-2	20.0	19.1
		con-all	23.8	30.4
	Concept Net	*direct*	31.7	10.2
		con-2	38.4	50.0
		con-all	37.6	50.8
AwA2		AZSL-D	23.9	6.5
	–	DGP	24.1	6.6
	–	ZSL-KG	9.38	14.18
	Labels	*direct*	29.2	12.0
		con-2	38.6	41.5
		con-all	24.6	23.4
	Concept Net	*direct*	32.7	9.5
		con-2	40.2	47.6
		con-all	23.1	19.1

the attribute-based classifier that exploits attributes from *ConceptNet* outperforms all baselines including the attribute-based classifier that makes use of the labels coming with the dataset. This is due to the fact that, among visual attributes, the KG also provides a set of non-visual attributes that help in linking semantically similar classes via alignments. Moreover, the attribute labels coming from the dataset are shared among different classes, which leaves only a few attributes discriminatively describing each class.

Example Alignments. We present the alignments computed by our method for the considered datasets in Fig. 7. One can observe that the alignments indeed contain attributes visually relevant to the respective images.

5.4   Reasoning over Multiple Networks

We analyze the usefulness of the neuron-attribute alignments for the task of joint reasoning over multiple networks without having to retrain or fine-tune them.

In this experiment we trained from scratch two ResNet50 networks net_1 and net_2, on *AwA2* as follows. net_1 was trained for 15 epochs on 8 classes, and net_2 for 15 epochs on the other 7 classes. Moreover, we trained another network net on all 15 classes for 16 epochs. We get for net_1 a test accuracy on seen classes of 74.2%, for net_2 of 86.4%, and for net 80.5%. For the test set, we have images from 5 unseen classes.

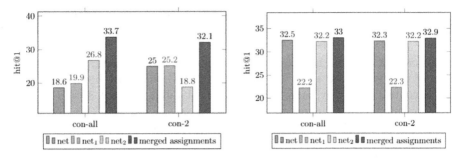

Fig. 6. Zero-shot learning using neuron-attribute alignments over multiple networks on *AwA2* (left) and *MITScenes* (right).

(n_1089, fur),
(n_779, black),(n_720, giant)

(n_1726, commuters),
(n_1608, tube),(n_534, track)

Fig. 7. Examples of neuron-attribute pairs computed by our method.

Figure 6 shows the results of the presented methods for reasoning over knowledge learned by multiple networks. For *AwA2* dataset, the attribute-based classifier that jointly considers neuron-attribute alignments from both net_1 and net_2 outperforms the attribute-based classifiers constructed separately for net_1, net_2 and net respectively. For the *MITScenes* dataset, a similar trend is observed with the exception that the attribute-based classifier constructed relying on net_2 significantly outperforms the one based on net_1 and has comparable performance to other classifiers. This is due to the fact that net_1 (resp. net_2) was trained on classes with many (resp. few) attributes in common with the unseen classes.

6 Related Work

Recently, there has been an increasing interest in understanding what deep learning models learn. Our work extends the earlier proposals on explaining individual neurons in deep representations [2,6,9,16,25]. However, in contrast to existing work, we do not rely on large amounts of training data, but instead exploit external knowledge graphs. In [25], semantic knowledge (in the form of ontologies) has also been considered for interpreting CNNs by generating explanations, yet this method again makes use of labeled and segmented images, unlike we do.

Our approach for aligning neurons and KG attributes is in the spirit of [8, 13], where data mining has been exploited for interpreting neural networks or forming concepts based solely on neurons, but KGs have not been considered in this context. Recently, many works have motivated the exploitation of KGs for enhancing the performance of image classifiers, e.g., [10,14,17,20] (see [4] for an overview). The direction of explaining the behavior of CNNs with semantic technologies has been also discussed as a valuable research stream in several works [15,21]. However, to the best of our knowledge, no concrete proposals for aligning individual neurons with KG entities exist to date.

Several works have considered graph neural networks (GNNs) for zero-shot learning [10,14,17,20]. These methods make use of graph-structured external knowledge, in which each class is represented by a single node and each inter-class link is represented by an edge. Given the external knowledge graph, its embedding representation is first computed using a GNN, and then exploited for the zero-shot learning task.

Some techniques [10,14] utilize convolutional layers with an additional dense connection layer to propagate features to distant nodes within the same net-work. The work [10] further introduced weighted aggregation as a method for emphasizing more significant neighboring nodes for class nodes. A key difference between these approaches and our work is that they do not aim at aligning neurons with KG entities like we do. Additionally, they explicitly include KG-based information about unseen classes during training, whereas we only exploit this knowledge at the inference phase. We observed that when knowledge about unseen classes is omitted from the information used for training, the performance of AZSL-D [10], DGP [17], and ZSL-KG [20] drops significantly (see Table 3).

7   Conclusion

This paper proposes a framework for aligning neurons of a neural network to attributes defined by external commonsense knowledge graphs. These alignments not only make NNs more interpretable (see Fig. 7 for examples), but are also useful in various applications, such as zero-shot classification (using multiple networks). Our framework does not require the knowledge about unseen classes to be used during training, but rather exploits it at inference stages. Our results demonstrate that commonsense KGs contain distinctive attributes relying on which CNNs tend to perform classification. This demonstrates the importance and usefulness of commonsense KGs for computer vision tasks.

Although we relied on ConceptNet KG in the experiments, our work is certainly not bound to it, and other KGs (or combinations of them) can likewise be exploited. We believe that our method has a broader impact, as it offers an interesting perspective for reducing machine learning tasks to those of reasoning over KGs.

Supplemental Material Statement: Supplemental material is available at https://github.com/boschresearch/feature-attribute-association.

Acknowledgements. We would like to thank Dr. Volker Fischer from Bosch Center for AI for providing helpful feedback on initial versions of this work.

References

1. Agrawal, R., Imielinski, T., Swami, A.N.: Mining association rules between sets of items in large databases. In: SIGMOD 1993, pp. 207–216 (1993)
2. Bau, D., Zhou, B., Khosla, A., Oliva, A., Torralba, A.: Network dissection: quantifying interpretability of deep visual representations. In: CVPR, pp. 3319–3327 (2017)
3. Brunner, T., Diehl, F., Knoll, A.: Copy and paste: a simple but effective initialization method for black-box adversarial attacks. In: 2019 IEEE/CVF Conference on Computer Vision and Pattern Recognition Workshops (CVPRW) (2019)
4. Chen, J., Geng, Y., Chen, Z., Horrocks, I., Pan, J.Z., Chen, H.: Knowledge-aware zero-shot learning: survey and perspective. In: IJCAI, pp. 4366–4373. ijcai.org (2021)
5. Cheng, X., Lu, J., Feng, J., Yuan, B., Zhou, J.: Scene recognition with objectness. Pattern Recogn. **74**, 474–487 (2018)
6. Dalvi, F., Nortonsmith, A., Bau, A., et al.: Neurox: a toolkit for analyzing individual neurons in neural networks. In: AAAI 2019, pp. 9851–9852 (2019)
7. Deng, J., Dong, W., Socher, R., Li, L., et al.: Imagenet: a large-scale hierarchical image database. In: CVPR 2009, pp. 248–255 (2009)
8. Endres, D., Földiák, P.: Interpreting the neural code with formal concept analysis. In: NIPS, pp. 425–432 (2008)
9. Fong, R., Vedaldi, A.: Net2vec: quantifying and explaining how concepts are encoded by filters in deep neural networks. In: CVPR, pp. 8730–8738 (2018)
10. Geng, Y., Chen, J., Zhiquan Ye, e.: Explainable zero-shot learning via attentive graph convolutional network and KGs. SW 12 (2021)
11. Goodfellow, I.J., Shlens, J., Szegedy, C.: Explaining and harnessing adversarial examples. In: ICLR 2015 (2015)
12. He, K., Zhang, X., Ren, S., Sun, J.: Deep residual learning for image recognition. In: Proceedings of the IEEE Conference on Computer Vision and Pattern Recognition, pp. 770–778 (2016)
13. Horta, V.A.C., Mileo, A.: Towards explaining deep neural networks through graph analysis. In: DB and Expert Systems Applications, pp. 155–165 (2019)
14. Kampffmeyer, M., Chen, Y., Liang, X., Wang, H., Zhang, Y., Xing, E.P.: Rethinking knowledge graph propagation for zero-shot learning. In: Proceedings of the IEEE/CVF Conference on Computer Vision and Pattern Recognition (CVPR) (2019)
15. Lécué, F.: On the role of knowledge graphs in explainable AI. Semant. Web **11**(1), 41–51 (2020)
16. Mu, J., Andreas, J.: Compositional explanations of neurons. Adv. Neural Inf. Process. Syst. **33**, 17153–17163 (2020)
17. Nayak, N.V., Bach, S.H.: Zero-shot learning with common sense knowledge graphs. CoRR abs/2006.10713 (2020)

18. Nguyen, A.M., Dosovitskiy, A., Jason Yosinski, e.: Synthesizing the preferred inputs for neurons in neural networks via deep generator networks. In: Neurips 2016, pp. 3387–3395 (2016)
19. Quattoni, A., Torralba, A.: Recognizing indoor scenes. In: 2009 IEEE Conference on Computer Vision and Pattern Recognition, pp. 413–420 (2009). https://doi.org/10.1109/CVPR.2009.5206537
20. Roy, A., Ghosal, D., Cambria, E., Majumder, N., Mihalcea, R., Poria, S.: Improving zero shot learning baselines with commonsense knowledge. CoRR abs/2012.06236 (2020)
21. Sarker, M.K., Xie, N., Doran, D., Raymer, M., Hitzler, P.: Explaining trained neural networks with semantic web technologies: first steps. In: NeSy (2017)
22. Selvaraju, R.R., et al.: Choose your neuron: incorporating domain knowledge through neuron-importance. In: ECCV (13), pp. 540–556 (2018)
23. Simonyan, K., Vedaldi, A., Zisserman, A.: Deep inside convolutional networks: visualising image classification models and saliency maps. In: ICLR 2014 (2014)
24. Simonyan, K., Zisserman, A.: Very deep convolutional networks for large-scale image recognition. In: ICLR 2015 (2015)
25. de Sousa Ribeiro, M., Leite, J.: Aligning artificial neural networks and ontologies towards explainable AI. In: AAAI 2021, pp. 4932–4940 (2021)
26. Speer, R., Chin, J., Havasi, C.: Conceptnet 5.5: an open multilingual graph of general knowledge. In: AAAI 2017, pp. 4444–4451 (2017)
27. Tandon, N., de Melo, G., Suchanek, F.M., Weikum, G.: Webchild: harvesting and organizing commonsense knowledge from the web. In: WSDM. ACM (2014)
28. Xian, Y., Lampert, C.H., Schiele, B., Akata, Z.: Zero-shot learning-a comprehensive evaluation. IEEE Trans. Pattern. Anal. Mach. Intell. **41**(9), 2251–2265 (2019)
29. Zhou, B., Khosla, A., Lapedriza, À., Oliva, A., Torralba, A.: Object detectors emerge in deep scene cnns. In: ICLR 2015 (2015)

Reproducibility Crisis in the LOD Cloud? Studying the Impact of Ontology Accessibility and Archiving as a Counter Measure

Johannes Frey[1]([✉]) [iD], Denis Streitmatter[1] [iD], Natanael Arndt[2] [iD],
and Sebastian Hellmann[1]

[1] Knowledge Integration and Linked Data Technologies (KILT/AKSW) DBpedia
Association/InfAI, Leipzig University, Leipzig, Germany
{frey,streitmatter,hellmann}@informatik.uni-leipzig.de
[2] eccenca GmbH, Leipzig, Germany
natanael.arndt@eccenca.com

Abstract. The reproducibility crisis is an ongoing problem that affects data-driven science to a big extent. The highly connected decentral Web of Ontologies represents the backbone for semantic data and the Linked Open Data Cloud and provides terminological context information crucial for the usage and interpretation of the data, which in turn is key for the reproducibility of research results making use of it.

In this paper, we identify, analyze, and quantify reproducibility issues related to capturing terminological context (e.g. caused by unavailable ontologies) and delineate the impact on the reproducibility crisis in the Linked Open Data Cloud. Our examinations are backed by a frequent and ongoing monitoring of online available vocabularies and ontologies that results in the DBpedia Archivo dataset. We also show the extent to which the reproducibility crisis can be countered with the aid of ontology archiving in DBpedia Archivo and the Linked Open Vocabularies platforms.

1 Introduction

The reproducibility crisis is an ongoing problem in science [2] that has a big impact on data centric disciplines as well [11,12,17]. Cockburn et al. and Miyakawa emphasize the importance of the availability of data and materials for research to be reproducible [5,15]. The Linked Open Data (LOD) cloud provides a huge amount of data relevant for data science. The semantic web architecture, as technological foundation for the LOD cloud and major driver for collecting and publishing globally interlinked knowledge, consists of instance data and terminological data. The terminological data is captured by vocabularies and ontologies that make up a common point of reference for the instance data. Reuse of terms across different ontologies and their formalization are crucial patterns for data engineering on the Web of Data and a major aspect to foster interoperability and data exchange. Accessing that ontological and terminological context information is crucial for the interpretation and use of the instance data. Often this context also formalizes implicit knowledge (e.g. subclass relationships) that is not explicitly materialized in the data itself.

Moreover, accessibility is one key aspect of the FAIR data principles [21] which also explicitly require the use of FAIR ontologies for FAIR (meta)data. Given the the best practice to reuse and derive from existing terms in ontology development, this typically leads to a recursive problem. If an ontology A, that is (re)used by an ontology B, becomes unavailable and therefore looses its FAIRness, then as a result B also looses its FAIRness. Subsequently, accessibility and reliability of vocabularies and ontologies are fundamental requirements for such a decentralized (FAIR) data architecture. Thus we argue that the reproducibility of research based on or utilizing LOD is influenced to a significant extent by the accessibility of the referenced vocabularies.

However, the accessibility of vocabularies and ontologies is subject to constant evolution and unavailability (link rot, "HTTP error 404"). Stakeholders, like *Ontology Users*, *Ontology Engineers*, and *Ontology Researchers* are affected by the unavailability of ontologies in their work to varying degrees. *Ontology Users* apply the terminology in their knowledge graphs and applications and are interested in having a consistently and permanently working application. *Ontology Engineers* create new ontologies by reusing existing terminology and are interested in the reliability of the ontologies they are reusing, as well as in the reliability of their own ontologies. *Ontology Researchers* retrieve data from the LOD cloud (typically according to schematic criteria, perform analyses or benchmarks using the data and ontologies; they are interested in the reproducibility and reliability of their results over a long period of time. Common to all of these stakeholders is, the demand for the availability of pre-existing ontologies and their own contribution in the future.

Based on these abstract requirements, we pursue four main research questions in this paper to further understand the reproducibility crisis on the LOD cloud with a focus on the ontological context.

RQ1 How does the reproducibility crisis look like in the Linked Open Data cloud in terms of accessing the ontological context?

RQ2 How big is **(a)** the problem of vocabulary and ontology accessibility issues and **(b)** the impact on the reproducibility crisis in the Linked Open Data cloud?

RQ3 How much of the terminology used in the Linked Open Data cloud is and is not **(a)** accessible in a formal way (i.e. RDFS/OWL ontologies or SKOS concept schemes) such that it can be automatically preserved, and **(b)** how much is preserved already.

RQ4 Can archiving contribute as a countermeasure to the accessibility issues of ontologies.

The contribution of this paper is subdivided into the following steps. We provide an analysis of the aspects contributing to the reproducibility crisis on the

Linked Open Data cloud. These aspects are then quantified with the aid of DBpedia Archivo (a unified online ontology interface and open augmented ontology archive). In this way we can depict the impact of the reproducibility crisis on the Linked Open Data cloud. Finally, based on the quantification, a categorization of the impacted vocabularies can be performed to indicate counter-measures, such as the automatic preservation, which leads to an evaluation of two archiving approaches to tackle the impact of the reproducibility crisis.

The remainder of the paper is structured as follows: Sect. 2 gives an overview what material and methods were used while Sect. 3 presents the results. In Sect. 4 we describe related work and Sect. 5 concludes the results and gives an overview over possible future work.

2 Material and Methods

In the following section we describe the tools and their methods which we selected for the analysis setup to answer the research questions. To perform the analysis, we were in need of unified access to, on the one hand a vast amount of ontologies published in the Web of Ontologies, and on the other hand datasets of the LOD cloud. We used the DBpedia Archivo Ontology archive and Linked Open Vocabularies for the former and LOD-a-lot for the latter, which are described in more detail in the next subsections.

The high level perspective on the analysis method is, that we analyze terminology reproducibility aspects on instance data using LOD-a-lot, and accessibility issues of ontologies in general using Archivo's accessibility statistics to get an impression of the dimension of the reproducibility crisis. We create an index on the terms contained in Archivo & LOV and another index on the terms in LOD-a-lot, that could in general be subject to accessibility issues. By joining the index information, it is possible to determine the minimal number of terms where accessibility issues can be countered by archiving (reproducibility support). In the term index for LOD-a-lot we incorporate frequency (triple) count information, to study the effects also weighted by term adoption. In contrast, we integrate information about the accessibility rate for every term in the Archivo index based the ontology that defines it. In a final step, we measure the effectiveness or impact of this theoretical reproducibility support of DBpedia Archivo by calculating the amount of LOD data (number of triples) that fall into different reliability classes. To complete the picture, we use Archivo's crawling engine in a sandboxed experiment to preserve terms that are not covered by Archivo and report on issues preventing an inclusion but also the potential of ontologies that could be included in the future.

2.1 DBpedia Archivo - Augmented Ontology Archive

DBpedia Archivo's initial vision was to create a fully automated, persistent ontology archive that can serve as a backbone for the Semantic Web [8] and to serve as a convenient and stable interface for ontology consumers [9].

Launched in May 2020, Archivo has meanwhile become one of the most exhaustive and recent ontology archives, providing alternative, persistent, and unified access to over 1,600 ontologies[1] in more than 5,000 versions. The daily checks for new ontology versions and automated tests monitor the evolution and accessibility of a huge portion of the ontologies used in the LOD cloud and allow to get a picture of the state of affairs on a global scale. As of September 2021 growth has not reached a plateau, yet and it is steadily growing at a pace of around 12.6 ontologies per week (6 month average, see Fig. 1) [10]. While more than 1440 ontologies were archived automatically via web-scale discovery mechanisms, Archivo also performed over 160 successful ontology inclusions suggested by the community (i.e. submitting the ontology URL manually at https://archivo.dbpedia.org/add). This fact and around 90 ontology downloads on an average day (plus 640 daily downloads from major bots) show that Archivo is already being adopted by the community.

2.2   Archivo Ontology Discovery and Monitoring

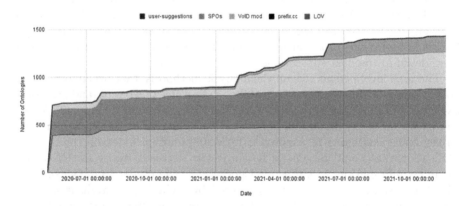

Fig. 1. Development of ontology archive growth, divided by discovery source (State of November 22nd 2021).

Archivo implements four generic approaches to discover RDFS & OWL[2] ontologies and SKOS[3] schemes to be archived. First, it queries already existing ontology repositories and catalogs (currently Linked Open Vocabularies [19] and prefix.cc). Second, it performs a vocabulary usage analysis of all RDF assets on the DBpedia Databus[4] utilizing VoID Mods that analyse the usage of classes and properties in the datasets. Moreover, it discovers (transitive) dependencies and imports ontologies from previous iterations of Archivo crawls. Finally, users can

---

[1] https://archivo.dbpedia.org/list.

[2] https://www.w3.org/TR/owl-overview/.

[3] https://www.w3.org/TR/skos-reference/.

[4] https://databus.dbpedia.org/.

request missing ontologies to be included in the automated runs via a Web inter-face. These approaches allow Archivo to have a good coverage of meaningful and relevant ontologies of the Semantic Web, while preventing the upload of incor-rect ontologies (ontology hijacking or spamming) by users. However, in order to ensure this, Archivo uses a strict technical definition of an ontology: it requires an RDF file that types the resolvable ontology (document) identifier with either `owl:Ontology` or `skos:ConceptScheme`. Note, that this requirement does not exclude RDFS ontologies, since these can be declared as an owl:Ontology but use plain RDFS semantics (a prominent example is the RDFS vocabulary itself).

2.3 Linked Open Vocabularies (LOV)

Linked Open Vocabularies [19] is a very prominent semi-automatically curated catalog of vocabularies that hosts snapshots of ontologies and provides an index to search for terms and vocabularies. New vocabularies are discovered by analyz-ing (re)use of terms from archived ontologies and can be suggested by users, but are subject to manual review and approval procedures. LOV provides an API[5] for easy access to the archived ontologies. Note, that the definition of an ontol-ogy slightly differs and that while Archivo uses the list of ontology identifiers in the LOV catalog, it performs its own automated crawling, access, versioning, monitoring, and approval strategies. As a consequence, there is no full overlap in terms of archived ontologies between the two approaches.

2.4 LOD Vocabulary Usage

In order to gain insight into the vocabulary usage of the Linked Open Data cloud, we utilized the LOD-a-lot HDT dump [4]. It contains more than 28.36 billion triples, 3.17 billion distinct objects, 3.21 billion distinct subjects, and 1,168,932 properties. Over 650,000 datasets are integrated summing up to 524 GB of compressed HDT [7] data. This dump data was crawled and cleaned by LOD-Laundromat [3]. A list of properties was retrieved by filtering the triples for predicates; a list of classes was retrieved by collecting all IRIs that occur in the object position of an `rdf:type` assertion.

3 Analysis

3.1 Ontology Accessibility Study

While it may be quite inconvenient if vocabularies are temporarily unavailable due to server failures, this unavailability leads to anomalies when using datasets built on top of them (e.g. varying or incomplete query results due to temporarily missing subclass axioms). Moreover, completely unreachable ontologies (e.g. due to publishers losing control over the domain) that are likely to be never accessible again, impede the reproducibility of existing work based on it significantly. In

---

[5] https://lov.linkeddata.es/dataset/lov/api.

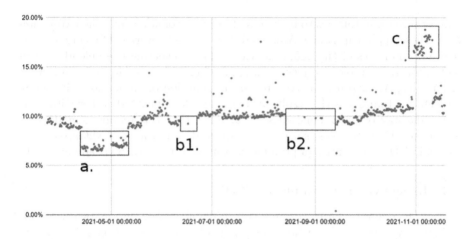

Fig. 2. Fraction of inaccessible ontologies per crawl from March to November 2021.

this first study we want to quantify how many ontologies are affected and how severely they are affected by unavailabilities.

Since Archivo runs multiple checks on every included ontology to potentially fetch new updates, three times a day, the Archivo logs[6] can be used to measure downtimes and outages of these ontologies. An outage occurs if a `HTTP-HEAD` request or the subsequent `HTTP-GET` request returns a status code ≥ 400 or reaches a timeout (Archivo waits 30 s for a response), the host name can not be resolved via the DNS, or if the RDF document is available but does not conform to the respective RDF syntax (i.e. if any error occurs when parsing the document[7]).

Figure 2 shows the outages in relation to the total number of included ontologies for the period of roughly eight months (240 days, from March 23rd to November 18th, 2021). While in average the total outage ratio is around 10%, four areas stand out, as denoted in the diagram:

a. April 12th - May 10th: the vocabularies hosted on the domain `vocab.deri.ie` were temporarily brought online but since then were unavailable again due to Linked Data configuration failures

b. June 11th - June 22nd and August 13th - September 14th: The Archivo crawling monitor had issues

c. October 29th - November 11th: A lot of vocabularies from `purl.org` were not available, but the problem was fixed eventually

Table 1 lists statistics of the downtimes of ontologies, measured over the same time period as Fig. 2. But unlike Fig. 2 it is aggregated per day and not per Archivo-Crawl, i.e. an ontology is considered as "down" for a particular day if it was inaccessible at least for one of the three crawling attempts that day. We

---

[6] See https://github.com/dbpedia/archivo/tree/master/paper-supplement/iswc2022.

[7] For this purpose Archivo uses the RaptorRDF library: https://librdf.org/raptor/.

excluded the days with crawling gaps from areas b1 and b2 as there is no reliable accessibility data (in total 29 days were excluded). The rows represent statistical values, i.e. *minimum, first quartile, median, third quartile, maximum, average, and total ontology count*. The columns stand for certain subsets of Archivo ontologies: *All onts* stand for the complete set of evaluated ontologies, *all failing* stands for all ontologies that fail at least once and *temp. failing* is the group of ontologies failing at least once, but excluding the vocabularies that fail over the whole monitoring period. The other four columns group the temporarily failing ontologies by downtime fractions, i.e. [0.01,5)% is the set of all ontologies being inaccessible 0.01% (included) up to 5% (excluded) of the time since their addition to Archivo.

Table 1. The distribution of downtimes of Archivo ontologies. Columns 1 to 3 group ontologies into failure classes. Columns 4 to 7 break down the temporarily failing ontologies into downtime intervals.

	Failure classes			Temp. failing classes			
	All onts	All failing	Temp. failing	[0.01,5)%	[5,25)%	[25,75)%	[75,100)%
Min	0.00%	0.50%	0.50%	0.50%	5.15%	26.87%	75.12%
Q1	0.00%	1.00%	1.00%	0.50%	6.47%	32.84%	88.56%
Med	0.50%	4.98%	3.72%	1.00%	7.46%	36.32%	88.56%
Q3	5.97%	12.19%	7.96%	1.99%	10.45%	69.40%	89.90%
Max	100.00%	100.00%	99.00%	4.98%	24.88%	74.62%	99.00%
Avg	10.64%	19.67%	12.20%	1.59%	9.17%	47.27%	88.90%
#	1439	775	709	394	224	51	40
% all	100.00%	53.86%	49.27%	27.38%	15.57%	3.54%	2.78%
% tmp	–	–	100.00%	55.57%	31.59%	7.19%	5.64%

Of all ontologies included during the evaluation (1439), Archivo detected no outages for 664 (∼46%) ontologies, showing that at least roughly a half of the ontologies are quite well maintained. On the other hand, 66 (∼5%) were inaccessible at every day Archivo crawled, which renders a huge problem for datasets depending on them. At least some of them are completely unmaintained and will likely continue to be inaccessible in the future. The rest (709) was inaccessible at least once (but not the whole time) in the time interval. Column 4 to 7 in Table 1 break down these temporarily inaccessible ontologies into smaller bits: more than half of them (∼56%) fall into the lowest category of outages (max. ∼5% downtime), with an average of 1.59% unavailability. Only 40 (∼6%) of the temporarily failing ontologies are in the worst category (inaccessible for more than 75% of measurement).

Overall, as it can be seen in Fig. 2 and Table 1, there is a total average of 10% downtime for all ontologies. This shows the clear need for a backup in form of an archive for ontologies, keeping track of older versions, and making backups of inaccessible ontologies easily accessible for reproducibility.

Table 2. LOD vocabulary term/namespace share.

Filter step	Properties			Classes		
	Terms	t. fract.	Triple fract.	Terms	t. fract.	Triple fract.
NONE	1,168,933	100.00%	100.00%	833,232	100.00%	100.00%
http(s) based	1,163,128	99.50%	100.00%	831,955	99.85%	99.99%
w/o dbr	1,090,550	93.29%	99.36%	785,351	94.25%	99.86%
w/o freebase	1,077,753	92.20%	99.08%	774,755	92.98%	99.57%
w/o dbp	145,820	12.47%	95.50%	–	–	–
w/o DBpYago	–	–	–	291,818	35.02%	98.19%
w/o Wikidata	142,424	12.18%	95.05%	291,555	34.99%	94.28%
w/o RDF-Seq	109,945	9.41%	94.35%	–	–	–
min 10 triples	52,721	4.51%	94.35%	145,870	17.51%	94.27%

3.2   LOD Term Usage Analysis

In a first step, we analyzed the used terminology of the LOD cloud based on
LOD-a-lot. We retrieved in total 1,168,933 terms that were used as predicate
identifier and 833,232 class identifiers used within instance type assertions (see
Table 2).

Although the LOD-a-lot data was subject to LOD-Laundromat cleaning procedures [3], we discovered more than 5,000 irretrievable identifiers that were
using a namespace that was not http(s) based. Typical representatives were
unexpanded namespace prefixes, file URI schemes, or URN schemes. We consider these types of identifiers as a burden for reproducibility since it is not
possible to automatically retrieve the semantics via Linked Data principles. Fortunately, these identifiers make up only less than half a percent of all terms and
are neglectable when it comes to the amount of filtered LOD triples affected.

During further investigation of the LOD term lists, we identified more terms
and namespaces that affect a meaningful outcome of the coverage study and
which we subsequently excluded in cascaded filtering steps and comment potential implication of these properties on the reproducibility. Table 2 reports how
many terms remain after each filtering step, as well as the remaining fraction
compared to the distinct number of terms and triples respectively.

A well-known error is to use DBpedia entity resource identifiers (namespace
prefix dbr) as a class reference, but surprisingly also as property identifier. These
triples are semantically incorrect and are therefore excluded. In the next step,
we additionally exclude Freebase identifiers, because these can be considered
as unreproducible, since Freebase did not publish an ontology. Furthermore the
project is deprecated and does not serve Linked Data anymore. We discovered
more prominent terms that are not captured systematically in an ontology. A
huge fraction (almost 80%) for property terms originates from the DBpedia
property (dbp) namespaces that are produced by the DBpedia Generic extraction [13] for each language version. These properties represent the raw value

of Wikipedia infobox parameters and therefore have no RDF or OWL semantics. The meaning can change over time and depend on the entity type, which
significantly affects reproducibility. So-called DBpedia-YAGO class identifiers
proxy the YAGO ontology but are neither captured in the DBpedia ontology
nor resolvable via Linked Data. This leads to reproducibility problems for more
than 57% of the class terms but less than 1.5% for the type statements. We
also pruned almost 4% of the Wikidata class assertions since Wikidata's class
hierarchy is not expressed using the common OWL/RDFS axioms and multiple
namespaces do not resolve via Linked Data (as of December 2021). As a consequence, in total, at least 87% of property and at least 65% of class terms have
issues in capturing the terminology context and semantics in an automatically
reproducible way. Fortunately, this only affects less than 6% of the data.

Additional 30 thousand `rdfs:ContainerMembershipPropertys` (e.g. used in
RDF sequences) can be excluded, since the semantics is specified in the RDF
standard, and this infinite set of properties is not materialized in the RDF(S)
ontology. From these over 109 thousand property terms and 291 thousand class
terms, we further filtered out all terms that had less than 10 occurrences in LOD.
We consider these terms as noise/errors and removing them has an impact of
less than 0.01% of ignored triples but cuts more than half the amount of terms
from the previous filter step.

The remaining 4.51% resp. 17.51% of terms occur following Zipf's Law in
around 94% of the LOD statements, which ensures that the reduced list of terms
still accurately represents a huge and relevant portion of LOD data.

3.3   Reproducibility Support and Archiving Impact Study

Based on the filtered term list we can evaluate how many terms are captured in
Archivo and LOV and the amount of LOD data that can be supported in terms
of a more robust reproducibility. We loaded the latest ontology snapshot of every
ontology contained in Archivo as of April 19th 2022 into a SPARQL endpoint to
verify if a term is defined in one of the archived ontologies. The same was done
with all archived ontologies of the LOV repository of that time by using its API
to fetch the latest version of each vocabulary.

We define a class as any subject that is typed as `rdfs:Class` or as a class
that is `rdfs:subClassOf` of `rdfs:Class`. Note that `owl:Class` is a subclass of
`rdfs:Class` and therefore OWL classes are included as well. The properties were
retrieved in a similar manner, only with the type being either `rdf:Property` or
any subclass of it[8]. These terms were then mapped to the frequency counts per
term measured in Sect. 3.2.

The results can be seen in Table 3 for properties and Table 4 for classes.
Out of the 52,721 property terms, 8.25% (4,350) were archived by Archivo and
9.23% by LOV, which in turn increases the reproducibility robustness for over
44% (almost 12 billion triples) respectively 52% for LOV out of the 26.76 billion
triples. In contrast, more than 80% (2.52 billion out of 3.13 billion triples) and

---

[8] See the Supplemental Material section at the end of the paper for further details.

74% of the type statements can be supported by Archivo resp. LOV. However, the support boost for individual class terms is on a similar level compared to property terms with approximately 10.82% (15,786 terms) in the case of Archivo but significantly lower with 2.41% in the case of LOV.

Although these numbers indicate that with LOV and Archivo the reproducibility of at least half of the LOD data is given, the effectiveness or impact of archiving as countermeasure is still unclear. All of these covered triples could have an ontological context defined in ontologies that are very reliable, such that the effect of archiving would be negligible at the current stage. In order to study RQ4, we therefore join the term frequency with the ontology accessibility monitoring information (as described in Sect. 2.2) of the ontology that defines the term. Figure 3 shows the impact of archiving ontologies by breaking down the fraction of triples that are covered by Archivo into the different accessibility categories of the ontology where the term is defined. The categories correspond with the ones in Table 1, Note that no data exists about the accessibility over time for ontologies only contained in LOV since the monitoring is a feature of Archivo. As a result this breakdown is only possible for terms that are covered by Archivo. We found that over 54% of these triples have their context in ontologies that did not show any problems in the monitoring time span (cf. Fig 2). However, from the remaining 46%, 15% would lack reproducibility without archiving, since the ontological context is permanently failing. The remaining 31% have temporary failures. These break down into 17% failing very often (75%–99.99% failure downtime), 2% often (25%–74.99%), 9% that fail sometimes (5%–24.99%), and 3% that fail rarely (0.01%–4.99%).

Table 3. LOD Property term coverage and reproducibility support of Archivo and LOV.

	Archivo		LOV	
	Count	Rep. factor	Count	Rep. factor
Terms covered	4,350	8.25%	4,865	9.23%
Studied terms	52,721	–	52,721	–
Triples covered	11,950,908,409	44.66%	14,025,673,856	52.41%
Studied triples	26,760,669,318	–	26,760,669,318	–

3.4   Archiving Potential and Barriers

Although Table 3 and Table 4 show that the fully automated ontology discovery, archiving, and evaluation of Archivo achieves all in all a similar performance for covering LOD terms compared to LOV, we wanted to study what major failure categories prevent an automatic retrieval and archiving of the corresponding ontologies (by Archivo) and whether there is a potential of ontologies that were not discovered yet but could be included. Therefore, we used the term list of the coverage study as input for the discovery and crawling mechanism in an

Table 4. LOD Class term coverage and reproducibility support of Archivo and LOV.

	Archivo		LOV	
	Count	Rep. factor	Count	Rep. factor
Terms covered	17,362	11.90%	3,516	2.41%
Studied terms	145,870	–	145,870	–
Triples covered	2,516,568,507	80.38%	2,322,889,414	74.19%
Studied triples	3,130,912,310	–	3,130,912,310	–

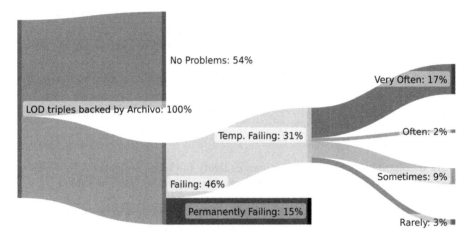

Fig. 3. Archivo Archiving Impact: Breakdown of LOD triples covered by Archivo, into the failure rate of the ontology defining the property/class term.

isolated, temporary Archivo instance. Table 6 and Table 5 show the results. In these tables, multiple reasons are given for ontologies not being accessible to Archivo. The percentage refers to the total number of terms resp. triples noted in Table 4/3. A minor reason for the outage for both classes and properties is that the crawling robot was not allowed to fetch the ontology. While this says nothing about the actual availability of the ontology, it completely prevents the ontology to be archived by Archivo and therefore no stable backup is provided. The by far most prominent reason for retrieval failure was the inaccessibility of any valid RDF at the term IRI. This could be due to link rot, server issues, losing control over the domain of the ontology, or providing unparseable RDF. This is the case for roughly 84% of uncovered properties and 59% of uncovered classes. If any RDF was discovered, the most common error was the missing ontology declaration statement, meaning the retrieved RDF document was not recognizable as an ontology and it does also not link to one. Interestingly, the share for this reason is far higher for classes (38%) than for properties (3%). Rather minor reasons were an error in the linked data deployment (the wrong identifier typed as ontology, or other errors in the RDF) or the ontology is contained in Archivo, but the term is not defined (usual typos in identifiers or deprecated terms). The last row denotes terms for which an ontology could be found and which could be archived permanently without problems, so these terms may be covered by Archivo in the future.

Table 5. Distribution of reasons for inaccessibility of properties not covered by Archivo. The percentage is based on the total number of terms/triples listed in Table 3.

	# of terms	% terms	# of triples	% triples
Total terms	48,371	91.75%	14,809,760,909	55.34%
Robots disallowed	2,336	4.43%	707,758,083	2.64%
No valid RDF accessible	40,851	77.49%	13,584,634,580	50.76%
Not linked to ontology/not recognizable	1,630	3.09%	112,504,895	0.42%
Ontology LD deployment error	729	1.38%	5,174,428	0.02%
Ontology in Archivo but term not defined	1,208	2.29%	300,318,286	1.12%
Coverable in the future	1,617	3.07%	99,370,637	0.37%

Table 6. Distribution of reasons for inaccessibility of classes not covered by Archivo. The percentage is based on the total number of terms/triples listed in Table 4.

	# of terms	% terms	# of triples	% triples
Total terms	128,508	88.10%	614,343,803	19.62%
Robots disallowed	1,894	1.30%	33,102,294	1.06%
No valid RDF accessible	76,409	52.38%	523,303,990	16.71%
Not linked to ontology/not recognizable	48,914	33.53%	5,093,624	0.16%
Ontology LD deployment error	280	0.19%	318,618	0.01%
Ontology in Archivo but term not defined	304	0.21%	29,854,614	0.95%
Coverable in the future	707	0.48%	22,670,663	0.72%

4   Related Work

Related and previous work can be grouped into three areas: archiving or mirroring of LOD-related data, data availability monitoring, and LOD evolution analysis studies.

Linked Open Vocabularies [19] (as described in Sect. 2.3) is a well-known, extensive cross-domain catalog for ontologies. There are also further efforts to host, archive, version, index, or catalog ontologies and vocabularies like OBO-Foundry [18] and BioPortal [20]. For an in-depth comparison of these approaches we refer the reader to [9].

LOD Laundromat [3] is a tool that crawls and cleans data from the LOD cloud. However, as of December 2021, the service http://lodlaundromat.org did not provide any access to the cleaned files anymore for several months and the GitHub page states that it is closed for maintenance since July 2021. Fortunately, a subset of the data is available in **LOD-a-lot** [4], that has been used for this analysis.

OpenLink's **LOD Cloud Cache** data space[9] is a SPARQL endpoint that gives access to data for a selected subset of the LOD cloud.

The **LOD Cloud**[10] website is a LOD metadata catalog which is also monitoring LOD datasets. The service provides a history for a set of accessibility crawls and the evolution of the catalog. Moreover, there is an effort to preserve LOD data on the IPFS filesystem [16]. The type of data being preserved on IPFS varies from dataset to dataset, ranging from metadata (e.g. VoID summary) to RDF snippets for example entities, but most importantly also ontologies and vocabularies.

The **LODStats** system[11] [6] lists 9,960 datasets that are monitored with regard to their accessibility and reports comprehensive statistics about its content. The statistics comprise the access methods to datasets, number of triples, issues when processing the datasets, the usage of classes, properties, datatypes, vocabularies, namespaces and many more. The datasets listed sum up to over 192 million triples, almost 50 thousand properties and 3,480 classes. The service provides insights into the accessibility and structure of the analyzed datasets, and also on the overall linked data cloud and the usage of the ontologies. However, the statistics shown on the website have some inconsistencies (e.g. almost 50 thousand properties overall are reported and the list shows only 32,634) and the project seems not active anymore, since the last update is reported over 6 years ago (as of July 2022). The fact that LOD-a-lot provides more data and access to the triples itself to calculate our own terminology usage statistics, were reasons why we picked LOD-a-lot.

A very simple LOD monitoring service is **LODservatory**[12], which reports the availability and service status of SPARQL interfaces of a list of endpoints (including ones from the LOD cloud) every hour. The **Dynamic Linked Data Observatory** (Dyldo) project [14] performs weekly crawls on Linked Open Data. Based on an IRI seed list it crawls and archives RDF data, subsequently all discovered IRIs are used to perform another crawl, finally the retrieved RDF data, HTTP headers, and redirections are persisted. This process captures also terms from ontologies or could even persist entire ontologies. However, there are no guarantees on completeness for terms and ontologies. Nevertheless, the availability and functioning of the Linked Data mechanisms for particular namespaces can be analyzed over time.

---

[9] http://vos.openlinksw.com/owiki/wiki/VOS/VirtuosoLODSampleTutorial.
[10] https://lod-cloud.net.
[11] https://lodstats.aksw.org/.
[12] https://github.com/SmartDataAnalytics/lodservatory.

An analysis on the evolution of vocabulary terms and their impact on the LOD Cloud has been carried out in [1]. The authors investigated to which extent changes in vocabularies were adopted in the evolution of three datasets (the Billion Triples Challenge datasets, the Dynamic Linked Data Observatory dataset, and Wikidata). The results show that the frequency of term changes was rather low, but a huge portion of deprecated terms was still used in the datasets.

To the best of our knowledge, this work is the first effort that specifically studies the accessibility of a huge corpus of ontologies for a longer period of time while also trying to analyze the potential impact of preserving this vocabularies for the LOD cloud to get a better picture of the state of affairs in terms of reproducibility of ontological context.

5   Discussion, Conclusion and Future Work

To conclude, we would like to summarize the results in terms of our research questions. Initially, we gathered reproducibility problems (RQ1) by looking at the namespaces, that are rooted in data or terminology representation itself: term identifiers were not using the HTTP protocol or not formalized with the standards RDFS, OWL or SKOS, formalization was not accessible as dump, or the dump file was not delivered or announced in a way to be accessed via Linked Data when resolving the term and ontology identifiers. Moreover, we discovered a huge portion of proxy identifiers. While it sounds alarming that these issues affected around 88% of the property and 65% of class terms used in LOD-a-lot, it fortunately affected less than 5% of the LOD-a-lot data. We excluded this portion of data from further being used in the studies, since the data or the ontological context modeling needs to be fixed in the first place, in order to be considered a meaningful amount of Linked Open Data.

In RQ2 we measured the problem from two angles. In RQ2a we were looking at the ontologies and in RQ2b at the data affected by the problem through their use of the ontologies. In terms of RQ2a we found that, while 46% of the Archivo-backed ontologies were fully reliable, 5% were permanently inaccessible. 3% of the ontologies were effectively inaccessible (more than 75% downtime) and around 4% were very unreliable (25–75% downtime). For the portion of LOD data, for which the Archivo-backed ontologies provide ontological context, we measured w.r.t. RQ2b that 46% of the statements are affected by accessability failures of ontologies. 15% of that data is affected by permanently failing ontologies, and 17% by the basically inaccessible ontologies. As a result 32% of data is impacted by ontologies with very severe accessability issues that make up a fraction of 8% of the backed ontologies. Surprisingly in contrast to that, the ontologies that are failing rarely (56%) only affected 3% of the data.

Based on the reduced and filtered LOD terms list, that excluded terms where we spotted general issues that affect the accessibility and reproducibility beforehand, we found with regard to RQ3b that only 8 to 9% of the property terms are covered, whereas for class terms around 12% are covered by Archivo and 2% by LOV. With the help of the Archivo crawling engine, we measured for over

77% of the property terms and over 52% of class terms that no RDF file could be retrieved (RQ3a). For around 3% of the property terms that are currently not covered by Archivo, we are optimistic that their ontologies can be preserved in future work by feeding them into the discovery mechanism. Additionally, 34% of the class terms are currently inaccessible to Archivo due to its strict protocol requirements. In the future, heuristics and more sophisticated crawling approaches could help here to also include these.

Fortunately in terms of RQ4, having these single digit fractions of terms preserved, covers a significant large amount of LOD triples. Around 50% of the statements are currently having a backup in Archivo or LOV. In the case of Archivo w.r.t. ontology properties for at least 44% of the LOD data and even 80% w.r.t. type assertions. Even more than half of the statements have reproducibility support by LOV for the property. For this portion of backed triples, we have shown that 46% were affected by accessability issues. When the percentages as shown in Fig. 3 are set into relation to the entire amount of LOD triples in the experiment (i.e. are divided by 2, since roughly half of the triples are covered), this translates into a rough estimate that Archivo could have provided failover for up to 23% of the statements, if data would have been requested at the time of inaccessibility. Subsequently, for roughly $\frac{15}{2}\% + \frac{17}{2}\% = 16\%$ of the LOD triples we effectively consider archiving as an important countermeasure since the ontological context would be not accessible for at least 75% of the time.

We conclude that the archiving approaches presented in this paper provide a foundation to work against the reproducibility crisis. As an approach that builds on top of Archivo and to counter the reproducibility crisis in the future, we plan to implement a transparent proxy tool for reasoners and other semantic tools, that allows reliable and deterministic repeatability and reproducibility of experiments referencing or accessing ontologies (ontology terms), by retrieving the correct, persistent ontology snapshot via Archivo. This approach would allow to fetch data via the original URL, but independent of the data that is actually returned when dereferencing it. Instead, the proxy could serve ontology versions that existed at a specific time span (like a time machine or wayback machine) or could serve as fail-over system if the current deployment of the ontology suffers from availability issues.

Supplemental Material Availability: Source code, scripts, queries and tables are available online. Please refer to https://purl.org/paper/iswc2022/archivo/material for further information and guidance.

Acknowledgments. This work was partially supported by grants from the German Federal Ministry for Economic Affairs and Climate Action (BMWK) to the projects LOD-GEOSS (03EI1005E), PLASS (01MD19003D), and CoyPu (01MK21007C).

References

1. Abdel-Qader, M., Scherp, A., Vagliano, I.: Analyzing the evolution of vocabulary terms and their impact on the LOD cloud. In: Gangemi, A., et al. (eds.) ESWC 2018. LNCS, vol. 10843, pp. 1–16. Springer, Cham (2018). https://doi.org/10.1007/978-3-319-93417-4_1
2. Baker, M.: 1,500 scientists lift the lid on reproducibility. Nature **533**, 452–454 (2016). https://doi.org/10.1038/533452a
3. Beek, W., Rietveld, L., Bazoobandi, H.R., Wielemaker, J., Schlobach, S.: LOD laundromat: a uniform way of publishing other people's dirty data. In: Mika, P., et al. (eds.) ISWC 2014. LNCS, vol. 8796, pp. 213–228. Springer, Cham (2014). https://doi.org/10.1007/978-3-319-11964-9_14
4. Beek, W., Fernández, J.D., Verborgh, R.: Lod-a-lot: a single-file enabler for data science. In: Hoekstra, R., Faron-Zucker, C., Pellegrini, T., de Boer, V. (eds.) Proceedings of the 13th International Conference on Semantic Systems, SEMANTICS 2017, Amsterdam, The Netherlands, 11–14 September 2017, pp. 181–184. ACM (2017). https://doi.org/10.1145/3132218.3132241
5. Cockburn, A., Dragicevic, P., Besançon, L., Gutwin, C.: Threats of a replication crisis in empirical computer science. Commun. ACM **63**, 70–79 (2020). https://doi.org/10.1145/3360311
6. Ermilov, I., Lehmann, J., Martin, M., Auer, S.: LODStats: the data web census dataset. In: Groth, P., et al. (eds.) ISWC 2016. LNCS, vol. 9982, pp. 38–46. Springer, Cham (2016). https://doi.org/10.1007/978-3-319-46547-0_5
7. Fernández, J.D., Martínez-Prieto, M.A., Gutiérrez, C., Polleres, A., Arias, M.: Binary RDF representation for publication and exchange (HDT). J. Web Semant. **19**, 22–41 (2013). https://doi.org/10.1016/j.websem.2013.01.002
8. Frey, J., Hellmann, S.: Fair linked data - towards a linked data backbone for users and machines. In: WWW Companion (2021). https://doi.org/10.1145/3442442.3451364
9. Frey, J., Streitmatter, D., Götz, F., Hellmann, S., Arndt, N.: DBpedia Archivo: a web-scale interface for ontology archiving under consumer-oriented aspects. In: Blomqvist, E., et al. (eds.) SEMANTICS 2020. LNCS, vol. 12378, pp. 19–35. Springer, Cham (2020). https://doi.org/10.1007/978-3-030-59833-4_2
10. Frey, J., Streitmatter, D., Hellmann, S.: DACOC3 - dbpedia archivo challenging ontology consistency check collection. In: Singh, G., Mutharaju, R., Kapanipathi, P. (eds.) Proceedings of the Semantic Reasoning Evaluation Challenge (SemREC 2021) co-located with the 20th International Semantic Web Conference (ISWC 2021), Virtual Event, 27 October 2021, CEUR Workshop Proceedings, vol. 3123, pp. 32–36. CEUR-WS.org (2021). https://ceur-ws.org/Vol-3123/paper4.pdf
11. Gundersen, O.E., Shamsaliei, S., Isdahl, R.: Do machine learning platforms provide out-of-the-box reproducibility? Future Gener. Comput. Syst. **126**, 34–47 (2022). https://doi.org/10.1016/j.future.2021.06.014
12. Haibe-Kains, B., et al.: Transparency and reproducibility in artificial intelligence. Nature **586**(7829), E14–E16 (2020). https://doi.org/10.1038/s41586-020-2766-y
13. Hofer, M., Hellmann, S., Dojchinovski, M., Frey, J.: The new dbpedia release cycle: increasing agility and efficiency in knowledge extraction workflows. In: Semantic Systems (2020). https://doi.org/10.1007/978-3-030-59833-4_1
14. Käfer, T., Abdelrahman, A., Umbrich, J., O'Byrne, P., Hogan, A.: Observing linked data dynamics. In: Cimiano, P., Corcho, O., Presutti, V., Hollink, L., Rudolph, S. (eds.) ESWC 2013. LNCS, vol. 7882, pp. 213–227. Springer, Heidelberg (2013). https://doi.org/10.1007/978-3-642-38288-8_15

15. Miyakawa, T.: No raw data, no science: another possible source of the reproducibility crisis. Molec. Brain **13** (2020). https://doi.org/10.1186/s13041-020-0552-2
16. Nasir, J.A., McCrae, J.P.: ilod: interplanetary file system based linked open data cloud. In: Orlandi, F., Graux, D., Vidal, M., Fernández, J.D., Debattista, J. (eds.) Proceedings of the 6th Workshop on Managing the Evolution and Preservation of the Data Web (MEPDaW) co-located with the 19th International Semantic Web Conference (ISWC 2020), Virtual event (instead of Athens, Greece), 1 November 2020, CEUR Workshop Proceedings, vol. 2821, pp. 27–32. CEUR-WS.org (2020). https://ceur-ws.org/Vol-2821/paper4.pdf
17. Pineau, J., et al.: Improving reproducibility in machine learning research (a report from the neurips 2019 reproducibility program). J. Mach. Learn. Res. **22**(164), 1–20 (2021). https://jmlr.org/papers/v22/20-303.html
18. Smith, B., et al.: The obo foundry: coordinated evolution of ontologies to support biomedical data integration. Nat. Biotechnol. **25**(11), 1251–1255 (2007)
19. Vandenbussche, P., Atemezing, G., Poveda-Villalón, M., Vatant, B.: Linked open vocabularies (LOV): a gateway to reusable semantic vocabularies on the web. Semant. Web **8**(3), 437–452 (2017). https://doi.org/10.3233/SW-160213
20. Whetzel, P.L., et al.: Bioportal: enhanced functionality via new web services from the NCBO to access and use ontologies in software applications. Nucl. Acids Res. **39**, 541–545 (2011). https://doi.org/10.1093/nar/gkr469
21. Wilkinson, M.D., et al.: The fair guiding principles for scientific data management and stewardship. Sci. Data **3**(1), 1–9 (2016)

HCL: Improving Graph Representation with Hierarchical Contrastive Learning

Jun Wang[1], Weixun Li[1], Changyu Hou[1], Xin Tang[2], Yixuan Qiao[1], Rui Fang[2],
Pengyong Li[3], Peng Gao[1], and Guotong Xie[1,4,5(✉)]

[1] Ping An Healthcare Technology, Beijing, China
[2] Ping An Property and Casualty Insurance Company, Shenzhen, China
deeplearning.pku@qq.com, xieguotong@pingan.com.cn
[3] School of Computer Science and Technology, Xidian University, Xian, China
lipy0628@163.com, lipengyong@xidian.edu.cn
[4] Ping An Health Cloud Company Limited, Shenzhen, China
[5] Ping An International Smart City Technology Company Limited, Shenzhen, China

Abstract. Contrastive learning has emerged as a powerful tool for graph representation learning. However, most contrastive learning methods learn features of graphs with fixed coarse-grained scale, which might underestimate either local or global information. To capture more hierarchical and richer representation, we propose a novel Hierarchical Contrastive Learning (HCL) framework that explicitly learns graph representation in a hierarchical manner. Specifically, HCL includes two key components: a novel adaptive Learning to Pool (L2Pool) method to construct more reasonable multi-scale graph topology for more comprehensive contrastive objective, a novel multi-channel pseudo-siamese network to further enable more expressive learning of mutual information within each scale. Comprehensive experimental results show HCL achieves competitive performance on 12 datasets involving node classification, node clustering and graph classification. In addition, the visualization of learned representation reveals that HCL successfully captures meaningful characteristics of graphs.

Keywords: Data mining · Graph learning · Contrastive learning

1 Introduction

Graph representation learning has recently attracted increasing research attention, because of broader demands on exploiting ubiquitous non-Euclidean graph data across various domains, including social networks, physics, and bioinformatics [13]. Along with the rapid development of graph neural networks (GNNs) [13, 18], GNNs have been reported as a powerful tool for learning expressive representation for various graph-related tasks. However, supervised training of GNNs usually requires faithful and labour-intensive annotations and relies on domain expert knowledge, which hinders GNNs from being adopted in practical applications.

Self-supervised learning has emerged as a powerful tool to alleviate the need for large labelled data. Among them, contrastive learning has recently achieved promising

---

J. Wang and W. Li—Equal contribution.

U. Sattler et al. (Eds.): ISWC 2022, LNCS 13489, pp. 108–124, 2022.
https://doi.org/10.1007/978-3-031-19433-7_7

results [14]. Contrastive learning techniques are used to train an encoder that builds discriminative representations by comparing positive and negative samples to maximize the mutual information (MI) [23].

Although the graph contrastive learning GCL methods have achieved significant success, they suffer all or partially from the following limitations. First, most contrastive learning methods like DGI [37], GCA [48], and GRACE [47], learn features of graphs with fixed fine-grained scale, which might underestimate either local or global information. However, each graph has multi-scale intrinsic structures, including the grouping of nodes into motifs, the further grouping of motifs into sub-graphs as well as the spatial layout of sub-graphs in the topology space. Such multi-scale intrinsic structures are more flexible and informative, and can provide important clues for graph representation learning. In most cases, a single level contrastive objective could merely capture limited characteristics of graphs [37,47,48]. Second, considering that existing GCL methods heavily rely on negative samples to avoid representation collapse, To alleviate this limitation, Grill et al. [11] propose the Bootstrap Your Own Latent (BYOL) framework to perform unsupervised representation learning on images by leveraging the bootstrapping mechanism with Siamese networks [5]. However, Siamese networks have not been well extended to graph domain yet. We argue that bootstrapping graphs with a multi-channel scheme would enable graph encoders to capture more powerful representation.

To address the aforementioned limitations, we propose a novel Hierarchical Contrastive Learning (HCL) framework, HCL constructs a cross-scale contrastive learning mechanism to learn hierarchical graph representation in an unsupervised manner. More specifically, the two key components of HCL including: (i) a Learning to Pool (L2Pool) method with topology-enhanced self-attention to recursively construct a series of coarser graphs during multi-scale contrastive learning and (ii) a contrastive objective term that preserves the mutual information with expressive multi-channel networks. The simple yet powerful framework can be optimized in an end-to-end manner to capture more comprehensive graph features for downstream tasks. To summarize, this work makes the following major contributions:

- We propose a novel Hierarchical Contrastive Learning (HCL) framework to learn graph representation by taking advantage of hierarchical MI maximization across scales and bootstrapping multi-channel contrastiveness across networks.
- We proposed a novel L2Pool method to form fine to coarse-grained graph and contrastive objective across scales, which explicitly preserves information concealed in the hierarchical topology of the graph.
- Extensive experiments indicate that HCL achieves superior or comparable results on various real-world 12 benchmarks involving both node-level and graph-level tasks. Moreover, visualization of nodes representation further reveals that HCL can capture more intrinsic patterns underlying the graph structures.

2   Related Works

2.1   Unsupervised Graph Learning

Traditional graph unsupervised learning methods are mainly based on graph kernel [25]. Compared to graph kernel, contrastive learning methods can learn explicit embedding,

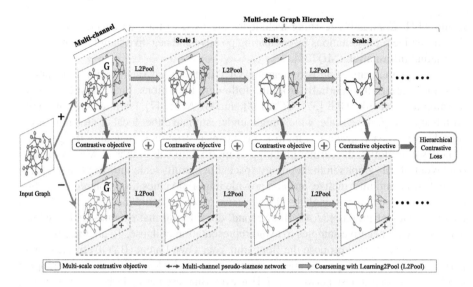

Fig. 1. Framework of the proposed Hierarchical Contrastive Learning (HCL) for graph representation.

and achieve better performance, which are the current state-of-the-art for unsupervised node and graph classification tasks [14,29]. Generally, current contrastive graph learning employs a node-node contrast [29,48] or node-graph contrast [14,37] to maximize the mutual information at single level. For example, DGI [37] employs the idea of Deep InfoMax [15] and consider both patch and global information during the discrimination. MVGRL [14] introduces augmented views to graph contrastive learning and optimizes the DGI-like objectives. Besides, GRACE [47], InfoGraph [35] and SUBG-CON [16], further extend the idea of graph MI maximization and conduct the discrimination across the node, sub-graph and graph. PHD [22] using graph-graph contrast reports impressive performances on graph classification, but not for the node-level tasks. Nevertheless, most of them contrast graphs with fixed scales, which might underestimate either local or global information. To address these issues, our HCL explicitly formulates multi-scale contrastive learning on graphs and enables capturing more comprehensive features for downstream tasks.

2.2 Multi-scale Graph Pooling

Early graph pooling methods use naive summarization to pool all the nodes [9], and usually fail to capture graph topology. Recently, multi-scale pooling methods have been proposed to address the limitations. Among them, graph-coarsening pooling methods like DiffPool [43] and StructPool [45] consider pooling as a node clustering problem, but the high computational complexity of these methods prevents them from being applied to large graphs. On the other hand, the node-selection pooling methods like gPool [7] and SAGPool [21] preserve representative nodes based on their importance, but tend to lose the original graph structures. Compared to previous works, the proposed HCL has two main differences: **1)** Apart from the common late fusion of features, HCL uses L2Pool and Pseudo-siamese network to intermediately aggregate richer contrastive objectives across scales, where the embeddings at various scales in each network layer are fused to enable richer contrasting in a hierarchical manner. **2)** The proposed L2Pool module is trained given an explicit optimization for node selection with topology-enhanced Transformer-style attention, hence effectively coarsen the original graph structure.

3   Methodology

3.1   Overview

The goal of HCL is to provide a framework to construct a multi-scale contrastive scheme that incorporate inherent hierarchical structures of the data to generate expressive graph representation. In this section, we introduce HCL and its main components in Fig. 1. First, given an input graph $G(X, A)$ with node features, $X \in \mathbb{R}^{N \times d}$, A is the adjacency matrix. We first generate positive (green) and negative (red) samples by attribute shuffling [37]. Specifically, We perform the row-wise shuffling on the feature matrix X, so the negative graph consists of the same nodes as the original graph, but they are located in different places in the graph, and therefore receive different contextual information. Second, for the positive branch above and the negative branch below, we both learn graph representations at multiple scales. We first employ a graph propagation layer on the input graph to initially embed the original scale of graph as $G_0(X_0, A_0)$ with $X_0 = X$, $A_0 = A$, where the graph propagation layer is implemented as a multi-channel pseudo-siamese network, with each channel using a graph convolution layer of the same structure but different weights [18]. We then recursively apply L2Pool for S times to obtain a series of coarser scales of graph $G_1(X_1, A_1), \ldots, G_S(X_S, A_S)$ where $|X_s| > |X_{s'}|$ for $\forall\ 1 \leq s < s' \leq S$. Thirdly, we learn the parameters through optimizing the fused multi-scale and multi-channel contrastive loss function. During the inference, we take the graph adjacency as inputs for downstream tasks.

To train our model end-to-end and learn multi-scale representation for downstream tasks, we jointly leverage cross-scale contrastive loss. Specifically, the overall objective function is defined as:

$$\mathcal{L} = \mathcal{L}_0 + \sum_{k'=1}^{k} \left(\left(\prod_{k'=1}^{k} \alpha_{p_{k'}} \right) * \mathcal{L}_{p_{k'}} \right), \tag{1}$$

where $\mathcal{L}_0$ is the contrastive loss at the first scale with all nodes, k is the total number of pool layers besides $\mathcal{L}_0$. The $\alpha_{p_{k'}}$ is the pooling ratio of $k' - th$ pooling scale, e.g., 0.9, etc. Then, $\mathcal{L}_{p_{k'}}$ is contrastive loss at $k' - th$ pooling scale.

3.2   Multi-scale Contrasting with L2Pool

In this section, in order to create graph contrasting at multiple scales, we propose a novel Learning to Pool method, namely L2Pool, to enable coarsening graph data and

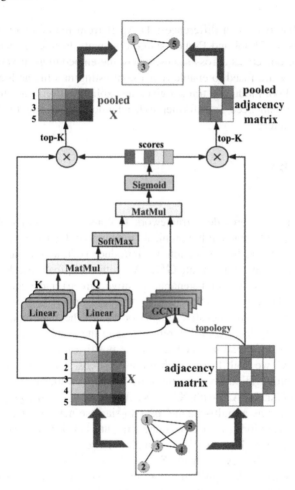

Fig. 2. An illustration of the proposed L2Pool using Transformer-style self-attention and topology information to select representative nodes and to coarsen into a graph hierarchy for cross-scale contrastive learning.

contrasting information interchange across scales explicitly. L2Pool adaptively creates graph representations at multiple scales, by selecting a subset of nodes to form a new but smaller graph with topology-enhanced attention.

As shown in Fig. 2, we implement a Transformer-style multi-head (MH) attention mechanism. While MH self-attention is superior to trivial pooling methods such as sum or mean, as it considers global dependencies among nodes. Moreover, note that for each node, the self-attention only calculates the semantic similarity between current node and other nodes, without considering the structural information of a graph reflected on the nodes and the relation between node pairs. To tackle this limitation, we define a novel multi-head attention enhanced with topological structure from GCNII [4]. Specifically, GCNII is a GCN model with two effective techniques: Initial residual and Identity mapping, GCNII relieves the problem of over-smoothing thus enables deeper networks. The input of the attention function (Att) consists of query $Q \in \mathbb{R}^{n_q \times d_k}$, key $K \in \mathbb{R}^{n \times d_k}$ and value $V \in \mathbb{R}^{n \times d_v}$, where n_q is the number of query vectors, n is the number of input nodes, d_k is the dimension of the key vector, and d_v is the dimension of the value vector. Then we compute the dot product of the query with all keys, to put more weights on the relevant values, namely nodes, as follows: $\text{Att}(Q, K, V) = \sigma(QK^T)V$, where σ is an activation function. The output of the multi-head attention function can be formulated as:

$$\text{MH}(Q, K, V) = [O_1, ..., O_h]W^o,$$
$$O_i = \text{Att}(QW_i^Q, KW_i^K, VW_i^V), \tag{2}$$
$$= \text{Att}(QW_i^Q, KW_i^K, \text{GCNII}_i^V(H, A)),$$

where the learning parameter matrices corresponding to Q, K and V are $W_i^Q \in \mathbb{R}^{d_k \times d_k}$, $W_i^K \in \mathbb{R}^{d_k \times d_k}$, and $W_i^V \in \mathbb{R}^{d_v \times d_v}$ respectively. Also, the output projection matrix is $W^O \in \mathbb{R}^{d_v \times d_{model}}$, where d_{model} is the output dimension for the multi-head attention function.

More specifically, we construct V using GCNII, to explicitly leverage the global structure and capture the interaction between nodes according to their structural dependencies. The multi-head self-attention enhanced by graph topology is defined as:

$$\text{GCNII}(H, A) = \sigma(((1 - \alpha)AH + \alpha H^0)((1 - \beta)I_n + \beta W)),$$
$$\text{Att}(Q, K, \text{GCNII}(H, A)) = \text{softmax}(\frac{QK^T}{\sqrt{d_k}})\text{GCNII}(H, A), \tag{3}$$

where α and β are hyperparameters and I_n is the identity matrix. Formally, given node embeddings $H \in \mathbb{R}^{n \times d}$ with their adjacency information A, we construct the value V using a 4-layer GCNII, to explicitly leverage the graph topology information (the equation for a single layer GCNII is given in above Eq. 3).

Specifically, we named the learnable score function as L2Pool at layer l, and select the high scored nodes $i^{(l+1)} \in \mathbb{R}^{n_{l+1}}$, to drop the unnecessary nodes, denoted as follows:

$$y^{(l)} = \text{L2Pool}(\text{Att}, H^{(l)}, A^{(l)}); \quad i^{(l+1)} = \text{top}_k(y^{(l)}), \tag{4}$$

where top_k function samples the top k nodes by dropping nodes with low scores $y^{(l)} \in \mathbb{R}^{n_l}$. In this way, HCL could preserve as much information as possible from the graph hierarchy and contrast in a multi-scale manner.

3.3 In-scale Bootstrapping Pseudo-Siamese Network

In HCL, we introduce a Pseudo-Siamese architecture to form the basic bootstrapping contrastiveness with multi-channel. Generally, the siamese network contains two identical subnetworks has been proved to be a common structure in unsupervised visual representation learning [5], but not been well extended to graph domain yet. Hence, we make a Pseudo-Siamese network with non-weight-sharing branches for multi-channel contrastive learning, which provides more flexibility and capacity than a restricted siamese network.

Inspired by above contrastive scheme, we train the GNN-encoder f_{GNN} to maximize the mutual information (MI) between node (fine-grain) representations, i.e., $\mathbf{H} = f_{GNN}(\mathbf{X}, \mathbf{A})$, and a global representation (summary of all representations). This encourages the encoder to prefer the information that is shared across all nodes. Since maximizing the precise value of mutual information is intractable, thus, a Jensen-Shannon MI estimator is often used [15,26], which maximizes MI's lower bound. The Jensen-Shannon-based estimator acts like a standard binary cross-entropy (BCE) loss, whose objective maximizes the expected log-ratio of the samples from the joint distribution (positive examples) and the product of marginal distributions (negative examples). The positive examples are pairings of s with $\mathbf{h}_i$ of the real input graph $\mathbf{G} = (\mathbf{X}, \mathbf{A})$, but the negatives are pairings of s with $\tilde{\mathbf{h}}_i$, which are obtained from a fake/generated input graph $\tilde{\mathbf{G}} = (\tilde{\mathbf{X}}, \tilde{\mathbf{A}})$ with $\tilde{\mathbf{H}} = f_{GNN}(\tilde{\mathbf{X}}, \tilde{\mathbf{A}})$. Then, a discriminator $\mathcal{D}_1 : \mathbb{R}^{F'} \times \mathbb{R}^{F'} \to \mathbb{R}$ is used to assign higher scores to the positive examples than the negatives, as in [15,26]. The Jensen-Shannon-based BCE objective with weighted sum of multi-channels across networks in $k - th$ pooling scale is expressed as:

$$
\begin{aligned}
\mathcal{L}_{p_k} = & \sum_{u=1}^{N} \mathbb{E}_{(X,A)} \left[\log \mathcal{D}_{p_k}(\boldsymbol{h}_u^{(1)} + \boldsymbol{h}_u^{(2)} * \delta_{p_k}, \boldsymbol{s}) \right] \\
& + \sum_{v=1}^{N} \mathbb{E}_{(\tilde{X},\tilde{A})} \left[\log \left(1 - \mathcal{D}_{p_k}(\tilde{\boldsymbol{h}}_v^{(1)} + \tilde{\boldsymbol{h}}_v^{(2)} * \delta_{p_k}, \boldsymbol{s}) \right) \right],
\end{aligned}
\tag{5}
$$

with $A \in \mathbb{R}^{N \times N}$ and $X \in \mathbb{R}^{N \times F}$, for simplicity. $\boldsymbol{h}_u^{(1)}$ and $\boldsymbol{h}_u^{(2)}$ represent the embedding of the first channel and the second channel of the pseudo siamese network, respectively. We use the average function over all node features to obtain the entire graph representation, $\boldsymbol{s} = \text{READOUT}(X_{p_k})$ is the summary vector represents the embedding of $k - th$ pooled graph. δ_{p_k} is the weighted sum parameter between multi-channels in the $k - th$ pooling scale. This approach effectively maximizes mutual information between summary vector $\boldsymbol{s}$ and $\boldsymbol{h}_u^{(1)} + \boldsymbol{h}_u^{(2)} * \delta_{p_k}$ in every pooling layer.

4   Experiments

In this section, we describe the experiments conducted to demonstrate the efficacy of proposed HCL for graph representation tasks. The experiments aim to answer the following five research questions:

- **RQ1.** How does HCL perform in node-level graph representation tasks?
- **RQ2.** How does HCL perform in graph-level representation tasks?
- **RQ3.** How does the hierarchical mutual information maximization mechanism improve the performance of HCL?
- **RQ4.** How do the difference parameter settings influence the performance of HCL?
- **RQ5.** Does HCL capture meaningful patterns and provide insightful representation?

Table 1. The statistics of the datasets.

	Dataset	Graphs	Nodes	Edges	Features	Classes
Node-level	Cora	1	2,708	5,429	1,433	7
	Citeseer	1	3,327	4,732	3,703	6
	Pubmed	1	19,717	44,338	500	3
	Amazon-C	1	13,752	245,861	767	10
	Amazon-P	1	7,650	119,081	745	8
	Coauthor-CS	1	18,333	81,894	6,805	15
	Coauthor-Phy	1	34,493	247,962	8,415	5
Graph-level	IMDB-B	1,000	19.77	193.06	–	2
	IMDB-M	1,500	13.00	65.93	–	3
	PTC-MR	344	14.29	14.69	–	2
	MUTAG	188	17.93	19.79	–	2
	Reddit-B	2,000	508.52	497.75	–	2

4.1 Datasets and Experimental Setup

Datasets. We evaluate the quality of learned node and graph embeddings on downstream tasks. According to the tasks, seven of them are utilized for node-level tasks, include node classification and clustering, while five of them are for graph-level classification task. Statistics of datasets used are shown in Table 1. For **node classification**, we adopt 3 citation networks including Cora, Citeseer, Pubmed [31], and 4 co-purchase and co-author networks including Amazon-Computers, Amazon-Photo, Coauthor-CS and Coauthor-Phy [32]. For **node clustering**, we adopt three benchmark datasets: Cora, Citeseer and Pubmed [31]. For **graph classification**, we use another five common datasets: MUTAG, PTC-MR [3], IMDB-B, IMDB-M and REDDIT-B [41].

Experimental Setup. We initialize the parameters using Xavier initialization [10] and train the model using Adam optimizer with an initial learning rate of 0.001 and an NVIDIA V100 GPU with 16G memory. For multi-channel configuration, the weight sum parameter δ is learned between -1 and 1. To have fair comparisons, we set the size of the hidden dimension of both node and graph representations to 512. Specifically, HCL has set up a total of 3 recursive pooling scales of 0.9-0.8-0.7, which preserves 90%(0.9), 72%(0.9*0.8) to 50.4%(0.9*0.8*0.7) nodes from the original graph, respectively. In the construction of multi-scale graphs, L2Pool is implemented with 4 attention heads and a 4-layer GCNII. **1) For node classification tasks**, we follow DGI [37] to use same GCN encoder for all methods, and report the mean classification accuracy with standard deviation on the test nodes after 50 runs of training followed by a linear model. On citation networks, we use the same training/validation/testing splits as [42] for training the classifier according to the node representations. Specifically, we use 20 labelled nodes per class as the training set, 20 nodes per class as the validation set, and the rest as the testing set. On co-purchase and co-author networks, we use 30 labelled nodes per class as the training set, 30 nodes per class as the validation set, and the rest as the testing set. For a fair comparison, the performances of all the methods are obtained on the same splits. The mean classification accuracy with standard deviation on the test nodes after 50 runs of training is reported. **2) For node clustering tasks,** we employ k-means on the obtained node representations, the clustering results averaged over 50 runs in terms of NMI and ARI are reported. **3) For graph classification tasks,** we follow InfoGraph [35] to fairly evaluate the performances of HCL. The graph embedding was obtained by averaging all embedding of nodes in the graph. The mean 10-fold cross validation accuracy with standard deviation after 5 runs followed by a linear SVM is reported. We follow InfoGraph to choose the number of GCN layers, number of epochs, batch size, and the C parameter of the SVM from $[2, 4, 8, 12]$, $[10, 20, 40, 100]$, $[32, 64, 128, 256]$, and $[10^{-3}, 10^{-2}, ..., 10^2, 10^3]$, respectively. The parameters of classifiers are independently tuned using cross validation on training folds of data, and the best average classification accuracy is reported for each method.

Table 2. Node classification accuracies (%) for supervised and unsupervised methods on different datasets. The best performance is highlighted in bold. The previous best performance is underlined. The Input column highlights the data available to each model during the model training process (X:features, A:adjacency matrix, D:diffusion matrix, Y:labels). * denotes model using Diffusion instead of Adjacency matrix as input. OOM indicates Out-Of-Memory on a 16 GB GPU. Some results without standard deviations are directly taken from [14].

Method	Input	Cora	Citeseer	Pubmed	Amazon-C	Amazon-P	Coauthor CS	Coauthor Phy
MLP	X,Y	58.2 ± 2.1	59.1 ± 2.3	70.0 ± 2.1	44.9 ± 5.8	69.6 ± 3.8	88.3 ± 0.7	88.9 ± 1.1
LogReg	X,A,Y	57.1 ± 2.3	61.0 ± 2.2	64.1 ± 3.1	64.1 ± 5.7	73.0 ± 6.5	86.4 ± 0.9	86.7 ± 1.5
LP	A,Y	68.0	45.3	63.0	70.8 ± 0.0	67.8 ± 0.0	74.3 ± 0.0	90.2 ± 0.5
Chebyshev	X,A,Y	81.2	69.8	74.4	62.6 ± 0.0	74.3 ± 0.0	91.5 ± 0.0	92.1 ± 0.3
GCN	X,A,Y	81.5	70.3	79.0	76.3 ± 0.5	87.3 ± 1.0	$\underline{91.8 \pm 0.1}$	92.6 ± 0.7
GAT	X,A,Y	$\underline{83.0 \pm 0.7}$	$\underline{72.5 \pm 0.7}$	79.0 ± 0.3	79.3 ± 1.1	86.2 ± 1.5	90.5 ± 0.7	91.3 ± 0.6
SGC	X,A,Y	81.0 ± 0.0	71.9 ± 0.1	78.9 ± 0.0	74.4 ± 0.1	86.4 ± 0.0	91.0 ± 0.0	90.2 ± 0.4
MoNet	X,A,Y	81.3 ± 1.3	71.2 ± 2.0	78.6 ± 2.3	$\underline{83.5 \pm 2.2}$	$\underline{91.2 \pm 1.3}$	90.8 ± 0.6	$\underline{92.5 \pm 0.9}$
DGI	X,A	81.7 ± 0.6	71.5 ± 0.7	76.9 ± 0.5	75.9 ± 0.6	83.1 ± 0.5	90.0 ± 0.3	91.3 ± 0.4
GMI	X,A	80.9 ± 0.7	71.1 ± 0.2	78.0 ± 1.0	76.8 ± 0.1	85.1 ± 0.1	91.0 ± 0.0	OOM
GRACE	X,A	80.0 ± 0.4	$\underline{71.7 \pm 0.6}$	$\underline{79.5 \pm 1.1}$	71.8 ± 0.4	81.8 ± 1.0	90.1 ± 0.8	92.3 ± 0.6
SUBG-CON	X,A	$\underline{82.5 \pm 0.3}$	70.9 ± 0.3	73.13 ± 0.5	OOM	OOM	OOM	OOM
GCA	X,A	80.5 ± 0.5	71.3 ± 0.4	78.6 ± 0.6	$\underline{80.8 \pm 0.4}$	$\underline{87.1 \pm 1.0}$	$\mathbf{91.3 \pm 0.4}$	$\underline{93.1 \pm 0.3}$
MVGRL	X,A	82.0 ± 0.7	70.7 ± 0.7	74.0 ± 0.3	76.2 ± 0.6	84.1 ± 0.3	83.6 ± 0.3	87.1 ± 0.2
HCL(Ours)	X,A	$\mathbf{82.5 \pm 0.6}$	$\mathbf{72.0 \pm 0.5}$	$\mathbf{79.2 \pm 0.6}$	$\mathbf{84.0 \pm 0.7}$	$\mathbf{87.5 \pm 0.4}$	91.1 ± 0.4	$\mathbf{93.3 \pm 0.5}$
GCA*	X,D	81.8 ± 0.8	72.0 ± 0.5	81.2 ± 0.7	81.5 ± 0.9	87.0 ± 1.2	91.6 ± 0.7	93.0 ± 0.5
MVGRL*	X,D	82.8 ± 1.0	72.7 ± 0.5	79.6 ± 0.8	82.9 ± 0.9	86.9 ± 0.5	91.0 ± 0.6	93.2 ± 1.0
HCL(Ours)*	X,D	$\mathbf{83.7 \pm 0.7}$	$\mathbf{73.3 \pm 0.4}$	$\mathbf{81.8 \pm 0.7}$	$\mathbf{83.4 \pm 0.5}$	87.3 ± 0.4	$\mathbf{91.7 \pm 0.3}$	$\mathbf{93.5 \pm 0.4}$

4.2 Evaluation on Node-Level Tasks (RQ1)

Node Classification. To evaluate node classification under the linear evaluation protocol, we compare results of our HCL with recent unsupervised models in Table 2, including DGI [37], GMI [29], MVGRL [14], GRACE [47], GCA [48]and SubGCON [16]. Moreover, we also compare our results with supervised models including MLP, Logistic Regression(LogReg), label propagation (LP) [46], Chebyshev [6], GCN, GAT [36], SGC [39] and mixture model networks (MoNet) [24]. The results show that our HCL achieves superior performances with respect to previous unsupervised models. For example, on Amazon-C dataset, we achieve 84.0% accuracy, which is a 3.1% relative improvement over previous state-of-the-art. Furthermore, inspired by MVGRL [14], employing Diffusion matrices other than Adjacency matrices has been shown to improve GNNs performance [19]. We also conducted experiments of HCL with Diffusion matrices D as input. Noting that, HCL with X and diffusion matrix D as input further yields even better performances than that of (X, A). HCL also outperforms both GCA and MVGRL using diffusion matrix in the same settings, which further denotes the superiority of HCL.

Node Clustering. To evaluate performance on node clustering task, we compare our HCL with models reported including: variational GAE (VGAE) [17], marginalized GAE (MGAE) [38], adversarially regularized GAE (ARGA) and VGAE (ARVGA) [27], GALA [28] and MVGRL [14]. The results in Table 3 suggest that our model achieves superior or comparable performance on NMI and ARI scores across most of the benchmarks. Besides, the improvements are more significant in terms of ARI compared to those of NMI. The results encourage that unsupervised clustering task prefers the representation containing the important and semantic feature due to the lack of supervised information. Meanwhile, HCL boosts the supervised classification with a larger margin, by adequately exploiting the labels and graph inherent characteristics. Thus, HCL tends to capture faithful and comprehensive information of the graph by enhancing the scheme of message passing.

4.3 Evaluation on Graph-Level Tasks (RQ2)

Besides node-level tasks, we further evaluate the performances of HCL and other baselines on graph classification under the linear evaluation protocol and answer the research question RQ2.

Graph Classifications. (1) We compare our results with five **graph kernel methods** including shortest path kernel (SP) [2], Graphlet kernel (GK) [34], Weisfeiler-Lehman sub-tree kernel (WL) [33], deep graph kernel (DGK) [41], and multi-scale Laplacian kernel (MLG) [20] reported in [35]. (2) We also compare with five **supervised GNNs** reported in [40] including GraphSAGE [13], GCN, GAT, and two variants of GIN: GIN-0 and GIN-ϵ. (3) Moreover, We compare the results with other **unsupervised methods** including random walk [8], node2vec [12], sub2vec [1], graph2vec [25], InfoGraph

Table 3. Performance on node clustering task reported in normalized MI (NMI) and adjusted rand index (ARI) measures. The best performance is highlighted in bold.

Method	Cora		Citeseer		Pubmed	
	NMI	ARI	NMI	ARI	NMI	ARI
K-means	0.321	0.230	0.305	0.279	0.001	0.002
Spectral	0.127	0.031	0.056	0.010	0.042	0.002
BigClam	0.007	0.001	0.036	0.007	0.006	0.003
GraphEncoder	0.109	0.006	0.033	0.010	0.209	0.184
DeepWalk	0.327	0.243	0.088	0.092	0.279	0.299
GAE	0.429	0.347	0.176	0.124	0.277	0.279
VGAE	0.436	0.346	0.156	0.093	0.229	0.213
MGAE	0.511	0.445	0.412	0.414	0.282	0.248
ARGA	0.449	0.352	0.350	0.341	0.276	0.291
ARVGA	0.450	0.374	0.261	0.245	0.117	0.078
GALA	0.577	0.531	0.441	0.446	0.327	0.321
MVGRL	0.572	0.495	0.469	**0.449**	0.322	0.296
HCL(Ours)	**0.586**	**0.536**	**0.472**	0.447	**0.332**	**0.329**

[35] , GCC [30], GraphCL [44] and MVGRL [14]. The results shown in Table 4 suggest that HCL achieves superior results with respect to unsupervised models. For example, on REDDIT-B, HCL achieves 91.9% accuracy, i.e., a 2.7% relative improvement over previous state-of-the-art. When compared to supervised baselines individually, our model outperforms GCN and GAT models in 3 out of 5 datasets, e.g., a 10.0% relative improvement over GAT on IMDB-M dataset.

Noting that HCL achieve superior and competitive performance on both node-level and graph-level tasks using a unified framework, unlike previous unsupervised models [35,37], we do not devise a specialized encoder for each task.

4.4 Components Analysis and Ablation of HCL (RQ3 and RQ4)

Due to computation complexity, we conduct the ablation studies of proposed HCL on node classification of Cora and Citeseer datasets. All the experiment details are the same as mentioned in Sect. 4.1. for fair comparison.

Effect of Multi-scale and Multi-channel Contrastiveness (RQ3). To validate the effectiveness of the two contrastive components (Multi-scale, Multi-channel), We use HCL with/without multi-channel and multi-scale to denote the ablated model with one of the key components removed. The experiments on Cora and Citeseer presented in Table 5 show that HCL with both components yielded best performance, which

Table 4. Mean 10-fold cross validation accuracies (%) on graph classification task. The best performance is highlighted in bold.

	Method	MUTAG	PTC-MR	IMDB-B	IMDB-M	REDDIT-B
KERNEL	SP	85.2 ± 2.4	58.2 ± 2.4	55.6 ± 0.2	38.0 ± 0.3	64.1 ± 0.1
	GK	81.7 ± 2.1	57.3 ± 1.4	65.9 ± 1.0	43.9 ± 0.4	77.3 ± 0.2
	WL	80.7 ± 3.0	58.0 ± 0.5	72.3 ± 3.4	47.0 ± 0.5	68.8 ± 0.4
	DGK	87.4 ± 2.7	60.1 ± 2.6	67.0 ± 0.6	44.6 ± 0.5	78.0 ± 0.4
	MLG	87.9 ± 1.6	63.3 ± 1.5	66.6 ± 0.3	41.2 ± 0.0	–
SUPERVISED	GraphSAGE	85.1 ± 7.6	63.9 ± 7.7	72.3 ± 5.3	50.9 ± 2.2	OOM
	GCN	85.6 ± 5.8	64.2 ± 4.3	74.0 ± 3.4	51.9 ± 3.8	50.0 ± 0.0
	GIN-0	89.4 ± 5.6	64.6 ± 7.0	75.1 ± 5.1	52.3 ± 2.8	92.4 ± 2.5
	GIN-ϵ	89.0 ± 6.0	63.7 ± 8.2	74.3 ± 5.1	52.1 ± 3.6	92.2 ± 2.3
	GAT	89.4 ± 6.1	66.7 ± 5.1	70.5 ± 2.3	47.8 ± 3.1	85.2 ± 3.3
UNSUPERVISED	random walk	83.7 ± 1.5	57.9 ± 1.3	50.7 ± 0.3	34.7 ± 0.2	OOM
	node2vec	72.6 ± 10.2	58.6 ± 8.0	OOM	OOM	OOM
	sub2vec	61.1 ± 15.8	60.0 ± 6.4	55.3 ± 1.5	36.7 ± 0.8	71.5 ± 0.4
	graph2vec	83.2 ± 9.6	60.2 ± 6.9	71.1 ± 0.5	50.4 ± 0.9	75.8 ± 1.0
	Infograph	89.0 ± 1.1	61.7 ± 1.4	73.0 ± 0.9	49.7 ± 0.5	82.5 ± 1.4
	GCC	86.4 ± 0.5	58.4 ± 1.2	–	–	88.4 ± 0.3
	GraphCL	86.8 ± 1.3	OOM	71.1 ± 0.4	OOM	89.5 ± 0.8
	MVGRL	$\mathbf{89.7 \pm 1.1}$	62.5 ± 1.7	74.2 ± 0.7	51.2 ± 0.5	84.5 ± 0.6
	HCL(Ours)	89.2 ± 1.2	$\mathbf{63.1 \pm 1.4}$	$\mathbf{74.3 \pm 0.6}$	$\mathbf{52.0 \pm 0.6}$	$\mathbf{91.9 \pm 0.7}$

Table 5. Ablation study of main components in HCL on Cora and Citeseer.

	Multi-scale	Multi-channel	Cora	Citeseer
HCL	✓	✓	$\mathbf{83.7 \pm 0.6}$	$\mathbf{73.3 \pm 0.4}$
HCL	✓	-	83.4 ± 0.7	72.9 ± 0.5
HCL	-	✓	83.0 ± 0.9	72.4 ± 0.7

demonstrates the effectiveness of our two contrastive schemes. Specifically, the relative improvements are fair to be prominent as: multi-scale & multi-channel, multi-scale, multi-channel are 2.2%, 1.8% and 1.3% on Cora, 2.1%, 1.5% and 0.8% on Citeseer, respectively (HCL without multi-scale and multi-channel can be considered as DGI with Diffusion matrices as input, it yielded only 81.9 on Cora and 71.8 on Citeseer). These improvements can be attributed to the comprehensive multi-scale and multi-channel contrastive learning scheme, which takes the advantage of more flexible contrastiveness and more sufficient feature exploration.

Effect of Pooling Settings (RQ4). To validate whether the multi-scale representation is useful at each of its scales in HCL, we conduct experiments on different scale settings. In the above part of Table 6, the experimental results suggested that removing scales decreased the graph learning performances. Each scale benefits from more multiplex self-supervision signals and empowered them to regularize each other. Moreover, we validate the advantages of the proposed L2Pool method on node classification task. We investigate three implementations for graph pooling methods: the proposed L2Pool, previous methods gPool [7] and SAGPool [21]. As shown in the below part of Table 6, the experiments indicate that L2Pool yields superior performance, demonstrating more effective and proper scoring functions of adaptive L2Pool enables constructing more reasonable multi-scale graphs, via reducing the size of a graph while maintaining essential properties.

Table 6. Ablation study of pooling scales and methods in HCL.

Pooling-settings	Cora	Citeseer
HCL (4 scales: 1.0-0.9-0.8-0.7)	83.7 ± 0.6	73.3 ± 0.4
HCL (3 scales: 1.0-0.9-0.8)	83.5 ± 0.8	73.0 ± 0.6
HCL (2 scales: 1.0-0.9)	83.2 ± 0.7	72.8 ± 0.5
HCL (1 scales: 1.0)	83.0 ± 0.9	72.4 ± 0.7
HCL_{L2Pool}	$\mathbf{83.7 \pm 0.6}$	$\mathbf{73.3 \pm 0.4}$
HCL_{gPool}	83.1 ± 0.7	72.5 ± 0.3
$HCL_{SAGPool}$	82.6 ± 0.8	72.2 ± 0.5

4.5   Further Analysis of Explainable Representation Visualization (RQ5)

In this subsection, we further investigate the power of HCL to provide insightful interpretations and produce representation with prominent patterns in different graphs and answer research question RQ5. As shown in Fig. 3, we visualize the node embeddings of Cora, Citeseer and Pubmed calculated by different baselines via the t-SNE algorithm. Our HCL exhibits a relatively more compact and discernible clustering than other baselines, like DGI [37], MVGRL [44] and GraphCL [44]. It suggests that the hierarchical contrastive learning scheme of HCL captures more meaningful and interpretable clusters, which provides high-quality representations for the downstream tasks. To our knowledge, most previous methods neglected to capture the hierarchical structure, hindered by operating on a fixed-size scale. HCL is the first to explicitly integrate the hierarchical node-graph contrastive objectives in multiple-granularity, demonstrating superiority over previous methods.

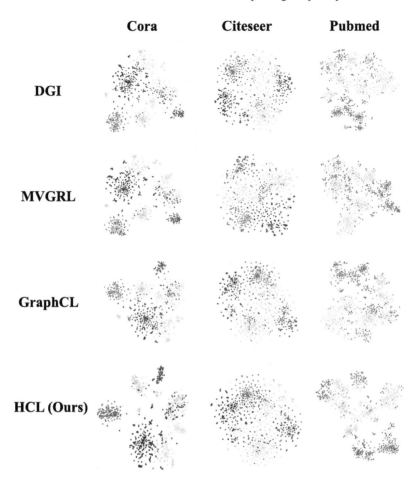

Fig. 3. t-SNE visualization of representation learned from different methods on Cora, Citeseer and Pubmed datasets.

5 Conclusions

In this work, we proposed a novel Hierarchical Contrastive Learning (HCL) framework for graph to explore more multiplex self-supervision signals and empowered them to regularize each other. Extensive experiments suggest that (i) HCL outperforms most state-of-the-art unsupervised learning methods on node classification, node clustering and graph classification tasks; (ii) the proposed L2Pool methods yield more reasonable graph hierarchy with learnable topology-enhanced multi-head attention scores; (iii) the nested contrastive objective across multi-scale and multi-channel leads to better performances. Therefore, HCL paves the way to a potential direction for unsupervised graph learning objective and superior architecture design. In particular, the composite multi-scale and multi-channel contrastive objective bridges the gap between prior contrasting and hierarchical representation learning objectives, hence introduces a more sufficient and effective graph mining. In the future, the proposed HCL framework could be effectively integrated with more GNN models and applied on more graph learning tasks, to explore richer feature interaction for intrinsic informative pattern capturing.

References

1. Adhikari, B., Zhang, Y., Ramakrishnan, N., Prakash, B.A.: Sub2vec: Feature learning for subgraphs. In: Pacific-Asia Conference on Knowledge Discovery and Data Mining, pp. 170–182 (2018)
2. Borgwardt, K.M., Kriegel, H.P.: Shortest-path kernels on graphs. In: IEEE International Conference on Data Mining, pp. 8–16 (2005)
3. Chen, J., Linstead, E., Swamidass, S.J., D. Wang, P.B.: ChemDB update-full-text search and virtual chemical space. Bioinformatics 23, 2348–2351 (2007)
4. Chen, M., Wei, Z., Huang, Z., Ding, B., Li, Y.: Simple and deep graph convolutional networks. In: International Conference on Machine Learning, pp. 1725–1735 (2020)
5. Chen, X., He, K.: Exploring simple Siamese representation learning. In: Conference on Computer Vision and Pattern Recognition (2021)
6. Defferrard, M., Bresson, X., Vandergheynst, P.: Convolutional neural networks on graphs with fast localized spectral filtering. Adv. Neural. Inf. Process. Syst. 29, 3844–3852 (2016)
7. Gao, H., Ji, S.: Graph U-nets. In: International Conference on Machine Learning, pp. 2083–2092 (2019)
8. Gärtner, T., Flach, P., Wrobel, S.: On graph kernels: hardness results and efficient alternatives. In: Learning Theory and Kernel Machines, pp. 129–143 (2003)
9. Gilmer, J., Schoenholz, S.S., Riley, P.F., Vinyals, O., Dahl, G.E.: Neural message passing for quantum chemistry. In: International Conference on Machine Learning, pp. 1263–1272 (2017)
10. Glorot, X., Bengio, Y.: Understanding the difficulty of training deep feedforward neural networks. In: Proceedings of the Thirteenth International Conference on Artificial Intelligence and Statistics, pp. 249–256 (2010)
11. Grill, J.B., et al.: Bootstrap your own latent-a new approach to self-supervised learning. Adv. Neural. Inf. Process. Syst. 33, 21271–21284 (2020)
12. Grover, A., Leskovec, J.: node2vec: scalable feature learning for networks. In: International Conference on Knowledge Discovery and Data Mining, pp. 855–864 (2016)
13. Hamilton, W., Ying, Z., Leskovec, J.: Inductive representation learning on large graphs. In: Advances in Neural Information Processing Systems, pp. 1024–1034 (2017)
14. Hassani, K., Ahmadi, A.H.K.: Contrastive multi-view representation learning on graphs. In: International Conference on Machine Learning, pp. 4116–4126 (2020)
15. Hjelm, R.D., et al.: Learning deep representations by mutual information estimation and maximization. In: International Conference on Learning Representations (2019)
16. Jiao, Y., et al.: Sub-graph contrast for scalable self-supervised graph representation learning. In: IEEE International Conference on Data Mining, pp. 222–231 (2020)
17. Kipf, T.N., Welling, M.: Variational graph auto-encoders. arXiv preprint arXiv:1611.07308 (2016)
18. Kipf, T.N., Welling, M.: Semi-supervised classification with graph convolutional networks. In: International Conference on Learning Representations (2017)
19. Klicpera, J., Weiß enberger, S., Günnemann, S.: Diffusion improves graph learning. In: Advances in Neural Information Processing Systems, pp. 13333–13345 (2019)
20. Kondor, R., Pan, H.: The multiscale Laplacian graph kernel. Adv. Neural. Inf. Process. Syst. 29, 2990–2998 (2016)

21. Lee, J., Lee, I., Kang, J.: Self-attention graph pooling. In: International Conference on Machine Learning, pp. 3734–3743 (2019)
22. Li, P., et al.: Pairwise half-graph discrimination: a simple graph-level self-supervised strategy for pre-training graph neural networks. In: International Joint Conference on Artificial Intelligence, pp. 2694–2700 (2021)
23. Liu, X., et al.: Self-supervised learning: generative or contrastive. arXiv preprint arXiv:2006.08218 (2020)
24. Monti, F., Boscaini, D., Masci, J., Rodola, E., Svoboda, J., Bronstein, M.M.: Geometric deep learning on graphs and manifolds using mixture model CNNs. In: Conference on Computer Vision and Pattern Recognition (2017)
25. Narayanan, A., Chandramohan, M., Venkatesan, R., Chen, L., Liu, Y., Jaiswal, S.: graph2vec: Learning distributed representations of graphs. arXiv preprint arXiv:1707.05005 (2017)
26. van den Oord, A., Li, Y., Vinyals, O.: Representation learning with contrastive predictive coding. arXiv preprint arXiv:1807.03748 (2018)
27. Pan, S., Hu, R., Long, G., Jiang, J., Yao, L., Zhang, C.: Adversarially regularized graph autoencoder for graph embedding. In: International Joint Conference on Artificial Intelligence, pp. 2609–2615 (2018)
28. Park, J., Lee, M., Chang, H.J., Lee, K., Choi, J.Y.: Symmetric graph convolutional autoencoder for unsupervised graph representation learning. In: International Conference on Computer Vision, pp. 6519–6528 (2019)
29. Peng, Z., et al.: Graph representation learning via graphical mutual information maximization. In: The Web Conference (2020)
30. Qiu, J., et al.: GCC: graph contrastive coding for graph neural network pre-training. In: Proceedings of the 26th ACM SIGKDD International Conference on Knowledge Discovery & Data Mining, pp. 1150–1160 (2020)
31. Sen, P., Namata, G., Bilgic, M., Getoor, L., Galligher, B., Eliassi-Rad, T.: Collective classification in network data. AI Mag. 29(3), 93–93 (2008)
32. Shchur, O., Mumme, M., Bojchevski, A., Günnemann, S.: Pitfalls of graph neural network evaluation. In: NeurIPS Relational Representation Learning Workshop (2018)
33. Shervashidze, N., Schweitzer, P., van Leeuwen, E.J., Mehlhorn, K., Borgwardt, K.M.: Weisfeiler-Lehman graph kernels. J. Mach. Learn. Res. 12, 2539–2561 (2011)
34. Shervashidze, N., Vishwanathan, S., Petri, T., Mehlhorn, K., Borgwardt, K.: Efficient graphlet kernels for large graph comparison. In: Artificial Intelligence and Statistics, pp. 488–495 (2009)
35. Sun, F., Hoffmann, J., Verma, V., Tang, J.: InfoGraph: unsupervised and semi-supervised graph-level representation learning via mutual information maximization. In: International Conference on Learning Representations (2020)
36. Veličković, P., Cucurull, G., Casanova, A., Romero, A., Liò, P., Bengio, Y.: Graph attention networks. In: International Conference on Learning Representations (2018)
37. Veličković, P., Fedus, W., Hamilton, W.L., Liò, P., Bengio, Y., Hjelm, R.D.: Deep graph infomax. In: International Conference on Learning Representations (2019)
38. Wang, C., Pan, S., Long, G., Zhu, X., Jiang, J.: MGAE: marginalized graph autoencoder for graph clustering. In: Conference on Information and Knowledge Management, pp. 889–898 (2017)
39. Wu, F., Souza, A., Zhang, T., Fifty, C., Yu, T., Weinberger, K.: Simplifying graph convolutional networks. In: International Conference on Machine Learning (2019)
40. Xu, K., Hu, W., Leskovec, J., Jegelka, S.: How powerful are graph neural networks? In: International Conference on Learning Representations (2019)
41. Yanardag, P., Vishwana, S.: Deep graph kernels. In: International Conference on Knowledge Discovery and Data Mining, pp. 1365–1374 (2015)

42. Yang, Z., Cohen, W., Salakhudinov, R.: Revisiting semi-supervised learning with graph embeddings. In: International Conference on Machine Learning, pp. 40–48 (2016)
43. Ying, R., You, J., Morris, C., Ren, X., Hamilton, W.L., Leskovec, J.: Hierarchical graph representation learning with differentiable pooling. In: Advances in Neural Information Processing Systems, pp. 4805–4815 (2018)
44. You, Y., Chen, T., Sui, Y., Chen, T., Wang, Z., Shen, Y.: Graph contrastive learning with augmentations. In: Advances in Neural Information Processing Systems (2020)
45. Yuan, H., Ji, S.: StructPool: structured graph pooling via conditional random fields. In: International Conference on Learning Representations (2020)
46. Zhu, X., Ghahramani, Z., Lafferty, J.D.: Semi-supervised learning using Gaussian fields and harmonic functions. In: International Conference on Machine Learning, pp. 912–919 (2003)
47. Zhu, Y., Xu, Y., Yu, F., Liu, Q., Wu, S., Wang, L.: Deep graph contrastive representation learning. In: ICML Workshop on Graph Representation Learning and Beyond (2020)
48. Zhu, Y., Xu, Y., Yu, F., Liu, Q., Wu, S., Wang, L.: Graph contrastive learning with adaptive augmentation. In: The Web Conference (2021)

How to Agree to Disagree
Managing Ontological Perspectives using Standpoint Logic

Lucía Gómez Álvarez[(✉)] [iD], Sebastian Rudolph [iD],
and Hannes Strass [iD]

Computational Logic Group, Faculty of Computer Science, TU Dresden, Dresden, Germany
{lucia.gomez_alvarez,sebastian.rudolph,
hannes.strass}@tu-dresden.de

Abstract. The importance of taking individual, potentially conflicting perspectives into account when dealing with knowledge has been widely recognised. Many existing ontology management approaches fully merge knowledge perspectives, which may require weakening in order to maintain consistency; others represent the distinct views in an entirely detached way.

As an alternative, we propose *Standpoint Logic*, a simple, yet versatile multimodal logic "add-on" for existing KR languages intended for the integrated representation of domain knowledge relative to diverse, possibly conflicting *standpoints*, which can be hierarchically organised, combined, and put in relation with each other.

Starting from the generic framework of *First-Order Standpoint Logic* (FOSL), we subsequently focus our attention on the fragment of *sentential* formulas, for which we provide a polytime translation into the standpoint-free version. This result yields decidability and favourable complexities for a variety of highly expressive decidable fragments of first-order logic. Using some elaborate encoding tricks, we then establish a similar translation for the very expressive description logic $\mathcal{SROIQb}_s$ underlying the OWL 2 DL ontology language. By virtue of this result, existing highly optimised OWL reasoners can be used to provide practical reasoning support for ontology languages extended by standpoint modelling.

Keywords: knowledge integration · ontology alignment · conflict management

1 Introduction

Artefacts of contemporary knowledge representation (ontologies, knowledge bases, or knowledge graphs) serve as means to conceptualise specific domains, with varying degrees of expressivity ranging from simple classifications and database schemas to fully axiomatised theories. Inevitably, such specifications reflect the individual points of view of their creators (be it on a personal or an institutional level) along with other contextual aspects, and they may also differ in modelling design decisions, such as the choice of conceptual granularity or specific ways of axiomatising information. This semantic heterogeneity is bound to pose significant challenges whenever the interoperability of independently developed knowledge specifications is required.

This paper proposes a way to address the interoperability challenge while at the same time preserving the varying perspectives of the original sources. This is particularly important in scenarios that require the simultaneous consideration of multiple, potentially contradictory, viewpoints.

© The Author(s) 2022
U. Sattler et al. (Eds.): ISWC 2022, LNCS 13489, pp. 125–141, 2022.
https://doi.org/10.1007/978-3-031-19433-7_8

Example 1. A broad range of conceptualisations and definitions for the notion of *forest* have been specified for different purposes, giving rise to diverging or even contradictory statements regarding forest distributions. Consider a knowledge integration scenario involving two sources adopting a *land cover* (LC) and a *land use* (LU) perspective on forestry. LC characterises a *forest* as a "forest ecosystem" with a minimum area (F1) where a *forest ecosystem* is specified as an ecosystem with a certain ratio of tree canopy cover (F2). LU defines a forest with regard to the purpose for which an area of land is put to use by humans, i.e. a forest is a maximally connected area with "forest use" (F3).[1]

Both sources LC and LU agree that forests subsume broadleaf, needleleaf and tropical forests (F4), and they both adhere to the Basic Formal Ontology (BFO, [1]), an upper-level ontology that formalises general terms, stipulating for instance that *land* and *ecosystem* are disjoint categories (F5). Using standard description logic notation and providing "perspective annotations" by means of correspondingly labelled box operators borrowed from multi-modal logic, the above setting might be formalised as follows:

(F1) $\Box_{\text{LC}}[\texttt{Forest} \equiv \texttt{ForestEcosystem} \sqcap \exists\texttt{hasLand.Area}_{\geq 0.5\text{ha}}]$

(F2) $\Box_{\text{LC}}[\texttt{ForestEcosystem} \equiv \texttt{Ecosystem} \sqcap \texttt{TreeCanopy}_{\geq 20\%}]$

(F3) $\Box_{\text{LU}}[\texttt{Forest} \equiv \texttt{ForestlandUse} \sqcap \texttt{MCON}] \wedge \Box_*[\texttt{ForestlandUse} \sqsubseteq \texttt{Land}]$

(F4) $\Box_{\text{LC} \sqcup \text{LU}}[(\texttt{BroadleafForest} \sqcup \texttt{NeedleleafForest} \sqcup \texttt{TropicalForest}) \sqsubseteq \texttt{Forest}]$

(F5) $(\text{LC} \preceq \text{BFO}) \wedge (\text{LU} \preceq \text{BFO}) \wedge \Box_{\text{BFO}}[\texttt{Land} \sqcap \texttt{Ecosystem} \sqsubseteq \bot]$

In the case of Example 1, *ecosystem* and *land* are disjoint categories according to the overarching BFO (F5), yet forests are defined as ecosystems according to LC (F1) and as lands according to LU (F3). These kinds of disagreements result in well-reported challenges in the area of Ontology Integration [6,21] and make ontology merging a non-trivial task, often involving a certain knowledge loss or weakening in order to avoid incoherence and inconsistency [22,28]. In Example 1, to merge LU and LC, there are two typical options to resolve the issue: (Opt-Weak) one may give up on the disjointness axiom (F5), or (Opt-Dup) one could duplicate all the conflicting predicates [20], in this case not only Forest (into Forest_LC and Forest_LU), but also the forest subclasses in (F4): BroadleafForest, NeedleleafForest and TropicalForest. In contrast, we advocate a multi-perspective approach that can represent and reason with many – possibly conflicting – standpoints, instead of focusing on combining and merging different sources into a single conflict-free conceptual model.

Standpoint logic [8] is a formalism inspired by the theory of supervaluationism [7] and rooted in modal logic that supports the coexistence of multiple standpoints and the establishment of alignments between them, by extending the base language with labelled modal operators. Propositions $\Box_{\text{LC}}\, \phi$ and $\Diamond_{\text{LC}}\, \phi$ express information relative to the *standpoint* LC and read, respectively: "according to LC, it is *unequivocal/conceivable* that ϕ". In the semantics, standpoints are represented by sets of *precisifications*,[2] such that $\Box_{\text{LC}}\, \phi$ and $\Diamond_{\text{LC}}\, \phi$ hold if ϕ is true in all/some of the precisifications in LC.

The logical statements (F1)–(F5), which formalise Example 1 by means of a standpoint-enhanced description logic, are not inconsistent, so all axioms can be jointly

---

[1] "Forest use" areas may qualify for logging and mining concessions as well as be further classified into, e.g. agricultural or recreational land use.

[2] Precisifications are analogous to the *worlds* of frameworks with possible-worlds semantics.

represented. Let us now illustrate the use of standpoint logic for reasoning with the individual perspectives. First, assume the following (globally agreed) facts about three instances, an ecosystem e, a parcel of land l, and a city c:

(F6) $\text{ForestEcosystem}(e)$ $\text{hasLand}(e, l)$ $\text{ForestlandUse}(l)$
(F7) $\text{Area}_{\geq 0.5\text{ha}}(l)$ $\text{MCON}(l)$ $\text{in}(l, c)$ $\text{City}(c)$

It is clear from (F1) that according to LC, e is a forest, written as $\square_{\text{LC}}[\text{Forest}(e)]$, since it is a forest ecosystem (F6) with an area larger than 0.5ha (F7). On the other hand, it is clear from (F3) that according to LU, l is a forest, $\square_{\text{LU}}[\text{Forest}(l)]$, since it has a forest land use (F6) and it is a maximally connected area (F7). More interestingly, we can also obtain *joint inferences*: assuming the (generally accepted) background knowledge expressed by $\text{hasLand} \circ \text{in} \sqsubseteq \text{in}$, we can infer

$$\square_{\text{LC} \cup \text{LU}}[(\text{City} \sqcap \exists\text{in}^{-}.\text{Forest})(c)],$$

which means that "according to both LC and LU there is some forest in City c." This holds for LU since l is a forest and is in c (F7); and it holds for LC because e is a forest in the land l, which is in turn in c.

In contrast to the options of the ontology merging approach, using standpoint logic prevents the multiplication (and corresponding "semantic detachment") of predicates from (Opt-Dup). It also avoids unintended consequences arising when knowledge sources are weakened just enough to maintain satisfiability: In the corresponding (Opt-Weak) scenario, after merging the knowledge sources of LU and LC and removing (F5), we can consistently infer $\text{Forest}(e)$ from the standpoint-free versions of (F1), (F6) and (F7) and $\text{Forest}(l)$ from (F3), (F6) and (F7), similar to the standpoint framework. But on top of that, reapplying (F1) and (F3) also yields "e is a forest, and its land l is also a forest and an ecosystem, and has some other associated land, bigger than 0.5ha" through the following derivable assertions:

$\text{Forest}(e)$ $\text{hasLand}(e, l)$ $\text{Forest}(l)$ $\text{ForestEcosystem}(l)$ $\exists\text{hasLand}.\text{Area}_{\geq 0.5\text{ha}}(l)$

This illustrates how, beyond the problem of inconsistency, naively merging different models of a domain may lead to erroneous reasoning. In fact, other non-clashing differences between the forest definitions (F1) and (F3) respond to relevant nuances that relate to each standpoint and should also not be naively merged. For instance, from the land cover perspective (F1), there is no spatial connectedness requirement, since there are "mosaic forest ecosystems" where the landscape displays forest patches that are sufficiently close to constitute a single ecosystem. On the other hand, for LU, there is no minimum tree canopy (F3), since a temporarily cleared area still has a "forest use".

Standpoint logic preserves the independence of the perspectives and escapes global inconsistency – without weakening the sources or duplicating entities – because its model theory (cf. Section 2.1) requires consistency only within standpoints and precisifications. Notwithstanding, it allows for the specification of structures of standpoints and alignments between them. Natural reasoning tasks over such multi-standpoint specifications include gathering unequivocal or undisputed knowledge, determining knowledge that is relative to a standpoint or a set of them, and contrasting the knowledge that can be inferred from different standpoints.

Let us get an idea of the expressivity of the proposed logic. In spite of its simple syntax, the language is remarkably versatile; it allows for specifying knowledge relative (a) to a standpoint, e.g. (F1), (b) to the global standpoint, denoted by $*$, e.g. (F3), and (c) to set-theoretic combinations of standpoints, e.g. (F4). Additional language features can be defined in terms of the former: $\mathcal{I}_{\mathsf{LC}}\phi$, which means that, "according to LC, it is inherently *indeterminate* whether ϕ" can be defined by $\mathcal{I}_{\mathsf{LC}}\phi := \Diamond_{\mathsf{LC}}\phi \wedge \Diamond_{\mathsf{LC}}\neg\phi$. The *sharper* operator $\preceq$ is used to establish hierarchies of standpoints and constraints on the structure of precisifications, e.g. (F5), and can be defined via $s_1 \preceq s_2 := \Box_{s_1 \setminus s_2}[\top \sqsubseteq \bot]$. Intuitively, $s_1 \preceq s_2$ expresses that standpoint s_1 inherits the propositions of s_2, by virtue of "$s_1 \subseteq s_2$" holding for the corresponding sets of precisifications. This type of statement comes handy to "import" background knowledge from some ontology, such as the foundational ontology BFO in our example. In combination, these modelling features allow for expressing further constraints useful for knowledge integration scenarios, e.g.,

(F8) $* \preceq (\mathsf{LC} \cup \mathsf{LU}) \wedge \Diamond_{\mathsf{LC}}[\top \sqsubseteq \top] \wedge \Diamond_{\mathsf{LU}}[\top \sqsubseteq \top],$

where the first conjunct allows us to specify that no interpretations beyond the standpoints of interest are under consideration, by stating that the universal standpoint is a subset of the union of LC and LU. The other two conjuncts enforce the non-emptiness of the standpoints of interest, LC and LU, ensuring that each standpoint by itself is coherent. To illustrate a use case, consider the statement $\Diamond_*[\mathtt{Forest}(f) \wedge \neg\mathtt{MCON}(f)]$, expressing that it is conceivable that f is a non-spatially-connected forest. From this, we can infer together with (F8) and the unfulfilled requirement of connectedness of LU (F3), that f must be conceivable for LC instead, and thus f must be a forest ecosystem (F1):

$$\Diamond_{\mathsf{LC}}[\mathtt{ForestEcosystem}(f) \wedge (\exists\mathtt{hasLand.Area}_{\geq 0.5\mathrm{ha}})(f)]$$

Gómez Álvarez and Rudolph [8] have introduced the standpoint framework over a propositional base logic. While they showed favourable complexity results (standard reasoning tasks are NP-complete just like for plain propositional logic), the framework is not expressive enough for knowledge integration scenarios employing contemporary ontology languages. In this paper, we widen the scope by (1) introducing the very general framework of *first-order* standpoint logic (FOSL) and (2) allowing for more modelling flexibility on the side of standpoint descriptions by introducing support for set-theoretical combinations of standpoints (Section 2). We provide the syntax and semantics of this generic framework, before focusing on the identification of FOSL fragments with beneficial computational properties. To this end, we define the *sentential* fragment, which imposes restrictions on the use of standpoint operators and guarantees a small model property (Section 2.2). Tailored to this case, we introduce a polynomial satisfiability-preserving translation (Section 2.3) that does not affect membership in diverse decidable fragments of FO. This allows us to immediately obtain decidability and tight complexity bounds for the standpoint versions of diverse FO fragments (e.g. the 2-variable counting fragment, the guarded negation fragment and the triguarded fragment) (Section 3). In addition, it provides a way to leverage off-the-shelf reasoners for practical reasoning in standpoint versions of popular ontology languages. We demonstrate this by extending our results to a standpoint logic based on the description logic $\mathcal{SROIQ}b_s$, a semantic fragment of FO closely related to the OWL 2 DL ontology language (Section 4). Finally, we revisit our example to discuss and illustrate properties of our proposal (Section 5). An extended version of this paper including proofs is available as a technical report [30].

2   First-Order Standpoint Logic

In this section we introduce the general framework of first order standpoint logic (FOSL) as well as its sentential fragment and establish model theoretic and computational properties. In addition to establishing various worthwhile decidability and complexity results, this approach also provides us with a clearer view on the underlying principles of our arguments, while avoiding distractions brought about by some peculiarities of expressive ontology languages, which we will address separately later on.

2.1   FOSL Syntax and Semantics

Definition 1. *The syntax of first-order standpoint logic* ($\mathbb{S}_{\mathrm{FO}}$) *is based on a* signature $\langle \mathcal{P}, \mathcal{C}, \mathcal{S} \rangle$, *consisting of* predicate symbols $\mathcal{P}$ *(each associated with an arity* $n \in \mathbb{N}$*), constant symbols* $\mathcal{C}$ *and* standpoint symbols $\mathcal{S}$, *usually denoted with* s, s', *as well as a set* $\mathcal{V}$ *of* variables, *typically denoted with* $x, y, \ldots$ *(possibly annotated). These four sets are assumed to be countably infinite and pairwise disjoint. The set* $\mathcal{T}$ *of* terms *contains all constants and variables, that is,* $\mathcal{T} = \mathcal{C} \cup \mathcal{V}$.

The set $\mathcal{E}_{\mathcal{S}}$ *of* standpoint expressions *is defined as follows:*

$$\mathsf{e}_1, \mathsf{e}_2 ::= * \mid \mathsf{s} \mid \mathsf{e}_1 \cup \mathsf{e}_2 \mid \mathsf{e}_1 \cap \mathsf{e}_2 \mid \mathsf{e}_1 \setminus \mathsf{e}_2$$

The set $\mathbb{S}_{\mathrm{FO}}$ *of FOSL* formulas *is then given by*

$$\phi, \psi ::= \mathrm{P}(t_1, \ldots, t_k) \mid \neg\phi \mid \phi \wedge \psi \mid \forall x \phi \mid \Box_{\mathsf{e}}\, \phi,$$

where $\mathrm{P} \in \mathcal{P}$ *is an k-ary predicate symbol,* $t_1, \ldots, t_k \in \mathcal{T}$ *are terms,* $x \in \mathcal{V}$, *and* $\mathsf{e} \in \mathcal{E}_{\mathcal{S}}$.

For a formula ϕ, we denote the set of all of its subformulas by $Sub(\phi)$. The *size* of a formula is $|\phi| := |Sub(\phi)|$. The connectives and operators $\mathbf{t}, \mathbf{f}, \phi \vee \psi, \phi \rightarrow \psi, \exists x \phi$, and $\Diamond_{\mathsf{e}}\, \phi$ are introduced as syntactic macros as usual. As further useful syntactic sugar, we introduce *sharpening* statements $\mathsf{e}_1 \preceq \mathsf{e}_2$ to denote $\Box_{\mathsf{e}_1 \setminus \mathsf{e}_2} \mathbf{f}$, the *indeterminacy operator* via $\mathcal{I}_{\mathsf{e}}\phi := \Diamond_{\mathsf{e}}\, \phi \wedge \Diamond_{\mathsf{e}}\, \neg\phi$, and the *determinacy operator* via $\mathcal{D}_{\mathsf{e}}\phi := \neg\mathcal{I}_{\mathsf{e}}\phi$.

Definition 2. *Given a signature* $\langle \mathcal{P}, \mathcal{C}, \mathcal{S} \rangle$, *a first-order standpoint structure* $\mathfrak{M}$ *is a tuple* $\langle \Delta, \Pi, \sigma, \gamma \rangle$ *where:*

- Δ *is a non-empty set, the* domain *of* $\mathfrak{M}$;
- Π *is the non-empty set of* precisifications;
- σ *is a function mapping each standpoint symbol from* $\mathcal{S}$ *to a set of precisifications (i.e., a subset of* Π*);*
- γ *is a function mapping each precisification from* Π *to an ordinary first-order structure* $\mathcal{I}$ *over the domain* Δ, *whose interpretation function* $\cdot^{\mathcal{I}}$ *maps:*
  - *each predicate symbol* $\mathrm{P} \in \mathcal{P}$ *of arity* k *to an k-ary relation* $\mathrm{P}^{\mathcal{I}} \subseteq \Delta^k$,
  - *each constant symbol* $a \in \mathcal{C}$ *to a domain element* $a^{\mathcal{I}} \in \Delta$.
  Moreover, for any two $\pi_1, \pi_2 \in \Pi$ *and every* $a \in \mathcal{C}$ *we require* $a^{\gamma(\pi_1)} = a^{\gamma(\pi_2)}$.

Note that all first-order structures in all precisifications implicitly share the same interpretation domain Δ given by the overarching first-order standpoint structure $\mathfrak{M}$, that is, we adopt the *constant domain assumption*.[3] Moreover, the last condition of Definition 2

---

[3] This is not a substantial restriction, as other variants – expanding domains, varying domains – can be emulated using constant domains [29, Theorem 6].

also enforces *rigid constants*, that is, constants denote the same objects in different standpoints (while clearly their properties could differ).

Definition 3. *Let* $\mathfrak{M} = \langle \Delta, \Pi, \sigma, \gamma \rangle$ *be a first-order standpoint structure for the signature* $\langle \mathcal{P}, \mathcal{C}, \mathcal{S} \rangle$ *and* $\mathcal{V}$ *be a set of variables. A* variable assignment *is a function* $v : \mathcal{V} \to \Delta$ *mapping variables to domain elements. Given a variable assignment* v, *we denote by* $v_{\{x \mapsto \delta\}}$ *the function mapping* x *to* $\delta \in \Delta$ *and any other variable* y *to* $v(y)$.

An interpretation function $\cdot^{\mathcal{I}}$ *and a variable assignment specify how to interpret terms by domain elements: We let* $t^{\mathcal{I},v} = v(x)$ *if* $t = x \in \mathcal{V}$, *and* $t^{\mathcal{I},v} = a^{\mathcal{I}}$ *if* $t = a \in \mathcal{C}$.

To interpret standpoint expressions, we lift σ *from* $\mathcal{S}$ *to all of* $\mathcal{E}_{\mathcal{S}}$ *by letting* $\sigma(*) = \Pi$ *and* $\sigma(e_1 \bowtie e_2) = \sigma(e_1) \bowtie \sigma(e_2)$ *for* $\bowtie \in \{\cup, \cap, \setminus\}$

The satisfaction relation for formulas is defined in the usual way via structural induction. In what follows, let $\pi \in \Pi$ *and let* $v : \mathcal{V} \to \Delta$ *be a variable assignment; we now establish the definition of the satisfaction relation* $\models$ *for first-order standpoint logic using pointed first-order standpoint structures:*

$$\mathfrak{M},\pi,v \models P(t_1, \ldots, t_k) \qquad \textit{iff } (t_1^{\gamma(\pi),v}, \ldots, t_k^{\gamma(\pi),v}) \in P^{\gamma(\pi)}$$

$$\mathfrak{M},\pi,v \models \neg\phi \qquad \textit{iff } \mathfrak{M},\pi,v \not\models \phi$$

$$\mathfrak{M},\pi,v \models \phi \wedge \psi \qquad \textit{iff } \mathfrak{M},\pi,v \models \phi \textit{ and } \mathfrak{M},\pi,v \models \psi$$

$$\mathfrak{M},\pi,v \models \forall x\phi \qquad \textit{iff } \mathfrak{M},\pi,v_{\{x \mapsto \delta\}} \models \phi \textit{ for all } \delta \in \Delta$$

$$\mathfrak{M},\pi,v \models \Box_e \phi \qquad \textit{iff } \mathfrak{M},\pi',v \models \phi \textit{ for all } \pi' \in \sigma(e)$$

$$\mathfrak{M},\pi \models \phi \qquad \textit{iff } \mathfrak{M},\pi,v \models \phi \textit{ for all } v : \mathcal{V} \to \Delta$$

$$\mathfrak{M} \models \phi \qquad \textit{iff } \mathfrak{M},\pi \models \phi \textit{ for all } \pi \in \Pi$$

As usual, $\mathfrak{M}$ is a *model* for a formula ϕ iff $\mathfrak{M} \models \phi$. As an aside, note that the modal-logic nature of FOSL may become more evident upon realizing that an alternative definition of its semantics via Kripke structures can be given (with $\Box_e$ interpreted in the standard way) by assigning every $e \in \mathcal{E}_{\mathcal{S}}$ the accessibility relation $\{(\pi, \pi') \mid \pi, \pi' \in \Pi, \pi' \in \sigma(e)\}$.

Later in this paper, we will consider cases where the number of precisifications is fixed. Thus, we conclude this section by a corresponding definition.

Definition 4. *For a natural number* $n \in \mathbb{N}$, *a FOSL formula* ϕ *is* n-satisfiable *iff it has a model* $\langle \Delta, \Pi, \sigma, \gamma \rangle$ *with* $|\Pi| = n$.

2.2 Small Model Property of Sentential Formulas

One interesting aspect of standpoint logic is that its simplified Kripke semantics brings about convenient model-theoretic properties that do not hold for arbitrary (multi-)modal logics. For propositional standpoint logic, it is known that standard reasoning tasks (such as checking satisfiability) are NP-complete [8], in contrast to PSPACE-completeness in related systems such as $K45_n$, $KD45_n$ and $S5_n$. This result is in fact linked to a *small model property*, according to which every satisfiable formula has a model with a "small" number of precisifications. This beneficial property only holds in the single-modal K45, KD45 and S5 [23] but applies to the multi-modal propositional standpoint logic because of its stronger modal interaction. Fortunately, it can also be shown to carry over to some fragments of FOSL and to the use of standpoint expressions. In particular, in this section, we will show that if we restrict the language to those formulas with no free variables in subformulas of the form $\Box_e\,\phi$, then we can indeed guarantee that every satisfiable FOSL formula has a model whose number of precisifications is linear in the size of the formula.

Definition 5. *Let ϕ be a formula of FOSL. We say that ϕ is* sentential *iff for all subformulas of ϕ of the form $\Box_e\,\psi$, all variables occurring in ψ are bound by a quantifier.*

Theorem 1. *A sentential FOSL formula ϕ is satisfiable iff it has a model with at most $|\phi|$ precisifications. That is, for sentential FOSL, satisfiability and $|\phi|$-satisfiability coincide.*

In the following, it will be convenient to assume that formulas are in *standpoint standard normal form* (SSNF), where no modal operator $\Box_e$ occurs inside the scope of another. Any FOSL formula ϕ can be transformed into SSNF in polynomial time.

2.3   Translation to Plain First-Order Logic

In this section, we present a translation Trans_n mapping any FOSL formula ϕ to a plain FO formula $\mathrm{Trans}_n(\phi)$ such that n-satisfiability of ϕ coincides with satisfiability of $\mathrm{Trans}_n(\phi)$. The translation will make explicit use of a fixed, finite set Π_n of precisifications with $|\Pi_n| = n$.

Our translation will map any ϕ into a formula of (standpoint-free) first-order logic. The basic idea is to "emulate" standpoint structures $\langle\Delta,\Pi_n,\sigma,\gamma\rangle$ in plain first-order structures over Δ by means of a "superposition" of all $\gamma(\pi)$, which requires to introduce n "copies" of the original set of predicates. To this end, we define our first-order vocabulary by $\mathbb{V}_{\mathrm{FO}}(\mathcal{P},\mathcal{C},\mathcal{S},\Pi_n) = \langle\mathcal{P}',\mathcal{C}\rangle$ where $\mathcal{P}'$ contains

- for each predicate $\mathsf{P}\in\mathcal{P}$ and precisification $\pi\in\Pi_n$, a predicate of the form P_π of the same arity as P, intuitively expressing that P_π should capture $\mathsf{P}^{\gamma(\pi)}$;
- for each standpoint constant $\mathsf{s}\in\mathcal{S}$ and every precisification $\pi\in\Pi_n$, a nullary predicate of the form s_π, intuitively expressing that $\pi\in\sigma(\mathsf{s})$.

The top-level translation is then defined to set:

$$\mathrm{Trans}_n(\phi) = \bigwedge\nolimits_{\pi\in\Pi_n}\mathrm{trans}_n(\pi,\phi)\ \wedge\ \bigwedge\nolimits_{\pi\in\Pi_n}*\pi,$$

where trans_n is inductively defined by

$$\mathrm{trans}_n(\pi,\mathsf{P}(t_1,\ldots,t_k)) = \mathsf{P}_\pi(t_1,\ldots,t_k)$$
$$\mathrm{trans}_n(\pi,\neg\psi) = \neg\mathrm{trans}_n(\pi,\psi)$$
$$\mathrm{trans}_n(\pi,\psi_1\wedge\psi_2) = \mathrm{trans}_n(\pi,\psi_1)\wedge\mathrm{trans}_n(\pi,\psi_2)$$
$$\mathrm{trans}_n(\pi,\forall x\psi) = \forall x(\mathrm{trans}_n(\pi,\psi))$$
$$\mathrm{trans}_n(\pi',\Box_e\,\psi) = \bigwedge\nolimits_{\pi\in\Pi_n}(\mathrm{trans}_\mathcal{E}(\pi,\mathsf{e})\rightarrow\mathrm{trans}_n(\pi,\psi))$$

Therein, $\mathrm{trans}_\mathcal{E}$ implements the semantics of standpoint expressions, providing for each expression $\mathsf{e}\in\mathcal{E}_\mathcal{S}$ a propositional formula $\mathrm{trans}_\mathcal{E}(\pi,\mathsf{e})$ over $\{s_\pi\mid\pi\in\Pi_n\}$ as follows:

$$\mathrm{trans}_\mathcal{E}(\pi,\mathsf{s}) = \mathsf{s}_\pi$$
$$\mathrm{trans}_\mathcal{E}(\pi,\mathsf{e}_1\cup\mathsf{e}_2) = \mathrm{trans}_\mathcal{E}(\pi,\mathsf{e}_1)\vee\mathrm{trans}_\mathcal{E}(\pi,\mathsf{e}_2)$$
$$\mathrm{trans}_\mathcal{E}(\pi,\mathsf{e}_1\cap\mathsf{e}_2) = \mathrm{trans}_\mathcal{E}(\pi,\mathsf{e}_1)\wedge\mathrm{trans}_\mathcal{E}(\pi,\mathsf{e}_2)$$
$$\mathrm{trans}_\mathcal{E}(\pi,\mathsf{e}_1\setminus\mathsf{e}_2) = \mathrm{trans}_\mathcal{E}(\pi,\mathsf{e}_1)\wedge\neg\mathrm{trans}_\mathcal{E}(\pi,\mathsf{e}_2)$$

A routine inspection of the translation ensures that it can be done in polynomial time and its output is of polynomial size, provided it is applied to formulas in SSNF.

Theorem 2. *A formula ϕ is n-satisfiable in FOSL if and only if the formula $\text{Trans}_n(\phi)$ is satisfiable in first-order logic.*

In fact, Theorem 2 provides us with a recipe for a satisfiability-preserving translation for any formula that comes with a "small model guarantee", whenever a bound on the number of precisifications can be computed upfront. In particular, leveraging Theorem 1, we obtain the following corollary.

Corollary 1. *A formula ϕ is satisfiable in sentential first-order standpoint logic if and only if the formula $\text{Trans}_{|\phi|}(\phi)$ is satisfiable in first-order logic.*

3   Expressive Decidable FOSL Fragments

We note that even for the sentential version, first-order standpoint logic is still a generalization of plain first-order logic, whence reasoning in it is undecidable. Therefore, we will next look into some popular decidable FO fragments and establish decidability and complexity results for reasoning in their sentential standpoint versions.

Definition 6. *Let $\mathcal{F}$ denote some FO fragment. Then the logic sentential Standpoint-$\mathcal{F}$, denoted $\mathbb{S}_{[\mathcal{F}]}$, contains the sentential FOSL formulas ϕ where:*

- *all variables inside ϕ are bound by some quantifier,*
- *for every subformula $\psi \in \text{Sub}(\text{SSNF}(\phi))$ preceded by a quantifier, $\psi \in \mathcal{F}$ holds.*

Fragment $\mathcal{F}$ is standpoint-friendly *iff every $\phi \in \mathbb{S}_{[\mathcal{F}]}$ satisfies $\text{Trans}_{|\phi|}(\text{SSNF}(\phi)) \in \mathcal{F}$.*

Lemma 1. *Let $\mathcal{F}$ be a standpoint-friendly fragment of FOL. Then the following hold:*

1. *Satisfiability for $\mathbb{S}_{[\mathcal{F}]}$ is decidable if and only if it is for $\mathcal{F}$.*
2. *If the satisfiability problem in $\mathcal{F}$ is at least NP-hard, then the satisfiability problem in $\mathbb{S}_{[\mathcal{F}]}$ is of the same complexity as in $\mathcal{F}$.*

It turns out that many popular formalisms are standpoint-friendly. For propositional logic (PL), this is straightforward: quantifiers and variables are absent altogether, which is also the reason why sentential Standpoint-PL and proper Standpoint-PL coincide. Thus, Lemma 1 yields an alternative argument for the NP-completeness of the latter, which was established previously [8].

On the expressive end of the logical spectrum, it is worthwhile to inspect fragments of FO that are still decidable (as a minimal requirement for the feasibility of automated reasoning). In fact, standpoint-friendliness can be established by structural induction for many of those. Notable examples are:

- the *counting 2-variable fragment* C^2 [10,24], which subsumes many *description logics* and serves as a mathematical backbone for related complexity results,
- the *guarded negation fragment* GNFO [2,3], which encompasses both the popular *guarded fragment* as well as the ubiquitous class of *(unions of) conjunctive queries* also known as *existential positive FO*, and

– the triguarded fragment TGF [14,27] (a more recent formalism subsuming both the two-variable and the guarded fragment without equality).

Intuitively, standpoint-friendliness for all these (and presumably many more) fragments follows from the fact that they are closed under Boolean combinations of sentences and that the transformation does not affect the structure of quantified formulas. We therefore immediately obtain that these four popular decidable fragments of FOL allow for accommodating standpoints without any increase in complexity.

Corollary 2. *The sentential FOSL fragments* $\mathbb{S}_{[PL]}$ $(= \mathbb{S}_{PL})$, $\mathbb{S}_{[C^2]}$, $\mathbb{S}_{[GNFO]}$, *and* $\mathbb{S}_{[TGF]}$ *are all decidable and the complexity of their satisfiability problem is complete for* NP, NExpTime, 2ExpTime, *and* N2ExpTime, *respectively.*

As an aside, we note that all these results remain valid when considering *finite satisfiability* (i.e., restricting to models with finite Δ), because for all considered fragments, companion results for the finite-model case exist and the equisatisfiability argument for our translation preserves (finiteness of) Δ.

4   Sentential Standpoint-$\mathcal{SROIQ}b_s$

We next present the highly expressive yet decidable logic *(Sentential) Standpoint-$\mathcal{SROIQ}b_s$*, which adds the feature of standpoint-aware modelling to $\mathcal{SROIQ}b_s$, a description logic (DL) obtained from the well-known DL $\mathcal{SROIQ}$ [13] by a gentle extension of its expressivity, allowing safe Boolean role expressions over simple roles [26].[4] The $\mathcal{SROIQ}$ family serves as the logical foundation of popular ontology languages like OWL 2 DL. In view of the fact that $\mathcal{SROIQ}b_s$ is a semantic fragment of FO, we can leverage the previously established results and present a satisfiability-preserving polynomial translation from Standpoint-$\mathcal{SROIQ}b_s$ into plain $\mathcal{SROIQ}b_s$ knowledge bases. On the theoretical side, this will directly provide us with favourable and tight complexity results for reasoning in Standpoint-$\mathcal{SROIQ}b_s$. On the practical side, this paves the way towards practical reasoning in "Standpoint-OWL", since it allows us to use highly optimised OWL 2 DL reasoners off the shelf.

4.1 $\mathcal{SROIQ}b_s$: Syntax and Semantics

Let $\mathcal{C}$, $\mathcal{P}_1$, and $\mathcal{P}_2$ be finite, mutually disjoint sets called *individual names*, *concept names* and *role names*, respectively. $\mathcal{P}_2$ is subdivided into *simple role names* $\mathcal{P}_2^s$ and *non-simple role names* $\mathcal{P}_2^{ns}$, the latter containing the *universal role* u and being strictly ordered by some strict order $\prec$. In the original definition of $\mathcal{SROIQ}b_s$, simplicity of roles and $\prec$ are not given a priori, but meant to be implicitly determined by the set of axioms. Our choice to fix them explicitly upfront simplifies the presentation without restricting expressivity. Then, the set $\mathcal{R}^s$ of *simple role expressions* is defined by

$$r_1, r_2 ::= s \mid s^- \mid r_1 \cup r_2 \mid r_1 \cap r_2 \mid r_1 \setminus r_2,$$

with $s \in \mathcal{P}_2^s$, while the set of (arbitrary) *role expressions* is $\mathcal{R} = \mathcal{R}^s \cup \mathcal{P}_2^{ns}$. The order $\prec$

---

[4] Focusing on the mildly stronger $\mathcal{SROIQ}b_s$ instead of the more mainstream $\mathcal{SROIQ}$ allows for a more coherent and economic presentation, without giving up the good computational properties and the availability of optimised algorithms and tools.

Table 1. $\mathcal{SROIQ}b_s$ role, concept expressions and axioms. $C \equiv D$ abbreviates $C \sqsubseteq D, D \sqsubseteq C$.

Name	Syntax	Semantics
inverse role	$\mathbf{s}^-$	$\{(\delta, \delta') \in \Delta \times \Delta \mid (\delta', \delta) \in \mathbf{s}^{\mathcal{I}}\}$
role union	$r_1 \cup r_2$	$r_1^{\mathcal{I}} \cup r_2^{\mathcal{I}}$
role intersection	$r_1 \cap r_2$	$r_1^{\mathcal{I}} \cup r_2^{\mathcal{I}}$
role difference	$r_1 \setminus r_2$	$r_1^{\mathcal{I}} \setminus r_2^{\mathcal{I}}$
universal role	$\mathbf{u}$	$\Delta^{\mathcal{I}} \times \Delta^{\mathcal{I}}$
nominal	$\{a\}$	$\{a^{\mathcal{I}}\}$
top	$\top$	$\Delta^{\mathcal{I}}$
bottom	$\bot$	$\emptyset$
negation	$\neg C$	$\Delta^{\mathcal{I}} \setminus C^{\mathcal{I}}$
conjunction	$C \sqcap D$	$C^{\mathcal{I}} \cap D^{\mathcal{I}}$
disjunction	$C \sqcup D$	$C^{\mathcal{I}} \cup D^{\mathcal{I}}$
univ. restriction	$\forall r.C$	$\{\delta \mid \forall y.(\delta, \delta') \in r^{\mathcal{I}} \rightarrow \delta' \in C^{\mathcal{I}}\}$
exist. restriction	$\exists r.C$	$\{\delta \mid \exists y.(\delta, \delta') \in r^{\mathcal{I}} \wedge \delta' \in C^{\mathcal{I}}\}$
Self concept	$\exists r.Self$	$\{\delta \mid (\delta, \delta) \in r^{\mathcal{I}}\}$
qualified number	$\leqslant n\,r.C$	$\{\delta \mid \#\{\delta' \in C^{\mathcal{I}} \mid (\delta, \delta') \in r^{\mathcal{I}}\} \leq n\}$
restrictions	$\geqslant n\,r.C$	$\{\delta \mid \#\{\delta' \in C^{\mathcal{I}} \mid (\delta, \delta') \in r^{\mathcal{I}}\} \geq n\}$

Name	Syntax	Semantics
concept assertion	$C(a)$	$a^{\mathcal{I}} \in C^{\mathcal{I}}$
role assertion	$r(a, b)$	$(a^{\mathcal{I}}, b^{\mathcal{I}}) \in r^{\mathcal{I}}$
equality	$a \doteq b$	$a^{\mathcal{I}} = b^{\mathcal{I}}$
inequality	$a \neq b$	$a^{\mathcal{I}} \neq b^{\mathcal{I}}$
general concept inclusion (GCI)	$C \sqsubseteq D$	$C^{\mathcal{I}} \subseteq D^{\mathcal{I}}$
role inclusion axioms (RIAs)	$r_1 \circ \ldots \circ r_n \sqsubseteq r$	$r_1^{\mathcal{I}} \circ \ldots \circ r_n^{\mathcal{I}} \subseteq r^{\mathcal{I}}$
	$r_1 \circ \ldots \circ r_n \circ r \sqsubseteq r$	$r_1^{\mathcal{I}} \circ \ldots \circ r_n^{\mathcal{I}} \circ r^{\mathcal{I}} \subseteq r^{\mathcal{I}}$
	$r \circ r_1 \circ \ldots \circ r_n \sqsubseteq r$	$r^{\mathcal{I}} \circ r_1^{\mathcal{I}} \circ \ldots \circ r_n^{\mathcal{I}} \subseteq r^{\mathcal{I}}$
	$r \circ r \sqsubseteq r$	$r^{\mathcal{I}} \circ r^{\mathcal{I}} \subseteq r^{\mathcal{I}}$

In RIAs, $\mathbf{r} \in \mathcal{P}_2^{\text{ns}}$, while $r_i \in \mathcal{R}$ and $r_i \prec \mathbf{r}$ for all $i \in \{1, \ldots, n\}$.

is then extended to $\mathcal{R}$ by making all elements of $\mathcal{R}^s$ $\prec$-minimal. The syntax of *concept expressions* is given by

$$C, D ::= \mathbf{A} \mid \{a\} \mid \top \mid \bot \mid \neg C \mid C \sqcup D \mid C \sqcup D \mid \forall r.C \mid \exists r.C \mid \exists r'.Self \mid \leqslant n\,r'.C \mid \geqslant n\,r'.C,$$

with $\mathbf{A} \in \mathcal{P}_1$, $a \in \mathcal{C}$, $r \in \mathcal{R}$, $r' \in \mathcal{R}^s$, and $n \in \mathbb{N}$. We note that any concept expression can be put in negation normal form, where negation only occurs in front of concept names, nominals, or *Self* concepts. The different types of $\mathcal{SROIQ}b_s$ sentences (called *axioms*) are given in Table 1.[5]

Similar to FOL, the semantics of $\mathcal{SROIQ}b_s$ is defined via interpretations $\mathcal{I} = (\Delta, \cdot^{\mathcal{I}})$ composed of a non-empty set Δ called the *domain of $\mathcal{I}$* and a function $\cdot^{\mathcal{I}}$ mapping individual names to elements of Δ, concept names to subsets of Δ, and role names to subsets of $\Delta \times \Delta$. This mapping is extended to role and concept expressions and finally used to define satisfaction of axioms (see Table 1).

4.2 Standpoint-$\mathcal{SROIQ}b_s$

The set $\mathbb{S}_{[\mathcal{SROIQ}b_s]}$ of *sentential Standpoint-$\mathcal{SROIQ}b_s$ sentences* is now defined inductively as follows:

- if $\mathbf{Ax}$ is a $\mathcal{SROIQ}b_s$ axiom then $\mathbf{Ax} \in \mathbb{S}_{[\mathcal{SROIQ}b_s]}$,
- if $\phi, \psi \in \mathbb{S}_{[\mathcal{SROIQ}b_s]}$ then $\neg\phi$, as well as $\phi \wedge \psi$ and $\phi \vee \psi$ are in $\mathbb{S}_{[\mathcal{SROIQ}b_s]}$,
- if $\phi \in \mathbb{S}_{[\mathcal{SROIQ}b_s]}$ and $e \in \mathcal{E}_S$ then $\Box_e\, \phi \in \mathbb{S}_{[\mathcal{SROIQ}b_s]}$ and $\Diamond_e\, \phi \in \mathbb{S}_{[\mathcal{SROIQ}b_s]}$.

The semantics of sentential Standpoint-$\mathcal{SROIQ}b_s$ is defined in the obvious way, by "plugging" the semantics of $\mathcal{SROIQ}b_s$ axioms into the semantics of $\mathbb{S}_{[\text{FO}]}$. We say a $\mathbb{S}_{[\mathcal{SROIQ}b_s]}$ sentence ϕ is in *negation normal form* (NNF), if negation occurs only inside or directly in front of $\mathcal{SROIQ}b_s$ axioms; obviously every Standpoint-$\mathcal{SROIQ}b_s$ sentence can be efficiently transformed into an equivalent one in NNF.

---

[5] The original definition of $\mathcal{SROIQ}$ contained more axioms (role transitivity, (a)symmetry, (ir)reflexivity and disjointness), but these are syntactic sugar in our setting.

4.3   Coping with Peculiarities of $\mathcal{SROIQ}b_s$

In the following, we will provide a polynomial translation, mapping any $\mathbb{S}_{[\mathcal{SROIQ}b_s]}$ sentence ϕ to an equisatisfiable set of $\mathcal{SROIQ}b_s$ axioms. This translation is very much in the spirit of the one presented for sentential FOSL, however, $\mathcal{SROIQ}b_s$ comes with diverse syntactic impediments that we need to circumvent. Thus, before presenting the translation, we will briefly discuss these issues and how to solve them.

First, $\mathcal{SROIQ}b_s$ does not provide nullary predicates (i.e., propositional symbols). As a surrogate, we use concept expressions of the form $\forall u.A$ which have the pleasant property of holding either for all domain individuals or for none. Second, $\mathcal{SROIQ}b_s$ does not directly allow for arbitrary Boolean combinations of axioms. For all non-RIA axioms, a more or less straightforward equivalent encoding is possible using nominals and the universal role; for instance the expression $\neg[r(a,b)] \vee [A \sqsubseteq B]$ can be converted into $\top \sqsubseteq \neg \exists u.(\{a\} \sqcap \exists r.\{b\}) \sqcup \forall u.(\neg A \sqcup B)$.

Dealing with RIAs requires auxiliary vocabulary; for negated RIAs, we introduce a fresh nominal, say $\{x\}$, to mark the end of a "violating" role chain, so $\neg[s \circ s \sqsubseteq r]$ essentially becomes $\top \sqsubseteq \exists u.((\exists s.\exists s.\{x\}) \sqcap (\neg \exists r.\{x\}))$.

Unnegated RIAs are even trickier. There is no way of converting them into GCIs, so we have to keep them, but we attach an additional "guard", which allows us to disable them whenever necessary. This guard can then be triggered from within a GCI. For an example, consider the expression $[t \circ t' \sqsubseteq r] \vee [t' \circ t \sqsubseteq r]$. Then, introducing fresh "guard roles" s_1 and s_2, we assert the three axioms $\top \sqsubseteq (\forall u.\exists s_1.Self) \sqcup (\forall u.\exists s_2.Self)$ as well as $s_1 \circ t \circ t' \sqsubseteq r$ and $s_2 \circ t' \circ t \sqsubseteq r$. With this arrangement, the first axiom will ensure that all domain elements carry an s_1-loop or all domain elements carry an s_2-loop. Depending on that choice, the corresponding RIA in the second line will behave like its original, unguarded version, while the other one may be entirely disabled.

The introduced strategy for handling positive RIAs has a downside: due to the restricted shapes of RIAs (governed by $\prec$), axioms of the shape $r \circ r \sqsubseteq r$ (expressing transitivity) cannot be endowed with guards. In order to overcome this nuisance, every nonsimple role r has to be accompanied by a subrole $\underline{r}$, which acts as a "lower approximation" of r and – whenever r is defined transitive – "feeds into" r via tail recursion. This way of reformulating $r \circ r \sqsubseteq r$ allows to attach the wanted guard, but requires adjustments in some axioms that mention r.

4.4   Translation into Plain $\mathcal{SROIQ}b_s$

We now assume a given $\mathbb{S}_{[\mathcal{SROIQ}b_s]}$ sentence ϕ, w.l.o.g. in NNF, and provide the formal definition of the translation. As before, we fix $\Pi_{|\phi|}$ and let our translation's vocabulary $\mathbb{V}_{[\mathcal{SROIQ}b_s]}(\phi)$ consist of all individual names inside ϕ, plus, for each $\pi \in \Pi_{|\phi|}$, the following symbols: (a) a concept name A^π for each $A \in \mathcal{P}_1$; (b) a simple role name s^π for each $s \in \mathcal{P}_2^s$; (c) non-simple role names r^π and $\underline{r}^\pi$ for each $r \in \mathcal{P}_2^{ns} \setminus \{u\}$; (d) a simple role name s_ρ^π for each unnegated RIA ρ inside ϕ; (e) a fresh constant name a_ρ^π for each negated RIA ρ inside ϕ; (f) a concept name M_π^s for each $s \in \mathcal{S}$. Thereby, the non-simple role names inherit their ordering $\prec$ from $\mathcal{P}_2^{ns}$ and we also let $\underline{r}^\pi \prec r^\pi$ for each $r \in \mathcal{P}_2^{ns} \setminus \{u\}$.

The translation $\text{Trans}(\phi)$ of ϕ is then a set of $\mathcal{SROIQ}$ axioms defined as follows: First, $\text{Trans}(\phi)$ contains the RIA $\mathbf{r}^\pi \sqsubseteq \mathbf{r}^\pi$ for every $\mathbf{r} \in \mathcal{P}_2^{\text{ns}} \setminus \{\mathbf{u}\}$ and each $\pi \in \Pi_{|\phi|}$. Second, for every unnegated RIA ρ inside ϕ and each $\pi \in \Pi_{|\phi|}$, $\text{Trans}(\phi)$ contains the RIA $BG_\pi(\rho)$, with BG_π defined by

$$r_1 \circ ... \circ r_n \sqsubseteq \mathbf{r} \mapsto \mathbf{s}_\rho^\pi \circ r_1^\pi \circ ... \circ r_n^\pi \sqsubseteq \mathbf{r}^\pi \qquad r_1 \circ ... \circ r_n \circ r \sqsubseteq \mathbf{r} \mapsto \mathbf{s}_\rho^\pi \circ r_1^\pi \circ ... \circ r_n^\pi \circ \underline{r}^\pi \sqsubseteq \mathbf{r}^\pi$$

$$r \circ r_1 \circ ... \circ r_n \sqsubseteq \mathbf{r} \mapsto \underline{r}^\pi \circ r_1^\pi \circ ... \circ r_n^\pi \circ \mathbf{s}_\rho^\pi \sqsubseteq \mathbf{r}^\pi \qquad r \circ r \sqsubseteq \mathbf{r} \mapsto \mathbf{s}_\rho^\pi \circ \underline{r}^\pi \circ r^\pi \sqsubseteq \mathbf{r}^\pi,$$

whereby the role expression r^π is obtained from r by substituting every role name $\mathbf{s}$ with $\mathbf{s}^\pi$ (except $\mathbf{u}$, which remains unaltered). Third and last, $\text{Trans}(\phi)$ contains the GCI

$$\top \sqsubseteq \bigsqcap_{\pi \in \Pi_{|\phi|}} \text{trans}(\pi, \phi) \sqcap \bigsqcap_{\pi \in \Pi_{|\phi|}} \forall \mathbf{u}.\mathsf{M}_\pi^*$$

where, by inductive definition,

$$\text{trans}(\pi, \mathbf{Ax}) = \text{trans}^+(\pi, \mathbf{Ax})$$

$$\text{trans}(\pi, \neg\mathbf{Ax}) = \text{trans}^-(\pi, \mathbf{Ax})$$

$$\text{trans}(\pi, \psi_1 \wedge \psi_2) = \text{trans}(\pi, \psi_1) \sqcap \text{trans}(\pi, \psi_2)$$

$$\text{trans}(\pi, \psi_1 \vee \psi_2) = \text{trans}(\pi, \psi_1) \sqcup \text{trans}(\pi, \psi_2)$$

$$\text{trans}(\pi', \Box_e \psi) = \bigsqcap_{\pi \in \Pi_{|\phi|}} (\neg\text{trans}_\mathcal{E}(\pi, e) \sqcup \text{trans}(\pi, \psi))$$

$$\text{trans}(\pi', \Diamond_e \psi) = \bigsqcup_{\pi \in \Pi_{|\phi|}} (\text{trans}_\mathcal{E}(\pi, e) \sqcap \text{trans}(\pi, \psi))$$

We next present the translation of unnegated and negated $\mathcal{SROIQ}$ axioms (ρ stands for an RIA $r_1 \circ ... \circ r_m \sqsubseteq \mathbf{r}$):

$$\text{trans}^+(\pi, \rho) = \forall \mathbf{u}.\exists \mathbf{s}_\rho^\pi.Self \qquad \text{trans}^-(\pi, \rho) = \exists \mathbf{u}.\left((\forall \mathbf{r}^\pi.\neg\{a_\rho^\pi\}) \sqcap (\exists \underline{r}_1^\pi...\exists \underline{r}_m^\pi.\{a_\rho^\pi\})\right)$$

$$\text{trans}^+(\pi, C \sqsubseteq D) = \forall \mathbf{u}.(\neg C \sqcup D)^\pi \qquad \text{trans}^-(\pi, C \sqsubseteq D) = \exists \mathbf{u}.(C \sqcap \neg D)^\pi$$

$$\text{trans}^+(\pi, C(a)) = \exists \mathbf{u}.(\{a\} \sqcap C^\pi) \qquad \text{trans}^-(\pi, C(a)) = \exists \mathbf{u}.(\{a\} \sqcap (\neg C)^\pi)$$

$$\text{trans}^+(\pi, r(a,b)) = \exists \mathbf{u}.(\{a\} \sqcap \exists \underline{r}^\pi.\{b\}) \qquad \text{trans}^-(\pi, r(a,b)) = \exists \mathbf{u}.(\{a\} \sqcap \forall r^\pi.\neg\{b\})$$

$$\text{trans}^+(\pi, a \doteq b) = \exists \mathbf{u}.(\{a\} \sqcap \{b\}) \qquad \text{trans}^-(\pi, a \doteq b) = \exists \mathbf{u}.(\{a\} \sqcap \neg\{b\})$$

Therein, for any role expression r, we let $\underline{r}$ denote $\mathbf{r}$ if $r = \mathbf{r}$ is a non-simple role name, and otherwise $\underline{r} = r$. Moreover, C^π denotes the concept expression that is obtained from C by transforming it into negation normal form, replacing concept names A with A^π and role expressions $\mathbf{r}$ by $\mathbf{r}^\pi$, and replacing every $\exists r$ for non-simple $\mathbf{r}$ with $\exists \underline{r}$.

As before, $\text{trans}_\mathcal{E}$ implements the semantics of standpoint expressions, but now adjusted to the new framework: each expression $e \in \mathcal{E}_S$ is transformed into a concept expression $\text{trans}_\mathcal{E}(\pi, e)$ over the vocabulary $\{\mathsf{M}_\pi^s \mid s \in \mathcal{S}, \pi \in \Pi_{|\phi|}\}$ as follows:

$$\text{trans}_\mathcal{E}(\pi, s) = \forall \mathbf{u}.\mathsf{M}_\pi^s$$

$$\text{trans}_\mathcal{E}(\pi, e_1 \cup e_2) = \text{trans}_\mathcal{E}(\pi, e_1) \sqcup \text{trans}_\mathcal{E}(\pi, e_2)$$

$$\text{trans}_\mathcal{E}(\pi, e_1 \cap e_2) = \text{trans}_\mathcal{E}(\pi, e_1) \sqcap \text{trans}_\mathcal{E}(\pi, e_2)$$

$$\text{trans}_\mathcal{E}(\pi, e_1 \setminus e_2) = \text{trans}_\mathcal{E}(\pi, e_1) \sqcap \neg\text{trans}_\mathcal{E}(\pi, e_2)$$

With all definitions in place, we obtain the desired result.

Theorem 3. *Given $\phi \in \mathbb{S}_{[\mathcal{SROIQb}_s]}$, the set $\text{Trans}(\phi)$ (i) is a valid $\mathcal{SROIQb}_s$ knowledge base, (ii) is equisatisfiable with ϕ, (iii) is of polynomial size wrt. ϕ, and (iv) can be computed in polynomial time.*

5   Example in the Forestry Domain

We consider an extension of Example 1 in Sentential Standpoint-$\mathcal{SROIQ}b_s$ to illustrate the main reasoning tasks in more detail. The following additional axiom specifies that forest land use and urban land use are disjoint subclasses of land (F9).

(F9) $\Box_*[\texttt{ForestlandUse} \sqcup \texttt{UrbanLandUse} \sqsubseteq \texttt{Land} \wedge \texttt{ForestlandUse} \sqcap \texttt{UrbanLandUse} \sqsubseteq \bot]$

Now, let us see how, through inferences in $\mathbb{S}_{[\mathcal{SROIQ}b_s]}$, we can gather unequivocal knowledge (Uneq), obtain knowledge that is relative to a standpoint (Rel), and contrast the knowledge that can be inferred from different standpoints (Cont). For unequivocal knowledge (Uneq), we can infer unambiguously that forests are no urban-use lands:

$$\Box_*[\texttt{Forest} \sqsubseteq \neg \texttt{UrbanLandUse}]$$

This holds because each precisification must comply with LC or LU (F8), and we have $\Box_{\textsf{LC}}[\texttt{Forest} \sqsubseteq \neg \texttt{UrbanLandUse}]$ from (F1) and (F5), and $\Box_{\textsf{LU}}[\texttt{Forest} \sqsubseteq \neg \texttt{UrbanLandUse}]$ from (F3) and (F9). Regarding relative (Rel) and contrasting (Cont) knowledge, if we now wanted to query our knowledge base for instances of forest, we would obtain

$$\Box_{\textsf{LC}}[\texttt{Forest}(e)] \wedge \Box_{\textsf{LC}}[\neg \texttt{Forest}(l)] \qquad \mathcal{I}_*[\texttt{Forest}(e)] \wedge \mathcal{I}_*[\texttt{Forest}(l)]$$

The first deduced formula contains knowledge relative to LC, showing its stance on whether the instances constitute a forest, which happens to be conclusive in both cases. The second formula states the global indeterminacy of both l's and e's membership to the concept Forest. This stems from the disagreement between the interpretations LC and LU, whose overall incompatibility ($\Box_{\textsf{LC} \sqcap \textsf{LU}}[\top \sqsubseteq \bot]$) can also be inferred.

Finally, it is worth looking at the limitations of the sentential fragment of Standpoint $\mathcal{SROIQ}b_s$. In a non-sentential setting, where modalities can be used at the concept level, "complex alignments" or bridges can be established between concepts according to possibly many standpoints. For instance, one can write

$$\Box_{\textsf{LU}}[\texttt{Forest}] \sqsubseteq \Box_{\textsf{LC}}[\exists \texttt{hasLand}^-.\texttt{Forest}] \sqcup \Box_*[\texttt{Cleared}]$$

to express that the areas classified as forest according to LU belong to a forest according to LC or have been cleared (in which case LC does not recognise them as forest). It is an objective of future work of ours to study decidable fragments for which the restrictions on the use of modalities are relaxed to express such kinds of axioms.

6   Related Work

A variety of formal representation systems have been proposed to model perspectives in rather diverse areas of research and with heterogeneous nomenclatures. Standpoint logic bears some similarities to *context logic* in the style proposed by McCarthy and Buvac [19], which has also been applied in a description logic setting [15]. This tradition treats contexts as "first-class citizens" of the logic, i.e., full-fledged formal objects over which one can express first-order properties. In contrast, standpoint logic is suitable when a formalisation of the contexts involved is unfeasible, or when the interest resides in the content of the standpoints rather than the context in which they occur.

Another related notion is that of *ontology views*, where some works consider potentially conflicting viewpoints [11,12,25]. Ribiére and Dieng [25] and Heman et al. [11,12]

implement the intuition of "viewpoints" via ad-hoc extensions of the syntax and semantics of description logics, in a style similar to the work on contextuality by Benslimane et al. [4]. Gorshkov et al. [9] implement them using named graphs. Instead, the standpoint approach extends the base language with modalities and provides a Kripke-style semantics for it. This leads to a simpler, more recognisable and more expressive framework that supports, for instance, hierarchies and combinations of standpoints, inferences of partial truths, the preservation of consistency with the established alignments and inferences about the standpoints themselves. On a technical level, first-order standpoint logic can be seen as a many-dimensional (multi-)modal logic [16], whence results from that area apply to our setting. In particular, the search for non-trivial fragments of first-order modal logics that are still decidable and even practically relevant is an important endeavour, for which we believe that standpoint logic can play useful role.

Finally, in the area of ontology modularity, different formalisms such as *DDL bridge rules* [5] and ε-*connections* [17, 18] have been proposed to specify the interaction between independent knowledge sources. These can be related to the present framework in that they provide mechanisms to establish links between conceptual models that do not need to be entirely coherent with each other. Yet the motivation is inherently different: while the standpoint framework focuses on integrating possibly overlapping knowledge into a global source (while preserving "standpoint-provenance" and thus enabling a peaceful coexistence of conflicting information), DDL bridge rules and ε-connections have been devised to establish a certain synchronisation between modules that are and will remain separate. DDL bridge rules could, however, be simulated within a standpoint framework.

7   Conclusions and Future Work

The diversity of human world views along with the semantic heterogeneity of natural language are at the heart of well-recognised knowledge interoperability challenges. As an alternative to the common strategy of merging, we proposed the use of a logical formalism based on the notion of *standpoint* that is suitable for knowledge representation and reasoning with sets of possibly conflicting characterisations of a domain.

Using first-order logic as an expressive underlying language, we proposed a multi-modal framework by means of which different agents can establish their individual standpoints (which typically involves specifying constraints and relations), but which also allows for combining standpoints and establishing alignments between them. Reasoning tasks over such multi-standpoint specifications include gathering unequivocal knowledge, determining knowledge that is relative to a standpoint or a set of them, and contrasting the knowledge that can be inferred from different standpoints.

Remarkably, the simplified Kripke semantics allows us to establish a small model property for the *sentential* fragment of FOSL. This result gave rise to a polynomial, satisfiability-preserving translation into the base logic, which also maintains membership in diverse decidable fragments, immediately implying that for a range of logics, reasoning in their standpoint-enhanced versions does not increase their computational complexity. This indicates that the framework can be applied to ontology alignment, concept negotiation, and knowledge aggregation with inference systems built on top of existing, highly optimised off-the-shelf reasoners.

Future work includes the study of the complexity of FOSL fragments allowing the presence of free variables within the scope of modalities. Note however that in the general case of FOSL, this leads to the loss of the small model property.

Example 2. Consider the following (non-sentential) FOSL sentence, axiomatising "better" (Btt) to be interpreted as a non-well-founded strict linear order and requiring for every domain element x (of infinitely many) the existence of some precisification where x is the (one and only) "best":

$$\forall xyz\big((\mathtt{Btt}(x,y) \wedge \mathtt{Btt}(y,z)) \rightarrow \mathtt{Btt}(x,z)\big) \quad \wedge \qquad \forall xy \neg(\mathtt{Btt}(x,y) \wedge \mathtt{Btt}(y,x)) \wedge$$

$$\forall xy\big(x \neq y \rightarrow (\mathtt{Btt}(x,y) \vee \mathtt{Btt}(y,x))\big) \qquad \wedge \quad \forall x \exists y \mathtt{Btt}(x,y) \wedge \forall x \Diamond_* \neg \exists y \mathtt{Btt}(y,x)$$

Obviously, this sentence is satisfiable, but only in a model with infinitely many precisifications; that is, the small model property is violated in the worst possible way.

On the other hand, it is desirable from a modelling perspective to allow for some interplay between FO quantifiers and standpoint modalities. E.g., the non-sentential FOSL sentence $\forall x_1 \cdots x_k\big(\mathtt{P}(x_1, \ldots, x_k) \rightarrow \Box_* \mathtt{P}(x_1, \ldots, x_k)\big)$ expresses the rigidity of a predicate P, thereby "synchronising" it over all precisifications.

Consequently, we will study how by imposing syntactic restrictions, we can guarantee the existence of small (or at least reasonably-sized) models for non-sentential standpoint formulas. Results in the field of many-dimensional modal logics [16] show that reasoning is decidable for diverse fragments of first-order modal logic such as the *monodic* fragment (where modalities occur only in front of formulas with at most one free variable). However, Example 2 already shows (by virtue of being within the monodic fragment) that we cannot hope for a small model property even for this slight extension of the sentential fragment. A detailed analysis of these issues as they apply to the simplified semantics of standpoint logic is the object of current work.

Additionally, we intend to implement the proposed translations and perform experiments to test the performance of the standpoint framework in scenarios of Knowledge Integration. While sentential standpoints can be added at no extra cost in complexity for the discussed fragments in this paper, we intend to run experiments to assess the runtime impact on large knowledge bases with off-the-shelf reasoners.

As another important topic toward the deployment of our framework, we will look into conceptual modelling aspects. Reviewing documented recurrent scenarios and patterns in the area of knowledge integration, we intend to establish guiding principles for conveniently encoding those by using novel strategies possible with structures of standpoints. Examples for such scenarios include the disambiguation of knowledge sources by using combinations of standpoints, and the establishment of bridge-like rules for alignment. For the latter we will investigate their relationship to similar constructs from other frameworks such as ε-connections, distributed description logics, and others.

Supplemental Material Statement: Proofs can be found in the extended version [30].

Acknowledgments. Lucía Gómez Álvarez was supported by the *Bundesministerium für Bildung und Forschung* (BMBF) in the Center for Scalable Data Analytics and Artificial Intelligence (ScaDS.AI). Sebastian Rudolph has received funding from the European Research Council (Grant Agreement no. 771779, DeciGUT).

References

1. Arp, R., Smith, B., Spear, A.D.: Building ontologies with basic formal ontology. MIT Press (2015)
2. Bárány, V., Benedikt, M., ten Cate, B.: Some model theory of guarded negation. Journal of Symbolic Logic **83**(4), 1307–1344 (2018)
3. Bárány, V., ten Cate, B., Segoufin, L.: Guarded negation. Journal of the ACM 62(3) (2015)
4. Benslimane, D., Arara, A., Falquet, G., Maamar, Z., Thiran, P., Gargouri, F.: Contextual ontologies. Motivations, challenges, and solutions. In: Procs. of the 4th Int. Conf. on Advances in Information Systems. pp. 168–176. Springer (2006)
5. Borgida, A., Serafini, L.: Distributed Description Logics: Assimilating information from peer sources. Journal on Data Semantics **2800**, 153–184 (2003)
6. Euzenat, J., Mocan, A., Scharffe, F.: Ontology alignments. In: Hepp, M., Leenheer, P.D., Moor, A.D., Sure, Y. (eds.) Ontology Management. Computing for Human Experience, vol. 7, pp. 177–206. Springer (2008)
7. Fine, K.: Vagueness, truth and logic. Synthese **30**(3–4), 265–300 (1975)
8. Gómez Álvarez, L., Rudolph, S.: Standpoint logic: Multi-perspective knowledge representation. In: Neuhaus, F., Brodaric, B. (eds.) Procs. of the 12th Int. Conf. on Formal Ontology in Information Systems. FAIA, vol. 344, pp. 3–17. IOS Press (2021)
9. Gorshkov, S., Kralin, S., Miroshnichenko, M.: Multi-viewpoint ontologies for decision-making support. In: Ngonga Ngomo, A.C., Křemen, P. (eds.) Knowledge Engineering and Semantic Web. pp. 3–17. Springer (2016)
10. Grädel, E., Otto, M., Rosen, E.: Two-variable logic with counting is decidable. In: Procs. of the 12th Annual IEEE Symposium on Logic in Computer Science. pp. 306–317. IEEE (1997)
11. Hemam, M.: An extension of the ontology web language with multi-viewpoints and probabilistic reasoning. Int. Journal of Advanced Intelligence Paradigms **10**(3), 247–265 (2018)
12. Hemam, M., Boufaïda, Z.: MVP-OWL: A multi-viewpoints ontology language for the Semantic Web. Int. Journal of Reasoning-based Intelligent Systems **3**(3–4), 147–155 (2011)
13. Horrocks, I., Kutz, O., Sattler, U.: The even more irresistible SROIQ. In: Doherty, P., Mylopoulos, J., Welty, C.A. (eds.) Procs. 10th Int. Conf. on Principles of Knowledge Representation and Reasoning. pp. 57–67. AAAI Press (2006)
14. Kieronski, E., Rudolph, S.: Finite model theory of the triguarded fragment and related logics. In: Procs. of the 36th Annual ACM/IEEE Symposium on Logic in Computer Science. pp. 1–13. IEEE (2021)
15. Klarman, S., Gutiérrez-Basulto, V.: Description logics of context. Journal of Logic and Computation **26**(3), 817–854 (2013)
16. Kurucz, A., Wolter, F., Zakharyaschev, M., Gabbay, D.M.: Many-Dimensional Modal Logics: Theory and Applications, 1st edn. Studies in Logics and the Foundations of Mathematics, Elsevier (2003)
17. Kutz, O., Lutz, C., Wolter, F., Zakharyaschev, M.: E-connections of description logics. Description Logics Workshop 81 (2003)
18. Kutz, O., Lutz, C., Wolter, F., Zakharyaschev, M.: E-connections of abstract description systems. Artificial intelligence **156**(1), 1–73 (2004)
19. McCarthy, J., Buvac, S.: Formalizing context (expanded notes). CSLI Lecture Notes 81, 13–50 (1998)
20. Osman, I., Ben Yahia, S., Diallo, G.: Ontology Integration: Approaches and Challenging Issues. Information Fusion **71**, 38–63 (2021)
21. Otero-Cerdeira, L., Rodríguez-Martínez, F.J., Gómez-Rodríguez, A.: Ontology matching: A literature review. Expert Systems with Applications 42(2) (2015)

22. Pesquita, C., Faria, D., Santos, E., Couto, F.M.: To repair or not to repair: Reconciling correctness and coherence in ontology reference alignments. In: Procs. of the 8th Int. Conf. on Ontology Matching. vol. 1111, pp. 13–24. CEUR (2013)
23. Pietruszczak, A.: Simplified Kripke style semantics for modal logics K45, KB4 and KD45. Bulletin of the Section of Logic **38**(3/4), 163–171 (2009)
24. Pratt-Hartmann, I.: Complexity of the two-variable fragment with counting quantifiers. Journal of Logic, Language, and Information **14**(3), 369–395 (2005)
25. Ribière, M., Dieng-Kuntz, R.: A viewpoint model for cooperative building of an Ontology. In: Procs. of the 10th Int. Conf. on Conceptual Structures. pp. 220–234. Springer (2002)
26. Rudolph, S., Krötzsch, M., Hitzler, P.: Cheap Boolean role constructors for description logics. In: Hölldobler, S., Lutz, C., Wansing, H. (eds.) Procs. of the 11th European Conf. on Logics in Artificial Intelligence. vol. 5293, pp. 362–374. Springer (2008)
27. Rudolph, S., Simkus, M.: The triguarded fragment of first-order logic. In: Barthe, G., Sutcliffe, G., Veanes, M. (eds.) Procs. of the 22nd Int. Conf. on Logic for Programming, Artificial Intelligence and Reasoning. EPiC Series in Computing, vol. 57, pp. 604–619 (2018)
28. Solimando, A., Jiménez-Ruiz, E., Guerrini, G.: Minimizing conservativity violations in ontology alignments. Knowledge and Information Systems 51(3) (2017)
29. Wolter, F., Zakharyaschev, M.: On the decidability of description logics with modal operators. In: Cohn, A.G., Schubert, L.K., Shapiro, S.C. (eds.) Procs. of the Sixth Int. Conf. on Principles of Knowledge Representation and Reasoning. pp. 512–523. Morgan Kaufmann (1998)
30. Álvarez, L.G., Rudolph, S., Strass, H.: How to Agree to Disagree: Managing Ontological Perspectives using Standpoint Logic. Tech. rep., https://arXiv.org/abs/2206.06793 (2022)

Context-Driven Visual Object Recognition Based on Knowledge Graphs

Sebastian Monka[1,2]([✉]), Lavdim Halilaj[1], and Achim Rettinger[2]

[1] Bosch Research, Renningen, Germany
{sebastian.monka,lavdim.halilaj}@de.bosch.com
[2] Trier University, Trier, Germany
rettinger@uni-trier.de

Abstract. Current deep learning methods for object recognition are purely data-driven and require a large number of training samples to achieve good results. Due to their sole dependence on image data, these methods tend to fail when confronted with new environments where even small deviations occur. Human perception, however, has proven to be significantly more robust to such distribution shifts. It is assumed that their ability to deal with unknown scenarios is based on extensive incorporation of contextual knowledge. Context can be based either on object co-occurrences in a scene or on memory of experience. In accordance with the human visual cortex which uses context to form different object representations for a seen image, we propose an approach that enhances deep learning methods by using external contextual knowledge encoded in a knowledge graph. Therefore, we extract different contextual views from a generic knowledge graph, transform the views into vector space and infuse it into a DNN. We conduct a series of experiments to investigate the impact of different contextual views on the learned object representations for the same image dataset. The experimental results provide evidence that the contextual views influence the image representations in the DNN differently and therefore lead to different predictions for the same images. We also show that context helps to strengthen the robustness of object recognition models for out-of-distribution images, usually occurring in transfer learning tasks or real-world scenarios.

Keywords: Neuro-symbolic · Knowledge graph · Contextual learning

1 Introduction

How humans perceive the real world is strongly dependent on the context [1,30]. Especially, in situations with poor quality of visual input, for instance caused by large distances, or short capturing times, context appears to play a major role in improving the reliability of recognition [43]. Perception is not only influenced by co-occurring objects or visual features in the same image, but also by experience and memory [39]. There is evidence that humans perceive similar images

© The Author(s), under exclusive license to Springer Nature Switzerland AG 2022
U. Sattler et al. (Eds.): ISWC 2022, LNCS 13489, pp. 142–160, 2022.
https://doi.org/10.1007/978-3-031-19433-7_9

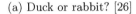

(a) Duck or rabbit? [26]   (b) Young lady or old woman? [2].

Fig. 1. The mental representation for ambiguous images can change based on the context, although the perceived image is still the same.

differently considering the given context [11]. A famous example are ambiguous figures as shown in Fig. 1.

Depending on the context, i.e. if it is Easter or Christmas [10], Fig. 1a can be either a duck or a rabbit. Likewise, influenced by own-age social biases [37], Fig. 1b can be either a young lady or an old woman. Humans categorize images based on various types of context. Known categories are based on visual features or semantic concepts [6], but may also be based on other information such as attributes describing their function. Accordingly, neuroscience has shown that the human brain encodes visual input into individual contextual object representations [16,18,49], namely visual, taxonomical, and functional [33]. Concretely, in a visual context, images of a drum and a barrel have a high similarity, as they share similar visual features. In a taxonomical context, a drum would be similar to a violin, as they both are musical instruments. And in a functional context, the drum would be similar to a hammer, since the same action of hitting can be performed with both objects [8].

Whereas there is much evidence that intelligent machines should also represent information in contextualized embeddings, deep neural networks (DNNs) form their object representations based only on the feature distribution of the image dataset [9,56]. Therefore, they fail if the objects are placed in an incongruent context that was not present in previous seen images [5].

For the scope of this work we investigate the following research questions:

- **RQ1** - Can context provided in form of a KG influence learning image representations of a DNN, the final accuracy, and the image predictions?
- **RQ2** - Can context help to avoid critical errors in domain changing scenarios where DNNs fail?

To enable standard DNNs to build contextual object representations, we provide the context using a knowledge graph (KG) and its corresponding knowledge graph embedding (h_{KG}). Similar to the process in the human brain, we conduct experiments with three different types of contexts, namely visual context, taxonomical context, and functional context 3. We provide two versions of knowledge infusion into a DNN and compare the induction of different contextual models in depth by quantitatively investigating their learned contextual embedding spaces using class-related cosine similarities. In addition we evaluate our approach quantitatively by comparing their final accuracy on object recognition tasks on source and target domains and provide insights and challenges. The structure of this paper is organized as follows: Sect. 6 outlines related work. In Sect. 3.1 we introduce the three different types of context and an option to model these views in a contextual knowledge graph. Section 3 shows two ways of infusing context into a visual DNN. In Sect. 4 we conduct experiments on seven image datasets in two transfer learning scenarios. In Sect. 5 we answer the research questions and summarize the main insights of our approach.

2   Preliminaries

Contextual Image Representations in the Brain. Cognitive and neuroscience research has recently begun to investigate the relationship between viewed objects and the corresponding fMRI scan activities of the human brain. It is assumed that the primate visual system is organized into two separate processing pathways in the visual cortex, namely, the *dorsal pathway* and the *ventral pathway*. While the dorsal pathway is responsible for the spatial recognition of objects as well as actions and manipulations such as grasping, the ventral pathway is responsible for recognizing the type of object based on its form or motion [52]. Bonner et al. [7] recently showed that the sensory coding of objects in the ventral cortex of the human brain is related to statistical embeddings of object or word co-occurrences. Moreover, these object representations potentially reflect a number of different properties, which together are considered to form an object concept [33]. It can be learned based on the context in which the object is seen. For example, an object concept may include the visual features, its taxonomy, or the function of the object [18,49].

Image Representations in the DNN. Recent work has shown that while the performance of humans, monkeys, and DNNs is quite similar for object-level confusions, the image-level performance does not match between different domains [49]. In contrast to visual object representations in the brain, which also include high level contextual knowledge of concepts and their functions, image representations of DNNs only depend on the statistical co-occurrence of visual features and a specific task. We consider the context extracted from the dataset as dataset bias. Even in balanced datasets, i.e., datasets containing the same number of images for each class, there still exists imbalance due to overlap of features between different classes. For instance, it must be taken into account that a cat and a dog have similar visual features and that in composite datasets certain classes can have different meta-information for the images, such as illumination, perspective or sensor resolution. This dataset bias leads to predefined neighborhoods in the visual embedding space, as well as predefined similarities between distinct classes. In a DNN, an *encoder network* $E(\cdot)$ maps images $\boldsymbol{x}$ to a visual embedding $\boldsymbol{h}_v = E(\boldsymbol{x}) \in \mathbb{R}^{d_E}$, where the activations of the final pooling layer and thus the representation layer have a dimensionality d_E, where d_E depends on the encoder network itself.

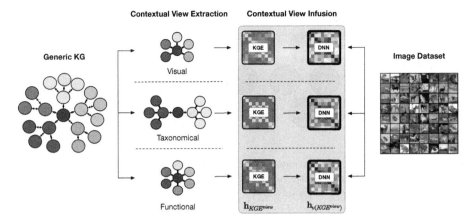

Fig. 2. Our approach to learn contextual image representations consists of two main parts: 1) the *contextual view extraction*; and 2) the *contextual view infusion*.

Contextual Representations in the KG. A knowledge graph is a graph of data aiming to accumulate and convey real-world knowledge, where entities are represented by nodes and relationships between entities are represented by edges [21]. We define a *generic knowledge graph* (*GKG*) as a graph of data that relates different classes of a dataset based on defined contextual properties. These contextual properties can be both learned and manually curated. They bring in prior knowledge about classes, even those that may not necessarily be present in the image dataset, and thus place them in contextual relationships with each other. A KG comprises a set of triples $G = H, R, T$, where H represents entities, $T \subseteq E \times L$ denotes entities or literal values and R, is a set of relationships connecting H and T.

3   Learning Contextual Image Representations

The framework, as shown in Fig. 2 consists of two main parts: 1) the *contextual view extraction*, where task relevant knowledge is extracted from a generic knowledge graph; and 2) the *contextual view infusion*, where the contextual view is infused into the DNN.

3.1   Contextual View Extraction

A knowledge graph can represent prior knowledge encoded with rich semantics in a graph structure. A *GKG* encapsulating n contextual views:

$$GKG \supseteq \{GKG^1, GKG^2, ..., GKG^n\}$$

is a collection of heterogeneous knowledge sources, where each contextual view defines specific relationships between encoded classes. However, for a particular

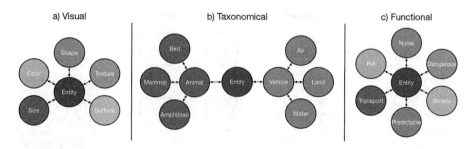

Fig. 3. Context can occur in various ways. Aligned to insights of how humans perceive the world, we present three contextual views of a generic knowledge graph, namely the visual, taxonomical, and functional view.

task only a specific part of a GKG can be relevant. Thus, a subgraph containing a single contextual view:

$$GKG^{view} = query(GKG; view)$$

or a combination of views is extracted from a GKG. Since object recognition models are deployed in the real world that differs from their training domain, it is necessary to encode prior knowledge that is not present in the dataset.

Based on image representations in our brain and on how humans tend to classify objects, we introduce three distinct types of contextual views as shown in Fig. 3. The first contextual view is based on visual, the second view is based on taxonomical, and the third view is based on functional properties.

Visual Context. The visual view (GKG^v) describes high-level visual properties of the classes, for instance properties describing color, shape, or texture. These properties may or may not be present in the image data set. For example if all horses in the dataset are white, we want to encode that horses can also occur in different colors.

Taxonomical Context. The taxonomical view (GKG^t) describes class relationships based on hierarchical schemes. A taxonomy is built by experts and can contain categories based on concepts from biology, living place, feeding method, etc. For instance, a biological taxonomy separate animals from vehicles and divides them into further subcategories.

Functional Context. The functional view (GKG^f) contains properties describing the function of a class. It is known that tools are categorized in the human brain based on their function [33]. In that sense properties as hit, rub, or drill would determine the category of a given tool. However, to broaden the scope, additional functional properties such as noise, transport, or smell can be introduced.

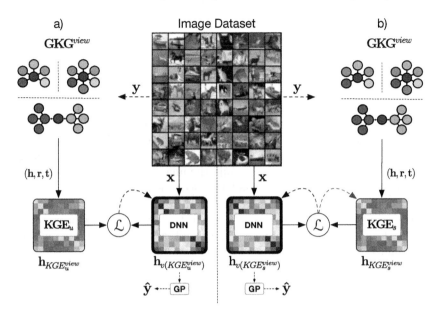

Fig. 4. Contextual view infusion. The contextual object recognition model (DNN) is trained in two different ways: a) using the KG as a trainer, where KGE_u uses no supervision of the image data; or b) using the KG as a peer, where KGE_s uses supervision of the image data. Images $\boldsymbol{x}$ are fed into the DNN, producing $\boldsymbol{h}_{v(KGE^{view})}$ which is compared with $\boldsymbol{h}_{KGE^{view}}$ using the KG-based contrastive loss. In a second step, a gaussian process (GP) or linear layer is trained to predict the class labels $\boldsymbol{y}$ of $\boldsymbol{x}$ based on the trained $\boldsymbol{h}_{v(KGE^{view})}$.

3.2   Contextual View Infusion

When transferring the knowledge from the GKG^{view} using a knowledge graph embedding method (KGE) into a knowledge graph embedding:

$$\boldsymbol{h}_{KGE^{view}} = KGE(GKG^{view})$$

graph based relationships are transferred into spatial relationships. Intuitively, a different context leads to a different representation in the vector space, where $\boldsymbol{h}_{KGE^{view}}$ reflects all relationships that are modelled in GKG^{view}.

As illustrated in Fig. 4, we present two different ways of learning a visual context embedding $\boldsymbol{h}_{v(GKG^{view})}$ following Monka et al. [34]. The first one is $DNN_{KGE_u^{view}}$, which uses the knowledge graph as a trainer [35] and thus learns $\boldsymbol{h}_{KGE_u^{view}}$ without any supervision of image data. The second version is $DNN_{KGE_s^{view}}$, which uses the knowledge graph as a peer and thus learns $\boldsymbol{h}_{v(KGE_s^{view})}$ and $\boldsymbol{h}_{KGE_s^{view}}$ jointly with additional supervision of image data.

Both versions use the contrastive loss to align the image embedding $\boldsymbol{h}_{v(KGE^{view})}$ of the images $\boldsymbol{x}$ and the DNN with the knowledge graph embedding $\boldsymbol{h}_{KGE^{view}}$ of the label information. A batch consists of N augmented training samples. The KG-based contrastive loss is constructed using the individual anchor losses as given by:

$$\mathcal{L}_{KGE^{view}} = \sum_{i=1}^{N} \mathcal{L}_{KGE^{view},i}.$$

Within a batch, an anchor image $i \in \{1...2N\}$ is selected that corresponds to a specific class label $\boldsymbol{y}_i$, where $\boldsymbol{y}_i$ points to its knowledge graph embedding $\boldsymbol{h}_{KGE^{view},i}$. Positive images j are all images of the batch that correspond to the same class label as the anchor i. The numerator in the loss function computes a similarity score between $\boldsymbol{h}_{KGE^{view},i}$ and the image embeddings $\boldsymbol{h}_{v(KGE^{view}),j}$. The denominator computes the similarity score between $\boldsymbol{h}_{KGE^{view},i}$ and the image embeddings $\boldsymbol{h}_{v(KGE),k}$ of all images of the other classes in the batch. As a similarity score, we choose the cosine similarity, which however can be replaced by others. $\mathbb{1}_{k \neq i} \in \{0,1\}$ is an indicator function that returns 1 iff $k \neq i$ evaluates as true, and $\tau > 0$ is a predefined scalar temperature parameter.

$$\mathcal{L}_{KGE^{view},i} = \frac{-1}{2N_{\boldsymbol{y}_i}-1} \sum_{j=1}^{2N} \mathbb{1}_{i \neq j} \cdot \mathbb{1}_{\boldsymbol{y}_i = \boldsymbol{y}_j} \cdot \log \frac{\exp\left(\boldsymbol{h}_{KGE^{view},i} \cdot \boldsymbol{h}_{v(KGE^{view}),j}/\tau\right)}{\sum_{k=1}^{2N} \mathbb{1}_{i \neq k} \exp\left(\boldsymbol{h}_{KGE^{view},i} \cdot \boldsymbol{h}_{v(KGE^{view}),k}/\tau\right)}$$

Prediction. To predict the class labels of unknown images it is common to train a linear layer (LL) or to use a gaussian process (GP) on top of $\boldsymbol{h}_{v(KGE^{view})}$. For GP, we run the whole training dataset through the trained DNN and calculate the mean and covariance matrices for all the classes in $\boldsymbol{h}_{v(KGE^{view})}$. GP and LL, both calculate decision boundaries in $\boldsymbol{h}_{v(KGE^{view})}$ for all the classes of the dataset. At inference, where the goal is to predict the class label of an unknown image, GP or LL assign probabilities if an image belongs to a specific class. The maximal probability is chosen to be the final prediction.

4   Experiments

The goal of our empirical investigations is to provide an answer to **RQ1** and **RQ2**. Therefore we conduct experiments with seven datasets in the two specific domain generalization settings, Cifar10 and Mini-ImageNet. For both experiments, we build separate GKGs that include three different contextual views, the visual (GKG^v), the taxonomical (GKG^t), and the functional (GKG^f) view, respectively. Based on the framework in Sect. 3, we use GKG^{view} to learn a contextual DNN in combination with image data. We evaluate and compare both versions of our approach, $DNN_{KGE_u^{view}}$ and $DNN_{KGE_s^{view}}$.

4.1   Implementation Details

For both experiments, we use a similar implementation of our approach. From the GKG, we extract various GKG^{view}s using respective SPARQL queries. A

ResNet-18 architecture is used as a DNN-backend, with a 128-dimensional MLP as the head. We train all configurations using an ADAM optimizer, a learning rate of 0.001, no weight decay, and a cosine annealing scheduler with a learning decay rate of 0.1. The images are augmented via random cropping, random horizontal flipping, color jittering, random grayscaling, and resizing to 32×32 pixels. All models are trained for 500 epochs. For a) $DNN_{KGE_u\,view}$ we transform GKG^{view} into vector space using a graph auto encoder (GAE) [28], which we denote as the $DNN_{GAE^{view}}$ model. Our GAE comprises two convolutional layers, with a hidden layer dimension of 128. We train the GAE using an ADAM optimizer with a learning rate of 0.01 for 500 epochs. For b) $DNN_{KGE_s^{view}}$, a graph attention network (GAT) [45] is trained in combination with the image data, denoted as the $DNN_{GAT^{view}}$ model. The GAT consists of two GAT-layers with 256 hidden dimensions, 8 heads, and an output dimension of 128. Training is performed via the same KG-based contrastive loss from the images in addition to the GKG^{view} input. We optimize the GAT using an ADAM optimizer with a learning rate of 0.001 and no weight decay.

4.2 Experiments on Cifar10

Dataset settings. The source domain Cifar10 [29] consists of 6000 32×32 color images for each of the 10 classes, namely airplane, bird, automobile, cat, deer, dog, horse, frog, ship, and truck. The target domain Stl10 [14] includes 500 96×96 color images for each of the 10 classes, namely airplane, bird, automobile, cat, deer, dog, horse, monkey, ship, and truck.

Knowledge graph construction. We build a GKG that includes the previously discussed three types of context, as shown in Fig. 3. GKG^v contains visual properties like: *hasBackground*: air, forest, water; *hasColor*: black, blue, brown; *hasPart*: eyes, legs, wings; *hasShape*: rectangular, ellipsoid, cross; *hasSize*: large, medium, small; or *hasTexture*: dotted, striped, uniform. GKG^t contains a taxonomy of the classes using the type-relation. For example, the class *Horse* is-a *Mammal* and is-an *Animal* or the class *Ship* is-a *Water-vehicle* and is-a *Vehicle*. GKG^f defines the function of the class, e.g. properties like: *hasMovement*: drive, fly, swim; *hasSound*: bark, meow, vroom; *hasSpeed*: fast, medium, slow; *hasWeight*: heavy, light, middle. Our GKG contains in total 34 classes, 16 object properties, and 65 individuals. Please note that our GKG is only an example and we are aware that there are unlimited possibilities of how and what type of knowledge can be modeled in a knowledge graph.

Evaluation. To evaluate our approach we first investigate the learned embeddings, if and how semantic relationships from GKG^{view} are reflected in $\boldsymbol{h}_{GKG^{view}}$. Second, we compare the individual class accuracies to see how these relationships influence the final object recognition. Figure 5 shows an analysis: a) the visual view; b) the taxonomical view; and c) the functional view. For every cell in $\boldsymbol{h}_{GAE^{view}}$ we calculate the cosine similarity between the corresponding nodes, i.e. the classes of the image dataset, and for $\boldsymbol{h}_{v(GAE^{view})}$ we calculate

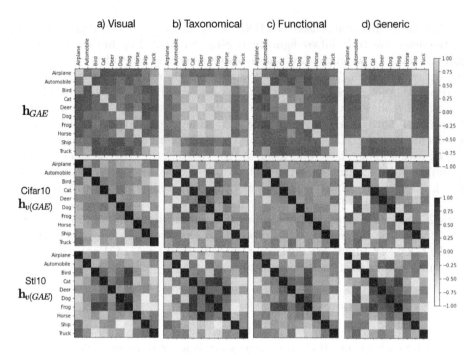

Fig. 5. We compare $h_{GAE^{view}}$ and $h_{v(GAE^{view})}$ based on: a) the visual view; b) the taxonomical view; c) the functional view; and d) the full generic KG. To investigate how the semantic relationships are reflected in the embeddings, we illustrate the individual cosine similarities between the classes of the Cifar10 and the Stl10 dataset.

the class-means of the image representations. Since the goal is to learn contextual image classifiers, we investigate if context is transferred to $h_{GKG^{view}}$ and $h_{v(GKG^{view})}$, respectively. It can be seen that semantic relationships provided by the GKG^{view} are reflected in $h_{GAE^{view}}$. In h_{GAE^v}, the airplane has the highest similarity to the truck and the bird, in h_{GAE^t}, the airplane has the highest similarity to the ship, in h_{GAE^f}, the airplane has the highest similarity to the automobile, and h_{GAE} the airplane has a high similarity to all vehicles. Further, one notices that taxonomical and generic h_{GAE} have two main distinctive groups in the embedding space. In h_{GAE^t} and h_{GAE} vehicles and animals have a high inter-cluster, but a small intra-cluster variance. For $h_{v(GAE^{view})}$, we observe that similarities in the GKG^{view} and $h_{GAE^{view}}$ are only partially reflected. All $h_{v(GAE^{view})}$ seem to have a similar underlying pattern of the class distribution, with minor differences. We think that implicit relations between class features interfere with the similarities given by h_{GAE} and the GKG. Further we retrieve different distributions for either Cifar10 or Stl10. This behaviour can be explained by the distribution shift between source and target domain. While the network attempts to separate classes in the training domain Cifar10, this separation is less successful in the testing domain Stl10.

Table 1. Comparison of the individual class accuracies for the Cifar10 dataset as training domain and the Stl10 dataset as testing domain. We compare the contextual view trained DNNs against their baseline SupSSL.

(a) Results on Cifar10

Cifar10	Airplane	Auto	Bird	Cat	Deer	Dog	Frog	Horse	Ship	Truck	All
SupSSL	95.1	97.0	91.8	83.9	92.9	85.7	96.0	93.5	96.8	95.9	92.9
ΔDNN_{GAE^v}	−1.2	**0.5**	−2.6	−0.2	**2.3**	−0.8	−0.2	−1.1	−0.5	−0.9	−0.5
ΔDNN_{GAE^t}	−0.9	−0.6	−1.2	−30.8	−29.8	−0.2	−2.2	−1.6	−1.5	−1.3	−7.0
ΔDNN_{GAE^f}	**1.0**	0.2	−1.1	**1.9**	0.1	0.6	**0.7**	1.2	−0.1	−0.4	**0.4**
ΔDNN_{GAE}	−0.7	0.0	−2.3	0.4	0.6	−0.6	−1.1	0.0	0.3	−1.8	−0.5
ΔDNN_{GAT^v}	−0.6	−0.3	**0.2**	0.3	0.1	−1.0	0.3	0.9	**0.7**	−0.8	−0.0
ΔDNN_{GAT^t}	−0.9	0.0	−1.7	1.8	0.1	1.0	0.4	0.5	−0.1	0.3	0.1
ΔDNN_{GAT^f}	−0.4	**0.5**	−3.0	1.7	1.5	−0.4	0.4	0.8	0.4	−0.1	0.1
ΔDNN_{GAT}	−1.0	0.3	−1.8	1.2	−0.3	**2.0**	−0.5	**1.7**	0.0	**0.7**	0.2

(b) Results on Stl10

Stl10	Airplane	Auto	Bird	Cat	Deer	Dog	Frog	Horse	Ship	Truck	All
SupSSL	85.4	86.9	82.4	56.6	91.5	60.5	−	76.5	84.5	74.1	77.6
ΔDNN_{GAE^v}	1.0	0.2	−2.6	**3.4**	**1.2**	−4.5	−	−4.8	−0.6	3.9	−0.3
ΔDNN_{GAE^t}	2.4	−1.0	−1.5	−10.1	−32.9	0.2	−	−0.5	−1.6	−1.6	−5.2
ΔDNN_{GAE^f}	1.9	−0.8	−1.3	1.4	−2.4	−0.5	−	**3.4**	0.9	3.3	**0.7**
ΔDNN_{GAE}	0.4	**0.5**	−1.9	1.8	−1.5	2.6	−	−1.4	−0.6	2.1	0.2
ΔDNN_{GAT^v}	0.5	−0.9	**2.6**	−0.6	−0.1	0.5	−	0.5	1.0	0.0	0.4
ΔDNN_{GAT^t}	1.0	−2.1	−0.5	1.9	−0.4	0.8	−	0.5	**1.6**	3.0	0.6
ΔDNN_{GAT^f}	**2.7**	−0.3	−1.5	−0.7	−1.0	−2.6	−	0.0	0.4	1.8	−0.1
ΔDNN_{GAT}	−1.6	−1.0	−2.6	−2.2	−1.2	**2.8**	−	3.1	1.2	**4.3**	0.3

In Table 1 we compare the final object recognition accuracy of the contextual DNNs, compared to their baseline SupSSL. SupSSL is the same model trained with the supervised contrastive loss [27] and without auxiliary context. We observe that for different contextual infusions the overall accuracy is not significantly impacted. For Cifar10 ΔDNN_{GAE^t} with −7.0 is the worst performing model, whereas ΔDNN_{GAE^f} with 0.4 is the best performing model. We marked the best performing model for every class in bold. It can be seen that for every class a different contextual model is outperforming the others. It also shows that context influences the focus a DNN puts on predicting a specific class. Table 1b shows the relative accuracies of the contextual models on the Stl10 dataset. Note that the models are only trained on Cifar10 data. The goal of that domain generalization scenario is to test the robustness of the models. When evaluated on the target domain, it can be observed that almost in every contextual model the relative accuracy is increased compared to the baseline with no contextual knowledge. In scenarios where the domain changes, we observe strange phenomena occurring such that the model with the second worst performance DNN_{GAE}^t for the class Aircraft of the Cifar10 dataset is the model with the second best performance for Aircraft on Stl10. However, for most of the classes, we see a

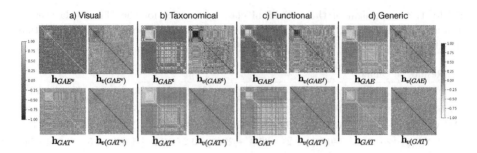

Fig. 6. We compare $h_{GAE^{view}}$ and $h_{v(GAE^{view})}$, as well as $h_{GAT^{view}}$ and $h_{v(GAT^{view})}$ based on, a) the visual view, b) the taxonomical view, c) the functional view, and d) the full generic KG. To investigate how the semantic relationships are reflected in the embeddings, we illustrate the individual cosine similarities between the classes of the Mini-ImageNet dataset.

trend that the best performing model for a class in Cifar10 tends to perform also better on the target domain.

4.3   Experiments on Mini-ImageNet

Dataset settings. We use Mini-ImageNet, a subset of the ImageNet dataset, as our training domain. It contains 100 classes, each having 600 images of size 84 × 84. As testing domain we use ImageNetV2 [40] comprising 10 new test images per class, ImageNet-Sketch [46] with 50 images per class, ImageNet-R [19], which has 150 images in the style of art, cartoons, deviantart, and ImageNet-A [20] with 7.500 unmodified real-world examples.

Knowledge Graph Construction. Our GKG is build using the three contextual views as depicted in Fig. 3. GKG^v contains visual properties, e.g. *hasColor*: black, blue, brown; *hasTexture*: dotted, striped, uniform; *hasSize*: large, medium-large, small; and *hasShape*: ellipsoid, quadratic, rectangular. GKG^t contains a taxonomy of the classes using the type-relation. Following DBpedia [3], the class *Malamute* is-a *Dog*, is-a *Mammal*, is-an *Animal*, is-an *Eukaryote*, and is-a *Species*. GKG^f defines the function of a class with properties like: *hasSpeed*: fast, static, slow; *hasWeight*: heavy, light, middle; or *hasTransportation*: goods, none, people. Our GKG contains in total 166 classes, 14 object properties, and 183 individuals.

Evaluation. Due to the difficulty of deeply investigating 100 × 100 class similarities, we provide a qualitative overview of the embedding spaces. Figure 6 shows a qualitative comparison of $h_{KGE^{view}}$ and $h_{v(KGE^{view})}$ of a) the visual view; b) the taxonomical view; c) the functional view; and d) the generic knowledge graph. Complementing the experiment in Sect. 4.2, we illustrate the class similarities of h_{GAT} and $h_{v(GAT)}$ learned using image data as supervision. Interestingly, it can be observed that the similarities in h_{GAT} and h_{GAE} follow a similar pattern, but h_{GAE} seems to have a stronger contrast. However, when investigating

Table 2. Comparison of the contextual view models and their SupSSL baseline on the Mini-ImageNet and its derivatives, Mini-ImageNet (Mini), ImageNetV2 (V2), ImageNet-Sketch (Sketch), ImageNet-R (R), and ImageNet-A (A).

ImageNet	Mini	V2	Sketch	R	A
SupSSL	58.6	43.0	20.3	4.3	1.2
ΔDNN_{GAE^v}	−0.3	0.0	−0.6	**0.2**	−0.2
ΔDNN_{GAE^t}	−19.6	−13.7	−8.8	−2.8	0.0
ΔDNN_{GAE^f}	−5.2	−3.3	−2.3	−0.7	**0.3**
ΔDNN_{GAE}	0.8	1.6	−0.6	−0.1	−0.1
ΔDNN_{GAT^v}	0.9	**2.3**	**0.2**	0.0	**0.3**
ΔDNN_{GAT^t}	**1.3**	0.6	0.1	0.1	0.0
ΔDNN_{GAT^f}	0.4	0.4	0.0	−0.1	−0.1
ΔDNN_{GAT}	0.5	0.6	0.1	0.0	0.0

Fig. 7. Contextual Predictions of DNN_{GAE} (GAE) and DNN_{GAT} (GAT) and their contextual view on Mini-ImageNet. The contextual view influences the image representation and therefore the final prediction for the same input image.

the learned image representations in $h_{v(GAT)}$ it is hard to spot the differences between the individual contextual models.

As depicted in Table 2 DNN_{GAE}^t and DNN_{GAE}^f are outperformed by the baseline $SupSSL$ and the other models with different contextual views by a large margin. In contrast to the Cifar10 experiment where the least performing model is only 8% worse than the baseline, in Mini-ImageNet the worst is around 34%. Further, we see that DNN_{GAT^t} does not suffer from constraints given by GKG^t. This finding confirms our assumption that a joint training can soften the constraints of the GKG.

Similar to the example of ambiguous figures in Fig. 1, our approach enables DNNs to interpret the same image in various ways using contextual views given by a knowledge graph. The results in Fig. 7 show that for out of distribution images the contextual views play a major role for giving reasonable predictions. The idea is that some class confusions are not that critical as others. In that sense, for some tasks it is uncritical to confuse a goose with a house finch as they are both part of the bird family, however confusing a music instrument (oboe), with a dog (malamute) could lead to problems. We also see that DNN_{GAE} (GAE) and DNN_{GAT} (GAT) do not necessarily predict the same image based on the given context. We believe that further research is needed w.r.t. investigating how to best incorporate context in combination with image data.

5   Discussion and Insights

With our work, we provided a method to infuse context in form of GKG^{view} into DNNs for visual object recognition. However, knowledge infusion is not straight-forward, as problems of machine learning, such as hyper-parameter selection, weight initialization, or dataset dependence, strongly influence the learned representations. Regarding **RQ1** - Can context provided in form of a KG influence learning image representations of a DNN, the final accuracy, and the image predictions? - we list the insights obtained from our investigations:

- GKG^{view} **defines class-relationships.** We showed that various contextual views can be extracted from a GKG and that different views lead to different relationships between classes of the dataset.

- $h_{KGE^{view}}$ **needs to reflect** GKG^{view}. The embedding method itself also influences the $h_{KGE^{view}}$ and the performance of the final prediction model. Context can get lost when transferring GKG^{view} into $h_{KGE^{view}}$. Hard constraints either in GKG^{view} or produced by the KGE-method, e.g. to represent dissimilar classes in $h_{KGE^{view}}$ together, can drastically reduce the prediction accuracy.

- $h_{GAE^{view}}$ **is only partially reflected in** $h_{v(GAE^{view})}$. Since data-driven approaches have a strong dependence on the dataset distribution, $h_{GAE^{view}}$ only influences $h_{v(GAE^{view})}$ to form a hybrid representation. We see that data augmentation weakens the dataset bias and helps to align $h_{v(GAE^{view})}$ with $h_{GAE^{view}}$.

- **Joint training reduces the impact of** GKG. Both the learned $h_{v(KGE_s)}$ and the achieved accuracy values are only slightly affected by the induced GKG. Neither the qualitative evaluation of $h_{v(KGE_s)}$ nor the quantitative evaluation based on accuracy show any significant contextual changes.

- **Context shifts the focus on learning specific classes.** We assume that the context constraints the DNN and its hypothesis space. It is known that DNNs tend to memorize spurious correlations that can lead to catastrophic errors in the real world. We think that the task of our contextual models is to prevent exactly these errors. In our experiments, we showed that specific contextual models performed better on specific classes. We assume that context can shift the overall interest of a DNN to predict a certain class.

- **Context rather influences individual image predictions.** Similar to the proposed motivation of how humans interpret ambiguous figures we see context influencing the prediction of difficult or undefinable images in the dataset. Regarding **RQ2** - Can context help to avoid critical errors in domain changing scenarios where DNNs fail?

- **Context makes more robust against domain changes.**

It can be seen that almost every contextual model increases its relative accuracy compared to the baseline when evaluated on the target domain. Moreover, contextual models that performed better on the source dataset tend to perform better if domain change occurs. We argue that GKG^{view} regularizes the strong dependency on the source domain and thus increases the performance on the target domain.

6 Related Work

Contextual information has always been of great interest for improving computer vision systems. We structure related work into implicit-contextual visual models, explicit-contextual visual models, and contextual knowledge graph embeddings.

Implicit-Contextual Visual Models. Contextualize relationships between visual features that occur in the image itself. They are used for object priming, where the context defines a prior on the detection parameters [43] or for object detection and segmentation, where boosting is used to relate objects in an image [44]. Wu et al. [51] improved object recognition by processing object regions and context regions in parallel. To overcome the drawback of small receptive fields from standard CNNs, extensions that incorporate visual features from far image regions [24,25] or alternative architectures, such as vision transformers (ViTs) [53] have been established recently. Moreover, Gao et al. [17] proposed that all modern DNNs are part of the implicit-contextual models since they aggregate contextual information over image regions.

Explicit-Contextual Visual Models. Use higher level information like object co-occurrences or semantic concept relationships. They induce additional contextual information that is either not in the dataset or cannot be automatically extracted by the DNN [22]. To create explicit context based on object relations, most methods use scene graphs which describe a scene based on symbolic representations of entities and their spatial and semantic relations. Scene graphs have been applied to the task of collective or group activity recognition [13,15], object recognition [55,56], object detection [12,32] and visual question answering [42]. Label graphs [23] apply fine-grained labels to an image and are used to improve object recognition and reasoning over object relationships [4]. Semantic scene graphs extend scene graphs by textual descriptions and fine-grained labels of a scene [31]. Context-aware zero-shot learning for object recognition [54] or compositional zero-shot learning methods [36] add observed visual primitive states (e.g. old, cute) to objects (e.g. car, dog) to build an embedding space based on visual context. However, scene correlations need to be addressed very carefully, as implicit-contextual models can heavily depend on learned contextual relationships that are only valid for a specific dataset configuration. Therefore, work was already done to decorrelate objects and their visual features to improve model generalization [41].

Contextual Knowledge Graph Embeddings. Whereas our approach extracts the contextual views in a previous step before the actual knowledge graph embedding, there exist works that create contextualized KG embeddings based on the full KG. Werner et al. [50] introduced a KG embedding over temporal contextualized KG facts. Their recurrent transformer enables to transform global KGEs into contextual embeddings, given the situation-specific factors of the relation and the subjective history of the entity. Ning et al. [38] proposed a lightweight framework for the usage of context within standard embedding methods. Wang et al. [47] presented a deep contextualized knowledge graph embedding method that learns representations of entities and relations from constructed contextual entity-relation chains. Wang et al. [48] introduced the contextualized KG embedding method (CoKE). They propose to take the contextual nature of KGs into account, by learning dynamic, flexible, and fully contextualized entity and relation embeddings.

7   Conclusion and Future Work

In this work, we proposed a framework for context-driven visual object recognition based on knowledge graphs. We qualitatively and quantitatively investigated how different contextual views, as well as their embedding and their infusion method, influence the learned DNN. Further, we have seen that contextual models tend to have a minor impact on the final accuracy, but a major impact on how individual classes or images are represented and predicted. In particular, for out of distribution data, where data-driven approaches suffer from less knowledge, contextual image representations help to constrain the hypothesis space, leading to more reasonable predictions. However, there are still challenges to be faced. We conducted intensive research about a possible context infusion approach and emerging challenges. On the one hand, we have the implementation of the infusion method, which itself heavily depends on modeling choices, weight initialization, as well as network and hyper-parameter selection. On the other hand, there is a strong dependence on the image data, which originally comes with an initial dataset bias. This dataset bias limits the ability to influence image data representations and thus predictions influenced by prior knowledge. However, our work showed that with deeper investigations of all the influencing parameters knowledge-infused learning is a promising approach to build context-driven and future intelligent systems.

Acknowledgement. This publication was created as part of the research project "KI Delta Learning" (project number: 19A19013D) funded by the Federal Ministry for Economic Affairs and Energy (BMWi) on the basis of a decision by the German Bundestag.

References

1. The role of context in object recognition. Trends in Cognitive Sciences (2007)
2. Attneave, F.: Multistability in perception. Sci. Am. **225**(6), 63–71 (1971)
3. Auer, S., Bizer, C., Kobilarov, G., Lehmann, J., Cyganiak, R., Ives, Z.G.: DBpedia: a nucleus for a web of open data. In: The Semantic Web - 6th International Semantic Web Conference ISWC (2007)
4. Battaglia, P.W., Pascanu, R., Lai, M., Rezende, D.J., Kavukcuoglu, K.: Interaction networks for learning about objects, relations and physics. In: Advances in Neural Information Processing Systems 29: Annual Conference on Neural Information Processing Systems (2016)
5. Beery, S., Van Horn, G., Perona, P.: Recognition in terra incognita. In: Ferrari, V., Hebert, M., Sminchisescu, C., Weiss, Y. (eds.) ECCV 2018. LNCS, vol. 11220, pp. 472–489. Springer, Cham (2018). https://doi.org/10.1007/978-3-030-01270-0_28
6. Biederman, I.: Recognition-by-components: a theory of human image understanding. Psychol. Rev. **94**(2), 115–147 (1987)
7. Bonner, M., Epstein, R.: Object representations in the human brain reflect the co-occurrence statistics of vision and language. Nat. Commun. **12**, 4081 (2021)
8. Bracci, S., Daniels, N., Op de Beeck, H.: Task Context Overrules Object- and Category-Related Representational Content in the Human Parietal Cortex. Cereb. Cortex **27**(1), 310–321 (2017)
9. Brendel, W., Bethge, M.: Approximating CNNs with bag-of-local-features models works surprisingly well on imageNet. In: 7th International Conference on Learning Representations, ICLR (2019)
10. Brugger, P., Brugger, S.: The Easter bunny in October: is it disguised as a duck? Percept. Mot. Skills **76**, 2 (1993)
11. Chambers, D., Reisberg, D.: Can mental images be ambiguous? J. Exp. Psychol. Human Perception Perform. **11**(3), 317–328 (1985)
12. Chen, X., Li, L., Fei-Fei, L., Gupta, A.: Iterative visual reasoning beyond convolutions. In: Conference on Computer Vision and Pattern Recognition, CVPR (2018)
13. Choi, W., Savarese, S.: A unified framework for multi-target tracking and collective activity recognition. In: Fitzgibbon, A., Lazebnik, S., Perona, P., Sato, Y., Schmid, C. (eds.) ECCV 2012. LNCS, vol. 7575, pp. 215–230. Springer, Heidelberg (2012). https://doi.org/10.1007/978-3-642-33765-9_16
14. Coates, A., Ng, A., Lee, H.: An analysis of single-layer networks in unsupervised feature learning. In: Proceedings of the Fourteenth International Conference on Artificial Intelligence and Statistics (2011)
15. Deng, Z., Vahdat, A., Hu, H., Mori, G.: Structure inference machines: recurrent neural networks for analyzing relations in group activity recognition. In: 2016 IEEE Conference on Computer Vision and Pattern Recognition, CVPR (2016)
16. DiCarlo, J.J., Cox, D.D.: Untangling invariant object recognition. Trends in Cogn. Sci. **11**(8), 333–341 (2007)

17. Gao, P., Lu, J., Li, H., Mottaghi, R., Kembhavi, A.: Container: context aggregation networks. In: Advances in Neural Information Processing Systems 34: Annual Conference on Neural Information Processing Systems (2021)
18. Greene, M.R., Hansen, B.C.: Disentangling the independent contributions of visual and conceptual features to the spatiotemporal dynamics of scene categorization. bioRxiv (2020)
19. Hendrycks, D., et al.: The many faces of robustness: a critical analysis of out-of-distribution generalization. arXiv preprint arXiv:2006.16241 (2020)
20. Hendrycks, D., Zhao, K., Basart, S., Steinhardt, J., Song, D.: Natural adversarial examples. arXiv preprint arXiv:1907.07174 (2019)
21. Hogan, A., et al.: Knowledge graphs. Synthesis Lectures on Data, Semantics, and Knowledge (2021)
22. Hoiem, D., Efros, A.A., Hebert, M.: Geometric context from a single image. In: International Conference on Computer Vision ICCV, Computer Society (2005)
23. Hu, H., Zhou, G., Deng, Z., Liao, Z., Mori, G.: Learning structured inference neural networks with label relations. In: IEEE Conference on Computer Vision and Pattern Recognition, CVPR, Computer Society (2016)
24. Hu, J., Shen, L., Albanie, S., Sun, G., Vedaldi, A.: Gather-excite: exploiting feature context in convolutional neural networks. In: Advances in Neural Information Processing Systems: Annual Conference on Neural Information Processing Systems (2018)
25. Hu, J., Shen, L., Albanie, S., Sun, G., Wu, E.: Squeeze-and-excitation networks. IEEE Trans. Pattern Anal. Mach, Intell. **42**, 1–34 (2020)
26. Jastrow, J.: Fact and fable in psychology. D Appleton & Company, New York (1900)
27. Khosla, P., et al.: Supervised contrastive learning. In: Advances in Neural Information Processing Systems: Annual Conference on Neural Information Processing Systems (2020)
28. Kipf, T.N., Welling, M.: Variational graph auto-encoders. arXiv preprint arXiv:1611.07308 (2016)
29. Krizhevsky, A.: Learning multiple layers of features from tiny images. Technology Reports (2009)
30. Lauer, T., Schmidt, F., Võ, M.: The role of contextual materials in object recognition. Sci. Rep. **11**, 21988 (2021)
31. Li, Y., Zhang, D., Mu, Y.: Visual-semantic matching by exploring high-order attention and distraction. In: IEEE/CVF Conference on Computer Vision and Pattern Recognition, CVPR (2020)
32. Liu, Y., Wang, R., Shan, S., Chen, X.: Structure inference net: Object detection using scene-level context and instance-level relationships. In: IEEE Conference on Computer Vision and Pattern Recognition, CVPR (2018)
33. Martin, A.: GRAPES—Grounding representations in action, perception, and emotion systems: how object properties and categories are represented in the human brain. Psychon. Bull. Rev. **23**(4), 979–990 (2016). https://doi.org/10.3758/s13423-015-0842-3
34. Monka, S., Halilaj, L., Rettinger, A.: A survey on visual transfer learning using knowledge graphs. Semantic Web **13**(3), 477–510 (2022)
35. Monka, S., Halilaj, L., Schmid, S., Rettinger, A.: Learning visual models using a knowledge graph as a trainer. In: The Semantic Web - 20th International Semantic Web Conference, ISWC (2021)

36. Naeem, M.F., Xian, Y., Tombari, F., Akata, Z.: Learning graph embeddings for compositional zero-shot learning. In: IEEE Conference on Computer Vision and Pattern Recognition, CVPR (2021)
37. Nicholls, M.E.R., Churches, O., Loetscher, T.: Perception of an ambiguous figure is affected by own-age social biases. Sci. Rep. **8**, 12661 (2018)
38. Ning, Z., Qiao, Z., Dong, H., Du, Y., Zhou, Y.: LightCAKE: a lightweight framework for context-aware knowledge graph embedding. In: Karlapalem, K., et al. (eds.) PAKDD 2021. LNCS (LNAI), vol. 12714, pp. 181–193. Springer, Cham (2021). https://doi.org/10.1007/978-3-030-75768-7_15
39. Rafetseder, E., et al.: Children struggle beyond preschool-age in a continuous version of the ambiguous figures task. Psychol. Res. **85**(2), 828–841 (2019). https://doi.org/10.1007/s00426-019-01278-z
40. Recht, B., Roelofs, R., Schmidt, L., Shankar, V.: Do imageNet classifiers generalize to imageNet? In: ICML (2019)
41. Singh, K.K., Mahajan, D., Grauman, K., Lee, Y.J., Feiszli, M., Ghadiyaram, D.: Don't judge an object by its context: Learning to overcome contextual bias. In: IEEE/CVF Conference on Computer Vision and Pattern Recognition, CVPR. Computer Vision Foundation (2020)
42. Teney, D., Liu, L., van den Hengel, A.: Graph-structured representations for visual question answering. In: IEEE Conference on Computer Vision and Pattern Recognition, CVPR (2017)
43. Torralba, A.: Contextual priming for object detection. Int. J. Comput. Vis. 53, 169–191 (2003). https://doi.org/10.1023/A:1023052124951
44. Torralba, A., Murphy, K.P., Freeman, W.T.: Contextual models for object detection using boosted random fields. In: Neural Information Processing Systems NIPS (2004)
45. Velickovic, P., Cucurull, G., Casanova, A., Romero, A., Liò, P., Bengio, Y.: Graph attention networks. In: International Conference on Learning Representations ICLR (2018)
46. Wang, H., Ge, S., Lipton, Z., Xing, E.P.: Learning robust global representations by penalizing local predictive power. In: NeurIPS (2019)
47. Wang, H., Kulkarni, V., Wang, W.Y.: Dolores: deep contextualized knowledge graph embeddings. In: Conference on Automated Knowledge Base Construction, AKBC 2020, Virtual, 22–24 June 2020 (2020)
48. Wang, Q., et al.: Coke: contextualized knowledge graph embedding (2019)
49. Wardle, S.G., Baker, C.I.: Recent advances in understanding object recognition in the human brain: deep neural networks, temporal dynamics, and context. F1000Res. **9**, 590 (2020)
50. Werner, S., Rettinger, A., Halilaj, L., Lüttin, J.: RETRA: recurrent transformers for learning temporally contextualized knowledge graph embeddings. In: Verborgh, R., et al. (eds.) ESWC 2021. LNCS, vol. 12731, pp. 425–440. Springer, Cham (2021). https://doi.org/10.1007/978-3-030-77385-4_25
51. Wu, K., Wu, E., Kreiman, G.: Learning scene gist with convolutional neural networks to improve object recognition. In: 52nd Annual Conference on Information Sciences and Systems CISS (2018)
52. Yang, X., Yan, J., Wang, W., Li, S., Hu, B., Lin, J.: Brain-inspired models for visual object recognition: an overview. Artificial Intelligence Review (2022)
53. Yu, Q., Xia, Y., Bai, Y., Lu, Y., Yuille, A., Shen, W.: Glance-and-gaze vision transformer (NeurIPS) (2021)

54. Zablocki, E., Bordes, P., Soulier, L., Piwowarski, B., Gallinari, P.: Context-aware zero-shot learning for object recognition. In: Proceedings of the 36th International Conference on Machine Learning ICML (2019)
55. Zhang, M., Feng, J., Montejo, K., Kwon, J., Lim, J.H., Kreiman, G.: Lift-the-flap: Context reasoning using object-centered graphs. arXiv preprint arXiv:1902.00163 (2019)
56. Zhang, M., Tseng, C., Kreiman, G.: Putting visual object recognition in context. In: IEEE/CVF Conference on Computer Vision and Pattern Recognition CVPR (2020)

EaT-PIM: Substituting Entities in Procedural Instructions Using Flow Graphs and Embeddings

Sola S. Shirai[1]([⊠]) and HyeongSik Kim[2]

[1] Rensselaer Polytechnic Institute, Troy, NY 12180, USA
shiras2@rpi.edu
[2] Robert Bosch LLC, Sunnyvale, CA, USA
Hyeongsik.Kim@us.bosch.com

Abstract. When cooking, it can sometimes be desirable to substitute ingredients for purposes such as avoiding allergens, replacing a missing ingredient, or exploring new flavors. More generally, the problem of substituting entities used in procedural instructions is challenging as it requires an understanding of how entities and actions in the instructions interact to produce the final result. To support the task of automatically identifying viable substitutions, we introduce a methodology to (1) parse instructions, using NLP tools and domain-specific ontologies, to generate flow graph representations, (2) train a novel embedding model which captures flow and interaction of entities in each step of the instructions, and (3) utilize the embeddings to identify plausible substitutions. Our embedding strategy aggregates nodes and dynamically computes intermediate results within the flow graphs, which requires learning embeddings for fewer nodes than typical graph embedding models. Our rule-based flow graph generation method shows comparable performance to machine learning-based work, while our embedding model outperforms baselines on a link-prediction task for ingredients in recipes.

Keywords: Procedural instructions · Cooking recipes · Information extraction · Ingredient substitution · Knowledge graph embedding

1 Introduction

Procedural instructions are a valuable source of information which provide descriptions of how to carry out a task or achieve some goal. Such instructions are typically presented in a stepwise fashion, breaking down the overarching task

---

S. S. Shirai—Part of this work was done while the author was an intern at Robert Bosch LLC.

Supplementary Information The online version contains supplementary material available at https://doi.org/10.1007/978-3-031-19433-7_10.

U. Sattler et al. (Eds.): ISWC 2022, LNCS 13489, pp. 161–178, 2022.
https://doi.org/10.1007/978-3-031-19433-7_10

into a series of individual steps. A prime example of this is a cooking recipe, which specifies a set of ingredients along with a number of steps describing how to combine and modify those ingredients to form the final dish.

When performing tasks that are described by such instructions, it is possible to modify the instructions to complete the task in a slightly different way while producing similar results. In cooking, this can be observed when people substitute ingredients in the recipe – many ingredients exist that can be replaced and result in a dish that is "close enough" to the original. However, it can be difficult to determine which modifications of the instructions are valid because it requires an understanding of the entities involved with the instructions, the actions taking place, and the outcomes produced by different actions.

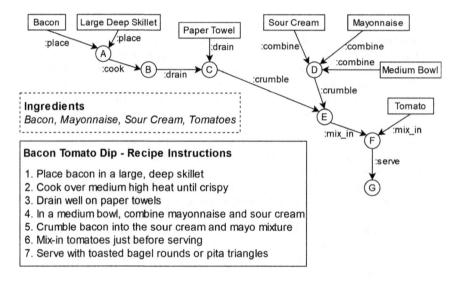

Fig. 1. A running example recipe and its flow graph. Intermediate nodes are labeled as A, B, etc. for convenience.

Gaining a comprehensive understanding about the entities and actions in procedural instructions presents a major challenge. Instructions often are not well structured or specific, as they rely on common sense. For example, given the instructions "(1) Place bacon in a skillet (2) Cook over medium heat", we infer that the instructions are telling us to cook the bacon that we just placed in the skillet. Correctly parsing these steps might also involve background knowledge, such as alternative names for similar entities (e.g., *pan* and *skillet*). Furthermore, steps are not necessarily completed sequentially, which requires us to identify branching instructions and co-references of similar entities from earlier steps.

One method that can help provide the structure necessary to represent this information and identify viable substitutions is to form a *flow graph* of the instructions. A flow graph can represent the instructions as a rooted, directed acyclic graph, with the root node representing the final result of the instructions (e.g., the dish produced by a recipe), leaf nodes representing the entities (e.g., the ingredients and equipment), and edges capturing the actions taking place to produce intermediate results (e.g., mixing flour and water to form a batter). Representing the procedural instructions in this form can then be utilized to further identify which modifications can be made to the instructions.

A running example recipe is illustrated in Fig. 1. We can see several steps that specify how to use the ingredients, as well as equipment such as the skillet and bowl, to make the recipe. The recipe's corresponding flow graph captures these ingredient and equipment entities as leaf nodes, and their usages – i.e., verbs such as "cook" and "drain" – are captured as edges.

In order to form such flow graphs from procedural text, it can also be beneficial to incorporate domain-specific information sources. For example, ontologies can provide authoritative knowledge about entities that has been manually curated by domain experts. This knowledge in turn can inform the information extraction process and augment the resulting flow graph.

In this paper, we present the **EaT-PIM** (Embedding and Transforming Procedural Instructions for Modification) methodology to extract information from domain-specific instructions – specifically, cooking recipes – to convert them into flow graphs. We then present an approach to learn embeddings for entities and actions that occur in the flow graphs such that we can use the embeddings to identify plausible modifications that can be made to the instructions. Intuitively, our approach aims to learn embeddings that capture the flow of entities and actions from the flow graph, which in turn can be used to dynamically compute the output of a recipe after performing an ingredient substitution.

Our contributions are as follows: **(1)** Present a rule-based method to generate flow graphs from instruction text, leveraging domain ontologies and dependency parsing tools. **(2)** Introduce a novel graph embedding strategy for flow graphs, which aggregates nodes to better capture instruction steps and dynamically calculates intermediate results. Our method requires learning embeddings for significantly fewer nodes compared to baseline graph embedding models while showing top performance at a link prediction task for cooking recipes. **(3)** Present a method to identify plausible entity substitutions in flow graphs using our embedding calculation approach. Further, this method can handle new combinations of entities and actions without additional training.

2   Problem Formulation

Here, we give a brief overview of our main problem formulation and definitions. While this work focuses specifically on recipes, the approach can be extended to procedural instructions in different domains in a similar manner.

2.1   Recipe Modeling

A recipe R contains two pieces of information – a list of steps in natural language, S_R, and the set of ingredients used in the recipe, I_R. $S_R = [S_i | i = 1..n]$ is a list of individual sentences, ordered sequentially as in recipe steps. Each ingredient $I_j \in I_R$ is a distinct ingredient defined by the recipe. We represent the ingredients and recipes following Resource Description Framework (RDF) standards to enable better integration with ontology and knowledge graph resources.

2.2   Flow Graph Representation

A key property of procedural instructions is that the main task of the instructions is to create an output entity through some combination and transformation of input entities. A recipe takes raw ingredients, applies transformations (such as cutting) to them, and combines them to form the final dish. Transformation that are applied may change properties of the original inputs (such as "diced tomatoes"), and the instructions provide us with a trace of how such intermediate results were formed. As such, it is sensible to consider representing instructions as a "flow" that captures how input items are processed through the instructions.

Our goal is to parse the instructions with the set of ingredients contained in R to form a flow graph. For this work, we define a flow graph as follows:

Definition 1. *A **flow graph** is an RDF graph of triples (h, r, t), denoting a relation r from entity h to entity t, with the following properties: (1) the graph contains no cycles; (2) the graph has a single output node that is reachable by all other nodes; (3) all incoming relations to a node have the same label; and (4) all domain-specific entities have no incoming relations.*

In our definition, we distinguish domain-specific entities as equipment or ingredients that are specified in the recipe text. All such entities act as leaf nodes in the flow graphs. Other nodes in the flow graph, which have incoming relations, are denoted as *intermediate nodes*. In turn, the relations in the flow graphs correspond to the actions taking place in the recipe instructions, and their connections and directions indicate how the entities and intermediate nodes are being processed through the flow graph.

Example 1. Consider our running example in Fig. 1. This flow graph contains no cycles and has a single output node G. All incoming relations to intermediate nodes also share the same label. Lastly, all entities corresponding to ingredients or cooking equipment are leaf nodes. We also can observe how the edge labels correspond to actions taking place in the recipe.

Our use of the terminology "flow graph" resembles that of some prior works [7,15,27], but we make several distinctions surrounding what information is captured and how it is represented. Our requirement that entities must be leaves in flow graphs is not shared by previous definitions. Additionally, prior models do not have restrictions that incoming edges must have the same label, and intermediate results (as we model in our flow graph definition) are not modeled.

We also note the omission of several details from our example recipe's instructions. For example, the details to cook the bacon "over medium high heat" and "until crispy" are omitted in our flow graph. For the scope of this work, we chose to focus on capturing and using the core information about actions and entities while dropping additional qualitative modifiers. Another point of omission is information about what role each entity plays in an action, as in how the bacon is being placed *into* the skillet. For the scope of this work, we simplify this information to only capture which entities were involved in the action. In these omissions, we opted to favor simplification of the flow graph at the cost of semantic accuracy due to the difficulty of correctly parsing the instructions.

Lastly, we omit information from sentences that are unrelated to cooking the actual recipe. Whenever ingredients that weren't included in the recipe's ingredient list occurred, we considered it extraneous information.

3   Flow Graph Generation from Instructions

To construct flow graphs, we make use of natural language processing (NLP) tools, a part-of-speech (PoS) tagger and dependency parser, as well as ontologies to provide knowledge about domain-specific entities. After using such tools to extract relations between entities and actions from each step in the recipe, the steps are combined together to form a flow graph. We note that our data and methods focus only on handling English recipe texts.

3.1   Parsing Instruction Text

The first step we apply is to perform dependency parsing and PoS tagging over each sentence in the recipe's instructions. Our goal is to find verbs and their associated nouns; these verbs are the actions taking place in the instructions. In our experiments, we perform this step using spaCy's [9] pretrained language models. An example of the dependency tree that is produced by spaCy can be seen in Fig. 2. Based on both the PoS and dependency tags produced by spaCy, we devised a rule-based method[1] to connect nouns and verbs occurring in each sentence to serve as the foundation for forming the recipe's flow graph.

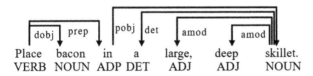

Fig. 2. An example dependency tree produced for a sentence using spaCy.

After processing each step in the recipe, we are left with a list of information pertaining to verbs and nouns that are directly interacting with each other in each step of the recipe. For example, from the example sentence in Fig. 2, we extract two tuples of verb-noun relations – ("place", "bacon"), and ("place",

---

[1] We refer to Sect. 1 in our supplemental material for further details on this process.

"large deep skillet"). The dependency relation between each verb and noun is retained for use in forming the flow graph. We discarded prepositions as well as adverbs to omit some details as noted in the previous section.

Correcting Parses: We found that parsing errors would occur frequently for sentences that were particularly terse or used implicit subjects (e.g., "Brown beef in the pot."). Such sentences have the subject (i.e., the person cooking the recipe) omitted, as is typical with many imperative sentences, and were ambiguous in how they should be parsed (e.g., "brown" may be a verb or an adjective).

We expect each sentence in the instructions to provide some meaningful action to perform, so in cases where no verb is found, we re-run the dependency parse with an augmented version of the sentence. Instructions are often presented as imperative sentences, and in English the imperative mood is typically (1) in the present tense and (2) in the second person. Based on this knowledge, in practice we found that simply adding a subject – the word "you" – to the beginning of the sentence resolved many such errors. For example, "you brown beef in the pot." resulted in correctly tagging "brown" as a verb.

Filtering. To better focus on modeling objects that are relevant to the instructions, we can use a domain-specific ontology to filter out extraneous information. In our experiments we use FoodOn [3], an ontology containing information about thousands of different foods and their relations, and filter out entities. We do this by matching noun-phrases from recipe texts to FoodOn classes based on their class labels, alternative names, and synonyms. We convert all noun-phrases and class names into one-hot vectors, weighted by TF-IDF measures, and calculate their cosine similarity to determine matches. In cases where a sufficiently high-confidence match was not found, we consider the noun irrelevant for our task and discard the information. We also retain links between ingredients in flow graphs and FoodOn classes for later use to train embeddings.

3.2   Forming Flow Graphs

After parsing instructions, we have a list of tuples containing verbs, nouns, and their relations in each step. We proceed to form a flow graph of the overall recipe by forming small graphs for the content of each step and then connecting the graphs for each step together into a single flow graph.

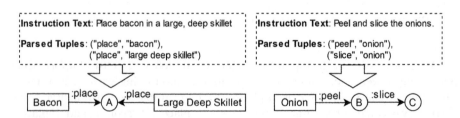

Fig. 3. Examples illustrating how two entities can form a single output (left) and how multiple verbs are applied sequentially to an entity (right).

First, to form minimal graphs from each step, we use verb-noun relations that were detected from the dependency parser. The verb is used as the edge label to connect the nouns to an output node. In cases where multiple verbs were used in the step, we assume that the noun and intermediate node content in the step are connected sequentially (as they occur in the step's sentence). An example of this step can be seen in Fig. 3.

Using the minimal graphs from each step in the instructions, we move on to connect each step together to form the overall flow graph. We consider 3 cases: (1) a step includes a reference to an entity that has been used in a previous step; (2) a step's dependency parse includes a verb with no direct subject or object; and (3) a step follows sequentially from the previous step.

Case 1: In the first case, we check for noun occurrences in each step to see if the same ingredient is being used. If such a situation exists, we connect the two steps together by adding an edge from the output of the earlier step to the first intermediate node in the later step. We check each step in order, prioritizing earlier steps when adding connections. An example demonstrating how two steps would be connected in this kind of case can be seen in Fig. 4.

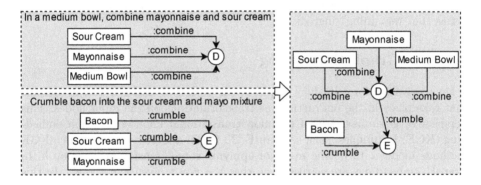

Fig. 4. An illustration connecting two steps in the running example together.

Case 2: For the second case, we use dependency relations between words that were obtained from the dependency parser. If the step includes a verb but has no relations to a direct subject or direct object, we infer that the verb is acting on the output of the previous step. An example of this situation can be seen in the first two steps of our running example, as "(1) Place bacon in a large, deep skillet", "(2) Cook over medium high heat until crispy". We can infer that the second step means we must cook the bacon – in the dependency parse result, "cook' in step 2 contains no direct subject or object.

Case 3: If either of the previous two cases do not apply, we simply connect steps together sequentially. In this case, the output node of each step is connected to the first intermediate node in the next step. The edge for this connection copies the same label as other incoming edges for that intermediate node, since we can assume that the output of the step is having the same actions applied as other entities in that step. Sequential connections have been shown to be a good baseline for creating flow graphs in the domain of cooking [10].

Recipe-Specific Cases: Another consideration for a recipe's flow graph is that we expect to see all of the ingredients specified by the recipe. While this some-times is trivial, there are often cases where ingredients are referred to by alternate names within the recipe steps or as a group of ingredients (e.g., instructions to "add herbs" rather than individually listing out each herb). In cases where not all relevant ingredients from the recipe have been included, we identify leaf nodes in the flow graph that are most similar to the missing ingredients. We used a mea-sure of semantic similarity, wpath [31], over FoodOn's ingredient class hierarchy to determine which node is the most similar.

We also must consider a recipe-specific special case for phrases such as "all ingredients" and "remaining ingredients." These phrases occur fairly often in recipes written by non-experts and rely on the assumption that we know all ingredients in the recipe ahead of time. They also rely on sequential knowledge about which ingredients have already been used in the recipe. When either of these cases occur, we check the flow graph for all instances of ingredient usage in prior steps and add new edges for any ingredients that have not been used yet as the "remaining" ingredients.

4   Flow Graph Embedding

A key motivation for using flow graphs in our work is to enable us to view actions that take place in the instructions as transformations on the input nodes. This perspective is similar that of common translational knowledge graph embed-ding (KGE) techniques, such as TransE [2]. Given a triplet (h, r, t), such KGE methods model t to be the result of applying some transformation r on h. In TransE, embeddings are learned such that $h + r \approx t$ given $h, r, t \in \mathbb{R}^k$. In this way, the relation r is used as a transformation on the entity h to produce the result entity t. Extending this idea to our flow graphs, our aim is to model our relations – i.e., actions such as "cook" or "crumble" – as transformations on the input ingredients to produce output intermediate nodes.

However, our flow graphs for procedural instructions are not well suited to directly apply KGEs that are trained over triplets of data. While KGE models view each triple independently as indicating a single factual statement, in our flow graphs *all* of the incoming nodes contribute to the output. Additionally, standard KGE model training over triples would require us to learn embeddings for all intermediate nodes, which is undesirable for our case as the number of unique intermediate nodes rapidly increases with the number of flow graphs.

4.1   Embedding Strategy

To address the aforementioned issues, we incorporate the idea of performing aggregation on incoming nodes in the flow graph. This aggregation should serve to provide additional context when training embeddings such that all ingredients involved in a recipe's step are considered while training. Additionally, we address the issue of handling intermediate nodes by calculating the output of applying transformations (based on relation embeddings) to entity embeddings during each training step. Figure 5 illustrates how entity embeddings are aggregated and calculated (calculations past node C are omitted for brevity). The aggregation is performed by taking the mean of the input nodes, while the output is calculated similar to TransE's $h + r = t$ formulation. Leveraging the fact that all incoming edge labels in our flow graphs are the same for a given intermediate node, each aggregation is treated as a single "head" entity in the KGE model's $(\mathbf{h}, \mathbf{r}, \mathbf{t})$ triplet, and the embeddings for intermediate nodes are calculated on the fly.

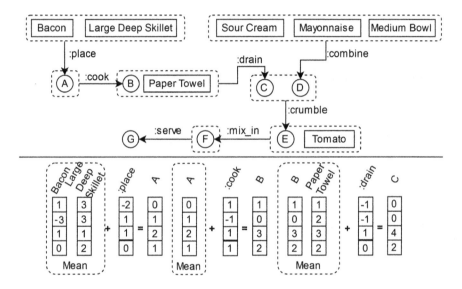

Fig. 5. An illustration of how we aggregate input nodes, within the dotted lines, and apply the embedding of the action to produce intermediate nodes.

Distance: We define the distance metric used during each training step in our model in a recursive fashion by defining a "triplet" (h_R, r_R, t_R), where $h_R, r_R, t_R \in \mathbb{R}^k$, for each recipe R. Our goal during training is to minimize the distance $|h_R + r_R - t_R|$, following from the distance formulation of TransE which minimizes the distance $|h + r - t|$.

Given a flow graph F_R, let I_v denote the set of nodes with incoming edges to node v and l_v denote the label for incoming edges to node v. For the flow graph F_R and its output node v_o, we can then define h_R as the output of Algorithm 1. For the given recipe, $r_R = r_{l_{v_o}}$ is then defined as the last action that takes place in the recipe, and $t_R = h_{v_o}$ is the embedding of the recipe's output node.

Example 2. Applying Algorithm 1 to our running example recipe, the output node v_o=G. The incoming nodes $I_G = [F]$, so we can calculate the recipe's embedding as $h_R = Aggregate([RecursiveAgg(F)])$. Stepping through the procedure for $RecursiveAgg$, we will reach line 5 where $Recursive\ Agg$ is called again on the incoming nodes to F, $I_F = [E, Tomato]$. Tomato is a leaf node, while E will once again enter a recursive call which we omit for brevity. Back to node F, in line 6 we will use node F's incoming edge ":mix_in" and its embedding $r_{:mix\_in}$, and return $h_R = r_{:mix\_in} + Aggregate(mean([h_{Tomato}, RecursiveAgg(E)]))$. This value is then used with the output node's incoming edge, $r_{:serve}$, to calculate $h_R + r_{:serve}$ as this recipe's calculated output embedding value.

Training Objectives: The distance between the recipe's calculated "triplet" (h_R, r_R, t_R) is then computed as $dist_R = |h_R + r_R - t_R|$. Following standard training for KGE models using this distance metric, the loss is optimized as $L_p = -\log \sigma(\gamma - dist_R)$, where γ is a fixed margin and σ is the sigmoid function.

Algorithm 1. Flow Graph Output Embedding Calculation Pseudocode

> **Input** A flow graph's output node v_o, incoming nodes I, incoming edge labels l
> **Output** Calculated head vector $h_R \in \mathbb{R}^k$

1: **function** RECURSIVEAGG(v)
2:     **if** v.isLeafNode **then**
3:         **return** h_v
4:     **else**
5:         inNodes = [RecursiveAgg(v_j) for $v_j \in I_v$]
6:         **return** Aggregate(inNodes) + r_{l_v}
7:     **end if**
8: **end function**
9: **function** AGGREGATE(EmbeddingList)
10:     **return** mean(EmbeddingList)
11: **end function**
12: h_R = Aggregate([RecursiveAgg(v_j) for $v_j \in I_{v_o}$])

We additionally follow best practices for training KGE models by utilizing negative sampling. For a given recipe R, negative sampling is performed for an incorrect tail entity $t_{R'} \neq t_R$ and an incorrect "head" flow graph $h_{R'} \neq h_R$. $t_{R'}$ entity points to another randomly selected recipe output, and $h_{R'}$ is constructed by randomly replacing input nodes in R's flow graph. k negative samples were collected for each training step, and the negative sampling loss was calculated for the negative head and tail samples as $L_n = -\frac{1}{k} \sum_1^k \log \sigma(|h_R + r_R - t_{R'}| - \gamma) - \frac{1}{k} \sum_1^k \log \sigma(|h_{R'} + r_R - t_R| - \gamma)$. The total loss is calculated as $L = L_p + L_n$.

By using our recursive aggregation strategy, we can calculate embeddings for intermediate nodes rather than learning them explicitly. The only nodes in our flow graph data that we learn embeddings for are the ingredient leaf nodes and the recipe's final output node v_o.

In order to incorporate external domain-specific knowledge, we also include triples from FoodOn to perform training. We connect classes from FoodOn to ingredients in our recipe dataset, identified during the flow graph generation stage, and perform normal training of the TransE model over this data.

4.2 Replacement Techniques

Once our entity embeddings $h \in \mathbb{R}^k$ and relation embeddings $r \in \mathbb{R}^k$ have been trained, we can apply the same aggregation techniques used during training – to calculate the "output" embedding, transforming the inputs – to perform modification and substitution of entities in a recipe.

Given a recipe's flow graph F_R, our model will have learned an embedding for the recipe's final output, h_{v_o}. Additionally, we can use the entity and relation embeddings for the nodes and edges in F_R to calculate the recipe's output as well (once again following from the intuition that the embeddings $h_R + r_R = t_R$). The original recipe's learned output node embedding, h_{v_o}, and the calculated output embedding of the original recipe's flow graph, t_R, can be used to identify plausible substitutions of ingredients by replacing nodes in F_R and calculating a new output embedding.

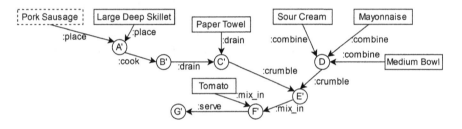

Fig. 6. Substituting "Bacon" with "Pork Sausage" in our running example recipe.

For an ingredient node $v \in F_R$ that we wish to replace, we simply can swap v with a new node v_s as seen in Fig. 6. We also replace all edges in F_R to which v was connected. Then, following the procedure from Algorithm 1, we can calculate a new output embedding for the flow graph with a node substitution as $t_{R'}$. To determine whether the substitution seems "good" or not, we can then compare the cosine similarity of the newly calculated embedding $t_{R'}$ with the original learned embedding h_{v_o} or the original calculated embedding t_R. This process can then be repeated over a number of substitute ingredient options to produce a ranking of which substitute is the "best" based on how similar the newly calculated result is to the original.

A result of our embedding and substitution strategy is that it is robust in its ability to handle previously unseen recipes. Assuming that embeddings have been learned for the relevant ingredients and actions, the output embedding for a new recipe's flow graph is dynamically calculated and would require no additional training. A completely novel recipe can therefore have an embedding representing its output, which in turn allows us to perform our substitution strategy.

5   Evaluation

5.1   Flow Graph Generation

We evaluate the quality of our flow graph generation method by comparing against a dataset of recipe annotations and flow graphs published by Yamakata et al. [27]. However, the level of detail, included concepts, and formulation of their flow graphs differs from that of our work. We therefore performed preprocessing, which included adjusting the graph's connections so that actions were edges rather than nodes.[2] After performing our preprocessing step, we evaluate F-measure by comparing edges in our generated graph versus the ground truth.

5.2   Embedding Flow Graphs

To evaluate the quality of our embeddings, we frame our problem as a knowledge graph completion task for individual flow graphs. Given a recipe flow graph and the learned embedding for its output node, we remove a single ingredient and then rank the ingredient that is most likely to fit in to the flow graph. Following our ingredient substitution procedure from Sect. 4.2, candidate ingredients are used as "substitutions" to calculate recipe output embeddings, and their similarity to the expected embedding of the recipe is used to rank ingredients. Our goal for this experiment is to demonstrate that our EaT-PIM method can effectively re-identify a missing ingredient from a recipe, which in turn would suggest that we might be able to identify plausible substitutions by selecting ingredients that are similar to the "missing" ingredient being replaced.

Dataset: We conduct our experiments using recipe data from Food.com [14]. We randomly selected a subset of the data consisting of 20,000 recipes, which included 6,142 distinct ingredients. We generated flow graphs for each recipe, and this data was further split into training, validation, and test data using a 70%, 15%, 15% split. Embeddings were trained using data from the training set as well as data from FoodOn [3], which similarly was split for training.

Baselines: Our first baseline uses a simplified problem setup, which omits the flow graph data and instead ranked missing ingredients based on ingredient co-occurrence in recipes (denoted COOC). The sum of co-occurrence probabilities between a candidate ingredient of all ingredients in a target recipe was used to produce a score, which was then used to rank the missing ingredient.

Our next set of baselines utilize standard KGE models. To enable training over triplets of data, we re-introduce explicit intermediate nodes for flow graphs in these baselines. We train two translational distance models, TransE [2] and RotatE [22], which are well suited for modeling compositional relations. We contrast these with two semantic matching models, DistMult [29] and ComplEx [23], which are better suited for modeling symmetric and antisymmetric

---

[2] We refer to Sect. 2 in our supplemental material for details on the preprocessing.

relations. RotatE and ComplEx also learn embeddings in complex vector space. These four baselines were trained using embedding sizes of 200, 300, and 400 dimensions, and the best results are reported. Lastly, we train a graph neural network (GNN)-based embedding model from [17] (denoted GNN (Nathani et al.)), which uses a Graph Attention Network [24] together with a convolutional layer [18] to perform link prediction. For each model, we perform link prediction for intermediate nodes connected to input ingredient and rank the missing ingredient to calculate performance. This ranking is performed in a filtered setting – i.e., the ranking is not penalized if a *true* triple is highly ranked.

For our final baseline, we introduce an additional TransE-based baseline that is trained in a similar manner to EaT-PIM (denoted TransE (flow graph path)). Rather than explicitly learning embeddings for intermediate nodes, this model is trained by using the path of edges between ingredients and the recipe output. This model differs from EaT-PIM in that no node aggregation is performed.

5.3   Results

Flow Graph Generation: EaT-PIM's methods to convert recipe texts to flow graphs yielded a precision of **0.638**, recall of **0.566**, and F1 score of **0.600** when comparing them to the ground-truth graphs. To give a rough comparison (albeit for a slightly different task[3]), the original results reported by Yamakata et al. [28] indicate an F1 of 0.433 for their full pipeline. Considering that our methods did not require any annotated training data, our results appear competitive with those presented in the original dataset publication.

Embedding Flow Graphs: Table 1 displays the mean reciprocal rank (MRR), HITS@3, HITS@5, and HITS@10 for our EaT-PIM method and the baselines. MRR is calculated as the average of $1/rank_t$, where $rank_t$ is the rank of the true entity t for each datapoint. HITS@K is calculated as the proportion of inputs for which the correct entity t is within the top K ranks.

Table 1. Results for ranking missing ingredients in recipe flow graphs.

Model	MRR	HITS@3	HITS@5	HITS@10
COOC	0.132	0.138	0.189	0.281
DistMult	0.012	0.012	0.015	0.021
ComplEx	0.017	0.018	0.023	0.032
RotatE	0.118	0.120	0.163	0.242
TransE	0.151	0.158	0.211	0.301
GNN (Nathani et al.)	0.068	0.068	0.88	0.124
TransE (flow graph path)	0.172	0.177	0.206	0.254
EaT-PIM (ours)	**0.286**	**0.355**	**0.437**	**0.520**

---

[3] Further details are discussed in Sect. 2 of our supplemental material.

EaT-PIM is able to outperform the baselines by a large margin for the task of re-identifying missing ingredients from recipes. Surprisingly, we find that the basic TransE model shows the best performance among our standard KGE baselines, followed by RotatE. The ability for these two models to capture compositional relations shows a stark contrast in performance compared to DistMult and ComplEx, which appear to be poorly suited for our task.

The TransE (flow graph path) baseline shows the second best performance. Compared to the standard TransE model, performing training and predictions based on the entire path from the ingredient to recipe output appears to have provided minor benefits. Our approach to perform aggregation improves upon this further – when applying the embedding trained through EaT-PIM to perform ingredient prediction only based on the path from the ingredient to the recipe, the MRR increases to 0.260. This suggests that EaT-PIM's approach to aggregate nodes was particulary useful to learn good embeddings, while applying EaT-PIM's substitution method to perform the link prediction granted an additional 10% increase in performance.

Discussion: EaT-PIM's ability to dynamically compute intermediate nodes allows it to learn embeddings for significantly fewer entities than standard KGEs require (40,500 entities in EaT-PIM versus 272,000 in baselines). This can be beneficial during training, as less memory is needed to load all of the embeddings. Additionally, EaT-PIM's simple model is less resource intensive compared to more advanced models such as the GNN. The GNN in our experiment required 190 MB of memory to store 50 dimensional embeddings of nodes along with the convolutional neural network, while EaT-PIM's 200 dimensional embeddings only needed 30 MB. This benefit would increase further if training is performed for more recipes, suggesting strong potential for scalability using EaT-PIM.

Table 2. Examples of top ranked substitutions in two recipes.

Recipe	Target ingredient	Top 3 substitutes
Pork marinate	Pork	Boneless pork, Rib, Pork loin roast
Mashed potatoes	Red potato	Dried thyme, all purpose flour, Chicken

Regarding our application of these embeddings to ingredient substitutions, while it is challenging to evaluate due to subjectivity issues, we observe that using EaT-PIM to rank substitutions generally produces reasonable results. Table 2 shows examples of ranking substitutions for a target ingredient in a specific recipe. The top substitutions for "Pork" are all varieties or names of pork. On the other hand, we observe some less desirable substitutes, such as thyme, for "Red Potato" in our example. While work remains to improve the consistency of substitution ranking, our methods can provide some utility by comparing substitutions across different recipes. For example, Table 3 displays the relative rankings of three potato substitutes[4] in different types of recipes.[5] While it is difficult to judge how *correct* these relative rankings are, it demonstrates that the suitability of each ingredient varies based on the recipe at hand.

Table 3. A comparison of relative rankings of potato substitutes in three recipes.

Recipe: **Mashed Potato**	Recipe: **Potato Gratin**	Recipe: **Healthy Soup**
Substitute Ranks	Substitute Ranks	Substitute Ranks
1. Jicama	1. Cauliflower	1. Rutabaga
2. Cauliflower	2. Jicama	2. Cauliflower
3. Rutabaga	3. Rutabaga	3. Jicama

6   Related Work

Ingredient Substitution: Previous works on ingredient substitution have explored methods such as rule-based substitutions in TAAABLE [5] and Intellimeal [21]. DIISH [20] applied a substitutability heuristic based on ingredient co-occurrence and similarity. A major limitation of such works was that they did not explicitly incorporate detailed information about cooking instructions.

Workflow Extraction: Extracting workflows instructions has been explored in the domain of cooking using methods such as frame- and pattern-based extraction [19] and case-based reasoning [4]. Semantic representations of procedural knowledge were proposed in [30], including annotations of pre-conditions, actions, and purpose. Outside of the cooking, explicit representations of procedural instructions have been investigated a variety of domains [1,6,12,16]. Our work shares some similarities to prior works in the use of ontologies to identify relevant entities. However, we do not rely on manually constructing templates to extract workflows, and the flow graph representation of our methods also differs.

Flow Graphs: The flow graphs modeled in our work shares similarities with past works such as [13,15,27,28]. Many previous works using recipe flow graphs use annotations [13,25,27], either by directly using the annotations or learning to predict labels and relations based on a training set, while our work does not rely on annotated data. A method demonstrated in [10] formed flow graphs in an unsupervised fashion, but it relied on an external parser to classify words.

Knowledge Graph Embedding: Beyond the baseline models applied in our experiments [2,22,23,29], a variety of distance metrics have been proposed for training KGE models [26]. Such models treat triples in the graph as independent facts, while our motivation of applying them to flow graphs would want to consider the combination of *multiple* triples together to produce an output.

---

[4] Jicama and rutabaga are often cited as healthy potato substitutes.

[5] We refer to Sect. 3 in our supplemental material for details on the example recipes.

Embedding graphs using graph neural networks (GNN), such as [8, 11, 24], have also gained traction in recent years. GNNs have demonstrated the benefits of aggregating information from neighboring nodes. Our embedding approach takes inspiration from such methods in that we also aim to aggregate input nodes.

7   Conclusion

We present EaT-PIM, which consists of two main methods. First, EaT-PIM converts procedural instructions into flow graphs using NLP tools and domain-specific ontologies. Using the generated flow graphs, EaT-PIM trains an embedding model using a strategy that allows us to aggregate input information and dynamically compute intermediate node representations within flow graphs. Our evaluations demonstrate strong performance of EaT-PIM in both generating flow graphs and performing link prediction for ingredients in recipes. Future work includes exploration of more intricate aggregation strategies in the embedding and applying EaT-PIM to instructions from different domains to explore substitutability for more diverse types of entities.

Supplemental Material Statement: Supplemental materials and source codes are made available at https://github.com/boschresearch/EaT-PIM.

Acknowledgements. We would like to express our thanks to the colleagues of Bosch's RTC-NA, the members of RPI's Tetherless World Constellation, and CMU's Naoki Otani for their feedback and reviews of this manuscript.

References

1. Agarwal, S., Atreja, S., Agarwal, V.: Extracting procedural knowledge from technical documents. ArXiv abs/2010.10156 (2020)
2. Bordes, A., Usunier, N., García-Durán, A., Weston, J., Yakhnenko, O.: Translating embeddings for modeling multi-relational data. In: NIPS (2013)
3. Dooley, D.M., et al.: Foodon: a harmonized food ontology to increase global food traceability, quality control and data integration. NPJ Science of Food 2 (2018)
4. Dufour-Lussier, V., Ber, F.L., Lieber, J., Meilender, T., Nauer, E.: Semi-automatic annotation process for procedural texts: an application on cooking recipes. ArXiv abs/1209.5663 (2012)
5. Gaillard, E., Lieber, J., Nauer, E.: Adaptation of taaable to the ccc'2017 mixology and salad challenges, adaptation of the cocktail names. In: ICCBR (Workshops), pp. 253–268 (2017)
6. Halioui, A., Valtchev, P., Diallo, A.B.: Ontology-based workflow extraction from texts using word sense disambiguation. bioRxiv (2016)
7. Hamada, R., Ide, I., Sakai, S., Tanaka, H.: Structural analysis of cooking preparation steps in Japanese. In: IRAL 2000 (2000)
8. Hamilton, W.L., Ying, Z., Leskovec, J.: Inductive representation learning on large graphs. In: NIPS (2017)

9. Honnibal, M., Montani, I., Van Landeghem, S., Boyd, A.: spacy: Industrial-strength natural language processing in python (2020)
10. Kiddon, C., Ponnuraj, G.T., Zettlemoyer, L., Choi, Y.: Mise en place: unsupervised interpretation of instructional recipes. In: EMNLP (2015)
11. Kipf, T., Welling, M.: Semi-supervised classification with graph convolutional networks. ICLR (2017)
12. Kulkarni, C., Xu, W., Ritter, A., Machiraju, R.: An annotated corpus for machine reading of instructions in wet lab protocols. In: NAACL (2018)
13. Maeta, H., Sasada, T., Mori, S.: A framework for procedural text understanding. In: IWPT (2015)
14. Majumder, B.P., Li, S., Ni, J., McAuley, J.: Generating personalized recipes from historical user preferences. In: EMNLP-IJCNLP, pp. 5976–5982. Association for Computational Linguistics, Hong Kong, China, November 2019
15. Mori, S., Maeta, H., Yamakata, Y., Sasada, T.: Flow graph corpus from recipe texts. In: LREC (2014)
16. Mysore, S., et al.: Automatically extracting action graphs from materials science synthesis procedures. CoRR abs/1711.06872 (2017). http://arxiv.org/abs/1711.06872
17. Nathani, D., Chauhan, J., Sharma, C., Kaul, M.: Learning attention-based embeddings for relation prediction in knowledge graphs. In: ACL (2019)
18. Nguyen, D.Q., Nguyen, T.D., Nguyen, D.Q., Phung, D.Q.: A novel embedding model for knowledge base completion based on convolutional neural network. In: NAACL (2018)
19. Schumacher, P., Minor, M., Walter, K., Bergmann, R.: Extraction of procedural knowledge from the web: a comparison of two workflow extraction approaches. WWW (2012)
20. Shirai, S.S., Seneviratne, O., Gordon, M.E., Chen, C.H., McGuinness, D.L.: Identifying ingredient substitutions using a knowledge graph of food. Front. Artif. Intell. **3**, 111 (2021)
21. Skjold, K., Øynes, M., Bach, K., Aamodt, A.: Intellimeal-enhancing creativity by reusing domain knowledge in the adaptation process. In: ICCBR (Workshops), pp. 277–284 (2017)
22. Sun, Z., Deng, Z., Nie, J.Y., Tang, J.: Rotate: Knowledge graph embedding by relational rotation in complex space. ICLR (2019)
23. Trouillon, T., Welbl, J., Riedel, S., Gaussier, É., Bouchard, G.: Complex embeddings for simple link prediction. In: ICML (2016)
24. Velickovic, P., Cucurull, G., Casanova, A., Romero, A., Lio', P., Bengio, Y.: Graph attention networks. ICLR (2018)
25. Wang, L., Li, Q., Li, N., Dong, G., Yang, Y.: Substructure similarity measurement in Chinese recipes. In: WWW (2008)
26. Wang, Q., Mao, Z., Wang, B., Guo, L.: Knowledge graph embedding: a survey of approaches and applications. IEEE Trans. Knowl. Data Eng. **29**, 2724–2743 (2017)
27. Yamakata, Y., Imahori, S., Maeta, H., Mori, S.: A method for extracting major workflow composed of ingredients, tools, and actions from cooking procedural text. In: 2016 IEEE International Conference on Multimedia Expo Workshops (ICMEW), pp. 1–6 (2016)
28. Yamakata, Y., Mori, S., Carroll, J.: English recipe flow graph corpus. In: LREC (2020)
29. Yang, B., tau Yih, W., He, X., Gao, J., Deng, L.: Embedding entities and relations for learning and inference in knowledge bases. CoRR abs/1412.6575 (2015)

30. Zhang, Z., Webster, P., Uren, V.S., Varga, A., Ciravegna, F.: Automatically extracting procedural knowledge from instructional texts using natural language processing. In: LREC (2012)
31. Zhu, G., Iglesias, C.A.: Computing semantic similarity of concepts in knowledge graphs. IEEE TKDE **29**(1), 72–85 (2017)

H²TNE: Temporal Heterogeneous Information Network Embedding in Hyperbolic Spaces

Qijie Bai[1,3], Jiawen Guo[2,3], Haiwei Zhang[1,2,3(✉)], Changli Nie[1,3], Lin Zhang[1,3], and Xiaojie Yuan[1,2,3]

[1] College of Computer Science, Nankai University, Tianjin, China
{qijie.bai,nie_cl}@mail.nankai.edu.cn
[2] College of Cyber Science, Nankai University, Tianjin, China
{zhhaiwei,yuanxj}@nankai.edu.cn
[3] TJ Key Laboratory of NDST, Nankai University, Tianjin, China
{guojiawen,zhanglin}@dbis.nankai.edu.cn

Abstract. *Temporal heterogeneous information network* (temporal HIN) embedding, aiming to represent various types of nodes of different timestamps into low-dimensional spaces while preserving structural and semantic information, is of vital importance in diverse real-life tasks. Researchers have made great efforts on temporal HIN embedding in Euclidean spaces and got some considerable achievements. However, there is always a fundamental conflict that many real-world networks show hierarchical property and power-law distribution, and are not isometric of Euclidean spaces. Recently, representation learning in hyperbolic spaces has been proved to be valid for data with hierarchical and power-law structure. Inspired by this character, we propose a *hyperbolic heterogeneous temporal network embedding* (H²TNE) model for temporal HINs. Specifically, we leverage a temporally and heterogeneously double-constrained random walk strategy to capture the structural and semantic information, and then calculate the embedding by exploiting hyperbolic distance in proximity measurement. Experimental results show that our method has superior performance on temporal link prediction and node classification compared with SOTA models.

Keywords: Temporal heterogeneous information networks · Hyperbolic geometry · Representation learning

1 Introduction

Heterogeneous information networks (HINs), which are seen as general and simplified knowledge graphs (KGs), are of a ubiquitous structure in various domains. HIN embedding has received great attention in recent years because of its powerful representation abilities for both structural and semantic information in real-world networks [4]. Different types of nodes are mapped into a low-dimension space for diverse downstream analytic tasks, such as pattern matching, node classification and link prediction, within lower time and space complexity [6].

Most existing HIN embedding methods focus on static networks. These methods are designed to preserve the topological structure and contextual semantics without

© The Author(s), under exclusive license to Springer Nature Switzerland AG 2022
U. Sattler et al. (Eds.): ISWC 2022, LNCS 13489, pp. 179–195, 2022.
https://doi.org/10.1007/978-3-031-19433-7_11

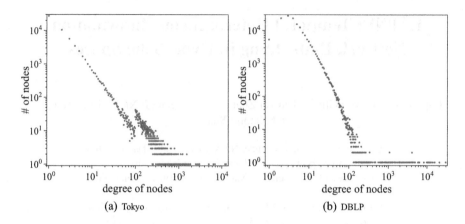

Fig. 1. The degree distributions of two real-world networks Tokyo and DBLP. The coordinate axes are logarithmic.

considering any temporal information. For example, PTE [29] embeds text data through heterogeneous text networks. HAN [32] and MAGNN [8] are proposed to capture the semantics involved in multiple types of nodes.

Complex real-world networks, however, are constantly evolving over time. As a result, how to capture temporal information in dynamic networks becomes more challenging. Many methods are proposed for temporal homogeneous networks like CTDNE [16], while studies on temporal HIN embedding are much less. Most of existing methods for temporal HIN embedding like DHNE [36], are non-incremental learning. They are designed to deal with snapshots rather than dynamic networks which keep changing by time. THINE [12] uses attention mechanism and metapath to capture heterogeneous information, and furthermore, Hawkes process is leveraged to simulate the evolution of temporal networks.

Although these embedding models have shown great performance in many areas, they are all built upon Euclidean spaces and their representation capacity is inherently limited by the dimension of embedding space. Recently, it has been noticed that complex real-world networks like social networks and many KGs always exhibit non-Euclidean structures [2]. As Fig. 1 shows, we find that the degrees of nodes follow power-law distributions in most real-world networks, in other words, indicate hyperbolic structures. Hyperbolic spaces are those of constant negative curvature and the areas of disks in hyperbolic spaces grow exponentially with their radius rather than polynomially in Euclidean spaces. Due to the exponential expansion property [15], the representation capacity and generalization ability of hyperbolic spaces for data with hierarchical structures or power-law distributions are potentially excellent [24]. In the past few years, researchers have made some progress in this domain [20,33,38]. Nevertheless, we find that none of them is designed for temporal HINs.

To this end, we propose H^2TNE, a novel hyperbolic heterogeneous temporal network embedding model. First, we leverage a temporally and heterogeneously double-constrained random walk strategy to capture the topological structure and contextual semantics over time. Then defined in hyperbolic spaces, our model maximizes the proximity between neighbors and minimizes it between negative samples. Moreover, we derive how the optimization process is calculated. Experiments on several real-world datasets show that our H^2TNE outperforms SOTA methods in two advanced analytic tasks temporal link prediction and node classification.

The contributions of this paper are summarized as follows:

- To our best knowledge, we are the first to study general temporal HIN embedding problem in hyperbolic spaces.
- We propose a novel temporal HIN embedding model H^2TNE, which leverages a temporally and heterogeneously double-constrained random walk strategy to capture the structural and semantic information, and exploits hyperbolic spaces to take full advantage of the power-law distributions for real-world networks.
- We conduct extensive experiments and the results show our model has better performance than several SOTA methods in node classification and link prediction tasks.

The rest of the paper is organized as follows. In Sect. 2, we make a brief but systematical review for related studies. Section 3 introduces necessary preliminaries and Sect. 4 presents our proposed H^2TNE from two key modules random walk sampling and hyperbolic embedding. Experiments are described in Sect. 5. Finally, we conclude our paper in Sect. 6.

2   Related Work

In this section, we systematically review the existing network embedding methods from three aspects, including traditional network embedding models, deep network embedding models and hyperbolic network embedding models.

Traditional Network Embedding Models. Network embedding aims to map nodes to a low-dimension space without losing structure and semantics of the network. In early researches, because of the unstructured character of networks, different sequential sampling strategies are proposed to simplify the data processing, e.g. Deepwalk [25] and node2vec [9]. LINE [30] learns node embeddings from the first-order and second-order neighbors. As the researches deepen, heterogeneous and temporal information are taken into account. Metapath2vec [7] leverages metapath-based random walks and achieves great performance. DynamicTriad [40] preserves structural information and evolution pattern on network snapshots by triadic closure process. Inspired of above two models, Change2vec [1] handles the difference between two snapshots by metapaths and triadic open/closure process.

Deep Network Embedding Models. With the development of deep learning, many GNN-based embedding models have emerged in recent years. GCN [14] aggregates messages from neighbors to update embeddings, and furthermore, GAT [31] introduces attention mechanism for aggregation and is competent on inductive tasks. M^2DNE [19] describes the temporal evolution of networks in terms of microscopic and macroscopic dynamics. DySAT [27] learns on snapshots by multi-head attention and achieves a great performance on link prediction. SHCF [17] jointly considers sequential information as well as high-order heterogeneous information. THINE [12] simulates the dynamic evolution of heterogeneous networks. LIME [23] incrementally trains on temporal HINs and significantly lowers memory resources and computational time.

Hyperbolic Network Embedding Models. Representation learning in hyperbolic spaces has been applied to network embedding due to the non-Euclidean structures of real-world networks. [20] learns hierarchical features of networks in the Poincaré ball, while [21] discovers pairwise hierarchical relations in Lorentz model. HHNE [33] is constructed in hyperbolic spaces on account of the power-law distribution of HINs. [18] proposes hyperbolic graph neural networks on graph classification problem, and HGCN [3] uses hyperbolic graph convolution networks for node embedding. HAT [38] exploits graph attention networks and devises a parallel strategy to improve the efficiency. Besides, h-MDS [26] provides a precision-dimension trade-off in hyperbolic embedding. [37] tells that hyperbolic models are more suited for sparse datasets and greatly outperform Euclidean models when the latent dimension number is small.

All above network embedding models are either built upon Euclidean spaces, or focused on only part of network features. In order to achieve better performance, we propose a hyperbolic embedding model with taking both temporal and heterogeneous information into account.

3 Preliminaries

In this section, we first define the temporal HINs and the problem of temporal HIN embedding. Then some critical properties of hyperbolic geometry are briefly introduced.

3.1 Temporal HIN Embedding

Following [5, 16, 28], HINs and temporal networks are defined traditionally as:

Definition 1 (HINs). *A heterogeneous information network is defined as $\mathcal{G} = (\mathcal{V}, \mathcal{E}, \phi, \varphi)$, in which $\mathcal{V}$ and $\mathcal{E}$ are the sets of nodes and edges. Each node $v \in \mathcal{V}$ and each edge $e \in \mathcal{E}$ are associated with mapping functions $\phi : \mathcal{V} \to \mathcal{L}_\mathcal{V}$ and $\varphi : \mathcal{E} \to \mathcal{L}_\mathcal{E}$. $\mathcal{L}_\mathcal{V}$ and $\mathcal{L}_\mathcal{E}$ denote the sets of node and edge types respectively and satisfy $|\mathcal{L}_\mathcal{V}| + |\mathcal{L}_\mathcal{E}| > 2$.*

Especially, a KG is a natural HIN since it contains different types of objects (e.g. subjects and objects) and links (e.g. properties) [39]. As a consequence, a general HIN model can be applied into KGs in most cases even with extra information like timestamps.

Definition 2 (Temporal Networks). *A temporal network is defined as $\mathcal{G} = (\mathcal{V}, \mathcal{E}, \tau)$, where $\mathcal{V}$ indicates the set of nodes and $\mathcal{E}$ indicates the set of edges. Each edge $e \in \mathcal{E}$ is associated with the mapping function $\tau : \mathcal{E} \to \mathcal{T}$, which maps edges to timestamps.*

It is worth noting that most existing temporal network models are designed for intermittent network snapshots, while our work studies the continuous-time dynamic networks. In other words, temporal networks in this paper can be seen as an edge stream and multiple edges may be established between two nodes at different timestamps. Based on Definition 1 and Definition 2, we formalize the temporal HINs as follows:

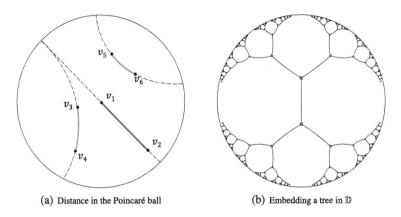

(a) Distance in the Poincaré ball   (b) Embedding a tree in $\mathbb{D}$

Fig. 2. (a) The colored curvatures $\widehat{v_1 v_2}$, $\widehat{v_3 v_4}$ and $\widehat{v_5 v_6}$ indicate the distances between nodes in the Poincaré ball. Geodesics are drawn as dashed curvatures. It's worth noting that the distance increases exponentially relative to Euclidean distances with the points being closer to the boundary. Best viewed in color. (b) Referred from [20]. It shows an example that a tree (a network with power-law distribution) is embedded into the Poincaré ball.

Definition 3 (Temporal HINs). *A temporal HIN can be formalized as $\mathcal{G} = (\mathcal{V}, \mathcal{E}, \phi, \varphi, \tau)$, in which $\mathcal{V}$ and $\mathcal{E}$ are the sets of nodes and edges. Mapping functions $\phi : \mathcal{V} \rightarrow \mathcal{L}_\mathcal{V}$ and $\varphi : \mathcal{E} \rightarrow \mathcal{L}_\mathcal{E}$ map nodes and edges into node types and edge types separately. $|\mathcal{L}_\mathcal{V}| + |\mathcal{L}_\mathcal{E}| > 2$ is satisfied. Another mapping function $\tau : \mathcal{E} \rightarrow \mathcal{T}$ maps edges to timestamps.*

In this paper, we aim to achieve the node embeddings of temporal HINs with consideration of not only temporal dynamics but also heterogeneous semantics. The problem is formally described as:

Problem (Temporal HIN embedding). *Given a temporal HIN $\mathcal{G} = (\mathcal{V}, \mathcal{E}, \phi, \varphi, \tau)$, the output is a node representation matrix $\mathbf{X} \in \mathbb{R}^{|\mathcal{V}| \times d}$. Each row of $\mathbf{X}$ is an embedding vector that corresponds to a node and $d \ll |\mathcal{V}|$ is the number of embedding dimensions. The representation matrix $\mathbf{X}$ needs to keep the influence of edge timestamps and node/edge types.*

3.2 Hyperbolic Geometry

Next, we introduce hyperbolic spaces. The n-dimensional hyperbolic space $\mathbb{H}^n$ is the unique simply connected n-dimensional complete Riemannian manifold with a constant negative sectional curvature. One critical property of hyperbolic spaces is that they expand exponentially, which means the areas of disks with radius r are of $O(e^r)$. This leads to the conclusion that data with power-law distribution is natural to be modeled in hyperbolic spaces [15]. Although hyperbolic spaces are not isometric to Euclidean spaces and difficult to perform operations on them consequently, there exist several well-known equivalent models of hyperbolic spaces defined on different Euclidean domains, such as the Klein model, the Poincaré ball model and the half-plane model. The Poincaré ball model is widely used because it is suitable for gradient-based optimization [20]. For an n-dimensional hyperbolic space with the curvature c, the definition domain of corresponding Poincaré ball model $\mathbb{D}$ is the point set

$$\mathbb{D} = \left\{ (x_1, x_2, \dots, x_n) : \sum_{i=1}^{n} x_i^2 < -\frac{1}{c} \right\}. \tag{1}$$

In this paper, let $c = -1$ if there are no special instructions. Under this circumstance, the Poincaré ball becomes an open unit ball. The distance between two points $\mathbf{u}$ and $\mathbf{v}$ in the ball is

$$d_{\mathbb{D}}(\mathbf{u}, \mathbf{v}) = arcosh \left(1 + \frac{2\|\mathbf{u} - \mathbf{v}\|^2}{(1 - \|\mathbf{u}\|^2)(1 - \|\mathbf{v}\|^2)} \right), \tag{2}$$

where $arcosh(x) = \ln(x + \sqrt{x^2 - 1})$ is the inverse hyperbolic cosine function. Note that the variation of distance is influenced by the location of $\mathbf{u}$ and $\mathbf{v}$. When $(1 - \|\mathbf{u}\|^2) \to 0$ and $(1 - \|\mathbf{v}\|^2) \to 0$, the points are close to the boundary of Poincaré ball and the distance between them is much larger than the case that they are closer to the center. See Fig. 2(a) for an illustration and Fig. 2(b) gives an example for embedding a tree-like network into the Poincaré ball.

4   Proposed Model

In this section, we describe our proposed H^{2}TNE in details. As Fig. 3 shows, H^{2}TNEfirst leverages a temporally and heterogeneously double-constrained random walk strategy [10] to capture both the topological structure and contextual semantics over time. Then, we propose a hyperbolic model defined in Poincaré ball to calculate the embeddings of nodes. Furthermore, we introduce how to optimize the model and analyze the time and space complexity.

4.1   The Double-Constrained Random Walk

In temporal networks, random walk over time is a natural choice. But in real world, one event may cause several additions of edges, and these edges share the same timestamp. This means local structures with the same timestamp always imply strong relations and semantics. Therefore, within the random walk going over time, a reasonable strategy needs to allow the next hop to stay at current timestamp. So how to make the trade-off between time going and staying becomes a challenge.

Non-decreasing temporal random walk is to run random walk process on a given temporal network $\mathcal{G}$ with the non-decreasing order on timestamps. Each generated node sequence $(v_1, v_2, \dots, v_l)$ conforms to the following rules:

1. For $i = 2, \dots, l - 1$, the timestamps between adjacent edges obey $\tau(v_{i-1}, v_i) \leq \tau(v_i, v_{i+1})$.

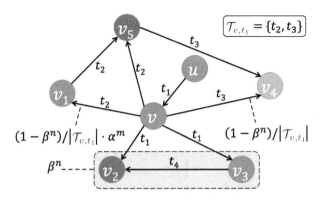

Fig. 3. The temporally and heterogeneously double-constrained random walk. Different colors refer to different node types and the timestamps are labeled on the edges. Last hop of the random walk is from node u to node v at timestamp t_1. Best viewed in color. (Color figure online)

2. The probability of $\tau(v_{i-1}, v_i) = \tau(v_i, v_{i+1})$, which means the timestamp of next hop equals to current timestamp, descends with the increase of hops staying at the same timestamp.

The latter tries to ensure that the random walk goes over time, and meanwhile keeps the possibility of staying at current timestamp. Let $t_i = \tau(v_{i-1}, v_i)$, then the probability of next hop staying at t_i is:

$$P\left(\tau(v_i, v_{i+1}) = t_i\right) = \begin{cases} \text{stop if } \mathcal{N}_{v_i}(t_i^*) = \varnothing, \\ 0 \quad \text{if } t_i \notin \mathcal{T}(\mathcal{N}_{v_i}), \\ \beta^n \quad \text{otherwise.} \end{cases} \tag{3}$$

Here, $\mathcal{N}_v$ is the universal neighbor set of node v, $\mathcal{N}_v(t^*)$ is the set of those connected with node v at timestamp t or later, $\mathcal{T}(\mathcal{N}_v)$ denotes the timestamp set of edges between node v and its neighbors. $\beta \in [0, 1]$ is the initial timestamp staying probability and n refers to the number of hops for which the random walk have been at current timestamp. First, in case that all the edges connected to node v_i are before timestamp t_i, we can only stop this random walk. Second, in case that there are no edges connected to node v_i at timestamp t_i, the next hop can only be chosen from the edges after t_i. Finally, if the timestamps of edges between node v_i and its neighbors contain both t_i and those after t_i, we probabilistically control the next hop staying at timestamp t_i with a probability β^n, and going to later timestamps otherwise. Adopting an exponential decay function here penalizes the cases that the random walk stays at the same timestamp for too long.

Taking Fig. 3 as an example, suppose that the random walk jumps from node u to v at timestamp t_1 in the last hop and it has been at t_1 for n hops. The probability of next hop staying at t_1, which means jumping to v_2 or v_3, is β^n. Let $\mathcal{T}_{v,t_1}$ denote the set of timestamps related to v after t_1. $\forall t \in \mathcal{T}_{v,t_1}$, the probability of the timestamp of next hop being t is $(1 - \beta^n)/|\mathcal{T}_{v,t_1}|$.

The random walks on temporal HINs need to satisfy two constraints: one is the non-decreasing principle for temporal information, and the other is for heterogeneous information. Taking node types into account, most existing methods use metapaths to guide the random walk sampling. However, in our model, overlaying the temporal constraint, metapaths are too strict to ensure the random walk process going continuously. Inspired by [13], we leverage a biased type choosing strategy based on historical walks. Suppose that we have chosen t_i to be the timestamp of next hop and currently the random walk is staying at node v_i of the node type l_i, then the probability of next hop still staying at node type l_i is:

$$P\left(\phi(v_{i+1}) = l_i; t_i\right) = \begin{cases} 0 & \text{if } \mathcal{N}_{v_i}(t_i) \cap \mathcal{N}_{v_i}(l_i) = \varnothing, \\ 1 & \text{if } \mathcal{N}_{v_i}(t_i) \subseteq \mathcal{N}_{v_i}(l_i), \\ \alpha^m & \text{otherwise.} \end{cases} \tag{4}$$

$\mathcal{N}_v(t)$ denotes the set of neighbors which connect to node v exactly at timestamp t, and $\mathcal{N}_v(l)$ refers to neighbors of the node type l. $\alpha \in [0,1]$ is the initial node type staying probability and m is the number of hops for which the random walk have been at node type l. Similar to the timestamp of next hop as aforementioned, we consider the following three cases. If any neighbors that connect to v_i at timestamp t_i are not of type l_i, the next hop will surely go to another node type. If all neighbors of v_i at timestamp t_i are of type l_i, the random walk can only stay at the same node type. If part of neighbors at timestamp t_i are of type l_i while others are not, the probability of next hop being at type l_i should be α^m. Similar to Eq. 3, we adopt the second exponential decay function to avoid the random walk staying at the same node type continuously.

Back to Fig. 3, suppose that the random walk has been staying at the same node type (in blue) for m hops. If we have chosen t_2 as the timestamp of next hop, according to Eq. 4, the probability of staying at current type is α^m. Overlaying the temporal constraint, the random walk will jump to node v_1 in next hop with the probability $(1 - \beta^n)/|\mathcal{T}_{v,t_1}| \cdot \alpha^m$.

With above constraints, we incrementally update the random walks when new edges come in order to lower the complexity of our model. In addition to newly added edges, historical random walks should also be processed appropriately. On the one hand, in real world, relations between entities are effected by historical events so they need to be preserved. On the other hand, their influence decreases gradually over time and recent events have greater importance for relations among entities.

The evolution of networks is manifested in the addition and deletion of nodes and edges. When evolution happens, nodes which directly connected to new nodes and edges are involved, and the random walks should be updated correspondingly. We consider the following four cases to incrementally update the node sequences of random walks when new edges come:

1. **Preserve uninvolved sequences.** If none of nodes in a sequence is involved, we keep the sequence unchanged.
2. **Remove invalid parts of sequences.** If the timestamps of front part of a sequence are too early, we treat this part as invalid and remove it.
3. **Continue involved sequences.** If the last node of a sequence is involved, continue the random walk with above strategy.
4. **Reverse new random walks from new timestamps.** When new edges and nodes come, to ensure that these changes are considered, reversed random walks from new timestamps backwards are processed.

With all above, we have captured the temporal and heterogeneous information of the networks and imply it into node sequences of random walks. Next, we'll explain how to embed these nodes into the hyperbolic space.

4.2 Hyperbolic Embedding

Defined in Poincaré ball, we exploit the hyperbolic distance in Eq. 2 to measure the proximity between nodes and calculate their probability of co-occurrence in random walks as following:

$$P(u|v) = \sigma\left(-d_{\mathbb{D}}(\mathbf{u}, \mathbf{v})\right), \tag{5}$$

where $\sigma(z) = \frac{1}{1+e^{-z}}$, $u|v$ denotes the co-occurrence of node u and v, and $\mathbf{u}$ and $\mathbf{v}$ denote the embedding vector of node u and v. For each node u, we randomly sample k negative nodes, each of which is denoted by n and each of whose corresponding embedding vector is denoted by $\mathbf{n}$, to speed up the training. The proximity between u and the co-occurrent node v is expected to be higher, so the optimization goal for each node u is:

$$\arg\max_{\Theta} \ \log\sigma\left(-d_{\mathbb{D}}(\mathbf{u}, \mathbf{v})\right) + \sum_{n} \log\sigma\left(d_{\mathbb{D}}(\mathbf{u}, \mathbf{n})\right). \tag{6}$$

Summing up all nodes and enhancing the ranking, the objective function of H^{2}TNE is written as:

$$\begin{aligned}
\mathcal{L} &= \arg\max_{\Theta} \sum_{u \in \mathcal{N}} \sum_{v;u|v} \log\sigma\left(-d_{\mathbb{D}}(\mathbf{u}, \mathbf{v})\right) + \sum_{u \in \mathcal{N}} \sum_{n;neg(u)} \log\sigma\left(d_{\mathbb{D}}(\mathbf{u}, \mathbf{n})\right) \\
&\sim \arg\max_{\Theta} \sum_{u \in \mathcal{N}} \sum_{v;u|v} \sum_{n;neg(u)} \log\sigma\left(d_{\mathbb{D}}(\mathbf{u}, \mathbf{n}) - d_{\mathbb{D}}(\mathbf{u}, \mathbf{v})\right),
\end{aligned} \tag{7}$$

where $neg(u)$ denotes the negative samples for node u.

Optimization. Due to the Riemannian manifold structure of Poincaré ball, the optimization is different from Euclidean models. Following [20], we primarily calculate the Euclidean gradients.

In training process, the parameters Θ are updated for each step of calculation. For $l = \log\sigma\left(d_{\mathbb{D}}(\mathbf{u}, \mathbf{n}) - d_{\mathbb{D}}(\mathbf{u}, \mathbf{v})\right)$,

$$\begin{aligned}
\frac{\partial l}{\partial \mathbf{u}} &= \left(1 - \sigma\left(d_{\mathbb{D}}(\mathbf{u}, \mathbf{n}) - d_{\mathbb{D}}(\mathbf{u}, \mathbf{v})\right)\right) \cdot \left(\frac{\partial d_{\mathbb{D}}(\mathbf{u}, \mathbf{n})}{\partial \mathbf{u}} - \frac{\partial d_{\mathbb{D}}(\mathbf{u}, \mathbf{v})}{\partial \mathbf{u}}\right), \\
\frac{\partial l}{\partial \mathbf{v}} &= \left(1 - \sigma\left(d_{\mathbb{D}}(\mathbf{u}, \mathbf{n}) - d_{\mathbb{D}}(\mathbf{u}, \mathbf{v})\right)\right) \cdot \left(-\frac{\partial d_{\mathbb{D}}(\mathbf{u}, \mathbf{v})}{\partial \mathbf{v}}\right), \\
\frac{\partial l}{\partial \mathbf{n}} &= \left(1 - \sigma\left(d_{\mathbb{D}}(\mathbf{u}, \mathbf{n}) - d_{\mathbb{D}}(\mathbf{u}, \mathbf{v})\right)\right) \cdot \left(\frac{\partial d_{\mathbb{D}}(\mathbf{u}, \mathbf{n})}{\partial \mathbf{n}}\right).
\end{aligned} \tag{8}$$

$\frac{\partial d_{\mathbb{D}}(\mathbf{u},\mathbf{v})}{\partial \mathbf{u}}$, $\frac{\partial d_{\mathbb{D}}(\mathbf{u},\mathbf{v})}{\partial \mathbf{v}}$, $\frac{\partial d_{\mathbb{D}}(\mathbf{u},\mathbf{n})}{\partial \mathbf{u}}$ and $\frac{\partial d_{\mathbb{D}}(\mathbf{u},\mathbf{n})}{\partial \mathbf{n}}$ is further derived:

$$
\begin{aligned}
\frac{\partial d_{\mathbb{D}}(\mathbf{u}, \mathbf{v})}{\partial \mathbf{u}} &= \frac{4}{\delta_v \sqrt{\gamma_{uv}^2 - 1}} \left(\frac{\|\mathbf{v}\|^2 - 2\langle \mathbf{u}, \mathbf{v}\rangle + 1}{\delta_u^2} \mathbf{u} - \frac{\mathbf{v}}{\delta_u} \right), \\
\frac{\partial d_{\mathbb{D}}(\mathbf{u}, \mathbf{v})}{\partial \mathbf{v}} &= \frac{4}{\delta_u \sqrt{\gamma_{uv}^2 - 1}} \left(\frac{\|\mathbf{u}\|^2 - 2\langle \mathbf{u}, \mathbf{v}\rangle + 1}{\delta_v^2} \mathbf{v} - \frac{\mathbf{u}}{\delta_v} \right), \\
\frac{\partial d_{\mathbb{D}}(\mathbf{u}, \mathbf{n})}{\partial \mathbf{u}} &= \frac{4}{\delta_n \sqrt{\gamma_{un}^2 - 1}} \left(\frac{\|\mathbf{n}\|^2 - 2\langle \mathbf{u}, \mathbf{n}\rangle + 1}{\delta_u^2} \mathbf{u} - \frac{\mathbf{n}}{\delta_u} \right), \\
\frac{\partial d_{\mathbb{D}}(\mathbf{u}, \mathbf{n})}{\partial \mathbf{n}} &= \frac{4}{\delta_u \sqrt{\gamma_{un}^2 - 1}} \left(\frac{\|\mathbf{u}\|^2 - 2\langle \mathbf{u}, \mathbf{n}\rangle + 1}{\delta_n^2} \mathbf{n} - \frac{\mathbf{u}}{\delta_n} \right),
\end{aligned}
\tag{9}
$$

where $\delta_u = 1 - \|\mathbf{u}\|^2$, $\delta_v = 1 - \|\mathbf{v}\|^2$, $\delta_n = 1 - \|\mathbf{n}\|^2$, $\gamma_{uv} = 1 + \frac{2}{\delta_u \delta_v}\|\mathbf{u} - \mathbf{v}\|^2$ and $\gamma_{un} = 1 + \frac{2}{\delta_u \delta_n}\|\mathbf{u} - \mathbf{n}\|^2$.

Next, combining with Riemannian gradient, a single embedding is updated as follows:

$$
\begin{aligned}
\mathbf{u}_{new} &\leftarrow \text{proj}\left(\mathbf{u}_{old} + lr\frac{(1 - \|\mathbf{u}_{old}\|^2)^2}{4} \frac{\partial l}{\partial \mathbf{u}} \right), \\
\mathbf{v}_{new} &\leftarrow \text{proj}\left(\mathbf{v}_{old} + lr\frac{(1 - \|\mathbf{v}_{old}\|^2)^2}{4} \frac{\partial l}{\partial \mathbf{v}} \right), \\
\mathbf{n}_{new} &\leftarrow \text{proj}\left(\mathbf{n}_{old} + lr\frac{(1 - \|\mathbf{n}_{old}\|^2)^2}{4} \frac{\partial l}{\partial \mathbf{n}} \right),
\end{aligned}
\tag{10}
$$

in which lr is the learning rate and $\text{proj}(\cdot)$ is a projection function that constrains the embeddings within the Poincaré ball:

$$
\text{proj}(\mathbf{x}) = \begin{cases} \mathbf{x}/(\|\mathbf{x}\| + \epsilon) & \text{if} \|\mathbf{x}\| \geq 1, \\ \mathbf{x} & \text{otherwise.} \end{cases}
\tag{11}
$$

Here $\epsilon = 10^{-7}$ is a small constant.

Time Complexity Analysis
The time complexity for random walk updating is $\mathcal{O}(|\mathcal{N}| \cdot \Delta_{l_{avg}})$, in which $\Delta_{l_{avg}}$ is the average length of updated part in random walks. The time complexity of hyperbolic embedding training is $\mathcal{O}(I \cdot k \cdot d \cdot |\mathcal{N}| \cdot \Delta_{l_{avg}})$, where I is the number of iterations, k is the number of negative samples for each node, and d is the dimension number of embedding space.

5   Experiments and Discussions

5.1   Experimental Setup

Datasets. We make extensive experiments on four real-world datasets Enron[1], DBLP[2], Tokyo [35] and MovieLens [11]. The statistics of these datasets are shown in Table 1.

---

[1] http://www.ahschulz.de/enron-email-data/.
[2] https://www.aminer.cn/citation.

Table 1. Statistics of the datasets.

Datasets	Enron	DBLP	Tokyo	MovieLens
# Nodes	115	164,174	64,151	9,940
# Edges	43,160	845,485	573,703	1,000,209
# Node types	9	2	2	2
# Timestamps	20	46	555,437	25,865

Table 2. Baselines.

Methods		Heterogeneous	Temporal
Shallow	Deepwalk [25]	×	×
	CTDNE [16]	×	✓
	ISGNS [22]	×	✓
	Change2vec [1]	✓	✓
	DHNE [36]	✓	✓
	HHNE [33]	✓	×
Deep	GCN [14]	×	×
	GAT [31]	×	×
	DySAT [27]	×	✓
	LIME [23]	✓	✓
	TGAT [34]	×	✓

Baselines and Experimental Details. Table 2 lists eleven SOTA network embedding methods, including six shallow models and five deep ones.

For all baselines, we take the recommended parameter settings except that the embedding size is set to be 128. For H^2TNE, we set the number of walks per node as 10, the maximum of walk length as 80, the number of negative samples per node as 5 and initial learning rate as 0.001. For the experimental results in Sect. 5.2, we set the values of α and β to be 0.9 and 0.3, and our method is trained on the dimensions both 16 and 128, denoted by H^2TNE_{16} and H^2TNE_{128}, respectively.

In order to validate the effectiveness of each part in our model, we further conduct ablation experiments on three different H^2TNE variants, in which H^2TNE_{-he} denotes ignoring heterogeneous information in random walk process, H^2TNE_{-te} denotes ignoring temporal information, and H^2TNE_{-hy} denotes embedding in Euclidean spaces. For fairness all of these three variants are evaluated with the dimension of 128.

We evaluate the performance of H^2TNE for temporal link prediction and node classification tasks on a server with $2 \times$ Intel Xeon Gold 6226R 16C 2.90GHz CPUs, $4 \times$ GeForce RTX 3090 GPUs and 256 GB memory. The experiments are run on Ubuntu 18.04 with CUDA 11.1.

5.2 Experimental Performance

We train the baselines shown in Table 2 in unsupervised manners on all datasets and evaluate them by two traditional tasks, temporal link prediction and node classification.

Table 3. Performance on temporal link prediction.

Dataset	Enron				Tokyo					
Timestamp	10	15	20	Avg	200k	300k	400k	500k	555k	Avg.
Deepwalk	0.9105	0.9199	0.9015	0.9106	0.7854	0.8695	0.8386	0.8565	0.8831	0.8466
CTDNE	0.8403	0.9269	0.9120	0.8931	0.7124	0.7621	0.7519	0.7695	0.8239	0.7640
ISGNS	0.9162	0.7392	0.7384	0.7979	0.7159	0.7315	0.6997	0.6706	0.5779	0.6791
Change2vec	0.7750	0.7796	0.7845	0.7797	0.5614	0.5266	0.5516	0.5164	0.4959	0.5304
DHNE	-	0.5751	0.5774	0.5763	-	0.5057	0.5005	0.5004	0.5002	0.5017
HHNE	0.8928	0.9135	0.8992	0.9018	0.6241	0.7225	0.7802	0.8513	0.8770	0.7710
GCN	0.8847	0.8916	0.8547	0.877	0.4944	0.4052	0.3626	0.3078	0.3004	0.3741
GAT	**0.9360**	0.8867	**0.9292**	0.9173	0.6911	0.6690	0.6518	0.7328	0.7086	0.6907
DySAT	-	0.7456	0.8305	0.7881	-	0.6576	0.6462	0.6473	0.6504	0.6504
LIME	0.5642	0.6296	0.5116	0.5685	0.5166	0.5144	0.5141	0.5107	0.5125	0.5137
TGAT	0.7224	0.6814	0.6799	0.6946	0.6432	0.6731	0.4647	0.6593	0.7365	0.6353
H^2TNE_{-he}	0.7886	0.9144	0.8994	0.8675	0.8753	0.8953	0.8848	0.8855	0.9008	0.8883
H^2TNE_{-te}	0.7172	0.8954	0.9044	0.8390	0.8773	0.8936	0.8839	0.8834	0.8980	0.8872
H^2TNE_{-hy}	0.9153	**0.9363**	0.9204	**0.9240**	0.7582	0.7907	0.7615	0.7779	0.8226	0.7822
H^2TNE_{16}	0.9052	0.9199	0.9060	0.9104	0.8432	0.8795	0.8702	0.8727	0.8921	0.8715
H^2TNE_{128}	0.9106	0.9233	0.9105	0.9148	**0.8795**	**0.8977**	**0.8871**	**0.8872**	**0.9032**	**0.8910**
Dataset	DBLP					MovieLens				
Timestamp	20	30	40	46	Avg	10k	15k	20k	25k	Avg.
Deepwalk	0.9290	0.8710	0.8422	0.8378	0.8700	0.8816	0.8482	0.8607	0.8310	0.8554
CTDNE	0.7381	0.5199	0.5657	0.5424	0.5915	0.3248	0.4165	0.4551	0.4577	0.4135
ISGNS	0.9321	0.8579	0.8414	0.7788	0.8526	0.8355	0.8030	0.8070	0.7771	0.8057
Change2vec	0.5482	0.5161	0.5025	0.4989	0.5164	0.8438	0.8455	0.8643	0.8446	0.8496
DHNE	-	0.5177	0.5002	0.5002	0.5060	-	0.5007	0.5004	0.4995	0.5002
HHNE	0.3487	0.5956	0.6987	0.7195	0.5906	0.8683	0.8881	0.8834	0.8837	0.8809
GCN	0.6550	0.6308	0.5706	0.5878	0.6111	0.2318	0.2343	0.2491	0.1816	0.2242
GAT	0.6722	0.7472	0.6474	0.5657	0.6581	0.4960	0.2448	0.3311	0.3889	0.3652
DySAT	-	0.5178	0.6046	0.6272	0.5832	-	0.7463	0.7429	0.7167	0.7353
LIME	0.5041	0.5353	0.5392	0.5385	0.5293	0.4801	0.4753	0.4764	0.4786	0.4776
TGAT	0.5091	0.6215	0.3311	0.5648	0.5066	0.4000	0.4567	0.5326	0.5161	0.4764
H^2TNE_{-he}	0.7270	0.8151	0.8376	0.8379	0.8044	0.8899	0.9276	0.9450	0.9292	0.9229
H^2TNE_{-te}	0.7681	0.6947	0.7849	0.8007	0.7621	0.6925	0.6870	0.6987	0.7156	0.6985
H^2TNE_{-hy}	0.7687	0.7989	0.7621	0.7573	0.7718	0.7448	0.5182	0.5385	0.5597	0.5903
H^2TNE_{16}	0.9302	0.8770	0.8757	0.8505	0.8834	0.9264	0.9433	0.9466	0.9377	0.9385
H^2TNE_{128}	**0.9349**	**0.8812**	**0.8770**	**0.8582**	**0.8878**	**0.9380**	**0.9475**	**0.9555**	**0.9435**	**0.9461**

* The best result is in bold, and the suboptimal result is underlined. The same applies to below tables.

Table 4. Performance on node classification.

Dataset	Enron		DBLP		Tokyo		MovieLens	
Metrics	Macro-f1	Micro-f1	Macro-f1	Micro-f1	Macro-f1	Micro-f1	Macro-f1	Micro-f1
Deepwalk	0.1832	0.3793	0.4999	0.9995	0.5208	0.9617	0.9446	0.9531
CTDNE	0.1277	0.2828	0.6552	0.9993	0.4915	0.9666	0.9862	0.9871
ISGNS	0.1084	0.3034	<u>0.7438</u>	0.9995	0.8501	0.9815	0.9903	0.9909
Change2vec	0.4482	0.6414	0.4997	0.9989	0.5229	0.9596	0.9415	0.9628
DHNE	0.0641	0.3448	0.4998	0.9994	0.4910	0.9648	0.4002	0.6036
HHNE	0.1497	0.2414	0.4997	0.9986	0.7953	<u>0.9889</u>	0.9906	0.9912
GCN	0.2957	0.4344	0.4999	0.9994	0.5280	0.9644	**0.9995**	**0.9995**
GAT	0.1824	0.2828	0.4998	0.9993	0.5723	0.9674	0.9599	0.9624
DySAT	0.0972	0.2069	0.6358	0.9977	<u>0.9095</u>	0.9816	0.9445	0.9478
LIME	0.0794	0.1538	0.4998	0.9955	0.4818	0.9299	0.8188	0.8317
TGAT	0.1018	0.2069	0.4998	0.9992	0.7381	0.9689	0.9459	0.9496
H^2TNE_{-he}	0.1241	0.3103	0.5907	0.9992	0.4908	0.9639	0.9866	0.9875
H^2TNE_{-te}	0.4215	0.5517	0.6199	0.9995	0.4903	0.9618	0.9880	0.9888
H^2TNE_{-hy}	0.1628	0.3172	**0.8023**	<u>0.9996</u>	**0.9469**	**0.9928**	0.8434	0.8523
H^2TNE_{16}	**0.8121**	**0.7931**	0.4999	**0.9997**	0.4916	0.9670	0.9873	0.9915
H^2TNE_{128}	<u>0.6783</u>	**0.7931**	0.6499	<u>0.9996</u>	0.4913	0.9659	**0.9995**	**0.9995**

Temporal Link Prediction. In this task, we divide Enron, DBLP, Tokyo and Movie-Lens into 4, 5, 6 and 5 snapshots evenly according to timestamps, and for the t-th snapshot except the first, the models are trained on the first $t-1$ snapshots and tested on the t-th snapshot. Noting that the Poincaré ball is a conformal model, which means that the angles in hyperbolic spaces are equal to corresponding ones in Euclidean spaces, we use the cosine similarity to calculate the proximity between nodes for fairness to all models. AUC is used to measure the performance in this task. The experimental results for all snapshots are shown in Table 3. In most cases, our method has the best performance and even 16-dimension embeddings of H^2TNE are better than previous models in dimension 128. On the dense dataset Enron, our method does not outperform other Euclidean models, suggesting that hyperbolic models are more suitable for sparse data, which is consistent with [37]. In addition, the results of ablation models show that performance of different variants mostly degrades. It proves that double-constrained random walk strategy does capture the temporal and heterogeneous information and the hyperbolic space does enhance the representation ability of our model.

Node Classification. In this task, we use 75% of node embeddings for each dataset to train a Logistic Regression classifier and the remains are treated as the test set. The results are evaluated by two metrics macro-f1 and micro-f1. As Table 4 shows, our method outperforms other models in most cases. It's worth noting that for most methods in datasets DBLP and Tokyo, the difference between macro-f1 and micro-f1 is very large, which is caused by the imbalance of various node types.

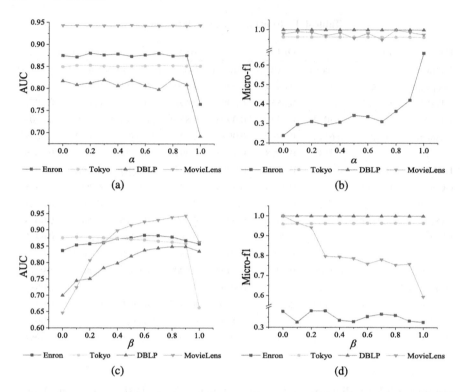

Fig. 4. The influence of parameters α and β for two experimental tasks in four datasets: (a) α for temporal link prediction, (b) α for node classification, (c) β for temporal link prediction, (d) β for node classification. The X-axis represents values of α and β, while the Y-axis represents AUC for temporal link prediction task and micro-f1 for node classification task. Best viewed in color. (Color figure online)

5.3   Parameter Analysis

We also analyze the influence of parameters α and β for two experimental tasks in four datasets. As Fig. 4 shows, no matter for temporal link prediction or node classification, datasets with multiple types of nodes (e.g. Enron) are more affected by α while those with fine temporal granularity (e.g. MovieLens) are more affected by β, which conforms to the control of random walk strategy. According to our experience, in temporal link prediction, both α and β are expected to be a larger value except 1 because this may lead to overly constraints and stop the random walk process too early. While in node classification, $\alpha = 1$ could keep random walks staying at the same type of nodes and strengthen the relations among them, which is especially important in multi-class classification tasks.

5.4   Visualizations

We further study the visualizations of all nodes. Figure 5 shows the embedding layouts, which are projected to 2 dimensions from 128 by t-SNE, on dataset MovieLens for

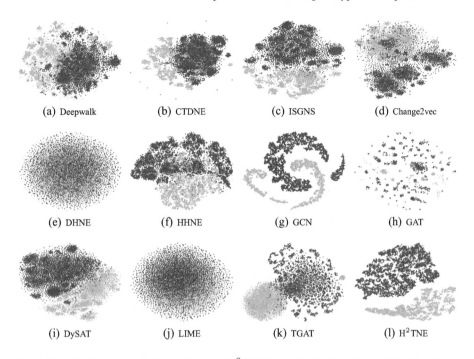

Fig. 5. The visualizations of all baselines and H^2TNE for node classification task in MovieLens. Different colors refer different types of nodes. Best viewed in color. (Color figure online)

eleven baselines and our proposed H^2TNE. Different colors refer different types of nodes. Obviously our method has the best capacity of discriminating different node types compared with other models.

6   Conclusion

In this paper, we propose a hyperbolic temporal HIN embedding model H^2TNE based on the power-law distribution of real-world networks. H^2TNE first leverages a temporally and heterogeneously double-constrained random walk strategy and then embeds nodes in achieved random walks into a hyperbolic space. Extensive experimental results prove the superior performance of our model.

Supplemental Material Statement: Section 5.1 has provided the detailed experimental hardware and software environments, parameter settings and provenances of all datasets. Source code is available from https://github.com/TaiLvYuanLiang/H2TNE.

Acknowledgements. This work is supported by the Chinese Scientific and Technical Innovation Project 2030 (2018AAA0102100), National Natural Science Foundation of China (U1936206, U1903128, 62172237) and the Fundamental Research Funds for the Central Universities (No. 63223046).

References

1. Bian, R., Koh, Y.S., Dobbie, G., Divoli, A.: Network embedding and change modeling in dynamic heterogeneous networks. In: Proceedings of the 42nd International ACM SIGIR Conference on Research and Development in Information Retrieval, pp. 861–864 (2019)
2. Bronstein, M.M., Bruna, J., LeCun, Y., Szlam, A., Vandergheynst, P.: Geometric deep learning: going beyond euclidean data. IEEE Signal Process. Mag. **34**(4), 18–42 (2017)
3. Chami, I., Ying, Z., Ré, C., Leskovec, J.: Hyperbolic graph convolutional neural networks. Advances in neural information processing systems 32 (2019)
4. Chen, F., Wang, Y.C., Wang, B., Kuo, C.C.J.: Graph representation learning: a survey. APSIPA Trans. Sig. Inf. Process. **9** (2020)
5. Chen, H., Perozzi, B., Al-Rfou, R., Skiena, S.: A tutorial on network embeddings. arXiv preprint arXiv:1808.02590 (2018)
6. Cui, P., Wang, X., Pei, J., Zhu, W.: A survey on network embedding. IEEE Trans. Knowl. Data Eng. **31**(5), 833–852 (2018)
7. Dong, Y., Chawla, N.V., Swami, A.: metapath2vec: Scalable representation learning for heterogeneous networks. In: Proceedings of the 23rd ACM SIGKDD International Conference on Knowledge Discovery and Data Mining, pp. 135–144 (2017)
8. Fu, X., Zhang, J., Meng, Z., King, I.: Magnn: Metapath aggregated graph neural network for heterogeneous graph embedding. In: Proceedings of the Web Conference 2020, pp. 2331–2341 (2020)
9. Grover, A., Leskovec, J.: node2vec: scalable feature learning for networks. In: Proceedings of the 22nd ACM SIGKDD International Conference on Knowledge Discovery and Data Mining, pp. 855–864 (2016)
10. Guo, J., Bai, Q., Lin, Z., Song, C., Yuan, X.: Dynamic heterogeneous network embedding based on non-decreasing temporal random walk. J. Comput. Res. Dev. **58**(8), 1624 (2021)
11. Harper, F.M., Konstan, J.A.: The movielens datasets: history and context. ACM Trans. Interactive Intell. Syst. (TIIS) **5**(4), 1–19 (2015)
12. Huang, H., Shi, R., Zhou, W., Wang, X., Jin, H., Fu, X.: Temporal heterogeneous information network embedding. In: The 30th International Joint Conference on Artificial Intelligence (2021)
13. Hussein, R., Yang, D., Cudré-Mauroux, P.: Are meta-paths necessary? revisiting heterogeneous graph embeddings. In: Proceedings of the 27th ACM International Conference on Information and Knowledge Management, pp. 437–446 (2018)
14. Kipf, T.N., Welling, M.: Semi-supervised classification with graph convolutional networks. In: International Conference on Learning Representations (2017)
15. Krioukov, D., Papadopoulos, F., Kitsak, M., Vahdat, A., Boguná, M.: Hyperbolic geometry of complex networks. Phys. Rev. E **82**(3), 036106 (2010)
16. Lee, J.B., Nguyen, G., Rossi, R.A., Ahmed, N.K., Koh, E., Kim, S.: Dynamic node embeddings from edge streams. IEEE Trans. Emerging Top. Comput. Intell. **5**(6), 931–946 (2020)
17. Li, C., Hu, L., Shi, C., Song, G., Lu, Y.: Sequence-aware heterogeneous graph neural collaborative filtering. In: Proceedings of the 2021 SIAM International Conference on Data Mining (SDM), pp. 64–72. SIAM (2021)
18. Liu, Q., Nickel, M., Kiela, D.: Hyperbolic graph neural networks. Advances in Neural Information Processing Systems 32 (2019)
19. Lu, Y., Wang, X., Shi, C., Yu, P.S., Ye, Y.: Temporal network embedding with micro-and macro-dynamics. In: Proceedings of the 28th ACM International Conference on Information and Knowledge Management, pp. 469–478 (2019)
20. Nickel, M., Kiela, D.: Poincaré embeddings for learning hierarchical representations. Advances in neural information processing systems 30 (2017)

21. Nickel, M., Kiela, D.: Learning continuous hierarchies in the lorentz model of hyperbolic geometry. In: International Conference on Machine Learning, pp. 3779–3788. PMLR (2018)
22. Peng, H., et al..: Dynamic network embedding via incremental skip-gram with negative sampling. Sci. China Inf. Sci. **63**(10), 1–19 (2020). https://doi.org/10.1007/s11432-018-9943-9
23. Peng, H., et al.: Lime: Low-cost incremental learning for dynamic heterogeneous information networks. IEEE Trans. Comput. (2021)
24. Peng, W., Varanka, T., Mostafa, A., Shi, H., Zhao, G.: Hyperbolic deep neural networks: a survey. IEEE Trans. Pattern Anal. Mach. Intell. (2021)
25. Perozzi, B., Al-Rfou, R., Skiena, S.: Deepwalk: online learning of social representations. In: Proceedings of the 20th ACM SIGKDD International Conference on Knowledge Discovery and Data Mining, pp. 701–710 (2014)
26. Sala, F., De Sa, C., Gu, A., Ré, C.: Representation tradeoffs for hyperbolic embeddings. In: International Conference on Machine Learning, pp. 4460–4469. PMLR (2018)
27. Sankar, A., Wu, Y., Gou, L., Zhang, W., Yang, H.: Dysat: deep neural representation learning on dynamic graphs via self-attention networks. In: Proceedings of the 13th International Conference on Web Search and Data Mining, pp. 519–527 (2020)
28. Shi, C., Li, Y., Zhang, J., Sun, Y., Philip, S.Y.: A survey of heterogeneous information network analysis. IEEE Trans. Knowl. Data Eng. **29**(1), 17–37 (2016)
29. Tang, J., Qu, M., Mei, Q.: Pte: Predictive text embedding through large-scale heterogeneous text networks. In: Proceedings of the 21th ACM SIGKDD International Conference on Knowledge Discovery and Data Mining, pp. 1165–1174 (2015)
30. Tang, J., Qu, M., Wang, M., Zhang, M., Yan, J., Mei, Q.: Line: large-scale information network embedding. In: Proceedings of the 24th International Conference on World Wide Web, pp. 1067–1077 (2015)
31. Veličković, P., Cucurull, G., Casanova, A., Romero, A., Liò, P., Bengio, Y.: Graph attention networks. In: International Conference on Learning Representations (2018)
32. Wang, X., et al.: Heterogeneous graph attention network. In: The World Wide Web Conference. pp. 2022–2032 (2019)
33. Wang, X., Zhang, Y., Shi, C.: Hyperbolic heterogeneous information network embedding. In: Proceedings of the AAAI Conference on Artificial Intelligence, vol. 33, pp. 5337–5344 (2019)
34. Xu, D., Ruan, C., Körpeoglu, E., Kumar, S., Achan, K.: Inductive representation learning on temporal graphs. In: International Conference on Learning Representations (2020)
35. Yang, D., Zhang, D., Zheng, V.W., Yu, Z.: Modeling user activity preference by leveraging user spatial temporal characteristics in lbsns. IEEE Trans. Syst. Man Cybern. Syst. **45**(1), 129–142 (2014)
36. Yin, Y., Ji, L.X., Zhang, J.P., Pei, Y.L.: Dhne: network representation learning method for dynamic heterogeneous networks. IEEE Access **7**, 134782–134792 (2019)
37. Zhang, S., Chen, H., Ming, X., Cui, L., Yin, H., Xu, G.: Where are we in embedding spaces? In: Proceedings of the 27th ACM SIGKDD Conference on Knowledge Discovery & Data Mining, pp. 2223–2231 (2021)
38. Zhang, Y., Wang, X., Shi, C., Jiang, X., Ye, Y.F.: Hyperbolic graph attention network. IEEE Trans. Big Data (2021)
39. Zheng, Y., Shi, C., Cao, X., Li, X., Wu, B.: Entity set expansion with meta path in knowledge graph. In: Kim, J., Shim, K., Cao, L., Lee, J.-G., Lin, X., Moon, Y.-S. (eds.) PAKDD 2017. LNCS (LNAI), vol. 10234, pp. 317–329. Springer, Cham (2017). https://doi.org/10.1007/978-3-319-57454-7_25
40. Zhou, L., Yang, Y., Ren, X., Wu, F., Zhuang, Y.: Dynamic network embedding by modeling triadic closure process. In: Proceedings of the AAAI Conference on Artificial Intelligence, vol. 32 (2018)

Facing Changes: Continual Entity Alignment for Growing Knowledge Graphs

Yuxin Wang[1], Yuanning Cui[1], Wenqiang Liu[3], Zequn Sun[1]●, Yiqiao Jiang[3], Kexin Han[3], and Wei Hu[1,2(✉)]●

[1] State Key Laboratory for Novel Software Technology, Nanjing University, Nanjing, China
whu@nju.edu.cn,yuxinwangcs@outlook.com,yncui.nju@gmail.com
[2] National Institute of Healthcare Data Science, Nanjing University, Nanjing, China
[3] Interactive Entertainment Group, Tencent Inc, Shenzhen, China
{masonqliu,gennyjiang,casseyhan}@tencent.com

Abstract. Entity alignment is a basic and vital technique in knowledge graph (KG) integration. Over the years, research on entity alignment has resided on the assumption that KGs are static, which neglects the nature of growth of real-world KGs. As KGs grow, previous alignment results face the need to be revisited while new entity alignment waits to be discovered. In this paper, we propose and dive into a realistic yet unexplored setting, referred to as continual entity alignment. To avoid retraining an entire model on the whole KGs whenever new entities and triples come, we present a continual alignment method for this task. It reconstructs an entity's representation based on entity adjacency, enabling it to generate embeddings for new entities quickly and inductively using their existing neighbors. It selects and replays partial pre-aligned entity pairs to train only parts of KGs while extracting trustworthy alignment for knowledge augmentation. As growing KGs inevitably contain non-matchable entities, different from previous works, the proposed method employs bidirectional nearest neighbor matching to find new entity alignment and update old alignment. Furthermore, we also construct new datasets by simulating the growth of multilingual DBpedia. Extensive experiments demonstrate that our continual alignment method is more effective than baselines based on retraining or inductive learning.

Keywords: Knowledge graphs · Continual entity alignment · Representation learning

1 Introduction

Entity alignment, also known as entity matching or entity resolution [22], has been a long-standing research topic in the Semantic Web and Database communities. The task aims at matching the identical entities with different URIs in different

U. Sattler et al. (Eds.): ISWC 2022, LNCS 13489, pp. 196–213, 2022.
https://doi.org/10.1007/978-3-031-19433-7_12

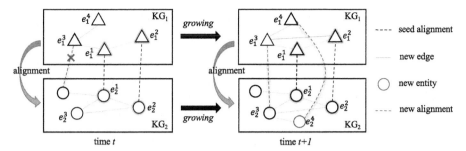

Fig. 1. Illustration of continual entity alignment. Given two pre-aligned entity pairs (e_1^1, e_2^1) and (e_1^2, e_2^2) between KG_1 and KG_2, we expect to find the identical counterparts for e_1^3 and e_1^4. At time t, due to the incompleteness of both KGs, e_1^3 can be falsely matched to a wrong entity, and the expecting counterpart of e_1^4 does not even appear yet. At time $t + 1$, as new triples emerge over time, e_1^3 and e_1^4 gain more chance to be correctly matched with richer supportive information.

knowledge graphs (KGs). For example, two entities http://dbpedia.org/resource/Hangzhou and http://zh.dbpedia.org/resource/杭州 from DBpedia [13] in different languages both refer to the same Chinese city, Hangzhou, which is the venue of ISWC 2022 conference. Early studies [11,22] mainly explore the literal similarities with probabilistic or semantic inference to match entities. However, these methods are hampered by the symbolic heterogeneity of different KGs, particularly the cross-lingual KGs. To resolve this issue, recent embedding-based methods strive to construct a unified vector space to represent different KGs, with entity embeddings used to infer entity similarity [24]. Furthermore, the embeddings from the unified space built by aligning various KGs are shown to be useful for downstream tasks, such as cross-lingual knowledge transfer and multi-lingual KG completion [7,20]. Thus, as a backbone of knowledge fusion and transfer, embedding-based entity alignment has received increasing attention [28,41,42].

However, existing embedding-based entity alignment methods assume an idealized scenario of static KGs, neglecting many real-world difficulties like alignment incompleteness, KG growth, and alignment growth. In this paper, we argue that entity alignment is not a one-time task. We propose and study a new setting, i.e., *continual entity alignment*, between growing and incomplete KGs. Our motivation comes from the growth and incompleteness nature of real-world KGs. For example, the release bot of DBpedia [13] extracts about 21 billion new triples per month [10], and Wikidata [30] releases data dumps in a weekly cycle.[1] The new entities and triples bring about new alignment to be found and provide new clues for correcting the previous alignment. Figure 1 presents an illustration.

This real scenario poses new challenges to embedding-based entity alignment. The first challenge is *how to learn embeddings for the new entities in an effective and efficient manner*. When KGs grow, the pre-trained entity alignment model sees new entities for the first time, as new triples bring structural changes to KGs.

---

[1] https://dumps.wikimedia.org/wikidatawiki/entities/.

To handle new entities, retraining the model from scratch is costly. Also, inductive entity embedding is less adaptable to changes of structure. Thus, it requires non-trivial updates of the pre-trained model to incorporate new entities and new triples. The second challenge is *how to capture the potential alignment of both old and new entities*. In real cases, KGs always contain unknown non-matchable entities [23], which necessitates a more reliable alignment retrieval strategy than simply ranking candidates from test sets. Furthermore, as new entities typically are few-linked [2], capturing the potential alignment for new entities becomes more difficult. The third challenge is *how to integrate the old predicted alignment with the new predictions*. In our setting, we output alignment results each time the KGs grow. The old and new alignment inevitably have conflicts. We need an effective integration strategy to combine them and update the final alignment.

As the first attempt to address these challenges, we propose a continual entity alignment method **ContEA**. Our key idea is to finetune the pre-trained model to incorporate new entities and triples, meanwhile capturing the potential entity alignment. Specifically, we use Dual-AMN [16], a prominent alignment model, as our basal encoder. To enable it to effectively handle new entities, we design an entity reconstruction objective, which allows the encoder to generate entity embeddings using solely neighboring subgraphs. To retrieve alignment from the embedding space, we propose a bidirectional nearest neighbor search strategy. Two entities are predicted to be aligned if and only if they are the nearest neighbors to each other. When new entities and triples emerge, ContEA finetunes the pre-trained model according to the changed structures. To capture potential entity alignment, we replay partial pre-known alignment to avoid knowledge oblivion and select high-confidence predictions for knowledge augmentation.

To support the research on this new and practical task, we build three new datasets based on the widely-used benchmark DBP15K [24], which contains three cross-lingual datasets, i.e., ZH-EN, JA-EN and FR-EN. For each dataset, we construct six snapshots (i.e., $t = 0, 1, 2, 3, 4, 5$) by adding new entities and new triples into the preceding snapshot, to simulate KGs' growth. We conduct extensive experiments on our datasets. Our method outperforms strong baselines that use retraining or inductive embedding techniques while at a lower time cost. Our datasets and source code are publicly available to foster future research.

2   Problem Statement

We define a KG as a 3-tuple $\mathcal{G} = \{\mathcal{E}, \mathcal{R}, \mathcal{T}\}$, where $\mathcal{E}$ and $\mathcal{R}$ denote the sets of entities and relations, respectively. $\mathcal{T} \subseteq \mathcal{E} \times \mathcal{R} \times \mathcal{E}$ is the set of relational triples. Given two KGs $\mathcal{G}_1 = \{\mathcal{E}_1, \mathcal{R}_1, \mathcal{T}_1\}$ and $\mathcal{G}_2 = \{\mathcal{E}_2, \mathcal{R}_2, \mathcal{T}_2\}$, *entity alignment* aims to identify entities in $\mathcal{G}_1$ and $\mathcal{G}_2$ that refer to the same real-world object, i.e., seeking a set of alignment $\mathcal{A} = \{(e_1, e_2) \in \mathcal{E}_s \times \mathcal{E}_t \mid e_1 \equiv e_2\}$, where "$\equiv$" indicates equivalence. A small set of seed entity alignment $\mathcal{A}_s \subset \mathcal{A}$ is usually provided as anchors (i.e., training data) beforehand to help align the remaining entities.

From time to time, new triples emerge and are added into KGs, which brings KGs' size growth. We propose the definition of *growing KGs* as follows:

Definition 1 (Growing knowledge graphs). *A growing KG $\mathcal{G}$ is a sequence of snapshots $\mathcal{G} = (\mathcal{G}^0, \mathcal{G}^1, \ldots, \mathcal{G}^T)$, where the superscript numbers denote different timestamps. For any two successive timestamps $\mathcal{G}^t = \{\mathcal{E}^t, \mathcal{R}^t, \mathcal{T}^t\}$ and $\mathcal{G}^{t+1} = \{\mathcal{E}^{t+1}, \mathcal{R}^{t+1}, \mathcal{T}^{t+1}\}$, there exist $\mathcal{E}^t \subseteq \mathcal{E}^{t+1}$, $\mathcal{R}^t = \mathcal{R}^{t+1}$ and $\mathcal{T}^t \subseteq \mathcal{T}^{t+1}$.*

In this definition, each newly added triple in $\Delta\mathcal{T}^{t+1}$ between t and $t+1$ contains zero, one, or two new entities. Considering that the set of relations in KGs is much less diverse than that of entities, we dismiss the emergence of new relations in this paper and assume that the relations in KGs are pre-defined.

To practice entity alignment on growing KGs. We propose the task of *continual entity alignment* and give its definition below:

Definition 2 (Continual entity alignment). *Given two growing KGs $\mathcal{G}_1$ and $\mathcal{G}_2$, and the seed entity alignment $\mathcal{A}_s$ at time $t = 0$, continual entity alignment at time t aims to find potential entity alignment $\mathcal{A}_p^t$ between $\mathcal{G}_1^t$ and $\mathcal{G}_2^t$ based on the currently learned KG embeddings and alignment model.*

In this definition, the size of $\mathcal{A}_s$ is constant, while $\mathcal{A}_p^t$ grows over time as new entities may bring new entity alignment to be found. Considering that the seed entity alignment is usually deficient and difficult to obtain [21], we do not assume that new snapshots bring new seed alignment to augment training data. That is to say, $\mathcal{A}_s$ of snapshot at time $t > 0$ is the same as that at time $t = 0$.

3   Methodology

In this section, we introduce the proposed continual entity alignment method ContEA. Figure 2 depicts its framework. It consists of two modules: the subgraph-based entity alignment module, and the embedding and alignment update module. The following is a brief overview of them:

- In the subgraph-based entity alignment module, the input is the two KGs at time $t = 0$ and the seed entity alignment across them. A graph neural network (GNN) is employed over the two KGs to represent entities based on their subgraph structures. The alignment learning objective is to minimize the embedding distance of similar entities while separating dissimilar ones. Additionally, an entity reconstruction design is used to encourage entities similar to their contexts. When the learning process is completed, the trustworthy alignment is predicted based on bidirectional nearest neighbor search.
- At time $t > 0$, the embedding and alignment update module first incorporates new entities into previously learned KG embeddings. It reconstructs new entities' embeddings based on their neighborhood subgraphs. Then, partial seed entity alignment and trustworthy alignment predicted in the previous snapshot are used for finetuning the GNN model. Last, after new alignment is predicted, we use it to update the previously-found old alignment.

We introduce the details of the two modules in the following two subsections.

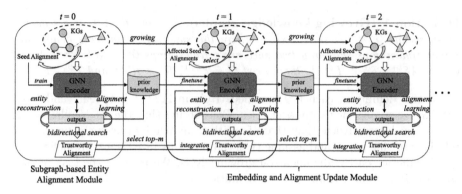

Fig. 2. Framework of the proposed continual entity alignment method ContEA.

3.1 Subgraph-Based Entity Alignment

This module is built upon a GNN that represents an entity by aggregating its neighborhood subgraph. The key assumption behind GNN is that the entities with similar neighborhoods appear to be close, which makes GNNs extensible to represent new entities. Please note that we do not focus on how to develop a powerful GNN for entity alignment, but on how to incorporate new entities and triples in an effective and efficient manner for continual entity alignment.

Subgraph Encoder. We adopt the GNN-based encoder of Dual-AMN [16] as our subgraph encoder for its effectiveness and simplicity. The encoder of Dual-AMN consists of an inner-graph layer (namely $\texttt{Aggregator}_1$) capturing the structural information within a single KG, and a cross-graph layer ($\texttt{Aggregator}_2$) capturing cross-graph matching information based on the outputs of $\texttt{Aggregator}_1$. Technically, $\texttt{Aggregator}_1$ is a 2-layered relation-aware GNN, and $\texttt{Aggregator}_2$ is a proxy attention network connecting entities with a list of proxy nodes. Overall, given an entity e, its representation after being encoded by Dual-AMN is

$$\texttt{Encoder}(e) = \texttt{Aggregator}_2\big(\texttt{Aggregator}_1(e, \mathcal{N}_e), \mathcal{E}_{\text{proxy}}\big), \tag{1}$$

where $\texttt{Aggregator}_1()$ aggregates the entity itself and its relational neighbors $\mathcal{N}_e$ to generate its embedding, and $\texttt{Aggregator}_2()$ combines the output embeddings with proxy nodes $\mathcal{E}_{\text{proxy}}$ to generate the final representations of entities. To save space, we do not present the detailed techniques of Dual-AMN here. Interested readers can refer to its original paper [16] for more details.

Entity Reconstruction. As KGs grow, the pre-trained GNN encoder encounters new entities and triples. The critical challenge is how to incorporate unseen entities into the encoder. Randomly initializing the embeddings of new entities could be detrimental to the previously optimized embedding space and cause representation inconsistency. A typical assumption in embedding-based entity alignment is that two entities are similar if their neighborhood subgraphs are similar (i.e., the two subgraphs have similar or pre-aligned entities). Motivated by this, we propose a self-supervised learning objective that enables the encoder to reconstruct an entity using its neighborhood subgraphs:

$$\mathcal{L}_{\text{reconstruct}} = \sum_{e \in \mathcal{E}} \left\| \mathbf{e} - \frac{1}{|\mathcal{N}_e|} \sum_{e' \in \mathcal{N}_e} \mathbf{e}' \right\|_2^2 . \tag{2}$$

Here, $\mathcal{N}_e$ denotes the set of one-hop neighbors of e. This objective minimizes the distance between an entity and its neighbor subgraph embedding (the mean vector of all neighbor embeddings).

Alignment Learning. Given the outputs of the encoder, alignment learning aims to gather similar entity pairs and distance dissimilar entity pairs. The dissimilar entity pairs is modeled by negative sampling. Following Dual-AMN [16], we also adopt the `LogSumExp` function to compute the loss:

$$\mathcal{L}_{\text{align}} = \log \left[1 + \sum_{(e_1,e_2) \in \mathcal{A}_s} \sum_{(e_1,e_2') \in \mathcal{A}_{e_1}^{\text{neg}}} \exp\left(\gamma(\lambda + \text{sim}(e_1, e_2) - \text{sim}(e_1, e_2')) \right) \right], \tag{3}$$

where $\mathcal{A}_{e_1}^{\text{neg}}$ denotes the negative alignment generated for entity e_1. γ is a scale factor, and λ is the margin for separating the similarities of seed alignment pairs and negative pairs. `Cosine` is used to compute embedding similarity, i.e., $\text{sim}(e_1, e_2) = \cos(\text{Encoder}(e_1), \text{Encoder}(e_2))$. We employ the in-batch negative generating method. Specifically, for entity e_1, other entities (e.g., e_2') in a training batch act as its negative counterparts to generate the negative pairs $\mathcal{A}_{e_1}^{\text{neg}}$. The final learning objective of subgraph-based entity alignment module $\mathcal{L}_1$ is a combination of $\mathcal{L}_{\text{align}}$ and $\mathcal{L}_{\text{reconstruct}}$ with a weight α on $\mathcal{L}_{\text{reconstruct}}$:

$$\mathcal{L}_1 = \mathcal{L}_{\text{align}} + \alpha \cdot \mathcal{L}_{\text{reconstruct}}. \tag{4}$$

Trustworthy Alignment Search. After the alignment learning is complete, we retrieve trustworthy entity alignment as predictions based on the optimized embedding space. Previous embedding-based entity alignment methods assume that each entity in one KG must have a counterpart in the other KG. A typical inference process is the nearest neighbor search, i.e., it seeks

$$\hat{e}_2 = \arg\min_{e_2 \in \mathcal{E}_2} \pi(\text{Encoder}(e_1), \text{Encoder}(e_2)), \tag{5}$$

where $\pi()$ is a measure for alignment search, and $\hat{e}_2$ is the predicted counterpart for e_1. However, such an "idealized" assumption may not stand in a realistic setting as there are many no-match entities in the two KGs [23]. To resolve this issue and improve alignment search, we propose a parameter-free strategy called bidirectional nearest alignment search. It searches for the nearest neighbor in one KG for the entities in the other. An alignment pair (e_1, e_2) is a trustworthy alignment if and only if $e_2 = \hat{e}_2$ and $e_1 = \hat{e}_1$. Other alignment pairs are discarded.

3.2 Embedding and Alignment Update

At time $t > 0$, the relational structure of KGs get changed as new triples come. It needs to generate embeddings for new entities while capturing the structure changes. To resolve this challenge, we propose to *finetune* the GNN encoder and new entity embeddings with partial seed alignment and selected trustworthy alignment. After finetuning, the new trustworthy entity alignment is retrieved based on the updated model and embeddings. The new predicted alignment is used to complete and update the old alignment discovered at time $t - 1$ using a heuristic strategy.

Encoder Finetuning. We initialize the encoder with the parameters learned in the previous module/time. Thanks to our entity reconstruction objective, the encoder is able to initialize the embedding of a new entity e as follows:

$$\texttt{Encoder}(e) = \texttt{Aggregator}_2\big(\texttt{Aggregator}_1(\texttt{MP}(\mathcal{N}'_e)), \mathcal{E}_{\text{proxy}}\big), \qquad (6)$$

where $\mathcal{N}'_e$ denotes the seen neighbors of the new entity e. $\texttt{MP}()$ is mean-pooling process to generate embedding for e using $\mathcal{N}'_e$.

Based on the output embeddings of new and existing entities, we finetune the GNN encoder. Specifically, we freeze the inner-graph layer $\texttt{Aggregator}_1$ while make the cross-graph $\texttt{Aggregator}_2$ learnable. For a single KG, the coming of new data does not change the neighbor aggregation pattern, as a KG's schema stays consistent (no new relations or entity domains). But the two KGs grow independently and asymmetrically in the proposed scenario. It is necessary to fine-tune the matching network to make adjustments and new discoveries.

For training data, considering that the potential entity alignment is more likely to occur near anchors [37], we replay only the affected seed entity alignment that contains anchors involved in new triples. This helps the alignment of new entities, which is originally difficult due to their low degrees. Also, to help align entities from wider and more dynamic areas, we select top-m predicted trustworthy alignment with the highest similarity scores and treat them as "new anchors".

We finetune the GNN encoder and new entity embeddings on the obtained affected seed alignment (ASA for short) and m selected trustworthy alignment (TA for short). We use a weight β on the learning loss over m trustworthy alignment to balance its importance. The final loss function $\mathcal{L}_2$ of finetuning is

$$\mathcal{L}_2 = \mathcal{L}_{\text{align}}(ASA) + \alpha \cdot \mathcal{L}_{\text{reconstruct}} + \beta \cdot \mathcal{L}_{\text{align}}(TA). \qquad (7)$$

Trustworthy Alignment Update. After finetuning, a new set of trustworthy alignment can be retrieved using the updated entity embeddings and model. It is necessary to combine it with the previously discovered trustworthy alignment because they are gathered from different snapshots and may complement each other to produce superior outcomes. Here, we carry out a heuristic strategy to integrate them. We keep new trustworthy alignment which is between two new entities. But for new ones that cause alignment conflicts [25] with the previous

---

Algorithm 1: Process of ContEA

Input : Two growing KGs G_1^t and G_2^t at time t, prior learned knowledge **K** (none for $t = 0$), seed alignment $\mathcal{A}_s$, previous trustworthy alignment TA (none for $t = 0$), hyperparameters α, β;

Output: Updated trustworthy alignment TA;

1 **if** $t = 0$ **then**
2 | Training encoder on G_1^0 and G_2^0 using $\mathcal{L}_1$ loss in Eq. (4);
3 | Generating TA though trustworthy alignment search;
4 **else**
5 | Initializing embeddings and encoder parameters using **K**, G_1^t and G_2^t;
6 | Selecting affected $\mathcal{A}_s$ as ASA and top-m TA with highest similarity;
7 | Finetuning encoder using $\mathcal{L}_2$ loss in Eq. (7);
8 | Updating TA with new trustworthy alignment;

---

trustworthy alignment (i.e., an entity is aligned with different entities), we decide to keep the alignment that has higher similarity scores. With KGs growing, the size of trustworthy entity alignment is accumulative.

3.3 Put It All Together

Algorithm 1 describes the training and finetuning details of ContEA for continual entity alignment. Lines 1–3 describe the process of the subgraph-based entity alignment module at time $t = 0$. Lines 4–8 describe the process of embedding and alignment updating modules at time $t > 0$.

4 Experiments

4.1 New Datasets for Continual Entity Alignment

Due to the lack of off-the-shelf benchmarks for proposed setting, we construct new datasets based on DBP15K [24]. For each DBP15K's cross-lingual entity alignment dataset, we use its two KGs as the first snapshots (i.e., $t = 0$). DBP15K only considers entity alignment between the head entities of triples and overlooks other entity alignment pairs. Hence, we first complete the reference entity alignment using the inter-language links in DBpedia[2], resulting in more than 15K reference alignment pairs in the first snapshot. Then, the reference entity alignment is divided into training, validation and test sets (i.e., $\mathcal{A}_s$, $\mathcal{A}_v$ and $\mathcal{A}_p^0$) with a ratio of 2 : 1 : 7. We further build five snapshots to simulate KGs' growth:

- At time $t > 0$, we first collect the relation triples from DBpedia that contain entities in $\mathcal{G}_1^{t-1}$ and $\mathcal{G}_2^{t-1}$. Then, among these triples we remove seen ones at time $t-1$, and sample new triples from the remaining with the size of 20% of the triples in previous snapshots. Adding the new triples into $\mathcal{G}_1^{t-1}$ and $\mathcal{G}_2^{t-1}$ and we create snapshots $\mathcal{G}_1^t$ and $\mathcal{G}_2^t$.

---

[2] We use the infobox-based relation triples (version 2016-10) following DBP15K.

Table 1. Statistics of the three datasets. Each consists of two growing KGs in six snapshots from consecutive timestamps. In a snapshot, $|T|$ is the current triple size, and $|\mathcal{A}_s|, |\mathcal{A}_v|, |\mathcal{A}_p|$ are the sizes of training, validation and test alignment, respectively.

	DBP$_{ZH\text{-}EN}$					DBP$_{JA\text{-}EN}$					DBP$_{FR\text{-}EN}$				
	$|T|_{ZH}$	$|T|_{EN}$	$|\mathcal{A}_s|$	$|\mathcal{A}_v|$	$|\mathcal{A}_p|$	$|T|_{JA}$	$|T|_{EN}$	$|\mathcal{A}_s|$	$|\mathcal{A}_v|$	$|\mathcal{A}_p|$	$|T|_{FR}$	$|T|_{EN}$	$|\mathcal{A}_s|$	$|\mathcal{A}_v|$	$|\mathcal{A}_p|$
$t=0$	70,414	95,142	3,623	1,811	12,682	77,214	93,484	3,750	1,875	13,127	105,998	115,722	3,727	1,863	13,048
$t=1$	103,982	154,833	3,623	1,811	14,213	112,268	150,636	3,750	1,875	15,079	148,274	184,132	3,727	1,863	15,875
$t=2$	137,280	213,405	3,623	1,811	16,296	147,097	207,056	3,750	1,875	18,092	191,697	251,591	3,727	1,863	20,481
$t=3$	173,740	278,076	3,623	1,811	18,716	185,398	270,469	3,750	1,875	21,690	239,861	326,689	3,727	1,863	25,753
$t=4$	213,814	351,659	3,623	1,811	21,473	227,852	341,432	3,750	1,875	25,656	293,376	411,528	3,727	1,863	31,564
$t=5$	258,311	434,683	3,623	1,811	24,678	274,884	421,971	3,750	1,875	29,782	352,886	507,793	3,727	1,863	37,592

- Then, we complete $\mathcal{G}_1^t$ and $\mathcal{G}_2^t$ by adding additional relation triples from DBpedia of which the head and tail entities are both in the snapshots, leading to more than 20% growth of triple size.
- Finally, we retrieve the new entity alignment pairs brought by the newly added entities, and add them into the test set $\mathcal{A}_p^t$ of snapshot t. The training set $\mathcal{A}_s$ or validation set $\mathcal{A}_v$ still follows that in the first snapshot at time $t = 0$. We do not assume that the new snapshot introduces new training data because obtaining seed alignment for emerging entities is usually more difficult than finding seed alignment for old entities in the real world.

The detailed statistics of our dataset are present in Table 1.

4.2   Baselines

We compare ContEA with two groups of entity alignment methods.

- **Retraining baselines.** Since most existing embedding-based EA methods are designed for static KGs, they need retraining each time new triples come. Here, we choose the representative translation-based method MTransE [6], and several state-of-the-art GNN-based methods, including GCN-Align [33], AlignE [25], AliNet [27], KEGCN [40] and Dual-AMN [16] as our baselines.
- **Inductive baselines.** The only entity alignment method focusing on KGs' growth is DINGAL [39]. We choose one of the proposed variants, DINGAL-O, as a baseline, which can handle our scenario. Additionally, since there are some inductive KG embedding (KGE) methods which can generate embeddings for new entities, we explore their combination with static methods to tackle our task. Here, we select two representative inductive KGE methods MEAN [8] and LAN [31] as the entity representation layer and incorporate them with Dual-AMN. We denote the two baselines by MEAN$^+$ and LAN$^+$.

4.3   Experiment Settings

Evaluation Metrics. At each time t, the bidirectional nearest neighbor search and alignment integration are used to obtain the final trustworthy alignment.

The details are described in Sect. 3.1 and Sect. 3.2. Then, we compare the final trustworthy alignment with gold test pairs $\mathcal{A}_p^t$. We report the precision, recall, and F1 scores as the evaluation metrics.

Implementation. We implement ContEA, Dual-AMN, MEAN$^+$ and LAN$^+$ using PyTorch. For other retraining baselines, we use the implementations in an open-source library.[3] We set the embedding dimensions to 100. The embedding similarity metric is CSLS [12]. We use grid search on hyperparameters and early stop to find the best performance. Specifically for ContEA, we set $\alpha = 0.1$, $\beta = 0.1$ and $m = 500$. More detailed hyperparameter settings can be found on our GitHub repository. For a fair comparison, all baselines only rely on KGs' structural information and do not use pre-trained models for initialization.

4.4   Results

General Results. We conduct experiments on the constructed datasets and present the results in Tables 2, 3 and 4. Compared with baselines, ContEA reaches the best performance in discovering potential entity alignment. Its F1 scores outperform the best baseline Dual-AMN by 27.1%, 19.4%, and 15.2% averagely on six snapshots of DBP$_{\text{ZH-EN}}$, DBP$_{\text{JA-EN}}$, and DBP$_{\text{FR-EN}}$, respectively. The superior performance of ContEA over retraining methods is because ContEA can iteratively leverage the prior knowledge (e.g., previously predicted alignment and model parameters) from the past snapshots. Also, ContEA collectively obtains predicted entity alignment by integrating new and old trustworthy alignment rather than totally neglecting old predictions in retraining. As for inductive baselines, MEAN$^+$ and LAN$^+$ perform worse than ContEA and Dual-AMN, which indicates that straightway adding the inductive KGE layer without adjusting the alignment network does not give satisfactory performance. DINGAL-O also shows unsatisfactory results, because it is purely inductive and does not update the alignment network. Besides, we can notice that the performance of all methods declines over time. This is due to the expansion of the searching space for alignment candidates, and the drop in the ratio of seed alignment against to-be-aligned alignment. Both of these increase the probability of entities being mismatched.

Ablation Study. To investigate the impact of each design of ContEA, also to give a fairer comparison between ContEA and baselines, we discard certain parts of ContEA and present three variants as follows:

- ContEA w/o TA. In the finetuning process, we discard the selected trustworthy entity alignment and only train on the affected seed alignment.
- ContEA w/o TA & ASA. We discard both the selected trustworthy alignment and the affected seed alignment. Thus, our method requires no finetuning and reduces to an inductive method. The entity reconstruction method generates embeddings for new entities using their neighbors.

---

[3] https://github.com/nju-websoft/OpenEA.

Table 2. Results of entity alignment on DBP$_{\text{ZH-EN}}$. NA stands for not applicable.

		$t = 0$	$t = 1$	$t = 2$	$t = 3$	$t = 4$	$t = 5$
		P / R / F1	P / R / F1	P / R / F1	P / R / F1	P / R / F1	P / R / F1
Retraining	MTransE	.552/.178/.269	.242/.111/.152	.159/.078/.105	.094/.054/.068	.080/.041/.055	.049/.030/.037
	GCN-Align	.550/.249/.343	.212/.152/.177	.133/.115/.123	.096/.091/.094	.076/.075/.076	.062/.062/.062
	AlignE	.721/.364/.484	.382/.272/.317	.282/.222/.248	.206/.173/.188	.191/.152/.169	.127/.112/.119
	AliNet	.641/.358/.459	.285/.311/.297	.195/.279/.230	.146/.244/.183	.129/.232/.166	.105/.199/.128
	KEGCN	.664/.200/.308	.315/.129/.183	.198/.093/.127	.160/.075/.102	.136/.064/.087	.120/.052/.072
	Dual-AMN	.834/.596/.695	.482/.443/.462	.357/.356/.356	.285/.286/.286	.249/.254/.251	.227/.227/.227
Induct.	MEAN$^+$	.828/.576/.679	.483/.422/.450	.357/.341/.349	.267/.264/.265	.225/.226/.225	.198/.197/.198
	LAN$^+$	.827/.576/.679	.488/.426/.455	.360/.345/.352	.274/.271/.272	.231/.229/.230	.205/.199/.202
	DINGAL-O	.497/.195/.280	.370/.158/.222	.315/.135/.189	.251/.111/.154	.229/.093/.132	.209/.080/.116
ContEA		**.843/.604/.703**	**.555/.539/.546**	**.444/.473/.458**	**.373/.421/.396**	**.324/.375/.348**	**.291/.336/.312**
w/o TA		NA / NA / NA	.543/.531/.537	.419/.469/.443	.357/.414/.384	.316/.371/.341	.286/.332/.307
w/o TA & ASA		NA / NA / NA	.543/.527/.535	.422/.463/.442	.352/.410/.379	.309/.365/.335	.278/.324/.300
Retraining		NA / NA / NA	.493/.455/.473	.364/.357/.361	.300/.301/.301	.265/.266/.265	.245/.240/.243

Table 3. Results of entity alignment on DBP$_{\text{JA-EN}}$. NA stands for not applicable.

		$t = 0$	$t = 1$	$t = 2$	$t = 3$	$t = 4$	$t = 5$
		P / R / F1	P / R / F1	P / R / F1	P / R / F1	P / R / F1	P / R / F1
Retraining	MTransE	.599/.200/.299	.293/.121/.172	.213/.082/.118	.151/.061/.087	.128/.046/.067	.117/.035/.054
	GCN-Align	.594/.279/.379	.263/.183/.216	.177/.142/.158	.140/.117/.127	.116/.099/.107	.099/.084/.091
	AlignE	.738/.359/.483	.433/.282/.342	.320/.218/.260	.270/.178/.214	.228/.148/.180	.193/.122/.149
	AliNet	.661/.364/.469	.305/.312/.308	.216/.270/.240	.167/.231/.194	.149/.215/.176	.126/.189/.151
	KEGCN	.663/.198/.305	.389/.153/.219	.280/.110/.157	.245/.087/.128	.200/.070/.104	.194/.063/.096
	Dual-AMN	**.861/.606/.711**	.517/.437/.474	.398/.347/.370	.348/.292/.318	.313/.251/.278	.300/.231/.261
Induct.	MEAN$^+$	.847/.571/.682	.528/.420/.468	.407/.330/.365	.330/.261/.292	.287/.221/.250	.265/.193/.223
	LAN$^+$	.845/.575/.684	.528/.424/.470	.410/.333/.368	.335/.265/.296	.296/.226/.257	.274/.200/.231
	DINGAL-O	.540/.227/.320	.391/.174/.241	.328/.137/.194	.271/.113/.159	.249/.092/.134	.231/.078/.116
ContEA		.858/**.610/.713**	**.586/.519/.551**	**.483/.440/.461**	**.417/.381/.398**	**.375/.336/.354**	**.344/.299/.320**
w/o TA		NA/NA/NA	.572/.518/.544	.466/.439/.452	.398/.377/.387	.357/.332/.344	.333/.294/.312
w/o TA & ASA		NA/NA/NA	.580/.514/.545	.466/.436/.450	.399/.374/.386	.359/.328/.343	.331/.291/.310
Retraining		NA/NA/NA	.530/.449/.486	.415/.356/.383	.369/.298/.330	.349/.272/.306	.327/.244/.280

Table 4. Results of entity alignment on DBP$_{\text{FR-EN}}$. NA stands for not applicable.

		$t = 0$	$t = 1$	$t = 2$	$t = 3$	$t = 4$	$t = 5$
		P / R / F1	P / R / F1	P /R / F1	P /R / F1	P /R/ F1	P /R/ F1
Retraining	MTransE	.570/.188/.283	.246/.100/.142	.145/.062/.087	.108/.040/.059	.104/.032/.049	.073/.024/.036
	GCN-Align	.561/.262/.357	.233/.161/.190	.148/.111/.127	.113/.086/.098	.089/.066/.076	.077/.056/.065
	AlignE	.757/.394/.518	.399/.274/.325	.305/.202/.243	.245/.154/.189	.210/.121/.154	.195/.104/.136
	AliNet	.653/.361/.465	.275/.289/.282	.187/.226/.205	.144/.180/.160	.124/.155/.138	.115/.138/.126
	KEGCN	.716/.214/.330	.344/.125/.184	.260/.090/.134	.237/.076/.115	.201/.058/.089	.169/.045/.071
	Dual-AMN	.862/.629/.727	.503/.443/.471	.394/.331/.359	.351/.273/.307	.322/.237/.273	.313/.214/.254
Induct.	MEAN$^+$	.840/.585/.690	.514/.415/.459	.387/.305/.341	.314/.235/.269	.273/.191/.225	.254/.169/.203
	LAN$^+$	.845/.594/.697	.506/.410/.453	.379/.300/.335	.304/.227/.260	.269/.188/.222	.247/.162/.195
	DINGAL-O	.540/.224/.317	.381/.165/.231	.329/.124/.180	.258/.092/.136	.247/.073/.112	.227/.061/.096
ContEA		**.866/.634/.732**	**.569/.520/.543**	**.453/.421/.436**	**.387/.351/.369**	**.351/.301/.324**	**.325/.265/.292**
w/o TA		NA/NA/NA	.559/.516/.537	.443/.417/.430	.379/.348/.363	.342/.299/.319	.315/.263/.287
w/o TA & ASA		NA/NA/NA	.548/.511/.528	.431/.413/.421	.367/.342/.354	.334/.293/.312	.311/.256/.281
Retraining		NA/NA/NA	.516/.437/.473	.409/.339/.370	.372/.284/.322	.348/.247/.289	.331/.224/.267

- ContEA retraining. Same as the retraining baselines, ContEA treats each snapshot as at $t = 0$. Old predicted entity alignment is totally replaced by newly predicted entity alignment rather than being integrated.

Table 5. Recall of the alignment containing new entities on DBP$_{\text{ZH-EN}}$.

		$t = 1$	$t = 2$	$t = 3$	$t = 4$	$t = 5$
Retraining	MTransE	.075	.055	.032	.023	.013
	GCN-Align	.049	.031	.028	.014	.012
	AlignE	.137	.099	.067	.057	.040
	AliNet	.148	.149	.118	.124	.085
	KEGCN	.059	.046	.026	.026	.021
	Dual-AMN	.204	.164	.128	.113	.094
Induct.	MEAN$^+$	.170	.142	.106	.098	.078
	LAN$^+$	.167	.140	.109	.095	.076
	DINGAL-O	.003	.007	.007	.008	.006
ContEA		**.205**	**.167**	**.140**	**.116**	**.095**

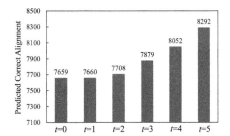

Fig. 3. Size growth of predicted correct alignment on DBP$_{\text{ZH-EN}}$.

We show the results of three variants in Tables 2, 3 and 4. The variants inherit the trained ContEA at $t = 0$ and perform respectively afterwards. We can notice a performance drop when discarding selected trustworthy alignment. Bigger declines are seen if further dropping the affected seed alignment. This demonstrates the effectiveness of both selected trustworthy alignment and affected seed alignment replay. For ContEA retraining, though it performs much worse than ContEA, it still outperforms all retraining baselines, including Dual-AMN, which indicates the effectiveness of entity reconstruction.

Discovering New Alignment. Next, we present the performance of ContEA on discovering alignment for new entities. At time $t = \{1, 2, 3, 4, 5\}$, we collect the final predicted alignment that involves new entities, and calculate the recall value by comparing it with the gold test alignment containing new entities. We show the results on DBP$_{\text{ZH-EN}}$ in Table 5. ContEA reaches the highest recall against all baselines, which indicates the advantage of our method in discovering alignment for new entities. We can also notice that the recalls on gold alignment about new entities are significantly lower than those on all gold alignment. This is because new entities tend to be sparsely-linked, which hinders the alignment models from matching them correctly. Also, Fig. 3 illustrates the growth of the total correctly predicted alignment of ContEA. At time t, the size of total correctly predicted alignment is calculated as $|\mathcal{A}_p^t| \times$ Recall (R in Table 2). The results show that ContEA can find an increasing size of correct entity alignment as KGs grow, which fulfills the proposal of continual entity alignment.

Efficiency. We compare the training efficiency of ContEA with retraining baselines. Note that, since inductive baselines have no training process as new triples come, we do not include them here. We run all experiments on a server outfitted with 512 GB memory, two Xeon Gold 6326 CPUs, and four RTX A6000 GPUs. Figure 4 depicts the average time cost on three datasets at different snapshots. We set the ceiling of vertical axis to 2,000 s for better presentation. We can see that ContEA has significantly less training time, which shows a part of its superiority in tackling the continual entity alignment task.

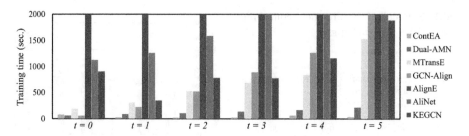

Fig. 4. Time cost comparison of ContEA and retraining baselines. We report the average time cost on the three datasets.

Table 6. F1 results comparison when incorporating name attribute of entities.

	DBP$_{ZH-EN}$						DBP$_{JA-EN}$						DBP$_{FR-EN}$					
	$t=0$	$t=1$	$t=2$	$t=3$	$t=4$	$t=5$	$t=0$	$t=1$	$t=2$	$t=3$	$t=4$	$t=5$	$t=0$	$t=1$	$t=2$	$t=3$	$t=4$	$t=5$
Google Translate	.550	.504	.473	.451	.434	.420	.677	.635	.617	.595	.587	.586	.749	.685	.658	.645	.636	.627
ContEA (fasttext)	.709	.556	.471	.411	.367	.334	.754	.615	.521	.456	.409	.374	.780	.613	.510	.446	.404	.368
ContEA ∪ G.T	.826	.645	.571	.506	.466	.441	.886	.742	.677	.637	.612	.604	.892	.740	.682	.650	.633	.623

4.5 Further Analysis

Incorporating Entity Names. Here we explore the advantage of leveraging entities' names. Practically, we use `fasttext` library to generate name embeddings for entities. Since the original word embedding dimension of `fasttext` is 300, to make the embedding space scalable, we reduce the dimension to 100 using the official dimension reducer.[4] Also, we involve Google Translate[5] (G.T.) as a competing method. For a cross-lingual dataset, we first translate entities from two KGs into the same language (both in English or non-English), and then calculate name similarity using Levenshtein distance, a popular measurement in linguistics [18] and ontology matching [4]. The bidirectional nearest neighbor search is also used later to obtain predicted trustworthy entity alignment, which are compared with the gold test set to calculate P, R, and F1 scores. We list the F1 results in Table 6. By utilizing name attributes, ContEA (`fasttext`) outperforms ContEA with a large margin. Google Translate gives satisfactory and robust performance over time, as powerful as expected. It performs more stably and is less sensitive to KGs' size, with outperforming ContEA (`fasttext`) on most snapshots of the three datasets except the first snapshot.

We further explore the combination of ContEA and Google Translate. To do so, we combine their predicted alignment when searching the nearest neighbor from one KG to the other, then take a bidirectional intersection to get the final combined predicted alignment. The results of this combination are shown in the last row. We can see that their combination outperforms both Google Translate and ContEA in almost all snapshots of three datasets. We believe that when Google Translate fails to align an entity, ContEA can be a practical alternative.

---

[4] https://fasttext.cc/docs/en/crawl-vectors.html.
[5] https://translate.google.com/.

Table 7. Case study on previously predicted alignment getting corrected.

	$t = 0$		$t = 5$	
	Predicted alignment	Sim.	Predicted alignment	Sim.
DBP$_{\text{ZH-EN}}$	(我是歌手, *Hunan Television*)	.204	(湖南卫视, *Hunan Television*)	.530
	(呼和浩特市, *Baotou*)	.243	(包头市, *Baotou*)	.541
DBP$_{\text{JA-EN}}$	(スウェーデン語, *Finnish language*)	.210	(フィンランド語, *Finnish language*)	.316
	(フランス人, *Spaniards*)	.265	(フランス人, *French people*)	.367
DBP$_{\text{FR-EN}}$	(*Révolution française, Réunion*)	.262	(*La Réunion, Réunion*)	.403
	(*Stade de Wembley, White Hart Lane*)	.302	(*Stade de Wembley, Wembley Stadium*)	.380

Case Study on Correcting Previous Alignment. Last, we present several cases in Table 7 about the previously predicted alignment getting corrected in later finetuning processes. We save the predicted alignment and their similarity scores at time $t = 0$ and $t = 5$, and juxtapose two alignment pairs from each time that involve the same entity. We manually check the list of juxtaposition and notice that the predicted alignment at $t = 0$ is usually incorrect with smaller similarity scores, while their counterparts at $t = 5$ are correct with higher similarity scores. This indicates the ability of ContEA on self-correction. Meanwhile, the two entities in falsely predicted alignment at $t = 0$ are not totally irrelevant. For example, in the second case from the DBP$_{\text{FR-EN}}$ dataset, both *Stade de Wembley* and *White Hart Lane* are Stadiums in London. In the first case from the DBP$_{\text{ZH-EN}}$ dataset, 我是歌手 is a popular TV show made by *Hunan Television*. And in the first case from the DBP$_{\text{JA-EN}}$ dataset, スウェーデン語 means Swedish language (Sweden and Finland are two neighboring Nordic countries). This gives an interesting insight on how ContEA predicts entity alignment with slight inaccuracy.

5   Related Work

Static Entity Alignment. Most existing embedding-based entity alignment methods focus on static KGs. They can usually be classified into two categories regarding the techniques of their KG encoders: translation-based [6,14,19,25,26,43] and GNN-based [16,17,27,33–36]. The former family adopts translation-based KG embedding (KGE) techniques [3,32] to embed entities, and map cross-graph entities into a unified space based on pre-aligned entity pairs. The encoder of GNN-based entity alignment methods learns a shared neighborhood aggregator to embed entities in different KGs. They have gained overwhelming popularity in recent years due to their strong ability to capture the structural information using a subgraph around an entity, rather than a single triple. For more details, there are several surveys [28,41] that comprehensively summarize the recent advances.

Dynamic Entity Alignment. As far as we know, DINGAL [39] is the only entity alignment method that addresses the dynamics of KGs. In its dynamic scenario, new triples are added into KGs as well as new pre-known alignment provided along with these new entities. A variant of DINGAL, named DINGAL-O, is also proposed in their work to handle a similar setting as ours where the pre-known alignment does not grow. DINGAL-O is an inductive method that leverages prior-learned model parameters to predict new alignment. Particularly, they use name attributes to generate word embeddings for entity initialization.

Inductive Knowledge Graph Embedding. The study on dynamic KG embedding has drawn lots of attention over the years. Powered by GNN, many inductive embedding methods for KG completion are proposed to generate embeddings for new entities. Early inductive methods either focus on semi-inductive settings where new entities are connected to existing KG and making inferences between new entities and existing entities [8,9,31,38], or fully-inductive settings where new entities form independent graphs and making inferences among new entities [5,29]. Later inductive method [15] intend to tackle both settings. Meanwhile, some inductive KG embedding methods focus on special tasks like few-shot learning [38] and hyper-relational KG completion [1]. Specifically, as the first inductive KG embedding method, MEAN [8] learns to represent entities using their neighbors by simply mean-pooling the information of neighboring entity-relation pairs. LAN [31] advances MEAN by incorporating a rule-based attention and a GNN-based attention on entity-relation pairs in the pooling process.

6   Conclusion and Future Work

In this paper, considering the growth nature of real-world KGs, we focus on an entity alignment scenario where both graphs are growing, and address a new task named continual entity alignment. We propose a novel method ContEA as a solution to the task. Also, we construct three datasets to imitate the scenario and conduct extensive experiments. The experimental results show the superiority of ContEA in terms of effectiveness and efficiency against a list of retraining and inductive baselines. For future work, there are many promising improvements and extensions to the current proposal. Regarding the setting, future studies can consider more complex scenarios such as the addition of new relations, the addition of new pre-known alignment, and even the deletion of entities and triples. As to the method, more reliable and comprehensive trustworthy alignment update strategies are necessary to handle intricate alignment conflict cases.

Supplemental Material Statement: The source code, detailed hyperparameters, and constructed datasets are available at our GitHub repository.[6]

Acknowledgments. This work was supported by National Natural Science Foundation of China (No. 61872172), Beijing Academy of Artificial Intelligence (BAAI),

---

[6] https://github.com/nju-websoft/ContEA.

and Collaborative Innovation Center of Novel Software Technology & Industrialization. Zequn Sun was also grateful for the support of Program A for Outstanding PhD Candidates of Nanjing University.

References

1. Ali, M., Berrendorf, M., Galkin, M., Thost, V., Ma, T., Tresp, V., Lehmann, J.: Improving inductive link prediction using hyper-relational facts. In: ISWC, pp. 74–92 (2021)
2. Baek, J., Lee, D.B., Hwang, S.J.: Learning to extrapolate knowledge: transductive few-shot out-of-graph link prediction. In: NeurIPS (2020)
3. Bordes, A., Usunier, N., García-Durán, A., Weston, J., Yakhnenko, O.: Translating embeddings for modeling multi-relational data. In: NIPS, pp. 2787–2795 (2013)
4. Cheatham, M., Hitzler, P.: String similarity metrics for ontology alignment. In: ISWC, pp. 294–309 (2013)
5. Chen, J., He, H., Wu, F., Wang, J.: Topology-aware correlations between relations for inductive link prediction in knowledge graphs. In: AAAI, pp. 6271–6278 (2021)
6. Chen, M., Tian, Y., Yang, M., Zaniolo, C.: Multilingual knowledge graph embeddings for cross-lingual knowledge alignment. In: IJCAI, pp. 1511–1517 (2017)
7. Chen, X., Chen, M., Fan, C., Uppunda, A., Sun, Y., Zaniolo, C.: Multilingual knowledge graph completion via ensemble knowledge transfer. In: Findings of EMNLP, pp. 3227–3238 (2020)
8. Hamaguchi, T., Oiwa, H., Shimbo, M., Matsumoto, Y.: Knowledge transfer for out-of-knowledge-base entities: a graph neural network approach. In: IJCAI, pp. 1802–1808 (2017)
9. He, Y., Wang, Z., Zhang, P., Tu, Z., Ren, Z.: Vn network: embedding newly emerging entities with virtual neighbors. In: CIKM, pp. 505–514 (2020)
10. Hofer, M., Hellmann, S., Dojchinovski, M., Frey, J.: The new DBpedia release cycle: increasing agility and efficiency in knowledge extraction workflows. In: Blomqvist, E., Groth, P., de Boer, V., Pellegrini, T., Alam, M., Käfer, T., Kieseberg, P., Kirrane, S., Meroño-Peñuela, A., Pandit, H.J. (eds.) SEMANTICS 2020. LNCS, vol. 12378, pp. 1–18. Springer, Cham (2020). https://doi.org/10.1007/978-3-030-59833-4_1
11. Jiménez-Ruiz, E., Grau, B.C.: LogMap: logic-based and scalable ontology matching. In: ISWC, pp. 273–288 (2011)
12. Lample, G., Conneau, A., Ranzato, M., Denoyer, L., Jégou, H.: Word translation without parallel data. In: ICLR (2018)
13. Lehmann, J., Isele, R., Jakob, M., Jentzsch, A., Kontokostas, D., Mendes, P.N., Hellmann, S., Morsey, M., van Kleef, P., Auer, S., Bizer, C.: DBpedia - a large-scale, multilingual knowledge base extracted from wikipedia. Semantic Web **6**(2), 167–195 (2015)
14. Lin, X., Yang, H., Wu, J., Zhou, C., Wang, B.: Guiding entity alignment via adversarial knowledge embedding. In: ICDM (2019)
15. Liu, S., Grau, B.C., Horrocks, I., Kostylev, E.V.: INDIGO: GNN-based inductive knowledge graph completion using pair-wise encoding. In: NeurIPS (2021)
16. Mao, X., Wang, W., Wu, Y., Lan, M.: Boosting the speed of entity alignment 10 ×: Dual attention matching network with normalized hard sample mining. In: WWW, pp. 821–832 (2021)

17. Mao, X., Wang, W., Xu, H., Lan, M., Wu, Y.: MRAEA: an efficient and robust entity alignment approach for cross-lingual knowledge graph. In: WSDM, pp. 420–428 (2020)
18. Medhat, D., Hassan, A., Salama, C.: A hybrid cross-language name matching technique using novel modified levenshtein distance. In: ICCES, pp. 204–209 (2015)
19. Pei, S., Yu, L., Zhang, X.: Improving cross-lingual entity alignment via optimal transport. In: IJCAI, pp. 3231–3237. IJCAI (2019)
20. Singh, H., Chakrabarti, S., Jain, P., Choudhury, S.R., Mausam: Multilingual knowledge graph completion with joint relation and entity alignment. In: AKBC (2021)
21. Song, Y., Karras, P., Xiao, Q., Bressan, S.: Sensitive label privacy protection on social network data. In: SSDBM, pp. 562–571 (2012)
22. Suchanek, F.M., Abiteboul, S., Senellart, P.: PARIS: probabilistic alignment of relations, instances, and schema. Proc. VLDB Endow. **5**(3), 157–168 (2011)
23. Sun, Z., Chen, M., Hu, W.: Knowing the no-match: Entity alignment with dangling cases. In: ACL, pp. 3582–3593 (2021)
24. Sun, Z., Hu, W., Li, C.: Cross-lingual entity alignment via joint attribute-preserving embedding. In: ISWC, pp. 628–644 (2017)
25. Sun, Z., Hu, W., Zhang, Q., Qu, Y.: Bootstrapping entity alignment with knowledge graph embedding. In: IJCAI, pp. 4396–4402 (2018)
26. Sun, Z., Huang, J., Hu, W., Chen, M., Guo, L., Qu, Y.: TransEdge: translating relation-contextualized embeddings for knowledge graphs. In: ISWC, pp. 612–629 (2019)
27. Sun, Z., et al.: Knowledge graph alignment network with gated multi-hop neighborhood aggregation. In: AAAI, pp. 222–229 (2020)
28. Sun, Z., Zhang, Q., Hu, W., Wang, C., Chen, M., Akrami, F., Li, C.: A benchmarking study of embedding-based entity alignment for knowledge graphs. Proc. VLDB Endow. **13**(11), 2326–2340 (2020)
29. Teru, K.K., Denis, E.G., Hamilton, W.L.: Inductive relation prediction by subgraph reasoning. In: ISWC (2020)
30. Vrandecic, D., Krötzsch, M.: Wikidata: a free collaborative knowledgebase. Commun. ACM **57**(10), 78–85 (2014)
31. Wang, P., Han, J., Li, C., Pan, R.: Logic attention based neighborhood aggregation for inductive knowledge graph embedding. In: AAAI, pp. 7152–7159 (2019)
32. Wang, Z., Zhang, J., Feng, J., Chen, Z.: Knowledge graph embedding by translating on hyperplanes. In: AAAI, pp. 1112–1119 (2014)
33. Wang, Z., Lv, Q., Lan, X., Zhang, Y.: Cross-lingual knowledge graph alignment via graph convolutional networks. In: EMNLP, pp. 349–357 (2018)
34. Wang, Z., Lv, Q., Lan, X., Zhang, Y.: Cross-lingual knowledge graph alignment via graph convolutional networks. In: ACL, pp. 349–357 (2018)
35. Wu, Y., Liu, X., Feng, Y., Wang, Z., Yan, R., Zhao, D.: Relation-aware entity alignment for heterogeneous knowledge graphs. In: IJCAI, pp. 5278–5284 (2019)
36. Wu, Y., Liu, X., Feng, Y., Wang, Z., Zhao, D.: Neighborhood matching network for entity alignment. In: ACL, pp. 6477–6487 (2020)
37. Xia, Y., Gao, J., Cui, B.: iMap: Incremental node mapping between large graphs using GNN. In: CIKM, pp. 2191–2200 (2021)
38. Xie, R., Liu, Z., Jia, J., Luan, H., Sun, M.: Representation learning of knowledge graphs with entity descriptions. In: AAAI, pp. 2659–2665 (2016)
39. , Yan, Y., Liu, L., Ban, Y., Jing, B., Tong, H.: Dynamic knowledge graph alignment. In: AAAI, pp. 4564–4572 (2021)
40. Yu, D., Yang, Y., Zhang, R., Wu, Y.: Knowledge embedding based graph convolutional network. In: WWW, pp. 1619–1628 (2021)

41. Zeng, K., Li, C., Hou, L., Li, J., Feng, L.: A comprehensive survey of entity alignment for knowledge graphs. AI Open **2**, 1–13 (2021)
42. Zhao, X., Zeng, W., Tang, J., Wang, W., Suchanek, F.: An experimental study of state-of-the-art entity alignment approaches. IEEE Trans. Knowl. Data Eng. (2020)
43. Zhu, H., Xie, R., Liu, Z., Sun, M.: Iterative entity alignment via joint knowledge embeddings. In: IJCAI, pp. 4258–4264 (2017)

Mapping Relational Database Constraints to SHACL

Ratan Bahadur Thapa and Martin Giese[(✉)]

Department of Informatics, University of Oslo, Oslo, Norway
{ratanbt,martingi}@ifi.uio.no

Abstract. Most structured data today is still stored in relational databases, which makes it important to provide a translation between relational and semantic data. A relational to RDF mapping, such as R2RML [13], provides a way to view existing relational data in the RDF data model through declarative mappings. While relational to RDF mapping translates relational instance data to RDF, it does not specify any translation of existing relational constraints such as primary and foreign key constraints. Since the introduction of R2RML, interest in RDF constraint languages has increased and SHACL [15] has been standardised. This raises the question of which SHACL constraints are guaranteed to be valid on a dataset produced by a relational to RDF mapping. For arbitrary SQL constraints and relational to RDF mappings, this is a hard problem, but we introduce a number of restrictions on the mappings that allow us to introduce a *constraint rewriting* for relational to RDF mappings that faithfully transfers SQL integrity constraints to SHACL constraints. We define and prove two fundamental properties, namely *maximal semantics preservation* and *monotonicity*.

1 Introduction

In relational database theory, one can restrict data to a set of relations that are considered to be useful to applications at hand by imposing relevant integrity constraints upon them, i.e., the semantics properties, also known as data dependencies, that the data in the database must obey. However, such integrity constraints of relational data are not explicit when mapped into RDF. A relational to RDF (R2R) mapping outputs an RDF graph that no longer contains the integrity constraints information. To overcome the problem, one can restore the semantic properties of R2R transformed data by using a semantics preserving constraint rewriting [7,23,26] that maps the integrity constraints of relational data into a well-behaved constraint formalism, which provides a closed-world description for the mapped RDF graph. The integrity constraints of the dataset that is being stored or represented in the RDF graph are a critical piece of information in practice, both to detect problems in the RDF dataset and provide data quality guarantees for RDF data exchange and interoperability.

In this paper, we study constraint rewriting for R2R mapping to make it more faithful by transforming the integrity constraints, such as primary and foreign keys, unique and not null integrity constraints as well as data types, from SQL database to RDF graph. In an attempt to transfer such integrity constraints of relational data, such as key constraints and functional dependency in *direct mapping* [2] to a larger perspective of

U. Sattler et al. (Eds.): ISWC 2022, LNCS 13489, pp. 214–230, 2022.
https://doi.org/10.1007/978-3-031-19433-7_13

relational constraints [1, Sect. 10] in more expressive *ontology-based mapping* [18] of relational data, into OWL DL axioms [20] as well as Epistemic DL axioms [14], the problem has recently been studied in [7,23] and [10,11,21] respectively. However, for our work, we follow the constraint rewriting technique proposed in [26] that explicitly transforms integrity constraints of SQL database into integrity constraints on the RDF graph, expressed in SHACL [15] as opposed to OWL/Epistemic DL axioms. Contrary to OWL, SHACL, the Shapes Constraint Language recommended by W3C since 2017, has a closed world semantics and uses the unique name assumption, which makes it a more suitable candidate than OWL for expressing as well as detecting the violations of integrity constraints on an RDF graph.

For arbitrary SQL constraints and relational to RDF mappings, constraint rewriting is a hard problem. For simplicity, we restrict ourselves to (a) the most common SQL constraints, namely keys, uniqueness and not null constraints, and (2) *simple* R2R mappings (Definition 4), which are restricted in such a way that the resulting RDF is structurally close enough to the source that it remains possible to analyse the propagation of source constraints to the target. Thus, once the SHACL descriptions of the mapped RDF graph are available, they can be used to validate that the facts in the graph are compatible with the constraints of the relational source and the mapping, using the SHACL validation engine. However, R2R mappings are also known for their mapping inconsistency and redundancy anomalies [9,16], thus one-to-one semantics correspondence such as *semantics preservation* proposed in [26, Defn. 6] and [23, Defn. 12] between the relational and the mapped RDF data can not be established in general [23,26, Prop. 1]. One of the prominent reasons behind such flaws is that R2R mappings often imply SHACL constraints that satisfy the mapped RDF graph with respect to database constraints even if the key constraints are violated in the source database, which can not be easily fixed as the mappings rely on the values of database keys to produce RDF terms [26, Exam. 4 and 5]. We can thus not hope for semantic *equivalence* between the SQL and SHACL constraints. In this work we instead define a notion of *maximal semantics preservation* to express that any additional SHACL constraints are either implied by the generated ones, or not implied by the SQL constraints.

Example 1. *Consider the following database instance $\mathcal{D}$ with schemas that describes students and their enrollment in courses being offered by a university:*

create table course *(C_id varchar primary key,* Title *varchar unique);*

create table student *(S_id integer primary key,* Name *varchar,* Code *varchar not null foreign key references* course(C_id)*);*

S_id	Name	Code
011	Ida	CS40
012		CS20

C_id	Title
CS40	Logic
CS20	Database
CS50	Data Eng

In general, an R2R mapping is an assertion of the form $Q \longrightarrow \psi$ that transforms a set of tuples projected by SQL query Q, called *source query*, over a relational source $\mathcal{D}$ into a set of RDF triples defined by graph triple patterns ψ. Assume an R2R mapping M to retrieve students and their enrollment in the university's courses,

Select S_id from student $\longrightarrow \langle \mathtt{iri}_1(\mathtt{S\_id}), \mathtt{rdf:type}, \mathtt{Student} \rangle$.

Select C_id from course $\longrightarrow \langle \mathtt{iri}_2(\mathtt{C\_id}), \mathtt{rdf:type}, \mathtt{Course} \rangle$.

Select S_id, C_id from student, course $\longrightarrow \langle \mathtt{iri}_1(\mathtt{S\_id}), \mathtt{enrolledFor}, \mathtt{iri}_2(\mathtt{C\_id}) \rangle$.

where student.Code = course.C_id

where iri_1 and iri_2 are injective functions that construct iris for students and courses from their respective id's. The mapping M yields the following RDF graph G (on the left) from the database instance $\mathcal{D}$:

$\langle iri_1(011), rdf:type, Student \rangle.$
$\langle iri_1(012), rdf:type, Student \rangle.$
$\langle iri_2(CS40), rdf:type, Course \rangle.$
$\langle iri_2(CS20), rdf:type, Course \rangle.$
$\langle iri_2(CS50), rdf:type, Course \rangle.$
$\langle iri_1(011), enrolledFor, iri_2(CS40) \rangle.$
$\langle iri_1(012), enrolledFor, iri_2(CS20) \rangle.$

```
:Student a sh:NodeShape, rdfs:Class;
    sh:property [ sh:path :enrolledFor;
        sh:maxCount 1;  sh:minCount 1;
        sh:nodeKind sh:IRI;  sh:class :Course ].
:Course a sh:NodeShape, rdfs:Class;
    sh:property [ sh:path [sh:inversePath
        :enrolledFor];
        sh:nodeKind sh:IRI;  sh:class :Student ].
```

Next, consider a SHACL document S (on the right), which consists of node shapes :Student and :Course with implicit target class[1] that define the constraints, intuitively, all students must be enrolled for exactly one course, and all courses must be enrolled by zero or more students. Now observe that the document S not only validates the graph G but also guarantee the validation of every RDF graphs that can be generated via mappings M from any valid instance $\mathcal{D}$ of the schemas in Example 1, i.e., semantics preservation. Moreover, any further restrictions on the property paths of S, such as all courses must be enrolled by at least one students, would easily be violated, meaning that a valid database instance $\mathcal{D}$ can be found such that mapped RDF graphs would not validate the document S. Thus, we say that S is a maximally implied set of SHACL shapes for the given relational source and the mappings M. For proof details, we refer the readers to the extended version [28].

Example 1 illustrates that an assessment of R2R mapping is necessary to guarantee whether the integrity constraints of relational data are maximally propagated via mappings to the RDF. We thus take the process of R2R transformation into account and define constraint rewriting as a function from constraints in SQL database to the sets of SHACL shapes over RDF graph. We first introduce two fundamental properties of constraint rewriting, namely maximal semantics preservation and monotonicity. Finally, we show that our proposed constraint rewriting is both maximal semantics preserving and monotone, even in the most general and practical scenario where relational databases contain null values. A constraint rewriting for R2R mappings is monotonic if it assures that the result of constraint rewriting that is already computed no longer requires alteration after the addition of new mappings.

2   Preliminaries

In this section, we fix notions and notations fundamental to the definition of R2R mapping, and SHACL constraints [15].

---

[1] https://www.w3.org/TR/shacl/#implicit-targetClass.

Databases. Let Δ be a countably infinite set of constants, including the reserved symbol null. A *relational schema* $\mathcal{R}$ is a finite set of relation names, known as *relation schemas*. We associate with each relation schema $R \in \mathcal{R}$ a finite, non-empty *set of named attributes*, denoted by att(R). An *instance* $\mathcal{D}$ of $\mathcal{R}$ assigns each relation schema $R \in \mathcal{R}$ a finite set of tuples $R^{\mathcal{D}}$, where each *tuple* $t \in R^{\mathcal{D}}$ is a function that assigns to each attribute in att(R) a value from domain Δ.

We write X as shorthand for a non-empty set $\{x_1, \ldots, x_n\}$ of attributes for $n \geq 1$, and $x \in X$ to say that x is one of the elements of the set. $|X| = n$ denotes the cardinality of the set. We further write $X \triangleleft R$ to denote that X is a non-empty subset of att(R). We write $t(x)$ to denote the restriction of a tuple $t \in R^{\mathcal{D}}$ to an attribute $x \in$ att(R), which can be extended to a set $X \triangleleft R$, i.e., $t(X)$. Finally, we define a *relational database* as a pair of $\mathcal{R}$ and $\mathcal{D}$, where $\mathcal{R}$ is a relational schema and $\mathcal{D}$ is a database instance of $\mathcal{R}$. The *active domain* $\Gamma_{\mathcal{D}}$ of a database is the set of constants appearing in $\mathcal{D}$, i.e., $\Gamma_{\mathcal{D}} \subseteq \Delta \setminus \{\text{null}\}$.

SQL Constraints. We consider declarations of the SQL: (a) *primary* (PK) and *foreign* (FK) keys, (b) *not null* (NN) and *unique* (UNQ) integrity, and (c) *data types*, constraints on the relational schema $\mathcal{R}$. We write Σ for the set of SQL constraints. NN, UNQ and PK constraints on a relational schema $\mathcal{R}$ are expressions of the form NN(X, R), UNQ(X, R) and PK(X, R), resp., for any $X \triangleleft R$ such that $R \in \mathcal{R}$. An instance $\mathcal{D}$ of $\mathcal{R}$ satisfies:

☐ NN(X, R) if for every $t \in R^{\mathcal{D}}$ and $x \in X$, $t(x) \neq$ null.
☐ UNQ(X, R) if for every $t, t' \in R^{\mathcal{D}}$, if $t(x) = t'(x) \neq$ null for every $x \in X$ then $t = t'$.
☐ PK(X, R) if: (a) for every $t \in R^{\mathcal{D}}$ and $x \in X$, $t(x) \neq$ null, and (b) for every $t, t' \in R^{\mathcal{D}}$, if $t(X) = t'(X)$ then $t = t'$.

An FK constraint on $\mathcal{R}$ is an expression of the form FK(X, R, Y, S) for any $X \triangleleft R$ and $Y \triangleleft S$ with $|X| = |Y|$ and $R, S \in \mathcal{R}$. An instance $\mathcal{D}$ of $\mathcal{R}$ satisfies FK(X, R, Y, S) if for every $t \in R^{\mathcal{D}}$: either (a) $t(x) =$ null for some $x \in X$, or (b) there exists a tuple $t' \in S^{\mathcal{D}}$ such that $t(X) = t'(Y)$. Next, to handle SQL data types, let the domain of an SQL data type v be a subset $\Delta_v \subseteq \Delta$. An SQL data type declaration on $\mathcal{R}$ is an expression of the form Type(x, v, R) for every $x \in$ att(R) such that $R \in \mathcal{R}$, where v is an SQL data type. An instance $\mathcal{D}$ of $\mathcal{R}$ satisfies Type(x, v, R) for an attribute $x \in$ att(R), if $t(x) \in \Delta_v$ for every $t \in R^{\mathcal{D}}$.

A *relational schema $\mathcal{R}$ with source constraints Σ* consists of the relational schema $\mathcal{R}$ and a set Σ of SQL constraints on $\mathcal{R}$, such that UNQ(Y, R) $\in \Sigma$ for all FK(X, R, Y, S) $\in \Sigma$, as usual in all SQL implementations. W.l.o.g., we also assume that for every $X \triangleleft R$: (a) if PK(X, R) $\in \Sigma$, then UNQ(X, R) $\in \Sigma$ and NN(X, R) $\in \Sigma$, (b) if NN(X, R) $\in \Sigma$, then NN(x, R) $\in \Sigma$ for every $x \in X$ and (c) if NN(x, R) $\in \Sigma$ for every $x \in X$, then NN(X, R) $\in \Sigma$. Finally, given a relational schema $\mathcal{R}$ with constraints Σ, and an instance $\mathcal{D}$ of $\mathcal{R}$, we call $\mathcal{D}$ a *legal instance* of $\mathcal{R}$ with Σ, denoted by $\mathcal{D} \models \Sigma$, if $\mathcal{D}$ satisfies all constraints in Σ.

Queries. Assume relational algebra with Selection $\sigma_{\neg\text{isNull}}$, Projection π, Equi Join $\bowtie_{\text{equality}}$, Right Outer Join $\bowtie^-_{\text{equality}}$, Left Outer Join $^-\!\bowtie_{\text{equality}}$ and Full Outer Join $\,^-\!\bowtie^-_{\text{equality}}$ operations as query language that corresponds to a sub-class of *basic fragment of SQL* standard. We use notation $\sigma_{\neg\text{isNull}}$ for the select condition 'IS NOT NULL' over an attribute as in SQL, which can be extended to a set of attributes. Assume that $\mathcal{R}$ is a relational schema, $\mathcal{D}$ is an instance of $\mathcal{R}$ and Q is a relational algebra expression over $\mathcal{R}$. Then att(Q), the set of attributes of Q, is recursively defined as follows, where we write $X \triangleleft Q$ to denote that X is a non-empty subset of att(Q):

1. If $Q = R$ such that $R \in \mathcal{R}$, then att(Q) = att(R).
2. If Q' is a relational algebra expression over $\mathcal{R}$, $X \triangleleft Q'$ and $Q = \sigma_{\neg\mathtt{isNull}(X)}(Q')$, i.e., $\sigma_{\neg\mathtt{isNull}(x_1)\wedge \ldots \wedge \neg\mathtt{isNull}(x_n)}(Q')$, then att($Q$) = att($Q'$).
3. If Q' is a relational algebra expression over $\mathcal{R}$, $X \triangleleft Q'$ and $Q = \pi_X(Q')$, then att(Q) = X.
4. Let Q_1, Q_2 be relational algebra expressions over $\mathcal{R}$ such that $X \triangleleft Q_1$ and $Y \triangleleft Q_2$ have compatible data types. If $Q = Q_1 \mathtt{OP}_{X=Y} Q_2$ s.t. OP $\in \{\bowtie, \bowtie:, :\bowtie, \bowtie\!\!\!\times\}$, then att($Q$) = att($Q_1$) $\cup$ att(Q_2).

The evaluation of Q over $\mathcal{D}$, a set of tuples denoted by $Q^{\mathcal{D}}$, is recursively defined as follows,

1. If $Q = R$ such that $R \in \mathcal{R}$, then $Q^{\mathcal{D}} = R^{\mathcal{D}}$.
2. If Q' is a relational algebra expression over $\mathcal{R}$, $X \triangleleft Q'$ and $Q = \sigma_{\neg\mathtt{isNull}(X)}(Q')$, then $Q^{\mathcal{D}} = \{t \in Q'^{\mathcal{D}} \mid t(x) \neq \mathtt{null}$ for every $x \in X\}$.
3. If Q' is a relational algebra expression over $\mathcal{R}$, $X \triangleleft Q'$ and $Q = \pi_X(Q')$ then, for every $t \in Q^{\mathcal{D}}$ there exists $t' \in Q'^{\mathcal{D}}$ such that $t(X) = t'(X)$.
4. Let Q_1, Q_2 be relational algebra expressions over $\mathcal{R}$ such that $X \triangleleft Q_1$ and $Y \triangleleft Q_2$ have compatible data types.
   a. If $Q = Q_1 \bowtie_{X=Y} Q_2$ then for every $t \in Q^{\mathcal{D}}$: (i) there exist $t_1 \in Q_1^{\mathcal{D}}$ and $t_2 \in Q_2^{\mathcal{D}}$ s.t. $t(x) = t_1(x) = t_2(y) \neq \mathtt{null}$ for every $x \in X$ and $y \in Y$, (ii) $t(u) = t_1(u)$ for every $u \in (\text{att}(Q_1)\backslash\text{att}(Q_2))$, and (iii) $t(v) = t_2(v)$ for every $v \in (\text{att}(Q_2)\backslash\text{att}(Q_1))$.
   b. If $Q = Q_1 :\bowtie_{X=Y} Q_2$ then for every $t \in Q^{\mathcal{D}}$: either (i) there exist $t_1 \in Q_1^{\mathcal{D}}$ and $t_2 \in Q_2^{\mathcal{D}}$ s.t. $t(x) = t_1(x) = t_2(y) \neq \mathtt{null}$ for every $x \in X$ and $y \in Y$, $t(u) = t_1(u)$ for every $u \in (\text{att}(Q_1) \backslash \text{att}(Q_2))$ and $t(v) = t_2(v)$ for every $v \in (\text{att}(Q_2) \backslash \text{att}(Q_1))$, or (ii) there exist $t_1 \in Q_1^{\mathcal{D}}$ s.t. $t(u) = t_1(u)$ for every $u \in (\text{att}(Q_1) \backslash \text{att}(Q_2))$ and $t(v) = \mathtt{null}$ for every $v \in (\text{att}(Q_2) \backslash \text{att}(Q_1))$.
   c. If $Q = Q_1 \bowtie:_{X=Y} Q_2$ then for every $t \in Q^{\mathcal{D}}$: either (i) there exist $t_1 \in Q_1^{\mathcal{D}}$ and $t_2 \in Q_2^{\mathcal{D}}$ s.t. $t(x) = t_1(x) = t_2(y) \neq \mathtt{null}$ for every $x \in X$ and $y \in Y$, $t(u) = t_1(u)$ for every $u \in (\text{att}(Q_1) \backslash \text{att}(Q_2))$ and $t(v) = t_2(v)$ for every $v \in (\text{att}(Q_2) \backslash \text{att}(Q_1))$, or (ii) there exist $t_2 \in Q_2^{\mathcal{D}}$ s.t. $t(v) = t_2(v)$ for every $v \in (\text{att}(Q_2) \backslash \text{att}(Q_1))$ and $t(u) = \mathtt{null}$ for every $u \in (\text{att}(Q_1) \backslash \text{att}(Q_2))$.
   d. If $Q = Q_1 \bowtie\!\!\!\times_{X=Y} Q_2$ then $Q^{\mathcal{D}} = Q_a^{\mathcal{D}} \cup Q_b^{\mathcal{D}}$ s.t. $Q_a = Q_1 :\bowtie_{X=Y} Q_2$ and $Q_b = Q_1 \bowtie:_{X=Y} Q_2$.

Henceforth, we denote by SP the relational expression containing only select-project relational operations, and SPJ the relational expression containing select-project-(outer)join relational operations, respectively.

Definition 1. *Let Q be a relational expression over a relational schema $\mathcal{R}$. Then, we say that the Q is a* valid query *if and only if there exist foreign key references between every two sets of attributes participating in an equality join condition in the Q.*

RDF Graphs. Assume that $\mathcal{I}, \mathcal{B}$ and $\mathcal{L}$ are countably infinite disjoint sets of *Internationalized Resource Identifiers* (IRIs), *Blank nodes* and *Literals*, respectively. The set of

RDF terms $\mathcal{T}$ is $I \cup \mathcal{L} \cup \mathcal{B}$. A *well-defined RDF triple* is defined as a triple $\langle s, p, o \rangle$ where $s \in I \cup \mathcal{B}$ is called the subject, $p \in I$ is called the predicate and $o \in \mathcal{T}$ is called the object. An RDF graph $G \subseteq (I \cup \mathcal{B}) \times I \times \mathcal{T}$ is a finite subset of RDF triples.

Definition 2. *The set of nodes of an RDF graph G is the set of subjects and objects of triples in the graph, i.e.,* $\{s, o \mid \langle s, p, o \rangle \in G\}$.

Assume a countably infinite set $\mathcal{V}$ of variables disjoint from $\mathcal{T}$. A triple pattern is defined as a triple in $(I \cup \mathcal{B} \cup \mathcal{V}) \times (I \cup \mathcal{V}) \times (\mathcal{T} \cup \mathcal{V})$. A *basic graph pattern (BGP)* is a finite set of triple patterns. The schema $sch(\psi)$ of a triple pattern ψ is the *RDF property and class* predicates [17] from the ψ.

Mappings. Formally, we adopt R2R mapping [6,22] that generate RDF triples from the active domain of a database $\Gamma_{\mathcal{D}}$. Assume countably infinite and disjoint sets $\mathbb{F}$ and $\mathbb{T}$ of iri-template and typing *functions* respectively, with each function $\alpha \in \mathbb{F} \cup \mathbb{T}$ has an associated arity $n > 0$. W.l.o.g., we assume that functions $\mathbb{F} \cup \mathbb{T}$ are injective, and map only null to null.

Definition 3. *We specify R2R-mapping $\mathcal{M}$, from relational database-to-RDF, partitioned into three disjoint sets:* $\mathcal{M}_C$, $\mathcal{M}_P$ *and* $\mathcal{M}_U$ *such that*

i. *$\mathcal{M}_C$ is a set of data-to-RDF concept mappings, each one of the form*

$$Q_X \longrightarrow \langle \mathbf{f}(X), \mathtt{rdf:type}, C \rangle,$$

where
   a. *Q_X is a source query Q over $\mathcal{R}$ with $X \triangleleft Q$,*
   b. *$\mathbf{f} \in \mathbb{F}$ and C is an RDF concept.*
ii. *$\mathcal{M}_P$ is a set of data-to-RDF object property mappings, each one of the form*

$$Q_{X,Y} \longrightarrow \langle \mathbf{f}(X), P, \mathbf{f}'(Y) \rangle,$$

where
   a. *$Q_{X,Y}$ is a source query Q over $\mathcal{R}$ with $X, Y \triangleleft Q$,*
   b. *$\mathbf{f}, \mathbf{f}' \in \mathbb{F}$ and P is an RDF object property.*
iii. *$\mathcal{M}_U$ is a set of data-to-RDF datatype property mappings, each one of the form*

$$Q_{X,Y} \longrightarrow \langle \mathbf{f}(X), U, \mathbf{t}(Y) \rangle,$$

where
   a. *$Q_{X,Y}$ is a source query Q over $\mathcal{R}$ with $X, Y \triangleleft Q$,*
   b. *$\mathbf{f} \in \mathbb{F}$, $\mathbf{t} \in \mathbb{T}$ and U is an RDF datatype property.*

Let m be a mapping $Q \longrightarrow \psi$ of a triple pattern ψ, as in Definition 3. The source query Q is the *body(m)* of m, whereas the triple pattern ψ is the *head(m)*. The schema $sch(\mathcal{M})$ of a mapping set $\mathcal{M}$ is the union of $sch(head(m))$ of each $m \in \mathcal{M}$. For any two mapping sets $\mathcal{M}$ and $\mathcal{M}'$ defined over a relational schema $\mathcal{R}$ with source constraint Σ, we write $\mathcal{M}' \subseteq \mathcal{M}$, if for every mapping definition m, if $m \in \mathcal{M}'$ then $m \in \mathcal{M}$.

Definition 4. *Let Q_C, Q_P and Q_U be the source queries of mappings of an RDF concept C, object property P and datatype property U, respectively. Then, we say that a mapping set M (according to Definition 3) is a* simple *mapping if: (a) M contains exactly one mapping definition per concept C, object property P and datatype property U predicates in sch(M); (b) each Q_P is a valid SPJ query with one join operation, (c) each Q_U is an SP query, d) if C and C' are the concepts whose instances are subject and object of an object property P, then the Q_C and $Q_{C'}$ are either equal to Q_P or SP queries with a projected set of attributes whose (tuple) values are mapped to instances of C and C', and (e) if C is the concept whose instances are the subject of a datatype property U, then Q_C is either equal to Q_U or an SP query with a projected set of attributes whose (tuple) values are mapped into the instances of C.*

Example 2. *Consider the mapping of object property 'EnrolledFor' in Example 1. Instances of concepts 'Student' and 'Course' are mapped to subject and object of the property 'EnrolledFor', respectively. Then, according to simple mapping in Definition 4, the source queries used in the mappings of those 'Student' and 'Course' concepts must be either the exact same source query used in the mapping of the property 'EnrolledFor' or the SP source queries as in Example 1. Thus, a distinct simple mapping could be defined for the same purpose that maps RDF concepts 'Student' and 'Course' using the same SPJ source query Q_P,*

$$Q_P ::= Select\ S\_id,\ C\_id\ from\ student, course$$
$$where\ student.Code = course.C\_id$$

as used in the mapping of object property 'EnrolledFor' as follows:

$$Q_P \longrightarrow \langle iri_1(S\_id), rdf:type, Student\rangle.$$
$$Q_P \longrightarrow \langle iri_2(C\_id), rdf:type, Course\rangle.$$
$$Q_P \longrightarrow \langle iri_1(S\_id), enrolledFor, iri_2(C\_id)\rangle.$$

Let $t \in Q^{\mathcal{D}}$ be a tuple of constants, and let $\mathbf{f}(X)$ be a term such that $\mathbf{f} \in \mathbb{F}$ and $X \triangleleft Q$. Then, $\mathbf{f}(t(X))$ is a ground term of $\mathbf{f}(X)$ obtained by substituting occurrence of every $x \in X$ with $t(x)$.

Definition 5. *Let $M_C \cup M_P \cup M_U$ be an R2R mapping set M defined over a relational schema $\mathcal{R}$, and $\mathcal{D}$ an instance of $\mathcal{R}$. Then, we call the set of well-defined RDF triple assertions $M(\mathcal{D})$, i.e.,*

$$M(\mathcal{D}) = \{\langle \mathbf{f}(t(X)), rdf:type, C\rangle \mid \{Q \longrightarrow \langle \mathbf{f}(X), rdf:type, C\rangle\} \in M_C, X \triangleleft Q\ and\ t \in Q^{\mathcal{D}}\}$$
$$\cup\ \{\langle \mathbf{f}(t(X)), P, \mathbf{f}'(t(Y))\rangle \mid \{Q \longrightarrow \langle \mathbf{f}(X), P, \mathbf{f}'(Y)\rangle\} \in M_P, X, Y \triangleleft Q\ and\ t \in Q^{\mathcal{D}}\}$$
$$\cup\ \{\langle \mathbf{f}(t(X)), U, \mathbf{t}(t(Y))\rangle \mid \{Q \longrightarrow \langle \mathbf{f}(X), U, \mathbf{t}(Y)\rangle\} \in M_U, X, Y \triangleleft Q\ and\ t \in Q^{\mathcal{D}}\},$$

the RDF graph projected by the mapping set M and the instance $\mathcal{D}$.

We recall that R2R mappings in Definition 3 generate RDF triples from the active domain of a database $\Gamma_{\mathcal{D}}$, i.e., null cannot appear in the output RDF triples. Therefore, in this paper, we explicitly consider that (a) mappings M is simple, and (b) w.l.o.g., source query Q of each mapping in M contains $\sigma_{\neg isNull(X)}$ and $\sigma_{\neg isNull(Y)}$ filters over every projected set of $X, Y \triangleleft att(Q)$.

SHACL. Our formal treatment of the *core constraints* of SHACL [15] is based on the approach of Corman et al. [12]. Each SHACL constraint is a set of conditions, usually referred to as shape, defined as a triple $\langle s, \tau_s, \phi_s \rangle$ consisting of a shape IRI s, a *target definition* τ_s, and a *constraint definition* ϕ_s. The τ_s and ϕ_s are expressions that determine for every RDF graph G and node n of G, whether n is a target of the shape, $G \models \tau_s(n)$, respectively, whether n satisfies the constraint, $G \models \phi_s(n)$. All shapes generated by our transformation have an 'implicit target class,' which means that s is also the IRI of a class and $G \models \tau(n)$ iff n is a SHACL instance of class s.[2] For the purpose of our work, the constraint ϕ_s is an expression defined according to the following grammar:

$$\phi ::= \phi \wedge \phi \mid \geq_n P^{\pm}.\alpha \mid \leq_n P^{\pm}.\alpha \mid \rhd_C P^{\pm} \tag{1}$$
$$\alpha ::= \top \mid \ell \mid \neg \ell \mid C \mid \neg C$$

where $\top$ stands for truth, ℓ is an XML schema datatype, C and P are an RDF concept and property names respectively, the superscript $\pm$ stands for a property or its inverse, $n \in \mathbb{N}$, $\neg$ for negation, $(\geq_n P^{\pm}.\alpha)$ means 'must have at least n $P^{\pm}$-successor verifying α' for any $n \in \mathbb{N}$ and $(\rhd_C P^{\pm})$ means 'all values of $P^{\pm}$-successor must be unique[3] among instances of concept C'. As syntactic sugar, we use $(=_n P^{\pm}.\alpha)$ for $(\geq_n P^{\pm}.\alpha) \wedge (\leq_n P^{\pm}.\alpha)$, $(\rhd_C P^{\pm}.\alpha)$ for $(\leq_1 P^{\pm}.\alpha) \wedge (\rhd_C P^{\pm})$ and $(\unrhd_C P^{\pm}.\alpha)$ for $(=_1 P^{\pm}.\alpha) \wedge (\rhd_C P^{\pm})$.

A SHACL document is a set of SHACL shapes. An RDF graph G validates against a shape $\langle s, \tau_s, \phi_s \rangle$ if for every nodes n of G, if $G \models \tau_s(n)$ then $G \models \phi_s(n)$. An RDF graph G validates against a SHACL document S, written $G \models S$, iff G validates against all shapes in S. The schema $sch(s)$ of a SHACL shape s is the set of RDF concept and property predicates [17] used in the target τ_s and constraint ϕ_s definition. The schema $sch(S)$ of a SHACL document S is the union of $sch(s)$ of every shape $s \in S$.

3   Constraint Rewriting: Definition and Properties

Our goal is to generate a set of SHACL constraints that is as strong as possible while being guaranteed to hold for all RDF graphs resulting from valid database instances. Let $\mathcal{M}$ be a mapping set defined over a relational schema $\mathcal{R}$ with source constraints Σ.

Definition 6. *A SHACL document S is an Σ-implied set of shapes with respect to $\mathcal{M}$, written as $\Sigma \models_{\mathcal{M}} S$, if for every instance $\mathcal{D}$ of $\mathcal{R}$:*

$$\mathcal{D} \models \Sigma \rightarrow \mathcal{M}(\mathcal{D}) \models S.$$

Definition 7. *Let $\Sigma \models_{\mathcal{M}} S$. Then, we say that S is a maximally Σ-implied set of shapes with respect to $\mathcal{M}$, written as $\Sigma \models^*_{\mathcal{M}} S$, if for every $\Sigma \models_{\mathcal{M}} S'$ s.t. $sch(S') \subseteq sch(\mathcal{M})$ and every RDF graph $\mathcal{G}$:*

$$\mathcal{G} \models S \rightarrow \mathcal{G} \models S'.$$

We now formalise a constraint rewriting and some desirable properties. Let $\mathbb{S}$ be the set of all SHACL shapes and $\mathbb{Q}$ be the set of all pairs $(\mathcal{M}, \Sigma)$ such that $\mathcal{M}$ is a mapping set defined over a relational schema $\mathcal{R}$ with source constraints Σ.

---

[2] https://www.w3.org/TR/shacl/#implicit-targetClass.
[3] `dash:uniqueValueForClassConstraintComponent` from http://datashapes.org.

Definition 8 (Constraint rewriting). *A constraint rewriting is a function* $\mathcal{T} : \mathbb{Q} \rightarrow \mathcal{P}(\mathbb{S})$.

We next introduce central properties of a constraint rewriting $\mathcal{T}$.

Definition 9 (Semantics preservation). *A constraint rewriting* $\mathcal{T}$ *is semantics preserving if for every mapping set* $\mathcal{M}$ *and every source constraints* Σ:

$$\Sigma \models_M \mathcal{T}(\mathcal{M}, \Sigma).$$

Definition 10 (Maximal semantics preservation). *A constraint rewriting* $\mathcal{T}$ *is maximal semantics preserving if for every mapping set* $\mathcal{M}$ *and every source constraints* Σ:

$$\Sigma \models_M^* \mathcal{T}(\mathcal{M}, \Sigma).$$

Definition 11 (Monotonicity). *A constraint rewriting* $\mathcal{T}$ *is monotone if for any mapping sets* $\mathcal{M}' \subseteq \mathcal{M}$ *defined over a relational schema* $\mathcal{R}$ *with source constraint* Σ *and every RDF graph* $\mathcal{G}$:

$$\mathcal{G} \models \mathcal{T}(\mathcal{M}, \Sigma) \rightarrow \mathcal{G} \models \mathcal{T}(\mathcal{M}', \Sigma).$$

4   View Constraint: Definitions

As introduced in Sect. 2, R2R mapping relies on database views based on a source query to compute RDF terms from the database values. As a first step of our constraint transformation, we have to analyse the propagation of database constraints to these views.

Let $\mathcal{R}$ be a relational schema with source constraints Σ, and $R \in \mathcal{R}$. The constraint Σ restricted to the set of att(R), denoted by $\Sigma|_R$, is the set of constraints such that for every constraint $\sigma \in \Sigma$ on any $X \triangleleft R$, there is $\sigma \in \Sigma|_R$. For example, if FK(X, R, Y, S) $\in \Sigma$ (resp., FK(Y, S, X, R) $\in \Sigma$) on any $X \triangleleft R$, then there is FK(X, R, Y, S) $\in \Sigma|_R$ (resp., FK(Y, S, X, R) $\in \Sigma|_R$).

Definition 12. *Let Q be a relational expression over a relational schema $\mathcal{R}$ with source constraints Σ. Then, the set Σ propagated to the set of* att(Q), *denoted by $\Sigma|_Q$, is recursively defined as follows,*

a. *If $Q = R$ such that $R \in \mathcal{R}$, then $\Sigma|_Q = \Sigma|_R$.*
b. *$Q = \sigma_{\neg isNull(X)}(Q')$ where $X \triangleleft Q'$, then $\Sigma|_Q = \Sigma|_{Q'}$.*
c. *If $Q = \pi_X(Q')$ where $X \triangleleft Q'$ then $\Sigma|_Q = \{PK(Y, R), UNQ(Y, R), NN(Y, R), FK(Y, R, Z, S),$ $FK(Z, S, Y, R) \in \Sigma|_{Q'} \mid Y \subseteq X$ and $R, S \in \mathcal{R}\}$.*
d. *If $Q = Q_1 \, OP_{X=Y} \, Q_2$ where $X \triangleleft Q_1$ and $Y \triangleleft Q_2$ have compatible data types, and $OP \in \{\bowtie, \bowtie\!\!\!\!\!\!\raisebox{-3pt}{\tiny=}, \bowtie\!\!\!\!\!\!\raisebox{3pt}{\tiny=}, \bowtie\!\!\!\!\!\!\raisebox{0pt}{\tiny><}\}$, then $\Sigma|_Q = \Sigma|_{Q_1} \cup \Sigma|_{Q_2}$.*

SQL constraints are not well suited to direct translation to SHACL, so we introduce an intermediate representation similar to functional dependencies. Let R be a relation name with $X, Y \triangleleft R$. Then, we write a functional dependency as an expression of the form $FD_{X \rightarrow Y}$, i.e., meaning $X \triangleleft R$ functionally determines $Y \triangleleft R$. Relational data dependencies, such as functional, multi-value and others, are originally defined on databases without null [3,5]. However, we need notions of data dependencies that also apply to databases with null, such as in [4], which we define as follows:

Definition 13. *Let Q be a source query over a relational schema $\mathcal{R}$ with source constraints Σ, $R \in \mathcal{R}$ a relation name and $\mathcal{D}$ an arbitrary instance of $\mathcal{R}$. Let V be the pair $(Q^{\mathcal{D}}, \Sigma|_Q)$ of projected view $Q^{\mathcal{D}}$ and propagated constraints $\Sigma|_Q$. Then, for any $X, Y \triangleleft Q$,*

a. *$V \models FP_{X \to Y}$ if for every $t, t' \in Q^{\mathcal{D}}$, if $t(X) = t'(X)$ then $t(Y) = t'(Y)$.*
b. *$V \models UF_{X \to Y}$ if $Q^{\mathcal{D}} \models FP_{X \to Y}$ and $Q^{\mathcal{D}} \models FP_{Y \to X}$.*
c. *$V \models FD_{X \to Y}$ if $Q^{\mathcal{D}} \models FP_{X \to Y}$ and $NN(X, R), NN(Y, R) \in \Sigma|_Q$.*
d. *$V \models UFD_{X \to Y}$ if $Q^{\mathcal{D}} \models FD_{X \to Y}$ and $Q^{\mathcal{D}} \models FD_{Y \to X}$.*

Henceforth, we will keep the SQL notations intuitively simple in examples, i.e., we write $NN(X) \in \Sigma|_{X \triangleleft R}$ instead of $NN(X, R) \in \Sigma|_{X \triangleleft R}$ for the propagated $NN(X, R) \in \Sigma$ to $\Sigma|_{X \triangleleft R}$.

Example 3. *Following Example 1, assume a mapping set $\mathcal{M}$ with $\mathbf{f}_S$ and $\mathbf{f}_C$ iri-templates and a typing function $\mathbf{t}_v$[4] as follows:*

a. *$\pi_{S\_id, Name} \sigma_{\neg isNull(S\_id) \wedge \neg isNull(Name)}(\text{student}) \longrightarrow \langle \mathbf{f}_S(S\_id), \text{hasName}, \mathbf{t}_v(Name) \rangle.$*
b. *$\pi_{C\_id, Title} \sigma_{\neg isNull(C\_id) \wedge \neg isNull(Title)}(\text{course}) \longrightarrow \langle \mathbf{f}_C(C\_id), \text{hasTitle}, \mathbf{t}_v(Title) \rangle.$*

Let $Q_1 = \pi_{S\_id, Name} \sigma_{\neg isNull(S\_id) \wedge \neg isNull(Name)}(\text{student})$, and $V_1 = (Q_1^{\mathcal{D}}, \Sigma|_{Q_1})$. Then,

- *$\text{att}(Q_1) = \{S\_id, Name\}$ and $\Sigma|_{\text{att}(Q_1)} = \{PK(S\_id), UNQ(S\_id), NN(S\_id), Type(S\_id, v), Type(Name, v)\}$, i.e., from assumption in Sect. 2, if $PK(S\_id)$ then $UNQ(S\_id)$ and $NN(S\_id)$.*
- *$V_1 \models FP_{S\_id \to Name}$ since for every $t, t' \in Q_1^{\mathcal{D}}$, if $t(S\_id) = t'(S\_id)$ then $t(Name) = t'(Name)$.*

Filter $\sigma_{\neg isNull(Name)}$ excludes tuples from $Q_1^{\mathcal{D}}$ that contains null for the Name $\in \text{att}(Q_1)$. Similarly, let $Q_2 = \pi_{C\_id, Title} \sigma_{\neg isNull(C\_id) \wedge \neg isNull(Title)}(\text{course})$, and $V_2 = (Q_2^{\mathcal{D}}, \Sigma|_{Q_2})$. Then,

- *$\text{att}(Q_2) = \{C\_id, Title\}$ and $\Sigma|_{\text{att}(Q_2)} = \{PK(C\_id), UNQ(C\_id), NN(C\_id), Type(C\_id, v), UNQ(Title), Type(Title, v), FK(Code, student, C\_id, course)\}$*
- *$V_2 \models FP_{C\_id \to Title}$ since for any $t, t' \in Q_2^{\mathcal{D}}$, if $t(C\_id) = t'(C\_id)$ then $t(Title) = t'(Title)$.*
- *$V_2 \models FP_{Title \to C\_id}$ since for any $t, t' \in Q_2^{\mathcal{D}}$, if $t(Title) = t'(Title)$ then $t(C\_id) = t'(C\_id)$.*
- *$V_2 \models UF_{C\_id \to Title}$ since $Q_2^{\mathcal{D}} \models FP_{C\_id \to Title}$ and $Q_2^{\mathcal{D}} \models FP_{Title \to C\_id}$.*

5   Source to View Constraint Implication

The next step is to determine which of the data dependencies from Definition 13 hold for the view defined by the source queries, i.e., they are implied by the propagated SQL constraints.

Let Q be a source query over a relational schema $\mathcal{R}$ with source constraints $\triangleleft \Sigma$. Then, we say that Σ implies a data dependency $\sigma_{X \to Y}$ s.t. $\sigma \in \{UFD, FD, UFP, FP\}$ on $X, Y \triangleleft Q$, denoted by $\Sigma_Q \Vdash \sigma_{X \to Y}$, if $V \models \sigma_{X \to Y}$ for every legal instance $\mathcal{D}$ of $\mathcal{R}$, where $V = (Q^{\mathcal{D}}, \Sigma|_Q)$ is the pair of projected view $Q^{\mathcal{D}}$ and propagated constraints $\Sigma|_Q$. We now concentrate on SP source queries.

---

[4] $\mathbf{t}_v$ specify XML Schema datatype of RDF literal $\mathbf{t}_v(d)$ corresponding to the SQL data type v of the database constant $d \in \Delta_v$, e.g., $\mathbf{t}_v$ is an xsd:string IRI term if v is varchar SQL data type.

Lemma 1. *Let Q be a source query $\pi_{X,Y}\sigma_{\neg\texttt{isNull}(X)\wedge\neg\texttt{isNull}(Y)}(R)$ over a relational schema $\mathcal{R}$ with source constraints Σ, $R \in \mathcal{R}$ a relation name and $\Sigma|_Q$ the set Σ propagated to set of* $\texttt{att}(Q)$. *Then, for any $X, Y \triangleleft Q$,*

a. $\Sigma_Q \Vdash FP_{X \to Y}$ *if* $UNQ(X, R) \in \Sigma|_Q$.
b. $\Sigma_Q \Vdash UF_{X \to Y}$ *if* $UNQ(X, R), UNQ(Y, R) \in \Sigma|_Q$.
c. $\Sigma_Q \Vdash FD_{X \to Y}$ *if* $UNQ(X, R) \in \Sigma|_Q$ *and* $NN(X, R), NN(Y, R) \in \Sigma|_Q$.
d. $\Sigma_Q \Vdash UFD_{X \to Y}$ *if* $UNQ(X, R), UNQ(Y, R) \in \Sigma|_Q$ *and* $NN(X, R), NN(Y, R) \in \Sigma|_Q$.

Corollary 1. *Let Q be a source query $\pi_{X,Y}\sigma_{\neg\texttt{isNull}(X)\wedge\neg\texttt{isNull}(Y)}(R)$ over a relational schema $\mathcal{R}$ with source constraints Σ, $R \in \mathcal{R}$ a relation name and $\Sigma|_Q$ the set Σ propagated to set of* $\texttt{att}(Q)$. *Then, for any $X, Y \triangleleft Q$,*

a. $\Sigma_Q \Vdash UFD_{X \to Y} \to \Sigma_Q \Vdash FD_{X \to Y}$ *and* $\Sigma_Q \Vdash FD_{X \to Y} \to \Sigma_Q \Vdash FP_{X \to Y}$
b. $\Sigma_Q \Vdash UFD_{X \to Y} \to \Sigma_Q \Vdash UF_{X \to Y}$ *and* $\Sigma_Q \Vdash UF_{X \to Y} \to \Sigma_Q \Vdash FP_{X \to Y}$

We next concentrate on SPJ source queries. An SPJ source query Q over a relational schema $\mathcal{R}$ with source constraints Σ is a relational algebra expression of the form,

$$Q := \pi_{X,Y}\sigma_{\neg\texttt{isNull}(X)\wedge\neg\texttt{isNull}(Y)}(R_1 \, OP_{U=V} \, R_2),$$

where $R_1, R_2 \in \mathcal{R}$ are relation names with $X, U \triangleleft R_1$ and $Y, V \triangleleft R_2$, $|U| = |V|$ and $OP \in \{\bowtie, \ltimes, \rtimes, \bowtie\}$. Since mapping in Definition 3 generates RDF triples from the active domain $\Gamma_D \subseteq \Delta \setminus \{\texttt{null}\}$ of the database, w.l.o.g., we equivalently express the stated SPJ source query Q, that yields the same set of RDF triples as the original Q, as follows,

$$\pi_{X,Y}\sigma_{\neg\texttt{isNull}(X)\wedge\neg\texttt{isNull}(Y)}(\sigma_{\neg\texttt{isNull}(X)\wedge\neg\texttt{isNull}(U)}(R_1) \, OP_{U=V} \, \sigma_{\neg\texttt{isNull}(V)\wedge\neg\texttt{isNull}(Y)}(R_2)).$$

Note that the SPJ query Q is valid if and only if $FK(U, R_1, V, R_2) \in \Sigma|_Q$ or $FK(V, R_2, U, R_1) \in \Sigma|_Q$, see Definition 1. Henceforth, we use symbol $\to^*$ to express dependency in the opposite direction of foreign key reference, i.e., we write $FD_{X \to^* Y}$ to state functional dependency from $X \triangleleft Q$ to $Y \triangleleft Q$ if $FK(Y, R_2, X, R_1) \in \Sigma|_Q$ or $FK(V, R_2, U, R_1) \in \Sigma|_Q$ s.t. $X, U \triangleleft R_1$ and $Y, V \triangleleft R_2$.

Lemma 2. *Let $\mathcal{R}$ be a relational schema with source constraints Σ, and let Q be an SPJ source query over $\mathcal{R}$,*

$$Q := \pi_{X,Y}\sigma_{\neg\texttt{isNull}(X)\wedge\neg\texttt{isNull}(Y)}(Q_1 \, OP_{U=V} \, Q_2)$$

s.t. Q_1 and Q_2 are SP expressions over $R_1 \in \mathcal{R}$ and $R_2 \in \mathcal{R}$ with $X, U \triangleleft Q_1$ and $Y, V \triangleleft Q_2$ respectively, $OP \in \{\bowtie, \ltimes, \rtimes, \bowtie\}$ and $FK(U, R_1, V, R_2) \in \Sigma|_Q$. Then, for any $X, Y \triangleleft Q$:

a. $\Sigma_Q \Vdash \sigma_{X \to Y}$ *if* $\Sigma_{Q_1} \Vdash \sigma_{X \to U}$ *and* $\Sigma_{Q_2} \Vdash \sigma_{V \to Y}$ *s.t.* $\sigma \in \{UFD, FD, UF\}$.
b. $\Sigma_Q \Vdash \sigma_{X \to Y}$ *if* $\Sigma_{Q_1} \Vdash UFD_{X \to U}$ *and* $\Sigma_{Q_2} \Vdash \sigma_{V \to Y}$ *s.t.* $\sigma \in \{FD, UF\}$.
c. $\Sigma_Q \Vdash \sigma_{X \to Y}$ *if* $\Sigma_{Q_1} \Vdash \sigma_{X \to U}$ *s.t.* $\sigma \in \{FD, UF\}$ *and* $\Sigma_{Q_2} \Vdash UFD_{V \to Y}$.
d. $\Sigma_Q \Vdash FP_{X \to Y}$ *if* $\Sigma_{Q_1} \Vdash FD_{X \to U}$ *and* $\Sigma_{Q_2} \Vdash UF_{V \to Y}$.
e. $\Sigma_Q \Vdash FP_{X \to Y}$ *if* $\Sigma_{Q_1} \Vdash UF_{X \to U}$ *and* $\Sigma_{Q_2} \Vdash FD_{V \to Y}$.
f. $\Sigma_Q \Vdash FP_{X \to Y}$ *if* $\Sigma_{Q_1} \Vdash FP_{X \to U}$.
g. $\Sigma_Q \Vdash FP_{X \to Y}$ *if* $\Sigma_{Q_1} \Vdash \sigma_{X \to U}$ *and* $\Sigma_{Q_2} \Vdash FP_{V \to Y}$ *s.t.* $\sigma \in \{UFD, FD, UF\}$.

h. $\Sigma_Q \Vdash \sigma_{Y\to^*X}$ if $\Sigma_{Q_1} \Vdash \sigma_{U\to X}$ and $\Sigma_{Q_2} \Vdash \sigma_{Y\to V}$ s.t. $\sigma \in \{UFD, UF\}$.

i. $\Sigma_Q \Vdash FP_{Y\to^*X}$ if $\Sigma_{Q_1} \Vdash \sigma_{U\to X}$ s.t. $\sigma \in \{UFD, FD, FP\}$ and $\Sigma_{Q_2} \Vdash UF_{Y\to V}$.

j. $\Sigma_Q \Vdash \sigma_{Y\to^*X}$ if $\Sigma_{Q_1} \Vdash \sigma_{U\to X}$ s.t. $\sigma \in \{FD, UF, FP\}$ and $\Sigma_{Q_2} \Vdash UFD_{Y\to V}$.

On the correctness of Lemma 2, e.g., assume the case (f). Then, $UNQ(V, R_2) \in \Sigma|_{Q_2}$ since $FK(U, R_1, V, R_2) \in \Sigma|_Q$. Thus, $\Sigma_{Q_2} \Vdash \sigma_{V\to Y}$ s.t. $\sigma \in \{UFD, FD, UF, FP\}$ is the set of all possible constraints implication. Hence, the case (f) of Lemma 2 covers the following possible cases of constraints implication:

- $\Sigma_Q \Vdash FP_{X\to Y}$ if $\Sigma_{Q_1} \Vdash FP_{X\to U}$ and $\Sigma_{Q_2} \Vdash \sigma_{V\to Y}$ s.t. $\sigma \in \{UFD, FD, UF, FP\}$.

Further, by applying similar arguments and the implication rules stated in Corollary 1 to the rest of cases in Lemma 2, the correctness proof of the Lemma can be enumerated.

Example 4. *Following Examples 1 and 4, assume an R2R mapping:*

$$Q \longrightarrow \langle \mathbf{f}_S(S\_id), \texttt{enrolledFor}, \mathbf{f}_C(C\_id)\rangle,$$

where Q is a source query $\pi_{S\_id, C\_id}\sigma_{\neg isNull(S\_id)\wedge\neg isNull(C\_id)}(Q_1 \bowtie_{Code=C\_id} Q_2)$ such that $Q_1 = \sigma_{\neg isNull(S\_id)\wedge\neg isNull(Code)}(\texttt{student})$ and $Q_2 = \sigma_{\neg isNull(C\_id)}(\texttt{course})$. Then,

a. *for SP expression Q_1 :*
   - $att(Q_1) = \{S\_id, Code\}$ *and* $\{UNQ(S\_id), NN(S\_id), NN(Code)\} \subseteq \Sigma|_{Q_1}$ *from Definition 12.*
   - $\Sigma_{Q_1} \Vdash FD_{S\_id\to Code}$ *from the case (c) of Lemma 1*
b. *for SP expression Q_2 :*
   - $att(Q_2) = \{C\_id\}$ *and* $\{UNQ(C\_id), NN(C\_id)\} \subseteq \Sigma|_{Q_2}$ *from Definition 12.*
   - $\Sigma_{Q_2} \Vdash UFD_{C\_id\to C\_id}$ *from the case (d) of Lemma 1*
c. *finally, for SPJ expression Q:*
   - $att(Q) = \{S\_id, C\_id\}$
   - $FK(Code, \texttt{student}, C\_id, \texttt{course}) \in \Sigma|_{Q_1} \cap \Sigma|_{Q_2}$, *i.e., Q is a valid SPJ query.*
   - $\Sigma_Q \Vdash FD_{S\_id\to C\_id}$ *from case (c) of Lemma 2, since*
     i. $\Sigma_{Q_1} \Vdash FD_{S\_id\to Code}$, *and*
     ii. $\Sigma_{Q_2} \Vdash FD_{C\_id\to C\_id}$ *from $\Sigma \Vdash UFD_{C\_id\to C\_id} \to \Sigma \Vdash FD_{C\_id\to C\_id}$ following the case (a) of Corollary 1*

6 The Constraint Rewriting

We now introduce a constraint rewriting Γ for a simple mapping $\mathcal{M}$ (Definition 4), and prove the properties defined in Sect. 3. The constraint rewriting Γ in Definition 15 transforms the view constraints implied by the relational source Σ (as introduced in Sects. 4 and 5) into sets of SHACL shapes. Since the semantic equivalence of generated SHACL constraints to the source constraints Σ also depends on the combination of source queries used in mappings of RDF triples, we first introduce the classification functions ι and κ to distinguish between the various cases that can occur.

Let $\mathbf{f}_C$ and $\mathbf{f}_{C'}$ be iri mapping templates for the respective RDF concepts C and C', and let $\mathbf{t}$ be an iri typing template. Let Q_C, Q_P and Q_U be the source queries of mapping Definition 3 of an RDF concept C, object property P and datatype property U, respectively.

Definition 14. *Let* M *be a simple mapping with RDF predicates* $C, C', P, U \in$ *sch*(M). *Let* ι *and* κ *be classification functions that take a triple pattern of the form* $\langle \mathbf{f}_C(X), P, \mathbf{f}_{C'}(Y) \rangle$ *and* $\langle \mathbf{f}_C(X), U, \mathbf{t}(Y) \rangle$ *respectively, and the mapping set* M *as input, and classifies the groups of the respective source queries* $(Q_C, Q_P, Q_{C'})$ *and* (Q_C, Q_U) *as follows,*

$$\iota(\langle \mathbf{f}_C(X), P, \mathbf{f}_{C'}(Y) \rangle, M) = \begin{cases} A & \text{if } Q_C \neq Q_P \\ B & \text{otherwise.} \end{cases} \text{ and } \kappa(\langle \mathbf{f}_C(X), U, \mathbf{t}(Y) \rangle, M) = \begin{cases} A & \text{if } Q_C \neq Q_U \\ B & \text{otherwise.} \end{cases}$$

Let Q be a source query over a relational schema $\mathcal{R}$ with source constraint Σ. Then, we write $\Sigma_Q \Vdash \sigma_{X \twoheadrightarrow Y}$ s.t. $\sigma \in \{\text{UFD}, \text{FD}, \text{UF}, \text{FP}\}$ to express the dependency that is either $\Sigma_Q \Vdash \sigma_{X \to Y}$ or $\Sigma_Q \Vdash \sigma_{X \to^* Y}$ on $X, Y \triangleleft Q$.

Definition 15 (Constraint rewriting Γ). *Let* M *be a simple mapping defined over a relational schema* $\mathcal{R}$ *with source constraint* Σ, *and let* ι *and* κ *be the classification functions. Then, the constraint rewriting* $\Gamma(M, \Sigma)$ *of* Σ *w.r.t.* M *is a set of SHACL shapes that for each RDF concept* C *with mapping* $Q_X \longrightarrow \langle \mathbf{f}_C(X), \text{rdf:type}, C \rangle$, *contains* $\langle C, \tau_C, \phi_C \rangle$ *with an implicit targetClass* τ_C *and conjunctive set of constraints* $\phi_C = \bigwedge_{1 \le i \le 3} \Phi_i$, *where*

1. for mapping m *of each object property* P *such as* $Q_{X,Y} \longrightarrow \langle \mathbf{f}_C(X), P, \mathbf{f}_{C'}(Y) \rangle$,

$$\Phi_1 = \begin{cases} (\le_0 P. \neg C') \wedge (\ge_0 P. C') \wedge (\bigwedge_{\Sigma_Q \Vdash \sigma} \lambda_1(\sigma)) & \text{if } \iota(\text{head}(m), M) = A \\ (\le_0 P. \neg C') \wedge (\ge_1 P. C') \wedge (\bigwedge_{\Sigma_Q \Vdash \sigma} \lambda_2(\sigma)) & \text{if } \iota(\text{head}(m), M) = B \end{cases}$$

where

$$\lambda_1(\sigma) = \begin{cases} (\unrhd_C P. C') & \text{if } \sigma = \text{UFD}_{X \to Y} \\ (=_1 P. C') & \text{if } \sigma = \text{FD}_{X \to Y} \\ (\rhd_C P. C') & \text{if } \sigma = \text{UF}_{X \to Y} \\ (\le_1 P. C') & \text{if } \sigma = \text{FP}_{X \to Y} \end{cases} \text{ and } \lambda_2(\sigma) = \begin{cases} (\unrhd_C P. C') & \text{if } \sigma = \text{UF}_{X \to Y} \\ (=_1 P. C') & \text{if } \sigma = \text{FP}_{X \to Y} \end{cases}$$

2. for mapping m *of each object property* P *such as* $Q_{X,Y} \longrightarrow \langle \mathbf{f}_{C'}(X), P, \mathbf{f}_C(Y) \rangle$,

$$\Phi_2 = \begin{cases} (\le_0 P^-. \neg C') \wedge (\ge_0 P^-. C') \wedge (\bigwedge_{\Sigma_Q \Vdash \sigma} \delta_1(\sigma)) & \text{if } \iota(\text{head}(m), M) = A \\ (\le_0 P^-. \neg C') \wedge (\ge_1 P^-. C') \wedge (\bigwedge_{\Sigma_Q \Vdash \sigma} \delta_2(\sigma)) & \text{if } \iota(\text{head}(m), M) = B \end{cases}$$

where

$$\delta_1(\sigma) = \begin{cases} (\unrhd_C P^-. C') & \text{if } \sigma = \text{UFD}_{X \to Y} \\ (=_1 P^-. C') & \text{if } \sigma = \text{FD}_{X \to Y} \\ (\rhd_C P^-. C') & \text{if } \sigma = \text{UF}_{X \to Y} \\ (\le_1 P^-. C') & \text{if } \sigma = \text{FP}_{X \to Y} \end{cases} \text{ and } \delta_2(\sigma) = \begin{cases} (\unrhd_C P^-. C') & \text{if } \sigma = \text{UF}_{X \to Y} \\ (=_1 P^-. C') & \text{if } \sigma = \text{FP}_{X \to Y} \end{cases}$$

3. for mapping m *of each datatype property* U *such as* $Q_{X,Y} \longrightarrow \langle \mathbf{f}_C(X), U, \mathbf{t}(Y) \rangle$,

$$\Phi_3 = \begin{cases} (\le_0 U. \neg \mathbf{t}) \wedge (\ge_0 U. \mathbf{t}) \wedge (\bigwedge_{\Sigma_Q \Vdash \sigma} \mu_1(\sigma)) & \text{if } \iota(\text{head}(m), M) = A \\ (\le_0 U. \neg \mathbf{t}) \wedge (\ge_1 U. \mathbf{t}) \wedge (\bigwedge_{\Sigma_Q \Vdash \sigma} \mu_2(\sigma)) & \text{if } \iota(\text{head}(m), M) = B \end{cases}$$

where

$$\mu_1(\sigma) = \begin{cases} (\unrhd_C U. \mathbf{t}) & \text{if } \sigma = \text{UFD}_{X \to Y} \\ (=_1 U. \mathbf{t}) & \text{if } \sigma = \text{FD}_{X \to Y} \\ (\rhd_C U. \mathbf{t}) & \text{if } \sigma = \text{UF}_{X \to Y} \\ (\le_1 U. \mathbf{t}) & \text{if } \sigma = \text{FP}_{X \to Y} \end{cases} \text{ and } \mu_2(\sigma) = \begin{cases} (\unrhd_C U. \mathbf{t}) & \text{if } \sigma = \text{UF}_{X \to Y} \\ (=_1 U. \mathbf{t}) & \text{if } \sigma = \text{FP}_{X \to Y} \end{cases}$$

Observe that in Definition 15, the first constraint components, such as $(\leq_0 \ P^{\pm}. \neg C')$ and $(\leq_0 \ U. \neg \mathbf{t})$ in the definitions of Φ_i, are implied by the restriction on the mapping set $\mathcal{M}$, i.e., by the fact that $\mathcal{M}$ contains exactly one mapping defining per object and datatype property predicates. The second constraint components, such as $(\geq_0 \ P^{\pm}. \neg C')$ or $(\geq_1 \ P^{\pm}. \neg C')$ and $(\geq_0 \ U. \neg \mathbf{t})$ or $(\geq_1 \ U. \neg \mathbf{t})$, in the Φ_i are implied by the combination of ι- and κ-classifications. Finally, the third constraints components $\bigwedge_{\Sigma_Q \Vdash \sigma} f(\sigma)$ s.t. $f \in \lambda_i \cup \delta_i \cup \mu_i$ for $1 \leq i \leq 2$ are implied by the source constraint Σ w.r.t. $\mathcal{M}$.

The constraint definition $\phi_C := (\leq_0 \ P^{\pm}. \neg C')$ requires all nodes n' in the graph that are reachable from a node n s.t. $\langle n, \mathtt{rdf:type}, C \rangle$ via property path $P^{\pm}$ to have a typing triple s.t. $\langle n', \mathtt{rdf:type}, C' \rangle$, which is exactly what we needed for the mapped object property paths $P^{\pm}$ in the RDF graph given the restriction that set $\mathcal{M}$ contains exactly one mapping definitions per object property predicates. Thus, to extend the constraint rewriting Γ Definition in 15 beyond the simple mapping $\mathcal{M}$, the rewriting Γ must: (i) not generate constraint components such as $(\leq_0 \ P^{\pm}. \neg C')$ and $(\leq_0 \ U. \neg \mathbf{t})$ when there exist more than one mapping definition per object P and datatype U properties, respectively, in the set $\mathcal{M}$, (ii) accommodate classification of all possible combinations of sources queries in the definitions of ι and κ, and (iii) revise the definitions of λ_i, δ_i and μ_i for additional consequences of Σ-implications w.r.t. the extended $\mathcal{M}$.

We now state the properties of the constraint Γ rewriting. Theorem 1 is a soundness statement that guarantees that all constraints produced by Γ will be validated by the RDF graph mapped from any valid database instance.

Theorem 1. *The constraint rewriting Γ is semantics preserving.*

Theorem 2 expresses the completeness of Γ, i.e., every SHACL constraint expressible with the schema $sch(\mathcal{M})$ of the mappings, and that is implied by Σ is implied by the generated shapes $\Gamma(\mathcal{M}, \Sigma)$. This does not hold in general for SHACL constraints on predicates not in $sch(\mathcal{M})$. Finally, Theorem 3 expresses that adding mappings will never invalidate generated constraints.

Theorem 2. *The constraint rewriting Γ is maximal semantics preserving.*

Theorem 3. *The constraint rewriting Γ is monotone.*

7 Discussion

We have presented a constraint rewriting Γ for simple R2R mapping that is useful in the context of relational to RDF data transformation [13,19,23] and data integration [22, 31]. Observe that simple R2R mappings can express a comprehensive catalog of useful mapping patterns studied in [8,24,25]. Simplifying simple R2R mapping further yields direct mapping [2] since that requires additional restrictions on Definition 4; therefore, the results for our constraint rewriting for simple mappings also seamlessly holds for direct mapping [2,23,27]. In future work, we believe that it would interesting to extend our constraint rewriting Γ in two different directions: (a) for arbitrary R2R mappings, e.g., admitting the full relational algebra or arbitrary SPJ expressions as the source query in mapping Definition 3, and (b) for a broader class of relational constraints such as (disjunctive) tuple and equality generating dependencies [1].

There are several approaches that map relational schemas and constraints to RDFS and OWL/Epistemic DL axioms since, with an appropriate closed world semantics, OWL can express integrity constraints. In particular, we first refer the reader to the implications of constraints in ontology-based data access platform under different names, such as protection and faithfulness in [10, 11], which is equivalent to relational constraints-to-OWL, i.e., to check whether the mapped RDF of every source dataset satisfying the source constraints can be extended to a model of the mapped $DL-Lite_A$ axioms, and OWL-to-relational constraints, i.e., opposite of former, constraints implication in [21]. Even though these proposals for combining OWL/Epistemic DL axioms with integrity constraints have some promising results for target constraints specification in the OBDA setting, there has been no unanimity on the correct semantics.

The problem of direct mapping of source schemas and constraints into RDFS/OWL axioms has been studied in [7, 23]. Sequeda et al. [23] attempted to capture the database constraints on the RDF graph resulting from direct mapping using OWL. However, the bootstrapped OWL axioms did not trigger the unsatisfiability of the directly mapped graph whenever keys are violated in the source database unless the database instance is explicitly encoded in the constraint rewriting. Further, Sequeda et al. [23, Theorem 3] established that the desirable monotonicity property of direct mapping is an obstacle to obtain a semantics preserving OWL axioms even if the database instance is explicitly encoded in the constraint rewriting. To accomplish the desired one-to-one semantics correspondence between legal relational data and RDF graph satisfying OWL axioms, Calvanese et al. [7] further extended the direct mapping of relational schemas into $DL-Lite_{RDFS}$ with disjointness - as constraints over mapped RDF graphs.

Finally, Thapa et al. [26] have studied the problem of translating database constraints into SHACL, instead of OWL/Epistemic DL, giving a direct transformation from SQL constraints to SHACL, preserving their semantics when source key constraints are satisfied [26, Theorem 2]. The present work improves on this by a) not being restricted to direct mappings, and b) lifting the requirement on satisfied key constraints.

8 Conclusion

In this paper, we study the problem of constraint rewriting for relational to RDF data transformation based on the central property of maximal semantics preservation. We translate standard SQL database constraints to shapes in the SHACL constraint language for RDF graphs. We show that our proposed rewriting Γ for the simple relational to RDF mappings satisfies the central properties of a constraint rewriting.

We believe that the propose constraint rewriting constitutes a core component of R2R mapping tools for the crucial task of constructing and maintaining a quality-assured RDF graph with SHACL constraints. The SHACL description of the generated RDF graph provides a data quality guarantee for data exchange, interoperability and query optimization. Hence, an important direction for future work will be the implementation and practical evaluation of our rewriting for relational to RDF data transformation and query optimization [30] in an ontology-based data access platform [29, 31].

Acknowledgements. This work is supported by the Norwegian Research Council via the SIR-IUS SFI (237898). We thank Egor Kostylev for many constructive suggestions.

References

1. Abiteboul, S., Hull, R., Vianu, V.: Foundations of Databases, vol. 8. Addison-Wesley, Reading (1995)
2. Arenas, M., Bertails, A., Prud'hommeaux, E., Sequeda, J.: A direct mapping of relational data to RDF. W3C Recommendation **27**, 1–11 (2012)
3. Armstrong, W.W.: Dependency structures of data base relationships. In: IFIP Congress, vol. 74, pp. 580–583. Geneva, Switzerland (1974)
4. Badia, A., Lemire, D.: Functional dependencies with null markers. Comput. J. **58**(5), 1160–1168 (2015)
5. Beeri, C., Fagin, R., Howard, J.H.: A complete axiomatization for functional and multivalued dependencies in database relations. In: Proceedings of the 1977 ACM SIGMOD International Conference on Management of Data, pp. 47–61 (1977)
6. Calvanese, D.: Ontologies and databases: the *DL-Lite* approach. In: Tessaris, S., et al. (eds.) Reasoning Web 2009. LNCS, vol. 5689, pp. 255–356. Springer, Heidelberg (2009). https://doi.org/10.1007/978-3-642-03754-2_7
7. Calvanese, D., Fischl, W., Pichler, R., Sallinger, E., Simkus, M.: Capturing relational schemas and functional dependencies in RDFS. In: Proceedings of the AAAI Conference on Artificial Intelligence, vol. 28 (2014)
8. Calvanese, D., Gal, A., Lanti, D., Montali, M., Mosca, A., Shraga, R.: Mapping patterns for virtual knowledge graphs. arXiv preprint arXiv:2012.01917 (2020)
9. Civili, C., Mora, J., Rosati, R., Ruzzi, M., Santarelli, V.: Semantic analysis of R2RML mappings for ontology-based data access. In: Ortiz, M., Schlobach, S. (eds.) RR 2016. LNCS, vol. 9898, pp. 25–38. Springer, Cham (2016). https://doi.org/10.1007/978-3-319-45276-0_3
10. Console, M., Lenzerini, M.: Data quality in ontology-based data access: the case of consistency. In: Proceedings of the AAAI Conference on Artificial Intelligence, vol. 28 (2014)
11. Console, M., Lenzerini, M.: Epistemic integrity constraints for ontology-based data management. In: Proceedings of the AAAI Conference on Artificial Intelligence, vol. 34, pp. 2790–2797 (2020)
12. Corman, J., Reutter, J.L., Savković, O.: Semantics and validation of recursive SHACL. In: Vrandečić, D., Bontcheva, K., Suárez-Figueroa, M.C., Presutti, V., Celino, I., Sabou, M., Kaffee, L.-A., Simperl, E. (eds.) ISWC 2018. LNCS, vol. 11136, pp. 318–336. Springer, Cham (2018). https://doi.org/10.1007/978-3-030-00671-6_19
13. Das, S., Sundara, S., Cyganiak, R.: R2RML: RDB to RDF mapping language, September 2012. http://www.w3.org/TR/2012/REC-r2rml-20120927/
14. Donini, F.M., Nardi, D., Rosati, R.: Description logics of minimal knowledge and negation as failure. ACM Trans. Comput. Logic (ToCL) **3**(2), 177–225 (2002)
15. Knublauch, H., Kontokostas, D.: Shapes constraint language (SHACL). W3C recommendation, W3C, July 2017. http://www.w3.org/TR/2017/REC-shacl-20170720/
16. Lembo, D., Mora, J., Rosati, R., Savo, D.F., Thorstensen, E.: Mapping analysis in ontology-based data access: algorithms and complexity. In: Arenas, M., Corcho, O., Simperl, E., Strohmaier, M., d'Aquin, M., Srinivas, K., Groth, P., Dumontier, M., Heflin, J., Thirunarayan, K., Staab, S. (eds.) ISWC 2015. LNCS, vol. 9366, pp. 217–234. Springer, Cham (2015). https://doi.org/10.1007/978-3-319-25007-6_13
17. Manola, F., Miller, E., McBride, B., et al.: RDF primer. W3C Recommendation **10**(1–107), 6 (2004)
18. Mecca, G., Rull, G., Santoro, D., Teniente, E.: Ontology-based mappings. Data Knowl. Eng. **98**, 8–29 (2015)

19. De Medeiros, L.F., Priyatna, F., Corcho, O.: MIRROR: automatic R2RML mapping generation from relational databases. In: Cimiano, P., Frasincar, F., Houben, G.-J., Schwabe, D. (eds.) ICWE 2015. LNCS, vol. 9114, pp. 326–343. Springer, Cham (2015). https://doi.org/10.1007/978-3-319-19890-3_21

20. Motik, B., Horrocks, I., Sattler, U.: Bridging the gap between OWL and relational databases. J. Web Semant. **7**(2), 74–89 (2009)

21. Nikolaou, C., Grau, B.C., Kostylev, E.V., Kaminski, M., Horrocks, I.: Satisfaction and Implication of Integrity Constraints in Ontology-based Data Access. In: IJCAI, pp. 1829–1835 (2019)

22. Poggi, A., Lembo, D., Calvanese, D., De Giacomo, G., Lenzerini, M., Rosati, R.: Linking data to ontologies. In: Spaccapietra, S. (ed.) Journal on Data Semantics X. LNCS, vol. 4900, pp. 133–173. Springer, Heidelberg (2008). https://doi.org/10.1007/978-3-540-77688-8_5

23. Sequeda, J.F., Arenas, M., Miranker, D.P.: On directly mapping relational databases to RDF and OWL. In: Proceedings of the 21st International Conference on World Wide Web, pp. 649–658 (2012)

24. Sequeda, J.F., Miranker, D.P.: Ultrawrap mapper: a semi-automatic relational database to RDF (RDB2RDF) mapping tool. In: International semantic web conference (posters & demos) (2015)

25. Juan, F., Sequeda, F.P., Villazón-Terrazas, B.: Relational database to RDF mapping patterns. In: WOP (2012)

26. Thapa, R.B., Giese, M.: A source-to-target constraint rewriting for direct mapping. In: Hotho, A., Blomqvist, E., Dietze, S., Fokoue, A., Ding, Y., Barnaghi, P., Haller, A., Dragoni, M., Alani, H. (eds.) ISWC 2021. LNCS, vol. 12922, pp. 21–38. Springer, Cham (2021). https://doi.org/10.1007/978-3-030-88361-4_2

27. Thapa, R.B., Giese, M.: A source-to-target constraint rewriting for direct mapping (extended version). Research Report 498, Dept. of Informatics, University of Oslo, September 2021. http://www.urn.nb.no/URN:NBN:no-90764

28. Thapa, R.B., Giese, M.: Mapping relational database constraints to SHACL (extended version). Research Report 503, Dept. of Informatics, University of Oslo, July 2022. http://www.urn.nb.no/URN:NBN:no-35645

29. Xiao, G., et al.: A survey. IJCAI Organization, Ontology-based data access (2018)

30. Xiao, G., Kontchakov, R., Cogrel, B., Calvanese, D., Botoeva, E.: Efficient handling of SPARQL OPTIONAL for OBDA. In: Vrandečić, D., Bontcheva, K., Suárez-Figueroa, M.C., Presutti, V., Celino, I., Sabou, M., Kaffee, L.-A., Simperl, E. (eds.) ISWC 2018. LNCS, vol. 11136, pp. 354–373. Springer, Cham (2018). https://doi.org/10.1007/978-3-030-00671-6_21

31. Xiao, G., Lanti, D., Kontchakov, R., Komla-Ebri, S., Güzel-Kalaycı, E., Ding, L., Corman, J., Cogrel, B., Calvanese, D., Botoeva, E.: The virtual knowledge graph system ontop. In: Pan, J.Z., Tamma, V., d'Amato, C., Janowicz, K., Fu, B., Polleres, A., Seneviratne, O., Kagal, L. (eds.) ISWC 2020. LNCS, vol. 12507, pp. 259–277. Springer, Cham (2020). https://doi.org/10.1007/978-3-030-62466-8_17

POSO: A Generic Positioning System Ontology

Maxim Van de Wynckel$^{(\boxtimes)}$ ⓘ and Beat Signer ⓘ

Web and Information Systems Engineering Lab, Vrije Universiteit Brussel,
Pleinlaan 2, 1050 Brussels, Belgium
{mvdewync,bsigner}@vub.be

Abstract. While satellite-based positioning systems are mainly used in outdoor environments, various other positioning techniques exist for different domains and use cases, including indoor or underground settings. The representation of spatial data via semantic linked data is well addressed by existing spatial ontologies. However, there is a primary focus on location data with its specific geographical context, but a lack of solutions for describing the different types of data generated by a positioning system and the used sampling techniques to obtain the data. In this paper we introduce a new generic Positioning System Ontology (POSO) that is built on top of the Semantic Sensor Network (SSN) and Sensor, Observation, Sample, and Actuator (SOSA) ontologies. With POSO, we provide missing concepts needed for describing a positioning system and its output with known positioning algorithms and techniques in mind. Thereby, we enable the improvement of hybrid positioning systems making use of multiple platforms and sensors that are described via the presented POSO ontology.

Keywords: Positioning system ontology · Positioning techniques · Positioning algorithms

1 Introduction

Whether we are developing a system for indoor or outdoor navigation or simply want to track the location of an object on a table, a positioning system that tracks the position based on one or multiple technologies and algorithms is needed. While outdoor positioning solutions mainly rely on satellite positioning systems such as the Global Positioning System (GPS), building-specific deployments and implementations using a wide variety of techniques [13,26] can be used indoors.

In order to facilitate the interoperability between different positioning systems or client applications, we need a vocabulary that is generic enough to cover various use cases. Expressing the position or movement in a geographical context is already well established using ontologies and vocabularies such as the Basic WGS84 vocabulary [3], the Location Ontology [10], GeoSPARQL [2] or

U. Sattler et al. (Eds.): ISWC 2022, LNCS 13489, pp. 231–247, 2022.
https://doi.org/10.1007/978-3-031-19433-7_14

the LinkedGeoData ontology [33]. However, positioning systems do not always need to operate within a geographical boundary and may even provide more contextual information that is relevant for other positioning systems that would like to make use of the data.

Interoperability between multiple positioning systems also covers the fusion of the data these systems provide. Work on linked data networks for IoT sensors already exists [9,11], allowing raw sensor data to be accessible by multiple platforms. Decision-level fusion of positioning data remains a lacking capability of positioning systems due to the missing knowledge on how the location data has been processed or obtained. The additional semantic information from these systems is often not available to other systems, making the *handover* of tracking [14] between systems difficult.

In this paper we introduce *POSO*, a generic positioning system ontology for expressing the techniques, algorithms and data handled by a positioning system. We demonstrate how POSO can be used by a positioning system and that we can perform decision-level sensor fusion of positioning data between multiple independent positioning systems when data is semantically defined based on POSO.

2   Ontology Design

The main goal of our *Positioning System Ontology* (POSO) is to offer a solution that can model different positioning systems, their deployments, techniques, algorithms and the real-time data they are providing. However, semantics on post-processed trajectory data lies beyond the scope of POSO.

In Fig. 1 we provide a general overview of a positioning system and related components. A positioning system is deployed at a particular location or area that is meant to be covered. This can be a building, an area outdoors or even an object-specific location such as a game board that does not have to be related to any geographical boundaries. Each positioning system uses a set of algorithms and technologies to help compute a position. Finally, with positioning systems modelled based on POSO, we aim to track the position, orientation and other properties of one or more entities. These properties can be anything that is of relevance to the system and are obtained using the techniques implemented by the positioning system. Spatial properties of a tracked entity are located within the deployment using an optionally defined reference system.

We designed POSO with the Semantic Sensor Network Ontology (SSN) as a top-level ontology [22] together with the Sensor, Observation, Sample and Actuator (SOSA) ontology [23]. Combined, SOSA and SSN provide an ontology for linking sensors, actuators, observations, samplers and the systems needed to process this sensor data to an output. This provides a stable core ontology that could enable the modelling of a positioning system with its deployment, the used sensors, procedures, the entities and as well as the observable properties of those entities. However, as these ontologies are meant to be used as core ontologies,

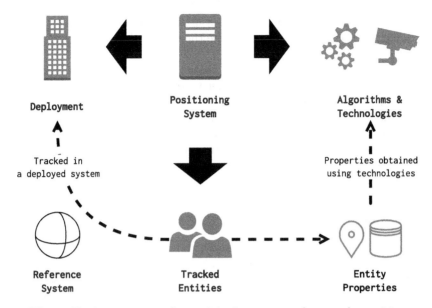

Fig. 1. Basic structure of a positioning system that tracks entities

they do not offer any semantics for expressing the accuracy of individual observations, the different types of algorithms that are relevant for positioning or how the results should be represented in order to be interoperable.

Our ontology has been designed with the common data requirements of various positioning system technologies [13,26], datasets [37,38,41] and frameworks [12,30,42] in mind to cover all types of systems without overcomplicating the modelling of the data. An initial validation has further been conducted based on the OpenHPS framework [39].

With our proposed ontology, we aim to support concepts for defining a generic position, orientation, velocity, acceleration and the sampling of this data. We extended the `sosa:ObservableProperty` to express different types of position, orientation, velocity and acceleration. For expressing observation-based sensor data, we use the SOSA ontology together with the QUDT ontology for expressing Units of Measure, Quantity Kinds, Dimensions and Data Types [16]. Each observable property defined in POSO can also be used as a result within a SOSA observation, with a set of predicates that express the result. This enables expressing a fixed position of a feature of interest as shown later in Listing 6. The proposed vocabulary should support the following three main goals:

- **Sensor fusion**: High- and low-level sensor fusion should be possible based on the data [8]. High-level fusion, also called decision-level fusion, consists of merging processed data from multiple sources, while low-level fusion is the use of multiple sources of raw sensor data. Both fusion levels require additional knowledge on how the data has been obtained and its quality. In the context of high-level fusion in a positioning system, the additional semantics includes the accuracy as well as the techniques used to obtain the data. Using this knowledge, other systems can prioritise the observations to be used.

- **Historical data**: Positioning systems make use of previous information to predict future movement [44]. These predictions can be used to improve the calculation of a next position. In order to support this technique, historical positioning data should be available.
- **Granularity**: The position of an entity should be offered with varying ranges of granularity without causing conflicts with the decision-level sensor fusion. This enables use cases where observations of a minimum or maximum accuracy can be separated in a different triple store, further enabling access control to these individual stores.

2.1   Positioning System

A positioning system is a system or mechanism that can determine the position of one or multiple objects based on some sensor data. Multiple positioning systems might track the same object either individually or simultaneously. These multiple systems can work independently from each other or combine information from other systems to provide an output. We identify five types of positioning systems based on the ISO 19116:2019 standard [20]. Each positioning system extends the `ssn:System` class of the SSN ontology:

- **Satellite positioning system**: A positioning system using satellites. Examples include the Global Positioning System, Galileo or GLONASS [17].
- **Integrated positioning system**: An integrated or hybrid positioning system can be used outdoors, indoors or in any other space. Despite the fact that many positioning systems are hybrid (e.g. Assisted GPS [7]), we explicitly specify it as a type in POSO to define a system that does not fall within other more specific categories. In POSO, we define an integrated positioning system as a system that must implement *at least one* sensor fusion procedure.
- **Optical positioning system**: A positioning system that uses optical sensors to determine a position. This includes positioning systems where objects are tracked externally (e.g. Multi-Target Multi-Camera Tracking [24]) or systems where the tracked object is the optical sensor observing the environment (e.g. Visual Simultaneous Localisation and Mapping [34]).
- **Inertial positioning system**: An inertial positioning system calculates the position based on its movement and an initial reference point [15].
- **Indoor positioning system**: Indoor positioning covers all systems and techniques that are deployed indoors as opposed to outdoor positioning where often satellite positioning is used [26].

Being able to determine whether a position was obtained using satellites, an inertial- or indoor positioning system enables the reasoning about the relevance of a position sampled by one of these systems. With this additional knowledge, a fusion technique can ignore the sampled position of a satellite positioning system if an indoor positioning system is able to determine that the tracked object is inside a building. Alternatively, an inaccurate inertial positioning system may provide useful context on the movement, rather than the position calculated using its algorithms.

Finally, we define a location-based service (LBS) as an `ssn:System` to categorise services with a black-box implementation of a positioning system. An example of such a service is the Geolocation API [29] that uses the techniques available by the underlying hardware. Note that an LBS might specify one or more positioning systems that it implements. In the `poso-common` extension discussed in Sect. 2.7, we provide a set of deployed satellite positioning systems, as these can be used as *subsystems*[1] in integrated positioning systems.

2.2 Positioning Algorithms and Techniques

The SOSA ontology describes a `sosa:Procedure` as a workflow, protocol, plan, algorithm or computational method to make an observation, sample or change the state of the world[2]. In a positioning system we identify a procedure as a workflow that processes sensor data to an intermediate result or observation.

A positioning system can use a broad range of techniques to calculate a position. While it might perform generic processing on raw sensor data, semantically describing the main techniques that are involved in the processing improves the reasoning that can be performed on the sampled data as well as its priority for decision-level sensor fusion. To illustrate this, we provide the example of an indoor positioning system (IPS) that uses simple QR codes for room check-ins and an IPS at the same location site that uses Bluetooth beacons. Without knowledge of the techniques used to determine a position, the accuracy of the position at a given time cannot be determined reliably. While the Bluetooth positioning provides a continuous output with varying accuracy, the QR scanning only provides a very high accuracy position when it is scanned; as the person will be near the code to scan it.

In POSO we subdivide a procedure over multiple different main categories that are based on the work of Liu et al. [26] and Gu et al. [13]:

- **Cell identification**: This covers all techniques that detect the position of an object when it is close to an object with a known position. Existing solutions range from radio frequency proximity to implicit position such as the act of scanning a QR code at a known fixed location.
- **Dead reckoning**: The velocity of an object can be used to determine its drift in space. This technique called dead reckoning can be a positioning system on its own, identified as an inertial positioning system [20], but can also form part of another technology such as Assisted GPS [7].
- **Fingerprinting**: Scene analysis techniques such as fingerprinting where sensor data is matched to a grid of positions can be used during the setup of the positioning system. Each scene analysis at a position is called a

---

[1] https://www.w3.org/TR/vocab-ssn/#SSNhasSubSystem.

[2] https://www.w3.org/TR/vocab-ssn/#SOSAProcedure.

fingerprint and is used during the online tracking stage to determine a position. The sensor data will be matched to the fingerprint that most closely resembles this data. POSO expresses a fingerprint as a subclass of `sosa:FeatureOfInterest` under the term `poso:Fingerprint` that requires to have a position in order to qualify as a fingerprint. This allows positioning systems that make use of this scene analysis to semantically describe the system's setup.

– **Odometry**: Positioning techniques that use sensor data to detect the change in position are classified as odometry. This can be sensor data from motion sensors, visual observations or other environmental data such as magnetic interference [32].
– **Simultaneous localisation and mapping**: In simultaneous localisation and mapping (SLAM), a sensor determines features that are tracked during movement. By tracking these features it can determine the drift while simultaneously using the features to construct a map of the environment [36]. SLAM can be subdivided into Visual SLAM [34] when image sensors are used to track features as opposed to LiDAR sensors.
– **Triangulation**: Subdivided into angulation and lateration, triangulation covers positioning techniques that use angles or linear distance indicators to determine a position between two or more landmarks with a known position.
– **Sensor fusion**: In order to specify how multiple positioning systems or sensors are used together, a sensor fusion procedure category defines procedures where observations from multiple different (sub)systems are merged. This fusion technique can further make use of additional available context.

As an extension of POSO, the `POSO-common` module introduced later in Sect. 2.7 provides several commonly used positioning algorithms and techniques. The different positioning systems, techniques and observable properties along with their hierarchical relation to the SOSA and SSN ontologies are illustrated in Fig. 2. Properties that only contain fixed results without multiple observations are also subclasses of `sosa:Result` defining a single result as shown in Listing 6.

2.3   Absolute and Relative Positions

Multiple definitions exist to indicate where a spatial object is located. Our decision for using the term *position* was based on the definitions in the English language, as well as its uses within real-world applications:

– **Place/Area**: The place or area of an entity is an existing semantic definition in many vocabularies [1]. However, it implies a space rather than a particular point within this space.
– **Pose**: Often used in robotics [4] or when describing the movement of a person [27], a pose contains the position and orientation of an object. In real-world applications such as the Robotics Operation System (ROS) [30] it is meant to indicate a position and orientation within 3D space. Not every positioning system might operate within three dimensions, in which case the *pose* terminology might not be appropriate.

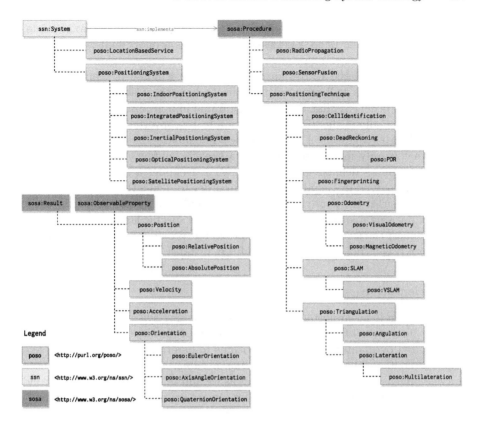

Fig. 2. Positioning systems and techniques in the POSO ontology

- **Location**: According to the Oxford English Dictionary which defines a location as *"a place where something happens or exists; the position of something"* we concluded that a location is a semantic description of either a vague place or accurate position. Because of this imprecision, we decided not to choose the term *location*.
- **Position**: A position can optionally also contain an orientation. It is the terminology used by most precise and generic positioning systems and location-based services [29].

Generic positioning systems make a distinction between absolute and relative positions [13,26]. An absolute position indicates a fixed point in space while a relative position is relative to another object or landmark. Such a relative position is a quantitative value relative in distance, angle or velocity, similar to the 'Best Practice 9' mentioned in [35].

When working with absolute positions in a geographical coordinate system, we make use of GeoSPARQL's geographical position representation by the Open Geospatial Consortium (OGC). However, for absolute positions that should not be expressed as geometric coordinates, we use the QUDT ontology [16] to express

Cartesian coordinates. POSO provides the concepts of `poso:xAxisValue`, `poso:yAxisValue` and `poso:zAxisValue` to express a `qudt:QuantityValue` in three dimensions.

Despite using simple Cartesian coordinates for a non-geographic position, a reference frame is still required to indicate how the Cartesian coordinates relate to each other. Similar to a reference frame in a geographical context, the reference frame allows the 2D or 3D position to be converted to other reference spaces such as a geographical context while still enabling the use of a positioning system that is only meant to operate in a specific context (i.e. an engineering reference frame as defined in ISO 19111 [21]). Defining a reference system is already well covered in GeoSPARQL [2]. In order to define the reference system of a `sosa:Result`, the `poso:hasSRS` or `poso:hasCRS` properties can be used.

For expressing a location that is covering a less specific larger 2D or 3D area, we still request the use of an absolute position, but provide the ability to indicate the accuracy as either a one-dimensional (i.e. distance) or polygonal coverage.

2.4 Orientation

An orientation is an important aspect of a positioning system. It does not only offer the final state of direction after a rotation of an object or person, but is also required by many positioning algorithms to determine a position. In a geographical context, the terminology *bearing*, *heading*, *course* or *azimuth* is used as a one-dimensional value [19]. However, as we aim to support use cases beyond geographical positioning and want to offer a more precise three-dimensional orientation, we resorted to mathematical concepts.

The commonly used mathematical definitions of an orientation are *Euler Angles*, *Axis Angles* and *Quaternions* [6]. Each mathematical definition has its advantages for a positioning system. Euler angles offer a well-known semantic description of a 3D rotation while still allowing the use of *yaw* only for expressing the heading in a 2D scenario. In robotics, quaternions are chosen since they avoid gimbal lock, as well as for their analytic properties.

As we aim to create a generic ontology, we have chosen to support any concept that can identify the orientation around three axes. POSO provides three extensions of the `poso:Orientation` class, including `poso:EulerOrientation`, `poso:AxisAngleOrientation` and `poso:QuaternionOrientation`.

2.5 Velocity and Acceleration

Active positioning systems make use of an object's velocity to determine a position and orientation based on its momentum. This procedure called dead reckoning uses an entity's last known location together with its angular and linear velocity to determine the new position and orientation at a later timestamp. POSO adds the concept of `poso:Velocity` with `poso:LinearVelocity` and `poso:AngularVelocity` as subclasses, as well as the momentary acceleration that is often returned by common Inertial Measurement Units (IMU).

2.6   Observations and Accuracy

Individual observations and different levels of granularity can be expressed for all properties. SSN-Systems [5], an extension of the SSN ontology, supports the description of a system's properties, capabilities and conditions. While this enables the semantic description of the potential properties (i.e. accuracy, precision and operating environment) of a positioning system, it does not provide information on the individual observations. For a positioning system, the spatial accuracy can vary depending on the implemented procedure, the amount of sensor data as well as the accuracy of that data.

The accuracy of any observation can be expressed via `poso:hasAccuracy`, a subproperty of `ssns:qualityOfObservation`[3] that can be applied to an observation or individual result. Alternatively, for expressing the accuracy of spatial data (i.e. absolute or relative position) the `geosparql:hasSpatialAccuracy` from the GeoSPARQL 1.1 draft [28] can be used to express a QUDT quantity value. Further, in order to express the aimed accuracy of an observable property, the `ssns:Accuracy` class can be used to indicate that the accuracy applies to the position.

Trajectories. Creating an observation for every calculated position provides context on historical data that can be used. Semantics of trajectories, such as segmentation, map matching and additional post-processing context [43] lies beyond the scope of our positioning system ontology. However, as each observation is a momentary timestamped result, they indirectly support the modelling of a trajectory space and time path [18].

A basic overview of how a person's speed, orientation and position in an office deployment might be modelled is shown in Fig. 3. The green objects and properties represent the concepts from SOSA and SSN(S), the blue objects and properties represent the concepts from POSO and the purple objects represent the example individuals. Note that the full POSO specification with all the available concepts can be found in [40].

2.7   Alignment Module

The `poso-common` alignment module provides individual common positioning algorithms, systems and data used in positioning systems categorised under the classes defined in POSO. It describes seven satellite positioning systems [17]; known platforms such as IndoorAtlas[4], Anyplace [12], OpenHPS [39,42], ROS [30] and individual algorithms for common positioning techniques. With the provided `poso-common` alignment module, we want to offer a foundation of algorithms and techniques that can easily be used to describe complete positioning systems. Future work should focus on expanding these algorithms, along with more detailed descriptions on their input and output shapes. In a hybrid

---

[3] `ssns:` is the prefix for SSN-Systems [5].

[4] https://www.indooratlas.com.

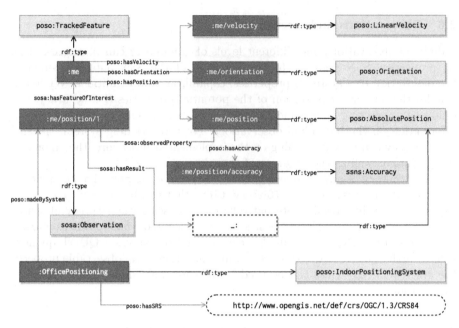

Fig. 3. Example of a positioning system with a position, orientation and velocity property

or integrated positioning system as described in Sect. 2.1, the use of these common algorithms can provide insights on what observations to use in the fusion process.

3   Usage

In order to demonstrate the use of POSO to semantically model multiple positioning systems, we provide an example of a campus positioning system for the indoor as well as outdoor tracking of students. Our fictional setup consists of three individual systems; an outdoor positioning system using GPS, an indoor positioning system using Wi-Fi fingerprinting as introduced in Sect. 2.2 and a hybrid position system that makes use of the indoor and outdoor tracking subsystems by using a high-level sensor fusion technique.

We start by semantically describing the technical setup of the fictional deployment of the three positioning systems on our campus. Additional domain-specific ontologies such as IndoorGML [25] can be used to describe the physical context of these deployments. Throughout our examples, we make use of the prefixes defined in Listing 1.

In Listing 2 we create an outdoor campus positioning system that uses GPS. Indoors, we deploy a system that uses k-NN fingerprinting for Wi-Fi access points. For the integrated positioning system on lines 15 to 18 that uses both the outdoor and indoor system, we add the two individual systems as subsystems

```
1   @prefix poso: <http://purl.org/poso/> .
2   @prefix poso-common: <http://purl.org/poso/common/> .
3   @prefix ssn: <http://www.w3.org/ns/ssn/> .
4   @prefix sosa: <http://www.w3.org/ns/sosa/> .
5   @prefix dbr: <http://dbpedia.org/resource/> .
6   @prefix geosparql: <http://www.opengis.net/ont/geosparql#> .
7   @prefix xsd: <http://www.w3.org/2001/XMLSchema#> .
8   @prefix qudt: <http://qudt.org/schema/qudt/> .
9   @prefix unit: <http://qudt.org/vocab/unit/> .
10  @prefix ssns: <http://www.w3.org/ns/ssn/systems/> .
11  @prefix schema: <http://schema.org/> .
```

Listing 1. Prefixes used in the demonstration examples

with an additional procedure on how the high-level fusion of these two systems is performed.

```
1   dbr:Some_Unversity a ssn:Deployment .
2   <deployment/building_a> a poso:IndoorDeployment, geosparql:Feature ;
3     rdfs:label "Building A"@en ;
4     geosparql:hasGeometry [
5       a geosparql:Geometry ;
6       geosparql:asWKT "..."^^geosparql:wktLiteral ] .
7   <system/OPS> a poso:LocationBasedService ;
8     rdfs:label "Outdoor campus positioning"@en ;
9     ssn:hasSubSystem poso-common:GPS ;
10    ssn:hasDeployment dbr:Some_University .
11  <system/IPS> a poso:IndoorPositioningSystem ;
12    rdfs:label "Indoor campus positioning"@en ;
13    ssn:hasDeployment <deployment/building_a> ;
14    ssn:implements poso-common:KNNFingerprinting .
15  <system/CampusPositioning> a poso:IntegratedPositioningSystem ;
16    rdfs:label "Hybrid campus positioning system"@en ;
17    ssn:hasSubSystem <system/OPS>, <system/IPS> ;
18    ssn:implements poso-common:WeightedAccuracyFusion .
```

Listing 2. Positioning system setup

The entity that is being tracked by the campus positioning system is configured in Listing 3. Each feature of interest, which we identify as our *tracked feature*, has multiple observable properties. A property predicate such as the poso:hasPosition on line 3 can be used multiple times to represent a position with different levels of granularity. In linked data front ends with data access control, such as Solid [31], these levels of granularity can control who is able to access a property with a certain accuracy. By specifying the accuracy of these properties along with possible other semantic information, the information can be used in queries to determine which property offers the required accuracy.

```
1   <me> a poso:TrackedFeature, foaf:Person ;
2     foaf:name "John Doe"@en ;
3     poso:hasPosition <me/position>, <me/approxposition> ;
4     poso:hasOrientation <me/orientation> .
5   <me/position> a poso:AbsolutePosition ;
6     rdfs:comment "Absolute position of John Doe"@en ;
7     poso:hasAccuracy <me/position/accuracy> .
8   <me/position/accuracy> a ssns:Accuracy ;
9     schema:maxValue "25.0"^^xsd:float ; schema:unitCode unit:CentiM .
```

Listing 3. Example setup of a tracked person and their properties

Further, in Listing 4 we show an observation created by the outdoor positioning system. The GPS provides a latitude and longitude that we output using the OGC GeoSPARQL 1.1 ontology [28] as a well-known text (WKT) representation on lines 9 to 11.

```
1   <position/1654350300000> a sosa:Observation ;
2     sosa:hasFeatureOfInterest <me> ;
3     sosa:observedProperty  <me/position> ;
4     sosa:resultTime "2022-06-04T15:55:00+02:00"^^xsd:dateTimeStamp ;
5     poso:usedSystem <system/OPS> ;
6     sosa:hasResult [ a geosparql:Geometry ;
7       geosparql:hasSpatialAccuracy [ a qudt:QuantityValue ;
8         qudt:unit unit:CentiM ; qudt:numericValue "28"^^xsd:float ] ;
9       geosparql:asWKT """
10        <http://www.opengis.net/def/crs/OGC/1.3/CRS84>
11        Point(4.888028 50.31397)"""^^geosparql:wktLiteral ;
12      geosparql:dimension 2 ] .
```

Listing 4. Example observation of the outdoor positioning system

Indoors, our system outputs an absolute Cartesian 3D position as illustrated in Listing 5. We identify that the 3D position is made inside a specific deployment on line 8, which contains information about its geometry and the reference system used to convert the coordinates to a common reference frame used by the campus positioning system. The technique used to obtain the result is defined using `sosa:usedProcedure` while the system where this technique is used is defined based on `poso:usedSystem`.

In previous example listings, we have shown how a positioning system might model the observations of an absolute position. With the example in Listing 6 we outline how a relative distance to a wireless access point (named `wap_1`) from our `TrackedFeature` can be expressed. Similar to an absolute position, we can have multiple observations of the relative distance. POSO requires the `poso:isRelativeTo` predicate on a relative position to indicate the feature of interest that the position is relative to.

```
1   <position/1647513000000> a sosa:Observation ;
2     sosa:hasFeatureOfInterest <me> ;
3     sosa:observedProperty  <me/position> ;
4     sosa:resultTime "2022-03-17T11:30:00+01:00"^^xsd:dateTimeStamp ;
5     sosa:usedProcedure poso-common:KNNFingerprinting ;
6     poso:usedSystem <system/IPS> ;
7     sosa:hasResult [ a poso:AbsolutePosition ;
8       poso:inDeployment <deployment/building_a> ;
9       poso:hasAccuracy [ a ssns:Accuracy ;
10        schema:maxValue "25.0"^^xsd:float ;
11        schema:unitCode unit:CentiM ] ;
12      poso:xAxisValue [ a qudt:QuantityValue ;
13        qudt:unit unit:M ; qudt:numericValue "5"^^xsd:double ] ;
14      poso:yAxisValue [ a qudt:QuantityValue ;
15        qudt:unit unit:M ; qudt:numericValue "6"^^xsd:double ] ;
16      poso:zAxisValue [ a qudt:QuantityValue ;
17        qudt:unit unit:M ; qudt:numericValue "3.5"^^xsd:double ] ] .
```

Listing 5. Example observation of the indoor positioning system

```
1   <landmark/wap_1> a poso:Landmark ;
2     rdfs:label "Wireless Access Point 1"@en ;
3     poso:hasPosition [ a poso:AbsolutePosition ;
4       poso:hasAccuracy [ ... ] ;
5       poso:xAxisValue [ ... ] ;
6       poso:yAxisValue [ ... ] ;
7       poso:zAxisValue [ ... ] ] .
8   <me/position/relative/wap_1> a poso:RelativeDistance ;
9     ssn:isPropertyOf <me> ; # Relative distance from <me> ...
10    poso:isRelativeTo <landmark/wap_1> ; # to <landmark/wap_1>
11    rdfs:comment "Relative position of John Doe to WAP_1"@en .
12  <position/relative/wap_1/1646891100000> a sosa:Observation ;
13    sosa:hasFeatureOfInterest <me>, <landmark/wap_1> ;
14    sosa:observedProperty  <me/position/relative/wap_1> ;
15    sosa:resultTime "2022-03-10T06:45:00+01:00"^^xsd:dateTimeStamp ;
16    poso:madeBySystem <system/IPS> ;
17    sosa:usedProcedure poso-common:LDPL ; # Log-distance path loss
18    sosa:hasResult [ a qudt:QuantityValue ;
19      qudt:unit unit:Meter ; qudt:value "3.7"^^xsd:double ] ;
20    sosa:hasResult [ a qudt:QuantityValue ;
21      qudt:unit unit:DeciB_M ; qudt:value "-82"^^xsd:integer ] .
```

Listing 6. Example observation of a relative position

As mentioned in the beginning of Sect. 2, each observable property can also be used to express a fixed result that does not consist of multiple observations. On lines 1 to 7 of Listing 6 we utilise this ability to express a fixed result to define the fixed position of a landmark rather than creating a single observation where the position is defined as a result. On lines 12 to 21, we have one observation of this observable relative distance obtained using our indoor positioning system. The result is expressed as a distance using a path loss algorithm and the raw signal strength expressed in decibel-milliwatts (*dBm*).

In order to provide a single output for the campus positioning system, we can use the observations from the indoor and outdoor positioning systems shown in Listing 5 and Listing 4 to compute a fused output based on the weighted accuracy fusion procedure that our campus positioning system implements in Listing 2. Using the knowledge about the accuracy, the systems that produced the results and the indoor positioning system deployments, we can perform a fusion with more context than only the self-reported accuracy of each individual subsystem.

4   Conclusions and Future Work

In this paper we introduced our new generic positioning system ontology called POSO for describing concepts relevant to a positioning system. These concepts include the different observable properties that can be obtained by a positioning system, the different categories of systems and the different algorithms and techniques these systems can implement to handle positioning. Further note that our generic positioning system ontology does not only focus on common geospatial and geographical concepts that are already described in various existing vocabularies [2,10,33] but also offers a novel vocabulary for describing generic data outputted by a positioning system. We expanded the SSN [22] and SOSA [23] ontologies by providing common procedures and observable properties. By further presenting the poso-common module, we illustrated how POSO can be expanded with a set of common algorithms, existing systems and platforms.

Finally, we illustrated the usage of POSO with a scenario containing two positioning systems and a hybrid positioning system using a high-level fusion technique. In this demonstration, we have shown how each positioning system might be modelled using POSO and how observational data can be expressed.

Future work will focus on adding additional positioning technique and algorithm procedures, further describing the input and output that each procedure provides. By using known input and output RDF shapes that are used in different positioning systems, we can further classify a positioning system's technologies and the output they provide. While we already offer procedures obtaining map information (i.e. Simultaneous Localisation and Mapping), we did not showcase how the raw observations generated by such an algorithm can be created.

Supplemental Material Statement: All the sources of POSO and poso-common, along with additional documentation[5] is available on GitHub [40].

---

[5] https://openhps.github.io/POSO/1.0/en/.

References

1. Abdelmoty, A.I., Smart, P., Jones, C.B.: Building place ontologies for the semantic web: issues and approaches. In: Proceedings GIR 2007, 4th ACM Workshop on Geographical Information Retrieval, pp. 7–12 (2007)
2. Battle, R., Kolas, D.: GeoSPARQL: enabling a geospatial semantic web. Semant. Web J. **3**(4) (2011)
3. Brickley, D.: W3C semantic web interest group: basic geo (WGS84 lat/long) vocabulary. W3C Working Group Note (2004)
4. Carbonera, J.L., et al.: Defining positioning in a core ontology for robotics. In: Proceedings of IROS 2013, IEEE/RSJ International Conference on Intelligent Robots and Systems, pp. 1867–1872 (2013). https://doi.org/10.1109/IROS.2013.6696603
5. Compton, M., et al.: The SSN ontology of the W3C semantic sensor network incubator group. J. Web Semant. **17** (2012). https://doi.org/10.1016/j.websem.2012.05.003
6. Diebel, J.: Representing attitude: euler angles, unit quaternions, and rotation vectors. Matrix **58**(15–16), 1–35 (2006)
7. Djuknic, G.M., Richton, R.E.: Geolocation and assisted GPS. Computer **34**(2) (2001). https://doi.org/10.1109/2.901174
8. Elmenreich, W.: An introduction to sensor fusion. Technical Report 47/2001, Vienna University of Technology (2002)
9. Elsaleh, T., Bermudez-Edo, M., Enshaeifar, S., Acton, S.T., Rezvani, R., Barnaghi, P.: IoT-stream: a lightweight ontology for internet of things data streams. In: Proceedings of GIoTS 2019, Global IoT Summit, pp. 1–6 (2019). https://doi.org/10.1109/GIOTS.2019.8766367
10. Flury, T., Privat, G., Ramparany, F.: OWL-based Location Ontology for context-aware services. In: Proceedings of AIMS 2004, International Workshop on Artificial Intelligence in Mobile Systems, pp. 52–57 (2004)
11. Ganzha, M., Paprzycki, M., Pawłowski, W., Szmeja, P., Wasielewska, K.: Semantic interoperability in the internet of things: an overview from the INTER-IoT perspective. J. Netw. Comput. Appl. **81**, 111–124 (2017). https://doi.org/10.1016/j.jnca.2016.08.007
12. Georgiou, K., Constambeys, T., Laoudias, C., Petrou, L., Chatzimilioudis, G., Zeinalipour-Yazti, D.: Anyplace: a crowdsourced indoor information service. In: Proceedings of MDM 2015, International Conference on Mobile Data Management, pp. 291–294 (2015). https://doi.org/10.1109/MDM.2015.80
13. Gu, Y., Lo, A., Niemegeers, I.: A survey of indoor positioning systems for wireless personal networks. IEEE Commun. Surv. Tutor. **11**(1) (2009). https://doi.org/10.1109/SURV.2009.090103
14. Hansen, R., Wind, R., Jensen, C.S., Thomsen, B.: Seamless indoor/outdoor positioning handover for location-based services in streamspin. In: Proceedings of MDM 2009, International Conference on Mobile Data Management, pp. 267–272 (2009). https://doi.org/10.1109/MDM.2009.39
15. Harle, R.: A survey of indoor inertial positioning systems for pedestrians. IEEE Commun. Surv. Tutor. **15**(3), 1281–1293 (2013). https://doi.org/10.1109/SURV.2012.121912.00075
16. Hodgson, R., Keller, P.J., Hodges, J., Spivak, J.: QUDT-Quantities, Units, Dimensions and Data Types Ontologies (2014). http://qudt.org
17. Hofmann-Wellenhof, B., Lichtenegger, H., Wasle, E.: GNSS-global navigation satellite systems: GPS, GLONASS, galileo, and more. Springer, Heidelberg (2007). https://doi.org/10.1007/978-3-211-73017-1

18. Hu, Y., et al.: A geo-ontology design pattern for semantic trajectories. In: Proceedings of COSIT 2013, International Conference on Spatial Information Theory, pp. 438–456 (2013). https://doi.org/10.1007/978-3-319-01790-7_24

19. ISO Central Secretary: Information Technology - Database Languages - SQL Multimedia and Application Packages - Part 3: Spatial. Standard ISO/IEC 13249–3:2016, International Organization for Standardization, Geneva, Switzerland (2016). https://www.iso.org/standard/60343.html

20. ISO Central Secretary: Geographic information - Positioning Services. Standard ISO 19116:2019, International Organization for Standardization (2019). https://www.iso.org/standard/70882.html

21. ISO Central Secretary: Geographic Information - Referencing by Coordinates. Standard ISO 19111:2019, International Organization for Standardization (2019). https://www.iso.org/standard/74039.html

22. Janowicz, K., Compton, M.: The stimulus-sensor-observation ontology design pattern and its integration into the semantic sensor network ontology. In: Proceedings of SSN 2010, International Workshop on Semantic Sensor Networks (2010)

23. Janowicz, K., Haller, A., Cox, S.J., Le Phuoc, D., Lefrançois, M.: SOSA: a lightweight ontology for sensors, observations, samples, and actuators. J. Web Semant. **56** (2019). https://doi.org/10.1016/j.websem.2018.06.003

24. Krumm, J., Harris, S., Meyers, B., Brumitt, B., Hale, M., Shafer, S.: Multi-camera multi-person tracking for easyliving. In: Proceedings of VS 2000, International Workshop on Visual Surveillance, pp. 3–10 (2000)

25. Lee, K., Lee, J., Kwan, M.P.: Location-based service using ontology-based semantic queries: a study with a focus on indoor activities in a university context. Comput. Environ. Urban Syst. **62** (2017). https://doi.org/10.1016/j.compenvurbsys.2016.10.009

26. Liu, H., Darabi, H., Banerjee, P., Liu, J.: Survey of wireless indoor positioning techniques and systems. IEEE Trans. Syst. Man Cybern. Part C (Appl. Rev.) **37**(6), 1067–1080 (2007). https://doi.org/10.1109/TSMCC.2007.905750

27. Perera, M., Haller, A., Rodríguez Méndez, S.J., Adcock, M.: HDGI: a human device gesture interaction ontology for the internet of things. In: Proceedings of ISWC 2020, International Semantic Web Conference, pp. 111–126 (2020). https://doi.org/10.1007/978-3-030-62466-8_8

28. Perry, M., et al.: OGC GeoSPARQL: A Geographic Query Language for RDF Data: GeoSPARQL 1.1 Draft. Technical report (2021). https://opengeospatial.github.io/ogc-geosparql/geosparql11/spec.html

29. Popescu, A.: Geolocation API Specification 2nd Edition. W3C Recommendation, W3C (2016). https://www.w3.org/TR/2016/REC-geolocation-API-20161108/

30. Quigley, M., et al.: ROS: an open-source robot operating system. In: Proceedings of the International Workshop on Open Source Software (2009)

31. Sambra, A.V., et al.: Solid: A platform for decentralized social applications based on linked data. Technical report, MIT CSAIL & Qatar Computing Research Institute (2016)

32. Skog, I., Hendeby, G., Gustafsson, F.: Magnetic odometry: a model-based approach using a sensor array. In: Proceedings of FUSION 2018, International Conference on Information Fusion, pp. 794–798 (2018). https://doi.org/10.23919/ICIF.2018.8455430

33. Stadler, C., Lehmann, J., Höffner, K., Auer, S.: LinkedGeoData: a core for a web of spatial open data. Semant. Web **3**(4), 333–354 (2012). https://doi.org/10.3233/SW-2011-0052

34. Sumikura, S., Shibuya, M., Sakurada, K.: OpenVSLAM: a versatile visual SLAM framework. In: Proceedings of MM 2019, International Conference on Multimedia. Nice, France (2019). https://doi.org/10.1145/3343031.3350539
35. Tandy, J., van den Brink, L., Barnaghi, P.: Spatial data on the web best practices. W3C Working Group Note (2017). https://www.w3.org/TR/sdw-bp/
36. Thrun, S.: Simultaneous localization and mapping. In: Robotics and Cognitive Approaches to Spatial Mapping, pp. 13–41. Springer (2007). https://doi.org/10.1007/978-3-540-75388-9_3
37. Torres-Sospedra, J., et al.: UJIIndoorLoc: a new multi-building and multi-floor database for wlan fingerprint-based indoor localization problems. In: Proceedings of IPIN 2014, International Conference on Indoor Positioning and Indoor Navigation, pp. 261–270 (2014). https://doi.org/10.1109/IPIN.2014.7275492
38. Torres-Sospedra, J., Rambla, D., Montoliu, R., Belmonte, O., Huerta, J.: UJIIndoorLoc-Mag: a new database for magnetic field-based localization problems. In: Proceedings of IPIN 2015, International Conference on Indoor Positioning and Indoor Navigation, pp. 1–10 (2015). https://doi.org/10.1109/IPIN.2015.7346763
39. Van de Wynckel, M., Signer, B.: OpenHPS: an open source hybrid positioning system. Technical Report WISE-2020-01, Vrije Universiteit Brussel (2020). https://doi.org/10.48550/ARXIV.2101.05198
40. Van de Wynckel, M., Signer, B.: POSO: A Generic Positioning System Ontology Repository (2022). https://github.com/OpenHPS/POSO/
41. Wang, S., Yue, J., Dong, Y., He, S., Wang, H., Ning, S.: A synthetic dataset for visual SLAM evaluation. Rob. Auton. Syst. **124**, 103336 (2020). https://doi.org/10.1016/j.robot.2019.103336
42. Van de Wynckel, M., Signer, B.: Indoor positioning using the OpenHPS framework. In: Proceedings of IPIN 2021, International Conference on Indoor Positioning and Indoor Navigation, pp. 1–8 (2021). https://doi.org/10.1109/IPIN51156.2021.9662569
43. Yan, Z., Macedo, J., Parent, C., Spaccapietra, S.: Trajectory ontologies and queries. Trans. GIS **12**, 75–91 (2008). https://doi.org/10.1111/j.1467-9671.2008.01137.x
44. Zampella, F., Ruiz, A.R.J., Granja, F.S.: Indoor positioning using efficient map matching, rss measurements, and an improved motion model. IEEE Trans. Veh. Technol. **64**(4) (2015). https://doi.org/10.1109/TVT.2015.2391296

Each Snapshot to Each Space: Space Adaptation for Temporal Knowledge Graph Completion

Yancong Li[1], Xiaoming Zhang[2(✉)], Bo Zhang[1], and Haiying Ren[3]

[1] School of Cyber Science and Technology, Beihang University, Beijing, China
[2] State Key Laboratory of Software Development Environment, Beihang University, Beijing 100191, People's Republic of China
`yolixs@buaa.edu.cn`
[3] School of Computer Science and Engineering, Beihang University, Beijing, China

Abstract. Temporal knowledge graphs (TKGs) organize and manage the dynamic relations between entities over time. Inferring missing knowledge in TKGs, known as temporal knowledge graph completion (TKGC), has become an important research topic. Previous models handle all facts with different timestamps in an identical latent space, even though the semantic space of the TKG changes over time. Therefore, they are not effective to reflect the temporality of knowledge. To effectively learn the time-aware information of TKGs, different latent spaces are adapted for temporal snapshots at different timestamps, which yields a novel model, i.e., Space Adaptation Network (SANe). Specifically, we extend convolutional neural networks (CNN) to map the facts with different timestamps into different latent spaces, which can effectively reflect the dynamic variation of knowledge. Meanwhile, a time-aware parameter generator is designed to explore the overlap of latent spaces, which endows CNN with specific parameters in term of the context of timestamps. Therefore, knowledge in adjacent time intervals is efficiently shared to boost the performance of TKGC, which can learn the validity of knowledge over a period of time. Extensive experiments demonstrate that SANe achieves state-of-the-art performance on four well-established benchmark datasets for temporal knowledge graph completion.

Keywords: Temporal knowledge graph · Temporal knowledge graph completion · Space adaptation · Parameter generation

1 Introduction

Knowledge Graphs (KGs) [1,3] organize and manage knowledge as structured information in the form of fact triples, which are crucial in various downstream tasks [14,33]. In KGs, nodes represent entities, and directed edges indicate relations between entities. Notably, most KGs are inherently incomplete, which motivates research on Knowledge Graph Completion (KGC). KGC aims to infer new facts from existing facts in KGs and is important to KG field. However, the

U. Sattler et al. (Eds.): ISWC 2022, LNCS 13489, pp. 248–266, 2022.
https://doi.org/10.1007/978-3-031-19433-7_15

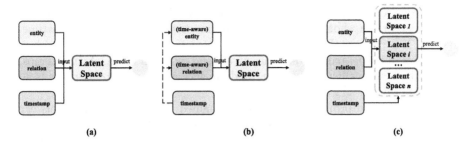

Fig. 1. Existing methods vs. our method. (a) Entities, relations and timestamps are learned to obtain independent representations [21,23,32,42]. (b) Temporal information is implicit in entities or relations to generate time-aware representations of entities or relations [13,41,44]. (c) A concise illustration of our model. Entities and relations are adapted into specific latent spaces that are produced based on timestamps.

facts are not always time-invariant, and the validity of triples is often time-aware. Traditional KGC methods are insensitive to temporal information, since they intuitively assume that triples in KGs are universally true. Therefore, these methods are not effective to predict the temporal facts.

Temporal Knowledge Graphs (TKGs), including ICEWS [5], YAGO3 [26], Wikidata [9], etc., are introduced to organize additional temporal aspects of facts. In TKGs, static triples are associated with timestamps, which reflect the temporal dynamics of facts in the form of quadruples. Knowledge in a TKG can be described by the evolution of snapshots over time. However, TKGs also suffer from incompleteness as with static KGs. Therefore, predicting missing knowledge with specific timestamps in TKGs, i.e., Temporal Knowledge Graph Completion (TKGC), has gained growing interest.

Recently, a variety of models have been proposed to handle TKGC. These models significantly outperform traditional KGC models by capturing the latent correlation between knowledge and temporal information. Previous works learn independent representations of entities, relations and timestamps [21,23,32,42] as shown in Fig. 1(a), or obtain time-aware representations by integrating temporal information into entities and relations [13,41,44] as shown in Fig. 1(b). These works model variable knowledge in an identical latent space, even though the semantic space of the TKG changes over time. Therefore, these methods are not effective to learn the temporality of knowledge. In practice, TKGs can be decomposed into two components, time-variability and time-stability, which are intrinsic and critical characteristics in TKGs. Time-variability denotes the dynamic knowledge which is varied in different snapshots. For example, the *president* of *USA* was *George W. Bush* on *2009-01-01*, but became *Barack Obama* on *2010-01-01*. On the other side, time-stability denotes the knowledge which remains unchanged for a period time. For example, (*Barack Obama, presidentOf, USA*) remains valid for a specific period from *2009-01-20* to *2017-01-20*. One of simple yet generic solution of TKGC is to encode the knowledge in different temporal snapshots into different latent spaces, such that the time-aware information at each snapshots can be captured effectively. Meanwhile, there is a part of knowledge remains unchanged during a interval. Therefore, knowledge sharing across adjacent snapshots is also required for knowledge accumulation over time. However, it is quite challenging to derive a latent space for each snapshot, since the number of model parameters linearly depend on the number of timestamps. In addition, how to efficiently gather valid knowledge from different spaces is an important problem as well.

In response, we propose a novel model named $\underline{S}$pace $\underline{A}$daptation $\underline{Ne}$twork (SANe) for TKGC as shown in Fig. 1(c). We establish the correlation between latent spaces and snapshots in terms of parameter generation, i.e., a time-specific network is produced for each snapshot, such that the facts with different timestamps are encoded into different spaces. Specifically, to model time-variability, a dynamic convolutional neural network (DCNN) is proposed to deal with the entities and relations with different parameters that are specific to the corresponding timestamps. Therefore, each temporal snapshot, i.e., knowledge graph with the same timestamp, is processed in a specific space. Essentially, TKGC is turn into the static KGC by handling different temporal snapshots in separate spaces. Thereby, this solution alleviates mutual interference of the knowledge with different timestamps. In addition, we explore how to produce the parameters with respect to timestamps to ensure time-stability. Thus, a time-aware parameter generator (TaPG) is designed to constrain the overlap of latent spaces according to the distance of timestamps, which allows adjacent snapshots to share different but similar latent spaces. In this way, valid knowledge across multiple snapshots within a time interval is preserved. The model is experimentally evaluated in detail on several recent standard benchmarks and achieves state-of-the-art performance compared to existing TKGC methods.

To summarize, our contributions are as follows:

- We propose a novel space adaptation network SANe for TKGC, where different latent spaces are adapted for different temporal snapshots. To the best of our knowledge, this is the first work to implement TKG completion from the perspective of space adaptation.
- By constraining the overlap of different spaces in terms of time intervals, the model strikes a balance between learning time-variability and adapting to time-stability.
- Experimental results on four benchmark datasets with rich temporal information demonstrate the superiority of our model[1]

2   Related Work

In this section, typical methods for static knowledge graph completion and temporal knowledge graph completion are introduced, and research advances on parameter generation in various fields are briefly reviewed.

Static Knowledge Graph Completion aims to infer missing facts in static KGs. Previous works can be broadly classified into translational, bilinear, and

---

[1] Our code will be publicly available at https://github.com/codeofpaper/SANe.

neural models. TransE [4] is a well-known translation-based model that regards relations as translations from head entities to tail entities. Later, several variants such as TransH [39], TransR [24] and TransD [16] have been proposed to improve the shortcomings of TransE. Bilinear models, such as RESCAL [29], ComplEx [37], and TuckER [2], represent relations as linear transformations acting on entity embeddings, and use bilinear functions to compute plausibility scores for facts. Neural models, such as ConvE [8], InteractE [38], and RGHAT [48], complement KGs with nonlinear neural networks and show great effectiveness. The above models have achieved promising results in addressing the incompleteness of KGs. However, they assume that the facts are static and thus cannot model the temporality in TKGs. For example, given two quadruples with timestamps: (*Barack Obama, presidentOf, USA, 2010-01-01*) and (*Barack Obama, presidentOf, USA, 2020-01-01*), the time-insensitive KGC models will output the same plausibility scores for these two quadruples. However, the second quadruple is invalid. To exploit temporal information to further improve the performance of KGC models, several studies have been conducted for temporal knowledge graph completion.

Temporal Knowledge Graph Completion extends KGC to support temporal information. Existing methods for temporal knowledge graph completion generally fall into two categories. The first line of researches models entities, relations, and timestamps independently in an identical latent space. TTransE [23], the variant of TransE [4], incorporates temporal representations into a distance-based scoring function. TComplEx [21] is a temporal extension of ComplEx [37] inspired by the canonical decomposition of order 4 tensors and provides a new regularization scheme. TeLM [42] improves on TComplEx by utilizing a linear temporal regularizer and multi-vector embeddings to perform 4th-order tensor factorization of TKGs. ChronoR [32] is a k-dimensional rotation based model that regards relations with timestamps as temporal rotations from head entities to tail entities. The another line argues that temporal information should be implicit in entities or relations, thus learning time-aware representations. ATiSE [44] incorporates temporal information into entities/relations by using additive time series decomposition and exploits the covariance of Gaussian distributions to represent temporal uncertainty. DE-SimplE [13] combines the static KGC model SimplE [19] with a diachronic embedding function that provides time-aware representations of entities, and utilizes the same scoring function as SimplE for temporal KGC. TIE [41] is a time-aware incremental embedding framework that combines representation learning, experience replay, and temporal regularization to improve model performance.

Parameter Generation has been explored in many research fields. Platanios et al. [31] proposed a neural translation model with a contextual parameter generator to generate parameters used by the encoder and decoder for the current sentence based on the source and target languages. N^3 [17] generates network parameters for image classification through natural language descriptions combined with pre-trained models. Nekvinda et al. [28] introduced a multilingual speech synthesis method that uses the meta-learning concept of contextual parameter generation to produce natural-sounding multilingual speech. According to our investigation, there is also work on parameter generation for static knowledge graph completion. CoPER [35] uses the embeddings of relations to generate model parameters that operate on the embeddings of head entities to allow for more complex interactions between entities and relations. ParamE [6] uses neural network parameters as relation embeddings to make the model more expressive and translational. However, CoPER and ParamE are time-agnostic and thus cannot capture the temporal dependencies of facts in TKGs.

3   Methodology

A temporal knowledge graph can be represented by a set of quadruples $\mathcal{G} = \{(h, r, t, \tau) \mid h, t \in \mathcal{E}, r \in \mathcal{R}, \tau \in \mathcal{T}\}$, where $\mathcal{E}$, $\mathcal{R}$, and $\mathcal{T}$ are sets of entities, relations, and timestamps, respectively. Each quadruple represents a time-dependent fact that a head entity h connects to a tail entity t with respect to the relation r at the timestamp τ. Given a query $(h, r, ?, \tau)$ or $(?, r, t, \tau)$, TKGC aims to predict the missing tail entity t or head entity h based on the observed temporal facts. For TKGC, we only focus on predicting missing facts at observed timestamps, i.e., interpolation task [18]. The extrapolation task that predicts future facts is not considered in this paper.

To tackle the challenges of TKGC, we propose a Space Adaptation Network (SANe), in which snapshots with different timestamps are adapted for different latent spaces. As shown in Fig. 2, SANe mainly consists of two modules, i.e., a Dynamic Convolutional Neural Network (DCNN), and a Time-aware Parameter Generator (TaPG). DCNN encodes entities and relations into different latent spaces in terms of convolutional layers equipped with different parameters. These parameters are produced by TaPG according to temporal information. TaPG transforms the timestamps into a set of DCNN parameters, where the timestamps dominate the overlap of multiple latent spaces in DCNN, such that the valid knowledge is shared across adjacent snapshots. Specifically, we denote by the d-dimensional vectors $\mathbf{h} \in \mathbb{R}^d$ and $\mathbf{r} \in \mathbb{R}^d$ the head entity and relation respectively. Given a query $(h, r, ?, \tau)$, DCNN f predicts the correct tail entity t based on generated parameters from TaPG g, i.e.,

$$\mathbf{t} = f(\mathbf{h}, \mathbf{r}; g(\boldsymbol{\tau})), \tag{1}$$

where $g(\boldsymbol{\tau})$ is the set of parameters of DCNN f, i.e., $\theta_f = g(\boldsymbol{\tau})$.

3.1   Dynamic Convolutional Neural Network

Convolutional neural networks (CNN) have shown expressiveness in static KGC methods [8,38], but have not been extensively explored in existing TKGC methods. We extend CNN to support TKGC by endowing CNN with specific parameters associated with temporal information. DCNN f consists of several dynamic convolutional layers and batch normalization, followed by a connected linear layer. Dynamic convolutional layer (DCL) is the important backbone of DCNN

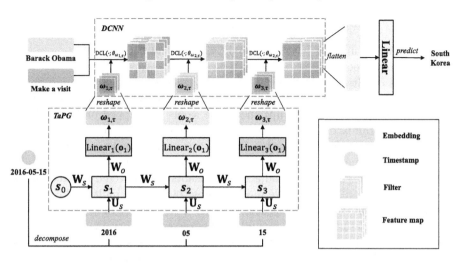

Fig. 2. The framework of our model SANe. DCNN is a multi-layer convolutional neural network for predicting missing entities, and its filter parameters are generated by TaPG based on temporal information.

that identifies the key feature from the inputs based on a filter. It differs from traditional convolutional layer that the parameters of DCL filter is dynamically produced from TaPG instead of fixed. Naturally, TaPG is a tremendous parameter pool and selects appropriate parameters for DCLs when dealing with different temporal facts. DCL pads and filters the input $\mathbf{X} \in \mathbb{R}^{C_i \times H \times W}$ to produce the feature map $\mathbf{X}' \in \mathbb{R}^{C_o \times H \times W}$ based on the filter $\omega_{p,\tau} \in \mathbb{R}^{C_o \times C_i \times k \times k}$ followed by the nonlinear activation function ReLU (i.e., Rectified Linear Unit [12]),

$$\mathbf{X}' = \mathsf{DCL}\left(\mathbf{X}; \theta_{\omega_{p,\tau}}\right) = \mathsf{ReLU}\left(\mathbf{X} \circledast \omega_{p,\tau}\right), \tag{2}$$

where $\circledast$ is the convolution operator, H and W are height and width, C_o and C_i are the size of input and output channels, and k is the kernel size. The filter $\omega_{p,\tau}$ is produced from TaPG according to the position p of DCL in DCNN and the timestamp τ, i.e., $\theta_{\omega_{p,\tau}} = g(\tau, p)$.

Multiple DCLs are stacked to handle the entities and relations in an effective way. In particular, we first reshape the entity $\mathbf{h}$ and the relation $\mathbf{r}$ into $\tilde{\mathbf{h}} \in \mathbb{R}^{H \times W}$ and $\tilde{\mathbf{r}} \in \mathbb{R}^{H \times W}$, respectively. To enhance the heterogenous interactions between entity $\tilde{\mathbf{h}}$ and relation $\tilde{\mathbf{r}}$ vectors, we perform feature permutation and checkered reshaping operations on the concatenation $\mathbf{X} \in \mathbb{R}^{2H \times W}$ of $\tilde{\mathbf{h}}$ and $\tilde{\mathbf{r}}$ inspired by the work [38]. Feature permutation shuffles each element in $\tilde{\mathbf{h}}$ and $\tilde{\mathbf{r}}$, while checkered reshaping ensures that every two adjacent cells in $\mathbf{X}$ are alternately occupied by elements in $\mathbf{h}$ and $\mathbf{r}$. The regularized input $\tilde{\mathbf{X}}$ after above operations is fed into P DCLs to produce the feature map $\mathbf{M}$.

To predict the correct tail entity, a scoring function is introduced to evaluate the score of correlation between the query $(h, r, ?, \tau)$ and candidate tail entity $\mathbf{t} \in \mathbb{R}^d$,

$$\psi_\tau(h, r, t) = \text{Linear}(\text{flatten}(\mathbf{M}))\mathbf{t}, \tag{3}$$

where $\text{Linear}(\cdot)$ is a linear layer activated by ReLU and $\text{flatten}(x)$ flattens x into a 1-dimensional vector.

The sets of filters of DCNN $\{\omega_{1,\tau}, \cdots \omega_{P,\tau}\}$ reflect the delivery and variation of knowledge at different snapshots in consecutive time. The spaces induced by DCNN at different timestamps should be same, overlapped or uncorrelated when the timestamps of facts are the same, adjacent and distant. In other words, the overlap of spaces at different timestamps constrains the range of knowledge sharing. This property ensures that the interfere from early snapshots is alleviated and the missing facts in adjacent snapshots are delivered to accumulate knowledge. Essentially, our SANe model stores the facts in multiple knowledge bases, i.e., multiple sets of parameters, depending on the time range. Thus, it can "index" the knowledge precisely by finding the "records" in parameters according to different timestamps. The next section will introduce the parameter generation of DCNN to preserve the valid knowledge and forget the mistaken in a time-aware way.

3.2   Time-Aware Parameter Generator

Usually, in the process of searching records by human, the searcher reduces the hunting zone by gradually indexing year, month and day. For example, if a person wants to query a record that are indexed by the timestamp, he needs to split timestamps into year, month and day to locate it. If the record is missing at the timestamp, the similar records around the timestamp should be returned. Based on the observation, the filter parameters $\omega_{1,\tau}$ of the first DCL in DCNN are required to establish a global "catalogue" of the year of τ. The catalogue encodes high-level contextual features with an annual perspective. After that, the second and third of DCLs predict the facts by supplementing more details of month and day information based on the parameters $\omega_{2,\tau}$ and $\omega_{3,\tau}$.

In this part, we introduce a time-aware parameter generator (TaPG) that "store" the knowledge in three sets of parameters that are associated with "year-month-day". Specifically, we first split and embed the timestamp τ as a fixed-length sequence $\overrightarrow{\tau} = (\tau_1, \tau_2, \tau_3)$, where $\tau_1, \tau_2, \tau_3 \in \mathbb{R}^{d_\tau}$ are the embeddings of year, month and day respectively. A recurrent neural network (RNN) is introduced to model the sequence data $\overrightarrow{\tau}$ that produces multiple outputs,

$$\{\mathbf{o}_1, \mathbf{o}_2, \mathbf{o}_3\} = \text{RNN}(\overrightarrow{\tau}), \tag{4}$$

$$\mathbf{o}_i = \sigma(\mathbf{W}_o \mathbf{s}_i + \mathbf{b}_o), \tag{5}$$

$$\mathbf{s}_i = \sigma(\mathbf{U}_s \tau_i + \mathbf{W}_s \mathbf{s}_{i-1} + \mathbf{b}_s), \tag{6}$$

where $\mathbf{W}_o$, $\mathbf{W}_s$ and $\mathbf{U}_s$ are RNN parameters, $\mathbf{s}_i$ and $\mathbf{o}_i$ are the hidden state and output at step i, and σ is the nonlinear activation function.

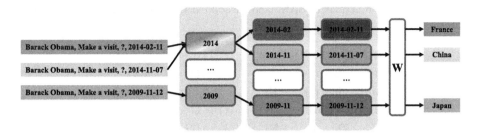

Fig. 3. The process of query prediction by DCNN. Queries with different timestamps are handled by different parameters, while queries with similar timestamps partially share model parameters.

Multiple fully connected layers $\{\text{Linear}_1, \text{Linear}_2, \text{Linear}_3\}$ are employed to transform the outputs of RNN into a set of parameters,

$$g(\tau) = \{\omega_{i,\tau}\} = \{\text{Linear}_i(\mathbf{o}_i)\}. \tag{7}$$

The linear layers $\{\text{Linear}_i\}$ are a parameter pool, which retrieves the parameters according to the context of timestamps. The 1-dimensional vectors produced by $\{\text{Linear}_i\}$ are reshaped into tensors in $\mathbb{R}^{C_o \times C_i \times k \times k}$, since the convolutional operations are involved. The scale of DCNN parameters is obviously irrelevant to the number of timestamps, which only depends on the size of the linear layers $\{\text{Linear}_i\}$.

As show in Fig. 3, the facts with the same year are dealt with the same filters $\omega_{1,\tau}$ and thus the valid knowledge during a interval is shared across adjacent snapshots. Compared to the works [40,45] that construct sparse snapshots at each timestamps explicitly, our implicit way enable the knowledge delivery at different snapshots. Of course, the facts that have long gap of timestamps are divided into two totally different models that avoids the interfere from early knowledge. Therefore, TaPG enables the ability of DCNN to tackle time-variability and time-stability in an efficient manner. Multiple spaces induced by the parameters output from TaPG are adapted for different temporal snapshots. The knowledge at different time is shared or separated during multiple spaces in term of the context from TaPG.

3.3   Training and Optimization

During training process, the score $\psi_\tau(h, r, t)$ is applied with the logistic sigmoid function $\sigma(\cdot)$ to obtain $p = \sigma(\psi_\tau(h, r, t))$. p indicates the predicted probability that the candidate tail entity t is the answer to query $(h, r, ?, \tau)$. The training objective is to minimize the negative log-likelihood loss as follows,

$$\mathcal{L}(y, p) = -\frac{1}{N} \sum_i (y_i \log(p_i) + (1 - y_i) \log(1 - p_i)), \tag{8}$$

Table 1. Scoring functions of SANe and several existing TKGC methods, and comparison of space complexity.

Model	Scoring Function	Space Complexity
TransE	$\|\mathbf{h} + \mathbf{r} - \mathbf{t}\|$	$\mathcal{O}\left(n_e d + n_r d\right)$
TTransE	$\|\mathbf{h} + \mathbf{r} + \tau - \mathbf{t}\|$	$\mathcal{O}\left(n_e d + n_r d + n_\tau d\right)$
HyTE	$\|P_\tau\left(\mathbf{h}\right) + P_\tau\left(\mathbf{r}\right) - P_\tau\left(\mathbf{t}\right)\|$	$\mathcal{O}\left(n_e d + n_r d + n_\tau d\right)$
ATiSE	$\mathcal{D}_{\mathcal{KL}}\left(\mathbf{P}_{h,\tau} - \mathbf{P}_{t,\tau}, \mathbf{P}_{r,\tau}\right)$	$\mathcal{O}\left(n_e d + n_r d\right)$
TeRo	$\|\mathbf{h}_\tau + \mathbf{r} - \bar{\mathbf{t}}_\tau\|$	$\mathcal{O}\left(n_e d + n_r d\right)$
SANe	$\text{Linear}(\text{flatten}(\text{CNN}(\mathbf{h}, \mathbf{r})))\mathbf{t}$	$\mathcal{O}\left(n_e d + n_r d + n_y d_\tau\right)$

where $y = 1$ for positive samples, i.e., $(h, r, t, \tau) \in \mathcal{G}$, otherwise $y = 0$. N indicates the number of training samples.

In Table 1, we summarize the scoring functions and space complexity of several TKGC methods. n_e, n_r, and n_τ are the number of entities, relations, and timestamps, respectively. d and d_τ are the dimensions of feature vectors. n_y is the number of years. CNN refers to the three-layer convolutional neural network in DCNN. In terms of space complexity, SANe is comparable to several existing methods.

4   Experiments

In this section, four TKGC benchmark datasets are used to demonstrate the effectiveness of SANe. The experimental setup is first explained in detail. Then, the experimental results are discussed. Ablation studies are also conducted to evaluate the importance of different components in SANe.

4.1   Experimental Setup

Datasets. The proposed model is evaluated on four public benchmarks, ICEWS14 [10], ICEWS05-15 [10], YAGO11k [7], and Wikidata12k [7]. ICEWS14 and ICEWS05-15 are subsets of the Integrated Crisis Early Warning System (ICEWS) [5] dataset, where ICEWS14 includes events that occurred in 2014, and ICEWS05-15 includes events that occurred in the period 2005 to 2015. ICEWS contains discrete time-annotated sociopolitical events, e.g. (*Barack Obama, Make a visit, South Korea, 2014-03-15*). YAGO11k and Wikidata12k are subsets of YAGO3 [26] and Wikidata [9], respectively. Facts in both YAGO11k and Wikidata12k contain time annotations, and each fact is formatted as a time interval. Following Dasgupta et al. [7], facts with time intervals are discretized into multiple quadruplets with a single timestamp. Meanwhile, month and day information is dropped, and year-level granularity is preserved. To process such datasets, timestamps are appended with constant fabricated months and days, e.g., 2015-*00-00*. Statistics for these four benchmarks are summarized in Table 2.

Table 2. Statistics of TKGC benchmark datasets. The unit of the time span is year.

Datasets	#Entities	#Relations	Time span	#Train	#Valid	#Test
ICEWS14	6,869	230	2014	72,826	8,941	8,963
ICEWS05-15	10,094	251	2005-2015	386,962	46,275	46,092
YAGO11k	10,623	10	-453-2844	16,408	2,050	2,051
Wikidata12k	12,554	24	1709-2018	32,497	4,062	4,062

Baselines. We compare with a wide selection of static and temporal KGC models: (1) static KGC models, including TransE [4], DistMult [46], ComplEx-N3 [22], RotatE [36], and QuatE^2 [47]; (2) temporal KGC models, including TTransE [23], HyTE [7], TA-TransE [10], TA-DistMult [10], DE-SimplE [13], ATiSE [44], TeRo [43], ChronoR [32], TimePlex [15], TComplEx [21], TeLM [42], and BoxTE [27]. Among them, ChronoR and BoxTE are not compared with SANe on YAGO11k and Wikidata12k, because their results are unobtainable.

Evaluation Protocols. For each quadruple (h, r, t, τ) in the test set, two queries $(h, r, ?, \tau)$ and $(?, r, t, \tau)$ are leveraged to optimize the model simultaneously. Note that in practice, each quadruple (h, r, t, τ) is added with a reciprocal relation (t, r^{-1}, h, τ). Thus, the query $(?, r, t, \tau)$ is replaced by $(t, r^{-1}, ?, \tau)$. Such operations do not result in a loss of generality [15,42]. MRR (Mean Reciprocal Rank, the average of the reciprocal values of all computed ranks) and Hits@N (the percentage of times that the true entity candidate appears in the top N of ranked candidates, where $N \in \{1, 3, 10\}$) are reported as evaluation metrics. Among them, MRR is an important evaluation index, which is less susceptible to outliers [10]. Higher MRR and Hits@N indicate better model performance. All evaluations are performed under the time-wise filtering setting widely adopted in previous work [43,44].

Implementation Details. The proposed model is implemented using PyTorch [30] and trained using a single NVIDIA GeForce RTX 3090 GPU. The values of the hyperparameters are determined based on the MRR performance on each validation set. The model parameters are initialized using Xavier initialization [11] and optimized by the Adam optimizer [20] with a learning rate of 0.001. During training, 256 mini-batches are created for each epoch. The negative sampling ratio is set to 1000, i.e., 1000 negative samples are created for each quadruple in the training set. The embedding dimension is set to $d = 200$ for all datasets except ICEWS05-15 which is set to $d = 300$. The number of convolution filters is fixed to 64. The kernel size is chosen from $k \in \{3, 5, 7\}$.

4.2   Main Results

The MRR and Hits@N results on ICEWS dataset, i.e., ICEWS14 and ICEWS05-15, are reported in Table 3. Some observations and analysis are listed as follows. (1) Most of TKGC models achieve significantly better results than static KGC

Table 3. Link prediction results on ICEWS14 and ICEWS05-15. *: results are taken from [10]. †: results are taken from [43]. ◇: results are taken from [42]. Dashes: results are unobtainable. Other results are taken from the original papers. The best results are marked in **bold**.

Datasets	ICEWS14				ICEWS05-15			
Metrics	MRR	Hits@1	Hits@3	Hits@10	MRR	Hits@1	Hits@3	Hits@10
TransE* [4]	.280	.094	–	.637	.294	.090	–	.663
DistMult* [46]	.439	.323	–	.672	.456	.337	–	.691
ComplEx-N3† [22]	.467	.347	.527	.716	.481	.362	.535	.729
RotatE† [36]	.418	.291	.478	.690	.304	.164	.355	.595
QuatE^{2†} [47]	.471	.353	.530	.712	.482	.370	.529	.727
TTransE† [23]	.255	.074	–	.601	.271	.084	–	.616
HyTE† [7]	.297	.108	.416	.655	.316	.116	.445	.681
TA-TransE* [10]	.275	.095	–	.625	.299	.096	–	.668
TA-DistMult* [10]	.477	.363	–	.686	.474	.346	–	.728
DE-SimplE† [13]	.526	.418	.592	.725	.513	.392	.578	.748
ATiSE [44]	.545	.423	.632	.757	.533	.394	.623	.803
TeRo [43]	.562	.468	.621	.732	.586	.469	.668	.795
ChronoR [32]	.625	.547	.669	.773	.675	.596	.723	.820
TimePlex [15]	.604	.515	–	.771	.640	.545	–	.818
TComplEx◇ [21]	.610	.530	.660	.770	.660	.590	.710	.800
TeLM◇ [42]	.625	.545	.673	.774	.678	.599	.728	.823
BoxTE [27]	.613	.528	.664	.763	.667	.582	.719	.820
SANe	**.638**	**.558**	**.688**	**.782**	**.683**	**.605**	**.734**	**.823**

methods. TKGC models leverage temporal information to constrain the similarity of facts, such that similar facts with different timestamps are separate efficiently. (2) SANe achieves the best performance for all metrics on link prediction, which suggests the effectiveness of adapting snapshots with different timestamps to different latent spaces. The facts are implicitly assigned to different CNN modules, and thus each snapshot at different timestamps is handled in term of a specific latent space. The results indicate that the parameter generation plays an important role in alleviating mutual interference of the knowledge across snapshots with different timestamps. (3) Facts in ICEWS are transient events, which usually happen and end in a moment. Compared to other TKGC methods, SANe is capable of remembering and inferring instant facts by recovering the CNN model from the parameter pool according to timestamps. The result in Table 3 further certifies that SANe is more effective to enable time-variability that inherent in TKGs.

Table 4 shows the prediction performance over Wikipedia-based datasets, i.e., YAGO11k and Wikidata12k. SANe achieves superior performance over previous methods by a large margin compared to the result on ICEWS. On MRR, a main

Table 4. Link prediction results on YAGO11k and Wikidata12k. *: results are taken from [44]. †: results are taken from [43]. ◇: results are taken from [42]. Dashes: results are unobtainable. Other results are taken from the original papers. The best results are marked in **bold**.

Datasets	YAGO11k				Wikidata12k			
Metrics	MRR	Hits@1	Hits@3	Hits@10	MRR	Hits@1	Hits@3	Hits@10
TransE* [4]	.100	.015	.138	.244	.178	.100	.192	.339
DistMult* [46]	.158	.107	.161	.268	.222	.119	.238	.460
ComplEx-N3* [22]	.167	.106	.154	.282	.233	.123	.253	.436
RotatE* [36]	.167	.103	.167	.305	.221	.116	.236	.461
QuatE²* [47]	.164	.107	.148	.270	.230	.125	.243	.416
TTransE† [23]	.108	.020	.150	.251	.172	.096	.184	.329
HyTE† [7]	.105	.015	.143	.272	.180	.098	.197	.333
TA-TransE† [10]	.127	.027	.160	.326	.178	.030	.267	.429
TA-DistMult† [10]	.161	.103	.171	.292	.218	.122	.232	.447
ATiSE [44]	.185	.126	.189	.301	.252	.148	.288	.462
TeRo† [43]	.187	.121	.197	.319	.299	.198	.329	.507
TimePlex [15]	.236	.169	–	.367	.334	.228	–	.532
TComplEx◇ [21]	.185	.127	.183	.307	.331	.233	.357	.539
TeLM◇ [42]	.191	.129	.194	.321	.332	.231	.360	.542
SANe	**.250**	**.180**	**.266**	**.401**	**.432**	**.331**	**.483**	**.640**

metric for the TKGC task, SANe outperforms by 6% and 29% dramatically compared with the state-of-the-art methods across the YAGO11k and Wikidata12k, respectively. The facts in Wikipedia-based datasets spans a period of hundreds of years, even around 3,000 years, while ICEWS only covers several years. The plenty of facts usually last for a long period of time different from ICEWS that events happen and end in a moment. The superior result of SANe reveals the necessity of designing a more principled parameter generation approach to produce multiple latent spaces that constrains the range of knowledge sharing based on timestamp distance. Multiple sets of parameters encode the context of timestamps that the knowledge in adjacent snapshots is delivered to accumulate knowledge. Therefore, the valid knowledge during a period can be preserved and shared efficiently. The models of learning independent representations [15,21,23,32,42] or incorporating timestamp into entities and relations [7,10,13,27,43,44] suffer from the interfere across snapshots particularly when the knowledge last for a long period. This is mainly because they handle all the facts in an identical latent space, and thus inevitably misremember and forget knowledge. The result in Table 4 further certifies that SANe is more effective to enable time-stability inherent in TKGs.

4.3   Analysis

Ablation Study. To better verify the effectiveness of the proposed model, several variants of SANe are investigated on ICEWS14. The results are shown in Table 5. The ✓ is used to indicate a component used in the experiment, and the ✗ is used to indicate the absence of the corresponding component. The SANe without time information means that TaPG returns a fixed set of parameters regardless of the timestamps. Based on the SANe without time information, the SANe without parameter generation also incorporates the temporal information into the entities, i.e., $\hat{\mathbf{h}} = \mathbf{h} \odot \tau$, where $\odot$ is Hadamard product as the work [34] does. The TaPG of SANe without time granularity produces the parameters directly in term of timestamp τ without RNN, i.e., $\{\mathsf{Linear}_i(\tau)\}$. It is found that (1) when the time information is not used, the model achieves the worst results, which reflects the importance of time information to SANe. (2) The parameter generator has a great influence on the model performance, which verifies the effectiveness of the time-aware parameter generator. (3) Decomposing timestamps into different time granularities is beneficial to the improvement of model performance. (4) Even if the timestamps are not decomposed into different granularities, the model achieves better results than previous TKGC methods, which confirms the superiority of the model.

Table 5. Results for different model variations on ICEWS14.

Time Information	Time Granularity	Parameter Generation	MRR	Hits@1	Hits@3	Hits@10
✗	✗	✗	.469	.350	.529	.703
✓	✗	✗	.608	.527	.656	.760
✓	✓	✗	.622	.536	.679	.778
✓	✗	✓	.630	.548	.683	.780
✓	✓	✓	**.638**	**.558**	**.688**	**.782**

Table 6. Generalization performance for queries with unseen timestamps on the ICEWS14 dataset.

Metrics	MRR	Hits@1	Hits@3	Hits@10
DistMult [46]	.410	.302	.462	.620
DE-SimplE [13]	.434	.333	.492	.624
TComplEx [21]	.443	.348	.492	.625
SANe	**.503**	**.394**	**.569**	**.709**

Generalizing to Unseen Timestamps. Since timestamps are decomposed at different time granularities in SANe, this allows queries with similar timestamps to share a part of filter parameters and temporal information. Therefore, SANe is expected to perform well on queries with unseen timestamps. Following Goel et al. [13], we re-split ICEWS14, taking all quadruplets except the 5th, 15th, and 25th day of each month as the training set, and using the excluded quadruplets to randomly split into validation and test sets. The obtained results in Table 6 indicate that SANe gains almost 14% MRR improvement over TComplEx [21], thus showing the effectiveness of our model to generalize to unseen timestamps.

Performance on Different Relations. Most of the time annotations in YAGO11k are time intervals, and the relations between entities may change after a period of time. We evaluate SANe on several relations (*worksAt, hasWonPrize, graduatedFrom,* and *isAffiliatedTo*) in YAGO11k, and reproduce ATiSE [44] and TimPlex [15] based on their given hyperparameters. These relations are usually created or disappeared between some entities at a certain point in time, and maintained for a period of time [44]. For example, a person may switch to another company after working for one company for a few months. SANe is expected to perform well in such relations. The comparisons in Fig. 4 show that SANe is superior in almost all metrics. This confirms our hypothesis that adapting different temporal snapshots to different latent spaces via parameter generation is beneficial for capturing the time-variability of knowledge. Likewise,

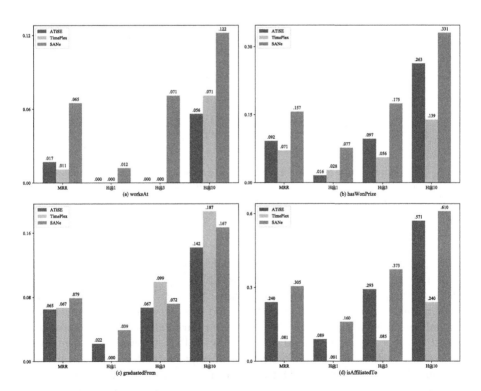

Fig. 4. Results obtained by ATiSE [44], TimPlex [15], and SANe on several relations in YAGO11k.

overlapping latent spaces by decomposing timestamps into different granularities facilitates knowledge sharing across adjacent snapshots, which is beneficial for modeling the time-stability of knowledge.

Visualization of Temporal Embeddings. Figure 5 shows a t-SNE [25] visualization of the temporal embeddings learned by SANe and its variant. Figure 5(a) visualizes the temporal embeddings learned by the variant of SANe. Timestamps are modeled independently by the variant of SANe rather than decomposed into different granularities. Figure 5(b) visualizes the temporal embeddings with granularity of 1 day learned by SANe. By comparison, it can be found that the temporal embeddings learned by SANe form good clusters in chronological order. In general, SANe effectively preserves time series information by decomposing timestamps into different granularities and processed by the time series model, which provides good geometric meanings for temporal embeddings, thus improving the model performance.

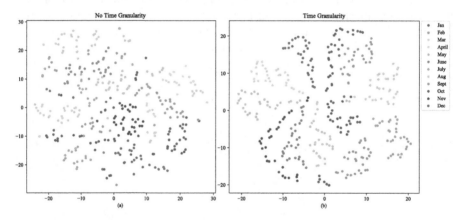

Fig. 5. The figure illustrates the t-SNE visualization of the temporal embeddings obtained by SANe and its variant after training on ICEWS14. Time points in different months are represented by different colors.

5   Conclusion and Future Work

In this paper, we shed a new light on the challenges of TKGC. For the first time, we proposed to investigate the problem of TKGC by adapting different latent spaces for snapshots at different timestamps. Specifically, we provided a novel model named SANe to process the entities and relations using a dynamic convolutional neural network equipped with different parameters, which are produced by TaPG according to temporal information. TaPG endowed with contextual timestamps gathers valid knowledge from multiple sets of parameters by constraining the overlap of spaces. Our model is different from existing works which learn the temporal KGs all the time in the same latent space. The experimental results demonstrate the benefits of constructing parameter-independent model implicitly for each temporal snapshot.

Supplemental Material Statement: Source code to reproduce the full experimental results is already available on the Easychair system and will be published on https://github.com/codeofpaper/SANe.

Acknowledgments. This work is supported by the Fund of the State Key Laboratory of Software Development Environment.

References

1. Auer, S., Bizer, C., Kobilarov, G., Lehmann, J., Cyganiak, R., Ives, Z.: DBpedia: a nucleus for a web of open data. In: Aberer, K., et al. (eds.) ASWC/ISWC -2007. LNCS, vol. 4825, pp. 722–735. Springer, Heidelberg (2007). https://doi.org/10.1007/978-3-540-76298-0_52
2. Balažević, I., Allen, C., Hospedales, T.: Tucker: tensor factorization for knowledge graph completion. In: Proceedings of the 2019 Conference on Empirical Methods in Natural Language Processing and the 9th International Joint Conference on Natural Language Processing (EMNLP-IJCNLP), pp. 5185–5194 (2019)
3. Bollacker, K., Evans, C., Paritosh, P., Sturge, T., Taylor, J.: Freebase: a collaboratively created graph database for structuring human knowledge. In: Proceedings of the 2008 ACM SIGMOD International Conference on Management of Data, pp. 1247–1250 (2008)
4. Bordes, A., Usunier, N., Garcia-Durán, A., Weston, J., Yakhnenko, O.: Translating embeddings for modeling multi-relational data. In: Proceedings of the 26th International Conference on Neural Information Processing Systems-Volume 2, pp. 2787–2795 (2013)
5. Boschee, E., Lautenschlager, J., O'Brien, S., Shellman, S., Starz, J., Ward, M.: Icews coded event data. Harvard Dataverse 12 (2015)
6. Che, F., Zhang, D., Tao, J., Niu, M., Zhao, B.: Parame: regarding neural network parameters as relation embeddings for knowledge graph completion. In: Proceedings of the AAAI Conference on Artificial Intelligence, vol. 34, pp. 2774–2781 (2020)
7. Dasgupta, S.S., Ray, S.N., Talukdar, P.: Hyte: hyperplane-based temporally aware knowledge graph embedding. In: Proceedings of the 2018 Conference on Empirical Methods in Natural Language Processing, pp. 2001–2011 (2018)
8. Dettmers, T., Minervini, P., Stenetorp, P., Riedel, S.: Convolutional 2d knowledge graph embeddings. In: Proceedings of the AAAI Conference on Artificial Intelligence, vol. 32 (2018)
9. Erxleben, F., Günther, M., Krötzsch, M., Mendez, J., Vrandečić, D.: Introducing wikidata to the linked data web. In: Mika, P., Tudorache, T., Bernstein, A., Welty, C., Knoblock, C., Vrandečić, D., Groth, P., Noy, N., Janowicz, K., Goble, C. (eds.) ISWC 2014. LNCS, vol. 8796, pp. 50–65. Springer, Cham (2014). https://doi.org/10.1007/978-3-319-11964-9_4
10. Garcia-Duran, A., Dumančić, S., Niepert, M.: Learning sequence encoders for temporal knowledge graph completion. In: Proceedings of the 2018 Conference on Empirical Methods in Natural Language Processing, pp. 4816–4821 (2018)
11. Glorot, X., Bengio, Y.: Understanding the difficulty of training deep feedforward neural networks. In: Proceedings of the Thirteenth International Conference on Artificial Intelligence and Statistics, pp. 249–256. JMLR Workshop and Conference Proceedings (2010)

12. Glorot, X., Bordes, A., Bengio, Y.: Deep sparse rectifier neural networks. In: Proceedings of the Fourteenth International Conference on Artificial Intelligence and Statistics, pp. 315–323. JMLR Workshop and Conference Proceedings (2011)

13. Goel, R., Kazemi, S.M., Brubaker, M., Poupart, P.: Diachronic embedding for temporal knowledge graph completion. In: Proceedings of the AAAI Conference on Artificial Intelligence, vol. 34, pp. 3988–3995 (2020)

14. Guo, Q., et al.: A survey on knowledge graph-based recommender systems. IEEE Trans. Knowl. Data Eng. (2020)

15. Jain, P., Rathi, S., Chakrabarti, S., et al.: Temporal knowledge base completion: New algorithms and evaluation protocols. In: Proceedings of the 2020 Conference on Empirical Methods in Natural Language Processing (EMNLP), pp. 3733–3747 (2020)

16. Ji, G., He, S., Xu, L., Liu, K., Zhao, J.: Knowledge graph embedding via dynamic mapping matrix. In: Proceedings of the 53rd Annual Meeting of the Association for Computational Linguistics and the 7th International Joint Conference on Natural Language Processing (volume 1: Long papers), pp. 687–696 (2015)

17. Jin, T., Liu, Z., Yan, S., Eichenberger, A., Morency, L.P.: Language to network: Conditional parameter adaptation with natural language descriptions. In: Proceedings of the 58th Annual Meeting of the Association for Computational Linguistics (2020)

18. Jin, W., Qu, M., Jin, X., Ren, X.: Recurrent event network: autoregressive structure inferenceover temporal knowledge graphs. In: Proceedings of the 2020 Conference on Empirical Methods in Natural Language Processing (EMNLP), pp. 6669–6683 (2020)

19. Kazemi, S.M., Poole, D.: Simple embedding for link prediction in knowledge graphs. In: Proceedings of the 32nd International Conference on Neural Information Processing Systems, pp. 4289–4300 (2018)

20. Kingma, D.P., Ba, J.: Adam: a method for stochastic optimization. In: Proceedings of 3rd International Conference on Learning Representations (2015)

21. Lacroix, T., Obozinski, G., Usunier, N.: Tensor decompositions for temporal knowledge base completion. In: International Conference on Learning Representations (2020)

22. Lacroix, T., Usunier, N., Obozinski, G.: Canonical tensor decomposition for knowledge base completion. In: International Conference on Machine Learning, pp. 2863–2872. PMLR (2018)

23. Leblay, J., Chekol, M.W.: Deriving validity time in knowledge graph. In: Companion Proceedings of the The Web Conference 2018, pp. 1771–1776 (2018)

24. Lin, Y., Liu, Z., Sun, M., Liu, Y., Zhu, X.: Learning entity and relation embeddings for knowledge graph completion. In: Twenty-Ninth AAAI Conference on Artificial Intelligence (2015)

25. Van der Maaten, L., Hinton, G.: Visualizing data using t-sne. J. Mach. Learn. Res. 9(11) (2008)

26. Mahdisoltani, F., Biega, J., Suchanek, F.: Yago3: a knowledge base from multilingual wikipedias. In: 7th Biennial Conference on Innovative Data Systems Research. CIDR Conference (2014)

27. Messner, J., Abboud, R., Ceylan, I.I.: Temporal knowledge graph completion using box embeddings. In: Proceedings of the AAAI Conference on Artificial Intelligence (2022)

28. Nekvinda, T., Dušek, O.: One model, many languages: meta-learning for multilingual text-to-speech. Proc. Interspeech **2020**, 2972–2976 (2020)

29. Nickel, M., Tresp, V., Kriegel, H.P.: A three-way model for collective learning on multi-relational data. In: Proceedings of the 28th International Conference on International Conference on Machine Learning, pp. 809–816 (2011)

30. Paszke, A., et al.: Pytorch: an imperative style, high-performance deep learning library. In: Proceedings of the 33rd International Conference on Neural Information Processing Systems, pp. 8026–8037 (2019)

31. Platanios, E.A., Sachan, M., Neubig, G., Mitchell, T.: Contextual parameter generation for universal neural machine translation. In: Proceedings of the 2018 Conference on Empirical Methods in Natural Language Processing, pp. 425–435 (2018)

32. Sadeghian, A., Armandpour, M., Colas, A., Wang, D.Z.: Chronor: rotation based temporal knowledge graph embedding. In: Proceedings of the AAAI Conference on Artificial Intelligence, vol. 35, pp. 6471–6479 (2021)

33. Saxena, A., Tripathi, A., Talukdar, P.: Improving multi-hop question answering over knowledge graphs using knowledge base embeddings. In: Proceedings of the 58th Annual Meeting of the Association for Computational Linguistics, pp. 4498–4507 (2020)

34. Shao, P., Zhang, D., Yang, G., Tao, J., Che, F., Liu, T.: Tucker decomposition-based temporal knowledge graph completion. Knowl.-Based Syst. **238**, 107841 (2022)

35. Stoica, G., Stretcu, O., Platanios, E.A., Mitchell, T., Póczos, B.: Contextual parameter generation for knowledge graph link prediction. In: Proceedings of the AAAI Conference on Artificial Intelligence, vol. 34, pp. 3000–3008 (2020)

36. Sun, Z., Deng, Z.H., Nie, J.Y., Tang, J.: Rotate: Knowledge graph embedding by relational rotation in complex space. In: International Conference on Learning Representations (2019)

37. Trouillon, T., Welbl, J., Riedel, S., Gaussier, É., Bouchard, G.: Complex embeddings for simple link prediction. In: Proceedings of the 33rd International Conference on International Conference on Machine Learning-Volume 48, pp. 2071–2080 (2016)

38. Vashishth, S., Sanyal, S., Nitin, V., Agrawal, N., Talukdar, P.: Interacte: improving convolution-based knowledge graph embeddings by increasing feature interactions. In: Proceedings of the AAAI Conference on Artificial Intelligence, vol. 34, pp. 3009–3016 (2020)

39. Wang, Z., Zhang, J., Feng, J., Chen, Z.: Knowledge graph embedding by translating on hyperplanes. In: Proceedings of the AAAI Conference on Artificial Intelligence, vol. 28 (2014)

40. Wu, J., Cao, M., Cheung, J.C.K., Hamilton, W.L.: Temp: temporal message passing for temporal knowledge graph completion. In: Proceedings of the 2020 Conference on Empirical Methods in Natural Language Processing (EMNLP), pp. 5730–5746 (2020)

41. Wu, J., Xu, Y., Zhang, Y., Ma, C., Coates, M., Cheung, J.C.K.: Tie: a framework for embedding-based incremental temporal knowledge graph completion. In: Proceedings of the 44th International ACM SIGIR Conference on Research and Development in Information Retrieval, pp. 428–437 (2021)

42. Xu, C., Chen, Y.Y., Nayyeri, M., Lehmann, J.: Temporal knowledge graph completion using a linear temporal regularizer and multivector embeddings. In: Proceedings of the 2021 Conference of the North American Chapter of the Association for Computational Linguistics: Human Language Technologies, pp. 2569–2578 (2021)

43. Xu, C., Nayyeri, M., Alkhoury, F., Yazdi, H.S., Lehmann, J.: Tero: a time-aware knowledge graph embedding via temporal rotation. In: Proceedings of the 28th International Conference on Computational Linguistics, pp. 1583–1593 (2020)

44. Xu, C., Nayyeri, M., Alkhoury, F., Yazdi, H., Lehmann, J.: Temporal knowledge graph completion based on time series gaussian embedding. In: Pan, J.Z., et al. (eds.) ISWC 2020. LNCS, vol. 12506, pp. 654–671. Springer, Cham (2020). https://doi.org/10.1007/978-3-030-62419-4_37
45. Xu, Y., et al.: Rtfe: a recursive temporal fact embedding framework for temporal knowledge graph completion. In: Proceedings of the 2021 Conference of the North American Chapter of the Association for Computational Linguistics: Human Language Technologies, pp. 5671–5681 (2021)
46. Yang, B., Yih, S.W.t., He, X., Gao, J., Deng, L.: Embedding entities and relations for learning and inference in knowledge bases. In: Proceedings of the International Conference on Learning Representations (ICLR) 2015 (2015)
47. Zhang, S., Tay, Y., Yao, L., Liu, Q.: Quaternion knowledge graph embeddings. In: Proceedings of the 33rd International Conference on Neural Information Processing Systems, pp. 2735–2745 (2019)
48. Zhang, Z., Zhuang, F., Zhu, H., Shi, Z., Xiong, H., He, Q.: Relational graph neural network with hierarchical attention for knowledge graph completion. In: Proceedings of the AAAI Conference on Artificial Intelligence, vol. 34, pp. 9612–9619 (2020)

Efficient Dependency Analysis
for Rule-Based Ontologies

Larry González[ID], Alex Ivliev[(✉)][ID], Markus Krötzsch[ID],
and Stephan Mennicke[ID]

Knowledge-Based Systems Group, TU Dresden, Dresden, Germany
{larry.gonzalez,alex.ivliev,markus.kroetzsch,
stephan.mennicke}@tu-dresden.de

Abstract. Several types of *dependencies* have been proposed for the
static analysis of existential rule ontologies, promising insights about computational properties and possible practical uses of a given set of rules, e.g.,
in ontology-based query answering. Unfortunately, these dependencies are
rarely implemented, so their potential is hardly realised in practice. We
focus on two kinds of rule dependencies – *positive reliances* and *restraints*
– and design and implement optimised algorithms for their efficient computation. Experiments on real-world ontologies of up to more than 100,000
rules show the scalability of our approach, which lets us realise several previously proposed applications as practical case studies. In particular, we
can analyse to what extent rule-based bottom-up approaches of reasoning can be guaranteed to yield redundancy-free "lean" knowledge graphs
(so-called *cores*) on practical ontologies.

Keywords: Existential rules · Chase algorithm · Rule dependencies ·
Acyclicity · Core stratification · Ontology-based query answering ·
Ontology reasoning

1 Introduction

Existential rules are a versatile knowledge representation language with relevance in ontological reasoning [1,5,6,10], databases [11,13,15], and declarative
computing in general [3,4,9]. In various semantic web applications, existential
rule engines have been used to process knowledge graphs and ontologies, often
realising performance advantages on large data sets [2,3,7,22].

Existential rules extend Datalog with the facility for *value invention*,
expressed by existentially quantified variables in conclusions. This ability to refer
to "unknown" values is an important similarity to description logics (DLs) and
the DL-based ontology standard OWL, and many such ontologies can equivalently be expressed in existential rules. This can be a practical approach for
ontology-based query answering [8,10]. For reasoning, many rule engines rely on
materialisation, where the input data is expanded iteratively until all rules are
satisfied (this type of computation is called *chase*). With existentials, this can
require adding new "anonymous" individuals – called *nulls* –, and the process

ⓒ The Author(s), under exclusive license to Springer Nature Switzerland AG 2022
U. Sattler et al. (Eds.): ISWC 2022, LNCS 13489, pp. 267–283, 2022.
https://doi.org/10.1007/978-3-031-19433-7_16

may not terminate. Several *acyclicity conditions* define cases where termination is ensured, and were shown to apply to many practical ontologies [10].

Nulls correspond to *blank nodes* in RDF, and – like bnodes in RDF [20] – are not always desirable. Avoiding nulls entirely is not an option in chase-based reasoning, but one can still avoid some "semantically redundant" nulls. For example, given a fact person(alice) and a rule $person(x) \rightarrow \exists y. parent(x, y)$, the chase would derive parent(alice, n) for a fresh null n. However, if we already know that parent(alice, bob), then this inference is redundant and can be omitted. In general, structures that are free of such redundancies are mathematically known as *cores*. An RDF-graph that is a core is called a *lean* graph [16]. Unfortunately, the computation of cores is expensive, and can in general not be afforded during the chase. Sometimes, however, when rules satisfy a condition known as *core stratification*, practical chase algorithms can also produce a core directly [17].

Interestingly, both of the previously mentioned types of conditions – acyclicity and core stratification – are detected by analysing *dependencies*[1] that indicate possible semantic interactions between rules. Early works focussed on cases where a rule ρ_2 *positively relies* on a rule ρ_1 in the sense that an application of rule ρ_1 might trigger an application of rule ρ_2. They are used to detect several forms of acyclity [1,11,21]. When adding negation, a rule might also inhibit another, and such *negative reliances* are used to define semantically well-behaved fragments of nonmonotonic existential rules [17,19]. A third kind of dependency are *restraints*, which indicate that the application of one rule might render another one redundant: restraints were used to define *core stratified rule sets* [17], and recently also to define a semantics for queries with negation [12].

Surprisingly, given this breadth of applications, rule dependencies are hardly supported in practice. To our knowledge, positive reliances are only computed by the Graal toolkit [2], whereas negative reliances and restraints have no implementation at all. A possible reason is that such dependency checks are highly intractable, typically Σ_2^P-complete, and therefore not easy to implement efficiently. This is critical since their proposed uses are often related to the choice of a rule-processing strategy, so that their computation adds to overall reasoning time. Moreover, as opposed to many other static analyses, dependency computation is not mainly an application of algorithms that are already used in rule reasoning. Today's use of dependencies in optimisation and analysis therefore falls short of expectations.

To address this problem, we design optimised algorithms for the computation of positive reliances and restraints. We propose *global* optimisations, reducing the number of relevant checks, and *local* optimisations, reducing the work needed to execute a specific check. The latter include an improved search strategy that often avoids the full exploration of exponentially many subsets of rule atoms, which may be necessary in the worst case. The underlying ideas can also be adapted to negative reliances and any of the modified definitions of positive reliances found in the literature.

---

[1] We use the term only informally, since *(tuple-generating) dependencies* are also a common name for rules in databases.

We implement our methods and conduct extensive experiments with over 200 real-world ontologies of varying sizes. Considering the effectiveness of our optimisations, we find that local and global techniques both make important contributions to overall performance, enabling various practical uses:

- We conduct the first analysis of the practical prevalence of *core stratification* [17] using our implementation of restraints. We find this desirable property in a significant share of ontologies from a curated repository and provide preliminary insights on why some rule sets are not core stratified.
- Comparing the computation of all positive reliances to Graal, we see speed-ups of more than two orders of magnitude. Our stronger definition yields an *acyclic graph of rule dependencies* [1] in more cases.
- The graph of positive reliances allows for showing how to speed up the expensive rule analysis algorithm *MFA* [10]. Compared to the MFA implementation of VLog [7], we observe speed-ups of up to four orders of magnitude.

2   Preliminaries

We build expressions from countably infinite, mutually disjoint sets $\mathbf{V}$ of *variables*, $\mathbf{C}$ of *constants*, $\mathbf{N}$ of *labelled nulls*, and $\mathbf{P}$ of *predicate names*. Each predicate name $p \in \mathbf{P}$ has an *arity* $\mathsf{ar}(p) \geq 0$. *Terms* are elements of $\mathbf{V} \cup \mathbf{N} \cup \mathbf{C}$. We use t to denote a list $t_1, \ldots, t_{|t|}$ of terms, and similar for special types of terms. An *atom* is an expression $p(t)$ with $p \in \mathbf{P}$, t a list of terms, and $\mathsf{ar}(p) = |t|$. *Ground* terms or atoms contain neither variables nor nulls. An *interpretation* $\mathcal{I}$ is a set of atoms without variables. A *database* $\mathcal{D}$ is a finite set of ground atoms.

Syntax. An *existential rule* (or just *rule*) ρ is a formula

$$\rho = \forall \boldsymbol{x}, \boldsymbol{y}. \, \varphi[\boldsymbol{x}, \boldsymbol{y}] \rightarrow \exists \boldsymbol{z}. \, \psi[\boldsymbol{y}, \boldsymbol{z}], \tag{1}$$

where φ and ψ are conjunctions of atoms using only terms from $\mathbf{C}$ or from the mutually disjoint lists of variables $\boldsymbol{x}, \boldsymbol{y}, \boldsymbol{z} \subseteq \mathbf{V}$. We call φ the *body* (denoted $\mathsf{body}(\rho)$) and ψ the *head* (denoted $\mathsf{head}(\rho)$). We may treat conjunctions of atoms as sets, and we omit universal quantifiers in rules. We require that all variables in $\boldsymbol{y}$ do really occur in φ (*safety*). A rule is *Datalog* if it has no existential quantifiers.

Semantics. Given a set of atoms $\mathcal{A}$ and an interpretation $\mathcal{I}$, a *homomorphism* $h \colon \mathcal{A} \rightarrow \mathcal{I}$ is a function that maps the terms occurring in $\mathcal{A}$ to the (variable-free) terms occurring in $\mathcal{I}$, such that: (i) for all $c \in \mathbf{C}$, $h(c) = c$; (ii) for all $p \in \mathbf{P}$, $p(t) \in \mathcal{A}$ implies $p(h(t)) \in \mathcal{I}$, where $h(t)$ is the list of h-images of the terms t. If (ii) can be strengthened to an "if, and only if", then h is *strong*. We apply homomorphisms to a formula by applying them individually to all of its terms.

A *match* of a rule ρ in an interpretation $\mathcal{I}$ is a homomorphism $\mathsf{body}(\rho) \rightarrow \mathcal{I}$. A match h of ρ in $\mathcal{I}$ is *satisfied* if there is a homomorphism $h' \colon \mathsf{head}(\rho) \rightarrow \mathcal{I}$ that agrees with h on all variables that occur in body and head (i.e., variables $\boldsymbol{y}$ in (1)). Rule ρ is *satisfied* by $\mathcal{I}$, written $\mathcal{I} \models \rho$, if every match of ρ in $\mathcal{I}$ is satisfied. A set of rules Σ is satisfied by $\mathcal{I}$, written $\mathcal{I} \models \Sigma$, if $\mathcal{I} \models \rho$ for all $\rho \in \Sigma$. We write $\mathcal{I} \models \mathcal{D}, \Sigma$ to express that $\mathcal{I} \models \Sigma$ and $\mathcal{D} \subseteq \mathcal{I}$. In this case, $\mathcal{I}$ is a *model* of Σ and $\mathcal{D}$.

Applying Rules. A rule ρ of form (1) is *applicable* to an interpretation $\mathcal{I}$ if there is an unsatisfied match h in $\mathcal{I}$ (i.e., h cannot be extended to a homomorphism $\psi \rightarrow \mathcal{I}$). Applying ρ for h yields the interpretation $\mathcal{I} \cup \psi[h'(\boldsymbol{y}), h'(\boldsymbol{z})]$, where h' is a mapping such that $h'(y) = h(y)$ for all $y \in \boldsymbol{y}$, and for all $z \in \boldsymbol{z}$, $h'(z) \in \mathbf{N}$ is a distinct null not occurring in $\mathcal{I}$. The *(standard) chase* is a reasoning algorithm obtained by applying rules to a given initial database, such that all applicable rules are eventually applied (fairness).

Core Models. A model $\mathcal{I}$ is a *core* if every homomorphism $h : \mathcal{I} \rightarrow \mathcal{I}$ is strong and injective. For finite models, this is equivalent to the requirement that every such homomorphism is an isomorphism, and this will be the only case we are interested in for this work. Intuitively, the condition states that the model does not contain a strictly smaller substructure that is semantically equivalent for conjunctive query answering.

Unification. For atom sets $\mathcal{A}$ and $\mathcal{B}$, partial function $m : \mathcal{A} \rightarrow \mathcal{B}$ is an *atom mapping*, where $\mathsf{dom}(m) \subseteq \mathcal{A}$ is the set of all atoms for which m is defined. A *substitution* is a function $\theta : \mathbf{C} \cup \mathbf{V} \cup \mathbf{N} \rightarrow \mathbf{C} \cup \mathbf{V} \cup \mathbf{N}$, such that $\theta(c) = c$ for all $c \in \mathbf{C} \cup \mathbf{N}$. Denote the application of θ to term t by $t\theta$, naturally extending to atoms and atom sets by term-wise application. The concatenation of substitutions σ and θ is $\sigma\theta$ where $t\sigma\theta = (t\sigma)\theta$. A substitution is a *unifier* for atom mapping m if for all $\alpha \in \mathsf{dom}(m)$, $\alpha\theta = (m(\alpha))\theta$. A unifier μ for m is a *most general unifier* (mgu) for m if for all unifiers ν of m, there is a substitution σ, such that $\mu\sigma = \nu$.

3   Dependencies and Their Naive Computation

We first introduce the two kinds of rule dependencies that we consider: *positive reliances* and *restraints*. Our definitions largely agree with the literature, but there are some small differences that we comment on.

Definition 1. *A rule ρ_2 positively relies on a rule ρ_1, written $\rho_1 \prec^+ \rho_2$, if there are interpretations $\mathcal{I}_a \subseteq \mathcal{I}_b$ and a function h_2 such that*

(a) $\mathcal{I}_b$ is obtained from $\mathcal{I}_a$ by applying ρ_1 for the match h_1 extended to h'_1,
(b) h_2 is an unsatisfied match for ρ_2 on $\mathcal{I}_b$, and
(c) h_2 is not a match for ρ_2 on $\mathcal{I}_a$.

Definition 1 describes a situation where an application of ρ_1 immediately enables a new application of ρ_2. Condition (b) takes into account that only unsatisfied matches can lead to rule applications in the standard chase. The same condition is used by Krötzsch [17], whereas Baget et al. [1, 2] – using what they call *piece-unifier* – only require h_2 to be a match. In general, weaker definitions are not incorrect, but may lead to unnecessary dependencies.

Example 1. Consider the following ontology. We provide three axioms in DL syntax (left-hand side) and their translation into existential rules (right-hand side).

$$A \sqsubseteq \exists R.B \qquad\qquad a(x) \rightarrow \exists v.\, r(x, v) \wedge b(v) \qquad (\rho_1)$$
$$R^- \circ R \sqsubseteq T \qquad\qquad r(y, z_1) \wedge r(y, z_2) \rightarrow t(z_1, z_2) \qquad (\rho_2)$$
$$\exists R^-.A \sqsubseteq B \qquad\qquad a(t) \wedge r(t, u) \rightarrow b(u) \qquad (\rho_3)$$

For this rule set, we find $\rho_1 \prec^+ \rho_2$ by using $\mathcal{I}_a = \{a(c)\}$, $\mathcal{I}_b = \{a(c), r(c, n)\}$, and $h_2 = \{y \mapsto c, z_1 \mapsto n, z_2 \mapsto n\}$. Note that ρ_3 does not positively rely on ρ_1 although the application of ρ_1 may lead to a new match for ρ_3. However, this match is always satisfied, so condition (b) of Definition 1 is not fulfilled.

The definition of restraints considers situations where the nulls introduced by applying rule ρ_2 are at least in part rendered obsolete by a later application of ρ_1. This obsolescence is witnessed by an *alternative match* that specifies a different way of satisfying the rule match of ρ_2.

Definition 2. *Let* $\mathcal{I}_a \subseteq \mathcal{I}_b$ *be interpretations such that* $\mathcal{I}_a$ *was obtained by applying the rule* ρ *for match* h *which is extended to* h'. *A homomorphism* $h^A \colon h'(\mathsf{head}(\rho)) \rightarrow \mathcal{I}_b$ *is an* alternative match *of* h' *and* ρ *on* $\mathcal{I}_b$ *if*

(1) $h^A(t) = t$ *for all terms* t *in* $h(\mathsf{body}(\rho))$, *and*
(2) there is a null n *in* $h'(\mathsf{head}(\rho))$ *that does not occur in* $h^A(h'(\mathsf{head}(\rho)))$.

Now ρ_1 restrains ρ_2 if it creates an alternative match for it:

Definition 3. *A rule* ρ_1 restrains *a rule* ρ_2, *written* $\rho_1 \prec^\square \rho_2$, *if there are interpretations* $\mathcal{I}_a \subseteq \mathcal{I}_b$ *such that*

(a) $\mathcal{I}_b$ *is obtained by applying* ρ_1 *for match* h_1 *extended to* h'_1,
(b) $\mathcal{I}_a$ *is obtained by applying* ρ_2 *for match* h_2 *extended to* h'_2,
(c) there is an alternative match h^A *of* h'_2 *and* ρ_2 *on* $\mathcal{I}_b$, *and*
(d) h^A *is no alternative match of* h'_2 *and* ρ_2 *on* $\mathcal{I}_b \setminus h'_1(\mathsf{head}(\rho_1))$.

Our definition slightly deviates from the literature [17], where (d) made a stronger requirement:

(d') h_2 *has no alternative match* $h'_2(\mathsf{head}(\rho_2)) \rightarrow \mathcal{I}_b \setminus h'_1(\mathsf{head}(\rho_1))$.

As we will see, our modification allows for a much more efficient implementation, but it also leads to more restraints. Since restraints overestimate potential interactions during the chase anyway, all formal results of prior works are preserved.

Example 2. For the rules $\rho_1 = r(y,y) \rightarrow \exists w. r(y,w) \wedge b(w)$ and $\rho_2 = a(x) \rightarrow \exists v. r(x,v)$, we find $\rho_1 \prec^\square \rho_2$ by Definition 3, where we set $\mathcal{I}_a = \{a(c), r(c, n_1)\}$, $\mathcal{I}_b = \mathcal{I}_a \cup \{r(c,c), r(c, n_2), b(n_2)\}$, and $h^A = \{c \mapsto c, n_1 \mapsto n_2\}$. However, these $\mathcal{I}_a$ and $\mathcal{I}_b$ do not satisfy the stricter condition (d'), since $h^B = \{c \mapsto c, n_1 \mapsto c\}$ is an alternative match, too. Indeed, when ρ_2 is applicable in such a way as to produce an alternative match w.r.t. an application of ρ_1, another one must have already existed.

Example 2 is representative of situations where (d) leads to different restraints than (d'): the body of the restraining rule ρ_1 must contain a pattern that enforces an additional alternative match (here: $r(y,y)$), while not being satisfiable by the conclusion of ρ_2 (here: $r(y, n_1)$). To satisfy the remaining conditions, head(ρ_1) must further produce a (distinct) alternative match. Such situations are very rare in practice, so that the benefits of (d) outweigh the loss of generality.

Checking for positive reliances and restraints is Σ_2^P-complete. Indeed, we can assume $\mathcal{I}_a$ and $\mathcal{I}_b$ to contain at most as many elements as there are distinct terms in the rule, so that they can be polynomially guessed. The remaining conditions can be checked by an NP-oracle. Hardness follows from the Σ_2^P-hardness of deciding if a rule has an unsatisfied match [15].

The existence of alternative matches in a chase sequence indicates that the resulting model may contain redundant nulls. Ordering the application of rules during the chase in a way that obeys the restraint relationship ($\prec^\square$) ensures that the chase sequence does not contain any alternative matches and therefore results in a core model [17].

Example 3. Consider again the rule set from Example 1. For the interpretation $\mathcal{I}_0 = \{a(c), r(c,d)\}$ all three rules are applicable. Disregarding $\rho_3 \prec^\square \rho_1$ and applying ρ_1 first results in $\mathcal{I}_1 = \mathcal{I}_0 \cup \{r(c,n), b(n)\}$, which leads to the alternative match $h^A = \{c \mapsto c, n \mapsto d\}$ after applying ρ_3. If we, on the other hand, start with ρ_3, we obtain $\mathcal{I}_1' = \mathcal{I}_0 \cup \{b(d)\}$. Rule ρ_1 is now satisfied and the computation finishes with a core model after applying ρ_2.

The ontology from Example 1 is an example of a *core stratified* rule set. A set of rules is *core stratified* if the graph of all $\prec^+ \cup \prec^\square$ edges does not have a cycle that includes a $\prec^\square$ edge. This property allows us to formulate a rule application strategy that respects the restraint relationship as follows: Given $\rho_1 \prec^\square \rho_2$, apply the restrained rule ρ_2 only if neither ρ_1 nor any of the rules ρ_1 directly or indirectly positively relies on is applicable.

4   Computing Positive Reliances

The observation that positive reliances can be decided in Σ_2^P is based on an algorithm that considers all possible sets $\mathcal{I}_a$ and $\mathcal{I}_b$ up to a certain size. This is not practical, in particular for uses where dependencies need to be computed as part of the (performance-critical) reasoning, and we therefore develop a more goal-oriented approach.

In the following, we consider two rules ρ_1 and ρ_2 of form $\rho_i = \mathsf{body}_i \to \exists \mathbf{z}_i. \mathsf{head}_i$, with variables renamed so that no variable occurs in both rules. Let $\mathbf{V}_\forall$ and $\mathbf{V}_\exists$, respectively, denote the sets of universally and existentially quantified variables in ρ_1 and ρ_2. A first insight is that the sets $\mathcal{I}_a$ and $\mathcal{I}_b$ of Definition 1 can be assumed to contain only atoms that correspond to atoms in ρ_1 and ρ_2, with distinct universal or existential variables replaced by distinct constants or nulls, respectively. For this replacement, we fix a substitution ω that maps each variable in $\mathbf{V}_\exists$ to a distinct null, and each variable in $\mathbf{V}_\forall$ to a distinct constant that does not occur in ρ_1 or ρ_2.

Algorithm 1: extend$^+$

Input: rules ρ_1, ρ_2, atom mapping m
Output: *true* iff the atom mapping can be extended successfully

1   **for** $i \in \{\mathtt{maxidx}(m) + 1, \ldots, |\mathsf{body}_2|\}$ **do**
2   **for** $j \in \{1, \ldots, |\mathsf{head}_1|\}$ **do**
3       $m' \leftarrow m \cup \{\mathsf{body}_2[i] \mapsto \mathsf{head}_1[j]\omega_\exists\}$
4   **if** $\eta \leftarrow \mathtt{unify}(m')$ **then**
5   **if** $\mathtt{check}^+(\rho_1, \rho_2, m', \eta)$ **then return** *true*

6   **return** *false*

A second insight is that, by (c), ρ_1 must produce some atoms that are relevant for a match of ρ_2, so that our algorithm can specifically search for a *mapped subset* $\mathsf{body}_2^m \subseteq \mathsf{body}_2$ and a substitution η such that $\mathsf{body}_2^m \eta \subseteq \mathsf{head}_1 \eta$. Note that η represents both matches h_1 and h_2 from Definition 1, which is possible since variables in ρ_1 and ρ_2 are disjoint. The corresponding set $\mathcal{I}_a$ then is $(\mathsf{body}_1 \cup (\mathsf{body}_2 \setminus \mathsf{body}_2^m))\eta\omega$. Unfortunately, it does not suffice to consider singleton sets for body_2^m, as shown by Example 4:

Example 4. Consider the rules from Example 1. Trying to map either one of the atoms of $\mathsf{body}(\rho_2)$ to $\mathsf{head}(\rho_1)$ yields an $\mathcal{I}_a = \{a(c), r(c, c')\}$, to which ρ_1 is not applicable. The correct $\mathcal{I}_a = \{a(c)\}$ as given in Example 1 is found by unifying both atoms of $\mathsf{body}(\rho_2)$ with (an instance of) $\mathsf{head}(\rho_1)$.

Therefore, we have to analyse all subsets $\mathsf{body}_2^m \subseteq \mathsf{body}_2$ for possible matches with head_1. We start the search from singleton sets, which are successively extended by adding atoms. A final important insight is that this search can often be aborted early, since a candidate pair for $\mathcal{I}_a$ and $\mathcal{I}_b$ may fail Definition 1 for various reasons, and considering a larger body_2^m is not always promising. For example, if η is a satisfied match for ρ_2 over $\mathcal{I}_b$ (b), then adding more atoms to body_2^m will never succeed.

These ideas are implemented in Algorithms 1 ($\texttt{extend}^+$) and 2 ($\texttt{check}^+$), explained next. For a substitution θ, we write $\theta_\forall$ ($\theta_\exists$, resp.), to denote the substitution assigning existential variables (universal variables, resp.) to themselves, and otherwise agrees with θ.

Function $\texttt{extend}^+$ iterates over extensions of a given candidate set. To specify how atoms of body_2 are mapped to head_1, we maintain an atom mapping $m \colon \text{body}_2 \to \text{head}_1$ whose domain $\text{dom}(m)$ corresponds to the chosen $\text{body}_2^m \subseteq \text{body}_2$. To check for the positive reliance, we initially call $\texttt{extend}^+(\rho_1, \rho_2, \emptyset)$. Note that ρ_1 and ρ_2 can be based on the same rule (a rule can positively rely on itself); we still use two variants that ensure disjoint variable names.

Algorithm 2: $\texttt{check}^+$

Input: rules ρ_1, ρ_2, atom mapping m with mgu η
Output: *true* if a positive reliance is found for m

7 $\text{body}_2^m \leftarrow \text{dom}(m)$
8 $\text{body}_2^\ell \leftarrow \{\text{body}_2[j] \in (\text{body}_2 \setminus \text{body}_2^m) \mid j < \texttt{maxidx}(m)\}$
9 $\text{body}_2^r \leftarrow \{\text{body}_2[j] \in (\text{body}_2 \setminus \text{body}_2^m) \mid j > \texttt{maxidx}(m)\}$
10 **if** $\text{body}_1\eta$ *contains a null* **then return** *false*
11 **if** $\text{body}_2^\ell\eta$ *contains a null* **then return** *false*
12 **if** $\text{body}_2^r\eta$ *contains a null* **then return** $\texttt{extend}^+(\rho_1, \rho_2, m)$
13 $\mathcal{I}_a \leftarrow (\text{body}_1 \cup \text{body}_2^\ell \cup \text{body}_2^r)\eta\omega$
14 **if** $\mathcal{I}_a \models \exists z_1. \text{head}_1\eta\omega_\forall$ **then return** $\texttt{extend}^+(\rho_1, \rho_2, m)$
15 **if** $\text{body}_2\eta\omega \subseteq \mathcal{I}_a$ **then return** $\texttt{extend}^+(\rho_1, \rho_2, m)$
16 $\mathcal{I}_b \leftarrow \mathcal{I}_a \cup \text{head}_1\eta\omega$
17 **if** $\mathcal{I}_b \models \exists z_2. \text{head}_2\eta\omega_\forall$ **then return** *false*
18 **return** *true*

We treat rule bodies and heads as lists of atoms, and write $\varphi[i]$ for the ith atom in φ. The expression $\texttt{maxidx}(m)$ returns the largest index of an atom in $\text{dom}(m)$, or 0 if $\text{dom}(m) = \emptyset$. By extending m only with atoms of larger index (L1), we ensure that each $\text{dom}(m)$ is only considered once. We then construct each possible extension of m (L3), where we replace existential variables by fresh nulls in head_1. In Line 4, $\texttt{unify}(m')$ is the most general unifier η of m' or undefined if m' cannot be unified. With variables, constants, and nulls as the only terms, unification is an easy polynomial algorithm.

Processing continues with $\texttt{check}^+$, called in Line 5 of $\texttt{extend}^+$. We first partition body_2 into the matched atoms body_2^m, and the remaining atoms to the left body_2^ℓ and right body_2^r of the maximal index of m. Only body_2^r can still be considered for extending m. Six if-blocks check all conditions of Definition 1, and *true* is returned if all checks succeed. When a check fails, the search is either stopped (L10, L11, and L17) or recursively continued with an extended mapping (L12, L14, and L15). The three checks in L10–L12 cover cases where $\mathcal{I}_a$ (L13) would need to contain nulls that are freshly introduced by ρ_1 only later. L10 applies, e.g., when checking $\rho_2 \prec^+ \rho_1$ for ρ_1, ρ_2 as in Example 2, where we would get $a(n) \in \mathcal{I}_a$ (note the swap of rule names compared to our present algorithm).

Further extensions of m are useless for L10, since they could only lead to more specific unifiers, and also for L11, where nulls occur in "earlier" atoms that are not considered in extensions of m. For case L12, however, moving further atoms from body_2^r to body_2^m might be promising, so we call $\mathtt{extend}^+$ there.

In L14, we check if the constructed match of ρ_1 on $\mathcal{I}_a$ is already satisfied. This might again be fixed by extending the mapping, since doing so makes body_2^r and hence $\mathcal{I}_a$ smaller. If we reach L15, we have established condition (a) of Definition 1. L15 then ensures condition (c), which might again be repaired by extending the atom mapping so as to make $\mathcal{I}_a$ smaller. Finally, L17 checks condition (b). If this fails, we can abort the search: unifying more atoms of body_2 with head_1 will only lead to a more specific $\mathcal{I}_b$ and η, for which the check would still fail.

Theorem 1. *For rules ρ_1 and ρ_2 that (w.l.o.g.) do not share variables, $\rho_1 \prec^+ \rho_2$ iff $\mathtt{extend}^+(\rho_1,\rho_2,\emptyset) = true$.*

5   Computing Restraints

We now turn our attention to the efficient computation of restraints. In spite of the rather different definitions, many of the ideas from Sect. 4 can also be applied here. The main observation is that the search for an alternative match can be realised by unifying a part of head_2 with head_1 in a way that resembles our unification of body_2 with head_1 in Sect. 4.

To realise this, we define a function $\mathtt{extend}^\square$ as a small modification of Algorithm 1, where we simply replace body_2 in L1 and L3 by head_2, and $\mathtt{check}^+$ in L5 by $\mathtt{check}^\square$, which is defined in Algorithm 3 and explained next.

Algorithm 3: $\mathtt{check}^\square$

Input: rules ρ_1, ρ_2, atom mapping m with mgu η
Output: *true* if a restraint is found for m

19 $\mathsf{head}_2^m \leftarrow \mathrm{dom}(m)$
20 $\mathsf{head}_2^\ell \leftarrow \{\mathsf{head}_2[j] \in (\mathsf{head}_2 \setminus \mathsf{head}_2^m) \mid j < \mathtt{maxidx}(m)\}$
21 $\mathsf{head}_2^r \leftarrow \{\mathsf{head}_2[j] \in (\mathsf{head}_2 \setminus \mathsf{head}_2^m) \mid j > \mathtt{maxidx}(m)\}$
22 **if** $x\eta \in \mathbf{N}$ *for some* $x \in \mathbf{V}_\forall$ **then return** *false*
23 **if** $z\eta \in \mathbf{N}$ *for some* $z \in \mathbf{V}_\exists$ *in* head_2^ℓ **then return** *false*
24 **if** $z\eta \in \mathbf{N}$ *for some* $z \in \mathbf{V}_\exists$ *in* head_2^r **then**
25   **return** $\mathtt{extend}^\square(\rho_1,\rho_2,m)$

26 **if** head_2^m *contains no existential variables* **then**
27   **return** $\mathtt{extend}^\square(\rho_1,\rho_2,m)$

28 $\tilde{\mathcal{I}}_a \leftarrow \mathsf{body}_2 \eta_\forall \omega_\forall$
29 **if** $\tilde{\mathcal{I}}_a \models \exists z_2. \mathsf{head}_2 \eta_\forall \omega_\forall$ **then return** *false*
30 $\mathcal{I}_a \leftarrow \tilde{\mathcal{I}}_a \cup \mathsf{head}_2 \eta_\forall \omega$
31 $\tilde{\mathcal{I}}_b \leftarrow \mathcal{I}_a \cup (\mathsf{body}_1 \cup \mathsf{head}_2^\ell \cup \mathsf{head}_2^r)\eta\omega$
32 **if** $\tilde{\mathcal{I}}_b \models \exists z_1. \mathsf{head}_1 \eta_\forall \omega_\forall$ **then return** $\mathtt{extend}^\square(\rho_1,\rho_2,m)$
33 **if** $\mathsf{head}_2 \eta\omega \subseteq \tilde{\mathcal{I}}_b$ **then return** $\mathtt{extend}^\square(\rho_1,\rho_2,m)$
34 **return** *true*

We use the notation for ρ_1, ρ_2, ω, $\mathbf{V}_\exists$, and $\mathbf{V}_\forall$ as introduced in Sect. 4, and again use atom mapping m to represent our current hypothesis for a possible match. What is new now is that unified atoms in $\mathsf{dom}(m)$ can contain existentially quantified variables, though existential variables in the range of m (from head_1) are still replaced by nulls as in Algorithm 1, L5. An existential variable in head_2 might therefore be unified with a constant, null, or universal variable of head_1. In the last case, where we need a unifier η with $z\eta = x\eta$ for $z \in \mathbf{V}_\exists$ and $x \in \mathbf{V}_\forall$, we require that $x\eta = z\eta \in \mathbf{V}_\forall$ so that η only maps to variables in $\mathbf{V}_\forall$. η simultaneously represents the matches h_1, h_2, and h^A from Definition 3.

Example 5. For rules $\rho_1 = r(x,y) \to s(x,x,y)$ and $\rho_2 = a(z) \to \exists v.\, s(z,v,v) \wedge b(v)$, and mapping $m = \{s(z,v,v) \mapsto s(x,x,y)\}$, we obtain a unifier η that maps all variables to x (we could also use y, but not the existential v). Let $x\omega = c$ be the constant that x is instantiated with. Then we can apply ρ_2 to $\tilde{\mathcal{I}}_a = \{a(z)\eta\omega\} = \{a(c)\}$ with match $h_2 = \{z \mapsto c, v \mapsto n\}$ to get $\mathcal{I}_a = \tilde{\mathcal{I}}_a \cup \{s(c,n,n), b(n)\}$, and ρ_1 to $\tilde{\mathcal{I}}_b = \mathcal{I}_a \cup \{r(c,c), b(c)\}$ with match $h_1 = \{x \mapsto c, y \mapsto c\}$ to get $\mathcal{I}_b = \tilde{\mathcal{I}}_b \cup \{s(c,c,c)\}$. Note that we had to add $b(c)$ to obtain the required alternative match h^A, which maps n to $v\eta\omega = c$ and c to itself.

As in the example, a most general unifier η yields a candidate h^A that maps every null of the form $v\omega_\exists$ to $v\eta_\exists\omega_\forall$. Likewise, for $i \in \{1,2\}$, $h_i = \eta_\forall\omega$ are the (extended) matches, while $\eta_\forall\omega_\forall$ are the body matches. The image of the instantiated $\mathsf{head}_2\eta_\forall\omega$ under the alternative match h^A is given by $\mathsf{head}_2\eta\omega$. The corresponding interpretations are $\mathcal{I}_a = \mathsf{body}_2\eta_\forall\omega_\forall \cup \mathsf{head}_2\eta_\forall\omega$ and $\mathcal{I}_b = \mathcal{I}_a \cup \mathsf{body}_1\eta_\forall\omega_\forall \cup \mathsf{head}_1\eta_\forall\omega \cup (\mathsf{head} \setminus \mathsf{dom}(m))\eta\omega$, where $(\mathsf{head}_2 \setminus \mathsf{dom}(m))\eta\omega$ provides additional atoms required for the alternative match but not in the mapped atoms of head_2. With these intuitions, Algorithm 3 can already be understood.

It remains to explain the conditions that are checked before returning *true*. As before, we partition $\mathsf{dom}(m)$ into mapped atoms head_2^m and left and right remainder atoms. Checks in L22–L24 ensure that the only variables mapped by η to nulls (necessarily from $\mathsf{head}_1\omega_\exists$) are existential variables in head_2^m: such mappings are possible by h^A. Extending m further is only promising if the nulls only stem from atoms in head_2^r.

Check L26 continues the search when no atoms with existentials have been selected yet. Selecting other atoms first might be necessary by our order, but no alternative matches can exist for such mappings (yet). Lines L29 and L32 check that the matches h_1 and h_2 are indeed unsatisfied. Extending m might fix L29 by making $\tilde{\mathcal{I}}_a$ smaller, whereas L32 cannot be fixed. Finally, L33 ensures condition (d) of Definition 3.

Example 6. Consider rules $\rho_1 = b(x,y) \to r(x,y,x,y) \wedge q(x,y)$, $\rho_2 = a(u,v) \to \exists w.\, r(u,v,w,w) \wedge r(v,u,w,w)$, and mapping $m = \{r(u,v,w,w) \mapsto r(x,y,x,y)\}$. We obtain unifier η mapping all variables to a single universally quantified variable, say x. We reach $\tilde{\mathcal{I}}_b = \{a(c,c), r(c,c,n,n), b(c,c), r(c,c,c,c)\}$, based on $\tilde{\mathcal{I}}_a = \{a(c,c)\}$ ($x\omega = c$), for which ρ_1 is applicable but $h^A = \{n \mapsto c, c \mapsto c\}$ is already an alternative match on $\tilde{\mathcal{I}}_b$, recognized by L33.

Theorem 2. *For rules ρ_1 and ρ_2 that (w.l.o.g.) do not share variables, $\rho_1 \prec^{\square} \rho_2$ holds according to Definition 3 for some $\mathcal{I}_a \neq \mathcal{I}_b$ iff* $\mathtt{extend}^{\square}(\rho_1, \rho_2, \emptyset) = true$.

The case $\mathcal{I}_a = \mathcal{I}_b$, which Theorem 2 leaves out, is possible [17, Example 5], but requires a slightly different algorithm. We can adapt Algorithm 3 by restricting to one rule, for which we map from atoms in head to atoms in head$\omega_\exists$. The checks (for head$_2$) of Algorithm 3 remain as before, but we only need to compute a single $\mathcal{I}$ that plays the role of $\mathcal{I}_a$ and $\mathcal{I}_b$. Check L33 is replaced by a new check

if head $\eta_\exists$ = head $\omega_\exists$ **then return** *false* ;

ensuring that at least one null is mapped differently in the alternative match. With these modifications, we can show an analogous result to Theorem 2 for the case $\mathcal{I}_a = \mathcal{I}_b$.

6   Implementation and Global Optimisations

We provide a C++ implementation of our algorithms, which also includes some additional optimisations and methods as described next. Our prototype is build on top of the free rule engine VLog (Release 1.3.5) [23], so that we can use its facilities for loading rules and checking MFA (see Sect. 7). Reasoning algorithms of VLog are not used in our code.

The algorithms of Sects. 4 and 5 use optimisations that are *local* to the task of computing dependencies for a single pair of rules. The quadratic number of potential rule pairs is often so large, however, that even the most optimised checks lead to significant overhead. We therefore build index structures that map predicates p to rules that use p in their body or head, respectively. For each rule ρ_1, we then check $\rho_1 \prec^+ \rho_2$ only for rules ρ_2 that mention some predicate from head(ρ_1) in their body, and analogously for $\rho_1 \prec^{\square} \rho_2$.

Specifically for large rule sets, we further observed that many rules share the exact same structure up to some renaming of predicates and variables. For every rule pair considered, we therefore create an abstraction that captures the co-occurrence of predicates but not the concrete predicate names. This abstraction is used as a key to cache results of prior computations that can be re-used when encountering rule pairs with the exact same pattern of predicate names.

Besides these optimisations, we also implemented unoptimised variants of the algorithms of Sects. 4 and 5 to be used as a base-line in experiments. Instead of our goal-directed check-and-extend strategy, we simply iterate over all possible mappings until a dependency is found or the search is completed.

7   Evaluation

We have evaluated our implementation regarding (1) efficiency of our optimisations and (2) utility for solving practical problems. The latter also led to the first study of so-called *core stratified* real-world rule sets. Our evaluation machine is a mid-end server (Debian Linux 9.13; Intel Xeon CPU E5-2637v4@3.50 GHz; 384 GB RAM DDR4; 960 GB SSD), but our implementation is single-threaded and did not use more than 2 GB of RAM per individual experiments.

Experimental Data. All experiments use the same corpus of rule sets, created from real-world OWL ontologies of the *Oxford Ontology Repository* (http://www.cs.ox.ac.uk/isg/ontologies/). OWL is based on a fragment of first-order logic that overlaps with existential rules. OWL axioms that involve datatypes were deleted; any other axiom was syntactically transformed to obtain a Horn clause that can be written as a rule. This may fail if axioms use unsupported features, especially those related to (positive) disjunctions and equality. We dropped ontologies that could not fully be translated or that required no existential quantifier in the translation. Thereby 201 of the overall 787 ontologies were converted to existential rules, corresponding largely to those ontologies in the logic Horn-$\mathcal{SRI}$ [18]. The corpus contains 63 small (18–1,000 rules), 90 medium (1,000–10,000 rules), and 48 large (10,000–167,351 rules) sets. Our translation avoided normalisation and auxiliary predicates, which would profoundly affect dependencies. This also led to larger rule bodies and heads, both ranging up to 31 atoms.

Table 1. Number of rule sets achieving a given order of magnitude of speed-up for computing $\prec^+$ (left) and $\prec^\square$ (right) from one variant to another; t.o. gives the number of avoided timeouts

	$=1$	<10	$<10^2$	$<10^3$	$\geq 10^3$	t.o.	$=1$	<10	$<10^2$	$<10^3$	$\geq 10^3$	t.o.
N/L	48	104	14	1	2	32	53	92	17	2	2	35
G/A	103	67	9	1	0	21	90	81	9	1	0	20
N/G	24	1	27	33	60	56	35	11	53	30	20	52
L/A	5	33	30	41	47	45	17	72	48	10	17	37

Optimisation Impact. We compare four software variants to evaluate the utility of our proposed optimisations. Our baseline N is the unoptimised version described in Sect. 6, while L uses the locally optimised algorithms of Sects. 4 and 5. Version G is obtained from N by enabling the global optimisations of Sect. 6, and A combines all optimisations of L and G. For each of the four cases, we measured the total time of determining all positive reliances and all restraints for each rule set. A timeout of 60sec was used. The number of timeouts for each experiment was as follows:

$\prec^+$	N	L	G	A		$\prec^\square$	N	L	G	A
	80	48	24	3			87	52	35	15

To present the remaining results, we focus on *speed-up*, i.e., the ratio of runtime of a less optimised variant over runtime of a more optimised one. Table 1 classifies the observed speed-ups in several scenarios by their order of magnitude. For example, in the left table, the number 14 in line N/L and column "$<10^2$" means that for 14 of the 201 rule sets, L was between 10–10^2 times faster than

N. Note that G/A shows the effect of adding *local* optimisations to G. Column
"=1" shows cases where both variants agree, and column "t.o." cases where the
optimisation avoided a prior timeout (the speed-up cannot be computed since
the timeout does not correspond to a time).

We conclude that both L and G can lead to significant performance gains
across a range of ontologies. Strong effects are seen against the baseline (N/L
and N/G), but also (to a slightly lesser extent) against variants with the other
optimisations (G/A and L/A). Overall, $\prec^{\square}$ turned out to be slower than $\prec^{+}$,
with the global optimisations being less effective.

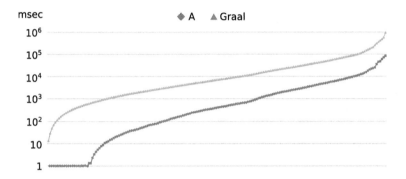

Fig. 1. Positive reliance computation in Graal (top) and our system (bottom)

Acyclic Positive Reliances. For rule sets where the graph of positive reliances
is acyclic, query answering is possible with many existing rule engines [1]. To
evaluate how our work compares to the state of the art in computing this graph,
we measure the time taken by Graal to find all positive reliances and compare
them to our prototype A from above. The results are shown in Fig. 1.

Our approach consistently outperformed Graal by about one order of magnitude. Overall, we can classify 178 ontologies in under 1 s, making this analysis
feasible at reasoning time. The difference in execution time is explained by our
optimisations: given two rules ρ_1 and ρ_2, Graal computes all (exponentially many
in the worst case) different ways to unify the $\mathsf{head}(\rho_1)$ with $\mathsf{body}(\rho_2)$ while our
implementation (1) stops when a positive reliance is discovered, (2) discards
atom mappings when a negative result is guaranteed, and (3) caches results of
previous computations. Recall that Graal uses a slightly weaker notion of positive reliance (cf. Sect. 3), which leads to more cycles: we find 36 acyclic sets in
Graal, but 70 such sets in our system.

Faster MFA. *Model-faithful acyclicity* (MFA) is an advanced analysis of rule
sets that can discover decidability of query answering in many cases, but is
2ExpTime-complete [10]. However, instead of performing this costly analysis
on the whole rule set, an equivalent result can be obtained by analysing each
strongly connected components of the $\prec^{+}$-graph individually. We measure the

times for both approaches using the MFA implementation of VLog and our optimised variant A, with a timeout of 30min per rule set. The two variants are denoted V (VLog MFA) and C (component-wise MFA).

Using C, 163 ontologies are classified as MFA, 33 fail MFA, and 5 cases time out. V times out in 10 cases, but agrees on all other outcomes. C is slower in three cases that still run in under 50 ms. The numbers of speed-ups, grouped by order of magnitude, are as follows:

Speed-up	$= 1$	< 10	$< 10^2$	$< 10^3$	$\geq 10^3$
V/C	0	85	54	41	11

We conclude that our optimised reliance computation is a feasible approach for speeding up MFA analysis.

Core Stratification. We can use our implementation to determine how common this favourable property (cf. Sect. 3) is among real-world ontologies. The analysis was feasible for 200 rule sets in our corpus, yielding 44 core stratified sets with up to 121,712 rules. One can improve this result by considering *pieces*, minimal subsets of rule heads where each two atoms refer to a common existentially quantified variable [1]. Each rule can then equivalently be replaced by several rules, each combining the original body with one of the pieces of the original head. Applying this transformation to our rule sets leads to more fine-grained dependencies that have fewer cycles over $\prec^\square$. With this modification, 75 rule sets are core stratified.

Our implementation fails in one case (ontology ID 00477), containing 167,351 rules like $A(x) \rightarrow \exists v.\, \mathsf{located\text{-}in}(x, v) \land B(v)$, for various A and B. The required $> 28 \times 10^9$ checks, though mostly cached, take very long. In spite of many $\prec^\square$-relations, the set is core-stratified as it describes a proper meronomy.

The remaining 125 rule sets are not core stratified. To validate the outcome, we have analysed these sets manually, and found several common reasons why ontologies were indeed not core stratified (and therefore correctly classified in our implementation). The following two examples explain two typical situations.

Example 7. In some cases, core stratification fails even though there is a natural rule application order that always leads to a core. Consider the rules $\rho_1 = a(x) \rightarrow \exists v.\, r(x, v) \land b(v)$, $\rho_2 = r(x, y) \rightarrow s(y, x)$, and $\rho_3 = s(x, y) \rightarrow r(y, x)$. This set is not core stratified since we have $\rho_1 \prec^+ \rho_3$, $\rho_2 \prec^+ \rho_3$, $\rho_3 \prec^+ \rho_2$, and $\rho_3 \prec^\square \rho_1$. However, prioritising ρ_2 and ρ_3 over ρ_1 (i.e., using a *Datalog-first* strategy [9]) always leads to a core. Indeed, the positive reliance $\rho_1 \prec^+ \rho_3$ over-estimates relevant rule applications, since no new atom produced by ρ_1 can (indirectly) lead to an application of ρ_3.

Example 8. In other cases, there is indeed no data-independent strategy for rule applications that would always lead to a core. Consider the rules $\rho_1 = a(x) \rightarrow \exists v.\, r(x, v) \land b(v)$ and $\rho_2 = r(x, y) \land r(y, z) \rightarrow r(x, z)$. Both are common in OWL ontologies with existential axioms and transitive roles. The rule set is not core stratified since $\rho_1 \prec^+ \rho_2$ and $\rho_2 \prec^\square \rho_1$.

Consider $\mathcal{I}_a = \{a(1), a(2), r(1,2)\}$. Applying ρ_1 over $\mathcal{I}_a$ to all matches yields $\mathcal{I}_b = \mathcal{I}_a \cup \{r(1,n), b(n), r(2,m), b(m)\}$, which makes ρ_2 applicable to obtain $\mathcal{I}_c = \mathcal{I}_b \cup \{r(1,m)\}$. Here we have the alternative match $h^A = \{1 \mapsto 1, 2 \mapsto 2, n \mapsto m\}$.

In contrast, applying ρ_1 only for the match $\{x \mapsto 2\}$ produces $\mathcal{I}_b' = \mathcal{I}_a \cup \{r(2,n), b(n)\}$. A subsequent application of ρ_2 yields $\mathcal{I}_c' = \mathcal{I}_b' \cup \{r(1,n)\}$, which is a core model. Indeed, core models could often be achieved in such settings, but require fine-grained, data-dependent strategies that cannot be found by static analysis (concretely: we could consider r as a pre-order and apply ρ_1 to the r-greatest elements first, followed by an exhaustive application of ρ_2).

Overall, our manual inspection supported the correctness of our computation and led to interesting first insights about core stratification in practical cases. Regarding the contribution of this work, our main conclusion of this evaluation is that our proposed algorithms are able to solve real-world tasks that require the computation of positive reliances and restraints over large ontologies.

8   Conclusions

We have shown that even the complex forms of dependencies that arise with existential rules can be implemented efficiently, and that doing so enables a number of uses of practical and theoretical interest. In particular, several previously proposed approaches can be made significantly faster or implemented for the first time at all. Our methods can be adapted to cover further cases, especially the *negative reliances*.

Our work opens up a path towards further uses of reliance-based analyses in practice. Already our experiments on core stratification – though primarily intended to evaluate the practical feasibility of our restraint algorithm – also showed that (a) core stratification does occur in many non-trivial real-world ontologies, whereas (b) there are also relevant cases where this criterion fails although a rule-based core computation seems to be within reach. This could be a starting point for refining this notion. It is also interesting to ask whether good ontology design should, in principle, lead to specifications that naturally produce cores, i.e., that robustly avoid redundancies. A different research path is to ask how knowledge of dependencies can be used to speed up reasoning. Indeed, dependencies embody characteristics of existential rule reasoning that are not found in other rule languages, and that therefore deserve further attention.

Supplemental Material Statement. We provide full proofs in the technical report published on arXiv [14]. Our source code, experimental data, instructions for repeating all experiments, and our own raw measurements are available on GitHub.

Acknowledgments. This work is partly supported by Deutsche Forschungsgemeinschaft (DFG, German Research Foundation) in project 389792660 (TRR 248, Center for Perspicuous Systems), by the Bundesministerium für Bildung und Forschung (BMBF, Federal Ministry of Education and Research) under European ITEA project 01IS21084   (InnoSale, Innovating Sales and Planning of Complex Industrial Products Exploiting Artificial Intelligence) and Center for Scalable Data Analytics and Artificial Intelligence (ScaDS.AI), by BMBF and DAAD (German Academic Exchange Service) in project 57616814 (SECAI, School of Embedded and Composite AI), and by the Center for Advancing Electronics Dresden (cfaed).

References

1. Baget, J.F., Leclère, M., Mugnier, M.L., Salvat, E.: On rules with existential variables: walking the decidability line. Artif. Intell. **175**(9–10), 1620–1654 (2011)
2. Baget, J.-F., Leclère, M., Mugnier, M.-L., Rocher, S., Sipieter, C.: Graal: a toolkit for query answering with existential rules. In: Bassiliades, N., Gottlob, G., Sadri, F., Paschke, A., Roman, D. (eds.) RuleML 2015. LNCS, vol. 9202, pp. 328–344. Springer, Cham (2015). https://doi.org/10.1007/978-3-319-21542-6_21
3. Bellomarini, L., Sallinger, E., Gottlob, G.: The vadalog system: datalog-based reasoning for knowledge graphs. Proc. VLDB Endow. **11**(9), 975–987 (2018)
4. Bourgaux, C., Carral, D., Krötzsch, M., Rudolph, S., Thomazo, M.: Capturing homomorphism-closed decidable queries with existential rules. In: Bienvenu, M., Lakemeyer, G., Erdem, E. (eds.) Proceedings of the 18th International Conference on Principles of Knowledge Representation and Reasoning (KR 2021), pp. 141–150. IJCAI (2021)
5. Calì, A., Gottlob, G., Lukasiewicz, T.: A general datalog-based framework for tractable query answering over ontologies. J. Web Semant. **14**, 57–83 (2012)
6. Calì, A., Gottlob, G., Pieris, A.: Towards more expressive ontology languages: the query answering problem. J. Artif. Intell. **193**, 87–128 (2012)
7. Carral, D., Dragoste, I., González, L., Jacobs, C., Krötzsch, M., Urbani, J.: VLog: a rule engine for knowledge graphs. In: Ghidini, C., et al. (eds.) ISWC 2019. LNCS, vol. 11779, pp. 19–35. Springer, Cham (2019). https://doi.org/10.1007/978-3-030-30796-7_2
8. Carral, D., Dragoste, I., Krötzsch, M.: The combined approach to query answering in Horn-$\mathcal{ALCHOIQ}$. In: Thielscher, M., Toni, F., Wolter, F. (eds.) Proceedings of 16th International Conference on Principles of Knowledge Representation and Reasoning (KR 2018), pp. 339–348. AAAI Press (2018)
9. Carral, D., Dragoste, I., Krötzsch, M., Lewe, C.: Chasing sets: how to use existential rules for expressive reasoning. In: Kraus, S. (ed.) Proceedings of 28th International Joint Conference on Artificial Intelligence (IJCAI 2019), pp. 1624–1631. ijcai.org (2019)
10. Cuenca Grau, B., et al.: Acyclicity notions for existential rules and their application to query answering in ontologies. J. Artif. Intell. Res. **47**, 741–808 (2013)
11. Deutsch, A., Nash, A., Remmel, J.B.: The chase revisited. In: Lenzerini, M., Lembo, D. (eds.) Proceedings of 27th Symposium on Principles of Database Systems (PODS 2008), pp. 149–158. ACM (2008)
12. Ellmauthaler, S., Krötzsch, M., Mennicke, S.: Answering queries with negation over existential rules. In: Proceedings of AAAI Conference on Artificial Intelligence, vol. 36, no. 5, pp. 5626–5633. AAAI Press (2022)

13. Fagin, R., Kolaitis, P.G., Miller, R.J., Popa, L.: Data exchange: semantics and query answering. Theoret. Comput. Sci. **336**(1), 89–124 (2005)
14. González, L., Ivliev, A., Krötzsch, M., Mennicke, S.: Efficient dependency analysis for rule-based ontologies. CoRR abs/2207.09669 (2022). https://arxiv.org/abs/2207.09669
15. Grahne, G., Onet, A.: Anatomy of the chase. Fundam. Inform. **157**(3), 221–270 (2018)
16. Hogan, A.: Canonical forms for isomorphic and equivalent RDF graphs: algorithms for leaning and labelling blank nodes. ACM Trans. Web **11**(4), 1–62 (2017). https://doi.org/10.1145/3068333
17. Krötzsch, M.: Computing cores for existential rules with the standard chase and ASP. In: Calvanese, D., Erdem, E., Thielscher, M. (eds.) Proceedings of 17th International Conference on Principles of Knowledge Representation and Reasoning (KR 2020), pp. 603–613. IJCAI (2020)
18. Krötzsch, M., Rudolph, S., Hitzler, P.: Complexities of Horn description logics. ACM Trans. Comput. Logic **14**(1), 2:1–2:36 (2013)
19. Magka, D., Krötzsch, M., Horrocks, I.: Computing stable models for nonmonotonic existential rules. In: Rossi, F. (ed.) Proceedings of 23rd International Joint Conference on Artificial Intelligence (IJCAI 2013), pp. 1031–1038. AAAI Press/IJCAI (2013)
20. Mallea, A., Arenas, M., Hogan, A., Polleres, A.: On blank nodes. In: Aroyo, L., et al. (eds.) ISWC 2011. LNCS, vol. 7031, pp. 421–437. Springer, Heidelberg (2011). https://doi.org/10.1007/978-3-642-25073-6_27
21. Meier, M., Schmidt, M., Lausen, G.: On chase termination beyond stratification. PVLDB **2**(1), 970–981 (2009)
22. Nenov, Y., Piro, R., Motik, B., Horrocks, I., Wu, Z., Banerjee, J.: RDFox: a highly-scalable RDF store. In: Arenas, M., et al. (eds.) ISWC 2015. LNCS, vol. 9367, pp. 3–20. Springer, Cham (2015). https://doi.org/10.1007/978-3-319-25010-6_1
23. Urbani, J., Jacobs, C., Krötzsch, M.: Column-oriented datalog materialization for large knowledge graphs. In: Schuurmans, D., Wellman, M.P. (eds.) Proceedings of 30th AAAI Conference on Artificial Intelligence (AAAI 2016), pp. 258–264. AAAI Press (2016)

Heterogeneous Graph Neural Network with Hypernetworks for Knowledge Graph Embedding

Xiyang Liu[1] ⓘ, Tong Zhu[1] ⓘ, Huobin Tan[1]([✉]) ⓘ, and Richong Zhang[2] ⓘ

[1] School of Software, Beihang University, Beijing, China
{liuxiyang,zhutong_software,thbin}@buaa.edu.cn
[2] SKLSDE, School of Computer Science and Engineering, Beihang University, Beijing, China
zhangrc@act.buaa.edu.cn

Abstract. Heterogeneous graph neural network (HGNN) has drawn considerable research attention in recent years. Knowledge graphs contain hundreds of distinct relations, showing the intrinsic property of strong heterogeneity. However, the majority of HGNNs characterize the heterogeneities by learning separate parameters for different types of nodes and edges in latent space. The number of type-related parameters will be explosively increased when HGNNs attempt to process knowledge graphs, making HGNNs only applicable for graphs with fewer edge types. In this work, to overcome such limitation, we propose a novel heterogeneous graph neural network incorporated with hypernetworks that generate the required parameters by modeling the general semantics among relations. Specifically, we exploit hypernetworks to generate relation-specific parameters of a convolution-based message function to improve the model's performance while maintaining parameter efficiency. The empirical study on the most commonly-used knowledge base embedding datasets confirms the effectiveness and efficiency of the proposed model. Furthermore, the model parameters have been shown to be significantly reduced (from 415M to 3M on FB15k-237 and from 13M to 4M on WN18RR).

Keywords: Knowledge graph embedding · Link prediction · Heterogeneous graph neural network

1 Introduction

Knowledge graphs (KGs), storing quantities of structured human knowledge in the form of triples (*subject entity*, *relation*, *object entity*), have been widely applied to many domains, such as question answering [4], recommendation systems [56], and dialog systems [29]. However, practical KGs, such as Freebase [3] and DBpedia [26], often suffer from incompleteness. As discussed in [10], 71% of people in Freebase have no known place of birth.

© The Author(s), under exclusive license to Springer Nature Switzerland AG 2022
U. Sattler et al. (Eds.): ISWC 2022, LNCS 13489, pp. 284–302, 2022.
https://doi.org/10.1007/978-3-031-19433-7_17

To infer missing links in KGs, numerous knowledge graph embedding (KGE) methods are proposed. Embedding models that represent entities and relations in low-dimensional vector spaces, can preserve the semantics and inherent structures of KGs. The early works of this line tend to employ simple, shallow models to learn the information contained in KGs, e.g., the translational distance models [5,51,58] and the tensor factorization-based models [35,53]. Methods such as ConvE [8] and RSN [14] apply deep neural networks to capture more expressive features. These approaches focus on capturing the semantics preserved in a single triple without explicitly encoding the graph structures.

To better model the structural information, there has been an increasing interest in leveraging graph neural networks (GNN) to incorporate the connectivity structures of KGs into the embedding space [40]. Most recent GNN-based models such as VR-GCN [54], CompGCN [46], and HRAN [27] first represent entities and relations as discretized embeddings with the same dimension size. Then, the embeddings of the connected entities and relations are combined into mixed embeddings which are subsequently processed by a graph convolution operation. However, relations play a critical role in knowledge graphs. For example, the average occurrence of entities in FB15k-237 [44], a subset of Freebase, is 37.4, while the average occurrence of relations reaches 1148. We argue that such a mechanism learns relation embeddings in the lower-level layers of models, which is sub-optimal for GNNs to extract the rich semantics of relations. In this paper, we consider building a HGNN that learns relational representations in higher-level layers of the architecture.

Although a bench of heterogeneous graph neural networks is proposed to achieve better performance than homogeneous GNNs in many tasks [18–20], most HGNNs are incapable of KGs. HGNNs typically define independent network parameters for different types of nodes and edges, where the number of parameters will be explosively increased with the kinds of types. Such fact limits HGNNs to handle graphs with fewer edge types and is not applicable for KGs with hundreds and even thousands of relations. For example, MAGNN [12] is a recent HGNN model of popular metapath-based methods. Assuming we leverage MAGNN to process a KG with 100 relations, the number of 2-order metapaths will be 10,000. Each metapath will be assigned separate parameters, which results in an immense number of trainable weights. Hence, MAGNN is suitable for datasets with serval kinds of edges, but it is not reasonable to apply the model to KGs without alteration. Similar issues broadly exist in other HGNN methods [18–20,50,55].

To solve the problems mentioned above, we believe that a key challenge in designing dedicated HGNNs for KGs is *how to effectively capture the high heterogeneity of relations while controlling the number of type-related parameters?*

In this paper, we propose a novel **H**eterogeneous **K**nowledge **G**raph neural **N**etwork (HKGN) incorporated with external networks called hypernetworks for parameter generation to resolve the aforementioned challenge. In our method, hypernetworks are effective at controlling the parameter counts through explicitly encoding the common information among relations. The rationale is that relations are not completely irrelevant, and there exist correlations among relations. Zhu et al. [58] found that there exists a low-rank structure over different relation embeddings. Specifically, we first introduce a primary HGNN utilized to process multiple single-relational subgraphs split from original KGs. We then incorporate external hypernetworks [15] into the primary HGNN to obtain essential parameters for graph convolution. To encode the rich information of relations, HKGN learns multiple independent representations of relations in different model layers. For each relation, we extend the linear transformation adopted in the message function to a convolution neural network for capturing the expressive feature combinations. To control the number of relation-specific parameters, hypernetworks are defined as mapping functions that take relational weight vectors with appropriate dimensions as input and output the corresponding parameters. HKGN eventually learns the abundant semantics of relations and reduces plentiful meaningless trainable parameters.

In summary, our main contributions are as follows:

- We present HKGN - a dedicated heterogeneous graph neural network for KGs which decouples relation embeddings as input of hypernetworks from entity embeddings as input of primary multi-relational graph convolution network. We leverage a relation-aware 2D convolution to promote the model's capability in learning representative information from neighbors, while external hypernetworks are introduced to keep parameters efficient.
- We conduct experiments on two benchmarks to evaluate the link prediction capability of HKGN and show that HKGN obtains better performance than state-of-the-art (SOTA) embedding models.

2   Related Work

2.1   Heterogeneous Graph Neural Network

Heterogeneous Graph Neural Networks are brought forward to handle ubiquitous heterogeneous graphs like academic network [18], product review network [19], and educational data [20]. HAN [50] applies node-level and semantic-level attention on metapath based graphs. HetGNN [55] aggregates node features transformed based upon node types sampled by random walks. HGT [18] designs a heterogeneous mutual transformer-like attention mechanism to propagate messages. These HGNNs outperform previous homogeneous GNNs like GCN [25] and GAT [47] on graph data with substantial heterogeneity. However, all these HGNNs are expected to handle heterogeneous graphs with few edge types and are not scalable to KGs in model complexity and computational demand.

2.2   Hypernetwork

Hypernetwork is a neural network trained to generate the weights for another network (called the primary network). Hypernetworks are first introduced for visual tasks like DFN [21] and SRCNN [38], in which the convolutional weights are dynamically generated dependent on input images. HyperRNN [15] uses a recurrent network to generate the parameters of another recurrent network.

Recently, hypernetworks have also been applied in graph neural networks. Nachmani and Wolf [30] utilize an MLP to get the GNN's weights. They find that the performance of the primary GNN can be improved when the first message and current message are combined as the input of the hypernetwork [31]. LGNN [28] employs dense layers to obtain node-level and edge-level localized weights. In this study, we incorporate hypernetworks into HGNNs to alleviate the problem of the count of heterogeneous parameters increasing explosively.

2.3 Knowledge Graph Embedding

Knowledge graph embedding has received considerable attention in recent years. Translation-based models treat relations as translations from subject entities to object entities, such as TransE [5] and TransH [51]. Tensor factorization-based methods regard a KG as a high-dimensional sparse tensor that can be factorized into smaller tensors, such as RESCAL [35] and DistMult [53]. HypER [1] proposes a hypernetwork to generate 1D relation-specific filters. CoPER [42] is a recent approach using relation embeddings to generate parameters of two basic models: ConvE [8] and MINERVA [7].

Graph neural network has been utilized in learning KGE, which has yielded promising performance [40]. However, many recent GNN-based works, such as VR-GCN [54], CompGCN [46], and KBGAT [32], learn relation embeddings in lower-level layers of the models. We argue that such a mechanism can lead to the limited representational power of GNNs.

3 Methodology

In this section, we elaborate on the details of the proposed HKGN. The knowledge graph is a collection of triples $(subject, relation, object)$ denoted as (s, r, o). All triples are connected to form a heterogeneous graph denoted as $\mathcal{G} = (\mathcal{E}, \mathcal{R}, \mathcal{T})$ with $\mathcal{E}$ as the entity set, $\mathcal{R}$ as the relation set, and $\mathcal{T}$ as the graph edge set. Following [40], a corresponding inverse triple (o, r^{-1}, s) is created with inverse relation r^{-1}, for each (s, r, o). To ensure that entities can receive information from themselves, we add self-connection $\top$ to each entity. In that case, the relation set and the graph edge set are extended as

$$\mathcal{R}' = \mathcal{R} \cup \{r^{-1} | r \in \mathcal{R}\} \cup \{\top\} \tag{1}$$

$$\mathcal{T}' = \mathcal{T} \cup \mathcal{T}^{-1} \cup \{s, \top, s \mid s \in \mathcal{E}\} \tag{2}$$

$$\mathcal{T}^{-1} = \{(o, r^{-1}, s) \mid (s, r, o) \in \mathcal{T}\} \tag{3}$$

Figure 1 illustrates an overview of HKGN. The architecture of HKGN follows the encoder-decoder scheme widely adopted by GNN-based KGE models. In the encoding phase, HKGN can be seen as an instantiation of the Message Passing Neural Network (MPNN) [13] framework. A message function is performed to encode the semantics of a single edge in latent space. Then, a multi-relational message propagation function is designed to contextualize entity embeddings with localized neighborhood structures by aggregating messages from neighbor edges. The relational parameters (also called heterogeneous parameters in this paper) utilized in this process are all generated by external hypernetworks. HKGN takes ConvE, one of the most generally used scoring functions, as the decoder to infer missing triples.

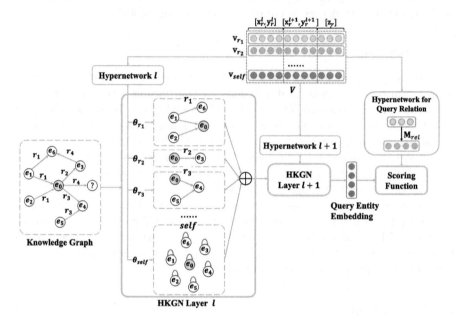

Fig. 1. An overview of HKGN. HKGN consists of two modules: the hypernetworks module used to obtain weights and the primary HGNN module utilized to process the multi-relational knowledge graph.

3.1 Hypernetworks for HGNNs

To flexibly control the number of trainable heterogeneous parameters in HGNNs, we evolve hypernetworks for parameter generation. A hypernetwork derived for HGNNs is a mapping function that takes the independent weights $\mathbf{w}_r^l$ of relation r as input and outputs the needed parameters $\boldsymbol{\theta}_r^l$:

$$\boldsymbol{\theta}_r^l = g^l(\mathbf{w}_r^l, \boldsymbol{\theta}_g^l) \tag{4}$$

- $\mathbf{w}_r^l$ describes the unique information about the structure of the weights specific to relation r. In this study, $\mathbf{w}_r^l$ is just considered as vectorized representations $\mathbf{v}_r^l \in \mathbb{R}^{d_r^l}$. d_r^l is the dimension of relation vector $\mathbf{v}_r^l$.

- $\boldsymbol{\theta}_g^l$ represents the global semantics shared among relations. Let n_g denote the number of parameters defined in $\boldsymbol{\theta}_g^l$.
- $g(\cdot)^l$ can be an arbitrary reasonable mapping function from relational input vector $\mathbf{v}_r^l$ to parameters required by HGNNs. A special case is adopting the lookup operation, which means there will be no $\boldsymbol{\theta}_g^l$ and the model is acting the same as normal HGNNs.
- l denotes the generated $\boldsymbol{\theta}_r^l$ utilized in layer l of HGNNs.

The above formulation compresses the heterogeneous parameter $\boldsymbol{\theta}_r^l$ into the vector $\mathbf{v}_r^l$. n_p^l denotes the parameter counts of $\boldsymbol{\theta}_r^l$. Assuming a knowledge graph with N_r relations, we can calculate a ratio q to assess the hypernetwork's ability in parameter reduction, omitting l for simplicity:

$$q = \frac{n_p \times N_r}{d_r \times N_r + n_g} = \frac{n_p}{d_r + \frac{n_g}{N_r}} \tag{5}$$

The effect of hypernetworks in controlling parameter counts is more significant with a bigger q value. Equation (5) shows that the impact of hypernetworks with the same architecture differs for KGs with various relation amounts. Knowledge graphs with more relations will be more likely affected by hypernetworks.

3.2   Message Construction with Hypernetworks

Keeping a separate weight matrix for each node or edge type is the most commonly applied mechanism for HGNNs to model the heterogeneity. For example, R-GCN [40] uses a relation-specific linear transformation to model the relational patterns. Given an edge (s, r, o), the representation of incoming message is learned as:

$$\mathbf{m}_{(r,o)} = \mathbf{W}_r \mathbf{e}_o \tag{6}$$

where $\mathbf{e}_o \in \mathbb{R}^d$ denotes the embedding of object entity o and $\mathbf{W}_r \in \mathbb{R}^{d' \times d}$ is the weight matrix assigned to r. Every element $\mathbf{m}^{[i]}$ in message embedding $\mathbf{m}$ is the weighted sum of all features from entity embedding $\mathbf{e}_o$:

$$\mathbf{m}_{(r,o)}^{[i]} = \sum_{j=0}^{d} \mathbf{W}_r^{[i,j]} \mathbf{e}_o^{[j]} \tag{7}$$

This type of transformation can implicitly lead to the restricted expressive capability of models because it has an intrinsic flaw in recognizing patterns that original features can be combined as a whole to contribute to messages. The importance of feature $\mathbf{e}_o^{[j]}$ is measured by coefficient $\mathbf{W}_r^{[i,j]}$ independently of other features to derive $\mathbf{m}_{(r,o)}^{[i]}$, as in Eq. (7). Nevertheless, some feature combinations may be prominent for relation r, and some other feature combinations play a pivotal role in another relation $\hat{r}$.

In this paper, we introduce a relational convolution layer to explore rich feature combinations:

$$\mathbf{c}_{(r,o)} = \sigma(Re2D(\mathbf{e}_o) * \boldsymbol{\omega}_r) \tag{8}$$

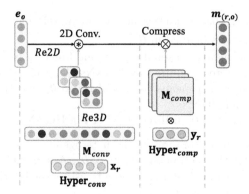

Fig. 2. An illustration of constructing messages incorporated with hypernetworks.

where $\mathbf{e}_o$ is reshaped into a 2D feature map and fed to a relation-aware 2D convolution layer with filters $\boldsymbol{\omega}_r \in \mathbb{R}^{f \times k_{size} \times k_{size}}$ to extract more interactions. As suggested in [8], compared with 1D convolution, one element in entity vector $\mathbf{e}_o$ can interact with distant elements rather than immediate elements by applying 2D convolution. The activation function $\sigma(\cdot)$ is chosen to be $tanh(\cdot)$. $\boldsymbol{\omega}_r$ interacts with diverse regions in $Re2D(\mathbf{e}_o)$ to generate different entries of $\mathbf{c}_{(r,o)}$. We notice that a range of convolution-based embedding methods like circular convolution [45], inception network [52], etc., can be adopted for further performance improvement.

To obtain embeddings with suitable dimensions for subsequent layers, a linear transformation operation is performed on $\mathbf{c}$ as:

$$\mathbf{m}_{(r,o)} = \mathbf{W}_r vec\left(\mathbf{c}_{(r,o)}\right) \tag{9}$$

where the resultant map is flattened into the 1D vector by vector concatenation operator $vec(\cdot)$ and $\mathbf{W}_r \in \mathbb{R}^{d' \times d^c}$ is the transformation matrix.

We have now defined convolution filters and weight matrix for each relation, which may incur a severe over-parameterization problem. To alleviate this issue, we exploit hypernetworks to improve the efficiency of heterogeneous parameters. The convolution filters are generated by the hypernetwork Hyper_{conv}:

$$\boldsymbol{\omega}_r = Re3D(\mathbf{M}_{conv}\mathbf{x}_r) \tag{10}$$

where $\mathbf{M}_{conv} \in \mathbb{R}^{f \cdot k_{size} \cdot k_{size} \times d_x}$ denotes the weight matrix and $\mathbf{x}_r \in \mathbb{R}^{d_x}$ is the relation vector. The transformed vector $\mathbf{M}_{conv}\mathbf{x}_r$ is reshaped into the 3D tensor $\boldsymbol{\omega}_r$ with the shape $f \times k_{size} \times k_{size}$. In practice, we have also experimented with employing a multi-layer perceptron $MLP(\cdot)$ to get $\boldsymbol{\omega}_r$. However, we found that the simple linear projection achieves the best results, which may be contributed to the better generalization of linear projection than $MLP(\cdot)$.

To limit the number of learnable parameters in $\mathbf{W}_r$, we introduce another hypernetwork Hyper_{comp}:

$$\mathbf{W}_r = <\mathbf{M}_{comp}, \mathbf{y}_r> \tag{11}$$

where $<,>$ denotes the tensor dot product between global tensor $\mathbf{M}_{comp} \in \mathbb{R}^{d' \times d^c \times d_y}$ and relation weight vector $\mathbf{y}_r \in \mathbb{R}^{d_y}$. The message construction approach applied in HKGN is depicted in Fig. 2.

In this paper, we let hypernetworks process all relation vectors in the same procedure. Hypernetworks can be arbitrary network architectures such as convolution neural networks or graph neural networks [31]. More carefully designed hypernetworks may let information flow among relations more reasonably. We defer this for future work.

3.3 Multi-relational Message Propagation

The central entity s can be surrounded by different neighboring triples, where the entities under the same relation are located in a single-relational graph. To aggregate information from the neighborhood, we first split neighboring triples into diverse single-relational subgraphs according to their relations. The same neighbor entity o located in different single-relational subgraphs will be processed by distinct message functions. Then we compute the new representation for each entity in the $(l+1)$-th layer by accumulating message embeddings learned in the l-th layer from single-relational graphs:

$$\mathbf{e}_s^{l+1} = \sigma \left(\sum_{r \in \mathcal{R}'} \sum_{o \in \mathcal{N}_s^r} \mathbf{m}_{(r,o)}^l \right) \tag{12}$$

where $\mathcal{N}_s^r$ is the set of neighboring entities under relation r.

To avoid mutual interference among network parameters of different GNN layers, we employ independent hypernetworks for each HKGN layer. So far, the parameter associated with relation r is a segmented vector:

$$\mathbf{v}_r = [\dots, \mathbf{x}_r^l, \mathbf{y}_r^l, \mathbf{x}_r^{l+1}, \mathbf{y}_r^{l+1} \dots, \mathbf{z}_r] \tag{13}$$

where $\mathbf{x}_r^l$ and $\mathbf{y}_r^l$ are the input weight vectors for hypernetworks Hyper_{conv}^l and Hyper_{comp}^l of the l-th layer, respectively. The length of $\mathbf{v}_r$ is agnostic to the dimension d of entity embedding. Each segment represents the distinct role of relation r during graph convolution and is non-interfering from each other.

$\mathbf{z}_r \in \mathbb{R}^{d_z}$ appeared in Eq. (13) is utilized by the hypernetwork Hyper_{rel} to generate the target relation embedding which is later used in the scoring function to estimate the probability of query triple $< h, r, ? >$:

$$\mathbf{q}_r = \mathbf{M}_{rel}\mathbf{z}_r \tag{14}$$

where $\mathbf{M}_{rel} \in \mathbb{R}^{d' \times d_z}$ is the global projection matrix.

3.4 Scoring Function

To estimate the probability of query triple (h, r, t), GNN-based methods typically employ convolution-based models as the scoring function like ConvE [8], ConvKB

[33], CapsE [34], etc. In this work, we utilize ConvE to validate our model's effectiveness. As revealed by [43], the evaluation process applied in ConvE is rigorous and fair when dealing with candidate triples with the same score. In contrast, the biased evaluation protocol adopted in ConvKB and CapsE can lead to inappropriate performance improvement.

Given query entity embeddings $\mathbf{e}_h^L$, $\mathbf{e}_t^L$ and relation embedding $\mathbf{q}_r$, the scoring function can be written formally as:

$$p = \sigma \left(f \left(vec \left(f([\overline{\mathbf{e}_h^L}; \overline{\mathbf{q}_r}] * \boldsymbol{\omega}) \right) \mathbf{W} \right) \mathbf{e}_t^L \right) \tag{15}$$

where $f(\cdot)$ and $\sigma(\cdot)$ are *ReLU* and *sigmoid* activation functions. $\overline{\mathbf{e}_h^L}$ and $\overline{\mathbf{q}_r}$ denote 2D reshapings of $\mathbf{e}_h^L$ and $\mathbf{e}_t^L$. $[;]$ represents the concatenation operation and W is the projection matrix. The model is trained using cross-entropy loss:

$$\mathcal{L} = -\frac{1}{N} \sum_i t_i log(p_i) + (1 - t_i) log(1 - p_i) \tag{16}$$

where t_i is the label of triple i and p_i is the corresponding score.

3.5   Training Strategy

In this study, two different training strategies are applied to the HKGN to make a trade-off between GPU memory footprints and learning time:

1. **Parallel**: Performing message construction and propagation functions of multiple single-relational graphs simultaneously. In this case, all triples in the KG will be assigned heterogeneous parameters based on their binary relations and be processed in parallel. The strategy leads to higher memory consumption and less training time.
2. **Iterative**: Processing single-relational subgraphs iteratively. Triples with one type of relation are handled during each iteration. The strategy requires a lower GPU memory footprint with a longer learning time.

HKGN adopts the 1-N scoring developed by ConvE [8], where all entity embeddings will be updated by message propagation in each training step. Though it has an expensive GPU memory requirement (as revealed in Sect. 4.6), we find that 1-N scoring achieves better results than 1-n (10, 100, etc.) scoring.

4   Experiment

4.1   Datasets

To evaluate the performance of HKGN on link prediction task, two commonly used benchmark datasets (FB15k-237 [44] and WN18RR [8]) are employed in this study. FB15k-237 and WN18RR are derived from FB15k and WN18 datasets [5], respectively, where original inverse relations are excluded to prevent the test leakage problem. The statistics of the two datasets are summarized in Table 1.

Table 1. Statistics of datasets.

	#Entities	#Relations	#Training	#Validation	#Test
FB15k-237	14,541	237	272,115	17,535	20,466
WN18RR	40,943	11	86,835	3,034	3,134

Note that we have added new inverse relation r^{-1} and self-loop $\top$ relation, as presented in Sect. 3. The "inverse relation" described here is different from that mentioned above. Because the inverse triples are created for train/valid/test set separately, no test leakage problem will be caused. In that case, HKGN handles 475 relations in FB15k-237 and 23 relations in WN18RR. The number of edge types is far more than those in graphs often analyzed by HGNNs, such as IMDB (2 edge types) [23], ACM (4 edge types) [57], and DBLP (3 edge types) [49].

4.2 Evaluation Protocol

Following the evaluation protocol applied broadly in previous works, each test triple (h, r, t) is estimated in two different scenarios: head entity prediction $(?, r, o)$ and tail entity prediction $(h, r, ?)$. The head entity prediction is performed in the form of $(t, r^{-1}, ?)$ with the corresponding inverse relation. The head or tail entity is replaced by every other entity $e' \in \mathcal{E}$, and then each candidate triple is assigned a predictive value by the scoring function. Subsequently, we sort these scores in descending order to obtain the exact rank of the correct triple in the candidates. Similar to most baselines, we report the experimental results using the *filtered* setting introduced by [5], where all true triples in KG are excluded before ranking. Three standard metrics are reported to evaluate performance, Mean Reciprocal Rank (MRR), Mean Rank (MR), and Top 1, 3, 10 (Hits@1, Hits@3 and Hits@10).

4.3 Baselines

Many studies on learning knowledge graph embedding have emerged. To demonstrate the effectiveness of our model, we compare it with SOTA baselines categorized as the following groups:

- Shallow KGE models with low time and space complexity, including TransE [5], DistMult [53], and DualE [6].
- Convolution-based methods like ConvE [8], ConvR [22], HypER [1] and CoPER [42].
- Methods utilizing graph neural networks, which include R-GCN [40], SACN [41], VR-GCN [54], A2N [2], KBGAT [32], CompGCN [46] and HRAN [27].

4.4 Hyper-parameter Settings

We evaluate the results of hyperparameter choices on the validation splits. In HKGN, the relation embedding size d_x of $\mathbf{x}_r$ is selected from $\{50, 100, 200, 300\}$,

d_y of $\mathbf{y}_r$ from $\{2, 4, 6, 8\}$, d_z of $\mathbf{z}_r$ from $\{50, 100, 200, 300\}$. Finally, we find that the following choices work well on both datasets: $d_x = 100$, $d_y = 2$ and $d_z = 100$. The initial entity embedding size is chosen to be 100. The number of convolution filters is set to 32 with kernel size 3×3. We use Adam [24] with an initial learning rate $lr = 0.001$ to optimize the model up to 1200 epochs. The number of HKGN layers L is set to 2, 1; the batch size b is set to 1024, 256 for FB15K-237 and WN18RR, respectively.

4.5   Results of Link Prediction

Table 2. Link prediction results of HKGN and baselines on FB15k-237 and WN18RR. Results of [△] are taken from [39], [◇] from [43]. CoPER [†] is reevaluated by using the authors' open-source code. Other results are taken directly from the corresponding original papers.

Model	FB15k-237					WN18RR				
	MRR	MR	Hits@N			MRR	MR	Hits@N		
			1	3	10			1	3	10
TransE [△]	0.313	-	0.221	0.347	0.497	0.228	-	0.053	0.368	0.520
DistMult [△]	0.343	-	0.250	0.378	0.531	0.452	-	0.413	0.466	0.530
DualE	0.330	-	0.237	0.363	0.518	0.482	-	0.440	0.500	0.561
ConvE [△]	0.339	-	0.248	0.369	0.521	0.442	-	0.411	0.451	0.504
ConvR	0.350	-	0.261	0.385	0.528	0.475	-	0.443	0.489	0.537
HypER	0.341	250	0.252	0.376	0.520	0.465	5798	0.436	0.477	0.522
CoPER [†]	0.320	390	0.234	0.351	0.491	0.442	5315	0.418	0.450	0.487
R-GCN	0.248	-	0.153	0.258	0.414	-	-	-	-	-
SACN	0.350	-	0.260	0.390	0.540	0.470	-	0.430	0.480	0.540
VR-GCN	0.248	-	0.159	0.272	0.432	-	-	-	-	-
A2N	0.317	-	0.232	0.348	0.486	0.450	-	0.420	0.460	0.510
KBGAT [◇]	0.157	270	-	-	0.331	0.412	**1921**	-	-	0.554
CompGCN	0.355	197	0.264	0.390	0.535	0.479	3533	0.443	0.494	0.546
HRAN	0.355	**156**	0.263	0.390	0.541	0.479	2113	**0.450**	0.494	0.542
HKGN	**0.365**	171	**0.272**	**0.402**	**0.552**	**0.487**	2468	0.448	**0.505**	**0.561**

Table 2 summarizes the results of link prediction of HKGN and baselines. Ruffinelli et al. [39] have recently performed extensive experiments using popular KGE model architectures and training strategies with a wide range of hyperparameter settings. They found that many shallow models can achieve competitive performance when trained appropriately. Here we take their reported results of TransE, DistMult, and ConvE. Sun et al. [43] investigated the inappropriate evaluation and test data leakage problem in KBGAT. Hence, we take the results of KBGAT from [43] when issues are fixed. The performance of DualE is reported without prior type constraints. CoPER is closely related to our method. Nevertheless, we find that the original model performance is just estimated in the tail prediction task. To ensure a fair comparison, we evaluate the performance of CoPER in head and tail prediction tasks and report the average results using the authors' open-source code[1].

From Table 2, we observe that: (i) HKGN consistently outperforms all baselines on most metrics in two benchmark datasets, demonstrating the effectiveness of our proposed method. Compared with HRAN, a recent HGNN model which introduces a heterogeneous relation attention mechanism to aggregate neighbor features, HKGN delivers better results. The improvement indicates HKGN's ability to model complex structures in heterogeneous KGs. (ii) HKGN outperforms HypER and CoPER, which also utilize hypernetworks in learning KGE, showing that the graph structure information is beneficial for link prediction.

Table 3. Experimental results on FB15k-237 by relation category.

		1-1(1.5%)	1-N(4.6%)	N-1(18.6%)	N-N(75.2%)
MRR	CoPER	0.427	0.249	0.409	0.297
	CompGCN	**0.469**	0.278	0.435	0.334
	HKGN	0.400	**0.282**	**0.452**	**0.345**
Hits@10	CoPER	0.526	0.360	0.494	0.501
	CompGCN	**0.593**	0.414	0.531	0.549
	HKGN	0.591	**0.416**	**0.562**	**0.561**

We investigate the performance of HKGN for different relation categories on FB15k-237. Following [51], all relations are categorized into four classes: 1-to-1, 1-to-N, N-to-1, and N-to-N. Table 3 presents the results of HKGN on different relation categories. We reproduce CompGCN[2] and CoPER based on publicly available source codes. Table 3 shows that the HKGN performs better for 1-to-N, N-to-1, and N-to-N relation categories, which shows that HKGN is effective at handling complex relations. We also notice that CompGCN outperforms our model on 1-to-1 relations. The phenomenon can be attributed to the reason that the characteristic information of 1-to-1 relations is corrupted by noises from other relations. It reminds us that the performance of HKGN may be boosted by introducing residual connection [17] or gate-based structures into hypernetworks to control the flow of information from other relations. Overall, triples with 1-to-1 relation cover only around 1.5% of all edges in the FB15k-237 training set. Hence, the stronger ability of HKGN in modeling complex relations makes it more applicable to KGs.

---

[1] https://github.com/otiliastr/coper.

[2] https://github.com/malllabiisc/CompGCN.

4.6   Ablation Study

Table 4 shows the results of the ablation study. Conv. denotes the relational convolution applied in the message function and Hyper. represents all hypernetworks adopted in HKGN.

Table 4. Ablation study on FB15k-237 and WN18RR.

Dataset	Model	q value	MRR	Hits@1	Hits@3	Hits@10	#param.
FB15k-237	w/o Conv.	150.9	0.355	0.264	0.39	0.536	1.64M
	w/o Hyper.	-	0.358	0.265	0.394	0.544	415.19M
	HKGN	212.3	0.365	0.272	0.402	0.552	3.40M
WN18RR	w/o Conv.	7.4	0.459	0.41	0.479	0.553	4.15M
	w/o Hyper.	-	0.483	0.444	0.497	0.558	13.52M
	HKGN	10.8	0.487	0.448	0.505	0.561	4.96M

Effect of Relational Convolution. As shown in Table 4, removing relational convolution leads to all metrics (MRR, Hits@1, 3, and 10) degradation on FB15k-237 and WN18RR datasets, demonstrating the effectiveness of capturing feature combinations. We further examine how the prediction results of entities with different degrees can be affected by the relational convolution. The entity with a larger degree is connected to more neighbor entities, and this kind of entity is expected to receive more semantic information from neighbors. For each entity e, we compute the degree (indegree and outdegree) $deg(e) = deg_{in}(e) + deg_{out}(e)$ by counting the corresponding training triples. Figure 3 presents the average results of Hits@10 for different sets of entities with different degree scopes. It can be observed that HKGN achieves better performance across all degree scopes by leveraging the relation-specific convolution. Along with the increase of degrees, the average value of Hits@10 increases initially but declines abruptly in a high-degree scope (e.g., $deg(e) \geq 1000$ in FB15k-237 and $deg(e) \geq 100$ in WN18RR). We conjecture this is primarily due to the representative information being covered by excessive messages from too many neighbors. One solution to this problem may be neighborhood sampling functions as in [16].

Effect of Hypernetworks. The empirical results in Table 4 show that the model eliminating hypernetworks obtains 122x (FB15k-237) and 2.7x (WN18RR) more parameters and simultaneously worse performance than the original HKGN. The significant parameter reduction and consistent performance improvement indicate that hypernetworks are powerful in keeping parameters efficient. The average training loss and MRR evaluated on the validation set for FB15k-237 during the training process are reported in Fig. 4. Obviously, the HKGN with hypernetworks achieves lower loss and higher MRR results. Using

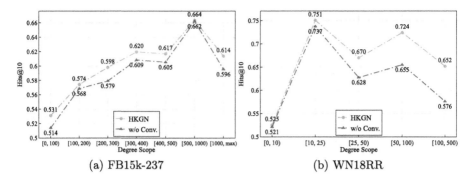

Fig. 3. Node degree study using FB15k-237 and WN18RR datasets.

hypernetworks helps reduce numerous network parameters and facilitates the weights converging to a more optimal solution. Without hypernetworks, the number of trainable parameters in the HKGN for handling FB15k-237 has reached 415M, which is even larger than some recent pre-trained language models, including GPT (110M) [37] and BERT (340M) [9]. Imagine we build HGNNs equipped with more complicated graph learning mechanisms such as transformer-style attention [18], metapath-based learning [12], and heterogeneous graph structure learning [57] to deal with web-scale knowledge graphs like Wikidata (4k relations) [48] and DBpedia (60k relations) [26], as summarized in [11]. There will be a blowup in the number of trainable parameters. Our experimental results suggest that it is possible to control the parameter counts and even boost performance by exploiting the underlying correlations among relations.

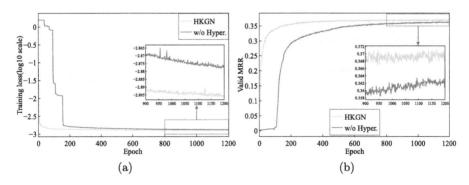

Fig. 4. Convergence results of HKGN and its counterpart without hypernetworks on FB15k-237 dataset.

The statistics of the maximum GPU memory allocated and the training time for HKGN with/without hypernetworks are shown in Table 5. The results are reported under the experimental environment with a single NVIDIA A100 GPU,

CUDA 11.2, and PyTorch [36] 1.8.0. With sufficient GPU memory, executing the message functions of multiple single-relational graphs in parallel gets nearly 12x and 3.8x speedup on FB15k-237 and WN18RR. When processing single-relational graphs iteratively, introducing hypernetworks into the HKGN does not slow the training speed because all hypernetworks are implemented linearly. Utilizing hypernetworks has a more prominent influence on GPU memory consumption. When we tried to run the model without hypernetworks in a parallel way, the procedure attempted to load 852 GB and 327 GB of memory for FB15k-237 and WN18RR, respectively, and got out of memory error. The memory consumption goes far beyond the limit of our resources and can be reduced remarkably to 21 GB (FB15k-237) and 5 GB (WN18RR) through applying hypernetworks. Also, the HKGN (iterative) with hypernetworks reduces up to 23.8% of memory footprint compared with its counterpart removing hypernetworks on FB15k-237.

Table 5. Statistics of the maximum GPU memory allocated (in GB) and training time (in seconds per epoch) of HKGN with/without hypernetworks on FB15k-237 and WN18RR datasets. OOM denotes the Out Of Memory error.

Dataset		FB15k-237 (2-layer)		WN18RR (1-layer)	
Training strategy	Models	Memory	Time	Memory	Time
Iterative	HKGN	14.6	960	2.8	260
	w/o Hyper.	19.2	970	2.9	260
Parallel	HKGN	21.5	80	5.5	68
	w/o Hyper.	OOM		OOM	

5   Conclusion and Future Work

In this paper, we propose HKGN, a novel heterogeneous graph neural network for learning KGE. HKGN introduces hypernetworks to alleviate the problem of the number of heterogeneous parameters in explosive growth, which is fundamental for the model to build a complicated convolution-based message construction function. The developed message function effectively improves prediction accuracy for entities with varying node degrees. As a result, HKGN achieves new SOTA on standard benchmark FB15k-237 and WN18RR. Experimental results show that the proposed hypernetworks significantly reduce the parameter counts and lead to lower GPU memory footprints. In the future, we intend to explore more variants of hypernetworks to make information flow among relations more reasonably. We would also like to combine hypernetworks with more advanced heterogeneous architectures to facilitate KGE learning.

Supplemental Material Statement: Source code for HKGN, detailed hyperparameter settings, datasets FB15k-237 and WN18RR, the data subsets divided by relation categories and entity degrees are available from Github[3].

Acknowledgements. This work was supported by the National Key Research and Development Program of China under Grant 2021YFB3500700.

References

1. Balažević, I., Allen, C., Hospedales, T.M.: Hypernetwork knowledge graph embeddings. In: Proceedings of the ICANN, Munich, Germany, pp. 553–565 (2019). https://doi.org/10.1007/978-3-030-30493-5_52
2. Bansal, T., Juan, D.C., Ravi, S., McCallum, A.: A2N: attending to neighbors for knowledge graph inference. In: Proceedings of the ACL, Florence, Italy, pp. 4387–4392 (2019). https://doi.org/10.18653/v1/P19-1431
3. Bollacker, K., Evans, C., Paritosh, P., Sturge, T., Taylor, J.: Freebase: a collaboratively created graph database for structuring human knowledge. In: Proceedings of the SIGMOD, Vancouver, BC, Canada, pp. 1247–1250 (2008). https://doi.org/10.1145/1376616.1376746
4. Bordes, A., Chopra, S., Weston, J.: Question answering with subgraph embeddings. In: Proceedings of the EMNLP, Doha, Qatar, pp. 615–620 (2014). https://doi.org/10.3115/v1/D14-1067
5. Bordes, A., Usunier, N., García-Durán, A., Weston, J., Yakhnenko, O.: Translating embeddings for modeling multi-relational data. In: Proceedings of the NIPS, Lake Tahoe, Nevada, United States, pp. 2787–2795 (2013)
6. Cao, Z., Xu, Q., Yang, Z., Cao, X., Huang, Q.: Dual quaternion knowledge graph embeddings. In: Proceedings of the AAAI, pp. 6894–6902 (2021)
7. Das, R., et al.: Go for a walk and arrive at the answer: reasoning over paths in knowledge bases using reinforcement learning. In: Proceedings of the ICLR, Vancouver, BC, Canada (2018)
8. Dettmers, T., Minervini, P., Stenetorp, P., Riedel, S.: Convolutional 2D knowledge graph embeddings. In: Proceedings of the AAAI, New Orleans, Louisiana, USA, pp. 1811–1818 (2018). https://doi.org/10.1609/aaai.v32i1.11573
9. Devlin, J., Chang, M.W., Lee, K., Toutanova, K.: BERT: pre-training of deep bidirectional transformers for language understanding. In: Proceedings of the NAACL-HIT, Minneapolis, Minnesota, pp. 4171–4186. Association for Computational Linguistics (2019). https://doi.org/10.18653/v1/n19-1423
10. Dong, X., et al.: Knowledge vault: a web-scale approach to probabilistic knowledge fusion. In: Proceedings of the SIGKDD, New York, NY, USA, pp. 601–610 (2014). https://doi.org/10.1145/2623330.2623623
11. Färber, M., Bartscherer, F., Menne, C., Rettinger, A.: Linked data quality of DBpedia, freebase, OpenCyc, Wikidata, and YAGO. Semant. Web **9**(1), 77–129 (2018). https://doi.org/10.3233/SW-170275
12. Fu, X., Zhang, J., Meng, Z., King, I.: MAGNN: metapath aggregated graph neural network for heterogeneous graph embedding. In: Proceedings of the WWW, New York, NY, USA, pp. 2331–2341 (2020). https://doi.org/10.1145/3366423.3380297

---

[3] https://github.com/liuxiyang641/HKGN.

13. Gilmer, J., Schoenholz, S.S., Riley, P.F., Vinyals, O., Dahl, G.E.: Neural message passing for quantum chemistry. In: Proceedings of the ICML, ICML 2017, pp. 1263–1272. JMLR.org (2017)

14. Guo, L., Sun, Z., Hu, W.: Learning to exploit long-term relational dependencies in knowledge graphs. In: Proceedings of the ICML, Long Beach, California, USA, vol. 97, pp. 2505–2514 (2019)

15. Ha, D., Dai, A., Le, Q.V.: Hypernetworks. In: Proceedings of the ICLR, Toulon, France (2017)

16. Hamilton, W.L., Ying, R., Leskovec, J.: Inductive representation learning on large graphs. In: Proceedings of the NIPS, pp. 1025–1035. Curran Associates Inc., Red Hook (2017)

17. He, K., Zhang, X., Ren, S., Sun, J.: Deep residual learning for image recognition. In: Proceedings of the CVPR, Las Vegas, NV, USA, pp. 770–778 (2016). https://doi.org/10.1109/CVPR.2016.90

18. Hu, Z., Dong, Y., Wang, K., Sun, Y.: Heterogeneous graph transformer. In: Proceedings of the Web Conference 2020, New York, NY, USA, pp. 2704–2710 (2020). https://doi.org/10.1145/3366423.3380027

19. Huang, Z., Li, X., Ye, Y., Ng, M.K.: MR-GCN: multi-relational graph convolutional networks based on generalized tensor product. In: Proceedings of the IJCAI, pp. 1258–1264 (2020). https://doi.org/10.24963/ijcai.2020/175

20. Jia, C., Shen, Y., Tang, Y., Sun, L., Lu, W.: Heterogeneous graph neural networks for concept prerequisite relation learning in educational data. In: Proceedings of the NAACL-HIT, pp. 2036–2047 (2021). https://doi.org/10.18653/v1/2021.naacl-main.164

21. Jia, X., De Brabandere, B., Tuytelaars, T., Gool, L.V.: Dynamic filter networks. In: Proceedings of the NIPS, Red Hook, NY, USA, vol. 29 (2016)

22. Jiang, X., Wang, Q., Wang, B.: Adaptive convolution for multi-relational learning. In: Proceedings of the NAACL-HIT, Minneapolis, Minnesota, pp. 978–987 (2019). https://doi.org/10.18653/v1/N19-1103

23. Jin, D., Huo, C., Liang, C., Yang, L.: Heterogeneous graph neural network via attribute completion. In: Proceedings of the Web Conference 2021, pp. 391–400. Association for Computing Machinery, New York (2021). https://doi.org/10.1145/3442381.3449914

24. Kingma, D.P., Ba, J.: Adam: a method for stochastic optimization. In: Proceedings of the ICLR, San Diego, CA, USA (2015)

25. Kipf, T.N., Welling, M.: Semi-supervised classification with graph convolutional networks. In: Proceedings of the ICLR, Toulon, France (2017)

26. Lehmann, J., et al.: DBpedia-a large-scale, multilingual knowledge base extracted from Wikipedia. Semant. Web 6(2), 167–195 (2015). https://doi.org/10.3233/SW-140134

27. Li, Z., Liu, H., Zhang, Z., Liu, T., Xiong, N.N.: Learning knowledge graph embedding with heterogeneous relation attention networks. IEEE Trans. Neural Netw. Learn. Syst. 1–13 (2021). https://doi.org/10.1109/TNNLS.2021.3055147

28. Liu, Z., Fang, Y., Liu, C., Hoi, S.C.H.: Node-wise localization of graph neural networks. In: Proceedings of the IJCAI, Montreal, Canada, pp. 1520–1526 (2021). https://doi.org/10.24963/ijcai.2021/210

29. Ma, Y., Crook, P.A., Sarikaya, R., Fosler-Lussier, E.: Knowledge graph inference for spoken dialog systems. In: Proceedings of the ICASSP, South Brisbane, Queensland, Australia, pp. 5346–5350 (2015). https://doi.org/10.1109/ICASSP.2015.7178992

30. Nachmani, E., Wolf, L.: Hyper-graph-network decoders for block codes. In: Proceedings of the NIPS, Vancouver, BC, Canada, pp. 2326–2336 (2019)
31. Nachmani, E., Wolf, L.: Molecule property prediction and classification with graph hypernetworks. Computing Research Repository arXiv:2002.00240 (2020)
32. Nathani, D., Chauhan, J., Sharma, C., Kaul, M.: Learning attention-based embeddings for relation prediction in knowledge graphs. In: Proceedings of the ACL, pp. 4710–4723. Florence, Italy (2019). https://doi.org/10.18653/v1/P19-1466
33. Nguyen, D.Q., Nguyen, T.D., Nguyen, D.Q., Phung, D.: A novel embedding model for knowledge base completion based on convolutional neural network. In: Proceedings of the NAACL-HIT, New Orleans, Louisiana, pp. 327–333 (2018). https://doi.org/10.18653/v1/N18-2053
34. Nguyen, D.Q., Vu, T., Nguyen, T.D., Nguyen, D.Q., Phung, D.: A capsule network-based embedding model for knowledge graph completion and search personalization. In: Proceedings of the NAACL-HIT, Minneapolis, Minnesota, pp. 2180–2189 (2019). https://doi.org/10.18653/v1/N19-1226
35. Nickel, M., Tresp, V., Kriegel, H.P.: A three-way model for collective learning on multi-relational data. In: Proceedings of the ICML, Bellevue, Washington, USA, pp. 809–816 (2011)
36. Paszke, A., et al.: Pytorch: an imperative style, high-performance deep learning library. In: Proceedings of the NIPS, Vancouver, BC, Canada, pp. 8024–8035 (2019)
37. Radford, A., Narasimhan, K., Salimans, T., Sutskever, I.: Improving language understanding by generative pre-training (2018)
38. Riegler, G., Schulter, S., Rüther, M., Bischof, H.: Conditioned regression models for non-blind single image super-resolution. In: Proceedings of the ICCV, Santiago, Chile, pp. 522–530 (2015). https://doi.org/10.1109/ICCV.2015.67
39. Ruffinelli, D., Broscheit, S., Gemulla, R.: You can teach an old dog new tricks! on training knowledge graph embeddings. In: Proceedings of the ICLR, Addis Ababa, Ethiopia (2020)
40. Schlichtkrull, M.S., Kipf, T.N., Bloem, P., van den Berg, R., Titov, I., Welling, M.: Modeling relational data with graph convolutional networks. In: Proceedings of the ESWC, Heraklion, Crete, Greece, vol. 10843, pp. 593–607 (2018). https://doi.org/10.1007/978-3-319-93417-4_38
41. Shang, C., Tang, Y., Huang, J., Bi, J., He, X., Zhou, B.: End-to-end structure-aware convolutional networks for knowledge base completion. In: Proceedings of the AAAI, Honolulu, Hawaii, USA, vol. 33, pp. 3060–3067 (2019). https://doi.org/10.1609/aaai.v33i01.33013060
42. Stoica, G., Stretcu, O., Platanios, E.A., Mitchell, T.M., Póczos, B.: Contextual parameter generation for knowledge graph link prediction. In: Proceedings of the AAAI, New York, NY, USA, pp. 3000–3008 (2020). https://doi.org/10.1609/aaai.v34i03.5693
43. Sun, Z., Vashishth, S., Sanyal, S., Talukdar, P., Yang, Y.: A re-evaluation of knowledge graph completion methods. In: Proceedings of the ACL, pp. 5516–5522 (2020). https://doi.org/10.18653/v1/2020.acl-main.489
44. Toutanova, K., Chen, D.: Observed versus latent features for knowledge base and text inference. In: Proceedings of the 3rd Workshop on CVSC, Beijing, China, pp. 57–66 (2015). https://doi.org/10.18653/v1/W15-4007
45. Vashishth, S., Sanyal, S., Nitin, V., Agrawal, N., Talukdar, P.P.: Interacte: improving convolution-based knowledge graph embeddings by increasing feature interactions. In: Proceedings of the AAAI, New York, NK, USA, pp. 3009–3016 (2020). https://doi.org/10.1609/aaai.v34i03.5694

46. Vashishth, S., Sanyal, S., Nitin, V., Talukdar, P.P.: Composition-based multi-relational graph convolutional networks. In: Proceedings of the ICLR, Addis Ababa, Ethiopia (2020)
47. Velickovic, P., Cucurull, G., Casanova, A., Romero, A., Liò, P., Bengio, Y.: Graph attention networks. In: Proceedings of the ICLR, Vancouver, BC, Canada (2018)
48. Vrandečić, D., Krötzsch, M.: Wikidata: a free collaborative knowledgebase. Commun. ACM **57**(10), 78–85 (2014)
49. Wang, P., Agarwal, K., Ham, C., Choudhury, S., Reddy, C.K.: Self-supervised learning of contextual embeddings for link prediction in heterogeneous networks. In: Leskovec, J., Grobelnik, M., Najork, M., Tang, J., Zia, L. (eds.) Proceedings of the Web Conference 2021, pp. 2946–2957. ACM/IW3C2, Virtual Event (2021). https://doi.org/10.1145/3442381.3450060
50. Wang, X., et al.: Heterogeneous graph attention network. In: Proceedings of the WWW, San Francisco, CA, USA, pp. 2022–2032 (2019). https://doi.org/10.1145/3308558.3313562
51. Wang, Z., Zhang, J., Feng, J., Chen, Z.: Knowledge graph embedding by translating on hyperplanes. In: Proceedings of the AAAI, Québec City, Québec, Canada, pp. 1112–1119 (2014). https://doi.org/10.1609/aaai.v28i1.8870
52. Xie, Z., Zhou, G., Liu, J., Huang, J.X.: ReInceptionE: relation-aware inception network with joint local-global structural information for knowledge graph embedding. In: Proceedings of the ACL, pp. 5929–5939 (2020). https://doi.org/10.18653/v1/2020.acl-main.526
53. Yang, B., Yih, W.t., He, X., Gao, J., Deng, L.: Embedding entities and relations for learning and inference in knowledge bases. In: Proceedings of the ICLR, San Diego, CA, USA (2015)
54. Ye, R., Li, X., Fang, Y., Zang, H., Wang, M.: A vectorized relational graph convolutional network for multi-relational network alignment. In: Proceedings of the IJCAI, Macao, China, pp. 4135–4141 (2019). https://doi.org/10.24963/ijcai.2019/574
55. Zhang, C., Song, D., Huang, C., Swami, A., Chawla, N.V.: Heterogeneous graph neural network. In: Proceedings of the SIGKDD, New York, NY, USA, pp. 793–803 (2019). https://doi.org/10.1145/3292500.3330961
56. Zhang, F., Yuan, N.J., Lian, D., Xie, X., Ma, W.Y.: Collaborative knowledge base embedding for recommender systems. In: Proceedings of the SIGKDD, New York, NY, USA, pp. 353–362 (2016). https://doi.org/10.1145/2939672.2939673
57. Zhao, J., Wang, X., Shi, C., Hu, B., Song, G., Ye, Y.: Heterogeneous graph structure learning for graph neural networks. In: Proceedings of the AAAI, pp. 4697–4705. AAAI Press (2021)
58. Zhu, J.-Z., Jia, Y.-T., Xu, J., Qiao, J.-Z., Cheng, X.-Q.: Modeling the correlations of relations for knowledge graph embedding. J. Comput. Sci. Technol. **33**(2), 323–334 (2018). https://doi.org/10.1007/s11390-018-1821-8

MultPAX: Keyphrase Extraction Using Language Models and Knowledge Graphs

Hamada M. Zahera[(✉)] [ID], Daniel Vollmers[ID], Mohamed Ahmed Sherif[ID],
and Axel-Cyrille Ngonga Ngomo[ID]

DICE Group, Department of Computer Science, Paderborn University,
Paderborn, Germany
{hamada.zahera,daniel.vollmers,mohamed.sherif,
axel.ngonga}@uni-paderborn.de

Abstract. Keyphrase extraction aims to identify a small set of phrases that best describe the content of text. The automatic generation of keyphrases has become essential for many natural language applications such as text categorization, indexing, and summarization. In this paper, we propose MultPAX, a multitask framework for extracting *present* and *absent* keyphrases using pre-trained language models and knowledge graphs. In particular, our framework contains three components: first, MultPAX identifies present keyphrases from an input document. Then, MultPAX links with external knowledge graphs to get more relevant phrases. Finally, MultPAX ranks the extracted phrases based on their semantic relatedness to the input document and return top-k phrases as a final output. We conducted several experiments on four benchmark datasets to evaluate the performance of MultPAX against different state-of-the-art baselines. The evaluation results demonstrate that our approach significantly outperforms the state-of-the-art baselines, with a significance t-test $p < 0.041$. Our source code and datasets are public available at https://github.com/dice-group/MultPAX.

Keywords: Present keyphrase extraction · Absent keyphrase generation · Knowledge graph · Pre-trained language models

1 Introduction

Keyphrase extraction is the process of extracting a small set of phrases that best describe a document. This process has been leveraged for several downstream applications, including text summarizing, organizing, and indexing [16]. In the literature, keyphrase extraction is divided into two sub-tasks: (i) detecting present keyphrases (PKE) that appear in a document, and (ii) generating absent keyphrases (AKG) that do not appear in the original document, but are essential for downstream applications (e.g., text summarization, indexing). Table 1 shows an example of extracting present and absent keyphrases from an input text.

Existing works mostly focus on extracting *present* keyphrases from an input text, including supervised learning (e.g., sequence labelling [22]), and unsupervised learning (e.g., TextRank [17], YAKE [4]). By contrast, generating *absent*

U. Sattler et al. (Eds.): ISWC 2022, LNCS 13489, pp. 303–318, 2022.
https://doi.org/10.1007/978-3-031-19433-7_18

Table 1. Example of present and absent keyphrase extraction from `Inspec` dataset. The predicted present keyphrases are in *italic, and the absent ones are highlighted in gray*

Input Text	*"This paper shows the importance that management plays in the protection of information and in the planning to handle a security breach when a theft of information happens. Recent thefts of information that have hit major companies have caused concern. These thefts were caused by companies' inability to determine risks associated with the protection of their data, and these companies lack of planning to properly manage a security breach when it occurs." quoted from [20]*
Ground-truth Keyphrases	security breach, risk analysis, management issue, theft of information
Predicted Keyphrases	*security breach, theft of information,* security management , security risk , data management

keyphrases (i.e., keyphrases that do not appear in a text) is a challenging task. According to the statistical study by [31], some benchmarking datasets (e.g., Inspec [9]) are missing up to 37.7% of *absent* keyphrases. To cope with this challenge, few studies have been proposed. For example, [15] employed a supervised sequence-to-sequence model with a *copy mechanism*, which allows copying important words directly from a source text, rather than decoding new words. However, this approach requires large-scale labelled data for training the model efficiently. In addition, the copy mechanism only generates one word at each time step and does not consider any dependencies between the selected words [33]. Another line of work aims to utilize external sources of knowledge to generate absent keyphrases. For example, [24] constructs a phrase bank consisting of all keyphrases in a text corpus. The authors assumed that absent keyphrases in one document might be found in other relevant documents. However, this approach requires creating a domain-specific phrase bank to generate absent keyphrases.

In this paper, we aim not only to *extract* present keyphrases from an input document, but also to *generate* absent keyphrases that are relevant and do not appear in the document. We reduce the effort required to develop a keyphrase model by employing pre-computed resources. In particular, we use *pre-trained language models* to extract present keyphrases and *knowledge graphs* (KGs) to generate absent keyphrases. Therefore, we propose an unsupervised multitask framework (dubbed MULTPAX) with the following pipeline: i) We tokenize an input document into n-grams phrases and embed both (*document and n-gram phrases*) as low-dimensional vectors into one semantic space. Then, we *extract* the top-k phrases that are close to the document's vector as candidates for present keyphrases. ii) We then *link* the extracted present keyphrases to find additional related terms (e.g., synonyms, hypernyms) from external KGs (e.g.,

DBPEDIA, BABELNET). For this purpose, we developed a new version of the MAG framework [18], which is optimized for linking keywords and extracting related terms. iii) Finally, we *rank* all keyphrases (i.e., *present* and *absent*) based on their semantic similarity to the input document. The top-k phrases are returned as the final keyphrases output.

Additionally, we propose an improved metric for evaluating predicted keyphrases based on their *semantic-matching* with ground-truth keyphrases. Existing studies [13,15,32] consider *precision, recall*, and F_1 based on the *exact-matching* between predicted and ground-truth keyphrases, which yields reasonable evaluation for present keyphrases that appear in text. However, in evaluating absent keyphrases, the exact-matching demonstrated an inefficient assessment of words that are semantically similar but are literally different [21]. As an example, assume *"Cryptocurrency"* as a ground-truth keyphrase, and a keyphrase model was able to generated *"Bitcoin"* as a predicted keyphrase. In this case, the exact-matching metric ignores the semantic relatedness between both words and considers them completely unrelated. By means of words embeddings, these words are similar and adjacent to each other in the embedding space. In this regard, we propose using an embedding-based F_1-score to evaluate keyphrases extraction in a more accurate semantic way.

To evaluate the performance of MULTPAX, we conducted several experiments on four benchmark datasets, where we study the performance of our system against different approaches. The evaluation results show that our approach significantly outperforms the state-of-the-art baselines with a significance t-test $p < 0.041$ and F_1-score up to 0.535. The main contributions in this paper can be summarized as follows:

- We propose an *unsupervised* multitask framework that not only extracts present keyphrases, but also generate absent ones.
- To the best of our knowledge, our approach is the first attempt that leverages existing *knowledge graphs* for keyphrases generation without the need to create keyphrases vocabularies or phrase banks.
- We introduce an *embedding-based* F_1 evaluation that considers semantic similarity between generated and ground-truth keyphrases rather than the existing *exact-matching*.
- We carried out several experiments on four benchmark datasets. The evaluation results showed that our approach proved to be more accurate compared with state-of-the-art baselines.

2   Related Work

In this section, we give an overview of the related approaches in *unsupervised keyphrase extraction* and *absent keyphrase generation*.

2.1   Unsupervised Keyphrase Extraction

Several approaches have recently been developed for extracting keyphrases in unsupervised setting without the need for annotated data. For example, statistical approaches such as TF-IDF and YAKE [4] compute statistical features (e.g., word frequencies and co-occurrences) to find important words as candidates for present keyphrases. Moreover, graph-based approaches like TextRank [17] construct a graph representation of text, where words are represented as nodes and their co-occurrences as edges. Thereafter, a node ranking algorithm (e.g., PageRank) is used to sort words, and return top-k words as candidate keyphrases. [3] proposed TopicRank, a graph-based approach similar to TextRank. In the first step, candidate phrases are clustered into topics and then ranked based on with their importance in the document.

Recent studies have demonstrated that embedding-based models can achieve significant results in extracting keyphrases. For example, EmbedRank [2] approach uses part-of-speech tags to extracts potential keyphrases from an input document. Then, EmbedRank uses a pre-trained embedding model to represent both phrases and an input document as low-dimensional vectors. Candidate keyphrases are then ranked based on their Cosine similarity scores to the document's embedding vector. Although pre-trained language models have shown promising performances for extracting present keyphrases, they have failed to generate absent keyphrases from their lexical corpus. Furthermore, [13] pointed out that embedding-based models ignore local information in a document. Accordingly, they developed a jointly-trained model to incorporate global and local context of a document. In the global view, their approach represented candidate keyphrases and the input document as low-dimensional vectors into one semantic space. After that, the similarity between each candidate keyphrase and the document is computed. In terms of the local context, the authors built a graph structure based on the document context, where nodes represent phrases and edges represent similarities between them. Finally, the output keyphrases are ranked based on this global and local information.

2.2 Absent Keyphrase Extraction

Many previous approaches have relied on *sequence-to-sequence* models—with encoder-decoder architecture—to generate absent keyphrases [6]. By doing so, sequence-to-sequence models are able to decode not only keyphrases that appear in source text, but also those that may be absent, i.e., the ones that are not explicitly mentioned in the text. However, additional mechanisms need to be integrated to improve the generation of absent keyphrases. For example, [31] applied a *Graph Neural Network* (GNN) to capture knowledge from related references in scholarly publications. A *neural topic model* is employed in [28] to expand the context of the decoding component to generate more absent keyphrases.

It is noteworthy that [32] achieved significant results in extracting keyphrases by dividing this task into two sub-tasks: present keyphrase extraction and absent keyphrase generation. Furthermore, the authors proposed a multitask approach to *select*, *guide*, and *generate* keyphrases. In the *select* module, the authors used a BiLSTM to predict whether a sentence has a keyphrase or not. Then, a *guider* network is employed to utilize the attention information and memorize the predictions of the *selector*. Finally, this information is fed to a *generator* network to generate absent keyphrases by selecting words from both the source text and a predefined vocabulary. In addition to these fully-supervised approaches, there are also some unsupervised methods that achieved promising results in generating keyphrases without the need for labelled data. [24] observed that many keyphrases absent from an input document appeared in other related documents. Therefore, they constructed a *phrase bank* of all keyphrases in a corpus. Then, they identified present keyphrases in relevant documents as candidates for absent keyphrases for the input document. In addition, they employed present keyphrases as *sliver labels* to train a sequence-to-sequence model. Finally, all keyphrases (both present and absent) were ranked based on their lexical and semantic similarity to an input document.

3   Our Approach

In this section, we present our approach for extracting *present* and *absent* keyphrases. Figure 1 depicts the architecture of our MULTPAX framework, including three components: i) *present keyphrase extraction* (PKE), ii) *absent keyphrase generation* (AKG), and iii) *Keyphrases Semantic Matching*.

3.1   Problem Formulation

Let $\mathcal{D}$ be an input document with $|S|$ sentences; each sentence $s \in S$ is a sequence of $|s|$ tokens $\mathcal{T} = \{t_1, t_2, \cdots, t_{|s|}\}$. Our goal is to build a keyphrase model that not only extracts *present keyphrases* $\mathcal{Y}^p = \{y_1^p, y_2^p, \cdots, y_{|\mathcal{Y}^p|}^p\}$ but also generates *absent keyphrases* $\mathcal{Y}^a = \{y_1^a, y_2^a, \cdots, y_{|\mathcal{Y}^a|}^a\}$ that are relevant to $\mathcal{D}$ by leveraging knowledge graphs such as DBPEDIA [1] and BABELNET [19].

Following previous works [8,22], we divide the task of keyphrase extraction into two sub-tasks: *Present Keyphrase Extraction* (PKE) and *Absent Keyphrase Generation* (AKG). Furthermore, we define the computation of final keyphrases as a *Semantic Matching* task. First, we consider PKE as a *ranking* problem, where candidate phrases are extracted and then ranked based on their similarities to the input document (see Sect. 3.2). Second, we formulate AKE as a *linking* problem to infer relevant information from external knowledge graphs. For this task, we employ an unsupervised *entity-linker* [23] that maps a present keyphrase ($\mathcal{Y}^p$) to its corresponding entity in a knowledge graph (i.e., DBPEDIA, BABEL-NET) and then get relevant terms (e.g., from `dct:subject`, `gold:hypernym` properties) as candidates for absent keyphrases. Finally, all keyphrases $\mathcal{Y}^p \cup \mathcal{Y}^a$ are ranked based on their similarities to $\mathcal{D}$, the top-k keyphrases are returned as the final output.

3.2   Present Keyphrase Extraction (PKE)

We employ the BERT language model [7] to extract present keyphrases based on their semantic similarity to a document. The main steps are as follows: (1) We tokenize an input document $\mathcal{D}$ into *n-gram phrases* and annotate each token

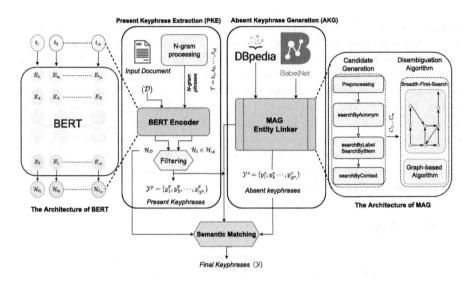

Fig. 1. The architecture of MultPAX framework with three components: *present keyphrase extraction, absent keyphrase generation* and *semantic matching*

with part-of-speech tags (e.g., ADJ: adjectives, NOUN: nouns, VERB: verbs). (2) Then, we remove stop words and keep noun phrases that consist of zero or more adjectives followed by one or multiple nouns [27]. (3) We employ the pre-trained language model (`BERT-Encoder`) to encode candidate keyphrases as low-dimensional vectors together with the input document into one embedding space.

A special preprocessing is applied to the input text of the `BERT-Encoder` as follows: a `[CLS]` token is added at the beginning of each sentence, which is then used to obtain the contextualized embeddings vector of a sentence. An additional token `[SEP]` is inserted to mark the end of a sentence. Afterward, the input is tokenized by *WordPiece* tokenizer [25]; each token t_i is associated with three types of embeddings: *token embeddings* (E_{t_i}) which represents the vocabulary index of each token, *segmentation embeddings* that distinguishes between input sentences $(E_A$ or $E_B)$, and *position embeddings* (E_i) to indicate the position of each word. The output of the `BERT-Encoder` is the sentence's representation matrix $\mathcal{H} = [h_0, h_1, \cdots h_{|s|}]$, where h_i denotes the embedding vector of token t_i. Formally, the embedding vector of a sentence s_j is

$$\mathcal{H}_j = \text{BERT-Encoder}(\{t_1, t_2, \cdots t_{|s|}\}). \tag{1}$$

Pooling is an essential operation for creating sentence and document embeddings [5]. It is commonly used to aggregate (e.g., mean, max) multiple representations (e.g., sentences) into one embedding vector. To obtain the document's embeddings $\mathcal{H}_\mathcal{D}$, we employ a `MaxPooling` layer on top of all sentences' representations. Formally,

$$\mathcal{H}_\mathcal{D} = \text{MaxPooling}(\{\mathcal{H}_1, \mathcal{H}_2, \cdots \mathcal{H}_{|S|}\}). \tag{2}$$

Finally, we use Cosine distance to compute similarities between the embedding vectors of candidate keyphrases $\mathcal{H}_i \in H_{|S|}$ and the document embedding $\mathcal{H}_\mathcal{D}$. We select the top-k keyphrases as candidates for present keyphrases.

3.3 Absent Keyphrase Generation (AKG)

To obtain absent keyphrases, we first link all present keyphrases $\mathcal{Y}^p$ to a knowledge graph and get additional surface forms (i.e., strings that could be synonyms or alternative names). We consider the DBPEDIA knowledge graph since it provides surface forms for a wide range of common entities. For *entity linking*, we follow a similar approach to the MAG framework [18].

MAG extracts entity links using two steps: *candidate generation* and *candidate disambiguation*. In the *candidate generation* step, MAG aims to find candidate links $(C_1, \ldots, C_n)$ for pre-marked entities in the search index [18]. To this end, MAG uses acronyms and labels in a knowledge graph to map premarked entity spans from the input text to candidate entities. Furthermore, MAG also relies on the Concise Bounded Description (CBD)[1] of the entities in a knowledge graph by comparing the context of the entity spans in the input document and the CBD of an entity in a knowledge graph [18]. We keep this candidate generation step from MAG and apply it to the extracted present keyphrases from the PKE component. In the *candidate disambiguation* step, MAG generates a local graph using a breadth-first-search method for all candidate entities on a knowledge graph. Then, MAG applies the HITS ranking algorithm [11] to jointly rank the candidate links for all entities in the local graph. HITS ranks the nodes in a directed graph based on incoming and outgoing edges. Authorities are seen as nodes, that carry important information, while hubs are nodes, that point to a large amount of authority nodes. So the authority score of a node n is calculated based on the hub score of the nodes, that have a directed edge to the node n, while the hub score of n is calculated based on the authority score of the nodes which are linked by n [11]. Formally, HITS calculates the authority score a_p for the node p as

$$a_p = \sum_{q:(q,p)\in G} h_q. \tag{3}$$

where h_q is the hub-score for the node q, given that a directed edge from node q to node p exists in the graph G. The hub-score h_p for a node p is calculated as

$$h_p = \sum_{q:(q,p)\in G} a_q. \tag{4}$$

where a_q is the authority-score for a node q, which is linked by node p [11]. a_q and h_p are initialized randomly and updated iteratively until convergence.

In contrast to MAG, we not only link present keyphrases, but also extract related terms for each linked keyphrase from a knowledge graph. Furthermore, we extract top-ranked candidates for each entity and n nodes with the highest

---

[1] https://www.w3.org/Submission/CBD/.

authority scores in the local graph, since their surface forms could be used as candidates for the absent keyphrases. In our approach, we use BABELNET to find *hypernyms* for the present keyphrases, in addition to the surface forms from DBPEDIA.

3.4   Keyphrases Semantic Matching

In the last component, we aim to identify top-k relevant keyphrases (*present and absent*), we set $k = \{5, 10, 20\}$ in our experiments. We regard this task as a semantic textual similarity [14]. To match similarities between a document $\mathcal{D}$ and candidate keyphrases, we embed them into one semantic space using a pre-trained embedding model. Then we employ Cosine distance to find top-k nearest keyphrases ($\mathcal{H}_i$) to the document's vector $\mathcal{H}_\mathcal{D}$ and return as final keyphrase predictions. Formally,

$$\mathrm{Cos}(\mathcal{H}_i, \mathcal{H}_\mathcal{D}) = \frac{\mathcal{H}_i \cdot \mathcal{H}_\mathcal{D}}{||\mathcal{H}_i|| \times ||\mathcal{H}_\mathcal{D}||}. \tag{5}$$

where $\mathcal{H}_i$ donates the embedding vector of candidate keyphrase (*present y_i^p* or *absent y_i^a*), and $\mathcal{H}_\mathcal{D}$ represents the embedding vector of the input document.

4   Experiments

We conducted our experiments to answer the following research questions:

Q_1. *How efficient is our approach in extracting present keyphrases compared to the state-of-the-art approaches?*

Q_2. *Are the existing exact-matching metrics (i.e., Precision, Recall and F_1-score) suitable for evaluating absent keyphrases?*

Q_3. *To what extent does each component in our framework contribute to the overall performance?*

Table 2. Statistics about the datasets (#Doc: number of documents, #Test: size of test set, #Avg. KP: average keyphrase per document, #Ratio%: percentage of absent keyphrase per dataset)

Dataset	#Doc	#Test	Avg. KP	Ratio%
Inspec	2k	500	7.65	37.7%
Krapivin	2.3k	460	3.03	15.3%
SemEval2010	144	100	7.15	11.3%
NUS	211	211	2.71	17.8%

4.1 Experimental Setup

Datasets. In our experiments, we used four benchmark datasets of English documents, namely, *Inspec* [9], *SemEval2010* [10], *Krapivin* [12], and *NUS* [26]. Table 2 provides a statistical overview of each dataset, including the total number of documents (#Doc.), the number of documents in the evaluation set (#Test), average keyphrases per document (Avg. KP) and the ratio of absent keyphrases in each dataset (Ratio%).

Baselines. We compared our approach with the following baselines for extracting keyphrases:

- **TextRank** [17] is an unsupervised approach that constructs a graph representation from a document, where nodes represent phrases and their edges are computed based on lexical similarities. Further, TextRank uses the *PageRank* algorithm to extract present keyphrases.
- **YAKE** [4] is a simple unsupervised method that extracts keywords automatically based on statistical features such as words co-occurrence and frequencies.
- **EmbedRank** [2] is an unsupervised method that employs words embeddings to identify relevant words to a document as candidate keyphrases. Furthermore, EmbedRank utilizes the *Maximum Marginal Relevance* algorithm to increase the diversity of the extracted keyphrases.
- **Supervised-CopyRNN** [15] is a supervised baseline that trains a sequence-to-sequence model with a *copy mechanism* on KP20K dataset [15]. We used this approach as a baseline for present keyphrases extraction as well as absent keyphrase generation to compare the performance of copy mechanism.
- **AutoKeyGen** [24] is an unsupervised approach that constructs a *phrase bank* by combining keyphrases from all documents into a corpus. Then, AutoKey-Gen considers lexical- and semantic-level similarities for selecting top candidate keyphrases (present and absent) for each input document.

Evaluation Metrics. We evaluated our approach using different metrics: *Precision*, *Recall*, and F_1 scores. The *Precision* is computed as the number of correctly-matched keyphrases over all predicted keyphrases.

Given a list of predicted keyphrases $\mathcal{Y} = (y_1, \ldots, y_{|\mathcal{Y}|})$, we select the top-$k$ ranked keyphrases $\mathcal{Y}_{:k} = (y_1, \ldots, y_{\min(k, |\mathcal{Y}|)})$ and compare with the top-k ranked keyphrases in the ground-truth set. We set $k = \{5, 10\}$ for present keyphrases and $k = \{10, 20\}$ for absent ones in our experiments. Following previous works [24,30], we use the *Porter Stemmer* from the NLTK library[2] v3.7 to compute exact-matching between the top-k predicted ($\mathcal{Y}_{:k}$) and the ground-truth ($\mathcal{Y}^{gold}$) keyphrases. The precision of the top-k predicted keyphrases is defined as

$$P@k = \frac{|\mathcal{Y}_{:k} \cap \mathcal{Y}^{gold}|}{|\mathcal{Y}_{:k}|}. \tag{6}$$

---

[2] https://www.nltk.org/index.html.

The *Recall* is calculated as how many correctly-matched keyphrases among all ground-truth keyphrases. Formally, the Recall is defined as

$$R@k = \frac{|\mathcal{Y}_{:k} \cap \mathcal{Y}^{gold}|}{|\mathcal{Y}^{gold}_{:k}|}. \tag{7}$$

and the $F_1@k$-score is defined as the harmonic mean of $P@k$ and $R@k$

$$F_1@k = 2 \times \frac{P@k \times R@k}{P@k + R@k}. \tag{8}$$

Although the *exact-matching* metric has been used widely in the literature [13], there is still a room for improvement regarding the absent keyphrases evaluation based on semantic similarity. Hence, we propose in Sect. 4.3 a semantic-based matching to evaluate the performance of generated absent keyphrases.

Hyperparameters. We performed a grid search to optimize the hyperparameters of our approach. We found the following values yield the best F_1-scores. In the PKE component, we tokenized the input text into phrases of 2–4 grams. Further, we considered the top-10 ranked phrases as candidates for present keyphrases. The full setup of our experiments is available at the GitHub repository.[3] For the baseline methods, the hyperparameters were set according to their original papers. In the MAG framework, we adapted the extraction of common entities to cover a larger set of entity types. In addition, we set the other hyperparameters values with the standard configuration[4] of the MAG framework.

Table 3. Evaluation results of *present* keyphrases prediction on `Inspec`, `SemEval2010`, `Krapivin`, and NUS datasets. $F_1@k$-scores are reported based on **exact-matching** between the predicted and ground-truth keyphrases. Best results are reported in bold

Model	Inspec		SemEval2010		Krapivin		NUS	
	$F_1@5$	$F_1@10$	$F_1@5$	$F_1@10$	$F_1@5$	$F_1@10$	$F_1@5$	$F_1@10$
TextRank	0.263	0.279	0.183	0.181	0.148	0.139	0.187	0.195
YAKE	0.027	0.038	0.050	0.242	0.013	0.020	0.013	0.020
EmbedRank	0.295	0.344	0.108	0.145	0.131	0.138	0.103	0.134
Supervised-CopyRNN	0.292	0.336	0.291	**0.296**	0.302	0.252	0.342	0.317
AutoKeyGen	0.303	**0.345**	0.187	0.240	0.171	0.155	0.218	0.233
MᴜʟᴛPAX	**0.371**	0.210	**0.449**	0.255	**0.384**	**0.334**	**0.535**	**0.344**

---

[3] https://github.com/dice-group/MultPAX.
[4] https://github.com/dice-group/AGDISTIS/blob/master/src/main/resources/config/agdistis.properties.

Table 4. *Absent* keyphrases evaluation (in terms of R@10, R@20). All results are reported based on **exact-matching** between the predicted and ground-truth keyphrases, except the last row shows Recall results based on **semantic-matching**

Model	Inspec		SemEval2010		Krapivin		NUS	
	R@10	R@20	R@10	R@20	R@10	R@20	R@10	R@20
Supervised-CopyRNN	0.051	0.068	0.049	0.057	0.116	0.142	0.078	0.10
AutoKeyGen-Bank	0.015	0.017	0.007	0.009	0.031	0.041	0.021	0.026
AutoKeyGen-Full	0.017	0.021	0.010	0.011	0.033	0.054	0.024	0.032
MULTPAX$_{\text{exact-Matching}}$	0.079	0.080	–	–	–	–	0.017	0.017
MULTPAX$_{\text{semantic-Matching}}$	0.696	0.584	–	–	–	–	0.608	0.669

4.2 Present Keyphrase Evaluation (Q_1)

To answer Q_1, we evaluated our approach (MULTPAX) vs. different baselines in extracting *present* keyphrases. As shown in Table 3, MULTPAX significantly outperforms all baselines by a large margin on most datasets with a significant *t-test* $p < 0.041$. This is due to, MULTPAX employs semantic similarity between candidate keyphrases and an input document using the state-of-the-art pre-trained language model in semantic textual matching [29]. In contrast, Copy-RNN [15] and AutoKeyGen [24] used sequence-to-sequence models to encode an input document as a low-dimensional vector and decode it back into a sequence of predicted keyphrases.

On the other hand, we find that YAKE does not perform well in detecting present keyphrases from short texts (e.g., papers' abstracts). Since YAKE relies on statistical features such as words co-occurrence and frequencies, which are efficiently computed only in long texts (e.g., full papers or news). Remarkably, the embedding-based baseline (EmbedRank) achieves comparable results; however, it fails to generate absent keyphrases. In our approach, we extract present keyphrases from text using contextualized embeddings and semantic matching. These findings answer Q_1; by employing pre-trained language models, we can not only efficiently identify present keyphrases from text without labelled data, but we also outperform the state-of-the-art approach (AutoKeyGen).

4.3 Absent Keyphrase Evaluation (Q_2)

We conduct further experiments to evaluate the performance of our approach against two baselines (namely, CopyRNN and AutoKeyGen) in generating absent keyphrases. Following previous work [24], we use the Recall metric (R@10, R@20) based on *exact-matching* for the performance evaluation as shown in Table 4. Since we used the same experimental setup of CopyRNN and AutoKeyGen approaches, we obtained the evaluation results from their papers [15, 24].

Regarding Q_2, we can clearly see that all approaches achieve poor performances when considering exact-matching between predicted and ground-truth keyphrases. For example, if two keyphrases are semantically similar, e.g., *"disaster relief organization"* and *"crisis responses institute"*, these keyphrases will not be considered as a *match* using the existing metrics. Hence, we found that such metrics are unsuitable for evaluating absent keyphrases. We propose an improved evaluation metric based on the *semantic-matching*. Formally, let $\mathcal{Y}^a$ be predicted keyphrases; $\mathcal{Y}^{gold}$ is ground-truth keyphrases. We first embed each keyphrase in $\mathcal{Y}^a$ and $\mathcal{Y}^{gold}$. Then, we use Cosine distance to compute similarities between the embedding of each keyphrase in $\mathcal{Y}$ and $\mathcal{Y}^{gold}$. We set a threshold (> 0.5) for similarities scores to consider semantic-matching between $\mathcal{Y}$ and $\mathcal{Y}^{gold}$. The two last rows in Table 4 show the evaluation results of R@10 and R@20 based on semantic-matching compared to exact-matching in absent keyphrase extraction.

The AutoKeyGen baseline demonstrates competitive performance in generating absent keyphrases on the NUS dataset. However, the generated keyphrases by AutoKeyGen are limited to the ones from the phrase bank of each dataset. In contrast, our approach leverages public knowledge graphs (such as DBPEDIA and BABELNET) to obtain relevant phrases as candidates for absent keyphrases.

Limitation of Our Work. In our experiment, we used the MAG framework to connect present keyphrases to DBPEDIA knowledge graph (see Sect. 3.3). In the SemEval2010 and Krapivin datasets, we were unable to link present keyphrases, due to the lack of coverage for these keyphrases in the DBPEDIA knowledge graph. That is the reason for the missing values shown in the last two rows of Table 4 for these datasets. In our future work, we plan to integrate other knowledge graphs (e.g., YAGO and WIKIDATA) to extend the coverage of entity linking in the MAG framework.

4.4   Ablation Study (Q_3)

To answer Q_3, we analysed the impact of each component of our framework on the overall performance. For this purpose, we set up four variants of our framework. The first variant MULTPAX-PKE was dedicated for only extracting present keyphrases, i.e., no absent keyphrase generation and thus no linking with knowledge graphs. We also created two variants of MULTPAX with the purpose of evaluating the generation of absent keyphrases, namely MULTPAX-AKE$_{DBpedia}$ and MULTPAX-AKE$_{BabelNet}$. Furthermore, we configured the MAG framework to link present keyphrases only with DBPEDIA in case of MULTPAX-AKE$_{DBpedia}$, and only with BABELNET for MULTPAX-AKE$_{BabelNet}$. Finally, we benchmarked the entire framework MULTPAX$_{Full}$ as our fourth variant.

Table 5 reports the evaluation results of each component in terms of *semantic-matching* F_1@5, and F_1@10 on the Inspec dataset, since it contains the highest ratio of absent keyphrases among the benchmark datasets. We can see that the performance of MULTPAX-PKE is improved when linking with knowledge graphs, e.g., MULTPAX-AKE$_{DBpedia}$ outperforms MULTPAX-PKE by $+0.41$ in F_1@10. In addition, we noticed that our approach could retrieve more terms from DBPEDIA than BABELNET, since DBPEDIA contains more semantic ontologies (approximately 3.5 millions instances) extracted from Wikipedia information boxes. Finally, our MULTPAX-$_{Full}$ showed an improved performance with

F_1-scores (0.911 in F_1@5, 0.763 in F_1@10) when incorporating both knowledge graphs (i.e., DBPEDIA and BABELNET) compared with individual variants. These findings conclude that each component of MULTPAX contributes to the overall performance of our framework and answers our last research question Q_3.

Table 5. Ablation Study of MULTPAX framework on `Inspec` dataset. F_1@K-scores are reported based on **semantic-matching** between the predicted and ground-truth keyphrases

MULTPAX-variant	F_1@5	F_1@10
MULTPAX-PKE	0.892	0.686
MULTPAX-AKE$_{BabelNet}$	0.907	0.701
MULTPAX-AKE$_{DBpedia}$	0.911	0.727
MULTPAX$_{Full}$	**0.911**	**0.763**

5   Conclusion

This paper presents MULTPAX framework, a multitask approach for extracting present and absent keyphrases, including three components: i) Present Keyphrase Extraction, ii) Absent Keyphrases Generation, and iii) Keyphrases Semantic Matching. In our approach, we employ a pre-trained language model (BERT) and knowledge graphs (DBPEDIA and BABELNET) in keyphrase extraction. Our experiments showed that pre-trained language models are capable of efficiently extracting present keyphrases. Furthermore, knowledge graphs proved to be valuable resources for generating keyphrases that are absent, especially in short text. In our future work, we plan to apply a bootstrapped approach for keyphrase extraction from DBPEDIA abstracts to find more relevant terms. In particular, we intend to apply MULTPAX recursively on the abstracts of DBPEDIA entities. In addition, we will experiment with other knowledge graphs (e.g., YAGO and WIKIDATA) to extend the coverage of entity link in the MAG framework.

Supplemental Material Statement. We implemented our framework in `Python 3.7`, the source code and how-to-run instructions can be found at the GitHub repository.[5] Furthermore, we used the benchmarking datasets available in the Dropbox drive.[6] For the baseline models, we used `OpenNMT library`[7], which enables us to benchmark different state-of-the-art baselines in our experiments. In addition, we used the pre-trained embedding of BERT model, namely `all-MiniLM-L6-v2` with 384 embedding dimension from the `huggingface`

---

[5] https://github.com/dice-group/MultPAX.
[6] https://www.dropbox.com/s/aluvkblymjs7i3r/MULTPAX-Datasets.zip?dl=0.
[7] https://github.com/memray/OpenNMT-kpg-release.

`library`[8] v4.16. For the hardware requirements, we used a computing server with 256 GB memory and `Xeon(R) CPU E5-2630 v4` with 2.20 GHz to run our experiments.

Acknowledgments. This work has been supported by the German Federal Ministry for Economic Affairs and Climate Action (BMWK) within the projects RAKI (grant no 01MD19012B) and SPEAKER (grant no 01MK20011U) as well as by the German Federal Ministry of Education and Research (BMBF) within the projects COLIDE (grant no 01IS21005D) and EML4U (grant no 01IS19080B). We are also grateful to Diego Moussallem for the valuable discussion on earlier drafts and Pamela Heidi Douglas for editing the manuscript.

References

1. Auer, S., Bizer, C., Kobilarov, G., Lehmann, J., Cyganiak, R., Ives, Z.: DBpedia: a nucleus for a web of open data. In: Aberer, K., et al. (eds.) ASWC/ISWC -2007. LNCS, vol. 4825, pp. 722–735. Springer, Heidelberg (2007). https://doi.org/10.1007/978-3-540-76298-0_52

2. Bennani-Smires, K., Musat, C., Hossmann, A., Baeriswyl, M., Jaggi, M.: Simple unsupervised keyphrase extraction using sentence embeddings. In: Proceedings of the 22nd Conference on Computational Natural Language Learning, pp. 221–229 (2018)

3. Bougouin, A., Boudin, F., Daille, B.: Topicrank: graph-based topic ranking for keyphrase extraction. In: Proceedings of the Sixth International Joint Conference on Natural Language Processing, pp. 543–551 (2013)

4. Campos, R., Mangaravite, V., Pasquali, A., Jorge, A., Nunes, C., Jatowt, A.: Yake! keyword extraction from single documents using multiple local features. Inf. Sci. **509**, 257–289 (2020)

5. Chen, Q., Ling, Z.H., Zhu, X.: Enhancing sentence embedding with generalized pooling. In: Proceedings of the 27th International Conference on Computational Linguistics, pp. 1815–1826 (2018)

6. Chen, W., Gao, Y., Zhang, J., King, I., Lyu, M.R.: Title-guided encoding for keyphrase generation. In: Proceedings of the AAAI Conference on Artificial Intelligence, vol. 33, pp. 6268–6275 (2019)

7. Devlin, J., Chang, M.W., Lee, K., Toutanova, K.: Bert: pre-training of deep bidirectional transformers for language understanding. arXiv preprint arXiv:1810.04805 (2018)

8. Gollapalli, S.D., Li, X.L., Yang, P.: Incorporating expert knowledge into keyphrase extraction. In: Proceedings of the AAAI Conference on Artificial Intelligence, vol. 31 (2017)

9. Hulth, A.: Improved automatic keyword extraction given more linguistic knowledge. In: Proceedings of the 2003 Conference on Empirical Methods in Natural Language Processing, pp. 216–223 (2003)

10. Kim, S.N., Medelyan, O., Kan, M.Y., Baldwin, T.: Semeval-2010 task 5: automatic keyphrase extraction from scientific articles. In: Proceedings of the 5th International Workshop on Semantic Evaluation, pp. 21–26 (2010)

---

[8] https://huggingface.co/sentence-transformers/all-MiniLM-L6-v2.

11. Kleinberg, J.M.: Authoritative sources in a hyperlinked environment. J. ACM (JACM) **46**(5), 604–632 (1999)
12. Krapivin, M., Autaeu, A., Marchese, M.: Large dataset for keyphrases extraction (2009)
13. Liang, X., Wu, S., Li, M., Li, Z.: Unsupervised keyphrase extraction by jointly modeling local and global context. In: Proceedings of the 2021 Conference on Empirical Methods in Natural Language Processing, pp. 155–164 (2021)
14. Majumder, G., Pakray, P., Gelbukh, A., Pinto, D.: Semantic textual similarity methods, tools, and applications: a survey. Comput. Sist. **20**(4), 647–665 (2016)
15. Meng, R., Zhao, S., Han, S., He, D., Brusilovsky, P., Chi, Y.: Deep keyphrase generation. In: Proceedings of the 55th Annual Meeting of the Association for Computational Linguistics (vol. 1: Long Papers), pp. 582–592 (2017)
16. Alami Merrouni, Z., Frikh, B., Ouhbi, B.: Automatic keyphrase extraction: a survey and trends. J. Intell. Inf. Syst. **54**(2), 391–424 (2019). https://doi.org/10.1007/s10844-019-00558-9
17. Mihalcea, R., Tarau, P.: Textrank: bringing order into text. In: Proceedings of the 2004 Conference on Empirical Methods in Natural Language Processing, pp. 404–411 (2004)
18. Moussallem, D., Usbeck, R., Röder, M., Ngonga Ngomo, A.C.: MAG: a multilingual, knowledge-base agnostic and deterministic entity linking approach. In: K-CAP 2017: Knowledge Capture Conference, p. 8. ACM (2017)
19. Navigli, R., Ponzetto, S.P.: Babelnet: the automatic construction, evaluation and application of a wide-coverage multilingual semantic network. Artif. Intell. **193**, 217–250 (2012)
20. Polstra III, R.M.: A case study on how to manage the theft of information. In: Proceedings of the 2nd Annual Conference on Information Security Curriculum Development, pp. 135–138 (2005)
21. Ray Chowdhury, J., Caragea, C., Caragea, D.: Keyphrase extraction from disaster-related tweets. In: The World Wide Web Conference, pp. 1555–1566 (2019)
22. Sahrawat, D., et al.: Keyphrase extraction as sequence labeling using contextualized embeddings. In: Jose, J.M., et al. (eds.) ECIR 2020. LNCS, vol. 12036, pp. 328–335. Springer, Cham (2020). https://doi.org/10.1007/978-3-030-45442-5_41
23. Shen, W., Wang, J., Han, J.: Entity linking with a knowledge base: issues, techniques, and solutions. IEEE Trans. Knowl. Data Eng. **27**(2), 443–460 (2014)
24. Shen, X., Wang, Y., Meng, R., Shang, J.: Unsupervised deep keyphrase generation. In: Proceedings of the AAAI Conference on Artificial Intelligence, vol. 36, pp. 11303–11311 (2022)
25. Song, X., Salcianu, A., Song, Y., Dopson, D., Zhou, D.: Fast wordpiece tokenization. In: Proceedings of the 2021 Conference on Empirical Methods in Natural Language Processing, pp. 2089–2103 (2021)
26. Vijayakumar, A.K., et al.: Diverse beam search: decoding diverse solutions from neural sequence models. arXiv preprint arXiv:1610.02424 (2016)
27. Wan, X., Xiao, J.: Single document keyphrase extraction using neighborhood knowledge. In: AAAI, vol. 8, pp. 855–860 (2008)
28. Wang, Y., Li, J., Chan, H.P., King, I., Lyu, M.R., Shi, S.: Topic-aware neural keyphrase generation for social media language. In: Proceedings of the 57th Annual Meeting of the Association for Computational Linguistics, pp. 2516–2526 (2019)
29. Xia, T., Wang, Y., Tian, Y., Chang, Y.: Using prior knowledge to guide bert's attention in semantic textual matching tasks. In: Proceedings of the Web Conference 2021, pp. 2466–2475 (2021)

30. Ye, H., Wang, L.: Semi-supervised learning for neural keyphrase generation. In: Proceedings of the 2018 Conference on Empirical Methods in Natural Language Processing, pp. 4142–4153 (2018)
31. Ye, J., Cai, R., Gui, T., Zhang, Q.: Heterogeneous graph neural networks for keyphrase generation. arXiv preprint arXiv:2109.04703 (2021)
32. Zhao, J., Bao, J., Wang, Y., Wu, Y., He, X., Zhou, B.: SGG: learning to select, guide, and generate for keyphrase generation. In: Proceedings of the 2021 Conference of the North American Chapter of the Association for Computational Linguistics: Human Language Technologies, pp. 5717–5726 (2021)
33. Zhao, Y., et al.: Deep keyphrase completion. arXiv preprint arXiv:2111.01910 (2021)

RT-KGD: Relation Transition Aware Knowledge-Grounded Dialogue Generation

Kexin Wang[1], Zhixu Li[2(✉)], Jiaan Wang[1], Jianfeng Qu[1(✉)], Ying He[3], An Liu[1], and Lei Zhao[1]

[1] School of Computer Science and Technology, Soochow University, Suzhou, China
{kxwang1,jawang1}@stu.suda.edu.cn, {jfqu,anliu,zhaol}@suda.edu.cn
[2] Shanghai Key Laboratory of Data Science, School of Computer Science,
Fudan University, Shanghai, China
zhixuli@fudan.edu.cn
[3] IFLYTEK Research, Suzhou, China
yinghe@iflytek.com

Abstract. Grounding dialogue system with external knowledge is a promising way to improve the quality of responses. Most existing works adopt knowledge graphs (KGs) as the external resources, paying attention to the contribution of entities in the last utterance of the dialogue for context understanding and response generation. Nevertheless, the correlations between knowledge implied in the multi-turn context and the transition regularities between relations in KGs are under-explored. To this end, we propose a Relation Transition aware Knowledge-Grounded Dialogue Generation model (RT-KGD). Specifically, inspired by the latent logic of human conversation, our model integrates dialogue-level relation transition regularities with turn-level entity semantic information. In this manner, the interaction between knowledge is considered to produce abundant clues for predicting the appropriate knowledge and generating coherent responses. The experimental results on both automatic evaluation and manual evaluation indicate that our model outperforms state-of-the-art baselines.

Keywords: Knowledge-Grounded Dialogue · Response generation · Relation transition regularity

1 Introduction

Knowledge-Grounded Dialogue Generation (KGD) aims at generating an informative response based on both dialogue context and external knowledge [6,9]. Current works typically utilize structured knowledge graphs (KGs) [16,32,38] or unstructured texts [9,36] as knowledge resources. Incorporating external knowledge related to the dialogue context has proven to alleviate generating meaningless and bland responses caused by traditional generative models, such as *"I don't know"* and *"You are right"* [11].

K. Wang and Z. Li—The first two authors made equal contributions to this work.

U. Sattler et al. (Eds.): ISWC 2022, LNCS 13489, pp. 319–335, 2022.
https://doi.org/10.1007/978-3-031-19433-7_19

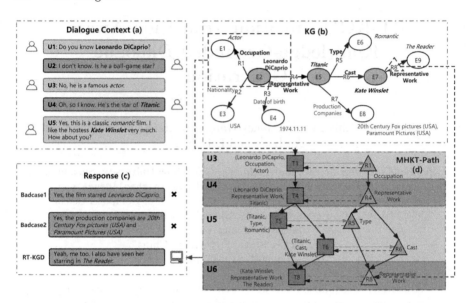

Fig. 1. An illustrative example from KdConv [39]. Based on the dialogue context (a) and the related KG (b), KGD is required to generate a response (c) guided by the MHKT-Path (d). The **bold** denotes the core entities in the dialogue, and the *Italic* denotes related knowledge values involved in the dialogue.

The existing works mainly focus on two aspects in KGD task: knowledge-enhanced context understanding [2,29] and knowledge-fused response generation [13,14]. Traditional efforts [2,6,39] simply treat the relevant external knowledge as the textual complementary to the dialogue context for both context understanding and response generation, neglecting considerable structural information in KGs. Some recent works [8,16,32] realize that the correlation between entities plays an important role in continuing dialogue, thus propose to excavate the valuable structural information between entities in the knowledge graph to predict the entities that might appear in the next response. The predicted entities are further used to guide the response generation. For example, DialKG Walker [16] treats the entities mentioned in the last utterance as the starting nodes and further retrieves relevant entities from KG within two hops. DuConv [30] pre-defines a topic goal including two entities for each dialogue, which guides the model to start with the first entity and gradually transition to the second one.

Despite their great contributions, there are two main drawbacks: on the one hand, the **entity-guided KGD** methods [16,32] consider the entities in the dialogue as the only guidance knowledge for context understanding and response generation, which neglects the importance of **relations** between entities in the KG. However, the regularity behind human conversation can be summarized as a sequence of topics, where each topic may correspond to a relation between entities rather than a single entity in the KG. On the other hand, the existing

KGD methods [8, 16] only care about the information in the last dialogue turn for predicting the subsequent knowledge, which is insufficient to learn how human transfer topics across a multi-turn dialogue. Taking Fig. 1 as an example, both badcase 1 and badcase 2 are flawed generated results based on the dialogue context. Badcase 1 demonstrates that the generated response might be redundant and incoherent without modeling multiple turns of knowledge, while badcase 2 reveals an abrupt transition in the topic since the latent relation transition path throughout the dialogue is ignored.

In this paper, we propose a novel KGD model: Relation Transition aware Knowledge-Grounded Dialogue Generation (RT-KGD), which models the knowledge transition across multi-turn dialogue by integrating dialogue-level relation transition regularities with turn-level entity semantic information. Specifically, we obtain all the relations and entities contained in the multi-turn dialogue context to construct a so-called Multi-turn Heterogeneous Knowledge Transition Path (MHKT-Path), which can be viewed as a subgraph of the external KG integrated with the sequential information of relations and entities in the multi-turn dialogue. Based on the constructed MHKT-Path, a knowledge prediction module is proposed to retrieve the triplets that might appear in the subsequent response from the external KG, and they are further fused for triplet prediction. Finally, the subsequent response is generated conditioned on both dialogue context and the predicted triplet. As the example shown in Fig. 1, the MHKT-Path grasps the latent conversation regularity of human beings, and the generated response based on the proposed RT-KGD is informative and coherent with the dialogue context.

The main contributions of this paper are concluded as follows:

- To the best of our knowledge, we are the first to incorporate the relation transition across multi-turn dialogue into the KGD task. In this manner, the regularity behind human conversation can be portrayed by integrating relation transition paths and entity semantic information.
- We propose to build a Multi-turn Heterogeneous Knowledge Transition Path (MHKT-Path) for each dialogue, which integrates the structure information of external KG and the sequential information of knowledge with the multi-turn dialogue. Based on MHKT-Path, our model then retrieves appropriate knowledge from the KG to guide the next response generation.
- The experimental results on a multi-domain knowledge-driven dialogue dataset (i.e., KdConv [39]) indicate that our model outperforms strong baseline models in both automatic and manual evaluation.

2   Related Work

According to whether to introduce knowledge, we categorize previous dialogue generation works into *Vanilla Dialogue Generation* and *Knowledge-grounded Dialogue Generation*.

Vanilla Dialogue Generation. Early dialogue systems typically employ Sequence-to-Sequence (Seq2Seq) models to generate responses [20,21,31], which is further improved with advanced context encoders [20,31] or more efficient response generation methods [2,33,37]. Recently, pre-trained generative models with the backbone of Transformer [25], such as GPT-2 [18] and BART [10], achieve promising performance in many text generation tasks. There is increasing work focusing on designing Transformer-based pre-trained dialogue models. Among them, Blender [19] enhances Transformer architecture and show their superiority in dialogue generation. DialoGPT [35] extends GPT-2 [18] for response generation. Besides, PLATO [3] pre-trains unified language models for both bi-directional encoding and uni-directional decoding. Nevertheless, they can only implicitly learn dialogue strategies and commonsense knowledge from dialogue corpora, resulting in limited transferability to other dialogue scenes.

Knowledge-Grounded Dialogue Generation. A promising way to generate meaningful and informative responses is to utilize external knowledge to guide the models. Generally, the external knowledge comes from textual corpora [9], commonsense knowledge graphs [29,32,38], and domain knowledge graphs [30,39]. To utilize the knowledge, [6,26] adapt the memory network [23] to store the relevant knowledge and then generate responses conditioned on both dialogue context and stored knowledge. Besides, [12,29] employ the posterior distribution of knowledge to guide its prior distribution, leading to accurate knowledge selection and high-quality generated responses. Furthermore, some work [13,14,29] leverages copy mechanism to copy words from knowledge sources directly and generate more informative responses. Although great progress has been made, the structural information of KG is neglected, which might lead to suboptimal responses.

To effectively excavate the structural information, some researchers attempt to utilize graph neural networks on KG to obtain its structure-aware representation that is further incorporated into dialogue generation [16,32,38]. AttnIO [8] leverages bi-direction attention flows to propagate messages from the entities appearing in the last utterance to their neighbor entities in KG. ConceptFlow [32] applies a graph attention mechanism to attend to appropriate concepts conditioning on dialogue context for responses generation, where the concepts are extracted from ConceptNet [22], a large-scale commonsense knowledge graph. Unlike previous research, our RT-KGD (1) refines the dialogue-level knowledge transition from different granularity; (2) incorporates the related knowledge based on the whole dialogue context rather than only the last utterance.

3 Methodology

In this section, we formally define the knowledge-ground dialogue generation task (Sect. 3.1) and then elaborate on four principal components of our RT-KGD model. As illustrated in Fig. 2, our model first constructs the multi-turn heterogeneous knowledge transition path (MHKT-Path) for the given dialogue context (Sect. 3.2) and then encodes the MHKT-Path by a knowledge encoder (Sect. 3.3).

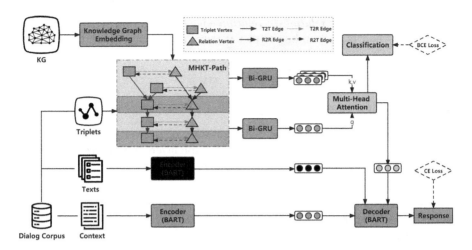

Fig. 2. The architecture of the proposed RT-KGD model.

Next, the predicted triplet from a knowledge prediction (Sect. 3.4) is finally incorporated into the subsequent response, which is generated by a knowledge-enhanced encoder-decoder (Sect. 3.5).

3.1 Task Formulation

Given a dialogue context $C = \{u_1, u_2, \cdots, u_{n-1}\}$, where u_i represents the i-th utterance. Each u_i corresponds to a knowledge triplet set $K_i = \{(h_{i_1}, r_{i_1}, t_{i_1}), (h_{i_2}, r_{i_2}, t_{i_2}), \cdots, (h_{i_{|K_i|}}, r_{i_{|K_i|}}, t_{i_{|K_i|}})\}$ $(|K_i| \geq 0)$, where (h, r, t) means that head entity h and tail entity t have a relation r, and a descriptive text set $S_i = \{s_{i_1}, s_{i_2}, \cdots, s_{i_{|S_i|}}\}$ $(|S_i| \geq 0)$. All knowledge triplets and descriptive texts are from domain knowledge graph $\mathcal{G}$ and corpus $\mathcal{O}$. The goal of knowledge-grounded dialogue systems is to generate a proper response u_n based on the dialogue context C, knowledge graph $\mathcal{G}$, and knowledge corpus $\mathcal{O}$.

3.2 Multi-turn Heterogeneous Knowledge Transition Path

To integrate dialogue-level relation transition regularities with turn-level entity semantic information, we utilize the knowledge triples associated with the given dialogue context, i.e., $K = K_1 \cup K_2 \cup \cdots \cup K_{n-1}$, to construct the multi-turn heterogeneous knowledge transition path, which is called MHKT-path. As shown in Fig. 2, MHKT-path contains two types of vertices, i.e., triplet vertices and relation vertices. In detail, each triplet vertex represents a knowledge triplet belonging to K, and corresponds with a relation vertex which is extracted from it. There are four types of edges in MHKT-Path: (1) the *triplet-to-triplet* edge links the triplet vertices associated in one utterance with others in the neighbor utterances; (2) the paired *triplet-to-relation* and (3) *relation-to-triplet* edges denote the bi-directional interaction between triplet vertices and their corresponding relation vertices; (4) the *relation-to-relation* edge links relation vertices with each other only if their corresponding triplet vertices are connected. In this manner, the knowledge transition of both turn-level triplets and dialogue-level relations is integrated into the MHKT-Path.

3.3 Knowledge Encoder

The knowledge encoder learns the representation of the vertices in MHKT-Path. Specifically, it contains vertex initializer and graph layers to initialize and update the vertex representations.

Vertex Initializer. Instead of directly using the average word embeddings of the flat texts in entities and relations, we employ a KG embedding algorithm (i.e., TransR [15]) to initialize the representation of vertices in our MHKT-Path[1]:

$$h_{e_i}^0 = \text{TransR}(e_i) \tag{1}$$

where $e_i \in \mathcal{K}$ denotes a KG element (e.g., entity or relation), $h_{e_i}^0$ means the initialized representation of e_i. TransR($\cdot$) represents the TransR KG embedding function, learned by projecting entities from entity space to different relation spaces and building translations between the projected entities. In this way, the learned representation of KG elements in $\mathcal{K}$ contain the global KG structural information due to their interaction in KG [4,15,34].

For relation vertex in MHKT-Path, we directly use $h_{e_i}^0$ as its initial representation. For triplet vertex (h_i, r_i, t_i), we calculate its representation as:

$$\text{TransR}(h_i) \oplus \text{TransR}(r_i) \oplus \text{TransR}(t_i) \tag{2}$$

where $\oplus$ denotes concatenation.

Graph Layers. Graph layers are used to update the vertex representations with the local structural information in the established MHKT-Path. Here, we employ the Heterogeneous Graph Transformer (HGT) [7] as the graph layers since it is aware of different types of vertices and edges. Given the MHKT-Path, the representation of each vertex v_i is updated by aggregating its neighbor information:

$$HGT(h_{v_i}^\ell) = \underset{\forall v_{src} \in N(v_i)}{\textbf{Aggregate}} \left(\textbf{Attention}(v_i^{\ell-1}, v_{src}^{\ell-1}) \cdot \textbf{Message}(v_{src}^{\ell-1}) \right) \tag{3}$$

where $N(v_i)$ is the neighbor vertices set of v_i, the **Aggregate**($\cdot$), **Attention**($\cdot$), and **Message**($\cdot$) are three basic operators in HGT:

- **Attention**($\cdot$) calculates the mutual attention of each vertex pair, where each type of vertex and edge has a unique linear projection.

---

[1] We also attempt to encode entities and relations based on word embedding, as suggested by [27,28], the results underperform that of using TransR.

- **Message**($\cdot$) transfers information from different types of neighbor vertices of each vertex v_i.
- **Aggregate**($\cdot$) integrates messages from neighbor vertices with attention weights to the core vertex v_i.

Finally, for vertex v_i, we concatenate the final node representation and the corresponding initial node representation with a simple linear projection:

$$h_{v_i}^{HGT} = W([h_{v_i}^0 \oplus h_{v_i}^L]) \tag{4}$$

where W is trainable parameters, L is the number of layers of HGT.

3.4 Knowledge Predictor

After obtaining the final representations of both triplet and relation vertices in MHKT-Path, the knowledge predictor is used to predict the knowledge which might be implied in the response. There are three parts to knowledge prediction, i.e., relation prediction, relation-aware triplet prediction, and multi-label triplet classification. Since the knowledge encoder aggregates only local neighborhood information, we further employ the bi-directional gated recurrent unit (Bi-GRU) [5] to enrich the sequential representations of relations and triplets.

In detail, we first treat the average vertices representation in dialogue order as the input of Bi-GRU. Suppose there are m relation vertices and m triplet vertices in turn i. The relation vertices in turn i are denoted as $\{r_{i,j}\}_{j=1}^m$, whose average representation is shown as follows:

$$R_i^0 = Mean(h_{r_{i,1}}^{HGT}, \cdots, h_{r_{i,m}}^{HGT}) \tag{5}$$

Similarly, the triplet vertices in turn i are denoted as $\{t_{i,j}\}_{j=1}^m \subset \mathcal{K}$, whose average representation is:

$$T_i^0 = Mean(h_{t_{i,1}}^{HGT}, \cdots, h_{t_{i,m}}^{HGT}) \tag{6}$$

Relation Prediction. The relation prediction part is to obtain the n-th relation hidden state $h_r^{GRU}(n)$ based on the previous $n-1$ turns relation representation. At step t of relation prediction, Bi-GRU generates the t-th relation hidden state as follows:

$$\begin{aligned} h_r^{GRU}(t) &= [h_r^{fw}(t); h_r^{bw}(t)] \\ &= [\overrightarrow{GRU}(R_t^0, h_r^{fw}(t-1)); \overleftarrow{GRU}(R_t^0, h_r^{bw}(t-1))] \end{aligned} \tag{7}$$

Relation Transition Aware Triplet Prediction. Different from the relation, we utilize Bi-GRU to obtain $n-1$ triplet hidden states $h_t^{GRU}(1), \cdots, h_t^{GRU}(n-1)$ based on the input $T^0 = T_1^0, \cdots, T_{n-1}^0$. For the i-th triplet, its hidden state is calculated as follows:

$$\begin{aligned} h_t^{GRU}(i) &= [h_t^{fw}(i); h_t^{bw}(i)] \\ &= [\overrightarrow{GRU}(T_i^0, h_T^{fw}(i-1)); \overleftarrow{GRU}(T_i^0, h_t^{bw}(i-1))] \end{aligned} \tag{8}$$

After obtaining the predicted n-th relation hidden state and $n-1$ triplet hidden states, we employ multi-head attention [25] to jointly attend to the information from both dialogue level and turn level. Thus the predicted triplet representation $h_{t_n}^{ATT}$ is calculated as follows:

$$\alpha_i = softmax_i \left(h_{r_n}^{GRU^T} h_{t_i}^{GRU} \right)$$

$$h_{t_n}^{ATT} = \overset{D}{\underset{d=1}{\|}} \sum_{i=1}^{n-1} \alpha_i^d h_{t_i}^{GRU}$$

(9)

where D denotes the number of attention heads.

Multi-label Triplet Classification. Since there might be multiple knowledge in the next response, the multi-label classification is adapted to map the predicted triplet representation to a label vector, where the number of labels is the total number of triplets in the knowledge graph $\mathcal{G}$.

Formally, let label $l = W_l(h_{t_n}^{ATT}) \in \mathcal{R}^{|\mathcal{K}|}$, where W_l is a trainable parameter and $|\mathcal{K}|$ is the total triplet size. The target label is denoted as $y \in \{0,1\}^{|\mathcal{K}|}$. Then we adapt the binary cross-entropy (BCE) loss to supervise the classification of triplets:

$$L_{BCE} = -\frac{1}{\mathcal{K}} \sum_{i=1}^{\mathcal{K}} \left[y_i log(\sigma(l_i)) + (1 - y_i)log(1 - \sigma(l_i)) \right]$$

(10)

where $\sigma(\cdot)$ is sigmoid function.

3.5 Knowledge-Enhanced Encoder-Decoder

We employ pre-trained BART [10] as the backbone of our KGD model, which aims to generate the final response based on dialogue context C, predicted triplet representation K and corresponding descriptive texts S. The input dialogue context is formed as "[CLS] u_1 [SEP] u_2 [SEP] $\cdots$ [SEP] u_{n-1} [SEP]", where [CLS] and [SEP] are two special tokens to indicate the utterance boundaries. Then, the input is automatically tokenized by the BART's tokenizer, followed by a stack of BART encoder layers. Next, the context-aware representation of each token is obtained from the output of the last encoder layer of BART:

$$h_1^C, \cdots, h_{|C_{inp}|}^C = BART_{enc}(C)$$

(11)

where $|C_{inp}|$ indicates the number of tokens in the input sequence, $BART_{enc}(\cdot)$ denotes the BART encoder, and h_i^C is the context-aware representation of the i-th token in the sequence.

Similarly, for the descriptive text set $S = \{S_1, S_2, \cdots, S_{n-1}\}$ corresponding to the context C, each S_i is encoded by the BART encoder, where the input is formed as "[CLS] S_{i_1} [SEP] S_{i_2} [SEP] $\cdots$ [SEP] $S_{i_{|S_i|}}$". We take the context-aware final representation of [CLS] as the sentence representation, and the encoded sentence embedding of the i-th turn is obtained as follows:

$$h_i^S = BART_{enc}(S_i) \tag{12}$$

Finally, the response is generated by the BART decoder, conditioning on the BART-encoded dialogue context $h_1^C, \cdots, h_{|C_{inp}|}^C$, descriptive sentences $h_1^S, h_2^S, \cdots, h_{|n-1|}^S$ and predicted triplets $h_{t_n}^{ATT}$:

$$G = BART_{dec}([h_1^C; h_2^C \cdots ; h_{|C_{inp}|}^C; h_1^S; h_2^S; \cdots ; h_{|n-1|}^S; h_{t_n}^{ATT};]) \tag{13}$$

where G is the representation of generated response, $BART_{dec}(\cdot)$ denotes the BART decoder, ; denotes the token boundaries.

Cross Entropy Loss. We guide the decoder with the ground-truth response $Y = u_n$ by computing the Cross-Entropy Loss:

$$L_{CE} = -\frac{1}{|Y|} \sum_{t=1}^{|Y|} log(P(G_t = Y_t)) \tag{14}$$

where G_t denotes the generated token at the decoding time step t, while Y_t is the t-th token of the ground-truth response. In summary, the final loss is defined by:

$$L_{total} = L_{CE} + \lambda \cdot L_{BCE} \tag{15}$$

where λ denotes the coefficients of the BCE loss.

4 Experiments

4.1 Dataset

To verify our model, two requirements should be met in the datasets: (1) each utterance is annotated with related knowledge triples, and (2) containing abundant utterances in each dialogue. Therefore, we conduct our experiments on KdConv [39], a Chinese multi-domain knowledge-driven dialogue dataset, which contains 4.5K dialogues together with 86K utterances from three domains (i.e., film, music, and travel). In KdConv, each dialogue contains 19.0 turns as well as 10.1 triplets on average. For domain-specific knowledge, both structured triplets and unstructured texts are provided. Specifically, the film, music, and travel domain knowledge contain 89K, 56K, and 10K triplets, together with 7.3K, 4.1K, and 1.1K descriptive sentences, respectively.

4.2 Settings

Baselines: We adopt both vanilla and knowledge-grounded (indicating by "+know") dialogue generation models as our baselines:

- **Seq2Seq** [24]: An encoder-decoder model augmented with attention mechanism [1].
- **Seq2Seq+know** [39] fuses the last hidden state of the encoder with the knowledge vector via the attention mechanism and feeds both of them into the Seq2Seq decoder.
- **HRED** [20]: A hierarchical recurrent encoder-decoder model which models utterances and context separately with different RNNs.
- **HRED+know** [39] fuses the context vector with the knowledge vector and treats the fused vector as the initial state of the HRED decoder.
- **BART** [10]: A pre-trained Transformer-based encoder-decoder model which achieves state-of-the-art performance on various text generation tasks.
- **BART+know** incorporates both knowledge entities and relations represented by the average word embeddings of the corresponding flat texts.
- **BART+know(TransR)** incorporates knowledge entities and relations represented by a knowledge graph embedding algorithm (i.e., TransR [15]).

Implementation: We implement the above models with PyTorch and Huggingface Transformers[2] libraries. In Seq2Seq and HRED baselines, we employ GRU architecture [5] as the encoder and the decoder with 200 hidden cells. In terms of word embeddings, we adapt Tencent AI Lab word embeddings of 200d[3]. When encoding context, all models treat the concatenation of the past $n-1$ utterances as the input of the encoder, while the target output of the decoder is the n-th utterance. n is set to 8 in our experiments suggested by KdConv [39]. All models are optimized with ADAM optimizer using an initial learning rate of 5e-5. The mini-batch size is set to 32.

For our RT-KGD, the embedding size of entities and relations is set to 200. The implementation of TransR is provided by *OpenKE*[4]. The knowledge encoder is Bi-GRU, the hidden size and the number of layers are set to 300 and 1, respectively. We choose the *Chinese BART*[5] as the baseline pre-training language model with the default hyper-parameter settings. When decoding the response, the beam search size of all models is set to 5. The λ is set to 1 in Eq. 15.

4.3 Evaluation Metrics

Automatic Evaluation: Following [39], we adopt perplexity (PPL), BLEU scores [17], and Distinct scores [11] as automatic metrics. In detail, PPL is used

---

[2] https://github.com/huggingface/transformers.
[3] https://ai.tencent.com/ailab/nlp/en/embedding.html.
[4] https://github.com/thunlp/OpenKE.
[5] https://huggingface.co/fnlp/bart-base-chinese.

Table 1. Automatic evaluation results on KdConv Corpus. The **bold** indicates the best performance. The "+know" means the models are enhanced by the knowledge base, and the knowledge words are encoded by word embeddings. ↑ indicates higher is better. ↓ indicates lower is better. † denotes the results reported by KdConv [39].

Model	PPL ↓	BLEU-1/2/3/4 ↑				Distinct-1/2/3/4 ↑			
Film									
Seq2Seq	$23.88^\dagger$	$26.97^\dagger$	$14.31^\dagger$	$8.53^\dagger$	$5.30^\dagger$	$2.32^\dagger$	$6.13^\dagger$	$10.88^\dagger$	$16.14^\dagger$
Seq2Seq+know	$25.56^\dagger$	$27.45^\dagger$	$14.51^\dagger$	$8.66^\dagger$	$5.32^\dagger$	$2.85^\dagger$	$7.98^\dagger$	$15.09^\dagger$	$23.17^\dagger$
HRED	$24.74^\dagger$	$27.03^\dagger$	$14.07^\dagger$	$8.30^\dagger$	$5.07^\dagger$	$2.55^\dagger$	$7.35^\dagger$	$14.12^\dagger$	$21.86^\dagger$
HRED+know	$26.27^\dagger$	$27.94^\dagger$	$14.69^\dagger$	$8.73^\dagger$	$5.40^\dagger$	$2.86^\dagger$	$8.08^\dagger$	$15.81^\dagger$	$24.93^\dagger$
BART	**2.66**	28.54	19.28	14.21	11.00	2.46	14.12	25.72	36.12
BART+know	2.85	29.38	20.18	15.02	11.74	2.55	15.26	28.01	39.45
BART+know(TransR)	2.82	29.68	20.43	15.26	11.97	2.50	15.12	27.96	39.56
RT-KGD(ours)	2.86	**32.11**	**22.21**	**16.68**	**13.18**	**3.05**	**16.34**	**31.36**	**44.68**
Music									
Seq2Seq	$16.17^\dagger$	$28.89^\dagger$	$16.56^\dagger$	$10.63^\dagger$	$7.13^\dagger$	$2.52^\dagger$	$7.02^\dagger$	$12.69^\dagger$	$18.78^\dagger$
Seq2Seq+know	$17.12^\dagger$	$29.6^\dagger$	$17.26^\dagger$	$11.36^\dagger$	$7.84^\dagger$	$3.93^\dagger$	$12.35^\dagger$	$23.01^\dagger$	$34.23^\dagger$
HRED	$16.82^\dagger$	$29.92^\dagger$	$17.31^\dagger$	$11.17^\dagger$	$7.52^\dagger$	$2.71^\dagger$	$7.71^\dagger$	$14.07^\dagger$	$20.97^\dagger$
HRED+know	$17.69^\dagger$	$29.73^\dagger$	$17.51^\dagger$	$11.59^\dagger$	$8.04^\dagger$	$3.80^\dagger$	$11.70^\dagger$	$22.00^\dagger$	$33.37^\dagger$
BART	2.46	31.65	23.04	18.22	15.05	2.80	13.69	24.73	34.59
BART+know	**2.40**	32.20	23.24	18.20	14.89	2.74	13.54	24.96	35.41
BART+know(TransR)	2.44	32.27	23.40	18.44	15.22	2.80	13.68	25.19	35.61
RT-KGD(ours)	2.47	**40.75**	**31.26**	**25.56**	**21.64**	**4.18**	**17.38**	**30.05**	**41.05**
Travel									
Seq2Seq	$10.44^\dagger$	$29.61^\dagger$	$20.04^\dagger$	$14.91^\dagger$	$11.74^\dagger$	$3.75^\dagger$	$11.15^\dagger$	$19.01^\dagger$	$27.16^\dagger$
Seq2Seq+know	$10.62^\dagger$	$37.04^\dagger$	$27.28^\dagger$	$22.16^\dagger$	$18.94^\dagger$	$4.25^\dagger$	$13.64^\dagger$	$24.18^\dagger$	$34.08^\dagger$
HRED	$10.90^\dagger$	$30.92^\dagger$	$20.97^\dagger$	$15.61^\dagger$	$12.30^\dagger$	$4.15^\dagger$	$12.01^\dagger$	$20.52^\dagger$	$28.74^\dagger$
HRED+know	$11.15^\dagger$	$36.87^\dagger$	$26.68^\dagger$	$21.31^\dagger$	$17.96^\dagger$	$3.98^\dagger$	$13.31^\dagger$	$24.06^\dagger$	$34.35^\dagger$
BART	1.83	34.77	29.11	25.69	23.33	2.70	13.39	21.92	29.53
BART+know	1.67	36.19	29.83	26.04	23.41	2.59	13.31	22.01	29.69
BART+know(TransR)	1.69	36.61	30.29	26.54	23.92	2.56	13.58	22.85	30.87
RT-KGD(ours)	**1.61**	**47.56**	**41.46**	**37.40**	**34.31**	3.58	**15.50**	**26.10**	**35.72**

to evaluate whether the generation result is grammatical and fluent. BLEU-n (n=1, 2, 3, or 4) estimates how many n-grams overlap between generated sentences and ground truth references. Distinct-n (n=1, 2, 3, or 4) evaluates the diversity of generated responses.

Human Evaluation: Considering the complexity of the knowledge-grounded dialogue generation task and the limitation of automatic evaluation, it is necessary to further conduct the human evaluation. Following KdConv [39], The criteria of human evaluation include two aspects: (1) Fluency evaluates whether the generated responses are reasonable and relevant to the given dialogue context. (2) Coherence measures how relevant the knowledge contained in the generated responses and the counterpart in the ground truth responses. We randomly select 100 dialogue contexts from KdConv in three domains, respectively, and then ask five well-educated evaluators to judge the generated responses by different models. The scoring adopts a 3-point scale.

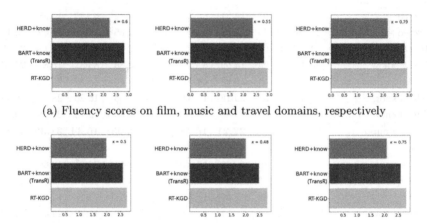

(a) Fluency scores on film, music and travel domains, respectively

(b) Coherence scores on film, music and travel domains, respectively

Fig. 3. Human evaluation in three domains, including means and variances of the Fluency (a) and Coherence (b). κ is the Fleiss' kappa value.

4.4   Experimental Results

Table 1 shows the automatic evaluation results. We analyze the results from the following perspectives:

(1) Comparison between models: Compared with all baseline models, RT-KGD achieves the best results on most of automatic metrics in three domains, which indicates that our knowledge-guided method is extremely effective in improving the coherence and diversity of generated responses. Specifically, compared with Seq2Seq-based and HRED-based models, our RT-KGD obtains not only lower PPL scores but also higher BLEU-n and Distinct-n scores in three domains. This is because we utilize the pre-trained language model to encode contexts and generate responses, which makes use of the implicitly learned knowledge from the pre-trained corpus. On the other hand, compared with BART-based models, our RT-KGD works better in terms of BLEU-n and Distinct-n scores, however worse on PPL scores. Based on our manual sampling analysis of the experimental results, the reason might be that our MHKT-Path takes the knowledge transition into consideration. At the same time, diverse knowledge information may result in responses that have never appeared in the corpus, thus reducing the PPL scores.

Moreover, it can be seen that all models with knowledge perform better than those without knowledge in terms of BLEU-n and Distinct-n, indicating the benefits of incorporating knowledge. However, the addition of knowledge works worse in PPL. The reason may be that the sentence with knowledge is less common and more difficult to understand for the model. We also observe that all models with "know(TransR)" obtain higher BLEU-n and Distinct-n scores than models with "know", demonstrating that introducing of knowledge graph embedding algorithm has a positive influence on generating high-quality responses. It is worth noting that in the music domain, BART performs better than BART+know in terms of Distinct-1 and Distinct-2 but worse in Distinct-3 and Distinct-4, which is due to that BART prefers to use individual words with low frequency rather than common phrases. Furthermore, it is possible to get a high Distinct-1 for putting together a response with entirely random words. The same analysis comparing *BART* and *BART+know* also applies to the travel domain.

(2) Comparison between domains: As we can see, models in the travel domain perform better than that in film and music domains on PPL and BLEU-k, while models in the film domain obtain higher Distinct-n scores than the same model in music and travel domains. The reason might be that there are more entities and relations in the film domain, which leads to more diverse knowledge tokens but a lower similarity with the ground-truth.

4.5 Human Study

Here, we estimate three knowledge-grounded dialogue generation models which perform better than other baselines. The experiment results are shown in Fig. 3. As can be seen, RT-KGD outperforms other models significantly on both metrics in all three domains, which indicates that our model can generate more human-like responses. Moreover, the performance gap between models behaves differently on different metrics. The fluency scores in the music domain (the middle one in Fig. 3(a)) are increased from 1.36 (HRED+know) to 1.93 (RT-KGD), while the coherence scores in the music domain (the middle one in Fig. 3(b)) are increased from 1.00 (HRED+know) to 1.77 (RT-KGD). We also show Fleiss' Kappa values of our human study. A higher score indicates higher agreements among evaluators. The kappa scores demonstrate a good inter-agreement among our evaluators.

4.6 Ablation Study

To analyze which components are driving the improvements, we further design three graph variants for detailed comparison and ablation study: (1) "w/o tri" removes the triplet vertices in MHKT-Path; (2) "w/o rel" removes the relation vertices in MHKT-Path; (3) "w/o edge" removes the edges between the triplet and the relation vertices in MHKT-Path.

Table 2 shows the results of ablation studies. First, we observed that models suffer the performance drop when removing any of the components, demonstrating the effectiveness of integrating triplets and relations. Second, the degree

Table 2. Ablation study on KdConv. The **bold** and underline denote the best and the worst performances, respectively.

Model	PPL ↓	BLEU-1/2/3/4 ↑				Distinct-1/2/3/4 ↑			
Film									
RT-KGD(ours)	2.86	**32.11**	**22.21**	**16.68**	**13.18**	**3.05**	**16.34**	**31.36**	**44.68**
- w/o tri	**2.85**	30.17	20.82	15.58	12.22	2.61	15.79	<u>29.28</u>	<u>41.16</u>
- w/o rel	<u>3.37</u>	<u>30.10</u>	<u>20.64</u>	<u>15.42</u>	<u>12.10</u>	2.56	<u>15.76</u>	29.31	41.44
- w/o edge	3.35	30.13	20.76	15.52	12.22	<u>2.53</u>	15.79	29.42	41.68
Music									
RT-KGD(ours)	2.47	**40.75**	**31.26**	**25.56**	**21.64**	**4.18**	**17.38**	**30.05**	**41.05**
- w/o tri	2.43	<u>32.22</u>	<u>23.24</u>	<u>18.22</u>	<u>14.94</u>	<u>2.74</u>	<u>13.17</u>	<u>24.26</u>	<u>34.42</u>
- w/o rel	<u>2.49</u>	32.53	23.66	18.67	15.44	2.85	14.12	26.28	37.22
- w/o edge	**2.42**	32.28	23.44	18.50	15.26	2.83	13.92	25.36	35.55
Travel									
RT-KGD(ours)	**1.61**	**47.56**	**41.46**	**37.40**	**34.31**	**3.58**	**15.50**	**26.10**	**35.72**
- w/o tri	1.70	<u>36.92</u>	30.69	26.95	24.33	2.71	13.89	23.32	31.76
- w/o rel	<u>1.84</u>	36.98	<u>30.59</u>	<u>26.74</u>	<u>24.06</u>	2.64	13.63	23.01	31.17
- w/o edge	1.82	37.39	31.02	27.21	24.55	<u>2.58</u>	<u>13.43</u>	<u>22.14</u>	<u>29.79</u>

of impact increases from the film domain to the travel domain after removing components. For example, the BLEU-n scores decrease by 1.4, 7.4, and 10.4 on average in film, music, and travel, respectively, which shows that our MHKT-Path plays a more significant role in the travel domain in improving the quality of generated response. Third, the contribution of each component is not equal in different domains. Specifically, if the triplet vertices are removed, BLEU-n and Distinct-n scores are dramatically dropped in the music domain, indicating that turn-level entity information is capable of enhancing knowledge comprehension. While removing the relation vertices, BLEU-n scores declined most significantly in film and travel domains, demonstrating the advantage of explicitly modeling dialogue-level relation transition regularities. Lastly, without the edges between the triplet and relation vertices, the performance of RT-KGD in all three domains is reduced to varying degrees. This is because the edge between triplet vertices and relation vertices effectively propagates the information between these two vertices.

4.7   Case Study

As shown in Fig. 4, we show the responses generated by HRED+know, BART+know(TransR) and RT-KGD. We can observe that given the context and corresponding knowledge triplets, HRED+know tends to generate generic or irrelevant responses, and BART+know(TransR) can generate coherent and

Dialogue (Film)		Knowledge		
		Head	Relation	Tail
Context	**User1:** Have you heard of **Andy Lau**?	Andy Lau	Occupation	Actor
	User2: Of course, he is an <u>actor</u>, <u>singer</u>, <u>lyricist</u> and <u>producer</u>.			Singer
				Lyricist
				Producer
	User1: Is he still a famous actor? Are there any representative works?		Representative Work	A World Without Thieves
	User2: Film and television works have <u>A World Without Thieves</u>, <u>Infernal Affairs</u>, <u>A Simple Life</u> and so on. Have you seen them?			Infernal Affairs
				A Simple Life
	User1: Oh, I've seen **A Simple Life**. Do you remember who starred in the film?	A Simple Life	Cast	Ye Dexian
Response	**Ground-Truth:** Starring <u>Ye Dexian</u>, <u>Andy Lau</u>, <u>Wang Fuli</u>, <u>Qin Hailu</u>, <u>Huang Qiusheng</u>, etc.			Andy Lau
	HRED+know: Yes, there's *Leonardo DiCaprio*. Do you remember who starred?			Wang Fuli
	BART+know(TransR): Of course, *Bradley Cooper*, *Christopher waltz*, *Melissa George* and so on. They all played very well!			Qin Hailu
	RT-KGD(Ours): Of course, there are <u>Ye Dexian</u>, <u>Andy Lau</u>, <u>Wang Fuli</u>, <u>Qin Hailu</u>, <u>Huang Qiusheng</u> and other co stars. Have you heard of them?			Huang Qiusheng

Fig. 4. Example dialogue cases. The **bold** is the core entity under discussion. <u>Underline</u> is the appropriate knowledge used in the dialogue. *Italic* is inconsistent with the context.

informative responses but utilizes the inconsistent knowledge. While our RT-KGD is superior to generating high-quality responses with appropriate knowledge.

5 Conclusion

In this paper, we proposed a novel KGD model: Relation Transition aware Knowledge-Grounded Dialogue Generation (RT-KGD), which models the knowledge transition across multi-turn dialogue by integrating dialogue-level relation transition regularities with turn-level entity semantic information. Furthermore, our RT-KGD model utilizes the predicted knowledge to generate a response given the dialogue context. According to automatic and manual evaluation, our model generates high-quality responses which utilize more appropriate knowledge and are closer to the responses given by humans.

Supplemental Material Statement: The KdConv dataset and part of the baselines in Sect. 4 are publicly available from Github[6]. Source codes for RT-KGD model are available at https://github.com/tigerwww-git/RT-KGD.

Acknowledgments. Zhixu Li and Jianfeng Qu are the corresponding authors. This research is supported by the National Natural Science Foundation of China (Grant No. 62072323, 62102276), the Natural Science Foundation of Jiangsu Province (Grant No.

---

[6] https://github.com/thu-coai/KdConv.

BK20191420, BK20210705, BK20211307), the Natural Science Foundation of Educational Commission of Jiangsu Province, China (Grant No. 21KJD520005), the Major Program of the Natural Science Foundation of Jiangsu Higher Education Institutions of China (Grant No. 19KJA610002), NH33714722 Youth Team on Interdisciplinary Research Soochow University - Research on Subjectivity and Reasoning Theory in Artificial Intelligence, the Priority Academic Program Development of Jiangsu Higher Education Institutions, Suda-Toycloud Data Intelligence Joint Laboratory, and the Collaborative Innovation Center of Novel Software Technology and Industrialization.

References

1. Bahdanau, D., Cho, K., Bengio, Y.: Neural machine translation by jointly learning to align and translate. In: ICLR (2015)
2. Bai, J., Yang, Z., Liang, X., Wang, W., Li, Z.: Learning to copy coherent knowledge for response generation. In: AAAI (2021)
3. Bao, S., He, H., Wang, F., Wu, H.: Plato: pre-trained dialogue generation model with discrete latent variable. In: ACL (2020)
4. Bordes, A., Usunier, N., García-Durán, A., Weston, J., Yakhnenko, O.: Translating embeddings for modeling multi-relational data. In: NIPS (2013)
5. Cho, K., et al.: Learning phrase representations using RNN encoder-decoder for statistical machine translation. In: EMNLP (2014)
6. Ghazvininejad, M., et al.: A knowledge-grounded neural conversation model. In: AAAI (2018)
7. Hu, Z., Dong, Y., Wang, K., Sun, Y.: Heterogeneous graph transformer. In: Proceedings of the Web Conference 2020 (2020)
8. Jung, J., Son, B., Lyu, S.: Attnio: knowledge graph exploration with in-and-out attention flow for knowledge-grounded dialogue. In: EMNLP (2020)
9. Kim, B., Ahn, J.H., Kim, G.: Sequential latent knowledge selection for knowledge-grounded dialogue. In: ICLR (2020)
10. Lewis, M., et al.: Bart: denoising sequence-to-sequence pre-training for natural language generation, translation, and comprehension. In: ACL (2020)
11. Li, J., Galley, M., Brockett, C., Gao, J., Dolan, W.B.: A diversity-promoting objective function for neural conversation models. In: NAACL (2016)
12. Lian, R., Xie, M., Wang, F., Peng, J., Wu, H.: Learning to select knowledge for response generation in dialog systems. In: IJCAI (2019)
13. Liang, Y., Meng, F., Zhang, Y., Chen, Y., Xu, J., Zhou, J.: Infusing multi-source knowledge with heterogeneous graph neural network for emotional conversation generation. In: AAAI, no. 15 (2021)
14. Lin, X.V., Jian, W., He, J., Wang, T., Chu, W.: Generating informative conversational response using recurrent knowledge-interaction and knowledge-copy. In: ACL (2020)
15. Lin, Y., Liu, Z., Sun, M., Liu, Y., Zhu, X.: Learning entity and relation embeddings for knowledge graph completion. In: AAAI (2015)
16. Moon, S., Shah, P., Kumar, A., Subba, R.: Opendialkg: Explainable conversational reasoning with attention-based walks over knowledge graphs. In: ACL (2019)
17. Papineni, K., Roukos, S., Ward, T., Zhu, W.J.: Bleu: a method for automatic evaluation of machine translation. In: ACL (2002)
18. Radford, A., Wu, J., Child, R., Luan, D., Amodei, D., Sutskever, I., et al.: Language models are unsupervised multitask learners. OpenAI blog (2019)

19. Roller, S., et al.: Recipes for building an open-domain chatbot. In: EACL (2021)
20. Serban, I., Sordoni, A., Bengio, Y., Courville, A.C., Pineau, J.: Building end-to-end dialogue systems using generative hierarchical neural network models. In: AAAI (2016)
21. Sordoni, A., et al.: A neural network approach to context-sensitive generation of conversational responses. In: NAACL (2015)
22. Speer, R., Chin, J., Havasi, C.: Conceptnet 5.5: an open multilingual graph of general knowledge. In: AAAI (2017)
23. Sukhbaatar, S., Szlam, A.D., Weston, J., Fergus, R.: End-to-end memory networks. In: NIPS (2015)
24. Sutskever, I., Vinyals, O., Le, Q.V.: Sequence to sequence learning with neural networks. In: NIPS (2014)
25. Vaswani, A., et al.: Attention is all you need. In: NIPS (2017)
26. Vougiouklis, P., Hare, J.S., Simperl, E.P.B.: A neural network approach for knowledge-driven response generation. In: COLING (2016)
27. Wang, J., et al.: Knowledge enhanced sports game summarization. In: WSDM (2022)
28. Wang, J., et al.: Incorporating commonsense knowledge into story ending generation via heterogeneous graph networks. In: Database Systems for Advanced Applications (2022)
29. Wu, S., Li, Y., Zhang, D., Zhou, Y., Wu, Z.: Diverse and informative dialogue generation with context-specific commonsense knowledge awareness. In: ACL (2020)
30. Wu, W., et al.: Proactive human-machine conversation with explicit conversation goal. In: ACL (2019)
31. Xing, C., Wu, W.Y., Wu, Y., Zhou, M., Huang, Y., Ma, W.Y.: Hierarchical recurrent attention network for response generation. In: AAAI (2018)
32. Zhang, H., Liu, Z., Xiong, C., Liu, Z.: Grounded conversation generation as guided traverses in commonsense knowledge graphs. In: ACL (2020)
33. Zhang, R., Guo, J., Fan, Y., Lan, Y., Xu, J., Cheng, X.: Learning to control the specificity in neural response generation. In: ACL (2018)
34. Zhang, T., et al.: Aligning internal regularity and external influence of multi-granularity for temporal knowledge graph embedding. In: Database Systems for Advanced Applications (2022)
35. Zhang, Y., et al.: Dialogpt: large-scale generative pre-training for conversational response generation. In: ACL (2020)
36. Zhao, X., Wu, W., Xu, C., Tao, C., Zhao, D., Yan, R.: Knowledge-grounded dialogue generation with pre-trained language models. In: EMNLP (2020)
37. Zheng, D., Xu, Z., Meng, F., Wang, X., Wang, J., Zhou, J.: Enhancing visual dialog questioner with entity-based strategy learning and augmented guesser. In: Findings of EMNLP 2021 (2021)
38. Zhou, H., Young, T., Huang, M., Zhao, H., Xu, J., Zhu, X.: Commonsense knowledge aware conversation generation with graph attention. In: IJCAI (2018)
39. Zhou, H., Zheng, C., Huang, K., Huang, M., Zhu, X.: KdConv: a Chinese multi-domain dialogue dataset towards multi-turn knowledge-driven conversation. In: ACL (2020)

LoGNet: Local and Global Triple Embedding Network

Giuseppe Pirrò$^{(\boxtimes)}$

Department of Computer Science, Sapienza University of Rome, Rome, Italy
pirro@di.uniroma1.it

Abstract. This paper introduces an end-to-end learning framework called LoGNet (Local and Global Triple Embedding Network) for triple-centric tasks in knowledge graphs (KGs). LoGNet is based on graph neural networks (GNNs) and combines local and global triple embedding information. Local triple embeddings are learned by treating triples as sequences. Global triple embeddings are learned by operating on the feature triple line graph $\mathcal{G}_L$ of a knowledge graph $\mathcal{G}$. The nodes of $\mathcal{G}_L$ are the triples of $\mathcal{G}$, edges are inserted according to subjects/objects shared by triples, and node and edge features are derived from the triples of $\mathcal{G}$. LoGNet brings a refreshing triple-centric perspective in learning from KGs and is flexible enough to adapt to various downstream tasks. We discuss concrete use-cases in triple classification and anomalous predicate detection. An experimental evaluation shows that LoGNet brings better performance than the state-of-the-art.

Keywords: Knowledge graphs · Triple embeddings

1 Introduction

Knowledge Graphs (KGs) are organized as a set of facts (or triples) of the form (s, p, o) where the predicate p represents a semantic relation holding between the subject entity s and the object entity o. As an example, the triple (M. Freeman, starring, Invictus) represents the fact that the actor *M. Freeman* was *starring* in the movie *Invictus*. Several approaches have focused on learning representations (aka embeddings), for both entities and predicates, in the form of low-dimensional vectors [5] to support knowledge discovery tasks. The problem of directly computing embeddings of entire triples has received little attention.

Related Work. We identify three main strands of related research. The first concerns node embeddings (e.g., RDF2Vec [27], metapath2vec [12], JUST [17], NESP [7]) and is based on first computing walks in KGs according to different strategies and feed them into language model techniques (e.g., Word2Vec [22]). Node embeddings can then be used in various downstream applications, including node classification and clustering (e.g., [7,17]). The second strand has focused on finding *both entity (node) and predicate (edge) embeddings* with the main goal to perform link prediction or knowledge graph completion (e.g., TransE [4], ComplexE [31], ConvE [11], RotatE [30]). The third strand leverages Graph neural networks (GNNs) [28] as a model that directly adapts to graphs in a variety of classification and prediction tasks (e.g., node-level, graph-level) and contexts, from drug discovery to neural translation. GNNs can be used to compute node, edge, and graph embeddings. We observe that *the problem of directly computing embeddings of entire triples has received little attention.* One *indirect way* to solve this problem would be to perform some operation (e.g., Hadamard product, concatenation, average) on the embeddings of the subject, object, and predicate in the triple. However, this approach is sub-optimal and fails to capture the essence of triple embeddings for two main reasons. First, it treats subject, predicate, and object (embeddings) as separate elements, disregarding that triples are inherently sequential. The second reason is that approaches based on entity/predicate embeddings aggregation fail to capture correlations among entire triples. Triple2Vec [13] is the only approach we are aware of that directly computes triple embeddings; it leverages the *triple line graph* $\mathcal{G}_L$ of a knowledge graph $\mathcal{G}$ where the nodes of $\mathcal{G}_L$ are the triples of $\mathcal{G}$ with edges between nodes inserted whenever the triples of $\mathcal{G}$ share an endpoint. Then, it uses walks computed on the triple line graph fed to word2vec to compute the embeddings of the nodes of $\mathcal{G}_L$ that correspond to the triples of $\mathcal{G}$.

Limitations of the State-of-the-Art. We identify some potential drawbacks for Triple2Vec: (i) Triple2Vec neither considers node nor edge features that may be derived in a KG, for instance, by looking at the semantics of predicates or node types. Besides, turning triples to nodes via the line graph transformation only considers topological information disregarding semantic relationships between triples; (ii) Triple2Vec is not trained in an end-to-end fashion; embeddings learned by Triple2Vec need to be fed to other learners (e.g., one-vs-rest logistic regressors) for downstream tasks. This approach requires to train additional modules on an objective unrelated to the initial task. *The goal of this paper is to present an end-to-end learning framework to compute triple embeddings.*

Challenges and Contributions. To accomplish the goal mentioned above, we address three main challenges. *The first concerns how to capture triple embedding information.* To solve this challenge, we note that triples in the input knowledge graph $\mathcal{G}$ have an inherently sequential nature and can be seen as three-word sentences; each triple is a sequence of subject→predicate→object (in the forward order) and object→predicate→subject (in the reverse order). We propose to learn *local* triple embeddings by using bidirectional recurrent neural networks [9], a class of neural networks specific for sequence learning. *The second challenge concerns node and edge features.* We have discussed that the state-of-the-art Triple2Vec neither considers node nor edge features. To initialize features one can consider, for instance, node degrees [15], random values [1] or position-based techniques [37]. Despite various approaches, it is unclear which kind of artificial feature initialization works best. To solve this challenge, we leverage semantic information carried by the triples of $\mathcal{G}$ to initialize both node and edge features of the $\mathcal{G}_L$. Specifically, the node features of $\mathcal{G}_L$ will be the local triple embeddings obtained from $\mathcal{G}$. The edge features are obtained by looking at the relatedness between the triples corresponding to adjacent nodes of $\mathcal{G}_L$. As an example, suppose that in the edge (n_i, n_j) of $\mathcal{G}_L$ node n_i and n_j correspond to the triples $s_k p_i o_j$ and $s_k p_k o_w$ in $\mathcal{G}$, respectively. We can consider a 3-dimensional feature vector where the first dimension represents the relatedness between the predicates [29] p_i and p_k while the second and third dimensions are the relatedness of the subject and object entity node types, respectively. *The third challenge concerns how to combine local, global, and neighbor triple embedding information.* To solve this challenge, we introduce the Local and Global Triple Embedding Network (LoGNet), a novel learning framework based on GNNs. LoGNet's underlying idea is to intertwine information from $\mathcal{G}$ (local triple embeddings) and $\mathcal{G}_L$ (global triple embeddings). In LoGNet message passing and aggregation relies on both node and edge features of the $\mathcal{G}_L$; LoGNet adopts a multi-channel convolution operator that weights the contributions of neighbor nodes to the representation of a target node. LoGNet is flexible enough for a variety of triple-centric downstream applications by providing an appropriate loss function and output layer.

Impact and Applications. Investigating triple-centric applications brings a refreshing perspective to a landscape dominated by node/edge-centric applications. Triple embeddings are good support for any path-based downstream application; here, the intuition is to embed paths as sequences of triple embeddings and then aggregate them. Examples are fact-checking [26] or user-item recommendation [13]. Triple embeddings are useful in sensitive data release scenarios where the same predicate may not be sensitive depending on the subject and object. Consider the triples (Joe, marriedTo, Val) and (Frank, marriedTo, Mary) extracted from a government document. It may be the case that the same predicate marriedTo may be considered sensitive for Val and not for Mary. Therefore, using the same predicate embedding in a data analysis scenario may be insufficient. In this paper, we will focus on *the predicate anomaly problem where both the subject and the object of a triple are legitimate entities, and the potential anomaly resides in the predicate linking them* [18]. Predicate anomaly is a fundamental problem as KGs are traditionally incomplete [10] and can have a considerable amount of incorrect triples [20]. We will show how LoGNet can be customized to tackle this task by adopting a margin-based loss function and an output layer, which returns a plausibility score for each triple.

Outline. We provide some preliminary definitions in Sect. 2. We outline in Sect. 3 LoGNet, which is a generic learning framework for triple-centric tasks in KGs. Section 4 shows how LoGNet can be adapted to solve the problem of anomalous predicate detection from the novel perspective of triple embeddings. In Sect. 5, we discuss an experimental evaluation. We conclude in Sect. 6.

2   Definitions and Background

A Knowledge Graph ($\mathcal{G}$) is a labeled directed multigraph $(\mathcal{V}_G, \mathcal{E}_G, \mathcal{T}_G)$ where $\mathcal{V}_G$ is a set of uniquely identified nodes representing entities (e.g., D. Lynch),

$\mathcal{E}_G$ a set of predicates (e.g., director) and $\mathcal{T}_G$ a set of triples of the form (s, p, o) representing directed labeled edges, where s, o $\in \mathcal{V}_G$ and p $\in \mathcal{E}_G$. Often, information in a $\mathcal{G}$ is organized according to an underlying schema defining, for instance, the types of the entity nodes (e.g., Person) and domain and range definitions for predicates stating what type of entity one should expect ad subject and object of a triple. We denote by type(e) the set of types of an entity e.

Entity and Predicate Embeddings. KG embedding approaches focus on learning vector representations $\mathbf{e} \in \mathbb{R}^{d_e}$ for each entity e $\in \mathcal{V}_G$ and possibly predicate embeddings $\mathbf{p} \in \mathbb{R}^{d_p}$ for each predicate p $\in \mathcal{E}_G$. Typically, KG embedding systems include an *embedding component* and a *scoring component*. The former maps each entity to its corresponding embedding while the latter learns a scoring function $\mathbf{f} \colon \mathcal{V}_G \times \mathcal{E}_G \times \mathcal{V}_G \to \mathbb{R}$ where $\mathbf{f}$(s, p, o)defines the score of the triple (s, p, o). Embeddings are obtained by defining a loss function (e.g., Logistic Loss) and solving an optimization problem where the score of a positive triple (s, p, o) is to be higher than that of a (corrupted) negative triple. As an example, in the popular TransE model [4], where predicates are modeled as vector translations, the scoring function is $s_p = d(\mathbf{s} + \mathbf{p}, \mathbf{o})$ where d is the euclidean distance. Other approaches capture more refined relations (see [5] for a survey).

Graph Neural Networks. We now introduce graph neural networks in a general form. To keep the presentation concise, we focus on undirected and unlabeled graph. Let $(\mathcal{V}_G, \mathcal{E}_G)$ be a graph with $N = |\mathcal{V}_G|$ nodes $v_i \in \mathcal{V}_G$, and edges $(e_i, e_j) \in \mathcal{E}_G$. Given a node u the set of neighbours is denoted by $\mathcal{N}(u)$. We denote by A the adjacency matrix where $A \in \mathbb{R}^{N \times N}$. Moreover, the matrix $H^{(0)} \in \mathbb{R}^{N \times D^0}$ is the initial node feature matrix and $h_i^{(0)}$ denotes the $D^{(0)}$-dimensional feature vector of node v_i. A GNN can be represented as:

$$h_i^{(l+1)} = \sigma\Big(\sum_{j=1}^{N} \alpha(v_i, v_j) \cdot h_j^{(l)} \cdot W^{(l)}\Big), \quad l = 0, \ldots, L-1 \qquad (1)$$

where $h_i^{(l)}$ is the embedding of node v_i at layer l. Moreover, $\alpha = (v_i, v_j) \in \mathbb{R}^{N \times N}$ is a weight matrix, $W^{(l)} \in \mathbb{R}^{D^{(l)}} \times D^{(l+1)}$ is the transformation matrix at layer l, and σ is the activation function. The weight $\alpha(v_i, v_j)$ (abbreviated as $\alpha_{i,j}$) is non-zero if the node v_j is a direct neighbor of node v_i, that is, $v_i \in \mathcal{N}(i)$. Different ways have been proposed when it comes to the weight matrix α. As an example, Kipf and Welling [19] define *fixed* weights as $\alpha = \tilde{D}^{-1}$ or $\alpha = \tilde{D}^{-1} \tilde{A} D^{-1}$, respectively, where $\tilde{A} = A + I$, and $\tilde{D}$ is the diagonal degree matrix of A. More sophisticated approaches, instead of assigning fixed weight, try to learn them via attention coefficients [32]. GATs [32] learn weights via attentive functions of the form $\alpha_{i,j} = \dfrac{\tilde{\alpha}_{i,j}(\theta)}{\sum_{v_k \in \mathcal{N}(i)} \tilde{\alpha}_{i,j}(\theta)}$; here, unnormalized attentions $\tilde{\alpha}_{i,j}(\theta)(exp(ReLU(\alpha^T [Wh_i || Wh_j])))$, are parametrized by $\theta = \{\alpha\}$ with $||$ denoting concatenation. For attention networks, the weights that are learned $\alpha_{i,j} \approx \tilde{\alpha_{i,j}}$ can be evaluated only given the unnormalized neighborhood weights.

3   The **LoGNet** Framework

We now describe the design of a learning framework called LoGNet to directly compute triple embeddings from a knowledge graph combining local and global triple embedding information. The intuition is that local triple embeddings can be complemented with global embeddings derived by scrutinizing the feature triple line graph structure. This structural information is independent of node features and can be derived solely based on the links between nodes of the feature triple line graph. Finally, integrating local embeddings with connectivity information is crucial to fully capture the essence of each node (triple) and thus of its embedding [3]. LoGNet computes local embeddings obtained from the triples of an input $\mathcal{G}$. However, local embeddings do not consider triples from a global perspective; notably, they do not consider dependencies among entire triples. We introduce an alternative view of triple information and discuss a GNN-based triple embedding module to cope with this issue.

3.1   Local Triple Embeddings

Triple Embedding via Aggregation. One simple way to compute triple embeddings is by aggregating the embeddings of the entities and predicate within. Given a triple $t = (s, p, o) \in \mathcal{G}$, the idea is to define a mapping function Emb_L: $Agg(Emb(s), Emb(p), Emb(o)){:}\mapsto \mathbb{R}^d$, where $Emb(\cdot)$ is an embedding function that maps entities or predicates into a D-dimensional vector. $Emb(\cdot)$ can be instantiated with a variety of techniques such as TransE [4], RotatE [30], and DistMul [36] that return embeddings for s, p, and o separately. As an example, TransE to learn entity and predicate embeddings utilizes the triple implausibility score $\mathbf{s} + \mathbf{p} \approx \mathbf{o}$ while DistMul considers $\langle \mathbf{p}, \mathbf{s}, \mathbf{o} \rangle$ where $\langle \cdot \rangle$ denotes the generalized dot product with $\mathbf{s}, \mathbf{p}, \mathbf{o} \in R^k$. Hence, triple embeddings can be obtained via an aggregation function $Agg(\cdot)$. Examples of aggregation include the average, maxpool, and Hadamard product.

Triple Embedding as Sequence Encoding. The approach based on aggregation suffers from some drawbacks. First, the usage of aggregation functions (e.g., mean, max) does not properly discern the contribution of each component of a triple to the final triple embedding. Second, as the approaches implementing the $Emb(\cdot)$ return an embedding for each entity and predicate in $\mathcal{G}$, triples sharing the same entity or predicate will share part of the final embedding, which does not allow to obtain a fine-grained triple embedding representation. Third, the approach based on aggregation mostly ignores the sequential nature of a triple, which has a relevant role in directed graphs as KGs. Therefore, we consider a second approach to obtain local triple representations, which treats a triple as a directed and ordered sequence $\mathbf{s} \rightarrow \mathbf{p} \rightarrow \mathbf{o}$ composed of three steps (i.e., s, p, o). To deal with this sequence of elements, we employ Recurrent Neural Networks and, in particular, Bidirectional Gated Recurrent Unit (BiGRU) [8]. This architecture offers performance comparable to the LSTM model [16] with the advantage of being more computationally efficient [9].

To fulfill our ultimate goal of learning triple embeddings, we need to consider the context of a triple in terms of neighbor triples. Missing contextual information will fail to capture potential correlation and dependencies among entire triples. Therefore, we introduce a global triple embedding computation mechanism in the next section.

3.2   Global Triple Embeddings

Correlation and dependencies among entire triples can be captured by looking at triples from a global perspective, where triples become first-class citizens.

Feature Line Graph. The notion of the line graph of a graph is well-known in graph theory [34]. Given an undirected graph $\mathcal{G} = (\mathcal{V}_G, \mathcal{E}_G)$, the corresponding line graph $\mathcal{G}_L$ is such that: (i) each node of $\mathcal{G}_L$ represents an edge of $\mathcal{G}$; (ii) two vertices of $\mathcal{G}_L$ are adjacent if, and only if, their corresponding edges in $\mathcal{G}$ have a node in common. This notion has been extended to multigraphs and directed graphs. The multigraph extension adds a different node in the line graph for each edge of the original multigraph. If the graph $\mathcal{G}$ is directed, the corresponding line graph $\mathcal{G}_L$ will also be directed; its vertices are in one-to-one correspondence to the edges of $\mathcal{G}$ and its edges represent two-length directed paths in $\mathcal{G}$. Triple2Vec [13] used the triple line graph of a knowledge graph. However, we note that such a triple line graph is unlabeled, and neither nodes nor edges are endowed with features, thus making difficult the usage of deep learning techniques at their full potential. For example, in the absence of node features, GNNs fail to differentiate between similar graph sub-structures within graphs [35]. A workaround would be to consider one-hot encoding instead of features. However, this will hinder using the model on new nodes. Other approaches could include the usage of random values [1] or positional features [37]. However, there is no transparent approach that works best in all scenarios. We overcome the lack of features in $\mathcal{G}_L$ by leveraging information from the triples of the original graph $\mathcal{G}$:

1. As nodes of $\mathcal{G}_L$ correspond to triple of $\mathcal{G}$, we can consider local triple embeddings (see Sect. 3.1) as the *initial* features of the nodes of $\mathcal{G}_L$.
2. An edge (n_i, n_j) of $\mathcal{G}_L$ links the two corresponding triples t_i and t_j in $\mathcal{G}$. However, each of such triple implicitly includes semantic information deriving, for instance, from the subject and object entity types or the type of predicate linking subject and object. As an example, the triples (M. Freeman, starring, Invictus) and (M. Damon, starring, Invictus) taken from the DBpedia knowledge graph tell us that type(M. Freeman) = {Person}, type(Invictus) = {Film} and that domain(starring) = Actor and range(starring) = Work. Our proposal is to introduce, for each edge $v_{i,j} \in \mathcal{E}_L$ a P-dimensional feature vector $\mathbf{v}_{i,j} \in \mathbb{R}^P$ where each dimension captures a different relatedness perspective between the elements of the triples t_i (corresponding to node $n_i \in \mathcal{V}_L$) and t_j (corresponding to the node $n_j \in \mathcal{V}_L$).

Therefore, we introduce a triple line graph with node and edge features that we refer to as *feature triple line graph*.

Definition 1. *(Feature Triple Line Graph). Given* $\mathcal{G} = (\mathcal{V}_G, \mathcal{E}_G, \mathcal{T}_G)$ *with* $N = |\mathcal{T}_G|$ *triples, the associated features triple line graph* $\mathcal{G}_L$ *is a graph* $(\mathcal{V}_L, \mathcal{E}_L, \mathcal{X}_V, \mathcal{X}_E)$, *where* $t_i \in \mathcal{T}_G \mapsto n_i \in \mathcal{V}_L$ *and* $|\mathcal{V}_L| = N$. *There exists an edge* $(i,j) \in \mathcal{E}_L$ *between* $n_i \leftharpoonup t_i = (s_1, p_1, o_1) \in \mathcal{T}_G$ *and* $n_j \leftharpoonup t_j = (s_2, p_2, o_2) \in \mathcal{T}_G$ *if* $\{s_1, o_1\} \cap \{s_2, o_2\} \neq \emptyset$. *Node features are represented by a matrix* $\mathcal{X}_V = N \times F$, *where* $\mathcal{X}_V(i,j)$ *gives the j-th entry of the F-dimensional feature vector of the i-th node in the feature triple line graph. Edge features are represented via a* $\mathcal{X}_E = N \times N \times P$ *tensor;* $\mathcal{X}_E(i,j,p)$ *is the p-th channel of the P-dimensional vector of the edge* (i,j).

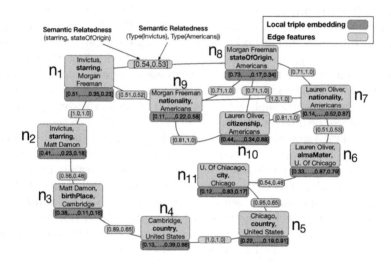

Fig. 1. Feature triple line graph.

Figure 1 shows an excerpt of feature triple line graph. We observe that nodes are endowed with features in the form of local triple embeddings, that is, embeddings computed by only looking at the triple elements (see Sect. 3.1). As for the edges, the figure shows a two-dimensional feature vector for each edge. The first dimension maintains the semantic relatedness between the predicates in the two neighbor nodes computed considering predicate co-occurrences in knowledge graph triples [25]. As an example, the relatedness between starring and stateOfOrigin is 0.54 while that between stateOfOrigin and nationality 0.71. The second dimension considers the relatedness between the type (e.g., Actor, Movie, Place) of entities not shared by neighbor nodes. As an example, for the node n_1 (Invictus, starring, M. Freeman) and n_2 (M. Freeman, stateOfOrigin, Americans) the not shared entities are Invictus[1] and Americans[2] whose type in the DBpedia KG are Film and Country, respectively. The semantic relatedness between these

---

[1] https://dbpedia.org/page/Invictus_(film).
[2] https://dbpedia.org/page/Americans.

types is 0.53 [29]. Note that the edge feature vector can be further extended to include additional dimensions considering, for instance, the cosine similarity between local triple embeddings or topological information such as the difference between node degrees. Going from the knowledge graph $\mathcal{G}$ to a feature-rich triple line graph $\mathcal{G}_L$, where triples are first-class-citizens, paves the way toward designing learning architectures that can leverage both node features, that in our context represent local triple embeddings obtained from $\mathcal{G}$, and edge features that capture different relatedness perspective between adjacent triples.

Triple Embeddings via Node and Edge Features. We introduced in the previous section a novel representation of the original knowledge graph $\mathcal{G}$ called feature triple line graph $\mathcal{G}_L$. We are now ready to show how LoGNet learns triple embeddings by intertwining information from $\mathcal{G}$ and $\mathcal{G}_L$. LoGNet is based on GNNs that learn node representations by recursively aggregating and transforming features of neighbor nodes [15]. In particular, as edge feature vectors in $\mathcal{G}_L$ include D-dimensions, LoGNet performs a separate weighted convolution operation for each dimension; the i-th feature value of dimension d is used to weight the contributions of node neighbors on that dimension. Concerning the general form of GNN outline in Sect. 2, we shall now make explicit the multi-dimensional edge feature vectors present in the feature triple line graph. For each dimension d of edge features, we consider the following formulation:

$$\hat{H}^{(l,d)} = \sigma\big(\tilde{E}_{i,j,d} \cdot H^{(l)} \cdot W^{(l,d)}\big), \tag{2}$$

where $\hat{H}^{(l,d)}$ denotes the matrix of embeddings at level l on dimension d, $\tilde{E}_{i,j,d}$ is the convolution coefficient matrix, $H^{(l)}$ the hidden state at layer l and $W^{(l,d)}$ a weight matrix. The D-dimensional information is is aggregated as follows:

$$H_i^{(l+1)} = \sigma\Big[\bigoplus_{d=1}^{D} (\hat{H}^{(l,d)})W_{\oplus}^{(d)}\Big] \tag{3}$$

where $\bigoplus$ is an aggregation function (e.g., average) and $W_{\oplus}^{(d)}$ learnable weights.

Edge Feature Aggregation. Edge features represent an important element of innovation for LoGNet and can be seen as driving a sort of edge-centered attention mechanism. Each of the D edge features can be seen as a different attention coefficient. Multiple ways (instantiations of the function $\oplus$) can be used to aggregate edge features along the D dimensions. When considering aggregation based on sum, that is, $\oplus = \sum$ we obtain:

$$H_i^{(l+1)} = \sigma\Big[\sum_{d=1}^{D} (\hat{H}^{(l,d)}) \cdot W_{sum}^{(d)}\Big] = \sigma\Big[\sum_{d=1}^{D} \Big(\sigma\Big(\sum_{j\in\mathcal{N}(i)} e_{i,j,d} \cdot h_j^{(l,d)} \cdot W^{(l,d)}\Big)\Big) \cdot W_{sum}^{(d)}\Big]$$

We underline that the architecture of LoGNet differs from the classical GNN models in one central respect. The GNN adjacency matrix A is either a binary matrix denoting node adjacency (as in GAT) or a positive matrix with only *one dimension* capturing edge features (as in GCN). Contrarily, the LoGNet model builds upon a D dimensional edge feature matrix obtained by investigating different types of relatedness between triples in the feature triple line graph.

4   Anomalous Predicate Detection

We apply the LoGNet framework to the task of anomalous predicate detection [18]. Given a triple (s, p, o), the goal is to check whether the predicate p correctly models the relation between the subject s and the object o. As an example, (I' m a looser, recordedIn, Abbey Road) would seem correct. However, when contextualizing the triple, by looking at the neighbor triples, it is immediate to see that the fact refers to the wrong entity Abbey Road; it refers to the street and not to the recording studio Abbey Road Studio [21]. This example shows the importance of considering both a local perspective (i.e., among the triple elements) and a global (i.e., wrt neighbor triples) to have a more refined assessment of the plausibility of the predicate.

Problem 1 *(Anomalous Predicate Detection). Given $G = (V_G, E_G, T_G)$ and the set of triple embeddings $\boldsymbol{T_G}$ associated with the triples T_G, our goal is to devise a scoring function $\boldsymbol{f_A}:(s, p, o) \mapsto \mathbb{R}$, which give an a triple $t \in T_G$ assigns a plausibility score to the predicate p.*

This section shows how LoGNet can be adapted to tackle this problem. *The main challenge that arises concerns how to combine local and global triple representations to find the plausibility of a predicate.* We introduce a local and global predicate plausibility score and optimize them to solve this challenge.

Local Plausibility Measure. To assess the plausibility of a predicate from a local perspective, we can readily use any of the existing scoring functions available from knowledge graph embedding techniques [5]. By considering TransE, the local plausibility of a triple can be measured as:

$$c_l(s, p, o) = \|\mathbf{h}_s + \mathbf{h}_p - \mathbf{h}_o\|_2 \tag{4}$$

where $\mathbf{h}_s$, $\mathbf{h}_p$, and $\mathbf{h}_o$ are either the embeddings of the triple elements found by the Emb($\cdot$) function or the hidden representations of the triple elements obtained from the BiGRU. The learning model can spot anomalous predicates from a local perspective by minimizing the above equation. Nevertheless, this approach does not consider the context of a triple in terms of neighbor predicates, which can fail to understand correlation and influence among triples. To this end, we also introduce a global plausibility measure.

Global Plausibility Measure. We compare information resulting from local triple embeddings, computed from $\mathcal{G}$, and global triple embeddings, computed from the feature triple line graph $\mathcal{G}_L$, to improve the overall plausibility check. In particular, minimizing the difference between local and global plausibility can point out anomalous predicates. More formally:

$$c_g(s, p, o) = \|\mathbf{z} - \mathbf{h}\|_2 \tag{5}$$

where $\mathbf{z}$ is the global triple embedding and $\mathbf{h}$ the local one.

Joint Optimization. We define the plausibility as a linear combination of the local and global plausibility:

$$c(\mathsf{s},\mathsf{p},\mathsf{o}) \;=\; \alpha c_l + \beta c_g \tag{6}$$

where the hyper-parameter α and β with $\beta = (1-\alpha)$ weight the importance of the two scores normalized. To optimize the model, we leverage a margin based loss function to distinguish between positive triples and negative ones:

$$\mathcal{L} \;=\; \sum_{(\mathsf{s},\mathsf{p},\mathsf{o})\in T_G^+} \sum_{(\mathsf{s}',\mathsf{p},\mathsf{o}')\in T_G^-} \Big[\theta + c(\mathsf{s},\mathsf{p},\mathsf{o}) - c(\mathsf{s}',\mathsf{p},\mathsf{o}')\Big] \tag{7}$$

where $\theta > 0$ is the margin hyper-parameter, T_G^+ is the set of positive triples, and T_G^- is the set of negative triples. At this point, with the model trained, we can assess the anomaly of a predicate in a triple $(\mathsf{s},\,\mathsf{p},\,\mathsf{o})$ as follows:

$$P_s(\mathsf{s},\mathsf{p},\mathsf{o}) \;=\; c(\mathsf{s},\mathsf{p},\mathsf{o}) \tag{8}$$

5   Experiments

We now report on the evaluation and comparison with related work in two tasks: anomalous predicate detection and triple classification. LoGNet[3] has been implemented using the DGL[4] library. We used Adam as an optimizer with a fixed batch size of 512 and initialized all model parameters via the Xavier initializer. We conducted a grid search to set the hyper-parameters learning rate, the weight of the plausibility scores, and the margin to their best values. All experiments have been conducted on an RTX6000 GPU and are the average of 5 runs (95% c.i). The goal of the evaluation is to answer the following research questions: **Q1**: How does LoGNet compare to the state-of-the-art in anomalous predicate detection? **Q2**: How does LoGNet compare with the state-of-the-art Triple2Vec? **Q3**: What is the impact of the plausibility on the quality of triple embeddings?

Datasets. For anomalous predicate detection, we used the following datasets: **NELL** [6]: it includes ~75K entities, 200 predicates and ~308K triples; **DBPE-DIA** (DBP) [29]: it is a KG extracted from Wikipedia. This is a subset of DBpedia with neither typing information nor literals. It includes ~2M entities, 661 predicates and ~1.2M triples; **DBPEDIA1M** (DBP1M): a subset of the dataset in [29], which includes 1M entities. For triple classification, we considered **DBLP** [33]: this is a subset of the DBLP database containing information about authors, papers, venues, and topics. Labels are provided for authors that are assigned one among four labels (i.e., database, data mining, machine learning, and information retrieval); **Foursquare** [17]: this dataset includes information about users, places, points of interests, and timestamps. Labels are available for points of interest that are given one among ten labels; **Yago** [33]: this dataset is a subset of the Yago KG[5] focused on the domain of movies. Here, labels are available for movies assigned one or more among five available labels.

---

[3] https://github.com/giuseppepirro/lognet.
[4] https://www.dgl.ai.
[5] http://yago-knowledge.org/.

5.1   Q1: Anomalous Predicate Detection

We evaluate the performance of LoGNet as compared to the state-of-the-art. We note that this paper does not aim to tackle anomalous predicate detection specifically; we aim to show novel applications of triple embeddings. We considered the following approaches: RotatE [30] and ConvE [11] node/predicate embeddings; KGist [2]: this approaches leverages rules to rule out incomplete and erroneous information in KGs; KGTtm [18]: this approach introduces a triple trustworthiness measure based on semantic information derived from triples along with global information; KBAT [23]: this approach uses an attention mechanism to capture features of the neighborhood of entities; Triple2Vec: we fed the triple embeddings obtained by Triple2Vec along with the labels to a one-vs rest logistic regressor. For LoGNet, we consider a three-layer model in two variants: (i) $LoGNet_E$ where local triple embeddings were obtained by concatenating the embeddings of the subject, predicate, and object obtained via ConvE[6]; (ii) $LoGNet_G$ where local triple embeddings were obtained via BiGRU. Moreover, we considered a 3-dimensional edge feature vector including predicate relatedness [29], subject and object type relatedness. We used $d = 128$ as embedding dimension.

Experimental Setting and Metrics. We used the NELL and DBpedia KGs. As there is no explicit information about anomalous predicates, we assumed that all triples available were correct and assigned them the label 1. To generate negative examples that were given a label 0, we adopted the same method as the state-of-the-art [18]. Given the true triple (Newton, nationality, England), a potential negative triple is (Newton, nationality, American) rather than (Newton, nationality, Google), which have been obtained by randomly replacing the object of the original triple. We considered different corruption percentages, that is, {0.05%, 1%, 2%, 3%, 5%} of the available true triples. The goal of the experiments is to identify triples that include anomalous predicates. To evaluate the performance of the systems, as done in the similar task of detecting incorrect facts (e.g., [29]), we considered the AUC score, which is useful to express the probability that a triple including a correct predicate receives a higher score than a triple including an anomalous one.

Results. From the results in Table 1 we observe: (1) Triple2Vec and LoGNet consistently outperform the competitors in the larger datasets (DBpedia, NELL). As ConvE, RotatE, KBAT, we observe the worst-performing results. The possible reason for such a behavior is that these systems were originally designed to tackle the KG completion task, different from anomalous predicate detection. Indeed, while KG completion aims to understand which part of a triple is missing, anomalous predicate detection is concerned with understanding whether the predicate in a triple makes sense. This underlines two aspects: (i) the need for specific techniques to face this task; (ii) the need to define triple embedding mechanisms alternative to those based on the aggregation of triple elements; (2) Approaches like KGTm and KGist that were designed to detect triple anomaly

---

[6] With RotatE and TransE we obtained inferior results.

Table 1. Anomalous predicate detection. The best AUC values are reported in bold.

KG	% Corr.	ConvE	RotatE	KGTtm	KBAT	KGist	T2Vec	LNet$_E$	LNet$_G$
DBP	0.05%	0.532	0.542	0.674	0.553	0.532	0.678	0.679	**0.684**
	1%	0.526	0.534	0.671	0.550	0.534	0.675	0.680	**0.691**
	2%	0.524	0.525	0.670	0.546	0.542	0.672	0.672	**0.687**
	3%	0.513	0.521	0.667	0.538	0.560	0.668	0.668	**0.671**
	5%	0.501	0.513	0.662	0.535	0.561	0.670	0.675	**0.680**
DBP1M	0.05%	0.543	0.567	0.687	0.561	0.547	0.6912	0.696	**0.702**
	1%	0.536	0.560	0.671	0.560	0.541	0.687	0.690	**0.696**
	2%	0.531	0.556	0.676	0.559	0.550	**0.678**	0.669	0.671
	3%	0.530	0.542	0.678	0.551	0.546	0.6751	0.677	0.679
	5%	0.526	0.534	0.674	0.541	0.576	0.671	0.673	0.681
NELL	0.05%	0.531	0.534	0.614	0.529	0.54	0.6214	0.621	**0.631**
	1%	0.5301	0.532	0.623	0.546	0.543	0.6245	0.625	**0.632**
	2%	0.523	0.521	0.638	0.543	0.542	0.641	0.631	**0.647**
	3%	0.513	0.516	0.622	0.526	0.552	0.623	0.624	**0.631**
	5%	0.502	0.512	0.637	0.518	0.553	0.6401	0.641	**0.655**

perform better than ConvE, RotatE, and KBAT. However, approaches based on triple embeddings performed consistently better. The reason may be the usage of the line graph construction. This novel structure plays a crucial role in better capturing the contextual structure of a triple wrt neighbor triples compared to learned rules or paths used by KGTtm and KGist. Moreover, the interplay between the local triple representation, learned by treating triples as bidirectional sequences, and the global triple representation provides a fine-grained mechanism to spot predicate anomalies. We observe that in the smallest dataset DBpedia1M, in one case Triple2Vec performs negligibly better than LoGNet; (3) Comparing LoGNet$_E$ and LoGNet$_G$, we observe that the latter performs consistently better. The reason for this behavior is that in the first case, local triple embeddings, representing the initial features of the nodes, are learned by aggregating the embeddings of the element of a triple. Consequently, triples sharing entities and predicates will also share portions of the local triple embeddings. On the other hand, in LoGNet$_G$ local triple embeddings are learned not only by considering the sequential nature of triples but also by the fact that a triple can be read in both forward and backward directions; (4) Comparing Triple2Vec and LoGNet both based on triple embeddings, we observe that the former performs worse than LoGNet. Although Triple2Vec deals with triples as a whole, it cannot spot anomalous predicate at a finer-grained level as LoGNet. This may be because LoGNet adopts a completely different approach based on a joint learning model leveraging local and global triple representations using node and edge features. We observe that triple embeddings offer good support for detecting anomalous predicates. The local triple representation obtained by modeling a triple as a sequence and the global representation constructed on the feature triple line graph where both nodes and edges have features and the context of a triple is obtained from neighbor triples is generally a valid alternative compared to approaches using rules or paths.

5.2   Q2: **LoGNet** vs **Triple2Vec**

We now shed more light on the differences between Triple2Vec and LoGNet. We want to answer the following questions: (i) how does LoGNet perform when using triple embeddings learned via Triple2Vec instead of local triple embeddings? (ii) how does the semantics relatedness-based weighting mechanism of the edges of the triple line graph used by Triple2Vec compare with LoGNet's approach?

Experimental Setting. We considered two variants of LoGNet. The first, denoted as LoGNet$_V$, leverages embeddings learned by Triple2Vec instead of local triple embeddings learned via BiGRU and still uses a 3-dimensional edge feature vector. In the second variant, denoted as LoGNet$_W$, instead of using the 3-dimensional feature vector, we only consider the relatedness between the predicates of neighbor triples (hence a 1-d feature vector).

Results. We report in Table 2 results for the anomalous predicate detection task and refer to LoGNet$_G$ as LoGNet. We make the following observations: (1) The usage of triple embeddings learned by Triple2Vec instead of local triple embeddings in LoGNet does not bring any tangible benefit. LoGNet$_V$ performs slightly worse than LoGNet in all experiments. The downside of using this approach is that it requires paying the training time cost for both

Table 2. Variants of LoGNet.

KG	% Corr. triples	LoGNet	LoGNet$_V$	LoGNet$_W$
DBP	0.05%	0.6842	0.6832	0.6124
	1%	0.6912	0.6879	0.6613
	2%	0.6873	0.6823	0.6731
	3%	0.6712	0.6689	0.6612
	5%	0.6803	0.6734	0.6352
DBP1M	0.05%	0.7022	0.6987	0.6825
	1%	0.6967	0.6823	0.6742
	2%	0.6712	0.6711	0.6531
	3%	0.6790	0.6732	0.6643
	5%	0.6816	0.6789	0.6703
NELL	0.05%	0.6312	0.6235	0.6124
	1%	0.6321	0.6256	0.6013
	2%	0.6476	0.6342	0.6235
	3%	0.6311	0.6211	0.6134
	5%	0.6553	0.6478	0.6391

Triple2Vec and LoGNet. Moreover, learning triple embeddings by looking at triples from their sequential perspective has an important role in the overall quality of triple embeddings; (2) Using a 1-d edge feature vector downgrades the performance of LoGNet. We also observe that LoGNet$_W$ performs worse than Triple2Vec (Table 1). The reason for this behavior may be found in the fact that Triple2Vec needs weights to find high-quality walks on the triple line graph that can correctly model node neighborhoods. The GNNs setting, where neighbor information is obtained via a message-passing scheme, brings some improvement.

Results on Triple Classification. We also compared LoGNet and Triple2Vec on the triple classification task in terms of Micro-F1 and Macro-F1 scores following the methodology described in Triple2Vec [13]. We considered the following competitors: metapath2vec [12], node2vec [14], and DeepWalk [24] configured with the best parameters reported in their respective papers. As these approaches compute embeddings for each node only (not for predicates), a triple embedding was obtained by using the *Hadamard operator over the embeddings of the triple endpoints* as it was the best performing; ConvE [11] and RotatE [30] configured with the best parameters reported in their respective paper and implemented. Triple embeddings were obtained by concatenating the embeddings of the triple endpoints and the predicate embedding. Figure 2 reports the results. We observe that the approaches based on triple embeddings consistently outperform competitors. This is especially true in the DBLP and Yago datasets. We also note that metapath2vec performs worse than node2vec and DeepWalk, although the former has been proposed to work on knowledge graphs. This may be explained by the fact that the metapaths used in the experiments and previously used by Hussein et al. [17] while being able to capture node embeddings, fail short in capturing triple embeddings.

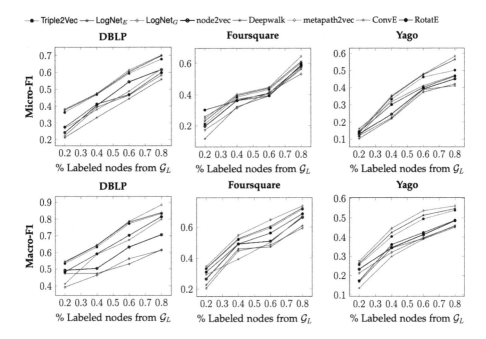

Fig. 2. Results on triple classification.

Moreover, for triple embeddings obtained via aggregation, we can see that the performance is even worse than those obtained by metapath2vec, node2vec, and Deepwalk, which did not consider the embeddings of predicates to compute triple embeddings. This may be due to two main reasons. First, the goal of these approaches is to learn entity and predicate embeddings for the link prediction task. Hence, the concatenation of entity and predicate embeddings does not correctly capture triple embeddings. Second, as these approaches compute a single predicate and node embedding, these embeddings will be shared by all triples in which they appear. As an example, the embeddings of the two triples (s, p, o) and (s, p, q) will only differ in the concatenation of the embedding of their object. This underlines the fact that a direct way to compute triple embeddings can capture better and discriminate the roles of the same predicate/entity in different triples; (3) LoGNet performs better than Triple2Vec, especially in the variant that computes local triple embeddings using the BiGRU (i.e., LoGNet$_G$). This may be due to three main reasons. First, the Triple2Vec's triple embeddings need to be fed into a one-vs-rest logistic regressor for triple classification; this additional optimization step is not related to the original task. On the other hand, LoGNet is directly trained to perform triple classification. Second, the BiGRU approach may provide better local triple embeddings as it considers the sequential nature of triples. Third, the LoGNet mechanism may be better able to weight the importance of neighbor triples (nodes of $\mathcal{G}_L$) than the weighting mechanism used by Triple2Vec based on predicate relatedness.

5.3   Q3: Ablation Study

We conducted an ablation study introducing two more variants of LoGNet: (i) LoGNet$_L$ with only local triple embeddings and the local plausibility measure in Eq. (6); (ii) LoGNet$_G$ with only global triple representation and the global plausibility in Eq. (6). Table 3 reports the results.

Results. We observe that the local plausibility score (LoGNet$_L$) seems to better capture anomalous predicates in triples. This comes as no surprise since local triple embeddings look at each triple from a finer-grained perspective, effectively analyzing the sequential nature of the triple and the dependency between subject, predicate, and object (reading the triple both forward and backward). On the other hand, LoGNet$_G$ can only rely on triple neighbor information aggre-

Table 3. Ablation study.

KG	% Corr. triples	LoGNet	LoGNet$_L$	LoGNet$_G$
DBP	0.05%	0.6842	0.6611	0.6132
	1%	0.6912	0.6712	0.6567
	2%	0.6873	0.6684	0.6648
	3%	0.6712	0.6701	0.6467
	5%	0.6803	0.6734	0.6212
DBP1M	0.05%	0.7022	0.6911	0.6674
	1%	0.6967	0.6856	0.6689
	2%	0.6712	0.6687	0.6511
	3%	0.6790	0.6701	0.6621
	5%	0.6816	0.6745	0.6687
NELL	0.05%	0.6312	0.6256	0.6073
	1%	0.6321	0.6301	0.5998
	2%	0.6476	0.6412	0.6278
	3%	0.6311	0.6287	0.6192
	5%	0.6553	0.6493	0.6398

gation, which cannot look into the triple. The fully-fledged LoGNet brings a clear improvement to the variants only considering either the local or global plausibility. This underlines that it is not convenient to separate local and global information.

6   Conclusions and Future Work

This paper showed how to compute triple embeddings by leveraging node and edge features derived from a KG. Our triple-centric embedding approach brings a refreshing perspective to a landscape dominated by node/edge-centric applications. It can support a variety of applications like path-based downstream applications where paths can be embedded as sequences of triple embeddings or data release scenarios where the same predicate may or not be considered sensitive depending on the subject and object like in the triples (Pat, marriedTo, Claire) and (Frank, marriedTo, Mary). Using the same predicate embedding to compute the embeddings of two triples may be counter-intuitive.

References

1. Abboud, R., Ceylan, İ.İ., Grohe, M., Lukasiewicz, T.: The surprising power of graph neural networks with random node initialization. In: Zhou, Z. (ed.) Proceedings of the Thirtieth International Joint Conference on Artificial Intelligence, IJCAI 2021, Virtual Event/Montreal, Canada, 19–27 August 2021, pp. 2112–2118 (2021)
2. Belth, C., Zheng, X., Vreeken, J., Koutra, D.: What is normal, what is strange, and what is missing in a knowledge graph: unified characterization via inductive summarization. In: Proceedings of the Web Conference 2020, pp. 1115–1126 (2020)
3. Bianconi, G., Pin, P., Marsili, M.: Assessing the relevance of node features for network structure. Proc. Natl. Acad. Sci. **106**(28), 11433–11438 (2009)
4. Bordes, A., Usunier, N., García-Durán, A., Weston, J., Yakhnenko, O.: Translating embeddings for modeling multi-relational data. In: Burges, C.J.C., Bottou, L., Ghahramani, Z., Weinberger, K.Q. (eds.) Advances in Neural Information Processing Systems 26: 27th Annual Conference on Neural Information Processing Systems 2013. Proceedings of a meeting held 5–8 December 2013, Lake Tahoe, Nevada, United States, pp. 2787–2795 (2013)
5. Cai, H., Zheng, V.W., Chang, K.C.C.: A comprehensive survey of graph embedding: problems, techniques, and applications. Trans. Knowl. Data Eng. **30**(9), 1616–1637 (2018)
6. Carlson, A., Betteridge, J., Kisiel, B., Settles, B., Hruschka Jr., E.R., Mitchell, T.M.: Toward an architecture for never-ending language learning. In: Proceedings of the AAAI Conference on Artificial Intelligence, vol. 5 (2010)
7. Chekol, M.W., Pirrò, G.: Refining node embeddings via semantic proximity. In: Pan, J.Z., et al. (eds.) ISWC 2020. LNCS, vol. 12506, pp. 74–91. Springer, Cham (2020). https://doi.org/10.1007/978-3-030-62419-4_5
8. Cho, K., et al.: Learning phrase representations using RNN encoder-decoder for statistical machine translation. In: Empirical Methods in Natural Language Processing (EMNLP) (2014)
9. Chung, J., Gulcehre, C., Cho, K., Bengio, Y.: Empirical evaluation of gated recurrent neural networks on sequence modeling. In: NIPS 2014 Deep Learning and Representation Learning Workshop (2014)
10. Darari, F., Nutt, W., Pirrò, G., Razniewski, S.: Completeness management for RDF data sources. ACM Trans. Web (TWEB) **12**(3), 1–53 (2018)
11. Dettmers, T., Minervini, P., Stenetorp, P., Riedel, S.: Convolutional 2D knowledge graph embeddings. In: Proceedings of the AAAI Conference, pp. 1811–1818 (2018)

12. Dong, X., Chawla, N.V., Swami, A.: metapath2vec: scalable representation learning for heterogeneous networks. In: Proceedings of International Conference on Information and Knowledge Management, pp. 135–144 (2017)
13. Fionda, V., Pirrò, G.: Learning triple embeddings from knowledge graphs. In: Proceedings of the AAAI Conference on Artificial Intelligence, vol. 34, pp. 3874–3881 (2020)
14. Grover, A., Leskovec, J.: node2vec: scalable feature learning for networks. In: Krishnapuram, B., Shah, M., Smola, A.J., Aggarwal, C.C., Shen, D., Rastogi, R. (eds.) Proceedings of the 22nd ACM SIGKDD International Conference on Knowledge Discovery and Data Mining, San Francisco, CA, USA, 13–17 August 2016, pp. 855–864. ACM (2016)
15. Hamilton, W.L., Ying, Z., Leskovec, J.: Inductive representation learning on large graphs. In: Guyon, I., et al. (eds.) Advances in Neural Information Processing Systems 30: Annual Conference on Neural Information Processing Systems 2017, 4–9 December 2017, Long Beach, CA, USA, pp. 1024–1034 (2017)
16. Hochreiter, S., Schmidhuber, J.: Long short-term memory. Neural Comput. **9**(8), 1735–1780 (1997)
17. Hussein, R., Yang, D., Cudré-Mauroux, P.: Are meta-paths necessary?: revisiting heterogeneous graph embeddings. In: Proceedings of the 27th ACM International Conference on Information and Knowledge Management, CIKM 2018, Torino, Italy, 22–26 October 2018, pp. 437–446. ACM (2018)
18. Jia, S., Xiang, Y., Chen, X., Wang, K.: Triple trustworthiness measurement for knowledge graph. In: Liu, L., et al. (eds.) The World Wide Web Conference, WWW 2019, San Francisco, CA, USA, 13–17 May 2019, pp. 2865–2871. ACM (2019)
19. Kipf, T.N., Welling, M.: Semi-supervised classification with graph convolutional networks. In: 5th International Conference on Learning Representations, ICLR 2017, Toulon, France, 24–26 April 2017, Conference Track Proceedings. OpenReview.net (2017)
20. Liang, J., Xiao, Y., Zhang, Y., Hwang, S.W., Wang, H.: Graph-based wrong ISA relation detection in a large-scarsescale lexical taxonomy. In: Proceedings of the Thirty-First AAAI Conference on Artificial Intelligence, pp. 1178–1184 (2017)
21. Melo, A., Paulheim, H.: Detection of relation assertion errors in knowledge graphs. In: Proceedings of the Knowledge Capture Conference, pp. 1–8 (2017)
22. Mikolov, T., Sutskever, I., Chen, K., Corrado, G.S., Dean, J.: Distributed representations of words and phrases and their compositionality. In: Proceedings of International Conference on Neural Information Processing, pp. 3111–3119 (2013)
23. Nathani, D., Chauhan, J., Sharma, C., Kaul, M.: Learning attention-based embeddings for relation prediction in knowledge graphs. In: 57th Annual Meeting of the Association for Computational Linguistics, pp. 4710–4723 (2019)
24. Perozzi, B., Al-Rfou, R., Skiena, S.: Deepwalk: online learning of social representations. In: The 20th ACM SIGKDD International Conference on Knowledge Discovery and Data Mining, KDD 2014, New York, NY, USA, 24–27 August 2014, pp. 701–710 (2014)
25. Pirrò, G.: Building relatedness explanations from knowledge graphs. Semant. Web **10**(6), 963–990 (2019)
26. Pirrò, G.: Fact-checking via path embedding and aggregation. In: Joint Proceedings of Workshops AI4LEGAL2020, NLIWOD, PROFILES 2020, QuWeDa 2020 and SEMIFORM2020 Colocated with the 19th International Semantic Web Conference (ISWC 2020), Virtual Conference, November 2020. CEUR Workshop Proceedings, vol. 2722, pp. 149–158. CEUR-WS.org (2020)

27. Ristoski, P., Paulheim, H.: RDF2Vec: RDF graph embeddings for data mining. In: Proceedings of International Semantic Web Conference, pp. 498–514 (2016)
28. Scarselli, F., Gori, M., Tsoi, A.C., Hagenbuchner, M., Monfardini, G.: The graph neural network model. IEEE Trans. Neural Networks **20**(1), 61–80 (2009)
29. Shiralkar, P., Flammini, A., Menczer, F., Ciampaglia, G.L.: Finding streams in knowledge graphs to support fact checking. In: 2017 IEEE International Conference on Data Mining (ICDM), pp. 859–864. IEEE (2017)
30. Sun, Z., Deng, Z.H., Nie, J.Y., Tang, J.: RotatE: knowledge graph embedding by relational rotation in complex space. In: Proceedings of International Conference on Learning Representations (2019)
31. Trouillon, T., Welbl, J., Riedel, S., Gaussier, É., Bouchard, G.: Complex embeddings for simple link prediction. In: Proceedings of International Conference on Machine Learning, pp. 2071–2080 (2016)
32. Veličković, P., Cucurull, G., Casanova, A., Romero, A., Lio, P., Bengio, Y.: Graph attention networks. In: Proceedings of International Conference on Learning Representations (2017)
33. Wang, X., Lu, Y., Shi, C., Wang, R., Cui, P., Mou, S.: Dynamic heterogeneous information network embedding with meta-path based proximity. IEEE Trans. Knowl. Data Eng. **34**(3), 1117–1132 (2022)
34. West, D.B., et al.: Introduction to Graph Theory, vol. 2. Prentice Hall, Hoboken (1996)
35. Xu, K., Hu, W., Leskovec, J., Jegelka, S.: How powerful are graph neural networks? In: 7th International Conference on Learning Representations, ICLR 2019, New Orleans, LA, USA, 6–9 May 2019. OpenReview.net (2019)
36. Yang, B., Yih, W., He, X., Gao, J., Deng, L.: Embedding entities and relations for learning and inference in knowledge bases. In: Bengio, Y., LeCun, Y. (eds.) 3rd International Conference on Learning Representations, ICLR 2015, San Diego, CA, USA, 7–9 May 2015, Conference Track Proceedings (2015)
37. You, J., Ying, R., Leskovec, J.: Position-aware graph neural networks. In: International Conference on Machine Learning, pp. 7134–7143. PMLR (2019)

An Analysis of Content Gaps Versus User Needs in the Wikidata Knowledge Graph

David Abián(✉) ⓘ, Albert Meroño-Peñuela ⓘ, and Elena Simperl ⓘ

King's College London, London, UK
{david.abian,albert.merono,elena.simperl}@kcl.ac.uk

Abstract. Content gaps in knowledge graphs impact downstream applications. Semantic Web researchers have studied them mainly in relation to data quality or ontology evaluation, for instance by proposing frameworks to capture various quality dimensions or methods to assess these dimensions, such as completeness, accuracy, or consistency. Less work has been done in framing these gaps in the context of user needs. This limits our ability to design processes and tools to help knowledge engineers tackle such gaps effectively. We propose a framework that: (i) captures core types of content gaps, informed by a literature review on peer-production systems; and, in the areas with such gaps, (ii) quantitatively compares the imbalances in the work on the knowledge graph with the imbalances in users' information needs to clarify the origin of the gaps. We operationalize the framework with gender, recency, geographic, and socio-economic gaps, and apply it to Wikidata by comparing edit metrics with Wikipedia pageviews between 2018 and 2021. We did not find gender or recency gaps endogenous to Wikidata's production. Only exceptionally, Wikidata editors work on under-represented entities (e.g. people from countries with lower Human Development Index) less than they should according to the volume of requests. We hope this study will provide a foundation for knowledge engineers to explore the causes of content gaps and address them if and when needed.

Keywords: Knowledge graphs · Content gaps · Wikidata · Data quality

1   Introduction

Content gaps in data sources are missed opportunities to meet information needs and achieve greater impact. They can also create or reinforce biases, for instance in artificial intelligence systems that rely heavily on data [27,43,49,65]. Ontologies [36] and knowledge graphs (KGs) such as Wikidata [54] show content imbalances that researchers have documented as harmful.

The Semantic Web community has studied content gaps in relation to data quality or ontology evaluation. Researchers have proposed ways to capture and assess various quality dimensions such as completeness, accuracy, or consistency

U. Sattler et al. (Eds.): ISWC 2022, LNCS 13489, pp. 354–374, 2022.
https://doi.org/10.1007/978-3-031-19433-7_21

[21,52,76]. There are also similar approaches for ontologies [42,69]. More often than not, these approaches deliver quantified accounts of quality, but struggle to put them in context, e.g. what does it mean that the completeness of a dataset has reached 80%? Is it worth aiming for more or is this a good enough result? Studying the evolution of quality indicators can help by putting numbers in perspective but is not enough to determine whether a dataset or ontology is *fit for use*, the litmus test to which most literature in this space refers [76].

We propose a framework that (i) captures core types of content gaps, informed by a literature review on peer-production systems; and, in the areas with such gaps (ii) quantitatively compares the imbalances in the work on the KG with the imbalances in users' information needs. This is valuable to clarify whether such gaps are endogenous to the KG and, therefore, whether they represent a fitness-for-use problem. We operationalize the framework with gender, recency, geographic, and socio-economic gaps, and apply it to Wikidata by comparing contribution metrics with Wikipedia pageviews between 2018 and 2021. We choose these gaps as they are among those that have attracted the most interest in the literature and, at the same time, are relevant to Wikidata [56]. We collect a representative random sample of each set of instances under study in the KG, enrich the samples with the contribution metrics and Wikipedia pageviews, and analyse the data to answer the following research questions:

RQ1 *Does the contribution to Wikidata show a gender gap that is misaligned with information needs?*

RQ2 *Does the contribution to Wikidata show a recency gap that is misaligned with information needs?*

RQ3 *Does the contribution to Wikidata show a geographic and socio-economic gap that is misaligned with information needs?*

We study the statistical significance and effect sizes of differences and correlations based on gender, years of birth and death, population of settlements, and several human development indicators with three different metrics of contribution and datasets about three different classes of entities (people, settlements, and countries). We find no evidence of gender or recency gaps in the contribution to Wikidata to a greater extent than in users' information needs or Wikipedia, which suggests that these gaps are exogenous to Wikidata's production processes. Only exceptionally, Wikidata editors work on under-represented entities (e.g. people from countries with lower Human Development Index) less than they should according to the volume of requests.

We hope this study will provide a foundation for knowledge engineers to explore the causes of content gaps and address them more effectively. In applying our framework to Wikidata, our findings also contribute towards Wikimedia's strategic goals to address content gaps [56] by pointing to potential biases in contribution patterns that impact the KG's quality.

2   Background and Related Work

Our work sits at the intersection between KGs and online peer-production systems. Consequently, we first explore related work on the quality of Wikidata, undertaken mainly by the Semantic Web community, and then we give an overview of literature from related fields (CSCW, social computing, computational social sciences) that have studied the relationship between digital artefacts (e.g. Wikipedia, OpenStreetMap) and their socio-technical ecosystems.

2.1   Wikidata Quality

Data quality is multidimensional and often conceived as the *fitness for use* for a task or application [76]. Researchers have proposed ways to capture and assess various quality dimensions, but have worked much less on framing these dimensions considering the actual use of the data. [52] surveyed 28 publications until 2018 about Wikidata quality, noting a prevalence of methods and tools for data completeness or accuracy. According to their data quality dimensions, our study addresses *completeness* and *timeliness*.

Wikidata Completeness. There are many ways to get a sense of the completeness of a KG. [2,8] compared similar Wikidata items to spot those missing information. [23] generated completeness assertions using rules, while [17,18,53] annotated Wikidata with completeness metadata and reasoned about the completeness of query results. [48] interpreted metrics on the coverage of scholarly literature on Wikidata, and [58] compared artefacts in Wikidata with other KGs. [40] estimated the completeness of a class in relation to a schema or ontology. [71] compared attribute completeness between different sets of items defined by other attributes (e.g. how complete the attribute "date of birth" is comparing between male computer scientists and female physicists), while [20] used visualizations and dimensional reduction to identify and explore subsets of items missing the same attributes. In 2019, Wikidata implemented Shape Expressions (ShEx)[1][2] [12,61], which allows checking the completeness of the data against a schema. Despite these developments, incompleteness remains an issue today.

Wikidata Timeliness. As [52] noted, Wikidata allows more frequent updates than other KGs because it is peer-produced. However, the literature on timeliness on Wikidata is limited. [21] studied three timeliness criteria, which Wikidata satisfied: timeliness frequency of the graph, specification of the modification date of statements, and specification of the validity period.

Our work complements these and compares content changes with users' information needs to understand the topics people ask for that the KG may not cover well enough. Furthermore, our framework allows exploring whether content gaps are endogenous to the socio-technical environment where the KG is produced or driven by externalities such as the requirements of the consumers of the graph.

---

[1] https://www.mediawiki.org/wiki/Extension:EntitySchema.
[2] https://www.wikidata.org/wiki/Wikidata:Schemas.

2.2   Content Gaps

Gaps are common in online peer production due to a multitude of reasons, including the motivations and interests of the participants, the ways tasks are allocated to participants and the degree to which they coordinate, as well as the technologies they use to contribute [13,19,28,56]. Researchers have documented several types of gaps in online peer production and explored how they come about. For example, [56] compiled a taxonomy that distinguishes between gaps based on characteristics of the contributing community, the users of the peer-produced artefact, and the artefact itself. Our study only addresses the latter, which we refer to as *content gaps*. The Wikimedia Foundation and the communities of Wikipedia and Wikidata have expressed concern about such gaps and have agreed to address them as a strategic priority [44,56].

In the following, we elaborate on the three types of gaps we address in the current implementation of our framework. We choose these as they are among those that have attracted the most interest in the literature and, at the same time, are relevant to Wikidata [56]. We provide an overview of prior studies of these gaps in the context of Wikipedia and Wikidata and, to a lesser extent, other popular systems.

RQ1: Gender Gap. The fact that Wikipedia and Wikidata cover more and better males than females is well documented [56]. However, its causes and the ways to mitigate it are still subject to ongoing discussions. [24] found significant gender differences in metadata, language, and network structure that partly attributed to the editors. In 2016, [70] concluded that Wikipedia articles about females were slightly more notable than their male counterparts. Furthermore, [75] found a systematic over-representation of men when comparing the labour market with the proportions of males with Wikipedia articles, redirects, images, and mentions. [78] suggested that the quality of Wikidata items on females was similar to the quality of those on males, and that Wikidata's proportions of females within each occupation were aligned with the professional societies' notability assessments. [37] found the creation of more articles on females (65.6%) than on males on the English Wikipedia, and [38] noted that the ratios of articles on females were rising exponentially. Finally, [74] commented that Wikipedia editors had over-corrected the content based on gender to the point of biases against males.

RQ2: Recency Gap. There is more content on Wikipedia and Wikidata on more recent events [11,34,35,56,60]. This *recentism*[3] significantly grew on Wikipedia throughout the 2000s [34]. Breaking news, such as incidents, crises, and deaths, quickly lead to a surge in edits [11,34,35]. Some researchers link this to users' information needs [56] rather than other factors endogenous to the Wikipedia ecosystem, based on engagement data that shows that e.g. references about recent events are more frequently hovered/clicked [51], or dates of birth in Wikidata and the historical human population are significantly correlated [38].

---

[3] https://en.wikipedia.org/wiki/Wikipedia:Recentism.

RQ3: Geographic and Socio-Economic Gap. On a wide range of websites, including Twitter, Flickr, Foursquare, Wikipedia, and OpenStreetMap, people tend to document urban and artificial entities earlier, better, and more often than rural, semi-natural, and natural entities, which are also more likely to be generated by bots rather than people interested in local topics [6,7,29,31,56]. The literature also notes Eurocentric, US-centric, pro-Western, and pro-Global North gaps on Wikipedia and OpenStreetMap [10,26,30,60,64]. These gaps are highly correlated with socio-economic factors such as wealth, literacy, and human development in general [30,38,64,81,82], so the geographic gap and socio-economic gap partially overlap. These global gaps are reported to be greater than the inequality in the global distribution of wealth [10], although Wikipedia editors have reduced them over time: Europe had 20 times more geotagged Wikipedia articles than Africa in 2010, but four times more than Africa in 2017 [25]. It is unclear in which cases these differences in content are linked to varying users' information needs.

3   Methods

We define a framework for quantitatively comparing the imbalances in the work on a KG with the imbalances in users' information needs. This allows us to clarify whether or not the content gaps studied are particular to the KG. We operationalize this framework for Wikidata and apply it to understand three families of potential gaps.

3.1   Framework of Analysis

Design Considerations. We want to: (r1) measure quantitatively, to understand the importance of each gap; (r2) measure imbalances introduced or maintained in a given period, to understand their evolution and be able to draw conclusions specific to the period of interest; (r3) measure imbalances based on any type of attribute, whether categorical (e.g. gender) or numerical (e.g. population), so that the framework applies to many domains; (r4) measure information needs in several representative languages, to avoid bias.

Dimensions and Metrics. We consider two families of metrics: proxies for the contribution to the KG, and proxies for the information needs, against which the former are compared. Metrics of information needs can be very diverse and context-specific. In contrast, from a comprehensive review of the literature on online peer production, we learned that contribution is mainly characterized and measured in four categories, which we will refer to as $CAPT$: (C) contributions (as a countable noun; e.g. edits in Wikipedia, edits and changesets in OpenStreetMap); (A) artefacts (e.g. Wikipedia articles, Wikidata items); (P) participants (e.g. Wikipedians or editors in Wikipedia, mappers in OpenStreetMap); and (T) time. A *contribution* is a documented change undertaken by a *participant* by applying a create, update or delete action to an *artefact* at a certain *time.* A participant or a unit of time can have any number of associated contributions, including zero, whereas an artefact should have one or more associated contributions. Contribution metrics can be calculated with filtering and aggregation operations on $CAPT$ entities. The most common aggregation operation is counting $CAPT$ entities of a certain type; the most common filtering operation, selecting a single value or $CAPT$ entity. The number of contributions is the most widely used contribution metric in the literature on online peer production [3,9,14,33,46,63]. The terminology may vary, including names such as "edit count" [4,32,39,47,57], "number of edits" [16,50,62,73,79,80], "quantity of edits" [63], "number of revisions" [59,67,72] and "number of user activities" [22], among others.

Measurement Criteria. We want to filter artefacts based on the attributes of interest (e.g. gender) and obtain metrics per artefact, so we can count three other types of $CAPT$ entities as the simplest contribution metrics: contributions, participants, and units of time. In several peer-production systems, most artefacts and participants have hardly any contributions, and most contributions are associated with a few artefacts and participants [5,41,46,62,72]. Participants can quickly add up large numbers of contributions by making many minor changes in a short time. This makes contributions a noisy metric because, in these cases, many contributions do not mean more value produced or more effort invested. To complement the number of contributions, it is possible to count units of time (e.g. hours, days, months) with contributions or consider the number of different participants with contributions. We also consider metrics linking contribution and information needs: the return on investment (ROI) ratios. We can calculate one of these ratios for each possible combination of contribution (c) metric and information need (n) metric by applying $n/(c+1)$. We assume that the potential content gaps against those artefacts with higher ROI ratios are more likely to be misaligned with information needs.

3.2   Operationalization for Wikidata

As per (r4), we decide to use the *pageviews from users* (not spiders or bots) of the Wikipedias corresponding to the top ten most spoken languages in the world in 2021 according to ethnologue.com[4]: English, Mandarin Chinese, Hindi, Spanish, French, Standard Arabic, Bengali, Russian, Portuguese, and Urdu. Pageviews are considered the "most important content consumption metric"[5] on Wikipedia, and studies and tools use it to identify "concepts with significant increase of the interest from the public" [15]. As each Wikidata item about an entity is linked to the titles of the Wikipedia articles about the same entity, it is possible to automatically enrich a dataset that contains identifiers of Wikidata items with their corresponding Wikipedia pageviews.

We choose the *number of contributions*, the *number of days with contributions* (operationalizing the number of units of time), and the *number of human*

---

[4] https://www.ethnologue.com/guides/ethnologue200.

[5] https://meta.wikimedia.org/wiki/Research:Page_view.

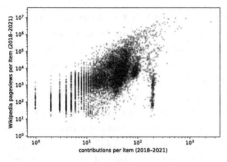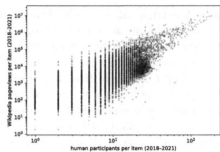

Fig. 1. Random sample of Wikidata items on settlements in two charts as a function of Wikipedia pageviews and two different contribution metrics: on the left, number of (manual and automatic) contributions, revealing clusters of similar entities that received the same automatic treatment (e.g. vertical line around 200 contributions); on the right, number of human editors, which does not provide this insight but better quantifies the actual effort invested and therefore better correlates with pageviews.

participants (operationalizing the number of participants). We consider only human participants for the latter metric because, according to [47], bots make around 85% of contributions to Wikidata items, but we do not discern noise generated by bots with the other two metrics. During our exploratory analysis (Fig. 1) we confirm that the combination of contribution metrics chosen is more informative and useful to operationalize contribution than any of the metrics individually.

For Wikidata we should measure the contribution made over at least a few years to avoid an excess of zeros [62]. At the same time, we seek to draw conclusions about the KG's current or most recent socio-technical context. Therefore, we set our study period to be the four years prior to the year of analysis: from 2018 to 2021.

Despite the existence of tools that allow querying Wikidata's edit history [32,66], we use simple random samples (see Sect. 4) instead of full sets of instances because: (a) the samples are sufficient to obtain conclusive results from the statistical analysis; and (b) we enrich the data with contribution metrics, but also with Wikipedia pageviews, so we have to combine two metadata sources,[6] the query of which would hardly scale to the full sets of instances.[7] Due to (r1), we choose hypothesis testing to confirm or reject a relationship between contribution and information needs with statistical significance for each potential gap studied. We quantify these relationships with the effect sizes. The unit of analysis is not the artefact, but the combination of the artefact and the attribute under study, as the latter may be multivalued. As per (r3), we choose two types of tests depending on the type of attribute under study: correlations, for numerical attributes (e.g. year of birth); and differences between groups, for

---

[6] The APIs https://www.wikidata.org/w/api.php and https://wikimedia.org/api/rest_v1/metrics/pageviews/, respectively. See supplemental material.

[7] We will extend the analysis to the full sets in future work.

categorical attributes (e.g. gender). To compare differences in numerical values between groups we use Mann-Whitney U tests; to check correlations between two numerical variables, Spearman's rank-order correlations. We choose these tests because they are non-parametric, are based on ranks, and do not assume normal distributions in the data. The literature has confirmed that contribution on peer-production websites, including Wikidata, does not follow normal distributions; instead, these distributions tend to be highly skewed, concentrated on a few participants and artefacts [5,41,46,62,72]. Our samples also show this property. In line with [55], we consider that a Spearman's rank-order correlation has a *negligible* strength and, therefore, we conclude that there is no correlation between variables, when $|\rho| < 0.1$. Similarly, we consider that a Mann-Whitney U test shows a *negligible* effect size, and conclude that there is no significant difference between groups, when $|r| < 0.1$. We reject the null hypothesis when $p \leq 0.01$.

3.3 Hypotheses About Wikidata

Note that we consider three contribution metrics, so we perform groups of three tests for comparing contribution and groups of three tests for comparing ROI ratios. Table 1 shows all the hypotheses tested, the tests used for each of them, and their correspondence to our research questions. For **H2–H4** and **H8–H11**, we consider both the set of all items and only those with links to articles in the Wikipedias studied, and both annually (2018, 2019, 2020, and 2021) and over the entire study period (2018–2021). For **H5** and **H6**, we consider *events* as births and as deaths. For **H7**, we consider both the set of all items and only those with links to articles in the Wikipedias studied, both annually (2018, 2019, 2020, and 2021) and over the entire study period (2018–2021), and considering *events* as births and as deaths.

4 Data

We generate and analyse three tabular datasets from Wikidata[8]: (a) 50,000 random items on people with, where defined, sex or gender, year of birth, year of death, occupation, and country of citizenship; (b) 50,000 random items on human settlements with population and, where defined, coordinates, continent, and country; and (c) all 374 items defined as instances of sovereign states.

For each item in each dataset we retrieve and include all the metrics described in Sect. 3.2, both from 2018 to 2021 and by year. We also include the pageviews broken down by Wikipedia and the corresponding title of the article, if any. The pageviews are quantified as zero for each Wikipedia without an article associated with a given item. We enrich all the datasets with the Human Development Index (HDI) per country and its base indicators according to [45]: Life Expectancy at birth (LE; in years); Expected Years of Schooling (EYS); Mean Years of Schooling (MYS); and Gross National Income per capita (GNIpc; in PPP $).

---

[8] The Python modules and SPARQL queries used to generate the datasets are available on https://github.com/davidabian/wikidata-gaps-vs-needs.

We analyse the gender and recency gaps based on the dataset about items on people, and the geographic and socio-economic gap based on the three datasets.

Table 1. Research questions, tests used, and hypotheses tested on Wikidata.

RQ1: GENDER GAP (TWO-SIDED FISHER'S EXACT TEST)
H1	The proportion of items with links to articles in the Wikipedias studied to all items is significantly different between the set of items on males and the set of items on females.

RQ1: GENDER GAP (MANN-WHITNEY U TESTS)
H2	($c_{male} > c_{female}$): The contribution metrics per item tend to be higher for items on males than for items on females.
H3	($pv_{male} > pv_{female}$): The pageviews per item tend to be higher for items on males than for items on females.
H4	($roi_{female} > roi_{male}$): The ROI ratios per item tend to be higher for items on females than for items on males.

RQ2: RECENCY GAP (MANN-WHITNEY U TESTS)
H5	The years of the events in items with links to articles in the Wikipedias studied tend to be different than those in items without links to articles in the Wikipedias studied.

RQ2: RECENCY GAP (SPEARMAN'S ρ RANK-ORDER CORRELATIONS)
H6	The last 500 years interpreted as numbers (1522–2021) are correlated with the proportions of Wikidata items that have the events in those years and links to articles in the Wikipedias studied relative to the Wikidata items that have the events in those years but no links to articles in the Wikipedias studied.
H7	The contribution metrics, pageviews, and ROI ratios per item are correlated with the years of the events.

RQ3: GEOGR. AND SOCIO-ECONOMIC GAP (SPEARMAN'S ρ RANK-ORDER CORRELATIONS)
H8	The contribution metrics, pageviews, and ROI ratios per item on a settlement are correlated with the average of its population values.
H9	The contribution metrics, pageviews, and ROI ratios per item on a person are correlated with the Human Development Index of the countries of citizenship.
H10	The contribution metrics, pageviews, and ROI ratios per item on a settlement are correlated with the Human Development Index of its country.
H11	The contribution metrics, pageviews, and ROI ratios per item on a state are correlated with its Human Development Index.

5 Results

In this section we present the results of the tests specified in Sect. 3.3 and Table 1, together with contextual information such as statistics and data visualizations. Many results of the tests based on metrics per item (H2–H4, H7–H11) are synthesized in Table 2 and not repeated in text.

5.1 RQ1: Gender Gap

- Around 36.4% of the items on males and 25.9% of the items on females had links to articles in the Wikipedias studied.
- ROI ratios were not higher for items on females than for items on males.
- An item on a male tended to receive more contribution than an item on a female in 2018, but this was no longer the case in 2021.

As of 30 January 2022, Wikidata had 9,608,862 items on people (instances of Q5), most of them (79.81%, 7,668,492) with some sex or gender defined. These

Table 2. Synthesis of the results of the Mann-Whitney U tests and Spearman's ρ rank-order correlations for hypotheses H2–H4 and H7–H11 based on contribution metrics (c), Wikipedia pageviews (pv), ROI ratios (roi), average of population figures in the item (pop), the Human Development Index of the country (HDI), and its core indicators Life Expectancy at birth (LE; in years), Expected Years of Schooling (EYS), Mean Years of Schooling (MYS), and Gross National Income per capita (GNIpc; in PPP \$). ✓ represents the acceptance of the hypothesis shown with a non-negligible effect size ($r \geq 0.1$) according to a metric; =, a conclusive result with a negligible effect size ($r < 0.1$); ?, an inconclusive result ($p > 0.01$); +, a positive correlation ($\rho \geq 0.1$); -, a negative correlation ($\rho \leq -0.1$); and 0, no correlation ($|\rho| < 0.1$ or $p > 0.01$).

RQ1: Gender Gap

items	tests	2018–21	2018	2019	2020	2021
all people	H2: $c_{male} > c_{female}$	✓==	✓✓✓	✓==	=??	???
	H3: $pv_{male} > pv_{female}$	✓	✓	✓	✓	=
	H4: $roi_{female} > roi_{male}$	???	???	???	???	???
people linked to Wikipedia	H1: $c_{male} > c_{female}$	???	???	???	???	???
	H3: $pv_{male} > pv_{female}$	?	?	?	?	?
	H4: $roi_{female} > roi_{male}$	===	✓✓✓	===	===	===

RQ3: Geographic and Socio-Economic Gap (Population)

items	tests	2018–21	2018	2019	2020	2021
all settlements	H8: corr(pop, contr)	+++	+++	+++	+++	+++
	H8: corr(pop, need)	+	+	+	+	+
	H8: corr(pop, ROI)	+++	+++	+++	+++	+++
settlements linked to Wikipedia	H8: corr(pop, contr)	+++	+++	+++	+++	+++
	H8: corr(pop, need)	+	+	+	+	+
	H8: corr(pop, ROI)	+++	+++	+++	+++	+++

RQ3: Geographic and Socio-Economic Gap (HDI)

items	tests	2018–21	2018	2019	2020	2021
all people	H9: corr(HDI, contr)	+++	++0	0++	+++	000
	H9: corr(HDI, need)	0	0	0	0	0
	H9: corr(HDI, ROI)	000	000	000	000	000
people linked to Wikipedia	H9: corr(HDI, contr)	+++	++0	+++	+++	000
	H9: corr(HDI, need)	0	0	0	0	0
	H9: corr(HDI, ROI)	000	000	000	000	000
all settlements	H10: corr(HDI, contr)	+++	+++	+++	+++	+++
	H10: corr(HDI, need)	+	+	+	+	+
	H10: corr(HDI, ROI)	+++	+++	+++	+++	+++
settlements linked to Wikipedia	H10: corr(HDI, contr)	+++	+++	+++	+++	+++
	H10: corr(HDI, need)	+	+	+	+	+
	H10: corr(HDI, ROI)	+++	+++	+++	+++	+++
all states	H11: corr(HDI, contr)	+++	0++	+++	+++	+++
	H11: corr(HDI, need)	+	+	+	+	+
	H11: corr(HDI, ROI)	+++	+++	+++	+++	+++
states linked to Wikipedia	H11: corr(HDI, contr)	+++	0++	+++	+++	+++
	H11: corr(HDI, need)	+	+	+	+	+
	H11: corr(HDI, ROI)	+++	+++	+++	+++	+++

RQ2: Recency Gap (Years Of Birth And Death)

items	tests	2018–21	2018	2019	2020	2021
all people	H7: corr(birth, c)	000	+00	++0	000	000
	H7: corr(birth, pv)	+	0	+	+	+
	H7: corr(birth, roi)	+++	000	+++	+++	+++
	H7: corr(death, c)	++0	+++	++0	000	000
	H7: corr(death, pv)	+	+	+	+	+
	H7: corr(death, roi)	+++	++0	+++	+++	+++
people linked to Wikipedia	H7: corr(birth, c)	000	000	000	000	000
	H7: corr(birth, pv)	+	0	+	+	+
	H7: corr(birth, roi)	+++	000	000	+++	+++
	H7: corr(death, c)	000	000	000	+++	+++
	H7: corr(death, pv)	0	0	0	0	0
	H7: corr(death, roi)	000	000	000	000	++0

RQ3: Geographic and Socio-Economic Gap (HDI), 2018–21

items	tests	HDI	LE	EYS	MYS	GNIpc
all people	H9: corr(contr, _)	+++	000	+++	+++	+++
	H9: corr(need, _)	0	-	0	0	0
	H9: corr(ROI, _)	000	---	000	000	000
people linked to Wikipedia	H9: corr(contr, _)	+++	+++	+++	+++	+++
	H9: corr(need, _)	0	0	0	0	0
	H9: corr(ROI, _)	000	---	000	000	000
all settlements	H10: corr(contr, _)	+++	+++	+++	+++	+++
	H10: corr(need, _)	+	+	+	+	+
	H10: corr(ROI, _)	+++	+++	+++	+++	+++
settlements linked to Wikipedia	H10: corr(contr, _)	+++	+++	+++	+++	+++
	H10: corr(need, _)	+	+	+	+	+
	H10: corr(ROI, _)	+++	+++	+++	+++	+++
all states	H11: corr(contr, _)	+++	+++	+++	+++	+++
	H11: corr(need, _)	+	+	+	+	+
	H11: corr(ROI, _)	+++	+++	+++	+++	+++
states linked to Wikipedia	H11: corr(contr, _)	+++	+++	+++	+++	+++
	H11: corr(need, _)	+	+	+	+	+
	H11: corr(ROI, _)	+++	+++	+++	+++	+++

included 5,819,674 items on males and 1,847,850 items on females, that is, 3.15 times more items on males than on females. Males and females accounted for 99.99% of all items with some sex or gender defined, with the remaining 0.01% of the values, in order of number of occurrences, being transgender female, non-binary, transgender male, eunuch, intersex, genderfluid, genderqueer, agender, transgender person, cisgender female, and many others.

H1. Out of 30,231 items on males and 9,540 items on females in the sample, 10,993 (36.36%) and 2,467 (25.86%) had links to articles in the Wikipedias studied, respectively. As hypothesized, these differences were statistically significant (Fisher's exact test, two-sided $p < .001$).

H2–H4, 2018–2021, all the Items. Small effect sizes ($r = 0.1$) for the numbers of human participants and pageviews.

H2–H4, 2018–2021, Items with Links to the Wikipedias Studied. None of the hypotheses were accepted.

H2–H4, Metrics per Year, all the Items. H2 ($c_{male} > c_{female}$) was only accepted for 2018, with small effect sizes, $r \in [0.1, 0.2]$; and for 2019, with a small effect size for the number of activity days, $r = 0.1$. Throughout the entire study period there was a negative monotonic evolution of effect sizes and a positive monotonic evolution of p-values. The differences in the average values of contribution between items on males and items on females also evolved monotonically (Fig. 2), starting in 2018 with higher average values of contribution to items on males than items on females and ending in 2021 with lower ones. H3 ($pv_{male} > pv_{female}$) was accepted for 2018, 2019, and 2020, with small effect sizes, $r = 0.1$.

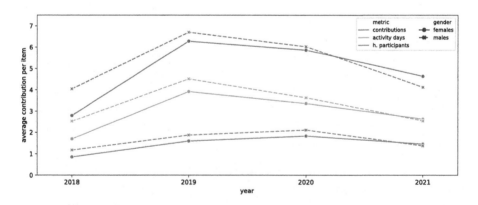

Fig. 2. Evolution of the average values of contribution metrics per item by gender.

H2–H4, Metrics per Year, Items with Links to the Wikipedias Studied. H4 ($roi_{female} > roi_{male}$) was accepted for 2018 with small effect sizes, $r = 0.1$.

5.2 RQ2: Recency Gap

> – People with items linked to articles in the Wikipedias studied tended to have more recent years of birth and death than the rest of the people with items.
> – The item on a person tended to have more pageviews and higher ROI ratios associated with it the more recent the years of birth and death were.

H5. As hypothesized, there were significant differences between the years of birth in items linked to articles in the Wikipedias studied ($n = 11963, \text{Med} = 1942$) and those that were not ($n = 15098, \text{Med} = 1927$), two-sided $p < .001, r = .13$. There were also significant differences between the years of death in items linked to articles in the Wikipedias studied ($n = 5843, \text{Med} = 1962$) and those that were not ($n = 7706, \text{Med} = 1942$), two-sided $p < .001, r = .15$.

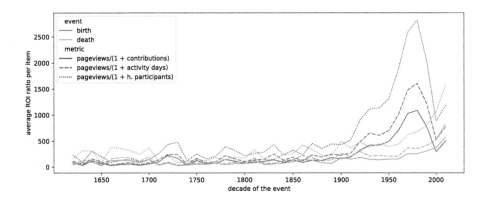

Fig. 3. Average ROI ratios per item by decade of the event.

H6. There was no conclusive (Spearman's ρ) rank-order correlation between years of birth between 1522 and 2021 and the proportions of Wikidata items with those years of birth that had links to articles in the Wikipedias studied, $\rho(493) = .10, p = .026$. The correlation was conclusive and positive for id. years of death $\rho(493) = .16, p < .001$.

H7, 2018–2021, all the Items. For years of birth, there were positive Spearman's correlations with pageviews and ROI ratios per item, with small effect sizes, $\rho \in [0.1, 0.2]$. For years of death, there were positive Spearman's correlations with activity days, human participants, pageviews, and ROI ratios per item, with small effect sizes, $\rho \in [0.1, 0.2]$. See Fig. 3.

H7, 2018–2021, Items with Links to the Wikipedias Studied. For years of birth, there were positive correlations with pageviews and ROI ratios per item. For years of death, there were no correlations.

H7, Metrics per Year, all the Items. Considering years of birth and Spearman's correlations with contribution per item, there were one positive correlation in 2018 and two in 2019; with pageviews per item, positive correlations in 2019, 2020, and 2021; and with ROI ratios, the three positive correlations in each of the years 2019, 2020, and 2021. Considering years of death and Spearman's correlations with contribution per item, there were the three positive correlations in 2018 and two in 2019; with pageviews per item, positive correlations for all years; and with ROI ratios, two positive correlations in 2018, and the three positive correlations in each of the years 2019, 2020, and 2021.

H7, Metrics per Year, Items with Links to the Wikipedias Studied. Considering years of birth and Spearman's correlations, there were positive correlations with pageviews per item in 2019, 2020, and 2021; and with ROI ratios, in each of the years 2020 and 2021. Considering years of death and Spearman's correlations with ROI ratios, there were two positive correlations in 2021.

5.3   RQ3: Geographic and Socio-Economic Gap

> – The more populated a settlement, the more contribution and pageviews, and the higher ROI ratios.
> – The higher the Human Development Index of a country or the country of a settlement, the more contribution and pageviews, and the higher ROI ratios.
> – The higher the Human Development Index of a person's country, the more contribution, but not the more pageviews or the higher ROI ratios.

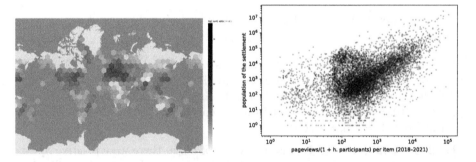

Fig. 4. Sum of contributions to items on settlements per area in logarithmic scale.

Fig. 5. Population of a settlement (y-axis, log) and the ROI ratio based on Wikipedia pageviews and number of human participants of the item (x-axis, log).

H8 (Population). For the entire period, the strength of the correlations (ρ) was 0.31–0.37 with contribution metrics and 0.55–0.58 with pageviews and ROI ratios (Fig. 5). Considering only those items linked to Wikipedia articles, the correlations with pageviews showed an increasing monotonic evolution, from 0.55 in 2018 to 0.60 in 2021; and ROI ratios as well, from 0.48–0.52 in 2018 to 0.60–0.61 in 2021.

H9 (HDI, People). There were positive correlations between the Human Development Index (HDI) of the countries of citizenship and the contribution metrics per item considering the entire study period (2018–2021), $\rho \in [0.1, 0.2]$. All HDI base indicators were positively correlated, except Life Expectancy at birth (LE) when considering all items. There was no correlation between HDI and pageviews or ROI ratios in any case. There were weak negative correlations between Life Expectancy at birth (LE) and ROI ratios when considering only items linked to Wikipedia articles, and between Life Expectancy at birth (LE) and both pageviews and ROI ratios when considering all items, $\rho \in [-0.1, -0.2]$.

H10 (HDI, Settlements). There were positive Spearman's ρ rank-order correlations between the Human Development Index (HDI) of the countries of settlements and the contribution metrics, pageviews, and ROI ratios per item. The strength of the correlations (ρ) was 0.4–0.5 with contribution metrics, 0.4 with pageviews, and 0.3 with ROI ratios. When considering only items linked to Wikipedia articles, the strength was 0.5–0.6 with contribution metrics, 0.5 with pageviews, and 0.3 with ROI ratios. See also Fig. 4.

H11 (HDI, Countries). There were positive Spearman's correlations between the Human Development Index (HDI) of the countries and the contribution metrics, pageviews, and ROI ratios per item. For the entire period, the strength of the correlations (ρ) was 0.31–0.51 with contribution metrics, 0.60 with pageviews, and 0.56–0.58 with ROI ratios.

6   Discussion

From the effect sizes we found that the influence of gender, time, and socio-economic factors on the contribution and information needs per item on a person was subtle. In contrast, the influence of geographic and socio-economic factors on the contribution and information needs associated with settlements and countries was considerable. We found no evidence of gender, recency, or urban imbalances in the contribution to Wikidata to a greater extent than in users' information needs or Wikipedia. This finding suggests that these content gaps are not endogenous to Wikidata, something consistent with previous literature. [1] documented that birth dates in DBpedia, sourced from Wikipedia, tended to be more recent than in Wikidata; and [75] found a systematic over-representation of males in Wikipedia compared to the labour market, whereas [78] found that Wikidata's representation of males was comparable to the professional societies' notability assessments. We did find a slightly larger socio-economic gap in the contribution to Wikidata than in users' information needs based on the development indices of the countries of citizenship of the people represented in Wikidata. This was not found in other classes of instances, such as settlements or the countries themselves. In summary, **the only content gaps we found that may be endogenous to Wikidata were subtle and related to socio-economic aspects of the people represented, whereas famous gaps such as gender and recency gaps could be explained by users' information needs, perhaps in conjunction with external systems** adjacent to Wikidata, e.g. Wikipedia and web search engines.

We argue that a KG's fine granularity and structure can act as equalizers of content differences between traditionally over- and under-represented groups. In Wikidata, **ontological properties (e.g. about people: place of birth/death, father, mother, etc.) leverage this fine granularity and can be understood as placeholders for information that is needed for the graph to be complete**, making missing information more explicit, and therefore helping to avoid gaps and biases. In contrast, it is not necessary, and generally not aligned with Wikipedia's policies, to create a Wikipedia article about e.g. a female just to mention her in the article about a male. [37] already considered that every Wikidata item on a "human without a Wikipedia article" was a "structural item" and exemplified that "a member of royalty without a Wikipedia article [...] is needed to make a family tree complete". The presence of pre-established properties and constraints (e.g. ShEx [12,61], Wikidata property constraints) with which to include the data, initially for making the KG ontologically predictable for software agents, can also help avoid bias, as it lets editors easily identify incompleteness at the KG entity level, and therefore solve it.

Meeting information needs is usually the purpose of a data source, and contribution is the form of resource investment through which a collaborative KG meets these needs. Therefore, the distance between the two is relevant and should be monitored. Nonetheless, distributing contribution solely on the basis of recorded information needs may not necessarily be the best decision. First, with this approach we estimate past needs and the extent to which contribution was aligned with them, but it would be preferable to determine which contribution will be able to meet future needs. Second, our metadata on information needs can only reflect the needs of the people who use the metadata source, Wikipedia in our case. However, not everyone consults Wikipedia for every information need, nor in the same cases, nor with the same frequency; in fact, access to Wikipedia has been banned or limited in entire countries [68,77]. Finally, not all information needs may be equally pressing, but our framework does not make such a distinction.

7   Conclusions

Despite the Semantic Web community's interest and progress in measuring and improving the quality of KGs such as Wikidata, differences in content coverage persist for unclear reasons. It is possible to learn more about the socio-technical grounds of such differences by comparing the imbalances in the work on the KG with the imbalances in information needs considering the problematic attributes (e.g. gender). In this work we have defined a quantitative framework to achieve this and applied it to gender, recency, and geographic and socio-economic gaps in Wikidata. Our results suggest that, in general, these gaps are not endogenous to Wikidata's production, although exceptions are possible, e.g. based on development indices of people's countries of citizenship.

We plan to continue analysing content gaps in KGs. With a greater investment of resources, we will use the full sets of instances in Wikidata instead of samples. We will analyse more attributes and classes of instances, which could reveal or rule out more content gaps with respect to information needs. It would also be helpful to implement software solutions to monitor possible content gaps in KGs with the proposed approach, probably considering a shorter period. Finally, imbalances in contribution and information needs separately are also relevant and impact downstream applications, so monitoring them and warning users about their existence would be beneficial, as well as completing the KGs based on these insights.

Supplemental Material Statement: The datasets, SPARQL queries, and code are available on https://github.com/davidabian/wikidata-gaps-vs-needs.

References

1. Abián, D., Bernad, J., Trillo-Lado, R.: Using contemporary constraints to ensure data consistency. In: Proceedings of the 34th ACM/SIGAPP Symposium on Applied Computing, pp. 2303–2310. ACM, Limassol, Cyprus, Apr 2019. https://doi.org/10.1145/3297280.3297509
2. Ahmeti, A., Razniewski, S., Polleres, A.: Assessing the completeness of entities in knowledge bases. In: Blomqvist, E., Hose, K., Paulheim, H., Ławrynowicz, A., Ciravegna, F., Hartig, O. (eds.) ESWC 2017. LNCS, vol. 10577, pp. 7–11. Springer, Cham (2017). https://doi.org/10.1007/978-3-319-70407-4_2
3. Anthony, D., Smith, S.W., Williamson, T.: Reputation and reliability in collective goods: the case of the online encyclopedia Wikipedia. Ration. Soc. **21**(3), 283–306 (2009). https://doi.org/10.1177/1043463109336804
4. Arazy, O., Lifshitz-Assaf, H., Balila, A.: Neither a Bazaar nor a cathedral: the interplay between structure and agency in Wikipedia's role system. J. Am. Soc. Inf. Sci. **70**(1), 3–15 (2019). https://doi.org/10.1002/asi.24076
5. Arazy, O., Lifshitz-Assaf, H., Nov, O., Daxenberger, J., Balestra, M., Cheshire, C.: On the "How" and "Why" of Emergent Role Behaviors in Wikipedia. Association for Computing Machinery, New York (2017)
6. Arsanjani, J.J., Helbich, M., Bakillah, M., Loos, L.: The emergence and evolution of OpenStreetMap: a cellular automata approach. Int. J. Digital Earth **8**(1), 74–88 (2015). https://doi.org/10.1080/17538947.2013.847125

7. Arsanjani, J.J., Mooney, P., Helbich, M., Zipf, A.: An exploration of future patterns of the contributions to OpenStreetMap and development of a contribution index. Trans. GIS **19**(6), 896–914 (2015). https://doi.org/10.1111/tgis.12139

8. Balaraman, V., Razniewski, S., Nutt, W.: Recoin: Relative completeness in Wikidata. In: Companion Proceedings of the World Wide Web Conference 2018 (www 2018), pp. 1787–1792. Association for Computing Machinery, New York (2018). https://doi.org/10.1145/3184558.3191641

9. Begin, D., Devillers, R., Roche, S.: Contributors' withdrawal from online collaborative communities: the case of OpenStreetMap. ISPRS Int. J. Geo Inf. **6**(11), 340 (2017). https://doi.org/10.3390/ijgi6110340

10. Beytía, P.: The positioning matters: estimating geographical bias in the multilingual record of biographies on Wikipedia. In: Companion Proceedings of the Web Conference WWW 2020, pp. 806–810. Association for Computing Machinery, New York, Apr 2020. https://doi.org/10.1145/3366424.3383569

11. Bubendorff, S., Rizza, C., Prieur, C.: Construction and dissemination of information veracity on French social media during crises: comparison of Twitter and Wikipedia. J. Contingencies Crisis Manag. **29**(2), 204–216 (2021). https://doi.org/10.1111/1468-5973.12351

12. Candela, G., Escobar, P., Sáez, M., Marco-Such, M.: A shape expression approach for assessing the quality of Linked Open Data in libraries. Semantic Web Preprint (Preprint), 1–21 (2021). https://doi.org/10.3233/SW-210441

13. Cho, H., Chen, M., Chung, S.: Testing an integrative theoretical model of knowledge-sharing behavior in the context of Wikipedia. J. Am. Soc. Inform. Sci. Technol. **61**(6), 1198–1212 (2010). https://doi.org/10.1002/asi.21316

14. Ciampaglia, G.L., Taraborelli, D.: MoodBar: increasing new user retention in Wikipedia through lightweight socialization. Association for Computing Machinery, New York (2015). https://doi.org/10.1145/2675133.2675181

15. Ciglan, M., Nørvåg, K.: WikiPop: personalized event detection system based on Wikipedia page view statistics. In: Proceedings of the 19th ACM International Conference on Information and Knowledge Management, CIKM 2010, pp. 1931–1932. Association for Computing Machinery, New York, Oct 2010. https://doi.org/10.1145/1871437.1871769

16. Clement, M., Guitton, M.J.: Interacting with bots online: users' reactions to actions of automated programs in Wikipedia. Comput. Hum. Behav. **50**, 66–75 (2015). https://doi.org/10.1016/j.chb.2015.03.078

17. Darari, F., Prasojo, R.E., Razniewski, S., Nutt, W.: COOL-WD: a completeness tool for Wikidata. In: SEMWEB (2017)

18. Darari, F., Razniewski, S., Prasojo, R.E., Nutt, W.: Enabling fine-grained RDF data completeness assessment. In: Bozzon, A., Cudre-Maroux, P., Pautasso, C. (eds.) ICWE 2016. LNCS, vol. 9671, pp. 170–187. Springer, Cham (2016). https://doi.org/10.1007/978-3-319-38791-8_10

19. Das, M., Hecht, B., Gergle, D.: The gendered geography of contributions to OpenStreetMap: complexities in self-focus bias. In: Chi 2019: Proceedings of the 2019 Chi Conference on Human Factors in Computing Systems. Association for Computing Machinery, New York (2019). https://doi.org/10.1145/3290605.3300793

20. Destandau, M., Fekete, J.D.: The missing path: analysing incompleteness in knowledge graphs. Inf. Vis. **20**(1), 66–82 (2021). https://doi.org/10.1177/1473871621991539

21. Faerber, M., Bartscherer, F., Menne, C., Rettinger, A.: Linked Data quality of DBpedia, Freebase, OpenCyc, Wikidata, and YAGO. Semantic Web **9**(1), 1–53 (2018)

22. Fraga, B.S., Couto da Silva, A.P., Murai, F.: Online Social Networks in Health Care: A Study of Mental Disorders on Reddit. IEEE, New York (2018). https://doi.org/10.1109/WI.2018.00-36

23. Galarraga, L., Razniewski, S., Amarilli, A., Suchanek, F.M.: Predicting completeness in knowledge bases. In: Wsdm 2017: Proceedings of the Tenth ACM International Conference on Web Search and Data Mining, pp. 375–383. Association for Computing Machinery, New York (2017). https://doi.org/10.1145/3018661.3018739

24. Graells-Garrido, E., Lalmas, M., Menczer, F.: First women, second sex: gender bias in Wikipedia. In: Proceedings of the 26th ACM Conference on Hypertext & Social Media, HT 2015, pp. 165–174. Association for Computing Machinery, New York, Aug 2015. https://doi.org/10.1145/2700171.2791036

25. Graham, M., Dittus, M.: Geographies of Digital Exclusion: Data and Inequality. Pluto Press (2022)

26. Graham, M., Hogan, B., Straumann, R.K., Medhat, A.: Uneven geographies of user-generated information: patterns of increasing informational poverty. Ann. Assoc. Am. Geogr. **104**(4), 746–764 (2014). https://doi.org/10.1080/00045608.2014.910087

27. Gumnishka, I.: Gender and racial bias in computer vision, Apr 2021. https://thegoodai.co/2021/04/14/gender-and-racial-bias-in-computer-vision/

28. Hecht, B., Gergle, D.: Measuring self-focus bias in community-maintained knowledge repositories. In: Proceedings of the Fourth International Conference on Communities and Technologies, C&T 2009 pp. 11–20. Association for Computing Machinery, New York, Jun 2009. https://doi.org/10.1145/1556460.1556463

29. Hecht, B., Stephens, M.: A Tale of Cities: Urban biases in volunteered geographic information. In: Proceedings of the International AAAI Conference on Web and Social Media, vol. 8(1), pp. 197–205 (May 2014). https://ojs.aaai.org/index.php/ICWSM/article/view/14554

30. Herfort, B., Lautenbach, S., de Albuquerque, J.P., Anderson, J., Zipf, A.: The evolution of humanitarian mapping within the OpenStreetMap community. Sci. Rep. **11**(1), 3037 (2021). https://doi.org/10.1038/s41598-021-82404-z

31. Johnson, I.L., Lin, Y., Li, T.J.J., Hall, A., Halfaker, A., Schöning, J., Hecht, B.: Not at home on the range: peer production and the urban/rural divide. In: Proceedings of the 2016 CHI Conference on Human Factors in Computing Systems, CHI 2016, pp. 13–25. Association for Computing Machinery, New York, May 2016. https://doi.org/10.1145/2858036.2858123

32. Kaffee, L.A., Endris, K.M., Simperl, E.: When Humans and Machines Collaborate: Cross-lingual Label Editing in Wikidata. Association for Computing Machinery, New York (2019). https://doi.org/10.1145/3306446.3340826

33. Kamptner, E., Kessler, F.: Small-scale crisis response mapping: comparing user contributions to events in OpenStreetMap. GeoJournal **84**(5), 1165–1185 (2018). https://doi.org/10.1007/s10708-018-9912-1

34. Keegan, B., Gergle, D., Contractor, N.: Hot off the Wiki: structures and dynamics of Wikipedia's coverage of breaking news events. Am. Behav. Sci. **57**(5), 595–622 (2013). https://doi.org/10.1177/0002764212469367

35. Keegan, B.C., Brubaker, J.R.: 'Is' to 'Was': Coordination and Commemoration on Posthumous Wikipedia Biographies. Association for Computing Machinery, New York (2015). https://doi.org/10.1145/2675133.2675238

36. Keet, C.M.: An exploration into cognitive bias in ontologies. In: Joint Ontology Workshops 2021 Episode VII: The Bolzano Summer of Knowledge, JOWO 2021, vol. 2969 (2021). https://pubs.cs.uct.ac.za/id/eprint/1474/

37. Klein, M., Gupta, H., Rai, V., Konieczny, P., Zhu, H.: Monitoring the Gender Gap with Wikidata Human Gender Indicators. Association for Computing Machinery, New York (2016). https://doi.org/10.1145/2957792.2957798
38. Konieczny, P., Klein, M.: Gender gap through time and space: a journey through Wikipedia biographies via the Wikidata Human Gender Indicator. New Media Soc. **20**(12), 4608–4633 (2018). https://doi.org/10.1177/1461444818779080
39. Lin, Y., Chen, Y.: Do less active participants make active participants more active? An examination of Chinese Wikipedia. Decis. Support Syst. **114**, 103–113 (2018). https://doi.org/10.1016/j.dss.2018.08.002
40. Luggen, M., Difallah, D., Sarasua, C., Demartini, G., Cudré-Mauroux, P.: Nonparametric class completeness estimators for collaborative knowledge graphs—the case of Wikidata. In: Ghidini, C., et al. (eds.) ISWC 2019. LNCS, vol. 11778, pp. 453–469. Springer, Cham (2019). https://doi.org/10.1007/978-3-030-30793-6_26
41. Ma, D., Sandberg, M., Jiang, B.: Characterizing the heterogeneity of the OpenStreetMap data and community. ISPRS Int. J. Geo Inf. **4**(2), 535–550 (2015). https://doi.org/10.3390/ijgi4020535
42. McDaniel, M., Storey, V.C.: Evaluating domain ontologies: clarification, classification, and challenges. ACM Comput. Surv. **52**(4), 70:1–70:44 (2019). https://doi.org/10.1145/3329124
43. Mehrabi, N., Morstatter, F., Saxena, N., Lerman, K., Galstyan, A.: A survey on bias and fairness in machine learning. ACM Comput. Surv. **54**(6), 115:1–115:35 (2021). https://doi.org/10.1145/3457607
44. Miquel Ribé, M., Vaidla, K., Fort, F., Torres, A.: Wikimedia 2030 movement strategy : How an inclusive open strategy process has placed people at the centre. BiD: textos universitaris de biblioteconomia i documentació (47), Dec 2021. https://doi.org/10.1344/BiD2021.47.05
45. Miščević, N.: United nations development programme, human development report 2020. the next frontier human development and the anthropocene. Croatian J. Phil. **21**(1 (61)), 231–235 (2021)
46. Mooney, P., Corcoran, P.: Analysis of Interaction and Co-editing patterns amongst OpenStreetMap Contributors. Trans. GIS **18**(5), 633–659 (2014). https://doi.org/10.1111/tgis.12051
47. Mueller-Birn, C., Karran, B., Lehmann, J., Luczak-Roesch, M.: Peer-production system or collaborative ontology engineering effort: What is Wikidata? Association for Computing Machinery. N. Y. (2015). https://doi.org/10.1145/2788993.2789836
48. Nielsen, F.Å., Mietchen, D., Willighagen, E.: Scholia, scientometrics and Wikidata. In: Blomqvist, E., Hose, K., Paulheim, H., Ławrynowicz, A., Ciravegna, F., Hartig, O. (eds.) ESWC 2017. LNCS, vol. 10577, pp. 237–259. Springer, Cham (2017). https://doi.org/10.1007/978-3-319-70407-4_36
49. Ntoutsi, E., et al.: Bias in data-driven artificial intelligence systems-An introductory survey. WIREs Data Mining Knowl. Dis. **10**(3), e1356 (2020). https://doi.org/10.1002/widm.1356, https://onlinelibrary.wiley.com/doi/abs/10.1002/widm.1356
50. Park, H., Park, S.J.: Communication behavior and online knowledge collaboration: evidence from Wikipedia. J. Knowl. Manag. **20**(4), 769–792 (2016). https://doi.org/10.1108/JKM-08-2015-0312
51. Piccardi, T., West, R., Redi, M., Colavizza, G.: Quantifying engagement with citations on Wikipedia. Nauchnye I Tekhnicheskie Biblioteki-Scientific and Technical Libraries (10), 77–86 (2020). https://doi.org/10.33186/1027-3689-2020-10-63-76
52. Piscopo, A., Simperl, E.: What we talk about when we talk about Wikidata quality: a literature survey. Association for Computing Machinery, New York (2019). https://doi.org/10.1145/3306446.3340822

53. Prasojo, R.E., Darari, F., Razniewski, S., Nutt, W.: Managing and consuming completeness information for Wikidata using COOL-WD. In: Proceedings of the 7th International Workshop on Consuming Linked Data (COLD) (2016). http://ceur-ws.org/Vol-1666/paper-02.pdf
54. Radstok, W., Chekol, M.W., Schaefer, M.T., et al.: Are knowledge graph embedding models biased, or is it the data that they are trained on? In: Wikidata Workshop 2021 co-located with the 20th International Semantic Web Conference (ISWC 2021) (2021)
55. Rea, L.M., Parker, R.A.: Designing and Conducting Survey Research: A Comprehensive Guide. Jossey-Bass Publishers (1992)
56. Redi, M., Gerlach, M., Johnson, I., Morgan, J., Zia, L.: A Taxonomy of Knowledge Gaps for Wikimedia Projects (Second Draft). arXiv:2008.12314 [cs] (Jan 2021)
57. Restivo, M., van de Rijt, A.: No praise without effort: experimental evidence on how rewards affect Wikipedia's contributor community. Inf. Commun. Soc. **17**(4), 451–462 (2014). https://doi.org/10.1080/1369118X.2014.888459
58. Ringler, D., Paulheim, H.: One knowledge graph to rule them all? Analyzing the differences between DBpedia, YAGO, Wikidata & co. In: Kern-Isberner, G., Fürnkranz, J., Thimm, M. (eds.) KI 2017. LNCS (LNAI), vol. 10505, pp. 366–372. Springer, Cham (2017). https://doi.org/10.1007/978-3-319-67190-1_33
59. Rizoiu, M.A., Xie, L., Caetano, T., Cebrian, M.: Evolution of Privacy Loss in Wikipedia. Association for Computing Machinery, New York (2016). https://doi.org/10.1145/2835776.2835798
60. Samoilenko, A., Lemmerich, F., Weller, K., Zens, M., Strohmaier, M.: Analysing timelines of national histories across Wikipedia editions: a comparative computational approach. In: Proceedings of the International AAAI Conference on Web and Social Media, vol. 11(1), pp. 210–219, May 2017. https://ojs.aaai.org/index.php/ICWSM/article/view/14881
61. Samuel, J.: ShExStatements: simplifying shape expressions for wikidata. In: Companion Proceedings of the Web Conference 2021, WWW 2021, pp. 610–615. Association for Computing Machinery, New York, Apr 2021. https://doi.org/10.1145/3442442.3452349
62. Sarasua, C., Checco, A., Demartini, G., Difallah, D., Feldman, M., Pintscher, L.: The evolution of power and standard Wikidata editors: comparing editing behavior over time to predict lifespan and volume of edits. Comput. Support. Coop. Work (CSCW) **28**(5), 843–882 (2018). https://doi.org/10.1007/s10606-018-9344-y
63. Schott, M., Grinberger, A.Y., Lautenbach, S., Zipf, A.: The impact of community happenings in OpenStreetMap-establishing a framework for online community member activity analyses. ISPRS Int. J. Geo Inf. **10**(3), 164 (2021). https://doi.org/10.3390/ijgi10030164
64. Sheehan, E., et al.: Predicting Economic Development using Geolocated Wikipedia Articles. Association for Computing Machinery, New York (2019). https://doi.org/10.1145/3292500.3330784
65. Stanczak, K., Augenstein, I.: A Survey on Gender Bias in Natural Language Processing. arXiv:2112.14168 [cs] (Dec 2021)
66. Pellissier Tanon, T., Suchanek, F.: Querying the edit history of Wikidata. In: Hitzler, P., et al. (eds.) ESWC 2019. LNCS, vol. 11762, pp. 161–166. Springer, Cham (2019). https://doi.org/10.1007/978-3-030-32327-1_32
67. Twyman, M., Keegan, B.C., Shaw, A.: Black Lives Matter in Wikipedia: Collaboration and Collective Memory around Online Social Movements. Association for Computing Machinery, New York (2017). https://doi.org/10.1145/2998181.2998232

68. Uzun, R.: National interest vs. online freedom of expression: the discussions of internet users on the blocking of 'Wikipedia' in Turkey. Etkileşim (5), 10–22 (2020). https://doi.org/10.32739/etkilesim.2020.5.82, https://dergipark.org.tr/en/pub/usuifade/issue/53630/715436

69. Vrandečić, D.: Ontology evaluation. In: Staab, S., Studer, R. (eds.) Handbook on Ontologies. IHIS, pp. 293–313. Springer, Heidelberg (2009). https://doi.org/10.1007/978-3-540-92673-3_13

70. Wagner, C., Graells-Garrido, E., Garcia, D., Menczer, F.: Women through the glass ceiling: gender asymmetries in Wikipedia. EPJ Data Sci. 5(1), 1–24 (2016). https://doi.org/10.1140/epjds/s13688-016-0066-4

71. Wisesa, A., Darari, F., Krisnadhi, A., Nutt, W., Razniewski, S.: Wikidata Completeness Profiling Using ProWD. Association for Computing Machinery, New York (2019). https://doi.org/10.1145/3360901.3364425

72. Wolfer, S., Mueller-Spitzer, C.: How many people constitute a crowd and what do they do? Quantitative analyses of revisions in the English and German Wiktionary editions. Lexikos 26, 347–371 (2016)

73. Yasseri, T., Kertesz, J.: Value production in a collaborative environment sociophysical studies of Wikipedia. J. Stat. Phys. 151(3–4), 414–439 (2013). https://doi.org/10.1007/s10955-013-0728-6

74. Young, A.G., Wigdor, A.D., Kane, G.C.: The gender bias tug-of-war in a cocreation community: core-periphery tension on Wikipedia. J. Manag. Inf. Syst. 37(4), 1047–1072 (2020). https://doi.org/10.1080/07421222.2020.1831773

75. Zagovora, O., Floeck, F., Wagner, C.: "(Weitergeleitet von Journalistin)": The Gendered Presentation of Professions on Wikipedia. Association for Computing Machinery, New York (2017). https://doi.org/10.1145/3091478.3091488

76. Zaveri, A., Rula, A., Maurino, A., Pietrobon, R., Lehmann, J., Auer, S.: Quality assessment for Linked Data: a survey. Semantic Web 7(1), 63–93 (2016). https://doi.org/10.3233/SW-150175

77. Zhang, A.F., Livneh, D., Budak, C., Robert, L., Romero, D.: Shocking the crowd: the effect of censorship shocks on Chinese Wikipedia. In: Proceedings of the International AAAI Conference on Web and Social Media, vol. 11(1), pp. 367–376, May 2017. https://ojs.aaai.org/index.php/ICWSM/article/view/14895

78. Zhang, C.C., Terveen, L.: Quantifying the gap: a case study of Wikidata gender disparities. In: 17th International Symposium on Open Collaboration, OpenSym 2021, pp. 1–12. Association for Computing Machinery, New York, Sep 2021. https://doi.org/10.1145/3479986.3479992

79. Zhang, X., Wang, C.: Network positions and contributions to online public goods: the case of Chinese Wikipedia. J. Manag. Inf. Syst. 29(2), 11–40 (2012). https://doi.org/10.2753/MIS0742-1222290202

80. Zhu, H., Kraut, R.E., Kittur, A.: Effectiveness of shared leadership in Wikipedia. Hum. Factors 55(6), 1021–1043 (2013). https://doi.org/10.1177/0018720813515704

81. Zia, M., Seker, D.Z., Cakir, Z.: Spatial evolution of Openstreetmap dataset in Turkey. In: Isikdag, U., Rahman, A.A., Castro, F.A., Karas, I.R. (eds.) 3rd International Geoadvances Workshop, vol. 42–52, pp. 169–172. Copernicus Gesellschaft Mbh, Gottingen (2016). https://doi.org/10.5194/isprs-archives-XLII-2-W1-169-2016

82. Zia, M., Cakir, Z., Seker, D.Z.: Turkey OpenStreetMap dataset - spatial analysis of development and growth proxies. Open Geosci. 11(1), 140–151 (2019). https://doi.org/10.1515/geo-2019-0012

Repairing SHACL Constraint Violations Using Answer Set Programming

Shqiponja Ahmetaj[1,2], Robert David[2,4(✉)], Axel Polleres[2,3],
and Mantas Šimkus[1,5]

[1] TU Wien, Vienna, Austria
shqiponja.ahmetaj@tuwien.ac.at
[2] WU Wien, Vienna, Austria
axel.polleres@wu.ac.at
[3] Complexity Science Hub Vienna, Vienna, Austria
[4] Semantic Web Company, Vienna, Austria
robert.david@semantic-web.com
[5] Umeå University, Umeå, Sweden
simkus@cs.umu.se

Abstract. The Shapes Constraint Language (SHACL) is a recent W3C recommendation for validating RDF graphs against *shape* constraints to be checked on *target nodes* of the data graph. The standard also describes the notion of *validation reports* for data graphs that violate given constraints, which aims to provide feedback on how the data graph can be fixed to satisfy the constraints. Since the specification left it open to SHACL processors to define such explanations, a recent work proposed the use of explanations in the style of database *repairs*, where a repair is a set of additions to or deletions from the data graph so that the resulting graph validates against the constraints. In this paper, we study such repairs for non-recursive SHACL, the largest fragment of SHACL that is fully defined in the specification. We propose an algorithm to compute repairs by encoding the explanation problem – using Answer Set Programming (ASP) – into a logic program, the answer sets of which correspond to (minimal) repairs. We then study a scenario where it is not possible to simultaneously repair all the targets, which may be often the case due to overall unsatisfiability or conflicting constraints. We introduce a relaxed notion of validation, which allows to validate a (maximal) subset of the targets and adapt the ASP translation to take into account this relaxation. Our implementation in Clingo is – to the best of our knowledge – the first implementation of a repair generator for SHACL.

Keywords: SHACL · Shapes Constraint Language · Database repairs · RDF Graphs · Semantic Web

1 Introduction

Semantic Web standards provide means to represent and link heterogeneous data sources in knowledge graphs [10], thereby potentially solving common data

U. Sattler et al. (Eds.): ISWC 2022, LNCS 13489, pp. 375–391, 2022.
https://doi.org/10.1007/978-3-031-19433-7_22

integration problems. Indeed, this approach became increasingly popular in enterprises for the consolidation of data silos in the form of so-called *enterprise knowledge graphs (EKG)*. However, in practice this flexible and expressive approach to data integration requires powerful tools for ensuring data quality, including ways to avoid creating invalid data and inconsistencies in the target EKGs. To this end, the W3C proposed the Shapes Constraint Language SHACL, in order to enable validation of RDF graphs against a set of shape constraints [1]. In this setting, the validation requirements are specified in a *shapes graph* (C, T) that consists of a collection C of validation rules (constraints) and a specification T of nodes to which various constraints should be applied. The result of validating an RDF graph (or, *data graph*) G against a shapes graph (C, T) is a *validation report*, which lists the constraint violations present in G. Unfortunately, validation reports, as specified in the SHACL standard, contain little information on what steps could be made to resolve those constraint violations. Since in many common scenarios (like the automated integration of heterogeneous data sources) inconsistencies appear very frequently, there is a need to *automatically* identify repairs that can be applied to the data graph in order to achieve consistency. A *repair* in our context is a collection of additions and deletions of facts that will cause the data to be consistent with the given constraints. Our contributions are as follows:

○ We propose to compute repairs of a data graph by encoding the problem into *Answer Set Programming (ASP)* [7]. In particular, we show how to transform a given data graph G and a SHACL shapes graph (C, T) into an ASP program P such that the answer sets (or, stable models) of P can be seen as a collection of plausible repairs of G w.r.t. the shapes graph (C, T). Since efficient ASP solvers exist (we use Clingo [9]), this provides a promising way to generate data repairs in practice. The repair generation task is challenging, because a given data graph might be repaired in many different ways. In fact, since fresh nodes could be introduced during the repair process, an infinite number of repairs is possible. This needs to be handled carefully and several design choices are possible.

○ We initially present the *basic encoding* of the repair task into ASP. In this encoding, the repair program tries to find a repair that satisfies *all* targets of the input shapes graph. This encoding employs a particular strategy for introducing new nodes in the data graph: when a value for a property needs to be added (e.g. for a violated *sh:minCount* constraint), a fresh value is always introduced. We argue that it is a reasonable strategy; it is also closely related to the standard notion of *Skolemization*. By using some of the features of ASP, we ensure that our repair program generates repairs that are minimal in terms of cardinality, which means that they contain only minimal modifications for resolving constraint violations. Our basic encoding is later extended to allow for the introduction of fresh nodes as well as the reuse of existing or previously introduced nodes.

○ We observe that requiring a repair to resolve violations for *all* specified targets may be too strong. In the context of the basic encoding, if the data graph has one inherently unfixable target (e.g., because of some erroneous constraint), then the repair program will have no answer sets at all and it will provide no guidance on how to proceed with fixing the data graph. To address this issue, we introduce the notion of *maximal repairs*, which repair the highest number of targets that is possible to repair. We show how our encoding can be augmented to generate repairs according to this new notion. This is done using the optimization features of Clingo as well as rules that allow to skip some targets.

○ We have implemented and tested these encodings using the Clingo ASP system, which showed that our approach is promising for providing quality control and quality improvements for RDF graphs for practical use.

Related Work. Our approach is inspired by previous work in the area of databases on computing repairs for violations of database integrity constraints (see, e.g., [5]) and reasoning about them. We adapt it for the RDF data model and SHACL constraints. Close to our work is [11], where database repairs are specified using disjunctive logic programs with the answer set semantics. These repairs modify a database to achieve conformance with a set of integrity constraints that are applied to a relational database. The repair program uses *annotations* to indicate which atoms should be added or deleted to satisfy the constraints. The program contains rules whose body identifies a violation of a constraint, while a disjunctive rule head describes the candidate actions (additions and deletions of tuples) that can potentially be used to resolve the identified violation. These repair rules can interact and possibly resolve conflicting constraints, eventually stabilizing into a minimal repair. The repair program contains constraints to prevent models with conflicting insertions and deletions. The so-called *interpretation* rules are then used to collect the actual additions and deletions corresponding to a possible database repair.

2   SHACL Validation and Answer Set Programming

In this section, we describe SHACL [1] and the notion of *validation* against RDF graphs. For an introduction to data validation, SHACL, and its close relative ShEx, we refer to [8]. We also describe answer set programming (ASP), which we use to implement the repair program.

SHACL Validation. We use the abstract syntax from [2] for RDF and SHACL. Note that in this work we focus on the fragment of SHACL 'Core Constraint Components' without path expressions (except for inverse roles), equality and disjoint operators.

Data Graph. We first define *data graphs*[1], which are RDF graphs to be validated against shape constraints. Assume countably infinite, mutually disjoint sets $\mathbf{N}$, $\mathbf{C}$, and $\mathbf{P}$ of *nodes* (or *constants*), *class names*, and *property names*, respectively. A *data graph* G is a finite set of *(ground) RDF atoms* of the form $B(c)$ and $p(c, d)$, where B is a class name, p is a property name, and c, d are nodes.

Syntax of SHACL. Let $\mathbf{S}$ be a countably infinite set of *shape names*, disjoint from $\mathbf{N}$, $\mathbf{C}$, and $\mathbf{P}$. A *shape expression* ϕ is of the form:

$$\phi, \phi' ::= \top \mid s \mid B \mid c \mid \phi \wedge \phi' \mid \neg\phi \mid \geq_n r.\phi \tag{1}$$

---

[1] https://www.w3.org/TR/shacl/#data-graph.

where $s \in \mathbf{S}$, $B \in \mathbf{C}$, $c \in \mathbf{N}$, n is a positive integer, and r is a property $p \in \mathbf{P}$ or an *inverse property* of the form p^- with $p \in \mathbf{P}$. In what follows, we may write $\phi \vee \phi'$ instead of $\neg(\neg\phi \wedge \neg\phi')$, $\exists r.\phi$ instead of $\geq_1 r.\phi$, and $\geq_n r$ instead of $\geq_n r.\phi$ if ϕ is $\top$. SHACL constraints are represented in the form of *(shape) constraints*, which are expressions of the form $s \leftarrow \phi$, with $s \in \mathbf{S}$ and ϕ a shape expression. A *shape atom* is an expression of the form $s(a)$, with s a shape name and a a node. A *shapes graph*[2] is a pair (C, T), where C is a set of shape constraints such that each shape name occurs exactly once on the left-hand side of a shape constraint, and T is a set of shape atoms, called *target set*, or simply *target*.

Non-recursive SHACL. We formally define non-recursive SHACL constraints as follows: a shape name s *directly refers* to a shape name s' in a set of constraints C, if C has a constraint $s \leftarrow \phi$ such that s' appears in ϕ. We say that s *refers* to s', if s directly refers to s', or there exists a shape name s'' such that s refers to s'', and s'' directly refers to s'. A set of SHACL constraints C is *non-recursive* if no shape name in C refers to itself.

Evaluation of Shape Expressions. A *(shape) assignment* for a data graph G extends G with a set L of shape atoms such that a occurs in G for each $s(a) \in L$. The evaluation of a shape expression ϕ over a data graph is defined in terms of a function $\llbracket \cdot \rrbracket^I$ that maps a (complex) shape expression to a set of nodes, and a property to a set of pairs of nodes. We refer to [3] for more details on the evaluation of shape expressions.

SHACL Validation. There are two semantics for SHACL validation, the classical (or supported) model semantics from [6] and the stable model semantics from [3]. Here, we only present the supported model semantics. It was shown in [3] that both semantics coincide on non-recursive SHACL. Assume a SHACL document (C, T) and a data graph G. An assignment I for G is a *(supported) model* of C if $\llbracket \phi \rrbracket^I = s^I$ for all $s \leftarrow \phi \in C$. The data graph G *validates* (C, T) if there exists an assignment $I = G \cup L$ for G such that (i) I is a model of C, and (ii) $T \subseteq L$.

Normal Form. To ease presentation, in the rest of the paper we focus on *normalized* sets of SHACL constraint. That is, each SHACL constraint can have one of the following normal forms:

(NF1) $s \leftarrow \top$	*(NF2)* $s \leftarrow B$	*(NF3)* $s \leftarrow c$
(NF4) $s \leftarrow s_1 \wedge \cdots \wedge s_n$	*(NF5)* $s \leftarrow \neg s'$	*(NF6)* $s \leftarrow \geq_n r.s'$

It was shown in [3], that a set of constrains C can be transformed in polynomial time into a set of constraints C' in normal form such that for every data graph G and target T, G validates (C, T) if and only if G validates (C', T). Further, the normalization may introduce fresh shape names, but it can easily be shown that C' is non-recursive if C is non-recursive.

Example 1. Assume a shape StudentShape (left) and a data graph (right), written in Turtle syntax:

---

[2] https://www.w3.org/TR/shacl/#shapes-graph.

```
: StudentShape a sh: NodeShape ;           : Ben : enrolledIn : C1 .
    sh: targetNode : Ben ;
    sh: property [
        sh: path : enrolledIn ;
        sh: qualifiedMinCount 1 ;
        sh: qualifiedValueShape [
        sh: class : Course ;]] .
```

The shape states that each StudentShape must be enrolled in at least one course and should be verified at node Ben. In the abstract syntax, we write the data graph $G = \{enrolledIn(Ben, C_1)\}$, the target $T = \{\text{StudentShape}(Ben)\}$, and C contains the constraint StudentShape $\leftarrow \exists enrolledIn.Course$ The normalized version C' of C contains the constraints StudentShape $\leftarrow \exists enrolledIn.s$ and $s \leftarrow Course$, where s is a fresh shape name. Clearly, extending G by assigning the shape name StudentShape to Ben does not satisfy the target StudentShape(Ben), since Ben is not enrolled in any $Course$. Hence, G does not validate (C, T).

Answer Set Programming. We introduce here some basic notation about Answer Set Programming (ASP) used throughout the paper and refer to [7] for more details on the language. We assume countably infinite, mutually disjoint sets **Preds** $\supset$ **C** $\cup$ **P** and **Var** of *predicate symbols*, and *variables*, respectively. A *term* is a variable from **Var** or a node from **N**. The notion of an *atom* is extended from RDF atoms here to include expressions of the form $q(t_1, \ldots, t_n)$, where $q \in$ **Preds** is an n-ary predicate symbol and $t_1, \ldots, t_n$ are terms; an atom is *ground* if its terms are nodes. A database is a set of ground atoms. An answer set program consists of a set of rules of the form $\psi \leftarrow \varphi$, where φ may be a conjunction of positive and negated atoms, and ψ is a (possibly empty) disjunction of atoms. We may call ψ the *head* of the rule and φ the *body* of the rule. We may write a rule $h_1, \ldots, h_n \leftarrow \varphi$ instead of a set of rules $h_1 \leftarrow \varphi, \ldots, h_n \leftarrow \varphi$. Roughly, a rule is satisfied by a database D in case the following holds: if there is a way to ground the rule by instantiating all its variables such that D contains the positive atoms in the body of the instantiated rule and does not contain the negative atoms, then it contains some atom occurring in the head of the rule. The semantics of answer set programs is given in terms of *stable models*. Intuitively, a stable model for (D, P), where D is a database and P a program, is a database D' that minimally extends D to satisfy all rules in P. We illustrate answer set programs with an example about 3-colorability.

Example 2. Let D $= \{\text{edge}(a, b), \text{edge}(b, c), \text{edge}(c, a), N(a), N(b), N(c)\}$ be a database storing a triangle over the nodes a, b, and c, and let P be a program with the following rules:

$$R(X) \vee B(X) \vee G(X) \leftarrow N(X) \qquad \leftarrow \text{edge}(X, Y), R(X), R(Y)$$
$$\leftarrow \text{edge}(X, Y), B(X), B(Y) \qquad \leftarrow \text{edge}(X, Y), G(X), G(Y).$$

P states that every node must be colored with red R, blue B, or green G and adjacent vertices must not be colored with the same color. Clearly, there are three possibilities to color the nodes and hence, three answer sets for (D, P)

that minimally extend D to satisfy the rules. E.g. one stable model is $M = D \cup \{R(a), B(b), G(c)\}$.

To implement the repair generator we selected Clingo[3], which provides additional features, like optimization functions, that will be present in the repair rules.

3   SHACL Repairs

In this section, we introduce the notion of repairs that we use in this work, analyze the kind of repairs that may be desirable in practice, and describe the design choices we will consider for the repair generator we propose. For repairs, we use the notion introduced in [2], where a repair is a set of facts that are added or removed from the input data graph so that the resulting graph validates the input shapes graph. We recall a slightly modified definition here.

Definition 1. *A repair problem is a tuple $\Psi = (G, C, T)$, where G is a data graph, and (C, T) is a shapes graph such that G does not validate (C, T). A repair for Ψ is a pair (A, D) of two sets of RDF atoms, where $D \subseteq G$, such that $(G \setminus D) \cup A$ validates (C, T).*

Note that the original definition of a repair problem in [2] includes a *hypothesis* set H, which allows to limit the space of possible additions by imposing the inclusion $A \subseteq H$. For simplicity, we do not limit the possible additions here, i.e. in the sense of [2], we simply let H to be the set of all possible RDF atoms.

When designing a repair generator, we need to make some choices. First, as also argued in [2], computing all possible repairs is not desirable: we naturally want the repairs to modify the data graph in a minimal way, i.e. additions and deletions that are not relevant for fixing the constraint violations should be excluded. For instance, the repair problem (G, C, T) in Example 1 can be solved, among other ways, by (i) adding to G the atom $Course(C1)$ (ii) by adding to G the atoms $Course(C2)$ and $enrolledIn(Ben, C2)$, or (iii) by adding to G the atoms $Course(C1)$ and $Course(C2)$. Observe that (i) is a repair that is minimal in terms of the *number* of modifications that are performed, i.e. cardinality-minimal. The repair (ii) can also be considered minimal, but in the sense of subset-minimality: observe that neither $Course(C2)$ nor $enrolledIn(Ben, C2)$ *alone* suffice to fix the constraint violation. The repair (iii) is not minimal in either sense, because the addition of $Course(C1)$ alone is sufficient to perform the repair.

Another issue is how to repair cardinality constraints of form (NF6). To satisfy them, we can either choose to generate new nodes, or we may try to reuse the existing nodes of the input data graph. There are scenarios where reusing nodes is not desired as we want to fix the violations while minimally changing the data graph. Reusing nodes may introduce wrong information from a real-world perspective and thus lower the quality of data. Consider the constraint

---

[3] https://potassco.org/clingo/.

StudentShape $\leftarrow$ $\exists hasStudID$ specifying that students must have a student ID and let the data graph have the atom $hasStudID(Ben, ID1)$. To validate the target $\{$StudentShape$(Ann)\}$, a meaningful repair would be to generate a new value $\_ID$ as placeholder and add $hasStudID(Ann, \_ID)$ instead of reusing $ID1$. Such placeholders can be replaced in a later step by the user with meaningful real-world values.

Unfortunately, forcing the repair generator to always introduce fresh values for cardinality constraints may sometimes leave out expected (minimal) repairs and even not produce any repairs at all. Consider the constraint RegisteredCitizen $\leftarrow$ $\exists MainAddress.Address \wedge \leq_1 MainAddress$, stating that registered citizens must have exactly one main address. Let $G = \{MainAddress(Ann, Ad1)\}$ and assume we want to validate that Ann is a RegisteredCitizen. We may attempt to satisfy the constraint by adding the atoms $MainAddress(Ann, n)$ and $Address(n)$ for a fresh node n. However, then Ann would have two main addresses, which is not allowed. The only way to fix the violation is to reuse the node $Ad1$ and add $Address(Ann, Ad1)$ to the initial data graph. Also, for the repair problem from Example 1, mentioned above, by forcing to introduce fresh values we would miss the intuitive minimal repair that simply adds $Course(C1)$. In conclusion, there are scenarios where reusing existing nodes may be desired and even necessary. However, to preserve the quality of the data as much as possible, we want to prioritize the introduction of fresh values whenever possible and reuse existing constants only when necessary. We study both versions. More precisely, in Sect. 4, we propose a repair generator that always introduces fresh values and in Sect. 5 we present the extended version that allows to reuse constants, but introduces fresh values whenever possible.

4   Generating Repairs

In this section, based on existing works in databases by Bertossi et al. (see e.g. [4] and references therein), we present an encoding of the repair problem for non-recursive SHACL to ASP. We are especially interested in minimal repairs. To ease presentation, we describe here the encoding for a restricted setting, where only existential constraints of the form $s \leftarrow_{\geq_1} r.s'$, i.e., a special case of cardinality constraints of form (NF6), are allowed; we label them with (NF6'). In particular, rules will always introduce fresh values to repair existential constraints. We refer to Sect. 5 for the extension that support unrestricted cardinality constraints of form (NF6) and allows to reuse constants from the input.

4.1   Encoding into ASP

For a repair problem $\Psi = (G, C, T)$, where C is a set of non-recursive SHACL constraints in normal form, we construct a program P_Ψ, such that the stable models of (G, P_Ψ) will provide repairs for Ψ. Following the standard notation for repairs as logic programs in databases [4], to annotate atoms we will use special constants: (i) t^{**} intuitively states that the atom is true in the repair

(ii) t^* states that the atom is true in the input data graph or becomes true by some rule (iii) t, states that the atom may need to be true and (iv) f states that the atom may need to be false. Intuitively, the repair program implements a top-down target-oriented approach, and starts by first making true all the shape atoms in the target. From this on, the rules for constraints specified by the shapes capture violations on the targets in the rule body and propose repairs in the rule head using the annotations described above. The rules will add annotated atoms which represent additions and deletions that can be applied to the data graph to fix the violations. Additions and deletions can interact, eventually stabilizing into a model that generates a (not necessarily minimal) repair.

For every constraint specified by a shape in the shapes graph, the repair program P_Ψ consists of four kinds of rules:

$P_{\text{Annotation}}$ consists of rules that collect existing atoms or atoms that are proposed to be in the repaired data graph.

P_{Repair} consists of rules that repair the constraints by proposing additions and deletions of atoms.

$P_{\text{Interpretation}}$ consists of rules that collect all the atoms that will be in the repaired data graph.

$P_{\text{Constraints}}$ consists of rules that filter out models that do not provide repairs.

We are ready to describe the repair program.

Adding the Shape Atoms in the Target as Facts. First, for each atom $s(a) \in T$, we add the rule $s_-(a, t^*) \leftarrow$, where s_- is a fresh binary relation.

$P_{\text{Annotation}}$. For each class name B and property name p occurring in G and C, we create a new binary predicate B_- and ternary predicate p_-, respectively. We add the following rules to P_Ψ:

$$B_-(X, t^*) \leftarrow B(X) \qquad\qquad p_-(X, Y, t^*) \leftarrow p(X, Y)$$
$$B_-(X, t^*) \leftarrow B_-(X, t) \qquad\qquad p_-(X, Y, t^*) \leftarrow p_-(X, Y, t)$$

P_{Repair}. We present here the rules that participate in P_{Repair}. For each constraint $s \leftarrow \phi$ in C, we add specific rules that consider in the body the scenarios where s at a certain node is suggested to be true in the repair program or false, and propose in the head ways to make ϕ true or false, respectively. We note that the presence of negation in constraints may enforce that a shape atom is false at specific nodes. We present the repair rules for each normal form that ϕ can take, that is for each type of constraint of the form (NF1) to (NF6') and add rules for both $s_-(X, t^*)$ and $s_-(x, f)$.

- If the constraint is of the form (NF1) or (NF3), then we do nothing here and treat them later as constraints.
- If ϕ is a class name B, that is of form (NF2), then we use the fresh binary predicate B_- and add the rules:

$$B_-(X, t) \leftarrow s_-(X, t^*) \qquad\qquad B_-(X, f) \leftarrow s_-(X, f)$$

- If ϕ is of the form $s_1 \wedge \cdots \wedge s_n$, that is of form (NF4), then we use fresh binary predicates s_{i-} and add the rules:

$$s_{1-}(X, t^*), \ldots, s_{n-}(X, t^*) \leftarrow s_-(X, t^*) \quad s_{1-}(X, f) \vee \cdots \vee s_{n-}(X, f) \leftarrow s_-(X, f)$$

- If ϕ is of the form $\neg s'$, that is of form (NF5), we add the rules:

$$s'_-(X, f) \leftarrow s_-(X, t^*) \qquad\qquad s'_-(X, t^*) \leftarrow s_-(X, f)$$

(*) If ϕ is of the form $\exists r.s'$, i.e., of form (NF6'), then we have to consider the scenarios where r is a property name p or an inverse property p^-. For the case where s is suggested to be true at X, i.e., for $s_-(X, t^*)$, we add a new p-edge from X to a fresh node and assign the node to s'. To this end, we use a function $@new(s, X, p)$, which maps a shape name s, a node X and a property name p to a new unique value Y. For the case where s is suggested to be false at X, i.e., for $s_-(X, f)$, we add disjunctive rules that, for all p-edges from X to some Y with s' true in Y, makes one of these atoms false. We add the rules for $r = p$. For $r = p^-$ the rules are analogously obtained by just swapping the variables in the argument of p.

$$s'_-(@new(s, X, p), t^*), p_-(X, @new(s, X, p), t) \leftarrow s_-(X, t^*)$$
$$p_-(X, Y, f) \vee s'_-(Y, f) \leftarrow s_-(X, f), p_-(X, Y, t^*)$$

$P_{\text{Interpretation}}$. For every class name B and property name p occurring in the input, we add the following rules:

$$B_-(X, t^{**}) \leftarrow B_-(X, t^*), not\ B(X, f)$$
$$p_-(X, Y, t^{**}) \leftarrow p_-(X, Y, t^*), not\ p(X, Y, f)$$

Intuitively, these rules will generate the atoms that will participate in the repaired data graph, that is the atoms that were added to the data graph, and those atoms from the data graph that were not deleted by the rules. $P_{\text{Constraints}}$.

We add to P_{Ψ} sets of rules that will act as constraints and filter out models that are not repairs.

(1) For each constraint of the form $s \leftarrow \top$, i.e., of form (NF1), we add $\leftarrow s_-(Y, f)$.
(2) For each constraint of the form $s \leftarrow c$, i.e., of form (NF3), we add the rules:

$$\leftarrow s_-(X, t^*), X \neq c \qquad\qquad \leftarrow s_-(c, f)$$

(3) For each class name B and property name p in the input, we add:

$$\leftarrow B_-(X, t), B_-(x, f) \qquad\qquad \leftarrow p_-(X, Y, t), p_-(X, Y, f)$$

Roughly (1) and (2) ensure that models preserve constraints of type (NF1) and (NF3) which cannot be repaired, and (3) ensures that no atom is *both inserted and deleted* from G.

The atoms marked with t^{**} in a stable model of P_Ψ form a repaired data graph that validates (C, T).

Theorem 1. *Assume a repair problem* $\Psi = (G, C, T)$. *For every stable model* M *of* (G, P_Ψ), *the data graph* G' *validates* (C, T), *where* G' *is the set of all atoms of the form* $B(a)$, $p(a, b)$ *such that* $B_-(a, t^{**})$ *and* $p_-(a, b, t^{**})$ *are in* M.

We note that this theorem carries over to all the extensions and the version with cardinality constraints and constants we propose in this paper. It is easy to see that, since the rules are non-recursive in essence[4], the number of fresh nodes that can be introduced in a stable model is in the worst-case exponential in the size of the input constraints. However, we do not expect to see this behavior often in practice. We illustrate the repair program with a representative example.

Example 3. Consider the repair problem $\Psi = (G, C', T)$ from Example 1, where C' is the normalized version of C. We construct the repair program Π_Ψ as follows.

For $P_{\text{Annotation}}$ we use fresh predicates $enrolledIn_-$ and $Course_-$. The rules for $Course_-$ are $Course_-(X, t^*) \leftarrow Course_-(X, t)$, and $Course_-(X, t^*) \leftarrow Course(X)$; the rules for $enrolledIn_-$ are analogous. Intuitively, these rules will initially add the atom $enrolledIn_-(Ben, C_1, t^*)$ to the stable model. For P_{Repair}, we add the following rules, where F stands for the function @$new(\mathsf{StudentShape}, X, enrolledIn)$.

$$enrolledIn_-(X, F, t), s_-(F, t^*) \leftarrow \mathsf{StudentShape}_-(X, t^*).$$
$$enrolledIn_-(X, Y, f) \vee s_-(Y, f) \leftarrow \mathsf{StudentShape}_-(X, f), enrolledIn_-(X, Y, t^*)$$
$$Course_-(X, t) \leftarrow s_-(X, t*)$$
$$Course_-(X, f) \leftarrow s_-(X, f)$$

Intuitively, these rules together with the ones in $P_{\text{Annotation}}$ will add to the stable model the atoms $enrolledIn_-(Ben, new_1, t^*)$ and $Course_-(new_1, t^*)$, for a fresh node new_1. For $P_{\text{Interpretation}}$, we add: $Course_-(X, t^{**}) \leftarrow Course_-(X, t^*)$, $not\ Course_-(X, f)$ for $Course_-$ and proceed analogously for $enrolledIn_-$. For $P_{\text{Constraints}}$, we add the (constraint) rule: $\leftarrow Course_-(X, t), Course_-(X, Y, f)$ for $Course_-$ and proceed analogously for $enrolledIn_-$. Since no atom labelled with 'f' is generated by the rules, then the three atoms mentioned above will be annotated with 't^{**}' by the rules in $P_{\text{Interpretation}}$.

Thus, there is one stable model with the atoms $enrolledIn_-(Ben, C_1, t^{**})$, $enrolledIn_-(Ben, new_1, t^{**})$, and $Course_-(new_1, t^{**})$. The corresponding atoms $enrolledIn(Ben, C_1)$, $enrolledIn(Ben, new_1)$ and $Course(new_1)$ will form the repaired data graph G' that validates (C', T). Hence, the only repair is $(A, \emptyset)$, where A contains $\{enrolledIn(Ben, new_1)$ and $Course_-(new_1)\}$.

Additions and Deletions. We want to represent repairs as sets of atoms that are added to and deleted from the input data graph. To achieve this, we use two

---

[4] Technically speaking, the repair rules above may be recursive. However, if the annotation constants t, f, t^*, t^{**} are seen as part of the predicate's name (instead of being a fixed value in the last position), then the rules are non-recursive.

fresh unary predicates *add* and *del*, and we add rules that "label" in a stable model with the label *add* all the atoms with 't^{**}' that were not in the data graph, and label with *del* all the atoms from the data graph that are annotated with 'f'. To this aim, for every class name B and property name p in the input, we introduce a function symbol (with the same name) whose arguments are the tuples of B and p, respectively. We show the rules for class names; the rules for property names are analogous.

$$add(B(X)) \leftarrow B_-(X, t^{**}), not\ B(X) \qquad del(B(X)) \leftarrow B_-(X, f), B(X)$$

4.2   Generating Minimal Repairs

We are interested to generate cardinality-minimal repairs, i.e. repairs that make the least number of changes to the original data graph. More formally, given a repair $\xi = (A, D)$ for Ψ, ξ is *cardinality-minimal* if there is no repair $\xi' = (A', D')$ for Ψ such that $|A| + |D| > |A'| + |D'|$. As noted already in Sect. 3, repairs produced by our repair program built so far may not be cardinality-minimal, and this holds already for constraints without existential quantification. Consider the following example.

Example 4. Let (G, C, T) be a repair problem, where G is empty, $T = \{s(a)\}$, and C contains the constraints: $s \leftarrow s1 \vee s2$, $s1 \leftarrow A$, and $s2 \leftarrow A \wedge B$, where A and B are class names, and $s, s1, s2$ are shape names. To ease presentation, the constraints are not in normal form and $s1 \vee s2$ is a shortcut for $\neg(\neg s1 \wedge \neg s2)$. Clearly, to validate the target $s(a)$ the repair program will propose to make $s1(a)$ or $s2(a)$ true. Hence, there will be two stable models: one generates a repair that adds $A(a)$, i.e., contains $add(A(a))$, and the other adds both $A(a)$ and, the possibly redundant fact, $B(a)$, i.e., contains $add(A(a))$ and $add(B(a))$.

To compute cardinality-minimal repairs, which minimize the number of additions and deletions, we introduce a post-processing step for our repair program that selects the desired stable models based on a cost function. We count the distinct atoms for additions and deletions and add a cost off each of them. The repair program should only return stable models that minimize this cost. More specifically, we add the $\#minimize\{1, W : add(W); 1, V : del(V)\}$ optimization rule to P_Ψ, which uses a cost 1 for each addition or deletion. We can also change the cost for additions and deletions depending on different repair scenarios, where one could have a higher cost for additions over deletions or vice versa.

4.3   Repairing Maximal Subsets of the Target Set

In this section, we discuss the situation where it is not possible to repair all of the target shape atoms, e.g., because of conflicting constraints in shape assignments to these target shape atoms or because of unsatisfiable constraints. Consider for instance the constraint $s \leftarrow B \wedge \neg B$, where B is a class name. Clearly, there is no repair for any shape atom over s in the target, since there is no way to repair the body of the constraint. Similarly, consider the constraints $s1 \leftarrow B$

and $s2 \leftarrow \neg B$ and targets $s1(a)$ and $s2(a)$; in this case adding $B(a)$ violates the second constraint and not adding it violates the first constraint. In both scenarios, the repair program will return no stable model, and hence, no repair. However, it still might be possible to repair a subset of the shape targets. In practice, we want to repair as many targets as possible. To support such a scenario, we introduce the concept of *maximal repairs*, which is a relaxation of the previous notion of repairs.

Definition 2. *Let $\Psi = (G, C, T)$ be a repair problem. A pair (A, D) of sets of atoms is called a* maximal repair *for Ψ if there exists $T' \subseteq T$ such that (i) (A, D) is a repair for (G, C, T'), and (ii) there is no $T'' \subseteq T$ with $|T''| > |T'|$ and (G, C, T'') having some repair.*

To represent this in the repair program, we add rules to non-deterministically select a target for repairing or skip a target if the repair program cannot repair it. This approach could be viewed similar in spirit to SHACL's *sh:deactivated* (https://www.w3.org/TR/shacl/#deactivated) directive that allows for deactivating certain shapes, with the difference that we"deactivate" *targets* instead of whole shapes which are automatically selected by the repair program based on optimization criteria. To this end, for each shape atom $s(a)$ in the input target set T, instead of adding all $s\_(a, t^*)$ as facts, we add rules to non-deterministically select or skip repair targets. If there are no conflicting or unsatisfiable constraints, then the stable models provide repairs for all the targets. However, if a repair of a target shape atom is not possible, because shape constraints advise t as well as f, then the repair program will skip this target shape atom and the stable models will provide repairs only for the remaining shape atoms in T. We introduce two predicates *actualTarget* and *skipTarget*, where *actualTarget* represents a shape atom in the target that will be selected to repair, whereas *skipTarget* represents a shape atom in the target that is skipped and will not be repaired. For each $s(a)$ in T we add the rules:

$$actualTarget(a, s) \vee skipTarget(a, s) \leftarrow s(a) \qquad s\_(a, t^*) \leftarrow actualTarget(a, s)$$

We want to first repair as many target shape atoms as possible, and then minimize the number of additions and deletions needed for these repairs. To this end, we add the $\#minimize\{1@3, X, s : skipTarget(X, s)\}$ optimization rule to P_Ψ to minimize the number of skipped targets and the $\#minimize\{1@2, W : add(W); 1@2, V : del(V)\}$ rule to minimize the additions and deletion. Note that we choose a higher priority level for minimizing the number of skipped targets (1@3) than for minimizing additions and deletions (1@2). This rule minimizes the *skipTarget* atoms and therefore maximizes the *actualTarget* atoms based on the cardinality.

Example 5. Let (G, C, T) be a repair problem, where $G = \{enrolledIn(Ben, C_1)\}$, $T = \{\mathsf{StudentShape}(Ben), \mathsf{TeacherShape}(Ben)\}$, and C contains $\mathsf{TeacherShape} \leftarrow \exists teaches \wedge \neg\mathsf{StudentShape}$ and $\mathsf{StudentShape} \leftarrow \exists enrolledIn.Course$. Thus, Ben is a target node for both $\mathsf{StudentShape}$ and $\mathsf{TeacherShape}$. However, the first constraint states that a node cannot be a $\mathsf{TeacherShape}$ and $\mathsf{StudentShape}$ at the same time, which causes a contradiction when applied to *Ben*. This causes the repair program to have no model. By applying the optimizations for maximal repairs, it will result in the target selection: *actualTarget*(*Ben*, StudentShape), and *skipTarget*(*Ben*, TeacherShape). The repair program skips the shape atom TeacherShape(*Ben*), so that we at least have a repair for StudentShape. For this repair program, this is the maximum possible number of targets. Changing the optimization cost to skip targets allows to specify a preference among targets or shapes, thereby adapting to different repair scenarios.

5   Extension with Cardinality Constraints and Constants

In Sect. 4, we proposed a repair program for a restricted setting with cardinality constraints of the form $s \leftarrow \geq_n r.s'$ with $n = 1$. We now explain the extension to support cardinality constraints with unrestricted n, i.e., of form (NF6). In addition to supporting the generation of new values, we now also allow to reuse existing constants from the input, which may even be necessary to generate some repair. E.g., consider an empty data graph G, the set of constraints $C = \{s \leftarrow \exists p.s', s' \leftarrow c\}$, and the target $T = \{s(a)\}$. Since the second constraint forces the selection of the constant c when generating a value for p, the only possible repair for (G, C, T) is to add the atom $p(a, c)$. However, we prioritize picking a fresh node over an existing one if the latter is not necessary. We construct a repair program P'_Ψ for a repair problem $\Psi = (G, C, T)$ whose stable models provide repairs for Ψ. In particular, P'_Ψ contains all the rules from P_Ψ, except for the rules marked with (*) in P_{Repair}, i.e., the rules for existential constraints, which will be replaced by the rules described here.

Repairing Cardinality Constraints. If ϕ is of the form $\geq_n p.s'$, that is of form (NF6), then for repairing the case $s_-(X, t^*)$ we need to insert at least n p-edges to nodes verifying s'. We first collect all nodes from C that are part of constraints to make sure that all necessary nodes are available to be picked for additions of property atoms. For every node c in C, we add: $const(c) \leftarrow$
   - For the case where s is suggested to be true at X, i.e., for $s_-(X, t^*)$, we add the following rules.

$$choose(s, X, p, 0) \vee \cdots \vee choose(s, X, p, n) \leftarrow s_-(X, t^*) \tag{2}$$
$$p_-(X, @new(s, X, p, 1..i), t) \leftarrow choose(s, X, p, i), i \neq 0 \tag{3}$$
$$0 \{p_-(X, Y, t) : const(Y)\} \, |const(Y)| \leftarrow s(X, t^*) \tag{4}$$
$$n \{s'(Y, t^*) : p_-(X, Y, t^{**})\} \, max(n, |const(Y)|) \leftarrow s(X, t^*) \tag{5}$$

In the following, we explain the rules (2) - (5) in detail. For adding atoms over p_- to satisfy $\geq_n p.s'$, we either generate fresh nodes using the function $@new$ or we pick from collected constants. For generating atoms with fresh nodes, we add a disjunctive rule (2) and use a fresh *choose* predicate, which is used to non-deterministically pick a number from 0 up to n for adding atoms over p_- to fix the cardinality constraint. To add the actual atoms, we add a rule (3) that produces this number of atoms using the @*new* function, which will generate a new unique value Y for every (s, X, p, i) tuple with s a shape name, p a property name, and $i \in \{1 \ldots n\}$. With these two rules, we can generate as many atoms over $p\_$ as necessary to satisfy the cardinality constraint. Similarly to adding atoms with fresh nodes, we can also pick constants from C. We add a rule (4) to pick a number of 0 up to the maximum number of constants – using Clingo's choice rules, which allow to be parameterised with a lower and upper bound of elements from the head to be chosen – which will only pick constants if either required, because of other constraints, or needed by the cardinal by adding optimization rules. In addition to adding atoms over p, we need to satisfy s' on a number of n nodes. We add a rule (5) to pick at least n, but might pick up to as many values as there are constants, so that we can satisfy the cardinality as well as any constraints that require specific constants. Note that an expression of the form $l \{W : V\} m$ intuitively allows to generate in the model a number between l and m W-atoms whenever V-atoms are also true.

- For the case where s is suggested to be false at X, i.e., for $s\_(X, f)$, we pick from all atoms $p(X, Y)$ to either delete the atom or falsify s' at Y. We add a disjunctive rule to pick one or the other (but not both).

$$ \ell \{\psi_1 \vee \psi_2\} \ \ell \leftarrow s\_(X, f), \#count\{Y : p\_(X, Y, t^*)\} = m, m > (n - 1) $$

where $\ell = m - (n - 1)$, ψ_1 is the expression $p\_(X, Y, f) : p(X, Y), not \ s'\_(Y, f)$ and ψ_2 is $s'\_(Y, f) : p\_(X, Y, t^*), not \ p\_(X, Y, f)$. To make $s\_$ false at X, we have two disjunctive options that we can falsify. The first option is to falsify the $p\_$ atom. This can only be selected if $s'\_$ was not falsified at node Y. The second option is to falsify the $s'\_$ at node Y, which in return should only be possible if the $p\_$ atom was not falsified. By picking $m - (n - 1)$ options, we make sure that only the maximum allowed cardinality will be in the repaired graph.

Constant Reuse Optimization. The rules above are allowed to pick from any constants that are needed to satisfy constraints in the current model. However, we want to pick a constant from C only if it is necessary to satisfy a constraint. To achieve this, for every constraint of the form $s \leftarrow_{\geq n} p.s'$, that is of form (NF6), we add the $\#minimize\{1@1, X, Y : p\_(X, Y, t), const(Y)\}$ optimization rule to P'_{ψ} that minimizes the use of constants among the different minimal repairs. We choose a lower priority level (1@1) for minimizing the use of constants after minimizing additions and deletions with a priority (1@2) and after minimizing the number of skipped target atoms (1@3). We first want to have minimal repairs and then among them to pick the ones with minimal number of constants. Note that this encoding may produce different repairs from the encoding in Sect. 3 on the same example as illustrated below.

Consider again Example 3. The repair program P'_{ψ} will generate three repairs. One repair will only add $Course(C_1)$. Intuitively, rule (2) adds $choose(s, X, p, 0)$ to the model, rule (3) and (4) will not add atoms, and rule (5) adds $s\_(C1, t^*)$ which together with the other rules treated in Example 3 add $Course\_(C1, t)$, and $Course(C1, t^{**})$, and hence . The second repair will add $enrolledIn(Ben, new_1)$ in addition to $Course(C_1)$ because of picking $i = 1$ in rule (2), and generating a fresh value new_1 in (3), and picking still $C1$ for s_-. The third repair will assign new_1 to s_-, thus resulting in the repair $(A, \emptyset)$ from Example 3. The optimization feature will return only the minimal repair that only adds $Course(C_1)$.

6   ASP Implementation

Repair Program. We developed a prototypical system for implementing SHACL repair programs using Java programming language and the ASP system Clingo. The prototype parses an RDF representation of a SHACL shapes graph and a data graph and transforms them into a repair program as a set of Clingo rules and facts. The repair program can then be executed using Clingo, which returns the stable models with (sub)sets of repaired shape target nodes and sets of additions and deletions as repairs for the data graph.

Unit Test Suite. To verify the implementation, we created a unit test suite with minimal examples that covers all the supported shape expressions. We grouped the test cases in four groups for class constraints, property constraints, value constraints and constraints with conflicts either within a shape or between multiple shape assignments. Each group includes expressions with conjunction, disjunction and negation. The unit test suite consist of a total of 43 test cases.

Data Shapes Test Suite. We applied the repair program to 16 selected test cases of the official SHACL data shapes test suite[5]. The selection was done based on the supported shape expressions of the repair program. All the selected tests were successful and repairs provided in the case of no conflicting constraints.[6]

7   Conclusion

We presented an approach to repair a data graph so that it conforms to a set of SHACL constraints. We first analyze the type of repairs that may be desirable in practice. To generate the repairs, inspired by existing work in databases, we encode the problem into an ASP program. We provide encodings for a restricted setting, which forces to introduce a new value to satisfy existential constraints, and for the extended setting that allows to reuse also existing constants. The optimizations as part of our approach were introduced with a view on practical scenarios, where we not only want to have minimal change, but also to avoid creating new data that is not sound from a real-world perspective. In case not all the shape targets can be repaired, we optimize to repair as many of them as possible. With the repair program and the ASP implementation, we have laid the foundation for bringing repairs into practical scenarios, and thus improving the quality of RDF graphs in practice.

---

[5] https://w3c.github.io/data-shapes/data-shapes-test-suite/.
[6] Our prototype, test suites, and statistics are available from the authors upon request.

Future Work. Several tasks remain for future work. For the practical side, the next step will be to select use-cases where we can apply the repairs and evaluate the practical feasibility and explore repair quality and scalability. For the more technical direction, we plan to extend the approach to support SHACL *property paths*. Another direction is to support *recursive* SHACL constraints. They are also challenging because recursion combined with the introduction of fresh nodes, may cause non-termination of the repair process, i.e. an infinite repair might be forced. A related direction is to extend our approach to the so-called *class-based* and *property-based* targets. These targets bring implicit recursion to the repair problem, even when the constraints are non-recursive as in this paper, which makes dealing with such targets as challenging as the full recursive case.

Acknowledgements. Supported by the Austrian Science Fund (FWF) and netidee SCIENCE project T 1349-N, and the FWF projects P30360 and P30873. Polleres is supported by funding in the European Commission's Horizon 2020 Research Program under Grant Agreement Number 957402 (TEAMING.AI).

References

1. Shapes constraint language (SHACL). Tech. rep., W3C, Jul 2017. https://www.w3.org/TR/shacl/
2. Ahmetaj, S., David, R., Ortiz, M., Polleres, A., Shehu, B., Simkus, M.: Reasoning about explanations for non-validation in SHACL. In: Bienvenu, M., Lakemeyer, G., Erdem, E. (eds.) Proceedings of the 18th International Conference on Principles of Knowledge Representation and Reasoning, KR 2021, Online event, 3–12 November 2021, pp. 12–21 (2021). https://doi.org/10.24963/kr.2021/2
3. Andresel, M., et al.: Stable model semantics for recursive SHACL. In: Proceedings of the Web Conference 2020, WWW 2020, pp. 1570–1580. ACM (2020). https://doi.org/10.1145/3366423.3380229
4. Bertossi, L.: Database Repairing and Consistent Query Answering. Morgan & Claypool Publishers (2011). https://doi.org/10.2200/S00379ED1V01Y201108DTM020
5. Bertossi, L.E.: Database Repairing and Consistent Query Answering. Synthesis Lectures on Data Management. Morgan & Claypool Publishers (2011). https://doi.org/10.2200/S00379ED1V01Y201108DTM020
6. Corman, J., Reutter, J.L., Savković, O.: Semantics and validation of recursive SHACL. In: Vrandečić, D., et al. (eds.) ISWC 2018. LNCS, vol. 11136, pp. 318–336. Springer, Cham (2018). https://doi.org/10.1007/978-3-030-00671-6_19
7. Eiter, T., Ianni, G., Krennwallner, T.: Answer set programming: a primer. In: Tessaris, S., et al. (eds.) Reasoning Web 2009. LNCS, vol. 5689, pp. 40–110. Springer, Heidelberg (2009). https://doi.org/10.1007/978-3-642-03754-2_2
8. Gayo, J.E.L., Prud'hommeaux, E., Boneva, I., Kontokostas, D.: Validating RDF Data. Synthesis Lectures on the Semantic Web: Theory and Technology. Morgan & Claypool Publishers (2017). https://doi.org/10.2200/S00786ED1V01Y201707WBE016
9. Gebser, M., Kaminski, R., Kaufmann, B., Schaub, T.: Multi-shot asp solving with clingo. Theory Pract. Logic Program. **19**(1), 27–82 (2019). https://doi.org/10.1017/S1471068418000054

10. Hogan, A., et al.: Knowledge Graphs. Synthesis Lectures on Data, Semantics, and Knowledge. Morgan & Claypool Publishers (2021). https://doi.org/10.2200/S01125ED1V01Y202109DSK022
11. Marileo, M.C., Bertossi, L.E.: The consistency extractor system: answer set programs for consistent query answering in databases. Data Knowl. Eng. **69**, 545–572 (2010). https://doi.org/10.1016/j.datak.2010.01.005

Entity Type Prediction Leveraging Graph Walks and Entity Descriptions

Russa Biswas[1,2]([✉])([ID]), Jan Portisch[3,4]([ID]), Heiko Paulheim[4]([ID]), Harald Sack[1,2]([ID]),
and Mehwish Alam[1,2]([ID])

[1] FIZ Karlsruhe – Leibniz Institute for Infromation Infrastructure, Karlsruhe,
Germany
{russa.biswas,harald.sack,mehwish.alam}@fiz-karlsruhe.de
[2] Karlsruhe Institute of Technology, Institute AIFB, Karlsruhe, Germany
[3] SAP SE, Walldorf, Germany
jan.portisch@sap.com
[4] Data and Web Science Group, University of Mannheim, Mannheim, Germany
{jan,heiko}@informatik.uni-mannheim.de

Abstract. The entity type information in Knowledge Graphs (KGs)
such as DBpedia, Freebase, etc. is often incomplete due to automated
generation or human curation. Entity typing is the task of assigning or
inferring the semantic type of an entity in a KG. This paper presents
GRAND, a novel approach for entity typing leveraging different graph
walk strategies in RDF2vec together with textual entity descriptions.
RDF2vec first generates graph walks and then uses a language model to
obtain embeddings for each node in the graph. This study shows that
the walk generation strategy and the embedding model have a significant
effect on the performance of the entity typing task. The proposed approach outperforms the baseline approaches on the benchmark datasets
DBpedia and FIGER for entity typing in KGs for both fine-grained and
coarse-grained classes. The results show that the combination of order-
aware RDF2vec variants together with the contextual embeddings of the
textual entity descriptions achieve the best results.

Keywords: Entity type prediction · RDF2vec · Knowledge graph
embedding · Graph walks · Language models

1 Introduction

Many efforts have been made towards the automated generation of Knowledge
Graphs (KGs) from heterogeneous resources such as text or images. One such
effort is the creation of cross-domain KGs such as DBpedia [1], Wikidata [32],
Freebase [4], etc. which are either extracted automatically from structured data,
generated using heuristics, or are human-curated. This leads to incomplete information in the KGs which can occur on factual level (e.g., missing entities and/or

---

R. Biswas and J. Portisch—The authors contributed equally to this paper.

U. Sattler et al. (Eds.): ISWC 2022, LNCS 13489, pp. 392–410, 2022.
https://doi.org/10.1007/978-3-031-19433-7_23

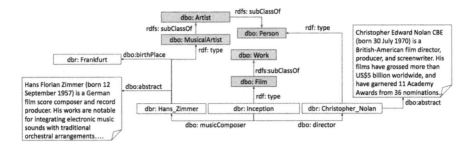

Fig. 1. Excerpt from DBpedia

relations between the entities) or on schema level (e.g., the missing entity type information). For instance, DBpedia version 2016-10 consists of 48 subclasses of *dbo:Person*; however, only 36.6% of the total number of entities belonging to *dbo:Person* are assigned to its subclasses. Moreover, 307,164 entities in the entire DBpedia 2016-10 version are assigned to *owl:Thing*.

To address the KG incompleteness on the factual level, a lot of models [5,6,28], etc. have been proposed. These models focus mainly on predicting the missing entities and relations in the KGs but not the entity types. However, the entity type information in KGs plays a vital role in various Natural Language Processing based applications such as question answering [31], relation extraction [10], recommendation, or system [33]. Following these lines, this paper focuses on the problem of entity typing which is the task of assigning or inferring the semantic type of an entity in a KG. Figure 1 shows an excerpt from DBpedia where the class *dbo:MusicalArtist* is a subclass of *dbo:Artist* which is a subclass of *dbo:Person*. *dbo:Artist* and *dbo:MusicalArtist*, respectively, are the fine-grained entity types for *dbr:Hans_Zimmer* and *dbo:Artist* is the missing type information. *dbo:Person* is the coarse-grained type.

Recent years have witnessed a few studies on entity typing approaches in KGs using heuristics [20] and machine learning based classification models [3,11,12,17,37]. These models predict entity types using different KG features such as the anchor text mentions in the textual entity descriptions, relations between the entities, entity names, and Wikipedia categories. They learn the representation of the entities from their KG structure by using translational models [15], GCN-based models [12], neighborhood based attention models [41] followed by the correlation between the entities and its types. These models exploit the neighborhood information only by the entities directly connected, i.e., the triple information of the entities. However, the large amount of contextual information of the entities captured in the graph walks remains unexplored. The work presented in this paper emphasizes on modeling the KG by taking advantage of the semantics of graph walks to predict the entity types with the help of different kinds of walk generation strategies, such as classic random walks, entity walks, and property walks. The paths generated by these graph walk strategies are used within the RDF2vec model [27] to generate different entity representations. Additionally, the textual entity descriptions in the KGs contain rich semantic information which is beneficial in predicting the missing entity types. For instance, as depicted in Fig. 1, the textual entity descriptions of the entities clearly mentions that *dbr: Christopher_Nolan* is a *director*, *dbr: Hans_Zimmer* is a *music composer*, and *dbr: Inception* is a *film*. Some of the existing baseline models such as MuLR [38] use non-contextual Neural Language Models (NLMs), whereas the other uses GCN model [12] on the words extracted from the entity descriptions. Therefore, to capture the contextual information of the textual entity description contextual NLM, is used to generate entity representations.

This paper presents a framework named **GRAND** (**G**raph Walks for **R**DF2vec **a**nd Entity **D**escriptions), which exploits different variants of the RDF2vec model based on different graph walk strategies together with textual entity descriptions to predict the missing entity types in a KG. In this work, the entity typing problem is modelled as a classification problem. A flat and a hierarchical classification model are deployed on the top of the feature vectors generated from the aforementioned entity representations to predict the missing entity types. The empirical results based on the extensive experiments on two benchmark datasets FIGER [37] and DBpedia630k [39] show that the proposed approach is robust and outperforms the state-of-the-art (SOTA) models. Further experiments show that *GRAND* performs considerably well on unseen entities. The main contributions of this work are:

- A framework which leverages different graph walk strategies based RDF2vec models and a contextual NLM for textual entity descriptions is proposed to predict the missing entity types.
- A generalized classification framework consisting of three different modules namely multi-class, multi-label, and hierarchical classification is introduced to predict the missing entity types on different levels of granularity. It can be easily deployed for predicting entity types on entity representations from any KGs.
- Extensive experiments are conducted on the benchmark datasets to study the impact of several combinations of entity representations generated from the RDF2Vec variants and the NLM. An analysis on the weights in the classification has been conducted for analyzing which entity representations are suitable in which entity typing situations. Furthermore, the impact of dimensionality reduction of the entity representations on the local and global level using Principle Component Analysis (PCA) is studied.

The rest of the paper is organized as follows: Sect. 2 gives an overview of the baseline approaches. Section 3 describes the proposed methodology, followed by experiments and results in Sect. 4. Finally, Sect. 5 provides the conclusion and an outlook of future work.

2   Related Work

This section discusses existing literature on entity typing and categorizes them based on their underlying methodology such as heuristics-based methods or machine learning based methods.

SDType [20] is a statistical heuristic model that exploits links between instances using weighted voting. The model is based on the assumption that certain relations occur only with particular types. SDType often does not perform well if two or more classes share the same sets of properties and also if specific relations are missing for the entities.

One of the recent models, Cat2Type [3], takes into account the semantics underlying the textual information in the Wikipedia categories using language models such as BERT. In order to consider the structural information of Wikipedia categories, a category-category network is generated which is then fed to Node2Vec for obtaining the category embeddings. The embeddings of both structural and textual information are combined for classifying entities into their types. In [2], different word embedding models, trained on triples, are leveraged together with a classification model to predict the entity types. Therefore, contextual information is not captured. In CUTE [36], a hierarchical classification model has been proposed which helps in cross-lingual entity typing by exploiting category, property, and property-value pairs. Another model has been proposed in [17] which performs type prediction using the Scalable Local Classifier per Node (SLCN) algorithm based on a set of incoming and outgoing relations. However, the entities with few relations are likely to be misclassified. MuLR [38] learns multi-level representations of entities via character, word, and entity embeddings followed by the hierarchical multi-label classification. Another model, namely FIGMENT [37], uses a global model and a context model. The global model predicts entity types based on the entity mentions from the corpus and the entity names. The context model calculates a score for each context of an entity and assigns it to a type. Therefore, it requires a large annotated corpus which is a drawback of the model. In APE [11], a partially labeled attribute entity-entity network is constructed containing structural, attribute, and type information for entities followed by deep neural networks to learn the entity embeddings. MRGCN [35] is a multi-modal message-passing network that learns end-to-end from the structure of KGs as well as from multimodal node features. In HMGCN [12], the authors propose a GCN-based model to predict the entity types considering the relations, textual entity descriptions, and the Wikipedia categories. ConnectE [40] and AttET [41] models find correlation between neighborhood entities to predict the missing types. However, unlike GRAND, these two models do not look for information far away from the source entity. They work on the principal of L2 distance in their embedding space to detect the types and therefore not compared with the proposed model. Also, in order to employ the hidden layer as latent features for entity representation, restricted Boltzman machines (RBMs) are used to learn a target distribution across the usage of relations of entities [34].

3   Entity Type Prediction: GRAND Framework

An overview of the GRAND framework is illustrated in Fig. 2. Component (A) represents the RDF2vec variants that use the different strategies for generating

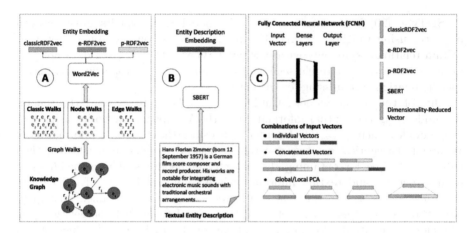

Fig. 2. Architecture of the GRAND framework

graph walks, i.e., classic walks, node walks, and property walks. Component (B) generates the representations of the entities from the textual entity description by using SBERT. Finally, component (C) shows combinations of the variants of entity representations used for flat as well as hierarchical classification. The rest of the section contains the explanation of the component details.

Preliminaries. We define a knowledge graph $\mathcal{G}$ as a labeled directed graph $\mathcal{G} = (\mathcal{V}, \mathcal{E})$, where $\mathcal{E} \subseteq \mathcal{V} \times \mathcal{R} \times \mathcal{V}$ for a set of relations $\mathcal{R}$. Vertices are subsequently also referred to as *entities* and edges as *predicates*.

3.1   Entity Representation

RDF2vec [27] is one of the first approaches to adopt statistical language modeling techniques to KGs. The key idea of RDF2vec is a two-step approach: first, random walks over the graph are executed, thereby collecting sequences of entities and relations. To employ language modeling techniques, these sequences are then considered as sentences where each entity and relation in the sequence are treated as words. In RDF2vec, those sentences are then processed by word2vec [18,19], where both variants of word2vec, i.e., continuous bag of words (CBOW) and skip-gram (SG), are possible.

One limitation of the word2vec algorithm is that it is not aware of the word order. For instance, for a window size of 4, the sentences "John ate a pizza" and "pizza ate a John" are equivalent. This is also the case with *RDF2vec*: For instance, the statements <Severus> <loves> <Lily> and <Lily> <loves> <Severus>, are considered equivalent even though <loves> is not a symmetric property. To overcome this limitation, an order-aware version of RDF2vec has been proposed [24] which has shown improved performance on multiple machine learning datasets. This order-aware variant of RDF2vec uses a *structured word2vec* model [16] which incorporates the positional information of the words in a sentence. The main advantage of the order-aware RDF2vec model over the classical RDF2vec model is that it respects the positional information of the entities and relations in the random walks, thereby learning embeddings which are better in terms of type separation.

Another type of RDF2vec extension is to explore different strategies for performing graph walks. These strategies have been explored using either variants of random walks (e.g., community hops [14], walklets [21], or hierarchical walks [29]), or by combining different random walk strategies, as the *ontowalk2vec* approach, which combines RDF2vec and node2vec walks [8]. In this paper, the aforementioned order-aware as well as different RDF2vec graph walk strategies [25] are leveraged to predict the missing types of the entities.

Graph Walk Generation Strategies. RDF2vec combines the notion of similarity and relatedness. This can be easily observed when printing the most related concepts for "Berlin" on DBpedia via KGvec2go [22], i.e., many people who are *related* to the city are identified as politicians. However, those are not really *similar* – they do not share properties with Berlin (which is a city rather than a living being). This leads to further exploration of RDF2vec for entity typing.

In this paper, six different RDF2vec configurations are presented and evaluated – stand alone as well as combinations. For the task of entity typing, three different walk generation strategies are applied: (1) classic walks (2) entity walks, and (3) predicate walks. Each strategy is explained below in more detail.

Classic Walks. The originally presented RDF2vec variant generates multiple random walks for each node in the graph. A random walk of length n (where n is an even number) is of the form

$$w = (w_{-\frac{n}{2}}, w_{-\frac{n}{2}+1}, ..., w_0, ..., w_{\frac{n}{2}-1}, w_{\frac{n}{2}}) \tag{1}$$

where $w_i \in \mathcal{V}$ if i is even, and $w_i \in \mathcal{R}$ if i is odd. For better readability, we stylize $w_i \in \mathcal{V}$ as e_i and $w_i \in \mathcal{R}$ as p_i:

$$w = (e_{-\frac{n}{2}}, p_{-\frac{n}{2}+1}, ..., e_0, ..., p_{\frac{n}{2}-1}, e_{\frac{n}{2}}) \tag{2}$$

Entity Walks (e-RDF2vec). An entity walk contains only entities without any other properties. Such an approach is also known as *e-RDF2vec*, given by

$$w_e = (e_{-\frac{n}{2}}, e_{-\frac{n}{2}+2}, ..., e_0, ..., e_{\frac{n}{2}-2}, e_{\frac{n}{2}}) \tag{3}$$

For an entity walk, all elements are entities, i.e., $w_{n_i} \in \mathcal{V}$.

Predicate Walks (p-RDF2vec). A predicate walk contains only one entity together with object properties known as *p-RDF2vec* and is defined as:

$$w_p = (p_{-\frac{n}{2}+1}, p_{-\frac{n}{2}+3}, ..., e_0, ..., p_{\frac{n}{2}-3}, p_{\frac{n}{2}-1}) \tag{4}$$

The different walk strategies are visualized in component (**A**) in Fig. 1.

Generating Entity Embeddings Using RDF2Vec Variants. An embedding model is trained for each set of walks using word2vec [18,19] and position-aware word2vec [16] (suffix *oa* in the following) which yields six sets of embeddings: (1) Classic RDF2vec (2) e-RDF2vec (3) p-RDF2vec (4) Classic RDF2vec$_{oa}$, (5) e-RDF2vec$_{oa}$, and (6) p-RDF2vec$_{oa}$. The proposed model, GRAND, is evaluated by using the configurations presented in 3.1 on their own as well as in a fused way. Concerning the fusion of vectors, three modes are employed: (1) Vector concatenation, (2) Local PCA (LPCA), and (3) Global PCA (GPCA). PCA is a technique for reducing the dimensionality of the vectors with minimal loss in encoded information. It is used for identification of a smaller number of uncorrelated variables known as principal components. The difference between (2) and (3) is that in the case of the LPCA, a principal component analysis is only performed for the subset of vectors that appear in the datasets (see Sect. 4) whereas for the GPCA, one all vectors generated from the KG using RDF2vec variants are considered. Each of these configurations can be used as vector within GRAND (see component Ⓒ in Fig. 2).

The main advantages of using different RDF2vec variants are: **(i)** With a growing length of walks and training window, they can take advantage of large entity context ranges by effectively treating every entity as being connected to all the others in the graph – this is in contrast to the baseline models which are based on local aggregation, i.e. they learn the representation of each entity based on its adjacent entities in the KG [12,41]. **(ii)** The graph walk strategies are effective, robust, and equitable, i.e., all relations and nodes are given equal importance in generating the embeddings. **(iii)** The walk strategies put emphasis on certain semantic aspects – namely *relatedness* and *similarity* [25]. **(iv)** RDF2vec is a very scalable embedding algorithm. **(v)** The experimental results from [42] show RDF2vec works better on the separability task compared to the other embedding models. The separability task aims at measuring if embeddings from different classes can be linearly separable and the evaluation is done on 10,000 pairs of classes from DBpedia. **(vi)** Any classification algorithm can be deployed on top of entity embeddings to predict the missing types.

3.2 Entity Description Representation

The textual descriptions of an entity provide rich semantic information. Sentence-BERT (SBERT) [26] fine-tunes the BERT [7] model using the siamese and triplet networks to update the weights such that the resulting sentence embeddings are semantically meaningful and semantically similar sentences are closely positioned in the embedding space. For one epoch, a 3-way softmax classifier objective function is used for the fine-tuning of the BERT model. In the training phase of SBERT, two input sentences are passed through the BERT model followed by a pooling layer namely, MEAN-strategy, and MAX-strategy. A fixed-size representation for the input sentences are generated by this pooling layer. Next, they are concatenated with the element-wise difference and multiplied with a trainable weight. The cross-entropy loss is used for optimization. In order to encode the semantics, the twin network is fine-tuned on Semantic

Textual Similarity data. SBERT model follows a two-step process in which it is first trained on Wikipedia via BERT and then fine-tuned on Natural Language Inference (NLI) data. NLI is a collection of 1,000,000 sentence pairs created by combining The Stanford Natural Language Inference (SNLI) and Multi-Genre NLI (MG.NLI) datasets.

In this work, the same approach is followed to extract the embedding of the textual entity descriptions as mentioned in the evaluation of the quality of sentence embeddings in [26]. Given be a textual entity description D_{e_i} denoted by a sequence of words $\{W_1, W_2, ..., W_n\}$, where W_j is the jth word in the entity description, and e_i is the corresponding entity. The entity description D_{e_i} is considered as a single sequence of words which is provided as an input to the SBERT model to get the embedding of the textual entity description $\mathbf{E_{D_i}}$. The pre-trained SBERT model used in GRAND is the SBERT-SNLI-STS-base model which is fine tuned on SNLI and STS datasets which outperforms the baseline models as shown in [26]. The MEAN pooling strategy is used in the pooling layer.

The main advantages of using pre-trained SBERT model are: (i) Since the pre-trained SBERT model is fine-tuned with two different datasets, the entity description embeddings obtained lose domain-specific knowledge and bias, and learn task-agnostic properties of the language. (ii) Unlike static word embedding models, such as word2vec, the contextual embedding model SBERT encodes semantics of the words differently based on different contexts. Therefore, the entity description embeddings capture the contextual information for the task of entity typing unlike the baseline models [12,38] (iii) They are computationally inexpensive as the model is pre-trained on huge amount of text and can be easily fine-tuned based on the information available. (iv) A representation of the entities can be obtained from the textual entity description for long-tailed entities in the KG, i.e., entities with no or few properties. (v) A task-specific classification model can be deployed on top of the entity description embeddings for entity typing task as illustrated in the proposed GRAND framework.

3.3   Entity Type Prediction

GRAND consists of three different classification modules: (1) Multi-class, (2) Multi-label, and (3) Hierarchical, that are discussion below.

Entity Representation. The aforementioned approaches generate entity embeddings from various RDF2vec variants and from the contextual embedding model SBERT, which are provided as input to the classification modules. The input entity vectors are generated by concatenating the different vectors generated by the embedding models as depicted in component Ⓒ in Fig. 2.

Classifiers. For *multi-class classification*, a Fully Connected Neural Network (FCNN) consisting of two dense layers with ReLU as an activation function is deployed on the top of the entity representation. A softmax classifier with a cross-entropy loss function is used in the last layer to calculate the probability of the entities belonging to different classes. Formally it is given by,

$$f(s)_i = \frac{e^{s_i}}{\sum_j^{C_T} e^{s_j}}, \quad \text{and} \quad CE_{loss} = -\sum_i^{C_T} t_i log(f(s)_i), \tag{5}$$

where s_j are the scores inferred for each class in C_T given in Eq. 5. t_i and s_i are the ground truth and the score for each class in C, respectively.

In *multi-label classification*, an entity can belong to more than one class or type. Therefore, a certain entity e_i belonging to one class c_i has no impact on the decision of it belonging to another class c_j, where $c_i, c_j \in C_T$. A FCNN with RELU as an activation function is used for the two dense layers. A sigmoid function with binary cross-entropy loss is used in the last layer which sets up a binary classification problem for each class in C_T and is given by,

$$CE_{loss} = -t_i log(f(s_i)) - (1 - t_i)log(1 - f(s_i)), \tag{6}$$

where s_i and t_i are the score and ground truth for i^{th} class in C_T.

Hierarchical Classification. can be broadly categorized into local and global classification. The local information in local classifier can be utilized in different ways leading to different types of local classifiers such as Local classifier Per Node (LPN), a Local classifier Per Parent Node (LPPN) and a Local classifier Per Level (LPL) [13]. The proposed framework GRAND uses LPL which consists of training a flat classifier for each level of the class hierarchy. A multi-class classifier is trained at each level of the class hierarchy is used to discriminate among the classes at that level. The two main advantages of the LPL model are: (i) It is computationally efficient compared to LPN for large KGs consisting of large number of classes as LPN model would have equal number of classifiers. The number of classifiers in LPL are restricted to the number of levels in the class hierarchy. (ii) Since a single classifier is trained at each level, it reduces the horizontal class prediction inconsistencies. In GRAND, a two-layered FCNN with ReLU activation function and cross-entropy loss has been deployed at each level of the class hierarchy. However, one of the drawbacks of LPL is that an entity can be classified as class 1 at one level and then it can be again classified as class 2.1 on the second level. Here, class 2.1 is not a subclass of 1 and the entity should be classified to a subclass of 1. In order to tackle such inconsistencies, in this work, the entity which is misclassified as 2.1 in level 2 will be typed as 1 as its entity type as it was correctly identified in level 1.

4 Experiments and Results

This section provides details on the benchmark datasets, experimental setup, analysis of the results obtained, and the ablation study.

Datasets. The two benchmark datasets FIGER [37] and DBpedia630k [39] are used to evaluate the performance of the GRAND framework against the baseline

Table 1. Statistics of the datasets

Parameters	DB-1	DB-2	DB-3	FIGER
#Entities	210,000	210,000	210,000	201,933
#Entities train	105,000	105,000	105,000	101,266
#Entities test	63,000	63,000	63,000	60,447
#Entities validation	42,000	42,000	42,000	40,220

models. DBpedia630k consists of 630,000 entities and 14 non-overlapping classes and FIGER consists of 201,933 entities with 102 classes from Freebase. The entities of the extended DBpedia630k dataset are split equally into three parts DB-1, DB-2, and DB-3, each containing 210,000 entities. Each DBpedia split is divided into a train, test and validation set with 50%, 30%, and 20% of the total entities respectively [12] as well as to 48 classes in the class hierarchy. There are no shared entities between the train, test, and validation sets for all the DBpedia630k splits and in FIGER. FIGER has been extended with triples from DBpedia as explained in [3,12]. The statistics is provided in Table 1. The code, and data are publicly available[1].

Experimental Setup. The experiments are conducted on six sets of embeddings: (1) Classic RDF2vec, (2) e-RDF2vec, (3) p-RDF2vec, (4) Classic RDF-2vec$_{oa}$, (5) e-RDF2vec$_{oa}$, and (6) p-RDF2vec$_{oa}$. The walks are generated with a depth of 8 and 500 walks per entity. Classic and OA embeddings are trained using SG with 200 dimensions and 5 epochs. For training the order aware variants (4–6), walks from the corresponding non-order aware variants (1–3) are reused. The training was performed using the jRDF2vec framework[2] [23]. All the classifiers are used with the batch size 64, 100 epochs, and adam optmizer. The vectors are publicly available.[3]

Results. In order to evaluate the proposed approach against the baseline models, Micro-averaged F_1 (Mi-F_1) and Macro-averaged F_1 (Ma-F_1) metrics are used along with the accuracy. Different variants of *RDF2vec* have been evaluated which serve as an ablation study. The baselines used for the experiments are: CUTE [36], MuLR [38], FIGMENT [37], APE [11], HMGCN [12], and CAT2Type [3]. The results of the proposed framework on two benchmark datasets and their comparison with the baseline models are depicted in Table 2. The results of GRAND as depicted in Table 2 can be obtained as follows: **(i)** *Coarse-grained setting:* For DBpedia splits, the original dataset consisting of 14 non-overlapping classes is used. For FIGER, the number of coarse-grained classes is 30 and they are non-overlapping as well. Since, none of the entities belong to more than one class, *multi-class* classification settings have been used here. **(ii)** *Fine-grained setting:* The original DBpedia630k dataset is expanded with

---

[1] https://shorturl.at/abJRW.

[2] https://github.com/dwslab/jRDF2Vec.

[3] https://bit.ly/3besaWF.

Table 2. Results of GRAND on benchmark datasets. The best result of each mode is printed in bold, the runner-up is underlined.

	Model	DB-1		DB2		DB3		FIGER	
		Ma-F1	Mi-F1	Ma-F1	Mi-F1	Ma-F1	Mi-F1	Ma-F1	Mi-F1
Baselines	CUTE [36]	0.679	0.702	0.681	0.713	0.685	0.717	0.743	0.782
	MuLR [38]	0.748	0.771	0.757	0.784	0.752	0.775	0.776	0.812
	FIGMENT [37]	0.740	0.766	0.738	0.765	0.745	0.769	0.785	0.819
	APE [11]	0.758	0.784	0.761	0.785	0.760	0.782	0.722	0.756
	HMGCN-no hier [12]	0.785	0.812	0.794	0.820	0.791	0.817	0.789	0.827
	CAT2Type-BERT [3]	<u>0.983</u>	<u>0.984</u>	<u>0.983</u>	<u>0.983</u>	<u>0.985</u>	<u>0.985</u>	<u>0.764</u>	<u>0.881</u>
GRAND Coarse-grained	Classic-RDF2vec$_{oa}$ $\oplus$ s-RDF2vec$_{oa}$ $\oplus$ p-RDF2vec$_{oa}$ $\oplus$ SBERT	**0.991**	**0.991**	**0.990**	**0.990**	**0.989**	**0.989**	**0.801**	**0.893**
	SBERT - only	0.972	0.972	0.97	0.97	0.97	0.97	0.648	0.844
Baselines Fine-grained	CAT2Type-BERT [3]	0.402	0.732	0.369	0.721	0.847	0.915	0.703	0.835
	CAT2Type-node2vec [3]	0.391	0.694	0.365	0.677	0.807	0.878	0.701	0.833
GRAND Fine-grained	Classic-RDF2vec$_{oa}$ $\oplus$ s-RDF2vec$_{oa}$ $\oplus$ p-RDF2vec$_{oa}$ $\oplus$ SBERT	**0.745**	**0.870**	**0.723**	**0.851**	**0.880**	**0.931**	**0.706**	**0.881**
Baseline Hierarchical	HMGCN-hier [12]	**0.794**	0.816	**0.796**	0.824	**0.798**	0.819	**0.798**	0.836
GRAND Hierarchical	classic-RDF2vec$_{oa}$ $\oplus$ s-RDF2vec$_{oa}$ $\oplus$ p-RDF2vec$_{oa}$	<u>0.731</u>	**0.882**	<u>0.729</u>	**0.881**	0.726	0.877	0.701	<u>0.880</u>
	classic-RDF2vec$_{oa}$ $\oplus$ s-RDF2vec$_{oa}$ $\oplus$ p-RDF2vec$_{oa}$ $\oplus$ SBERT	<u>0.731</u>	0.875	0.718	0.869	**0.935**	**0.946**	<u>0.712</u>	**0.883**

the DBpedia hierarchy to 37 fine-grained classes and these are non-overlapping classes. Therefore, a *multi-class* classification model is used here as well. On the other hand, the FIGER dataset consists of overlapping fine-grained classes, i.e., one entity can belong to multiple classes. Therefore, a *multi-label* classification is used for fine-grained FIGER dataset. **(iii)** For *Hierarchical Classification*, a classifier on each level of the hierarchy is deployed. For DBpedia splits, it is a multi-class classification model and for FIGER it is a multi-label classification model at each level of the hierarchy. The baseline models which use a non-hierarchical classification such as CAT2Type [3] also use a multi-class classification for DBpedia splits and a multi-label one for FIGER dataset. The SOTA model for hierarchical classification HMGCN [12] uses multi-label classification model. The results show that GRAND outperforms the SOTA model CAT2Type with an improvement of 0.8% on $Ma\text{-}F_1$ and 0.7% on $Mi\text{-}F_1$ for DB-1, 0.7% and 0.4% on both the metrics for DB-2 and DB-3 respectively for the coarse-grained classes. The original dataset with 14 classes which do not contain the hierarchy is used for this coarse-grained non-hierarchical variant. Furthermore, for hierarchical classification, the proposed model significantly outperforms the SOTA HMGCN-hier model with an increment of 6.6% for DB-1, 5.7% for DB-2, and 12.7% for DB-3 on the $Mi\text{-}F_1$ measure. For FIGER, the coarse-grained approach is a multi-class classification whereas the fine-grained approach is a multi-label classification. GRAND achieves the best results for FIGER on the coarse-grained approach which outperforms the baseline models. Moreover, with the multi-label fine-grained settings it achieves comparable results with the non-hierarchical baseline model CAT2Type and significantly outperforms the other non-hierarchical model HMGCN. One advantage of GRAND over CAT2Type is that it can be applied to any KGs and is not restricted to KGs containing information on Wikipedia Categories. Table 3 and Table 4 show the experimental results of the proposed approach for the coarse-grained and fine-grained classes respectively with different variants of RDF2vec and their combinations. Experiments using *Single* strategy show that *all* order-aware RDF2vec embeddings significantly outperform their classic counterparts. Hence, the fusion strategies only focus on position-aware embeddings reducing the combinatorial complexity.

Impact of RDF2vec Variants on Coarse-Grained Entity Typing. Table 3 shows the results of the experiment for coarse-grained entity typing. On the DB1 Split of the dataset, the best results for GRAND are obtained where the models are combined, i.e., $classic\text{-}RDF2vec_{oa} \oplus p\text{-}RDF2vec_{oa} \oplus e\text{-}RDF2vec_{oa}$ (*concat*) outperforms $HMGCN$ for $Ma\text{-}F_1$ by 0.1744 and for $Mi\text{-}F_1$ by 0.148 and achieves comparable results with CAT2Type. However, e-RDF2vec configurations perform the weakest on their own but introduces additional value when combined with other approaches as depicted in the concat model. The best performing configuration includes the entity embeddings. Given the data, it appears that the PCA discards too much valuable information for DBpedia splits but not for FIGER. Overall, it can be observed that the performance differences between p-RDF2vec and classic-RDF2vec are minor. Nonetheless, the embeddings encode different information which is visible when combining the embeddings. Therefore, it can be concluded that the contextual information of the entities in form of path captures the characteristics features of the entities. Similar observation has been made for both DB2, DB3 split and FIGER. A detailed analysis of the impact of different vector components is provided in Sect. 4.

Impact of RDF2vec variants on Fine-Grained Entity Typing. GRAND is compared with the two best variants of CAT2Type namely BERT and node2vec as shown in Table 2 and results show that the proposed model significantly outperforms the CAT2Type model for all DBpedia splits and FIGER. In general, it is observed for uneven class distribution the evaluation metric $Ma\text{-}F_1$ achieves lower values compared to $Mi\text{-}F_1$. However, the $Ma\text{-}F_1$ results of GRAND for DB1 and DB2 splits are much better than that of CAT2Type. It strengthens the fact that the representation of entities obtained using strategic graph walks and contextual embedding of entity descriptions contain more information about entities compared to the embeddings used in CAT2Type.

Impact of RDF2vec on Hierarchical classification. Table 5 shows the results of the hierarchical classification of the GRAND framework on different levels of the class hierarchy. The performance is computed for only $classic\text{-}RDF2vec_{oa} \oplus p\text{-}RDF2vec_{oa} \oplus e\text{-}RDF2vec_{oa}$ since it is the highest performing model based on experiments discussed in previous sections. The results show

Table 3. Evaluation of single classifier results on the coarse-grained dataset. The best result of each mode is printed in bold, the runner-up is underlined. The overall best configuration for each dataset is bold and underlined.

Dataset	Mode	Model	DB-1			DB-2			DB-3			FIGER		
			ACC	Ma-F$_1$	Mi-F$_1$	ACC	Ma-F$_1$	Mi-F$_1$	ACC	Ma-F$_1$	Mi-F$_1$	ACC	Ma-F$_1$	Mi-F$_1$
Coarse-Grained	Single	classic-RDF2vec	0.9163	0.9150	0.9163	0.9062	0.9043	0.9062	0.9123	0.9109	0.9123	0.931	0.431	0.778
		classic-RDF2vec$_{oa}$	0.9448	0.9439	0.9448	0.9346	0.9330	0.9346	0.9457	0.9449	0.9457	0.933	0.419	0.781
		e-RDF2vec	0.7352	0.7318	0.7352	0.7250	0.7308	0.7250	0.7357	0.7304	0.7357	0.927	0.421	0.771
		e-RDF2vec$_{oa}$	0.7665	0.7651	0.7665	0.7625	0.7453	0.7625	0.7694	0.7650	0.7694	0.927	0.422	0.771
		p-RDF2vec	0.8949	0.8946	0.8949	0.8999	0.8914	0.8999	0.8882	0.887	0.8882	0.922	0.426	0.778
		p-RDF2vec$_{oa}$	0.9412	0.9404	0.9412	0.9332	0.9303	0.9332	0.9430	0.9421	0.9430	0.928	0.422	0.779
	Concat	e-RDF2vec$_{oa}$ ⊕ p-RDF2vec$_{oa}$	0.9518	0.9512	0.9518	0.9482	0.9412	0.9482	0.9502	0.9495	0.9502	0.912	0.414	0.77
		e-RDF2vec$_{oa}$ ⊕ classic-RDF2vec$_{oa}$	0.9450	0.9444	0.9450	0.9450	0.9144	0.9450	0.9452	0.9482	0.9452	0.908	0.418	0.772
		classic-RDF2vec$_{oa}$ ⊕ p-RDF2vec$_{oa}$	0.9564	0.9555	0.9563	0.9560	0.9546	0.9560	0.9582	0.9513	0.9592	0.92	0.429	0.774
		classic-RDF2vec$_{oa}$ ⊕ p-RDF2vec$_{oa}$ ⊕ e-RDF2vec$_{oa}$	0.9600	0.9594	0.9600	0.9667	0.9544	0.9667	0.9572	0.9564	0.9574	0.924	0.424	0.772
	Local PCA	e-RDF2vec$_{oa}$ ⊕ p-RDF2vec$_{oa}$	0.8855	0.8845	0.8855	0.8757	0.8770	0.8757	0.8918	0.8905	0.8918	0.921	0.422	0.769
		e-RDF2vec$_{oa}$ ⊕ classic-RDF2vec$_{oa}$	0.9323	0.9314	0.9324	0.9314	0.9122	0.9314	0.9015	0.9000	0.9015	0.919	0.419	0.770
		classic-RDF2vec$_{oa}$ ⊕ p-RDF2vec$_{oa}$	0.9471	0.9466	0.9472	0.9442	0.9300	0.9442	0.9378	0.9217	0.9378	0.92	0.421	0.724
		classic-RDF2vec$_{oa}$ ⊕ p-RDF2vec$_{oa}$ ⊕ e-RDF2vec$_{oa}$	0.9405	0.9395	0.9405	0.9551	0.9195	0.9551	0.9413	0.9402	0.9413	0.925	0.428	0.778
	Global PCA	e-RDF2vec$_{oa}$ ⊕ p-RDF2vec$_{oa}$	0.9325	0.9316	0.9325	0.9412	0.9330	0.9412	0.9321	0.9310	0.9321	0.923	0.428	0.778
		e-RDF2vec$_{oa}$ ⊕ classic-RDF2vec$_{oa}$	0.9413	0.9405	0.9414	0.9322	0.9311	0.9322	0.9416	0.9405	0.9416	0.925	0.428	0.776
		classic-RDF2vec$_{oa}$ ⊕ p-RDF2vec$_{oa}$	0.9499	0.9490	0.9499	0.9356	0.9212	0.9356	0.9490	0.9482	0.9490	0.927	0.427	0.767
		classic-RDF2vec$_{oa}$ ⊕ p-RDF2vec$_{oa}$ ⊕ e-RDF2vec$_{oa}$	0.9476	0.9468	0.9476	0.9568	0.9412	0.9568	0.9489	0.9481	0.9489	0.929	0.433	0.779

Table 4. Evaluation of Single Classifier Results on the Fine-Grained Dataset. The best result of each mode is printed in bold, the runner-up is underlined. The overall best configuration for each dataset is bold and underlined.

Dataset	Mode	Model	DB-1			DB-2			DB-3			FIGER		
			ACC	Ma-F_1	Mi-F_1	ACC	Ma-F_1	Mi-F_1	ACC	Ma-F_1	Mi-F_1	ACC	Ma-F_1	Mi-F_1
Fine-Grained	Single	classic-RDF2vec	0.6716	0.374	0.672	0.6635	0.363	0.663	0.8402	0.736	0.840	0.991	0.467	0.774
		classic-RDF2vec$_{oa}$	0.704	0.386	0.704	0.701	0.356	0.701	0.871	0.774	0.871	0.987	0.469	0.778
		e-RDF2vec	0.564	0.297	0.5643	0.5231	0.3164	0.5231	0.6709	0.5632	0.6709	0.946	0.445	0.721
		e-RDF2vec$_{oa}$	0.5831	0.3064	0.5831	0.5542	0.3174	0.5442	0.6926	0.5747	0.6926	0.951	0.452	0.722
		p-RDF2vec	0.6500	0.3549	0.6499	0.6504	0.3449	0.6504	0.7848	0.6513	0.7848	0.949	0.467	0.77
		p-RDF2vec$_{oa}$	0.706	0.384	0.706	0.702	0.381	0.7022	0.847	0.732	0.8471	0.951	0.459	0.772
	Concat	e-RDF2vec$_{oa}$ ⊕ p-RDF2vec$_{oa}$	0.699	0.378	0.6996	0.698	0.388	0.698	0.877	0.784	0.877	0.949	0.454	0.774
		e-RDF2vec$_{oa}$ ⊕ classic-RDF2vec$_{oa}$	0.698	0.374	0.6978	0.701	0.384	0.7011	0.881	0.7811	0.881	0.96	0.512	0.781
		classic-RDF2vec$_{oa}$ ⊕ p-RDF2vec$_{oa}$	0.707	0.386	0.707	0.719	0.396	0.719	0.887	0.781	0.881	0.955	0.519	0.778
		classic-RDF2vec$_{oa}$ ⊕ p-RDF2vec$_{oa}$ ⊕ e-RDF2vec$_{oa}$	0.703	0.393	0.720	0.7204	0.3912	0.720	0.890	0.801	0.8908	0.961	0.519	0.783
	Local PCA	e-RDF2vec$_{oa}$ ⊕ p-RDF2vec$_{oa}$	0.653	0.358	0.6538	0.648	0.385	0.648	0.806	0.695	0.8060	0.948	0.457	0.778
		e-RDF2vec$_{oa}$ ⊕ classic-RDF2vec$_{oa}$	0.6865	0.3683	0.6865	0.6952	0.3682	0.6952	0.8746	0.7770	0.8746	0.951	0.501	0.779
		classic-RDF2vec$_{oa}$ ⊕ p-RDF2vec$_{oa}$	0.7006	0.3902	0.7006	0.7116	0.3907	0.7116	0.8774	0.7801	0.8774	0.950	0.504	0.771
		classic-RDF2vec$_{oa}$ ⊕ p-RDF2vec$_{oa}$ ⊕ e-RDF2vec$_{oa}$	0.6936	0.3839	0.6936	0.7122	0.3438	0.7123	0.864	0.764	0.864	0.958	0.514	0.781
	Global PCA	e-RDF2vec$_{oa}$ ⊕ p-RDF2vec$_{oa}$	0.6845	0.3716	0.6844	0.66125	0.3189	0.6612	0.855	0.7525	0.8547	0.942	0.449	0.772
		e-RDF2vec$_{oa}$ ⊕ classic-RDF2vec$_{oa}$	0.6908	0.3879	0.6908	0.67143	0.3119	0.67143	0.8677	0.7686	0.8677	0.945	0.449	0.769
		classic-RDF2vec$_{oa}$ ⊕ p-RDF2vec$_{oa}$	0.6981	0.3778	0.6981	0.6881	0.3241	0.6881	0.8754	0.7771	0.8754	0.956	0.457	0.771
		classic-RDF2vec$_{oa}$ ⊕ p-RDF2vec$_{oa}$ ⊕ e-RDF2vec$_{oa}$	0.7005	0.3768	0.7004	0.7014	0.3228	0.7014	0.8709	0.7780	0.8709	0.961	0.498	0.784

Table 5. Results of the GRAND-LPL classification model at each level

Level	#classes	DB1		DB2		DB3	
		$Ma\text{-}F_1$	$Mi\text{-}F_1$	$Ma\text{-}F_1$	$Mi\text{-}F_1$	$Ma\text{-}F_1$	$Mi\text{-}F_1$
1	5	**0.961**	**0.962**	**0.960**	**0.960**	**0.959**	**0.959**
2	11	0.744	0.925	0.747	0.929	0.744	0.924
3	12	0.857	0.934	0.851	0.926	0.859	0.935
4	17	0.361	0.705	0.358	0.702	0.359	0.674

higher performances on level 1 since the number of classes is lesser i.e., 5, as compared to other levels. GRAND outperforms the baseline model $HMGCN\text{-}withHier$ for $Mi\text{-}F_1$ metric as depicted in Table 2.

Impact of Textual Entity Descriptions. To analyze the impact of entity descriptions, a multi-class classification was performed on the entity embeddings generated from the SBERT model. As shown in Table 2, GRAND with only SBERT performs better than all the baseline models except CAT2Type. Therefore, it can be concluded that contextual embeddings using SBERT provide the necessary relevant information as compared to the triple-based baseline models.

Analysis of Vector Component Weight. In the experiments, it can be seen that the concatenation of embeddings achieves the best result. Therefore, it is further evaluated (1) which components are the most and the least important for the predictions and (2) whether there is a difference in the weights given the coarse-grained and the fine-grained prediction tasks.

Experimental Setup. In order to analyze the weights each vector component receives in the neural network, a FCNN with one layer was trained on the combination of all ordered aware RDF2vec (depicted in 1st 2 rows in coarse-grained and 1st 2 rows in fine-grained in Table 6) and also with SBERT. It is noted that the overall goal of this setup is to analyze how much weight each of the four vector groups receive. Therefore, the sum of absolute weights in the network given to each vector is calculated for the first, and the tenth epoch.

Results. The relative weights can be found in Table 6. It is observed that the highest overall impact is independent of the dataset, achieved using the p-RDF2vec embeddings. This is followed by the classic RDF2vec embeddings. The least impact is achieved by the e-RDF2vec embeddings. Interestingly, a weight-shift occurs when switching from the coarse-grained entity typing to fine-grained entity typing, i.e., it is visible that the classic and the entity embeddings are more important for fine-grained predictions. The results suggest that p-RDF2vec is helpful for coarse-grained type prediction – an intuitive finding given that p-RDF2vec encodes structural similarity. However, the more fine-grained the task gets, the more important are the *actual* neighbor vertices.

Table 6. Relative network weights of each vector component group for DB-1 split.

Dataset	Epoch	SBERT	Classic RDF2vec$_{oa}$	p-RDF2vec$_{oa}$	e-RDF2vec$_{oa}$
Coarse-grained	1	–	35.5%	44.4%	20.0%
	10	–	32.9%	49.9%	17.1%
	1	58.04%	14.6%	16.28%	11.08%
	10	47.9%	18.5%	22.8%	10.8%
Fine-grained	1	–	35.4%	42.1%	22.5%
	10	–	33.6%	46.4%	20.0%
	1	56.7%	15.36%	16.84%	11.1%
	10	51.19%	16.83%	19.5%	12.48%

5   Summary and Future Directions

This paper proposes a novel entity type prediction framework, named **GRAND** based on RDF2vec variants and textual entity descriptions. The variants are constructed by different walk generation strategies and a new order-aware variant of word2vec. GRAND is evaluated on DBpedia630k and FIGER datasets. The results show that GRAND considerably outperforms all the baseline models. Also, given the weight analysis, further experimentation on more fine-granular type systems – such as in YAGO [30] or CaLiGraph [9] is to be conducted.

References

1. Auer, S., Bizer, C., Kobilarov, G., Lehmann, J., Cyganiak, R., Ives, Z.: DBpedia: a nucleus for a web of open data. In: Aberer, K., et al. (eds.) ASWC/ISWC -2007. LNCS, vol. 4825, pp. 722–735. Springer, Heidelberg (2007). https://doi.org/10.1007/978-3-540-76298-0_52
2. Biswas, R., Sofronova, R., Alam, M., Sack, H.: Entity type prediction in knowledge graphs using embeddings. arXiv pp. arXiv-2004 (2020)
3. Biswas, R., Sofronova, R., Sack, H., Alam, M.: Cat2type: Wikipedia category embeddings for entity typing in knowledge graphs. In: Gentile, A.L., Gonçalves, R. (eds.) K-CAP 2021: Knowledge Capture Conference, Virtual Event, USA, 2–3 December 2021, pp. 81–88. ACM (2021). https://doi.org/10.1145/3460210.3493575
4. Bollacker, K., Evans, C., Paritosh, P., Sturge, T., Taylor, J.: Freebase: a collaboratively created graph database for structuring human knowledge. In: ACM SIGMOD International Conference on Management of Data (2008)
5. Bordes, A., Weston, J., Collobert, R., Bengio, Y.: Learning structured embeddings of knowledge bases. In: Proceedings of the Twenty-Fifth AAAI Conference on Artificial Intelligence (2011)
6. Dettmers, T., Pasquale, M., Pontus, S., Riedel, S.: Convolutional 2d knowledge graph embeddings. In: Proceedings of the 32th AAAI Conference on Artificial Intelligence (2018)

7. Devlin, J., Chang, M., Lee, K., Toutanova, K.: BERT: pre-training of deep bidirectional transformers for language understanding. In: Conference of the North American Chapter of the Association for Computational Linguistics: Human Language Technologies (2019)

8. Gkotse, B.: Ontology-based Generation of Personalised Data Management Systems: an Application to Experimental Particle Physics. Ph.D. thesis, Université Paris sciences et lettres (2020)

9. Heist, N., Paulheim, H.: Entity extraction from Wikipedia list pages. In: Harth, A., et al. (eds.) ESWC 2020. LNCS, vol. 12123, pp. 327–342. Springer, Cham (2020). https://doi.org/10.1007/978-3-030-49461-2_19

10. Jain, P., Kumar, P., Chakrabarti, S., et al.: Type-sensitive knowledge base inference without explicit type supervision. In: Proceedings of the 56th Annual Meeting of the Association for Computational Linguistics, vol. 2: Short Papers, pp. 75–80 (2018)

11. Jin, H., Hou, L., Li, J., Dong, T.: Attributed and predictive entity embedding for fine-grained entity typing in knowledge bases. In: 27th International Conference on Computational Linguistics (2018)

12. Jin, H., Hou, L., Li, J., Dong, T.: Fine-grained entity typing via hierarchical multi graph convolutional networks. In: Empirical Methods in Natural Language Processing and the 9th International Joint Conference on Natural Language Processing (2019)

13. Jr., C.N.S., Freitas, A.A.: A survey of hierarchical classification across different application domains. Data Min. Knowl. Discov. **22**(1–2), 31–72 (2011). https://doi.org/10.1007/s10618-010-0175-9

14. Keikha, M.M., Rahgozar, M., Asadpour, M.: Community aware random walk for network embedding. Knowl.-Based Syst. **148**, 47–54 (2018)

15. Lin, Y., Liu, Z., Sun, M., Liu, Y., Zhu, X.: Learning entity and relation embeddings for knowledge graph completion. In: Twenty-ninth AAAI Conference on Artificial Intelligence (2015)

16. Ling, W., Dyer, C., Black, A.W., Trancoso, I.: Two/too simple adaptations of word2vec for syntax problems. In: NAACL HLT 2015, pp. 1299–1304. ACL (2015)

17. Melo, A., Paulheim, H., Völker, J.: Type prediction in RDF knowledge bases using hierarchical multilabel classification. In: WIMS (2016)

18. Mikolov, T., Chen, K., Corrado, G., Dean, J.: Efficient estimation of word representations in vector space. arXiv preprint arXiv:1301.3781 (2013)

19. Mikolov, T., Sutskever, I., Chen, K., Corrado, G., Dean, J.: Distributed representations of words and phrases and their compositionality. arXiv preprint arXiv:1310.4546 (2013)

20. Paulheim, H., Bizer, C.: Type inference on noisy RDF data. In: ISWC (2013)

21. Perozzi, B., Kulkarni, V., Chen, H., Skiena, S.: Don't walk, skip! online learning of multi-scale network embeddings. In: Proceedings of the 2017 IEEE/ACM International Conference on Advances in Social Networks Analysis and Mining 2017, pp. 258–265 (2017)

22. Portisch, J., Hladik, M., Paulheim, H.: Kgvec2go - knowledge graph embeddings as a service. In: Calzolari, N., et al. (eds.) Proceedings of The 12th Language Resources and Evaluation Conference, LREC 2020, Marseille, France, 11–16 May 2020, pp. 5641–5647. European Language Resources Association (2020). https://aclanthology.org/2020.lrec-1.692/

23. Portisch, J., Hladik, M., Paulheim, H.: Rdf2vec light - A lightweight approach for knowledge graph embeddings. In: Taylor, K.L., Gonçalves, R.S., Lécué, F.,

Yan, J. (eds.) Proceedings of the ISWC 2020 Demos and Industry Tracks: From Novel Ideas to Industrial Practice co-located with 19th International Semantic Web Conference (ISWC 2020), Globally online, 1–6 Nov 2020 (UTC). CEUR Workshop Proceedings, vol. 2721, pp. 79–84. CEUR-WS.org (2020). http://ceur-ws.org/Vol-2721/paper520.pdf

24. Portisch, J., Paulheim, H.: Putting rdf2vec in order. In: Seneviratne, O., Pesquita, C., Sequeda, J., Etcheverry, L. (eds.) Proceedings of the ISWC 2021 Posters, Demos and Industry Tracks: From Novel Ideas to Industrial Practice co-located with 20th International Semantic Web Conference (ISWC 2021), Virtual Conference, 24–28 October 2021. CEUR Workshop Proceedings, vol. 2980. CEUR-WS.org (2021). http://ceur-ws.org/Vol-2980/paper352.pdf

25. Portisch, J., Paulheim, H.: Walk this way! entity walks and property walks for rdf2vec. CoRR abs/2204.02777 (2022)

26. Reimers, N., Gurevych, I.: Sentence-bert: Sentence embeddings using siamese bert-networks. In: Proceedings of the 2019 Conference on Empirical Methods in Natural Language Processing and the 9th International Joint Conference on Natural Language Processing, EMNLP-IJCNLP (2019)

27. Ristoski, P., Rosati, J., Noia, T.D., Leone, R.D., Paulheim, H.: Rdf2vec: RDF graph embeddings and their applications. Semantic Web **10**(4), 721–752 (2019). https://doi.org/10.3233/SW-180317

28. Schlichtkrull, M., Kipf, T.N., Bloem, P., Van Den Berg, R., Titov, I., Welling, M.: Modeling relational data with graph convolutional networks. In: Proceedings of the European Semantic Web Conference (2018)

29. Schlötterer, J., Wehking, M., Rizi, F.S., Granitzer, M.: Investigating extensions to random walk based graph embedding. In: 2019 IEEE International Conference on Cognitive Computing (ICCC), pp. 81–89. IEEE (2019)

30. Suchanek, F.M., Kasneci, G., Weikum, G.: Yago: a core of semantic knowledge. In: Williamson, C.L., Zurko, M.E., Patel-Schneider, P.F., Shenoy, P.J. (eds.) Proceedings of the 16th International Conference on World Wide Web, WWW 2007, Banff, Alberta, Canada, 8–12 May 2007, pp. 697–706. ACM (2007). https://doi.org/10.1145/1242572.1242667

31. Tong, P., Zhang, Q., Yao, J.: Leveraging domain context for question answering over knowledge graph. Data Sci. Eng. **4**, 323–335 (2019)

32. Vrandečić, D., Krötzsch, M.: Wikidata: a free collaborative knowledgebase. Commun. ACM **57**, 78–85 (2014)

33. Wang, X., Wang, D., Xu, C., He, X., Cao, Y., Chua, T.S.: Explainable reasoning over knowledge graphs for recommendation. In: Proceedings of the AAAI Conference on Artificial Intelligence (2019)

34. Weller, T., Acosta, M.: Predicting instance type assertions in knowledge graphs using stochastic neural networks. In: Proceedings of the 30th ACM International Conference on Information & Knowledge Management, pp. 2111–2118 (2021)

35. Wilcke, W., Bloem, P., de Boer, V., van't Veer, R., van Harmelen, F.: End-to-end entity classification on multimodal knowledge graphs. arXiv (2020)

36. Xu, B., Zhang, Y., Liang, J., Xiao, Y., Hwang, S., Wang, W.: Cross-lingual type inference. In: Database Systems for Advanced Applications - 21st International Conference, DASFAA (2016)

37. Yaghoobzadeh, Y., Adel, H., Schütze, H.: Corpus-level fine-grained entity typing. J. Artif. Intell. Res. **61** (2018)

38. Yaghoobzadeh, Y., Schütze, H.: Multi-level representations for fine-grained typing of knowledge base entities. In: 15th Conference of the European Chapter of the Association for Computational Linguistics (2017)

39. Zhang, X., Zhao, J.J., LeCun, Y.: Character-level convolutional networks for text classification. In: Advances in Neural Information Processing Systems 28: Annual Conference on Neural Information Processing Systems (2015)

40. Zhao, Y., Zhang, A., Xie, R., Liu, K., Wang, X.: Connecting embeddings for knowledge graph entity typing. In: Proceedings of the 58th Annual Meeting of the Association for Computational Linguistics, pp. 6419–6428 (2020)

41. Zhuo, J., Zhu, Q., Yue, Y., Zhao, Y., Han, W.: A neighborhood-attention fine-grained entity typing for knowledge graph completion. In: Proceedings of the Fifteenth ACM International Conference on Web Search and Data Mining, pp. 1525–1533 (2022)

42. Zouaq, A., Martel, F.: What is the schema of your knowledge graph? leveraging knowledge graph embeddings and clustering for expressive taxonomy learning. In: Proceedings of the International Workshop on Semantic Big Data, pp. 1–6 (2020)

Strabo 2: Distributed Management of Massive Geospatial RDF Datasets

Dimitris Bilidas[1]([⊠]), Theofilos Ioannidis[1], Nikos Mamoulis[2], and Manolis Koubarakis[1]

[1] National and Kapodistrian University of Athens, Athens, Greece
{d.bilidas,tioannid,koubarak}@di.uoa.gr
[2] University of Ioannina, Ioannina, Greece
nikos@cs.uoi.gr

Abstract. We present STRABO 2, a distributed geospatial RDF store able to process GeoSPARQL queries over massive RDF datasets. STRABO 2 is based on robust technologies, able to scale on TBs of data distributed on hundreds of nodes. Specifically, we use the Spark framework, enhanced with the geospatial library SEDONA, for distributed in-memory processing on Hadoop clusters, and Hive for compact persistent storage of RDF data. STRABO 2 employs a flexible design that can store and partition thematic RDF data using different relational schemas, and spatial data in a separate Hive table, by taking into consideration the GeoSPARQL vocabulary. STRABO 2 is cluster friendly both memory and disk-wise, since it compresses triples using a partial encoding technique in addition to Parquet data file format compression schemes. GeoSPARQL queries are translated into the Spark SQL dialect, enhanced with the spatial functions and predicates offered by SEDONA. During this process the system takes into consideration SEDONA's capabilities for both spatial selections and spatial joins, in order to apply optimizations that result in efficient query processing. We experimentally test STRABO 2 on an award winning Hadoop based cluster environment and exhibit STRABO 2's excellent scalability while handling massive synthetic and real world datasets. We also show that STRABO 2 clearly outperforms state of the art centralized engines in a single server setup, once the dataset size increases beyond few GBs.

1 Introduction

As the spatial information in the web of linked data has been increasing steadily over the past decade, many systems that perform geospatial processing over RDF graphs have been developed, mainly targeting the GeoSPARQL vocabulary and query language, an OGC standard for representing and querying spatial information in RDF. At the same time, as large RDF datasets become available, the need for distributed processing of SPARQL queries has lead to the development of many RDF query engines that rely on big data tools and technologies for storing and processing massive RDF data. Some of the most prominent approaches

U. Sattler et al. (Eds.): ISWC 2022, LNCS 13489, pp. 411–427, 2022.
https://doi.org/10.1007/978-3-031-19433-7_24

rely on distributed in-memory big data frameworks, mainly Apache Spark, like for example S2RDF [23] and PRoST [7].

However, despite the importance of the spatial dimension of these massive datasets, to the best of our knowledge none of the distributed RDF engines supports execution of spatial queries. This leads to a lack of spatial RDF engines able to scale to the continously increasing spatial information in the linked data cloud. For example, the state-of-the art geospatial RDF store Strabon can only handle up to 100GBs of point data and still be able to answer simple geospatial queries (selections over a rectangular area) efficiently (in a few seconds). Competitor systems like GraphDB perform similarly. If the complexity of geometries in the dataset increases (i.e., we have multi-polygons), not even the aforementioned performance can be achieved for both Strabon and GraphDB.

Reviewing benchmarks with big geospatial semantic datasets [15] for mature centralized RDF stores reveal the shortcomings of this category of systems handling large datasets (range of few GBs of size). In sum, the main shortcomings of such systems include: i) high bulk loading times, with mostly single threaded reading, usually one file at a time, followed by single-thread re-indexing. ii) only DBMS-based RDF stores seem to be able to marginally handle spatial selections and spatial joins against datasets of several GBs size and this depends very much on the DMBS tuning and iii) mostly single-threaded implementations of algorithms [18] and components, leaves unexploited the potential of these systems to vertically scale to the maximum of their potential on a regular multi-core server-grade single node. This is even more true for open source or free versions of these systems. Some commercial systems offer limited parallelization only in some of their components, i.e., bulk loaders in Ontotext GraphDB Free and offer full multi-threaded capabilities in their licensed product versions.

To address the above limitations, the main contributions of this work are:

- We present STRABO 2, the first distributed system that is able to process GeoSPARQL queries over massive geospatial RDF datasets on Spark clusters.
- We present a flexible design that can store thematic RDF data using different relational schemas, and spatial data in a separate Hive table, by taking into consideration the GeoSPARQL vocabulary. We use the query translation mechanism of Ontop-spatial in order to obtain the final set of spatial SQL queries from the initial GeoSPARQL query.
- We optimize the translation process based on spatial joins and also use the spatial partitioning and indexing capabilities of the Apache Sedona library in order to achieve efficient query execution.
- We present an extensive experimental evaluation in order to examine the scalability of the system with respect to different query characteristics, like the spatial and thematic selectivities. We also compare the system with state of the art centralized solutions for smaller datasets that can be ingested and processed by single-node installations.

2   Related Work

In this section we present related work. The examination of the capabilities and design choices of the systems we presented were taken into consideration in the definition of the architecture of the STRABO 2 distributed GeoSPARQL engine.

Centralized GeoSPARQL Query Processing. Strabon is one of the first systems offering GeoSPARQL support. Strabon extends the well-known RDF store Sesame and uses the PostGIS spatially-enabled DBMS as the backend. GraphDB[1] is a semantic graph database enhanced with geospatial capabilities. For its geospatial capabilities, it relies on a uSeekM implementation and Lucene Spatial. The spatial index mechanism is controlled through an optional GeoSPARQL plugin. Other geospatial RDF stores include: Parliament [3] which uses a standard R-tree as its spatial index and concentrates on optimizing query patterns (using the Topology Vocabulary extension of GeoSPARQL) while it omits optimization for functions in the filter clause of a query, Oracle Spatial and Graph which supports the GeoSPARQL standard and also uses an R-Tree and Stardog, a popular knowledge graph platform that allows the use of custom connectors in order to enable geospatial support.

A detailed comparative study of centralized geospatial RDF stores is [14], where different systems were benchmarked and evaluated with datasets of up to 90 GB size. Strabon [19] achieves the best overall score in most scenarios, such as the macro and scalability, whereas GraphDB[2] also performed very well on bulk loading and certain types of queries. These results motivated us to use Strabon and GraphDB as the baseline systems for the performance comparison with the new distributed implementation we are presenting in Sect. 3.

Apart from triple stores that store and query RDF graphs, GeoSPARQL querying is also supported in the context of Ontology-Based Data Access (OBDA), where data are stored in a spatially-enabled RDBMS, and GeoSPARQL to SQL translation is performed by the system in order to delegate query processing to the underlying database. Ontop-spatial [4], a geospatial extension of Ontop [6], was the first OBDA system able to answer GeoSPARQL queries on top of geospatial relational databases, performing on-the-fly GeoSPARQL-to-SQL translation using ontologies and mappings. The aim of Ontop-spatial is to allow integrating multiple geospatial sources, without converting, materializing and persisting original data as RDF. More recently, support for the GeoSPARQL query language has also been added to the main Ontop branch since version 4.1[3].

SPARQL Query Processing in the Cloud. The increasing size of available RDF data has exceeded the capacity of single node systems. As a result, a large number of approaches for querying RDF graphs in the cloud rely on existing robust and widely used distributed data processing frameworks [17]. Among these systems, in-memory distributed data processing frameworks, and especially Spark,

---

[1] http://graphdb.ontotext.com/documentation/free/.

[2] http://graphdb.ontotext.com/documentation/free/.

[3] https://ontop-vkg.org/guide/releases.html#_4-1-0-february-28-2021.

are amongst the most prominent and fast solutions for SPARQL processing. For example S2RDF [23] uses Spark to precompute specific semi-joins, PRoST [7] explores different storage strategies for RDF data as tabular data used by Spark, such as a single triples table, vertical partitioning and property tables. [2] extend the work of PRoST by examining several processing option in Spark. SPAR-QLGX [11] compiles triple patterns of a SPARQL query into operations over Spark's resilient distributed datasets (RDDs). S2RDF and PRoST are the more relevant systems to our approach, as they employ query translation in order to transform each SPARQL query into an SQL query that is executed using the corresponding API offered by Spark.

Parallel and Distributed Geospatial Query Processing. The first systems for distributed spatial query processing on the Hadoop ecosystem were implemented as extensions of the MapReduce paradigm, such as SpatialHadoop [9], Hadoop-GIS [1], and Parallel Secondo [20]. Hadoop provides a fault tolerant environment for parallel execution, but storing intermediate results to disk according to MapReduce increases the execution time for spatial operations. Hence, the in-memory execution model of Spark became very popular as it reduces the execution time drastically, compared to MapReduce jobs [12]. Following this trend, many Spark-based systems included geospatial support, most notable of which are the systems STARK [13], GeoSpark/Sedona [26,27], Magellan [24] and Spatial-Spark [25]. In the context of this work, we will only consider the Spark-based systems as they reportedly achieve better performance [12,13] than the Hadoop-based systems. Eldawy and Mokbel have presented a survey paper and tutorial on these systems [8,10].

The above systems have also been compared regarding their functionality in [22]. GeoSpark/Sedona is found to be the most complete system, both in terms of functionality and performance, as it now offers support for spatial datatypes such as points, rectangles, polygons and lines, and spatial operations such as different kinds of spatial joins (e.g., contains, intersects, touches, overlaps) and distance-based joins. It supports several partitioning techniques such as Equal-grid, Hilbert, R-Tree, Voronoi and Quad-Tree. Spatial indexes like R-Tree or Quad-Tree are provided in the Spatial Query Processing layer. Sedona's index can be persisted either in memory or in disk for later use from the same program. It can be used via its Java or Scala API and also via an SQL interface that expands Spark SQL. Finally, Sedona is currently an Apache incubating project[4] and it is actively maintained and enhanced[5].

Finally, to the best of our knowledge, the only system that deals with a form of distributed spatial RDF processing is the DiStRDF system [21]. DistRDF accepts SPARQL queries, along with a set of spatial and temporal constraints for each query. DistRDDF does not support the GeoSPARQL language, it only considers point geometries and the user can only express a spatial range query for a given box or circle. In contrast, STRABO 2 accepts GeoSPARQL queries,

---

[4] https://sedona.apache.org/.
[5] https://github.com/apache/incubator-sedona/.

supports different kinds of geometries, and besides spatial range queries, it also supports spatial joins and distance-based joins queries defined in the GeoSPARQL language.

3   The Strabo 2 System for Distributed GeoSPARQL Processing

In this section we present the technical details of the Strabo 2 system, starting with its architecture, which is shown in Fig. 1.

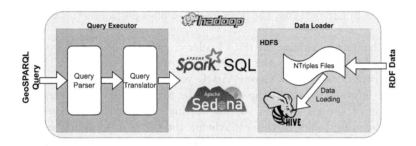

Fig. 1. Architectural overview of Strabo 2

The system consists of two main modules: the data loader and the query executor. The data loader is shown in the right part of Fig. 1 and is responsible for reading and importing into a HIVE database the RDF files from the file system. The query executor module accepts the input GeoSPARQL queries, and it performs query translation. The result of this process is a series of Spark SQL queries that also contain spatial functions provided by the Sedona library.

3.1   Data Loader

The Strabo 2 data loader imports RDF graphs encoded with N-Triples serialization, in Text or Parquet files located in multiple folders. The tool works very well with partitioned files (Text or Parquet) which further speeds up ingestion. The output of the loading process is a set of tables in a Hive database.

The parameters of the data loader are the following: (i) The name of the output Hive database. (ii) Selecting the relational schema for the thematic data. Currently only vertical partitioning and a single triples table are supported. (iii) Optional physical partitioning on the columns of the created tables. (iv) Using HiveQL or Spark SQL dataframe API as the data definition language. (v) Hive table format: Parquet is the default file format, as it is highly efficient and also uses columnar compression, which results in decreased size. (vi) A JSON file with common IRI namespace prefixes related to the ingested dataset.

The Common Prefixes JSON file is constructed manually per imported dataset. This file guides the partial dictionary encoding of the IRIs at a later stage and, at the very least, it should contain common namespace prefixes from XML, RDF, RDFS and GeoSPARQL vocabularies which are encountered in many datasets. The data loader uses the common namespace prefixes in `nsprefixes`, it applies partial dictionary encoding on all IRIs of thematic and spatial RDDs. This effectively simulates the main part of an N-Triples to Turtle conversion with the emphasis being on achieving a substantial first-level compression of the ingested dataset. After the initial parsing to Spark RDD, the data loader proceeds with the inference of the geospatial WKT serialization predicates which are consequently persisted to the `aswktprops(value)` Hive table. The process involves searching for triples matching the triple pattern (`?s rdfs:subPropertyOf geo:asWKT`) and using the matching subject `?s` as a geospatial property. Finally, using the common namespace prefixes in `nsprefixes`, the data loader applies partial dictionary encoding on all IRIs.

After the initial loading, the data loader creates the *geometry linking tables*, aiming to achieve efficient spatial processing during query execution. These tables take into consideration the GeoSPARQL vocabulary in order to store in the same table information about the entities, the corresponding geometries and the serialization of the geometries, so that during query execution joins between the corresponding tables of the VP schema (or the corresponding self joins on the single triples table) can be avoided. Also, during this step, for these tables, the loader creates the binary geometry column from the serializations, using the `ST_GeomFromText` function of Sedona. The geometry linking tables are created as follows. For each VP table that corresponds to some subproperty of the GeoSPARQL `hasGeometry` property, we compute the object-subject join with any other table that corresponds to some subproperty of the GeoSPARQL `hasSerialization` property.

As an example consider the following triples, where we have omitted the full IRIs for ease of presentation. The example comes from a sea ice mapping using satellite images application that we have implemented using STRABO 2 in the context of European project ExtremeEarth[6]. *Drift ice* is sea ice that is not attached to the shoreline or any other fixed object (shoals, grounded icebergs, etc.). Unlike fast ice, which is "fastened" to a fixed object, drift ice is carried along by winds and sea currents, hence its name.[7]

```
Ice1 type IceObservation .      Ice1 hasCT "Drift Ice" .
Ice1 observationGeom Geo1 .     Geo1 asWKT "POINT (10 10)" .
Img1 type SatelliteImage .      Img1 imageGeom Geo2 .
Geo2 asWKT "POLYGON (8 8, 12 8, 12 12, 8 12, 8 8 )" .
```

According to the VP schema, a separate table corresponding to each distinct predicate will be created in Hive. These are the first five tables shown in Fig. 2. Also, in this example, the properties `imageGeom` and `observationGeom` are subproperties of the GeoSPARQL `hasGeometry` property, and the property `asWKT` is a GeoSPARQL property that is subproperty of `hasSerialization`. As a result,

---

[6] https://earthanalytics.eu/.

[7] https://en.wikipedia.org/wiki/Drift_ice.

the geometry linking tables `observationGeom-asWKT` and `imageGeom-asWKT` will also be created.

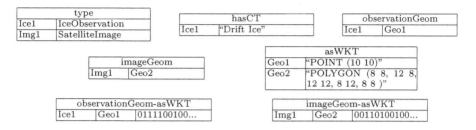

Fig. 2. Tables created in Hive

After data loading, during system startup, we also create in-memory spatial indexes on the geometry columns of the geometry linking tables. Due to the fact that clustered indexes cannot be defined when accessing Sedona from the SQL interface, we use the Scala/RDD interface. The following code is executed for each geometry linking table:

```
var spatialDf = _sqlContext.sql("SELECT entity,
    geometry, binary_geometry FROM observationGeom-asWKT")
spatialDf.registerTempTable(tableStat.tName)
spatialRDD = Adapter.toSpatialRdd(spatialDf, "binary_geometry")
spatialRDD.buildIndex(IndexType.QUADTREE, false)
spatialRDD.indexedRawRDD.persist(StorageLevel.MEMORY_AND_DISK);
```

3.2 Query Executor

The second module of STRABO 2 is the query executor shown in the left part of Fig. 1. The query executor accepts GeoSPARQL queries from the user, and transforms them to a series of Spark SQL queries that access the Hive tables (and in some cases the spatial RDD indexes) created by the loader. The spatial operators of GeoSPARQL are translated to corresponding spatial functions and predicates offered by the Apache Sedona library, which operates on top of the Spark engine. The translation mechanism of the query executor depends on the Ontop-spatial system [5]. Ontop-spatial is a system for GeoSPARQL-to-SQL query translation over arbitrary relational schemas, through the means of mappings defined in the W3C recommendation mapping language R2RML[8], that construct RDF terms from the database values.

In order to use Ontop-spatial for query translation in the query executor module of STRABO 2, we had to perform several modifications and improvements in order to use Spark as a backend and work with the RDF data stored in Hive. First of all, as in our case the data loader stores the data according to

---

[8] https://www.w3.org/TR/r2rml/.

a specific storage schema, we had to provide mappings that reconstruct the original RDF triple for each tuple in the Hive tables. In the normal setup of Ontop-spatial, the user has to manually construct the mappings. In our case, as the Hive schema is predetermined from the loader, we can avoid this process and instead, during system startup, automatically construct the mappings for the thematic and the geometry linking tables. As an example, consider the table hasCT of Fig. 2 constructed from the data loader. The following mapping is generated and provided as input to the Ontop-spatial translation mechanism:

```
{subject} hasCT "{object}"^^<http://www.w3.org/2001/XMLSchema#string> <-
    SELECT subject, object FROM hasCT
```

The right-hand side of the mapping is a SQL query that can be executed by Spark, whereas the left-hand side is a template that defines how triples should be generated, using the output columns of the SQL query within curly brackets. Ontop-spatial takes as input a set of such mappings and accesses the metadata of the database in order to gather necessary information that will guide the query translation. Again, as Spark is not compatible with the Ontop-spatial system, we provide the specific metadata automatically, during system start-up, using information from the Hive created tables. This information includes the tables that reside in the database, the data types of each column and information about primary keys. As in the case of the mappings, this information is constructed automatically by STRABO 2.

Once Ontop-spatial has been provided with the set of mappings and the metadata, it is ready to accept GeoSPARQL queries. The input GeoSPARQL query is initially parsed and transformed in an intermediate form, based on logic programs, and finally into SQL queries on the dialect of Spark SQL. During this procedure, the spatial operators of GeoSPARQL are transformed to spatial functions and predicates provided by Apache Sedona. Currently, we support the translation of all simple features relations of GeoSPARQL, and also of the GeoSPARQL functions, including the distance function, that corresponds to distance based joins in Sedona. In order to demonstrate query translation, consider the following initial GeoSPARQL query:

```
SELECT ?img WHERE {
?observation type IceObservation .
?observation hasCT "Drift Ice"^^<http://www.w3.org/2001/XMLSchema#string> .
?observation observationGeom ?obsGeo .   ?g1 geo:asWKT ?obsWKT .
?img type SatelliteImage .   ?img imageGeom ?imgGeo .   ?imgGeo asWKT ?imgWKT .
FILTER (geof:sfIntersects(?obsWKT, ?imgWKT)). }
```

This query asks for satellite images, such that the geometry of the image intersects with the geometry of an observation that has class type drift ice. The query uses the GeoSPARQL topological relation geof:sfIntersects with arguments the corresponding geometries. Default query translation will produce the following query that will be sent for execution to the Spark engine, where function ST_Intersects is defined in the Apache Sedona library:

```
SELECT qview5.subject AS img
FROM  type qview1, hasCT qview2, observationGeom qview3, asWKT qview4,
      type qview5, imageGeom qview6, asWKT qview7
WHERE
 qview1.object = 'IceObservation' AND qview2.object = 'Drift Ice' AND
 qview1.subject = qview2.subject AND qview1.subject = qview3.subject AND
 qview3.object = qview4.subject AND qview5.object = 'SatelliteImage' AND
 qview5.subject = qview6.subject AND qview6.object = qview7.subject AND
 ST_Intersects(ST_GeoFromText(qview4.object),ST_GeoFromText(qview7.object))
```

Using Geometry Linking Tables. The default translation only uses the tables of the VP schema. In order to obtain a more efficient query, during translation we identify joins between subproperties of hasGeometry and hasSerialization. According to the GeoSPARQL vocabulary, in order to access the geometry serialization of an entity, the query needs to contain two triple patterns. The first pattern relates the entity with its geometry though the hasGeometry property (or a subproperty), and the second pattern relates the geometry with a serialization through the hasSerialization property (or a subproperty). By taking advantage of the fact that such joins between triple patterns usually occur in GeoSPARQL queries, and having computed the corresponding geometry linking tables during import, we can save one join if we replace the access to the two tables, with access to the corresponding geometry linking table. In our example query, we identify two such cases, one for the join between observationGeom and asWKT, and the second one for the join between imageGeom and asWKT. The optimized SQL query is shown below, and it contains two less joins from the default translation.

```
SELECT qview4.subject AS img
FROM type qview1, hasCT qview2, observationGeom-asWKT qview3,
     type qview4, imageGeom-asWKT qview5
WHERE
qview1.object = 'IceObservation' AND qview2.object = 'Drift Ice' AND
qview1.subject = qview2.subject AND qview1.subject = qview3.entity AND
qview4.object = 'SatelliteImage' AND qview4.subject = qview5.entity AND
ST_Intersects(qview3.binary,qview5.binary)
```

Pushing Thematic Processing Before Spatial Joins. The query produced so far is optimized in the sense that it avoids extra thematic joins between the geometry related tables, but it still contains a spatial join that poses a potentially heavy burden on the execution engine. The reason for that is that in order to perform the spatial join, Sedona will either perform a distributed GSJoin algorithm, where it will spatially partition the two input operands of the join, and also create a local spatial index at each partition, or, if the datasets are small, it will perform a broadcast join algorithm, where it will partition the larger input, and it will replicate the smaller [27]. In any case, the spatial join will lead to data shuffling and computationally heavy processing. Also, the Spark catalyst optimizer treats the spatial UDF as a black box, as it does not take into consideration the cost of the spatial partitioning and indexing, and in many cases it will not optimally optimize the produced query with respect to the join order of the operators. For this reason, in STRABO 2 query translator we follow a heuristic that aims at minimizing the size of input operands of the spatial join. Specifically, we push thematic processing before the spatial join operators in the final produced query. The rationale is that thematic processing on each side of the spatial join input will limit the size of the intermediate result that has to be spatially partitioned and indexed. In our example query, for the input that corresponds to ice observations, we will first apply the filter that ensures that we only need resources about ice observations, we will perform the thematic join corresponding to the hasCT predicate and also the filter that ensures that the classification result is drift ice. This will limit the number of geometries that need to be processed, in contrast with a bad execution plan, where, for example, we first partition all geometries and then perform the join corresponding to the hasCT predicate and filter out the observations that correspond to drift ice. In order to ensure the execution plan according to our heuristic, we identify spatial joins during the translation process, and then we decompose the result in different subqueries, that are sequentially sent for execution. In our example, we will first produce two subqueries that create temporary views corresponding to the two inputs of the spatial join, and one final query that performs the spatial join between these two intermediate results:

```
CREATE TEMPORARY VIEW TEMP1 AS
SELECT qview3.binary as qview3_binary
FROM type qview1, hasCT qview2, observationGeom-asWKT qview3,
WHERE
qview1.object = 'IceObservation' AND qview2.object = 'Drift Ice' AND
qview1.subject = qview2.subject AND qview1.subject = qview3.entity

CREATE TEMPORARY VIEW TEMP2 AS
SELECT qview5.binary as qview5_binary, qview4.subject as qview4_subject
FROM type qview4, imageGeom-asWKT qview5
WHERE
qview4.object = 'SatelliteImage' AND qview4.subject = qview5.entity

SELECT TEMP2.qview4_subject AS img
FROM TEMP1, TEMP2
WHERE ST_Intersects(TEMP1.qview3_binary,TEMP2.qview5_binary)
```

Using Persistent Spatial Indexing and Partitioning. As described in Sect. 3.1, both thematic and spatial RDF data are stored in disk in a Hive database according to the specified schema and the geometry linking tables of the dataset. During query execution, the Spark execution engine loads the necessary fragments of thematic data in memory. Geometries have the same treatment. In case of spatial selection, we have to read the geometries from the disk, build an in-memory spatial index and/or partitioning during query execution time and discard this index/partitioning afterwards. If the next query is again a spatial selection, this process has to be repeated. Unfortunately, this is an inherent issue of Apache Sedona when we access it from the SQL interface, due to the fact that clustered indexes cannot be defined in Spark SQL. In order to take advantage of persistent spatial indexes and partitioning, we have implemented a hybrid translation to both the SQL and RDD/Scala interface, that accesses the cached spatial RDDs that have been created during import. Then, for each query, we modify the intermediate translation that is in the form of a logic program rule, before the final translation into SQL, by identifying spatial FILTER clauses that can be evaluated efficiently using the spatial index, and then by replacing the atoms corresponding to the specific spatial operation by temporary atoms that correspond to the intermediate result after accessing the persistent spatial structure. As an example, consider a query that asks for ice observations and the class name assigned to them, such that their geometries intersect a given polygon:

```
SELECT ?x ?ctName
WHERE { ?x type IceObservation . ?x hasCT ?ctName .
        ?x hasGeometry ?geo1 .   ?geo1 asWKT ?wkt .
FILTER(geof:sfIntersects(?wkt,"POLYGON((1 0,3 0,4 4,1 0))"^^geo:wktLiteral)).}
```

The translation result without using the spatial RDD that has been created during import, is the following:

```
SELECT qview1.subject AS x, qview2.object AS ctName
FROM type qview1, hasCT qview2, observationGeom-asWKT qview3,
WHERE
qview1.object = 'IceObservation' AND qview1.subject = qview2.subject AND
qview1.subject = qview3.entity AND
ST_Intersects(qview3.binary,POLYGON((1 0,3 0,4 4,1 0)))
```

By identifying the spatial filter during the transaltion, we can see that we can use the spatialRDD for its evaluation. In order to do that, we are replacing access to table `observationGeom-asWKT` with a new temporary table, that corresponds to the result of the access to the spatial index. First, we access the spatial index and take the result of the intersection with the given polygon, transform the result into a dataframe and save it in the temporary table with name `temp`.

```
val rangeQueryWindow = wktReader.read("POLYGON((1 0,3 0,4 4,1 0))")
val considerBoundaryIntersection = true
val usingIndex = true
var queryResult = RangeQuery.SpatialRangeQuery(spatialRDD,
        rangeQueryWindow,considerBoundaryIntersection, usingIndex)
Adapter.toDf(queryResult).createGlobalTempView("temp")
```

Finally, we issue the following SQL query, that accesses the temporary result instead of the table `observationGeom-asWKT`:

```
SELECT qview1.subject AS x, qview2.object AS ctName
FROM type qview1, hasCT qview2, temp qview3,
WHERE qview1.object = 'IceObservation'
AND qview1.subject = qview2.subject AND qview1.subject = qview3.entity
```

4   Experimental Results

In this section we present the experimental evaluation of STRABO 2, with three main objectives. First, we evaluate the system as a whole, including the ability to scale with respect to the cluster and dataset size. Second, we evaluate specific aspects of the system, and importantly the impact of the improvements and optimizations. Last, as STRABO 2 is the first distributed system able to handle geospatial queries on RDF graphs, we compare the performance of STRABO 2 with that of existing centralized GeoSPARQL processing systems in a single server environment.

4.1   Datasets and Queries

We have used the following datasets and queries: (i) *Scalability Workload.* This is a real-world dataset based on Open Street Maps from the Geographica 2 benchmark, which features a set of increasingly larger datasets (up tom 500M triples) and a queryset of 3 queries: 1 spatial selection (SC1) and 2 spatial joins (SC2, SC3). (ii) *PregenSynthetic Workload.* This is based on the synthetic workload of the Geographica 2 benchmark, but it has been modified so that it now uses a distributed Spark-based generator. (iii) *ExtremeEarth Workload.* This is a real-world dataset accompanied by 12 GeoSPARQL queries that were produced after analyzing end-user needs from the use cases of the project. The queries use a combination of spatial selections and spatial joins (including distance joins). The dataset has a size of 32 GB in N-Triples format.

4.2   Results in Distributed Environment

The experiments were carried out in a cluster provided by CREODIAS[9] consisting of 53 virtual processing cores and 164 GB of RAM. The Hopsworks platform v. 2.1.0 was used as the execution environment[10] providing access to an underlying Hadoop v. 3.2.0 installation with Spark v. 2.4.3 and Hive v. 3.0.0. Hopsworks is an open-source platform that provides an execution environment for distributed data science and data engineering tasks and extends Hadoop with an optimized distributed metadata architecture [16]. In the experiments, we set the number of shuffle partitions in STRABO 2 (Spark parameter `spark.sql.shuffle.partitions`) to be 5x the number of virtual cores in each setting.

As a first experiment, we determined the largest possible PregenSynthetic dataset that can be generated and imported in STRABO 2 using the aforementioned cluster, in order to stress the system given the available resources. As a result, we have generated the dataset for scaling factor 16384 and we have generated all the thematic tags. The size of the dataset is 156 GB in compressed Parquet format, which corresponds to an initial size of **1.16 TB** in N-Triples

---

[9] https://creodias.eu/.
[10] https://www.hopsworks.ai/.

text format. We have also generated 72 queries with spatial selectivities of 1%, 0.1% and 0.01% and thematic selectivities corresponding to values 4096, 8192 and 16384 (a thematic selectivity with value M means that one every M entitites is annotated with a thematic tag that has the corresponding value). We have used 22 executors with 6120 MB of memory and 2 virtual cores per executor. The data loader finished import in **4.5** hours. It is worth mentioning that, according to our experiments, this size of input datasets is much larger from what centralized geospatial RDF stores can ingest using a setup similar to the one described in Sect. 4.3. The total execution time for the 72 queries is **7711** seconds, which gives an average execution time of **107** seconds per query. The queries and the execution time for each query can be found in the supplemental material. We have also used 12 executors with 2 virtual cores with 4096 MB memory each, in order to execute the 12 queries from the ExtremeEarth dataset. The data loader in this case executed the import in **34** minutes. The average execution time was **122** seconds.

In further experiments, and in order to evaluate the specific aspects and improvements in query execution we have used the PregenSynthetic generator to generate a dataset with scale factor 1024 and queries for spatial selectivities of 1%, 0.1% and 0.01% and thematic selectivities corresponding to values 256, 512 and 1024. As before, we generate all thematic tags. In total we have generated 72 queries. We use 4 worker nodes, each one with 2 virtual cores and 4096 MB of memory. First, in order to evaluate the impact of the hybrid translation with persistent spatial index and partitioning, as described in Sect. 3.2, we have executed the 18 queries that contain a spatial selection with and without the spatial index. The total execution time when using the persistent spatial index and partitioning, drops from **111 s to 54 s**, leading to a reduction in execution time of more than 50%. The exact execution times are included in the supplemental material.

We also executed the spatial join queries using the default translation, in order to compare it with the optimized translation that pushes the thematic processing before spatial joins. In all cases the optimized translation was much faster, in some cases, especially for queries with few results, more than **10x**. The reason for that is that the Spark catalyst optimizer, when it takes as input the default translation query, it chooses to partition and index all the geometries on the geometry linking tables for the left side of the spatial join. We have also executed queries with thematic selectivity equal to 1. In this case the thematic processing does not filter out any values. In this extreme scenario, the default translation performs similarly with the optimized one.

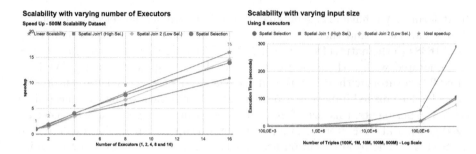

Fig. 3. Scalability of STRABO 2 with varying number of executors (left) and varying dataset size (right)

Regarding the ability of the system to scale in the distributed setting, we used the Scalability Workload and the results are presented in Fig. 3. In the left side of the picture we have used the 500M dataset and executed the three queries with 1, 2, 4, 8 and 16 executors. In the right side we use 8 executors with the datasets from 100K to 500M triples. In both cases each executor had two cores and 6600 MB of memory. In the plots we also show the ideal speedup/linear scalability. In both experiments STRABO 2 exhibits very good behavior for both spatial selection and spatial join queries as in both scenarios, the spatial selection and the low selectivity join exhibit scaling very close to linear. The most difficult query to scale is the high selectivity join where large intermediate results needs to be saved, but even in this case the improvement as we add more executors is substantial.

4.3   Results in Centralized Environment

In order to perform a comparison between centralized RDF stores and STRABO 2, we selected the two most competitive systems from the Geographica 2 benchmark, namely Strabon and GraphDB. For Strabon we used v3.3.2-SNAPSHOT and for GraphDB v9.10.3. The test server was a Dell Inc PowerEdge R820 with 128 GB, with an Intel(R) Xeon(R) CPU E5-4603 v2 @ 2.20 GHz with 32 execution threads, running Ubuntu 18.04.6 LTS. The system also features a PostgreSQL v12.10 installation as it is required by Strabon and was appropriately tuned. For disk-based centralized systems we report both warm cache and cold cache times. For GraphDB the `Preload` loading tool was used for all repositories. For STRABO 2 we used Spark 2.4.5 and Hive 2.3.6. We also used all available processing threads and we set 116 GB of memory available to Spark, although even for the 500M dataset half of this amount was enough.

In this set of experiments we have used the Scalability Workload and the PregenSynthetic workload. For the latter, four increasingly bigger datasets were generated, with scaling factor N in {512, 768, 1024, 2048}. For each dataset the corresponding query set had two thematic tags to help achieve the least and maximum thematic selectivity and the spatial selectivity list was fixed to

(100%, 10%, 1%). The execution results for the scalability workload are shown in Fig. 4. From the two centralized systems, Strabon exhibits better performance. In comparison with Strabon, STRABO 2 performs worse for the small datasets, but once the datasets size is increased, especially for the 100M and 500M, STRABO 2 in most cases outperforms the centralized solutions. An important point is that both centralized systems scale poorly when we increase the dataset size beyond 10M triples. As an example, even in the warm cache setting for spatial join 1, where Strabon performs faster than STRABO 2 with execution time of 133.29 s, we have an increase of 10x in execution time from the 100M case, whereas the corresponding increase for STRABO 2 is 6x. Due to space limitation we omit the full results for the PregenSynthetic workload, which are available at the supplemental material, but the systems exhibit similar behaviour. Especially for the dataset with scaling factor of 2048, from the total 28 queries, GraphDB had **12 timeouts** and an average time of **82** and **45** seconds (cold and warm cache) for the 16 succeeded queries, whereas Strabon and STRABO 2 had no timeouts with average execution time of **134** and **105** seconds (cold and warm cache) from Strabon and only **28** seconds for STRABO 2.

Dataset	Query	GraphDB		Strabon		Strabo 2
		Cold (sec)	Warm (sec)	Cold (sec)	Warm (sec)	
100K	Spatial Selection	2.44	0.93	1.54	0.39	0.78
1M		10.60	7.62	5.84	3.83	1.08
10M		68.07	55.32	28.10	22.11	2.78
100M		553.37	556.03	246.82	165.70	15.54
500M		2,876.22	2,895.70	983.50	753.41	99.46
100K	Spatial Join 1 (High Selectivity)	52.39	53.58	0.67	0.08	2.35
1M		454.36	440.52	1.64	0.45	5.21
10M		3,941.93	3,972.95	7.26	2.34	12.54
100M		> 2h	-	50.30	13.75	28.44
500M		> 2h	-	575.94	133.29	172.80
100K	Spatial Join 2 (Low Selectivity)	21.41	20.45	0.59	0.08	2.15
1M		20.26	19.17	1.70	0.48	4.47
10M		87.21	84.80	10.67	2.57	6.54
100M		312.70	311.64	95.60	22.63	14.22
500M		> 2h	-	962.29	457.16	75.12

Fig. 4. Execution results for scalability workload

5   Conclusions and Future Work

We presented STRABO 2, the first distributed geosaptial RDF store, able to handle massive datasets beyond the capabilities of centralized systems. Through experimental evaluation, we showed that STRABO 2 is faster even in a single server environment, once the dataset size reaches several GBs, by taking advantage the parallel multi-threaded execution carried out by Spark. For future work we plan to cover the GeoSPARQL RCC8 and Egenhofer topological relations and the Query Rewrite Extension.

Supplemental Material Statement: STRABO 2 source code and exprimental results are publicly available[11]. Scalability and Synthetic workloads are avail-

---

[11] https://github.com/db-ee/Strabo-2.

able at the Geographica 2 website. ExtremeEarth datasets and queries can be found at the GitHub repository of the project[12].

Acknowledgements. This work has received funding from the European Union's Horizon 2020 research and innovation programme under GA No. 825258 (ExtremeEarth), GA No. 101016798 (AI4Copernicus), EU Horizon Europe GA No. 101070122 (STELAR), and from the Hellenic Foundation for Research and Innovation (H.F.R.I.) under the "First Call for H.F.R.I. Research Projects to support Faculty members and Researchers and the procurement of high-cost research equipment grant" (Project Number: HFRI-FM17-2351 GeoQA)

References

1. Aji, A., et al.: Hadoop GIS: a high performance spatial data warehousing system over mapreduce. Proc. VLDB Endowment **6**(11), 1009–1020 (2013)
2. Arrascue Ayala, V.A., et al.: Relational schemata for distributed SPARQL query processing. In: Proceedings of the International Workshop on Semantic Big Data, pp. 1–6 (2019)
3. Battle, R., Kolas, D.: Enabling the geospatial Semantic Web with Parliament and GeoSPARQL. Semantic Web **3**(4), 355–370 (2012)
4. Bereta, K., Koubarakis, M.: Ontop of geospatial databases. In: Groth, P., et al. (eds.) ISWC 2016. LNCS, vol. 9981, pp. 37–52. Springer, Cham (2016). https://doi.org/10.1007/978-3-319-46523-4_3
5. Bereta, K., Xiao, G., Koubarakis, M.: Ontop-spatial: ontop of geospatial databases. J. Web Semantics **58**, 100514 (2019)
6. Calvanese, D., et al.: Ontop: answering SPARQL queries over relational databases. Semantic Web **8**(3), 471–487 (2017)
7. Cossu, M., Färber, M., Lausen, G.: PRoST: distributed execution of SPARQL queries using mixed partitioning strategies. arXiv preprint arXiv:1802.05898 (2018)
8. Eldawy, A., Mokbel, M.F.: The era of big spatial data: a survey. Inf. Media Technol. **10**(2), 305–316 (2015)
9. Eldawy, A., Mokbel, M.F.: SpatialHadoop: a MapReduce framework for spatial data. In: 2015 IEEE 31st International Conference on Data Engineering, pp. 1352–1363. IEEE (2015)
10. Eldawy, A., Mokbel, M.F.: The era of big spatial data. In: Proceedings of the VLDB Endowment (2017)
11. Graux, D., Jachiet, L., Genevès, P., Layaïda, N.: SPARQLGX: efficient distributed evaluation of SPARQL with apache spark. In: Groth, P., et al. (eds.) ISWC 2016. LNCS, vol. 9982, pp. 80–87. Springer, Cham (2016). https://doi.org/10.1007/978-3-319-46547-0_9
12. Hagedorn, S., Götze, P., Sattler, K.U.: Big spatial data processing frameworks: feature and performance evaluation. In: EDBT, pp. 490–493 (2017)
13. Hagedorn, S., Räth, T.: Efficient spatio-temporal event processing with STARK. In: Proceedings of the 20th International Conference on Extending Database Technology, EDBT 2017, Venice, Italy, 21–24 March 2017, pp. 570–573 (2017). https://doi.org/10.5441/002/edbt.2017.72

---

[12] https://github.com/ExtremeEarth-Project.

14. Ioannidis, T., Garbis, G., Kyzirakos, K., Bereta, K., Koubarakis, M.: Evaluating geospatial RDF stores using the benchmark Geographica 2. arXiv preprint arXiv:1906.01933 (2019)
15. Ioannidis, T., Garbis, G., Kyzirakos, K., Bereta, K., Koubarakis, M.: Evaluating geospatial RDF stores using the benchmark geographica 2. J. Data Semantics **10**, 189–228 (2021)
16. Ismail, M., Gebremeskel, E., Kakantousis, T., Berthou, G., Dowling, J.: Hopsworks: improving user experience and development on hadoop with scalable, strongly consistent metadata. In: 2017 IEEE 37th International Conference on Distributed Computing Systems (ICDCS), pp. 2525–2528. IEEE (2017)
17. Kaoudi, Z., Manolescu, I.: RDF in the clouds: a survey. VLDB J. **24**(1), 67–91 (2015)
18. Kyzirakos, K., Alvanaki, F., Kersten, M.: In memory processing of massive point clouds for multi-core systems. In: Proceedings of the 12th International Workshop on Data Management on New Hardware, pp. 1–10 (2016)
19. Kyzirakos, K., Karpathiotakis, M., Koubarakis, M.: Strabon: a semantic geospatial DBMS. In: Cudré-Mauroux, P., et al. (eds.) ISWC 2012. LNCS, vol. 7649, pp. 295–311. Springer, Heidelberg (2012). https://doi.org/10.1007/978-3-642-35176-1_19
20. Lu, J., Güting, R.H.: Parallel secondo: boosting database engines with hadoop. In: 2012 IEEE 18th International Conference on Parallel and Distributed Systems, pp. 738–743. IEEE (2012)
21. Nikitopoulos, P., Vlachou, A., Doulkeridis, C., Vouros, G.A.: Parallel and scalable processing of spatio-temporal RDF queries using spark. GeoInformatica **25**(4), 623–653 (2021)
22. Pandey, V., Kipf, A., Neumann, T., Kemper, A.: How good are modern spatial analytics systems? Proc. VLDB Endowment **11**(11), 1661–1673 (2018)
23. Schätzle, A., Przyjaciel-Zablocki, M., Skilevic, S., Lausen, G.: S2RDF: RDF querying with SPARQL on spark. PVLDB **9**(10), 804–815 (2016)
24. Sriharsha, R.: Magellan: Geospatial Analytics Using Spark. https://github.com/harsha2010/magellan. Accessed 04 Nov 2019
25. You, S., Zhang, J., Gruenwald, L.: Large-scale spatial join query processing in cloud. In: 2015 31st IEEE International Conference on Data Engineering Workshops, pp. 34–41. IEEE (2015)
26. Yu, J., Wu, J., Sarwat, M.: Geospark: a cluster computing framework for processing large-scale spatial data. In: Proceedings of the 23rd SIGSPATIAL International Conference on Advances in Geographic Information Systems, p. 70. ACM (2015)
27. Yu, J., Zhang, Z., Sarwat, M.: Spatial data management in apache spark: the GeoSpark perspective and beyond. GeoInformatica **23**(1), 37–78 (2018). https://doi.org/10.1007/s10707-018-0330-9

Controlled Query Evaluation in OWL 2 QL: A "Longest Honeymoon" Approach

Piero Bonatti[1], Gianluca Cima[2], Domenico Lembo[3],
Lorenzo Marconi[3]([✉]), Riccardo Rosati[3], Luigi Sauro[1],
and Domenico Fabio Savo[4]

[1] Università di Napoli Federico II, Naples, Italy
{pab,luigi.sauro}@unina.it
[2] University of Bordeaux, CNRS, Bordeaux INP, LaBRI, Bordeaux, France
gianluca.cima@u-bordeaux.fr
[3] Sapienza Università di Roma, Rome, Italy
{lembo,marconi,rosati}@diag.uniroma1.it
[4] Università degli Studi di Bergamo, Bergamo, Italy
domenicofabio.savo@unibg.it

Abstract. Controlled Query Evaluation (CQE) has been recently studied in the context of Semantic Web ontologies. The goal of CQE is concealing some query answers so as to prevent external users from inferring confidential information. In general, there exist multiple, mutually incomparable ways of concealing answers, and previous CQE approaches choose in advance which answers are visible and which are not. In this paper, instead, we study a *dynamic* CQE method, namely, we propose to alter the answer to the current query based on the evaluation of previous ones. We aim at a system that, besides being able to protect confidential data, is maximally cooperative, which intuitively means that it answers affirmatively to as many queries as possible; it achieves this goal by delaying answer modifications as much as possible. We also show that the behavior we get cannot be intensionally simulated through a static approach, independent of query history. Interestingly, for OWL 2 QL ontologies and policy expressed through denials, query evaluation under our semantics is first-order rewritable, and thus in AC^0 in data complexity. This paves the way for the development of practical algorithms, which we also preliminarily discuss in the paper.

Keywords: Ontologies · Data protection · Description logics · First-order rewritability

1 Introduction

Semantic Web technologies are increasingly used to represent and link together different sources of information coming from public organizations as well as private citizens. This information may include sensitive knowledge, e.g. medical records or social network activities, whose disclosure may affect the privacy of

U. Sattler et al. (Eds.): ISWC 2022, LNCS 13489, pp. 428–444, 2022.
https://doi.org/10.1007/978-3-031-19433-7_25

individuals if not adequately protected [8, 16]. Furthermore, OWL 2 ontologies allow one to infer implicit information from explicit data, which amplifies the risk of information leakage.

One goal of confidentiality-preserving data publishing is to prevent the disclosure of sensitive information to unauthorized users while being as cooperative as possible, that is, answering queries honestly whenever this does not harm confidentiality. Specifically, in controlled query evaluation (CQE) [3, 4] the data protection policy is declaratively specified through logical formulas and is enforced by altering query answers through so-called censors, which either refuse to answer some queries or lie when this is needed to protect some secrets. In general, there exist multiple, mutually incomparable ways of concealing answers, i.e., mutually incomparable censors. Different works have proposed static CQE methods, where a censor is constructed (or approximated) beforehand, establishing once and for all which queries should be answered truthfully [8, 11, 13, 15, 17]. In several cases, such approaches are not fully cooperative, because the secure view of the data is chosen without taking the users' interests into account.

Conversely, following the work of Biskup and Bonatti [5], in this paper we introduce a dynamic CQE (dynCQE) method that progressively decides whether being truthful or lying, based on the specific stream of queries. Roughly speaking, the dynamic CQE approach selects, at each step, as many censors as possible, coherently with the previous answers. By doing so, it maximizes the possibility of answering the next query honestly by choosing from the current pool of censors those that allow to answer the query truthfully (if any).

We will prove that this method satisfies the so-called "longest honeymoon" property, which means that, given a sequence of queries, dynCQE returns the longest possible sequence of honest answers before lying. This property can be supported with several arguments. First, without any specific model of the users' intentions, the order in which queries are posed allegedly reflects their importance. Secondly, since we cannot foresee which nor how many queries are coming in the future, answering honestly the current query (if possible) is the most cooperative possible strategy. We will prove also that dynCQE is optimal in a more classical sense: the set of queries honestly answered by dynCQE is always maximal under set containment.

After introducing the dynCQE framework and formally investigating its general properties (Sect. 3), the paper focuses on ontologies in OWL 2 QL [19], a tractable profile of OWL 2 designed for data-intensive applications. For this setting, in Sect. 4, we first show that the behavior of dynCQE cannot be simulated by static CQE through data-independent modifications of the intensional components of the framework, i.e., the ontology (TBox) and the formulas representing the data protection policy. It is thus necessary to devise specific techniques to implement the dynamic approach. To this aim, we provide a tailored query rewriting algorithm through which we show that dynCQE query processing in OWL 2 QL is *first-order rewritable*, which implies that its data complexity is in AC^0 (like the evaluation of first-order sentences, i.e., SQL, queries). Towards practical implementations, in Sect. 5, we present a first optimization of the query reformulation technique used to prove the first-order rewritability result, based on the information acquired by the system during the interaction with users; we also present a possible approximation of the approach, should the sequence of queries become too long for our rewriting technique. A section on related work and one on final remarks conclude the paper.

2   Preliminaries

For the technical treatment we resort to Description Logics (DLs), which are decidable fragments of First-Order (FO) logic underpinning the OWL 2 standard. We introduce here the basic notions needed in this work and refer the reader to [1] for further details. The languages of our interest are built from an alphabet Γ that consists of unary predicates (a.k.a. *atomic concepts*), binary predicates (a.k.a. *atomic roles*), constants (a.k.a. *individual names*), and a countably infinite supply of variables. An atom is a formula of the form $A(t)$ or $P(t_1, t_2)$, where A is an atomic concept, P is an atomic role, and the terms t, t_1, t_2 are either variables or constants. An atom is *ground* if all its terms are constants.

A DL ontology $\mathcal{O} = \mathcal{T} \cup \mathcal{A}$ is constituted by a TBox $\mathcal{T}$ and an ABox $\mathcal{A}$, specifying intensional and extensional knowledge, respectively. In particular, in this paper we assume that the ABox is a set of ground atoms. A *model* of an ontology $\mathcal{O} = \mathcal{T} \cup \mathcal{A}$ is a FO interpretation that satisfies all axioms in $\mathcal{T}$ and $\mathcal{A}$. $\mathcal{O}$ is *consistent* if it has at least one model, *inconsistent* otherwise, and *entails* an FO sentence ϕ, denoted $\mathcal{O} \models \phi$, if ϕ is true in every model of $\mathcal{O}$. Given an ABox $\mathcal{A}$ and a FO sentence ϕ, we say that ϕ *evaluates to true in* $\mathcal{A}$ if the evaluation of ϕ in the Herbrand model of $\mathcal{A}$ is true [18], otherwise we say that ϕ *evaluates to false in* $\mathcal{A}$. In the paper, we often refer to the set of ground atoms entailed by $\mathcal{T} \cup \mathcal{A}$, which we denote with $\mathsf{cl}_\mathcal{T}(\mathcal{A})$.

In this work, we focus on ontologies expressed in *DL-Lite$_R$* [9], which is the logical counterpart of OWL 2 QL [19]. In this DL, a role R is an atomic role P or its inverse P^-, whereas a concept B takes the form A, $\exists P$, or $\exists P^-$. The concepts $\exists P$ and $\exists P^-$ denote the domain and the range of a role P, respectively. A *DL-Lite$_R$* TBox $\mathcal{T}$ is a set of *positive inclusions* of the form $B_1 \sqsubseteq B_2$ or $R_1 \sqsubseteq R_2$, and *negative inclusions* of the form $B_1 \sqsubseteq \neg B_2$ or $R_1 \sqsubseteq \neg R_2$.

By $conj(\vec{x})$ we mean a conjunction $\alpha_1 \wedge \ldots \wedge \alpha_n$ of atoms where $\vec{x}$ indicates all the variables occurring in it. Then, a Boolean Conjunctive Query (BCQ) is an existentially quantified conjunction of atoms $\exists \vec{x}(conj(\vec{x}))$ and a Boolean Union of Conjunctive Queries (BUCQ) is a disjunction $q_1 \vee \ldots \vee q_n$ of BCQs. Sometimes we write $q \in q'$ to indicate that the BCQ q is one of the BCQs of the BUCQ q'. Note that a ground atom can be seen as a BCQ with no variables, and that a BCQ is a BUCQ with only one disjunct.

Given a BCQ q, *Atoms(q)* is the set of atoms occurring in q. Given two BUCQs $q_1 = q_1^1 \vee \ldots \vee q_1^n$ and $q_2 = q_2^1 \vee \ldots \vee q_2^m$, we denote by $q_1 \wedge q_2$ the BUCQ

$$(q_1^1 \wedge q_2^1) \vee \ldots \vee (q_1^1 \wedge q_2^m) \vee$$
$$\vdots$$
$$(q_1^n \wedge q_2^1) \vee \ldots \vee (q_1^n \wedge q_2^m).$$

We recall that entailment of BUCQs in $DL\text{-}Lite_R$ is FO rewritable, i.e., for every $DL\text{-}Lite_R$ TBox $\mathcal{T}$ and BUCQ q, it is possible to compute an FO query q_r, called the *perfect reformulation of q with respect to $\mathcal{T}$*, such that, for each ABox $\mathcal{A}$, $\mathcal{T} \cup \mathcal{A} \models q$ iff q_r evaluates to true in $\mathcal{A}$. We will use the algorithm *PerfectRef* presented in [9], which uses only positive inclusions in $\mathcal{T}$ as rewriting rules to compute perfect reformulations. We point out that the reformulation returned by *PerfectRef* is a BUCQ. The following proposition is from [9].

Proposition 1. *Let $\mathcal{T} \cup \mathcal{A}$ be a consistent $DL\text{-}Lite_R$ ontology and let q be a BUCQ. Then, $\mathcal{T} \cup \mathcal{A} \models q$ iff PerfectRef$(q, \mathcal{T})$ evaluates to true in $\mathcal{A}$.*

Furthermore, a *policy* $\mathcal{P}$ is a (finite) set of *denials*, i.e., sentences of the form $q \rightarrow \perp$, where q is a BCQ. An interpretation satisfies a denial $q \rightarrow \perp$ iff it does not satisfy the BCQ q. We denote by $q(\mathcal{P})$ the BUCQ $\bigvee_{q \rightarrow \perp \in \mathcal{P}} q$.

The following proposition follows from the definition of satisfaction of a denial and from Proposition 1.

Proposition 2. *Let $\mathcal{T} \cup \mathcal{A}$ be a consistent $DL\text{-}Lite_R$ ontology and let $\mathcal{P}$ be a policy. Then, $\mathcal{T} \cup \mathcal{P} \cup \mathcal{A}$ is a consistent FO theory iff PerfectRef$(q(\mathcal{P}), \mathcal{T})$ evaluates to false in $\mathcal{A}$.*

Our complexity results refer to data complexity, i.e., the complexity computed with respect to the size of the ABox only.

3   Framework

We now introduce our framework. All definitions and properties given in this section apply to any DL language.

A *CQE specification* is a pair $\langle \mathcal{T}, \mathcal{P} \rangle$, where $\mathcal{T}$ is a TBox and $\mathcal{P}$ is a policy, such that $\mathcal{T} \cup \mathcal{P}$ is consistent. A CQE instance is a triple $\mathcal{E} = \langle \mathcal{T}, \mathcal{P}, \mathcal{A} \rangle$, where $\langle \mathcal{T}, \mathcal{P} \rangle$ is a CQE specification, and $\mathcal{A}$ is an ABox such that $\mathcal{T} \cup \mathcal{A}$ is consistent.

Censors specify which consequences of an ontology can be disclosed without violating the policy. The following definition is adapted from [11, Definition 1].[1]

Definition 1 (Censor). *Let $\mathcal{E} = \langle \mathcal{T}, \mathcal{A}, \mathcal{P} \rangle$ be a CQE instance. A censor for $\mathcal{E}$ is an ABox $\mathcal{C} \subseteq cl_{\mathcal{T}}(\mathcal{A})$ such that $\mathcal{T} \cup \mathcal{P} \cup \mathcal{C}$ is consistent.*

Given a CQE instance $\mathcal{E}$ and a censor $\mathcal{C}$ for $\mathcal{E}$, we say that $\mathcal{C}$ is *optimal* if there exists no censor $\mathcal{C}'$ for $\mathcal{E}$ such that $\mathcal{C} \subset \mathcal{C}'$. We denote by $OptCens(\mathcal{E})$ the set of all the optimal censors for $\mathcal{E}$. We observe that a censor for a CQE instance $\mathcal{E}$ always exists,[2] and thus $OptCens(\mathcal{E}) \neq \emptyset$. Given a BUCQ q, we denote by $OptCens(\mathcal{E}, q)$ the set of optimal censors that, together with $\mathcal{T}$, entail q:

$$OptCens(\mathcal{E}, q) = \{\mathcal{C} \in OptCens(\mathcal{E}) \mid \mathcal{T} \cup \mathcal{C} \models q\}$$

---

[1] Other definitions of censors have been considered in the literature, for example in [15, 17]. Definition 1 is chosen because it yields several important properties, such as *indistinguishability* (cf. Sect. 6), and it has been thoroughly investigated in various settings (e.g., in [10, 11]).

[2] Trivially, the empty set is a censor for any CQE instance $\mathcal{E}$.

The following notion of *protection state* captures the history of queries submitted by the users to a CQE instance.

Definition 2 (State). *Let $\mathcal{E} = \langle \mathcal{T}, \mathcal{P}, \mathcal{A} \rangle$ be a CQE instance. A protection state of $\mathcal{E}$ (or simply state of $\mathcal{E}$) is a pair $\mathcal{S} = \langle \mathcal{E}, \mathcal{Q} \rangle$, where $\mathcal{Q} = \langle q_1, \ldots, q_n \rangle$ (with $n \geq 0$) is a sequence of BUCQs.*

Below we formalize our idea of dynamic CQE (dynCQE), i.e., a CQE that takes into account the sequence of queries that have been already processed. In what follows, given a CQE instance $\mathcal{E}$, a sequence $\mathcal{Q}_n = \langle q_1, \ldots, q_n \rangle$ of BUCQs, and any integer $i \in [0, n]$, we denote with $\mathcal{Q}_i$ the sequence $\langle q_1, \ldots, q_i \rangle$ and with $\mathcal{S}_i$ the state $\langle \mathcal{E}, \mathcal{Q}_i \rangle$ of $\mathcal{E}$, with the convention that $\mathcal{Q}_0$ is the empty sequence $\langle \rangle$.

Definition 3. (Dynamic CQE – dynCQE). *Let $\mathcal{E} = \langle \mathcal{T}, \mathcal{P}, \mathcal{A} \rangle$ be a CQE instance, and let $\mathcal{Q}_n = \langle q_1, \ldots, q_n \rangle$ (with $n \geq 0$) a sequence of BUCQs. The set $StCens(\mathcal{S}_n)$ of censors of $\mathcal{S}_n$ is inductively defined as follows:*

- $StCens(\mathcal{S}_0) = OptCens(\mathcal{E})$;
- $StCens(\mathcal{S}_{i+1}) = \begin{cases} StCens(\mathcal{S}_i) & \text{if } StCens(\mathcal{S}_i) \cap OptCens(\mathcal{E}, q_{i+1}) = \emptyset, \\ StCens(\mathcal{S}_i) \cap OptCens(\mathcal{E}, q_{i+1}) & \text{otherwise,} \end{cases}$
  for every $0 \leq i \leq n-1$.

For each BUCQ q_i occurring in $\mathcal{Q}_n$, we say that q_i is entailed by $\mathcal{S}_n$, denoted by $\mathcal{S}_n \models q_i$, if $\mathcal{T} \cup \mathcal{C} \models q_i$ for every $\mathcal{C} \in StCens(\mathcal{S}_n)$. We denote by $EntQ(\mathcal{S}_n)$ the set of queries of $\mathcal{Q}_n$ entailed by $\mathcal{S}_n$, i.e., $EntQ(\mathcal{S}_n) = \{q \in \mathcal{Q}_n \mid \mathcal{S}_n \models q\}$.

One can see that, for any $i = 1, \ldots, n$, the set of censors of a state $\mathcal{S}_i$ is always non-empty and consists of a subset of the set of censors in its predecessor state $\mathcal{S}_{i-1}$, i.e. $StCens(\mathcal{S}_{i-1}) \supseteq StCens(\mathcal{S}_i) \supset \emptyset$. This also means that $EntQ(\mathcal{S}_{i-1}) \subseteq EntQ(\mathcal{S}_i)$ holds for any $i = 1, \ldots, n$.

Informally speaking, each set $StCens(\mathcal{S}_i)$ (with $1 \leq i \leq n$) in the above definition progressively selects the optimal censors of $\mathcal{E}$ that agree with $EntQ(\mathcal{S}_i)$. If none of the surviving optimal censors in $StCens(\mathcal{S}_i)$ entails (together with $\mathcal{T}$) a query q_{i+1}, then $\mathcal{S}_{i+1} \not\models q_{i+1}$, so we have that $StCens(\mathcal{S}_{i+1}) = StCens(\mathcal{S}_i)$. Conversely, if at least one of the censors in $StCens(\mathcal{S}_i)$, together with the TBox, entails q_{i+1}, then, according to dynCQE, we have a positive answer, and $StCens(\mathcal{S}_{i+1})$ keeps only the censors in $StCens(\mathcal{S}_i)$ that agree with such answer.

As a result, the stream of queries is processed greedily, answering the truth as long as some of the censors in $StCens(\mathcal{S}_n)$ allows to do it (*longest honeymoon approach* [5]), as we will formally show below.

Note that, by Definition 3, given a state $\mathcal{S} = \langle \mathcal{E}, \mathcal{Q} \rangle$ and a query q occurring in $\mathcal{Q}$, we have that either $\mathcal{T} \cup \mathcal{C} \models q$ for every $\mathcal{C} \in StCens(\mathcal{S})$, or $\mathcal{T} \cup \mathcal{C} \not\models q$ for every $\mathcal{C} \in StCens(\mathcal{S})$. This means that $\mathcal{S} \models q$ if and only if there exists a censor $\mathcal{C} \in StCens(\mathcal{S})$ such that $\mathcal{T} \cup \mathcal{C} \models q$.

Example 1. Some pharmaceutical products may reveal with high accuracy which kind of disease is affecting a person. For instance, drugs that contain phenytoin, or that are classified as anti-seizure medications, indicate some form of epilepsy. Let $\mathcal{E} = \langle \mathcal{T}, \mathcal{P}, \mathcal{A} \rangle$ be a CQE instance, where:

$\mathcal{T} = \{\text{Abc} \sqsubseteq \text{Antiseizure}\}$;
$\mathcal{P} = \{\exists x, y(\text{buy}(x, y) \wedge \text{Antiseizure}(y)) \rightarrow \bot,$
$\qquad \exists x, y(\text{buy}(x, y) \wedge \text{contain}(y, \text{phenytoin})) \rightarrow \bot\}$;
$\mathcal{A} = \{\text{buy}(\text{john}, m_a), \text{Abc}(m_a), \text{buy}(\text{alice}, m_b), \text{contain}(m_b, \text{phenytoin})\}$.

In words, the TBox states that Abc is an anti-seizure medication, while the policy conceals the presence of patients suffering from epilepsy.

Let us start by considering an empty sequence of BUCQs. By definition, we have that $StCens(\langle \mathcal{E}, \langle \rangle \rangle)$ coincides with the set of the optimal censors for $\mathcal{E}$:

- $\mathcal{C}_1 = \{\text{buy}(\text{john}, m_a), \text{buy}(\text{alice}, m_b)\}$;
- $\mathcal{C}_2 = \{\text{buy}(\text{john}, m_a), \text{contain}(m_b, \text{phenytoin})\}$;
- $\mathcal{C}_3 = \{\text{Abc}(m_a), \text{Antiseizure}(m_a), \text{buy}(\text{alice}, m_b)\}$;
- $\mathcal{C}_4 = \{\text{Abc}(m_a), \text{Antiseizure}(m_a), \text{contain}(m_b, \text{phenytoin})\}$.

Let $q_1 = \text{buy}(\text{john}, m_a)$ be the first query. The censors $\mathcal{C}_1$ and $\mathcal{C}_2$ agree with answering *true* to this query. All the censors that disagree with such answer are then removed, obtaining $StCens(\langle \mathcal{E}, \langle q_1 \rangle \rangle) = StCens(\langle \mathcal{E}, \langle \rangle \rangle) \cap OptCens(\mathcal{E}, q_1) = \{\mathcal{C}_1, \mathcal{C}_2\}$. Then, let $q_2 = \text{Abc}(m_a)$ be a new query in the sequence. Since neither $\mathcal{T} \cup \mathcal{C}_1$ nor $\mathcal{T} \cup \mathcal{C}_2$ entail q_2, then $StCens(\langle \mathcal{E}, \langle q_1, q_2 \rangle \rangle) = StCens(\langle \mathcal{E}, \langle q_1 \rangle \rangle)$. Now, consider to add $q_3 = \exists x \text{buy}(x, m_b)$ to the sequence. Since $\mathcal{T} \cup \mathcal{C}_1 \models q_3$ while $\mathcal{T} \cup \mathcal{C}_2 \not\models q_3$, we have $StCens(\mathcal{S}) = \{\mathcal{C}_1\}$, where $\mathcal{S} = \langle \mathcal{E}, \mathcal{Q} \rangle$ with $\mathcal{Q} = \langle q_1, q_2, q_3 \rangle$. Clearly, $\mathcal{S} \models q_1$ and $\mathcal{S} \models q_3$, but $\mathcal{S} \not\models q_2$. □

Let $\mathcal{E} = \langle \mathcal{T}, \mathcal{P}, \mathcal{A} \rangle$ be a CQE instance. For all states $\mathcal{S}$ of $\mathcal{E}$, our dynamic CQE method is *optimal with respect to* $\mathcal{S}$, in the sense that we have that $EntQ(\mathcal{S})$ is never strictly contained in the set of queries of $\mathcal{S}$ entailed by any censor $\mathcal{C}$ for $\mathcal{E}$. In order to formalize this property, for all states $\mathcal{S} = \langle \mathcal{E}, \mathcal{Q} \rangle$ and all censors $\mathcal{C}$ for $\mathcal{E}$, let $EntQ(\mathcal{Q}, \mathcal{C}, \mathcal{T})$ be the subset of queries of $\mathcal{Q}$ entailed by $\mathcal{C} \cup \mathcal{T}$, i.e. $EntQ(\mathcal{Q}, \mathcal{C}, \mathcal{T}) = \{q \in \mathcal{Q} \mid \mathcal{T} \cup \mathcal{C} \models q\}$.

Proposition 3. *Let* $\mathcal{E} = \langle \mathcal{T}, \mathcal{P}, \mathcal{A} \rangle$ *be a CQE instance,* $\mathcal{Q} = \langle q_1, \ldots, q_n \rangle$ *(with* $n \geq 0$*) be a sequence of BUCQs, and* $\mathcal{S} = \langle \mathcal{E}, \mathcal{Q} \rangle$*. There exists no censor* $\mathcal{C} \in OptCens(\mathcal{E})$ *such that* $EntQ(\mathcal{S}) \subset EntQ(\mathcal{Q}, \mathcal{C}, \mathcal{T})$*.*

Proof. By contradiction, let such a censor $\mathcal{C}$ exist and let i be the least index such that $\mathcal{T} \cup \mathcal{C} \models q_i$ and $q_i \notin EntQ(\mathcal{S})$. By the minimality of i we have that, for all $j \in \{1, \ldots, i-1\}$, $\mathcal{T} \cup \mathcal{C} \models q_j$ iff $q_j \in EntQ(\langle \mathcal{E}, \langle q_1, \ldots, q_{i-1} \rangle \rangle)$. It follows that $\mathcal{C} \in StCens(\langle \mathcal{E}, \langle q_1, \ldots, q_{i-1} \rangle \rangle)$. But then, by definition, we should have that $\mathcal{C} \in StCens(\langle \mathcal{E}, \langle q_1, \ldots, q_i \rangle \rangle)$, and, consequently, that $q_i \in EntQ(\langle \mathcal{E}, \langle q_1, \ldots, q_i \rangle \rangle) \subseteq EntQ(\mathcal{S})$ (a contradiction). □

Moreover, dynCQE is the *only* way to guarantee that such optimality is preserved in the future. One might object that answering the current query q honestly may prevent the system from answering honestly another set of queries $\mathcal{Q}'$ in the future. However, the queries in $\mathcal{Q}'$ might never be submitted, so any censor that conceals the answer to q now might remain sub-optimal in the future. This may happen no matter how many additional queries are submitted by the users. Formally, we have:

Proposition 4. *Let $\mathcal{E} = \langle \mathcal{T}, \mathcal{P}, \mathcal{A} \rangle$ be a CQE instance, $\mathcal{Q} = \langle q_1, \ldots, q_n \rangle$ be a sequence of BUCQs, and $\mathcal{S} = \langle \mathcal{E}, \mathcal{Q} \rangle$. For all BUCQs q_{n+1}, and for all censors $\mathcal{C}$ in $StCens(\mathcal{S}) \setminus StCens(\langle \mathcal{E}, \mathcal{Q} \circ \langle q_{n+1} \rangle \rangle)$[3], there exist queries $q_{n+2}, q_{n+3}, \ldots, q_{n+k}, \ldots$ such that $EntQ(\langle q_1, \ldots, q_i \rangle, \mathcal{C}, \mathcal{T}) \subset EntQ(\langle \mathcal{E}, \langle q_1, \ldots, q_i \rangle \rangle)$ for all $i > n$.*

In the above proposition, the hypothesis $\mathcal{C} \in StCens(\mathcal{S}) \setminus StCens(\langle \mathcal{E}, \mathcal{Q} \circ \langle q_{n+1} \rangle \rangle)$ implies that q_{n+1} can be given a positive answer without disclosing any protected data, but $\mathcal{C}$ does not allow a positive answer to q_{n+1}.

Another property of dynamic CQE is that the first answer modification occurs as late as possible (*longest honeymoon* property). The following notion of maximal cooperativity implies and strengthens the longest honeymoon property.

Definition 4 (Cooperativity). *Let $\mathcal{E} = \langle \mathcal{T}, \mathcal{P}, \mathcal{A} \rangle$ be a CQE instance, $\mathcal{Q} = \langle q_1, \ldots, q_n \rangle$ (with $n \geq 0$) a sequence of BUCQs, and $\mathcal{C}$ and $\mathcal{C}'$ two censors for $\mathcal{E}$. We say that $\mathcal{C}$ is more cooperative than $\mathcal{C}'$ with respect to $\mathcal{Q}$ if there exists a non-negative natural number $m < n$ such that*

- $\mathcal{T} \cup \mathcal{C} \models q_i \iff \mathcal{T} \cup \mathcal{C}' \models q_i$ *for every* $1 \leq i \leq m$*, and*
- $\mathcal{T} \cup \mathcal{C} \models q_{m+1}$ *and* $\mathcal{T} \cup \mathcal{C}' \not\models q_{m+1}$*.*

We also say that $\mathcal{C}$ is maximally cooperative with respect to $\mathcal{Q}$ if there does not exist any censor $\mathcal{C}''$ for $\mathcal{E}$ that is more cooperative than $\mathcal{C}$.

The following intermediate result shows that a state of a CQE instance cannot discriminate between two optimal censors if they have answered all the queries posed so far in the same way.

Lemma 1. *Let $\mathcal{E} = \langle \mathcal{T}, \mathcal{P}, \mathcal{A} \rangle$ be a CQE instance, $\mathcal{Q} = \langle q_1, \ldots, q_n \rangle$ (with $n \geq 0$) be a sequence of BUCQs, and $\mathcal{C}$ and $\mathcal{C}'$ be two optimal censors for $\mathcal{E}$ such that $\mathcal{T} \cup \mathcal{C} \models q_i \iff \mathcal{T} \cup \mathcal{C}' \models q_i$, for all $i \in \{1, \ldots, n\}$. Then, $\mathcal{C} \in StCens(\langle \mathcal{E}, \mathcal{Q} \rangle)$ iff $\mathcal{C}' \in StCens(\langle \mathcal{E}, \mathcal{Q} \rangle)$.*

Proof. The proof is by induction on the length of $\mathcal{Q}$.

Case $n = 0$. Since $\mathcal{Q}$ is empty, both $\mathcal{C}$ and $\mathcal{C}'$ are in $StCens(\langle \mathcal{E}, \mathcal{Q} \rangle)$.

Case $n \geq 1$. In this case $\mathcal{Q} = \mathcal{Q}' \circ \langle q_n \rangle$, where $\mathcal{Q}' = \langle q_1, \ldots, q_{n-1} \rangle$. From the assumption $\mathcal{T} \cup \mathcal{C} \models q_i$ iff $\mathcal{T} \cup \mathcal{C}' \models q_i$, for all $i \in \{1, \ldots, n\}$, the following two facts hold: (*i*) $\mathcal{C} \in OptCens(\mathcal{E}, q_n)$ iff $\mathcal{C}' \in OptCens(\mathcal{E}, q_n)$; (*ii*) by IH, $\mathcal{C} \in StCens(\langle \mathcal{E}, \mathcal{Q}' \rangle)$ iff $\mathcal{C}' \in StCens(\langle \mathcal{E}, \mathcal{Q}' \rangle)$. Then, since $StCens(\langle \mathcal{E}, \mathcal{Q} \rangle)$ is by Definition 3 equal either to $StCens(\langle \mathcal{E}, \mathcal{Q}' \rangle)$ or to $StCens(\langle \mathcal{E}, \mathcal{Q}' \rangle) \cap OptCens(\mathcal{E}, q_n)$, we have the thesis. $\square$

Then, we prove that for all states $\mathcal{S} = \langle \mathcal{E}, \mathcal{Q} \rangle$ of a CQE instance, the set $StCens(\mathcal{S})$ coincides with the set of all censors that are maximally cooperative with respect to $\mathcal{Q}$.

Theorem 1. *Let $\mathcal{E} = \langle \mathcal{T}, \mathcal{P}, \mathcal{A} \rangle$ be a CQE instance, and $\mathcal{Q} = \langle q_1, \ldots, q_n \rangle$ (with $n \geq 0$) be a sequence of BUCQs. A censor $\mathcal{C}$ for $\mathcal{E}$ is maximally cooperative with respect to $\mathcal{Q}$ iff $\mathcal{C} \in StCens(\langle \mathcal{E}, \mathcal{Q} \rangle)$.*

---

[3] With $\mathcal{Q} \circ \langle q_{n+1} \rangle$ we denote the sequence $\langle q_1, \ldots, q_n, q_{n+1} \rangle$.

Proof. We start by showing that every $C \in StCens(\langle \mathcal{E}, \mathcal{Q} \rangle)$ is maximally cooperative with respect to $\mathcal{Q}$. Let $\mathcal{S}_h = \langle \mathcal{E}, \langle q_1, \ldots, q_h \rangle \rangle$, with $h \leq n$, and assume by contradiction that, for some $C \in StCens(\mathcal{S}_n)$, there exists an optimal censor C' and a number $m < n$ such that (i) $\mathcal{T} \cup C \models q_i \Longleftrightarrow \mathcal{T} \cup C' \models q_i$, for each $i \leq m$, and (ii) $\mathcal{T} \cup C \not\models q_{m+1}$ and $\mathcal{T} \cup C' \models q_{m+1}$.

Note that the sets $StCens(\mathcal{S}_h)$ form by construction a descending $\subseteq$-chain, hence C is in $StCens(\mathcal{S}_m)$. Then, from (i) and Lemma 1, $C' \in StCens(\mathcal{S}_m)$ too.

From (ii) we have that C' occurs in $OptCens(\mathcal{E}, q_{m+1})$ whereas C does not. Then, on the one hand, since $C' \in StCens(\mathcal{S}_m) \cap OptCens(\mathcal{E}, q_{m+1})$, $StCens(\mathcal{S}_{m+1})$ is equal by definition to $StCens(\mathcal{S}_m) \cap OptCens(\mathcal{E}, q_{m+1})$. On the other hand, $StCens(\mathcal{S}_{m+1})$ does not contain C, as C is not in $OptCens(\mathcal{E}, q_{m+1})$. But this means that also $StCens(\mathcal{S}_n)$ does not contain C, a contradiction.

Now, we show that if a censor C for $\mathcal{E}$ is maximally cooperative w.r.t. $\mathcal{Q}$, then $C \in StCens(\langle \mathcal{E}, \mathcal{Q} \rangle)$. By contradiction, assume that $C \notin StCens(\langle \mathcal{E}, \mathcal{Q} \rangle)$. So, there exists in $\mathcal{Q} = \langle q_1, \ldots, q_n \rangle$ a query q_i such that $C \in StCens(\langle \mathcal{E}, \langle q_1, ..., q_{i-1} \rangle \rangle) \setminus StCens(\langle \mathcal{E}, \langle q_1, ..., q_i \rangle \rangle)$. Hence, there exists a censor $C' \in StCens(\langle \mathcal{E}, \langle q_1, ..., q_i \rangle \rangle)$ such that $\mathcal{T} \cup C' \models q_i$, while $\mathcal{T} \cup C \not\models q_i$ and such that $\mathcal{T} \cup C' \models q_j \Longleftrightarrow \mathcal{T} \cup C \models q_j$ for every $1 \leq j \leq i-1$. So, by Definition 4, C' is more cooperative than C, which contradicts the fact that C is maximally cooperative. $\square$

We conclude this section by comparing our new semantics of entailment with some other semantics from the literature. A first proposed strategy is arbitrarily choosing an optimal censor [6,13,14]. In this case, it might happen, as also stated by Proposition 4, that one looses optimality with respect to the state $\mathcal{S}$. For instance, if one arbitrarily picks censor C_2 in Example 1, then $EntQ(\mathcal{Q}, C_2, \mathcal{T}) \subset EntQ(\mathcal{S})$. On the other hand, when the chosen censor C turns out to be optimal with respect to a state $\mathcal{S}$, then, due to Theorem 1, either $C \in StCens(\mathcal{S})$ or C is not maximally cooperative with respect to $\mathcal{Q}$.

Other two CQE semantics proposed in literature are: (i) *skeptical reasoning* [13,17], where a query q is entailed by a CQE instance $\mathcal{E} = \langle \mathcal{T}, \mathcal{P}, \mathcal{A} \rangle$, denoted by $\mathcal{E} \models q$, if it is entailed by all the optimal censors for $\mathcal{E}$ together with the TBox, i.e., $\mathcal{T} \cup C \models q$ for each $C \in OptCens(\mathcal{E})$, and (ii) its approximation, called IGA semantics [10], under which q is entailed – in symbols, $\mathcal{E} \models_{\mathsf{IGA}} q$ – if it is entailed by $\mathcal{T} \cup C_{\mathsf{IGA}}$, where C_{IGA} is the intersection of all the optimal censors for $\mathcal{E}$, i.e., $C_{\mathsf{IGA}} = \bigcap_{C \in OptCens(\mathcal{E})} C$. The following proposition shows that skeptically reasoning over all optimal censors is always a sound approximation of dynCQE.

Proposition 5. *Let $\mathcal{E} = \langle \mathcal{T}, \mathcal{P}, \mathcal{A} \rangle$ be a CQE instance, $\mathcal{Q} = \langle q_1, \ldots, q_n \rangle$ (with $n \geq 0$) be a sequence of BUCQs, and q be a BCQ in $\mathcal{Q}$. We have that $\mathcal{E} \models_{\mathsf{IGA}} q \implies \mathcal{E} \models q \implies \langle \mathcal{E}, \mathcal{Q} \rangle \models q$. The converse does not necessarily hold.*

Proof. Suppose that $\mathcal{E} \models_{\mathsf{IGA}} q$. By [10, Proposition 1], we already know that $\mathcal{E} \models q$. Now, since $\mathcal{E} \models q$ by definition means that $\mathcal{T} \cup C \models q$ holds for each $C \in StCens(\mathcal{S}) \subseteq OptCens(\mathcal{E})$, we trivially have that $\langle \mathcal{E}, \mathcal{Q} \rangle \models q$.

As for the converse, consider Example 1. We have that $\langle \mathcal{E}, \mathcal{Q} \rangle \models q_1$ but $\mathcal{E} \not\models q_1$ (and thus, also $\mathcal{E} \not\models_{\mathsf{IGA}} q_1$) because $\mathcal{T} \cup C_3 \not\models q_1$. $\square$

4   First-Order Rewritability of Query Entailment

We now move to the study of computational complexity of query entailment. In this investigation, we focus on $DL\text{-}Lite_R$ CQE specifications, i.e., whose TBox and ABox are expressed in $DL\text{-}Lite_R$.

A first way to solve query entailment in a state might consist in finding a reduction to the stateless CQE approach, for which algorithms are already known. It turns out, however, that the behavior of dynCQE cannot be intensionally simulated by a stateless CQE instance, independent of query history.

Theorem 2. *There exist a $DL\text{-}Lite_R$ CQE specification $\langle T, P \rangle$ and a BUCQ q such that there exist no $DL\text{-}Lite_R$ CQE specification $\langle T', P' \rangle$ such that, for every ABox A, $OptCens(\langle T', P', A \rangle) = StCens(S)$, where $S = \langle\langle T, P, A \rangle, \langle q \rangle\rangle$.*

Proof. Let $T = \emptyset$, let $P = \{C(x) \wedge D(x) \rightarrow \bot\}$, and let $q = \exists x C(x)$. By contradiction, suppose there exist a TBox T' and a policy P' such that, for every ABox A, $OptCens(\langle T', P', A \rangle) = StCens(S)$.

Now consider the ABox $A = \{C(a_1), C(a_2), D(a_1), D(a_2)\}$, where a_1, a_2 are individual names that do not appear in P'. The optimal censors for $\langle T, P, A \rangle$ are $C_1 = \{C(a_1), C(a_2)\}$, $C_2 = \{C(a_1), D(a_2)\}$, $C_3 = \{D(a_1), C(a_2)\}$, $C_4 = \{D(a_1), D(a_2)\}$. Among such optimal censors, only C_4 does not satisfy q. Therefore, $StCens(S) = \{C_1, C_2, C_3\}$. Since by hypothesis $StCens(S) = OptCens(\langle T', P', A \rangle)$, it follows that $T' \cup P' \cup C_4$ is inconsistent and $T' \cup P' \cup C_3$ is consistent. Consequently, by Proposition 2, $PerfectRef(q(P'), T')$ evaluates to true in C_4 and evaluates to false in C_3.

On the other hand, it is immediate to see that, for every BUCQ q that does not mention individual names in A, q evaluates to true in C_4 only if q evaluates to true in C_3. Consequently, $PerfectRef(q(P'), T')$ evaluates to true in C_4 only if $PerfectRef(q(P'), T')$ evaluates to true in C_3. Thus we get a contradiction.   □

We now study the data complexity of the query entailment problem in a state, i.e., given a state $S = \langle \mathcal{E}, \mathcal{Q} \rangle$ of a CQE instance $\mathcal{E} = \langle T, P, A \rangle$, the problem of checking whether a BUCQ q in $\mathcal{Q}$ belongs to $EntQ(S)$. In particular, we prove that this problem is FO rewritable, and, so, that it is in AC^0 in data complexity.

We start by showing a fundamental property of query entailment in a state, which holds for all DLs.

Theorem 3. *Let $\mathcal{E} = \langle T, P, A \rangle$ be a CQE instance, $\mathcal{Q} = \langle q_1, \ldots, q_n \rangle$ be a sequence of BUCQs, and let $S = \langle \mathcal{E}, \mathcal{Q} \rangle$. For every i such that $1 \leq i \leq n$, $q_i \in EntQ(S)$ iff there exists a censor C for $\mathcal{E}$ such that*

$$T \cup C \models (\bigwedge_{q \in EntQ(S_{i-1})} q) \wedge q_i$$

Proof. ($\Leftarrow$:) Suppose there exists a censor C for $\mathcal{E}$ such that $T \cup C \models (\bigwedge_{q \in EntQ(S_{i-1})} q) \wedge q_i$. Then, it follows immediately that there exists an optimal censor C' for $\mathcal{E}$ such that $C' \supset C$, consequently $T \cup C' \models (\bigwedge_{q \in EntQ(S_{i-1})} q) \wedge q_i$. Hence, by Definition 3, $C' \in StCens(\langle \mathcal{E}, \langle q_1, \ldots, q_i \rangle \rangle)$. Therefore, $q_i \in EntQ(S)$.

($\Rightarrow$:) Suppose $q_i \in EntQ(\mathcal{S})$. Now, let $\mathcal{C}'$ be an optimal censor for $\mathcal{E}$ such that $\mathcal{C}' \in StCens(\mathcal{S})$. We have that $\mathcal{T} \cup \mathcal{C}' \models q$ for every $q \in EntQ(\mathcal{S})$, and since $q_i \in EntQ(\mathcal{S})$ and $EntQ(\mathcal{S}_{i-1}) \subseteq EntQ(\mathcal{S})$, it follows that $\mathcal{T} \cup \mathcal{C}' \models (\bigwedge_{q \in EntQ(\mathcal{S}_{i-1})} q) \wedge q_i$, thus proving the thesis. $\qquad\square$

Given a BUCQ q and an ABox $\mathcal{A}$, we say that an *image of q in $\mathcal{A}$* is a minimal subset $\mathcal{A}'$ of $\mathcal{A}$ such that $\mathcal{A}' \models q$. Furthermore, given a BUCQ q, a TBox $\mathcal{T}$ and an ABox $\mathcal{A}$, we say that an *image of q in $\mathcal{A}$ with respect to $\mathcal{T}$* is a minimal subset $\mathcal{A}'$ of $\mathcal{A}$ such that $\mathcal{T} \cup \mathcal{A}' \models q$.

Theorem 4. *Let $\mathcal{E} = \langle \mathcal{T}, \mathcal{P}, \mathcal{A} \rangle$ be a DL-Lite$_R$ CQE instance and $\mathcal{Q} = \langle q_1, \ldots, q_n \rangle$ (with $n \geq 0$) be a sequence of BUCQs. For every i such that $1 \leq i \leq n$, $q_i \in EntQ(\mathcal{S})$ iff there exists an image IM of PerfectRef$((\bigwedge_{q \in EntQ(S_{i-1})} q) \wedge q_i, \mathcal{T})$ in $cl_{\mathcal{T}}(\mathcal{A})$ such that PerfectRef$(q(\mathcal{P}), \mathcal{T})$ evaluates to false in IM.*

Now observe that: (i) $cl_{\mathcal{T}}(\mathcal{A})$ can be computed in PTIME w.r.t. data complexity; (ii) every image of a BUCQ q has a size that is not larger than the length of the longest BCQ in q; (iii) such a maximum length is a constant w.r.t. data complexity; (iv) all the conditions in the theorem can be verified in PTIME with respect to data complexity [9]. This implies that the entailment problem in a state can be decided in PTIME w.r.t. data complexity.

In the following, we provide a tighter upper bound, showing that this entailment problem is in AC^0 in data complexity. We do so by proving that the problem is FO rewritable. That is, for every BUCQ q of the state, there exists an FO query q' that does not depend on the ABox and is such that q is entailed in the state iff q' evaluates to true in the ABox.

To this purpose, we will find an FO query that depends on the intensional part of the state, i.e., the TBox, the policy and the sequence of queries, and such that its evaluation on the ABox is true if and only if the condition expressed in Theorem 4 holds (Theorem 7). We will make two intermediate steps towards this result: first (Theorem 5), given a query q on a *DL-Lite$_R$* CQE specification $\langle \mathcal{T}, \mathcal{P} \rangle$, we will find a query denoted by $BraveRef(q, \mathcal{T}, \mathcal{P})$ whose evaluation on $cl_{\mathcal{T}}(\mathcal{A})$ corresponds to checking the existence of an optimal censor $\mathcal{C}$ for the CQE instance $\langle \mathcal{T}, \mathcal{P}, \mathcal{A} \rangle$ such that $\mathcal{T} \cup \mathcal{C} \models q$; then (Theorem 6), we will find an FO query such that its evaluation on $cl_{\mathcal{T}}(\mathcal{A})$ is true if and only if the condition expressed in Theorem 4 holds.

Given two BCQs q and q', a *mapping of q' into q* is a function $h : Atoms(q') \rightarrow Atoms(q)$ such that there exists a most general unifier σ_h such that, for every atom $\alpha \in Atoms(q')$, $\sigma_h(\alpha) = \sigma_h(h(\alpha))$. Such a most general unifier (variable substitution) assigns variables occurring either in q' or in q to either variables of q or constants. We denote by $Map(q', q)$ the set of all the mappings of q' into q.

Furthermore, we denote by $\sigma_h[q]$ the variable substitutions of σ_h limited to variables occurring in q. For instance, if $q = \exists x, y, z R(x, y, z)$, $q' = \exists x' R(x', x', a)$ (where a is a constant and all other arguments are variables), then $\sigma_h = \{x' \leftarrow x, y \leftarrow x, z \leftarrow a\}$ and $\sigma_h[q] = \{y \leftarrow x, z \leftarrow a\}$.

Given two BCQs q and q', we denote by $Unify(q,q')$ the formula:

$$\bigvee_{h \in Map(q',q)} \left(\bigwedge_{x \leftarrow t \, \in \sigma_h[q]} x = t \right)$$

Definition 5. *Given a BUCQ q, a DL-Lite$_R$ TBox T and a policy P, we define BraveRef(q, T, P) as the FO sentence:*

$$\bigvee_{q_r \in PerfectRef(q,T)} \exists \vec{x}_r \left(conj_r(\vec{x}_r) \wedge \neg \left(\bigwedge_{q_d \in PerfectRef(q(P),T)} Unify(q_r, q_d) \right) \right)$$

(where we assume $q_r = \exists \vec{x}_r (conj_r(\vec{x}_r))$).

We now establish the fundamental property of the above query reformulation function *BraveRef*.

Theorem 5. *Let $\langle T, P \rangle$ be a DL-Lite$_R$ CQE specification. For every ABox A, there exists an optimal censor C for $\langle T, P, A \rangle$ such that $T \cup C \models q$ iff BraveRef(q, T, P) evaluates to true in $cl_T(A)$.*

Then, we use *BraveRef* to define the new query reformulation function *StateRef* as follows.

Definition 6. *Let $\mathcal{E} = \langle T, P, A \rangle$ be a DL-Lite$_R$ CQE instance, $\mathcal{Q} = \langle q_1, \ldots, q_n \rangle$ (with $n \geq 0$) be a sequence of BUCQs, let i be such that $1 \leq i \leq n$, and let $I \subseteq \{1, \ldots, i-1\}$: I represents the set of indexes of the queries that precede query q_i in $\mathcal{Q}$ and that are guessed to be true in the state $\mathcal{S} = \langle \mathcal{E}, \mathcal{Q} \rangle$. We define StateRef$(\mathcal{S}, i, I)$ as the FO sentence:*

$$\left(\bigwedge_{\substack{1 \leq j \leq i-1 \\ \wedge \, j \notin I}} \neg BraveRef\left(\left(\bigwedge_{\ell \in I \wedge \ell < j} q_\ell \right) \wedge q_j, T, P \right) \right) \wedge BraveRef\left(\left(\bigwedge_{\ell \in I} q_\ell \right) \wedge q_i, T, P \right)$$

As an example, consider the *DL-Lite$_R$* CQE instance $\mathcal{E} = \langle T, P, A \rangle$ and the query sequence $\mathcal{Q} = \langle q_1, q_2, q_3 \rangle$ of Example 1, and let us set $i = 3$ and $I = \{1\}$. We have that $StateRef(\langle \mathcal{E}, \mathcal{Q} \rangle, i, I)$ is the FO sentence $\neg BraveRef(q_1 \wedge q_2, T, P) \wedge BraveRef(q_1 \wedge q_3, T, P) = \neg(\mathsf{buy}(\mathsf{john}, \mathsf{m}_a) \wedge \mathsf{Abc}(\mathsf{m}_a) \wedge \neg(\exists z, w(\mathsf{buy}(z, w) \wedge \mathsf{Abc}(w) \wedge z = \mathsf{john} \wedge w = \mathsf{m}_a))) \wedge \exists x(\mathsf{buy}(\mathsf{john}, \mathsf{m}_a) \wedge \mathsf{buy}(x, \mathsf{m}_b))$.

The query reformulation function *StateRef* allows for reducing query entailment in a state to evaluating an FO query, as stated by the following property.

Theorem 6. *Let $\mathcal{E} = \langle T, P, A \rangle$ be a DL-Lite$_R$ CQE instance, $\mathcal{Q} = \langle q_1, \ldots, q_n \rangle$ (with $n \geq 0$) be a sequence of BUCQs. For every i such that $1 \leq i \leq n$, $q_i \in EntQ(\mathcal{S})$ iff the following FO sentence evaluates to true in $cl_T(A)$:*

$$\bigvee_{I \in \wp(\{1, \ldots, i-1\})} StateRef(\mathcal{S}, i, I),$$

where $\wp(\{1, \ldots, i-1\})$ denotes the powerset of $\{1, \ldots, i-1\}$.

The last two theorems show the FO rewritability of the problems studied on $cl_{\mathcal{T}}(\mathcal{A})$. We now modify the respective reformulations to evaluate them directly on the ABox $\mathcal{A}$ and thus produce "genuine" FO rewritability results.

In what follows we will make use of the algorithm *AtomRewr* provided in [13], that we now briefly describe. Given an FO sentence ϕ and a *DL-Lite$_R$* TBox $\mathcal{T}$, $AtomRewr(\phi, \mathcal{T})$ computes the FO sentence obtained from ϕ by replacing every atom $\alpha = p(\vec{x})$ (where $\vec{x}$ are all the variables occurring in α) with the disjunction of atoms corresponding to the perfect rewriting of the non-Boolean atomic query $q_\alpha = \{\vec{x} \mid p(\vec{x})\}$ with respect to $\mathcal{T}$.

For our purposes, we recall the key property of *AtomRewr* provided in [13].

Proposition 6. *For every FO sentence ϕ, DL-Lite$_R$ TBox $\mathcal{T}$, and ABox $\mathcal{A}$, ϕ evaluates to true in $cl_{\mathcal{T}}(\mathcal{A})$ iff AtomRewr($\phi, \mathcal{T}$) evaluates to true in $\mathcal{A}$.*

Now, Proposition 6 and Theorem 6 immediately imply the next property.

Theorem 7. *Let $\mathcal{E} = \langle \mathcal{T}, \mathcal{P}, \mathcal{A} \rangle$ be a DL-Lite$_R$ CQE instance, $\mathcal{Q} = \langle q_1, \ldots, q_n \rangle$ be a sequence of BUCQs. For every i such that $1 \leq i \leq n$, $q_i \in EntQ(\mathcal{S})$ iff the following FO sentence evaluates to true in $\mathcal{A}$:*

$$AtomRewr\left(\bigvee_{I \in \wp(\{1,\ldots,i-1\})} StateRef(\mathcal{S}, i, I), \mathcal{T} \right)$$

The previous theorem shows the FO rewritability of the problem of entailment of BUCQs in a state.

Example 2. Let $\mathcal{E}$ and $\mathcal{Q} = \langle q_1, q_2, q_3 \rangle$ be as in Example 1. According to Theorem 7, the query $q_3 = \exists x\, buy(x, \mathsf{m}_b)$ belongs to $EntQ(\langle \mathcal{E}, \mathcal{Q} \rangle)$ if and only if the FO sentence below evaluates to true in $\mathcal{A}$ (f_I denotes the sub-formula considering the guess I of the indexes of the queries that precede the query q_3):

$$
\begin{array}{l|l}
& AtomRewr(\bigvee_{I \in \wp(\{1,2\})} StateRef(\langle \mathcal{E}, \mathcal{Q} \rangle, i, I), \mathcal{T}) = \\
f_{I=\emptyset} & \neg BraveRef(q_1, \mathcal{T}, \mathcal{P}) \wedge \neg BraveRef(q_2, \mathcal{T}, \mathcal{P}) \wedge BraveRef(q_3, \mathcal{T}, \mathcal{P}) \vee \\
f_{I=\{1\}} & \neg BraveRef(q_1 \wedge q_2, \mathcal{T}, \mathcal{P}) \wedge BraveRef(q_1 \wedge q_3, \mathcal{T}, \mathcal{P}) \vee \\
f_{I=\{2\}} & \neg BraveRef(q_1, \mathcal{T}, \mathcal{P}) \wedge BraveRef(q_2 \wedge q_3, \mathcal{T}, \mathcal{P}) \vee \\
f_{I=\{1,2\}} & BraveRef(q_1 \wedge q_2 \wedge q_3, \mathcal{T}, \mathcal{P}) = \\
f_{I=\emptyset} & \neg buy(john, \mathsf{m}_a) \wedge \neg Abc(\mathsf{m}_a) \wedge \exists x\, buy(x, \mathsf{m}_b) \vee \\
f_{I=\{1\}} & \neg(buy(john, \mathsf{m}_a) \wedge Abc(\mathsf{m}_a) \wedge \neg(\exists z, w(buy(z, w) \wedge Abc(w) \wedge \\
& z = john \wedge w = \mathsf{m}_a))) \wedge \exists x(buy(john, \mathsf{m}_a) \wedge buy(x, \mathsf{m}_b)) \vee \\
f_{I=\{2\}} & \neg(buy(john, \mathsf{m}_a)) \wedge (\exists x(Abc(\mathsf{m}_a) \wedge buy(x, \mathsf{m}_b))) \vee \\
f_{I=\{1,2\}} & \exists x(buy(john, \mathsf{m}_a) \wedge Abc(\mathsf{m}_a) \wedge buy(x, \mathsf{m}_b)) \wedge \\
& \neg(\exists z, w(buy(z, w) \wedge Abc(w) \wedge z = john \wedge w = \mathsf{m}_a))
\end{array}
$$

which, indeed, evaluates to true in $\mathcal{A}$ thanks to $f_{I=\{1\}}$.   □

5   Towards Practical Techniques and Approximations

We now provide a simplification of the query rewriting presented in Theorem 7. In particular, in a real maximally collaborative CQE system, the answers to the queries already executed (i.e., the queries belonging to the state) can obviously be stored and re-used when the next query is submitted. This allows for greatly simplifying the structure of the FO reformulation of the query defined in Theorem 7, as shown in the following.

Theorem 8. *Let* $\mathcal{E} = \langle \mathcal{T}, \mathcal{P}, \mathcal{A} \rangle$ *be a DL-Lite$_R$ CQE instance,* $\mathcal{Q} = \langle q_1, \ldots, q_n \rangle$ *be a sequence of BUCQs, let* $\mathcal{S} = \langle \mathcal{E}, \mathcal{Q} \rangle$*, let* q_{n+1} *be a BUCQ, and let* $\mathcal{S}' = \langle \mathcal{E}, \langle q_1, \ldots, q_n, q_{n+1} \rangle \rangle$*. Then,* q_{n+1} *is entailed by* $\mathcal{S}'$ *iff the following FO sentence evaluates to true in* $\mathcal{A}$*:*

$$AtomRewr(BraveRef((\bigwedge_{q_i \in EntQ(\mathcal{S})} q_i) \wedge q_{n+1}, \mathcal{T}, \mathcal{P}), \mathcal{T})$$

Proof. Suppose $\mathcal{S}' \models q_{n+1}$, i.e. $EntQ(\mathcal{S}') = EntQ(\mathcal{S}) \cup \{q_{n+1}\}$. By Theorem 7, the sentence $\psi = AtomRewr(StateRef(\mathcal{S}', n+1, I), \mathcal{T})$ evaluates to true in $\mathcal{A}$, where $I = \{i \mid q_i \in EntQ(\mathcal{S}')\}$. Consequently, the sentence $AtomRewr(BraveRef((\bigwedge_{q_i \in EntQ(\mathcal{S})} q_i) \wedge q_{n+1}, \mathcal{T}, \mathcal{P}), \mathcal{T})$ is equal to the last conjunct of ψ, and therefore evaluates to true in $\mathcal{A}$ as well.

Suppose now $\mathcal{S}' \not\models q_{n+1}$. From Theorem 7, we have that the sentence $AtomRewr(StateRef(\mathcal{S}', n+1, I), \mathcal{T})$ evaluates to false in $\mathcal{A}$, where $I = \{i \mid q_i \in EntQ(\mathcal{S})\}$. Since $EntQ(\mathcal{S})$ is the set of BUCQ from $\langle q_1, \ldots, q_n \rangle$ entailed by $\mathcal{S}$, all the conjuncts of $AtomRewr(StateRef(\mathcal{S}', n+1, I), \mathcal{T})$ except the last one evaluate to true in $\mathcal{A}$. This means that its last conjunct evaluates to false in $\mathcal{A}$. Such a conjunct is equal to the sentence $AtomRewr(BraveRef((\bigwedge_{q_i \in EntQ(\mathcal{S})} q_i) \wedge q_{n+1}, \mathcal{T}, \mathcal{P}), \mathcal{T})$, which proves the thesis. □

Example 3. Let $\mathcal{E}$ and the queries q_1, q_2, and q_3 be as in Example 1. Consider the sequence of queries $\mathcal{Q} = \langle q_1, q_2 \rangle$. From Example 1, we know that only $q_1 = \mathsf{buy}(\mathsf{john}, \mathsf{m}_a)$ belongs to $EntQ(\langle \mathcal{E}, \mathcal{Q} \rangle)$. Hence, according to Theorem 8, the query $q_3 = \exists x \mathsf{buy}(x, \mathsf{m}_b)$ is entailed by the state $\langle \mathcal{E}, \mathcal{Q} \circ \{q_3\} \rangle$ if and only if the FO sentence $\exists x (\mathsf{buy}(\mathsf{john}, \mathsf{m}_a) \wedge \mathsf{buy}(x, \mathsf{m}_b))$ evaluates to true in $\mathcal{A}$. □

An issue that the query rewriting technique of Theorem 8 does not solve is the scalability w.r.t. the number of submitted queries, which might become too large to make the FO query produced by the rewriting executable in practice. On the other hand, Theorem 2 shows that it is not always possible to intensionally simulate dynCQE by using a stateless CQE specification, i.e., through an ABox-independent transformation of the intensional part of a CQE instance.

To overcome the above issue, a possible approach is to materialize a censor $\mathcal{C}$ of the current state $\mathcal{S}$ of the CQE instance, and then evaluate the next queries over the ontology $\mathcal{T} \cup \mathcal{C}$. If the current state $\mathcal{S}$ has multiple censors, evaluating a query over $\mathcal{T} \cup \mathcal{C}$ is only an approximation of the query entailment through dynCQE, i.e., in the corresponding state. More precisely: as long as the materialized system processes only queries entailed by $\mathcal{T} \cup \mathcal{C}$ (i.e., it always answers "yes"), it returns exactly the same answers provided by dynCQE. The first time it processes a query q non-entailed by $\mathcal{T} \cup \mathcal{C}$ (i.e., it answers "no"), its behaviour might differ from the dynamic approach, where q might be either entailed or not entailed (depending on how the censors of the states evolve). After the first negative answer, the system using $\mathcal{C}$ might answer "yes" (resp. "no") to a subsequent query q even if the state does not entail (resp. entail) q. Obviously, if the state $\mathcal{S}$ has the only censor $\mathcal{C}$, then $\mathcal{T} \cup \mathcal{C}$ and the dynCQE system will have the same behaviour. Below we describe how to materialize a censor of a state.

1. Split the FO query of Theorem 8, execute only one $q' \in PerfectRef(EntQ(\mathcal{S})\cup \{q\}, \mathcal{T})$ at a time, and turn all the variables appearing in $AtomRewr(q', \mathcal{T})$ as free variables.
2. As soon as one of such queries is true in $\mathcal{A}$, we can construct (through the corresponding binding of the free variables of the query) an image of this query in $\mathcal{A}$. Let $\mathcal{A}'$ be such a subset of $\mathcal{A}$.
3. $\mathcal{P} \cup \mathcal{A}'$ is consistent, so there exists at least one censor $\mathcal{C}$ of $\mathcal{S}$ that contains $\mathcal{A}'$. One such censor can be computed by first setting $\mathcal{C} = \mathcal{A}'$, and then, as long as it possible, by iteratively adding to $\mathcal{C}$ ground atoms γ from $cl_{\mathcal{T}}(\mathcal{A}) \setminus \mathcal{A}'$ such that $\mathcal{T} \cup \mathcal{P} \cup \mathcal{C} \cup \{\gamma\}$ is consistent.

6 Related Work

As shown in [11], the censors introduced in Definition 1 enjoy the *indistinguishability property*, that is, for all CQE instances $\mathcal{E} = \langle \mathcal{T}, \mathcal{P}, \mathcal{A} \rangle$ and all censors $\mathcal{C}$ for $\mathcal{E}$, there exists an ABox $\mathcal{A}'$ that entails no secrets, such that $\mathcal{C}$ is also a censor for $\mathcal{E} = \langle \mathcal{T}, \mathcal{P}, \mathcal{A}' \rangle$. Such censors are called *indistinguishability-based* (IB) because the instances with $\mathcal{A}$ and $\mathcal{A}'$ cannot be distinguished based on the answers allowed by $\mathcal{C}$. IB censors are secure against attackers that know the censor's algorithm. In particular, even if the attackers could compute the ABoxes that yield $\mathcal{C}$, using their knowledge about the algorithm, the ABox $\mathcal{A}'$ would prevent them from inferring any secret.

Benedikt et al. [2] provide, for OBDA settings, a systematic complexity analysis of confidentiality preserving query answering based on indistinguishability. They do not address the issue of selecting a secure data disclosure among the available ones. IB censors in OBDA are also considered in [10], where a practical approach to skeptical reasoning in CQE is presented. Differently from our approach, in [10] censors do not take into account the history of the users' queries.

In [13], IB censors are compared with so-called *confidentiality preserving* (CP) censors, that in general do not enjoy the indistinguishability property. Moreover, [13] introduces algorithms and complexity results for skeptical reasoning in CQE, i.e., the problem of computing only the query answers that are returned by *all* IB censors. By definition, the skeptical CQE method is generally less cooperative than the dynamic method introduced and analyzed in this paper (Theorem 5). In [12], policies have been extended with numerical restrictions, and it is proved that this extension preserves FO rewritability.

The first IB CQE method for Description Logics was introduced in [8]. Its confidentiality model is more robust and general, as it takes into account both object-level and meta-level background knowledge of the attacker. However, CQ answering and FO rewritability are not addressed. Moreover, the *secure views* of

[8] are constructed from a sequence of queries that covers *all* possible relevant queries, while the properties we investigate here hold for arbitrary (possibly non-exhaustive) sequences of queries submitted by the users.

The issue of how to select an optimal censor has been tackled in [11]. The selection criterion is based on explicit preferences over predicates, that are specified together with the CQE instance. This approach, in general, is neither maximally cooperative nor optimal w.r.t. a given state, because the optimal censor is selected statically, in a stateless fashion. Moreover, the given preferences are not always able to select a single optimal censor.

Other CQE approaches based on censors, such as CP censors, in general do not enjoy the indistinguishability property [15,17], which makes them vulnerable to attacks based on knowledge of the CQE algorithm. Moreover, they do not address dynamic query-based censor selection. See [8] for a list of earlier approaches with similar features focused on publishing secure subsets of the ontology. Two nice abstract analyses of censors properties can be found in [21,22].

Finally, Cuenca Grau et al. [16] introduce and investigate an anonymization framework for knowledge graphs based on substituting nodes with blanks.

7   Conclusions

In this paper, we have presented a maximally cooperative approach to controlled query evaluation in OWL and Description Logic ontologies. We have shown that the approach is computationally not harder than the previous static and less cooperative approaches to CQE. Moreover, we have defined a new query rewriting algorithm to solve the query entailment problem in this framework.

The present work can be extended in several interesting directions. First, while the presented results indicate the possibility of a query rewriting approach to dynamic CQE, more work is still needed to define a practical query answering technique and to extend it to non-Boolean UCQs.

Then, the policy language adopted in this paper (set of denials) can be extended to encompass more expressive data protection policies. One step towards this direction, although in the context of static CQE, has been presented e.g. in [12]: it would be interesting to see whether dynCQE can also be extended in a similar way. Finally, it would be interesting to study the computational properties of dynamic CQE in ontology languages different from OWL 2 QL and *DL-Lite$_R$*, in particular in the other lightweight profiles of OWL 2.

Supplemental Material Statement: For complete proofs of our results we refer the reader to an extended version of the present paper [7].

Acknowledgements. This work was partly supported by the EU within the Horizon Europe Programme under the Glaciation project (ref. no. 101070141) and within the H2020 Programme - ERA-NET Cofund ICT-AGRI-FOOD under the ADCATER Project (ref. no. 862665).

References

1. Baader, F., Calvanese, D., McGuinness, D., Nardi, D., Patel-Schneider, P.F. (eds.): The Description Logic Handbook: Theory, Implementation and Applications. Cambridge University Press, Cambridge (2003)
2. Benedikt, M., Cuenca Grau, B., Kostylev, E.V.: Logical foundations of information disclosure in ontology-based data integration. Artif. Intell. **262**, 52–95 (2018)
3. Biskup, J.: For unknown secrecies refusal is better than lying. Data Knowl. Eng. **33**(1), 1–23 (2000)
4. Biskup, J., Bonatti, P.: Controlled query evaluation for enforcing confidentiality in complete information systems. Int. J. Inf. Secur. **3**(1), 14–27 (2004). https://doi.org/10.1007/s10207-004-0032-1
5. Biskup, J., Bonatti, P.A.: Controlled query evaluation for known policies by combining lying and refusal. Ann. Math. Artif. Intell. **40**(1–2), 37–62 (2004)
6. Biskup, J., Bonatti, P.A.: Controlled query evaluation with open queries for a decidable relational submodel. Ann. Math. Artif. Intell. **50**(1–2), 39–77 (2007)
7. Bonatti, P., et al.: CQE in OWL 2 QL: A "longest honeymoon" approach (extended version). arXiv:2207.11155 (2022)
8. Bonatti, P.A., Sauro, L.: A confidentiality model for ontologies. In: Alani, H., et al. (eds.) ISWC 2013. LNCS, vol. 8218, pp. 17–32. Springer, Heidelberg (2013). https://doi.org/10.1007/978-3-642-41335-3_2
9. Calvanese, D., De Giacomo, G., Lembo, D., Lenzerini, M., Rosati, R.: Tractable reasoning and efficient query answering in description logics: the DL-Lite family. J. Autom. Reason. **39**(3), 385–429 (2007)
10. Cima, G., Lembo, D., Marconi, L., Rosati, R., Savo, D.F.: Controlled query evaluation in ontology-based data access. In: Pan, J.Z., et al. (eds.) ISWC 2020. LNCS, vol. 12506, pp. 128–146. Springer, Cham (2020). https://doi.org/10.1007/978-3-030-62419-4_8
11. Cima, G., Lembo, D., Marconi, L., Rosati, R., Savo, D.F.: Controlled query evaluation over prioritized ontologies with expressive data protection policies. In: Hotho, A., et al. (eds.) ISWC 2021. LNCS, vol. 12922, pp. 374–391. Springer, Cham (2021). https://doi.org/10.1007/978-3-030-88361-4_22
12. Cima, G., Lembo, D., Marconi, L., Rosati, R., Savo, D.F., Sinibaldi, D.: Controlled query evaluation over ontologies through policies with numerical restrictions. In: Proceedings of AIKE 2021, pp. 33–36. IEEE (2021)
13. Cima, G., Lembo, D., Rosati, R., Savo, D.F.: Controlled query evaluation in description logics through instance indistinguishability. In: Proceedings of IJCAI 2020, pp. 1791–1797 (2020)
14. Cuenca Grau, B., Kharlamov, E., Kostylev, E.V., Zheleznyakov, D.: Controlled query evaluation over OWL 2 RL ontologies. In: Alani, H., et al. (eds.) ISWC 2013. LNCS, vol. 8218, pp. 49–65. Springer, Heidelberg (2013). https://doi.org/10.1007/978-3-642-41335-3_4
15. Cuenca Grau, B., Kharlamov, E., Kostylev, E.V., Zheleznyakov, D.: Controlled query evaluation for datalog and OWL 2 profile ontologies. In: Proceedings of IJCAI 2015, pp. 2883–2889 (2015)
16. Cuenca Grau, B., Kostylev, E.V.: Logical foundations of linked data anonymisation. J. Artif. Intell. Res. **64**, 253–314 (2019)
17. Lembo, D., Rosati, R., Savo, D.F.: Revisiting controlled query evaluation in description logics. In: Proceedings of IJCAI 2019, pp. 1786–1792 (2019)

18. Lloyd, J.W.: Foundations of Logic Programming (Second, Extended). Springer, Heidelberg (1987). https://doi.org/10.1007/978-3-642-83189-8
19. Motik, B., Cuenca Grau, B., Horrocks, I., Wu, Z., Fokoue, A., Lutz, C.: OWL 2 Web Ontology Language profiles (second edition). W3C Recommendation, W3C, December 2012. http://www.w3.org/TR/owl2-profiles/
20. Motik, B., Fokoue, A., Horrocks, I., Wu, Z., Lutz, C., Cuenca Grau, B.: OWL Web Ontology Language profiles. W3C Recommendation, W3C, October 2009. http://www.w3.org/TR/owl-profiles/
21. Studer, T.: No-go theorems for data privacy. CoRR, abs/2005.13811 (2020)
22. Studer, T., Werner, J.: Censors for boolean description logic. Trans. Data Privacy 7(3), 223–252 (2014)

A Survey of Syntactic Modelling Structures in Biomedical Ontologies

Christian Kindermann[(⊠)] and Martin G. Skjæveland

Department of Informatics, University of Oslo, Oslo, Norway
{chrikin,martige}@ifi.uio.no

Abstract. Despite the large-scale uptake of semantic technologies in the biomedical domain, little is known about common modelling practices in published ontologies. OWL ontologies are often published only in the crude form of sets of axioms leaving the underlying design opaque. However, a principled and systematic ontology development life cycle is likely to be reflected in regularities of the ontology's emergent syntactic structure. To develop an understanding of this emergent structure, we propose to reverse-engineer ontologies taking a syntax-directed approach for identifying and analysing regularities for axioms and sets of axioms. We survey BioPortal in terms of syntactic modelling trends and common practices for OWL axioms and class frames. Our findings suggest that biomedical ontologies only share simple syntactic structures in which OWL constructors are not deeply nested or combined in a complex manner. While such simple structures often account for large proportions of axioms in a given ontology, many ontologies also contain non-trivial amounts of more complex syntactic structures that are not common across ontologies.

1 Introduction

The uptake of OWL in the biomedical domain has lead to the development of a large number of ontologies as well as tools providing support for ontology construction and maintenance. While some ontologies are documented to follow pattern-based design principles, e.g., [19,21], little is known about what kind of design choices, principles, and patterns are widely-used, how they impact ontology engineering in practice. Comparing ontologies in terms of their design rationales is often challenging because different ontology are developed and maintained using a wide range of methodologies, techniques, and tools. Moreover, ontologies are often published as a single file with scarce to no documentation. Yet, a principled and systematic ontology design is likely to be reflected in regularities of the ontology's emergent syntactic structure.

So, to develop an understanding of common practices in ontology engineering, we propose to *reverse-engineer* ontologies in terms of syntactic regularities. Identified regularities may then be analysed and compared to distil common modelling structures both within and across ontologies. In this work, we focus on the syntactic structure of logical expressions in OWL ontologies. In particular, we analyse the way they are composed and combined. The contributions are as follows: (i) we adapt and simplify the formal framework for identifying syntactic regularities originally proposed in [9,10], (ii) we extend this framework by developing methods for analysing such regularities

U. Sattler et al. (Eds.): ISWC 2022, LNCS 13489, pp. 445–461, 2022.
https://doi.org/10.1007/978-3-031-19433-7_26

w.r.t. their underlying syntactic structures, and (iii) we conduct an empirical study to characterise the syntactic structure of axioms and class frames in biomedical ontologies.

This paper is accompanied by a technical report [11] providing more detailed examples, an in-depth discussion about differences between this and prior work, and a more elaborate presentation of both the motivation and potential impact of our work.

2   Preliminaries

We assume the reader to be familiar with Description Logics (DL) [1] and the Web Ontology Language (OWL) [5]. We use DL notation for the sake of readability but interpret logical constructors as specified by OWL. Furthermore, we use both infix and prefix notation for presentational purposes, e.g., $SubClassOf(A, B)$ may be written as $A \sqsubseteq B$ or $\sqsubseteq(A, B)$. We disregard OWL annotations, i.e., axioms with and without annotations are indistinguishable.

A directed labelled *graph* g is an ordered pair (N, E, L) where N is a set of nodes, L is a set of labels, and $E \subseteq N \times L \times N$ is a set of edges. A graph $s = (N', E', L')$ is a *subgraph* of g, written $s \lesssim g$, if $N' \subseteq N$ an $E' \subseteq E$. A *graph isomorphism* between two graphs $g_1 = (N_1, E_1, L_1)$ and $g_2 = (N_2, E_2, L_2)$ is a bijection $f : N_1 \cup L_1 \rightarrow N_2 \cup L_2$ s.t. $(n, l, n') \in E_1$ iff $(f(n), f(l), f(n')) \in E_2$. Two graphs are isomorphic if there exists an isomorphism between them. A *contraction* of an edge $e = (n_1, l, n_2) \in E$ with $n_1 \neq n_2$ is an operation that first removes e from E and replaces both n_1 and n_2 with a single node n' and then makes any node (originally) adjacent to either n_1 or n_2 adjacent to n'. A minor of a graph is a graph obtained by (iteratively) contracting edges, removing edges, or removing nodes without adjacent nodes.

3   Framework for Syntax-Directed Analysis of OWL Ontologies

3.1   Syntactic Regularities

We analyse structures in OWL ontologies using a syntax-directed approach based on their abstract representation according to the structural specification for OWL 2 [16]. This abstract representation can be captured by abstract syntax trees (AST).

Definition 1 (OWL Abstract Syntax Tree). *Let φ be an OWL expression. Then, the abstract syntax tree for $T(\varphi)$ is defined as follows:*

- *if φ is atomic, then $T(\varphi)$ is a node labelled with φ,*
- *if $\varphi = C(\psi_1, \ldots, \psi_n)$, where C is an OWL constructor and $\psi_1, \ldots, \psi_n$ are OWL expressions, then $T(\varphi) =$*

$$
\begin{array}{c}
C \\
\ell(\varphi, 1) \diagup \quad \diagdown \ell(\varphi, n) \\
T(\psi_1) \quad \cdots \quad T(\psi_n)
\end{array}
$$

where ℓ is a labelling function for branches s.t. $\ell(\varphi, i)$ specifies how a subexpression ψ_i at position i is used in relation to C.

The labelling function ℓ is used to treat abstract syntax trees for OWL expressions uniformly as *unordered* trees even in cases where the order of arguments for OWL constructors matters. Consider for example the AST of $SubClassOf(\mathsf{A}, \mathsf{B})$. Here the branches to A and B would be labelled with "Subclass" and "Superclass" respectively. In the following, we will not distinguish between OWL axioms and their ASTs, i.e., an axiom will be referred to simply as a tree (meaning its AST) and vice versa. Similarly, an ontology can be understood as a set of trees.

Given the notion of OWL abstract syntax trees, we can formulate syntax-directed *transformations* for OWL abstract syntax trees that highlight specific syntactic properties of OWL expressions. In particular, we can highlight *shared* syntactic properties between OWL axioms to identify recurring expressions. Consider the axioms $\alpha_1 = \mathsf{A}_1 \sqsubseteq \exists \mathsf{P}.\mathsf{A}_2$ and $\alpha_2 = \mathsf{B}_1 \sqsubseteq \exists \mathsf{Q}.\mathsf{B}_2$. While both axioms differ in terms of named classes and properties, they coincide otherwise. This structural similarity can be highlighted via a syntax-directed transformation that *abstracts* over syntactic properties in which two axioms differ. For example, with a transformation G that replaces atomic entities with a placeholder symbol, say $*$, we have $G(\alpha_1) = G(\alpha_2) = * \sqsubseteq \exists * . * $. Put differently, α_1 and α_2 exhibit the same syntactic structure that is preserved under the *abstraction* G. An abstraction is intuitively understood as an operation that *hides* some level of detail. This intuition can be captured for transformations of ASTs by restricting them to the removal of branches and nodes.

Definition 2 (Language Abstraction). *An* abstraction *for a tree language $\mathcal{L}$ into a tree language $\mathcal{L}'$ is defined by a function $A \colon \mathcal{L} \to \mathcal{L}'$ such that*

1. *there exist $t, t' \in \mathcal{L}$ s.t. $t \neq t'$ with $A(t) = A(t')$,*
2. *for $t \in \mathcal{L}$ there exists a graph minor t_m that is isomorphic to $A(t)$.*

The second condition formalises the idea of only allowing the removal of a tree's branches and nodes whereas the first condition requires that an abstraction hides some kind of information so that two syntax trees become *indistinguishable*. Coming back to the earlier observation that $G(\alpha_1) = G(\alpha_2)$, we note that axiom equality under a given abstraction gives rise to an equivalence relation w.r.t. the syntactic structure of axioms in an ontology. We refer to corresponding equivalence classes as *syntactic regularities*.

Definition 3 (Syntactic Regularity for Axioms). *A syntactic regularity for axioms in an ontology $\mathcal{O}$ is an equivalence class $[\alpha]_A = \{\alpha_i \in \mathcal{O} \mid A(\alpha_i) = A(\alpha)\}$, where A is a language abstraction.*

While axioms are the primary building blocks in OWL ontologies, an entity is often not represented by single axiom but by a *set* of axioms. So, in addition to regularities for axioms, we are also interested in regularities for sets of axioms. We defer the discussion of how to group related axioms into sets until Sect. 3.2. Here, we only note that the notion of syntactic regularities for axioms can be lifted to sets of axioms in a straightforward way. By abuse of notation, we write $A(S)$ to denote a language abstraction on *forests* of syntax trees S rather than syntax trees only.

Definition 4 (Syntactic Regularity for Sets of Axioms). *Let $\mathcal{S} = \{S_1, \ldots, S_n\}$ be a family of sets of axioms in an ontology $\mathcal{O}$. A syntactic regularity for sets of axioms in $\mathcal{O}$ w.r.t. $\mathcal{S}$ is an equivalence class $[S]_A = \{S_i \in \mathcal{S} \mid A(S) = A(S_i)\}$ where A is a language abstraction.*

$$\mathcal{O} = \{ \ \alpha_1 = \mathsf{A} \sqsubseteq \sqcap(\mathsf{A}_1, \mathsf{A}_2),$$
$$\alpha_2 = \mathsf{B} \sqsubseteq \sqcap(\mathsf{B}_1, \mathsf{B}_2),$$
$$\alpha_3 = \mathsf{C} \sqsubseteq \sqcap(\mathsf{C}_1, \mathsf{C}_2, \mathsf{C}_3) \ \}$$

$$[\alpha_1]_G = \{\alpha_1, \alpha_2\}$$
$$[\alpha_3]_G = \{\alpha_3\}$$

$$[\alpha_1]_I = \{\alpha_1, \alpha_2, \alpha_3\}$$

(a)   (b)   (c)

Fig. 1. Example of the language abstractions G and I applied to a sample ontology, and their associated modelling structures: (a) shows the sample ontology (of three axioms) and its syntactic regularities under G and I, (b) displays the two modelling structures for $\mathcal{O}$ under G, while (c) shows the single modelling structure for $\mathcal{O}$ under I. Branch labels are not shown.

3.2 Modelling Structures

A syntactic regularity w.r.t. a language abstraction is uniquely determined by an abstract syntactic structure, namely the abstract syntax tree or forest that each of its elements are mapped to under the used language abstraction. We will refer to these abstract structures as *modelling structures*.

Definition 5 (Modelling Structure). *Let $\mathcal{O}$ be an OWL ontology, $\alpha \in \mathcal{O}$, and $S \subseteq \mathcal{O}$, and A a language abstraction. Then $A(\alpha)$ and $A(S)$ are modelling structures for α and S under A respectively.*

So, a language abstraction gives rise to syntactic regularities in an ontology and each syntactic regularity is associated with a modellling structure. In the following, we provide concrete examples for these notions. We already mentioned the language abstraction G that highlights structural similarities between axioms by abstracting over atomic entities. We will refer to this abstraction as the ground generalisation.

Definition 6 (Ground Generalisation). *Let t be an OWL abstract syntax tree. The Ground Generalisation $G(t)$ of t is a language abstraction defined by a function G that replaces the label of each leaf node in t with the label $*$.*

The example ontology in Fig. 1(a) has two syntactic regularities w.r.t. G, namely $[\alpha_1]_G = \{\alpha_1, \alpha_2\}$ and $[\alpha_3]_G = \{\alpha_3\}$, which each give rise to a modelling structure under G, shown in Fig. 1(b): $G(\alpha_1) = G(\alpha_2) = * \sqsubseteq \sqcap(*, *)$ and $G(\alpha_3) = * \sqsubseteq \sqcap(*, *, *)$. Note that we use prefix notation for the n-ary constructor $\sqcap$ to avoid notational ambiguity. However, all three axioms in the example can be characterised in terms of the nesting of OWL constructors, i.e., all three are subsumption axioms with a conjunction on the right-hand side. The nesting of constructors in OWL axioms can be distilled with a transformation that removes all leaf nodes (and corresponding branches) from the axiom's associated abstract syntax tree. We will refer to the nesting structure of OWL constructors as an axiom's internal tree structure.

Definition 7 (Internal Tree Structure). *Let t be an OWL abstract syntax tree. The internal tree structure $I(t)$ of t is a language abstraction defined by a function I that removes all leaf nodes and corresponding branches from t.*

The example ontology in Fig. 1(a) has only one syntactic regularity w.r.t. I, shown in Fig. 1(c), since $I(\alpha_1) = I(\alpha_2) = I(\alpha_3)$. Intuitively, the abstraction I abstracts over more syntactic properties compared to G which leads to fewer but larger syntactic regularities (where the size of a regularity is the number of its elements, i.e., axioms).

As already mentioned in Sect. 3.1, conceptual models for domain-specific entities are, more often than not, represented with a *set of axioms* rather than with a single axiom. The notion of a *class frame* is widely used for grouping conceptually related axioms in OWL ontologies [7,18].

Definition 8 (Class Frame). *A* class frame $CF(\mathsf{C}, \mathcal{O})$ *for a class expression* C *in an ontology* $\mathcal{O}$ *is defined as the set:* $CF(\mathsf{C}, \mathcal{O}) = \{\alpha \in \mathcal{O} \mid \alpha = SubClassOf(\mathsf{C}, \mathsf{C}'), \text{ or } \alpha = EquivalentClasses(\mathsf{C}, \mathsf{C}_1, \ldots, \mathsf{C}_n)\}, \text{ or } \alpha = DisjointClasses(\mathsf{C}, \mathsf{C}_1, \ldots, \mathsf{C}_n)\}, \text{ or } \alpha = DisjointUnion(\mathsf{C}, \mathsf{C}_1, \ldots, \mathsf{C}_n)\}.$

The abstractions I and G for abstract syntax trees of axioms can be lifted to forests of abstract syntax trees in a straightforward manner.

Definition 9 (Multiset Lifting of Language Abstractions). *Let F be a forest of OWL abstract syntax trees and A a language abstraction for OWL abstract syntax trees. Then the image $A(F)$ of F under A is defined as the multiset $A(F) = \{A(t) \mid t \in F\}$.*

We define $A(F)$ as a multiset to account for repetitions of axioms with the same modelling structure. Consider the set $F = \{SubClassOf(\mathsf{C}, \mathsf{B}), SubClassOf(\mathsf{C}, \mathsf{D})\}$. Using a set for the lifting of G would yield $\{SubClassOf(*, *)\}$ instead of the desired multiset. We write α^x to denote the x-fold repetition of modelling structure α. So, $\{SubClassOf(*, *)^2\}$ denotes the multiset $\{SubClassOf(*, *), SubClassOf(*, *)\}$.

3.3 Relations Between Modelling Structures

The intention of G with regards to syntactic regularities is to group OWL axioms or sets of axioms based on the way OWL constructors are combined and nested. In particular, any difference between axioms in terms of used OWL constructors will be captured by different syntactic regularities. Consider the axioms $\alpha_1 = \mathsf{A} \sqsubseteq \exists\, \mathsf{R}.\mathsf{B}$ and $\alpha_2 = \mathsf{A} \sqsubseteq \exists\, \mathsf{R}.(\exists\, \mathsf{R}.\mathsf{B})$. Clearly, $G(\alpha_1) \neq G(\alpha_2)$. Note, however, that the nesting of OWL constructors in α_1, i.e., its internal tree structure $I(\alpha_1)$, occurs as a *substructure* in α_2. We can formalise this substructure relationship via subgraphs in modelling structures.

Definition 10 (Structure Containment). *Let t and t' be two OWL abstract syntax trees. Then, t structurally contains t', written $t \lesssim^G_I t'$, if*

1. $I(t) \lesssim I(t')$ *and* $I(t) \neq I(t')$, *or*
2. $G(t) \lesssim G(t')$ *and* $I(t) = I(t')$.

The two cases in the definition for structure containment are owed to n-ary constructors. In the case of two OWL expressions e and e' that only involve constructors with a fixed arity we have that $I(e) = I(e')$ implies $G(e) = G(e')$. However, this is not the case for expressions involving n-ary constructors. Consider for example the axioms

$\alpha_1 = A \sqsubseteq \sqcap(C_1, C_2)$ and $\alpha_2 = A \sqsubseteq \sqcap(C_1, C_2, C_3)$. Here, we have $I(\alpha_1) = I(\alpha_2)$ but $G(\alpha_1) \neq G(\alpha_2)$. So, defining the substructure containment between OWL abstract syntax trees only in terms of their internal tree structures would ignore structural information about n-ary constructors. The second case in Definition 10 rectifies this so that α_2 structurally contains α_1. The structure containment relation defines a partial order on OWL abstract syntax trees and thus induces a partial order on syntactic regularities for axioms.

Lemma 1 (Partial Order on Ground Generalisations). *Let $[t_1]_G, \ldots, [t_n]_G$ be syntactic regularities for axioms w.r.t. G in an ontology $\mathcal{O}$. Then the relation $\lesssim_I^G$ induces a partial order on $[t_1]_G, \ldots, [t_n]_G$.*

Similarly, we can induce a partial order on syntactic regularities for class frames w.r.t. G by defining a containment relation based on a notion of subsets for multisets. That is, for each number of axioms with the same ground generalisation in one class frame there needs to exist at least as many axioms with an identical ground generalisation in the other class frame.

Definition 11 (Class Frame Containment). *Let C and C' be class frames in an ontology $\mathcal{O}$. If there exists an injective mapping $m: C \to C'$ s.t. $t \in C$ implies that $G(t) = G(m(t))$, then C' contains C, written $C \lesssim_G C'$.*

Lemma 2 (Partial Order on Class Frames). *Let $[C_1], \ldots, [C_n]$ be syntactic regularities for class frames in an ontology $\mathcal{O}$. Then the relation $\lesssim_G$ for class frames induces a partial order on $[C_1], \ldots, [C_n]$.*

4   Methods

Research Questions. To develop a first understanding of syntactic structures in published ontologies, we focus on properties related to OWL constructors for class expressions. In particular, we investigate to what extent such constructors are nested and combined to give rise to more complex structures. Furthermore, we aim to identify and characterise common structures within and across ontologies. Lastly, we investigate to what extent distinct syntactic structures are related by shared substructures.

Experimental Design. Since we are interested in the way OWL constructors are used in OWL ontologies, we will investigate syntactic regularities w.r.t. the language abstraction G proposed in Sect. 3.2. So, we will refer to syntactic regularities based on G (for axioms and class frames) simply as regularities (for axioms and class frame respectively) unless stated otherwise. Likewise, we will not explicitly specify that modelling structures for regularities are based on G unless the context is ambiguous. Our investigation consists of five experiments. In the following, we give a brief description for each of these experiments and describe the construction of the experimental corpus of ontologies using BioPortal. We refer the interested reader to the technical report [11] for a discussion of using BioPortal for the purposes of this study.

1. Number of Syntactic Regularities. We determine to what extent ontologies give rise to different regularities, i.e., contain different syntactic structures.

2. *Size of Syntactic Regularities.* We give an account of the size of syntactic regularities. Since a regularity is a set, its size is defined by the number of its elements.
3. *Characteristics of Common Modelling Structures.* We determine what kind of modelling structures are common within and across ontologies. For this purpose, we inspect the three largest syntactic regularities in each ontology and qualify their associated modelling structures in terms of the nesting and combination of OWL constructors. Furthermore, we compare the modelling structures associated with large regularities across ontologies to identify structures of a general nature.
4. *Size and Depth of Modelling Structures.* We determine to what extent OWL constructors are nested and combined in modelling structures. For this purpose, we report on the maximal size and depth of modelling structures in ontologies. Since a modelling structure for axioms is a tree, its depth is defined as its tree depth, i.e., the longest path from its root to a child. In the case of modelling structures for class frames, their depth is defined as the maximal depth of its axioms.
5. *Interrelations between Syntactic Regularities.* We determine to what extent syntactic regularities in ontologies are structurally related. So, we analyse the partially ordered sets of syntactic regularities w.r.t. the notions of structural containment (cf. Sect. 3.3). In particular, we construct the Hasse diagrams associated with said posets for each ontology and report on their longest paths, i.e., their depth, as well as their maximal branching factors.

Ontology Corpus. We work with a recent (February 2022) snapshot of BioPortal created in the same way as described in [14]. The data set of ontologies encompasses a total of 736 ontologies. We use the OWL API[1] (v.5.1.15) to orchestrate all experiments. Therefore, we restrict the experimental corpus to ontologies that can be loaded with the OWL API. We load ontologies without their imports closure to avoid double counting syntactic structures that are imported by different ontologies. Furthermore, we exclude ontologies that do not contain class expression axioms because our experiments are restricted to class expression axioms. Lastly, we exclude ontologies for which we could not compute all syntactic regularities and their interrelations within one hour. This procedure results in an experimental corpus of 657 ontologies.

In our experiments, we distinguish between three kinds of ontologies. First, ontologies that consist of atomic axioms only, i.e., $SubClassOf$ and $EquivalentClasses$ axioms that have only named classes as arguments. Second, ontologies expressible in $\mathcal{EL}^{++}$. And third, ontologies not expressible in $\mathcal{EL}^{++}$. We refer to these three kinds of ontologies as atomic, $\mathcal{EL}^{++}$, and rich ontologies respectively. Figure 2 shows the size of an ontology's TBox as well as the size of its subset of class expression axioms. We order ontologies within a category by size and assign each ontology an index in ascending order starting with atomic ontologies as shown in Fig. 2. The corpus contains 94 atomic ontologies, 90 $\mathcal{EL}^{++}$ ontologies, and 473 rich ontologies.

5   Results

We present results for the five experiments as specified in Sect. 4 in separate subsections. We remind the reader that our experimental design distinguishes between three

---

[1] http://owlcs.github.io/owlapi/.

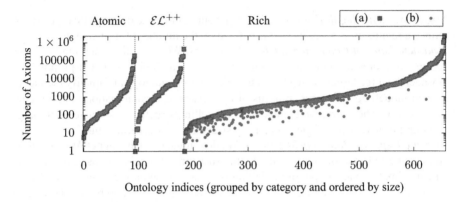

Fig. 2. Number of TBox axioms (a) and class expression axioms (b).

categories of ontologies (atomic, $\mathcal{EL}^{++}$, and rich) and that we have two experimental conditions for all three categories, namely, (a) regularities for axioms and (b) regularities for class frames.

5.1   Experiment 1: Number of Syntactic Regularities

The number of different syntactic regularities for (a) axioms and (b) class frames are shown in Fig. 3 for all three categories of ontologies.

The data reveals that atomic and $\mathcal{EL}^{++}$ ontologies give rise to mostly only one or two regularities for axioms whereas rich ontologies give rise to varying numbers of regularities for axioms. While the largest number of regularities can be found in large rich ontologies, it is not the case that all large ontologies give rise to many regularities.

Even though atomic and $\mathcal{EL}^{++}$ ontologies exhibit only a few regularities for axioms and thus contain mostly axioms of the same syntactic structure, these axioms are combined in many ontologies to give rise to a comparatively larger number of regularities for class frames. For example, the $\mathcal{EL}^{++}$ ontology RH-MESH at index 183 has only two regularities for axioms but 65 regularities for class frames. Similarly, most rich ontologies, especially larger ones beyond index 351 (with about 350 axioms), often give rise to considerably more regularities for class frames compared to regularities for axioms. For example, the rich ontology FMA at index 652 gives rise to 99 regularities for axioms and 3487 regularities for class frames.

5.2   Experiment 2: Size of Syntactic Regularities

The results of Experiment 1 show that many rich ontologies give rise to a fair number of regularities for axioms. In [10], the same result was found for an older snapshot of BioPortal and it was reported that only a few of these regularities for axioms are large. In particular, in the case of regularities for axioms, it was determined that 90% of axioms in many ontologies can be covered by one to three regularities in all three ontology categories. However, the same could not be reported for regularities of class

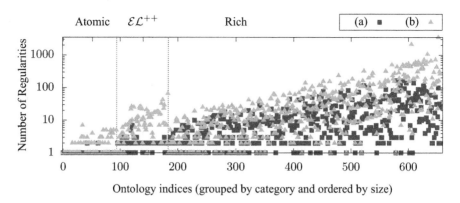

Fig. 3. Number of regularities (with respect to G) for (a) axioms and (b) class frames in atomic, $\mathcal{EL}^{++}$, and rich ontologies.

Table 1. Number of ontologies giving rise to a minimal number of regularities (both for axioms and class frames) with a minimal size of 10, 100, and 1000.

Min. Regularities	Min. Size	Number of Ontologies					
		Regularities for Axioms			Regularities for Class Frames		
		Atomic	$\mathcal{EL}^{++}$	Rich	Atomic	$\mathcal{EL}^{++}$	Rich
5	10	–	–	127	1	37	189
	100	–	–	35	1	6	64
	1000	–	–	8	–	1	21
10	10	–	–	45	–	9	108
	100	–	–	7	–	1	34
	1000	–	–	–	–	–	5

frames; especially for larger rich ontologies. In the case of class frames, it was reported that often more than ten regularities are required to account for 90% of axioms in a given ontology.

While this finding gives some indication for the size of the three largest regularities in ontologies, it is important to keep in mind that many ontologies in our experimental corpus contain several thousands of axioms and that small relative proportions of an ontology can still correspond to many axioms. So, to give an account of the size of regularities in terms of absolute numbers, we report on the number of ontologies that contain at least five or ten regularities with a minimal size of (i) ten, (ii) a hundred or (iii) a thousand elements in Table 1.

It transpires that mostly rich ontologies give rise to multiple regularities of non-trivial sizes within a given ontology. In the case of regularities for axioms, for example, there are 35 rich ontologies with at least 5 regularities that have at least 100 elements. In the case of regularities for class frames, there are even 34 rich ontologies with at least 10 regularities that have at least 100 elements. This confirms to some extent the hypothesis that there exist ontologies with more than three regularities of non-trivial size. However, increasing either the number of minimal regularities, e.g., to ten, or the number of minimal elements, e.g., to 1000, reveals that there are only a few ontologies with many regularities of considerable size.

Lastly, we note that many rich ontologies *do not* give rise to at least 5 regularities with a minimal size of ten. This is interesting in the context of the total number of ontologies (cf. Sect. 5.1) that give rise to 5 or more regularities. In the case of regularities for axioms, there are 285 such rich ontologies which means that $285 - 127 = 158$ ontologies contain only a few large regularities despite giving rise to 5 or more. Similarly, in the case of regularities for class frames, there are $364 - 189 = 175$ such ontologies.

5.3   Experiment 3: Characteristics of Common Modelling Structures

We remind the reader that each syntactic regularity is associated with a unique modelling structure. So, we can identify common syntactic structures *within* an ontology by inspecting the modelling structures of the ontology's largest regularities. Furthermore, we can identify common syntactic structures *across* ontologies by comparing modelling structures associated with the largest regularities within ontologies.

The three largest regularities for axioms across atomic, $\mathcal{EL}^{++}$, and rich ontologies give rise to 2, 11, and 103 distinct modelling structures respectively. Table 2 lists those modelling structures[2] that occur across at least 20 different ontologies. The values in the last three columns of Table 2 reveal the actual number of ontologies in which a given modelling structure is associated with one of the three largest regularities, e.g., the modelling structure $EquivalentClasses(*, *)$ is associated with one of the three largest regularities in two atomic ontologies, two $\mathcal{EL}^{++}$ ontologies, and 24 rich ontologies.

Overall, it transpires that only a few modelling structures for axioms are common both within and across ontologies. Furthermore, these modelling structures are fairly simple in regards to the way OWL constructors are nested and combined. Nevertheless, it is important to keep in mind that rich ontologies exhibit a large variety of modelling structures that are associated with their respective largest regularities. It is also important to mention that many such structures are more complex compared to the ones shown in Table 2. For example, the second largest regularity in the ontology HOOM with 78738 elements is associated with the modelling structure.

$$EquivalentClasses(*, ObjectIntersectionOf(ObjectSomeValuesFrom(*,*),$$
$$ObjectSomeValuesFrom(*,*), ObjectSomeValuesFrom(*,*),$$
$$ObjectSomeValuesFrom(*,*), DataHasValue(*,*))).$$

So, while common modelling structures for axioms *across* ontologies are mostly simple, common modelling structures *within* ontologies can also be rather complex.

The three largest regularities for class frames across atomic, $\mathcal{EL}^{++}$, and rich ontologies give rise to 6, 28, and 209 distinct modelling structures respectively. Table 3 lists

---

[2] The prefix "Object" in some OWL expressions is abbreviated with the capital letter "O" for presentational purposes.

Table 2. Common modelling structures across ontologies. A modelling structure is considered common in a given ontology if it associated with one of its three largest regularities. Ordered by total number of ontologies.

Row	Modelling Structure	Atomic	$\mathcal{EL}^{++}$	Rich
1	$SubClassOf(*,*)$	94	88	466
2	$SubClassOf(*,OSomeValuesFrom(*,*))$	–	68	270
3	$DisjointClasses(*,*)$	–	–	103
4	$EquivalentClasses(*,OIntersectionOf(*,OSomeValuesFrom(*,*)))$	–	1	70
5	$SubClassOf(*,OAllValuesFrom(*,*))$	–	–	44
6	$EquivalentClasses(*,*)$	2	2	24
7	$SubClassOf(*,OExactCardinality(*,*,*))$	–	–	20

Table 3. Number of ontologies in which its the three largest regularities for class frames is associated with a given modelling structure. Ordered by total number of ontologies.

Row	Modelling Structure	Atomic	$\mathcal{EL}^{++}$	Rich
1	$\{SubClassOf(*,*)^1\}$	94	67	431
2	$\{SubClassOf(*,*)^2\}$	37	32	106
3	$\{SubClassOf(*,*)^3\}$	16	15	20
4	$\{SubClassOf(*,OSomeValuesFrom(*,*))^1\}$	-	22	12
5	$\{EquivalentClasses(*,OIntersectionOf(*,OSomeValuesFrom(*,*)))^1\}$	-	1	62
6	$\{DisjointClasses(*,*)^1\}$	-	-	22
7	$\{SubClassOf(*,*)^1, SubClassOf(*,OSomeValuesFrom(*,*))^1\}$	-	35	157
8	$\{SubClassOf(*,*)^1, SubClassOf(*,OSomeValuesFrom(*,*))^2\}$	-	9	50
9	$\{SubClassOf(*,*)^1, SubClassOf(*,OSomeValuesFrom(*,*))^3\}$	-	15	8
10	$\{SubClassOf(*,*)^1, DisjointClasses(*,*)^1\}$	-	-	58
11	$\{SubClassOf(*,*)^1, EquivalentClasses(*,*)^1\}$	2	-	19

those modelling structures for class frames that occur across at least 20 different ontologies in the same manner as Table 2 lists modelling structures for axioms. The results are similar to the case for regularities for axioms in the sense that common modelling structures for class frames across ontologies are mostly simple, i.e., the class frames consist of only a few axioms and the axioms are not deeply nested. Likewise, there are also many ontologies in which the largest three regularities for class frames are associated with more complex modelling structures involving more axioms or more deeply nested OWL constructors (see regularities in CLO for example). However, such more complex modelling structures are only common within ontologies and not across.

5.4 Experiment 4: Size and Depth of Modelling Structures

In this section, we shed some light on the most complex modelling structures in ontologies. We start with the size of modelling structures, i.e., their number of nodes. Figure 4 shows the size of the largest modelling structures in ontologies for both (a) axioms and (b) class frames. We will first highlight some details about the size of modelling structures for axioms before we compare them to modelling structures for class frames.

The maximal size of modelling structures for axioms in atomic ontologies is three because they only contain the modelling structures $* \sqsubseteq *$ and $* \equiv *$. Similarly, the size of modelling structures in most $\mathcal{EL}^{++}$ ontologies is three or five because they only contain the modelling structures $* \sqsubseteq *$ and $* \sqsubseteq \exists *.*$. There are only four ontologies containing modelling structures with a size larger than five. The largest one is found in the ontology CHIRO with size 11 and has the form $* \equiv * \sqcap (\exists *.(* \sqcap (\exists *.*)))$. However, about half of rich ontologies (211 out of 473) contain modelling structures for axioms with a size larger than ten. Interestingly, the maximal size of modelling structures in ontologies appears be independent of the ontologies' overall size, i.e., modelling structures of different sizes occur in ontologies of different sizes.

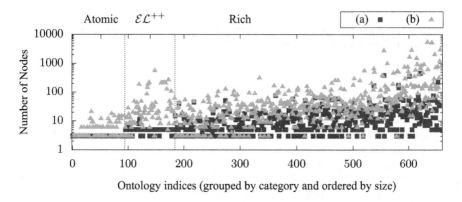

Fig. 4. Number of nodes in the largest modelling structures associated with regularities for (a) axioms and (b) class frames.

The maximal size of modelling structures for class frames is often considerably larger compared to the maximal size of modelling structures for axioms, especially for $\mathcal{EL}^{++}$ and rich ontologies that have more than about 350 axioms. This is to be expected if class frames consist of combinations of many axioms. In this regard, it transpires that class frames in many atomic ontologies and many rich ontologies of smaller size consist of only single axioms. On the right-hand side of Table 4, we summarise how many ontologies contain class frames up to a maximal number axioms. It appears that $\mathcal{EL}^{++}$ and rich ontologies contain class frames with more than three axioms whereas many atomic ontologies only contain class frames with one or two axioms.

In addition to the size of modelling structures, we also investigate their depth. Note that the depth of a class frame is defined in terms of the maximal depth of its axioms. So, the maximal depth of modelling structures for both axioms and class frames is the same and we will not distinguish between the two in the following. On the left-hand side of Table 4, we summarise how many ontologies contain modelling structures up to a maximal depth. There are 167 rich ontologies that contain modelling structures with a depth of at least four. This shows that many rich ontologies not only contain fairly large modelling structures but that modelling structures also involve non-trivial nestings of OWL constructors.

5.5   Experiment 5: Interrelations Between Syntactic Regularities

Table 5 shows the depth and maximal branching factor of Hasse diagrams corresponding to partially ordered sets for syntactic regularities for axioms and class frames w.r.t. $\lesssim_I^G$ and $\lesssim_G$ respectively. It transpires that more than half of the ontologies in our experimental corpus (365 out of 657) give rise to Hasse diagrams with a depth of at least 4. Moreover, 110 ontologies even bring about Hasse diagrams with a depth of 10 or more. The numbers for the maximal branching factor are comparable.

A long path in a Hasse diagram for regularities of class frames means that corresponding modelling structures for class frames are based on the same constituent components since $\lesssim_G$ is defined in terms of a subset relation for multisets. A large branching factor, on the one hand, means that many class frames share a common substructure, namely the modelling structure of their parent. But, on the other hand, it also means that siblings of that parent vary in terms of the modelling structures.

Similarly, a long path in a Hasse diagram for regularities for axioms (as in the case of many rich ontologies) means that many regularities are based on the same nesting of OWL constructors. And a large branching factor signifies that there is a good amount of variablitiy in term of the nesting of OWL constructors on some nesting level.

6   Related Work and Discussion

While there are many surveys of properties of existing ontologies, e.g., [4,13,23,24], there is only little research on the topic of discovering ontology patterns or reverse-engineering an ontology's design. However, two approaches in this direction are motivated on similar grounds to the ones put forward in this work.

The first approach is based on agglomerative clustering to identify commonalities for named entities in an ontology based on similar syntactic representations [15]. Similarities between these representations are distilled in the form of sets of axioms with variables. While these representations bear some similarities to the notion of modelling structures in the context of this work, there are subtle differences with regards to the underlying notion of regularity. The approach using agglomerative clustering identifies regularities for named entities, whereas the approach based on language abstractions identifies regularities for axioms (or sets of axioms). So, the former approach is primarily concerned with regularities for elements of an ontology's domain-specific vocabulary, whereas the latter focuses on regularities for syntactic structures based on an ontology's underlying formal language, e.g., OWL.

The second approach is based on frequent subtree mining over OWL axioms [12]. By interpreting OWL axioms as syntax trees, well-known subtree mining algorithms can be used to identify frequent tree structures. Furthermore, a notion for regularities for class frames is motivated that is based on identified regularities for syntax trees of axioms. For example, regularities for subsumption axioms with the same and non-variable left-hand side are grouped into a set to give rise to a new regularity for sets. In cases where the left-hand side is a variable, frequent itemset mining is proposed to identify co-occurring axioms as regularities for class frames. While the approach based on frequent subtree mining bears a resemblance to the approach based language abstractions, there are both technical differences as well as conceptual differences.

Table 4. Maximal nesting depth of modelling structures (left-hand side) and maximal number of axioms in class frames (right-hand side).

Max Depth	Atomic	$\mathcal{EL}^{++}$	Rich
1	94	16	107
2	-	71	116
3	-	1	83
4	-	1	36
5–9	-	1	118
≥ 10	-	-	13

Max CF Axioms	Atomic	$\mathcal{EL}^{++}$	Rich
1	54	7	43
2	21	14	46
3	6	11	49
4–9	13	35	174
10–19	-	5	73
≥ 20	-	18	88

Table 5. Depth and maximal branching factor of Hasse diagrams for posets.

Depth	Axioms			Class Frames		
	Atomic	$\mathcal{EL}^{++}$	Rich	Atomic	$\mathcal{EL}^{++}$	Rich
1	94	21	96	54	8	47
2	-	67	136	21	14	53
3	-	2	56	9	15	71
4–9	-	-	139	10	33	212
10–19	-	-	41	-	17	61
≥ 20	-	-	5	-	3	29

Branching	Axioms			Class Frames		
	Atomic	$\mathcal{EL}^{++}$	Rich	Atomic	$\mathcal{EL}^{++}$	Rich
0	94	21	96	54	8	47
1	-	66	123	40	34	64
2	-	2	55	-	43	51
3–9	-	1	174	-	5	179
10–19	-	-	25	-	-	70
≥ 20	-	-	-	-	-	62

First and foremost, it is important to recognise that frequent subtree mining aims at identify regularities based on some notion of *frequency*. A tree structure is considered frequent if it satisfies some threshold criterion. However, regularities based on language abstractions are *independent* of any notion of frequency; or any other notion depending on a threshold for that matter. The importance of this needs to be emphasised because regularities based on thresholds are generally not suitable for analysing an ontology's design as a whole. The simple reason for this is that such notions, by definition, do not account for structures that do not satisfy the threshold criterion. For example, variations in the reuse of a single pattern in an ontology's design may give rise to many slightly different syntactic structures. If none of the variant reuses of the pattern gives rise to frequent structures, then no regularity (based on frequency) is identified.

In any case, any conclusion or claim about an ontology's underlying design based on syntactic regularities has to be made with due diligence regardless of the used approach. Consider for example the case of a pattern-based ontology design. A *pattern* in the context of ontology engineering often denotes a rather distinctive notion. An example of this are *Ontology Design Patterns* (ODP) that are proposed as well-proven modelling solution to common modelling problems and often provide a reusable component such as a set of axioms [2,3]. While such a reusable component is often associated with a syntactic structure, e.g., a set of axioms, the converse is not necessarily the case. Meaning, a reusable component of a pattern cannot be equated with the pattern itself and the presence of axioms associated with a pattern's reusable component cannot be equated with an actual reuse of the pattern. So, even though the discovery of regularities can be helpful to detect structures that are indicative of an ODP's reuse, a domain expert's assessment of an identified regularity in an ontology is required to gauge whether the regularity is connected to an ODP.

Even though the idea of reusable components has been popularised by the ODP community, there is no standard mechanism or de facto practice for reusing a given ODP. Despite the development of frameworks and tool support for ODPs reuse [8, 17, 22, 25], little is known about what kind of features are needed to facilitate pattern-based ontology engineering in practice [6]. Developing an understanding of compositional aspects of syntactic structures in ontologies w.r.t. syntactic abstractions may provide a way of informing and evaluating the design of tools and frameworks in this direction.

As an example, consider the Galen Ontology [20] in which the classes Current-BloodPressureLevel and RecentBloodPressureLevel are represented via almost identical $EquivalentClasses$ axioms. Both use the following expression (written in infix notation):

LevelState ⊓ (∃isSpecificAnswerOf.(InvestigationAct ⊓ (∃hasTimeOfOccurrence.
(TimeOfOccurrence ⊓ (∃hasAbsoluteState $atTime$))) ⊓ (∃isToDetermine.BloodPressure)))

where the variable $atTime$ is set to Now and RecentPast respectively. Here, the use of the variable $atTime$ can be seen as an abstraction over differences between the representations of CurrentBloodPressureLevel and RecentBloodPressureLevel. In this case, a simple templating mechanism allowing for the *instantiation of parametrised representations*, e.g. CurrentBloodPressureLevel ≡ BloodPressureLevel(Now), would be suitable to capture this abstract structure in an arguably meaningful way. So, research into the discovery of meaningful abstractions as well as suitable ways of encoding them promises to have a great impact on pattern-based ontology engineering.

7   Conclusion

In this paper, we adapted and extended a formal framework for analysing syntactic regularities in ontologies originally proposed in [9, 10]. The framework is based on a syntax-directed approach that decomposes an ontology into equivalence classes of syntactic structures, where two syntactic structures are considered equivalent if they are indistinguishable under a formal notion of abstraction. We proposed the notion of a modelling structure for the purpose of analysing and characterising syntactic regularities. Furthermore, we proposed formal relations between such modelling structures so that they can be organised in terms of a partial order that captures a notion of substructure containment. Finally, we used these notions to conduct a large-scale empirical investigation of syntactic modelling structures in biomedical ontologies.

We find that most ontologies contain primarily axioms of a simple syntactic structure. However, such axioms seem to be combined in various ways to give rise to comparatively many modelling structures for class frames. This suggests that class frames play a crucial role in the representation of many entities in the biomedical domain.

Our findings on common modelling structures across biomedical ontologies reveal that only comparatively simple syntactic structures for both axioms and class frames reoccur. However, the results obtained on the maximal size and depth of modelling structures indicate that many rich ontologies also contain highly complex modelling structures in which OWL constructors are deeply nested and combined. Moreover, such complex structures are also highly interrelated w.r.t. shared substructures in many ontologies. While our investigation provides proof of structural complexities in ontologies, further research is needed to qualify underlying design rationales.

Supplemental Material Statement: Source code is available at https://github.com/ckindermann/iswc-2022.

References

1. Baader, F., Calvanese, D., McGuinness, D.L., Nardi, D., Patel-Schneider, P.F. (eds.): The Description Logic Handbook: Theory, Implementation, and Applications. Cambridge University Press, Cambridge (2003)
2. Blomqvist, E., Sandkuhl, K.: Patterns in ontology engineering: classification of ontology patterns. In: ICEIS (3), pp. 413–416 (2005)
3. Gangemi, A.: Ontology design patterns for semantic web content. In: Gil, Y., Motta, E., Benjamins, V.R., Musen, M.A. (eds.) ISWC 2005. LNCS, vol. 3729, pp. 262–276. Springer, Heidelberg (2005). https://doi.org/10.1007/11574620_21
4. Glimm, B., Hogan, A., Krötzsch, M., Polleres, A.: OWL: yet to arrive on the web of data? In: LDOW. CEUR Workshop Proceedings, vol. 937. CEUR-WS.org (2012)
5. Grau, B.C., Horrocks, I., Motik, B., Parsia, B., Patel-Schneider, P.F., Sattler, U.: OWL 2: The next step for OWL. J. Web Semant. **6**(4), 309–322 (2008)
6. Hammar, K., et al.: Collected research questions concerning ontology design patterns. In: Ontology Engineering with Ontology Design Patterns, Studies on the Semantic Web, vol. 25, pp. 189–198. IOS Press (2016)
7. Horridge, M., Patel-Schneider, P.F.: Manchester syntax for OWL 1.1. In: OWLED (Spring). CEUR Workshop Proceedings, vol. 496. CEUR-WS.org (2008)
8. Iannone, L., Rector, A., Stevens, R.: Embedding knowledge patterns into OWL. In: Aroyo, L., et al. (eds.) ESWC 2009. LNCS, vol. 5554, pp. 218–232. Springer, Heidelberg (2009). https://doi.org/10.1007/978-3-642-02121-3_19
9. Kindermann, C.: Analysing patterns and regularities in ontologies. Ph.D. thesis, University of Manchester, UK (2022)
10. Kindermann, C., Parsia, B., Sattler, U.: Syntactic regularities based on language abstractions. In: Advances in Pattern-Based Ontology Engineering, vol. 51, p. 312 (2021)
11. Kindermann, C., Skjæveland, M.G.: A survey of syntactic modelling structures in biomedical ontologies. CoRR abs/2207.14119 (2022). https://arxiv.org/abs/2207.14119
12. Lawrynowicz, A., Potoniec, J., Robaczyk, M., Tudorache, T.: Discovery of emerging design patterns in ontologies using tree mining. Semantic Web **9**(4), 517–544 (2018). https://doi.org/10.3233/SW-170280
13. Matentzoglu, N., Bail, S., Parsia, B.: A snapshot of the OWL web. In: Alani, H., et al. (eds.) ISWC 2013. LNCS, vol. 8218, pp. 331–346. Springer, Heidelberg (2013). https://doi.org/10.1007/978-3-642-41335-3_21
14. Matentzoglu, N., Parsia, B.: BioPortal Snapshot 30.03.2017, March 2017. https://doi.org/10.5281/zenodo.439510
15. Mikroyannidi, E., Iannone, L., Stevens, R., Rector, A.: Inspecting regularities in ontology design using clustering. In: Aroyo, L., et al. (eds.) ISWC 2011. LNCS, vol. 7031, pp. 438–453. Springer, Heidelberg (2011). https://doi.org/10.1007/978-3-642-25073-6_28
16. Motik, B., et al.: OWL 2 Web Ontology Language: Structural Specification and Functional-Style. WC3 Recommendation, January 2008

17. Noppens, O., Liebig, T.: Ontology patterns and beyond - towards a universal pattern language. In: WOP. CEUR Workshop Proceedings, vol. 516. CEUR-WS.org (2009)
18. Noy, N.F., Musen, M.A., Jr Mejino, J.L.V., Rosse, C.: Pushing the envelope: challenges in a frame-based representation of human anatomy. Data Knowl. Eng. **48**(3), 335–359 (2004)
19. Osumi-Sutherland, D., Courtot, M., Balhoff, J.P., Mungall, C.J.: Dead simple OWL design patterns. J. Biomed. Semant. **8**(1), 18:1-187 (2017)
20. Rector, A., Rogers, J.: Ontological and practical issues in using a description logic to represent medical concept systems: experience from GALEN. In: Barahona, P., Bry, F., Franconi, E., Henze, N., Sattler, U. (eds.) Reasoning Web 2006. LNCS, vol. 4126, pp. 197–231. Springer, Heidelberg (2006). https://doi.org/10.1007/11837787_9
21. Sarntivijai, S., et al.: CLO: the cell line ontology. J. Biomed. Semant. **5**, 37 (2014)
22. Skjæveland, M.G., Lupp, D.P., Karlsen, L.H., Forssell, H.: Practical ontology pattern instantiation, discovery, and maintenance with reasonable ontology templates. In: Vrandečić, D., et al. (eds.) ISWC 2018. LNCS, vol. 11136, pp. 477–494. Springer, Cham (2018). https://doi.org/10.1007/978-3-030-00671-6_28
23. Sváb-Zamazal, O., Svátek, V.: Analysing ontological structures through name pattern tracking. In: Gangemi, A., Euzenat, J. (eds.) EKAW 2008. LNCS (LNAI), vol. 5268, pp. 213–228. Springer, Heidelberg (2008). https://doi.org/10.1007/978-3-540-87696-0_20
24. Wang, T.D., Parsia, B., Hendler, J.: A survey of the web ontology landscape. In: Cruz, I., et al. (eds.) ISWC 2006. LNCS, vol. 4273, pp. 682–694. Springer, Heidelberg (2006). https://doi.org/10.1007/11926078_49
25. Warrender, J.D., Lord, P.: A Pattern-driven Approach to Biomedical Ontology Engineering. In: SWAT4LS. CEUR Workshop Proceedings, vol. 1114. CEUR-WS.org (2013)

HybridFC: A Hybrid Fact-Checking Approach for Knowledge Graphs

Umair Qudus[(✉)][iD], Michael Röder[iD], Muhammad Saleem[iD],
and Axel-Cyrille Ngonga Ngomo[iD]

DICE Group, Department of Computer Science, Universität Paderborn, Paderborn, Germany
{umair.qudus,michael.roeder,axel.ngonga}@uni-paderborn.de,
saleem@mail.uni-paderborn.de
https://dice-research.org/

Abstract. We consider fact-checking approaches that aim to predict the veracity of assertions in knowledge graphs. Five main categories of fact-checking
approaches for knowledge graphs have been proposed in the recent literature,
of which each is subject to partially overlapping limitations. In particular, current text-based approaches are limited by manual feature engineering. Path-
based and rule-based approaches are limited by their exclusive use of knowledge graphs as background knowledge, and embedding-based approaches suffer
from low accuracy scores on current fact-checking tasks. We propose a hybrid
approach—dubbed HybridFC—that exploits the diversity of existing categories
of fact-checking approaches within an ensemble learning setting to achieve a significantly better prediction performance. In particular, our approach outperforms
the state of the art by 0.14 to 0.27 in terms of Area Under the Receiver Operating
Characteristic curve on the FactBench dataset. Our code is open-source and can
be found at https://github.com/dice-group/HybridFC.

Keywords: Fact checking · Ensemble learning · Knowledge graph veracity

1 Introduction

Knowledge graphs (KGs) are an integral part of the Web. A recent crawl of 3.2 billion
HTML pages found over 82 billion RDF statements distributed over roughly half of
the Web pages that were crawled.[1] The increasing adoption of RDF at Web scale is
further corroborated by the Linked Open Data cloud, which now contains over 10,000
KGs with more than 150 billion assertions and 3 billion entities.[2] Large-scale KGs like
WikiData [30], DBpedia [2], Knowledge Vault [13], and YAGO [43] contain billions
of assertions, and describe millions of entities. They are being used as background
knowledge in a growing number of applications, including healthcare [26], autonomous
chatbots [1], and in-flight entertainment [31]. However, it is well established that current
KGs are partially incorrect. For example, roughly 20% of DBpedia's assertions are

---

[1] http://webdatacommons.org/structureddata/2021-12/stats/stats.html.
[2] https://lod-cloud.net/.

© The Author(s), under exclusive license to Springer Nature Switzerland AG 2022
U. Sattler et al. (Eds.): ISWC 2022, LNCS 13489, pp. 462–480, 2022.
https://doi.org/10.1007/978-3-031-19433-7_27

assumed to be false in the literature [20,39]. Fostering the further uptake of KGs at Web scale hence requires the development of highly accurate approaches that are able to predict the veracity of the assertions found in KGs in an automated fashion. We call such approaches fact-checking approaches.

In general, fact checking can be understood as the task of computing the likelihood that a given assertion is true [6]. Various categories of automatic approaches have been proposed for this task. These categories include but are not limited to text-based [20, 46], path-based [9,19,41,45,48], rule-based [16,17,27], and embedding-based [7,29] approaches. State-of-the-art instantiations of these categories of approaches are faced with a set of common limitations. In particular,

(1) Current text-based approaches rely on manual feature engineering [20,39,46], which is time-consuming, and has been shown to be suboptimal w.r.t. their prediction performance by representation learning approaches [5].
(2) Path-based approaches rely on the availability of (short) paths in the KG between the entities that are part of the given assertion [48].
(3) Approaches that rely on KGs as background knowledge, i.e., path-, rule- and embedding-based approaches, have to take the open-world assumption (OWA) into account when determining the veracity of the given assertion [48].
(4) Embedding-based approaches [42] encounter limitations with respect to their accuracy [22] as well as their scalability [50].

We alleviate these limitations by exploiting the principles of diversity and accuracy known from ensemble learning. Our approach, dubbed HybridFC, overcomes the drawbacks of individual categories of approaches by leveraging the advantages of other categories of approaches. For example, we replace the manual feature engineering of the text-based approaches by exploiting embeddings. To the best of our knowledge, we are the first to propose the combination of text-, path- and embedding-based fact-checking approaches in an ensemble learning setting.

The contributions of this work are as follows:

- We use pre-trained KG embedding and sentence transformer models, and take advantage of transfer learning to reuse them for the task of fact checking.
- We study the performance of different fact-checking approaches in isolation and in combination, and show that the joint use of multiple categories of approaches within an ensemble learning setting often leads to an improved performance.
- We benchmark our approach on two recent fact-checking datasets, i.e., FactBench and BirthPlace/DeathPlace (BD). Our experiments suggest that our hybrid approach outperforms other text-, path-, rule- and embedding-based approaches by at least 0.14 area under the curve (AUROC) on average on the FactBench dataset. It is ranked 3rd on the smaller BD dataset.

The rest of this paper is structured as follows. In Sect. 2, we introduce the notation required to understand the rest of the paper. In Sect. 3, we give related work and motivate our work using a real-world example. In Sect. 4, we present HybridFC. Thereafter, the evaluation datasets and metric used are presented in Sect. 5. We then discuss our results in Sect. 6. In Sect. 7, we present an ablation study of our approach. Finally, we conclude and discuss potential future work in Sect. 8.

2 Preliminaries

In this section, we define the terminology and notation used throughout this paper. We build upon the definition of fact checking for KGs suggested in [46]:

Definition 1 (Fact Checking). *Given an assertion, a reference KG G, and/or a reference corpus, fact checking is the task of computing the likelihood that the given assertion is true or false [46].*

Throughout this work, we rely on RDF KGs:

Definition 2 (RDF Knowledge Graph). *An RDF KG G is a set of RDF triples $G \subseteq (\mathbb{E} \cup \mathbb{B}) \times \mathbb{P} \times (\mathbb{E} \cup \mathbb{B} \cup \mathbb{L})$, where each triple $(s, p, o) \in G$ comprises a subject s, a predicate p, and an object o. $\mathbb{E}$ is the set of all RDF resource IRIs, $\mathbb{B}$ the set of all blank nodes, $\mathbb{P} \subseteq \mathbb{E}$ the set of all RDF predicates, and $\mathbb{L}$ the set of all literals [47].*

In our approach, we use multiple representations of RDF KGs. In addition to their representation as sets of assertions, we also exploit representations in continuous vector spaces, called embeddings [10,50].

Definition 3 (KG Embeddings). *A KG embedding function φ maps a KG G to a continuous vector space. Given an assertion (s, p, o), $\varphi(s), \varphi(p)$, and $\varphi(o)$ stand for the embedding of the subject, predicate, and object, respectively. Some embedding models map the predicate embedding into a vector space that differs from the space wherein $\varphi(s)$ and $\varphi(o)$ are mapped. For those models, we use $\varphi^*(p)$ to denote predicate embeddings.*

Different embedding-based approaches use different scoring functions to compute embeddings [50]. The approaches considered in this paper are shown in Table 1.

Table 1. Scoring functions of different embedding-based approaches used in this paper. $\otimes$ stands for the quaternion multiplication, $\mathbb{R}$ for the space of real numbers, $\mathbb{H}$ for the space of quaternions, $\mathbb{C}$ for the complex numbers, Re for the real part of a complex number, Im for the imaginary part of a complex number, conv for the convolution operator, $\overline{\varphi(o)}$ for the complex conjugate of $\varphi(o)$, q is the length of embedding vectors, $\cdot$ for the dot product and $\|\cdot\|_2$ for the L2 norm.

Approach	Scoring function	VectorSpace	Regularizer
TransE	$\|(\varphi(s) + \varphi(p)) - \varphi(o)\|_2$	$\varphi(s), \varphi(p), \varphi(o) \in \mathbb{R}^q$	L2
ComplEx	$\mathrm{Re}\left(< \varphi(s), \varphi(p), \overline{\varphi(o)} >\right)$	$\varphi(s), \varphi(p), \varphi(o) \in \mathbb{C}^q$	Weighted L2
QMult	$\varphi(s) \otimes \varphi(p) \cdot \varphi(o)$	$\varphi(s), \varphi(p), \varphi(o) \in \mathbb{H}^q$	Weighted L2
ConEx	$\mathrm{Re}(\langle \mathrm{conv}(\varphi(s), \varphi(p)), \varphi(s), \varphi(p), \overline{\varphi(o)} \rangle)$	$\varphi(s), \varphi(p), \varphi(o) \in \mathbb{C}^q$	Dropout, BatchNorm

Definition 4 (Sentence Embedding Model). *A sentence embedding model maps the natural language sentence t to a continuous vector space [37]. Let b be the embedding function and let $T = (t_1, \ldots, t_k)$ be a list of k sentences. We create the embedding vector for T by concatenating the embedding vectors of the single sentences.*

3 Related Work

We divide the existing fact-checking approaches into 5 categories: text-based [20,46], path-based [41,47], rule-based [16,17,27], KG-embedding-based [7,24,29], and hybrid approaches [14,15,28]. In the following, we give a brief overview of state-of-the-art approaches in each category along with their limitations.

3.1 Text-Based Approaches

Approaches in this category validate a given assertion by searching for evidence in a reference text corpus. FactCheck [46] and DeFacto [20] are two instantiations of this category. Both approaches search for pieces of text that can be used as evidence to support the given assertion by relying on RDF verbalisation techniques. TISCO [39] relies on a temporal extension of DeFacto. All three approaches rely on a set of manually engineered features to compute a vectorial representation of the texts they retrieved as evidence. This manual feature engineering often leads to a suboptimal vectorial representation of textual evidence [5]. In contrast, we propose the use of embeddings to represent pieces of evidence gathered from text as vectors. First, this ensures that our approach is aware of the complete piece of textual evidence instead of the fragment extracted by previous approaches. Second, it removes the need to engineer features manually and hence reduces the risk of representing text with a possibly suboptimal set of manually engineered features.

3.2 Path-Based Approaches

Path-based approaches generally aim to validate the input assertion by first computing short paths from the assertion's subject to its object within the input KG. These paths are then used to score the input assertion. Most of the state-of-the-art path-based approaches, such as COPAAL [47], Knowledge stream [41], PRA [19], SFE [18], and KG-Miner [40] rely on RDF semantics (e.g., class subsumption hierarchy, domain and range information) to filter useful paths. However, the T-Box of a large number of KGs provides a limited number of RDFS statements. Furthermore, it may also be the case that no short paths can be found within the reference KG, although the assertion is correct [47]. In these scenarios, path-based approaches fail to predict the veracity of the given assertion correctly.[3]

3.3 Rule-based Approaches

State-of-the-art rule-based models such as KV-Rule [25], AMIE [16,17,27], OP [8], and RuDiK [34] extract association rules to perform fact checking or fact prediction on KGs. To this end, they often rely on reasoning [27,44]. These approaches are limited by the knowledge contained within the KG, and mining rules from large-scale KGs can be a very slow process in terms of runtime (e.g., OP takes $\geq$ 45 hours on DBpedia [27]).

---

[3] For the assertion *award_00135* from the FactBench, COPAAL produces a score of 0.0 as it is unable to find a path between the assertion's subject and its object.

3.4   Embedding-Based Approaches

Embedding-based approaches use a mapping function to represent the input KG in a continuous low-dimensional vector space [7,12,21,24,29,42,49]. For example, Esther [42] uses compositional embeddings to compute likely paths between resources. TKGC [21] checks the veracity of assertions extracted from the Web before adding them to a given KG. The veracity of assertions is calculated by creating a KG embedding model and learning a scoring function to compute the veracity of these assertions. In general, embedding-based approaches are mainly limited by the knowledge contained within the continuous representation of the KG. Therefore, these approaches encounter limitations with respect to their accuracy in fact-checking scenarios [22] as well as their scalability when applied to large-scale KGs [50].

3.5   Hybrid Approaches

While the aforementioned categories have their limitations, they also come with their own strengths. Consider the assertion in Listing 1.1. The text-based approach FactCheck cannot find evidence for the assertion. A possible reason might be that West Hollywood is not mentioned on the Wikipedia page of Johnny Carson. However, COPAAL finds evidence in the form of corroborative paths that connect the subject and the object in DBpedia. For example, the first corroborative path in this particular example from FactBench [20] encodes that if two individuals share a death place, then they often share several death places. While this seems counter-intuitive, one can indeed have several death places by virtue of the part-of relation between geo-spatial entities, e.g., one's death places can be both the Sierra Towers and West Hollywood. In our second example shown in Listing 1.2, COPAAL is not able to find any relevant paths between the subject and the object. This shows one of the weaknesses of COPAAL which does not perform well for rare events, e.g., when faced with the :award property [47]. In contrast, TransE [7] is able to classify the assertion as correct. These examples support our hypothesis that there is a need for a hybrid solution in which the limitations of one approach can be compensated by the other approaches.

Listing 1.1. Example 1 (correct, `death-00129.ttl` in the FactBench dataset [20]).

```
PREFIX dbr:   <http://dbpedia.org/resource/>
PREFIX dbo:   <http://dbpedia.org/ontology/>
Assertion:    dbr:Johnny_Carson dbo:deathPlace dbr:West_Hollywood,_California

FactCheck Result: Score: 0.0
Proofs: [no proofs found]
========================================================
COPAAL Result: Score: 0.99
Proofs: evidence paths:[
evidence path 1: "predicate path: dbo:deathPlace/^dbo:deathPlace/dbo:deathPlace",
evidence path 2: "predicate path: dbo:deathPlace/^dbo:recordedIn/dbo:recordedIn",
...]
```

Listing 1.2. Example 2 (correct, `award-00135.ttl` in the FactBench dataset [20]).

```
Assertion:   dbr:T._S._Eliot dbo:award dbr:Nobel_Prize_in_Literature

COPAAL Result: Score: 0.0
Proofs: evidence paths: [no paths found]
========================================================
TransE Result: Score: 0.90
```

FACTY [28], ExFaKT [15], and Tracy [14] are hybrid approaches that exploit structured as well as textual reference knowledge to find the human-comprehensible explanations for a given assertion. ExFaKT and Tracy[4] make use of rules mined from the KG. A given assertion is assumed to be correct if it fulfills all conditions of one of the mined rules. These conditions can be fulfilled by facts from the KG or by texts retrieved from the Web. The output of these approaches is not a veracity score. Rather, they produce human-comprehensible explanations to support human fact-checkers. Furthermore, these approaches are not designed for ensemble learning settings. They incorporate a text search merely to find support for the rules they generate. As such, they actually address different problem statements than the one addressed herein. FACTY leverages textual reference and path-based techniques to find supporting evidence for each triple, and subsequently predicts the correctness of each triple based on the found evidence. Like Tracy and ExFaKT, FACTY only combines two different categories and mainly focuses on generating human-comprehensible explanations for candidate facts. To the best of our knowledge, our approach is the first approach that uses approaches from three different categories with the focus on automating the fact-checking task.

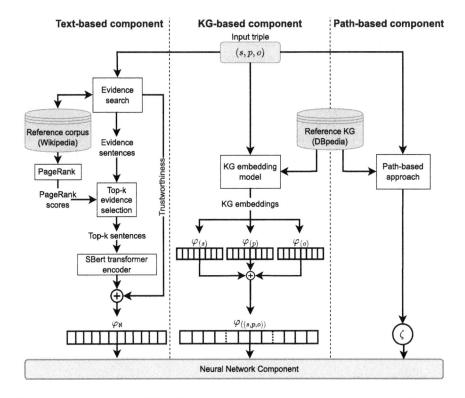

Fig. 1. Architecture of HybridFC. The purple color represents reference knowledge. The green color marks the input assertion. KG stands for knowledge graph. (Color figure online)

---

[4] https://www.mpi-inf.mpg.de/impact/exfakt#Tracy.

4 Methodology

The main idea behind our approach, HybridFC, is to combine fact-checking approaches from different categories. To this end, we created components for a text-based, a path-based and a KG embedding-based fact-checking algorithm. Figure 1 depicts a high-level architecture of our approach. We fuse the results from the three components and feed them into a neural network component, which computes a final veracity score. In the following, we first describe the three individual components of our approach in detail. Thereafter, we describe the neural network component that merges their results.

4.1 Text-Based Component

Text-based approaches typically provide a list of scored text snippets that provide evidence for the given assertion, together with a link to the source of these snippets and a trustworthiness score [20,46]. The next step is to use machine learning on these textual evidence snippets to evaluate a given assertion. In HybridFC, we refrain from using the machine learning module of text-based approaches. Instead, we compute an ordering for the list of text snippets returned by text-based approaches. To this end, we first determine the PageRank scores for all articles in the reference corpus [35] and select evidence sentences. Our evidence sentence selection module is based on the following hypothesis: "Documents (websites) with higher PageRank score provide better evidence sentences". Ergo, once provided with scored text snippets by a text-based approach, we select the top-k evidence sentences coming from documents with top-k PageRank scores. To each text snippet, we assign the PageRank score of its source article. Then, we sort the list of text snippets and use the k snippets with the highest PageRank score.

We convert each of the selected snippets t_i into a continuous vector representation using a sentence embedding model. We concatenate these sentence embeddings along with the trustworthiness scores [32] of their respective sources to create a single vector $\varphi_\aleph$. In short:

$$\varphi_\aleph = \bigoplus_{i=1}^{k} \left(b(t_i) \oplus \tau_i \right), \tag{1}$$

where $\oplus$ stands for the concatenation of vectors, $b(t_i)$ is the sentence embeddings of t_i and τ_i is the trustworthiness score of t_i. Our approach can make use of any text-based fact-checking approach that provides text snippets and a trustworthiness score, and allows us to compute PageRank score. Moreover, we can use any sentence embedding model. For our experiments, we adapt the state-of-the-art text-based approach FactCheck [46] as a text-based fact checking approach, and make use of a pre-trained SBert Transformer model for sentence embeddings [37].

4.2 Path-Based Component

Path-based approaches determine the veracity of a given assertion by finding evidence paths in a reference KG. Our path-based component can make use of any existing path-based approach that takes the given assertion as input together with the reference KG and creates a single veracity score ζ as output. This veracity score is the result of our path-based component. Within our experiments, we use the state-of-the-art unsupervised path-based approach COPAAL [48].

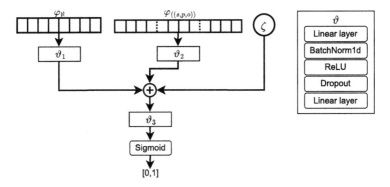

Fig. 2. Left: Overview of the architecture of HybridFC's neural network component. Right: Every ϑ_i is a multi-layer perceptron module.

4.3 KG Embedding-Based Component

KG embedding-based approaches generate a continuous representation of a KG using a mapping function. Based on a given KG embedding model, we create an embedding vector for a given assertion (s, p, o) by concatenating the embedding of its elements and define the embedding mapping function for assertions $\varphi((s, p, o))$ as follows:

$$\varphi((s, p, o)) = \varphi(s) \oplus \varphi(p) \oplus \varphi(o). \tag{2}$$

In our approach, we can make use of any KG embedding approach that returns both entities and relations embeddings. However, only a few approaches provide pre-trained embeddings for large-scale KGs (e.g., DBpedia). We use all approaches that provide pre-trained embeddings for DBpedia entities and relations in our experiments.

4.4 Neural Network Component

The output of the three components above is the input to our neural network component. As depicted in Fig. 2, the neural network component consists of three multi-layer perceptron modules that we name ϑ_i.[5] Each of these modules consists of a Linear layer, a Batch Normalization layer, a ReLU layer, a Dropout layer and a final Linear layer. The output of the text-based component $\varphi_\aleph$ is fed as input to the first module. The output of the KG embedding-based component $\varphi((s, p, o))$ is fed to the second module. The output of the 2 modules and the veracity score ζ of the path-based component are concatenated and fed to the third module. The result of the third module is used as input to

---

[5] During a first evaluation a simpler approach with only one multi-layer perceptron module (i.e., without ϑ_1 and ϑ_2) showed an insufficient performance.

a sigmoid function σ, which produces a final output in the range $[0, 1]$. The calculation of the final veracity ω score for the given assertion can be formalized as follows:

$$\omega = \sigma\left(w_\sigma^T \vartheta_3\left(\vartheta_1(\varphi_\mathbf{N}) \oplus \vartheta_2(\varphi((s, p, o))) \oplus \zeta\right)\right), \tag{3}$$

where w_σ is a weight vector that is multiplied with the output vector of the third module. Each of the three multi-layer perceptron modules (ϑ_i) is defined as follows for an input vector x:

$$\vartheta_i = W_{5,i} \times D_p(ReLU(W_{3,i} \times (BN(W_{1,i} \times x)))), \tag{4}$$

where x is an input vector, $W_{j,i}$ is the weight matrix of an affine transformation in the j-th layer of the multi-layer perceptron, $\times$ represents the matrix multiplication, ReLU is an activation function, D_p stands for a Dropout layer [51], and BN represents the Batch Normalization [23]. The latter is defined in the following equation:

$$BN(x') = \beta + \gamma \frac{x' - \mathrm{E}[x']}{\sqrt{\mathrm{Var}[x']}}, \tag{5}$$

where, x' is the output vector of the first Linear layer and the input to the Batch Normalization, and $\mathrm{E}[x']$ and $\mathrm{Var}[x']$ are the expected value and variance of x', respectively. β and γ are weight vectors, which are learned during the training process via backpropagation to increase the accuracy [23]. Furthermore, given the output of the Linear layer x as input to the Dropout layer D_p, the output $\bar{x}$ is computed as:

$$\begin{cases} \bar{x} &= D_p(x) \\ \bar{x}_i &= \delta_i x_i, \end{cases} \tag{6}$$

where each δ_i follows the Bernoulli distribution of parameter p, i.e., δ is 1 with probability p, and 0 otherwise.

5   Experimental Setup

We evaluate our approach by comparing it with seven state-of-the-art fact-checking approaches. In the following, we first describe the datasets we rely upon. Then, we describe our experimental setting.

5.1   Datasets

Fact-Checking Datasets. In our experiments, we use two recent fact-checking datasets that are often used in the literature [20,46,47]: FactBench and BirthPlace/DeathPlace (BD). We use these datasets because they comprise entities of DBpedia, which is (i) large, and (ii) for which multiple pre-trained embedding models are available.

We only use a subset of the original FactBench dataset because it was created in 2014, and is based on DBpedia version 3.9 [20]. Ergo, some of the facts it contains are outdated. For example, (:B.Obama, :presidentOf, :USA) was a correct assertion when the benchmark was created but is currently incorrect (without the date information). We performed the following list of changes to obtain the benchmark used herein:

Table 2. Overview of all correct facts used in our experiments. The train and test sets (train/test) are from the 2 benchmark datasets FactBench and BD from [46].

	Property	|Sub|	|Obj|	Comment
FactBench	:birthPlace	75/75	67/65	Birth place (city)
	:deathPlace	75/75	54/48	Death place (city)
	:award	75/75	5/5	Winners of nobel prizes
	:foundationPlace	75/75	59/62	Foundation place and timeof software companies
	:author	75/75	75/73	Authors of science fiction books (one book/author)
	:spouse	74/74	74/74	Marriages between actors(after 2013/01/01)
	:starring	22/21	74/74	Actors starring in a movie
	:subsidiary	54/50	75/75	Company acquisitions
BD	:birthPlace	51/52	45/35	Birth place (city)
	:deathPlace	52/51	42/38	Death place (city)

Table 3. Overview of the number of wrong assertions in the different categories of the train and test set (train/test) from the 2 benchmark datasets FactBench and BD [46].

	Category	|Assertions|	Comment
FactBench	Domain	1000/985	Replacing s with another entity in the domain of p
	Range	999/985	Replacing o with another entity in the range of p
	DomainRange	990/989	Replacing s or o based on the domain and range of p, resp
	Property	1032/997	Replacing s and o based on p connectivity
	Random	1061/1031	Randomly replacing o or s with other entities
	Mix	1025/1024	Mixture of above categories
BD	type-based	206/206	Replacing s or o of different RDF type

- We removed the date category from wrong assertions.
- We removed all assertions with Freebase entities.
- We removed the : *team* predicate, because there were many false positives in this category of assertions, since nearly all players changed their teams meanwhile.

Our second evaluation dataset, dubbed BirthPlace/DeathPlace (short DB) [46], aims to overcome a limitation of the FactBench dataset. It only contains assertions pertaining to birth and death places. The dataset was created based on the observation that some fact-checking approaches only check if the subject and object have a relation to each other while the type of the relation, i.e., whether it matches the property of the given assertion, is not always taken into account. Hence, all subjects and objects within the BD dataset have a relation to each other. This ensures that an approach only performs well on this dataset if it takes the type of the relation in assertions into account.

An overview of the two benchmarking datasets used in our evaluation in terms of the number of true and false assertions in training and testing sets, predicates, and some details about the generation of those assertions are presented in Tables 2 and 3. Note that both datasets were designed to be class-balanced. Hence, we do not need to apply any method to alleviate potential class imbalances in the training and test data. However, we want to point out that the BD dataset provides less training examples than FactBench.

Reference Corpus. Our text-based component makes use of a reference corpus. We created this corpus by extracting the plain text snippets from all English Wikipedia articles and loading them into an Elasticsearch instance. We used the dump from March 7th, 2022. For the Elasticsearch[6] index, we used a cluster of 3 nodes with a combined storage of 1 TB and 32 GB RAM per node.

5.2   Evaluation Metric

As suggested in the literature, we use the area under the receiver operator characteristic curve (AUROC) to compare the fact-checking results [25,46,47]. We compute this score using the knowledge-base curation branch of the GERBIL framework [33,36].

5.3   Setup Details and Reproducibility

Within the sentence embedding module, we use a pre-trained SBert model.[7] Furthermore, we set $k = 3$ in the sentence selection module. The size of the sentence embedding vectors generated by SBert is 768, and the trustworthiness score values against each sentence vector, which leads to $|\varphi_N| = (3 \times 768) + 3 = 2307$.

We use embeddings from 5 KG embedding models, where pre-trained DBpedia embeddings are available[8]. These models include: TransE [7], ConEx [12], QMult [11], ComplEx [49], and RDF2Vec [38]. For the FactBench dataset, we do not include experiments using RDF2Vec embeddings, because these embeddings were generated using a different version of DBpedia (i.e., 2015-10) and missing embeddings of multiple entities (i.e., 40/1800).[9] However, we included RDF2Vec embedding in the BD dataset comparison. Different KG embedding models provide embedding vectors with different lengths. For example, the TransE model used within our experiment maps each entity and each relation to a vector with 100 dimensions. This leads to a total size for $\varphi_{(s,p,o)}$ of 300.

We use the Binary Cross Entropy (BCE) as loss function for training our neural network component. We set the maximum number of epochs to 1000 with a batch size of 1/3 of the training data size. The training may have to be stopped earlier in case the neural network component starts to overfit. To this end, we calculate the validation

---

[6] https://www.elastic.co/.

[7] We ran experiments with all available pre-trained models (not shown in the paper due to space limitations) from the SBert homepage (https://www.sbert.net/docs/pretrained_models. html) and found that `nq-distilbert-base-v1` worked best for our approach.

[8] A large number of KG embedding algorithms [12,42,49] has been developed in recent years. However, while many of them show promising effectiveness, their scalability is often limited. For many of them, generating embedding models for the whole DBpedia is impractical (runtimes > 1 month). Hence, we only considered the approaches for which pre-trained DBpedia embeddings are available.

[9] Fair comparison could not be possible with missing entities, which constitute many assertions.

loss every 10th epoch and if this loss does not decrease for 50 epochs, the training is stopped.

All experiments are conducted on a machine with 32 CPU cores, 128 GB RAM and an NVIDIA GeForce RTX 3090. We provide hyperparameter optimization, training, and evaluation scripts on our project page for the sake of reproducibility.

5.4 Competing Approaches

We compare HybridFC in different configurations to FactCheck [46], COPAAL [47], and KV-Rule [25], which are the state-of-the-art approaches of the text-, path- and rule-based categories, respectively. We also compare our results to those four KG embedding-based approaches for which pre-trained DBpedia embedding models are available. We employ these models for fact checking by training the neural network module ϑ_2 of our approach based only on the output of the KG-based component. The output of this neural network module is then directly used as input for the final sigmoid function. We do not compare our results with results of the hybrid approaches mentioned in Sect. 3 because ExFaKT and Tracy mainly focus on generating human-comprehensible explanations and do not produce the veracity score, and FACTY focuses on calculating the veracity of assertions containing long-tail vertices (i.e., entities from less popular domains, for example, cheese varieties).

6 Results and Discussion

Tables 4 and 5 show the AUROC scores for the different hybrid and competing approaches on the FactBench train and test datasets, respectively. We can see that HybridFC performs best when it uses the TransE embedding model. This is not unexpected as TransE is one of the simplest embedding models that supports property composition: Given two properties p_1 and p_2, TransE entails that $\varphi(p_1 \circ p_2) \approx \varphi(p_1) + \varphi(p_2)$. With TransE as its embeddings model, HybridFC significantly outperforms all competing approaches on the test data.[10].

Note that FactCheck does not achieve the performance reported in [46] within our evaluation. This is due to (i) the use of a different English Wikipedia as reference corpus—Syed et al. showed that they achieve better results with the larger ClueWeb corpus—and (ii) the fact that we had to remove triples from the FactBench dataset.

The overall performance of COPAAL is better than the performance of FactCheck, ConEx, QMult and KV-Rule on the test set. However, we observe large performance differences with respect to the different properties. While COPAAL achieves the second best AUROC scores after HybridFC for 6 out of the 8 properties it struggles to achieve good results for :award and :author. These experimental results suggest that our approach makes good use of the diversity of the performance of the approaches it includes. In particular, it seems to rely on COPAAL's good performance on most of the properties while being able to complement COPAAL's predictions with that of other algorithms for properties on which COPAAL does not perform well.

---

[10] We use a Wilcoxon signed rank test with a significance threshold $\alpha = 0.05$.

Table 4. Area under the curve (AUROC) score on different categories of FactBench train sets. T stands for text-based approach, P for path-based approach, R for rule-based approaches, and KG-emb for KG-embedding-based approaches.

		Domain	Range	DomainRange	Mix	Random	Property	Avrg.
T	FactCheck [46]	0.69	0.69	0.68	0.65	0.68	0.57	0.66
P	COPAAL [47]	0.67	0.67	0.68	0.65	0.69	0.68	0.67
R	KV-Rule [25]	0.57	0.57	0.58	0.58	0.63	0.63	0.59
KG-emb	TransE [7]	0.67	0.61	0.78	0.66	0.92	0.97	0.76
	ConEx [12]	0.64	0.67	0.68	0.86	0.96	0.88	0.78
	ComplEx [49]	0.78	0.66	0.74	0.80	0.98	0.97	0.82
	QMult [11]	0.83	0.73	0.75	0.86	0.97	0.98	0.85
HybridFC	TransE	**0.94**	**0.94**	**0.96**	**0.90**	**0.99**	**0.99**	**0.95**
	ConEx	0.81	0.79	0.81	0.74	0.82	0.80	0.79
	ComplEx	0.94	0.94	0.94	0.86	0.95	0.97	0.93
	QMult	0.90	0.89	0.89	0.81	0.91	0.94	0.89

Table 5. Area under the curve (AUROC) score on different categories of FactBench test sets; the abbreviations are: T/Text-based approaches, P/Path-based approaches, R/Rule-based approaches, and KG-emb/KG embedding-based approaches.

		Domain	Range	DomainRange	Mix	Random	Property	Avrg.
T	FactCheck [46]	0.67	0.67	0.66	0.61	0.66	0.59	0.64
P	COPAAL [47]	0.67	0.68	0.68	0.65	0.69	0.69	0.68
R	KV-Rule [25]	0.57	0.57	0.57	0.58	0.61	0.62	0.59
KG-emb	TransE [7]	0.63	0.60	0.63	0.64	0.87	0.96	0.72
	ConEx [12]	0.50	0.50	0.50	0.52	0.60	0.60	0.54
	ComplEx [49]	0.58	0.58	0.52	0.62	0.86	0.95	0.69
	QMult [11]	0.57	0.62	0.55	0.69	0.84	0.93	0.70
HybridFC	TransE	**0.80**	**0.80**	**0.81**	**0.78**	**0.95**	**0.99**	**0.86**
	ConEx	0.77	0.78	0.79	0.71	0.80	0.70	0.75
	ComplEx	0.75	0.76	0.74	0.72	0.93	0.97	0.81
	QMult	0.69	0.73	0.71	0.69	0.91	0.94	0.77

On the BD dataset, KV-rule outperforms all other approaches on the test split (Table 6). COPAAL achieves the second best score, closely followed by the TransE-based HybridFC variant. The results confirm that the unsupervised fact-checking approaches COPAAL and KV-rule achieve good results for the :birthPlace and :deathplace properties. A closer look at the results reveals two main reasons for the lower result of the TransE-based HybridFC variant on the test dataset. First, FactCheck fails to extract pieces of evidence for most of the assertions. Second, FactCheck, the embedding-based approaches as well as the HybridFC variants are supervised approaches and suffer from the small size of the train split of the BD dataset. This is

Table 6. Area under the curve (AUROC) scores on the BD dataset; the abbreviations are: T stands for text-based approaches, P for path-based approaches, R for rule-based approaches, KG-emb for KG-embedding-based approaches.

	T	P	R	KG-emb					HybridFC				
	FactCheck [46]	COPAAL [47]	KV-Rule [25]	TransE [7]	ConEx [12]	ComplEx [49]	QMult [11]	RDF2Vec [38]	TransE	ConEx	ComplEx	QMult	RDF2Vec
Train	0.51	0.67	0.76	0.69	0.50	0.73	0.60	0.67	0.80	0.51	0.74	0.60	0.74
Test	0.49	0.70	**0.81**	0.54	0.50	0.54	0.55	0.62	0.69	0.50	0.57	0.58	0.68

Table 7. Results of our ablation study on the FactBench test set and BD dataset. D stands for Domain, R for Range, DR for DomainRange, Ran. for Random, Prop. for Property, and Avg. for average. TC stands for text-based component, PC for path-based component, EC for embedding-based component, and the symbol + indicates the combination of 2 components. Best performances are bold, second-best are underlined.

(a) FactBench test set

	D	R	DR	Mix	Ran.	Prop.	Avg.
TC	0.76	0.77	0.76	0.69	0.77	0.64	0.73
PC	0.68	0.69	0.69	0.65	0.70	0.69	0.68
EC	0.63	0.61	0.62	0.64	0.86	0.97	0.72
TC+EC	0.76	<u>0.78</u>	0.76	<u>0.74</u>	<u>0.92</u>	<u>0.98</u>	<u>0.82</u>
TC+PC	<u>0.77</u>	0.77	<u>0.77</u>	0.7	0.79	0.67	0.74
PC+EC	0.71	0.7	0.69	0.72	0.89	0.97	0.78
HybridFC	**0.80**	**0.80**	**0.81**	**0.78**	**0.95**	**0.99**	**0.86**

(b) BD dataset

	Train	Test
TC	0.59	0.56
PC	0.67	**0.70**
EC	0.69	0.56
TC+EC	<u>0.79</u>	0.65
TC+PC	0.67	0.64
PC+EC	0.74	0.66
HybridFC	**0.80**	<u>0.69</u>

confirmed by our observation that the neural network component tends to overfit during the training phase.

7   Ablation Study

Our previous experiments suggest that HybridFC performs best in combination with TransE. Hence, we use it as default setting throughout the rest of the paper and overload HybridFC to mean HybridFC with TransE embeddings. To evaluate the contribution of the different components of HybridFC to its performance, we rerun our evaluation for each component (i.e., text-based (TC), path-based (PC), and embedding-based (EC)) individually and as pairwise combination of different components (TC+PC, TC+EC, PC+EC). The results for the FactBench test and the BD datasets are shown in Tables 7a and 7b.[11] The results suggest that the individual path-based and embedding-based components achieve results similar to those of COPAAL and TransE, respectively. Our text-based component achieves better results than FactCheck. On the FactBench test datasets, the combination of two components leads to better results than the single components. Similarly, HybridFC, i.e., the combination of all three components, leads to significantly better results than all pairwise combinations, where significance is measured using a Wilcoxon signed rank test with a p-value threshold of 0.05. Here, our null hypothesis is that the performances of the approaches compared are sampled from the same distribution. For the BD dataset, the pairwise combinations of components suffer from the same overfitting problem as HybridFC. Overall, our results in Table 7a suggest that our text component commonly achieves the highest average performance on datasets that provide enough training data. The text component is best supplemented by the embedding-based component. HybridFC outperforming all combinations of two components on FactBench suggests that in cases in which HybridFC is trained with enough training data, each of the three components contributes to the better overall performance of HybridFC.

8   Conclusion

In this paper, we propose HybridFC–a hybrid fact-checking approach for KGs. HybridFC aims to alleviate the problem of manual feature engineering in text-based approaches, cases in which paths between subjects and objects are unavailable to path-based approaches, and the poor performance of pure KG-embedding-based approaches by combining these three categories of approaches. We compare HybridFC to the state of the art in fact checking for KGs. Our experiments show that our hybrid approach is able to outperform competing approaches in the majority of cases. As future work, we will exploit the modularity of HybridFC by integrating rule-based approaches. We also plan to explore other possibilities to select the best evidence sentences.

Supplemental Material Statement

- The source code of HybridFC, the scripts to recreate the full experimental setup, and the required libraries can be found on GitHub.[12]
- Datasets used in this paper and the output generated by text-based and path-based approaches on these datasets are available at Zenodo [3].
- Pre-trained embeddings for these datasets are also available at Zenodo [4].

Acknowledgments. The work has been supported by the EU H2020 Marie Skłodowska-Curie project KnowGraphs (no. 860801), the German Federal Ministry for Economic Affairs and Climate Action (BMWK) funded project RAKI (no. 01MD19012B), and the German Federal Ministry of Education and Research (BMBF) funded EuroStars projects 3DFed (no. 01QE2114B) and FROCKG (no. 01QE19418). We are also grateful to Daniel Vollmers and Caglar Demir for the valuable discussion on earlier drafts.

---

[11] Due to space limitation we exclude the results of FactBench train set. These results are available on our GitHub page.

[12] Source code: https://github.com/dice-group/HybridFC.

References

1. Athreya, R.G., Ngonga Ngomo, A.C., Usbeck, R.: Enhancing community interactions with data-driven chatbots-the dbpedia chatbot. In: Companion Proceedings of the The Web Conference 2018, pp. 143–146. WWW 2018, International World Wide Web Conferences Steering Committee, Republic and Canton of Geneva, CHE (2018). https://doi.org/10.1145/3184558.3186964
2. Auer, S., Bizer, C., Kobilarov, G., Lehmann, J., Cyganiak, R., Ives, Z.: DBpedia: a nucleus for a web of open data. In: Aberer, K., et al. (eds.) ASWC/ISWC -2007. LNCS, vol. 4825, pp. 722–735. Springer, Heidelberg (2007). https://doi.org/10.1007/978-3-540-76298-0_52
3. Authors, A.: Mypublications dataset. https://doi.org/10.5281/zenodo.6523389
4. Authors, A.: Pre-trained embeddings for fact-checking datasets. https://doi.org/10.5281/zenodo.6523438
5. Bengio, Y., Courville, A., Vincent, P.: Representation learning: a review and new perspectives. IEEE Trans. Pattern Anal. Mach. Intell. 35(8), 1798–1828 (2013)
6. Boland, K., Fafalios, P., Tchechmedjiev, A., Dietze, S., Todorov, K.: Beyond facts - a survey and conceptualisation of claims in online discourse analysis, March 2021. https://hal.mines-ales.fr/hal-03185097, working paper or preprint
7. Bordes, A., Usunier, N., Garcia-Durán, A., Weston, J., Yakhnenko, O.: Translating embeddings for modeling multi-relational data. In: Proceedings of the 26th International Conference on Neural Information Processing Systems - Volume 2. NIPS 2013, pp. 2787–2795, Curran Associates Inc., Red Hook, NY, USA (2013)
8. Chen, Y., Goldberg, S., Wang, D.Z., Johri, S.S.: Ontological pathfinding: mining first-order knowledge from large knowledge bases. In: Proceedings of the 2016 International Conference on Management of Data. SIGMOD 2016, New York, NY, USA, pp. 835–846. Association for Computing Machinery (2016). https://doi.org/10.1145/2882903.2882954
9. Ciampaglia, G.L., Shiralkar, P., Rocha, L.M., Bollen, J., Menczer, F., Flammini, A.: Computational fact checking from knowledge networks. PLoS ONE 10(6), 1–13 (2015). https://doi.org/10.1371/journal.pone.0128193
10. Dai, Y., Wang, S., Xiong, N.N., Guo, W.: A survey on knowledge graph embedding: approaches, applications and benchmarks. Electronics 9(5) (2020). https://doi.org/10.3390/electronics9050750
11. Demir, C., Moussallem, D., Heindorf, S., Ngomo, A.C.N.: Convolutional hypercomplex embeddings for link prediction. In: Asian Conference on Machine Learning, pp. 656–671. PMLR (2021)
12. Demir, C., Ngomo, A.-C.N.: Convolutional complex knowledge graph embeddings. In: Verborgh, R., et al. (eds.) ESWC 2021. LNCS, vol. 12731, pp. 409–424. Springer, Cham (2021). https://doi.org/10.1007/978-3-030-77385-4_24
13. Dong, X.L., et al.: Knowledge vault: a web-scale approach to probabilistic knowledge fusion. In: The 20th ACM SIGKDD International Conference on Knowledge Discovery and Data Mining, KDD 2014, New York, NY, USA, 24–27 August, pp. 601–610, 2014 (2014). http://www.cs.cmu.edu/nlao/publication/2014.kdd.pdf, evgeniy Gabrilovich Wilko Horn Ni Lao Kevin Murphy Thomas Strohmann Shaohua Sun Wei Zhang Geremy Heitz
14. Gad-Elrab, M.H., Stepanova, D., Urbani, J., Weikum, G.: Exfakt: a framework for explaining facts over knowledge graphs and text. In: Proceedings of the Twelfth ACM International Conference on Web Search and Data Mining. WSDM 2019, New York, NY, USA, pp. 87–95. Association for Computing Machinery (2019). https://doi.org/10.1145/3289600.3290996
15. Gad-Elrab, M.H., Stepanova, D., Urbani, J., Weikum, G.: Tracy: tracing facts over knowledge graphs and text. In: The World Wide Web Conference. WWW 2019, pp. 3516–3520, New York, NY, USA. Association for Computing Machinery (2019). https://doi.org/10.1145/3308558.3314126

16. Galárraga, L., Teflioudi, C., Hose, K., Suchanek, F.M.: Fast rule mining in ontological knowledge bases with AMIE+. VLDB J. **24**(6), 707–730 (2015). https://doi.org/10.1007/s00778-015-0394-1
17. Galárraga, L.A., Teflioudi, C., Hose, K., Suchanek, F.: Amie: association rule mining under incomplete evidence in ontological knowledge bases. In: Proceedings of the 22nd International Conference on World Wide Web. WWW 2013, pp. 413–422, New York, NY, USA. Association for Computing Machinery (2013). https://doi.org/10.1145/2488388.2488425
18. Gardner, M., Mitchell, T.: Efficient and expressive knowledge base completion using subgraph feature extraction. In: Proceedings of the 2015 Conference on Empirical Methods in Natural Language Processing, pp. 1488–1498 (2015)
19. Gardner, M., Talukdar, P., Krishnamurthy, J., Mitchell, T.: Incorporating vector space similarity in random walk inference over knowledge bases. In: Proceedings of the 2014 Conference on Empirical Methods in Natural Language Processing (EMNLP), pp. 397–406, Doha, Qatar. Association for Computational Linguistics, October 2014. https://doi.org/10.3115/v1/D14-1044
20. Gerber, D., et al.: Defacto-temporal and multilingual deep fact validation. Web Semant. **35**(P2), 85–101 (2015). https://doi.org/10.1016/j.websem.2015.08.001
21. Huang, J., et al.: Trustworthy knowledge graph completion based on multi-sourced noisy data. In: Laforest, F., et al. (eds.) WWW 2022: The ACM Web Conference 2022, Virtual Event, Lyon, France, April 25–29, 2022, pp. 956–965. ACM (2022). https://doi.org/10.1145/3485447.3511938
22. Huynh, V.P., Papotti, P.: Towards a benchmark for fact checking with knowledge bases. In: Companion Proceedings of the The Web Conference 2018, pp. 1595–1598. WWW 2018, Republic and Canton of Geneva, CHE. International World Wide Web Conferences Steering Committee (2018). https://doi.org/10.1145/3184558.3191616
23. Ioffe, S., Szegedy, C.: Batch normalization: Accelerating deep network training by reducing internal covariate shift. In: Proceedings of the 32nd International Conference on International Conference on Machine Learning - Volume 37. ICML 2015, pp. 448–456. JMLR.org (2015)
24. Ji, G., He, S., Xu, L., Liu, K., Zhao, J.: Knowledge graph embedding via dynamic mapping matrix. In: Proceedings of the 53rd Annual Meeting of the Association for Computational Linguistics and the 7th International Joint Conference on Natural Language Processing (Volume 1: Long Papers), pp. 687–696. Association for Computational Linguistics, Beijing, China, July 2015. https://doi.org/10.3115/v1/P15-1067
25. Kim, J., Choi, K.s.: Unsupervised fact checking by counter-weighted positive and negative evidential paths in a knowledge graph. In: Proceedings of the 28th International Conference on Computational Linguistics, pp. 1677–1686. International Committee on Computational Linguistics, Barcelona, Spain (Online), December 2020. https://doi.org/10.18653/v1/2020.coling-main.147
26. Kotonya, N., Toni, F.: Explainable automated fact-checking for public health claims. arXiv preprint arXiv:2010.09926 (2020)
27. Lajus, J., Galárraga, L., Suchanek, F.: Fast and exact rule mining with AMIE 3. In: Harth, A., et al. (eds.) The Semantic Web, pp. 36–52. Springer, Cham (2020). https://doi.org/10.1007/978-3-030-49461-2_3
28. Li, F., Dong, X.L., Langen, A., Li, Y.: Knowledge verification for long-tail verticals. Proc. VLDB Endow. **10**(11), 1370–1381 (2017). https://doi.org/10.14778/3137628.3137646
29. Lin, Y., Liu, Z., Sun, M., Liu, Y., Zhu, X.: Learning entity and relation embeddings for knowledge graph completion. In: Proceedings of the AAAI Conference on Artificial Intelligence, vol. 29 (2015)
30. Malyshev, S., Krötzsch, M., González, L., Gonsior, J., Bielefeldt, A.: Getting the most out of Wikidata: semantic technology usage in Wikipedia's knowledge graph. In: Vrandečić, D.,

et al. (eds.) The Semantic Web - ISWC 2018, pp. 376–394. Springer, Cham (2018). https://doi.org/10.1007/978-3-030-00668-6_23

31. Malyshev, S., Krötzsch, M., González, L., Gonsior, J., Bielefeldt, A.: Getting the most out of wikidata: semantic technology usage in Wikipedia's knowledge graph. In: Vrandečić, D., et al. (eds.) ISWC 2018. LNCS, vol. 11137, pp. 376–394. Springer, Cham (2018). https://doi.org/10.1007/978-3-030-00668-6_23

32. Nakamura, S., et al.: Trustworthiness analysis of web search results. In: Kovács, L., Fuhr, N., Meghini, C. (eds.) ECDL 2007. LNCS, vol. 4675, pp. 38–49. Springer, Heidelberg (2007). https://doi.org/10.1007/978-3-540-74851-9_4

33. Ngonga Ngomo, A.C., Röder, M., Syed, Z.H.: Semantic web challenge 2019. Website (2019). https://github.com/dice-group/semantic-web-challenge.github.io/. Accessed 30 March 2022

34. Ortona, S., Meduri, V.V., Papotti, P.: Rudik: rule discovery in knowledge bases. Proc. VLDB Endow. **11**(12), 1946–1949 (2018). https://doi.org/10.14778/3229863.3236231

35. Page, L., Brin, S., Motwani, R., Winograd, T.: The pagerank citation ranking: Bringing order to the web. Technical Report 1999–66, Stanford InfoLab, November 1999. http://ilpubs.stanford.edu:8090/422/, previous number = SIDL-WP-1999-0120

36. Paulheim, H., Ngonga Ngomo, A.C., Bennett, D.: Semantic web challenge 2018. Website (2018). http://iswc2018.semanticweb.org/semantic-web-challenge-2018/index.html. Accessed 30 March 2022

37. Reimers, N., Gurevych, I.: Sentence-BERT: sentence embeddings using Siamese BERT-networks. In: Proceedings of the 2019 Conference on Empirical Methods in Natural Language Processing and the 9th International Joint Conference on Natural Language Processing (EMNLP-IJCNLP), pp. 3982–3992. Association for Computational Linguistics, Hong Kong, China, November 2019. https://doi.org/10.18653/v1/D19-1410

38. Ristoski, P., Paulheim, H.: RDF2Vec: RDF graph embeddings for data mining. In: Groth, P., et al. (eds.) ISWC 2016. LNCS, vol. 9981, pp. 498–514. Springer, Cham (2016). https://doi.org/10.1007/978-3-319-46523-4_30

39. Rula, A., et al.: Tisco: temporal scoping of facts. Web Semant. **54**(C), 72–86 (2019). https://doi.org/10.1016/j.websem.2018.09.002

40. Shi, B., Weninger, T.: Discriminative predicate path mining for fact checking in knowledge graphs. Know.-Based Syst. 104(C), 123–133 (2016). https://doi.org/10.1016/j.knosys.2016.04.015

41. Shiralkar, P., Flammini, A., Menczer, F., Ciampaglia, G.L.: Finding streams in knowledge graphs to support fact checking. In: 2017 IEEE International Conference on Data Mining (ICDM), pp. 859–864 (2017). https://doi.org/10.1109/ICDM.2017.105

42. da Silva, A.A.M., Röder, M., Ngomo, A.-C.N.: Using compositional embeddings for fact checking. In: Hotho, A., et al. (eds.) ISWC 2021. LNCS, vol. 12922, pp. 270–286. Springer, Cham (2021). https://doi.org/10.1007/978-3-030-88361-4_16

43. Suchanek, F.M., Kasneci, G., Weikum, G.: Yago: a core of semantic knowledge. In: Proceedings of the 16th International Conference on World Wide Web, pp. 697–706. ACM (2007)

44. Sultana, T., Lee, Y.: Efficient rule mining and compression for RDF style kb based on horn rules. J. Supercomput. (2022). https://doi.org/10.1007/s11227-022-04519-y

45. Sun, Y., Barber, R., Gupta, M., Aggarwal, C.C., Han, J.: Co-author relationship prediction in heterogeneous bibliographic networks. In: 2011 International Conference on Advances in Social Networks Analysis and Mining, pp. 121–128 (2011). https://doi.org/10.1109/ASONAM.2011.112

46. Syed, Z.H., Röder, M., Ngonga Ngomo, A.C.: Factcheck: validating RDF triples using textual evidence. In: Proceedings of the 27th ACM International Conference on Information and Knowledge Management. CIKM 2018, New York, NY, USA, pp. 1599–1602. Association for Computing Machinery (2018). https://doi.org/10.1145/3269206.3269308

47. Syed, Z.H., Srivastava, N., Röder, M., Ngomo, A.C.N.: Copaal - an interface for explaining facts using corroborative paths. In: ISWC Satellites (2019)
48. Syed, Z.H., Srivastava, N., Röder, M., Ngomo, A.N.: COPAAL - an interface for explaining facts using corroborative paths. In: Suárez-Figueroa, M.C., Cheng, G., Gentile, A.L., Guéret, C., Keet, C.M., Bernstein, A. (eds.) Proceedings of the ISWC 2019 Satellite Tracks (Posters & Demonstrations, Industry, and Outrageous Ideas) co-located with 18th International Semantic Web Conference (ISWC 2019), Auckland, New Zealand, October 26–30, 2019. CEUR Workshop Proceedings, vol. 2456, pp. 201–204. CEUR-WS.org (2019). http://ceur-ws.org/Vol-2456/paper52.pdf
49. Trouillon, T., Welbl, J., Riedel, S., Gaussier, E., Bouchard, G.: Complex embeddings for simple link prediction. In: International Conference on Machine Learning, pp. 2071–2080 (2016)
50. Wang, Q., Mao, Z., Wang, B., Guo, L.: Knowledge graph embedding: a survey of approaches and applications. IEEE Trans. Knowl. Data Eng. **29**(12), 2724–2743 (2017). https://doi.org/10.1109/TKDE.2017.2754499
51. Watt, N., du Plessis, M.C.: Dropout algorithms for recurrent neural networks. In: Proceedings of the Annual Conference of the South African Institute of Computer Scientists and Information Technologists, New York, NY, USA, pp. 72–78. SAICSIT 2018, Association for Computing Machinery (2018). https://doi.org/10.1145/3278681.3278691

GNNQ: A Neuro-Symbolic Approach to Query Answering over Incomplete Knowledge Graphs

Maximilian Pflueger[1]([✉]) [ID], David J. Tena Cucala[1] [ID], and Egor V. Kostylev[2] [ID]

[1] University of Oxford, Oxford OX1 2JD, UK
{maximilian.pflueger,david.tena.cucala}@cs.ox.ac.uk
[2] University of Oslo, Problemveien 7, 0315 Oslo, Norway
egork@ifi.uio.no

Abstract. Real-world knowledge graphs (KGs) are usually incomplete—that is, miss some facts representing valid information. So, when applied to such KGs, standard symbolic query engines fail to produce answers that are expected but not logically entailed by the KGs. To overcome this issue, state-of-the-art ML-based approaches first embed KGs and queries into a low-dimensional vector space, and then produce query answers based on the proximity of the candidate entity and the query embeddings in the embedding space. This allows embedding-based approaches to obtain expected answers that are not logically entailed. However, embedding-based approaches are not applicable in the inductive setting, where KG entities (i.e., constants) seen at runtime may differ from those seen during training. In this paper, we propose a novel neuro-symbolic approach to query answering over incomplete KGs applicable in the inductive setting. Our approach first symbolically augments the input KG with facts representing parts of the KG that match query fragments, and then applies a generalisation of the Relational Graph Convolutional Networks (RGCNs) to the augmented KG to produce the predicted query answers. We formally prove that, under reasonable assumptions, our approach can capture an approach based on vanilla RGCNs (and no KG augmentation) using a (often substantially) smaller number of layers. Finally, we empirically validate our theoretical findings by evaluating an implementation of our approach against the RGCN baseline on several dedicated benchmarks.

Keywords: Query answering · Knowledge graphs · Graph neural networks · Neuro-symbolic AI

1 Introduction

Knowledge graphs (KGs) are databases where information is represented as a collection of *entities* and *relations* between them [13], or, equivalently, as a set of (function-free) first-order facts. *Query answering* is a fundamental reasoning

© The Author(s) 2022
J. P.. A. Sattler et al. (Eds.): ISWC 2022, LNCS 13489, pp. 481–497, 2022.
https://doi.org/10.1007/978-3-031-19433-7_28

task on KGs, which requires identifying all (tuples of) entities in a KG that satisfy a specific formal expression, called a *query*. For example, (conjunctive) query $q(x) = \exists y_1, y_2.\, \mathsf{almaMater}(x, y_1) \wedge \mathsf{professorAt}(y_1, y_2)$ finds, in a KG, all the universities that are the alma maters of persons working as professors.

Queries can be answered over KGs using symbolic logic-based engines, such as SPARQL and Cypher [16]. This approach, however, is challenged by the problem that many real-life KGs are *incomplete*, in the sense that there are true facts missing in the KG that may be relevant for answering a particular query. For example, if a KG contains the fact $\mathsf{professorAt}(edith, berkeley)$, representing that Edith is a professor at UC Berkeley, but it is missing the fact $\mathsf{almaMater}(melbourne, edith)$, representing that the University of Melbourne is the alma mater of Edith, then *melbourne* will not be returned as an answer for the above query, even though this answer may be expected by the user.

Query Embedding (QE) approaches have been proposed as a way to overcome this limitation [4,9,11,17,18,20]. QE approaches embed KGs and monadic conjunctive queries jointly in a low dimensional vector space, and then they evaluate the likelihood of candidate answers according to their distance to the query embedding in the embedding space. These methods can produce answers that may be of interest to the user, even if they correspond to parts of the KG that only partially match the query. However, to the best of our knowledge, existing QE approaches are only applicable in the *transductive* setting, where trained models can only process KGs that mention only entities seen during training. An increasing number of applications, however, require an *inductive* setting [10,14,23,25], where unseen entities are also allowed.

Relational Graph Convolutional Networks (RGCNs) [19] are a class of graph neural networks (GNNs) which take as input directed labelled multigraphs—in particular, graphs with nodes connected by coloured edges and annotated with real-valued feature vectors. When applied to such a multigraph, an RGCN updates, in each layer, the feature vector of each node by combining, by means of learned parameters, the node's feature vector in the previous layer with the previous-layer vectors of the node's neighbours. If the vector in the final layer is a single Boolean value, then the RGCN can be seen as a (binary) node classifier. RGCNs can be used to answer monadic queries on a KG: first, encode the KG as a directed multigraph with a node for each entity in the KG; then, run a trained RGCN on the multigraph to predict whether each entity is an answer to the query or not (similar approaches have been used for the related problem of KG completion [10,14,22–24]). This method has three properties making it suitable for answering queries on incomplete KGs in an inductive setting.

1. *Inductive Capabilities.* RGCNs do not use entity-specific parameters, so they can be applied to KGs mentioning entities not seen during training.
2. *Expressivity.* Recent theoretical analysis of RGCNs [5] shows that, for every monadic tree-shaped conjunctive query, there exists an RGCN that exactly *captures* this query—that is, for each KG, the answers provided by the RGCN on the KG are the same as the real query answers over the KG.

3. *Noise Tolerance.* Similarly to other ML approaches, RGCNs can produce relevant query answers even if such answers do not have exact matches in the input KG (e.g., due to missing information).

A key limitation of using RGCNs for query answering over KGs, however, is that, in order to recognise a part of the KG relevant to a query answer, any RGCN requires at least as many layers as the length of the longest (simple) path in the query to an answer variable. Empirical results have shown, however, that GNNs with many layers often fail to learn long-range dependencies and suffer from several problems, such as over-smoothing [12]. This problem persists even if the input KGs have no missing information.

To address this limitation, we propose in this paper a novel neuro-symbolic approach to inductive query answering over incomplete KGs. Our approach first augments an input KG using a set of logical (i.e., symbolic) rules extracted from the query. The application of a rule to a KG adds new facts that represent (complete) parts of the KG matching connected query fragments. Then the approach encodes the augmented KG as a coloured *hypergraph*, and processes this hypergraph using a novel neural architecture called *Hyper-Relational Graph Convolutional Network* (*HRGCN*), which generalises vanilla RGCNs to be applicable to coloured hypergraphs. We then provide a proof that, under mild and reasonable assumptions, our approach can emulate the baseline approach that relies on vanilla RGCNs (without KG augmentation) using significantly less layers. Finally, we present an implementation of our approach in a system called GNNQ and evaluate it on nine novel benchmarks for inductive query answering over incomplete KGs against a baseline without augmentation. Our results show that instances of GNNQ can be effectively trained and deployed in practice; moreover, they outperform the baselines, even if the latter use more layers.

2 Preliminaries

In this paper, we rely on a standard formalisation of knowledge graphs (and related concepts) in first-order logic.

Let us consider disjoint countable sets of *predicates, constants*, and *variables*, where each predicate is assigned a natural number called *arity*. A k-ary *atom*, with $k \in \mathbb{N}$, is an expression of the form $P(\bar{t})$, where P is a k-ary predicate and $\bar{t} = t_1, \ldots, t_k$ is a k-tuple of constants and variables. A *fact* is a variable-free atom. A *dataset* is a finite set of facts. A *knowledge graph* (*KG*) is a dataset containing only unary and binary facts. So, entities in a KG are represented by constants, while classes of entities and relations between them are represented by unary and binary facts, respectively. Let $\mathsf{Const}(\mathcal{D})$ and $\mathsf{Pred}(\mathcal{D})$ denote the constants and predicates mentioned in a dataset $\mathcal{D}$, respectively.

A *conjunctive query* (CQ) with (a tuple of) *answer* variables $\bar{x}$, is a formula $q(\bar{x}) = \exists \bar{y}. \phi(\bar{x}, \bar{y})$, where the *body* $\phi(\bar{x}, \bar{y})$ is a conjunction of atoms over variables $\bar{x}, \bar{y}$. A tuple $\bar{a}$ of constants is an *answer* to $q(\bar{x})$ over a dataset $\mathcal{D}$ if there is a *homomorphism* from $q(\bar{a})$ to $\mathcal{D}$—that is, an assignment of constants to $\bar{y}$ such that each atom in $\phi(\bar{a}, h(\bar{y}))$ is in $\mathcal{D}$. Let $q[\mathcal{D}]$ denote the set of all answers to

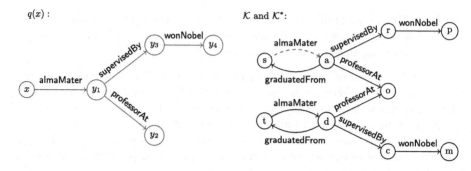

Fig. 1. Representation of tree-CQ $q(x)$ and KG $\mathcal{K}$ with completion $\mathcal{K}^*$ from Example 1: the single completion fact is drawn as a dashed line, constants are shown by first letter.

$q(\bar{x})$ over $\mathcal{D}$. In this paper, we concentrate on *tree-shaped* CQs (*tree-CQs*)—that is, constant-free CQs over unary and binary predicates with one answer variable such that the primal pseudograph of the CQ's body is a tree; here, the *primal pseudograph* of a conjunction of atoms is the undirected pseudograph whose nodes are the variables of the conjunction and which has an edge between (not necessary distinct) z_1 and z_2 for each binary atom $R(z_1, z_2)$ in the conjunction. We call a primal pseudograph *primal tree* if it is a tree. The *height* of a tree-CQ is the height of its primal tree with the answer variable as the root.

3   Inductive Query Answering over Incomplete KGs

We are interested in the problem of finding the answers to a given (known in advance) tree-CQ over KGs that may be incomplete—that is, missing (relevant) information. In particular, we assume that each KG has a *completion*—that is, a larger (or identical) KG that may include additional facts, which are 'missing' in the original KG. We consider the setting where all the constants in the completion facts are already mentioned in the original KG. However, we assume that the function that maps a KG to its completion is unknown; instead, only partial knowledge about this function is provided to a system in the form of examples, each of which consists of a KG, a constant, and a Boolean value, which tells whether the constant is an answer to the tree-CQ over the completion of the KG. Finally, our setting is *inductive* [10,14,23,25], which means that there exists a finite, known-in-advance set of predicates used in all KGs, their completions, and the tree-CQ, but the constants in different KGs may be different.

We are now ready to formalise the ML task of inductive tree-CQ answering over incomplete KGs, which we call the *IQA task* for brevity.

Definition 1. *Given a finite set* Pred *of unary and binary predicates, and a tree-CQ $q(x)$ that uses only predicates from* Pred, *let us assume a hidden completion function $\cdot^*$ mapping each KG $\mathcal{K}$ with* Pred($\mathcal{K}$) $\subseteq$ Pred *to another KG*

$\mathcal{K}^*$ with $\mathsf{Pred}(\mathcal{K}^*) \subseteq \mathsf{Pred}$, *called the* completion *of* $\mathcal{K}$, *such that* $\mathcal{K} \subseteq \mathcal{K}^*$ *and* $\mathsf{Const}(\mathcal{K}^*) = \mathsf{Const}(\mathcal{K})$. *Then, the* IQA *task is to learn a function* g_q *mapping each KG* $\mathcal{K}$ *with* $\mathsf{Pred}(\mathcal{K}) \subseteq \mathsf{Pred}$ *to the set* $q[\mathcal{K}^*]$ *of answers to* $q(x)$ *over* $\mathcal{K}^*$.

Example 1. Let $q(x)$ be the tree-CQ

$$\exists y_1, y_2, y_3, y_4.\, \mathsf{almaMater}(x, y_1) \wedge \mathsf{professorAt}(y_1, y_2) \wedge$$
$$\mathsf{supervisedBy}(y_1, y_3) \wedge \mathsf{wonNobel}(y_3, y_4),$$

which asks for all universities that are the *alma maters* of professors who were supervised by Nobel Prize winners, and let $\mathcal{K}$ be the KG

$$\{\mathsf{supervisedBy}(alice, roger), \mathsf{supervisedBy}(daniel, carol),$$
$$\mathsf{wonNobel}(roger, physics), \mathsf{wonNobel}(carol, medicine),$$
$$\mathsf{professorAt}(alice, oxford), \mathsf{professorAt}(daniel, oxford),$$
$$\mathsf{graduatedFrom}(alice, shanghai), \mathsf{graduatedFrom}(daniel, toronto),$$
$$\mathsf{almaMater}(toronto, daniel)\}$$

with $\mathcal{K}^* = \mathcal{K} \cup \{\mathsf{almaMater}(shanghai, alice)\}$ (see Fig. 1). The desired function g_q for $q(x)$ should return the set $\{shanghai, toronto\}$ of answers when applied to $\mathcal{K}$, because both *toronto* and *shanghai* are answers to $q(x)$ over $\mathcal{K}^*$. Note, however, that *shanghai* is not an answer to $q(x)$ over $\mathcal{K}$, since the fact $\mathsf{almaMater}(shanghai, alice)$ is missing from $\mathcal{K}$.

4 Neuro-Symbolic Approach to the IQA Task

In this section, we describe our approach for solving the IQA task. For the remainder of this section, let us fix a (possibly empty) set $\mathsf{Pred}_1 = \{A_1, \ldots, A_m\}$ of unary predicates, a finite set Pred_2 of binary predicates, and a tree-CQ $q(x) = \exists \bar{y}.\, \phi(x, \bar{y})$ over predicates in $\mathsf{Pred}_1 \cup \mathsf{Pred}_2$. For technical reasons, we assume that the variables $x, \bar{y}$ are ordered following a breadth-first traverse of the primal tree of $\phi(x, \bar{y})$. This assumption is without loss of generality, since given an arbitrary tree-CQ, we can always construct a semantically equivalent query that satisfies our requirement by reordering $\bar{y}$. Finally, for each $R \in \mathsf{Pred}_2$, we consider a fresh binary predicate $\bar{R}$, which we call the *inverse* of R, and we let Pred_2^+ denote the set $\mathsf{Pred}_2 \cup \{\bar{R} \mid R \in \mathsf{Pred}_2\}$.

Our approach is divided in three steps. In the first step, described in Sect. 4.1, the input KG is augmented with new facts that will assist our ML model in recognising parts of the input KG that match selected query fragments. In the second step, described in Sect. 4.2, our approach encodes the augmented KG into a data structure suitable for our ML model, namely, a coloured labelled (multi-)hypergraph, where nodes correspond to constants in the KG and edges to non-unary atoms. In the third and final step, described in Sect. 4.3, the approach processes the coloured hypergraph by means of a generalisation of RGCNs. The output of this process is a Boolean value for each node in the hypergraph, representing whether the constant associated to this node is predicted as an answer to $q(x)$ over the completion of the input KG or not.

4.1 Augmentation of Knowledge Graphs

As discussed in the introduction, vanilla RGCNs with Boolean outputs can be used to solve the IQA task by first encoding the input KG as a directed multi-graph and then applying a trained RGCN to the encoding. Such RGCNs, however, may require a large number of layers to adequately capture the target function. However, training RGCNs with many layers is expensive; moreover, the resulting models may have poor performance due to over-smoothing [12]. To address these issues, our procedure first augments the input KG with facts representing (complete) parts of the KG matching query fragments. As we prove in Sect. 5, this allows us to solve the IQA task using significantly less layers.

The KG augmentation relies on a set of logical rules, which correspond to fragments of the tree-CQ. These rules are applied to the KG to infer new facts, which are added to the KG. To formalise this step, we need some terminology.

A (projection-free) *rule* is an expression of the form $H(\bar{z}) \leftarrow \psi(\bar{z})$, where the *head* $H(\bar{z})$ is an atom over a $|\bar{z}|$-ary predicate H, and the *body* $\psi(\bar{z})$ is a conjunction of atoms using variables $\bar{z}$ (i.e., each variable in $\bar{z}$ appears in at least one atom in $\psi(\bar{z})$, and there are no other variables in these atoms). The *application* of a set $\mathcal{R}$ of rules to a dataset $\mathcal{D}$ is a dataset $\mathcal{R}(\mathcal{D})$ that extends $\mathcal{D}$ with each fact $H(\bar{a})$ such that there is a rule $H(\bar{z}) \leftarrow \psi(\bar{z})$ in $\mathcal{R}$ with every fact in $\psi(\bar{a})$ belonging to $\mathcal{D}$. Note that in what follows we will only apply a rule to datasets that do not mention the head predicate of the rule.

Next, we associate a set $\mathcal{R}_q$ of rules to our fixed tree-CQ $q(x)$. Specifically, we define $\mathcal{R}_q$ as the set of all the rules $H(\bar{z}) \leftarrow \psi(\bar{z})$, where $\psi(\bar{z})$ is a sub-conjunction of $\phi(x, \bar{y})$ with the same order of variables in $\bar{z}$ as their order in $x, \bar{y}$, such that

- the primal pseudograph of $\psi(\bar{z})$ is connected (and hence it is a tree) and
- the height of this tree is at least 2,

and where H is a fresh $|\bar{z}|$-ary predicate uniquely associated to $\psi(\bar{z})$. Subsequently, we use Pred_q to denote the set of head predicates of the rules in $\mathcal{R}_q$. Note that, by our assumptions on the order of variables, the first variable in $\bar{z}$ will always be the one closest to x in the primal tree of $\phi(x, \bar{y})$ rooted at x. Moreover, the assumptions ensure that $\mathcal{R}_q$ does not contain rules with the same body and head predicate, but different heads; this eliminates redundancy by preventing augmentation with multiple facts identifying the same sub-KGs.

As discussed in Sect. 6.1, in our experiments we observe that it is often better not to use all rules in $\mathcal{R}_q$ in the augmentation step. We believe that there are two main reasons for this: first, increasing the number of augmentation facts appears to have diminishing returns, since different facts can represent similar parts of the input KG (satisfying similar query fragments); second, having a large number of augmentation facts mentioning the same constant can produce problems similar to over-smoothing. Therefore, we consider KG augmentations with full $\mathcal{R}_q$ and augmentations with subsets of $\mathcal{R}_q$.

Definition 2. *The* partial augmentation *of a KG $\mathcal{K}$ over* $\mathsf{Pred}_1 \cup \mathsf{Pred}_2$ *for the tree-CQ $q(x)$ with respect to rules $\mathcal{R}'_q \subseteq \mathcal{R}_q$ is the dataset $\mathcal{R}'_q(\mathcal{K})$. The (full) augmentation of $\mathcal{K}$ is the partial augmentation with respect to all $\mathcal{R}_q$.*

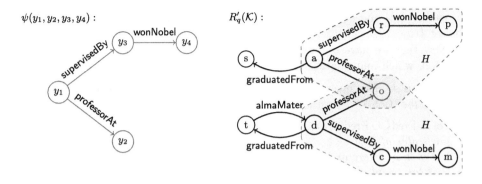

Fig. 2. Representation of ψ, $\mathcal{K}$, and augmentation $\mathcal{R}'_q(\mathcal{K})$ from Example 2

Example 2. Consider KG $\mathcal{K}$, tree-CQ $q(x)$ in Example 1, and the subconjunction

$$\psi(y_1, y_2, y_3, y_4) = \mathsf{professorAt}(y_1, y_2) \wedge \mathsf{supervisedBy}(y_1, y_3) \wedge \mathsf{wonNobel}(y_3, y_4),$$

of the body of $q(x)$ (see Fig. 2); its primal pseudograph is a tree of height 3. So, $\mathcal{R}_q$ contains rule $r = H(y_1, y_2, y_3, y_4) \leftarrow \psi(y_1, y_2, y_3, y_4)$ for a fresh predicate H, and the partial augmentation of $\mathcal{K}$ for $q(x)$ with respect to $\mathcal{R}'_q = \{r\}$ is $\mathcal{K} \cup \{H(alice, oxford, roger, physics), H(daniel, oxford, carol, medicine)\}$.

4.2 Encoding of Knowledge Graphs

We now describe our encoding of datasets into directed (multi-)hypergraphs where hyperedges are coloured and nodes are labelled by real-valued vectors. Specifically, our encoding introduces a hypergraph node for each constant in the input dataset; then, each fact of arity greater than 1 is encoded into a hyperedge of the colour corresponding to the fact's predicate, and each fact of arity 1 is encoded as a component of the feature vector labelling the corresponding node. Furthermore, for each binary fact in the original dataset with a predicate R, the encoding introduces, besides the R-coloured edge, an $\bar{R}$-coloured edge in the reverse direction; such edges will ensure that our ML model propagates information in both directions whenever a binary fact connects two constants.

Definition 3. *Given a finite set* Col *of colours with fixed arities greater than 1 and a dimension $\delta \in \mathbb{N}$, a* (Col, δ)-*hypergraph G is a triple $(\mathcal{V}, \mathcal{E}, \lambda)$ where $\mathcal{V}$ is a finite set of nodes, $\mathcal{E}$ is a set of directed hyperedges of the form $(v, c, (u_1, \dots, u_k))$ with $c \in$ Col of arity $k+1$, $\{v, u_1, \dots, u_k\} \subseteq \mathcal{V}$, and λ is a labelling function that assigns a vector $\lambda(v) \in \mathbb{R}^\delta$ to every $v \in \mathcal{V}$. Hypergraph G is* Boolean *if $\delta = 1$ and $\lambda(v) \in \{0, 1\}$ for every $v \in \mathcal{V}$.*

Given a (Col, δ)-*hypergraph* $G = (\mathcal{V}, \mathcal{E}, \lambda)$, we denote, for brevity, the vector $\lambda(v)$ for a node v with $\mathbf{v}$, and we refer to its ith element as $(\mathbf{v})_i$. Furthermore, for each $v \in V$ and $c \in \mathsf{Col}$, we define the *c-neighbourhood* $N_G^c(v)$ of v in G as the set $\{(u_1, \dots, u_k) \mid (v, c, (u_1, \dots, u_k)) \in \mathcal{E}\}$.

Now that we have our target graph structure, we can define our encoding function, which maps datasets (including augmented KGs) to hypergraphs.

Definition 4. *The* encoding *of a dataset $\mathcal{D}$ over predicates $\mathsf{Pred}_1 \cup \mathsf{Pred}_2 \cup \mathsf{Pred}_q$ is the (Col, δ)-hypergraph $G_{\mathcal{D}} = (V, \mathcal{E}, \lambda)$ such that*

- $\mathsf{Col} = \mathsf{Pred}_2^{\pm} \cup \mathsf{Pred}_q$ *(i.e., the binary predicates, their inverses, and the head predicates of $\mathcal{R}_q$),*
- $\delta = m + 1$ *(where m is the number $|\mathsf{Pred}_1|$ of unary predicates),*
- V *is the set of constants in $\mathcal{D}$,*
- $\mathcal{E}$ *includes $(a, R, (b_1, \dots, b_k))$ for every $R(a, b_1 \dots, b_k) \in \mathcal{D}$ with $k > 1$,*
- $\mathcal{E}$ *includes $(b, \bar{R}, (a))$ for every $R(a, b) \in \mathcal{D}$ with $R \in \mathsf{Pred}_2$, and*
- λ *is the labelling that assigns, to each $a \in V$, the vector $\mathbf{a} \in \mathbb{R}^\delta$ such that $(\mathbf{a})_i = 1$ if $A_i(a) \in \mathcal{D}$ or $i = m + 1$, and $(\mathbf{a})_i = 0$ otherwise.*

Note that the $(m + 1)^{\text{th}}$ element of each vector $\mathbf{a}$ is always 1; this element is needed to cover the case $m = 0$—that is, when there are no unary predicates.

4.3 Hyper-Relational Graph Convolutional Networks

We now introduce a generalised version of the RGCN [19] architecture that can process (Col, δ)-hypergraphs; we call this generalisation *Hyper-Relational Graph Convolutional Network (HRGCN)*. Our approach uses a HRGCN to process the hypergraphs that are encodings of augmented KGs.

Definition 5. *Given a finite set Col of colours with fixed arities and $\delta \in \mathbb{N}$, a (Col, δ)-HRGCN $\mathfrak{S}$ with $L \geq 1$ layers and dimensions $(\delta_0, \dots, \delta_L)$, for $\delta_0 = \delta$, is*

$$(\{\mathsf{Aggr}^\ell\}_{\ell=1}^L, \{\mathsf{Comb}^\ell\}_{\ell=1}^L, \mathsf{Cls}),$$

where

- *each* aggregation *function Aggr^ℓ, $1 \leq \ell \leq L$, maps a multiset of tuples of the form $(c, \mathbf{u}_1, \dots, \mathbf{u}_k)$ with $c \in \mathsf{Col}$ and each $\mathbf{u}_i$ in $\mathbb{R}^{\delta^{\ell-1}}$ to a vector in $\mathbb{R}^{\delta^{\ell-1}}$;*
- *each* combination *function Comb^ℓ, $1 \leq \ell \leq L$, maps two vectors in $\mathbb{R}^{\delta^{\ell-1}}$ to a vector in $\mathbb{R}^{\delta^\ell}$;*
- *classification* function Cls *maps a vector in $\mathbb{R}^{\delta^L}$ to a value in $\{0, 1\}$.*

Given a (Col, δ)-hypergraph $G = (V, \mathcal{E}, \lambda)$, HRGCN $\mathfrak{S}$ induces the sequence $\lambda^0, \dots, \lambda^L$ of labellings such that $\lambda^0 = \lambda$, and, for each $\ell \in \{1, \dots, L\}$ and $v \in V$, the value of $\lambda^\ell(v) = \mathbf{v}^\ell$ is defined as

$$\mathbf{v}^\ell = \mathsf{Comb}^\ell\left(\mathbf{v}^{\ell-1}, \mathsf{Aggr}^\ell\left(\{\{(c, \mathbf{u}_1^{\ell-1}, \dots, \mathbf{u}_k^{\ell-1}) \mid (u_1, \dots, u_k) \in N_G^c(v), c \in \mathsf{Col}\}\}\right)\right).$$

The result $\mathfrak{S}(G)$ of applying $\mathfrak{S}$ to G is the (Col, δ)-hypergraph $(V, \mathcal{E}, \lambda_{bool})$, where λ_{bool} is the labelling of every node $v \in V$ by $\mathsf{Cls}(\mathbf{v}^L)$. Subsequently, $\mathfrak{S}(G, v)$ denotes $\mathbf{v}^L$ and $\mathfrak{S}_{\text{true}}[G]$ denotes the set of all $v \in V$ with $\lambda_{bool}(v) = 1$.

Then, a (Col, δ)-*RGCN* is a (Col, δ)-HRGCN for Col with no colours of arity greater than 2 (this is essentially the standard definition of RGCNs [19]).

5   Advantages of Knowledge Graph Augmentation

As discussed in the introduction, the main motivation for KG augmentation is to help ML models easily recognise parts of the input KG that match complete connected fragments of the query. In this section, we present a theorem that makes this conjecture precise. To this end, we assume a natural and broad class of completion functions, which arguably captures those one may expect to find in practice. Then, we will show that, for each (big enough) tree-CQ q, if there is an instance of our approach capturing the goal function g_q without using KG augmentation, then there exists an instance of the approach that also captures g_q using (full) KG augmentation, but whose HRGCN has significantly less layers.

Definition 6. *A completion function* $\cdot^*$ *over a set of predicates* Pred *is*

- monotonic under homomorphisms *if for every KGs $\mathcal{K}_1$ and $\mathcal{K}_2$ over* Pred *and each homomorphism h from $\mathcal{K}_1$ to $\mathcal{K}_2$, h is also a homomorphism from $\mathcal{K}_1^*$ to $\mathcal{K}_2^*$, where a homomorphism h from $\mathcal{K}_1$ to $\mathcal{K}_2$ is a mapping from $\mathsf{Const}(\mathcal{K}_1)$ to constants such that $h(\mathcal{K}_1) \subseteq \mathcal{K}_2$;*
- s-local, *for $s \in \mathbb{N}$, if for every KG $\mathcal{K}$ over* Pred *and every fact $\alpha \in \mathcal{K}^*$ there is $\mathcal{K}_\alpha \subseteq \mathcal{K}$ such that $\alpha \in \mathcal{K}_\alpha^*$ and $\mathcal{K}_\alpha$ contains an undirected path (through constants and binary facts) from each constant in $\mathcal{K}_\alpha$ to each constant in α of length at most s;*
- k-incomplete *for a tree-CQ $q(x)$ if for each KG $\mathcal{K}$ over* Pred *and each answer $a \in q[\mathcal{K}^*]$ there is $\mathcal{K}_a$ such that $\mathcal{K} \subseteq \mathcal{K}_a \subseteq \mathcal{K}^*$, $a \in q[\mathcal{K}_a]$, and $|\mathcal{K}_a \setminus \mathcal{K}| \leq k$.*

The intuition under these notions is as follows. Monotonicity under homomorphisms requires that every fact in the completion of a KG should also appear (in a suitable form) in the completion of any KG that has the same structure as the original KG. Locality reflects the intuition that every fact in the completion is a consequence of a small neighbourhood of the fact in the original KG. Finally, incompleteness for a query means that, for every answer to the query, only a small number of facts can be missing in any 'witness' of it—that is, any part of the KG completion (fully) matching the query. We will now state our main result; its proof can be found in the supplemental material.

Theorem 1. *Let* Pred$_1$ *and* Pred$_2$ *be finite sets of unary and binary predicates, respectively, and let* Pred$_2^+$ = Pred$_2 \cup \{\bar{R} \mid R \in$ Pred$_2\}$ *and* Pred = Pred$_1 \cup$ Pred$_2$. *Let $q(x)$ be a tree-CQ of height h over* Pred *and $\cdot^*$ be a completion function over* Pred *that is monotonic under homomorphisms, s-local, and k-incomplete for $q(x)$. If there is an L-layer (Pred$_2^+, \delta$)-RGCN $\mathfrak{R}$, for $\delta \in \mathbb{N}$, such that $\mathfrak{R}_{\mathsf{true}}[G_\mathcal{K}] = q[\mathcal{K}^*]$ for each KG $\mathcal{K}$ over* Pred, *then there is a $(k(s+1)+1)$-layer (Pred$_2^+ \cup$ Pred$_q, \delta$)-HRGCN $\mathfrak{S}$ such that $\mathfrak{S}_{\mathsf{true}}[G_{\mathcal{R}_q(\mathcal{K})}] = q[\mathcal{K}^*]$ for each KG $\mathcal{K}$ over* Pred.

We emphasise that many completion functions that one may find in practice will have small values of s and k, thus making $k(s+1)+1$ significantly smaller than L. Therefore (for large enough L) KG augmentation allows us to reduce the number of layers that an HRGCN instance in our approach requires to capture the goal function g_q—that is, to capture query q on incomplete KGs.

Table 1. Benchmark statistics, where $||q||$ and $h(q)$ are the number of atoms and height of the tree-CQ, and 'pos./neg.' stands for 'number of positive / negative examples'

Benchmark	|Pred|	$||q||$ /$h(q)$	train: pos./neg.	test: pos./neg.
WATDIV-Q1	158	8 / 4	2114 / 699699	1085 / 349877
WATDIV-Q2	158	8 / 3	3258 / 698396	1769 / 349119
WATDIV-Q3	158	8 / 3	1520 / 700276	798 / 350165
WATDIV-Q4	158	10 / 4	2397 / 698986	1226 / 349546
WATDIV-Q5	158	10 / 4	6338 / 693988	2866 / 347570
WATDIV-Q6	158	10 / 4	7545 / 692439	3744 / 346290
FB15K237-Q1	237	7 / 4	1185 / 1180	395 / 395
FB15K237-Q2	237	7 / 4	650 / 660	220 / 220
FB15K237-Q3	237	5 / 4	860 / 870	290 / 290

6   Implementation and Evaluation

We have implemented our approach to the IQA task over incomplete KGs using Python 3.8.10, RDFLIB 6.1.1, and PyTorch 1.11.0 in a system called GNNQ. We then evaluated several instances $GNNQ_L$ of GNNQ using KG augmentation, parametrised by the number L of layers of the underlying HRGCN, on a number of benchmarks. To the best of our knowledge, no existing system can solve the IQA task (in particular, can deal simultaneously with KG incompleteness, complex queries, and the inductive setting); thus, we compared the instances $GNNQ_L$ against instances $GNNQ_L^-$ of GNNQ that do not use KG augmentation, which we treat as baselines. Our experiments show that the $GNNQ_L$ instances significantly outperform the $GNNQ_L^-$ instances, even if the RGCNs underlying the latter use more layers. Thus, we conclude that KG augmentation can provide a significant advantage in solving the IQA task in practice. All experiments were performed on a machine equipped with an Intel® Core™ i9-10900K CPU, 64GB of RAM, running Ubuntu 20.04.4, and a Nvidia GeForce RTX 3090 GPU.

6.1   Benchmarks

The existing benchmarks for query answering on KGs used in the QE literature [4,9,11,17,18,20] are designed for the transductive setting, so we cannot use them for an informative comparison of systems addressing the IQA task. Thus, in order to evaluate GNNQ instances, we have designed nine novel IQA benchmarks. Six of these, called WATDIV-Qi, for $i \in \{1, \ldots, 6\}$, are based on synthetic KGs generated with the WatDiv framework [3], and the remaining three, called FB15K237-Qi, for $i \in \{1, 2, 3\}$, are based on subgraphs of FB15k-237 [6], a real-life KG commonly used in benchmarks for evaluation of KG completion and QE systems. Each of our benchmarks provides the following:

- a set Pred of unary and binary predicates and a tree-CQ over Pred;
- sets of examples for training (including validation) and testing; each example is of the form $(\mathcal{K}, a, Ans)$ where $\mathcal{K}$ is a KG over Pred, a is a constant, and $Ans \in \{0, 1\}$ is the ground-truth answer.

The benchmarks are constructed so that the ground-truth answer of an example is 1 if and only if $a \in q[\mathcal{K}^*]$, where $\cdot^*$ is a hidden completion function over Pred, which is not given as part of the benchmark. For all our benchmarks, $\cdot^*$ is defined by appropriately constructed Datalog rules [2]; such an approach allows us to capture structural dependencies of KGs, which are best-fitted for the inductive setting [23]. Table 1 summarises the statistics of our nine benchmarks. Further details about the selection of queries, completion functions, and examples for each benchmark are provided in the supplemental material.

6.2   GNNQ Implementation

Using a set of predicates Pred and a tree-CQ $q(x)$ as parameters, each $GNNQ_L$ processes a KG $\mathcal{K}$ over Pred and a candidate constant $a \in \mathsf{Const}(\mathcal{K})$ by performing the following steps, implementing (and specifying) our approach.

Step 1. Each $GNNQ_L$ computes a partial augmentation $R'_q(\mathcal{K})$ of $\mathcal{K}$ with respect to some subset $\mathcal{R}'_q \subseteq \mathcal{R}_q$ specified as follows: for the FB15k237-Q_i benchmarks, we take $\mathcal{R}'_q = \mathcal{R}_q$; in contrast, for the WATDIV-Q_i benchmarks, we take $\mathcal{R}'_q$ as the subset of all rules in $\mathcal{R}_q$ with at most 4 variables. We selected such $\mathcal{R}'_q$ because, on the one hand, the FB15k237-Q_i benchmarks are relatively irregular, so we expect that even with full augmentation only a relatively small number of augmentation facts will be generated; on the other hand, the WATDIV-Q_i benchmarks are highly regular, which suggests that performance may be hampered if we perform full augmentation, as this will derive many similar facts, which may cause problems analogous to over-smoothing. Each $GNNQ_L$ then encodes $\mathcal{R}'_q(\mathcal{K})$ as a (Col, δ)-hypergraph $G_{\mathcal{R}'_q(\mathcal{K})}$ with appropriate Col and δ (see Sect. 4.2).

Step 2. Each $GNNQ_L$ applies, to $G_{\mathcal{R}'_q(\mathcal{K})}$, a (Col, δ)-HRGCN $\mathfrak{I}$ with L layers, dimensions $(\delta^0, \ldots, \delta^L)$ such that $\delta^0 = \delta$ and $\delta^L = 1$, and the following components. Functions Aggr^ℓ and Comb^ℓ for each layer $\ell \in \{1, \ldots, L\}$ of $\mathfrak{I}$ are defined so that the feature vector of each node v is updated as

$$\mathbf{v}^\ell = \sigma^\ell \left(\mathbf{C}^\ell \mathbf{v}^{(\ell-1)} + \sum_{c \in \mathsf{Col}} \sum_{(u_1, \ldots, u_{k_c}) \in N^c_{G_{\mathcal{R}'_q(\mathcal{K})}}(v)} \frac{\mathbf{A}^\ell_c [\mathbf{u}_1^{(\ell-1)}, \ldots, \mathbf{u}_{(k_{c-1})}^{k_c}]}{|N^c_{G_{\mathcal{R}'_q(\mathcal{K})}}(v)|} + \mathbf{b}^\ell \right),$$

where σ^ℓ is a element-wise leaky ReLU for each $\ell \in \{1, \ldots, L-1\}$ and the element-wise sigmoid function if $\ell = L$; where every $\mathbf{C}^\ell$ and $\mathbf{A}^\ell_c$, for each colour $c \in \mathsf{Col}$, are (learnable) real-valued matrices of dimension $\delta^\ell \times \delta^{\ell-1}$ and $\delta^l \times (k_c \delta^{(l-1)})$, respectively, for $k_c + 1$ the arity of c, and each $\mathbf{b}^\ell$ is a (learnable) real-valued *bias* vector of dimension δ^ℓ; and where $[\mathbf{u}_1^\ell, \ldots, \mathbf{u}_{k_c}^\ell]$ is the vector obtained by concatenating $\mathbf{u}_1^\ell, \ldots, \mathbf{u}_{k_c}^\ell$. The classification function maps $x \in \mathbb{R}$

Table 2. Results for WATDIV-Qi benchmarks in the format precision/recall/AP

	WATDIV-Q1	WATDIV-Q2	WATDIV-Q3	WATDIV-Q4	WATDIV-Q5	WATDIV-Q6
GNNQ$^-_{h-1}$	.648/ .646/ .678	.655/ .722/ .661	.652/ .731/ .729	.660/ .590/ .653	.733/ .724/ .780	.555/ .614/ .578
GNNQ^-_h	.742/ .707/ .771	.819/ .852/ .881	.680/ .787/ .784	**.791**/ .700/ .798	.696/**.933**/ .860	.625/ .840/ .733
GNNQ$^-_{h+1}$	.621/**.856**/ .750	**.919/.920/.969**	.742/**.835**/ .807	.770/ .804/**.829**	.865/ .924/**.925**	**.852/.815/.877**
GNNQ$_{h-1}$	.737/ .721/ .815	.779/ .820/ .858	.700/ .806/ .793	.717/ .783/ .806	.743/ .833/ .885	.736/ .619/ .700
GNNQ$_h$	**.806/ .772/.870**	.821/ .830/ .906	**.797/ .791/.847**	.714/**.839**/ .827	**.876**/ .852/ .924	.763/ .705/ .784

to 1 if and only if $x \geq 0.5$. The feature vector dimensions $\delta^1 = \cdots = \delta^{L-1}$ and the negative slope of the ReLU activations are tuneable hyperparameters.

Step 3. The model returns 1 if $a \in \Im_{\text{true}}[G_{\mathcal{R}'_q(\mathcal{K})}]$ and 0 otherwise.

The baselines $GNNQ^-_L$ follow the same procedure, except that they skip KG augmentation and use $\mathcal{K}$ instead of $\mathcal{R}'_q(\mathcal{K})$, thus relying on vanilla RGCNs [19].

For each benchmark, we trained and evaluated the $GNNQ_L$ instances for each $L \in \{h-1, h\}$ and the $GNNQ^-_L$ instances for each $L \in \{h-1, h, h+1\}$, where h is the height of the benchmark's tree-CQ. Before training, we randomly split the benchmark's training-and-validation set of examples into training and validation sets with ratio 1:1 or 2:1, in case of a WATDIV or a FB15k237 benchmark, respectively. In each training run (on the training set), we trained all model parameters for 250 epochs using the Adam optimiser and a standard binary cross-entropy loss computed using the value of the (1-dimensional) feature vector in the last layer of the model as the prediction value (i.e., without applying the classification function). Each training run is specified by hyperparameters: the learning rate from $\{.0001, .0006, \ldots, .1001\}$, the negative slope of the leaky-ReLU activation functions from $\{.001, .006, \ldots, .101\}$, and the latent feature vector dimension from $\{8, 9, \ldots, 64\}$. We report results for the hyperparameter values maximising the *average precision* on the validation set, which are found by means of 100 training runs using Optuna (MedianPruner) with 5 warm-up runs, 30 warm-up epochs in every run, and step size 25.

6.3 Performance Metrics

For each benchmark, we evaluated all the (best of the) trained models over the test set. For each model, we recorded the numbers tp, tn, fp, fn of true positives, true negatives, false positives, and false negatives, respectively, and report the *precision* $tp/(tp + fp)$ and *recall* $tp/(tp + fn)$ metrics. Furthermore, to test the robustness of our models under variations to the threshold used in the classification, we modified each learned model by removing the application of the classification function, so that each modified model returns the real value labelling the node for the candidate constant in the last layer. We then applied the modified models to the test set, and used the outputs to compute the *average precision* (*AP*), which is the area under the precision-recall curve.

Table 3. Results for the FB15K237-Qi benchmarks in the format precision/recall/AP

	FB15K237-Q1	FB15K237-Q2	FB15K237-Q3
GNNQ$_{h-1}^-$	.582/ .451/ .554	.569/ .618/ .544	.550/ .648/ .518
GNNQ$_h^-$	.606/ .382/ .581	.603/ .559/ .557	.588/ .621/ .579
GNNQ$_{h+1}^-$	.766/ .597/ .742	.624/ .505/ .580	.556/ .731/ .593
GNNQ$_{h-1}$	.903/ .873/ .958	.641/ .650/**.757**	.766/ .769/ .889
GNNQ$_h$	**.919/.922/.976**	**.643/.664/** .670	**.822/.828/.933**

6.4   Results

We report the results of our experiments for the WATDIV-Qi and FB15K237-Qi benchmarks in Tables 2 and 3, respectively. As one can see, the GNNQ$_L$ instances outperform the GNNQ$_L^-$ instances on almost all benchmarks, when comparing instances whose HRGCN has the same number of layers. Furthermore, the GNNQ$_L$ instances with the smallest number of layers outperformed all *GNNQ$^-$* instances by a significant margin on the FB15K237-Qi benchmarks. We attribute this to the fact that the real-world KGs are more noisy than the synthetic ones, and the baselines are more vulnerable to noise since they must learn longer dependencies. These results confirm our hypothesis that augmenting input KGs with facts representing the parts of the KG that satisfy connected query fragments can lead to improved empirical performance in the IQA task.

7   Related Work

KG Completion, which predicts missing facts in a KG, is a central soft reasoning task on KGs. Existing KG completion approaches can be classified in two categories. *Transductive* KG completion models learn an *embedding* function that maps constants and predicates in a fixed KG to elements of a vector space. At inference time, a missing target fact can then be verified by first applying the embedding function to the predicate and constants used in the target fact, and then applying a fixed *scoring* function to the resulting embeddings [1,6,7,21,27]. *Inductive* KG completion assumes only a fixed set of predicates, and a trained model can be applied to any KG over these predicates. Many inductive KG completion approaches use GNNs [10,14,23,24], which can reason over the structure of KGs and are therefore inductive by design.

Query Embedding (QE) aims to answer monadic queries from various classes over the completion of an arbitrary but fixed KG. Common QE approaches are inspired by embedding-based KG completion methods [4,9,11,17,18,20]. To produce query answers that are not logically entailed, such QE models usually jointly learn embedding functions for constants and for queries during training. At inference time, a QE model first embeds the input query using the learnt embedding functions and then scores constants as potential answers based on the distance of their embeddings to the query embedding. Thus QE approaches aim to answer arbitrary queries over the predicates and constants of a fixed KG. This is orthogonal to our inductive setting, which assumes a fixed query but is applicable to arbitrary KGs (over a predefined set of predicates).

Connection of Logic and GNNs. The increasing interest in GNNs across different domains has motivated the theoretical analysis of the expressiveness and limitations of GNNs. For example, it is trivial to see that GNNs cannot distinguish between two non-isomorphic k-regular graphs of the same size with uniform node features. Further analysis connected GNNs to the family of well-known Weisfeiler-Lehman (WL) graph isomorphism tests; in particular, Xu et al. [26] and Morris et al. [15] independently showed that the most expressive GNNs can distinguish the same nodes as the 1-dimensional WL test and hence between the same nodes as formulas in FOC_2, the two-variable fragment of the first-order logic with counting quantifiers. Further deep connections between various logics and GNNs have recently followed these works [5,8,22], and we anticipate that these results are paving a path for future efficient neuro-symbolic AI approaches to many tasks in data and knowledge management.

8   Conclusion and Future Work

In this paper, we presented a novel neuro-symbolic approach to query answering over incomplete KGs. In contrast to existing embedding-based approaches, which assume a fixed KG, our approach is inductive—that is, it only relies on a fixed set of predicates and is thus applicable to arbitrary KGs over these predicates. Our approach proceeds in three phases. First, it uses symbolic rules to augment the input KG with facts representing subgraphs that match connected fragments of the query. Second, it encodes the augmented KG into a hypergraph with vector-labelled nodes. Third, it processes the hypergraph using a Hyper-Relational Graph Convolutional Network (HRGCN), a novel GNN architecture which generalises the well-known RGCN architecture. We then provided a theorem showing that the KG augmentation phase can considerably reduce the number of layers a HRGCN-based system needs to produce correct answers to a query on every KG. Finally, we implemented our approach in the GNNQ system and evaluated it on several novel benchmarks. Our experiments showed that KG augmentation indeed leads to improved empirical performance in the IQA task. The main challenge for future work is extending our approach to support more expressive queries. We shall also investigate the queries and completion functions that can be perfectly captured by our approach and its potential extensions.

Supplemental Material Statement. A proof of Theorem 1 as well as details about the creation of the benchmark datasets can be found in the supplementary material. This material, together with the source code of GNNQ, the benchmarks, and the instructions for the reproduction of our experiments are accessible through Github (https://github.com/KRR-Oxford/GNNQ).

Acknowledgements. This work was supported by Siemens AG, the AIDA project (Alan Turing Institute, EP/N510129/1), the SIRIUS Centre for Scalable Data Access (Research Council of Norway, project number 237889), Samsung Research UK, and the EPSRC projects ConCur (EP/V050869/1), OASIS (EP/S032347/1) and UK FIRES (EP/S019111/1). For the purpose of Open Access, the author has applied a CC BY public copyright licence to any Author Accepted Manuscript (AAM) version arising from this submission.

References

1. Abboud, R., Ceylan, I., Lukasiewicz, T., Salvatori, T.: Boxe: a box embedding model for knowledge base completion. In: Advances in Neural Information Processing Systems, vol. 33 (2020)
2. Abiteboul, S., Hull, R., Vianu, V.: Foundations of Databases. Addison Wesley, Boston (1995)
3. Aluç, G., Hartig, O., Özsu, M.T., Daudjee, K.: Diversified stress testing of RDF data management systems. In: Mika, P., et al. (eds.) ISWC 2014. LNCS, vol. 8796, pp. 197–212. Springer, Cham (2014). https://doi.org/10.1007/978-3-319-11964-9_13
4. Arakelyan, E., Daza, D., Minervini, P., Cochez, M.: Complex query answering with neural link predictors. In: International Conference on Learning Representations (2021). https://openreview.net/forum?id=Mos9F9kDwkz
5. Barceló, P., Kostylev, E.V., Monet, M., Pérez, J., Reutter, J., Silva, J.P.: The logical expressiveness of graph neural networks. In: International Conference on Learning Representations (2019)
6. Bordes, A., Usunier, N., Garcia-Duran, A., Weston, J., Yakhnenko, O.: Translating embeddings for modeling multi-relational data. In: Advances in Neural Information Processing Systems, pp. 2787–2795 (2013)
7. Dettmers, T., Pasquale, M., Pontus, S., Riedel, S.: Convolutional 2d knowledge graph embeddings. In: Proceedings of the 32th AAAI Conference on Artificial Intelligence, pp. 1811–1818, February 2018 https://arxiv.org/abs/1707.01476
8. Grohe, M.: The logic of graph neural networks. In: 2021 36th Annual ACM/IEEE Symposium on Logic in Computer Science (LICS), pp. 1–17. IEEE (2021)
9. Guu, K., Miller, J., Liang, P.: Traversing knowledge graphs in vector space. arXiv preprint arXiv:1506.01094 (2015)
10. Hamaguchi, T., Oiwa, H., Shimbo, M., Matsumoto, Y.: Knowledge transfer for out-of-knowledge-base entities : A graph neural network approach. In: Proceedings of the Twenty-Sixth International Joint Conference on Artificial Intelligence, pp. 1802–1808. AAAI Press (2017)
11. Hamilton, W.L., Bajaj, P., Zitnik, M., Jurafsky, D., Leskovec, J.: Embedding logical queries on knowledge graphs. In: Advances in Neural Information Processing Systems, pp. 2026–2037 (2018)
12. Hamilton, W.L.: Graph representation learning. In: Synthesis Lectures on Artificial Intelligence and Machine Learning, vol. 14(3), pp. 1–159 (2021)
13. Hogan, A., et al.: Knowledge Graphs. ACM Computing Surveys **54**(4), 71:1-71:37 (2021)
14. Liu, S., Cuenca Grau, B., Horrocks, I., Kostylev, E.V.: Indigo: GNN-based inductive knowledge graph completion using pair-wise encoding. In: NeurIPS (2021)

15. Morris, C., et al.: Weisfeiler and leman go neural: higher-order graph neural networks. In: Proceedings of the AAAI Conference on Artificial Intelligence, vol. 33, pp. 4602–4609 (2019)
16. Motik, B., Nenov, Y., Piro, R., Horrocks, I., Olteanu, D.: Parallel Materialisation of datalog programs in centralised, main-memory RDF systems. In: Proceedings of the 28th AAAI Conference on Artificial Intelligence (AAAI 2014), pp. 129–137 (2014)
17. Ren, H., Hu, W., Leskovec, J.: Query2box: reasoning over knowledge graphs in vector space using box embeddings. In: International Conference on Learning Representations (2020)
18. Ren, H., Leskovec, J.: Beta embeddings for multi-hop logical reasoning in knowledge graphs (2020)
19. Schlichtkrull, M., Kipf, T.N., Bloem, P., van den Berg, R., Titov, I., Welling, M.: Modeling relational data with graph convolutional networks. In: Gangemi, A., et al. (eds.) ESWC 2018. LNCS, vol. 10843, pp. 593–607. Springer, Cham (2018). https://doi.org/10.1007/978-3-319-93417-4_38
20. Sun, H., Arnold, A.O., Bedrax-Weiss, T., Pereira, F., Cohen, W.W.: Faithful embeddings for knowledge base queries. In: Advances in Neural Information Processing Systems, vol. 33 (2020)
21. Sun, Z., Deng, Z.H., Nie, J.Y., Tang, J.: Rotate: Knowledge graph embedding by relational rotation in complex space. In: International Conference on Learning Representations (2019). https://openreview.net/forum?id=HkgEQnRqYQ
22. Tena Cucala, D.J., Cuenca Grau, B., Kostylev, E.V., Motik, B.: Explainable GNN-based models over knowledge graphs. In: International Conference on Learning Representations (2022). https://openreview.net/forum?id=CrCvGNHAIrz
23. Teru, K., Denis, E.G., Hamilton, W.L.: Inductive relation prediction by subgraph reasoning. In: International Conference on Machine Learning, pp. 9448–9457. PMLR (2020)
24. Wang, H., Ren, H., Leskovec, J.: Entity context and relational paths for knowledge graph completion. arXiv preprint arXiv:2002.06757 (2020)
25. Wang, P., Han, J., Li, C., Pan, R.: Logic attention based neighborhood aggregation for inductive knowledge graph embedding. In: The Thirty-Third AAAI Conference on Artificial Intelligence, AAAI 2019, pp. 7152–7159. AAAI Press (2019)
26. Xu, K., Hu, W., Leskovec, J., Jegelka, S.: How powerful are graph neural networks? CoRR abs/1810.00826 (2018), http://arxiv.org/abs/1810.00826
27. Yang, B., Yih, W., He, X., Gao, J., Deng, L.: Embedding entities and relations for learning and inference in knowledge bases (2015)

Radar Station: Using KG Embeddings for Semantic Table Interpretation and Entity Disambiguation

Jixiong Liu[1,2], Viet-Phi Huynh[1], Yoan Chabot[1(✉)], and Raphael Troncy[2]

[1] Orange, Belfort, France
yoan.chabot@orange.com
[2] EURECOM, Sophia-antipolis, France

Abstract. Relational tables are widely used to store information about entities and their attributes and they are the de-facto format for training AI algorithms. Numerous Semantic Table Interpretation approaches have been proposed in particular for the so-called cell-entity annotation task aiming at disambiguating the values of table cells given reference knowledge graphs (KGs). Among these methods, heuristic-based ones have demonstrated to be the ones reaching the best performance, often relying on the column types and on the inter-column relationships aggregated by voting strategies. However, they often ignore other column-wised semantic similarities and are very sensitive to error propagation (e.g. if the type annotation is incorrect, often such systems propagate the entity annotation error in the target column). In this paper, we propose Radar Station, a hybrid system that aims to add a semantic disambiguation step after a previously identified cell-entity annotation. Radar Station takes into account the entire column as context and uses graph embeddings to capture latent relationships between entities to improve their disambiguation. We evaluate Radar Station using several graph embedding models belonging to different families on Web tables as well as on synthetic datasets. We demonstrate that our approach can lead to an accuracy improvement of 3% compared to the heuristics-based systems. Furthermore, we empirically observe that among the various graph embeddings families, the ones relying on fine-tuned translation distance show superior performance compared to other models.

Keywords: Cell-entity annotation · Graph embeddings · Semantic Table Interpretation · Entity disambiguation

1 Introduction

Tabular data is one of the most commonly used formats. This condensed representation of information offers a compact visualisation of the data that is easy for users to access and use. Among the wide variety of tabular data, relational tables organise entity attributes into columns and are used extensively in enterprise data repositories and on the Web for storing information and for training

© The Author(s), under exclusive license to Springer Nature Switzerland AG 2022
U. Sattler et al. (Eds.): ISWC 2022, LNCS 13489, pp. 498–515, 2022.
https://doi.org/10.1007/978-3-031-19433-7_29

AI algorithms. We argue that adding a semantic layer on top of such rich data source using KGs can be beneficial to several downstream tasks such as datasets indexing [2], KG enrichment [25], or dataset recommendation [32]. This process of automatically understanding what tabular data is about is named Semantic Table Interpretation (STI). Cell-entity annotation [16] (CEA) is one of the fundamental tasks for STI. This task is often performed by retrieving and scoring possible entity candidates (from a target KG) to disambiguate a cell value. Next, the result is used as input for performing Column-Type Annotation (CTA) and Columns-Property Annotation (CPA) [1,6,13,21]. However, associating a mention contained in a cell with an entity in a KG is a complex task requiring the resolution of several issues including handling properly the syntactic heterogeneity of mentions (e.g. the Wikidata entity "France" (Q142) may be referenced in a table by mentions like "The Republic of France" or "FRA"), the polysemy of terms (e.g. "Apple" can refer to a fruit or a company), and the diversity and complexity of table formats and layouts (e.g. matrices, relational table with hidden subjects, etc.).

Numerous approaches have been proposed for handling these issues. Among these methods, heuristic-based iterative approaches [1,6,13,21] aim to leverage the column types and the inter-column relationships aggregated by voting strategies for disambiguating cell annotations. They have demonstrated to be the methods reaching the best performance in the SemTab challenge series [9,16,17]. However, one drawback of these strategies is related to error propagation. Often, such systems propagate the entity annotation error in the target column. Furthermore, they also often ignore other column-wised semantic similarities: for example, books appearing in the same column may share the same topic.

To address these limitations, we propose a new hybrid disambiguation system called Radar Station that takes advantage of both an iterative disambiguation pipeline and semantic disambiguation using graph embedding similarities. Radar Station takes as input CEA annotations and associated confidence scores that quantify the level of certainty associated with each result. Our approach uses an ambiguity detection module that detects cases where the cell annotation is potentially wrong due to error propagation. In the following steps, the use of graph embeddings allows Radar Station to potentially fix the wrong annotations by taking into account semantic proximities (e.g. geometric proximity of entities representing books) that are not directly encoded and captured in the sole content of table columns. We evaluate Radar Station using several graph embedding models belonging to different families on Web tables as well as on synthetic datasets, and we provide a thorough analysis of the performance among the graph embeddings models and the datasets.

The remainder of this paper is structured as follows. In Sect. 2, we introduce some definitions and the assumptions we made in this study. Next, we review the many approaches that have been proposed for cell annotations and discuss their limitations (Sect. 3). In Sect. 4, we present the Radar Station system and the use of embeddings for cell-entity disambiguation. Then, we present our experimental settings in Sect. 5 and the evaluation using existing gold standards in Sect. 6. Finally, we conclude and outline future work in Sect. 7.

2 Preliminaries

In this paper, we focus on relational tables since they are the most used type of tabular data. Relational tables geometrically translate subjects from the same topic and their attributes accordingly to a given orientation. More specifically, in a horizontal table, a row describes the attributes of a given entity, and a column contains the values of a given attribute for all entities contained in the table. For example, Table 1 provides an example of relational table from the Limaye dataset [19]. The last row describes the book "Ylesia" with its attributes, including the published year ("2002") and the platform ("e-book"). We assume that the orientation of the input table is known and is either horizontal or vertical. We also assume that a cell value does not contain more than a single entity and that the system knows the target columns containing the entities to annotate. Radar Station assumes that a table cell can always be correctly annotated with an entity w.r.t this KG. Given the above assumptions, Radar Station is a system that aims to improve cell disambiguation from annotations produced by an STI system using a target KG (Wikidata, in our experiments). Given Table 1, Radar Station annotates the cell "Traitor" with the entity "Q7833036", the science fiction book, using the table context, while often, traditional STI system will disambiguate this cell with the anti-war romance novel "Q21161161" which has the same label.

Table 1. Table file405599_0_cols1_rows23.csv from Limaye dataset, row 13–17

2002	Enemy Lines : Rebel Dream	
2002	Enemy Lines : Rebel Stand	
2002	Traitor	
2002	Destiny's Way	
2002	Ylesia	e - book

3 Related Work

STI covers five main tasks: CEA, CTA, CPA [16], row-to-instance annotation and table topic annotation [24]. Radar Station aims to improve the CEA disambiguation. Thus, this section reviews the current state-of-the-art methods for the CEA task on relational tables. We classify them into three groups: heuristic-based approaches, iterative disambiguation, and graph embeddings approaches, and we discuss their strengths and limitations [20].

3.1   Heuristic-Based Approaches

Starting from a basic lookup service that generates target candidates for a given cell mention, heuristic-based approaches leverage diverse methods interpreting the table context to filter unreliable candidates and to produce a final annotation. Based on heuristic candidate generation and string similarities measures, [19] is one of the first works on STI. It constructs a graph-based algorithm that exploits learnable features from column context, row context, and relation context to construct a confidence function for each candidate for annotating a cell. TabEL [3] introduces a hybrid system that leverages probabilities to build a graphical model for representing the interactions between cells, columns, and headers. ADOG [22] generates features from string similarities, frequencies of properties, and the normalized Elasticsearch score. Then, these features are calibrated with the candidate's TF-IDF score according to entities' types in the same column. Our approach takes as input a list of CEA candidate annotations together with their scores (generated by such an existing CEA annotation tool), and detects the presence of potential ambiguities in order to select the right candidate from this closed set.

3.2   Candidate Disambiguation

Adding a disambiguation process on top of a heuristic-based approach can significantly improve the performance of an annotation system. Iterative processing is one of the most commonly-used methods for improving pre-annotated results. The iteration loop aims to collect the results of several annotation tasks, mutually improving the compatibility between annotations (e.g. taking into account the type of a column produced by the CTA to choose the right CEA candidates), and increasing the scores of candidates that would not have been chosen in the first place. For example, [35] uses a loop that exploits the CTA annotation of a given column to select candidate cells that feature that type and then redefines a new CTA annotation for the column by exploiting the entities selected. Regarding the CEA disambiguation, we identified two classes of iterative systems. First, T2K [25] and TableMiner+ [33] introduce a loop in the pipeline that ends when the result becomes stable. The other iterative systems [1,6,13,21] provide a predefined pipeline with sequential modules (e.g. the pipeline of LinkingPark [6] is composed of a CEA pre-scoring, then a CPA step, and finally the use of the CPA annotations to generate the final CEA annotations).

Radar Station uses the output scores of an existing STI system. It currently supports the DAGOBAH-SL [13,14], MTab [21] and BBW [27] systems which have all competed during the SemTab Challenge series [9,17] and are selected as baseline systems during the evaluation of Radar Station. These systems use string similarity in the scoring system and leverage table's global information carried out by the CTA and CPA annotations to generate more precise CEA annotations. For cell annotations, they evaluate whether a candidate entity $e_c \in \mathcal{E}_c(e_m)$

retrieved from the KG is a good representation of the corresponding table cell e_m by incorporating the table context of e_m and KG context of e_c in the score of e_c. Although these approaches show great performance for datasets like BioTable and HardTable from SemTab, they still have limitations as described in Sect. 1. First, the use of a unique column type or columns pairs relationship potentially propagates type (resp. relation) annotation error through cell annotations. Second, leveraging only entities' type (resp. relations) result does not allow to take into account more attributes and properties in the disambiguation process. For example, a column type may not bring necessary information such as a person's nationality, building localization, or object ownership for disambiguating entities. Facing these challenges, Radar Station first activates an ambiguity detection module that detects cases where the cell annotation is potentially wrong. Meanwhile, it considers entities' embeddings to leverage more similarity measures inside a given column.

3.3 Usage of Graph Embeddings

Methods applying graph embeddings for STI focus on entity-level in which the models learn embedding representations for entities of a table cell instead of the cell itself. Specifically, KG embedding techniques are used to encode the entities and their relationships into a vector space. STI approaches using deep learning models are based on the intuition that the entities in the same column should exhibit semantic similarities. Hence, they should be close to each other in the embedding space w.r.t. a cosine similarity distance [11] or an Euclidean distance [5].

Vasilis et al. [11] provide different methods. One of them assumes that the correct CEA candidates in a column should be semantically close. From this assumption, a weighted correlation subgraph in which a node represents a CEA candidate is constructed. The edges are weighted by the cosine similarity between two related nodes. The best candidates are the ones whose accumulated weights over all incoming and outcoming edges are the highest. In addition, a hybrid system combining a correlation subgraph method and an ontology matching system, is also introduced, which considerably improves the final result. Yasamin et al. [12] further enhance this approach by taking the header of the table into account for ontology matching and giving more weights to unique cell candidates when calculating embeddings Page-Rank. DAGOBAH-Embedding [5] follows the same assumption that all entities in the same column of the table should be close to each other in the embeddings space. Consequently, the correct candidates are assumed to belong to a few clusters. They apply a K-means clustering using TransE pre-trained KG embeddings to cluster the entity candidates. The good clusters with high coverage are selected by a weighted voting strategy. Experimental results prove that they have successfully improved the accuracy of the CTA task. However, the system is also misled by incorrect candidates during the CEA task when correct candidates are not in selected clusters. TURL [10] leverages the BERT model for STI and table augmentation with the help of a visibility matrix for capturing table structure. Although TURL introduces entity embeddings as one of the inputs to its model to assign information to entities, the entity embeddings do not embed properties about the entities in the graph, such as the fact that neighbouring nodes are missing in them.

The contributions of our approach are as follows. First, we use embeddings only during the disambiguation step to benefit from both the iterative disambiguation and the embeddings disambiguation. Second, we provide a new scoring mechanism that takes into account the scores generated by CEA approaches and the distance between the entities in the embedding space.

4   System Description

Radar Station is not a standalone annotation system. It is built on top of a given annotation system and resolves ambiguities detected in the annotated results. We choose to use DAGOBAH-SL [26] as the base annotation system to illustrate the process of Radar Station. We motivate the need for Radar Station observing that pure string-based matching and iterative scoring methods are limited in situations where: i) the target KG is incomplete; ii) the matching mechanism failed; iii) the CTA or CPA disambiguation can not provide enough information in very ambiguous cases (e.g. candidates belonging to the same type or no property identified). These situations also cover cases with limited row numbers that can annotate a unique column type (resp. unique columns relationship) by majority voting. For example, voting for a common type given only the two cell mentions "Apple" and "Blackberry" may lead to randomly select the company or the fruit.

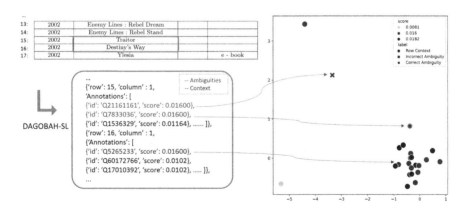

Fig. 1. Illustration of Radar Station with DAGOBAH-SL results. The plot is generated with RotatE embeddings after dimension reduction by T-SNE.

Figure 1 provides an example where DAGOBAH-SL is not able to handle properly an ambiguous case: two potential candidates with the same score for the cell "Traitor". The ambiguity comes from an unsuccessful matching between the column "2002" with literal information "30 July 2002" of candidate "Q7833036" for entity scoring and CPA disambiguation. CTA disambiguation does not work in this case since these two candidates are books with the type "literary work" ("Q7725634"). "Q21161161" is a science fiction novel and "Q7833036" is an anti-wars romance novel.

We do not aim at improving the performance of the system by relying on clever string matching methods. Instead, we expect to find more semantic similarities using the full column as context with the help of the scores generated from the row context. In this example, one could identify that the correct entity is "Q7833036" since the topic of this table is the science fiction series "The New Jedi Order" from Star Wars. This relationship is missing in the table cells, but it still could be beneficial for the disambiguation steps. Radar Station aims to leverage graph embeddings to dig similarities alongside the entity types and common relationships inside the tables. The architecture of Radar Station is illustrated in Fig. 2 and the modules are described in the following sections. Table 2 summarizes the notation used in the Radar Station approach.

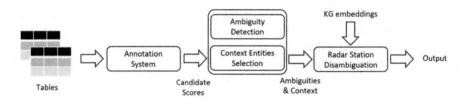

Fig. 2. Overview of the Radar Station pipeline.

Table 2. Summary of the notation used to define Radar Station

Notation	Description
$\mathcal{C}$	The collection of cells from the target column
$\mathcal{E}_c$	The collection of the context entities representing the column $\mathcal{C}$
$\mathcal{A}m_{c_i}$	The collection of the ambiguous entities extracted from the cell c_i
$\mathcal{S}c(e)$	The initial score for the candidate e generated from the previous annotation system, in our case, DAGOBAH-SL
$\mathcal{E}m(e)$	The embedding of a given entity e
$\mathcal{E}_k$	The collection of K nearest context entities of an ambiguous candidate $am \in \mathcal{A}m_{c_i}$ for the target column $\mathcal{C}$, $\mathcal{E}_k \in \mathcal{E}_c$

4.1   Input Data Structure

Before running Radar Station, the information required by the system includes the index of the cell in the table (row number and column number), and information about all candidates for each cell without filtering the candidates. This information includes an identification of each candidate and their confidence score. The confidence score evaluates how compatible a candidate is with the context information given by the table (e.g. row values, column type, columns-pair relations).

4.2   Context Entities Selection

The row context has already been interpreted by DAGOBAH-SL and is used to compute the confidence score of each candidate. The first step of Radar Station is to build a column-wised context to support the disambiguation process. We collect entities with the highest confidence score from all cells of a given column $\mathcal{C}$ as the context entities set. In case of ambiguity, that is, multiple candidates (n candidates) sharing the same highest score, we collect all of them, and the score is divided by n. Other candidates are not taken into account to maximize the trust for "sure" annotation from DAGOBAH-SL (e.g., only one candidate with the highest score) and to avoid noise inside this column. For example, for the row 15 in Fig. 1, both "Q7833036" and "Q21161161" are collected into the context set with a score "0.008" (0.016/2), and for row 16, only "Q5265233" is collected with a score "0.016". The collected context entities set for the column $\mathcal{C}$ are noted as $\mathcal{E}_c$.

4.3   Ambiguity Detection

Radar Station detects ambiguous cells that are worthy to be disambiguated given a tolerance t. Intuitively, t enables to relax the constraints one wants to have in looking up candidates potentially matching a cell mention. Once a candidate's score is larger than $t * Max(scores)$, it is selected as one of the "top candidates". For example, if we set $t = 1$, "Q7833036" and "Q21161161" for row 15 of Fig. 1 will be among the top candidates. If we relax the tolerance t to 0.7, "Q1536329" will also be considered as a top candidate. We denote "Ambiguities" as Am for the case that the size of the top candidates is greater than or equal to two. Radar Station is activated in this case and it will annotate the cell with one of the candidates from the ambiguities. When there is no ambiguity inside a cell, we directly output the single top candidate as the annotation.

4.4 Radar Station Disambiguation

Algorithm 1. Radar Station disambiguation algorithm

Input: Cell index $\mathcal{C}$ and ambiguities for each cell $\mathcal{A}m_{c_i}$, $c_i \in \mathcal{C}$ where the collected
context entities (or senders) of the target column is $\mathcal{E}_c$.
Candidate scores from the annotation system $\{Sc(e_i)\}$, $e_i \in \mathcal{E}_c$.
Candidate embeddings $\{Em(e_i)\}$, $e_i \in \mathcal{E}_c$.
Output: Entity annotation selected by Radar Station.
 1: build a KD-tree with all candidates' embeddings $\{Em(e_i)\}$
 2: $K \leftarrow min(|\mathcal{E}_f|, 20)$
 3: **for** each cell c_i from $\mathcal{C}$ **do**
 4:     **if** there is an ambiguity in $\mathcal{A}m_{c_i}$ **then**
 5:         $\mathcal{E}_c \leftarrow$ filter entities from the same cell in $\mathcal{E}_c$
 6:         **for** each ambiguous entity am_i in $\mathcal{A}m_{c_i}$ **do**
 7:             find the K nearest candidates of the ambiguous entity $\mathcal{E}_k$ in the KD-tree by ignoring candidates from the same cell.
 8:             $RadarScore_{am_i} \leftarrow 0$
 9:             **for** each neighboring entity $e_j \in \mathcal{E}_k$ **do**
10:                 $RadarScore_{am_i} \leftarrow RadarScore_{am_i} + \frac{Sc(e_j)}{distance(am_i, e_j)}$
11:             **end for**
12:             $RadarScore_{am_i} \leftarrow \frac{RadarScore_{am_i}}{K}$
13:             $g(am_i) \leftarrow \alpha RadarScore_{am_i} + Sc(e_j)$
14:         **end for**
15:         the annotation is the ambiguous entity with the highest $g(am_i)$
16:     **end if**
17: **end for**

In our approach, we leverage KG embeddings to uncover the entities' co-relationship from a table to improve the disambiguation step. The principle of the Radar Station approach is inspired by radar station signal emissions. The receiving signal power of a signal station depends on both the initial power strength from the sending station and the distance between the sender and the receiver. That is, the receiving signal will be stronger when the initial power from the sender is stronger, and this receiving signal strength will decrease as the distance increases. In our approach, we treat each context entity from the same column as a signal sender, and receivers are the ambiguities to be resolved. One ambiguous candidate captures signals from multiple neighbouring context entities (i.e. senders) and the sum of the receiving signals is the confidence score of the candidate. The disambiguation pseudo-code is presented in Algorithm 1.

We consider only the K nearest context entities to computer the final score of an annotation in order to avoid noise and to optimize the performance. The system first constructs a KD tree of all context entities for each column, and then calls this KD tree to drop the K nearest context entities during the prediction (lines 1–2). We set that the maximum K value is 20 (line 2). We set the initial sender power strength with the confidence score generated by DAGOBAH-SL.

One ambiguous candidate am_i detects K received signals from the surrounding senders $e_j \in \mathcal{E}_c$ (or context candidates) to generate the confidence score $f(am_i)$ with the Function 1 (line 3–12), where $Sc(e_j)$ denotes DAGOBAH-SL scores of the sender e_j and $distance(am_i, e_j)$ denotes the Euclidean distance between the sender e_j and the receiver am_i.

In detail, for a target am_i, we collect its top-K nearest neighbors from $\mathcal{E}_c$, where each context entity c_j belongs to $\mathcal{E}_c$. We have each context entity's scores $Sc(c_j)$ and the distance with the target candidate $distance(am_i, c_j)$. We then apply the Function 1. Like this, we could generate a confidence score for each of those two target candidates. We divide each of their context entities' confidence score by the distance between those two candidates and then calculate the sum to compare.

$$f(am_i) = \frac{1}{K} \sum_{j<K} \left(\frac{Sc(e_j)}{distance(am_i, e_j)} \right) \tag{1}$$

The final result $g(am_i)$ for an ambiguous entity is the combination of Radar Station score $f(am_i)$ and the initial DAGOBAH-SL confidence score $Sc(am_i)$ introduced in Function 2 (line 13).

$$g(am_i) = \alpha f(am_i) + Sc(am_i) \tag{2}$$

Our initial experiments showed that the average distance in the embedding space between the target ambiguity and its top K nodes is approximately 1. According to the Function 1, we know that $f(am_i)$ and $S_c(am_i)$ are roughly in the same order of magnitude. Since we expect to disambiguate candidates with a tolerance between 0.7 and 1, we need the value of the discrepancy caused by $f(am_i)$ to be roughly within $S_c(am_i) * 0.3$. We originally set α to 0.3 and we tested the following α values (0,3, 0.2, 0.1, 0.05, and 0.01). We empirically observed that 0.05 gives the best results.

5 Experiments

In our experiments, we consider Wikidata as the target KG. We first rely on the DAGOBAH-SL system to lookup for candidates for each entity cell. We only consider the top 100 candidates according to the string similarity on entity label and aliases. We evaluate the result on four different gold standard datasets: T2D [25], Limaye [19], Tough Tables version 2 [8] and ShortTables.

5.1 Knowledge Graph Embeddings

Pre-trained KG embeddings can provide additional information for table understanding beyond the table context. Entities inside the same table column should be somehow co-related, which means they may share the same entity type, similar topics, or even attributes. In order to have the most suitable embeddings given the latest version of Wikidata, we use the PyTorch-BigGraph framework [18] for training embeddings. The triples used for the training are collected from a

Wikidata dump published in May 2021[1]. Before the training, the triples with literal values and Wikimedia disambiguation page entities (e.g. "Q1151870") are filtered out. The selection of the final embeddings is made given our empirical evaluation of Radar Station after fine-tuning the hyper-parameters. We consider two representative translational distance models (TransE [4] and RotatE [28]) and two semantic matching models (DistMult [31] and ComplEx [29]) following the classification of [30].

Translational distance models study the geometric distance between entities inside the vector space. TransE [4] considers both entities and relations from the same vector space. The training intends to adjust the three vectors from a given triple (h, r, t) to the synchronized state until $h + r \approx t$. In Pytorch-BigGraph, we use the $\boxed{\text{translation}}$ operator for generating the TransE model. Unlike TransE's translation, RotatE [28] regards the relation as a rotational degree between heads and tails. It introduces a loss function based on $h \circ r \approx t$ for simulating the relation translation. We use the GraphVite's [34] pre-trained RotatE embeddings in our experiments.

Semantic matching models measure the similarity between entities and relations during the training. DistMult [31] is based on a bilinear scoring function $h^T M_r t$, where M_r is the relation matrix built on top of the entity. ComplEx [29] can be seen as a constrained variant of RESCAL [15] that leverages fewer relation dimensions inside a complex space. The ComplEx score is defined as $Re(h^T diag(r)\bar{t})$. In Pytorch-Biggraph training, we use the $\boxed{\text{diagonal}}$ operator for generating DistMult embeddings and iterations between $\boxed{\text{complex\_diagonal}}$ and $\boxed{\text{dot}}$ operators for ComplEx embeddings.

5.2 Datasets

We evaluate Radar Station on three popular gold standards: T2D[2], Limaye[3], and Tough Tables version 2[4]. The original T2D and Limaye datasets contain some annotation errors that we have corrected. As T2D and Limaye are gold standards based on DBpedia and Radar Station is a Wikidata-based annotation system, we translate the DBPedia entities given in the gold standards into Wikidata entities through the "Wikidata item" hyperlink from Wikipedia pages of DBpedia entities. We manually corrected this translation when it was failing. Since the number of entities in Wikidata is larger than the number of entities in DBpedia [23], the annotation based on Wikidata is also harder with more candidates to disambiguate. We publish the new resulting ground truth on Zenodo (see

---

[1] https://archive.org/details/wikibase-wikidatawiki-20210521.
[2] http://webdatacommons.org/webtables/goldstandardV2.html.
[3] http://websail-fe.cs.northwestern.edu/TabEL/.
[4] https://zenodo.org/record/6211551.

Table 3. Gold standard datasets for evaluating STI approaches. The ambiguities are based on DAGOBAH-SL scores

Gold standard	#Tables	Avg. #Rows	Avg. #Col	#Entities	Ambiguities (t = 1)	Ambiguities (t = 0.9)
Limaye	437	37	2	5,143	181 (3.52%)	685 (13.31%)
T2D	762	157	5	18,589	2,322 (12.49%)	8,852 (47.62%)
2T_v2	180	1080	5	661,297	30,686(4.64%)	86,739(13.11%)
ShortTables	2237	2	5	4,474	1422 (31.78%)	1822 (40.72%)

the supplementary material). ShortTables is a new dataset we built from T2D, in such a manner that each table only contains two rows. The aim of creating such a dataset is to simulate extreme cases where voting strategies lack electors (i.e. row entities) for a correct CTA (resp. CPA) annotation. The provenance of T2D and Limaye is Web tables. We also consider a synthetic dataset named Tough Tables version 2 (2T_2) to evaluate on more data types. We provide the statistics of these gold standard datasets in Table 3.

6   Evaluation

We evaluate Radar Station with these four datasets varying the embeddings and the tolerance threshold. A random selection of the highest scoring candidates is considered as our baseline and noted as the original system name. We show the overall result for t equals to 1, 0.95, and 0.9 based on DAGOBAH-SL scores on four datasets with different embeddings in Table 4 and the fine-tuned result based on DAGOBAH-SL, MTab and BBW with Limaye and T2D in Table 5.

6.1   Evaluation Settings

We aim to evaluate the performance of Radar Station on the ambiguity lists and how it can influence the global annotations. Thus, we use three indicators including Ambiguity quality (AP), Precision inside ambiguities (PA), and Global precision (GP). AP (Eq. 3) shows the quality of generated ambiguity list after the Ambiguity Detection step, that is, how many ambiguous cells contain a ground truth in its top candidates. It indicates the extreme precision that we could achieve in all ambiguous annotations, which is PA in Eq. 4. GP (Eq. 5) is the overall precision in all labelled cells considering annotations generated with or without Radar Station.

$$AP = \frac{\#Correct\ candidates\ in\ the\ candidate\ set\ of\ ambiguities}{\#\ Ambiguities} \quad (3)$$

$$PA = \frac{\#\ Correct\ ambiguity\ disambiguations}{\#\ Ambiguities} \quad (4)$$

Table 4. Radar Station evaluation based on DAGOBAH-SL scores. AP: Ambiguity quality, PA: Precision inside ambiguities, GP, Global precision

t	Methods	Limaye			T2D			2T_v2			ShortTables		
		AP	PA	GP	AP	PA	GP	AP	PA	GP	AP	PA	GP
1	DAGOBAH-SL	0.647	0.168	0.853	0.308	0.053	0.785	0.067	0.023	0.870	0.672	0.194	0.654
	RS + TransE		0.630	0.870		0.294	0.813		0.041	0.871		0.355	0.673
	RS + RotatE		0.636	0.870		0.289	0.812		0.044	0.871		0.363	0.673
	RS + DistMult		0.391	0.861		0.163	0.798		0.034	0.870		0.229	0.658
	RS + ComplEx		0.57	0.869		0.171	0.798		0.036	0.870		0.235	0.659
0.95	DAGOBAH-SL	0.614	0.296	0.853	0.332	0.180	0.785	0.327	0.208	0.870	0.671	0.302	0.654
	RS + TransE		0.528	0.872		0.312	0.815		0.230	0.872		0.414	0.673
	RS + RotatE		0.542	0.873		0.312	0.815		0.235	0.872		0.418	0.674
	RS + DistMult		0.377	0.860		0.230	0.797		0.213	0.870		0.328	0.659
	RS + ComplEx		0.435	0.864		0.233	0.798		0.219	0.870		0.334	0.660
0.9	DAGOBAH-SL	0.653	0.432	0.853	0.336	0.241	0.785	0.500	0.300	0.870	0.714	0.414	0.654
	RS + TransE		0.570	0.872		0.323	0.815		0.313	0.872		0.532	0.684
	RS + RotatE		0.578	0.873		0.322	0.814		0.318	0.872		0.536	0.684
	RS + DistMult		0.475	0.860		0.274	0.797		0.303	0.870		0.466	0.668
	RS + ComplEx		0.494	0.862		0.275	0.798		0.306	0.870		0.471	0.669

Table 5. Gold standard datasets for evaluating STI approaches with RotatE embeddings. AP: Ambiguity quality, PA: Precision inside ambiguities, GP, Global precision

Dataset	System	t	AP	Original output		Radar Station	
				PA	GP	PA	GP
Limaye	DAGOBAH-SL	0.9	0.653	0.432	0.853	0.578 (+0.146)	0.873 (+0.020)
	MTab	0.83	0.820	0.705	0.857	0.787 (+0.082)	0.875 (+0.018)
	BBW	0.65	0.587	0.359	0.563	0.507 (+0.148)	0.597 (+0.034)
T2D	DAGOBAH-SL	0.95	0.332	0.180	0.785	0.312 (+0.132)	0.815 (+0.030)
	MTab	0.71	0.385	0.295	0.837	0.346 (+0.051)	0.857 (+0.020)
	BBW	0.65	0.263	0.192	0.364	0.253 (+0.061)	0.382 (+0.018)

$$GP = \frac{\#Correct\ annotations}{\#Total\ labels} \tag{5}$$

We also use the Cohen's Kappa coefficient [7] to evaluate the independence of the annotation from different embeddings models (*kappa* equals to 1 means that two datasets are the same).

6.2 Analysis

Overall Result. We first observe from Table 4 that all the chosen embeddings contribute to a significant improvement for PA in the ambiguous cases with the chosen tolerance values and GP. We also notice that Radar Station brings more improvements to GP for the Limaye (Max. 0.02), T2D (Max. 0.03), and

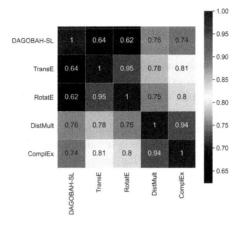

Fig. 3. Illustration of the Kappa test between different outputs on all datasets, $t = 0.95$.

ShortTables (Max. 0.03) than for 2T_v2 (Max. 0.002). This drop for 2T_v2 is due to the distribution of the scores of the top candidates: i) as we can see, after relaxing the tolerance from 1 to 0.9, AP for 2T_v2 has dramatically increased in comparison to the other datasets. Hence, there is no clear boundary between top candidates and bad candidates for the 2T_v2 dataset. That leads to a relatively lousy context embedding for the disambiguation. This scoring distribution is impacted by row number with DAGOBAH-SL mechanism, that is, the more rows we have, the more balanced the scoring would be; ii) the other reason is that 2T_v2 is a synthetic dataset generated with types from a KG. Thus, other column-wised semantic similarities are not obvious in this dataset. Hence, we recommend that future synthetic datasets should consider the inclusion of common themes from these tables to simulate other real-world use cases.

We introduce ShortTables for simulating the extreme cases where the very limited number of rows does not allow existing systems to generate correct CTA and CPA annotations. Bad CTA or CPA may propagate the error to the cell annotations. Thus, we expected to have a more significant GP improvement for ShortTables compared to T2D. However, from our evaluation, the contribution of Radar Station is close in these two datasets (Max 0.03). We analyze that a small number of rows can decrease the quality of type annotation and more likely propagate error with type disambiguation: therefore, it provides more chances for semantic disambiguation. At the same time, the limited number of rows also limits the content of the context entity set that has been used for semantic disam-biguation. We argue that these two effects cancel each other in this experiment. We have implemented Radar Station on two other systems and evaluated its performance with two Web table datasets. The result shown in Table 5 indicates that Radar Station benefits to all input annotation systems.

Analysis on Embeddings. Regarding the two families of embeddings (TransE and RotatE are translational distance models, DistMult and ComplEx are semantic matching models), the GP for embeddings from the same family achieves similar results inside our trained embeddings. From the result of Cohen's kappa shown in Fig. 3, we observe that the output is similar for embeddings from the same family. For example, the kappa value for TransE and RotatE is much higher than TransE with other outputs (same for DistMult and ComplEx). This similarity could also be seen in the precision shown in Table 4. We also observe that translational distance models are generally better than semantic matching models in our trained embeddings. That may be because we leverage geometric distance inside Radar Station, which is compatible with the training strategy of translational distance models. Globally, RotatE embeddings outperform all other models for all datasets.

Tolerance. Relaxing the tolerance has for effect to include more candidate entities and thus has the potential to increase the probability that the correct candidate is in the candidate set. However, such an operation also puts more noise into the candidate list. In Fig. 4, we illustrate how the tolerance influences the performance of the system on Limaye and T2D. It shows that relaxing the tolerance with TransE and RotatE improves the quality of the annotation (performance peak at $t = 0.95$ in Fig. 4). In our observation, largely relaxing the tolerance may decrease the accuracy since more noise is included during the disambiguation. This is therefore a delicate tradeoff to generalize across datasets.

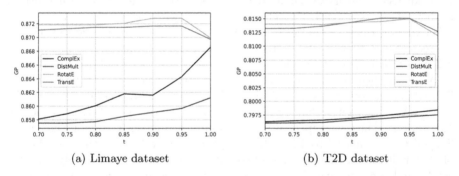

(a) Limaye dataset   (b) T2D dataset

Fig. 4. The GP evaluation on Limaye and T2D with t from 0.7 to 1 based on DAGOBAH-SL.

7   Conclusion and Future Work

In this paper, we analyze the current limitations of STI systems with relational tables and we introduce Radar Station, a new disambiguation method that makes use of pre-trained KG embeddings to strengthen the performance. We evaluate the system with different embeddings methods and we prove that this optimization can be beneficial. In the future, we aim to process more table types such as entity tables or matrix tables for enhancing the coverage and robustness of the system. We also seek to leverage language models to take more contextual information into account. We finally aim to plug Radar Station on top of other competitive STI systems.

Supplemental Material Statement. The source code for Radar Station is available at https://github.com/Orange-OpenSource/radar-station. The RotatE Embeddings, TransE embeddings, DAGOBAH-SL scores, Ground Truth and other required datasets are available from Zenodo at https://zenodo.org/record/6522985 while the ComplEx and DistMult embeddings are available at https://zenodo.org/record/6522921.

References

1. Abdelmageed, N., Schindler, S.: JenTab: matching tabular data to knowledge graphs. In: Semantic Web Challenge on Tabular Data to Knowledge Graph Matching (SemTab), pp. 40–49 (2020)
2. Bhagavatula, C.S., Noraset, T., Downey, D.: Methods for exploring and mining tables on Wikipedia. In: ACM SIGKDD Workshop on Interactive Data Exploration and Analytics, pp. 18–26 (2013)
3. Bhagavatula, C.S., Noraset, T., Downey, D.: TabEL: entity linking in web tables. In: Arenas, M., et al. (eds.) ISWC 2015. LNCS, vol. 9366, pp. 425–441. Springer, Cham (2015). https://doi.org/10.1007/978-3-319-25007-6_25
4. Bordes, A., Usunier, N., Garcia-Duran, A., Weston, J., Yakhnenko, O.: Translating embeddings for modeling multi-relational data. In: International Conference on Advances in Neural Information Processing Systems (NIPS), vol. 26 (2013)
5. Chabot, Y., Labbe, T., Liu, J., Troncy, R.: DAGOBAH: an end-to-end context-free tabular data semantic annotation system. In: Semantic Web Challenge on Tabular Data to Knowledge Graph Matching (SemTab), pp. 41–48 (2019)
6. Chen, S., et al.: LinkingPark: an integrated approach for semantic table interpretation. In: Semantic Web Challenge on Tabular Data to Knowledge Graph Matching (SemTab) (2020)
7. Cohen, J.: Weighted kappa: nominal scale agreement provision for scaled disagreement or partial credit. Psychol. Bull. **70**(4), 213 (1968)
8. Cutrona, V., Bianchi, F., Jiménez-Ruiz, E., Palmonari, M.: Tough tables: carefully evaluating entity linking for tabular data. In: Pan, J.Z., et al. (eds.) ISWC 2020. LNCS, vol. 12507, pp. 328–343. Springer, Cham (2020). https://doi.org/10.1007/978-3-030-62466-8_21
9. Cutrona, V., et al.: Results of SemTab 2021. In: Semantic Web Challenge on Tabular Data to Knowledge Graph Matching (SemTab), pp. 1–12. CEUR Workshop Proceedings (2022)
10. Deng, X., Sun, H., Lees, A., Wu, Y., Yu, C.: TURL: table understanding through representation learning. arXiv:2006.14806 (2020)
11. Efthymiou, V., Hassanzadeh, O., Rodriguez-Muro, M., Christophides, V.: Matching web tables with knowledge base entities: from entity lookups to entity embeddings. In: d'Amato, C., et al. (eds.) ISWC 2017. LNCS, vol. 10587, pp. 260–277. Springer, Cham (2017). https://doi.org/10.1007/978-3-319-68288-4_16

12. Eslahi, Y., Bhardwaj, A., Rosso, P., Stockinger, K., Cudré-Mauroux, P.: Annotating web tables through knowledge bases: a context-based approach. In: 7th Swiss Conference on Data Science (SDS), pp. 29–34. IEEE (2020)

13. Huynh, V.P., et al.: DAGOBAH: table and graph contexts for efficient semantic annotation of tabular data. In: Semantic Web Challenge on Tabular Data to Knowledge Graph Matching (SemTab) (2021)

14. Huynh, V.P., Liu, J., Chabot, Y., Labbé, T., Monnin, P., Troncy, R.: DAGOBAH: enhanced scoring algorithms for scalable annotations of tabular data. In: Semantic Web Challenge on Tabular Data to Knowledge Graph Matching (SemTab) (2020)

15. Jenatton, R., Le Roux, N., Bordes, A., Obozinski, G.: A latent factor model for highly multi-relational data. In: International Conference on Advances in Neural Information Processing Systems (NIPS), pp. 3176–3184 (2012)

16. Jiménez-Ruiz, E., Hassanzadeh, O., Efthymiou, V., Chen, J., Srinivas, K.: SemTab 2019: resources to benchmark tabular data to knowledge graph matching systems. In: Harth, A., et al. (eds.) ESWC 2020. LNCS, vol. 12123, pp. 514–530. Springer, Cham (2020). https://doi.org/10.1007/978-3-030-49461-2_30

17. Jiménez-Ruiz, E., Hassanzadeh, O., Efthymiou, V., Chen, J., Srinivas, K., Cutrona, V.: Results of SemTab 2020. In: Semantic Web Challenge on Tabular Data to Knowledge Graph Matching (SemTab), vol. 2775, pp. 1–8 (2020)

18. Lerer, A., et al.: Pytorch-biggraph: a large scale graph embedding system. In: Conference on Machine Learning and Systems (MLSys), vol. 1, pp. 120–131 (2019)

19. Limaye, G., Sarawagi, S., Chakrabarti, S.: Annotating and searching web tables using entities, types and relationships. Proc. VLDB Endow. **3**(1–2), 1338–1347 (2010)

20. Liu, J., Chabot, Y., Troncy, R., Huynh, V.P., Labbé, T., Monnin, P.: From tabular data to knowledge graphs: a survey of semantic table interpretation tasks and methods. J. Web Semant. (2022), under revision

21. Nguyen, P., Yamada, I., Kertkeidkachorn, N., Ichise, R., Takeda, H.: Mtab4wikidata at SemTab 2020: tabular data annotation with Wikidata. In: Semantic Web Challenge on Tabular Data to Knowledge Graph Matching (SemTab) (2020)

22. Oliveira, D., d'Aquin, M.: ADOG-annotating data with ontologies and graphs. In: Semantic Web Challenge on Tabular Data to Knowledge Graph Matching (SemTab) (2019)

23. Ringler, D., Paulheim, H.: One knowledge graph to rule them all? Analyzing the differences between DBpedia, YAGO, Wikidata & co. In: Kern-Isberner, G., Fürnkranz, J., Thimm, M. (eds.) KI 2017. LNCS (LNAI), vol. 10505, pp. 366–372. Springer, Cham (2017). https://doi.org/10.1007/978-3-319-67190-1_33

24. Ritze, D., Bizer, C.: Matching web tables to DBpedia - a feature utility study. In: International Conference on Extending Database Technology (EDBT), pp. 210–221 (2017)

25. Ritze, D., Lehmberg, O., Bizer, C.: Matching HTML tables to DBpedia. In: 5th International Conference on Web Intelligence, Mining and Semantics, pp. 1–6 (2015)

26. Sarthou-Camy, C., et al.: DAGOBAH UI: a new hope for semantic table interpretation. In: 19th European Semantic Web Conference (ESWC), Poster and Demo Track. Springer (2022). https://doi.org/10.1007/978-3-031-11609-4_20

27. Shigapov, R., Zumstein, P., Kamlah, J., Oberländer, L., Mechnich, J., Schumm, I.: bbw: Matching CSV to Wikidata via meta-lookup. In: Semantic Web Challenge on Tabular Data to Knowledge Graph Matching (SemTab) (2020)

28. Sun, Z., Deng, Z.H., Nie, J.Y., Tang, J.: RotatE: knowledge graph embedding by relational rotation in complex space. arXiv:1902.10197 (2019)
29. Trouillon, T., Welbl, J., Riedel, S., Gaussier, É., Bouchard, G.: Complex embeddings for simple link prediction. In: International Conference on Machine Learning (ICML), pp. 2071–2080. PMLR (2016)
30. Wang, Q., Mao, Z., Wang, B., Guo, L.: Knowledge graph embedding: a survey of approaches and applications. IEEE Trans. Knowl. Data Eng. **29**(12), 2724–2743 (2017)
31. Yang, B., Yih, W.T., He, X., Gao, J., Deng, L.: Embedding entities and relations for learning and inference in knowledge bases. arXiv:1412.6575 (2014)
32. Zhang, S., Balog, K.: Recommending related tables. arXiv:1907.03595 (2019)
33. Zhang, Z.: Effective and efficient semantic table interpretation using TableMiner+. Semant. Web **8**(6), 921–957 (2017)
34. Zhu, Z., Xu, S., Tang, J., Qu, M.: GraphVite: a high-performance CPU-GPU hybrid system for node embedding. In: The World Wide Web Conference (WWW), pp. 2494–2504 (2019)
35. Zwicklbauer, S., Einsiedler, C., Granitzer, M., Seifert, C.: Towards disambiguating web tables. In: International Semantic Web Conference (ISWC), Posters & Demos Track, pp. 205–208 (2013)

CRNet: Modeling Concurrent Events over Temporal Knowledge Graph

Shichao Wang[1,2], Xiangrui Cai[1,2(✉)], Ying Zhang[2,3], and Xiaojie Yuan[2,3]

[1] College of Cyber Science, Nankai University, Tianjin, China
wangshichao@dbis.nankai.edu.cn, caixr@nankai.edu.cn
[2] Tianjin Key Laboratory of Network and Data Security Technology, Tianjin, China
[3] College of Computer Science, Nankai University, Tianjin, China
{yingzhang,yuanxj}@nankai.edu.cn

Abstract. Temporal knowledge graph (TKG) reasoning, which aims to extrapolate missing facts in TKGs, is vital for many significant applications, such as event prediction. Previous studies have attempted to equip entities and relations with temporal information in historical timestamps and have achieved promising performance. While ignoring the likelihood that future occurrences would occur simultaneously, they independently forecast the missing data. However, there are complicated connections between future concurrent events that might correlate with and influence one another. Therefore, we propose our **C**oncurrent **R**easoning **Net**work (CRNet) to leverage event concurrency in both historical and future timestamps for TKG reasoning. Specifically, we select the top-k candidate events for each missing event and construct a candidate graph based on the candidate events of all missing events at the future timestamp. The candidate graph connects missing facts by sharing the same entities. Furthermore, we employ a novel relational graph attention network to represent the interactions of candidate events. We evaluate our proposal by the entity prediction task on three well-known public event-based TKG datasets. Extensive experimental results show that our CRNet complete future missing facts with a 15–20% improvement over MRR. (The source code is available at https://github.com/shichao-wang/CRNet-ISWC2022.)

Keywords: Temporal knowledge graph · Temporal reasoning · Concurrent events

1 Introduction

Each fact in the TKGs is a quadruple $(subject, relation, object, timestamp)$. Grouping quadruples by timestamps results in a sequence of KGs. Nodes represent entities in the real world, and the labeled edges represent related events between entities. TKG reasoning attempts to predict missing future facts like (s, r,?, t). Reasoning over TKGs forecasts emerging events, which is helpful for

© The Author(s), under exclusive license to Springer Nature Switzerland AG 2022
U. Sattler et al. (Eds.): ISWC 2022, LNCS 13489, pp. 516–533, 2022.
https://doi.org/10.1007/978-3-031-19433-7_30

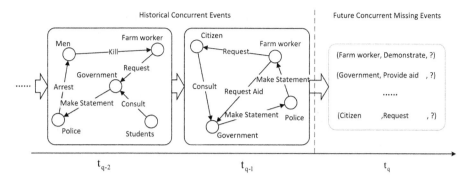

Fig. 1. An illustration of temporal reasoning over TKGs. The concurrent events exist in history and the future.

many real-world applications, including product recommendation [32] and event prediction [13, 28].

On the one hand, historical events happened concurrently and are relevant to TKG reasoning. As shown in Fig. 1, for the missing events *(Farmworker, Demonstrate, ?)* a good TKG reasoning method should learn from previous concurrent events *(Government, Make statement, Police)* and *(Police Make statement, Farmworker)*. Previous studies, such as RE-Net [13] and CyGNet [40], attempt to retrieve query-related information from historical events. Some methods such as RE-GCN [19], CEN [17] and EvoKG [24], employ recurrent neural networks (RNNs) to learn a dynamic representation from historical KGs. These methods adopt relational graph convolution networks (RGCNs) to learn the concurrent events at historical timestamps. Limited by the traditional RGCN diagram, which regards the head and tail entities separately, they cannot exploit the complete semantics of event triplets or leverage the different importance of neighbors.

On the other hand, there are also complex dependencies among the concurrent events at future timestamps [21, 39], which all the previous studies neglect. As shown in Fig. 1, the prediction results will influence each other. For the query *(Government, Provide aid, ?)*, a possible object would be *Farm worker*, since there are two events *(Farmworker, Request, Government)* and *(Farmworker, Request Aid, Government)* at the previous timestamps. However, when there is the event *(Farmworker, Demonstrate, Government)* at future timestamp. The government would not provide aid to farmworkers somehow, since they are antagonistic to each other. Thus, combining the concurrent events at future timestamp is suitable for real world application and enables predicting missing events.

In this paper, we propose the **C**oncurrent **R**esoning **Net**work (CRNet) for TKG reasoning, which exploits the concurrent events at historical and future timestamps. For the historical concurrent events, we develop a novel relational graph attention network, namely EventRGAT, which passes the complete event message, rather than nodes or edges, to neighbors and aggregates them adaptively. We also propose a two-stage framework to model the interactions among future concurrent events. Using true events at future timestamps directly will result in information leakage and is not suitable for real-world application, so we first collect the top-k candidates for every missing event at future timestamp and build the candidate events graph together. Nodes and edges in the candidate graph are the entities and the candidate events. Then, we employ our novel RGAT to encode the interaction among the candidate events and enhance the representations with concurrent dependencies. In summary, our contributions are in three folds:

- We formulate and address the problem of concurrent events for the TKG reasoning in historical and future timestamps, which is fit with the concurrent nature of events and suitable for real world application.
- For the historical concurrent events, we develop EventRGAT to aggregate related events adaptively. For future concurrent events, we propose a two-stage framework, which builds a candidate graph for concurrent missing events, to capture their interactions.
- Extensive experimental results demonstrate that our CRNet achieves significant improvement (15%–20% on MRR) on event-based TKG benchmarks. A thorough case study is carried out to verify the effectiveness of our proposal.

2   Related Works

This section first discusses two the difference between reasoning over temporal knowledge graph and the static knowledge graph. Then, we review the temporal knowledge graph reasoning under two different settings, e.g., interpolative and extrapolative.

2.1   Static Knowledge Graph Reasoning

The static knowledge graph reasoning aims to predict the missing facts in the KG. Recent researches focus on learning the low-dimensional representation for entity and relations in KGs to solve the problem. The representation learning methods can be categorized into translational and semantic-matching. The translational models, such as TransE [1] and its variants [20,29,34], measure the distance between the head and tail entities in the subspace translated by the relation. RESCAL [23], DistMult [37], NTN [26] and ConvE [5] are semantic matching methods, which measure the plausibility of facts by matching the semantics of entities and relations in the vector space. Graph neural networks (GNNs) have also extended for the relational-aware representation learning on KGs, such as R-GCN [30], HAN [33]. However, these methods are developed for static KGs, and they are not capable of modeling the dynamic evolutional patterns in TKGs directly.

Table 1. Important notations and their descriptions.

Notations	Description
G_t, $\mathcal{V}$, $\mathcal{R}$, $\mathcal{E}_t$	Event knowledge graph at timestamp t, and its node set, relation set and events set
$\boldsymbol{h}_i$ $\boldsymbol{h}_j$, $\boldsymbol{r}_k$	Embedding vector for Entity e_i, Entity e_j, and Relation r_k
$\boldsymbol{h}_t$	Embedding vector for Entity e and the matrix at timestamp t
$\boldsymbol{H}_t$, $\boldsymbol{R}$	Embedding matrix for entities at timestamp t and relations
s, r, o	The subject, relation, and object of a event
$\boldsymbol{s}_t$, $\boldsymbol{r}_t$, $\boldsymbol{o}_t$	The subject, relation, and object embedding vector at timestamp t
Q_t, Q_q	The missing events sets at timestamp t and q

2.2   Temporal Knowledge Graph Reasoning

There are two settings for reasoning over TKGs, interpolation, and extrapolation. The interpolative TKG reasoning task assumes that there are missing facts in the historical timestamps. It attempts to completing the missing facts through contextual KGs [6,7,11,12,14,35,36]. For example, Jiang et al. [12] adopt the temporal order of the happening time of facts to constrain the transformation between time-sensitive relations. TimePlex [11] embeds the entities, relations, and timestamps into a uniform compatible space. RTFE [36] treats the sequence of graphs as a Markov chain and tracks the state transition recursively. These methods cannot obtain the representations for entities and relations at future timestamps. Thus, they are not able to tackle the extrapolative TKG reasoning.

On the contrary, the extrapolative reasoning, which this paper focuses on, attempts to predict the facts at future timestamps through historical KGs. These methods can be categorized into two: Query-specific methods and evolution representation learning methods [17]. The query-specific methods retrieve contextual information from the question, such as subject and relation, from the historical KGs. For example, RE-Net [13] aggregates the historical neighbors for the queried subject and predicts its future interactions. CyGNet [40] utilizes the copy mechanism to collect the object distribution given a specific subject and relation. xERTE [8] build the sub-graph from the historical facts for the query. TITer [27] and CluSTeR [18] employ the reinforcement learning to find query-related paths. The evolution representation learning methods update the embedding for every entity and relation based on the historical KGs. RE-GCN [19] learns the evolution representation at a fixed length. CEN [17] extends it for the dynamic lengths. DynamicGCN [3] and Glean [4] enrich the representation with text features.

3   Problem Formulation and Notations

A temporal knowledge graph (TKG) $\mathcal{G} = \{G_1, G_2, \ldots, G_t, \ldots\}$ is a multi-relational directed graph. $G_t = (\mathcal{V}, \mathcal{R}, \mathcal{E}_t)$ denotes a set of events happened at time t, where $\mathcal{V}$ is the set of entities, $\mathcal{R}$ is the set of relations (a.k.a.

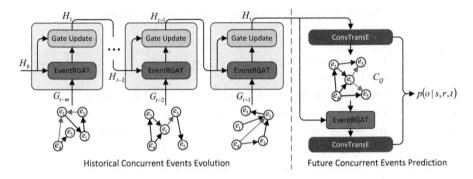

Fig. 2. The overview of our proposed CRNet model architecture. CRNet consists of two parts, e.g., the historical concurrent evolution module and the future concurrent prediction module. Edges in different colors denote different events between entities.

events) and $\mathcal{E}_t$ is the set of facts at timestamp t. A fact in TKG can be represented by a quadruple (s, r, o, t), where $s, o \in \mathcal{V}$, $r \in \mathcal{R}$ represent the subject, object, and relation respectively. The quadruple describes the subject s interacts with the object o with an event of r at time t. For every quadruple in the testing set, the extrapolative TKG reasoning task aims to complete the missing facts $(s, r, ?, t_q)$ and $(?, r, o, t_q)$ with a sequence of historical KGs $G_{q-m:q-1} = \{G_{q-m}, G_{q-m+1}, \ldots, G_{q-1}\}$. Taking the object prediction as an example, the conditional probability of an object given the subject s, relation r, and history $G_{q-m:q-1}$ is $p(o|s, r, G_{q-m:q-1})$. We denote it as $p_i(o|s, r, q)$ in the rest of paper.

In this paper, we conduct the concurrent reasoning over TKGs. Comparing with traditional TKG reasoning our concurrent reasoning diagram considers the concurrent missing events at future timestamp. We denote all the missing facts at future timestamp t_q as $Q_q = \{(s, r)|(s, r, o) \in G_q\}$. The conditional probability for object o given the subject s and relation r is $p(o|s, r, G_{q-m:q-1}, Q_q)$. We denote it as $p_c(o|s, r, q)$ in the rest of paper.

The important mathematical notations are described in Table 1

4   Methodology

This section introduces our proposal, CRNet. Figure 2 depicts the overview of our CRNet, which consists of the historical concurrent evolution module and the future concurrent prediction module. In the historical concurrent evolution module, the evolution embeddings for all entities are learned from historical KGs. In the future concurrent prediction module, we collect the missing facts to build a candidate graph and conduct concurrent prediction.

4.1   Historical Concurrent Events Evolution

To capture the concurrent interactions for entities, we use the historical KG G_t to update the entity embeddings. Give an entity representation $\boldsymbol{h}_i$ at timestamp

t, the adaptive triplet message passing module aims to collect the structural interactions $\boldsymbol{h}_i'$ for it. To obtain the triplet message, we perform a linear transformation over the concatenated triplet (e_i, r_k, e_j) embedding [22].

$$\boldsymbol{t}_{ijk} = \boldsymbol{W}_1 \left[\boldsymbol{h}_i \| \boldsymbol{r}_k \| \boldsymbol{h}_j \right] \tag{1}$$

where $\boldsymbol{t}_{ijk}$ is the representation for the event triplet (e_i, r_k, e_j). $[\cdot\|\cdot]$ is the concatenation operation. $\boldsymbol{h}_i$ and $\boldsymbol{h}_j$ are the embeddings for e_i and e_j, and $\boldsymbol{r}_k$ for the relation r_k respectively. $\boldsymbol{W}_1 \in \mathbb{R}^{h \times 3h}$ is the learnable parameter matrix. To learn the different importance α_{ijk} for message aggregation, we first adopt a linear transformation parameterized by a vector $\boldsymbol{w}_2$ followed by a LeackyReLU to compute the absolute score for every message, which is similar to the architecture proposed in GAT [31].

$$s_{ijk} = \mathrm{LeackyReLU} \left(\boldsymbol{w}_2 \boldsymbol{t}_{ijk} \right) \tag{2}$$

To get the relative attention value for aggregation, we apply softmax over s_{ijk} shown in Eq. (2).

$$\begin{aligned} \alpha_{ijk} &= \mathrm{softmax}_{jk}(s_{ijk}) \\ &= \frac{\exp\left(s_{ijk}\right)}{\sum_{n \in \mathcal{N}_i} \sum_{r \in \mathcal{R}_{i,n}} \exp\left(s_{inr}\right)} \end{aligned} \tag{3}$$

where $\mathcal{N}_i$ is the neighborhood node set for entity e_i, $\mathcal{R}_{i,n}$ represents the connected relation sets for entity e_i and e_n. The neighbor message is finally adaptively aggregated following Eq. (4).

$$\boldsymbol{h}_i^{l+1} = \sigma \left(\sum_{j \in \mathcal{N}_i} \sum_{k \in \mathcal{R}_{i,j}} \alpha_{ijk}^l \boldsymbol{t}_{ijk}^l + \boldsymbol{W}_3^l \boldsymbol{h}_i^l \right) \tag{4}$$

where $\boldsymbol{h}_i^l$ is the embedding for e_i learned at l^{th} layer. σ is the RReLU [15] activation function. As suggested in GAT [31], we also employ the multi-head mechanism to collect multiple information from neighborhoods and stabilize the learning process. We employ M independent attention heads to calculate the embeddings from M different subspaces. We average the embeddings from subspaces resulting in the final representation. Note that, there are no parameters shared across heads or layers.

The final interaction information for entity e_i is the aggregated results after L layers, $\boldsymbol{h}_i' = \boldsymbol{h}_i^L$. We treat L and M as empirical hyper-parameters. We denote relational graph attention network above as $\boldsymbol{H}' = \mathrm{EventRGAT}(G, \boldsymbol{H}, \boldsymbol{R})$, where $\boldsymbol{H}, \boldsymbol{R}$ is the embedding matrix for all entities and relations respectively. We will employ it to model the concurrent events again at the future timestamp.

Temporal Evolution. After gathering the interaction information in a specific timestamp t. We need to update the representation for the next timestamp.

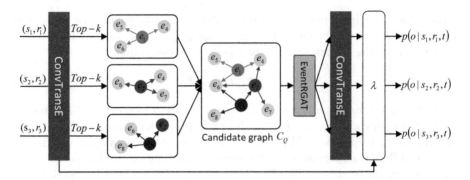

Fig. 3. The architecture of future concurrent events prediction module. There are three concurrent missing events to predict, namely (e_1, r_1), (e_2, r_2), (e_3, r_3). For each missing event, we select top-k (k = 3) candidates to build the candidate graph $\mathcal{C}_Q$. The final predict score is an average of p_c and p_i with the balance term λ.

We denote $\boldsymbol{h}_t$ and $\boldsymbol{h}_t'$ as the entity embedding and interaction information at timestamp t. We employ the gate mechanism to update the entity embedding.

$$u = \sigma \left(W_3 \left[h_t' || h_t \right] + b \right) \tag{5}$$

$$h_{t+1} = u \odot h_t' + (1 - u) \odot h_t \tag{6}$$

where $\sigma(\cdot)$ is the sigmoid function which controls the gate value in vector $\boldsymbol{u} \in \mathbb{R}^d$ ranges 0 to 1. $\odot$ is the vector element-wise dot operation.

4.2   Future Concurrent Events Prediction

This subsection introduces our two-stage concurrent prediction framework Fig. 3. We first use ConvTransE [25] to predict all entities' probability score p_i.

$$p_i (o|s, r, t) = o_t \text{ConvTransE}_1(s_t, r_t) \tag{7}$$

where $\boldsymbol{s}_t$, $\boldsymbol{r}_t$, $\boldsymbol{o}_t$ are the corresponding subject, relation and object embedding vectors at timestamp t respectively.

$$\text{ConvTransE}(s, r) = f \left(vec(M(s, r)) W_4 \right) \tag{8}$$

where $M(s, r)$ are aligned output vectors from the convolution kernels. $vec(\cdot)$ converts the feature map matrix into a vector. $f(\cdot)$ denotes the ReLU activation function here.

Candidate Graph Construction. Q_q is the set of concurrent missing events at future timestamp q. For every $(s_i, r_i) \in Q_q$, we select k candidate triplets with highest probability score $p_i(o|s, r, t)$. We then union all queries and their k candidates to build the candidate graph $\mathcal{C}_Q = (\mathcal{V}, \mathcal{R}, \mathcal{E}_Q)$, where $\mathcal{E}_Q$ is the candidate event triplet set for all queries. Thus, it results in $|Q_q| \times k$ edges in the candidate graph, where $|Q_q|$ is the number of missing facts.

Algorithm 1. Batch training procedure of CRNet

Input: Historical knowledge graph sequence $\{G_{t-m}, ..., G_{t-2}, G_{t-1}\}$,
Concurrent missing facts at future timestamp t Q_t
Output: Reasoning score for each query in Q_t
 1: Generate Evolutional Embedding from historical KGs. Eq. (4) and (6).
 2: **for** each $(s, r) \in Q_t$ **do**
 3:    Calculate the prediction score $p_i(o|s, r, t)$ without concurrent context Eq. (7).
 4:    Generate top-k candidate events. $\mathcal{E}_{s,r}^{k}$ with the k highest prediction score.
 5:    Add $\mathcal{E}_{s,r}^{k}$ to candidate graph $\mathcal{C}_Q$.
 6: **end for**
 7: Enrich entity embeddings with concurrent events based on $\mathcal{C}_Q$ Eq. (9).
 8: Calculate the predict score with concurrent context $p_c(o|s, r, t)$ Eq. (10).
 9: Predict missing object by jointing two prediction scores. Eq. (11).
10: Update model parameters by minimizing cross-entropy loss. Eq. (12).

Concurrent Events Prediction. After the candidate graph construction, we employ our novel relational graph attention network EventRGAT to model the interactions among candidate events. The entity representation after future concurrent interactions $\hat{H}$ follows:

$$\hat{H}_t = \text{EventRGAT}(\mathcal{C}_Q, H_t, R) \tag{9}$$

The probability score for entities with concurrent events p_c can be calculated as follows:

$$p_c(o|s, r, t) = \hat{H}_t \text{ConvTransE}_2(\hat{s}_t, r_t) \tag{10}$$

where $\hat{s}$ is the enhanced entity embedding for subject s. The final probability score is a combination of p_i and p_c with a balance term λ.

$$p(o|s, r, t) = \lambda \cdot p_i(o|s, r, t) + (1 - \lambda) \cdot p_c(o|s, r, t) \tag{11}$$

The entity prediction task can be seen as a multi-label classification problem. We employ the cross-entropy loss at future KG G_q:

$$\mathcal{L} = \sum_{(s,r,o)\in G_q} -\log p(o|s, r, t) \tag{12}$$

The training procedure for a batch of data is detailed in Algorithm 1. The training procedure will stop with the early stopping strategy with patience of 5.

5 Experiments

This section demonstrates the effectiveness of our proposal on the TKG reasoning. We first declare our experimental settings in detail, including datasets, baseline methods and evaluation metrics. Secondly, we compare the performance between CRNet and baseline methods on the link prediction and discussed the experimental results. After that, we analyze the influence of important hyperparameters in CRNet. Finally, we carry out a case study to explain the effectiveness intrinsically.

Table 2. Statistics of temporal knowledge graph (TKG) datasets.

Dataset	# Train	# Valid	# Test	# Nodes	# Relations	Granularity
ICEWS18	746,036	91,990	99,090	23,033	256	24 h
ICEWS14	74,845	8,514	7,371	6,869	230	24 h
GDELT	1,734,399	238,765	305,241	7,691	240	15 min

5.1 Experimental Setup

Datasets. We use three real-word event-based TKGs that have been widely used in previous studies: ICEWS18 [2], ICEWS14 [28] and GDELT [16]. Datasets are divided into training (80%), validation (10%) and testing (10%) sets by timestamps following [13]. ICEWS and GDELT are event-based TKGs. Detailed statistics of the aforementioned datasets are listed in Table 2.

Baselines. We compare our proposed method with the following state-of-the-art reasoning methods for temporal knowledge graphs, including

- RE-Net Jin et al. [13] propose an auto-regressive architecture for predicting future missing facts.
- xTERTE Han et al. [8] propose a temporal relational attention network and a reverse representation update strategy to guide the query-specific sub-graph extraction.
- CyGNet Zhu et al. [40] employ a time-aware copy-generation mechanism to identify facts with repetition.
- HIP He et al. [10] develop the historical information passing network to pass information from temporal, structural and repetitive perspectives.
- TANGO Han et al. [9] extends the idea of neural ordinary differential equations (ODEs). TANGO encodes both temporal and structural information into dynamic embeddings.
- TITer Sun et al. [27] define an abstract agent to search the answer from historical KGs. They also design a Dirichlet distribution-based time-shaped reward for reinforcement learning.
- CluSTeR Li et al. [18] propose a clue searching and temporal reasoning two-stage framework to predict future facts with reinforcement learning.
- RE-GCN Li et al. [19] employ a recurrent architecture to learn the evolutional representations of entities and relations following the KG sequence.
- EvoKG Park et al. [24] joint learns the time prediction task and link prediction task in an effective framework.
- CEN Li et al. [17] employ a length-aware decoder and the curriculum learning strategy to mine the complex evolutional pattern from length diversity and time-variability aspects.

Evaluation Metrics. We evaluate our model on TKG reasoning, which is a link prediction task at future timestamps. We adopt Mean Reciprocal Rank

(MRR), Hits@1, Hits@3 Hits@10 as our evaluation metrics. Note that, the same as previous works, we add reciprocal relation for every quadruple in the dataset, i.e., we add (o, r^{-1}, s, t) for every (s, r, o, t). For each quadruple (s, r, o, t) in the testing set, we predict two facts, e.g.$(s, r, ?, t)$ and $(o, r^{-1}, ?, t)$. We also employ the time-aware filtered setting which removes all the valid facts that appear in the ranking list of time-specific corrupted facts. Taking the query $(s, r, ?, t_1)$ with the answer o_1 and two ground truths (s, r, o_2, t_1), (s, r, o_3, t_2) as an example, under the time-aware setting, we consider the (s, r, o_2, t_1) as the corrupted fact and remove it from the ranking list.

5.2   Implementation Details

There are several empirical hyperparameters in our proposal. For all the entity and relation embeddings, their dimension d is set to 200. We also constrain the embedding vector with $L2$ normalization [38]. The number of layers of the relational graph attention network L is set to 2. The number of attention head M is set to 4. We fix the length of historical length m to 3 over all datasets. We adopt the Adam optimizer with $1e-3$ learning rate and $1e-4$ weight decay to optimize the model parameters. We employ the grid search algorithm to find the optimal number of candidate k and the balance term λ from the validation set according to MRR. The optimal k are 20,35,10 for ICEWS18, ICEWS14 and GDELT, respectively. The optimal balance term λ are 0.5,0.5,0.9 for ICEWS18, ICEWS14 and GDELT, respectively. We analyze their influence in Sect. 5.4. We use all the missing facts available to conduct the concurrent prediction. We also study its influence in Sect. 5.4.

5.3   Performance Comparison

Table 3 reports the entity prediction results of CRNet and baseline methods on the three event-based TKG datasets. The first group of baselines are query-specific methods, they search context for queries from historical timestamps. They fail to capture the global environment for event evolution, so they obtain a relatively poor performance. The second group consists of methods using reinforcement learning. They design an abstract agent to 'walk' through historical timestamps. The agent usually starts with a query, but 'walks' with a specific strategy, so they will not limit themselves by the query and obtain a better performance. However, reinforcement learning methods require a large number of computational resources and can not fit with large datasets, such as GDELT. The last group of baselines are evolution representation learning methods, which update entities or relations following historical timestamps. They learn entities' interactions from historical concurrent events but fail to capture the concurrent events at the future timestamp. As we can observe, our CRNet outperforms the baselines of all metrics on ICEWS18 and GDELT datasets and achieves an improvement of 14.62% and 19.57% on MRR, respectively. On the ICEWS14, CRNet obtains the best performance on most of the metrics except for Hits@10. CluSTeR searches explicit clues from historical KGs, but is unable to specify

Table 3. The performance of entity prediction with time-aware filtered metrics. Some methods do not report their performance under the time-aware filter setting, we use their public implementation to generate results and denote them with †.

Method	ICEWS18				ICEWS14				GDELT			
	MRR	H@1	H@3	H@10	MRR	H@1	H@3	H@10	MRR	H@1	H@3	H@10
RE-Net	28.81	19.05	32.44	47.51	36.93	26.83	39.51	54.78	19.60	12.03	20.56	33.89
CyGNet	24.93	15.90	28.28	42.61	35.05	25.73	39.01	53.55	†18.79	†11.83	†19.84	†32.31
TANGO	28.97	19.51	32.61	47.51	26.25	17.30	29.07	44.18	–	–	–	–
HIP	†29.20	†20.12	†32.27	†47.60	†40.84	†31.60	†40.54	†56.02	†20.08	†12.78	†20.15	†33.62
xERTE	29.31	21.03	33.51	46.48	40.79	32.06	45.67	57.30	–	–	–	–
TITer	29.98	22.05	33.46	44.83	41.73	32.28	46.46	58.44	–	–	–	–
CluSTeR	32.30	20.60	–	55.90	46.00	33.80	–	71.20	18.30	11.60	–	31.90
EvoKG	29.28	–	33.94	50.09	27.18	–	30.84	47.76	19.28	–	20.55	34.44
RE-GCN	30.58	21.01	34.34	48.75	40.39	30.66	44.96	59.21	†19.72	†12.46	†20.99	†33.92
CEN	31.50	21.70	35.44	50.59	42.20	32.08	47.46	61.31	†21.16	†13.43	†22.71	†36.38
CRNet	**37.81**	**26.12**	**43.10**	**61.01**	**48.37**	**38.21**	53.79	67.79	**25.32**	15.39	27.82	44.07

the most significant clue, thus it achieves high Hits@10 but ordinary Hits@1 or MRR.

5.4 Ablation Studies

To investigate the influence of concurrent event prediction and verify the robustness of our proposal, we conduct several ablation studies for CRNet. We first analyze the influence of important hyperparameters in CRNet, e.g. k and λ. After that, we study the influence of the number of concurrent missing facts.

Influence of k Candidates. k is the number of candidate selected for each missing fact. Figure 4 demonstrates the influence of k ranges from 1 to 50. The metric values reported in the line chart are collected from validation set. As we can observe, for the k ranges from 1 to 10, the performance increase with higher k. The larger k results in more edges in the candidate graph and will have more interactions among candidates. On the other hand, the larger k will more likely to retrieve correct prediction and rank better. However, the larger k does not mean better performance. More candidate facts will lead to a more complex environment for concurrent prediction and decrease the predicting performance. Thus, every datasets have their own optimal k. We choose the optimal k based on the MRR, e.g., 20 for ICEWS18, 35 for ICEWS14 and 10 for GDELT. We think the optimal k is relevant to the scale of dataset, since the GDELT and the ICEWS14 are the largest and smallest dataset, respectively.

Influence of the Balance Term λ. λ is the balance term between $p_i(o|s,r,t)$ and $p_c(o|s,r,t)$. The larger λ lead our CRNet to predict missing facts more on concurrent context $p_c(o|s,r,t)$. We evaluate the effectiveness with λ in a range of 0.0, 0.1, 0.3, 0.5, 0.7, 0.9 and 1.0. $\lambda = 0.0$ and $\lambda = 1.0$ are two special cases, in which CRNet predict the missing facts purly by $p_i(o|s,r,t)$ or

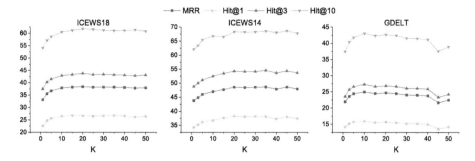

Fig. 4. The influence of the number of candidates k on three event-based TKG datasets. The black, red, blue, and green line represent MRR, Hits@1, Hits@3, and Hits@10. (Color figure online)

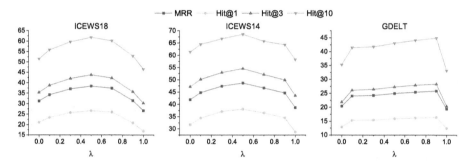

Fig. 5. Influence of balance term λ on three event-based datasets. The black, red, blue, and green line represent MRR, Hits@1, Hits@3, and Hits@10. (Color figure online)

$p_c(o|s,r,t)$. Figure 5 illustrates the influence of different λ. As we can observe from Fig. 5, ICEWS14, ICEWS18 and GDELT have their own optimal λ. Since the ICEW14 and ICEWS18 share similar collecting procedure, they have the same $\lambda = 0.5$. GDELT obtain the best performance with $\lambda = 0.9$. The metric values with $\lambda = 0.0$ and $\lambda = 1.0$ obtain a relatively poor performance comparing with any joint prediction model, which means our proposed concurrent context $p_c(o|s,r,t)$ complement with $p_i(o|s,r,t)$ well. However, the pure predict metrics of $p_c(o|s,r,t)$ are worse than $p_i(o|s,r,t)$. This means that our candidate graph not only create the interactions between future missing facts, but also introduce some distractive information. We leave this problem in our future work.

Influence of the Number of Concurrent Missing Facts. As we introduced in Sect. 4.2, we build our candidate sub-graph from the concurrent missing fact set Q_q. Therefore, the number of missing facts affects the scale of candidate sub-graph, and influence the performance further. Since the number of the concurrent missing facts varies from datasets and future timestamps, we split the missing facts into several partitions, i.g., 1, 2, 3, 4 and 5, to analysis how the number of

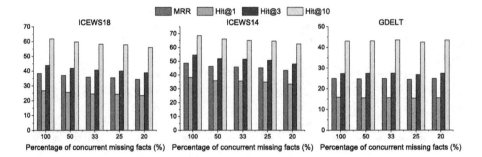

Fig. 6. MRR and Hit@3 performance with different ratio of concurrent missing facts at ICEWS18, ICEWS14 and GDELT datasets. All the metrics are obtained from validation set.

concurrent missing facts affect the performance. Figure 6 illustrates the performance difference from different ratio of concurrent missing facts. In ICEWS18 and ICEWS14 datasets, all metric values drop with smaller scale of concurrent missing facts significantly. On the contrary, the performance of different number of missing facts are almost the same and the best performance is obtained with 33% missing facts in GDELT dataset. This is because the GDELT has a relatively low performance and has more concurrent missing facts comparing with the other datasets. Thus, GDELT samples can not benefit from concurrent missing facts well.

5.5   Case Studies

To evaluate the effectiveness of concurrent missing events, we visualize 4 typical cases in the testing set of ICEWS14 in Fig. 7. More concretely, we group the missing events in the same topic and compare the prediction results of CRNet with RE-GCN, which can not leverage the concurrent context.

In case 1, there are two highly related missing events, *(China, Express intent to meet, ?)* and *(Japan Express intent to meet, ?)*. The traditional methods will easily predict the events with object *South Korea*, because there are two related events, such as *(South Korea, Make statement, China)* and *(South Korea, Make statement, Japan)* events in historical context. The *Express intent to meet* is seen as a evolution result of *Make statement*. However, the *Express intent to meet* event usually happens to each other. Our CRNet can discover the relationship between concurrent events *(China Express intent to meet, ?)* and *(Japan Express intent to meet, ?)*, and make correct predictions.

For case 2, there are two opposite events *Make visit* and *Host visit*, which usually happen concurrently at the same timestamp. In the historical context, *Envoy (US)* makes a visit to the *South Korea*, and the *South Korea* also host a visit for *Envoy (US)* as a response. When it comes to the missing events *(South Korea, Host visit, ?)* at a future timestamp, previous methods will fill the object with *Envoy (US)* according to the historical context. On the contrary,

Case 1

Historical context	Concurrent missing events	RE-GCN	CRNet
(South Korea, Make statement, China)	(China, Make statement, ?)	Japan	Japan
(South Korea, Make statement, Japan)	(China Express intent to meet, ?)	South Korea	Japan
	(Japan Express intent to meet, ?)	South Korea	China
	(Japan Diplomatic cooperation, ?)	South Korea	China

Case 2

Historical context	Concurrent missing events	RE-GCN	CRNet
(Envoy (US), Make visit, South Korea)	(North Korea, Make visit, ?)	South Korea	South Korea
	(South Korea, Make statement, ?)	Envoy (US)	Envoy (US)
(South Korea Host visit, Envoy (US))	(South Korea Host visit, ?)	Envoy (US)	North Korea

Case 3

Historical context	Concurrent missing events	RE-GCN	CRNet
	(Protester, Protest, ?)	Police	Police
	(Protester, Demonstrate, ?)	Police	Police
-	(Police, Use military force, ?)	Protester	Protester
	(Police, Repress, ?)	Protester	Protester
	(Protester, Make a request, ?)	Police	Student
	(Student, Express intent to yield, ?)	Protester	Police

Case 4

Historical context	Concurrent missing events	RE-GCN	CRNet
	(Government, Intent to diplomatic coop., ?)	Citizen	Citizen
	(Government, Expel individuals, ?)	Citizen	Citizen
-	(Citizen, Accuse, ?)	Government	Government
	(Citizen, Make request, ?)	The Judiciary	The Judiciary
	(Citizen, Appeal economic aid, ?)	Government	The Judiciary

Fig. 7. Four typical cases in the testing set of ICEWS14.

our CRNet considers the concurrent future event, such as *(North Korea, Make visit, ?)*, and predict them jointly with concurrent context. With the help of concurrent context *(North Korea, Make vist, South Korea)*, CRNet completes the missing event *(North Korea, Make visit, ?)* with the object *North Korea*.

The latter two cases are two emergencies, in which historical context cannot provide enough information to model the actors' behavior concretely.

In case 3, there is a conflict between the protester and the police. RE-GCN can predict the events between the police and the protester by transferring knowledge learned from previous conflicts. However there is a new participant *Student* in the happening conflict (obtained from *(Student, Express intent to yield, ?)*. RE-GCN limits itself with the participant of *Police* and *Protester* and cannot leverage the relationship between *Student* and *Protester*, which exists in the concurrent context.

In case 4, previous studies intend to predict the missing event *(Citizen, Appeal economic aid, ?)* with *Government*, since *Citizen* usually reach out to *Government* for help according to previous events. However, the *Citizen* and the

Government are in poor relationship which can be learned from the concurrent events. The *Citizen* are not likely to request economic aid from the *Government*.

In summary, concurrent missing events at future timestamps are important for TKG reasoning. Our proposal can mine the relationship between concurrent missing events and complete missing events more accurately.

6   Conclusion

We formulate and address the problem of concurrent events int TKG reasoning task in historical and future timestamps. Our proposal, CRNet, is consisted of two parts. For the historical concurrent events, we propose a novel relational graph attention network, EventRGAT, to model the interactions among events in a specific timestamp. For the future concurrent events, we propose a two-stage frame work, in which we build a candidate graph and model the interactions among future candidate events. Extensive experiments on three event-based TKG benchmarks demostrate the effectiveness of our CRNet. We also investigate into cases to study the influence of concurrent missing facts. The results indicate the concurrent context at future timestamp is informative for predicting missing events.

Supplemental Material Statement: Source code for our proposal is attached with the submission on EasyChair and will be available to public after acceptance. The datasets we used is adopt from the repository of RE-GCN. and have been submitted in the supplemental material. The raw data used to generate Table 3, Fig. 4, Fig. 5, and Fig. 6 are attached on EasyChair.

Acknowledgements. We would like to thank all anonymous reviewers for their insightful comments. This research is supported by the NSFC-General Technology Joint Fund for Basic Research (No. U1936206), the NSFC-Xinjiang Joint Fund (No. U1903128), the Natural Science Foundation of China (No. 62002178, No. 62172237), and the Fundamental Research Funds for the Central Universities (No. 63223046).

References

1. Bordes, A., Usunier, N., Garcia-Duran, A., Weston, J., Yakhnenko, O.: Translating embeddings for modeling multi-relational data. In: NeurIPS, vol. 26. Curran Associates, Inc. (2013)
2. Boschee, E., Lautenschlager, J., O'Brien, S., Shellman, S., Starz, J., Ward, M.: ICEWS Coded Event Data (2015). https://doi.org/10.7910/DVN/28075
3. Deng, S., Rangwala, H., Ning, Y.: Learning dynamic context graphs for predicting social events. In: KDD, pp. 1007–1016. KDD 2019. Association for Computing Machinery, New York, NY, USA, July 2019. https://doi.org/10.1145/3292500. 3330919
4. Deng, S., Rangwala, H., Ning, Y.: Dynamic knowledge graph based multi-event forecasting. In: KDD, pp. 1585–1595. ACM, Virtual Event CA USA, August 2020. https://doi.org/10.1145/3394486.3403209

5. Dettmers, T., Minervini, P., Stenetorp, P., Riedel, S.: Convolutional 2D knowledge graph embeddings. In: Proceedings of the Thirty-Second AAAI Conference on Artificial Intelligence and Thirtieth Innovative Applications of Artificial Intelligence Conference and Eighth AAAI Symposium on Educational Advances in Artificial Intelligence, pp. 1811–1818. AAAI 2018/IAAI 2018/EAAI 2018. AAAI Press, 2 Feb 2018

6. García-Durán, A., Dumančić, S., Niepert, M.: Learning sequence encoders for temporal knowledge graph completion. In: EMNLP, pp. 4816–4821. Association for Computational Linguistics, Brussels, Belgium, October 2018. https://doi.org/10.18653/v1/D18-1516

7. Han, Z., Chen, P., Ma, Y., Tresp, V.: DyERNIE: dynamic evolution of riemannian manifold embeddings for temporal knowledge graph completion. In: EMNLP, pp. 7301–7316. Association for Computational Linguistics, Online, November 2020. https://doi.org/10.18653/v1/2020.emnlp-main.593

8. Han, Z., Chen, P., Ma, Y., Tresp, V.: Explainable subgraph reasoning for forecasting on temporal knowledge graphs. In: ICLR, 28 September 2020

9. Han, Z., Ding, Z., Ma, Y., Gu, Y., Tresp, V.: Learning neural ordinary equations for forecasting future links on temporal knowledge graphs. In: Proceedings of the 2021 Conference on Empirical Methods in Natural Language Processing, pp. 8352–8364. Association for Computational Linguistics (2021). https://doi.org/10.18653/v1/2021.emnlp-main.658

10. He, Y., Zhang, P., Liu, L., Liang, Q., Zhang, W., Zhang, C.: HIP network: historical information passing network for extrapolation reasoning on temporal knowledge graph. In: IJCAI, vol. 2, pp. 1915–1921, 9 August 2021. https://doi.org/10.24963/ijcai.2021/264

11. Jain, P., Rathi, S., Mausam, Chakrabarti, S.: Temporal knowledge base completion: new algorithms and evaluation protocols. In: EMNLP, pp. 3733–3747. Association for Computational Linguistics, Online, November 2020. https://doi.org/10.18653/v1/2020.emnlp-main.305

12. Jiang, T., et al.: Encoding temporal information for time-aware link prediction. In: Proceedings of the 2016 Conference on Empirical Methods in Natural Language Processing, pp. 2350–2354. Association for Computational Linguistics, Austin, Texas, November 2016. https://doi.org/10.18653/v1/D16-1260

13. Jin, W., Qu, M., Jin, X., Ren, X.: Recurrent event network: autoregressive structure inference over temporal knowledge graphs. In: EMNLP, pp. 6669–6683. Association for Computational Linguistics, November 2020. https://doi.org/10.18653/v1/2020.emnlp-main.541

14. Jung, J., Jung, J., Kang, U.: Learning to walk across time for interpretable temporal knowledge graph completion. In: Proceedings of the 27th ACM SIGKDD Conference on Knowledge Discovery & Data Mining, pp. 786–795. KDD 2021. Association for Computing Machinery, New York, NY, USA, August 2021. https://doi.org/10.1145/3447548.3467292

15. Khalid, M., Baber, J., Kasi, M.K., Bakhtyar, M., Devi, V., Sheikh, N.: Empirical evaluation of activation functions in deep convolution neural network for facial expression recognition. In: 2020 43rd International Conference on Telecommunications and Signal Processing (TSP), pp. 204–207, July 2020. https://doi.org/10.1109/TSP49548.2020.9163446

16. Leetaru, K., Schrodt, P.A.: GDELT: global data on events, location, and tone, 1979–2012. In: ISA Annual Convention, vol. 2, pp. 1–49. Citeseer (2013). https://www.gdeltproject.org/

17. Li, Z., et al.: Complex evolutional pattern learning for temporal knowledge graph reasoning. In: ACL, 20 March 2022

18. Li, Z., et al.: Search from history and reason for future: two-stage reasoning on temporal knowledge graphs. In: ACL, pp. 4732–4743. Association for Computational Linguistics, Online (2021). https://doi.org/10.18653/v1/2021.acl-long.365

19. Li, Z., et al.: Temporal knowledge graph reasoning based on evolutional representation learning. In: SIGIR, pp. 408–417. ACM, 11 July 2021. https://doi.org/10.1145/3404835.3462963

20. Lin, Y., Liu, Z., Sun, M., Liu, Y., Zhu, X.: Learning entity and relation embeddings for knowledge graph completion. In: Proceedings of the Twenty-Ninth AAAI Conference on Artificial Intelligence, pp. 2181–2187. AAAI 2015. AAAI Press, 25 January 2015

21. Matsubara, Y., Sakurai, Y., Faloutsos, C., Iwata, T., Yoshikawa, M.: Fast mining and forecasting of complex time-stamped events. In: Proceedings of the 18th ACM SIGKDD International Conference on Knowledge Discovery and Data Mining, pp. 271–279. KDD 2012. Association for Computing Machinery, New York, NY, USA, August 2012. https://doi.org/10.1145/2339530.2339577

22. Nathani, D., Chauhan, J., Sharma, C., Kaul, M.: Learning attention-based embeddings for relation prediction in knowledge graphs. In: Proceedings of the 57th Annual Meeting of the Association for Computational Linguistics, pp. 4710–4723. Association for Computational Linguistics, Florence, Italy, July 2019. https://doi.org/10.18653/v1/P19-1466

23. Nickel, M., Tresp, V., Kriegel, H.P.: A three-way model for collective learning on multi-relational data. In: Proceedings of the 28th International Conference on International Conference on Machine Learning, pp. 809–816. ICML 2011, Omnipress, 28 June 2011

24. Park, N., Liu, F., Mehta, P., Cristofor, D., Faloutsos, C., Dong, Y.: EvoKG: jointly modeling event time and network structure for reasoning over temporal knowledge graphs. In: WSDM, 16 February 2022. https://doi.org/10.1145/3488560.3498451

25. Shang, C., Tang, Y., Huang, J., Bi, J., He, X., Zhou, B.: End-to-End structure-aware convolutional networks for knowledge base completion. In: Proceedings of the AAAI Conference on Artificial Intelligence, vol. 33, pp. 3060–3067, 17 July 2019. https://doi.org/10.1609/aaai.v33i01.33013060

26. Socher, R., Chen, D., Manning, C.D., Ng, A.: Reasoning with neural tensor networks for knowledge base completion. In: Advances in Neural Information Processing Systems, vol. 26. Curran Associates, Inc. (2013)

27. Sun, H., Zhong, J., Ma, Y., Han, Z., He, K.: TimeTraveler: reinforcement learning for temporal knowledge graph forecasting. In: EMNLP, September 2021

28. Trivedi, R., Dai, H., Wang, Y., Song, L.: Know-Evolve: deep temporal reasoning for dynamic knowledge graphs. In: ICML, pp. 3462–3471. PMLR, 17 July 2017

29. Trouillon, T., Welbl, J., Riedel, S., Gaussier, E., Bouchard, G.: Complex embeddings for simple link prediction. In: Proceedings of the 33rd International Conference on International Conference on Machine Learning - Volume 48, pp. 2071–2080. ICML 2016, JMLR.org, 19 June 2016

30. Vashishth, S., Sanyal, S., Nitin, V., Talukdar, P.: Composition-based multi-relational graph convolutional networks. In: ICLR, 25 September 2019

31. Velickovic, P., Cucurull, G., Casanova, A., Romero, A., Lio', P., Bengio, Y.: Graph Attention Networks. ICLR (2018). https://doi.org/10.17863/CAM.48429

32. Wang, R., et al.: RETE: retrieval-enhanced temporal event forecasting on unified query product evolutionary graph. In: WWW, February 2022

33. Wang, X., et al.: Heterogeneous graph attention network. In: The World Wide Web Conference, pp. 2022–2032. WWW 2019. Association for Computing Machinery, 13 May 2019. https://doi.org/10.1145/3308558.3313562
34. Wang, Z., Zhang, J., Feng, J., Chen, Z.: Knowledge graph embedding by translating on hyperplanes. In: Proceedings of the Twenty-Eighth AAAI Conference on Artificial Intelligence, pp. 1112–1119. AAAI 2014, AAAI Press, 27 July 2014
35. Xu, C., Chen, Y.Y., Nayyeri, M., Lehmann, J.: Temporal knowledge graph completion using a linear temporal regularizer and multivector embeddings. In: NAACL, pp. 2569–2578. Association for Computational Linguistics, Online, June 2021. https://doi.org/10.18653/v1/2021.naacl-main.202
36. Xu, Y., et al.: RTFE: a recursive temporal fact embedding framework for temporal knowledge graph completion. In: NAACL, pp. 5671–5681. Association for Computational Linguistics, Online, June 2021. https://doi.org/10.18653/v1/2021.naacl-main.451
37. Yang, B., Yih, S.W.T., He, X., Gao, J., Deng, L.: Embedding entities and relations for learning and inference in knowledge bases. In: Proceedings of the International Conference on Learning Representations (ICLR) 2015 (2015)
38. Yang, M., Meng, Z., King, I.: FeatureNorm: L2 feature normalization for dynamic graph embedding. In: ICDM (2020). https://doi.org/10.1109/ICDM50108.2020.00082
39. Zhao, L.: Event prediction in the big data era: a systematic survey. ACM Comput. Surveys **54**(5), 94:1–94:37 (2021). https://doi.org/10.1145/3450287
40. Zhu, C., Chen, M., Fan, C., Cheng, G., Zhang, Y.: Learning from history: modeling temporal knowledge graphs with sequential copy-generation networks. In: AAAI, vol. 35, pp. 4732–4740, May 2021

Resources Track

LODChain: Strengthen the Connectivity of Your RDF Dataset to the Rest LOD Cloud

Michalis Mountantonakis[1,2](✉) and Yannis Tzitzikas[1,2]

[1] Institute of Computer Science - FORTH-ICS, Heraklion, Greece
{mountant,tzitzik}@ics.forth.gr
[2] Computer Science Department, University of Crete, Heraklion, Greece

Abstract. It is not an easy task for a data owner to publish a dataset as Linked Data with connections to existing datasets since there are too many datasets, thus it is hard to find the related ones, to download them and to check their content (let alone to apply entity matching over them). However, the connections with other datasets are important for discoverability, browsing, and querying in general. To alleviate this problem in this paper we introduce LODChain, a service that can help a provider to strengthen the connections between his/her dataset and the rest of datasets. LODChain finds the common entities, schema elements and triples among the dataset at hand and hundreds of LOD Datasets and through equivalence reasoning it suggests to the user various inferred connections, as well as related datasets. In addition, it detects erroneous mappings, and offers various content-based dataset discovery services, for enabling the enrichment of datasets' content. The key difference with the existing approaches is that they are metadata-based, while what we propose is data-based. We present an implementation of LODChain, and we report various experimental results over real and synthetic datasets.

Keywords: Linked data · Connectivity · Dataset search · Data discovery

Resource Type: Software Service.
Resource URL: https://demos.isl.ics.forth.gr/LODChain.
Permanent URL: https://doi.org/10.5281/zenodo.6467419.

1 Introduction

An increasing number of datasets are published through Linked Open Data (LOD) principles, i.e., over 10,000 datasets [24]. For making a new RDF dataset more discoverable and reusable, for improving its trustworthiness and for enriching its content, several tasks should be executed before its actual publishing to the web. Indeed, it is a prerequisite to discover existing datasets, to create connections with them, through *equivalence relationships* such as owl:sameAs, to

U. Sattler et al. (Eds.): ISWC 2022, LNCS 13489, pp. 537–555, 2022.
https://doi.org/10.1007/978-3-031-19433-7_31

check the quality of such relationships and to create rich metadata. These tasks can be assisted at large scale through existing approaches; for discovering and exporting relevant datasets through metadata-based services like http://lod-cloud.net [19] or Google Dataset Search [6], for transforming and querying data [11,34], for creating schema and instance mappings [8,30], for quality assessment [28,48], for finding all the URIs of a given entity [22,39] and others.

However, the huge volume of LOD datasets makes it difficult to discover every possible relevant dataset, especially given that a) existing approaches for publishing RDF datasets do not favor their discoverability and reusability; e.g., [10] states that "up till now, data consumers could, painfully, crawl or search the LOD cloud diagram for a potential dataset", and b) Dataset Search engines rely on metadata and ignore the actual content of datasets [7]. Also, even if one has discovered and fetched the content of all the datasets, it would be very costly and time consuming to find commonalities with these datasets at scale, to create mappings and to check their quality. Such Data Integration tasks usually require manual work, thus huge human effort, if applied at scale, as well as high storage and computational capacity, which can be prohibitively expensive [24].

Due to these limitations, the major target of LOD, i.e., linking and integration [5], has not been yet reached. Indeed, LOD Cloud is sparsely linked; publishers tend to connect their datasets with few and popular datasets and ontologies [2,22], and "LOD Cloud is at risk of becoming a museum for datasets" [10]. Hence, there is a high need for services that can strengthen the connectivity of a dataset to the rest of LOD Cloud. To alleviate this problem, we introduce the research prototype LODChain, which receives a dataset, e.g., before its actual publishing, computes the transitive and symmetric closure of its owl:sameAs (for entities), owl:equivalentProperty (for properties) and owl:equivalentClass (for classes) relationships with hundreds of LOD datasets, i.e., those indexed by LODsyndesis KB [25], and offers connectivity and enrichment services. For a new dataset, say D_{new}, LODChain a) spots errors in equivalence mappings, b) infers new mappings, connections and all the common elements, e.g., entities and triples, between D_{new} and LOD datasets, c) discovers its K most relevant datasets, and d) enriches D_{new}, e.g., for offering advanced query capabilities.

Comparing to large-scale services, like LODsyndesis [22,25] or LODlaundromat [34], to the best of our knowledge LODChain is the first service for strengthening the connectivity of an RDF dataset to the rest of LOD Cloud, at any time, even before its actual publishing. In [26], we described a preliminary version of LODChain providing analytics only for the entities of Cultural Heritage datasets. In this paper, we introduce the current version of LODChain, which also leverages the schema and the triples of a dataset of any domain and offers more connectivity analytics and services. We present use cases showcasing its impact for the discoverability, reusability and trustworthiness of a dataset, and the process of LODChain, including methods for computing the owl:sameAs closure between a new dataset and the precomputed inference (of 45 million owl:sameAs mappings) from hundreds of LOD datasets. Finally, we provide comparative results for the effectiveness and the efficiency by using 5 real and 2 synthetic datasets, indicatively, we obtained at least 450% increase to the connections of real datasets.

The rest of the paper is organized as follows. Section 2 introduces the related work, whereas Sect. 3 presents several use cases by using the real dataset *WW1LOD* [18] containing historical data about World War I. Section 4 presents the process of LODChain, while Sect. 5 provides comparative results for its efficiency and effectiveness. Finally, Sect. 6 concludes the paper and identifies directions for future research.

2   Related Work

Several approaches have been proposed for aiding the creation, integration and publication of an RDF dataset, see a recent survey [24] for more details. Here, we focus on a) large scale services for hundreds or even thousands of RDF datasets, b) dataset search and discovery approaches and c) data enrichment approaches, which can be exploited for strengthening the connectivity of a dataset.

Large Scale Services for Multiple RDF Datasets. First, LODLaundromat [34] offers data cleaning and transformation for thousands of RDF documents, whereas LOD-a-lot [11] provides a single integrated file containing the documents of LODLaundromat, for enabling their reusability and for offering more advanced query capabilities. Moreover, there are services for finding all the datasets of a given URI, e.g., WIMU [39] and LODsyndesis [23,25], all the equivalent URIs of a given URI, such as MetaLink [3] and LODsyndesis, i.e., by computing the transitive closure of millions of owl:sameAs mappings, and approaches for detecting erroneous owl:sameAs links [31,40]. Such services can be exploited from the publisher of a new dataset, for enriching the connectivity of their dataset, e.g., by adding inferred links, and for checking its quality.

RDF Dataset Search and Discovery. Existing services, such as LOD Cloud (http://lod-cloud.net), Google Dataset Search [7], LODatio [12] and LODAtlas [32], provide metadata-based search for discovering relevant RDF datasets, whereas [44] evaluates different snippet generation algorithms that can be used for performing RDF Dataset Search for thousands of datasets. Furthermore, [29] introduces a framework for content-based similarity dataset discovery, by using external knowledge bases (e.g., Wikidata), whereas LODsyndesis offers content-based dataset discovery for finding the most relevant datasets to a given one.

RDF Dataset Enrichment. There are several approaches introducing methods (and their importance) for enriching the content of datasets for several domains, e.g., for tourism [35,46], for Open City Data [4] or for marine domain [37]. Additionally, one can enrich the data for a given entity, by visiting dereferencable equivalent URIs, e.g., through services like Metalink or LODsyndesis, by using instance matching tools, e.g., Silk [42], by exploiting link-traversal queries [38], or through SPARQL queries to the endpoints of relevant datasets. A catalog of SPARQL endpoints is available from SPARQLES [41] and SpEnD [47].

Comparison with Existing Approaches. Concerning the mentioned works, a) the process of large-scale services (e.g., [25,34]) is done periodically for a high number of open datasets, i.e., it is infeasible to exploit the offered services for unpublished data or for closed linked data, as big organizations/companies maintain (e.g., [14]), b) the dataset search services (e.g., [7,32]) are metadata-based, and c) the data enrichment approaches are either domain specific (e.g., [35,37]), or require additional effort for discovering enriched data (e.g., [3]). On the contrary, to the best of our knowledge, LODChain is the first service that can be used by a publisher at any time, for strengthening the connectivity of a dataset (of any domain) by providing content-based connectivity analytics and enrichment to the rest of LOD datasets. Thereby, it can be used for unpublished or "closed" data, without needing to download any software or to fetch any RDF dataset.

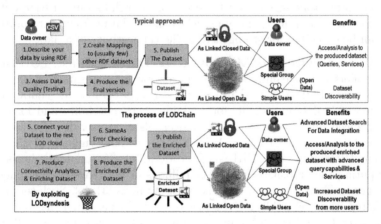

Fig. 1. Typical approach versus the LODChain approach for publishing an RDF dataset

3   Data Publishing - Typical Approach Versus LODChain

We define the user categories that can have access to a given RDF dataset: i) data owners (publishers), i.e., people, organizations, universities, etc., that are the creators and owners of a given dataset, ii) a special group of interest, i.e., certain individuals, e.g., people, services, within an organization, a research project, etc., iii) users (or services), i.e., any user on the web like publishers of other datasets, or services that have access or/and reuse the content of a dataset. This category is a superset of the previous two, i.e., publishers and special group of interest. Figure 1 shows the typical approach of publishing an RDF dataset. Indeed, a data owner describes the desired data in RDF format, creates mappings with usually few RDF datasets and after assessing its quality, e.g., through competency queries [45], he/she produces the final version. For achieving this target, more steps are usually required, e.g., data conversion, transformation, etc. [24]. Afterwards, the final version is published, either to an open domain (e.g., to LOD Cloud) which can be publicly accessible, discoverable and reusable from any user/service on the web (for performing an analysis, for creating an application, etc.), or to a closed domain, i.e., these benefits are provided to a special group of interest.

Concerning the process of LODChain (lower part of Fig. 1), it receives an RDF dataset, e.g., before its actual publishing, for checking and improving its connectivity to the LOD Cloud and for enriching its content (by exploiting LODsyndesis). The target is to increase the benefits of publishing a dataset for any category of users. Below, we present how LODChain can contribute to these benefits (lower right side of Fig. 1), by showing a scenario with a real dataset.

Benefits of LODChain for Data Publishing (Use Cases). We describe use cases by following the steps of the lower side of Fig. 1. For the introduced scenario, we use the small real dataset $WW1LOD$ [18]. It contains data about World War I and includes 47,616 triples and 547 sameAs mappings to 5 RDF datasets, including popular ones, such as DBpedia [16] and GeoNames (more statistics are given in §5). For checking more cases, we use a synthetic version of $WW1LOD$, say $WW1LOD_{synt}$, where we have added 50 erroneous owl:sameAs mappings. The scenario starts when the data owner decides to use LODChain for improving the connectivity of his dataset, before its actual publishing. We suppose that the first version of the dataset is $WW1LOD_{synt}$ (upper left side of Fig. 2). We show how the lifecycle of $WW1LOD_{synt}$ can be changed by using LODChain, and for each *Use Case* (UC) we indicate its potential impact. The use cases are also presented in an online video (https://youtu.be/Kh9751p32tM).

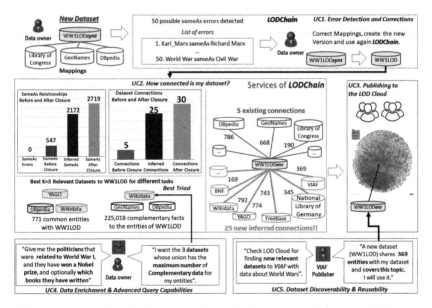

Fig. 2. A scenario with 5 use cases by uploading a new dataset to LODChain

UC1. Error Detection and Corrections. The publisher uploads the version $WW1LOD_{synt}$ to LODChain, which informs the publisher that there are 50

possible erroneous mappings, and provides a list containing these errors (upper side of Fig. 2). The publisher downloads the list for correcting the mappings and for creating the version *WW1LOD*. Without checking the quality of equivalence relationships, which is quite difficult at scale [24], it can result in erroneous relationships, which can negatively affect the trustworthiness of a publisher.

UC2. How Connected is My Dataset? The scenario continues by uploading the version *WW1LOD*. LODChain analyzes the dataset, informs the publisher that there are no errors, and it offers several connectivity analytics. Some of these real results are shown in UC2 of Fig. 2, i.e., we inferred 2,172 owl:sameAs relationships (397% increase), which resulted to 25 new connections, i.e., 500% increase, since the initial version had only 5 connections. In Fig. 2 (and also in Fig. 1) the inferred connections are depicted as edges/nodes with green color and the old connections with red color, whereas the label of each edge indicates the number of their common entities. Except for finding new connections with popular datasets (e.g., Wikidata [43], YAGO [33]), which is expected due to transitivity (they share millions of entities with DBpedia), it is feasible to discover connections with not so popular datasets that were unknown to the publisher. As regards dataset discovery and selection, indicatively Fig. 2 shows the best triad of datasets offering a) the most common entities and b) the most complementary triples for *WW1LOD* entities. We suppose that the publisher exports all the inferred data and analytics for reusing them (i.e., version $WW1LOD_{enr}$), although one can decide to use any subset of these enriched data.

UC3. Publishing the Enriched Dataset to LOD Cloud. Suppose that the publisher decides to upload the enriched version $WW1LOD_{enr}$, including all the inferred equivalence mappings and connectivity analytics, to LOD Cloud (see UC3 in Fig. 2). Below, we explain the possible impact for any users' category.

UC4. Advanced Query Capabilities, Enrichment and Verification. We mention the benefits of using LODChain for the data owner or/and for a special group of interest. By enriching *WW1LOD* through multiple datasets, more complex queries can be answered, such as the following: "Give me the politicians that were related to first World War, they have won a Nobel prize and optionally information for the books that they have written" (UC4 in Fig. 2). That query requires data from several datasets, e.g., for "Theodore Roosevelt", which is a possible answer, the first part can be answered from *WW1LOD* (http://ldf. fi/ww1lod/96403a6a), the second (nobel prizes) from Wikidata (https://www. wikidata.org/wiki/Q33866), and the third (books) from the National Library of Germany (http://d-nb.info/gnd/118749633). Although *WW1LOD* was not connected to Wikidata and the National Library of Germany (Fig. 2), LODChain inferred and added these connections in the enriched version.

However, it is not always feasible to export and use all the relevant datasets due to huge data volume, thereby, LODChain also offers services for selecting the K most relevant datasets for a desired task. For example, two possible tasks are to find the combination of K = 3 datasets providing i) "the most complementary triples for the entities of *WW1LOD*" (UC4 in Fig. 2), i.e., for data enrichment, or ii) "the most common entities with *WW1LOD*", i.e., for data verification. From the 30 connected datasets, there exists 4,060 combinations of 3 datasets, thereby, it is quite expensive to check any possible combination. However, by exploiting the precomputed results of LODChain, one can find very fast the $K = 3$ most relevant datasets for a task (e.g., UC4 in Fig. 2). These examples indicate the impact of LODChain for the dataset selection process, i.e., the K most relevant datasets differ according to the desired needs, even for the same dataset.

UC5. Dataset Search, Discoverability and Reusability. Here, we mention the benefits for any user/service (in case of open data). Suppose that publishers of other datasets periodically check the LOD Cloud for discovering relevant datasets to their dataset, that were recently published, or an automated service informs them when a new dataset is connected with their dataset. E.g., in UC5 of Fig. 2, the publisher of VIAF desires to find datasets having a) common entities with VIAF and b) information about World Wars, i.e., for enriching or for verifying their content. They observe that *WW1LOD* not only covers this topic, but also has 369 common entities with VIAF, thereby they decide to use it. Without LODChain, it would be extremely difficult for most publishers (25 out of 30) to discover that *WW1LOD* is relevant to their dataset (and to reuse it), e.g., the first version of *WW1LOD* did not have links to VIAF.

4   LODChain: Connecting Your Dataset to the LOD Cloud

First, we describe LODsyndesis (which is used from LODChain), and then the steps of LODChain, by showing a running example of how to strengthen the connectivity of a new dataset, i.e., D_{new} (upper left part of Fig. 3). For finding new connections for D_{new}, it is prerequisite D_{new} to contain links to at least one dataset, e.g., in Fig. 3, D_{new} is connected with 2 datasets: DBpedia and Wikidata. Indeed, we do not perform instance and schema matching, but we infer new connections by computing the closure of equivalence mappings among D_{new} and the rest of LOD datasets. Finally, the data of D_{new} are saved temporarily in LODsyndesis indexes for a user session for producing the desired output.

4.1   LODsyndesis Aggregated Knowledge Graph

LODChain is based on LODsyndesis [25], which is an *Aggregated Knowledge Graph* derived by *aggregating* the content of datasets, computing the transitive and symmetric closure of 45 million *equivalence relationships*, and offering *semantics-aware indexes and services* for over 412 million entities and 2 billion triples from 400 LOD datasets. Concerning the quality of the mentioned closure, it has been evaluated in a semi-manual way in our past work [20]. Afterwards, LODsyndesis keeps a unique representation for each real world entity, property and class, while also storing their provenance. The lower right side of Fig. 3 shows a graph representation of the LODsyndesis data about the Greek composer "Mikis Theodorakis". LODsyndesis has precomputed the owl:sameAs closure for "Mikis Theodorakis" URIs, has stored their provenance, and has replaced all these URIs by a single internal URI (see the single node for M. Theodorakis). The same process has been done for all the entities (e.g., "Paris"), properties (e.g., "bornYear") and so forth. Regarding the triples (i.e., facts), it stores at the same place in the index, all the triples of an entity occurring either as a subject or as an object, and their provenance. Thereby, triples having entities as objects are stored twice in the index. The lower right side of Fig. 3 shows the triples for M. Theodorakis and their provenance (see the bold text under each node).

4.2 The Steps of LODChain

Step A. Input. LODChain supports many formats: NTriples, NQuads, RDF/XML and Turtle (by using the RDF4J library https://rdf4j.org/). The publishers just give a link of their dataset in one of these formats. They can optionally type the title and domain of their dataset and can select to perform the process only for a subset of their dataset (e.g., 10,000 triples) for having a very fast overview.

Step B. Computation of Equivalence Relationships Closure and Provenance. The objective is to detect which real world objects are a) common in D_{new} and LODsyndesis, b) unique in D_{new}, and to detect c) errors in the equivalence relationships of D_{new}. LODChain reads the triples of D_{new}, collects all the owl:sameAs, owl:equivalent Property and owl:equivalentClass relationships and partitions the URIs in three sets: entities, properties and classes.

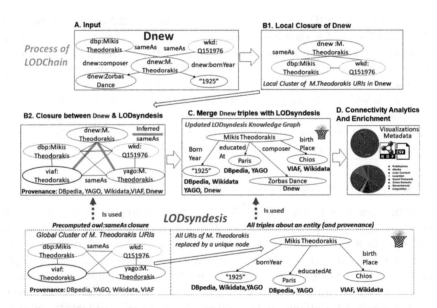

Fig. 3. Running example. The steps of LODChain for a new dataset D_{new}

B1. Local Computation of Closure in D_{new}. For each type of these URIs and *equivalence relationships*, we use the signature-based algorithm proposed in [22], for computing the transitive and symmetric closure of the equivalence relationships of D_{new}. Then we store all the URIs of D_{new} referring to the same real world object in the same local "cluster" (i.e., class of equivalence). At the end, the set $C(D_{new})$ is created, which includes all the "local" clusters of D_{new} (which are pairwise disjoint). For an entity e in D_{new} we shall use $loc(e) \in C(D_{new})$ to denote the local cluster including the URIs of e, e.g. the local cluster of "M. Theodorakis" (Step B1 of Fig. 3) contains 3 URIs, $loc(e) = \langle$dnew:M. Theodorakis, dbp:Mikis Theodorakis, wkd:Q151976$\rangle$. Finally, for the URIs that are not part of any equivalence relationship, their cluster contains a single URI, e.g., in Fig. 3 for the entity "Zorbas Dance", $loc(e) = \{dnew : Zorbas\_Dance\}$.

B2. Computation of Closure Between D_{new} and LODsyndesis. Here, we merge the local "clusters" of D_{new}, with the results of the precomputed closure of LODsyndesis. We shall use $C(LOD)$ to denote the set of all the clusters of LODsyndesis (which are pairwise disjoint), and $glob(e) \in C(LOD)$ to denote the cluster of entity e in LODsyndesis, e.g., for "Mikis Theodorakis" $glob(e) = \{$dbp:Mikis Theodorakis, wkd:Q151976, viaf:Theodorakis, yago:M. Theodorakis$\}$ (lower left side of Fig. 3). Moreover, $prov(e)$ denotes the provenance of e in LODsyndesis, e.g., for the mentioned entity $prov(e) = \{$DBpedia,YAGO,Wikidata, VIAF$\}$. Each $loc(e) \in C(D_{new})$ belongs to exactly one of the three below rules:

Rule 1. No Match Between Clusters: New Entities. Here, $loc(e)$ does not match with any global cluster of LODsyndesis, thereby the corresponding entity exists only in D_{new}, i.e., for a given $loc(e) \in C(D_{new})$, $\nexists\ glob(e') \in C(LOD)$ s.t. $loc(e) \cap glob(e') \neq \emptyset$. In such a case, we add $loc(e)$ to $C(LOD)$.

Algorithm 1: Computation of Closure between D_{new} and LODsyndesis

---

Input: Local Closure $C(D_{new})$ and global closure $C(LOD)$
Output: The common and unique entities, and errors in `owl:sameAs` mappings

```
 1  uniqEnt ← ∅, cmnEnt ← ∅, errors ← ∅
 2  forall loc(e) ∈ C(D_new) do                          // for each local cluster
 3      glob_new(e) ← ∅                                  // init. the new global cluster of e
 4      forall u ∈ loc(e) do                             // For each URI u of local cluster
 5          if u ∈ glob(e'), glob(e') ∈ C(LOD) then      // If u in LODsyndesis
 6              if glob_new(e) ≡ ∅ then                  // 1st global cluster for e
 7                  glob_new(e) ← glob(e')               // Store the global cluster
 8              else if glob_new(e) ≠ glob(e') then      // 2nd global cluster for e
 9                  delete glob_new(e)                   // Delete e, matches 2 glob. clusters
10                  errors ← errors ∪ {loc(e)}           // Add loc(e) to errors
11                  break and go to line 2               // Continue with the next loc(e)
            // After finishing with all the URIs of loc(e)
12
13      if glob_new(e) ≡ ∅ then                          // No global cluster found
14          glob_new(e) ← loc(e)                         // loc(e) is the global cluster of e
15          uniqEnt ← uniqEnt ∪ {e}                      // Add e to unique entities
16          prov(e) ← D_new                              // Store its provenance
17      else if glob_new(e) ≠ ∅ then                     // A single global cluster found
18          glob_new(e) ← glob_new(e) ∪ loc(e)           // Update global cluster of e
19          cmnEnt ← cmnEnt ∪ {e}                        // Add e to common entities
20          prov(e) ← prov(e) ∪ {D_new}                  // Update its provenance
21  return cmnEnt, uniqEnt, errors
```

Rule 2. Single Match Between Clusters: Inferring New Relationships.
If a given $loc(e) \in C(D_{new})$ matches with exactly one $glob(e')$, i.e. if $\exists! glob(e') \in C(LOD)$ s.t. $glob(e') \cap loc(e) \neq \emptyset$, then we assume that $e \equiv e'$, and we perform the following operation: $loc(e) \cup glob(e')$. In step B1 of Fig. 3, two URIs of the local cluster, i.e., dbp:Mikis Theodorakis and wkd:Q151976, belong also to the same global cluster in LODsyndesis (see the lower side of Fig. 3). By merging these clusters (step B2 of Fig. 3), we inferred two new `owl:sameAs` mappings for the URI "dnew:M. Theodorakis", we updated its provenance, and we managed to discover two new connections for D_{new}, i.e., VIAF and YAGO.

Rule 3. Cluster Conflicts: Detecting Possible Errors. If a $loc(e) \in C(D_{new})$ matches with two or more clusters of LODsyndesis, i.e., if $\exists glob(e_1), glob(e_2) \in C(LOD)$. s.t. $glob(e_1) \cap loc(e) \neq \emptyset$, $glob(e_2) \cap loc(e) \neq \emptyset$, $glob(e_1) \neq glob(e_2)$, then this is an indication of error. For instance, suppose that we have added the following erroneous mapping in D_{new}: ⟨dnew:M. Theodorakis, `owl:sameAs`, dbp:Theodore Roosevelt⟩. Due to closure, in Step B1 the result would be $loc(e)=\{$dnew:M. Theodorakis, dbp:Mikis Theodorakis, wkd:Q151976, dbp:Theodore Roosevelt$\}$. However, by proceeding to Step B2, $loc(e)$ would match with two clusters of LODsyndesis, i.e., the URIs dbp:Mikis Theodorakis and dbp:Theodore Roosevelt refer to different entities and belong to different global clusters. `LODChain` identifies such cases and informs the user.

Algorithm for Step B2. Algorithm 1 detects if there is zero, one or more global clusters, that match with the URIs of $loc(e)$, for finding common and unique entities, and errors in the `owl:sameAs` mappings. Algorithm 1 reads each $loc(e)$ separately and iterates over all its URIs (lines 2–11). For each URI u, it performs a binary search in LODsyndesis index (see line 5), for checking if it occurs in a global cluster (i.e., if it exists in LODsyndesis). Concerning the rules, for the local clusters belonging to Rule 1, the lines 6–11 will never be executed, since there is not a global cluster containing at least one URI of $loc(e)$. On the contrary, the lines 13–16 will be executed and the entity e will be stored as unique. Regarding Rule 2, the first time that we find a URI of $loc(e)$ that belongs to a global cluster, we retrieve and store the corresponding global cluster (lines 5–7). In case of finding another URI(s) of $loc(e)$ belonging to the same global cluster, we just continue with the next URI of $loc(e)$. At the end, lines 17–20 are executed for updating the global cluster of e (i.e., $glob_{new}(e)$) and its provenance, and for storing the entity as a common one. Concerning Rule 3, in case of detecting a second different global cluster that matches $loc(e)$, lines 8–11 are executed exactly one time, $loc(e)$ is stored as an error and we continue with the next $loc(e)$. Finally, Algorithm 1 returns the common and unique entities, and the `sameAs` errors.

This algorithm reads each URI u of D_{new} once (i.e., each URI of D_{new} exists in exactly one local cluster), and then it performs a binary search for u in LODsyndesis index. Therefore, its time complexity is $\mathcal{O}(|U_{D_{new}}| * log(|U_{LOD}|))$, where $U_{D_{new}}$ are all the URIs of D_{new}, U_{LOD} are all the URIs in LODsyndesis, and $log(|U_{LOD}|)$ is the cost of the binary search in LODsyndesis. On the other hand, it keeps in memory all the updated global clusters, containing the entities of D_{new}, i.e., its space complexity is $\mathcal{O}(\sum_{\forall loc(e) \in C(D_{new})} |glob_{new}(e)|)$.

How to Reduce the Number of Index Reads? A limitation is that $|U_{LOD}|$ can be huge, i.e., LODsyndesis contains more than 412 million URIs. Although we use a binary search (which is logarithmic in scale), we desire to further decrease the cost of searching to the index of LODsyndesis. For this reason, we exploit the prefixes of URIs, i.e., they usually indicate the company or university that publishes the dataset (data owner). For instance, the prefix of the URI "http://dbpedia.org/resource/Mikis_Theodorakis" is "http://dbpedia. org/". We use the prefix index of LODsyndesis [22], which contains all the prefixes for the URIs that are indexed in LODsyndesis, for checking very fast if a URI occurs in at least one existing dataset. Indeed, we know that if the prefix of a URI does not exist in the prefix index, the URI cannot be found in LODsyndesis [22].

How to Use the Prefix Index: Since the size of the prefix index is quite small compared to the index of LODsyndesis, i.e., it contains less than 1 million prefixes, before executing the line 5 of Algorithm 1, we can search if the prefix of URI u occurs in the prefix index (of LODsyndesis), and only if it is true, we can perform a binary search for u in the index of LODsyndesis. Otherwise, we just continue with the next URI. For further reducing the cost, even for searching in the prefix index, and since prefixes are highly repeated in a given dataset (e.g., in our experiments, each dataset has on average only 23.6 prefixes), we keep in memory the prefixes that we have already seen. As it is shown in §5, it can highly reduce the execution time, i.e., even more than 5× for real datasets.

Algorithm 2: Merging the triples (facts) of D_{new} with LODsyndesis

---

Input: The common entities $cmnEnt$ and their triples in D_{new}
Output: Common and unique triples of D_{new} entities to LODsyndesis datasets

1 $uniqTriples \leftarrow \emptyset$, $cmnTriples \leftarrow \emptyset$
2 **forall** $e \in cmnEnt$ **do**   // Read each common entity e
3   **forall** $\langle s, p, o \rangle \in T(D_{new}, e)$ **do**   // Read each triple of e in D_{new}
4   **if** $\langle s, p, o \rangle \in T(LOD, e)$ **then**   // If triple exists in LODsyndesis
5              $prov(\langle s, p, o \rangle) \leftarrow prov(\langle s, p, o \rangle) \cup \{D_{new}\}$ // Update provenance
6              $cmnTriples \leftarrow cmnTriples \cup \{\langle s, p, o \rangle\}$ // Add to $cmnTriples$
7   **else**   // Triple is offered only from D_{new}
8              $prov(\langle s, p, o \rangle) \leftarrow \{D_{new}\}$ // Store its provenance
9              $uniqTriples \leftarrow uniqTriples \cup \{\langle s, p, o \rangle\}$ // Add to $uniqTriples$
10             $T(LOD, e) \leftarrow T(LOD, e) \cup \{\langle s, p, o \rangle\}$ // Add to LODsyndesis
11 **return** $uniqTriples, cmnTriples$

Step C. Merging Triples of D_{new} with LODsyndesis. Here, we merge the triples for the common entities of D_{new} to LODsyndesis, for finding common and unique facts, and possibly complementary facts from other LOD datasets (data enrichment). This is performed only for the common entities (Rule 2), since for the entities belonging only to D_{new} (Rule 1), we know that all their triples are unique. We denote all triples having an entity e either as a subject or as an object, in LODsyndesis as $T(LOD, e)$ and in D_{new} as $T(D_{new}, e)$. We desire to find for each common entity e, a) the common triples in LODsyndesis, i.e., $T(LOD, e) \cap T(D_{new}, e)$, b) the unique triples of D_{new}, i.e., $T(D_{new}, e) \setminus T(LOD, e)$, and optionally c) the complementary triples to D_{new}, i.e., $T(LOD, e) \setminus T(D_{new}, e)$.

Algorithm for Step C. Algorithm 2 shows how to compute the unique and common triples. It receives as input the common entities ($cmnEnt$), and $\forall e \in cmnEnt$, it accesses its entry in LODsyndesis index through a random access file mechanism. The pointer of the entry of each entity (in the index) has been obtained from the binary search of the previous step (i.e., line 5 of Algorithm 1). Then, for each triple in $T(D_{new}, e)$, it checks if it occurs in LODsyndesis (lines 3–10). If it is true, we update the provenance and we store the triple as common (lines 4–6), otherwise, we add the unique triple to $T(LOD, e)$ (lines 7–10). In the worst case, i.e., all the entities of D_{new} are part of LODsyndesis, we iterate and keep in memory all the entities and triples of D_{new}, i.e., time and space complexity is $\mathcal{O}(|cmnEnt| + |T(D_{new})|)$. For finding complementary facts, we can extend Algorithm 2 by also iterating over $T(LOD, e)$. However, since it can be expensive, for producing connectivity analytics we can use pre-computed posting lists containing the provenance of each triple of e [25]. In step C of Fig. 3, we updated the triples and we found common, complementary and unique facts for D_{new}, e.g., the fact "M. Theodorakis, bornYear, 1925" is verified from 3 other datasets, the fact "M. Theodorakis, educatedAt, Paris" is complement to D_{new} and the fact "M. Theodorakis, composer, Zorbas Dance" is offered only by D_{new}.

Step D. Connectivity Analytics and Enrichment Services. By using the updated (temporal) LODsyndesis indexes and specialized lattice-based algorithms (presented in [22, 25]), we provide both connectivity and dataset discovery content-based measurements (e.g., see Step D of Fig. 3). The algorithms exploit the posting lists of an index (i.e., containing information about the provenance of entities, triples, etc.) for computing content-based metrics among any combination of datasets, by solving the corresponding maximization problems [22, 25]. LODChain offers connectivity analytics and data discovery services for the input dataset, through several visualizations and HTML tables (e.g., UC2 of Fig. 2).

First, LODChain provides a list of possible errors in case of detecting erroneous owl:sameAs mappings (Rule 3 of step B2), that can be used for correcting the mappings. Second, a plenty of connectivity metrics are computed and visualized, i.e., a) the inferred equivalence mappings, b) common, unique and complementary elements, i.e., how many entities, schema elements and triples of D_{new} exist in ≥ 1 other datasets, how many only in D_{new}, and how many complementary triples exist for the entities of D_{new}, c) connections of D_{new} due to closure, i.e., the datasets having common entities with D_{new} before and after the computation of closure, d) top-10 connections of D_{new} (separately for entities, schema and triples), and many others. Regarding *Dataset Discovery*, LODChain finds the K most relevant datasets to D_{new} with common or complementary elements. Third, it offers an enriched version of D_{new} in RDF format having:

all the common elements and their provenance, the inferred `owl:sameAs` mappings, complementary triples, and rich metadata, created through VoID [1] and VoIDWH [21], that describe through triples the results of connectivity analytics.

Accessing LODChain and Sustainability Plan. `LODChain` is available in https://demos.isl.ics.forth.gr/LODChain and is running on a common machine with 8 cores, 8 GB memory and 60 GB disk space in *okeanos* service [13]. There is no need to download any software for using it, and sample datasets are offered in the webpage. Regarding its sustainability plan, `LODChain` can be used with any updated version of LODsyndesis' indexes, thereby, one major plan is to investigate ways for aiding the update of LODsyndesis at least periodically.

5   Experimental Evaluation

The objective is to measure the efficiency of `LODChain` and to provide connectivity analytics. We use a common machine with 8 cores and 8 GB memory, which contains the indexes of LODsyndesis. These indexes include over 2 billion triples and 412 million URIs from 400 RDF datasets, i.e., statistics are given in [24,25]. Concerning the datasets, we use the 5 real and 2 synthetic RDF datasets of Table 1. The real datasets include from 3K to 1.5M of triples, they contain links to few other datasets, i.e., see more statistics in Sect. 5.2, and only a few number of unique prefixes, i.e., on average 23.6 prefixes. Indeed, most of their URIs contain a prefix that cannot be found in LODsyndesis. In the worst case for real datasets, only 26.4% of URIs contain a prefix that occurs in LODsyndesis. We also use two synthetic datasets having the same number of triples, URIs and `owl:sameAs` mappings, for evaluating two cases. In the first one (HiConn), most URIs are part of LODsyndesis (highly connected), whereas in the second (LowConn), most URIs and their prefix are new (almost disconnected from LODsyndesis).

Table 1. The 7 evaluation RDF datasets (5 Real and 2 Synthetic)

ID	Dataset (abbreviation)	Domain	# of Triples	# of sameAs	# of URIs	# of URIs with prefix in LODsyndesis
R1	GReek Children Art Museum (**GRC**) [15]	User content	2,212	0	452	58 (12.8%)
R2	Geological TimeScale (**GTS**) [9]	Geography	13,271	173	1,206	181 (15.0%)
R3	World War 1 LOD (**WW1LOD**) [18]	Publication	47,616	547	11,690	2,191 (18.7%)
R4	MuziekWeb (**MW**) [17]	Media	506,582	10,563	153,538	105,548 (6.8%)
R5	Persons of National Library of Netherlands (**PNLN**) [36]	Publication	1,500,000	268,861	636,230	168,444 (26.4%)
S1	Synthetic 1 (**HiConn**)	–	1,000,000	181,105	425,500	400,697 (94.1%)
S2	Synthetic 2 (**LowConn**)	–	1,000,000	181,105	425,500	1,020 (2.3%)

Table 2. Total execution time for each dataset, with and without prefix index

Dataset	w/o Prefix index	With prefix index	Achieved speedup
GRC	7.47 s	5.26 s	1.41×
GTS	10.37 s	7.11 s	1.45×
WW1LOD	79.74 s	39.04 s	2.04×
MW	779.10 s	143.11 s	5.44×
PNLN	3,881.02 s	2,110.12 s	1.83×
LowConn	1,960.08 s	62.80 s	31.11×
HiConn	2,531.00 s	2,446.41 s	1.03×

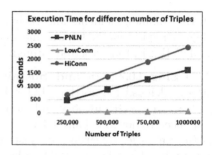

Fig. 4. Execution time with different number of triples for the same dataset

5.1 Efficiency

We measure the execution time i) for the whole process, ii) for the different steps of LODChain, and iii) by using a different number of triples for the same dataset.

Execution Time - The Gain of Prefix Index. Concerning the real datasets (first five rows of Table 2), as the size of the dataset grows, the execution time increases. However, by exploiting the prefix index, the execution time highly decreases for all the real datasets, i.e., we achieved a speedup from 1.41× to 5.44×. Since these datasets contain a high percentage of URIs with new prefixes (that are not part of LODsyndesis) we managed to reduce the reads to LODsyndesis indexes (and thus the execution time). By using that approach, we needed for the first four real datasets from 5 s to 2.5 min, whereas for the largest dataset, i.e. PNLN, we needed 35 min. For the synthetic datasets (last two rows of Table 2), the execution time is extremely different in case of using the prefix index, although they contain the same number of triples, URIs and owl:sameAs mappings. For the LowConn dataset, we achieved a 31.11× speedup by exploiting the prefix index, while for the whole process 1 min was needed, although the dataset contains 1 million triples. On the contrary, for the HiConn, which consists of the same number of triples, we needed 40 min to complete the process, even by using the prefix index, which is rational, since most URIs of HiConn contain a prefix that is common in LODsyndesis.

Execution Time for Different Numbers of Triples/URIs. Figure 4, shows the execution time for different numbers of triples (and URIs), by using the three largest datasets (including the two synthetic datasets). We can see that as the number of triples (and URIs) grows, the execution time linearly increases, which is expected, since the time complexity of the most time consuming tasks (results are presented in the next paragraph), i.e., computation of closure and merging of triples with LODsyndesis are linearithmic and linear, respectively (see Sect. 4).

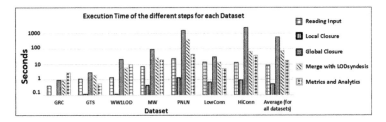

Fig. 5. Execution time for the different steps for each dataset (log scale with base 10)

Table 3. Connectivity Analytics for each real dataset to 400 other LOD datasets

ID	Measurement	GRC	GTS	WW1LOD	MW	PNLN
1	# of `owl:sameAs`	–	173	547	10,563	268,861
2	# of inferred `owl:sameAs`	–	548	2,172	26,113	309,134
3	Increase % of `owl:sameAs`	–	316%	397%	247%	114%
4	# of detected errors in `owl:sameAs`	–	0	0	1	20
5	# of unique entities	411	902	10,271	54,089	297,091
6	# of common entities	39	130	825	3,066	75,181
7	common entities percentage	8.6%	12.5%	7.4%	5.3%	20.1%
8	# of connections before `LODChain`	2	2	5	5	3
9	# of inferred connections	17	9	25	26	33
10	# of connections after `LODChain`	19	11	30	31	36
11	Increase % of connections	850%	450%	500%	520%	1100%
12	# of unique properties	19	21	65	19	4
13	# of common properties	23	58	81	8	14
14	common properties percentage	54.7%	73.4%	55.4%	29.6%	77.7%
15	# of unique classes	1	20	52	8	0
16	# of common classes	1	8	23	2	1
17	common classes percentage	50.0%	28.5%	30.6%	20.0%	100%
18	# of unique facts	2,897	16,908	53,505	611,750	1,231,972
19	# of common facts	0	25	368	7,935	193,248
20	common facts percentage	0%	0.1%	0.6%	1.2%	13.5%
21	# of new facts for D_{new} entities	26,658	17,632	362,339	597,475	3,632,412
22	% of facts enrichment for D_{new} entities	920%	104%	672%	96%	254%
23	Dataset with most common entities	Wikidata	DBpedia	Wikidata	Wikidata	VIAF
24	Dataset with most common facts	–	Opencyc	YAGO	Wikidata	VIAF
25	Dataset with most complementary facts	Wikidata	DBpedia	GeoNames	Freebase	VIAF

Execution Time of Different Steps. Figure 5 depicts in log scale (with base 10) the execution time of the different steps of `LODChain` for each single dataset and also the average time (of all the datasets) by using the approach with the prefix index. The most time-consuming task is the computation of closure among the URIs of a new dataset and LODsyndesis (i.e., global closure), e.g., for PNLN dataset, it requires the 76.4% of the time, whereas the process of merging the triples can require enough time in case of having a high number of common entities, e.g., for PNLN it requires 20.2% of the total time. On the contrary, the rest of steps are quite fast in any case, i.e., less than 50 s even in the worst case. In general, datasets with high connectivity require more time to be processed, i.e., for datasets having a lot of common entities with other datasets (such as PNLN), we need to access more times the indexes of LODsyndesis.

5.2   Connectivity Analytics Over Real Datasets

Table 3 provides connectivity analytics for the 5 real datasets. We can see (IDs 1–3) the high increase (even 397%) in the number of owl:sameAs mappings. On the contrary, we detected only a very few number of sameAs errors (ID 4), e.g., only 0.007% for PNLN dataset. Concerning the entities, each dataset shares several common entities with existing datasets, i.e., from 5.3% to 20.1% of their total entities (IDs 5–7). Due to the inference, we obtain a high increase in the number of connections after using LODChain, i.e., from 450% to 1100% (IDs 8–11). Indeed, the initial versions of the datasets included mappings to few LOD datasets (from 2 to 5), whereas LODChain discovered many inferred connections (from 9 to 33). Concerning the schema elements (IDs 12–17), most datasets use existing ontologies, and have several common properties (even 77.7%). In some cases we obtained a high number of common facts (IDs 18–20) with other datasets, i.e., 13.5% for PNLN, which can be used for data verification. Also, we found a high number of complementary facts (IDs 21–22) for the entities of each dataset, which can aid data enrichment, e.g., 254% more facts were discovered for PNLN entities. Also, popular datasets like Wikidata and DBpedia offer several common entities, common and complementary facts for the input datasets (IDs 23–25). All the datasets, and the results of even more analytics are online in [27].

6   Conclusion and Future Work

Since the current way of publishing an RDF dataset does not favor its connectivity, and thus its discoverability, reusability and content enrichment, we proposed a novel service, called LODChain, for strengthening the connections of any RDF dataset (even before its actual publishing) to the rest of LOD cloud. For showcasing its potential impact, we described use cases involving different categories of users, and we detailed its process, which includes methods for computing the equivalence reasoning among the input dataset and hundreds of LOD datasets. For evaluating its impact and efficiency we used 5 real and 2 synthetic datasets; LODChain produced connectivity analytics for datasets with thousands of triples even in less than 1 min, whereas the connections of real datasets increased from 450% to 1100%. As a future research, work and long-term plan, we want to a) investigate ways to parallelize LODChain (by extending the techniques of [23]), b) improve the GUI and perform a usability evaluation with dataset owners, c) support entity matching for finding connections for totally disconnected RDF datasets, and d) create an evaluation benchmark for such connection services.

Resource Availability Statement: The source code and URL of LODChain, the datasets and the experimental results are available in [27]. A tutorial video presenting LODChain is available in https://youtu.be/Kh9751p32tM.

Acknowledgments. This work has received funding from the European Union's Horizon 2020 coordination and support action 4CH (Grant agreement No 101004468).

References

1. Alexander, K., Cyganiak, R., Hausenblas, M., Zhao, J.: Describing linked datasets with the VoID vocabulary (2011)
2. Asprino, L., Beek, W., Ciancarini, P., Harmelen, F.V., Presutti, V.: Observing LOD using equivalent set graphs: it is mostly flat and sparsely linked. In: International Semantic Web Conference, pp. 57–74. Springer (2019). https://doi.org/10.1007/978-3-030-30793-6_4
3. Beek, W., Raad, J., Acar, E., van Harmelen, F.: MetaLink: a travel guide to the LOD cloud. In: Harth, A., et al. (eds.) ESWC 2020. LNCS, vol. 12123, pp. 481–496. Springer, Cham (2020). https://doi.org/10.1007/978-3-030-49461-2_28
4. Bischof, S., Harth, A., Kämpgen, B., Polleres, A., Schneider, P.: Enriching integrated statistical open city data by combining equational knowledge and missing value imputation. J. Web Semant. **48**, 22–47 (2018)
5. Bizer, C., Heath, T., Berners-Lee, T.: Linked data: the story so far. In: Semantic Services, Interoperability and Web Applications: Emerging Concepts, pp. 205–227. IGI global (2011)
6. Brickley, D., Burgess, M., Noy, N.: Google dataset search: building a search engine for datasets in an open web ecosystem. In: The World Wide Web Conference, pp. 1365–1375 (2019)
7. Chapman, A., et al.: Dataset search: a survey. VLDB J. **29**(1), 251–272 (2019). https://doi.org/10.1007/s00778-019-00564-x
8. Christophides, V., Efthymiou, V., Palpanas, T., Papadakis, G., Stefanidis, K.: An overview of end-to-end entity resolution for big data. ACM Comput. Surv. (CSUR) **53**(6), 1–42 (2020)
9. Cox, S.J.D., Richard, S.M.: A geologic timescale ontology and service. Earth Sci. Inf. **8**(1), 5–19 (2014). https://doi.org/10.1007/s12145-014-0170-6
10. Debattista, J., Attard, J., Brennan, R., O'Sullivan, D.: Is the LOD cloud at risk of becoming a museum for datasets? Looking ahead towards a fully collaborative and sustainable LOD cloud. In: Proceedings of WWW Conference, pp. 850–858 (2019)
11. Fernández, J.D., Beek, W., Martínez-Prieto, M.A., Arias, M.: LOD-a-lot. In: International Semantic Web Conference, pp. 75–83. Springer (2017). https://doi.org/10.1007/978-3-319-68204-4_7
12. Gottron, T., Scherp, A., Krayer, B., Peters, A.: LODatio: a schema-based retrieval system for linked open data at web-scale. In: Extended Semantic Web Conference, pp. 142–146. Springer (2013). https://doi.org/10.1007/978-3-642-41242-4_13
13. GRNET: Okeanos cloud computing service. https://okeanos.grnet.gr. Accessed 25 July 2022
14. Hubauer, T., Lamparter, S., Haase, P., Herzig, D.M.: Use cases of the industrial knowledge graph at siemens. In: International Semantic Web Conference (P&D/Industry/BlueSky) (2018)

15. Kotis, K., Angelis, S., Chondrogianni, M., Marini, E.: Children's art museum collections as linked open data. Int. J. Metadata Semant. Ontol. **15**(1), 60–70 (2021)
16. Lehmann, J., et al.: Dpedia-a large-scale, multilingual knowledge base extracted from Wikipedia. Semant. Web **6**(2), 167–195 (2015)
17. Weigl, D.M., et al.: Interweaving and enriching digital music collections for scholarship, performance, and enjoyment. In: 6th International Conference on Digital Libraries for Musicology, pp. 84–88 (2019)
18. Mäkelä, E., Törnroos, J., Lindquist, T., Hyvönen, E.: WW1LOD: an application of CIDOC-CRM to world war 1 linked data. IJDL **18**(4), 333–343 (2017)
19. McCrae, J.P., et al.: The linked open data cloud. Lod-cloud. net (2019)
20. Mountantonakis, M.: Services for Connecting and Integrating Big Numbers of Linked Datasets, vol. 50. IOS Press (2021)
21. Mountantonakis, M., et al.: Extending VoID for expressing connectivity metrics of a semantic warehouse. In: PROFILES@ ESWC (2014)
22. Mountantonakis, M., Tzitzikas, Y.: On measuring the lattice of commonalities among several linked datasets. Proc. VLDB **9**(12), 1101–1112 (2016)
23. Mountantonakis, M., Tzitzikas, Y.: Scalable methods for measuring the connectivity and quality of large numbers of linked datasets. J. Data Inf. Qual. (JDIQ) **9**(3), 1–49 (2018)
24. Mountantonakis, M., Tzitzikas, Y.: Large-scale semantic integration of linked data: a survey. CSUR **52**(5), 1–40 (2019)
25. Mountantonakis, M., Tzitzikas, Y.: Content-based union and complement metrics for dataset search over RDF knowledge graphs. ACM JDIQ **12**(2), 1–31 (2020)
26. Mountantonakis, M., Tzitzikas, Y.: How your cultural dataset is connected to the rest linked open data. In: Proceedings of the TMM-CH2021, Communications in Computer and Information Science, Athens, Greece, pp. 12–15 (2021)
27. Mountantonakis, M., Tzitzikas, Y.: LODChain, April 2022. https://doi.org/10.5281/zenodo.6467419
28. Nayak, A., Božić, B., Longo, L.: Linked data quality assessment: a survey. In: International Conference on Web Services, pp. 63–76. Springer (2021). https://doi.org/10.1007/978-3-030-96140-4_5
29. Nečaskỳ, M., Škoda, P., Bernhauer, D., Klímek, J., Skopal, T.: Modular framework for similarity-based dataset discovery using external knowledge. Data Technol. Appl. **56**(4), 506–535 (2022)
30. Otero-Cerdeira, L., et al.: Ontology matching: a literature review. Expert Syst. Appl. **42**(2), 949–971 (2015)
31. Paris, P.-H.: Assessing the quality of owl:sameAs links. In: Gangemi, A., et al. (eds.) ESWC 2018. LNCS, vol. 11155, pp. 304–313. Springer, Cham (2018). https://doi.org/10.1007/978-3-319-98192-5_49
32. Pietriga, E., et al.: Browsing linked data catalogs with LODAtlas. In: International Semantic Web Conference, pp. 137–153. Springer (2018). https://doi.org/10.1007/978-3-030-00668-6_9
33. Rebele, T., Suchanek, F., Hoffart, J., Biega, J., Kuzey, E., Weikum, G.: YAGO: a multilingual knowledge base from Wikipedia, Wordnet, and Geonames. In: Groth, P., et al. (eds.) ISWC 2016. LNCS, vol. 9982, pp. 177–185. Springer, Cham (2016). https://doi.org/10.1007/978-3-319-46547-0_19
34. Rietveld, L., Beek, W., Schlobach, S.: LOD Lab: experiments at LOD scale. In: Arenas, M., et al. (eds.) ISWC 2015. LNCS, vol. 9367, pp. 339–355. Springer, Cham (2015). https://doi.org/10.1007/978-3-319-25010-6_23

35. Sabou, M., Onder, I., Brasoveanu, A.M.P., Scharl, A.: Towards cross-domain data analytics in tourism: a linked data based approach. Inf. Technol. Tour. **16**(1), 71–101 (2016). https://doi.org/10.1007/s40558-015-0049-5

36. Sierman, B., Teszelszky, K.: How can we improve our web collection? An evaluation of webarchiving at the KB national library of the Netherlands (2007–2017). Alexandria **27**(2), 94–107 (2017)

37. Tzitzikas, Y., et al.: Methods and tools for supporting the integration of stocks and fisheries. In: International Conference on Information and Communication Technologies in Agriculture, Food & Environment, pp. 20–34. Springer (2017). https://doi.org/10.1007/978-3-030-12998-9_2

38. Umbrich, J., Hogan, A., Polleres, A., Decker, S.: Link traversal querying for a diverse web of data. Semant. Web **6**(6), 585–624 (2015)

39. Valdestilhas, A., Soru, T., Nentwig, M., Marx, E., Saleem, M., Ngomo, A.-C.N.: Where is My URI? In: Gangemi, A., et al. (eds.) ESWC 2018. LNCS, vol. 10843, pp. 671–681. Springer, Cham (2018). https://doi.org/10.1007/978-3-319-93417-4_43

40. Valdestilhas, A., Soru, T., Ngomo, A.C.N.: CEDAL: time-efficient detection of erroneous links in large-scale link repositories. In: Proceedings of the International Conference on Web Intelligence, pp. 106–113 (2017)

41. Vandenbussche, P.Y., Umbrich, J., Matteis, L., Hogan, A., Buil-Aranda, C.: SPARQLES: monitoring public SPARQL endpoints. Semant. Web **8**(6), 1049–1065 (2017)

42. Volz, J., Bizer, C., Gaedke, M., Kobilarov, G.: Silk-a link discovery framework for the web of data. In: LDOW (2009)

43. Vrandečić, D., Krötzsch, M.: Wikidata: a free collaborative knowledge base. Commun. ACM **57**(10), 78–85 (2014)

44. Wang, X., Cheng, G., Pan, J.Z., Kharlamov, E., Qu, Y.: BANDAR: benchmarking snippet generation algorithms for (RDF) dataset search. IEEE Trans. Knowl. Data Eng. (2021). https://ieeexplore.ieee.org/document/9477056

45. Wiśniewski, D., Potoniec, J., Ławrynowicz, A., Keet, C.M.: Analysis of ontology competency questions and their formalizations in SPARQL-OWL. J. Web Semant. **59**, 100534 (2019)

46. Yochum, P., Chang, L., Gu, T., Zhu, M.: Linked open data in location-based recommendation system on tourism domain: a survey. IEEE Access **8**, 16409–16439 (2020)

47. Yumusak, S., Dogdu, E., Kodaz, H., Kamilaris, A., Vandenbussche, P.Y.: SpEnD: linked data SPARQL endpoints discovery using search engines. IEICE Trans. Inf. Syst. **100**(4), 758–767 (2017)

48. Zaveri, A., Rula, A., Maurino, A., Pietrobon, R., Lehmann, J., Auer, S.: Quality assessment for linked data: a survey. Semant. Web **7**(1), 63–93 (2016)

WDV: A Broad Data Verbalisation Dataset Built from Wikidata

Gabriel Amaral[(✉)] [iD], Odinaldo Rodrigues[iD], and Elena Simperl[iD]

King's College London, London WC2R 2LS, UK
{gabriel.amaral,odinaldo.rodrigues,elena.simperl}@kcl.ac.uk

Abstract. Data verbalisation is a task of great importance in the current field of natural language processing, as there is a clear benefit in the transformation of our abundant structured and semi-structured data into human-readable formats. Verbalising Knowledge Graph (KG) data focuses on converting interconnected triple-based claims, formed of subject, predicate, and object, into text. Although KG verbalisation datasets exist for some KGs, there are still limitations in their applicability to many scenarios. This is especially true for Wikidata, where available datasets either loosely couple claim sets with textual information or heavily focus on predicates around biographies, cities, and countries. To address these gaps, we propose WDV, a large KG claim verbalisation dataset built from Wikidata, with a tight coupling between triples and text, covering a wide variety of entities and predicates. We also evaluate the quality of our verbalisations through a reusable workflow for measuring human-centred fluency and adequacy scores. Our data (https://doi.org/10.6084/m9.figshare.17159045.v1) and code (https://github.com/gabrielmaia7/WDV) are openly available in the hopes of furthering research towards KG verbalisation.

Keywords: Crowdsourcing · Knowledge graphs · Data verbalisation

1 Introduction

Data verbalisation, a facet of Natural Language Generation (NLG), is a task that has great importance in the current field of natural language processing [10,14,15,32,35,44], as there is great benefit in the transformation of our abundant structured and semi-structured data into human-readable formats. It is important in its own right, as well as as a step toward larger tasks such as open-domain question-answering [23] and automated fact checking [40,41]. One large source of semi-structured data that would benefit greatly from verbalisation is collaborative Knowledge Graphs (KG) like DBpedia[1] and Wikidata.[2]

The verbalisation of KGs data consists of converting sets of claims into natural language text. Each claim consists of a triple, formed of subject, predicate,

---
[1] https://www.dbpedia.org/.
[2] https://www.wikidata.org.

© The Author(s), under exclusive license to Springer Nature Switzerland AG 2022
U. Sattler et al. (Eds.): ISWC 2022, LNCS 13489, pp. 556–574, 2022.
https://doi.org/10.1007/978-3-031-19433-7_32

and object, and each claim set shares subjects and objects; the verbalisation then has to deal with expressing and linking these pieces of information. Although KG verbalisation datasets, mapping claim sets to text, exist for some popular KGs [2,6,11], they are not without their limitations.

Wikidata, the web's largest collaborative KG, has very few such datasets [6, 38], and existing ones rely on distant supervision to prioritise the sheer number of couplings in exchange for coupling tightness. They also disproportionately represent specific entity types from Wikidata (e.g. people and locations) when Wikidata covers a much wider variety of information. Finally, data verbalisation performance is mainly measured via algorithms, such as BLEU [27], which have been the target of many criticisms when applied to NLG [25,31,33].

We propose WDV, a large KG verbalisation dataset with 7.6k Wikidata entries. WDV addresses limitations in coverage disproportion, verbalisation coupling, and algorithmically measured quality, respectively, given that:

1. WDV is built from a much wider variety of entity types and predicates than similar datasets, and is intended as a benchmarking dataset for data verbalisation models applied on Wikidata;
2. WDV supports a tight coupling between single claims and text directly associating a triple-based claim and a natural language sentence;
3. 1.4k entries of WDV have been annotated by a collective of humans, allowing for the evaluation and future improvement of our verbalisations, as well as establishing a non-algorithmic baseline for other verbalisation models.

Additionally, we create a reproducible crowdsourcing workflow for capturing human evaluations of fluency and adequacy in graph-to-text NLG. All used code and gathered data are available in this paper's GitHub repository.

The remainder of the paper is structured as follows. Section 2 positions our dataset in regards to existing datasets. Section 3 presents our dataset construction, including quality annotations. Section 4 describes our verbalisation model. Finally, Sects. 5 and 6 reinforce and summarise our contributions.

2   Background and Related Work

Verbalising KGs consists of generating grammatically correct natural language based on structured and semi-structured data from a KG, maintaining the original meaning. This data is encoded in triples (claims), consisting of a subject, a predicate, and an object; all three components model aspects of knowledge, such as entities, classes, attributes, and relationships. Examples of popular KGs are DBpedia, Wikidata, Yago,[3] and Freebase.[4] Their verbalisation is an important task on its own, but is also a key step in downstream tasks [23,36,40,41].

Datasets that align KG claims to text are vital for creating and evaluating KG verbalisation approaches. While several have been created, they are not

---

[3] https://github.com/yago-naga/yago3.
[4] https://developers.google.com/freebase.

without their limitations. The *NYT-FB* [24, 42] dataset aligns text from the New York Times with triples from Freebase through named entity linking and keyword matching against Freebase labels. This leads to a disproportional coverage of news-worthy entities and topics, such as geography and politics, and from a specific period in time, limiting its usefulness in broader scenarios. The same narrow scope is seen in the *TACRED* dataset [43], which covers only 41 relationships about people and organisations, such as age, spouse, shareholders, etc., as its data does not stem from any specific KG, but rather annotated newswire and web text from the TAC KBP corpora [5]. Also, its texts often contain much more information than their aligned triples, making it a resource not fully suited for NLG. The *FB15K-237* dataset [34] aligns Freebase triples to synsets instead of text, making it unusable for NLG without text grounding. Additionally, both NYT-FB and FB15K-237 rely on Freebase, which was discontinued and its data moved to Wikidata [28], compromising these datasets' usability and upkeep.

More recent datasets attempt to remedy some of these limitations. Pavlos et al. [37, 38] propose two large corpora that align Wikidata and DBpedia claims to Wikipedia text. However, they focus on verbalisations of multiple claims at a time, which limits its usefulness for important tasks e.g. automated fact-checking in favour of others e.g. summarisation. Even more critically, they are based on distant supervision techniques, providing a loose alignment between sets of triples and text; triple sets consist of numerous claims that are very likely - but not guaranteed - to be expressed in the text, and the text contains information that is not assured to exist in the claims. The same is true for *T-REx* [6], which aligns Wikidata claims to Wikipedia abstracts, making it unreliable for NLG from KG claims while perfectly preserving their sense. Our dataset bridges this gap by focusing on a tight alignment between Wikidata claims and text.

The coverage issue seen in NYT-FB and TACRED is also present, although less so, in T-REx. It covers many unique predicates, yet they are disproportionately represented: the top 7.7% of its unique predicates represent 90% of its unique triples, and these mostly express information on people and places, with the country predicate alone representing over 11% of triples. The *WebNLG* [11] dataset remedies this by defining a list of very broad DBpedia classes and then collecting separate and balanced sets of claims from entities in each class. However, WebNLG also focuses on sets of multiple claims at a time.

We follow WebNLG's approach to resolving predicate and theme bias. However, we build WDV out of Wikidata instead, expanding the entity classes defined by WebNLG, as Wikidata lacks verbalisation datasets that cover its wide range of predicates and themes. To provide a better view of how WDV compares to other datasets mentioned in this Section, refer to Table 1.

3   WDV: An Annotated Wikidata Verbalisation Dataset

This section describes the construction of the WDV dataset, including crowd-sourced annotations, as well as details of its structure. Figure 1 illustrates the entire process with numbered steps, which we cover in this Section. In a nutshell, it consists of first defining 20 large pools of filtered Wikidata claims, each

Table 1. Comparison between WDV and other KG verbalisation datasets. 'Entity Classes' shows in how many distinct themes the claims might be organised by, if at all. 'Text Alignment' refers to whether all text corresponds to aligned triples (Tight) or not (Distant). *Avail.* stands for Availability.

	Source graph	Aligned documents	Unique predicates	Unique triples	Entity classes	Text alignment	Avail
NYT-FB	Freebase	1.8M	258	39K	n.a	Distant	Partial
TACRED	n.a	106K	41	21K	n.a	Distant	Closed
FB15K-237	Freebase	2.7M	237	2.7M	n.a	Tight	Public
T-REx	Wikidata	6.2M	642	11M	n.a	Distant	Public
WebNLG	DBpedia	39K	412	3.2K	16	Tight	Public
WDV	Wikidata	7.6K	439	7.6K	20	Tight	Public

corresponding to a Wikidata class (steps 1–4). Then, we obtain a sample of claims from each pool such that predicates are represented as equally as possible (step 5). Lastly, we obtain aligned verbalisations and human annotations (steps 6 and 7). Throughout this entire construction process, data was extracted from a Wikipedia JSON dump from August 2021. The JSON format was used since the later stages of the pipeline i.e. crowdsourcing and verbalisation either require or greatly benefit from that input format. We also release WDV in this format as it targets ML practitioners and developers, who are very familiar with it.

To improve comprehensibility, transparency, and repeatability, we follow two recently proposed sets of guidelines. The first, by Gebru et al. [13], pertains to the effective documentation of machine learning datasets, supporting the transparency and reproducibility of their creation process. The second, by Ramirez et al. [30], pertains to the detailing of crowdsourcing experiments to guarantee clarity and repeatability. It ensures the impact of task design, data processing, and other factors on our conclusions, as well as their validity, can be assessed.

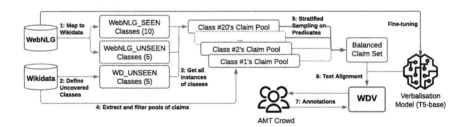

Fig. 1. Overview of WDV's construction workflow, starting with WebNLG's structure and Wikidata's contents, finishing with WDV and crowd annotations.

3.1 Balanced Claim Set Collection

WDV adapts and expands on WebNLG's partition and class structure to fit Wikidata. Firstly, this ensures a balanced representation of Wikidata entities and predicates of various natures. Secondly, our data verbalisation model, used later in the workflow, is fine-tuned with WebNLG; keeping the same class composition thus reduces the chances of low-quality verbalisations. WebNLG has two partitions: SEEN, with 15 classes, and UNSEEN, with five, as seen in Table 2.

We start by mapping WebNLG's 15 DBpedia classes to their Wikidata equivalents (**step 1**). Some of Wikidata's most populous classes are not at all covered by these 15. Thus, from these uncovered classes, we select the five largest to compose an additional partition WD_UNSEEN (**step 2**); we do not consider ontological or scientifically complex classes (e.g. proteins). Next, we extract from Wikidata all entities that can be considered as instances or examples of these 20 classes or their subclasses (**step 3**), composing 20 large groups of entities.

From each class' extracted group of entities, we retrieve all claims that we deem suitable for verbalisation, based on the following exclusion criteria (**step 4**): we exclude deprecated claims, as they might contain incorrect or invalid values; claims with objects of datatypes that are hard to represent in natural language are excluded e.g. external database identifiers, URLs, images, mathematical formulas, etc.; we exclude claims that serve taxonomic or ontological purposes e.g. subclass of (P31), Topic's main category (P910), See also (P1659) etc.; and finally, claims whose objects are the special values *no value* or *some value*. The claims remaining after these exclusions compose 20 distinct pools of claims, or *themes*, from which we will next sample a set of claims.

These themes have very unbalanced distributions of claims over predicates e.g. over 50% of the claims in the *Airport* and *Mountain* themes have the patronage (P3872) and country (P17) predicates, respectively. A simple random sample would build a dataset that ignores the vast majority of Wikidata predicates. Hence, we opt for a stratified sampling of claims (**step 5**).

For each theme t, we determine the representative sample size N_t needed, considering its total number of claims, a 95% confidence interval, and a 5% margin of error. We start the sampling process by grouping each theme's claims by predicate, discarding very rare predicates (0.3% to 1.7% of total claims in a theme), and defining each theme's remaining M_t predicate groups as a stratum. For each theme t, we attempt to sample an equal amount of claims (N_t/M_t) from each stratum. If a stratum in theme t has less than N_t/M_t claims, we select all its claims and compensate by oversampling other strata in t, so that total sample size is still N_t. We keep track of all sampling weights in order to adjust any estimated statistic to account for the stratification. The resulting balanced claim set consists of statistically representative sets of claims from all 20 themes (7.6k claims in total), where predicates are as equally present as possible.

3.2 Text Alignment

WDV tightly aligns each claim to a natural language text i.e. each claim corresponds exactly to one sentence (and vice-versa), such that both hold the same meaning and the sentence is grammatically well-written. This is so that NLG is directly supported (as explored in Sect. 2) and also because WDV is the first step towards future research into automating fact checking for Wikidata.

To achieve this alignment (**step 6**), we first collect subject, predicate, and object labels (preferably in English) for each claim in the balanced claim set. We also collect aliases and descriptions, which play a part later in crowdsourcing. The collection is done by querying Wikidata's SPARQL engine.[5] In cases such as timestamps and measurements with units, label templates are used.

For each claim, its three labels are given to a verbalisation model, which outputs an English sentence that attempts to communicate the same information. The model itself, including its training and validation, is detailed in Sect. 4. This results in 7.6k claim-verbalisation pairings.

These claim-verbalisation pairings, alongside ontological attributes and the aggregated crowdsourced annotations (see Sect. 3.3), constitute WDV. Its detailed structure, an exemplary record, and some descriptive statistics are given in Sect. 3.4. Section 3.5 explores insights obtained from crowd annotations.

3.3   Crowdsourced Annotations

To measure how much of the claims' meanings are kept (i.e. adequacy) by the verbalisations and how much they resemble text written by humans (i.e. fluency), as well as to support the dataset's refining and correction, we crowdsource human annotations (**step 7**). These annotations are collected for a portion of WDV (20% of total claims) due to budget constraints, randomly selected among those claims having all labels in English, while keeping a proportional representation of each theme. Claim components not labelled in English are a minority that would represent a hurdle for crowd workers [22] and bias results.

Experimental Design. Before crowdsourcing, the WDV data goes through two pre-processing steps: *golden data generation* and *task composition*. Golden data is a small data subset that is manually annotated and used as a reference to discern between good and bad workers. We calculate how much golden data is necessary by minimizing, based on available data from similar studies [1], the probability of a regular worker finding a repeated set of golden data in two different tasks, which plateaus near 100% with 90 golden data annotations.

We take 45 random records from the sampled WDV data and set them aside as golden data for both fluency and adequacy tasks. We manually generate another 90 uniquely identified pairs to represent poor model performance: 45 for the fluency task by writing different levels of gibberish, and 45 for adequacy by randomly shuffling their verbalisations. We annotate golden data by defining, for each pair, what would represent reasonable scores for fluency and adequacy.

Task composition consists of: first, grouping the sampled WDV data plus the golden data such that each group (a *task set*) has two random golden data pairs and four random non-annotated pairs; then, attributing to each task a unique identifier; and lastly, sending the task set to the crowd embedded in an HTML script to be solved by at least five different workers.

---

[5] https://query.wikidata.org/.

Pilots were run in August 2021, and main tasks were run between September and October of the same year. Pilots helped us measure median time spent by workers to define fair payment, and collect general feedback to adjust task design. We calculated pay based on double the US's minimum hourly wage of USD7.25, in order to properly account for good workers that need more time than the median. We paid USD0.50 per fluency task and USD1.00 per adequacy task. Workers rated our tasks as having fair pay on TurkerView.[6] Before starting the task, workers are made aware of the pay and conditions and are told that continuing with the task means consenting to both.

Crowd. Crowd workers were selected from Amazon Mechanical Turk (AMT), the demographics of which have been explored in several papers [3,4,18]. We limited the tasks only to workers that had a good grasp of English by including an English grammar screening quiz before each task. Secondly, we only allowed workers that had done over 1000 tasks with over 80% acceptance rate to work on our tasks. We analysed contributions from the pilot, identifying workers that exhibited malicious behaviour and banning them from the main tasks.

Tasks. Task sets are sent to be annotated embedded in HTML pages. There is one for *fluency* and one for *adequacy* annotation tasks. Before starting either task type, workers are shown a description of that task, rules, and instructions they should follow. They also see many examples of acceptable answers with explanations. Workers can access this information at all times during the task.

In the fluency task, workers are shown only the verbalisation and are asked to rate its fluency with a score from 0 to 5, 0 being the worst and 5 being the best. In the adequacy task, workers are shown both the verbalisation and the claim, as well as labels, aliases, and descriptions, and are asked whether they convey the same information. They can reply *Yes* (giving it a score of 0), *No* (score of 1), and *Not Sure* (score of 2). Answering *No* and *Not Sure* prompts a question as to the reason; workers can blame the verbalisation, each component in the triple, a combination, or select *Other* and give a new justification. These tasks were released on AMT after receiving ethical approval.

Quality Control. Multiple quality control techniques were applied. The small randomized grammar quiz at the start of the task serves as an attention check, discouraging spammers. Our gold data is used to measure worker quality during the task, alongside other checks such as time spent per pair and whether all questions were answered. Failing these checks alerts the user and asks them to reevaluate their annotations. Failing three times closes the task without submission. Workers are told these details before engaging with the task.

Task Code and Raw Data. All the code and data for our crowdsourcing are in this paper's GitHub repository, including detailed descriptions of each task's

---

[6] https://turkerview.com/.

execution and the exact HTML code sent to each anonymous worker alongside instructions, agreement terms, and examples. It also includes all retrieved data before it was processed and aggregated back into WDV.

3.4 WDV Composition

WDV consists of a large partially annotated dataset of over 7.6k entries that align a broad collection of Wikidata claims with their respective verbalisations. An example of an annotated record can be seen in Fig. 2. The attributes seen there consist of: attributes describing the claim, such as its Wikidata ID (*claim_id*) and its *rank* (normal, deprecated or preferred); attributes from the claim's components (subject, predicate, and object), including their Wikidata IDs (e.g. *subject_id*), labels (e.g. *subject_label*), descriptions (e.g. *subject_desc*), and aliases (e.g. *subject_alias*); a JSON representation of the *object* alongside its type (*object_datatype*) as defined by Wikidata; attributes from the claim's theme such as its root class' Wikidata ID (theme_root_class_id) and label (theme_label); the aligned *verbalisation*, before and after replacement of tokens unknown to the model (*verbalisation_unk_replaced*); the *sampling weight* from the stratified sampling process; and the crowdsourced *annotations* and their aggregations, for those entries (∼1.4k) that are annotated.

Our schema is different from the Wikipedia dumps' JSON schema. Firstly, the latter is entity-centered: each entry is an entity and claims are components hierarchically encoded as elements. As WDV is centered on claim-verbalisation alignments, we flatten this structure. Secondly, information on the claims' components is spread over their respective JSON objects. Our schema organises all relevant data about the claim-verbalisation pair in a single JSON object.

WDV is a 3 star dataset according to the 5 star deployment scheme for Linked Data.[7] It is available on the web in a structured, machine-readable, and non-proprietary format. Making it 4 star by converting it into RDF is our immediate next step. Wikidata already has a well-documented RDF representation schema,[8] reified based on n-ary relationships [7]. We will make use of this schema to express the data about the claim and its components (e.g. ids, rank, labels, descriptions, values, etc.), as they are already explicitly supported by it, and it is an effective way to represent Wikidata in RDF [17]. We will then complement it with custom vocabulary in order to express the verbalisations and their crowdsourced annotations. We can do this by linking the statements, expressed in Wikidata's RDF schema as nodes, to a verbalisation node through a `wdv:verbalisation` predicate, which then is linked to its crowdsourced annotations through fitting predicates, e.g. `wdv:fluencyScore` and `wdv:adequacyScore`. We can also reuse existing vocabularies, such as LIME [9]).

Table 2 shows a breakdown of WDV. In the first column, we can identify the SEEN and UNSEEN partitions from WebNLG, as well as our added WD_-UNSEEN partition built from other Wikidata classes. The second column divides

---

[7] https://www.w3.org/2011/gld/wiki/5_Star_Linked_Data.

[8] https://www.mediawiki.org/wiki/Wikibase/Indexing/RDF_Dump_Format.

```
{    "claim_id": "Q55425899$D1CB6CEC-33E4-41DF-9244-3277C2BE1FA5"
     "rank" : "normal",
     "subject_id" : "Q55425899",
     "property_id" : "P6216",
     "subject_label" : "Spring in Jølster",
     "property_label" : "copyright status",
     "object_label" : "public domain",
     "subject_desc" : "painting by Nikolai Astrup",
     "property_desc" : "copyright status for intellectual creations like
     ↪ works of art, publications, software, etc.",
     "object_desc" : "works that are no longer in copyright term or were
     ↪ never protected by copyright law",
     "subject_alias" : "no-alias",
     "property_alias" : ["copyright restriction"],
     "object_alias" : ["PD", "out of copyright", "DP"],
     "object_datatype" : "wikibase-item",
     "object" : { "value": {"entity-type": "item", "numeric-id": 19652,
     ↪ "id": 'Q19652'}, "type": "wikibase-entityid" },
     "theme_root_class_id" : "Q3305213",
     "theme_label" : "Painting",
     "verbalisation" : "Spring in J <unk> lster is in the public domain.",
     "verbalisation_unk_replaced" : "Spring in Jølster is in the public
     ↪ domain.",
     "sampling_weight" : 3538.615384615385,
     "annotations": { "fluency_scores" : [5, 4, 4, 2, 1],
                      "fluency_mean" : 3.2,
                      "fluency_median" : 4.0,
                      "adequacy_scores" : [0, 0, 1, 0, 0],
                      "adequacy_majority_voted" : 0,
                      "adequacy_percentage" : 0.8 }
}
```

Fig. 2. Example of an annotated record from WDV in JSON format

them into component themes (or pools of claims). For each theme, it then shows the number of unique properties (predicates), unique claims (calculated as N_t, as described in Sect. 3.1), and how many were annotated.

3.5   Crowd Data and Risk Analysis

Crowdsourced annotations were aggregated and added to WDV as attributes, as depicted in Sect. 3.4. In this section, we analyse these aggregated annotations and draw conclusions on the quality and reliability of WDV.

Aggregation and Reliability. Fluency scores were aggregated by calculating both median and mean, in case more or less weight, respectively, needs to be given to workers who disagree greatly with their peers. Adequacy was aggregated by majority voting, and also by calculating the percentage of workers that voted *Yes*, which we call *adequacy percentage*.

Table 2. Total number of unique properties, unique claims, and annotated claims, per partition and themes in WDV.

Partition	Theme	Properties	Claims	Annotated claims
WebNLG_SEEN	Airport	27	382	76
	Astronaut	57	351	71
	Building	67	385	63
	City	72	383	73
	ComicsCharacter	79	376	76
	Food	64	368	67
	Monument	62	380	51
	SportsTeam	49	383	75
	University	62	378	75
	WrittenWork	21	385	66
WebNLG_UNSEEN	Artist	65	384	78
	Athlete	53	385	80
	CelestialBody	25	385	83
	MeanOfTransportation	58	376	71
	Politician	56	385	75
WD_UNSEEN	ChemicalCompound	33	383	81
	Mountain	23	380	69
	Painting	29	385	50
	Street	21	384	66
	Taxon	27	385	80
ALL	ALL	439	7607	1426

Fluency has been fair to very high in most verbalisations. A fluency score of 3 indicates "Comprehensible text with minor grammatical errors", and over 96% of verbalisations find themselves with median fluency equal to or above 3. This shows our verbalisation model produces fluent text from Wikidata triples. The model also maintains very well the meaning of Wikidata claims after verbalising. Almost 93% of verbalisations are majority-voted as adequate.

The reliability of aggregated crowdsourced data can be indicated by statistical inter-annotator agreement metrics [26] such as Krippendorff's Alpha [16]. The alpha measured for the fluency scores is 0.4272, and for the adequacy scores it is 0.4583; both indicate moderate agreement, according to the interpretations recommended by Landis & Koch [21].

Variations in Scores and Agreement. Next, we see how fluency, adequacy, and agreement might vary across the partitions and themes shown in Table 2.

We can calculate fluency and adequacy scores for each theme by making use of the sampling weights, accounting for any bias introduced by stratification. Figure 3a shows the adjusted median fluency per theme: all have from fair (above 3) to excellent (above 4) fluency, with complex and scientific themes in the lower half. Figure 3b shows the adjusted adequacy percentage per theme, ranging from 85.7% to 99.8%.

For a bigger-picture view, we calculate the average aggregated fluency and adequacy per partition. This does not consider the sampling weights, as they are not translatable across differently stratified populations. In all aggregated metrics (i.e. mean fluency, median fluency, adequacy percentage, and majority-voted adequacy) WebNLG_SEEN performs the best, followed by WebNLG_UNSEEN, and then WD_UNSEEN. Exact metrics can be seen in Table 3. This is in line with how the model was trained and validated. However, the differences are small, signalling excellent generalisation to themes unseen both in training and validation, and also whose provenance is from an entirely different KG.

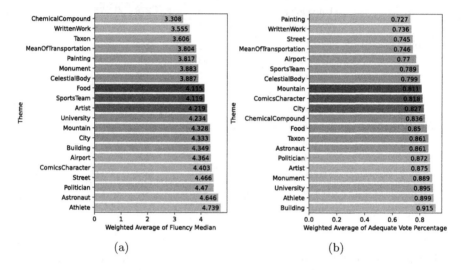

(a)   (b)

Fig. 3. Median fluency (a) and adequacy percentage (b) per theme after adjusting for stratification by considering sampling weights.

Table 3. Aggregated scores and agreement per partition. Mean fluency, median fluency and adequacy percentage were averaged. Majority-Adequate Perc. is the percentage of claims whose majority-voted adequacy score was *Yes*.

	WD_UNSEEN	WebNLG_UNSEEN	WebNLG_SEEN
Mean fluency	3.684	3.884	3.91
Median fluency	3.848	4.103	4.148
Adequacy percentage	80.3%	80.6%	82%
Majority-adequate perc.	92.5%	92.8%	93.1%
Fluency scores agreement	0.466761	0.508015	0.496089
Adequacy scores agreement	0.659174	0.649527	0.654175

We calculate the agreement for each theme and partition. All themes show agreement above 0.4 on the fluency task, and above 0.6 on the adequacy task.

Fluency and adequacy agreement metrics per theme have a substantial correlation (0.63 Pearson correlation). Agreement did not vary substantially between partitions (see Table 3), showing that whether or not the model was trained or validated on a partition did not impact the workers' abilities to judge it.

4   Verbalisation Model

Our dataset relies on a pre-trained and fine-tuned data verbalisation model for its text alignment. In this section, we describe the model we have chosen and all reasons for it, as well as its training approach and hyperparameters used. We finish by evaluating its fitness for use with examples from our dataset.

4.1   Approach, Training, and Validation

Many state-of-the-art KG data verbalisation models take the graph structure into consideration [10,35,44]. GTR-LSTM [35] and DualEnc [44] both encode the graph by combining graph neural networks and recurrent sequential neural networks. Working with single-claim data, we do not need to maintain the graph's structure. Large pre-trained language models have achieved state-of-the-art results when fine-tuned and evaluated on WebNLG [14,15,32], mainly the T5 [29]. They can disregard most structure and can be applied to one or many claims at a time. Hence, we utilise the T5 (base version) as our verbalisation model, following training and evaluation methods from these works.

The T5 converts input text into output text based on a given task, such as summarisation, specified through natural language as a prefix to the input. It can also learn new tasks by being fine-tuned with new data and a new prefix [29]. Our model has been fine-tuned on WebNLG [12]. The SEEN partition is used for both training and validation/testing, while the UNSEEN partition is kept for testing only. We follow the training setup from Ribeiro et al. [32] by specifying a new prefix "translate from Graph to Text" and adding three new tokens ($\langle H \rangle$, $\langle R \rangle$, and $\langle T \rangle$) that precede the claim's subject, predicate, and object, respectively.

Each entry in the training data consists of a set aligning multiple triples to multiple sentences. We train the model by concatenating all triples in the set in a random order, marked with the new tokens, and choosing one of the verbalisations at random (as long as they were tagged as *good* by WebNLG).

Some of the hyperparameters used in the model were: a 3e-5 learning rate on a linear scheduler with no warmup steps, an Adam [19] optimiser with no weight decay and 1e-8 epsilon, a cross-entropy loss function, 100 epochs of training with early stopping patience of 15, batch size of four for both training and evaluation, and text generation was done via beam search with 3 beams. The T5 was obtained from HuggingFace [39] and trained with PyTorch Lightning [8]. A full list of hyperparameters is available in this paper's GitHub repository.

We benchmarked our model in two ways. Firstly, by evaluating aggregated crowdsourced metrics, covered in Sect. 3.5. Secondly, by calculating the BLEU score [27] for both the SEEN and UNSEEN partitions to make sure our model matches current state-of-the-art [32]. BLEU scores were calculated with Moses [20]. The model achieved 65.51 on SEEN, 51.71 on UNSEEN, and 59.41 on ALL. We refer to Ribeiro et al. [32] for a comparison with results from other methods.

4.2 Evaluation and Output Examples

Comparisons between the model employed by us (T5-base), other language models, and other mentioned approaches to verbalising the WebNLG dataset have been carried by other authors [2,32] and are out of the scope of our paper, as well as an analysis of language variability and complexity.

To evaluate our model's fitness for use, we will now look at cases in which it performed well and poorly for fluency or adequacy. This allows us to understand how the model could improve, and in which situations its use is and is not effective. Table 4 shows a few examples of the model's inputs and outputs.

Table 4. Examples of claims verbalised by the model. From left to right, we see: the claims, their components' labels, the verbalisations, and their aggregated metrics of fluency (median) and adequacy (adequacy percentage).

Subject	Predicate	Object	Verbalisation	Flu.	Ade.
Eve Towards the Light	Height	268 centimetre	Eve Towards the Light is 268 centimetres high	2.0	1.0
Bydgoszcz	Flag	Flag of Bydgoszcz	The flag of Bydgoszcz is the flag of Bydgoszcz	0.0	1.0
Marawi	Köppen climate classification	Tropical climate	City of the Philippines and capital of the province of Lanao del Sur	4.0	0.4
Decius	Child	Hostilian	Decius is a child of Hostilian	4.0	0.4
UCAC2 28288086	Surface gravity	9 centimetre per square second	UCAC2 28288086 has a surface gravity of 9 centimetres per square second	4.0	1.0
Casa Batlló	Fabrication method	Trencadís	Casa Batlló is made using the Trencadís method	5.0	0.8

We consider a low fluency score to be under 3, when grammatical errors are not minor or text is not comprehensible. Out of over 1.4k annotated claim-verbalisation pairs, 55 had low fluency. A considerable amount of them (41%) suffer due to subject or object labels having complex syntaxes, such as IUPAC chemical nomenclatures, names of astronomical bodies, and full titles of scientific papers. These are challenging both for the model and for workers with no context or knowledge of how to use these names in a sentence. This potential misinterpretation is evidenced by 38% of all low-fluency verbalisations being simply misinterpreted by the crowd; the sentences are fluent, but have non-trivial or non-English terms that throw workers off e.g. "Eve Towards the Light is 268 centimetres high", which describes a painting. Around a third (32%) of cases were the model's fault, either by failure to structure the predicate or by corrupting or inverting subject and object labels. However, 21% of cases could be solved by improving predicates and entity labels, or rethinking how information is stored in Wikidata; some predicates are vague or depend on qualifiers to make complete sense e.g. `inception` and `different from`, and some claims have redundant data e.g. "The flag of Bydgoszcz is the flag of Bydgoszcz".

Low adequacy is when the majority-voted option for adequacy was *No*. This corresponds to 78 verbalisations. Almost half (46.15%) consists of claims either for which the model could not properly structure the predicate e.g. "Köppen climate classification" or for which subject and predicate had complex or non-English labels. Over a third (38.4%) of these were adequate claims that were misunderstood by the crowd e.g. "Craig-y-llyn is designated as a Site of Special Scientific Interest". Somewhat often (17.9%), vague predicates and badly written labels were also to blame. Lastly, the model would sometimes (11.5%) either shift subject with object, infer information not seen in the claim (delusions), or translate words between English and German (one of T5's other learned tasks).

These cases show us that the verbalisation model can be improved either by design or through data curation. For instance, predicates that rely on qualifiers can have that information communicated to the model if the model can properly link them to specific components of the claim. We can avoid inversion of subject and object by adding direction either on the predicate labels (e.g. *child* to *has child*) or through the model's encoding. We managed to help the model understand certain predicates and entities by using alternative labels (e.g. *conflict* to *participated in conflict*), but which aliases to use is very context dependent.

Some issues are less trivial to address. Entities with syntactically complex labels hardly have simpler aliases. Vague predicates might be solved by using aliases, but this is extremely context-sensitive, and there might be good reasons why these predicates unite multiple senses under a common abstraction (e.g. `facet of` and `inception`). Finally, redundant information can emerge from Wikidata's predicates. For instance, an entity exists for the city of Bydgoszcz, and another for its flag, containing information such as its appearance. They are linked by the `flag` predicate. This makes ontological sense, but no verbal sense, as one would express this relationship as either "Bydgoszcz has a flag" or "Bydgoszcz's flag is Bydgoszcz's flag"; this is either redundant or inadequate.

5   Addressing Review Criteria

Here, we further strengthen the argument that the resources presented are not only of interest to Semantic Web researchers, but have a provable claim to adoption by them and the Wikidata research community. These resources support a line of research by the same authors on the quality of Wikidata references, which proposes crowdsourcing and computational methods to assess different dimensions of reference quality. The first part of the work assessed reference accessibility, relevance and authoritativeness based on features that are not directly related to the content of the reference themselves. It has been recently awarded the Wikimedia Research Paper of the Year 2022, from among 230 peer-reviewed papers. The judges highlighted the importance of the research problem (reference quality) and the value of the solution proposed, especially in a multilingual setting. WDV directly builds on top of this, by feeding into computational methods that allow us to assess reference quality also in terms of the actual content in the reference source. It has already made possible the authors' efforts toward automated fact verification in Wikidata.

Wikidata recognises references as essential in its own guidelines, stating that "Wikidata is not a database that stores facts about the world, but a secondary knowledge base that collects and links to references to such knowledge".[9] They promote reference quality assurance efforts, as many open phabricator tickets show.[10,11] The Wikidata editing community also discusses at length the need for automated techniques for reference quality assessment.[12,13]

6 Conclusion

In this paper, we have presented WDV: a large dataset for the verbalisation of single triple-based claims from Wikidata (a collaborative KG). It directly aligns claims to natural language sentences that aim at being grammatically well-written and transmitting the same meaning. WDV was created to provide a data-to-text resource that covers a wide range of entities, topics, and predicates in Wikidata. More importantly, it does so in a balanced manner, so that specific themes are not overly represented. We also presented and carried an evaluation workflow of the fluency and adequacy of its natural language sentences, concluding that they have very high levels of both metrics.

We believe this dataset constitutes a valuable step towards understanding how to efficiently carry the verbalisation of triple claims from Wikidata and KGs in general. Bridging the gap between labelled triple components and natural language is crucial to implementing downstream NLP tasks in the KG. One such task that can be helped immensely by this resource is the automated fact-checking of KG claims based on the textual information found in the references they cite. Finally, WDV, alongside the annotation workflow we have defined, can promote the evaluation, through a human perspective, of NLG models performances without relying on algorithmic metrics. WDV's construction process can also be extended to include languages other than English by using multilingual LMs and training data akin to WebNLG.

Acknowledgements. This research received funding from the European Union's Horizon 2020 research and innovation programme under the Marie Skłodowska-Curie grant agreement no. 812997.

---

[9] https://www.wikidata.org/wiki/Help:Statements.

[10] https://phabricator.wikimedia.org/T90881.

[11] https://phabricator.wikimedia.org/T156389.

[12] https://www.wikidata.org/wiki/Property_talk:P1456.

[13] https://www.wikidata.org/wiki/Wikidata:Project_chat/Archive/2017/10# Proposal_on_citation_overkill.

References

1. Amaral, G., Piscopo, A., Kaffee, L.A., Rodrigues, O., Simperl, E.: Assessing the Quality of sources in Wikidata across languages: a hybrid approach. J. Data Inf. Qual. **13**(4) (2021). https://doi.org/10.1145/3484828
2. Bosc, T., Cabrio, E., Villata, S.: DART: a dataset of arguments and their relations on Twitter. In: Proceedings of the Tenth International Conference on Language Resources and Evaluation (LREC 2016), pp. 1258–1263. European Language Resources Association (ELRA), Portorož, Slovenia, May 2016
3. Burnham, M.J., Le, Y.K., Piedmont, R.L.: Who is Mturk? Personal characteristics and sample consistency of these online workers. Mental Health Relig. Cult. **21**(9–10), 934–944 (2018). https://doi.org/10.1080/13674676.2018.1486394
4. Difallah, D., Filatova, E., Ipeirotis, P.: Demographics and dynamics of mechanical turk workers. In: Proceedings of the Eleventh ACM International Conference on Web Search and Data Mining, pp. 135–143. WSDM 2018. Association for Computing Machinery, New York, NY, USA (2018). https://doi.org/10.1145/3159652. 3159661
5. Ellis, J., Getman, J., Graff, D., Strassel, S.: TAC KBP Comprehensive English Source Corpora 2009–2014 (2018). https://doi.org/11272.1/AB2/VC89SM
6. Elsahar, H., et al.: T-REx: a large scale alignment of natural language with knowledge base triples. In: Proceedings of the Eleventh International Conference on Language Resources and Evaluation (LREC 2018). European Language Resources Association (ELRA), Miyazaki, Japan, May 2018
7. Erxleben, F., Günther, M., Krötzsch, M., Mendez, J., Vrandečić, D.: Introducing Wikidata to the linked data web. In: Mika, P., et al. (eds.) ISWC 2014. LNCS, vol. 8796, pp. 50–65. Springer, Cham (2014). https://doi.org/10.1007/978-3-319-11964-9_4
8. Falcon, W.: The PyTorch Lightning team: PyTorch Lightning, March 2019. https://doi.org/10.5281/zenodo.3828935, https://github.com/Lightning-AI/lightning
9. Fiorelli, M., Stellato, A., McCrae, J.P., Cimiano, P., Pazienza, M.T.: LIME: The metadata module for OntoLex. In: Gandon, F., Sabou, M., Sack, H., d'Amato, C., Cudré-Mauroux, P., Zimmermann, A. (eds.) The Semantic Web. Latest Advances and New Domains, pp. 321–336. Springer International Publishing, Cham (2015). https://doi.org/10.1007/978-3-319-18818-8_20
10. Gao, H., Wu, L., Hu, P., Xu, F.: RDF-to-Text generation with graph-augmented structural neural encoders. In: Bessiere, C. (ed.) Proceedings of the Twenty-Ninth International Joint Conference on Artificial Intelligence, IJCAI-20, pp. 3030–3036. International Joint Conferences on Artificial Intelligence Organization, July 2020. https://doi.org/10.24963/ijcai.2020/419, main track
11. Gardent, C., Shimorina, A., Narayan, S., Perez-Beltrachini, L.: Creating training corpora for NLG micro-planners. In: Proceedings of the 55th Annual Meeting of the Association for Computational Linguistics (Volume 1: Long Papers), pp. 179–188. Association for Computational Linguistics, Vancouver, Canada, July 2017. https://doi.org/10.18653/v1/P17-1017
12. Gardent, C., Shimorina, A., Narayan, S., Perez-Beltrachini, L.: Creating training corpora for NLG micro-planners. In: Proceedings of the 55th Annual Meeting of the Association for Computational Linguistics (Volume 1: Long Papers), pp. 179–188. Association for Computational Linguistics, Vancouver, Canada, July 2017. https://doi.org/10.18653/v1/P17-1017

13. Gebru, T., Morgenstern, J., Vecchione, B., Vaughan, J.W., Wallach, H., au2, H.D.I., Crawford, K.: Datasheets for Datasets (2020)
14. Guo, Q., et al.: P^2: a plan-and-pretrain approach for knowledge graph-to-text generation. In: Proceedings of the 3rd International Workshop on Natural Language Generation from the Semantic Web (WebNLG+), pp. 100–106. Association for Computational Linguistics, Dublin, Ireland (Virtual), December 2020. https://aclanthology.org/2020.webnlg-1.10
15. Harkous, H., Groves, I., Saffari, A.: Have your text and use it too! End-to-End neural data-to-text generation with semantic fidelity. In: Proceedings of the 28th International Conference on Computational Linguistics, pp. 2410–2424. International Committee on Computational Linguistics, Barcelona, Spain (Online), December 2020. https://doi.org/10.18653/v1/2020.coling-main.218
16. Hayes, A.F., Krippendorff, K.: Answering the call for a standard reliability measure for coding data. Commun. Methods Meas. **1**(1), 77–89 (2007). https://doi.org/10.1080/19312450709336664
17. Hernández, D., Hogan, A., Krötzsch, M.: Reifying RDF: What works well with Wikidata? In: SSWS@ISWC (2015)
18. Huff, C., Tingley, D.: "Who are these people?" Evaluating the demographic characteristics and political preferences of MTurk survey respondents. Res. Polit. **2**(3) (2015). https://doi.org/10.1177/2053168015604648
19. Kingma, D.P., Ba, J.: Adam: a method for stochastic optimization. CoRR abs/1412.6980 (2015)
20. Koehn, P., et al.: Moses: open source toolkit for statistical machine translation. In: Proceedings of the 45th Annual Meeting of the Association for Computational Linguistics Companion Volume Proceedings of the Demo and Poster Sessions, pp. 177–180. Association for Computational Linguistics, Prague, Czech Republic, June 2007
21. Landis, J.R., Koch, G.G.: The measurement of observer agreement for categorical data. Biometrics **33**(1), 159–174 (1977). http://www.jstor.org/stable/2529310
22. van der Lee, C., Gatt, A., van Miltenburg, E., Krahmer, E.: Human evaluation of automatically generated text: current trends and best practice guidelines. Comput. Speech Lang. **67**, 101151 (2021). https://doi.org/10.1016/j.csl.2020.101151
23. Ma, K., Cheng, H., Liu, X., Nyberg, E., Gao, J.: Open Domain Question Answering over Virtual Documents: A Unified Approach for Data and Text (2021)
24. Mintz, M., Bills, S., Snow, R., Jurafsky, D.: Distant supervision for relation extraction without labeled data. In: Proceedings of the Joint Conference of the 47th Annual Meeting of the ACL and the 4th International Joint Conference on Natural Language Processing of the AFNLP, pp. 1003–1011. Association for Computational Linguistics, Suntec, Singapore, August 2009. https://aclanthology.org/P09-1113
25. Novikova, J., Dušek, O., Curry, A.C., Rieser, V.: Why we need new evaluation metrics for NLG. In: Proceedings of the 2017 Conference on Empirical Methods in Natural Language Processing, pp. 2241–2252. Association for Computational Linguistics, Copenhagen, Denmark, September 2017. https://doi.org/10.18653/v1/D17-1238
26. Nowak, S., Rüger, S.: How reliable are annotations via crowdsourcing: a study about inter-annotator agreement for multi-label image annotation. In: Proceedings of the International Conference on Multimedia Information Retrieval, pp. 557–566. MIR 2010. Association for Computing Machinery, New York, NY, USA (2010). https://doi.org/10.1145/1743384.1743478

27. Papineni, K., Roukos, S., Ward, T., Zhu, W.J.: BLEU: a method for automatic evaluation of machine translation. In: Proceedings of the 40th Annual Meeting on Association for Computational Linguistics, pp. 311–318. ACL 2002 (2002). https://doi.org/10.3115/1073083.1073135
28. Tanon, T.P., Vrandečić, D., Schaffert, S., Steiner, T., Pintscher, L.: From freebase to Wikidata: the great migration. In: Proceedings of the 25th International Conference on World Wide Web, pp. 1419–1428. WWW 2016, International World Wide Web Conferences Steering Committee, Republic and Canton of Geneva, CHE (2016). https://doi.org/10.1145/2872427.2874809
29. Raffel, C., et al.: Exploring the Limits of Transfer Learning with a Unified Text-to-Text Transformer. CoRR abs/1910.10683 (2019). http://arxiv.org/abs/1910.10683
30. Ramírez, J., et al.: On the state of reporting in crowdsourcing experiments and a checklist to aid current practices. Proc. ACM Hum.-Comput. Interact. **5**(CSCW2) (2021). https://doi.org/10.1145/3479531
31. Reiter, E.: A structured review of the validity of BLEU. Comput. Linguist. **44**(3), 393–401 (2018). https://doi.org/10.1162/coli_a_00322
32. Ribeiro, L.F.R., Schmitt, M., Schütze, H., Gurevych, I.: Investigating pretrained language models for graph-to-text generation. In: Proceedings of the 3rd Workshop on Natural Language Processing for Conversational AI, pp. 211–227. Association for Computational Linguistics, Online, November 2021. https://aclanthology.org/2021.nlp4convai-1.20
33. Sulem, E., Abend, O., Rappoport, A.: BLEU is not suitable for the evaluation of text simplification. In: Proceedings of the 2018 Conference on Empirical Methods in Natural Language Processing, pp. 738–744. Association for Computational Linguistics, Brussels, Belgium, October 2018. https://doi.org/10.18653/v1/D18-1081
34. Toutanova, K., Chen, D.: Observed versus latent features for knowledge base and text inference (2015)
35. Trisedya, B.D., Qi, J., Zhang, R., Wang, W.: GTR-LSTM: a triple encoder for sentence generation from RDF data. In: Proceedings of the 56th Annual Meeting of the Association for Computational Linguistics (Volume 1: Long Papers), pp. 1627–1637. Association for Computational Linguistics, Melbourne, Australia, July 2018. https://doi.org/10.18653/v1/P18-1151
36. Vlachos, A., Riedel, S.: Identification and verification of simple claims about statistical properties. In: Proceedings of the 2015 Conference on Empirical Methods in Natural Language Processing, pp. 2596–2601. Association for Computational Linguistics, Lisbon, Portugal, September 2015. https://doi.org/10.18653/v1/D15-1312
37. Vougiouklis, P., et al.: Neural Wikipedian: generating textual summaries from knowledge base triples. J. Web Semant. **52–53**, 1–15 (2018). https://doi.org/10.1016/j.websem.2018.07.002
38. Vougiouklis, P., Maddalena, E., Hare, J., Simperl, E.: Point at the triple: generation of text summaries from knowledge base triples (extended abstract). In: Bessiere, C. (ed.) Proceedings of the Twenty-Ninth International Joint Conference on Artificial Intelligence, IJCAI-20, pp. 5080–5084. International Joint Conferences on Artificial Intelligence Organization, July 2020. https://doi.org/10.24963/ijcai.2020/711, journal track
39. Wolf, T., et al.: Transformers: state-of-the-art natural language processing. In: Proceedings of the 2020 Conference on Empirical Methods in Natural Language Processing: System Demonstrations, pp. 38–45. Association for Computational Linguistics, Online, October 2020

40. Yang, X., Nie, F., Feng, Y., Liu, Q., Chen, Z., Zhu, X.: Program Enhanced fact verification with verbalization and graph attention network. In: Proceedings of the 2020 Conference on Empirical Methods in Natural Language Processing (EMNLP), pp. 7810–7825. Association for Computational Linguistics, Online, November 2020. https://doi.org/10.18653/v1/2020.emnlp-main.628

41. Yang, X., Zhu, X.: Exploring Decomposition for Table-based Fact Verification (2021)

42. Yao, L., Haghighi, A., Riedel, S., McCallum, A.: Structured relation discovery using generative models. In: Proceedings of the 2011 Conference on Empirical Methods in Natural Language Processing, pp. 1456–1466. Association for Computational Linguistics, Edinburgh, Scotland, UK, July 2011. https://aclanthology.org/D11-1135

43. Zhang, Y., Zhong, V., Chen, D., Angeli, G., Manning, C.D.: Position-aware attention and supervised data improve slot filling. In: Proceedings of the 2017 Conference on Empirical Methods in Natural Language Processing, pp. 35–45. Association for Computational Linguistics, Copenhagen, Denmark, September 2017. https://doi.org/10.18653/v1/D17-1004

44. Zhao, C., Walker, M., Chaturvedi, S.: Bridging the structural gap between encoding and decoding for data-to-text generation. In: Proceedings of the 58th Annual Meeting of the Association for Computational Linguistics, pp. 2481–2491. Association for Computational Linguistics, Online, July 2020. https://doi.org/10.18653/v1/2020.acl-main.224

Machine Learning-Friendly Biomedical Datasets for Equivalence and Subsumption Ontology Matching

Yuan He[1]([⊠]) , Jiaoyan Chen[1] , Hang Dong[1] , Ernesto Jiménez-Ruiz[2,3] , Ali Hadian[4], and Ian Horrocks[1]

[1] Department of Computer Science, University of Oxford, Oxford, UK
{yuan.he,jiaoyan.chen,hang.dong,ian.horrocks}@cs.ox.ac.uk
[2] City, University of London, London, UK
ernesto.jimenez-ruiz@city.ac.uk
[3] University of Oslo, Oslo, Norway
[4] Samsung Research, Staines, UK
a.hadian@samsung.com

Abstract. Ontology Matching (OM) plays an important role in many domains such as bioinformatics and the Semantic Web, and its research is becoming increasingly popular, especially with the application of machine learning (ML) techniques. Although the Ontology Alignment Evaluation Initiative (OAEI) represents an impressive effort for the systematic evaluation of OM systems, it still suffers from several limitations including limited evaluation of subsumption mappings, suboptimal reference mappings, and limited support for the evaluation of ML-based systems. To tackle these limitations, we introduce five new biomedical OM tasks involving ontologies extracted from Mondo and UMLS. Each task includes both equivalence and subsumption matching; the quality of reference mappings is ensured by human curation, ontology pruning, etc.; and a comprehensive evaluation framework is proposed to measure OM performance from various perspectives for both ML-based and non-ML-based OM systems. We report evaluation results for OM systems of different types to demonstrate the usage of these resources, all of which are publicly available as part of the new BIO-ML track at OAEI 2022.
Resource type: Ontology Matching Dataset
License: CC BY 4.0 International
DOI: https://doi.org/10.5281/zenodo.6510086
Documentation: https://krr-oxford.github.io/DeepOnto/#/om_resources
OAEI track: https://www.cs.ox.ac.uk/isg/projects/ConCur/oaei/

Keywords: Ontology Alignment · Equivalence matching · Subsumption matching · Evaluation resource · Biomedical ontology · OAEI

© The Author(s), under exclusive license to Springer Nature Switzerland AG 2022
U. Sattler et al. (Eds.): ISWC 2022, LNCS 13489, pp. 575–591, 2022.
https://doi.org/10.1007/978-3-031-19433-7_33

1   Introduction

Ontology Alignment (a.k.a. Ontology Matching (OM)) is the task of identifying inter-ontology entity pairs that are semantically related. A primary OM setting is matching *named classes* with semantic *equivalence* or *subsumption* relationships, with the aim of integrating knowledge from different ontologies. A matched pair of named classes is known as an equivalence or subsumption mapping. A successful OM case study is the Mondo Disease Ontology[1] [27], which integrates disease concepts from various biomedical ontologies through mappings. OM can also support interoperability among ontologies, and help to construct a unified terminology that extends the coverage of each individual ontology. For example, given two classes about "Desosom" in the FMA (Foundational Model of Anatomy) ontology and the SNOMED CT (SNOMED Clinical Terms) ontology that are matched with equivalence, the subclass of the "Desosom" class named "Autodesosome" in FMA can be further inferred as a subclass of the "Desosom" class in SNOMED CT, thus augmenting SNOMED CT with more fine-grained knowledge. However, as ontologies evolve over time and become larger, it is unfeasible to have human beings annotating all the mappings; hence (semi-)automatic OM systems are urgently needed [28].

Classical OM systems typically exploit text (e.g., labels and synonyms), structure (e.g., class hierarchies), and/or logical inference for class matching, and focus mostly on equivalence mappings. For example, LogMap [15] iteratively conducts lexical matching, structure-based mapping extension and logic-based mapping repair; while AML [9] implements a matcher that considers various string-based heuristics, followed by mapping extension and repair. Recently, machine learning (ML)-based OM systems have become increasingly popular as they can go beyond surface-form string comparison by encoding ontology entities into vectors. For example, DeepAlignment [17] adopts *counter-fitting* to refine word embeddings for better representation of class labels; VeeAlign [14] proposes a *dual encoder* to encode both textual and path information of classes; and BERTMap [12] derives mappings through dynamic contextual text embeddings from the pre-trained language model BERT.

For evaluation, the Ontology Alignment Evaluation Initiative[2] (OAEI) has been organizing a yearly evaluation campaign including several tracks (datasets) mainly comparing Precision, Recall, and F-score. Meanwhile, some recent OM studies, especially the ML-based ones, have proposed non-standard metrics and/or datasets with very incomplete gold standards. For example, Chen et al. used LogMap-ML [6] to match the food ontology FoodOn with the health and lifestyle ontology HeLiS, and measured approximate Precision and Recall based on partial reference mappings, sampling and manual checking; and Neutel and de Boer [21] measured coverage and MRR (Mean Reciprocal Rank) on industrial data with human judgement.

---

[1] https://mondo.monarchinitiative.org/.

[2] http://oaei.ontologymatching.org/.

Despite the impressive community effort around the OAEI, the evaluation campaign still suffers from several limitations:

1. **Limited evaluation metrics.** The prevalent evaluation metrics, Precision, Recall, and F-score, are of limited value when the reference mappings are incomplete, and can even stifle development by penalising advanced systems with high Recall that find correct mappings that are missing from the reference set. Some other metrics, such as approximate Precision and Recall based on sampling and human checking [6] or based on consensus by multiple systems [11], and Accuracy on distinguishing one positive mapping from few loosely constructed negative mappings [22], may also be inaccurate and/or not sufficiently general.

2. **Suboptimal reference mappings.** The reference mappings of many OM datasets are quite incomplete and/or incorrect. Such mappings are sometimes called *silver standards* to distinguish them from (supposedly) complete gold standard mappings. The use of silver standards often leads to unfair comparisons among OM systems. For example, DeepAlignment [17] exhibited better performance than LogMap and AML when evaluated using silver standard mappings between the Schema.org and DBPedia ontologies. In this study AML achieved zero Recall, but closer examination of the results reveals that it actually retrieved some reasonable mappings that were not in the reference set. In the OAEI LargeBio track, some reference mappings are removed (or marked as "ignore") by an algorithm that repairs logical unsatisfiability resulting from the integration of the relevant ontologies [23]; however, the mappings may still be correct according to human experts.

3. **Ignoring subsumption mappings.** The majority of existing resources are for equivalence matching. However, there are often more subsumption mappings than equivalence mappings between real-world ontologies, and the former could play an important role in knowledge integration and ontology curation. With the blooming research and application of ML and text understanding techniques, systems for subsumption matching (e.g., BERTSubs [4]) will likely become more feasible and widely investigated.

4. **Lack of support for ML-based Systems.** Most existing OM resources, including OAEI tracks, are not well suited to ML-based systems. They often do not consider hold-out validation sets required for tuning hyper-parameters (even non-ML-based systems may need such a validation set for adjusting parameters) and/or for training in supervised or semi-supervised settings. Moreover, during the development of an ML-based system, Precision, Recall and F-score are not very useful, because computing the full output mappings is rather time-consuming and often does not directly reflect the capabilities of different ML modules or settings. Ranking-based metrics are more suitable for ML development and are widely used in investigations of ML tasks such as knowledge graph completion [18,25], but they are rarely considered in the OM community. These issues often lead to non-standardized and inconvenient evaluation set-ups for ML-based OM systems.

To address the aforementioned issues, in this paper, we present new large-scale OM resources based on Mondo and UMLS (Unified Medical Language System)[3], and propose a unified evaluation framework suitable for both ML-based and non-ML-based OM systems. This OM resource and evaluation framework is the basis for a new BIO-ML track in the OAEI 2022 campaign, which should be especially useful in attracting ML-based OM systems. With Mondo, we create two OM tasks involving the OMIM (Online Mendelian Inheritance in Man), ORDO (Orphanet Rare Disease Ontology), NCIT (National Cancer Institute Thesaurus) and DOID (Human Disease Ontology) ontologies, which are tailored to the disease domain with high quality mappings curated by human experts. With UMLS, we use the semantic types (categories) of UMLS concepts to create multiple category-relevant tasks that involve the SNOMED CT, FMA, and NCIT ontologies. Briefly, our contributions can be summarized as follows:

1. We have constructed an OM resource from Mondo which includes high quality manually curated mappings for the disease domain.
2. We propose ontology *pruning* to *(i)* improve the relative completeness of reference mappings w.r.t. the pruned ontologies, and *(ii)* obtain ontologies of various sizes to evaluate OM systems with different computational characteristics. In particular, for UMLS ontologies, we present a semantic-type-based pruning method for category-specific ontologies.
3. We have developed an approach to generate reference subsumption mappings from reference equivalence mappings. By deleting the classes involved in a given equivalence mapping, we ensure that the resulting subsumption mapping cannot be directly inferred from the equivalence mapping.
4. We have formulated a unified evaluation framework which includes MRR (Mean Reciprocal Rank) and Hits@K as *local ranking* metrics, which measure a system's ability to distinguish correct mappings from (non-trivial) false mappings; and Precision, Recall and F-score as *global matching* metrics, which compare a system's final output mappings with the reference mappings. Our framework also includes standard data splitting: mappings are divided into validation and testing sets for unsupervised systems, and into training, validation and testing sets for (semi-)supervised systems.
5. We present preliminary evaluation results on our datasets for multiple OM systems of different types.

All the resources are open access, and we are setting up a new BIO-ML track within OAEI 2022 to promote their use and to attract more participation from the ML community.

2   Resource Construction

In this section, we introduce how our OM resources are constructed from the original ontology data shown in Table 1. The resulting equivalence and subsumption matching datasets are presented in Table 2 and 3, respectively.

---

[3] https://www.nlm.nih.gov/research/umls/index.html.

Table 1. Information of the source ontologies used for creating the OM resources.

Mapping source	Ontology	Ontology source & Version	#Classes
Mondo	OMIM	Mondo[a]	44,729
	ORDO	BioPortal, V3.2	14,886
	NCIT	BioPortal, V18.05d	140,144
	DOID	BioPortal, 2017-11-28	12,498
UMLS	SNOMED	UMLS, US.2021.09.01[b]	358,222
	FMA	BioPortal, V4.14.0	104,523
	NCIT	BioPortal, V21.02d	163,842

[a]Created from OMIM texts by Mondo's pipeline tool available at: https://github.com/monarch-initiative/omim.
[b]Created by the official snomed-owl-toolkit available at: https://github.com/IHTSDO/snomed-owl-toolkit, which keeps 350K classes of all the 490K classes in the original SNOMED CT.

Table 2. Statistics of each Mondo or UMLS equivalence matching task (dataset), including its two ontologies, its category (semantic type) for ontology pruning, its scale (named class and reference mapping sizes), the numbers of class annotations like labels, synonyms and definitions, and the average depth of named classes (depth is the minimum number of subclass hops from a named class to owl:Thing)). "Body", "Pharm", and "Neoplas" denote semantic types of "Body Part, Organ, or Organ Components", "Pharmacologic Substance", and "Neoplastic Process" in UMLS, respectively.

	Ontology pair	Category	#Classes	#Refs ($\equiv$)	#Annot.	AvgDepths
Mondo	OMIM-ORDO	Disease	9,642–8,838	3,721	34K–34K	1.44–1.63
	NCIT-DOID	Disease	6,835–8,848	4,684	80K–38K	2.04–6.85
UMLS	SNOMED-FMA	Body	24,182–64,726	7,256	39K–711K	1.86–9.32
	SNOMED-NCIT	Pharm	16,045–15,250	5,803	19K–220K	1.09–3.26
	SNOMED-NCIT	Neoplas	11,271–13,956	3,804	23K–182K	1.15–1.68

Table 3. Statistics of each Mondo or UMLS subsumption matching task (dataset), including its two ontologies, its category (semantic type) for ontology pruning, its scales (named class and mapping sizes). Note that **#Classes** of the target ontology (right side) is smaller than the corresponding one in Table 2 as some classes are deleted when constructing subsumption mappings.

	Ontology pair	Category	#Classes	#Refs ($\sqsubseteq$)
Mondo	OMIM-ORDO	Disease	9,642–8,735	103
	NCIT-DOID	Disease	6,835–5,113	3,339
UMLS	SNOMED-FMA	Body	24,182–59,567	5,506
	SNOMED-NCIT	Pharm	16,045–12,462	4,225
	SNOMED-NCIT	Neoplas	11,271–13,790	213

2.1   Mondo Datasets

Our first two datasets are based on the cross-references in Mondo which is an integrated disease ontology with each of its classes matched to classes of some source ontologies [27]. When constructing Mondo, curators first gathered reference mappings from various sources such as UMLS, MeSH (Medical Subject Headings), ICD (International Classification of Diseases). These mappings are deemed as semantically loose because there is no guarantee that they can be merged into a logically coherent ontology. Curators then adopted an ontology construction tool named k-BOOM to merge various source ontologies based on logical reasoning and Bayesian inference [20], and further invited domain experts for manual correction. The merged ontology forms a more comprehensive terminology for rare diseases [10].

As suggested by the Mondo team, we selected two ontology pairs, OMIM-ORDO and NCIT-DOID, which are relatively up-to-date in Mondo. OMIM is the primary online source of genes, genetic phenotypes, and gene-phenotype relations, based on manual curation from biomedical literature [2]. The maximum class depth of the OMIM ontology is 2, making it a typical example of "flat" ontology. Such ontologies have limited structural information, thus posing challenges to OM systems. ORDO, the Orphanet Rare Disease Ontology, includes a classification of rare diseases and relationships between diseases, genes and epidemiologic features; the ontology is derived from the Orphanet database, which is populated by literature curation and validated by international experts [30]. Many rare diseases are genetic disorders, therefore ORDO has a prominent overlap with OMIM, which is cross-referenced in ORDO and integrated in Mondo. NCIT (or NCIt) is a large ontology composed of various cancer-related concepts including cancer diseases, findings, drugs, anatomy, abnormalities, etc. [29], therefore it has a relatively smaller overlap with Mondo. DOID (or DO) stands for Human Disease Ontology, a regularly maintained source of human diseases [26], and most of its concepts are incorporated in Mondo. Matching NCIT and DOID will, in principle, identify the shared cancer-related diseases. The versions of the selected ORDO, NCIT, and DOID ontologies (see Table 1) are the closest to the most recent update of the Mondo mappings, according to Mondo's documentation[4]. With the Mondo mapping data and these original ontologies, we create our OM datasets as follows:

Ontology Preprocessing. For each ontology, we conduct two preprocessing operations: *(i)* removing obsolete or deprecated classes because they usually have up-to-date alternatives or are not in use anymore; *(ii)* removing annotation properties that indicate cross-references to other data sources (e.g., `obo:hasDbXref`) because they could leak hints about the reference alignment to the OM systems. Unlike the OAEI LargeBio track where some annotation properties are selected

---

[4] Mondo was working on official versioning, the information of current mappings is based on the preliminary release at: https://github.com/monarch-initiative/mondo/tree/master/src/ontology/mappings.

and merged into `rdfs:label`, we keep the rest of annotation properties and leave their interpretation to the OM systems.

Ontology Pruning. Since the Mondo cross-references mainly aim at disease concepts, we prune each ontology by preserving disease classes and their contexts. Specifically, if a class c in an ontology is matched to a Mondo concept through the `skos:exactMatch` property, we preserve c; otherwise, we remove c as well as all the axioms involving c, and at the same time directly assert its children as subclasses of each of its parents for keeping the hierarchy. Pruning not only leads to OM tasks with ontologies of reasonable scale, but also improves the completeness of the reference mappings w.r.t. the pruned ontologies.

Equivalence Mapping Extraction. We extract equivalence mappings from the cross-references of each Mondo class, i.e., each pair of classes that are linked to the same Mondo class through the `skos:exactMatch` property is transformed to an equivalence mapping[5]. For example, `NCIT:C27518`[6] and `DOID:4321` form an equivalence mapping because they are both mapped to the Mondo concept, `MONDO:0002961` ("Large Cell Acanthoma").

Subsumption Mapping Extraction. We construct subsumption reference mappings based on the equivalence reference mappings. Given an equivalence mapping (c, c'), we extract a subsumption mapping (c, c'') where c'' is an asserted subsumer of c' in the ontology of c'. Taking the example of `DOID:4321` ("Large Cell Acanthoma"), which is equivalently matched to `NCIT:C27518`; since one of its parent classes is `DOID:174` ("Acanthoma"), a potential subsumption mapping is (`NCIT:C27518`, `DOID:174`). Note that both c and c' could have multiple asserted and inferred subsumers; considering all of them could lead to excessively many subsumption mappings for each equivalence mapping. Our solution simply selects one of the most specific subsumers of c'. This leads to challenging but incomplete subsumption mappings. Thus, when evaluating subsumption matching, we do not consider Recall (see Sect. 3). To evaluate a system's ability on directly inferring cross-ontology subsumptions, we prevent it from utilizing the original equivalence mapping (c, c') by deleting c'. As in ontology pruning, after deleting c', its parent classes are asserted to be subsumers of each of its child classes, so as to preserve the class hierarchy. It is possible that the deleted class appears in some other equivalence mappings to process, or some subsumption mappings that have been created. For the former, we skip such equivalence mappings, while for the later, we remove such subsumption mappings.

2.2   UMLS Datasets

UMLS is one of the most comprehensive mapping efforts, and integrates over 200 vocabularies to create a biomedical metathesaurus [3]. As an integrated ontology, it incorporates well-known ontologies such as SNOMED CT, FMA, NCIT,

---

[5] We exclude mappings involving missing class ids.
[6] Compact IRI of a class in the form of `ontology_prefix:class_ID`.

and GO (Gene Ontology). It describes millions of biomedical concepts, and relationships among them. Each concept is classified into one or more hierarchical *semantic types* (or categories) such as "Finding", "Chemicals", and "Substance".

To construct OM datasets from UMLS, we selected its latest version 2021AB at the time of doing experiments, and downloaded three of its corresponding ontologies—SNOMED CT, FMA and NCIT, all of which are large biomedical ontologies with over 100K named classes (see Table 1 for more information). SNOMED CT[7] has a more general and comprehensive coverage of clinical terms to support electronic healthcare systems and clinical applications [7,8], while FMA [24] and NCIT (as introduced previously) are mainly about human anatomy and cancer, respectively.

We first performed the same preprocessing as described in Sect. 2.1, and then established category-specific alignment tasks by pruning the ontologies via semantic types, i.e., we preserve classes of a chosen semantic type, delete the other classes, and preserve the hierarchy of the superclasses and subclasses of each deleted class as in ontology pruning for Mondo. The equivalence reference mappings are extracted from cross-ontology classes that are matched to the same UMLS concept [16], and the subsumption reference mappings are constructed from the equivalence mappings in the same way as for Mondo.

3   Evaluation Framework

We propose a comprehensive OM evaluation framework with different metrics of *local ranking* and *global matching* under both *unsupervised* (fully automatic) and *semi-supervised* settings. Metrics of local ranking are to measure a system's capability on distinguishing true mappings and (hard) false mappings; while metrics of global matching are to measure whether a system can output a set of mappings close to the reference mappings. The semi-supervised setting enables the evaluation of some ML-based systems that require training mappings.

3.1   Local Ranking

Given a reference mapping $m = (c, c')$, where c and c' are two classes from the to-be-aligned ontologies $\mathcal{O}$ and $\mathcal{O}'$, respectively, an OM system is required to distinguish m from its corresponding set of negative mappings (denoted as $\mathcal{M}_m$) by assigning m with a higher matching score. $\mathcal{M}_m := \{(c, c'')|c'' \in \mathcal{C}_{neg}\}$ is constructed by combining c with a set of mismatched (negative) candidate classes (denoted as $\mathcal{C}_{neg}$) from $\mathcal{O}'$. With the mapping scores, we adopt ranking-based evaluation metrics $Hits@K$ ($H@K$ in short) and MRR (Mean Reciprocal Rank), which are computed as follows:

$$Hits@K = \frac{|m \in \mathcal{M}_{ref} \mid Rank(m) \leq K)\}|}{|\mathcal{M}_{ref}|}$$

---

[7] The license to access UMLS is global and can be used to access SNOMED CT. We obtained SNOMED CT (and UMLS) after signing up to the UTS account and license following SNOMED and UMLS licensing in https://www.nlm.nih.gov/healthit/snomedct/snomed_licensing.html.

$$MRR = \frac{\sum_{m \in \mathcal{M}_{ref}} Rank(m)^{-1}}{|\mathcal{M}_{ref}|}$$

where $\mathcal{M}_{ref}$ denotes the set of reference mappings, $Rank(m)$ returns the ranking position of m among $\mathcal{M}_m \cup \{m\}$ according to their scores, K (often set to 1, 5 and 10) denotes the ranking position that is concerned. We could consider all the classes in $\mathcal{O}'$ for constructing $\mathcal{M}_m$, but this frequently results in excessive evaluation time, especially for large-scale ontologies. To ensure the evaluation efficiency, which is particularly important for ML-based model comparison/selection, we sample challenging negative candidates with heuristics introduced as follows.

Negative Candidate Generation. Given a reference mapping $m = (c, c')$, we consider three strategies to construct $\mathcal{C}_{neg}$ from $\mathcal{O}'$.

1. **IDFSample** (text similarity-based). This strategy is to introduce hard negative candidates that are ambiguous to the ground truth class at text level (i.e., with similar labels[8]). We first build a sub-word inverted index [12] for the labels of all the classes of $\mathcal{O}'$ using a sub-word tokenizer pre-trained on biomedical texts [1]. With this index, we select top-N classes from $\mathcal{O}'$ according to the *idf* (inverted document frequency) scores in descending order:

$$s(c', c'') = \sum_{t \in Tok(c') \cap Tok(c'')} \log_{10} \frac{|C'|}{|I(t)|}$$

   where $Tok(\cdot)$ gives all sub-word tokens of a class's labels, $I(t)$ returns classes of $\mathcal{O}'$ whose labels contain the token t, and C' denotes all the classes of $\mathcal{O}'$.

2. **NeighbourSample** (graph context-based). This strategy is to introduce hard negative candidates that are close to the ground truth class along class hierarchy. With the asserted subsumption axioms in an ontology, we can establish an *undirected* graph with named classes as nodes and subclass (`rdfs:subClassOf`) relations as edges. We adopt breadth-first search (BFS) over the subclass edges (bidirectional) to add the neighbouring classes of c' as candidates. The search starts from one-hop away neighbours, then goes to two-hop away neighbours, and so forth. It terminates when the number of neighbours (candidates) exceeds the required number N or the preset maximum number of hops has been reached. It is possible to obtain more than N candidates by adding all r-hop away neighbours; in this case, we sample among these r-hop candidates randomly to meet the number. Note that we exclude the root class `owl:Thing` from BFS. This restricts the candidates within the branch of c', leading to high quality negative candidates and significantly improving the searching efficiency.

3. **RandomSample**. This strategy is to randomly select negative candidates from the classes of $\mathcal{O}'$, as a complement to the above two strategies.

---

[8] Labels are extracted from annotation properties concerning synonyms of the class name, e.g., `rdfs:label`, `fma:synonym`, `skos:prefLabel`, etc.

To ensure we always get the required number of negative candidates with no duplicates, we combine the above three strategies with a Negative Candidate Generation algorithm (see Algorithm 1) which has the following characteristics:

1. The above strategies could occasionally generate positive candidates, i.e., classes that can be matched to c. These classes are pre-computed (in Line 1, denoted as $\mathcal{T}(m)$) and excluded from negative candidates. For subsumption matching, $\mathcal{T}(m)$ further incorporates the asserted and inferred subumers of c' since their combinations with c are not negative subsumption mappings.
2. At i^{th} iteration, only when strategy $\mathcal{S}_i$ cannot generate N_i ($N_i << |C'|$) *new* candidates will RandomSample be used to amend the number. The reason for sampling $|\mathcal{G}(m)| + |\mathcal{T}(m)| + N_i$ raw candidates first (in Line 3; the current set of negative candidates is denoted as $\mathcal{G}(m)$) is that in the worst case scenario, all the generated candidates are either duplicated or invalid. Therefore, the algorithm samples $|\mathcal{G}(m)| + |\mathcal{T}(m)|$ more than required first to preserve as many candidates as possible.

Algorithm 1. Negative Candidate Generation

Input: A reference mapping, $m = (c, c')$; Generation strategies $\{\mathcal{S}_1, \mathcal{S}_2, ..., \mathcal{S}_n\}$, and their corresponding numbers of negative candidates to generate $\{N_1, N_2, ..., N_n\}$
Output: Negative candidates for m, $\mathcal{G}(m)$
1: $\mathcal{T}(m) \leftarrow$ invalid candidates for m
2: Initialize the set of negative candidates: $\mathcal{G}(m) \leftarrow \{\}$
3: **for** $i \leftarrow 1$ to n **do**
4:      Generate unique $|\mathcal{G}(m)| + |\mathcal{T}(m)| + N_i$ raw samples with strategy $\mathcal{S}_i$ as $\mathcal{G}_i(m)$
5:      Remove those have been sampled and invalid: $\mathcal{G}_i(m) \leftarrow \mathcal{G}_i(m) \setminus (\mathcal{G}(m) \cup \mathcal{T}(m))$
6:      Truncate $\mathcal{G}_i(m)$ to first N_i (ranked) samples if $|\mathcal{G}_i(m)| > N_i$
7:      **while** $|\mathcal{G}_i(m)| < N_i$ **do**
8:          Randomly select $N_i - |\mathcal{G}_i(m)|$ unique candidates as $\mathcal{R}$
9:          $\mathcal{G}_i(m) \leftarrow (\mathcal{G}_i(m) \cup \mathcal{R}) \setminus (\mathcal{G}(m) \cup \mathcal{T}(m))$
10:     $\mathcal{G}(m) \leftarrow \mathcal{G}(m) \cup \mathcal{G}_i(m)$
11: **return** $\mathcal{G}(m)$

Overall, for each reference mapping $m = (c, c')$, we sample $\sum_{i=1}^{n} N_i$ (defined in Input of Algorithm 1) unique negative candidates and add c' as the only positive candidate; we then compute the ranking-based metrics for each OM system that supports class pair (mapping) scoring.

3.2   Global Matching

To eventually determine the output mappings, an OM system requires not only a mapping scoring module (which can be evaluated by local ranking), but also other components such as mapping searching, blocking, extension and repair. The prevalent metrics for measuring the final output mappings are Precision (P), Recall (R), and F-score:

$$P = \frac{|\mathcal{M}_{out} \cap \mathcal{M}_{ref}|}{|\mathcal{M}_{out}|}, \quad R = \frac{|\mathcal{M}_{out} \cap \mathcal{M}_{ref}|}{|\mathcal{M}_{ref}|}, \quad F_\beta = (1 + \beta^2) \cdot \frac{P \cdot R}{\beta^2 \cdot P + R}$$

where $\mathcal{M}_{out}$ and $\mathcal{M}_{ref}$ correspond to mappings computed by an OM system and the reference mappings, respectively; β, often set to 1, is a weighting for Precision and Recall. The global matching evaluation can demonstrate the overall performance of an OM system, but it is not well applicable for developing the ML-based mapping scoring module that has been widely considered in OM research in recent years, since (i) the output mappings depend on several other modules besides mapping scoring, and (ii) computing all the mappings is rather time-consuming (the naive traversal has a quadratic mapping search space), leading to very inefficient evaluation for ML models. Meanwhile, when the reference mappings are incomplete, we are essentially penalizing OM systems with good Recall. The local ranking evaluation can address these issues and thus, it is a good complement to the global matching evaluation.

3.3 Data Splitting

For both evaluation schemes, we consider two settings for reference mapping splitting. The first setting splits the reference mappings into 10% hold-out validation set for hyperparameter tuning or model selection, and 90% testing set for final evaluation. Such setting can be used for comparing fully automatic non-ML-based OM systems and unsupervised ML-based OM systems. The second setting splits the reference mappings into 20%, 10%, and 70%, corresponding to training, validation, and testing sets, respectively. Such a setting can evaluate those ML-based OM systems that are able to (or have to) use a small portion of given mappings for training. Note that the prevalent (fully) supervised learning data split with large portion of training data is not applicable for OM because of the extreme positive-negative imbalance, i.e., the number of correct mappings is of several orders smaller than the incorrect ones.

It is worth mentioning when calculating Precision, Recall and F-score on a particular set (validation or testing) of the reference mappings, we need to exclude reference mappings that are not in this set from the system output mappings; e.g., Precision on the validation set $\mathcal{M}_{val}$ is computed as:

$$P_{val} = \frac{|\mathcal{M}_{out} \cap \mathcal{M}_{val}|}{|\mathcal{M}_{out} \setminus (\mathcal{M}_{ref} \setminus \mathcal{M}_{val})|}.$$

4 Evaluation Results

4.1 Equivalence Matching

For equivalence matching, we evaluated the following OM systems (methods):

1. **EditSim**[9]. Many of the equivalent concepts have a similar naming and therefore, measuring class similarity based on simple edit distance between class

---

[9] EditSim and BERTMap codes: https://github.com/KRR-Oxford/DeepOnto.

labels is a reasonable baseline. Specifically, this method computes the matching score between two classes using the maximum of the normalized edit similarity scores among the combinations of their labels (See footnote 5). Note that the normalized edit similarity score is defined as *1 − normalized edit distance*.

2. **LogMap**[10] **& AML**[11]. LogMap and AML are two classical OM systems based on lexical matching, mapping extension and repair. They are leading OM systems in many equivalence matching tasks including those in the OAEI.

Table 4. Results of equivalence matching.

Task	System	90% Test mappings					70% Test mappings				
		P	R	F1	MRR	H@1	P	R	F1	MRR	H@1
OMIM-ORDO (Disease)	EditSim	0.819	0.499	0.620	0.776	0.729	0.781	0.507	0.615	0.777	0.727
	LogMap	0.827	0.498	0.622	0.803	0.742	0.788	0.501	0.612	0.805	0.744
	AML	0.749	0.510	0.607	NA	NA	0.702	0.517	0.596	NA	NA
	BERTMap	0.730	0.572	0.641	0.873	0.817	0.762	0.548	0.637	0.877	0.823
NCIT-DOID (Disease)	EditSim	0.912	0.776	0.838	0.904	0.884	0.889	0.771	0.826	0.903	0.883
	LogMap	0.918	0.667	0.773	0.559	0.364	0.896	0.661	0.761	0.559	0.363
	AML	0.873	0.773	0.820	NA	NA	0.841	0.770	0.804	NA	NA
	BERTMap	0.912	0.829	0.868	0.967	0.953	0.823	0.887	0.854	0.968	0.955
SNOMED-FMA (Body)	EditSim	0.976	0.660	0.787	0.895	0.869	0.970	0.665	0.789	0.897	0.871
	LogMap	0.702	0.581	0.636	0.545	0.330	0.646	0.580	0.611	0.542	0.328
	AML	0.841	0.776	0.807	NA	NA	0.805	0.779	0.792	NA	NA
	BERTMap	0.997	0.639	0.773	0.954	0.930	0.811	0.708	0.756	0.967	0.950
SNOMED-NCIT (Pharm)	EditSim	0.979	0.432	0.600	0.836	0.760	0.973	0.429	0.595	0.835	0.758
	LogMap	0.915	0.612	0.733	0.820	0.695	0.893	0.609	0.724	0.821	0.699
	AML	0.940	0.615	0.743	NA	NA	0.924	0.609	0.734	NA	NA
	BERTMap	0.966	0.606	0.745	0.919	0.876	0.941	0.724	0.818	0.963	0.941
SNOMED-NCIT (Neoplas)	EditSim	0.815	0.709	0.759	0.900	0.876	0.775	0.713	0.743	0.900	0.876
	LogMap	0.823	0.547	0.657	0.824	0.747	0.783	0.547	0.644	0.821	0.743
	AML	0.747	0.554	0.636	NA	NA	0.696	0.552	0.616	NA	NA
	BERTMap	0.655	0.777	0.711	0.960	0.939	0.575	0.784	0.664	0.965	0.947

3. **BERTMap** (See footnote 9). BERTMap is a ML-based OM system which uses class labels (See footnote 5) to fine-tune a pre-trained language model for synonym classification, and then aggregates the synonym scores as the mapping score. For efficient prediction, it exploits the sub-word inverted index for candidate selection and uses EditSim to filter mappings whose two classes have a common class label. Note that we employ the same candidate selection method for EditSim.

The validation set is used for tuning hyperparameters such as the mapping filtering threshold of BERTMap and EditSim, and the selection of annotation

---

[10] https://github.com/ernestojimenezruiz/logmap-matcher.
[11] https://github.com/AgreementMakerLight/AML-Project.

properties. The numbers of negative candidates using IDFSample and NeighbourSample are both set to 50, and RandomSample is used only for compensating the number. In total, for each reference mapping, the systems need to rank 100 negative candidates plus 1 ground truth class.

The equivalence matching results are shown in Table 4. The columns of "90% Test Mappings" and "70% Test Mappings" correspond to the unsupervised and semi-supervised data splitting settings, respectively. From the global matching results, we can see that OMIM-ORDO (Disease) is the most challenging task (with the lowest average F1), while NCIT-DOID (Disease) is the least challenging. BERTMap attains the highest F1 on OMIM-ORDO (Disease), NCIT-DOID (Disease), SNOMED-NCIT (Pharm), whereas AML is ranked first on SNOMED-NCIT (Body). Surprisingly, the naive EditSim method gets the highest F1 score on SNOMED-NCIT (Neoplas), possibly because the ontologies of this task has relatively less hierarchical information to utilize. For the local ranking results, we do not report results of AML because it has no interface for scoring input class pairs. BERTMap consistently outperforms EditSim and LogMap, which is expected because of the advanced BERT-based ML module.

4.2 Subsumption Matching

For subsumption matching, we evaluated the following OM systems (methods)[12]:

1. **Word2Vec + Random Forest (RF)**. This method encodes each class by the average of the token vectors of its label defined by `rdfs:label`. We use a Word2Vec model [19] trained by a Wikipedia English article dump accessed in 2018. Given a subsumption, the vectors of its two classes are concatenated and fed to a RF classifier which outputs a mapping score. The classifier is trained by the asserted intra-ontology subsumptions in both ontologies for matching in the unsupervised setting. In the semi-supervised setting, these subsumptions are merged with the training mappings for training.

2. **OWL2Vec* + RF**. This method is similar to Word2Vec + RF, except that it encodes each class by an ontology embedding model named OWL2Vec* [5] which is a Word2Vec model trained on corpora extracted from the ontology with different kinds of semantics concerned. We tested different corpus settings with the best results reported.

3. **BERTSubs with Isolated Class (IC)**. BERTSubs with the IC setting [4] has the same architecture as BERTMap, but it fine-tunes the BERT model by the declared subsumptions in the two ontologies for matching. The current results are based on the labels defined by `rdfs:label`. We will evaluate the other settings that consider surrounding classes in the new OAEI track.

The setting for negative candidates is the same as in equivalence matching (N is set to 50; RandomSample is used only when IDFSample or NeighbourSample

---

[12] BERTSubs codes: https://gitlab.com/chen00217/bert_subsumption; Word2Vec (or OWL2Vec*) + RF codes are in the folder `Inter_Ontology/baselines/` of the this repository.

Table 5. Results of subsumption matching.

Task	System	90% Test mappings				70% Test mappings			
		MRR	H@1	H@5	H@10	MRR	H@1	H@5	H@10
OMIM-ORDO (Disease)	Word2Vec+RF	0.191	0.106	0.223	0.362	0.193	0.110	0.233	0.315
	OWL2Vec*+RF	0.270	0.160	0.362	0.521	0.284	0.151	0.411	0.534
	BERTSubs (IC)	0.299	0.108	0.473	0.613	0.295	0.139	0.472	0.667
NCIT-DOID (Disease)	Word2Vec+RF	0.306	0.206	0.390	0.510	0.363	0.263	0.448	0.566
	OWL2Vec*+RF	0.388	0.285	0.485	0.604	0.422	0.315	0.524	0.647
	BERTSubs (IC)	0.601	0.460	0.777	0.877	0.618	0.496	0.758	0.862
SNOMED-FMA (Body)	Word2Vec+RF	0.558	0.415	0.731	0.850	0.629	0.503	0.792	0.886
	OWL2Vec*+RF	0.668	0.540	0.836	0.911	0.743	0.626	0.900	0.944
	BERTSubs (IC)	0.589	0.422	0.816	0.939	0.622	0.490	0.788	0.878
SNOMED-NCIT (Pharm)	Word2Vec+RF	0.488	0.335	0.687	0.852	0.526	0.402	0.663	0.834
	OWL2Vec*+RF	0.524	0.364	0.738	0.870	0.579	0.446	0.747	0.893
	BERTSubs (IC)	0.504	0.321	0.762	0.920	0.476	0.281	0.715	0.900
SNOMED-NCIT (Neoplas)	Word2Vec+RF	0.512	0.368	0.694	0.834	0.577	0.433	0.773	0.880
	OWL2Vec*+RF	0.603	0.461	0.782	0.860	0.666	0.547	0.827	0.880
	BERTSubs (IC)	0.530	0.333	0.786	0.948	0.638	0.463	0.859	0.953

outputs less than N candidates). The results are shown in Table 5. We can find that OWL2Vec* leads to better performance than Word2Vec in all the five tasks when their class embeddings are fed to RF. BERTSubs (IC) has higher scores than OWL2Vec* + RF on tasks of OMIM-ORDO and NCIT-DOID for all the four metrics; while on SNOMED-FMA (Body), SNOMED-NCIT (Pharm) and SNOMED-NCIT (Neoplas), BERTSubs (IC) has lower MRR and H@1 scores, but it often has higher H@10 scores than OWL2Vec* + RF. We can also observe that the results under the semi-supervised setting are usually better than their correspondences under the unsupervised setting, which matches our assumption that adding some training mappings bridges the gap between the intra-ontology subsumptions for training and the inter-ontology subsumptions (mappings) for testing. Meanwhile, we can find that subsumption matching by BERTSubs (IC) has much lower MRR and H@1 than equivalence matching by BERTMap in each task. Although BERTSubs (IC) only uses one class label, this in some degree verifies that subsumption matching is more challenging.

5   Conclusion and Discussion

In this paper, we proposed evaluation resources for five biomedical OM tasks that consider both equivalence matching and subsumption matching, with many new features for supporting the evaluation and development of both ML-based and non-ML-based OM systems. The quality of the reference mappings is ensured by selecting reliable mapping sources (e.g., the human curated mappings from Mondo) and pruning the ontologies. Subsumption reference mappings are constructed from equivalence reference mappings, where a class deletion algorithm is employed to prevent OM systems from directly inferring the subsumptions through the equivalence mappings. We also proposed a comprehensive evaluation framework which includes local ranking and global matching, providing metrics from various perspectives, as well as unsupervised and semi-supervised mapping splitting settings. Several typical OM systems have been evaluated to demonstrate the application of these resources and some interesting results and observations have been reported.

While we only constructed datasets for five OM tasks, the resource construction approach is reproducible for constructing more datasets from Mondo and UMLS for different tasks and settings. Most of our techniques, such as category-specific ontology pruning, subsumption mapping construction, and negative candidate generation, are also applicable to general OWL ontologies beyond the biomedical domain, and other tasks beyond OM such as ontology completion.

As for the evaluation, bringing in local ranking amends some key features not properly considered in previous works, thus forming a more comprehensive evaluation framework on assessing both OM systems and mappings. First, most OM systems, especially those ML-based, rely on a mapping scoring module as well as some other modules for mapping searching (e.g., task blocking, candidate mapping selection and mapping repair). If an OM system often performs well in local ranking but performs poorly in global matching, then the mapping searching modules need to be debugged and improved. Second, even when reference mappings are rather incomplete, local ranking can still provide a fair comparison, especially towards the mapping scoring module, whereas global matching will underestimate Precision of an OM system that has good Recall. Actually, local ranking itself simulates some real-world OM applications, such as querying a list of matched classes in a target ontology for a given class in a source ontology. Third, when many representative OM systems attain high ranking scores but low matching scores on the same set of reference mappings, it is likely that the reference mappings themselves are not complete.

We are running a new BIO-ML track in the OAEI 2022 edition with the proposed datasets. This new track is superseding the current OAEI *largebio* and *phenotype* tracks and, among other objectives, aims at attracting more ML-based systems to the OAEI, which has been highlighted as a key challenge within the OM community. We will also consider adapting our evaluation framework into MELT (Matching EvaLuation Toolkit) [13], especially the MELT-ML module for ML-based OM systems, to hold a public evaluation for the OM participants. Meanwhile, we will also develop and extend our current OM systems BERTMap and BERTSubs based on these new resources, and further consider feeding high-quality system output mappings to the UMLS and Mondo communities.

Acknowledgments. This work was supported by the SIRIUS Centre for Scalable Data Access (Research Council of Norway, project 237889), eBay, Samsung Research UK, Siemens AG, and the EPSRC projects OASIS (EP/S032347/1), UK FIRES (EP/S019111/1) and ConCur (EP/V050869/1). We would like to to thank the Mondo team, especially Nicolas Matentzoglu and Joe Flake, for their great help in creating the Mondo datasets.

References

1. Alsentzer, E., et al.: Publicly available clinical BERT embeddings. ArXiv abs/1904.03323 (2019)
2. Amberger, J.S., Bocchini, C.A., Schiettecatte, F., Scott, A.F., Hamosh, A.: OMIM. org: Online Mendelian Inheritance in Man (OMIM®), an online catalog of human genes and genetic disorders. Nucleic Acids Res. **43**(D1), D789–D798 (2015)
3. Bodenreider, O.: The Unified Medical Language System (UMLS): integrating biomedical terminology. Nucl. Acids Res. (2004)
4. Chen, J., He, Y., Jimenez-Ruiz, E., Dong, H., Horrocks, I.: Contextual semantic embeddings for ontology subsumption prediction. arXiv preprint arXiv:2202.09791 (2022)
5. Chen, J., Hu, P., Jimenez-Ruiz, E., Holter, O.M., Antonyrajah, D., Horrocks, I.: OWL2Vec*: embedding of OWL ontologies. Mach. Learn. **110**(7), 1813–1845 (2021)
6. Chen, J., Jiménez-Ruiz, E., Horrocks, I., Antonyrajah, D., Hadian, A., Lee, J.: Augmenting ontology alignment by semantic embedding and distant supervision. In: European Semantic Web Conference, pp. 392–408. Springer (2021). https://doi.org/10.1007/978-3-030-77385-4_23
7. Coiera, E.: Guide to Health Informatics, chap. Chapter 23 Healthcare Terminologies and Classification Systems, pp. 381–399. CRC Press (2015)
8. Donnelly, K., et al.: SNOMED-CT: the advanced terminology and coding system for ehealth. In: Medical and Care Compunetics 3, Studies in health technology and informatics, vol. 121, pp. 279–290. IOS Press (2006)
9. Faria, D., Pesquita, C., Santos, E., Palmonari, M., Cruz, I.F., Couto, F.M.: The agreement maker light ontology matching system. In: OTM Conferences (2013)
10. Haendel, M., et al.: How many rare diseases are there? Nat. Rev. Drug Disc. **19**(2), 77–78 (2020)
11. Harrow, I., et al.: Matching disease and phenotype ontologies in the ontology alignment evaluation initiative. J. Biomed. Semant. **8**(1), 1–13 (2017)
12. He, Y., Chen, J., Antonyrajah, D., Horrocks, I.: BERTMap: a BERT-based ontology alignment system. In: AAAI (2022)
13. Hertling, S., Portisch, J., Paulheim, H.: Melt - matching evaluation toolkit. In: SEMANTiCS (2019)
14. Iyer, V., Agarwal, A., Kumar, H.: VeeAlign: multifaceted context representation using dual attention for ontology alignment. In: EMNLP (2021)
15. Jiménez-Ruiz, E., Grau, B.C.: LogMap: logic-based and scalable ontology matching. In: International Semantic Web Conference (2011)
16. Jiménez-Ruiz, E., Grau, B.C., Horrocks, I., Berlanga, R.: Logic-based assessment of the compatibility of UMLS ontology sources. J. Biomed. Semant. **2**(1), 1–16 (2011)
17. Kolyvakis, P., Kalousis, A., Kiritsis, D.: DeepAlignment: unsupervised ontology matching with refined word vectors. In: NAACL (2018)
18. Lin, Y., Liu, Z., Sun, M., Liu, Y., Zhu, X.: Learning entity and relation embeddings for knowledge graph completion. In: AAAI (2015)
19. Mikolov, T., Chen, K., Corrado, G., Dean, J.: Efficient estimation of word representations in vector space. arXiv preprint arXiv:1301.3781 (2013)
20. Mungall, C.J., Koehler, S., Robinson, P.N., Holmes, I.H., Haendel, M.A.: k-BOOM: a Bayesian approach to ontology structure inference, with applications in disease ontology construction. F1000Research (2016)

21. Neutel, S., de Boer, M.: Towards automatic ontology alignment using BERT. In: AAAI Spring Symposium: Combining Machine Learning with Knowledge Engineering (2021)
22. Nguyen, V., Yip, H.Y., Bodenreider, O.: Biomedical Vocabulary Alignment at Scale in the UMLS Metathesaurus. In: Proceedings of the Web Conference 2021, pp. 2672–2683 (2021)
23. Pesquita, C., Faria, D., Santos, E., Couto, F.M.: To repair or not to repair: reconciling correctness and coherence in ontology reference alignments. In: Proceedings of the 8th International Workshop on Ontology Matching, pp. 13–24 (2013)
24. Rosse, C., Mejino, J.L.: The foundational model of anatomy ontology. In: Anatomy Ontologies for Bioinformatics, pp. 59–117. Springer (2008). https://doi.org/10.1007/978-1-84628-885-2_4
25. Rossi, A., Firmani, D., Matinata, A., Merialdo, P., Barbosa, D.: Knowledge graph embedding for link prediction: a comparative analysis. ACM Trans. Knowl. Discov. Data **15**, 14:1–14:49 (2021)
26. Schriml, L.M., et al.: Human disease ontology 2018 update: classification, content and workflow expansion. Nucl. Acids Res. (2018)
27. Shefchek, K.A., et al.: The monarch Initiative in 2019: an integrative data and analytic platform connecting phenotypes to genotypes across species. Nucl. Acids Res. (2020)
28. Shvaiko, P., Euzenat, J.: Ontology matching: state of the art and future challenges. IEEE Trans. Knowl. Data Eng. **25**, 158–176 (2013)
29. Sioutos, N., de Coronado, S., Haber, M.W., Hartel, F.W., Shaiu, W.L., Wright, L.W.: NCI Thesaurus: a semantic model integrating cancer-related clinical and molecular information. J. Biomed. Inform. **40**(1), 30–43 (2007). bio*Medical Informatics
30. Vasant, D., et al.: ORDO: an ontology connecting rare disease, epidemiology and genetic data. In: Proceedings of ISMB, vol. 30 (2014)

The DLCC Node Classification Benchmark for Analyzing Knowledge Graph Embeddings

Jan Portisch[1,2](✉) and Heiko Paulheim[2]

[1] SAP SE, Walldorf, Germany
`jan.portisch@sap.com`
[2] Data and Web Science Group, University of Mannheim, Mannheim, Germany
{`jan,heiko`}`@informatik.uni-mannheim.de`

Abstract. Knowledge graph embedding is a representation learning technique that projects entities and relations in a knowledge graph to continuous vector spaces. Embeddings have gained a lot of uptake and have been heavily used in link prediction and other downstream prediction tasks. Most approaches are evaluated on a single task or a single group of tasks to determine their overall performance. The evaluation is then assessed in terms of how well the embedding approach performs on the task at hand. Still, it is hardly evaluated (and often not even deeply understood) what information the embedding approaches are *actually* learning to represent.

To fill this gap, we present the DLCC (Description Logic Class Constructors) benchmark, a resource to analyze embedding approaches in terms of which kinds of classes they can represent. Two gold standards are presented, one based on the real-world knowledge graph DBpedia and one synthetic gold standard. In addition, an evaluation framework is provided that implements an experiment protocol so that researchers can directly use the gold standard. To demonstrate the use of DLCC, we compare multiple embedding approaches using the gold standards. We find that many DL constructors on DBpedia are actually learned by recognizing different correlated patterns rather than those defined in the gold standard; we further find that specific DL constructors, such as cardinality constraints, are particularly hard to be learned for most embedding approaches.

Keywords: Knowledge graph embedding · Node classification · Description logics · Benchmark · Evaluation framework

1 Introduction

Knowledge graph embeddings are projections of entities and relations to continuous vector spaces. They have been proposed for various purposes and are typically evaluated on task-specific gold standards such as FB15k and WN18 [3] for link prediction, kgbench for node classification [2], or GEval [9,10] for machine learning tasks such as classification, regression, or clustering. The benchmarks frequently come with their own evaluation protocol.

© The Author(s), under exclusive license to Springer Nature Switzerland AG 2022
U. Sattler et al. (Eds.): ISWC 2022, LNCS 13489, pp. 592–609, 2022.
https://doi.org/10.1007/978-3-031-19433-7_34

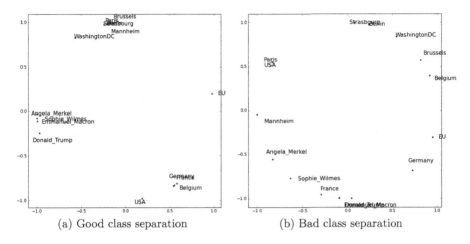

Fig. 1. Two example embeddings. The left-hand side embedding shows a good class separation of persons, countries, and cities, whereas the right-hand side one does not.

Independent of the original benchmark task, knowledge graph embeddings are generally versatile so that they can be used for multiple tasks [11]. While the performance of embeddings in downstream tasks is often superior to other entity representation techniques, most, if not all, embedding approaches have in common that it is not ultimately clear *what* is learned. For example, both for link prediction and for node classification, it is required that classes can be separated (e.g., persons, countries, and cities are clustered in the embedding space) [11], but so far, it has not been systematically evaluated which embedding methods can learn which kinds of class separations. Figure 1 shows an example of two embedding spaces with different qualities of class separation.

In this paper, we present the DLCC (for *Description Logic Class Constructors*) dataset and an evaluation framework that help to better analyze and understand embedding approaches for specific DL constructors. There are four contributions of this paper: (1) A framework for the DLCC gold standard creation is presented, (2) two concrete gold standards are provided – a real graph-based gold standard and one based on synthetic knowledge graphs, (3) an evaluation framework is provided to easily evaluate and compare the class separation capabilities of embeddings, and (4) a preliminary analysis for different state of the art embedding approaches is provided.

2   Related Work

In the area of link prediction (or knowledge base completion), the two well-known evaluation datasets FB15k and WN18 [3] are both based on real datasets: FB15k is based on the Freebase dataset, and WN18 is based on WordNet [5]. They were presented in the context of link prediction: Given a triple in the form *(head, relation, tail)*, two prediction tasks *(head, relation, ?)* and *(?, relation, tail)* are created. The evaluation is performed by calculating the mean rank/HITS@10 for a list of proposals. Since it has been remarked that those datasets contain too many simple inferences due to inverse relations, the more challenging variants FB15k-237 [21] and WN18RR [4] have been proposed. More recently, evaluation sets based on larger knowledge graphs, such as YAGO3-10 [4] and DBpedia50k/DBpedia500k [19], have been introduced.

Bloem et al. [2] introduce *kgbench*, a node classification benchmark for knowledge graphs, which, like DLCC, comes with datasets in different sizes and predefined train/test splits. Unlike DLCC, kgbench is based on real-world datasets. Therefore, it is suitable to evaluate and compare the quality of different embedding approaches on real-world tasks but does not provide any insights into what these embedding approaches are capable of representing.

Alshagari et al. [1] present a framework for ontological concepts covering three aspects: (i) categorization, (ii) hierarchy, and (iii) logic validation. The framework can be used for language models and for knowledge graph embeddings. The work presented in this paper differs in that it goes beyond explicit DBpedia types. The evaluation of this paper is, therefore, of analytical rather than descriptive nature. Moreover, the task sets of DLCC are significantly larger and more comprehensive.

Ristoski et al. [17] provide a collection of benchmarking datasets for machine learning, including classification, clustering, and regression tasks. Later, the GEval framework [9,10] was introduced to provide a standardized evaluation protocol for this dataset. The evaluation datasets are based on DBpedia. Internally, the embeddings are processed by different downstream classification, regression, or clustering algorithms. The evaluation framework presented in this paper is similar to GEval in that it also evaluates multiple classifiers given a concept vector input.

Melo and Paulheim [8] provide a method for synthesizing benchmark datasets for link and entity type prediction, which are used in conjunction with a fixed ontology. Their goal is to mimic the characteristic of existing knowledge graphs in terms of distributions and patterns.

3   Covered DL Constructors

The aim of this paper is to provide a benchmark for analyzing which kinds of constructs in a knowledge graph can be recognized by different embedding methods. To that end, we define class labels using different DL constructors. Later on, we apply classification algorithms to analyze how well the differently labeled classes can be separated using different embedding algorithms.

Ingoing and Outgoing Relations. All entities that have a particular outgoing or ingoing relations (e.g., *everything that has a location*).

$$\exists r. \top \tag{1}$$

$$\exists r^{-1}.\top \tag{2}$$

$$\exists r.\top \sqcup \exists r^{-1}.\top \tag{3}$$

where r is bound to a particular relation.[1]

Relations to Particular Individuals. All entities that have a relation (in any direction) to a particular individual (e.g., *everything that is related to New York City*).

$$\exists R.\{e\} \sqcup \exists R^{-1}.\{e\} \tag{4}$$

where R is *not* bound to a particular relation. Those relations can also span two (or more[2]) hops):

$$\exists R_1.(\exists R_2.\{e\}) \sqcup \exists R_1^{-1}.(\exists R_2^{-1}\{e\}) \tag{5}$$

Particular Relations to Particular Individuals. All entities that have a particular relation to a particular individual (e.g., *movies directed by Steven Spielberg*).

$$\exists r.\{e\} \tag{6}$$

Qualified Restrictions. All entities that have a particular relation to an individual of a given type (e.g., *all people married to soccer players*).

$$\exists r.T \tag{7}$$

$$\exists r^{-1}.T \tag{8}$$

If types are modeled as a normal relation in the graph (i.e., `rdf:type` is yet another relation), we can reformulate Eq. 7 and 8 to

$$\exists r.(\exists \mathtt{rdf:type}.T) \tag{7a}$$

$$\exists r^{-1}.(\exists \mathtt{rdf:type}.T) \tag{8a}$$

In that case, it behaves equally to a chained variant of Eq. 6.

Cardinality Restrictions of Relations. All entities that have at least or at most n relations of a particular kind (e.g., *people who have at least two citizenships*). Here, we depict only the *lower bound* variant because the corresponding decision problem is between the two variants (entities that fall below the bound, i.e., adhere to the upper bound, are in the negative example set).[3]

$$\geq 2r.\top \tag{9}$$

$$\geq 2r^{-1}.\top \tag{10}$$

---

[1] We use r to denote a particular relation, whereas R denotes *any* relation.

[2] For reasons of scalability, we restrict the provided gold standard to two hops.

[3] The fact that most KGs follow the open-world assumption is neglected here since we test for the presence/absence of patterns.

Table 1. Overview of the test cases

Test case	DL expression
tc01	$\exists r.\top$
tc02	$\exists r^{-1}.\top$
tc03	$\exists r.\top \sqcup \exists r^{-1}.\top$
tc04	$\exists R.\{e\} \sqcup \exists R^{-1}.\{e\}$
tc05	$\exists R_1.(\exists R_2.\{e\}) \sqcup \exists R_1^{-1}.(\exists R_2^{-1}\{e\})$
tc06	$\exists r.\{e\}$
tc07	$\exists r.T$
tc08	$\exists r^{-1}.T$
tc09	$\geq 2r.\top$
tc10	$\geq 2r^{-1}.\top$
tc11	$\geq 2r.T$
tc12	$\geq 2r^{-1}.T$

Qualified Cardinality Restrictions. Qualified cardinality restrictions combine qualified restrictions with cardinalities (e.g., people who have published at least two science fiction novels).

$$\geq 2r.T \tag{11}$$

$$\geq 2r^{-1}.T \tag{12}$$

Table 1 summarizes the DL constructors for which test cases were built.

4   Approach

For the twelve test cases in Table 1, we create positive examples (i.e., those which fall into the respective class) and those which do not (under closed-world semantics). For example, for tc01, we would generate a set of positive instances for which $\exists r.\top$ holds and a set of negative instances for which $\not\exists r.\top$ holds. We then evaluate how well these two classes can be separated, given the embedding vectors of the positive and negative instances. For that, we split the examples into a training and testing partition, we train binary classifiers on the training subset of the examples, and evaluate their performance on the test subset.

The approach is visualized in Fig. 2: A gold standard generator generates a set of positive and negative URIs, as well as a fixed train/test split. The approach presented in this paper allows to generate custom gold standards – however, a contribution of this paper is also to provide a pre-calculated gold standard. This pre-calculated gold standard can be used to guarantee reproducibility. Officially published gold standards are versioned to allow for future improvements. In this paper, we present version v1 of the gold standard.

A user provides embeddings in a simple textual format and provides them together with the training data as input to the evaluator. The evaluator trains multiple classifiers and evaluates them on the selected gold standard using the provided vectors as classification input. The program then calculates multiple statistics in the form of CSV files that can be further analyzed in a spreadsheet program or through data analysis frameworks such as pandas[4]. These analyses help the user to understand how well the provided vectors are performing on a particular DL constructor.

4.1 Gold Standard Generator

The gold standard generator is publicly available[5]. It is implemented as a Java maven project. The generator can generate either a DBpedia benchmark (see Subsect. 5.1) or a synthetic one (see Subsect. 5.2). Any DBpedia version can be used; the user merely needs to provide a SPARQL endpoint. A comprehensive set of unit tests ensures a high code quality. The generator automatically generates a fixed train-test split for the evaluation framework or any other downstream application. The split is configurable; for the pre-generated gold standards, an 80–20 split is used. The resulting gold standard is balanced – i.e., the number of positives equals the number of negatives – and the train and test partitions are stratified. Hence, any classifier which achieves an accuracy significantly above 50% is capable of learning the test case's problem type from the vectors to some extent.

It is important to note that the generator only needs to be run by users who want to build their own gold standards. The typical user would merely download[6] the official gold standard files online. We recommend using the pre-calculated gold standards to ensure comparability across publications.

4.2 Evaluation Framework

The evaluator is publicly available[7] as well together with usage examples. It is implemented in Python and can be easily used in a Jupyter notebook. A comprehensive set of unit tests ensures a high code quality.

The standard user can directly download the gold standard and use the evaluation framework. To test class separability, the evaluation framework currently runs six machine learning classifiers:[8] (1) decision trees, (2) naïve Bayes, (3) KNN, (4) SVM, (5) random forest, and (6) a multilayer perceptron network. The framework uses the default configurations of the sklearn library[9].

After training and evaluation, the framework persists multiple CSV files per test case as well as higher-level aggregate CSV files. Examples of such CSV files

---

[4] https://pandas.pydata.org/.

[5] https://github.com/janothan/DL-TC-Generator.

[6] DOI: 10.5281/zenodo.6509715; GitHub link for the latest version. https://github.com/janothan/DL-TC-Generator/tree/master/results.

[7] https://github.com/janothan/dl-evaluation-framework.

[8] The evaluation framework is not restricted to the set of classifiers listed here. New classifiers can be easily added if desired.

[9] https://scikit-learn.org/stable/index.html.

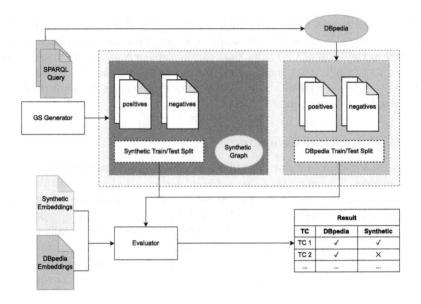

Fig. 2. Overview of the approach

are a file listing the accuracy per classifier and per test case or a file listing the accuracy of the best classifier per test case. In the case of DBpedia, test cases are created for multiple domains, and the results can be analyzed on the level of each domain separately or in an aggregated manner on the level of the test case.

5   Benchmarks

We currently provide two benchmarks, while the framework described above allows for generating customized benchmarks.

5.1   DBpedia Benchmark

We use the DBpedia knowledge graph to create test cases.[10] We created SPARQL queries for each test case (see Table 1) to generate positives, negatives, and hard negatives. The latter are meant to be less easily distinguishable from the positives and are created by variations such as softening the constraints in the class constructor or switching subject and object in the constraint. For example, for qualified relations, a positive example would be a person playing in a team which is a basketball team. A simple negative example would be any person not playing in a basketball team, whereas a hard negative example would be any person playing in a team that is not a basketball team.

---

[10] We used DBpedia version 2021-09. The generator can be configured to use any DBpedia SPARQL endpoint if desired.

Query examples for every test case in the people domain are provided in Table 2. The framework uses slightly more involved queries to vary the size of the result set and to better randomize results.

In total, we used six different domains: people (P), books (B), cities (C), music albums (A), movies (M), and species (S). This setup yields more than 200 hand-written SPARQL queries, which are used to obtain positives, negatives, and hard negatives; they are available online[11] and can be easily extended, e.g., to add an additional domain. For each test case, we created differently sized (50, 500, 5000) balanced test sets.[12]

5.2 Synthetic Benchmark

The previous benchmark is realistic and well suited to compare approaches on differently typed DL constructors.

However, the following aspects have to be considered: (1) DBpedia is a large knowledge graph; not every embedding approach can be used to learn an embedding for it (or not every researcher has the computational means to do so, respectively). (2) Depending on the DL constructor and the domain, not enough examples can be found on DBpedia. (3) It cannot be precluded that patterns correlate; therefore, the fact that an embedding approach can learn a particular class can only be an indicator that it *might* learn the underlying constructor pattern, but the results are not conclusive. Correlating properties, type biases for entities, etc., may lead to surprising results in some domains (see Sect. 6.3).

Therefore, we complement the DBpedia-based gold standard with a synthetic benchmark. The idea is to generate a graph that contains the DL constructors (positive and negative) of interest. The graph can be constructed to resemble the DBpedia graph statistically but can be significantly smaller (and contain a sufficient number of positives and negatives), and, by construction, side effects and correlations which exist in DBpedia can be mitigated to a large extent.

The configurable parameters are `numClasses`, `numProperties`, `numInstances`, `branchingFactor`, `maxTriplesPerNode`, and `numNodesInterest` (all parameters are integers). The overall process is depicted in Algorithm 1: First, a class tree with `numClasses` classes is constructed in a way that each class has at most `branchingFactor` children. Then, `numproperties` properties are generated. Each property is assigned to a range and domain from the class tree, whereby the first property has the root node as domain and range type so that every node can be involved in at least one triple statement. A skew can be introduced so that domain and range refer with a higher probability to a more general class than to a specific one. Lastly, we generate instances and assign them to a class as type, which is depicted in Algorithm 1.

Once the ontology is created, `numNodesInterest` positives and negatives are generated (adhering to domain/range restrictions). Each class constructor is

---

[11] https://github.com/janothan/DL-TC-Generator/tree/master/src/main/resources/queries.

[12] The desired size classes can be configured in the framework.

Table 2. Exemplary SPARQL queries for class `Person`

TC	Query Positive	Query Negative	Query Negative (hard)

tc01	`SELECT DISTINCT(?x) WHERE {`
	 `  { ?x a dbo:Person .`
	 `    ?x dbo:child ?y . }`
		`SELECT DISTINCT(?x) WHERE {`
		 `  ?x a dbo:Person .`
		 `  FILTER(NOT EXISTS {`
		 `    ?x dbo:child ?z})}`
			`SELECT DISTINCT(?x) WHERE {`
			 `  ?x a dbo:Person .`
			 `  ?y dbo:child ?x.`
			 `  FILTER(NOT EXISTS {`
			 `    ?x dbo:child ?z})}`

tc02	Analogous to tc01 (inverse case).		

tc03	`SELECT DISTINCT(?x) WHERE {`
	 `{ ?x a dbo:Person .`
	 `  ?x dbo:child ?y} UNION`
	 `{ ?x a dbo:Person .`
	 `  ?y dbo:child ?x}}`
		`SELECT COUNT(?x) WHERE {`
		 `  ?x a dbo:Person .`
		 `  FILTER(NOT EXISTS{`
		 `    ?x dbo:child ?y}`
		 `  AND NOT EXISTS {`
		 `    ?z dbo:child ?x})}`
			–

tc04	`SELECT DISTINCT(?x) WHERE {`
	 `{ ?x a dbo:Person .`
	 `  ?x ?y dbr:New_York_City}`
	 `UNION`
	 `{ ?x a dbo:Person .`
	 `  dbr:New_York_City ?y ?x}}`
		`SELECT DISTINCT(?x) WHERE {`
		 `  ?x a dbo:Person .`
		 `  FILTER(NOT EXISTS{`
		 `    ?x ?y dbr:New_York_City}`
		 `  AND NOT EXISTS {`
		 `    dbr:New_York_City ?y`
		 `  ?x})}`
			`SELECT DISTINCT(?x) WHERE {{`
			 `  ?x a dbo:Person .`
			 `  ?x ?y1 ?z .`
			 `  ?z ?y2 dbr:New_York_City }`
			 `UNION {`
			 `  ?x a dbo:Person .`
			 `  ?z ?y1 ?x .`
			 `  dbr:New_York_City ?y2 ?z }`
			 `FILTER(NOT EXISTS`
			 `  {?x ?r dbr:New_York_City}`
			 `AND NOT EXISTS`
			 `  {dbr:New_York_City ?s`
			 `?x})}`

tc05	Analogous to tc04 (inverse case).		

tc06	`SELECT DISTINCT(?x) WHERE {`
	 `  ?x a dbo:Person .`
	 `  ?x dbo:birthPlace`
	 `    dbr:New_York_City }`
		`SELECT DISTINCT(?x) WHERE {`
		 `  ?x a dbo:Person .`
		 `  FILTER(NOT EXISTS{`
		 `    ?x dbo:birthPlace`
		 `      dbr:New_York_City })}`
			`SELECT DISTINCT(?x) ?r WHERE`
			 `{{`
			 `    ?x a dbo:Person .`
			 `    ?x dbo:birthPlace ?y .`
			 `    dbr:New_York_City ?r ?x .`
			 `    FILTER(?y!=dbr:New_York_City)}`
			 `UNION {`
			 `    ?x a dbo:Person .`
			 `    ?x dbo:birthPlace ?y .`
			 `    ?x ?r dbr:New_York_City .`
			 `    FILTER(?y!=dbr:New_York_City)}}`

tc07	`SELECT DISTINCT(?x) WHERE {`
	 `  ?x a dbo:Person .`
	 `  ?x dbo:team ?y .`
	 `  ?y a dbo:BasketballTeam`
	 `}`
		`SELECT DISTINCT(?x) WHERE {`
		 `  ?x a dbo:Person .`
		 `  FILTER(NOT EXISTS{`
		 `    ?x dbo:team ?y .`
		 `    ?y a`
		 `dbo:BasketballTeam})}`
			`SELECT DISTINCT(?x) WHERE {`
			 `  ?x a dbo:Person .`
			 `  ?x dbo:team ?z1 .`
			 `  ?x ?r ?z2 .`
			 `  ?z2 a dbo:BaseballTeam`
			 `  FILTER(NOT EXISTS{`
			 `    ?x dbo:team ?y .`
			 `    ?y a dbo:BasketballTeam`
			 `})}`

tc08	Analogous to tc07 (inverse case).		

tc09	`SELECT DISTINCT(?x) WHERE {`
	 `  ?x a dbo:Person .`
	 `  ?x dbo:award ?y1.`
	 `  ?x dbo:award ?y2.`
	 `  FILTER(?y1!=?y2)}`
		`SELECT DISTINCT(?x) WHERE {`
		 `  ?x a dbo:Person .`
		 `  FILTER(NOT EXISTS{`
		 `    ?x dbo:award ?y1.`
		 `    ?x dbo:award ?y2.`
		 `    FILTER(?y1!=?y2)})}`
			`SELECT DISTINCT(?x) WHERE {`
			 `  ?x a dbo:Person .`
			 `  ?x dbo:award ?y .`
			 `  FILTER(NOT EXISTS{`
			 `    ?x dbo:award ?z.`
			 `    FILTER(?y!=?z)})}`

tc10	Analogous to tc09 (inverse case).		

tc11	`SELECT DISTINCT(?x) WHERE {`
	 `  ?x a dbo:Person .`
	 `  ?x dbo:recordLabel ?y1 .`
	 `  ?y1 a dbo:RecordLabel .`
	 `  ?x dbo:recordLabel ?y2 .`
	 `  ?y2 a dbo:RecordLabel .`
	 `  FILTER(?y1!=?y2)}`
		`SELECT DISTINCT(?x) WHERE {`
		 `  ?x a dbo:Person .`
		 `  FILTER(NOT EXISTS{`
		 `    ?x dbo:recordLabel ?y1`
		 `  .`
		 `    ?y1 a dbo:RecordLabel .`
		 `    ?x dbo:recordLabel ?y2`
		 `  .`
		 `    ?y2 a dbo:RecordLabel .`
		 `    FILTER(?y1!=?y2)})}`
			`SELECT DISTINCT(?x) WHERE {`
			 `  ?x a dbo:Person .`
			 `  ?x dbo:recordLabel ?y1 .`
			 `  ?y1 a dbo:RecordLabel .`
			 `  FILTER(NOT EXISTS{`
			 `    ?x dbo:recordLabel ?y2 .`
			 `    ?y2 a dbo:RecordLabel .`
			 `    FILTER(?y1!=?y2)})}`

tc12	Analogous to tc11 (inverse case).		

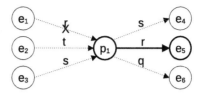

Fig. 3. Illustration of the instance generation, using the class constructor $\exists r.T$. First, the pattern is instantiated for the positive example p_1 with the edge (p_1, r, e_5). Then, random edges are inserted (dashed lines). The edge (e_1, r, p_1) is removed, because it would turn e_1 into an additional positive example.

first initialized explicitly for the positive examples. Then, for each entity e in the graph (i.e., positive and negative examples), $rand(n) \in [1, maxTriplesPerNode]$ random triples are generated, which have e as a subject and adhere to the domain and range definitions, whereby it is checked that no additional positives are created, and no negatives are turned into positives accidentally (see Fig. 3).

For version v1 of the gold standard, `numClasses = 760`, `numProperties = 1355`, `numInstances = 10,000`, `branchingFactor = 5`, `maxTriplesPerNode = 11`, and `numNodesInterest = 1000` were chosen. The parameters were chosen to form graphs which are smaller than DBpedia but resemble the DBpedia graph statistically. Therefore, the statistical properties of the DBpedia ontology calculated by Heist et al. [6] were used.

6   Exemplary Analysis

In order to demonstrate the use of the DLCC benchmark, we compare two flavors of RDF2vec [16], two flavors of TransE [3], as well as TransR [7] and ComplEx [22] embeddings with respect to their capability of separating the classes in the different datasets.

6.1   Configurations

For DBpedia, we use version 2021-09. We train RDF2vec in the variants SG and its order-aware counterpart SG_{oa} [14]. The embedding files are available via KGvec2go [12].[13] For the DBpedia embeddings, we used 500 random, duplicate free walks per entity, with a depth of 4, a window of 5, 5 epochs, and a dimension of 200. We used the same parameters for the synthetic gold standard with the exception of $dimension = 100$ and $walks = 100$ to account for the smaller gold standard size. The embeddings were trained using the jRDF2vec[14] framework [13].

For TransE, we use the variants using the L1 and L2 norm [3]. TransE, TransR, and ComplEx were trained using the DGL-KE framework[15] [23], using

---

[13] http://data.dws.informatik.uni-mannheim.de/kgvec2go/dbpedia/2021-09/.
[14] https://github.com/dwslab/jRDF2Vec.
[15] https://github.com/awslabs/dgl-ke.

Algorithm 1. Ontology Creation

---

procedure GENERATECLASSTREE(numClasses, branchingFactor)
    $clsURIs \leftarrow$ GENERATEURIS(numClasses)
    $root \leftarrow$ RANDOMDRAW(clsURIs)
    $i \leftarrow 0$
    $workList \leftarrow$ NEWLIST( )
    $result \leftarrow$ NEWTREE( )
    $currentURI \leftarrow root$
    for $clsURI$ in $clsURIs$ **do**
        if $clsURI = root$ **then**
            CONTINUE
        end if
        if $i = branchingFactor$ **then**
            $currentURI \leftarrow workList.removeFirst()$
            $i \leftarrow 0$
        end if
        $result.addLeaf(currentURI, clsURI)$
        $i \leftarrow i + 1$
        $workList.add(clsURI)$
    end for
    return $result$
end procedure

procedure GENERATEPROPERTIES(numProperties, classTree)
    $properties \leftarrow$ GENERATEURIS(numProperties)
    for $property$ in $properties$ **do**
        $property.addDomain($ DRAWDOMAINRANGE(classTree, 0.25))
        $property.addRange($ DRAWDOMAINRANGE(classTree, 0.25))
    end for
    return $properties$
end procedure

procedure DRAWDOMAINRANGE(classTree, p)
    $result \leftarrow classTree.randomClass()$
    while $Random.nextDouble > p \wedge \neg(classTree.getChildren(result) == \emptyset)$ **do**
        $result \leftarrow randomDraw(classTree.getChildren(result))$
    end while
end procedure

procedure POPULATECLASSES(numInstances, classTree)
    $instances \leftarrow$ GENERATEURIS(numInstances)
    for $instance$ in $instances$ **do**
        $instance.type(classTree.randomClass())$
    end for
    return $instances$
end procedure

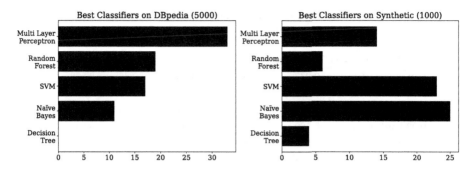

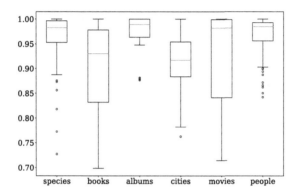

Fig. 4. Best classifiers on the DBpedia and synthetic gold standards. It is important to note that the total number of test cases varies between the two gold standards – therefore, two separate plots were drawn.

Fig. 5. Domain complexity of the DBpedia gold standard (size class 5000)

the respective default parameters, with 200 dimensions for DBpedia and 100 for the synthetic datasets, as for RDF2vec. The models are publicly available.[16]

6.2   Results and Interpretation

The results on the DBpedia gold standard (class size 5,000) and the synthetic gold standard (class size 1,000) are depicted in Tables 3 and 4. For each model and test case, six classifiers were trained (192 classifiers in total). The tables present the results of the best classifiers. We performed significance tests (approximated one-sided binomial test) for each test case and approach with $\alpha = 0.05$ to determine whether the accuracy is significantly higher than 0.5 (random guessing). Since multiple classifiers were trained for each test case, we applied a Bonferroni correction [18] of α to account for the multiple testing problem. On the DBpedia gold standard, all results are significant; on the synthetic gold standard, more insignificant results are observed, particularly for TransR and ComplEx.

---

[16] http://data.dws.informatik.uni-mannheim.de/kgvec2go/dbpedia/2021-09/non-rdf2vec/.

Table 3. Results on the DBpedia gold standard. The best result for each test case is printed in bold. Listed are the results of the best classifier for each task and model.

TC	RDF2vec	RDF2vec$_{oa}$	TransE-L1	TransE-L2	TransR	ComplEx
tc01	0.915	0.937	0.842	**0.947**	0.858	0.862
tc01 hard	0.681	0.891	0.799	**0.916**	0.744	0.651
tc02	0.953	0.961	0.852	**0.970**	0.832	0.853
tc02 hard	0.637	0.780	0.780	**0.849**	0.693	0.608
tc03	0.949	**0.958**	0.821	0.933	0.856	0.874
tc04	0.960	0.968	0.934	0.986	0.973	**0.990**
tc04 hard	0.963	**0.984**	0.814	0.912	0.855	0.935
tc05	0.986	**0.992**	0.867	0.948	0.881	0.905
tc06	0.957	0.963	0.929	0.985	0.976	**0.991**
tc06 hard	0.863	0.936	0.823	0.779	**0.964**	0.933
tc07	0.938	0.955	0.930	**0.987**	0.978	0.966
tc08	0.961	**0.966**	0.898	0.964	0.870	0.888
tc09	0.902	0.901	0.884	**0.938**	0.879	0.883
tc09 hard	0.785	0.793	0.749	**0.848**	0.758	0.776
tc10	0.947	0.958	0.957	**0.984**	0.898	0.931
tc10 hard	0.740	0.737	**0.775**	0.774	0.656	0.739
tc11	0.932	0.897	0.917	**0.960**	0.930	0.946
tc11 hard	0.725	0.737	0.712	**0.806**	0.753	0.723
tc12	0.955	0.938	0.961	**0.984**	0.879	0.894
tc12 hard	0.714	0.717	0.762	**0.765**	0.659	0.710

Figure 4 shows the aggregated number of the best classifiers for each embedding on each test case. It is visible that on DBpedia, MLPs work best, followed by random forests and SVMs. On the synthetic gold standard, naïve Bayes works best most of the time, followed by SVMs and MLPs. The differences can partly be explained by the different size classes of the training sets (MLPs and random forests typically work better on more data).

Figure 5 depicts the complexity per domain of the DBpedia gold standard in a box-and-whisker plot. The complexity was determined by using the accuracy of the best classifier of each embedding model without hard test cases (since not every domain has an equal amount of hard test cases). We observe that all domain test cases are similarly hard to solve, whereby the albums, people, and species domain are a bit simpler to solve than the books and cities domain.

In general, we can observe that the results on the DBpedia gold standard are much higher than on the synthetic gold standard. While on the DBpedia gold standard, all but five tasks can be solved with an accuracy above 0.9 (although the cases with hard variants are actually harder than the non-hard ones, and all the five problems with a best accuracy below 0.9 are hard cases), the synthetic gold standard has quite a few tasks (tc07–tc12) which are obviously much harder. For example, it is hardly possible for any of the approaches to learn classes whose

Table 4. Results on the synthetic gold standard. The best result for each test case is printed in bold; statistically insignificant results are printed in italics. Listed are the results of the best classifier for each task and model.

TC	RDF2vec	RDF2vec$_{oa}$	TransE-L1	TransE-L2	TransR	ComplEx
tc01	**0.882**	0.867	0.767	0.752	0.712	0.789
tc02	**0.742**	0.737	0.677	0.677	*0.531*	*0.549*
tc03	0.797	**0.812**	*0.531*	0.581	*0.554*	*0.536*
tc04	**1.000**	0.998	0.790	0.898	0.685	*0.553*
tc05	**0.892**	0.819	0.691	0.774	0.631	0.726
tc06	0.978	0.963	0.898	0.978	0.888	**1.000**
tc07	0.583	0.583	*0.540*	0.615	**0.673**	*0.518*
tc08	0.563	0.585	0.585	**0.613**	*0.540*	*0.523*
tc09	0.610	**0.628**	0.588	*0.543*	*0.525*	*0.545*
tc10	**0.638**	0.623	0.588	0.573	*0.518*	*0.510*
tc11	**0.633**	0.580	0.583	0.590	0.573	0.590
tc12	**0.644**	0.614	0.618	*0.550*	*0.513*	*0.540*

definitions involve cardinalities. RDF2vec can produce results slightly above the baseline here because the frequencies of properties appearing in random walks can reflect cardinalities to a certain extent.

Furthermore, we can observe that it seems easier to predict patterns involving outgoing edges than those involving ingoing edges (cf. tc02 vs. tc01, tc08 vs. tc07, tc10 vs. tc09, tc12 vs. tc11), at least for the DBpedia case. Even though the tasks are very related, this can be explained by the learning process, which often emphasizes outgoing directions: In RDF2vec, random walks are performed in forward direction; similarly, TransE is directed in its training process.

For constructors involving a particular entity (tc04 and tc05), we can observe that RDF2vec is clearly better than embedding approaches for link prediction, at least on the synthetic gold dataset. Those tasks refer to *entity relatedness*, for which RDF2vec has been shown to be more adequate [14,15]. The picture is more diverse for the other cases.

6.3   DBpedia Gold Standard vs. Synthetic Gold Standard

The results reveal great differences between the gold standards. Many class constructors that are easily learnable on the DBpedia gold standard are hard on the synthetic one. Moreover, the previously reported superiority of RDF2vec$_{oa}$ over standard RDF2vec [11,14] cannot be observed on the synthetic data.

Figure 6 shows an excerpt of DBpedia, which we will use to illustrate these deviations. The instance `dbr:LeBron_James` is a positive example for task tc07 in Table 2. At the same time, 95.6% of all entities in DBpedia fulfilling the positive query for positive examples also fall in the class $\exists$`dbo:position`.$\top$ (which is

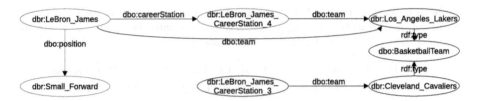

Fig. 6. Excerpt of DBpedia

a tc01 problem), but only 13.6% of all entities fulfilling the query for trivial negatives. Hence, on a balanced dataset, this class can be learned with an accuracy of 0.91 by any approach that can learn classes of type tc01. As a comparison to the synthetic dataset shows, the results on the DBpedia test set for tc07 actually overestimate the capability of many embedding approaches to learn classes constructed with a tc07 class constructor. Such correlations are quite frequent in DBpedia but vastly absent in the synthetic dataset.

The example can also explain the advantage of RDF2vec$_{oa}$ on DBpedia. Unlike standard RDF2vec, this approach would distinguish the appearance of dbo:team as a direct edge of dbr:LeBron_James as well as an indirect edge connected to dbr:LeBron_James_CareerStation_N, where the former denotes the current team, whereas the latter also denotes all previous teams. Those subtle semantic differences of distinctive usages of the same property in various contexts also do not exist in the synthetic gold standard. Hence, the order-aware variant of RDF2vec does not have an advantage here.

7   Conclusion and Future Work

In this paper, we presented DLCC, a resource to analyze embedding approaches in terms of which kinds of classes they are able to represent. DLCC comes with an evaluation framework to easily evaluate embeddings using a reproducible protocol. All DLCC components, i.e., the gold standard, the generation framework, and the evaluation framework, are publicly available.[17]

We have shown that many patterns using DL class constructors on DBpedia are actually learned by recognizing patterns with other constructors correlating with the pattern to be learned, thus yielding misleading results. This effect is less prominent in the synthetic gold standard. We showed that certain DL constructors, such as cardinality constraints, are particularly hard to learn.

In the future, we plan to extend the systematic evaluation to more embedding approaches, including the flavors of RDF2vec, which were published more recently [14,15,20]. The synthetic dataset generator also allows for more interesting experiments: We can systematically analyze the scalability of existing approaches or study how variations in the synthetic gold standard (e.g., larger and smaller ontologies) influence the outcome.

---

[17] Dataset DOI: 10.5281/zenodo.6509715.

References

1. Alshargi, F., Shekarpour, S., Soru, T., Sheth, A.P.: Metrics for evaluating quality of embeddings for ontological concepts. In: Martin, A., Hinkelmann, K., Gerber, A., Lenat, D., van Harmelen, F., Clark, P. (eds.) Proceedings of the AAAI 2019 Spring Symposium on Combining Machine Learning with Knowledge Engineering (AAAI-MAKE 2019) Stanford University, Palo Alto, California, USA, March 25–27, 2019, Stanford University, Palo Alto, California, USA, 25–27 March 2019. CEUR Workshop Proceedings, vol. 2350. CEUR-WS.org (2019). https://ceur-ws.org/Vol-2350/paper26.pdf
2. Bloem, P., Wilcke, X., van Berkel, L., de Boer, V.: kgbench: a collection of knowledge graph datasets for evaluating relational and multimodal machine learning. In: Verborgh, R., et al. (eds.) ESWC 2021. LNCS, vol. 12731, pp. 614–630. Springer, Cham (2021). https://doi.org/10.1007/978-3-030-77385-4_37
3. Bordes, A., Usunier, N., García-Durán, A., Weston, J., Yakhnenko, O.: Translating embeddings for modeling multi-relational data. In: Burges, C.J.C., Bottou, L., Ghahramani, Z., Weinberger, K.Q. (eds.) Advances in Neural Information Processing Systems 26: 27th Annual Conference on Neural Information Processing Systems 2013. Proceedings of a meeting held December 5–8, 2013, Lake Tahoe, Nevada, United States. pp. 2787–2795 (2013). https://proceedings.neurips.cc/paper/2013/hash/1cecc7a77928ca8133fa24680a88d2f9-Abstract.html
4. Dettmers, T., Minervini, P., Stenetorp, P., Riedel, S.: Convolutional 2D knowledge graph embeddings. In: McIlraith, S.A., Weinberger, K.Q. (eds.) Proceedings of the Thirty-Second AAAI Conference on Artificial Intelligence (AAAI-18), the 30th innovative Applications of Artificial Intelligence (IAAI-2018), and the 8th AAAI Symposium on Educational Advances in Artificial Intelligence (EAAI-2018), New Orleans, Louisiana, USA, 2–7 February 2018, pp. 1811–1818. AAAI Press (2018). https://www.aaai.org/ocs/index.php/AAAI/AAAI18/paper/view/17366
5. Fellbaum, C. (ed.): WordNet: An Electronic Lexical Database. Language, Speech, and Communication, MIT Press, Cambridge (1998). https://doi.org/10.7551/mitpress/7287.001.0001, https://doi.org/10.7551/mitpress/7287.001.0001
6. Heist, N., Hertling, S., Ringler, D., Paulheim, H.: Knowledge graphs on the web - an overview. In: Tiddi, I., Lécué, F., Hitzler, P. (eds.) Knowledge Graphs for eXplainable Artificial Intelligence: Foundations, Applications and Challenges, Studies on the Semantic Web, vol. 47, pp. 3–22. IOS Press (2020). https://doi.org/10.3233/SSW200009, https://doi.org/10.3233/SSW200009
7. Lin, Y., Liu, Z., Sun, M., Liu, Y., Zhu, X.: Learning entity and relation embeddings for knowledge graph completion. In: Bonet, B., Koenig, S. (eds.) Proceedings of the Twenty-Ninth AAAI Conference on Artificial Intelligence, 25–30 January 2015, Austin, Texas, USA, pp. 2181–2187. AAAI Press (2015). https://www.aaai.org/ocs/index.php/AAAI/AAAI15/paper/view/9571
8. Melo, A., Paulheim, H.: Synthesizing knowledge graphs for link and type prediction benchmarking. In: Blomqvist, E., Maynard, D., Gangemi, A., Hoekstra, R., Hitzler, P., Hartig, O. (eds.) ESWC 2017. LNCS, vol. 10249, pp. 136–151. Springer, Cham (2017). https://doi.org/10.1007/978-3-319-58068-5_9
9. Pellegrino, M.A., Altabba, A., Garofalo, M., Ristoski, P., Cochez, M.: GEval: a modular and extensible evaluation framework for graph embedding techniques. In: Harth, A., et al. (eds.) ESWC 2020. LNCS, vol. 12123, pp. 565–582. Springer, Cham (2020). https://doi.org/10.1007/978-3-030-49461-2_33

10. Pellegrino, M.A., Cochez, M., Garofalo, M., Ristoski, P.: A configurable evaluation framework for node embedding techniques. In: Hitzler, P., et al. (eds.) ESWC 2019. LNCS, vol. 11762, pp. 156–160. Springer, Cham (2019). https://doi.org/10.1007/978-3-030-32327-1_31

11. Portisch, J., Heist, N., Paulheim, H.: Knowledge graph embedding for data mining vs. knowledge graph embedding for link prediction - two sides of the same coin? Seman. Web **13**(3), 399–422 (2022). https://doi.org/10.3233/SW-212892, https://doi.org/10.3233/SW-212892

12. Portisch, J., Hladik, M., Paulheim, H.: Kgvec2go - knowledge graph embeddings as a service. In: Calzolari, N., et al. (eds.) Proceedings of The 12th Language Resources and Evaluation Conference, LREC 2020, Marseille, France, 11–16 May 2020. pp. 5641–5647. European Language Resources Association (2020). https://aclanthology.org/2020.lrec-1.692/

13. Portisch, J., Hladik, M., Paulheim, H.: Rdf2vec light - a lightweight approach for knowledge graph embeddings. In: Taylor, K.L., Gonçalves, R.S., Lécué, F., Yan, J. (eds.) Proceedings of the ISWC 2020 Demos and Industry Tracks: From Novel Ideas to Industrial Practice co-located with 19th International Semantic Web Conference (ISWC 2020), Globally online, November 1–6, 2020 (UTC). CEUR Workshop Proceedings, vol. 2721, pp. 79–84. CEUR-WS.org (2020). https://ceur-ws.org/Vol-2721/paper520.pdf

14. Portisch, J., Paulheim, H.: Putting RDF2vec in order. In: Seneviratne, O., Pesquita, C., Sequeda, J., Etcheverry, L. (eds.) Proceedings of the ISWC 2021 Posters, Demos and Industry Tracks: From Novel Ideas to Industrial Practice co-located with 20th International Semantic Web Conference (ISWC 2021), Virtual Conference, 24–28 October 2021. CEUR Workshop Proceedings, vol. 2980. CEUR-WS.org (2021). https://ceur-ws.org/Vol-2980/paper352.pdf

15. Portisch, J., Paulheim, H.: Walk this way! entity walks and property walks for RDF2vec. CoRR abs/2204.02777 (2022). 10.48550/arXiv. 2204.02777, https://doi.org/10.48550/arXiv.2204.02777

16. Ristoski, P., Rosati, J., Noia, T.D., Leone, R.D., Paulheim, H.: Rdf2vec: RDF graph embeddings and their applications. Seman. Web **10**(4), 721–752 (2019). https://doi.org/10.3233/SW-180317, https://doi.org/10.3233/SW-180317

17. Ristoski, P., de Vries, G.K.D., Paulheim, H.: A collection of benchmark datasets for systematic evaluations of machine learning on the semantic web. In: Groth, P., et al. (eds.) The Semantic Web - ISWC 2016–15th International Semantic Web Conference, Kobe, Japan, 17–21 October 2016, Proceedings, Part II. LNCS, vol. 9982, pp. 186–194 (2016). https://doi.org/10.1007/978-3-319-46547-0_20, https://doi.org/10.1007/978-3-319-46547-0_20

18. Salzberg, S.: On comparing classifiers: Pitfalls to avoid and a recommended approach. Data Min. Knowl. Discov. **1**(3), 317–328 (1997). https://doi.org/10.1023/A:1009752403260, https://doi.org/10.1023/A:1009752403260

19. Shi, B., Weninger, T.: Open-world knowledge graph completion. In: McIlraith, S.A., Weinberger, K.Q. (eds.) Proceedings of the Thirty-Second AAAI Conference on Artificial Intelligence, (AAAI-2018), the 30th Innovative Applications of Artificial Intelligence (IAAI-2018), and the 8th AAAI Symposium on Educational Advances in Artificial Intelligence (EAAI-2018), New Orleans, Louisiana, USA, 2–7 February 2018, pp. 1957–1964. AAAI Press (2018). https://www.aaai.org/ocs/index.php/AAAI/AAAI18/paper/view/16055

20. Steenwinckel, E., et al.: Walk extraction strategies for node embeddings with RDF2vec in knowledge graphs. In: Kotsis, G., et al. (eds.) DEXA 2021. CCIS, vol. 1479, pp. 70–80. Springer, Cham (2021). https://doi.org/10.1007/978-3-030-87101-7_8

21. Toutanova, K., Chen, D.: Observed versus latent features for knowledge base and text inference. In: Proceedings of the 3rd Workshop on Continuous Vector Space Models and Their Compositionality, pp. 57–66 (2015). https://doi.org/10.18653/v1/W15-4007, https://www.doi.org/10.18653/v1/W15-4007

22. Trouillon, T., Welbl, J., Riedel, S., Gaussier, É., Bouchard, G.: Complex embeddings for simple link prediction. In: Balcan, M., Weinberger, K.Q. (eds.) Proceedings of the 33nd International Conference on Machine Learning, ICML 2016, New York City, NY, USA, June 19–24, 2016. JMLR Workshop and Conference Proceedings, vol. 48, pp. 2071–2080. JMLR.org (2016). https://proceedings.mlr.press/v48/trouillon16.html

23. Zheng, D., et al.: DGL-KE: training knowledge graph embeddings at scale. In: Huang, J., et al. (eds.) Proceedings of the 43rd International ACM SIGIR conference on research and development in Information Retrieval, SIGIR 2020, Virtual Event, China, July 25–30, 2020. pp. 739–748. ACM (2020). https://doi.org/10.1145/3397271.3401172, https://doi.org/10.1145/3397271.3401172

μKG: A Library for Multi-source Knowledge Graph Embeddings and Applications

Xindi Luo[1], Zequn Sun[1] , and Wei Hu[1,2(✉)]

[1] State Key Laboratory for Novel Software Technology, Nanjing University,
Nanjing, China
xdluo.nju@gmail.com, zqsun.nju@gmail.com, whu@nju.edu.cn
[2] National Institute of Healthcare Data Science, Nanjing University, Nanjing, China

Abstract. This paper presents μKG, an open-source Python library for representation learning over knowledge graphs. μKG supports joint representation learning over multi-source knowledge graphs (and also a single knowledge graph), multiple deep learning libraries (PyTorch and TensorFlow2), multiple embedding tasks (link prediction, entity alignment, entity typing, and multi-source link prediction), and multiple parallel computing modes (multi-process and multi-GPU computing). It currently implements 26 popular knowledge graph embedding models and supports 16 benchmark datasets. μKG provides advanced implementations of embedding techniques with simplified pipelines of different tasks. It also comes with high-quality documentation for ease of use. μKG is more comprehensive than existing knowledge graph embedding libraries. It is useful for a thorough comparison and analysis of various embedding models and tasks. We show that the jointly learned embeddings can greatly help knowledge-powered downstream tasks, such as multi-hop knowledge graph question answering. We will stay abreast of the latest developments in the related fields and incorporate them into μKG.

Resource Type: Software
License: GPL-3.0 License
GitHub Repository: https://github.com/nju-websoft/muKG

Keywords: Multi-source knowledge graphs · Representation learning · Link prediction · Entity alignment · Entity typing

1 Introduction

Knowledge graphs (KGs), such as Freebase [4], DBpedia [21], Wikidata [45], and YAGO [25], store rich structured knowledge about the real world. They have been widely used in a variety of knowledge-driven applications, including semantic search, question answering, and logic reasoning [19]. Learning vector

---

X. Luo and Z. Sun—Equal contributors.

U. Sattler et al. (Eds.): ISWC 2022, LNCS 13489, pp. 610–627, 2022.
https://doi.org/10.1007/978-3-031-19433-7_35

representations (a.k.a. embeddings) of KGs has become critical to support these intelligent applications. In the past ten years, various KG embedding models such as TransE [5], ConvE [12], RotatE [41] and TuckER [3] were proposed and achieved promising performance. Please refer to the recent surveys [31, 46] for an overview. With these applications becoming more and more popular and diverse, they put forward higher demands to KGs in terms of coverage, richness and multilingualism. Oftentimes, a single KG cannot meet all these demands. This difficulty calls for the integration of multiple KGs. Learning from multi-source KGs with entity alignment has drawn a lot of attention in recent years [10, 36]. The joint KG embeddings have demonstrated useful for a variety of downstream tasks such as entity typing and multi-source KG completion [11, 35].

Table 1. Comparison of existing KG embedding libraries and ours.

Libraries	Multi-KG support	Deep learning libraries		KG tasks			
		PyTorch	TensorFlow	LP	EA	ET	Multi-LP
OpenKE [16] [a]	✗	✓	TF1	✓	✗	✗	✗
DGL-KE [57] [b]	✗	✓	✗	✓	✗	✗	✗
Pykg2vec [53] [c]	✗	✓	TF2	✓	✗	✗	✗
PyKEEN [1,2] [d]	✗	✓	✗	✓	✗	✗	✗
TorchKGE [6] [e]	✗	✓	✗	✓	✗	✗	✗
LibKGE [7] [f]	✗	✓	✗	✓	✗	✗	✗
OpenEA [40] [g]	✓	✗	TF1	✗	✓	✗	✗
EAkit [54] [h]	✓	✓	✗	✗	✓	✗	✗
NeuralKG [56] [i]	✗	✓	✗	✓	✗	✗	✗
μKG (Ours)	✓	✓	TF2	✓	✓	✓	✓

[a] https://github.com/thunlp/OpenKE.
[b] https://github.com/awslabs/dgl-ke.
[c] https://github.com/Sujit-O/pykg2vec.
[d] https://github.com/pykeen/pykeen.
[e] https://github.com/torchkge-team/torchkge.
[f] https://github.com/uma-pi1/kge.
[g] https://github.com/nju-websoft/OpenEA.
[h] https://github.com/THU-KEG/EAkit.
[i] https://github.com/zjukg/NeuralKG.

To support the easy use of KG embeddings and foster reproducible research into KG embedding techniques, much effort has been dedicated to developing KG embedding libraries, including OpenKE [16], DGL-KE [57], Pykg2vec [53], PyKEEN [1,2], TorchKGE [6], LibKGE [7], OpenEA [40], EAkit [54] and NeuralKG [56]. The majority of these libraries concentrates on the typical KG embedding task of link prediction. Only OpenEA and EAkit support multi-source KG embedding and the corresponding task entity alignment. Besides, most of them only support one deep learning library, especially PyTorch. No one supports another prominent deep learning library TensorFlow2 (TF2 for short). This limits the contexts in which these libraries can be used. Facing these limitations of existing work and being aware of the effectiveness of multi-source KG embeddings, we develop a new scalable library, namely μKG, for multi-source KG embeddings and applications. Table 1 compares μKG with the existing popular KG embedding libraries. In summary, μKG has the following features:

- **Comprehensive.** μKG is a full-featured Python library for representation learning over a single KG or multi-source KGs. It is compatible with the two widely-used deep learning libraries PyTorch and TF2, and can therefore be easily integrated into downstream applications. It integrates a variety of KG embedding models and supports four KG tasks including link prediction, entity alignment, entity typing, and multi-source link prediction.
- **Fast and Scalable.** μKG provides advanced implementations of KG embedding techniques with the support of multi-process and multi-GPU parallel computing, making it fast and scalable to large KGs.
- **Easy-to-Use.** μKG provides simplified pipelines of KG embedding tasks for easy use. Users can interact with μKG through both methods APIs and command line. It also has high-quality documentation.
- **Open-Source and Continuously Updated.** The source code of μKG is publicly available. Our team will keep up-to-date on new related techniques and integrate new (multi-source) KG embedding models, tasks, and datasets into μKG. We will also keep improving existing implementations.

Our experiments on several benchmark datasets demonstrate the effectiveness and efficiency of our library μKG. Moreover, we carefully design two new tasks, multi-source link prediction and multi-source knowledge graph question answering (KGQA), with experiments to demonstrate the potential of multi-source KG embeddings:

- For **Multi-source Link Prediction**, we can convert the multiple KGs into a joint graph by merging their aligned entities, on which we learn joint KG embeddings for link prediction over each KG. This differs from the traditional link prediction, which first trains the model on a single KG and then predicts links for the same KG. In our joint learning setting, to avoid the test set of a KG's link prediction task having overlap with other KGs' training set, we do not consider relation alignment in multi-source KGs, and also remove these overlapping triples from the training set if they exist. Our experiment on DBP15K [36] shows that the joint trained TransE [5] outperforms its separately trained variant by 122% on *Hits*@1.
- For **multi-source KGQA**, as a downstream application of KGs, we have attempted to use multi-source KG embeddings to aid in the task of multi-hop question answering over a KG. The typical pipeline of using KG embeddings to answer natural language questions [32] is learning to align the question representation (encoded by a pre-trained language model like BERT [13]) with the answer entity's embedding (encoded by a KG embedding model like ComplEx [44]). Conventional methods and datasets only consider QA over a single KG. We introduce an additional KG for joint embedding with the

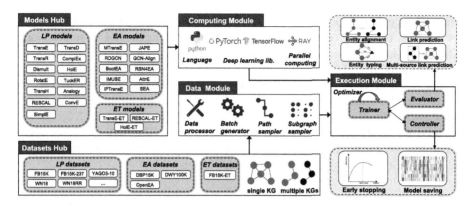

Fig. 1. Framework overview of μKG.

target KG using μKG. The embeddings of the target KG from the joint space are used for QA. Our results on WebQuestionsSP [52] show that joint KG embeddings can improve the accuracy by 8.6% over independently trained embeddings on a single KG.

Overall, these experiments show that the multi-source KG embeddings are able to promote knowledge fusion and transfer, and therefore benefit downstream tasks. We hope that our μKG library can encourage the use of multi-source KG embeddings and promote their applications.

2   μKG

μKG is a scalable library for multi-source KG embeddings and applications. It also supports representation learning over a single KG. Its architecture is shown in Fig. 1. μKG supports a variety of link prediction, entity alignment, and entity typing models, as well as the datasets that go with them. It consists of three modules. The *data module* converts the input single KG or multi-source KGs into the training data format (e.g., triples, paths or subgraphs) used by the embedding model. The *computing module* supports the execution module with neural computation and parallel training solutions. As a result, the *execution module* can be used for large-scale KGs and is compatible with the widely-used deep learning libraries PyTorch and TensorFlow. The execution module trains a KG embedding model with the training data produced by the data module. The *controller* keeps track of and records the training process. The *evaluator* employs the pre-trained embedding model to perform KG tasks, such as link prediction, entity alignment, entity typing, and multi-source link prediction.

2.1   Data Module

We hereby introduce the data module of μKG.

Data Processor. The goal of the *data processor* is to generate numerical IDs for entities, relations, and attributes from the input single KG or multi-source KGs in the Datasets Hub. The numerical ID is the identifier of a resource in an embedding model. The data processor first reads the original relation triples and attribute triples from the txt or ttl files. Then, it assigns an ID to each entity, relation, and attribute. It currently provides two ID generation algorithms. The *unique-ID algorithm* generates a unique ID for each resource in KGs. It can be used for both single KG and multi-source KGs. The *shared-ID algorithm* generates the same ID for aligned entities in different KGs. In this way, the multiple KGs are merged as a "single" joint graph.

Batch Generator. The *batch generator* takes as input KG triples and divides the complete data into multiple fixed-size batches for model training. If the model requires relational paths or subgraphs for training, the batch generator would first call the path or subgraph sampler to convert triples. The batch generator also includes several negative sampling methods to randomly generate negative examples (e.g., negative alignment pairs or negative triples) for each positive example. The positive and negative examples are used in the embedding model for contrastive embedding learning. The *uniform negative sampling* method replaces an entity in a triple or an alignment pair with another randomly-sampled entity to generate a negative example. It gives each entity the same replacement probability. Such uniform negative sampling has the problem of inefficiency since many sampled negative samples are obviously false as training goes on, which does not provide any meaningful information. μKG also supplies the self-adversarial negative sampling method [41] and the truncated negative sampling method [37] that seek to generate hard negative examples.

Path Sampler. The *path sampler* is to support some embedding models that are built by modeling the paths of KGs, such as IPTransE [58] and RSN [15]. It can generate three types of paths based on random walks. The first is the relational path like $(e_1, r_1, e_2, r_2, e_3)$, where e_i stands for an entity and r_j denotes a relation. It is an entity-relation chain. The second is the entity path like (e_1, e_2, e_3), and the third is the relation path like (r_1, r_2).

Subgraph Sampler. The *subgraph sampler* is to support GNN-based embedding models like GCN-Align [49] and AliNet [39]. It can generate both first-order (i.e., one-hop) and high-order (i.e., multi-hop) neighborhood subgraphs of entities. The GNN-based models represent an entity by aggregating the embeddings of its neighbors in the subgraphs.

2.2   Execution Module

This module carries out the training task of embedding models.

Trainer. The *trainer* directs the model training and evaluation based on the detailed configurations of users. It manages the model's training progress. μKG configures trainers for entity alignment models, link prediction models, and entity typing models, respectively. The *trainer* provides three optimizers, including the standard stochastic gradient descent, Adagrad, and Adam. It implements four loss functions, including the mean-squared loss, marginal ranking loss, limit-based loss, and noise-contrastive estimation loss.

Evaluator. The *evaluator* is to assess the performance of the trained model on specific test data. For (joint) link prediction, it uses the energy function to compute the plausibility of a candidate triple. For entity alignment or typing, it provides several metrics to measure entity embedding similarities, such as the cosine, inner, Euclidean distance, and cross-domain similarity local scaling. The evaluation process can be accelerated using multi-processing. The implemented metrics for assessing the performance of embedding tasks include $Hits@K$, mean rank (MR) and mean reciprocal rank (MRR). $Hits@K$ measures the percentage of the test cases in which the correct counterpart is ranked in the top k. MR calculates the mean of these ranks. MRR is the average of the reciprocal ranks of results. Higher $Hits@K$ and MRR or lower MR values indicate better performance.

Controller. The *controller* is in charge of the trainer. During the training process, the controller calls the evaluator to assess the model performance on validation data. If the performance begins to drop continuously, the controller would terminate the training (i.e., early stopping). After that, the controller saves the model and embeddings for further use.

2.3 Computing Module

In this section, we introduce the computing module.

Support of PyTorch and TF2. The computing module uses PyTorch and TF2 as the backbone for neural computing. Users can choose one of the backbones to run μKG or carry on secondary development based on μKG. If no backbone is specified by the user, μKG can automatically detect which backbone has already been installed in the Python environment.

Multi-GPU and Multi-processing Computation. Scalability is a key consideration when we develop μKG, because KGs in real-world applications are typically very large. Although PyTorch and TensorFlow both provide interfaces for parallel computing, they differ greatly in implementation and are difficult for users to use. Hence, we use Ray[1] to provide a uniform and easy-to-use interface

---

[1] https://www.ray.io/.

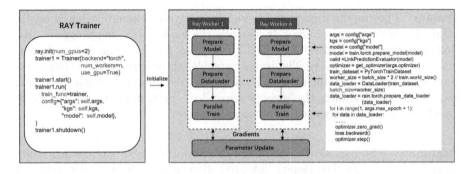

Fig. 2. Code snippet for training KG embedding models in the parallel mode.

```
PS D:\Knower\src\py> python main_args.py -t lp -m transe -o train -d data/FB15K

PS D:\Knower\src\py> python main_args.py -t lp -m transe -o train -d data/FB15K -r gpu:2 -w 2
```

Fig. 3. Command line for using μKG.

for multi-GPU and multi-processing computation. Fig. 2 shows our Ray-based implementation for parallel computing and the code snippet to use it. Users can set the number of CPUs or GPUs used for model training.

2.4   User Interface

μKG gives users two options for running KG embedding models. For users that are unfamiliar with μKG, they can run a model on a dataset with the command line, as shown in Fig. 3. For advanced users, they can modify the configurations of a model and call the model's running function in their Python code.

3   Experiments

In this section, we report our experiments to evaluate the effectiveness and efficiency of μKG. The source code is available at our GitHub repository.[2]

3.1   Experiments on Effectiveness

To evaluate the effectiveness, we compare the results produced by our library with the corresponding official results reported in the models' papers. We consider one single-KG task *link prediction*, and three multi-KG tasks *entity alignment*, *entity typing* and *multi-source link prediction*.

---

[2] https://github.com/nju-websoft/muKG.

Table 2. LP results on FB15K.

Models		Hits@1	Hits@10	MRR
RESCAL	Original	–	0.284	–
	Ours	0.129	0.342	0.202
TransE	Original	–	0.471	–
	Ours	0.194	0.647	0.353
TransH	Original	–	0.585	–
	Ours	0.188	0.604	0.332
TransD	Original	–	0.742	–
	Ours	0.214	0.595	0.345

Table 3. LP results on FB15K-237.

Models		Hits@1	Hits@10	MRR
TransE	Original	–	0.465	0.294
	Ours	0.174	0.463	0.270
ConvE	Original	0.237	0.501	0.325
	Ours	0.237	0.514	0.327
RotatE	Original	0.205	0.480	0.297
	Ours	0.172	0.456	0.260
TuckER	Original	0.266	0.544	0.358
	Ours	0.254	0.535	0.346

Link Prediction. We choose two benchmark datasets, FB15K [5] and FB15K-237 [42], for link prediction evaluation. FB15K-237 was created from FB15K to ensure that the testing and evaluation datasets do not have inverse relation test leakage. Recent link prediction models use FB15K-237 for evaluation. On FB15K, we compare the $Hits@1$, $Hits@10$ and MRR results of four old but popular models in Table 2, including RESCAL [29], TransE [5], TransH [48], and TransD [18]. "–" denotes the unreported results. We can see that our implemented RESCAL, TransE and TransH can achieve better results than the original code due to our modern implementations. We also notice that the implemented TransD shows lower Hits@10 performance than its original version. The reason lies in the different evaluation settings. The original TransD removes the corrupted triplets in the training, validation and test sets before ranking. But our implementation only removes those in the training set following other methods because this is more reasonable. On FB15K-237, we compare TransE and other three recent models including ConvE [12], RotatE [41],[3] and TuckER [3] in Table 3. The results of TransE on FB15K-237 are taken from [41] because TransE was not evaluated on this dataset. As we can see, our implementations of TransE and ConvE in μKG perform very similarly to their original code. As for RotatE and TuckER, the performance of our implementations is slightly lower than the original results, but also in the range of acceptance. This is due to different hyperparameter settings. In consideration of GPU resources, we do not set the embedding dimension to 1,000, which is used in their original papers but would cost too much GPU memory. Generally, a large dimension leads to good performance. In summary, our implementations of link prediction models can basically reproduce the reported results.

Entity Alignment. We use the recent benchmark dataset OpenEA [40] for entity alignment evaluation. OpenEA also provides the implementations of several entity alignment models using TensorFlow 1.12. We choose three structure-based entity alignment models GCN-Align [49], SEA [30] and BootEA [37], as

---

[3] We use uniform negative sampling for a fair comparison with other models.

Table 4. Entity alignment results on EN-DE and EN-FR 15K.

Models	Backends	EN-DE			EN-FR		
		$Hits@1$	$Hits@10$	MRR	$Hits@1$	$Hits@10$	MRR
GCN-Align	OpenEA	0.481	0.753	0.571	0.338	0.680	0.451
	TF2 (ours)	0.480	0.754	0.571	0.335	0.670	0.446
	PyTorch (ours)	0.460	0.747	0.560	0.337	0.671	0.453
SEA	OpenEA	0.530	0.796	0.617	0.280	0.642	0.328
	TF2 (ours)	0.536	0.806	0.624	0.281	0.630	0.304
	PyTorch (ours)	0.561	0.834	0.650	0.321	0.679	0.439
BootEA	OpenEA	0.675	0.865	0.740	0.507	0.794	0.603
	TF2 (ours)	0.671	0.866	0.737	0.503	0.786	0.597
	PyTorch (ours)	0.662	0.884	0.738	0.493	0.811	0.599
IMUSE	OpenEA	0.580	0.778	0.647	0.569	0.777	0.638
	TF2 (ours)	0.567	0.672	0.636	0.571	0.777	0.640
	PyTorch (ours)	0.596	0.804	0.670	0.564	0.776	0.640

well as an attribute-enhanced model IMUSE [17], as baselines. We compare their $Hits@1$, $Hits@10$ and MRR results on OpenEA's EN-DE and EN-FR 15K settings with our PyTorch-based implementations and TF2-based implementations in Table 4. We can see that the two implementations of a model in μKG achieve similar performance. For SEA and IMUSE, PyTorch-based implementations perform better than TF2-based implementations. We think this is caused by the difference between the two backbones. When compared to the results of OpenEA, μKG achieves comparable results. This demonstrates the efficacy of our implementations for entity alignment models.

Entity Typing. Entity typing can be seen as a special link prediction task across an instance KG and an ontological KG. For example, given ("Michael Jackson", "rdf:type", _), the task is to predict the target type "/music/artist". We use the FB15K-ET dataset for evaluation [26]. FB15K-ET is an expansion of FB15K with entity types. We follow [26] to implement two baselines, RESCAL-ET and HolE-ET, for entity typing. The two models are built based on the link prediction models RESCAL [29] and HolE [28], respectively. We compare our results with those in [26] in Table 5. We can observe that our implementations achieve similar or even better performance than those in [26], demonstrating the effectiveness of μKG in entity typing.

Multi-source Link Prediction. This is a new task that we propose, which is inspired by both link prediction in a single KG and entity alignment between two KGs. We believe that training embeddings solely on a KG for link prediction is ineffective because the KG may be very incomplete. We introduce another background KG with entity alignment to the target KG for joint KG embedding learning. We use the shared-ID generation method in μKG to merge the two

Table 5. Entity typing results on FB15K-ET.

Models		$Hits@1$	$Hits@10$	MRR
RESCAL-ET	Original	0.097	0.376	0.190
	Ours	0.128	0.456	0.236
HolE-ET	Original	0.133	0.382	0.220
	Ours	0.129	0.522	0.252

KGs and learn embeddings of the joint KG with a KG embedding model such as TransE [5]. When the learning progress is completed, only the embeddings of the target KG are used to participate in link prediction. For evaluation, we choose DBP15K$_{ZH-EN}$ [36]. It is an entity alignment dataset, and we denote the two KGs in DBP$_{ZH-EN}$ by DBP$_{ZH}$ and DBP$_{EN}$, respectively. Following TransE [5], we divide triples into training, validation and test sets. Specifically, DBP$_{ZH}$ has $63,372$ training triples, $3,522$ validation triples and $3,520$ test triples, while DBP$_{EN}$ has $85,627$, $4,758$ and $4,757$, respectively. Conventional link prediction is usually carried out on a single KG. However, for multi-source link prediction with entity alignment, it would be interesting to see the performance of link prediction based on the jointly-trained KG embeddings. Based on μKG, we train a TransE model over the joint graph of DBP$_{ZH}$ and DBP$_{EN}$. We choose three translational models TransE [5], TransH [48] and TransD [18]; four semantic matching models DistMult [51], HolE [28], ComplEx [44] and Analogy [23]; as well as two neural models ProjE [34] and ConvE [12], as baselines. From Table 6, we can see that μKG (TransE) outperforms the translational and semantic matching models. ConvE achieves better results than our method, but its model complexity is also much higher than TransE. By encoding alignment information, μKG (TransE) greatly outperforms TransE. The results demonstrate the joint training is effective to improve the separately-trained models on link prediction. We think that this is because the alignment information between two KGs can complement the incomplete relational structures of each other.

3.2 Experiments on Efficiency

In this section, we evaluate the efficiency of the proposed library μKG. The experiments were conducted on a server with an Intel Xeon Gold 6240 2.6GHz CPU, 512GB of memory and four NVIDIA Tesla V100 GPUs.

Efficiency of Multi-GPU Training. Figure 4 compares the training time of RotatE and ConvE on FB15K-237 when using different numbers of GPUs. As we can see, using multiple GPUs for parallel computing can significantly accelerate training. The final link prediction results are not affected by parallel computing.

Table 6. Link prediction results with joint KG embeddings.

Models	DBP$_{ZH}$			DBP$_{EN}$		
	Hits@1	Hits@10	MRR	Hits@1	Hits@10	MRR
TransE	0.100	0.529	0.248	0.099	0.512	0.241
TransH	0.103	0.519	0.274	0.125	0.535	0.263
TransD	0.097	0.506	0.237	0.114	0.517	0.251
DistMult	0.095	0.375	0.188	0.100	0.385	0.195
HolE	0.114	0.327	0.186	0.122	0.405	0.221
ComplEx	0.174	0.374	0.245	0.195	0.435	0.279
Analogy	0.145	0.363	0.220	0.169	0.375	0.241
ProjE	0.257	0.613	0.317	0.265	0.629	0.323
ConvE	0.291	0.597	0.398	0.322	0.631	0.429
μKG (TransE)	0.222	0.549	0.331	0.252	0.585	0.363

For example, the Hits@1 scores of ConvE when using 1, 2, and 4 GPUs for computing are 0.241, 0.239 and 0.227, respectively. This experiment shows the efficiency of our multi-GPU training.

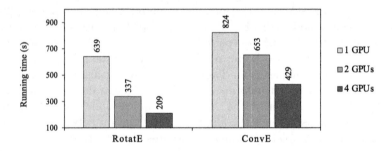

Fig. 4. Running time comparison on FB15K-237 with multi-GPU training.

Efficiency Comparison Against LibKGE and PyKEEN. We further compare the training time used by μKG with LibKGE [7] and PyKEEN [1]. They are both PyTorch-based libraries for efficient training, evaluation, and optimization of KG embeddings. The backbone of μKG in this experiment is also PyTorch. Table 7 gives the training time of ConvE and RotatE on FB15K-237 with a single GPU for calculation. For a fair comparison, we use the same hyper-parameter settings (e.g., batch size and maximum training epochs) for each model in the three libraries. We discover that μKG costs less time than LibKGE and PyKEEN to train a KG embedding model, which demonstrates its efficiency.

Table 7. Running time on FB15K-237 with a GPU.

Models	μKG	LibKGE	PyKEEN
RotatE	**639** s	3,260 s	1,085 s
ConvE	**824** s	1,801 s	961 s

4   Application to Multi-hop KGQA

We hereby report the experimental results on the downstream task, i.e., multi-hop KGQA, using our proposed joint embeddings.

Settings. We follow EmbedKGQA [32], a recent popular embedding-based KGQA method, to build a QA pipeline with our μKG. EmbedKGQA consists of three modules. The KG embedding module learns embeddings for the input KG. Existing KG embedding models such as TransE [5] and ComplEx [44] can be chosen. The question embedding module encodes natural language questions with the help of the pre-trained language model RoBERTa [24], which is a new training recipe that improves on BERT and is widely used for encoding natural language text. The answer selection module chooses the final answer based on the question and relation similarity scores. Using KG embeddings to answer natural language questions can make it more effective in handling the relational sparsity in KGs. The KG embedding model used in EmbedKGQA is ComplEx. In our pipeline for QA, we use μKG (the embedding model is also ComplEx) to learn joint embeddings based on the target KG and another background KG Wikidata5M [47], which is a subset of Wikidata with million-scale entities. For a fair comparison, we keep other modules in our pipeline the same as those in EmbedKGQA.

Dataset. We choose the popular multi-hop QA benchmark WebQuestionsSP [52] as the dataset. There are 4,737 questions in total. This dataset contains 1-hop and 2-hop questions that may be answered using Freebase entities [4]. Following EmbedKGQA, we limit the KG to a subset of Freebase that contains all relational triples within 2-hops of any entity specified in the WebQuestionsSP questions. We refine it further to include only those relations that are stated in the dataset. There are a total of 1.8 million entities and 5.7 million triples in this selected KG (denoted as FB4QA in this paper) to support these questions. The number of entity links between Wikidata5M and FB4QA is 493,987.

Results. Table 8 presents the QA accuracy. To study the effect of KG sparsity on QA performance, following EmbedKGQA, the FB4QA is used for two settings: Half-FB4QA and Full-FB4QA. The former randomly drops half of the triples in FB4QA to simulate an incomplete KG. The latter uses the full FB4QA to learn entity embeddings. Besides, in the Full-FB4QA w/ rel. pruning setting,

Table 8. QA accuracy on WebQuestionsSP.

	EmbedKGQA [32]	EmbedKGQA + Wikidata5M
Half-FB4QA	0.485	0.547
Full-FB4QA	0.587	0.646
Full-FB4QA w/rel. pruning	0.666	0.723

a relation pruning strategy is employed to reduce the candidate answer space by filtering out the dissimilar relations with the key entity in the question. We can see from the table that EmbedKGQA + Wikidata outperforms the baseline EmbedKGQA in all three settings. This is because our learned embeddings of FB4QA can benefit from the background KG, and thus are more expressive than those in EmbedKGQA. Both our method and EmbedKGQA in the Full-KG setting achieve better accuracy than the corresponding result in the Half-KG setting. This demonstrates that KG incompleteness degrades the quality of KG embeddings, and thus causes a decrease in performance. Our method can improve the incompleteness issue in KGs through knowledge transfer from other background KGs. We also consider extending LibKGE [7] for this new task. We merge two KGs into a large graph and use LibKGE to learn KG embeddings. The accuracy is 0.718 in the setting of Full-FB4QA w/ rel. pruning, a similar performance compared with our μKG. This result further shows the effectiveness of our library and the potential of multi-source KG embeddings. In summary, this experiment demonstrates that multi-source KG embeddings are also effective in improving KG-related downstream tasks, and knowledge transfer between multi-source KGs is an alternative for boosting performance in real-world applications.

5   Related Work

In this section, we review the related work on KG embedding models and tasks, as well as existing libraries for KG embedding.

5.1   Knowledge Graph Embedding Tasks and Models

Link Prediction. TransE [5] introduces translational KG embeddings. It defines the score function $f_{\text{TransE}}(\tau) = ||\mathbf{h} + \mathbf{r} - \mathbf{t}||^4$ to measure the plausibility of relational triple $\tau = (h, r, t)$, where h, r and t denote the head entity, relation and tail entity, respectively. Boldfaced letters denote the corresponding vector representations. Although TransE performs well for modeling one-to-one relations, it encounters issues when dealing with more complex relations. For example, if (h, r, t_1) and (h, r, t_2) hold for a one-to-many relation r, we have $\mathbf{h} + \mathbf{r} \approx \mathbf{t}_1$ and $\mathbf{h} + \mathbf{r} \approx \mathbf{t}_2$, then $\mathbf{t}_1 \approx \mathbf{t}_2$. If (h, r_1, t) and (h, r_2, t) hold for h and t, we have $\mathbf{r}_1 \approx \mathbf{r}_2$. To resolve these problems, several improved translational

---

[4] Hereafter, $|| \cdot ||$ denotes the L_2 vector norm.

models, such as TransH [48], TransR [22], and TransD [18], have been proposed. They enable entities to have relation-specific embeddings. For example, TransH interprets a relation as a translation vector on a hyperplane, while TransR and TransD embed entities and relations in distinct vector spaces. RotatE [41] is an improved variant in the complex vector space. Besides, semantic matching-based models exploit similarity-based functions to score relational triples. The scores are computed using bilinear functions in RESCAL [29], DistMult [51], ComplEx [44] and SimplE [20], while HolE [28] replaces dot product with circular correlation. Embeddings are given analogical qualities in Analogy [23]. Recently, neural network-based models, including ProjE [34], ConvE [12], R-GCN [33], ConvKB [27], KBGAN [8] and LinkNBed [14], achieve superior link prediction performance. μKG currently supports TransE, TransR, TransH, TransD, TuckER, DisMult, ComplEx, HolE, Analogy, RESCAL, RotatE, SimplE and ConvE.

Entity Alignment. Embedding-based entity alignment models usually consist of two modules, i.e., KG embedding and alignment learning. For KG embedding based on relational facts, many models including MTransE [10], IPTransE [58], JAPE [36], KDCoE [9], BootEA [37], SEA [30], AttrE [43], MultiKE [55] and TransEdge [38] adopt TransE [5] or its improved variants. Most of other models like GCN-Align [49], RDGCN [50] and AliNet [39] adopt GCN due to its powerful representation learning ability. Other models like RSN [15] use recurrent neural networks for KG embedding, respectively. In addition to relational facts, some models such as KDCoE, AttrE, MultiKE, RDGCN and IMUSE [17] also exploit entity attributes for KG embedding and achieve good results. For alignment learning, IPTransE and KDCoE use the pair loss. Besides, JAPE, BootEA, AttrE, RSN and MultiKE let aligned entities in seed alignment share the same or similar embeddings by some tailored data processing skills, which can be also regarded as a special case of the pair loss. GCN-Align and RDGCN use the marginal ranking loss and AliNet uses the limit-based loss. To achieve better performance, some models including IPTransE, BootEA, KDCoE and TransEdge further employ semi-supervised learning. μKG currently supports MTransE, AttrE, SEA, GCN-Align, RDGCN, IPTransE, JAPE, BootEA, RSN and IMUSE.

Entity Typing. Entity typing seeks to predict the "type entities" of an instance entity. It can be regarded as a special link prediction task across an instance KG and an ontological KG. μKG currently supports TransE-ET, HolE-ET and RESCAL-ET. Please refer to [26] for more details.

5.2 Knowledge Graph Embedding Libraries

As summarized in Table 1, most of existing libraries for KG embeddings only focus on link prediction, a common KG embedding task. Multi-source KG embedding and entity alignment are only supported by OpenEA [40] and EAkit [54].

Only OpenKE [16], OpenEA and Pykg2vec [53] are developed with TensorFlow, other libraries only support PyTorch. LibKGE [7] is a recent library for link prediction with a high degree of modularity. DGL-KGE [57] is developed based on DGL. It supports PyTorch and XMNet, but not TensorFlow. NeuralKG [56] is a recent Python-based library for diverse representation learning of KGs, but it mainly focuses on rule-based link prediction models. By contrast, our library is more comprehensive than existing work.

6 Conclusion and Future Work

In this paper, we present a new scalable library, μKG, for multi-source KG embeddings and applications. It facilitates joint representation learning across multi-source KGs. It supports PyTorch and TensorFlow2, and can perform multiple tasks, including link prediction, entity alignment, entity typing, and multi-source link prediction, with advanced implementations of the corresponding embedding models. Extensive experiments validate the effectiveness and efficiency of μKG. We further demonstrate how jointly learned embeddings can greatly aid KG-powered downstream tasks such as multi-hop KGQA. We show that knowledge transfer in multi-source KGs is an efficient way to improve the performance of KG-powered tasks.

Best Practices of KG Embedding Libraries. The proposed μKG supports multiple tasks, while few libraries support entity typing and multi-source link prediction. For users who want to carry out these two tasks, μKG is the best choice. μKG provides many popular methods in both TensorFlow and PyTorch implementations. If the official code of a model only has one implementation but users need another, μKG is a good choice. μKG is still in its early stages, and a few methods do not achieve optimal results. In this case, the original works are more suitable. For the models that μKG currently does not implement, users can try other libraries, e.g., LibKGE [7] and PyKEEN [1] for link prediction, or OpenEA [40] and EAkit [54] for entity alignment.

Future Work. We plan to integrate more KG embedding models and multi-source KG tasks. We also plan to continually improve our implementations.

Acknowledgments. This work was supported by National Natural Science Foundation of China (No. 61872172), Beijing Academy of Artificial Intelligence (BAAI), and Collaborative Innovation Center of Novel Software Technology & Industrialization. Zequn Sun was also grateful for the support of Program A for Outstanding PhD Candidates of Nanjing University.

References

1. Ali, M., et al.: PyKEEN 1.0: a python library for training and evaluating knowledge graph embeddings. J. Mach. Learn. Res. **22**, 82:1–82:6 (2021)

2. Ali, M., Jabeen, H., Hoyt, C.T., Lehmann, J.: The KEEN universe - an ecosystem for knowledge graph embeddings with a focus on reproducibility and transferability. In: ISWC, pp. 3–18 (2019)
3. Balazevic, I., Allen, C., Hospedales, T.M.: TuckER: tensor factorization for knowledge graph completion. In: EMNLP, pp. 5184–5193 (2019)
4. Bollacker, K., Evans, C., Paritosh, P., Sturge, T., Taylor, J.: Freebase: a collaboratively created graph database for structuring human knowledge. In: SIGMOD, pp. 1247–1250 (2008)
5. Bordes, A., Usunier, N., García-Durán, A., Weston, J., Yakhnenko, O.: Translating embeddings for modeling multi-relational data. In: NIPS, pp. 2787–2795 (2013)
6. Boschin, A.: TorchKGE: knowledge graph embedding in python and pytorch. CoRR abs/2009.02963 (2020)
7. Broscheit, S., Ruffinelli, D., Kochsiek, A., Betz, P., Gemulla, R.: LibKGE - a knowledge graph embedding library for reproducible research. In: EMNLP (Demonstration), pp. 165–174 (2020)
8. Cai, L., Wang, W.Y.: KBGAN: adversarial learning for knowledge graph embeddings. In: NAACL, pp. 1470–1480 (2018)
9. Chen, M., Tian, Y., Chang, K., Skiena, S., Zaniolo, C.: Co-training embeddings of knowledge graphs and entity descriptions for cross-lingual entity alignment. In: IJCAI, pp. 3998–4004 (2018)
10. Chen, M., Tian, Y., Yang, M., Zaniolo, C.: Multilingual knowledge graph embeddings for cross-lingual knowledge alignment. In: IJCAI, pp. 1511–1517 (2017)
11. Chen, X., Chen, M., Fan, C., Uppunda, A., Sun, Y., Zaniolo, C.: Multilingual knowledge graph completion via ensemble knowledge transfer. In: Findings of EMNLP, pp. 3227–3238 (2020)
12. Dettmers, T., Minervini, P., Stenetorp, P., Riedel, S.: Convolutional 2D knowledge graph embeddings. In: AAAI, pp. 1811–1818 (2018)
13. Devlin, J., Chang, M., Lee, K., Toutanova, K.: BERT: pre-training of deep bidirectional transformers for language understanding. In: NAACL, pp. 4171–4186 (2019)
14. Faloutsos, C., Trivedi, R., Sisman, B., Dong, X.L., Ma, J., Zha, H.: Linknbed: multigraph representation learning with entity linkage. In: ACL, pp. 252–262 (2018)
15. Guo, L., Sun, Z., Hu, W.: Learning to exploit long-term relational dependencies in knowledge graphs. In: ICML (2019)
16. Han, X., et al.: OpenKE: an open toolkit for knowledge embedding. In: EMNLP (Demonstration), pp. 139–144 (2018)
17. He, F., et al.: Unsupervised entity alignment using attribute triples and relation triples. In: DASFAA, pp. 367–382 (2019)
18. Ji, G., He, S., Xu, L., Liu, K., Zhao, J.: Knowledge graph embedding via dynamic mapping matrix. In: ACL, pp. 687–696 (2015)
19. Ji, S., Pan, S., Cambria, E., Marttinen, P., Yu, P.S.: A survey on knowledge graphs: representation, acquisition, and applications. EEE Trans. Neural Netw. Learn. Syst. **33**(2), 494–514 (2022)
20. Kazemi, S.M., Poole, D.: Simple embedding for link prediction in knowledge graphs. In: NeurIPS, pp. 4289–4300 (2018)
21. Lehmann, J., et al.: DBpedia - a large-scale, multilingual knowledge base extracted from Wikipedia. Seman. Web J. **6**(2), 167–195 (2015)
22. Lin, Y., Liu, Z., Sun, M., Liu, Y., Zhu, X.: Learning entity and relation embeddings for knowledge graph completion. In: AAAI, pp. 2181–2187 (2015)
23. Liu, H., Wu, Y., Yang, Y.: Analogical inference for multi-relational embeddings. In: ICML, pp. 2168–2178 (2017)

24. Liu, Y., et al.: RoBERTa: a robustly optimized BERT pretraining approach. CoRR abs/1907.11692 (2019)
25. Mahdisoltani, F., Biega, J., Suchanek, F.M.: YAGO3: a knowledge base from multilingual wikipedias. In: CIDR (2015)
26. Moon, C., Jones, P., Samatova, N.F.: Learning entity type embeddings for knowledge graph completion. In: CIKM, pp. 2215–2218 (2017)
27. Nguyen, D.Q., Nguyen, T.D., Nguyen, D.Q., Phung, D.Q.: A novel embedding model for knowledge base completion based on convolutional neural network. In: NAACL, pp. 327–333 (2018)
28. Nickel, M., Rosasco, L., Poggio, T.A.: Holographic embeddings of knowledge graphs. In: AAAI, pp. 1955–1961 (2016)
29. Nickel, M., Tresp, V., Kriegel, H.: A three-way model for collective learning on multi-relational data. In: ICML, pp. 809–816 (2011)
30. Pei, S., Yu, L., Hoehndorf, R., Zhang, X.: Semi-supervised entity alignment via knowledge graph embedding with awareness of degree difference. In: WWW, pp. 3130–3136 (2019)
31. Rossi, A., Barbosa, D., Firmani, D., Matinata, A., Merialdo, P.: Knowledge graph embedding for link prediction: a comparative analysis. Trans. Knowl. Discov. Data 15(2), 14:1–14:49 (2021)
32. Saxena, A., Tripathi, A., Talukdar, P.P.: Improving multi-hop question answering over knowledge graphs using knowledge base embeddings. In: ACL, pp. 4498–4507 (2020)
33. Schlichtkrull, M.S., Kipf, T.N., Bloem, P., van den Berg, R., Titov, I., Welling, M.: Modeling relational data with graph convolutional networks. In: ESWC, pp. 593–607 (2018)
34. Shi, B., Weninger, T.: ProjE: embedding projection for knowledge graph completion. In: AAAI, pp. 1236–1242 (2017)
35. Singh, H., Chakrabarti, S., Jain, P., Choudhury, S.R., Mausam: multilingual knowledge graph completion with joint relation and entity alignment. In: AKB (2021)
36. Sun, Z., Hu, W., Li, C.: Cross-lingual entity alignment via joint attribute-preserving embedding. In: ISWC, pp. 628–644 (2017)
37. Sun, Z., Hu, W., Zhang, Q., Qu, Y.: Bootstrapping entity alignment with knowledge graph embedding. In: IJCAI, pp. 4396–4402 (2018)
38. Sun, Z., Huang, J., Hu, W., Chen, M., Guo, L., Qu, Y.: Transedge: translating relation-contextualized embeddings for knowledge graphs. In: ISWC (2019)
39. Sun, Z., et al.: Knowledge graph alignment network with gated multi-hop neighborhood aggregation. In: AAAI (2020)
40. Sun, Z., et al.: A benchmarking study of embedding-based entity alignment for knowledge graphs. In: PVLDB, vol. 13, pp. 2326–2340 (2020)
41. Sun, Z., Deng, Z., Nie, J., Tang, J.: RotatE: knowledge graph embedding by relational rotation in complex space. In: ICLR (2019)
42. Toutanova, K., Chen, D.: Observed versus latent features for knowledge base and text inference. In: CVSC (2015)
43. Trisedya, B.D., Qi, J., Zhang, R.: Entity alignment between knowledge graphs using attribute embeddings. In: AAAI (2019)
44. Trouillon, T., Welbl, J., Riedel, S., Gaussier, É., Bouchard, G.: Complex embeddings for simple link prediction. In: ICML, pp. 2071–2080 (2016)
45. Vrandečić, D., Krötzsch, M.: Wikidata: a free collaborative knowledgebase. Commun. ACM 57(10), 78–85 (2014)

46. Wang, Q., Mao, Z., Wang, B., Guo, L.: Knowledge graph embedding: a survey of approaches and applications. IEEE Trans. Knowl. Data Eng. **29**(12), 2724–2743 (2017)
47. Wang, X., et al.: KEPLER: a unified model for knowledge embedding and pre-trained language representation. Trans. Assoc. Comput. Linguistics **9**, 176–194 (2021)
48. Wang, Z., Zhang, J., Feng, J., Chen, Z.: Knowledge graph embedding by translating on hyperplanes. In: AAAI, pp. 1112–1119 (2014)
49. Wang, Z., Lv, Q., Lan, X., Zhang, Y.: Cross-lingual knowledge graph alignment via graph convolutional networks. In: EMNLP, pp. 349–357 (2018)
50. Wu, Y., Liu, X., Feng, Y., Wang, Z., Yan, R., Zhao, D.: Relation-aware entity alignment for heterogeneous knowledge graphs. In: IJCAI (2019)
51. Yang, B., Yih, W., He, X., Gao, J., Deng, L.: Embedding entities and relations for learning and inference in knowledge bases. In: ICLR (2015)
52. Yih, W., Richardson, M., Meek, C., Chang, M., Suh, J.: The value of semantic parse labeling for knowledge base question answering. In: ACL (2016)
53. Yu, S., Chhetri, S.R., Canedo, A., Goyal, P., Faruque, M.A.A.: Pykg2vec: a python library for knowledge graph embedding. J. Mach, Learn. Res **22**, 16:1–16:6 (2021)
54. Zeng, K., Li, C., Hou, L., Li, J., Feng, L.: A comprehensive survey of entity alignment for knowledge graphs. AI Open **2**, 1–13 (2021)
55. Zhang, Q., Sun, Z., Hu, W., Chen, M., Guo, L., Qu, Y.: Multi-view knowledge graph embedding for entity alignment. In: IJCAI (2019)
56. Zhang, W., et al.: NeuralKG: an open source library for diverse representation learning of knowledge graphs. CoRR abs/2202.12571 (2022)
57. Zheng, D., et al.: DGL-KE: training knowledge graph embeddings at scale. In: SIGIR, pp. 739–748 (2020)
58. Zhu, H., Xie, R., Liu, Z., Sun, M.: Iterative entity alignment via joint knowledge embeddings. In: IJCAI, pp. 4258–4264 (2017)

IMGT-KG: A Knowledge Graph for Immunogenetics

Gaoussou Sanou[1,2]($\boxtimes$) (iD), Véronique Giudicelli[1](iD), Nika Abdollahi[1](iD),
Sofia Kossida[1](iD), Konstantin Todorov[2](iD), and Patrice Duroux[1](iD)

[1] IGH/University of Montpellier/CNRS, Montpellier, France
{gaoussou.sanou,veronique.giudicelli,nika.abdollahi,sofia.kossida,
patrice.duroux}@igh.cnrs.fr
[2] LIRMM/University of Montpellier/CNRS, Montpellier, France
{gaoussou.sanou,konstantin.todorov}@lirmm.fr

Abstract. Knowledge graphs are emerging as one of the most popular means for data federation, transformation, integration and sharing, promising to improve data visibility and reusability. Immunogenetics is the branch of life sciences that studies the genetics of the immune system. Although the complexity and the connected nature of immunogenetics data make knowledge graphs a prominent choice to represent and describe immunogenetics entities and relations, hence enabling a plethora of applications, little effort has been directed towards building and using such knowledge graphs so far. In this work, we present the IMGT Knowledge Graph (IMGT-KG), the first of its kind FAIR knowledge graph in immunogenetics. IMGT-KG acquires and integrates data from different immunogenetics databases, hence creating links between them. Consequently, IMGT-KG provides access to 79 670 110 triplets with 10 430 268 entities, 673 concepts and 173 properties. IMGT-KG reuses many existing terms from domain ontologies or vocabularies and provides external links to other resources of the same domain, as well as a set of rules to guide inference on nucleotide sequence positions by applying Allen Interval Algebra. Such inference allows, for example, reasoning about genomics sequence positions. IMGT-KG fills in the gap between genomics and protein sequences and opens a perspective to effective queries and integrative immuno-omics analyses. We make openly and freely available IMGT-KG with detailed documentation and a Web interface for access and exploration.

Keywords: Immunogenetics and immunoinformatics · Ontology · Knowledge graphs · SPARQL endpoint · Reasoning rules · Semantic web

1 Introduction

Immunogenetics has the mission to decrypt the genetics of the immune system and immune responses. To take an example, immunogenetics plays a crucial role

U. Sattler et al. (Eds.): ISWC 2022, LNCS 13489, pp. 628–642, 2022.
https://doi.org/10.1007/978-3-031-19433-7_36

in the current context marked by the COVID-19 pandemic. The genetic basis of the immune response in COVID-19 cases may explain the inter-individual disease variability and provide a way to classify patients in different severity profiles according to the presence or absence of genetic variants [16]. In addition, the understanding of such genetics bases contributes to the rapid development of vaccines.

IMGT®, the *International ImMunoGeneTics Information System* ®, is an international data reference in the immunogenetics field, particularly in the management of the adaptive immune response data [13,14]. Over the past 30 years, IMGT elaborated several high-quality databases, web resources and tools for understanding and cracking the adaptive immune response, now considered as a reference in the field. IMGT® offers a knowledge management system, that allows for a standardised annotation of immunogenetics entities from genomic to protein data by using a formal vocabulary: the IMGT-ONTOLOGY [12]. Based on the type of the immunogenetics entity (genomic or protein), IMGT® provides five different databases: two genomic databases (IMGT/LIGM-DB, IMGT/GENE-DB) and three protein databases (IMGT/2Dstructure-DB, IMGT/3Dstructure-DB and IMGT/mAb-DB), described in the following section in more detail. These databases are freely accessible via different query form-like interfaces[1] [13,14]. According to the connected nature of immunogenetics information, federating and integrating different entities in a central knowledge base will not only give a way to make integrative analyses (via expressive, complete and rich queries like, for example, *"find all proteins with their gene and alleles with a particular genomic reference sequence"*), but will also provide a way to discover new facts like, for example, the particular genomic sequence associated to a protein structure.

To fill in this gap, we introduce IMGT-KG, the first Findable, Accessible, Interoperable and Reusable (FAIR) knowledge graph (KG) in immunogenetics, which provides access to structured immunogenetics data based on the IMGT® resources. IMGT-KG is built and published following the W3C recommendations and best practices [4]. The data model of IMGT-KG is an extended version of the IMGT-ONTOLOGY [12]. For interoperability purposes, IMGT-KG also reuses terms from various biomedical resources. To generate the IMGT-KG, we collect and lift data from the IMGT databases and instantiate the data model, applying a reasoner to check its consistency and to enrich it by inferring new facts. In addition, we use a set of rules based on Allen's interval algebra [1], to infer the different spatial relations between sequence features.[2] Hence, IMGT-KG enables advanced exploration of immunogenetics data via queries such as *"Find all protein chains, domains, the associated allele and its genomic reference sequence"* or *"find the epitopes on the Immune Epitope Database (IEDB) which are in interaction with a particular structure of IMGT-KG"* or *"Find the structure that interacts with the COVID-19 spike and their associated chains,*

---

[1] https://www.imgt.org/.

[2] A feature is a region in a sequence—a succession of nucleotide or amino acids—with coordinates (start and end value) and a label.

genes, alleles and genomic reference sequences". Currently, IMGT-KG contains data from IMGT/LIGM-DB, IMGT/GENE-DB, IMGT/2Dstructure-DB, IMGT/3Dstructure-DB. It provides access to 79 670 110 triplets with 10 430 268 entities, 673 concepts and 173 properties. We make openly and freely available IMGT-KG with adequate documentation.[3]

In Sect. 2, we provide basic background in biology. We describe the IMGT® resources and databases used to generate IMGT-KG in Sect. 3. In Sect. 4, we detail the construction of the KG, while Sect. 5 gives examples of use-cases. We present related resources in Sect. 6, before we conclude in Sect. 7.

2   Background

This section lays down some fundamentals in molecular biology, needed for the understanding of our work.

Our body is constituted of tissues and tissues are made of cells. Every cell has a kernel that contains chromosomes. Each chromosome contains deoxyribonucleic acid (DNA), which is coded with nucleotides represented by four letters: A,T,C,G. The DNA has a double helix structure and can be considered as the cell manual. The information contained in one DNA helix is transcribed to RNA (ribonucleic acid), what is known as a transcription process. The RNA is then translated to a protein chain or polypeptide,[4] known as a translation process. The protein chains will fold to create a 3D conformation: protein structure. The processes of transcription and translation are depicted in Fig. 1. A protein is coded by one or more genes and is made with a succession of residues or amino acids. A protein can have different units called chains and a chain can be constituted by domains and regions. A gene is a DNA sequence (genomics level) that can be potentially transcribed and/or translated (protein level). A gene can have multiple versions marked by mutations[5] called alleles. A gene is localised in a particular place on a chromosome called a locus.

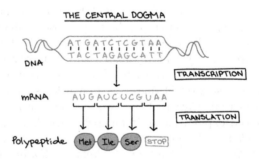

Fig. 1. Central dogma of molecular biology (from biocore).

---

[3] https://www.imgt.org/imgt-kg/, gives access to the entire IMGT®database.

[4] Successions of amino acids.

[5] Either an insertion of nucleotide, either a deletion of nucleotide or substitution of nucleotide.

When an organism that can produce a disease, known as a pathogen, enters our body, a defensive strategy is put in place: our immune response produces proteins thanks to the B cells, called immunoglobulins (IG) or antibodies and thanks to the T cells, called T cell receptors (TR). These proteins recognise the pathogen thanks to their motifs (epitopes) and trigger their destruction. Each produced antibody will be specific to the pathogen. This is the so-called adaptive immune response.

3   IMGT®: A Knowledge Management System for Immunogenetics Data

IMGT® is an information system specialised in the management of the diversity and complexity of the immunoglobulins or antibodies, T cell receptors, major histocompatibility (MH) and superfamilies of IG (IgSF) of MH (MhSF) and immune system proteins (RPI) [13,14]. It manages immunogenetics data through 3 axes:

- the first axis aims to decipher the IG and TR loci, genes and alleles in the genome of jawed vertebrates.
- the second axis concerns the exploration and analysis of the expressed IG and TR repertoires based on comparison with IMGT reference directories in normal and pathological situations.
- the third axis aims to analyse the amino acid changes and functions of 2D and 3D structures of engineered antibody and TR.

IMGT® provides a standard way to represent immunogenetics data based on the IMGT-ONTOLOGY [12] a vocabulary that describes immunogenetics data from genomics (nucleotide) data level to protein (three-dimensional structure) level. This vocabulary allows IMGT®, to build a rich knowledge system with 7 databases in total, 17 tools and more than 20,000 web pages and documents [13, 14]. The vocabulary terms allow for the identification, description, classification, localisation, orientation, acquisition and numbering of immunogenetics data. The databases of interest for this study are:

- IMGT/LIGM-DB[6] [10] and IMGT/GENE-DB[7] [11]. The former (246951 entries) provides standardised terms to annotate immunogenetics data including IG, TR and MH nucleotide sequences from human and other vertebrate species. The latter (9089 entries) stores the IG and TR genes curated with all IMGT identified alleles.
- IMGT/3Dstructure-DB and IMGT/2Dstructure-DB,[8] [8] and the monoclonal antibodies database IMGT/mAb-DB.[9] The structure databases (8260 entries) provide an access to protein structures and their related chains and domains. IMGT/mAb-DB is a monoclonal antibody database (1257 entries) for therapeutic purposes.

---

[6] https://www.imgt.org/ligmdb/.
[7] http://www.imgt.org/genedb/.
[8] https://www.imgt.org/3Dstructure-DB/.
[9] https://www.imgt.org/mAb-DB/.

4   IMGT-KG Construction

IMGT-KG is constructed by using an extended version of the IMGT-ONTOLO-GY [12] as data model and the IMGT® genomic and protein databases as data sources. The construction comprises three steps, as illustrated in Fig. 2: i) defining a data model based on the IMGT-ONTOLOGY by reusing existing terms when possible and linking equivalent terms with the sameAs property, ii) instantiating the model and generating the KG, iii) checking the consistency of the KG by the help of a reasoning engine and completing the KG with newly inferred facts.

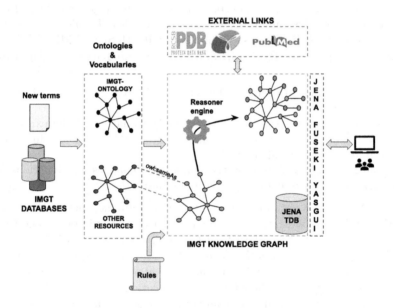

Fig. 2. Pipeline of IMGT-KG construction

The KG is built by using W3C best practices and standards.[10] We generate URIs[11] for the IMGT-KG by using the existing URI pattern of the IMGT-ONTOLOGY: http://www.imgt.org/imgt-ontology#. The implementation of IMGT-KG is made by the means of the Apache Jena framework.[12] To take advantage of existing terms, we use OntoFox, a web-based application, that allows the extraction of terms from an ontology by keeping their related properties, annotations and classes [19].[13] It provides also a means to serialise the extracted terms in the W3C recommendation format. To interact with the

---

[10] RDF, RDFS, and OWL.
[11] Uniform Resource Identifier.
[12] https://jena.apache.org/.
[13] http://ontofox.hegroup.org.

IMGT® databases, we use an Object-Relational Mapping (ORM) model to map the relational database to an object model, then we access to the data with a Java Persistence API (JPA). In order to check the consistency of the KG, we use Pellet[14] an OWL2 DL (Description Logic) reasoner. Additionally, we make OWL2 DL inference with the latter and use the Jena rule engine to compute deductions of a defined rule set.

4.1 IMGT-KG Data Model's Definition and (Re-)used Ontologies and Vocabularies

The IMGT-KG data model provides the necessary vocabulary and axioms to describe immunogenetics entities and their relations. We updated the previous version of the IMGT-ONTOLOGY and defined new terms (identification, description, classification, localisation, orientation, acquisition and numbering) for structuring immunogenetics data following the W3C recommendations. In order to enhance interoperability and link our KG with other external resources [3,5], we reuse existing terms when it is possible and make equivalence links with certain Sequence Ontology (SO) terms.[15] Major parts of these terms come from the OBO foundry ontologies (see Figs. 3 and 4):[16]

- Relation Ontology (RO) [18] provides more than 400 terms for defining relations across a variety of domains.
- Feature Annotation Location Description Ontology (FALDO) [6] provides terms to describe a sequence based on location (position/coordinates) of its different features. This is particularly useful to annotate a position or coordinates of a feature.
- Genotype Ontology (GENO) is an ontology that provides terms covering genotype description and genetic variations in model organisms.[17]
- NCI Thesaurus (NCIt) is a reference terminology and core biomedical ontology, providing 120,000 key biomedical concepts with a rich set of terms, codes, 115,000 textual definitions, and over 400,000 inter-concept relationships.[18]
- NCBI Taxonomy provides terminology that covers classification and organisms nomenclature.[19]
- Sequence Ontology (SO) [9] provides a controlled and standardised vocabulary for sequence annotation, aiming to unify all sequence annotations. SO uses the concept of feature in sequence annotation, and provides links that point to some IMGT labels [12]. In fact, 64 terms of SO have synonyms in IMGT labels.

---

[14] https://github.com/stardog-union/pellet.

[15] http://www.sequenceontology.org/.

[16] https://oboundry.org/.

[17] https://github.com/monarch-initiative/GENO-ontology.

[18] https://ncit.nci.nih.gov/ncitbrowser/.

[19] https://www.ncbi.nlm.nih.gov/taxonomy.

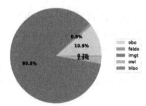

Fig. 3. Concepts in IMGT-KG (Color figure online)

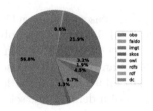

Fig. 4. Properties in IMGT-KG (Color figure online)

Figure 5 describes the IMGT-KG data model. We use the following colour code in the figure representing the model:

- The light blue colour represents the Gene and its associated knowledge. In fact, a Gene can be a member of (obo:RO_0002350) IMGT Group, SubGroup and/or Clan. A Clan or a SubGroup can also be a member of a Group. A concept of Gene is associated with a type (variable, diversity, joining, constant, conventional) and a structure type. A Gene has at least one Allele (obo:GENO_0000413) and an Allele can have a functionality type that states its functionality (functional, Open Reading Frame (ORF) or pseudogene). An allele is associated to a coding region (faldo:Region), this region can be a reference sequence or a sequence from the literature. Each Gene is ordered in a Locus and belongs to a taxon (obo:NCBITaxon_1).
- At the locus level (orange), a Locus has a location type (major locus, orphon set etc.), it is also member of a given chromosome (obo:SO_0000340) for a given taxon. This chromosome is member of a given assembly (obo:SO_0001248) and the assembly has a version number (obo:SWO_0004000), data origin (obo:NCIT_C103167) and belongs to a taxon.
- Light green colour represents the sequence features and their related description. A feature is a sequence Region (faldo:Region) with a location (faldo:ExactPosition) and an IMGT label. Every location has a start value (obo:GENO_0000894) and an end value (obo:GENO_0000895). A gene feature part of (obo:BFO_0000050) a genomic sequence (obo:GENO_0000960) with an accession number (obo:NCIT_C25402). The feature with associated IMGT prototype label (e.g. V-GENE) contains other small features thanks to the imgt:isInPrototype relation and is related to a genomics sequence with the imgt:isPrototypeInSeq. Also, the feature with the IMGT cluster label contains the features with IMGT prototype labels thanks to imgt:isInCluster relation and is related to a genomics sequence with the imgt:isClusterInSeq.
- The pink colour introduces to the protein level and characterises the protein Chain and its related properties. A chain (obo:NCIT_C41207) can have protein domains (obo:NCIT_C13303) with a domain type. It has also regions and residues (obo:NCIT_C48795) with the associated amino acid (obo:CHEBI_33709) and an IMGT numbering. Every protein chain domain has an IMGT label and a location. The associated region of a Chain is the

reference sequence of an Allele with a similarity score. Chains belong to a taxon and a structure (obo:NCIT_C13303).

– The white colour represents the protein Structure and its associated description. A Structure (obo:NCIT_C13303) that can belong to a complex (NCIT_C19398), having IMGT label and a molecular component. A Structure is attached to an entry of an amino-acid sequence (obo:GENO_0000720). This sequence has an accession number, a related bibliographic reference and an acquisition experiment.

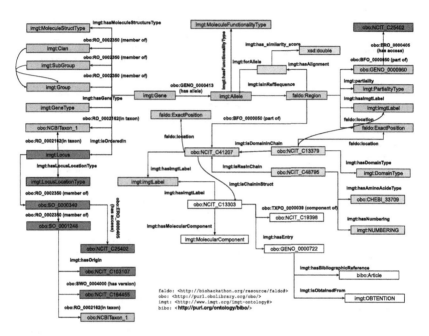

Fig. 5. An overview of the IMGT-KG data model without annotation properties. Details are given on the KG interface: https://www.imgt.org/imgt-kg/kgdescription. html.

4.2   IMGT-KG Data Model's Population

Once we have the schema of our knowledge graph, we proceed to populate it, i.e. add facts to the graph by using data from the IMGT databases described above thanks to the ORM model and the JPA. In the genomic level, we do JPQL queries in IMGT/GENE-DB in order to retrieve information about genes including their classification (group, subgroup, clan, allele), their localisation (locus, chromosome, assembly) and their identification (gene type, molecule type etc.) and we associate the description (IMGT labels) of their genomic nucleotide sequence thanks to the information from IMGT/LIGM-DB.[20] On protein level,

---

[20] Java Persistence Query Language.

we query the Structure databases in order to retrieve information about structures, chains, domains, regions, residues, alleles and other related properties and we associate the alleles of structure databases to alleles in IMGT/GENE-DB. Thanks to the JPA, we harvest the result of these queries and instantiate the data model with Jena Ontology API, then we serialise the data in the turtle format.

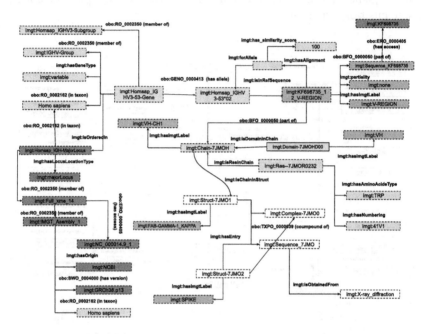

Fig. 6. Instances in the IMGT-KG related to the COVID-19 SPIKE protein of the structure 7JMO

As an example, Fig. 6 shows the representation of the SPIKE protein in the COVID-19 case. We have the structure 7JMO2 annotated with the SPIKE IMGT label; it is a component of the 7JMO0 complex and is associated to the 7JMO amino acid sequence obtained from X-ray diffraction. We have also the 7JMO1 structure which belongs to the same complex and has the same amino acid. The 7JMO1 labelled with FAB-GAMMA-1_KAPPA, contains the 7JMOH chain (VH-CH1), this chain has 7JMOHD00 domain (VH), a tryptophan residue at position 41 and a coding region KF698735_12_V-REGION. This region is not partial and is part of the genomic sequence KF698735. The region is also a reference sequence of an allele Homsap_IGHV3-53*02 with an alignment similarity score of 100. The allele is a variant of a joining gene Homsap_IGHV3-53-Gene which is member of the IGHV-Group and the Homsap_IGHV3-Subgroup. This gene belongs to *Homo sapiens (human)* taxon and is ordered in the major locus Homsap_IGH-MajorLocus. This locus belongs to the same taxon and is member of the chromosome 14. The chromosome comes from a NCBI assembly of the same human taxon.

We generated a KG with 79 670 110 triplets, 10 430 268 entities, 15 848 105 distinct subjects, 21 861 727 distinct objects, 673 distinct concepts or classes and 171 distinct properties or relations. The top 10 instantiated concepts and properties are presented in Fig. 7, 8.

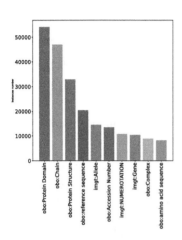

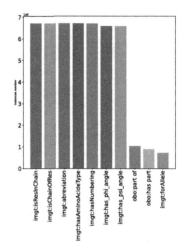

Fig. 7. Top 10 instantiated concepts in IMGT-KG

Fig. 8. Top 10 instantiated properties in IMGT-KG

4.3   IMGT-KG Enrichment: Rules, Consistency and Inference

After the KG is generated, we make sure that no data model violation is encountered in the KG using Pellet for consistency check. We formalise a set of rules in order to make deduction on the spatial position of sequence by the means of Jena rule engine API, then we apply Pellet reasoner in order to deduce new facts in the KG.

Allen's Interval Algebra and Rules. In 1989, Allen et al. provided a way to formalise and reason over the time interval [1]. Called Allen's Logic Interval, this powerful tool allows reasoning over time events. For example, suppose the start of event A is the end of another event B, then event A meets event B. Thus, 13 decidable relations were formalised by Allen to describe all types of events that may occur over time interval [1]. Similarly, we transpose this logic on genomic sequence positions (Fig. 9). In fact, the genomic sequence spatial position can be considered as interval with a start and end point, consequently Allen's Logic Interval turns out to be the most suitable to make automatic deductions in our genomic sequence position. Hence, we formalise a set of rules in order to reason over genomic sequence position.

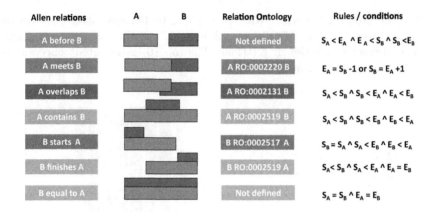

Fig. 9. Allen's interval rules adaptation, S = start and E = end.

For example, the Fig. 10 shows an example of a prototype (V-GENE) which is a topological model to describe a nucleotide sequence architecture[21]. The prototype allows the annotation of IMGT® genomic data. The application of the defined rules in Fig. 9 on the V-GENE sequence allows to infer or deduce that the L-PART2 meets (obo:RO_0002220) the V-INTRON and FR1-IMGT and it starts (obo:RO_0002517) the V-EXON and finishes (obo:RO_0002519) the L-INTRON-L.

Being able to make these deductions allows not only to do spatial reasoning over genomic sequences but also to verify if all features in a genomic sequence are well positioned in order to detect annotation errors.

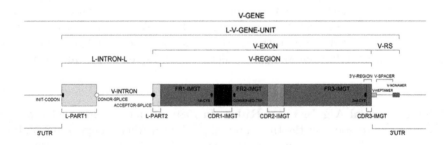

Fig. 10. A V-GENE prototype [12].

Reasoning on IMGT-KG. Once we formalised Allen rule set, we inject them in the KG and compute automatic deductions on genomic sequence positions by the means of the Jena rule engine API. Then, we apply Pellet reasoner to not only check the consistency of the KG but also to infer or complete the KG with inferred fact.

---

[21] A nucleotide sequence consists of many features with a position and IMGT label.

We built IMGT-KG, an enriched and FAIR KG that integrates a high-quality immunogenetics data harvested from five IMGT® databases. We use Jena triple-store TDB2[22] to store our triplets and we provide an access endpoint thanks to a SPARQL server: Fuseki2.[23] IMGT-KG provides access to over 79 million of triplets without inferences and more than 97 million with inferences.

5   IMGT-KG in Use

The IMGT® resources are largely adopted by the international immunogenetics scientific community, establishing themselves as the main reference in the field over the past 30 years. Therefore, IMGT-KG, which integrates and builds on top of these resources, also targets this community, enhancing the adoption of semantic web technologies to a field which is currently underrepresented.[24]

The IMGT-KG fills the gap between different IMGT® databases and consequently unifies the genomics and proteins data. Hence, the centralisation of the IMGT® databases in a FAIR KG allows for more query possibilities and enables the discovery of new knowledge. We provide free access to our KG via a well-documented web interface. This interface allows the user to explore different facets of IMGT-KG. The welcome page introduces users to IMGT-KG and provides information about the IMGT-KG team. The IMGT-KG Description page provides details on the KG data model. We also provide a description of the IMGT-KG dataset via the VoID Vocabulary.[25] The IMGT-KG Statistics page provides detailed statistics and chart plots about the KG. The IMGT-KG Data Access page, powered by YASGUI,[26] provides open access to the resource. There, users will find various SPARQL query examples. The IMGT-KG Model documentation and visualisation page provides useful documentation and a taxonomy visualisation of our data model. These pages are generated with Ontospy.[27]

We provide a set of use-case scenarios. The corresponding queries for each of the scenarios can be found on IMGT-KG's webpage: https://www.imgt.org/imgt-kg/kgyasgui.html.

Scenario 1: Assume that a user searches information on the genes/alleles functionality and why they are not functional. She/he must first select the alleles/genes of interest, the associated reference sequence and its belonging entity, the functionality (here P for pseudogene). To explain the absence of some functionality, she/he must check the qualifier associated to the entity with the imgt:has_imgt_qualifier and filter based on the qualifier that contains "pseudo" terms for example.

Scenario 2: Suppose an immunogenetics researcher wants to explore a specific structure and the associated external links, for example find some structures

---

[22] https://jena.apache.org/documentation/tdb/.

[23] https://jena.apache.org/documentation/fuseki2/index.html.

[24] We plan to communicate our results and resources to the biological community.

[25] https://www.w3.org/TR/void/.

[26] https://yasgui.triply.cc/.

[27] http://lambdamusic.github.io/Ontospy/.

and their related bibliographies with the PUBMED identifier, the associated visualisation of the structure, the same structure in the Protein Database (PDB) and the probable epitope of the structure. For that, the user must first select the entry associated to the structure, the related properties of the entry (pdb_link, jmol_visualisation, bibliography properties), then select the related properties of the structure (epitope, name).

Scenario 3: Suppose a clinician wants to find the structures that interact with the COVID-19 spike and their associated chains, genes, alleles and genomics reference sequences. For that, the user can select the structures having an IMGT label SPIKE, their related properties (complex, IEDB epitope, entry) and the complementary structure of the SPIKE protein which has also the same entry and belong to the same complex. Subsequently, the user can select the related properties of entry, like the PDB link. For the associated gene and allele, the user must select the regions associated to the chain of the complementary structure and, associated to these regions, their respective allele. These alleles are used to find the related reference sequence, the entity of the reference sequence and the gene.

6 Related Resources: The OBO Foundry

Considering the complexity of the biological field, there has been a growing effort to provide structured data and models in the field, mainly driven by the OBO (Open Biological and Biomedical Ontologies) community. OBO fosters research in biological and life sciences by making available ontologies and vocabularies. Although not specialised for the immunogenetics field, some of these resources provide general terms to describe: **proteins:** Protein Ontology PRO allows the representation of protein-related entities: from protein families to proteoforms to complexes [7];[28] **genes:** Gene Ontology GO provides resources to enhance the scientific knowledge about the functions of genes from different organisms [2];[29] **sequences:** Sequence Ontology SO [9] provides a controlled and standardised vocabulary for sequence annotation, aiming to unify all sequence annotations. In addition to being more general than IMGT-KG, to our knowledge, none of the resources developed in OBO provide access to integrated immunogenetics data, where IMGT-KG comes to fill exactly this gap.

7 Conclusion

Given the complexity of dealing with adaptive immune response from genome (set of genes) to proteome (set of proteins), there is a need for knowledge sharing and advanced data access in this field to facilitate future and ongoing research. Nowadays, responding to many health and sanitary challenges requires a combination of different studies in different domains, for example the understanding of

---

[28] https://lod.proconsortium.org/.
[29] http://geneontology.org/.

the COVID-19 virus and the development of a vaccine to counter its spread are both powered by immunogenetics research such as the genetics basis, the main protein implied in the COVID-19 disease.

To face these challenges, we built IMGT-KG, the first FAIR KG in the domain of immunogenetics containing over 79 million triplets. The core model of IMGT-KG is an extended version of the IMGT-ONTOLOGY and the data to populate the KG come from IMGT® databases - established reference data sources for immunogenetics containing both *genomics* and *protein* data. Hence IMGT-KG unifies in a unique manner these two levels of knowledge. This unification gives more query possibilities and opens a way to the discovery of new scientific knowledge. To take an example, among other applications, the IMGT-KG may help to improve knowledge about the coronavirus proteins potentially targeted by the adaptive immune system.

In future work, we will enrich the KG by integrating the IMGT/mAb-DB, the dedicated database to engineered monoclonal antibodies for clinical applications [14], then connect it to related resources like PRO and GO . Subsequently, we will apply representation learning models on the graph in order to predict or discover new links in our data by embedding the KG [15,17]. A named entity recognition system relying on IMGT-KG's entities is currently under construction, aiming to enable the automatic text annotation (e.g. from scientific articles) with IMGT-KG entities.

Resource Availability Statement:

- IMGT-KG web interface: https://www.imgt.org/imgt-kg/
- IMGT-KG fuseki server: https://www.imgt.org/fuseki/#/
- IMGT-KG data model: https://doi.org/10.5281/zenodo.6511279
- Query scenarios: https://doi.org/10.5281/zenodo.6674479
- VoID description: https://www.imgt.org/imgt-kg/kgvoid.html

References

1. Allen, J.F., Hayes, P.J.: Moments and points in an interval-based temporal logic. Comput. Intell. **5**(3), 225–238 (1989). https://doi.org/10.1111/j.1467-8640.1989.tb00329.x
2. Ashburner, M., et al.: Gene ontology: tool for the unification of biology (2000). https://doi.org/10.1038/75556, http://www.flybase.bio.indiana.edu, http://fruitfly.bdgp.berkeley.edu, http://www.genome.stanford.edu, http://www.informatics.jax.org
3. Berners-Lee, T.: Linked Data's rule (2006). https://www.w3.org/DesignIssues/LinkedData.html
4. Berners-Lee, T., Hendler, J., Lassila, O.: The semantic web. Sci. Am. **284**(5), 34–43 (2001). https://doi.org/10.1038/scientificamerican0501-34
5. Bizer, C., Heath, T., Berners-Lee, T.: Linked data - the story so far. Int. J. Semant. Web Inf. Syst. **5**(3), 1–22 (2009). https://doi.org/10.4018/jswis.2009081901
6. Bolleman, J.T., et al.: FALDO: a semantic standard for describing the location of nucleotide and protein feature annotation. J. Biomed. Seman. **7**(1), 1–12 (2016). https://doi.org/10.1186/s13326-016-0067-z

7. Chen, C., et al.: Protein ontology on the semantic web for knowledge discovery. Sci. Data **7**(1) (2020). https://doi.org/10.1038/s41597-020-00679-9

8. Ehrenmann, F., Giudicelli, V., Duroux, P., Lefranc, M.P.: IMGT/collier de perles: IMGT standardized representation of domains (IG, TR, and IgSF variable and constant domains, MH and MhSF groove domains). Cold Spring Harb. Protoc. **6**(6), 726–736 (2011). https://doi.org/10.1101/pdb.prot5635

9. Eilbeck, K., et al.: The sequence ontology: a tool for the unification of genome annotations. Genome Biol. **6**(5) (2005). https://doi.org/10.1186/gb-2005-6-5-r44

10. Giudicelli, V.: IMGT/LIGM-DB, the IMGT(R) comprehensive database of immunoglobulin and T cell receptor nucleotide sequences. Nucleic Acids Res. **34**(90001), D781–D784 (2006). https://doi.org/10.1093/nar/gkj088

11. Giudicelli, V., Chaume, D., Lefranc, M.P.: IMGT/GENE-DB: a comprehensive database for human and mouse immunoglobulin and T cell receptor genes. Nucleic Acids Res. **33**(Database Iss.), 256–261 (2005). https://doi.org/10.1093/nar/gki010

12. Giudicelli, V., Lefranc, M.P.: IMGT-Ontology 2012. Front. Genet. **3**(May), 1–16 (2012). https://doi.org/10.3389/fgene.2012.00079

13. Lefranc, M.P., et al.: IMGT R, the international ImMunoGeneTics information system R 25 years on. Nucleic Acids Res. **43**(D1), D413–D422 (2015). https://doi.org/10.1093/nar/gku1056. http://www.imgt.org

14. Manso, T., et al.: IMGT® databases, related tools and web resources through three main axes of research and development. Nucleic Acids Res. **50**(D1), D1262–D1272 (2022). https://doi.org/10.1093/nar/gkab1136

15. Nguyen, D.Q.: A survey of embedding models of entities and relationships for knowledge graph completion. In: Graph-Based Natural Language Processing (TextGraphs 2020), pp. 1–14 (2021). https://doi.org/10.18653/v1/2020.textgraphs-1.1

16. Pojero, F., et al.: The role of immunogenetics in covid-19 (2021). https://doi.org/10.3390/ijms22052636

17. Rossi, A., Barbosa, D., Firmani, D., Matinata, A., Merialdo, P.: Knowledge graph embedding for link prediction: a comparative analysis. ACM Trans. Knowl. Discov. Data **15**(2) (2021). https://doi.org/10.1145/3424672, http://arxiv.org/abs/2002.00819

18. Smith, B., et al.: Relations in biomedical ontologies. Genome Biol. **6**(5) (2005). https://doi.org/10.1186/gb-2005-6-5-r46

19. Xiang, Z., Courtot, M., Brinkman, R.R., Ruttenberg, A., He, Y.: OntoFox: web-based support for ontology reuse. BMC Res. Notes **3** 175 (2010). https://doi.org/10.1186/1756-0500-3-175, http://www.biomedcentral.com/1756-0500/3/175

REBench: Microbenchmarking Framework for Relation Extraction Systems

Manzoor Ali[1]([⊠]) [iD], Muhammad Saleem[2] [iD],
and Axel-Cyrille Ngonga Ngomo[1] [iD]

[1] DICE Group, Department of Computer Science, Paderborn University,
Paderborn, Germany
manzoor@campus.uni-paderborn.de, axel.ngonga@upb.de
[2] AKSW Research Group, University of Leipzig, Leipzig, Germany
saleem@informatik.uni-leipzig.de
https://www.dice-research.org/

Abstract. In recent years, several relation extractions (RE) models have been developed to extract knowledge from natural language texts. Accordingly, several benchmark datasets have been proposed to evaluate these models. These RE datasets consisted of natural language sentences with a fixed number of relations from a particular domain. Albeit useful for general-purpose RE benchmarking, they do not allow the generation of customized microbenchmarks according to user-specified criteria for a specific use case. Microbenchmarks are key to testing the individual functionalities of a system and hence pinpoint component-based insights. This article proposes REBench, a framework for microbenchmarking RE systems, which can select customized relation samples from existing RE datasets from diverse domains. The framework is flexible enough to choose relation samples of different sizes and according to the user-defined criteria on essential features to be considered for RE benchmarking. We used various clustering algorithms to generate microbenchmarks. We evaluated the state-of-the-art RE systems using different RE benchmarking samples. The evaluation results show that specialized microbenchmarking is crucial for identifying the limitations of various RE models and their components.

Resource Type: Evaluation benchmarks or Methods
Repository: https://github.com/dice-group/REBench
License: GNU General Public License v3.0

Keywords: Microbenchmark · Relation extraction · Clustering algorithm

1 Introduction

Relation extraction (RE) systems extract the relationship between two named entities from natural language texts. The named entities are often pre-annotated,

© The Author(s), under exclusive license to Springer Nature Switzerland AG 2022
U. Sattler et al. (Eds.): ISWC 2022, LNCS 13489, pp. 643–659, 2022.
https://doi.org/10.1007/978-3-031-19433-7_37

and the task is to determine the relationship between the entities. There have a wide range of applications of RE including knowledge base creation [25], event generation [14], and question-answering approaches [33]. In recent years, several novel approaches have been proposed to extract relations, including rule-based [22] and machine learning [11,26,27] approaches. These approaches operate in different environments, such as supervised, semi-supervised, distant-supervised, and unsupervised [17].

Research Gap: Several datasets such as NYT-FB [18], TACRED [36], WEB-NLG [8], Wikidata RE [21], and SemEval-2010 [10] have been proposed to benchmark RE systems. These datasets (Table 1) contain a fixed number of relations from a particular domain and are sufficient to test the overall performance of the RE system in terms of precision and recall. However, they do not allow generation of use-case-specific benchmarking based on user specified-criteria. For example, a user may be interested in testing a given RE system using a benchmark containing only binary relations with a fixed number of sentences and more than three named entities in each sentence. Such customized microbenchmarks are essential for performing use-case specific benchmarking and detailed component-based testing to demonstrate their strengths and weaknesses.

To the best of our knowledge, there is no RE benchmarking framework that allows users to generate customized microbenchmarks according to user-defined criteria. Furthermore, the existing RE datasets are generally designed for specific purpose. For example, the primary purpose of the NYT-FB [18] dataset is distant supervision and is specialized for RE tasks that are based on distant supervision. Similarly, the WEB-NLG [8] dataset primarily targets natural language generation, and supervised RE systems are the main objective of the TACRED [36] dataset. The main task of the Wikidata-RE [21] dataset is to extract overlapping or multiple relationships. Consequently, no benchmark dataset is curated from multiple sources (most of the datasets have Wikipedia as a source). Riedal et al. [18] mentioned the problems caused by considering only a single source for RE systems. Finally, the RE systems reported a significant difference in the F scores for the different datasets (see Table 2).

Our Proposal: The performance of RE systems is significantly affected by various sentence and relations-level features, such as the number of tokens in the sentences, named entities, tokens around the mentioned entities, tokens in the entities, exact string match of the entities, and number of punctuations [1,4,22,26]. We propose REBench, an RE benchmarking framework that allows users to generate customized microbenchmarks according to user-defined criteria on various sentence and relations-level features. We use state-of-the-art clustering algorithms in REBench to cluster more representative relations and select divers microbenchmarks.

REBench selects microbenchmarks from the RELD-RDF dataset, created from six – WEB-NLG [8], NYT-FB [18], Wikidata RE [21], SemEval2010 [10], Google-RE [15], and FewRel [9], – state-of-the-art RE datasets. In RELD-RDF, we model

Table 1. State-of-the-art benchmark datasets, its primary tasks and source of extraction.

Benchmark	Primary task	Underlying Corpus	Availability
NYT-FB	Distant supervision	New york times article	Partially available
Wikidata-RE	Overlaping RE	Wikipedia	Open
WEB-NLG	Natural language Generaion	Crowdsourced	Open
SEMEval-2010	RE classification	Web	Open
Google-RE	Relation Extraction	Wikipedia	Open
TACRED	Supervised RE	TAC-KBP	Closed
DocRED	Document RE	Wikipedia	Open

Table 2. Basic statistics of well-known relation extraction benchmark datasets, ^{D} represents documents instead of sentences.

Benchmark	# training Sentences	# Relation	Best F1	# NA relation
NYT-FB	561,95	24	92.5	x
Wikidata-RE	372,059	353	83	0%
WEB-NLG	501,9	246	93	0%
SEMEval-2010	10,717	9	91	17.4%
Google-RE	5528	3	87.2	0%
TACRED	106,264	41	75.2	80%
DocRED	3053^D	96	67.28	0%

all these datasets (which were in different formats) into a single ontology. RELD-RDF provides a unified format for data access along with various annotations which are required for training different types of relation extraction systems. The RELD-RDF resulted in the largest (to the best of our knowledge) RDF knowledge graphs of relations, containing 55.54 million triples describing 824 relations and 2 million sentences.

Our main contributions are as follows:

- REBench allows users to generate customized benchmarks according to user-defined criteria on important sentences and relation-level features. The framework completely abides by Semantic Web technologies: it uses the RDF dataset as input and makes use of SPARQL queries for sample selection and clustering.
- RELD-RDF is an assorted dataset constructed from well-known RE datasets extracted from various domains. This enables REBench to select a microbenchmark from multiple sources to avoid single-source problems [18].
- We evaluated state-of-the-art RE tools on a customized benchmark generated by REBench. The evaluation results show that baseline systems can be changed using more diverse benchmarks.

The rest of the paper is organized as follows: In Sect. 2, we describe the RDF dataset we used and the approach to building REBench. Section 3 presents the performance of different RE systems on the REBench. The importance and impact of the resource are explained in Sect. 4, and Sect. 5 presents resource availability, reusability and sustainability. Related work, conclusion and future work are presented in Sects. 6, and 7, respectively.

2   REBench

This section first discusses the RDF dataset used as an input for the REBench relation sample generation framework. We then discuss the relation sampling process and microbenchmark generation framework in detail.

2.1   RELD-RDF Dataset

As mentioned previously, our framework selects a customized relation sample from the RELD-RDF dataset. The RELD-RDF dataset consists of six datasets that are commonly used to train and evaluate different types of RE systems. For example, WEB-NLG, NYT-FB, and Wikidata datasets are commonly used for sentential RE, Google-RE and DocRED are used for document-based RE, the FewRel dataset is used for Few-shot RE, and the SemEval2010 dataset is commonly used for casual RE[1]. In RELD-RDF, each relation contains 23 features (more than the source datasets) divided into two main categories: relation-level and sentence-level features. Features related to relations include its natural language representation; source; other representations of the relationship such as *P569, date of birth, birthDate, and /people/person/date_of_birth* all represent the same relation; and distribution (training, testing, validation). Similarly, the features related to sentences include the number of tokens, number of entities, direction of relation, position of the subject and object entity[2] in the sentence. Figure 1 summarizes the features attached to each relation. A sample RDF representation of a relationship in RELD-RDF is presented in Listing 1.1. The RELD-RDF is publicly available from the SPARQL endpoint http://reld.cs.upb.de:8890/sparql.

2.2   Relation Sample Generation for Microbenchmarking

In this section, we first define the relation sampling generation problem, followed by the generation process. We define our relation sampling generation problem as follows:

Definition 1 (Sampling problem). *Let S be a set of input relations. Our aim is to choose a set of $\mathcal{R}$ relations that best represents S with more diverse features $\mathcal{R} << |S|$.*

---

[1] For the details about different types of RE system see Sect. 6.

[2] Subject and object entities sometimes also named as head and tail entities.

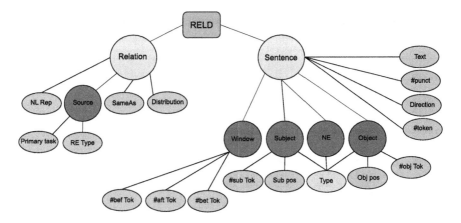

Fig. 1. A summary tree of features attached to relations and sentences in RELD-RDF dataset.

The relation sample generation process is carried out in four main steps, as shown in Fig. 2. As a prerequisite, the user provides the RELD-RDF dataset as input, the required number of relation $\mathcal{R}$, and the selection criteria (as SPARQL query) to be considered in the RE sampling for microbenchmarking. The sampling process is carried out in four steps. (1) The relation selection step selects all relations with required features from the RELD-RDF dataset. (2) The vector representation step generates feature vectors and normalization of them for the selected relationships. (3) The model generates an $\mathcal{R}$ number of clusters from the selected relations in the clustering step. (4) Final relation selection, the model selects the most representative relation from each cluster to be included in the final sample requested by the user. We now discuss these four steps in more detail.

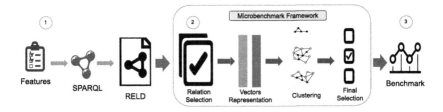

Fig. 2. REBench sampling process from input to output.

Listing 1.1. An example RELD-RDF representation of a relation with associated data sentences properties and associated data of sentences.

```
@prefix dataset: <https://reld.dice-research.org/> .
@prefix dbo: <http://dbpedia.org/ontology/> .
@prefix dc: <http://purl.org/dc/elements/1.1/> .
@prefix freebase: <http://rdf.freebase.com/ns> .
@prefix owl: <http://www.w3.org/2002/07/owl#> .
@prefix ps: <http://www.wikidata.org/prop/statement/> .
@prefix rdf: <http://www.w3.org/1999/02/22-rdf-syntax-ns#> .
@prefix rdfs: <http://www.w3.org/2000/01/rdf-schema#> .
@prefix reldr: <https://reld.dice-research.org/resource/> .
@prefix reldv: <https://reld.dice-research.org/schema/> .
@prefix xml: <http://www.w3.org/XML/1998/namespace> .
@prefix xsd: <http://www.w3.org/2001/XMLSchema#> .
# Dataset #
dataset:NYT-FB reldv:hasRelation reldr:R-4001,
      reldr:Dataset_2 dc:title reldr:NYT-FB .
      reldr:NYT-FB dc:source reldr:text_freebase ;
      reldv:primaryTask reldr:distant_supervision ;
      reldv:reType reldr:ternary .
# Relation #
reldr:R-4001 rdfs:label "place_of_birth" ;
    owl:equivalentProperty reldr:placeOfBirth ;
    owl:sameAs <http://rdf.freebase.com/ns/people/person/place_of_birth>,
        ps:P19, reldr:R-2, reldr:R-3001, reldr:R-5001 ;
    reldv:distribution "test"^^xsd:string,
        "train"^^xsd:string,
        "valid"^^xsd:string ;
    reldv:hasSentence reldr:S_NYT-FB_103382,
    ...
        reldr:S_NYT-FB_106692.
# Sentence #
reldr:S_NYT-FB_103382 reldv:direction false ;
    reldv:hasNamedEntity reldr:ne_n559817, reldr:ne_n559818,
        reldr:ne_n559819, reldr:ne_n559820;
    reldv:hasObject reldr:object_55 ;
    reldv:hasSubject reldr:subject_50 ;
    reldv:hasText "Or as Heather Marks ,
    the 17-year-old Vogue favorite from Calgary , puts it : ''
    It could be that Canada is just having a moment like Brazil and
    Russia did ."@en ;
    # Sentnece Properties #
    reldv:numAftToken 21 ;
    reldv:numBefToken 2 ;
    reldv:numBetToken 6 ;
    reldv:numOfObjToken 1 ;
    reldv:numOfPunctuations 3 ;
    reldv:numOfRelation 3 ;
    reldv:numOfSubToken 2 ;
    reldv:numOfTokens 32 ;
    reldv:objPos 10 ;
    reldv:subPos 2 .
# Subject & Object #
reldr:subject_50 reldv:subject reldr:Heather_Marks .
reldr:object_55 reldv:object reldr:Calgary .
# Named Entities #
reldr:ne_n559817 a dbo:GPE ;
    rdfs:label "calgary"@en .
reldr:ne_n559818 a dbo:GPE ;
    rdfs:label "canada"@en .
reldr:ne_n559819 a dbo:GPE ;
    rdfs:label "brazil"@en .
reldr:ne_n559820 a dbo:GPE ;
    rdfs:label "russia"@en .
```

Relations Selection: There can be potentially many relations in the REDL-RDF dataset that pass the user criteria for microbenchmarks. The sampling framework fetches all relevant relations along with the required annotated features from the `RELD-RDF` dataset using a single SPARQL query. An example of a SPARQL query is presented in Listing 1.2. This SPARQL query retrieves all relations from the dataset along with the following features in the sentences: total number of tokens, named entities, and number of punctuations in a sentence. The user can select any number of features that are considered important for microbenchmarking. The result of this query execution is stored in a map that is used in subsequent sampling steps. In the following sections, we show how this query can be modified to select customized samples for microbenchmarking.

Feature Vectors: The clustering step (explained next) requires measures of distances between relations. Each relation that was retrieved in the relation selection step from the `RELD-RDF` dataset is mapped to a vector representation. The length of the vector is equal to the number of selected features. The vector stores the corresponding relation features that were retrieved along with the given relations. Once feature vectors are created from relations, the next step is to normalize all values in the vectors between 0 and 1 to avoid bias owing to high values in the vector. The normalization of vectors for particular features is performed as follows: each of the individual values in every feature vector is divided by the overall maximal value (across all vectors) for that feature. This ensures that all the relations are located in a unit hypercube.

Clustering: Given a set of normalized vectors, the next step is to group them into the required $\mathcal{R}$ number of clusters. For this, we draw a normalized vector in the multidimensional space and used existing well-known distance-based clustering namely FEASIBLE [20], FEASIBLE Exemplars [20], KMeans++, DBSCAN+KMeans++ (Combination of DBSCAN and KMeans where DBSCAN remove outliers while KMeans generate the required number of clusters) [7], and Random selection. The `REBench` framework is not limited to these clustering methods; it is sufficiently flexible to be extended to other clustering algorithms that allow the generation of a fixed number of clusters.

Listing 1.2. SPARQL Query for selection of relations from NYT-FB from `RELD-RDF` dataset using named entity, number of punctuation and number of token features.

```
PREFIX reld: <https://reld.dice-research.org/schema/>
SELECT DISTINCT ?rId (AVG(?nToken) as ?avgToken) (count(?ne) as ?NE) (AVG(?
    numPunc) as ?avgPunc)
FROM <http://reld.dice-research.org/NYT-FB>
WHERE{
?rId reld:hasSentence ?sentence.
?sentence reld:hasSubject ?sub.
?sentence reld:hasObject ?obj.
?sentence reld:numOfTokens ?nToken.
?sentence reld:numOfPunctuations ?numPunc.
?sentence reld:hasNamedEntity ?ne.
}
```

Final Selection of Most Representative Relations: For this step, we adopt the exact approach of FEASIBLE [20] as follows: For each cluster C finds the centroid c which is the average of the feature vectors of all queries in the vectors in C. Next, we determine the distance between each relation in C and the centroid c. The final selection criterion is the minimum distance between the relationship and c. The output of our framework is an RDF file containing the selected relations, along with a list of features. This RDF output can be queried directly using a SPARQL query. The input for state-of-the-art RE systems is different, and we provide a generic script to convert the output into JSON format. The user can also convert the output into the desired style with minimum effort. REBench contains CLI options for benchmark generation that are available from the resource homepage.

Listing 1.3. Personalized query for selection of relations and corresponding sentences along with required features from RELD-RDF dataset having balanced number of sentences.

```
Prefix reld: <https://reld.dice-research.org/schema/>
SELECT   DISTINCT ?rId  (AVG(?nToken) as ?avgToken)  (AVG(?befT) as ?
    avgBeforeTokens) (AVG(?aftT) as ?avgAfterToken)
{
?rId   reld:hasSentence ?sentence.
?sentence reld:numOfTokens ?nToken.
?sentence reld:numBefToken ?befT.
?sentence reld:numAftToken ?aftT.

} Group by ?rId having (count(?sentence) = 700)
```

2.3 Relation Sample Personalization

As mentioned previously, our framework allows users to generate customized benchmarks according to user requirements. For example, a user might be interested in generating a Few-Shot (a benchmark with a balanced number of sentences for each relation) microbenchmark with 700 sentences each. To do so, the user can simply personalize the SPARQL query given in Listing 1.2 by adding SPARQL Group By, and Having clauses as shown in Listing 1.3.

2.4 Diversity of Relation Sample

Like any benchmark, the relations included in an RE benchmark should be diverse in terms of the features that affect the performance of RE systems. We define the diversity of the benchmark generated by REBench as follows.

Definition 2 (Sample Diversity)
Let S be a relation sample extracted from a set of relations L. The diversity score D is the average standard deviation of the relation features k included in the relation sample S:

$$D = \frac{1}{k} \sum_{i=1}^{k} (\sigma_i(S)) \tag{1}$$

where μ_i and σ_i represent mean and standard deviation, respectively. Where i represents the ith feature of the said distribution. In the next section, we present the diversity scores of the microbenchmarks generated using different clustering methods included in the REBench.

3   Evaluation and Results

This section describes the experimental setup and evaluation results.

3.1   Experimental Setup

We used three microbenchmarks in our evaluation: (1) A 15 relations sample was extracted from the RELD-RDF NYT-FB sub-graph to evaluate the systems trained on the NYT-FB dataset. We used the personalized query in Listing 1.2 to select these relations.

(2) To evaluate the Few-shot relation extraction model, we used listing 1.3 to extract relations with a balanced number of sentences in the RELD-RDF datasets. We selected 40 relations from the RELD-RDF dataset by keeping the number of sentences equal to 700. (3) Bootstrapping-based RE approaches are more likely to be sensitive to the features in a sentence; therefore, we choose two 100 relation benchmarks with features such as the number of tokens in a sentence, the number of tokens around the entities, and the direction property. We kept the direction property true in one benchmark and false in the second benchmark to observe the effect of direction of the entities during evaluation. We selected all these benchmarks using FEASIBLE-Exemplars because of their highest diversity score. The systems we chose for evaluation did not accept data directly in the RDF format; therefore, we converted the selected data according to the requirements of a particular RE system we chose for the evaluation.

3.2   Selected RE Systems for Evaluation

We selected those RE systems for evaluation that carry out the following criteria:

- Availability of open source implementation
- State-of-the-art baseline results
- Designed for sentence-based relation extraction

We chose three types of RE systems for the evaluation: supervised, bootstrapping, and unsupervised. Supervised systems include Partition Filter Network (PFN) [29] and Relation Extraction By End-to-end Language generation (REBEL) [11]. In addition, we selected Distributional Similarity for Relation Learning (Matching the Blanks) [2] system to evaluate on a balanced benchmark. For bootstrapping-based systems, we selected BREDS [4], and from the unsupervised category, we selected Revisiting Unsupervised Relation Extraction (URE) [26].

3.3   Results

Diversity Scores: First, we wanted to check which clustering method included in REBench generates more diverse benchmarks. To this end, we generated five microbenchmarks with a number of relations equal to 4, 24, 80, 200, and 350 using supported clustering methods. The diversity scores of these benchmarks are shown in Fig. 3 for each supported clustering method. It is observed that FEASIBLE-Exemplars generates the most diverse benchmarks, followed by FEASIBLE, KMean++, DBSCAN+KM++, and Random selection, respectively. The reason for FEASIBLE-Exemplars high diversity is due to its clustering method: it selects exemplars based on the longest distances from each other. FEASIBLE and KMeans++ are centroid-based, instead of selecting samples based on the longest distance. The removal of outliers by DBSCAN reduced the overall diversity score. Finally, random selection does not follow a particular method for the selection of relations; therefore, its diversity score is the lowest.

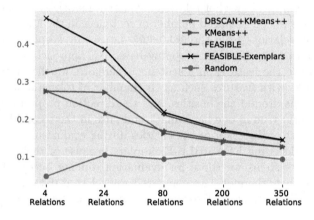

Fig. 3. Diversity score for five different algorithms using benchmarks of different size.

F Measures: We now compare the performance of the selected RE systems in terms of standard precision, recall, and F measures. The evaluation results are listed in Table 3. In the supervised category, PFN slightly outperformed REBEL (in terms of F scores 92.4 vs 91.7) while using the original benchmark dataset, i.e., NYT-FB. However, REBEL clearly outperformed PFN (F score 89.9 vs 82) for REBench. One possible reason for the fluctuation in the results is that PFN considers a single token named entity. The results change when the number of tokens in the entity changes. This indicates that the results of an RE system depend on the diversity of the samples selected for evaluation and the different sentence and relation-level features such as the number of named entities, tokens in the sentences, can change the ranking of the tested RE systems. It is highly possible that an RE system might be tuned well for a particular type of sentence length and style, but performed worse when applied to sentences with high veracity.

Table 3. Precision, Recall and F-score of different types of RE systems on `REBench` and the original benchmark dataset, we observed fluctuation in the values and shows new baseline. * represents average F-score, while ^{F} and ^{T} represent a direction feature in a benchmark as False and True, respectively.

Type	RE Systems	Dataset	P	R	F
Supervised	REBEL (micro)	NYT-FB	91.5	92.0	91.7
	PFN(micro)		**92.3**	**92.5**	**92.4**
	REBEL (micro)	REBench	**90.4**	**89.6**	**89.9**
	PFN(micro)		84.2	80.0	82.0
Bootstrapping	BREDS	News Articles	0.79	0.80	0.79*
		REBench ^{F}	**0.84**	**0.87**	**0.85**
		REBench ^{T}	0.66	0.73	0.69
Unsupervised	URE	NYT-FB	0.31	0.63	0.41
		REBench ^{F}	**0.32**	**0.70**	**0.44**
		REBench ^{T}	0.29	0.55	0.38

Similarly, bootstrapping and unsupervised RE systems are sensitive to the structure of the sentences from which the relations are extracted. For example, our results show that simply changing the subject and object position in sentences significantly affects the F scores of the BREDS and URE RE systems. This change in results indicate the importance of customized microbenchmarks for performing diverse stress testing. Furthermore, we evaluate a Few-shot RE system [2] on Listing 1.3; the overall F-score remains almost the same as that reported in the paper (`F-score = 88.9`). The reported F-score from the original paper is based on 80 relations, while we chose the 40 most representative relations. The results indicate that our framework can select the most representative sample from the population.

4   Impact

This study provides an open source, easily extendable, and reusable resource for microbenchmarking of RE components and models. We constructed an RDF dataset from existing RE datasets, which are in different formats. We added additional features to each relation that are important to perform RE benchmarking. This dataset is publicly available and can be queried via SPARQL. The proposed dataset can be used for various NLP tasks such as relation extraction, and named entity recognition. To the best of our knowledge, no microbenchmarking framework is available for RE systems. Our proposed framework completely abides by semantic web technologies. We hope that REBench will be used by the NLP community to perform use-case specific benchmarking and pinpoint component-level pros and cons of RE systems.

5   Availability, Reusability and Sustainability

The resource is publicly available for reuse under the licence of GNU General Public V3.0. A detailed usage manual for reusing and adapting resources is available in our public GitHub repository. The code and usage instructions are both documented and available on the project homepage (see Sect. 7). The resource uses Semantic Web technologies which makes its usage extendable, as well as the potential to add new clustering algorithms to the core REBench framework. In addition, the proposed RELD-RDF dataset can be extended to include more RE datasets. We provided instructions on how to reuse our code to extend the RDF dataset, as well as the REBench framework. All future extensions will be reflected on the same GitHub page. In addition, REBench will be sustained via the Paderborn Center for Parallel Computing PC^2, which provides computing resources as well as consulting regarding their usage to research projects at Paderborn University and also to external research groups. The Information and Media Technologies Centre (IMT) at Paderborn University also provides permanent IT infrastructure to host the REBench project.

6   Related Work

Many benchmarking datasets are available for relation extraction systems. Most of these benchmarks target a specific type of RE task. In this section, we divide them according to the target RE task.

Sentence Level Relation Extraction Benchmarks: The highly explored method of relation extraction is sentence-level RE. In this type of RE, a system attempts to find the relationship between a pair of entities in a natural language sentence. A single sentence can contain one or more relations or no relation at all; similarly, a sentence can contain any number of entities. Several benchmark datasets are available for the training and evaluation of sentence-level RE systems.

NYT-FB [18]: This dataset was extracted from the New York Times and aligned to freebase [5] entities. The dataset contains 24 relations and, 56195 sentences. The dataset was initially curated for distant-supervision tasks. Some reported shortcomings of this dataset are that the dataset does not contain overlapping sentences [35], it suffers from the problem of long-tailed distribution of sentences and imbalanced relations in terms of sentence annotation [23], and Wang et al. [27] found a problem related to NER format and only the last word annotation, which directly affects the performance. Wei et al. [28] reported that a single relation annotation in NYT-FB degrades the overall performance. *TACRED* [35]: is a well-known benchmark dataset for RE systems. The datasets contained 41 relations, which also include NA (no relation). The dataset is not available as open source. Sample imbalance, a high noise rate, and incorrect annotations have been reported in TACRED [13,16,37].

Wikipedia-Wikidata-RE: This is a comparatively large dataset in terms of relations and number of sentences. Sentences were extracted from Wikipedia and aligned to the entities of Wikidata. The dataset contains 353 relations and 372,059 training sentences. There is a high difference in the macro and micro evaluation on these datasets [3] Furthermore, some relations are sparse [38] that significantly affect the overall performance.

WEB-NLG: A natural language generation dataset containing 5019 crowd-sourced training sentences and 246 relations. It is a widely used dataset for RE and has achieved human-level accuracy. Researchers have identified multiple problems regarding this dataset such as long-tail distribution, last word annotation, confusing relation labels, noisy sentences, and issue related to NER [23,24,27,32].

Apart from these benchmark datasets, there are other datasets which target sentence-level RE, such as SciERC [12], Trex [6] and, CoNLL2004 [19].

Document Level Relation Extraction Benchmarks: A relation in natural language may or may not explicitly exist in a single sentence, but comes from the context of other surrounding sentences. Therefore, sentence-level relation benchmarks do not fulfil this requirement. Document-level relation extraction benchmarks like DocRED [31] and Google-RE [15] are used for this purpose [34]. One of the main disadvantages of these benchmarks is that the source of the sentences is mostly Wikipedia. The Google-RE dataset only contains four relations and the primary task is not document-based relation extraction, while DocRED consists of 96 relations.

Causal Relation Extraction Benchmarks: A relationship between two entities e1 and e2, such that the occurrence of e1 results in the occurrence of e2, is known as a cause-effect relation or causal relation extraction [30]. SemEval 2010 Task 8 and TACRED, contain causality relationships (1331 in SemEval 2010 Task 8 and 269 in TACRED). The main disadvantage of these benchmarks is the size (in terms of number of sentences) of the benchmarks.

None of the above benchmarking datasets provide a customized microbenchmark; neither of them uses Semantic Web technologies such as SPARQL querying. Our proposed framework `REBench` overcomes these problems and provides task specific, component-level microbenchmarks according to the user requirements.

7 Conclusion and Future Work

In this article, we describe a resource for generating samples of relations and sentences for microbenchmarking of relation extraction systems. Our resource uses different clustering algorithms to create more diverse clusters of samples to evaluate the relation extraction task. Users can select personalized samples for microbenchmarks based on the required features. The results indicate that diversity in the benchmark sample is key to performing fine-grained evaluations of RE systems. Microbenchmarking is key to performing such fine-grained component-level performance evaluations. Using our resources, the NLP community can evaluate their relation extraction systems based on their specific needs. We aim to extend our work to other natural language processing tasks, such as named entity disambiguation and Named Entity recognition.

Resource Availability Statement:

- Source code, usage instruction, evaluation results, JSON conversion code and code for generation of Fig. 3 of `REBench` is available from our GitHub repository[3]
- Details about the `RELD-RDF` dataset is available on the GitHub Repository[4]
- Online endpoint of the data used in `REBench` is available on[5]

Acknowledgments. This work has been supported by the BMWK-funded project RAKI (01MD19012B), SPEAKER (01MK20011U), BMBF-funded EuroStars project PORQUE (01QE2056C), 3DFed (01QE2114B) and partially supported by DFG within the Collaborative Research Centre SFB 901 (160364472) and the University of Malakand Pakistan.

References

1. Agichtein, E., Gravano, L.: Snowball: Extracting relations from large plain-text collections. In: Proceedings of the fifth ACM conference on Digital libraries, pp. 85–94 (2000)
2. Baldini Soares, L., FitzGerald, N., Ling, J., Kwiatkowski, T.: Matching the blanks: Distributional similarity for relation learning. In: Proceedings of the 57th Annual Meeting of the Association for Computational Linguistics, pp. 2895–2905. Association for Computational Linguistics, Florence, Italy (2019). https://doi.org/10.18653/v1/P19-1279
3. Bastos, A., et al.: RECON: relation extraction using knowledge graph context in a graph neural network. In: Proceedings of the Web Conference 2021, pp. 1673–1685 (2021)

---

[3] https://github.com/dice-group/REBench.
[4] https://github.com/dice-group/RELD.
[5] http://reld.cs.upb.de:8890/sparql.

4. Batista, D.S., Martins, B., Silva, M.J.: Semi-supervised bootstrapping of relation-ship extractors with distributional semantics. In: Proceedings of the 2015 Conference on Empirical Methods in Natural Language Processing, pp. 499–504. Association for Computational Linguistics, Lisbon, Portugal (2015). https://doi.org/10.18653/v1/D15-1056

5. Bollacker, K., Evans, C., Paritosh, P., Sturge, T., Taylor, J.: Freebase: a collaboratively created graph database for structuring human knowledge. In: Proceedings of the 2008 ACM SIGMOD international conference on Management of data, pp. 1247–1250 (2008)

6. Elsahar, H., et al.: T-REx: a large scale alignment of natural language with knowledge base triples. In: Proceedings of the Eleventh International Conference on Language Resources and Evaluation (LREC 2018). European Language Resources Association (ELRA), Miyazaki, Japan (2018)

7. Ester, M., et al.: A density-based algorithm for discovering clusters in large spatial databases with noise. In: KDD, vol. 96, pp. 226–231 (1996)

8. Gardent, C., Shimorina, A., Narayan, S., Perez-Beltrachini, L.: Creating training corpora for NLG micro-planners. In: Proceedings of the 55th Annual Meeting of the Association for Computational Linguistics (Volume 1: Long Papers), pp. 179–188. Association for Computational Linguistics, Vancouver, Canada (2017). https://doi.org/10.18653/v1/P17-1017

9. Han, X., et al.: FewRel: a large-scale supervised few-shot relation classification dataset with state-of-the-art evaluation. In: Proceedings of the 2018 Conference on Empirical Methods in Natural Language Processing, pp. 4803–4809. Association for Computational Linguistics, Brussels, Belgium (2018). https://doi.org/10.18653/v1/D18-1514

10. Hendrickx, I., et al.: SemEval-2010 task 8: multi-way classification of semantic relations between pairs of nominals. In: Proceedings of the 5th International Workshop on Semantic Evaluation, pp. 33–38. Association for Computational Linguistics, Uppsala, Sweden (2010)

11. Huguet Cabot, P.L., Navigli, R.: REBEL: relation extraction by end-to-end language generation. In: Findings of the Association for Computational Linguistics: EMNLP 2021, pp. 2370–2381. Association for Computational Linguistics, Punta Cana, Dominican Republic (2021). https://doi.org/10.18653/v1/2021.findings-emnlp.204

12. Luan, Y., He, L., Ostendorf, M., Hajishirzi, H.: Multi-task identification of entities, relations, and coreference for scientific knowledge graph construction. In: Proceedings of the 2018 Conference on Empirical Methods in Natural Language Processing, pp. 3219–3232. Association for Computational Linguistics, Brussels, Belgium (2018). https://doi.org/10.18653/v1/D18-1360

13. Lyu, S., Chen, H.: Relation classification with entity type restriction. In: Findings of the Association for Computational Linguistics: ACL-IJCNLP 2021, pp. 390–395. Association for Computational Linguistics, Online (2021). https://doi.org/10.18653/v1/2021.findings-acl.34

14. Ning, Q., Feng, Z., Roth, D.: A structured learning approach to temporal relation extraction. In: Proceedings of the 2017 Conference on Empirical Methods in Natural Language Processing, pp. 1027–1037. Association for Computational Linguistics, Copenhagen, Denmark (2017). https://doi.org/10.18653/v1/D17-1108

15. Orr, D.: Research Blog: 50,000 lessons on how to read: a relation extraction corpus, 11 (2013)

16. Park, S., Kim, H.: Improving sentence-level relation extraction through curriculum learning. arXiv e-prints arXiv:2107.09332 (2021)

17. Pawar, S., Palshikar, G.K., Bhattacharyya, P.: Relation extraction: a survey. arXiv preprint arXiv:1712.05191 (2017)
18. Riedel, S., Yao, L., McCallum, A.: Modeling relations and their mentions without labeled text. In: Balcázar, J.L., Bonchi, F., Gionis, A., Sebag, M. (eds.) ECML PKDD 2010. LNCS (LNAI), vol. 6323, pp. 148–163. Springer, Heidelberg (2010). https://doi.org/10.1007/978-3-642-15939-8_10
19. Roth, D., Yih, W.t.: A linear programming formulation for global inference in natural language tasks. In: Proceedings of the Eighth Conference on Computational Natural Language Learning (CoNLL-2004) at HLT-NAACL 2004, pp. 1–8. Association for Computational Linguistics, Boston, Massachusetts, USA (2004)
20. Saleem, M., Mehmood, Q., Ngonga Ngomo, A.-C.: FEASIBLE: a feature-based SPARQL benchmark generation framework. In: Arenas, M., et al. (eds.) ISWC 2015. LNCS, vol. 9366, pp. 52–69. Springer, Cham (2015). https://doi.org/10.1007/978-3-319-25007-6_4
21. Sorokin, D., Gurevych, I.: Context-aware representations for knowledge base relation extraction. In: Proceedings of the 2017 Conference on Empirical Methods in Natural Language Processing, pp. 1784–1789. Association for Computational Linguistics, Copenhagen, Denmark (2017). https://doi.org/10.18653/v1/D17-1188
22. Stolcke, A., et al.: Dialogue act modeling for automatic tagging and recognition of conversational speech. Comput. Linguist. **26**(3), 339–374 (2000)
23. Sui, D., Chen, Y., Liu, K., Zhao, J., Zeng, X., Liu, S.: Joint entity and relation extraction with set prediction networks. arXiv preprint arXiv:2011.01675 (2020)
24. Sun, K., Zhang, R., Mensah, S., Mao, Y., Liu, X.: Recurrent interaction network for jointly extracting entities and classifying relations. In: Proceedings of the 2020 Conference on Empirical Methods in Natural Language Processing (EMNLP), pp. 3722–3732. Association for Computational Linguistics, Online (2020). https://doi.org/10.18653/v1/2020.emnlp-main.304
25. Surdeanu, M., Tibshirani, J., Nallapati, R., Manning, C.D.: Multi-instance multi-label learning for relation extraction. In: Proceedings of the 2012 Joint Conference on Empirical Methods in Natural Language Processing and Computational Natural Language Learning, pp. 455–465. Association for Computational Linguistics, Jeju Island, Korea (2012)
26. Tran, T.T., Le, P., Ananiadou, S.: Revisiting unsupervised relation extraction. In: Proceedings of the 58th Annual Meeting of the Association for Computational Linguistics, pp. 7498–7505. Association for Computational Linguistics, Online (2020). https://doi.org/10.18653/v1/2020.acl-main.669
27. Wang, Y., Yu, B., Zhang, Y., Liu, T., Zhu, H., Sun, L.: TPLinker: single-stage joint extraction of entities and relations through token pair linking. In: Proceedings of the 28th International Conference on Computational Linguistics, pp. 1572–1582. International Committee on Computational Linguistics, Barcelona, Spain (Online) (2020). https://doi.org/10.18653/v1/2020.coling-main.138
28. Wei, Z., Su, J., Wang, Y., Tian, Y., Chang, Y.: A novel cascade binary tagging framework for relational triple extraction. In: Proceedings of the 58th Annual Meeting of the Association for Computational Linguistics, pp. 1476–1488. Association for Computational Linguistics, Online (2020). https://doi.org/10.18653/v1/2020.acl-main.136
29. Yan, Z., Zhang, C., Fu, J., Zhang, Q., Wei, Z.: A partition filter network for joint entity and relation extraction. In: Proceedings of the 2021 Conference on Empirical Methods in Natural Language Processing, pp. 185–197. Association for Computational Linguistics, Online and Punta Cana, Dominican Republic (2021). https://doi.org/10.18653/v1/2021.emnlp-main.17

30. Yang, J., Han, S.C., Poon, J.: A survey on extraction of causal relations from natural language text. Knowl. Inf. Syst. **64**(5), 1161–1186 (2022). https://doi.org/10.1007/s10115-022-01665-w
31. Yao, Y., et al.: DocRED: a large-scale document-level relation extraction dataset. In: Proceedings of the 57th Annual Meeting of the Association for Computational Linguistics, pp. 764–777. Association for Computational Linguistics, Florence, Italy (2019). https://doi.org/10.18653/v1/P19-1074
32. Ye, H., et al.: Contrastive triple extraction with generative transformer (2020). https://doi.org/10.48550/ARXIV.2009.06207
33. Yu, M., Yin, W., Hasan, K.S., dos Santos, C., Xiang, B., Zhou, B.: Improved neural relation detection for knowledge base question answering. In: Proceedings of the 55th Annual Meeting of the Association for Computational Linguistics (Volume 1: Long Papers), pp. 571–581. Association for Computational Linguistics, Vancouver, Canada (2017). https://doi.org/10.18653/v1/P17-1053
34. Zaporojets, K., Deleu, J., Develder, C., Demeester, T.: DWIE: an entity-centric dataset for multi-task document-level information extraction. Inf. Process. Manage. **58**(4), 102563 (2021). https://doi.org/10.1016/j.ipm.2021.102563
35. Zeng, X., Zeng, D., He, S., Liu, K., Zhao, J.: Extracting relational facts by an end-to-end neural model with copy mechanism. In: Proceedings of the 56th Annual Meeting of the Association for Computational Linguistics (Volume 1: Long Papers), pp. 506–514. Association for Computational Linguistics, Melbourne, Australia (2018). https://doi.org/10.18653/v1/P18-1047
36. Zhang, Y., Zhong, V., Chen, D., Angeli, G., Manning, C.D.: Position-aware attention and supervised data improve slot filling. In: Proceedings of the 2017 Conference on Empirical Methods in Natural Language Processing, pp. 35–45. Association for Computational Linguistics, Copenhagen, Denmark (2017). https://doi.org/10.18653/v1/D17-1004
37. Zhou, W., Chen, M.: An improved baseline for sentence-level relation extraction (2021). https://doi.org/10.48550/ARXIV.2102.01373
38. Zhu, H., Lin, Y., Liu, Z., Fu, J., Chua, T.S., Sun, M.: Graph neural networks with generated parameters for relation extraction. In: Proceedings of the 57th Annual Meeting of the Association for Computational Linguistics, pp. 1331–1339. Association for Computational Linguistics, Florence, Italy (2019). https://doi.org/10.18653/v1/P19-1128

ISSA: Generic Pipeline, Knowledge Model and Visualization Tools to Help Scientists Search and Make Sense of a Scientific Archive

Anne Toulet[1], Franck Michel[2(✉)], Anna Bobasheva[3], Aline Menin[3],
Sébastien Dupré[1], Marie-Claude Deboin[1], Marco Winckler[3],
and Andon Tchechmedjiev[4]

[1] CIRAD (French Agricultural Research Centre for International Development),
Ales, France
{anne.toulet,sebastien.dupre,marie-claude.deboin}@cirad.fr
[2] University Côte d'Azur, CNRS, Inria, Ales, France
franck.michel@inria.fr
[3] University Côte d'Azur, Inria, CNRS, Ales, France
{anna.bobasheva,aline.menin,marco.winckler}@inria.fr
[4] Euromov Digital Health in Motion,
Univ Montpellier, IMT Mines Ales, Ales, France
andon.tchechmedjiev@mines-ales.fr

Abstract. Faced with the ever-increasing number of scientific publications, researchers struggle to keep up, find and make sense of articles relevant to their own research. Scientific open archives play a central role in helping deal with this deluge, yet keyword-based search services often fail to grasp the richness of the semantic associations between articles. In this paper, we present the methods, tools and services implemented in the ISSA project to tackle these issues. The project aims to (1) provide a generic, reusable and extensible pipeline for the analysis and processing of articles of an open scientific archive, (2) translate the result into a semantic index stored and represented as an RDF knowledge graph; (3) develop innovative search and visualization services that leverage this index to allow researchers, decision makers or scientific information professionals to explore thematic association rules, networks of co-publications, articles with co-occurring topics, etc. To demonstrate the effectiveness of the solution, we also report on its deployment and user-driven customization for the needs of an institutional open archive of 110,000+ resources. Fully in line with the open science and FAIR dynamics, the presented work is available under an open license with all the accompanying documents necessary to facilitate its reuse. The knowledge graph produced on our use-case is compliant with common linked open data best practices.

Keywords: Data indexing · Scientific literature · Information retrieval · Linked open data · Knowledge graph

© The Author(s) 2022
U. Sattler et al. (Eds.): ISWC 2022, LNCS 13489, pp. 660–677, 2022.
https://doi.org/10.1007/978-3-031-19433-7_38

1   Searching Scientific Literature: Beyond Keywords

In recent years, several evolutions have drastically transformed the way researchers interact with scientific literature. First, the number and pace of articles published are skyrocketing, such that it is increasingly difficult to keep up, find relevant articles or even identify potential collaborators. The use of social networks such as Twitter to monitor scientific advances, results in an echo chamber highlighting laboratories and researchers that are already visible and recognized. Second, most scientific literature repositories offer simple search capabilities that typically rely on keyword matches or author names. Such an approach commonly fails to grasp the richness of the semantic relationships that hold between articles, leaving to the user a cumbersome filtering of search results. Finally, the ultra-specialization of research communities makes it difficult to discover cross-disciplinary knowledge, yet essential to meet the growing demand of funding agencies for pluri- or inter-disciplinarity. It is therefore essential to **offer tools that allow researchers, as well as scientific and technical information (STI) professionals, to find their way in and make sense of this mass of knowledge.** There exists a variety of methods and tools designed to process the content of text documents, extract knowledge, and provide advanced services. However, to the best of our knowledge, these tools are either domain-specific or address specific steps but do not provide an end-to-end, integrated pipeline.

In this paper, we present the methods, tools and services implemented in the ISSA project [3] to tackle these needs. ISSA aims to (1) provide **a generic, reusable and extensible pipeline for the analysis and processing of an open scientific archive,** (2) translate the results into a **semantic index in the form of an RDF knowledge graph** (KG); (3) develop **innovative search and visualization services exploiting the index**, aimed at researchers, decision makers, or STI professionals. Geared towards genericity and reusability, the proposed solution adheres to the FAIR principles [35] and the open science guidelines. Furthermore, ISSA adopts a pragmatic approach that strives to rely on robust, industry-proven, scalable solutions, and integrate them into a coherent, easily deployable pipeline.

The processing pipeline, depicted in Fig. 1, involves various artificial intelligence techniques: natural language processing, knowledge engineering, semantic web and linked data. Publications' metadata and full text are processed in order to extract thematic descriptors[1] and named entities (NE). To allow services to reason upon the extracted knowledge while leveraging terminological references such as ontologies or thesauri, thematic descriptors and NEs are linked with resources such as Wikidata, DBpedia and GeoNames. The resulting KG serves as a keystone able to support the development of services such as search and visualization. In particular, the Arviz [24] and MGExplorer [25] visualization tools make it possible to explore and visualize thematic association rules, networks

---

[1] Thematic descriptors are keywords linked to reference vocabularies, thesauri or ontologies that characterize an article as a whole. Unlike keywords provided by authors, they are extracted automatically using text classification methods.

of co-publications, or of articles with co-occurring topics, in order to concretely answer competency questions. These visualization tools are highly configurable and can be tailored to a wide range of scenarios.

To demonstrate the effectiveness of the proposed solution, we deployed it for the needs of a real-world use case, Agritrop [1], CIRAD[2]'s open archive of 110,000+ resources (i.e., book, book chapter, article, thesis, etc.). By drawing on the outcome of interviews conducted with CIRAD researchers and documentalists, we show the ability of these services to meet user needs and competency questions with relevant answers.

In the rest of this paper, Sect. 2 provides an overview and a comparison with related work. Section 3 describes the pipeline spanning metadata retrieval, extraction and linking of thematic descriptors and NEs, and construction of the KG. Then, Sect. 4 presents the exploitation and visualization tools and how they were configured in the Agritrop use-case. Section 5 provides further information about the accessibility of the pipeline and the KG generated in the case of Agritrop. Finally, Sect. 6 discusses the impact and reuse of this work in various communities, and Sect. 7 draws conclusions and suggests future works.

2   Related Works

For over twenty years, the open science movement has aimed at making scientific research results freely accessible, considerably transforming the landscape of scientific production. Initiatives such as **Research Data Alliance** [6] (RDA) that federates working groups on **FAIR principles**, metadata standards, and semantic resources (ontologies, thesauri, etc.); or **Go Fair** [2] and **European Open Science Cloud** (EOSC) [11], have laid the ground work for the implementation of the FAIR principles for open science. In this context, the role of open archives and of how to exploit them are central questions: many projects, including the ISSA project, have taken up this dimension, covering complementary aspects.

The **OpenMinted** [5] project aimed at creating a generic Software As A Service EU infrastructure for text mining, based on a modular architecture, that researchers could use by contributing their use-cases. After 5 years of development, the project fell short of delivering a fully functional prototype, merely laying the foundational components of the infrastructure. The related **Visa TM** project [7] was to be the core knowledge extraction component, integrating thesauri and ontologies from many domains, but only achieved a very preliminary integration [20]. In contrast, the ISSA project adopts a more modest but focused and pragmatic approach, proposing a generic pipeline adaptable to multiple domains, based on the integration of robust, industry-proven and scalable existing tools, and deployable by each community. ISSA also has a strong focus on using Linked Open Data and FAIR principles, which are absent from OpenMinted.

---

[2] CIRAD is the French Agricultural Research Centre for International Development https://www.cirad.fr/en.

The ISTEX infrastructure, which was meant to be the corpus provider for OpenMinted [20], has goals related to ISSA in that it aims at constituting corpora of scientific publications and providing research communities with tools to explore relevant subsets of the curated corpora. However, the main focus is to allow the creation and download of subsets of corpora through very precise criteria, extract terminology and provide a descriptive visualization of the results through the LODEX tool [10]. The indexing and consolidated KG aspects of ISSA are absent. The more recent **Covid-on-the-Web** project [28] has the most in common with ISSA, providing researchers with ways to access, extract and query knowledge from literature related to the coronavirus family, by building and exploiting a KG describing the concepts and arguments extracted from 100,000+ scientific articles, but stopping short of an end-to-end, reusable pipeline like in ISSA.

In summary the overall scope of ISSA includes something absent from all those initiatives: a generic end-to-end pipeline, that is easy to deploy and customize.

3   From an Open Scientific Archive to the ISSA Pipeline and Knowledge Graph

The ISSA pipeline harnesses existing tools to analyze and index the articles of a scientific archive, drawing meaningful links between the articles and the Web of Data, and following Semantic Web standards. Figure 1 describes the pipeline: (1) Metadata is retrieved from the open archive API, (2) translated into RDF with Morph-xR2RML and stored in a Virtuoso OS server. (3) Full text is extracted with Grobid and for each article, (4) Thematic descriptors and NEs are extracted from the text and linked to Wikidata, DBPedia and optionally domain-specific thesauri (unsupervised linking and disambiguation). (5) Descriptors and

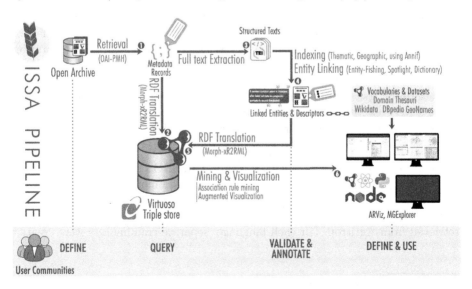

Fig. 1. ISSA pipeline: resources, services and applications.

entities are translated into a unified RDF dataset and stored in Virtuoso along metadata records. (6) The KG is exploited to propose augmented visualization applications.

3.1   Text Classification of Articles for Their Thematic Indexing

Thematic descriptors are keywords (typically 5 or 6) or expressions that characterize an article as a whole and that are linked to a standardized vocabulary. In some institutions, documentalists manually annotate articles with descriptors, which yields accurate annotations but is time consuming, such that it is usually not performed retroactively for older publications, possibly leaving behind a large set of legacy publications.

Provided that there exists a large enough corpus annotated with a domain vocabulary, one can train a specialized supervised classification model to automatically assign thematic descriptors to publications. The ISSA pipeline includes such a classification system through the integration of Annif [32], a framework developed by the National Library of Finland. Annif does not propose any new methods per se, but provides a framework and API to integrate existing machine learning models and tools to index corpora of scientific publications. In addition to the integration of multiple supervised and unsupervised models (TensorFlow deep net, Omikuji, fastText and Gensim), Annif supports multiple vocabulary formats, comes with standardized evaluation protocols and metrics, and supports multiple languages. In the ISSA pipeline, a corpus is extracted per language and split into training, validation and testing sets, in order to train the Annif model. The recreation of new models can be triggered independently from the pipeline, either manually or automatically at fixed intervals. The trained models are used in the pipeline to classify each article. For articles already manually indexed we end up with two sets of descriptors, one set corresponding to manual annotation and one set corresponding to automatic annotation.

Thematic descriptors are represented in RDF as annotations using the Web Annotation Vocabulary [34] (`issa:ThematicDescriptorAnnotation` is a subclass of `oa:Annotation`). An example is given in Listing 1.1 (lines 7–13). The annotation points to the annotated article (the target) and the resource that the descriptor links to (the body). It also provides the confidence of the extraction and linking of the descriptor, its rank in the list of descriptors ordered by descending confidence. Using PROV-O[3], the annotation keeps track of whether a thematic descriptor was retrieved from the article metadata or extracted by Annif.

Application to Agritrop. CIRAD curators annotate newly submitted articles with terms from AGROVOC [13], a standard SKOS thesaurus in the agronomy and agriculture domains. To train Annif to annotate new articles with AGROVOC terms, we extracted a corpus of approximately 12,000 English and French open-access articles. Descriptors manually annotated by curators were retrieved from Agritrop. For each language, separate training sets were created

---

[3] https://www.w3.org/TR/prov-o/.

```
 1 @prefix dct:      <http://purl.org/dc/terms/> .
 2 @prefix issa:     <http://data-issa.cirad.fr/> .
 3 @prefix issapr:   <http://data-issa.cirad.fr/property/> .
 4 @prefix oa:       <http://www.w3.org/ns/oa#> .
 5 @prefix prov:     <http://www.w3.org/ns/prov#> .
 6 @prefix schema:   <http://schema.org/> .
 7 # Thematic descriptor "sustainable development"
 8 [] a                       prov:Entity , issa:ThematicDescriptorAnnotation ;
 9    issapr:confidence       0.4556 ;
10    issapr:rank             6 ;
11    oa:hasBody              <http://aims.fao.org/aos/agrovoc/c_35332> ;
12    oa:hasTarget            <http://data-issa.cirad.fr/article/543654> ;
13    prov:wasAttributedTo issa:AnnifSubjectIndexer .
14 # Named entity "banana"
15 [] a                       prov:Entity , oa:Annotation ;
16    schema:about            <http://data-issa.cirad.fr/article/543654> ;
17    issapr:confidence 0.5939 ;
18    oa:hasBody              <http://www.wikidata.org/entity/Q503> ;
19    oa:hasTarget [
20      oa:hasSource          <http://data-issa.cirad.fr/article/543654#body_text> ;
21      oa:hasSelector        [
22        a oa:TextPositionSelector , oa:TextQuoteSelector ;
23        oa:exact "banana" ; oa:start 12750; oa:end 12756 ]] ;
24    prov:wasAttributedTo issa:EntityFishing .
```

Listing 1.1. Representation of a thematic descriptor extracted by Annif and linked to AGROVOC, and a named entity extracted from the article's body by Entity-fishing, and linked to Wikidata.

based on automatic language detection[4]. We experimented with different available models and chose the best performing one, namely an ensemble of lexical matching (MLLM) [32] and a tree-based machine learning algorithm [30].

3.2 Extraction and Linking of Named Entities

The ISSA pipeline relies on three tools to identify, disambiguate and link NEs from the articles (title, abstract and body) of the scientific archive:

- DBpedia Spotlight [15] annotates text in eight different languages with DBpedia entities. Disambiguation is carried out by entity linking using a generative model with maximum likelihood.
- Entity-fishing [31] identifies and disambiguates NEs against Wikidata. It relies on FastText word embeddings to generate candidates and ranks them with gradient tree boosting and features derived from relations and context.
- Dictionary projection annotation performs in-domain NEs with pyclinrec[5] and disambiguation is performed with EigenThemes [9] using hyperbolic graph embeddings [14] computed from the corresponding domain thesauri.

For each article, the pipeline invokes each of the three tools and translates their respective outputs into an RDF representation. An additional post-processing step specifically identifies geographic entities by looking for GeoNames mappings in the corresponding Wikidata concepts.

---

[4] https://pypi.org/project/pycld2/.
[5] https://github.com/twktheainur/pyclinrec.

Like thematic descriptors, NEs are modelled in RDF as annotations, as exemplified in Listing 1.1 (lines 14–23). The annotation points to the annotated article (property `schema:about`). The matched text fragment is described in the annotation target that points to the article part wherein the NE was recognized (title, abstract or body), and locates it with start and end offsets. The annotation body is the URI of the resource that the NE links to (Wikidata and Geonames in the example). The annotation includes the extraction and linking confidences, and provenance information regarding the tool used to extract the NE.

Application to the Agritrop Use Case. The only specific part concerns the annotation of articles with the AGROVOC thesaurus. Since no gold standard is available, we used the dictionary projection approach with unsupervised entity disambiguation. The integration of disambiguation is still ongoing at the time of writing: Eignethemes must be adapted to compute arbitrary graph embeddings for any standardized SKOS thesaurus, with a technique suited for hierarchies [14].

3.3   Articles Metadata

In addition to text processing steps, the ISSA pipeline requires obtaining the articles' metadata and translating them into RDF. The metadata must contain a URL to download the PDF file of each article, and may contain an identifier, title, authors, date, journal, license, DOI, etc. Depending on the considered archive, metadata may be obtained using various interfaces, commonly a REST API. Therefore, this step will usually require (1) writing a connector to adjust to the archive's API specifics, and (2) adjusting the mapping that lifts the archive-specific metadata to the target RDF model. The ISSA pipeline comes with a connector compatible with the Open Archives Initiative Protocol for Metadata Harvesting (OAI-PMH)[6] that is largely adopted in scientific data sharing [16].

We have defined an RDF model that represents articles' metadata and content using well-adopted vocabularies: DCMI[7], FRBR-aligned Bibliographic Ontology (FaBiO) [29], Bibliographic Ontology[8], FOAF [18] and Schema.org [19]. A comprehensive description of the RDF representation together with examples are provided in the pipeline's Github repository.[9]

Application to the Agritrop Use Case. In Agritrop, OAI-PMH is used to retrieve the common metadata as well as the abstract and thematic descriptors defined by the curators, that are mapped to RDF using the model described in Sect. 3.1. Given that the text and abstract extracted from the PDF files by Grobid can be of poor quality, we provide a mechanism to coalesce title and abstract retrieved from the metadata with those extracted from full text.

---

[6] https://www.openarchives.org/pmh/.

[7] https://www.dublincore.org/specifications/dublin-core/dcmi-terms/.

[8] http://bibliontology.com/specification.html.

[9] https://github.com/issa-project/issa-pipeline/blob/main/doc/.

3.4   Integrating All Building Blocks into a Comprehensive Pipeline

Running the Extractors. The pipeline's Github repository provides multiple scripts[10] that orchestrate and automate the processing steps from downloading articles to yielding the resulting RDF KG. To facilitate the deployment, third-party tools Grobid, Annif, Entity-fishing and DBpedia Spotlight are dockerized using official Docker images. In addition, DBpedia Spotlight[11] and Entity-fishing are deployed using pre-trained English and French models.

Generation and Publication of the KG. The translation into RDF of the outputs of each step is carried out using Morph-xR2RML,[12] an implementation of the xR2RML mapping language [27] for MongoDB databases. Thus, the next steps consist of importing the outputs into MongoDB, pre-processing them to filter out unneeded or invalid data, and apply the translation rules with Morph-xR2RML. Lastly, the produced RDF files are loaded into a dockerized Virtuoso OS server deployed using an official Docker image. An additional customizable RDF Turtle file[13] describes the generated RDF dataset using the DCAT [22], VOID [8] and SPARQL-SD [33] vocabularies.

Incremental Updates. After initial publication, periodic invocation of the pipeline can be scheduled to incrementally update the KG with new documents and retrain the Annif models.

Application to the Agritrop Use Case. In the case of Agritrop, the pipeline processed the 12,000 open-access articles in English and French. Annif and the NE extractors were deployed on a virtual machine with 12 CPU cores (2.3 GHz) and 32 GB RAM, the processing took 11 h. MongoDB and Morph-xR2RML were deployed on the same virtual machine. The upload in MongoDB of the documents produced by the NE and descriptor extractors, their pre-processing, the generation of RDF files and their loading into Virtuoso took 1 h 05 m. Additional insights into the dataset generated for Agritrop are given in Sect. 5.

Pipeline Reusability. The pipeline can be customized to meet the needs of any scientific archive and community. The OAI-PMH protocol is very common among scientific archives, such that connecting to archives implementing it should be straightforward. The comprehensive metadata model relies on standard vocabularies and is fully generic. The pipeline is delivered with pre-integrated tools to perform entity-linking against DBpedia, Wikidata, and GeoNames. Yet, new processing steps can easily be defined to leverage other tools and vocabularies suited to specific needs. Finally, the automatic thematic indexing relies on Annif

---

[10] https://github.com/issa-project/issa-pipeline/tree/main/pipeline.

[11] https://sourceforge.net/projects/dbpedia-spotlight/files/2016-10/en/.

[12] https://github.com/frmichel/morph-xr2rml/.

[13] https://github.com/issa-project/issa-pipeline/blob/main/dataset/dataset.ttl.

that supports numerous models and can be used with arbitrary vocabularies and languages.

4   Visualization and Exploration Services

4.1   Augmented Visualization of Metadata Records

The primary role of an open archive is to provide access to the bibliographic records of the resources it contains. The ISSA prototype meets this need by **enabling users to access an enriched bibliographic view of each open access article in the database.** Beyond merely presenting common article metadata, this service (exemplified in Fig. 2 for the case of Agritrop) visualizes the article abstract where extracted NEs are highlighted and point to the associated knowledge bases (Wikidata, DBpedia, GeoNames, . . .). Thematic descriptors automatically extracted with text classification and linked to the considered thesaurus (e.g. AGROVOC) are also shown, along with a cartographic visualization of the places mentioned in the article, linked to GeoNames. Technically, the service consists of a React.js-based web interface and a Node.js server that carries out queries to the semantic index, and is fully generic: adapting the CSS stylesheets suffices to match any other graphical chart.

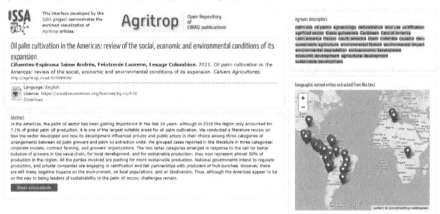

Fig. 2. Augmented visualization of an article's bibliographic records.

4.2   Extraction and Visualization of Association Rules

An association rule is an implication of the form $X \rightarrow Y$, where X is an antecedent itemset and Y is a consequent itemset: transactions containing items in set X tend to contain items in set Y. Each rule is described through its *confidence*, which defines the probability of finding Y in a transaction knowing that X is in the same transaction, and *interestingness*, which defines the serendipity of a rule by penalizing rules with high incidence of antecedent and/or consequent items. Association rule mining is widely used to discover correlations, frequent patterns, associations or casual structures, and can assist researchers in narrowing down the search for scientific publications.

Using the algorithm proposed in [12], we extract association rules linking the articles' thematic descriptors extracted as described in Sect. 3.1. The mining process casts scientific publications as transactions and thematic descriptors as itemsets. Although the approach helps to reduce and focus the exploration of a dataset, researchers are still confronted with a large set of rules. Therefore, we leverage the potential of visualization to assist the exploration of these rules and thus the discovery of hidden knowledge in the database. In particular, we explore the data using ARViz[14] (Fig. 3), a generic tool designed to support the exploration of association rules via three complementary visualization techniques (i.e. a scatter plot, a chord diagram, and an association graph) providing the distribution of rules over the measures of interest and a focused exploration of (i) **items**, to find and/or describe the rules involving a particular item, and (ii) **rules**, to detect distinguishable association rules that are worth saving for knowledge acquisition.

Application to the Agritrop Use Case. In the analysis, we considered the 3,610 thematic descriptors mentioned in 21,013 articles[15]. To keep only relevant rules, we dropped rules with confidence and interestingness below a given threshold (empirically set to 0.7 and 0.3, respectively), as well as redundant rules (i.e. a rule $A, B, C \rightarrow D$ is redundant if $Conf(A, B \rightarrow D) \geq Conf(A, B, C \rightarrow D)$). The resulting set consists of 20,697 association rules that can be explored using ARViz. Given a antecedent or consequent concept, ARViz dynamically identifies and displays all the relevant associated concepts. For instance, in the current context of the COVID-19 pandemics, researchers might be interested in knowing how strongly the disease relates to other concepts in publications. Thus, we use the association graph view in ARViz to display all the rules involving the concept COVID-19 (Fig. 3b). The graph provides an intuitive portrayal of antecedent and consequent items involved in the rules (Fig. 3a), where items are represented over on the left and right sides of the screen, and rules are encoded as diamond-shaped nodes placed between the items, which color encodes the measures of interest. This example reveals that COVID-19 is associated to three consequent concepts: the family Coronavirinae of viruses, pandemics, and economic crises. For the latter, the associated references indeed reveal publications on the resilience of the food sector and agricultural response to the COVID-19 crisis. Concepts co-occurring with COVID-19 share one or more consequent concepts. This is the case of food security that occurs in publications concerned with economic crises and pandemics.

4.3   Exploring Descriptors Co-occurrence

We present below a complementary visualization tool, LDViz[16] [26] which can meet other types of exploration needs and solve complex competency questions.

---

[14] Accessible at http://dataviz.i3s.unice.fr/arviz/issa.

[15] This includes the 12,000 articles processed by the pipeline, together with articles for which we only have metadata with curator-provided descriptors.

[16] Accessible at http://dataviz.i3s.unice.fr/ldviz.

Use Case 1. The *One Health* initiative [21,23] seeks to unify public, animal and environmental health themes to better understand the development of pandemics and the spread of emerging diseases. In the current context of global climate change, CIRAD researchers wish to figure out publications in the Agritrop open archive that mention both climate change and health (including sub-concepts such as human health, public health, animal health, plant health, etc.), and the time period when these links appeared in CIRAD's research work. To this end, we explore the ISSA semantic index using the LDViz tool which leverages SPARQL queries to explore relevant data through the multiple perspectives delivered by the MGExplorer graphic library. In particular, the tool supports the exploration of relationships within data in cluster and pairwise manners and their distribution over time.

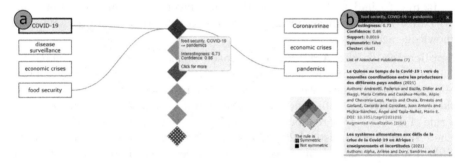

Fig. 3. Visual exploration of (a) association rules involving the COVID-19 concept using ARViz and (b) the publications mentioning the concepts COVID-19, food security and pandemics.

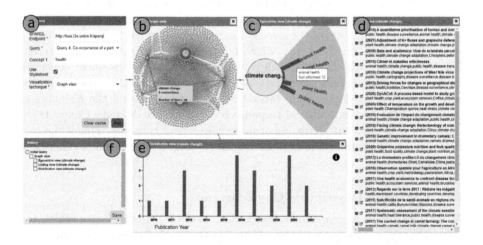

Fig. 4. Visual exploration of health and climate change relationship using LDViz.

To solve the task at hand, we defined a SPARQL query that retrieves the set of articles mentioning `climate change` together with `health` or any narrower or related concept. LDViz proposes a query panel where domain experts can select predefined queries (Fig. 4a) and explore the data through complementary visualization techniques. The exploration starts with a graph view where nodes represent concepts linked together through the scientific publications where they co-occur (Fig. 4b). We continue the exploration with an egocentric view focused on the `climate change` concept since we want to know how it is related to `health`. This shows the different concepts linked to `climate change` and the number of publications where they co-occur. For instance, we can see in Fig. 4c that `climate change` co-occurs mostly with `animal health` in 12 publications. Then, the listing view (Fig. 4d) shows the publications that co-mention `climate change` and `health`, which we can further explore using the other visualizations presented in Sect. 4. Finally, we explore the temporal distribution of those publications (Fig. 4e) where we observe a slightly more intense joint use of those concepts in 2016 and 2020.

Use Case 2. This second use case exemplifies how these tools can be used at institutional and decision-making levels. Public policies are a relevant research subject in CIRAD, as it helps in steering and supporting public decision-making. Thus, we explore the CIRAD publications through the perspective of the `policies` concept to (i) identify the major research areas around public policies, (ii) the ones that are absent or poorly covered, and (iii) the predominant topics across time, which can be contextualized via historical events. We begin the exploration with a graph where green nodes depict the `policies` concept and its narrowers. These are linked to other concepts (in orange) when they co-occur in publications (Fig. 5a). This visualization reveals that CIRAD's major public policy research topic is agricultural policies (central green node). These are strongly linked to `development policies` (Fig. 5d), in line with CIRAD's mandate, as well as to `land policies`. Concepts `water` (Fig. 5c), `food` (Fig. 5b), `forestry` (Fig. 5e) and `environmental policies` (Fig. 5f) are present to a lesser extent while being all related to `agricultural policies`. The time distribution of publications dealing with `environmental policies` reveals a growing interest of research at CIRAD in this field, confirming that their evolution is correlated with relevant world events such as the World Development program (UN) in 2016, the Paris Agreement in 2015, its fifth anniversary in 2020, or the COVID-19 pandemic in 2020.

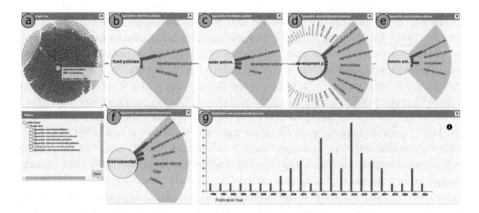

Fig. 5. Visual exploration of scientific publications mentioning any concept of the "Policies" family of descriptors.

5   Source Code, Dataset, Documentation

Source Code Availability. From a technical perspective, ISSA consists of several software components integrated together. Third-party components such as Annif, Grobid, DBpedia Spotlight and Entity-fishing are obtained through their official Docker image distributions on DockerHub.[17] The components developed within the ISSA project are available on Github repositories, licensed under the open-source, free-software Apache 2.0 license, and assigned a DOI that guarantees long-term availability. This information is summarized in Table 1. In particular, the processing pipeline's repository provides multiple scripts that orchestrate and automate the different steps from downloading the articles to running the triple store, together with documentation including deployment instructions, licensing and RDF modelling description.

Sustainability Plan. In the short term, CIRAD wishes to dedicate efforts to the deployment of the ISSA pipeline and visualization tools for production use. This will be the opportunity to assess the quality of the deployment procedure and documentation, and improve them when necessary. Furthermore, a key motivation of the ISSA project is to provide a solution generic enough to be reused with various scientific archives. Therefore, we intend to provide support to communities showing interest in this solution and willing to experiment with it for their own needs. Depending on further funding opportunities, this may range from a best-effort support to more substantial collaborations.

---

[17] https://hub.docker.com/.

Table 1. Source code developed or adapted for ISSA.

Name	License	DOI	Repository
Processing pipeline	Apache 2.0	10.5281/zenodo.6513983	https://github.com/issa-project/issa-pipeline
Arviz and association rules mining	Apache 2.0	10.5281/zenodo.6511786 10.5281/zenodo.6511146	https://github.com/Wimmics/arviz https://github.com/Wimmics/association-rules-mining
MGExplorer	Apache 2.0	10.5281/zenodo.6511782	https://github.com/Wimmics/ldviz
Article visualization	Apache 2.0	10.5281/zenodo.6510031 10.5281/zenodo.6510029	https://github.com/issa-project/web-visualization https://github.com/issa-project/web-backend

ISSA Agritrop Dataset. The dataset generated by the pipeline for the Agritrop archive is available as a downloadable, DOI-identified RDF dump, and through a Virtuoso OS triple store and SPARQL endpoint. This information is summarized in Table 2 along with basic statistics. The RDF model underlying the dataset is provided in the Github repository.[18] At the time of writing, the URIs are not yet dereferenceable due to on-going security validation procedures required by CIRAD's administrators. In line with best practices [17], the dataset comes with a thorough self-description, comprising (1) licensing, authorship and provenance information, used vocabularies, interlinking and access information, described with Dublin Core Metadata Information, DCAT, VOID and SPARQL-SD.

Table 2. Main facts and statistics about the ISSA Agritrop dataset.

Dataset DOI	10.5281/zenodo.6505847
Downloadable RDF dump	https://doi.org/10.5281/zenodo.6505847
Public SPARQL endpoint	http://issa.i3s.unice.fr/sparql
Documentation	https://github.com/issa-project/issa-pipeline/blob/main/doc/
URIs namespace	http://data-issa.cira.fr/
Dataset URI	http://data-issa.cirad.fr/issa-agritrop
# extracted entities	Named entities: 3.65M, thematic descriptors: 350K
# links to external resources	Wikidata: 2.17M, DBpedia: 1.47M, GeoNames: 152K, AGROVOC: 314K
# RDF triples	66.0M

Dataset Licensing. Being derived from the Agritrop open archive, different licenses apply to the different subsets of the ISSA Agritrop dataset. Articles metadata is provided under the Agritrop open licence[19]. By contrast, article content is ruled by various licenses that consequently also apply to the full text content extracted from the articles and stored in the ISSA dataset. The additional data produced by mining the articles (thematic descriptors, NEs) is published under the Open Data Commons Attribution License 1.0 (ODC-By).[20]

---

[18] https://github.com/issa-project/issa-pipeline/blob/main/doc.

[19] https://agritrop.cirad.fr/mention_legale.html.

[20] ODC-By license: http://opendatacommons.org/licenses/by/1.0/.

6   Potential Impact and Reusability

Target Audiences and Expected Uses. The ISSA project addresses a widely expressed need in communities that manage open archives, in particular libraries and STI services: provide users with powerful, accurate services to find articles relevant for their goals. The ISSA pipeline not only allows the automatic indexing of articles, but also offers services to find relevant articles by exploiting the richness of their semantic associations. Moreover, adhering to the FAIR principles, the solution can be reused by any community adopting these principles while leaving them free to use terminological references suited to their field. It is therefore aimed at both researchers and specialists in STI, and will be of interest to any person or group in charge of institutional management.

Potential for Reuse. The processing pipeline and visualization services are concrete contributions delivered by the project, designed to be as generic as possible, and successfully tested and deployed in the context of an institutional open archive in production. This technical achievement is a positive indicator of the solution's reusability, and we believe that transferring it to other communities should require only marginal development and adaptation. The adaptation of thematic descriptors extraction may require more substantial work in the absence of a corpus to train supervised models: one should start with an unsupervised model and perform manual validation to bootstrap an annotated corpus of sufficient size for supervised approaches. Furthermore, in line with the dynamics of open science, all developed software is available under an open license, along with all the necessary documentation. Finally, in order to inform, share and transfer our results to other communities, a dissemination workshop was organized in Strasbourg in June 2022 [4].

Impact Assessment. Being the institution that publishes and maintains the Agritrop open archive, CIRAD intends to set up the ISSA pipeline in production as soon as the project will complete (September 2022). This underlines the interest of CIRAD users in the services offered by ISSA, and results from a joint work on application scenarios submitted by CIRAD researchers and scientific information specialists to the ISSA project team. The outcome of this work demonstrates the relevance and flexibility of the prototype for answering competency questions, and the benefit provided compared to traditional search tools integrated into document management platforms. Thus, we are confident that the solution delivered by ISSA can accommodate multiple open archives concerned with similar issues and needs, and help them improve their service offerings.

7   Conclusion and Perspectives

In this article, we have highlighted the challenge of finding relevant publications in the ever-growing body of scientific literature, and presented concrete methods and tools implemented in the ISSA project to deliver services that address this challenge. Leveraging robust, industry-proven tools, we designed a generic, reusable pipeline for the analysis and processing of articles from an open scientific archive, to produce a semantic index in the form of an RDF knowledge graph. We developed innovative search and visualization services that leverage this semantic index to allow researchers, decision makers or scientific information professionals to explore thematic association rules, co-publication networks, networks of articles with co-occurring topics, etc. We demonstrated the ability of these services to provide answers to real competency questions submitted by researchers.

In the short and middle terms, we plan to continue this work in several ways. First, in terms of data quality evaluation. In particular, evaluating the quality of the text classification models trained with Annif is not trivial. Because of the subjectivity inherent to annotation of documents, the common quality metrics are not so relevant. However we can calculate the similarity metrics between human and machine annotations. Secondly, we intend to apply association rules mining, not only to descriptors, but also to extracted named entities, and assess the quality and usability of these rules. We also wish to enrich our service offering, in particular in terms of bibliometrics and information retrieval, and apply the pipeline to another scientific archive so as to confirm its reusability. Finally, we plan to conduct dissemination activities so that other communities can take up our work and adapt it to their own needs. In the longer term, we believe that the proposed solution could serve as a framework to integrate additional tools and methods, and eventually extract richer, machine-processable knowledge from the mass of human-readable knowledge inherent in scientific archives.

Acknowledgments. This ISSA project is supported by the research infrastructure CollEx-Persée (https://www.collexpersee.eu/projet/issa/).

References

1. Agritrop Portal (2022). https://agritrop.cirad.fr/
2. GO-FAIR Initiative (2022). https://www.go-fair.org/
3. ISSA Project Website (2022). https://issa.cirad.fr/en
4. ISSA Workshop, June 2022 (2022). https://t.co/iYVf7xcdhR
5. OpenMINTED project website (2022). http://openminted.eu/
6. RD Alliance project website (2022). https://www.rd-alliance.org/
7. VisaTM Project Website (2022). https://www.ouvrirlascience.fr/projet-visa-tm/
8. Alexander, K., Cyganiak, R., Hausenblas, M., Zhao, J.: Describing Linked Datasets with the VoID Vocabulary. W3C Recommendation (2011). http://www.w3.org/TR/2011/NOTE-void-20110303/
9. Arora, A., Garcia-Duran, A., West, R.: Low-rank subspaces for unsupervised entity linking. In: Proceedings of the 2021 Conference on Empirical Methods in Natural Language Processing, pp. 8037–8054. Association for Computational Linguistics, Online and Punta Cana, Dominican Republic, November 2021. https://aclanthology.org/2021.emnlp-main.634
10. Benedetti, F., Bergamaschi, S., Po, L.: Lodex: a tool for visual querying linked open data, January 2015
11. Budroni, P., Claude-Burgelman, J., Schouppe, M.: Architectures of knowledge: the European open science cloud. ABI Technik **39**(2), 130–141 (2019). https://doi.org/10.1515/abitech-2019-2006

12. Cadorel, L., Tettamanzi, A.G.B.: Mining RDF data of COVID-19 scientific literature for interesting association rules. In: Proceedings of the WI-IAT'20-IEEE/WIC/ACM International Joint Conference on Web Intelligence and Intelligent Agent Technology, 14–17 December 2020, Melbourne, Australia (2020). https://hal.inria.fr/hal-03084029

13. Caracciolo, C., et al.: The AGROVOC linked dataset. Semant. Web - Interoper. Usabil. Appl. **4**(3), 341–348 (2013). http://content.iospress.com/articles/semantic-web/sw106

14. Chami, I., Wolf, A., Juan, D.C., Sala, F., Ravi, S., Ré, C.: Low-dimensional hyperbolic knowledge graph embeddings. In: Proceedings of the 58th Annual Meeting of the Association for Computational Linguistics, pp. 6901–6914. Association for Computational Linguistics, Online, July 2020. https://aclanthology.org/2020.acl-main.617

15. Daiber, J., Jakob, M., Hokamp, C., Mendes, P.N.: Improving efficiency and accuracy in multilingual entity extraction. In: Proceedings of the 9th International Conference on Semantic Systems, pp. 121–124 (2013)

16. Devarakonda, R., Palanisamy, G., Green, J.M., Wilson, B.E.: Data sharing and retrieval using OAI-PMH. Earth Sci. Inform. **4**(1) (2010). https://www.osti.gov/biblio/990230

17. Farias Lóscio, B., Burle, C., Calegari, N.: Data on the web best practices. W3C Recommandation (2017). https://www.w3.org/TR/2017/REC-dwbp-20170131/

18. Graves, M., Constabaris, A., Brickley, D.: FOAF: connecting people on the semantic web. Catalog. Classif. Q. **43**(3–4), 191–202 (2007)

19. Guha, R.V., Brickley, D., Macbeth, S.: Schema. Org: Evolution of Structured Data on the Web. Commun. ACM **59**(2), 44–51 (2016). https://doi.org/10.1145/2844544

20. Kettani, F., et al.: Projet VisaTM : l'interconnexion OpenMinTeD - AgroPortal - ISTEX, un exemple de service de Text et Data Mining pour les scientifiques français. In: Ranwez, S. (ed.) IC: Ingénierie des Connaissances, pp. 247–249. Nancy, France, July 2018. https://hal.archives-ouvertes.fr/hal-01839626

21. Lerner, H., Berg, C.: The concept of health in one health and some practical implications for research and education: what is one health? Infect. Ecol. Epidemiol. **5**, 25300 (2015)

22. Maali, F., Erickson, J., Archer, P.: Data catalog vocabulary (DCAT). W3C Recommendation, January 2014. https://www.w3.org/TR/2014/REC-vocab-dcat-20140116/

23. Mackenzie, J.: The one health approach-why is it so important? Tropical Med. Infect. Disease **4**, 88 (2019)

24. Menin, A., Cadorel, L., Tettamanzi, A.G.B., Giboin, A., Gandon, F., Winckler, M.: ARViz: interactive visualization of association rules for RDF data exploration. In: Proceedings of the 25th International Conference Information Visualisation (IV), vol. 25, pp. 13–20. Melbourne/Virtual, Australia (2021). https://hal.archives-ouvertes.fr/hal-03292140

25. Menin, A., Cava, R., Dal Sasso Freitas, C.M., Corby, O., Winckler, M.: Towards a visual approach for representing analytical provenance in exploration processes. In: Proceedings of the 25th International Conference Information Visualisation (IV), vol. 25, pp. 21–28. Melbourne/Virtual, Australia (2021). https://hal.archives-ouvertes.fr/hal-03292172

26. Menin, A., Faron Zucker, C., Corby, O., Dal Sasso Freitas, C.M., Gandon, F., Winckler, M.: From linked data querying to visual search: towards a visualization pipeline for LOD exploration. In: WEBIST 2021–17th International Conference on Web Information Systems and Technologies. Proceedings of the 17th International Conference on Web Information Systems and Technologies (WEBIST), Online Streaming, France, October 2021. https://hal.archives-ouvertes.fr/hal-03404572

27. Michel, F., Djimenou, L., Faron-Zucker, C., Montagnat, J.: Translation of relational and non-relational databases into RDF with xR2RML. In: Proceeding of the 11th International Conference on Web Information Systems and Technologies (WebIST), pp. 443–454. Lisbon, Portugal (2015)

28. Michel, F., et al.: Covid-on-the-web: knowledge graph and services to advance COVID-19 research. In: Pan, J.Z., et al. (eds.) ISWC 2020. LNCS, vol. 12507, pp. 294–310. Springer, Cham (2020). https://doi.org/10.1007/978-3-030-62466-8_19

29. Peroni, S., Shotton, D.: FaBiO and CiTO: ontologies for describing bibliographic resources and citations. J. Web Semant. **17**, 33–43 (2012). https://www.sciencedirect.com/science/article/pii/S1570826812000790

30. Prabhu, Y., Kag, A., Harsola, S., Agrawal, R., Varma, M.: Parabel: partitioned label trees for extreme classification with application to dynamic search advertising. In: Proceedings of the 2018 World Wide Web Conference. WWW 2018, pp. 993–1002. International World Wide Web Conferences Steering Committee, Republic and Canton of Geneva, CHE (2018). https://doi.org/10.1145/3178876.3185998

31. Science-Miner: entity-fishing (2016–2022). https://github.com/kermitt2/entity-fishing

32. Suominen, O.: Annif: DIY automated subject indexing using multiple algorithms. LIBER Q. **29**(1), 1–25 (2019). https://doi.org/10.18352/lq.10285

33. W3C: Sparql 1.1 service description. W3C Recommendation (2013). https://www.w3.org/TR/2013/REC-sparql11-service-description-20130321/

34. W3C: Web annotation vocabulary. W3C Recommendation (2017). https://www.w3.org/TR/annotation-vocab/

35. Wilkinson, M., et al.: The fair guiding principles for scientific data management and stewardship. Sci. Data **3** (2016)

CS-KG: A Large-Scale Knowledge Graph of Research Entities and Claims in Computer Science

Danilo Dessí[1]([envelope]) [ID], Francesco Osborne[2,3] [ID], Diego Reforgiato Recupero[1] [ID], Davide Buscaldi[4] [ID], and Enrico Motta[2] [ID]

[1] Department of Mathematics and Computer Science, University of Cagliari, Cagliari, Italy
`{danilo.dessi,diego.reforgiato}@unica.it`
[2] Knowledge Media Institute, The Open University, Milton Keynes, UK
`{francesco.osborne,enrico.motta}@open.ac.uk`
[3] Department of Business and Law, University of Milano Bicocca, Milan, Italy
[4] LIPN, CNRS (UMR 7030), Université Sorbonne Paris Nord, Villetaneuse, France
`davide.buscaldi@lipn.univ-paris13.fr`

Abstract. In recent years, we saw the emergence of several approaches for producing machine-readable, semantically rich, interlinked description of the content of research publications, typically encoded as knowledge graphs. A common limitation of these solutions is that they address a low number of articles, either because they rely on human experts to summarize information from the literature or because they focus on specific research areas. In this paper, we introduce the Computer Science Knowledge Graph (CS-KG), a large-scale knowledge graph composed by over $350M$ RDF triples describing $41M$ statements from $6.7M$ articles about $10M$ entities linked by 179 semantic relations. It was automatically generated and will be periodically updated by applying an information extraction pipeline on a large repository of research papers. CS-KG is much larger than all comparable solutions and offers a very comprehensive representation of tasks, methods, materials, and metrics in Computer Science. It can support a variety of intelligent services, such as advanced literature search, document classification, article recommendation, trend forecasting, hypothesis generation, and many others. CS-KG was evaluated against a benchmark of manually annotated statements, yielding excellent results.

Keywords: Knowledge graph · Scholarly data · Information extraction · Natural language processing · Semantic Web · Artificial Intelligence

1 Introduction

In the last few years, we have witnessed a paradigm shift towards Open Science, greatly increasing the availability of scientific articles, datasets, software,

Resource Type: Knowledge Graph - **Resource URI:** http://w3id.org/cskg.

and other research outcomes. This represents an historical opportunity to support researchers with new tools enabling more sophisticated search, exploration, and analytical services than the ones currently available. However, the current document-centric scholarly communication paradigm does not enable scholars to efficiently explore, categorize, and reason on this knowledge [17]. Scientists need instead to find and manually analyze large number of static PDF files in order to gain a (often incomplete) understanding about recent research advancements [9].

In recent years, we saw the emergence of several solutions for producing machine-readable, semantically rich, interlinked descriptions of the content of research publications, typically encoded as knowledge graphs [12,22,36,40,46]. For instance, the Open Research Knowledge Graph[1] [22] offers an infrastructure for describing articles in a structured manner, making it easy to find and compare them. The resulting knowledge graph includes about 10K articles, 4.5K research problems, and 3.3K datasets. Similarly, Nanopublications[2] [19] allow users to represent scientific facts as knowledge graphs and have recently been used to support "living literature reviews", which can be continuously amended with new findings [46]. A common drawback of these solutions is that they are limited to a relatively low number of articles, either because they rely on human experts to summarize information from the literature [22,24] or because they focus on very specific domains (e.g., computational linguistics [16], intrusion detection [48]).

In order to address this issue, in 2020 we released the Artificial Intelligence Knowledge Graph (AI-KG) [15], the first automatically generated large-scale knowledge graph of AI, which included 1.2M statements about 820K research entities. This resource was an important first step in the large-scale generation of scientific knowledge graphs, inspiring further work in this direction [6,31] and supporting several methods for classifying and recommend scientific papers [8,21, 25]. However, AI-KG still suffers from a number of significant limitations, which emerged clearly during discussions with its users. First and most important, it only covers about 330K articles in AI: sizable compared to alternative solutions, but not quite representative of the millions of articles published in Computer Science. Second, the methodology for integrating different lexical variations of entities did not always work, resulting in multiple versions of the same entity (e.g., *recommendation_system* and *recommendation_framework*). Finally, the mapping schema used for recognizing a relations (e.g., *aikg-ont:supportsMethod*) from verbal predicates in the articles (e.g., *support, enable, foster*) was quite limited. As a result, sentences using less frequent predicates were not considered.

In this paper, we introduce the Computer Science Knowledge Graph (CS-KG), a large-scale knowledge graph composed by over $350M$ RDF triples describing $41M$ statements from $6.7M$ articles about $10M$ entities (e.g., tasks, methods, materials, metrics) linked by 179 semantic relations. Our objective is to make available and maintain a comprehensive representation of all the significant concepts in this field, in order to support a variety of intelligent services, such as

---

[1] https://www.orkg.org/.

[2] https://nanopub.org/.

advanced search, article recommendation, trend forecasting, hypothesis generation, and many others.

CS-KG is an order of magnitude larger than AI-KG. Specifically, it is 34 times larger in terms of number of statements and 20 times larger in terms of number of articles. It was generated by applying an improved version of the AI-KG pipeline [14] which includes the following advancements: 1) a novel module to merge different lexical representations of the same entity based on transformers [32], 2) a new methodology to map verbal predicates to relations which exploits VerbNet [38], and 3) a richer domain ontology describing 179 semantic relations. CS-KG was evaluated on a benchmark of 1, 200 manually annotated statements, yielding excellent results in comparison with alternative solutions.

CS-KG is licensed under a Creative Commons Attribution 4.0 International License (CC BY 4.0). It available as a dump[3] or via a SPARQL endpoint[4].

In summary, the main contributions of this resource paper are:

- The CS-KG knowledge graph, which includes $41M$ statements about $10M$ entities in Computer Science.
- An improved pipeline for knowledge graph generation from research articles.
- An analysis of the entities and statements extracted from $6.7M$ articles.
- A ground truth[5] of 1200 manually annotated statements, which can be used as a benchmark for statements validation.

The remainder of this paper is organized as follows. Section 2 discusses the related work, pointing out the existing gaps. Section 3 describes CS-KG and its user cases. The pipeline used for its generation is discussed in Sect. 4. Section 5 reports several statistics about CS-KG and Sect. 6 describes the evaluation. Finally, Sect. 7 concludes the paper, discusses the limitations, and defines future directions of research.

2   Related Work

Knowledge extraction from scientific and academic texts is a relatively recent task in which structured information is mined from research publications, patents, and similar texts [35,39]. The interest in this task has been also fostered by the continuous growth of the number of scientific articles available online; in some fields the growth is such that researchers trying to perform assessment of scientific literature are overwhelmed [33].

Existing scientific knowledge graphs (sometimes also named scholarly knowledge graphs) can be categorized into two main types: i) knowledge graphs

---

[3] CS-KG dump - http://w3id.org/cskg/downloads/cskg.zip.

[4] CS-KG SPARQL endpoint - http://w3id.org/cskg/sparql. It contains about $740M$ RDF triples because, for the sake of performance, we materialize some statements entailed by the ontology (e.g., inverse relations).

[5] http://w3id.org/cskg/downloads/ML1200.csv.

based only on meta-information such as authors, titles, organizations and citations (e.g., the Microsoft Academic Graph [44], ArnetMiner [49], OpenAlex[6], AIDA [2]) and ii) knowledge graphs that also represent the content of papers at a fine-grained level. In this paper, we focus on the second category. One of such knowledge graphs is ORKG [22], where articles are associated with the relevant topics, approaches, datasets, and evaluation methodologies. Nanopublications [19] enable users to represent in a minimalistic way various facts from academic publications. One of the drawbacks of both ORKG and Nanopub is that they are manually curated resources, where the representations of research articles are filled by crowdsourcing. Therefore, they cover a limited number of articles and require an important manual effort.

Biology is the only field offering some sizable and high-quality knowledge bases of relevant entities, such as UMLS[7]. Other research areas, including Computer Science, are very lacking in this respect. Some recent efforts focused on producing methods and tools able to automatically extract fine-grained semantic information from the content of the papers. For instance, Luan at al. [27] implemented a deep architecture that carries out multitask learning on top of shared span representations to build a knowledge graph on a dataset of $110K$ papers. Jiang et al. [23] used instead a recurrent neural network model to carry out joint entity and relation extraction. In their work, they extract also "conditional" tuples that represent constraints on other statements: they assume that some facts are not universally valid but depend on the context of application. Their final resource contains 756 fact tuples and 654 condition tuples. Wang at al. [45] targeted specifically articles on Covid-19. Specifically, they adapted an entity recognition tool to extract 75 different types of entities, using distant supervision. The advantage of distant supervision is that it does not require expensive human annotation. However, relations are not extracted from text, but are defined in a handcrafted ontology. Overall, there is still a significant lack of large-scale resources that offer a granular representation of claims and entities in research literature.

3   The Computer Science Knowledge Graph

The Computer Science Knowledge Graph (CS-KG) includes over $350M$ RDF triples that describe $41M$ statements and $10M$ entities extracted from a collection of $6.7M$ scientific papers in the period 2010–2021. These articles were selected by considering all papers from 2010 to 2019 with at least 1 citation (as of December 2021) and all the papers in 2020-2021 period from the set of articles from MAG [44] associated with the Field of Study "Computer Science". Since MAG has been decommissioned in 2021, the following versions will adopt OpenAlex, which offers a comparable publication coverage.

---

[6] OpenAlex - https://openalex.org/.
[7] UMLS - https://www.nlm.nih.gov/research/umls/index.html.

The CS-KG ontology is available at https://scholkg.kmi.open.ac.uk/cskg/ontology and builds on top of SKOS[8] and PROV-O[9]. Its documentation is available at https://scholkg.kmi.open.ac.uk/cskg/ontology.html. The current schema in CS-KG uses the namespaces http://scholkg.kmi.open.ac.uk/cskg/ontology# to refer to elements that belong to the ontology (prefix *cskg-ont*), and http://scholkg.kmi.open.ac.uk/cskg/resource/ for the instances (prefix *cskg*). The ontology defines 179 relations (e.g., *cskg-ont:usesMethod, cskg-ont:solvesTask*) between five entity types: *cskg-ont:Task, cskg-ont:Method, cskg-ont:Material, cskg-ont:Metric, cskg-ont:OtherEntity*.

In order to design the object properties, we started from a set of 39 high level predicates (e.g., *uses, analyzes, includes*) produced by the knowledge graph generation pipeline (see Sect. 4.2). We then associate specific domain and range constraints to them, which are used to drive and correct the automatic extraction process. For example, since a *Method* or a *Task* can use a *Material*, the predicate *uses* was used to create the object property *cskg-ont:usesMaterial* which has *cskg:Method* and *cskg:Task* in its domain as well as *cskg:Material* as its range. We instead considered incorrect to claim that a *cskg:Material* uses a *cskg:Method*, and therefore, the domain of the property *cskg-ont:usesMethod* does not include the class *cskg:Material*.

A statement in CS-KG refers to a specific claim extracted from a research article, defining a relationship between two entities, e.g., `<cskg:web_ontology_language, skos:broader, cskg:semantic_web_standard_technology>`. Naturally, it is not possible to verify the objective truth of every claim. As a consequence, within CS-KG and its potential use cases, a claim should be considered correct only in the context of the research papers linked to it. We also associate the statement with metadata about the original articles and other provenance information. Each statement in CS-KG includes:

- *rdf:subject, rdf:predicate*, and *rdf:object*, which provide the reification of triples within a *rdf:Statement*;
- *cskg-ont:hasSupport*, which reports the number of articles that contributed to create the statement (support);
- *provo:wasDerivedFrom*, which provides provenance information and lists the MAG IDs (now OpenAlex IDs) of the articles from which the statement was extracted;
- *provo:wasGeneratedBy*, which provides provenance and versioning information of the tools used to detect the statement.

The support score can be used to select subsets of statements that are supported by a good number of articles, and thus are typically more reliable (see evaluation in Sect. 6).

---

[8] SKOS - https://www.w3.org/2004/02/skos/.
[9] PROV-O - https://www.w3.org/TR/prov-o/.

In the following we report an exemplary statement:

```
cskg:statement_4508242 a cskg-ont:Statement, provo:Entity;
        rdf:subject          cskg:web_ontology_language;
        rdf:predicate        skos:broader;
        rdf:object           cskg:semantic_web_standard_technology;
        cskg-ont:hasSupport 6;
        provo:wasDerivedFrom cskg:2913757079,
                             cskg:2145844448,
                             ...,
                             cskg: 1551604567;
        provo:wasGeneratedBy cskg:DyGIEpp.
```

This statement describes a claim which is extracted from 6 papers (MAG IDs *2913757079, 2145844448*, etc.), by the tool *DyGIEpp*.

Following the best practices of Linked Data, entities in CS-KG are associated with a set of alternative labels that are used to refer them in the scientific literature. For example, the entity *cskg:recurrent_neural_network* is associated with the labels *recurrent neural network, recurrent trainable neural network*, and *recurrent neural network paradigm*. CS-KG also provides $31K$ *owl:sameAs* links to DBPedia [4], $27K$ links to Wikidata[10], and $6K$ to the Computer Science Ontology (CSO) [37]. For instance the entity *cskg:feedforward_neural_network* is linked to the CSO topic *cso:feedforward_neural_network*, to the DBpedia entity *dbpedia:Feedforward_neural_network*, and to the Wikidata entity *wd:Q5441227*.

CS-KG can support several intelligent services that require a high quality representation of research concepts and currently rely on alternative knowledge bases which cover a smaller number of publications (e.g., AI-KG, ORKG, Nanopublications) or offer a less granular conceptualization of the domain (SemanticScholar, OpenAlex, AIDA). These include systems for supporting machine-readable surveys [30,46], tools for generating research hypothesis [20] and detecting contradictory research claims [3], ontology-driven topic models (e.g., CoCoNoW [5]), recommender systems for articles (e.g., SBR [41]) and video lessons [7], visualisation frameworks (e.g., ScholarLensViz [26], ConceptScope [47]), scholarly knowledge graph embeddings (e.g., Trans4E [29]), tools for identifying domain experts (e.g., VeTo [42]), and systems for predicting research impact (e.g., ArtSim [13]).

We plan to keep maintaining and updating CS-KG in the following several years. We thus created a fully automatic pipeline that we will run every six months to produce new versions of CS-KG that will include recent papers from OpenAlex. Indeed, one of the advantage of our solution is that it does not require heavy workload for the maintainers. In order to cope with the ever increasing number of papers, we are also embedding big data technologies within the pipeline. We also plan to keep evolving the ontology by including new predicates according to patterns emerging from the data and the community feedback.

---

[10] https://www.wikidata.org/wiki/Wikidata:Main_Page.

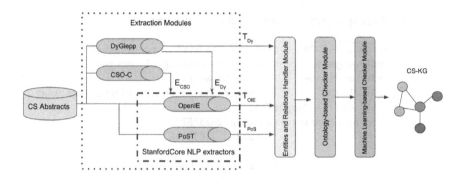

Fig. 1. Architecture of the automatic generation pipeline.

4 Automatic Generation of CS-KG

This section briefly describes the methodology that we applied to build the CS-KG. It builds on top of the pipeline introduced in [14], which has already been successfully employed to build the Artificial Intelligence Knowledge Graph (AI-KG) [15]. Our new approach is more scalable, allowing to efficiently compute the much larger set of articles used for CS-KG. It also extends significantly the range of semantic relations extracted from the literature by using VerbNet [38] to semi-automatically enrich the domain ontology. Finally, it can extract multiple relationships between a pair of entities, while the previous solution was limited to one. Figure 1 shows an overview of the automatic extraction pipeline.

4.1 Extraction Modules

The proposed methodology employs four complementary tools to extract entities and relationships from plain text (typically the titles and abstracts of the articles). These tools are:

- **DyGIEpp** [43]. This tool extracts a set of entities E_{Dy} of six pre-defined types (*Method, Task, Material, Metric, Other-Scientific-Term*, and *Generic*) and seven kinds of relationship (*Used-for, Hyponym-Of, Compare, Part-of, Conjunction, Feature-of, Evaluate-for*). It is used to yield a set of entities E_{Dy} and a set of triples among them, T_{Dy}.
- **Computer Science Ontology Classifier (CSO-C)** [34]. CSO-C is a classifier which exploits syntactic and semantic similarity to map text spans to topics in CSO. It extracts the set of entities E_{CSO}.
- **OpenIE** of the Stanford Core NLP suite [1]. This tool is used to extract open domain relationships from plain texts of the input dataset among the entities in the sets E_{Dy} and E_{CSO}. The module considers only triples whose relations are composed by only one verb and yields the set of triples T_{OIE}.

- **PoS Tagger (PoST)**. This module is built on top of the Stanford Core
  NLP suite [28]. It uses part-of-speech (PoS) tags to find all verbs that exist in
  sentences between pairs of entities. For example, given a sentence s and two
  entities in it e_i and e_j where $e_i, e_j \in E_{Dy} \cup E_{CSO}$, this module builds triples
  $<e_i, v, e_j>$, where v is a verb in s between e_i and e_j. This module uses a
  window of size 15 as the maximum number of tokens that can occur between
  two entities to extract verb relations. It returns the set of triples T_{PoS}.

The sets T_{Dy}, T_{OIE}, and T_{PoS} are given as an input to the *Entities and
Relations Handler Module*.

4.2   Entities and Relations Handler Module

This module has been developed to integrate and clean up entities and relationships from the different tools, in order to reduce noise and redundancies.

Entities Handler. This module: (i) lemmatizes all entities to group singulars
and plurals forms of the same entities; (ii) solves acronyms by exploiting the fact
that they are usually placed in brackets near entities in the text; (iii) removes
entities which appear in a handcrafted blacklist; (iv) removes generic entities
which have an information content provided by WordNet equal to or lower than
an empirically defined threshold of 5. In order to not discard key entities for the
this domain, the module uses a whitelist of research entities which includes the
'Fields of Study' from MAG.

Next, a sentence transformer model is used to detect and merge entities with
the same meaning.

Given the set of all entities, let us say E, the module creates an index based
on the tokens contained by the entities. The index links each token to all the
entities that include it. Then, it compares two entities $e_i, e_j \in E$ if they share at
least one token. The comparison is performed by using the state-of-the-art framework *SentenceTransformers* [32] and encoding the entities with the *paraphrase-
distilroberta-base-v2*[11] transformer model. Entities which have a cosine similarity
equal to or greater than a threshold $th_{merge} = 0.9$ (empirically calculated) are
merged together. For example, if the entity e_i and e_j have a cosine similarity
greater than 0.9, then the module chooses e_i as representative entity for both e_i
and e_j, and uses e_j as an alternative label of e_i.

Relationships Handler. The sets T_{Dy}, T_{OIE}, and T_{PoS} may contain several
redundant triples that use different predicates (e.g., *includes*, *embeds*, *contains*)
to convey the same meaning. We address this issue by mapping similar verbs
to the same predicate. The mapping schema has been built by enriching our
previous handcrafted mapping [15] with VerbNet [38], which offers a complete
and coherent semantic representations of verbs [10]. Verbnet is a taxonomy of

---

[11] https://huggingface.co/sentence-transformers/paraphrase-distilroberta-base-v2.

English verbs organized in classes whose verbs share syntactic and semantic coherence. It enables to build new taxonomies with domain-specific jargon while holding as a core the most common use of verbs based on their semantics in more general contexts. Specifically, we associated the extracted verbs with the high-level predicates of the previous mapping as well as relevant VerbNet classes. We then manually refined this schema to produce a final set of 39 representative predicates mapped to 464 verbs from the articles[12]. These same predicates were also used to produce the relevant relations in the CS-KG ontology.

All verbs of sets T_{OIE}, and T_{PoS} are mapped using this schema. The relations generated by *DyGIEpp* in the set T_{Dy} are also mapped to the same representative predicates[13]. For example, two triples which share the same entities such as <a, embeds, b> and <a, contains, b> will be merged in a single triple <a, includes, b>, given that embeds and contains are mapped to includes. After mapping all the relations of the sets T_{Dy}, T_{OIE}, and T_{PoS}, the module yields the set of triples T.

4.3 Ontology-Based Checker Module

In this phase, the CS-KG ontology is used to integrate entities from different tools and discard triples that do not comply with domain and range of the relations. All triples of the set T are then represented according to the CS-KG ontology. The types of entities returned by the *DyGIEpp* tool are mapped to the relevant classes in the ontology. Specifically, methods, tasks, materials, and metrics are mapped to the homonymous classes in the ontology (e.g., material is mapped to the class *cskg-ont:Material*), while other-scientific-terms and generic entities are mapped to *cskg-ont:OtherEntity*. The predicates are mapped to the ontology object properties. For instance, <cskg:semantic_interoperability, uses, cskg:ontology_matching>, considering that <cskg:ontology_matching, rdf:type, cskg-ont:Task>, becomes <cskg:semantic_interoperability, cskgont:usesTask, cskg:ontology_matching>.

In this phase, triples which do not comply with the semantics of the ontology are discarded. For example the triple <cskg:utk_face_dataset,uses, cskg:deep_learning>, where *cskg:utk_face_ dataset* is a *cskg-ont:Material* and *cskg: deep_ learning* is a *cskg-ont:Method*, is discarded because the class *cskg-ont: Material* is not in the domain of the property *cskg-ont:usesMethod*.

4.4 Machine Learning-Based Checker Module

Triples obtained from several articles are typically of good quality, since the probability of extracting the same incorrect claim from multiple papers is fairly low. On the other hand, triples which appear in one or very few papers are more noisy and less reliable. We can thus use the number of papers associated with a triple, which we label *support*, to distinguish between *reliable* and *uncertain*

---

[12] http://w3id.org/cskg/downloads/SKG-predicates-new-VerbNet-equivCSKG.csv.

[13] http://w3id.org/cskg/downloads/SKG-dygiepp-Mapping.csv.

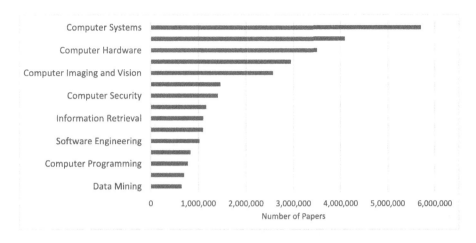

Fig. 2. Distribution of the research areas in terms of relevant papers.

triples. However, we do not want to automatically discard all *uncertain* triples, since many of them may be valid. Therefore, this module uses a classifier to decide which triples need to be included in the knowledge graph. It first splits T in two disjoint sets: $T_{reliable}$ (*support* ≥ 3) and $T_{uncertain}$ (otherwise). The set $T_{reliable}$ is employed to train a Multi-Layer Perceptron classifier which implements a function $\theta : t \rightarrow \{0, 1\}$ that, given an input triple t, predicts 1 if the triple t is correct and can be included in the knowledge graph, and 0 if the triple t should be discarded. In order to generate negative triples for the training phase, each triple $t \in T_{reliable}$ is corrupted by a triple $t'|t' \notin T$ by replacing the head or the tail with a random chosen entity. The set of the triples $\{t'_0, \ldots, t'_n\}$ constitutes the set of negative triples $T_{negative}$. Therefore the set $T_{reliable} \cup T_{negative}$ is actually used to train the model. The rationale behind this solution is to use the classifier to identify high quality triples in the set $T_{uncertain}$ which is consistent with triples of the set $T_{reliable}$. The set of triples for which the classifier predicts 1 is referred as $T_{consistent}$. Finally, the triples in sets $T_{reliable}$ and $T_{consistent}$ as well as all associated information (e.g., support, relevant articles, and so on) are refied into statements and encoded as RDF in order to generate CS-KG.

5   Statistics About CS-KG

This section discusses several analytics about the current version of CS-KG. The first two subsections report statistics about entities and statements, respectively. The third one compares CS-KG to AI-KG according to several quantitative metrics. A major novelty of CS-KG is that include a variety of fiends across all Computer Science. Figure 2 shows the top 15 high-level topics (direct sub-topics of Computer Science in CSO) associated with the articles within CS-KG.

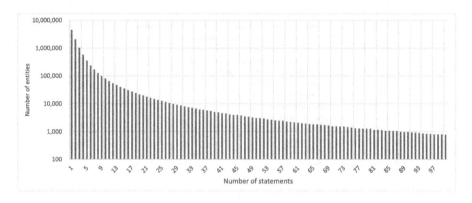

Fig. 3. Entities distribution over number of statements in logarithmic scale. For space constraints, we show only entities appearing in less than 100 statements.

5.1   Entity Statistics

CS-KG contains 10M entities distributed among the five exclusive entity types. About 3.9M entities are classified as *Methods* (e.g., *cskg:spiking_ neural_ network, cskg:latent_ topical_ skip_ gram, cskg:secret_ key_ generation_ approach*); this reflects the fact that a large number of articles in the Computer Science literature present or reuse methods. CS-KG also includes 1.3M *Tasks* (e.g., *cskg: identity_ authentication, cskg:face_ recognition, cskg:natural_ language_ generation*) , 450K *Materials* (e.g., *cskg:freebase, cskg:dbpedia, cskg:image_ data*), and 215K *Metrics* (e.g., *cskg:accuracy_ rate, cskg:network_lifetime, cskg:storage_ efficiency*). Finally, 4M entities are associated with the type *OtherEntity*, which includes all entities that were not assigned to the other classes. In future work we plan to further investigate and characterize more accurately the entities currently associated to this class.

Figure 3 shows the distribution of the entities according to the number of statements in which they appear. For example, $79K$ entities appear in *exactly* 10 statements. CS-KG contains a large number entities associated with multiple statements. For instance, a total of $820K$ entities appear in at least 10 statements (i.e., the sum of the y values corresponding to $x \geq 10$ in Fig. 3). This allows users to chose different compromises between the number of entities and the richness of their description. For instance, in some use cases it may be advisable to consider a smaller set of entities associated with a lot of information.

Very common entities are often associated to several CS subdomain, such as *cskg:quality_ of_ service* (6, 141 statements), *cskg:feedforward_ neural_ network* (1, 747 statements), *cskg:cskg:simulation_ based_ environment* (1, 711 statements), *cskg:computing_ time* (1, 228 statements). Conversely, entities that appear only in a lower number of statements suggests are either very recent or only used for specific purposes or CS sub-areas. For example, the entities *cskg:fingerprint_ image_ encryption_ scheme* and *cskg:gene_ ontology_ tool*, that only appear 6 and 5 times, respectively, are specific to their sub-areas.

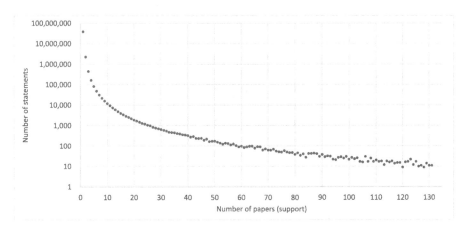

Fig. 4. The distribution of the statements over the support in logarithmic scale.

5.2 Statement Statistics

Figure 4 reports the distribution of all statements over the number of articles from which they were extracted. Most of the statements are associated to one or few scientific papers. This indicates the importance of including a mechanism to validate low supported statements such as the one described in Sect. 4.4. The chart also suggests that CS-KG includes both broad knowledge, which is supported by a large community consensus, and very fine-grained information, appearing in few articles.

The distribution of high supported statements can be better observed in Fig. 5, where each bar represents the number of statements supported by a minimum amount of papers. For instance, $100K$ statements are supported by at least 5 articles. Some examples of this category are `<cskg:ontology_engineering, cskg:usesMethod, cskg:description_logic>`, `<cskg:web_ontology_langua-ge, skos:broader, cskg:semantic_web_standard_technology>`, and `<cskg: sparql, cskg-ont:queriesMaterial, cskg:rdf_data>` which represent general knowledge about the Semantic Web domain.

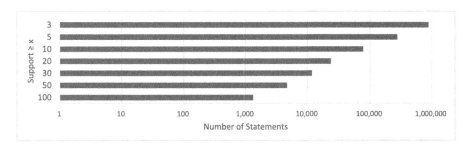

Fig. 5. The distribution of the statements over the minimum level of support in logarithmic scale.

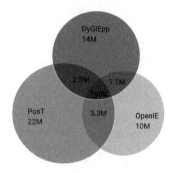

Fig. 6. The number of statements produced by each extractor tool.

The tools used to extract statements from the articles contributed differently to CS-KG: PoST yielded $22M$ statements, DyGIEpp $14M$, and OpenIE $10M$. The Venn diagram in Fig. 6 shows the number of statements extracted from each tool, as well as their intersections. The relatively small size of the intersections suggest that these solutions are highly complementary. Finally, Fig. 7 shows the distribution of the 20 most frequent relations over the number of relevant statements. We can appreciate the variety of significant relations in CS-KG: 19 relations are associated with at least 500K statements and 64 with over 100K statements. The most common relations are *cskg:usesMethod*, *cskg:includesMethod*, *cskg:includesOtherEntity*, and *skos:broader* which are associated respectively with $6.6M$, $4.4M$, $3.5M$, and $2.0M$ statements.

5.3   Comparison Between CS-KG and AI-KG

Table 1 compares CS-KG and AI-KG according to different characteristics. CS-KG is a major improvement according to all metrics. Specifically, it is 34 times

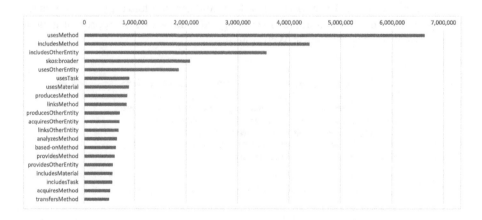

Fig. 7. The number of statements of the 20 most frequent relationships.

Table 1. Comparison between CS-KG and AI-KG.

Feature	CS-KG	AI-KG	Difference
Number of entities	10M	820K	+1,119%
Number of statements	41M	1.2M	+3,316%
Number of covered scientific papers	6.7M	333K	+1,930%
Multiple relationships between two entities	Yes	No	N.A
Number of ontology axioms	2,213	321	+901%
Number of object properties	179	27	+562%
Links to DBpedia	31K	0	N.A
Links to Wikidata	27K	19K	+42%

larger in terms of number of statements, 20 times larger in terms of number of articles, and 12 times bigger in terms of number of entities. The ontological schema is also much more comprehensive, including a larger number of object properties and axioms such as *cskg-onto:executesMethod*, *cskg-ont:basedonMethod*, and *cskg-ont:producesMaterial*. CS-KG is also better connected to external knowledge graphs, including about 65K *owl:sameAs* links against the 25K of AI-KG.

6   Evaluation

In order to evaluate the automatic methodology used for producing CS-KG, we measured its performance on a manually annotated gold standard. To this purpose, we first selected 1200 statements which contain as subject or object one of sub-topics of *Machine Learning*[14] according to CSO. More specifically, the set of statements was created by aggregating: 1) 200 statements whose support is greater than 5, 2) 200 statements whose support is equal to or greater than 3, 3) 200 statements whose support is lower than 3, 4) 400 statements discarded by the methodology, and 5) 200 randomly generated statements that are not part of CS-KG. The latter were produced by replacing the subject or the object of a statement from CS-KG.

This set was then manually annotated by 3 senior computer science researchers. For each triple, the experts were asked to return 1 if a triple was correct, i.e., it appeared in literature, and 0 otherwise. They were also allowed to use online tools to check if a triple was consistent with the scientific literature. The Fleiss' kappa agreement [18] between the annotators was 0.435, indicating a moderate agreement. The majority vote schema was employed to generate the gold standard. In order to show the advantage of our hybrid method that builds on top of multiple tools, we compared our full methodology against DyGIEpp [43], OpenIE [1], PoST [28], and against the union of their results

---

[14] https://cso.kmi.open.ac.uk/topics/machine_learning.

Table 2. Precision (P) Recall (R) and F-measure (F1) over 1,200 annotated statements.

Extraction tools	P	R	F1
DyGIEpp	0.67	0.37	0.47
OpenIE	0.60	0.24	0.34
PoST	0.56	0.46	0.51
DyGIEpp + OpenIE + PoST	0.55	**0.93**	0.69
CS-KG pipeline	**0.76**	0.77	**0.76**

(DyGIEpp + OpenIE + PoST). Table 2 reports the results of the evaluation in terms of precision, recall, and f-measure. The CS-KG pipeline outperforms all the other tools yielding a overall f-measure of 0.76. This demonstrates how the checker modules (described in Sects. 4.3 and 4.4) are able to increase significantly the accuracy of the statements (+21% in precision), paying a relatively low price in recall. An inspection of the results shows also that 86% of the statements with support greater than 5 are correct, consistently with the intuition that support is an indicator of a triple correctness. The method which aggregates all the basic tools (DyGIEpp+OpenIE+PoST) performs second best (0.69), highlighting the value of an hybrid approach that combines both unsupervised and supervised methods. Finally, DyGIEpp, OpenIE, and PoST obtain f-measures in the 0.47-0.51 range. Among them, DyGIEpp has the highest precision (0.67), while PoST has the highest recall (0.46).

In summary, the evaluation suggests that i) CS-KG offers good quality statements, in particular when associated to a good support, ii) the performance of each of the three tools is unsatisfactory and, therefore, it is worth to produce a pipeline that is able to combine them, and iii) the components of the CS-KG pipeline used to discriminate valid statements (i.e., the *Machine Learning-based Checker Module* and the *Ontology-based Checker Module*) play an important role in improving the overall quality and reducing noisy and incorrect statements.

7   Conclusions

In this paper, we introduce the Computer Science Knowledge Graph (CS-KG), a new knowledge graph including over $350M$ RDF triples that describes $41M$ statements about $10M$ entities automatically extracted from over $6.7M$ articles. CS-KG offers a much more comprehensive representation of research concepts in Computer Science than alternative knowledge bases and can support a wide variety of intelligent services. CS-KG will replace AI-KG, now deprecated. We plan to keep maintaining and updating it in the following years. To this purpose we developed an automatic pipeline that we will run every six months.

The main limitation of CS-KG is that it was produced with a fully automatic methodology, so the specific statements are not revised by humans, as in manually crafted knowledge graphs. We are thus investigating ways to allow users to correct and give feedback on specific statements, either by supporting wiki-like portals (e.g., the CSO Portal, Semantic Wikis [11]) or more complex platforms for editing machine-readable representations of the literature (e.g., ORKG). We are also working on developing an entity linking tool for automatically mapping documents (e.g., articles, patents, educational material) to entities and statements in CS-KG. Finally, we plan to further extend the ontology and the entity typing process, in particular by providing a more granular categorization of entity types.

References

1. Angeli, G., Premkumar, M.J.J., Manning, C.D.: Leveraging linguistic structure for open domain information extraction. In: Proceedings of the 53rd Annual Meeting of the Association for Computational Linguistics and the 7th International Joint Conference on Natural Language Processing (Volume 1: Long Papers), pp. 344–354 (2015)
2. Angioni, S., Salatino, A., Osborne, F., Recupero, D.R., Motta, E.: AIDA: a knowledge graph about research dynamics in academia and industry. Quant. Sci. Stud. **2**(4), 1356–1398 (2021)
3. Asif, I., Tiddi, I., Gray, A.J.: Using nanopublications to detect and explain contradictory research claims. In: 2021 IEEE 17th International Conference on eScience (eScience), pp. 1–10. IEEE (2021)
4. Auer, S., Bizer, C., Kobilarov, G., Lehmann, J., Cyganiak, R., Ives, Z.: DBpedia: a nucleus for a web of open data. In: Aberer, K., et al. (eds.) ASWC/ISWC -2007. LNCS, vol. 4825, pp. 722–735. Springer, Heidelberg (2007). https://doi.org/10.1007/978-3-540-76298-0_52
5. Beck, M., Rizvi, S.T.R., Dengel, A., Ahmed, S.: From automatic keyword detection to ontology-based topic modeling. In: Bai, X., Karatzas, D., Lopresti, D. (eds.) DAS 2020. LNCS, vol. 12116, pp. 451–465. Springer, Cham (2020). https://doi.org/10.1007/978-3-030-57058-3_32
6. Blagec, K., Barbosa-Silva, A., Ott, S., Samwald, M.: A curated, ontology-based, large-scale knowledge graph of artificial intelligence tasks and benchmarks. arXiv preprint arXiv:2110.01434 (2021)
7. Borges, M.V.M., dos Reis, J.C.: Semantic-enhanced recommendation of video lectures. In: 2019 IEEE 19th International Conference on Advanced Learning Technologies (ICALT), vol. 2161, pp. 42–46. IEEE (2019). https://doi.org/10.1109/ICALT.2019.00013
8. Brack, A., Hoppe, A., Ewerth, R.: Citation recommendation for research papers via knowledge graphs. In: Berget, G., Hall, M.M., Brenn, D., Kumpulainen, S. (eds.) TPDL 2021. LNCS, vol. 12866, pp. 165–174. Springer, Cham (2021). https://doi.org/10.1007/978-3-030-86324-1_20
9. Brack, A., Hoppe, A., Stocker, M., Auer, S., Ewerth, R.: Analysing the requirements for an open research knowledge graph: use cases, quality requirements, and construction strategies. Int. J. Digit. Libr. **23**(1), 33–55 (2022)
10. Brown, S.W., Bonn, J., Kazeminejad, G., Zaenen, A., Pustejovsky, J., Palmer, M.: Semantic representations for NLP using VerbNet and the generative lexicon. Front. Artif. Intell. **5** (2022). https://doi.org/10.3389/frai.2022.821697, https://www.frontiersin.org/article/10.3389/frai.2022.821697
11. Buffa, M., Gandon, F., Ereteo, G., Sander, P., Faron, C.: SweetWiki: a semantic wiki. J. Web Semant. **6**(1), 84–97 (2008)

12. Buscaldi, D., Dessì, D., Motta, E., Osborne, F., Reforgiato Recupero, D.: Mining scholarly publications for scientific knowledge graph construction. In: The Semantic Web: ESWC 2019 Satellite Events, pp. 8–12 (2019)

13. Chatzopoulos, S., Vergoulis, T., Kanellos, I., Dalamagas, T., Tryfonopoulos, C.: ArtSim: improved estimation of current impact for recent articles. In: Bellatreche, L., et al. (eds.) TPDL/ADBIS -2020. CCIS, vol. 1260, pp. 323–334. Springer, Cham (2020). https://doi.org/10.1007/978-3-030-55814-7_27

14. Dessì, D., Osborne, F., Recupero, D.R., Buscaldi, D., Motta, E.: Generating knowledge graphs by employing natural language processing and machine learning techniques within the scholarly domain. Futur. Gener. Comput. Syst. **116**, 253–264 (2021)

15. Dessì, D., Osborne, F., Reforgiato Recupero, D., Buscaldi, D., Motta, E., Sack, H.: AI-KG: an automatically generated knowledge graph of artificial intelligence. In: Pan, J.Z., et al. (eds.) ISWC 2020. LNCS, vol. 12507, pp. 127–143. Springer, Cham (2020). https://doi.org/10.1007/978-3-030-62466-8_9

16. D'Souza, J., Auer, S.: Pattern-based acquisition of scientific entities from scholarly article titles. In: Ke, H.-R., Lee, C.S., Sugiyama, K. (eds.) ICADL 2021. LNCS, vol. 13133, pp. 401–410. Springer, Cham (2021). https://doi.org/10.1007/978-3-030-91669-5_31

17. Fathalla, S., Auer, S., Lange, C.: Towards the semantic formalization of science. In: Proceedings of the 35th Annual ACM Symposium on Applied Computing, pp. 2057–2059 (2020)

18. Fleiss, J.L., Nee, J.C., Landis, J.R.: Large sample variance of kappa in the case of different sets of raters. Psychol. Bull. **86**(5), 974 (1979)

19. Groth, P., Gibson, A., Velterop, J.: The anatomy of a nanopublication. Inf. Serv. Use **30**(1–2), 51–56 (2010)

20. de Haan, R., Tiddi, I., Beek, W.: Discovering research hypotheses in social science using knowledge graph embeddings. In: Verborgh, R., et al. (eds.) ESWC 2021. LNCS, vol. 12731, pp. 477–494. Springer, Cham (2021). https://doi.org/10.1007/978-3-030-77385-4_28

21. Hoppe, F., Dessì, D., Sack, H.: Deep learning meets knowledge graphs for scholarly data classification. In: Companion Proceedings of the Web Conference 2021, pp. 417–421 (2021)

22. Jaradeh, M.Y., Oelen, A., Farfar, K.E., et al.: Open research knowledge graph: next generation infrastructure for semantic scholarly knowledge. In: Proceedings of the 10th International Conference on Knowledge Capture, pp. 243–246 (2019)

23. Jiang, T., Zhao, T., Qin, B., Liu, T., Chawla, N., Jiang, M.: The role of "condition": a novel scientific knowledge graph representation and construction model. Proceedings of the 25th ACM SIGKDD International Conference on Knowledge Discovery and Data Mining (2019)

24. Kuhn, T., Chichester, C., Krauthammer, M., Queralt-Rosinach, N., Verborgh, R., et al.: Decentralized provenance-aware publishing with nanopublications. PeerJ Comput. Sci. **2**, e78 (2016)

25. Li, X., Daoutis, M.: Unsupervised key-phrase extraction and clustering for classification scheme in scientific publications. arXiv preprint arXiv:2101.09990 (2021)

26. Löffler, F., et al.: ScholarLensViz: a visualization framework for transparency in semantic user profiles. In: Taylor, K., Gonçalves, R., Lecue, F., Yan, J. (eds.) Proceedings of the ISWC 2020 Demos and Industry Tracks: From Novel Ideas to Industrial Practice co-located with 19th International Semantic Web Conference (ISWC 2020), Globally Online, 1–6 November 2020 (UTC) (2020)

27. Luan, Y., He, L., Ostendorf, M., Hajishirzi, H.: Multi-task identification of entities, relations, and coreference for scientific knowledge graph construction. In: Proceedings of the EMNLP 2018 Conference, pp. 3219–3232 (2018)
28. Manning, C.D., Surdeanu, M., Bauer, J., Finkel, J.R., et al.: The Stanford CoreNLP natural language processing toolkit. In: Proceedings of 52nd Annual Meeting of the Association for Computational Linguistics: System Demonstrations, pp. 55–60 (2014)
29. Nayyeri, M., et al.: Trans4e: link prediction on scholarly knowledge graphs. Neurocomputing (2021). https://doi.org/10.1016/j.neucom.2021.02.100
30. Oelen, A., Stocker, M., Auer, S.: SmartReviews: towards human- and machine-actionable reviews. In: Berget, G., Hall, M.M., Brenn, D., Kumpulainen, S. (eds.) TPDL 2021. LNCS, vol. 12866, pp. 181–186. Springer, Cham (2021). https://doi.org/10.1007/978-3-030-86324-1_22
31. Pramanik, P., Jana, R.K.: Identifying research trends of machine learning in business: a topic modeling approach. Meas. Bus. Excell. (2022)
32. Reimers, N., Gurevych, I.: Sentence-BERT: sentence embeddings using Siamese BERT-networks. In: Proceedings of the 2019 Conference on Empirical Methods in Natural Language Processing. Association for Computational Linguistics, November 2019. https://arxiv.org/abs/1908.10084
33. Ronzano, F., Saggion, H.: Knowledge extraction and modeling from scientific publications. In: González-Beltrán, A., Osborne, F., Peroni, S. (eds.) SAVE-SD 2016. LNCS, vol. 9792, pp. 11–25. Springer, Cham (2016). https://doi.org/10.1007/978-3-319-53637-8_2
34. Salatino, A., Osborne, F., Motta, E.: CSO classifier 3.0: a scalable unsupervised method for classifying documents in terms of research topics. Int. J. Digit. Libr. **23**(1), 91–110 (2022)
35. Salatino, A.A., Osborne, F., Thanapalasingam, T., Motta, E.: The CSO classifier: ontology-driven detection of research topics in scholarly articles. In: Doucet, A., Isaac, A., Golub, K., Aalberg, T., Jatowt, A. (eds.) TPDL 2019. LNCS, vol. 11799, pp. 296–311. Springer, Cham (2019). https://doi.org/10.1007/978-3-030-30760-8_26
36. Salatino, A.A., Osborne, F., Birukou, A., Motta, E.: Improving editorial workflow and metadata quality at springer nature. In: Ghidini, C., et al. (eds.) ISWC 2019. LNCS, vol. 11779, pp. 507–525. Springer, Cham (2019). https://doi.org/10.1007/978-3-030-30796-7_31
37. Salatino, A.A., Thanapalasingam, T., Mannocci, A., Osborne, F., Motta, E.: The computer science ontology: a large-scale taxonomy of research areas. In: ISWC, pp. 187–205 (2018)
38. Schuler, K.K.: VerbNet: a broad-coverage, comprehensive verb lexicon. University of Pennsylvania (2005)
39. Souili, A., Cavallucci, D., Rousselot, F.: Natural language processing (NLP) - a solution for knowledge extraction from patent unstructured data. Procedia Eng. **131**, 635–643 (2015)
40. Tennant, J.P., Crane, H., Crick, T., Davila, J., et al.: Ten hot topics around scholarly publishing. Publications **7**(2), 34 (2019)
41. Thanapalasingam, T., Osborne, F., Birukou, A., Motta, E.: Ontology-based recommendation of editorial products. In: Vrandečić, D., et al. (eds.) ISWC 2018. LNCS, vol. 11137, pp. 341–358. Springer, Cham (2018). https://doi.org/10.1007/978-3-030-00668-6_21

42. Vergoulis, T., Chatzopoulos, S., Dalamagas, T., Tryfonopoulos, C.: VeTo: expert set expansion in academia. In: Hall, M., Merčun, T., Risse, T., Duchateau, F. (eds.) TPDL 2020. LNCS, vol. 12246, pp. 48–61. Springer, Cham (2020). https://doi.org/10.1007/978-3-030-54956-5_4

43. Wadden, D., Wennberg, U., Luan, Y., Hajishirzi, H.: Entity, relation, and event extraction with contextualized span representations. In: Proceedings of the 2019 Joint Conference EMNLP-IJCNLP, pp. 5788–5793 (2019)

44. Wang, K., Shen, Z., Huang, C., Wu, C.H., Dong, Y., Kanakia, A.: Microsoft academic graph: when experts are not enough. Quant. Sci. Stud. 1(1), 396–413 (2020)

45. Wang, Q., et al.: Covid-19 literature knowledge graph construction and drug repurposing report generation. arXiv abs/2007.00576 (2021)

46. Wijkstra, M., Lek, T., Kuhn, T., Welbers, K., Steijaert, M.: Living literature reviews. arXiv preprint arXiv:2111.00824 (2021)

47. Zhang, X., Chandrasegaran, S., Ma, K.L.: ConceptScope: organizing and visualizing knowledge in documents based on domain ontology. In: Proceedings of the 2021 CHI Conference on Human Factors in Computing Systems, pp. 1–13 (2021)

48. Zhang, Y., Wang, M., Saberi, M., Chang, E.: From big scholarly data to solution-oriented knowledge repository. Front. Big Data, p. 38 (2019)

49. Zhang, Y., Zhang, F., Yao, P., Tang, J.: Name disambiguation in AMiner: clustering, maintenance, and human in the loop. In: Proceedings of the 24th ACM SIGKDD International Conference on Knowledge Discovery and Data Mining, pp. 1002–1011 (2018)

RMLStreamer-SISO: An RDF Stream Generator from Streaming Heterogeneous Data

Sitt Min Oo[1]([✉])[iD], Gerald Haesendonck[1][iD], Ben De Meester[1][iD],
and Anastasia Dimou[2,3][iD]

[1] IDLab, Department of Electronics and Information Systems,
Ghent University – imec, Ghent, Belgium
{x.sittminoo,gerald.haesendonck,ben.demeester}@ugent.be
[2] Department of Computer Science, KULeuven, Leuven, Belgium
anastasia.dimou@kuleuven.be
[3] AI – Flanders Make, Lommel, Belgium

Abstract. Stream-reasoning query languages such as CQELS and C-SPARQL enable query answering over RDF streams. Unfortunately, there currently is a lack of efficient RDF stream generators to feed RDF stream reasoners. State-of-the-art RDF stream generators are limited with regard to the velocity and volume of streaming data they can handle. To efficiently generate RDF streams in a scalable way, we extended the RMLStreamer to also generate RDF streams from dynamic heterogeneous data streams. This paper introduces a scalable solution that relies on a dynamic window approach to generate RDF streams with low latency and high throughput from multiple heterogeneous data streams. Our evaluation shows that our solution outperforms the state-of-the-art by achieving millisecond latency (compared to seconds that state-of-the-art solutions need), constant memory usage for all workloads, and sustainable throughput of around 70,000 records/s (compared to 10,000 records/s that state-of-the-art solutions take). This opens up the access to numerous data streams for integration with the semantic web.
Resource type: Software
License: MIT License
URL: https://github.com/RMLio/RMLStreamer/releases/tag/v2.3.0

Keywords: RML · Stream processing · Window joins · Knowledge graph generation

1 Introduction

An increasing portion of data are continuous in nature, e.g., sensor events, user activities on a website, or financial trade events. This type of data is known as data streams; sequences of unbounded tuples generated continuously in different rates and volumes [3]. Due to the temporal nature of data streams, low latency

U. Sattler et al. (Eds.): ISWC 2022, LNCS 13489, pp. 697–713, 2022.
https://doi.org/10.1007/978-3-031-19433-7_40

computation of analytical results is needed to timely react in different use cases, e.g., fraud detection [9]. Thus, stream processing engines must efficiently handle low latency computation of varying velocity and volume.

On the one hand, different frameworks were proposed to handle data streams, e.g., Flink, Spark or Storm [6,19,26]. On the other hand, RDF stream processing (RSP) engines, e.g., CQELS and C-SPARQL [1,5,16], were widely studied and perform high-throughput analysis of RDF streams with low memory footprints [16]. Yet, these stream processing frameworks are not substantially used in the domain of RDF graph generation from streaming data sources, despite the demand of these mature RSP engines for more RDF streams.

Between data processing frameworks and stream processing engines, there are tools to generate RDF streams from heterogeneous data streams (e.g. SPARQL-Generate [17], RDFGen [21], TripleWave [18], Cefriel's Chimera [22]). However, some of these tools are inefficient when the data stream starts to scale in terms of volume and velocity, such as TripleWave, and SPARQL-Generate. While other tools are not open sourced nor suitable for the mapping of streaming data, such as RDFGen, and Cefriel's Chimera respectively. Overall, there are no RDF stream generators that keep up with the needs of stream reasoning engines while taking advantage of data processing frameworks to efficiently produce RDF streams.

In this paper, we present the RMLStreamer-SISO, a parallel, vertically and horizontally scalable stream processing engine to generate RDF streams from heterogeneous data streams of any format (e.g. JSON, CSV, XML, etc.). We extended previous preliminary work [13] of heterogeneous data stream mapping solution: an open source implementation on top of Apache Flink [6], available under MIT license, which generates high volume RDF data from high volume heterogeneous data. RMLStreamer-SISO extends RMLStreamer to also support any input data streams and export RDF streams (Stream-In-Stream-Out (SISO)). RMLStreamer-SISO now supports a much larger part of the RML specification[1], including all features of RML but relational databases.

The RMLStreamer-SISO outperforms the state-of-the-art tools when handling high velocity data stream, increasing the throughput it could handle while maintaining low latency. The RMLStreamer-SISO achieves millisecond latency, as opposed to seconds that state-of-the-art solutions need, constant memory usage for all workloads, and sustainable throughput of around 70,000 records/s, compared to 10,000 records/s that state-of-the-art solutions take.

Through the utilization of a low-latency tool like RMLStreamer-SISO, legacy streaming systems could exploit the unique characteristics of real-life streaming data, while enabling analysts to exploit the semantic reasoning using knowledge graphs in real-time and have access to more reliable data.

The contributions presented in this paper are: (i) an algorithm to generate the RDF streams from heterogeneous streaming data; (ii) its implementation, the RMLStreamer-SISO, as an extension of RMLStreamer; and (iii) an evaluation demonstrating that the RMLStreamer-SISO outperform the state-of-the-art. The paper is structured as follows: Sect. 2 discusses related work, Sect. 3

---

[1] Implementation report of RML: https://rml.io/implementation-report/.

the approach and its implementation, Sect. 4 the evaluation of RMLStreamer-SISO against state-of-the-art, Sect. 5 the results of our evaluations, and Sect. 7 concludes our work with possible future works.

2 Related Works

Streaming RDF mapping engines transform heterogeneous data streams to RDF data streams. Several solutions exist in the literature for generating RDF from persistent data sources [2,13,14,23], but only few generate RDF from data streams [17,18,21]. Although the implementations details are elaborated in these works, their evaluations are designed without considering the different data stream behaviours nor the resource contention between different evaluation components.

TripleWave [18] generates RDF streams from streaming or static data sources using R2RML mappings, and publishes them as RDF stream. However, the R2RML mappings of TripleWave are invalid according to the specifications of R2RML and it does not support joins. Although it is purported to support several input sources, the user has to write the code to process the input data and iterate over them before using the tool. This can result in poor performance from improper implementation. Last, it is not designed to support distributed parallel processing, resulting in limited scaling with data volume and velocity.

RDF-Gen [21] generates static or streaming RDF data from static or streaming data sources. A Data connector communicates with the data source, iterates over its data entries, and converts every entry to a record of values. These records are converted to RDF using a graph template: a listing of RDF-like statements with variables bound to the record values coming from data connectors. RDF-Gen generates RDF on a per record basis, theoretically allowing a distributed parallel processing set-up. However, the current implementation and documentation show no indication of a clustered setup nor how to run it.

SPARQL-Generate [17] extends SPARQL 1.1 syntax to support mapping of heterogeneous data to RDF data. SPARQL-Generate could be implemented on top of any SPARQL query engine, and knowledge engineers with SPARQL experience could use it with ease. The reference implementation of SPARQL-Generate[2] generates RDF streams from data streams, even though it is not reported in the original paper. Although joining data from multiple sources is supported, SPARQL-Generate waits for one of the data streams to end first before consuming other data sources to join the data. Thus, joins with unbounded streaming data sources are not supported. The implementation is based on single machine setup without scaling with data volume and velocity.

Cefriel's Chimera [22] is an integration framework based on Apache Camel[3] split into four "blocks" of components to map heterogeneous data to RDF data: lifting block, data enricher, inference enricher, and lowering block.

---

[2] SPARQL-Generate: https://github.com/sparql-generate/sparql-generate.
[3] Apache Camel: https://camel.apache.org/.

Chimera aims to be modular and allows each block to be replaced with custom implementations. The current implementation uses a modified version of RMLMapper[4] in the lifting block for data stream processing. However, the whole RML mapping process is recreated with each incoming message which could lead to high performance overhead in a highly dynamic data stream environment.

3   Stream In - Stream Out (SISO)

We extend RMLStreamer's architecture for generating RDF from persistent big data sources [13] to also generate RDF streams from heterogeneous data streams with high data velocity and volume, while keeping the latency low. The RDF mapping language (RML) [10], a superset of R2RML, expresses customized mapping from heterogeneous data sources to RDF datasets. We illustrate the concepts of RML with the example RML document in Listing 1.2.

We break the process of generating RDF from a data stream into tasks and subtasks (Fig. 1). Each task or subtask is a stream processing operator acting on an incoming data stream. They could be chained one after the other to form a pipeline of operators and result in one or more outgoing data streams. This approach introduces parallelism on both data and processing level, enabling each data stream and operator to be processed and executed respectively in parallel.

To illustrate RMLStreamer-SISO's pipeline, we use the examples in Listing 1.1 and 1.2. The mapping document in Listing 1.2 is used to join and map JSON data (Listing 1.1) from websocket streams to RDF with dynamic window join.

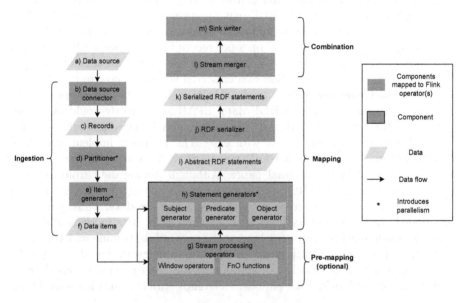

Fig. 1. Workflow of RMLStreamer. Data flows from the *Data Source* at the top through all the components pipeline to the *Sink writer* at the bottom.

---

[4] RMLMapper: https://github.com/RMLio/rmlmapper-java.

Listing 1.1. Data records from 2 data streams "Flow" & "Speed".

```
1  // data records from Speed stream
2  {"speed":123.0,"time":"14:42:00","id":"lane1"}
3  // data records from Flow stream
4  {"flow":1680,"time":"14:42:00","id":"lane1"}
```

Listing 1.2. Example RML Mapping file to generate streaming RDF from the streaming heterogeneous data of Listing 1.1.

```
1  # prefix definitions omitted
2  _:ws_source_ndwSpeed a td:Thing ;
3    td:hasPropertyAffordance [ td:hasForm [
4      hctl:hasTarget "ws://data-streamer:9001" ; # URL and content type
5      hctl:forContentType  "application/json" ; # Data format
6      hctl:hasOperationType "readproperty" ] ] . # Read only
7  _:ws_source_ndwFlow a td:Thing ;
8    td:hasPropertyAffordance [ td:hasForm [
9      hctl:hasTarget "ws://data-streamer:9000" ;
10     hctl:forContentType  "application/json" ;
11     hctl:hasOperationType "readproperty" ] ] .
12 <JoinConfigMap> a rmls:JoinConfigMap ;
13   rmls:joinType rmls:TumblingJoin .           # Trigger/eviction type
14 <NDWSpeedMap> a rr:TriplesMap ;
15   rml:logicalSource [                         # Describes data source
16     rml:source _:ws_source_ndwSpeed ;
17     rml:referenceFormulation ql:JSONPath ;    # JSONPath iterator
18     rml:iterator "$" ] ; # Iterates the data as JSON root object
19   rr:subjectMap [         # Generation of the subject IRI
20     rr:template "speed={speed}&time={time}" ] ;
21   rr:predicateObjectMap [ # Describes how predicate and object are generated
22     rr:predicate <http://example.com/laneFlow> ;
23     rr:objectMap [
24       rr:parentTriplesMap <NDWFlowMap> ;      # TripleMap to be joined with
25       rmls:joinConfig <JoinConfigMap> ;       # Configuration of join window
26       rmls:windowType  rmls:TumblingWindow ; # Type of join window
27       rr:joinCondition [ # Attributes on which the data records are joined
28         rr:child "id" ; rr:parent "id" ; ] ] ] .
29 <NDWFlowMap> a rr:TriplesMap ;
30   rml:logicalSource [
31     rml:source _:ws_source_ndwFlow ;
32     rml:referenceFormulation ql:JSONPath ;
33     rml:iterator "$" ] ;
34   rr:subjectMap [ rr:template "flow={flow}&time={time}" ] .
```

3.1   RDF Stream Generation Workflow

Our approach consists of a workflow with four tasks (see Fig. 1):

Ingestion. The ingestion task captures data streams and prepares the data records for the mapping task. Each data stream triggers one ingestion task that can run in parallel with the other ingestion tasks spawned by the other data streams. The ingestion task can be divided in three subtasks:

1. *Data source connector* (Fig. 1, *(b)*): This subtask is responsible for connecting to a (streaming) data source (a). It reads data records from the source and passes these records (c) on to the stream partitioner.

2. *Stream partitioner (d)*: The stream of data records is optionally partitioned in disjoint partitions to be fed to the next subtask. The partitioning depends on the order's maintenance. If the exact order of the incoming data records is not important to be maintained, then these records can be distributed evenly among multiple instances of the next subtask, increasing parallelism. If the order of generating RDF statements needs to correspond with the order of the incoming data records, then the stream is not distributed at this stage.

3. *Item generator (e)*: One data record can lead to zero or more RDF statements. This subtask splits a data record in zero or more items of internal representation called *data items* (f), according to the logical iterators defined in the mapping document, before the actual mapping task takes place. Using the sample data and the mapping document from Listing 1.1 and 1.2 respectively, this subtask will use the logical iterator '$', a JSONPath[5], to generate data items from each data record shown in Listing 1.1. In this case, the logical iterator is the JSON root object, so the data item is the same as the incoming data records. Otherwise, if the data record contains a list of sub-records, and the logical iterator is specified over the list (e.g., `$.list[*]`), each of these sub-records are turned into *data items*.

Pre-mapping (Optional). Before the data items are mapped to RDF, the data items may be processed with custom data transformations defined with FnO [8], or the window operators, such as joins, aggregates, and reduce. The FnO functions could be as simple as changing letters to uppercase or as complex as the window joins. This stage is optional and omitted if the RML document does not define pre-mapping functions. The pre-mapping task (g) is right before the mapping task since the data fields requiring preprocessing can be more than the data fields needed for mapping to RDF data. For example, with the given inputs and mapping document (Listing 1.2), the data items (Listing 1.1) from the two input streams, "`Flow`" and "`Speed`", are first buffered inside a window, and then joined based on their `internalId` value. Data records, having the same value for the "`id`", are joined pairwise. If windows joins were implemented after the mapping stage, the verbosity of RDF would substantially increase the network bandwidth. More, to fully map the data before joining, RMLStreamer-SISO needs to know all attributes present in the raw data records which would be infeasible.

To support joining with windows, RML was extended. New vocabulary terms were defined to support windowing operations with RML. We defined two new properties: *rmls:windowType* to provide the type of window to be used when joining and *rmls:joinConfig* when joining the *Child* and *Parent Triple Map* to define how the trigger, and eviction are fired inside the window.

Section 3.2 details the dynamic windowing algorithm and Sect. 3.3 elaborates on the design choice and windows' implementation for RMLStreamer-SISO.

Mapping. RDF statements are generated from data items coming from the ingestion task and the pre-mapping task.

---

[5] JSONPath documentation: https://goessner.net/articles/JsonPath/index.html.

1. *Statement generator (h)*: Each data item leads to one or more RDF statements in this sub task. Each statement is generated in parallel as an abstract RDF statement (i) which could be fed to the next subtask for serialization.
2. *RDF serializer (j)*: The abstract RDF statements are serialized into various RDF serialisations based on the configuration given to the RMLStreamer.

Combination. This task brings back together all streams of RDF statements (l) into one final RDF stream which will be written out using the sink writer (m).

3.2   Heterogeneous Data Streams Join in RDF Streams

Supporting *joins* in RMLStreamer-SISO and any streaming RDF generator, is not trivial as windowing techniques are required for unbounded and unsynchronized streaming data. Unlike batch processing where data is bounded, processing whole data streams in memory is unsustainable due to the continuous and infinite characteristics of streaming data. Therefore, stream processing engines use buffers called *windows* to hold the most recent stream of records in memory. The windows' lifetime is measured in terms of time interval, thus, the *window interval* determines the size of the window and their operation behaviour is defined by the trigger, and the eviction events [12]. A *trigger event* occurs when an operator is executed to process the data records inside the window interval. An *eviction event* occurs when the window evicts the data records inside its buffer.

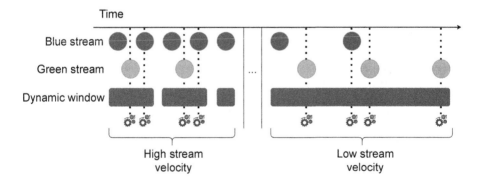

Fig. 2. Behaviour of the dynamic window under high, and low stream velocities. The cogwheels are the *trigger* events representing the moment when the data records are processed. In this figure, the *trigger* events are fired with every new data record, and only when there is at least one data record from each data stream.

We opted for an eager trigger implementation to lower the latency of RML-Streamer's responses for the windowed joins' implementation. The joined results are emitted as soon as possible without waiting for the eviction event to occur. We designed a dynamic window which adapts its window intervals according to the velocity of the incoming data streams. Adaptive windowing [27] was studied in the context of batch stream processing with a positive impact on the stream processing job's performance: lower latency, and higher throughput. We opted for a simple cost metric based on the data records' number to keep the memory and latency low in a real-time stream processing environment where the time constraint is more stringent.

The algorithm is inspired by the additive-increase, and multiplicative decrease algorithm of TCP congestion control [7]. Figure 2 shows the high level behaviour of our dynamic window for the two different stream velocities. When the data stream velocity is high, the window size shrinks to process the data records as fast as possible, keeping the latency low and throughput high. When the data stream velocity is low, the size of the window grows to wait for more data records and process them. This ensures that the window do not miss the records due to short window size. We elaborate the details of the algorithm below. For each window, the following configuration parameters are provided:

1. $|W|$: The window interval
2. ϵ_u & ϵ_l: Upper and lower threshold limit for total cost metric
3. U & L: Upper and lower limit for the window interval
4. $Limit(List_P)$ & $Limit(List_C)$: Upper limit size for parent and child stream

---

Algorithm 1: Dynamic window *onEviction* routine

Data: $|W|, \epsilon_u, \epsilon_l, U, L, Limit(List_P), Limit(List_C), S_P, S_C$

1   $cost(List_P) = |S_P|/Limit(List_P)$
2   $cost(List_C) = |S_C|/Limit(List_C)$
3   total cost $m = cost(List_P) + cost(List_C)$
    // adapts window size based on cost
4   **if** $m > \epsilon_u$ **then**
5 | $|W| = |W|/2$
6 | $Limit(List_P) = Limit(List_P) * cost(List_P) * 1.5$
7 | $Limit(List_C) = Limit(List_C) * cost(List_C) * 1.5$

8   **else if** $m < \epsilon_l$ **then**
9 | $|W| = |W| * 1.1$
10 | $Limit(List_P) = Limit(List_P) * cost(List_P) * 1.5$
11 | $Limit(List_C) = Limit(List_C) * cost(List_C) * 1.5$

12   clean both $List_C$ and $List_P$
13   clip $|W|$ in the range of $[L, U]$

Since we implement the join operator with eager execution, the trigger event is fired when the current record r_c arrives inside the window. We denote the current window as W with interval size $|W|$. The streams are denoted as S_p and S_c with the corresponding states $List_p$ and $List_c$, for the parent and child stream respectively (the parent and child stream follows the RML specification for joining triples maps). The states contain the records from their respective streams inside the window with for example $|S_p|$ denoting the number of records from S_p. $List_p$ and $List_c$ are only used in cost calculation to determine if the window interval needs to be changed; they do not limit the amount of records that could be buffered inside the window.

At each eviction trigger, we calculate the cost for each list states $List_p$ and $List_c$. For example, the cost for $cost(List_P) = |S_p|/Limit(List_P)$. The total cost is $m = cost(List_p) + cost(List_c)$ and it is checked against the thresholds ϵ_l and ϵ_u to adjust the window interval accordingly. We assume the stable zone to be achieved if the total cost fulfils the predicate: $\epsilon_l \leq m \leq \epsilon_u$. Algorithm 1 shows the pseudo-code for the eviction algorithm we just elaborated.

3.3 Implementation

RMLStreamer-SISO is released as version 2.3 of RMLStreamer to utilize Flink's parallelism for horizontal scaling (via distributed processing in a network and vertical scaling (via multi-threaded execution of tasks). The update brings the windowing support for joining multiple data streams, the dynamic windowing algorithm, and FnO [8] as an extension point for joins execution. The code and usage instructions for RMLStreamer-SISO are available online at the Github repository: https://github.com/RMLio/RMLStreamer.

Windowing support is implemented through the use of Flink's windowing API[6] for common types of window, e.g., Tumbling Window. We implemented the *KeyedCoProcessFunction* provided by Flink's low-level stream processing API to manage the different states required for the algorithm (Algorithm 1) of the dynamic window. We implemented the dynamic windowed join before the mapping stage, to group input streams and reduce network bandwidth usage. The generated RDF stream could be windowed by the RDF stream processing engines consuming the output.

Currently, FnO functions jar files have to be compiled together as part of the RMLStreamer-SISO jar. Examples on github[7] show the working of RMLStreamer-SISO with TCP data stream. We also provide an extensive documentation on RMLStreamer-SISO in a containerized environment with docker[8].

4 Evaluation

An extensive evaluation was conducted focused on variable data stream velocity, volume and variety of data formats to emulate the real-life workloads as close as possible. The code for the evaluation is available on github[9]. Since RMLStreamer-SISO is situated between traditional stream processing and RSP, state-of-the-art approaches for benchmarking in these domains are combined:

---

[6] Window: https://nightlies.apache.org/flink/flink-docs-release-1.14/docs/dev/datastream/operators/windows/.

[7] RMLStreamer-SISO: https://github.com/RMLio/RMLStreamer.

[8] Docker: https://docker.com.

[9] Benchmark: https://github.com/s-minoo/rmlstreamer-benchmark-rust.

architectural design of RSPLab [25], workload design of Open Stream Processing Benchmark [11], and measurement strategies of Karimov et al. [15].

We compare the RMLStreamer-SISO with the state-of-the-art streaming RDF generator, SPARQL-Generate, which is actively maintained, used and supports the same features as RMLStreamer-SISO. The other tools were not considered for different reasons: TripleWave requires a custom implementation to process each data stream and feed it in TripleWave which means it cannot be used as-it-is. More, TripleWave is meant purely for feeding RDF streams to RDF stream processing engines without performing joins, therefore it would have been an unfair comparison both in terms of features and scope. RDF-Gen's source code is not available, but only a jar is available without any instructions to run it. Both TripleWave and RDF-Gen are also not actively maintained. Finally, Cefriel's Chimera restarts the RDF mapping engine with every data record, which means that the processing of the input and mapping is not performed in a true streaming manner; the comparison would not be meaningful.

Data Source. The input data used in the evaluation comes from time annotated traffic sensor data from the Netherlands provided by NDW (Nationale Databank Wegverkeersgegevens)[10], and also used by Van Dongen et al. [11]. It contains around 68,000 rows of CSV data with two different measurements across different lanes on a highway: number of cars (flow), and their average speed. The two measurements are streamed through a websocket data streaming server.

Metrics. Stream processing frameworks are typically evaluated using two main metrics: latency and throughput [15]. Latency can be further distinguished into two types: processing-time latency, and event-time latency. *Processing time latency* is the interval between the data record's arrival time at the input and the emission time at the output of the streaming engine [15]. *Event-time latency* is the interval between the creation time, and the emission time at the streaming engine's output, of the data record [15]. Latency measurement requires to consider the effect of coordinated occlusion, where the queueing time, a part of the event-time, is ignored [15]. Therefore, we consider event-time latency as our latency measurement to take the effect of coordinated occlusion in consideration.

For our evaluation, we considered the event-time latency of each record, the throughput as number of consumed records per second, the memory and CPU usage of the engine's docker container. The measurements are captured on a machine separate from the host machine of the System Under Test (SUT), where memory and CPU usage are measured using cAdvisor[11]. By treating the SUTs as a blackbox, we ensure that the measurement of the metrics incurs no performance penalty nor resource contention with the SUTs during the evaluation.

Evaluation Set Up. The architectural design is a modification of RSPLab with a custom data streaming component (Fig. 3). It consists of three components: a) the data streamer, b) the system under test, and c) the monitoring system.

---

[10] NDW: https://www.ndw.nu/.

[11] cAdvisor: https://github.com/google/cadvisor.

With the proposed architecture where each components is isolated, we aim to reduce the influence of the benchmark components on the engine during the evaluation process. The modularity of the setup also increases the flexibility of configuring the evaluation environment with minimal changes for the engines.

Workload Design. To evaluate the performance of the engines under different data characteristics and processing scenarios, we devise three different workloads: (i) throughput measurement, (ii) periodic burst, and (iii) scalability measurement. As SPARQL-Generate is unable to join unbounded streaming data (it expects data streams with an end, Sect. 2), we evaluated the two workloads (throughput measurement and periodic burst) without joining functionality to compare.

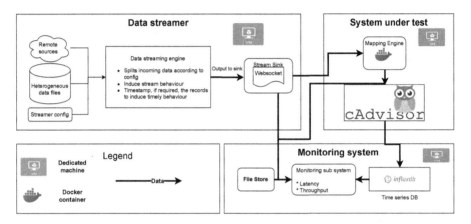

Fig. 3. Benchmark architecture to evaluate the different engines, inspired by RSPLab.

- throughput measurement: the data stream throughput is constant and steadily increases with each run to determine the engine's *sustainable throughput* [15]. CPU, latency and memory usage are measured.
- periodic burst: a burst of data records is emitted periodically to mimic fluctuations in data streams; CPU, memory, latency and throughput are measured.
- scalability measurement: RMLStreamer-SISO is evaluated in two modes: centralised mode without parallelism and distributed mode with parallelizable data to measure the impact of parallelism on its scalability. In both modes, data from two input streams are joined and latency is measured.

System Specifications. We ran the evaluation on a single machine with multiple docker containers to emulate the communication between the data streaming source and the mapping engine in a streaming network environment. The machine has Intel i7 CPU with 8 cores at 4.8 GHz, 16 GB RAM, and 200 GB hard disk space. The data streamer and the monitoring system docker containers (Fig. 3) have access to 4 of the cores, and the SUT docker container has access to the leftover 4 cores. This prevents CPU resource contention between the SUT and the other components used for running the evaluation.

To evaluate horizontal scaling, the data streamer component is replaced with Apache Kafka to support parallel ingestion of data streams by RMLStreamer-SISO. Apache Kafka is configured with default settings and the data (Sect. 4) is streamed into two topics[12]; "ndwFlow", and "ndwSpeed" containing the records about the number, and the average speed of the cars respectively.

5 Results

In this section, we discuss the results of our evaluation using different workloads.

Workload for Throughput Measurement. For the throughput measurement workload, we ran the evaluation multiple times with increasing input data throughput for each run to evaluate the sustainable throughput of the SUTs.

In the first few runs of the evaluation, the RMLStreamer fared a bit worse than SPARQL-Generate in all three measurements. This is due to the overhead of having a distributed task manager for executing, and managing the different tasks and subtasks of mapping heterogeneous data (Fig. 1). However, when the throughput starts increasing beyond 10,000 records per second, RMLStreamer-SISO outperforms SPARQL-Generate in terms of latency and memory usage.

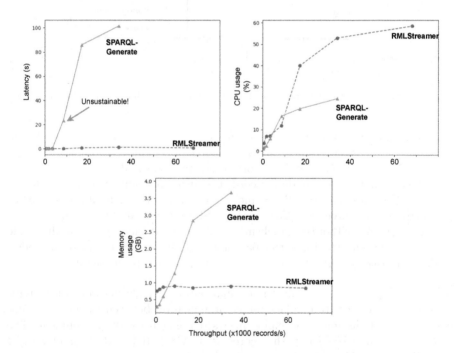

Fig. 4. SUTs performance under different data stream velocity for sustainable throughput measurement. The last run for SPARQL-Generate was omitted because it took more than 1 h instead of the expected 30 min to process the whole data stream.

<hr />

[12] Kafka topics: https://developer.confluent.io/learn-kafka/apache-kafka/topics/.

Compared to RMLStreamer-SISO, SPARQL-Generate became unsustainable when the throughput of the input data streams passes 10,000 records per second with 20 s latency (Fig. 4). To the contrary, RMLStreamer-SISO has a consistent low latency of 1 s for all runs of the workload having 100x magnitude lower latency than SPARQL-Generate in later runs.

Regarding CPU usage, RMLStreamer-SISO has on average 20% more CPU usage for the overhead of Apache Flink managing the distributed tasks.

In terms of memory usage, RMLStreamer-SISO uses significantly lower memory than SPARQL-Generate at around 900 MB compared to 3 GB by SPARQL-Generate. Based on the previous observations, we conclude that RMLStreamer-SISO outperforms SPARQL-Generate at higher throughput with lower latency and memory usage. Even though, RMLStreamer-SISO's CPU usage is around 30% higher than SPARQL-Generate in the last run, it effectively copes with the increase in data stream velocity to maintain low latency processing.

Workload for Periodic Burst. The periodic burst workload studies the adaptability of the engine to the recurring sudden burst of data stream. We used the measurements from the last minute of the evaluation, when the engines are *stable* without warm-up overheads, to better visualize their performance during the periodic burst of data (Fig. 5). In Fig. 5, we see a periodic increase, and drop in the throughput metrics measurements, which is an expected behaviour in the engines when consuming a data stream input with periodic burst of data. Every 10 s we see a burst of around 35,000 messages. Both engines behave as expected for the throughput metrics measurement.

The spikes for latency measurement of SPARQL-Generate (Fig. 5) have a wider base than those of RMLStreamer-SISO. This indicates that SPARQL-Generate takes a longer time to recover from processing periodic workload than RMLStreamer-SISO by a few seconds. RMLStreamer-SISO's peak latency is around 500 ms whereas SPARQL-Generate has a peak latency of around 3.5 s. Although RMLStreamer-SISO uses more CPU than SPARQL-Generate to process data burst, it adapts to the sudden burst of data and recover more quickly than SPARQL-Generate. The latency of RMLStreamer-SISO is also 7 times lower than SPARQL-Generate due to the record-based processing capabilities. We conclude that RMLStreamer-SISO is better adapted to workloads with periodic burst of data with faster recovery period, lower latency and memory usage while maintaining the same throughput capabilities as SPARQL-Generate.

Workload for Scalability Measurement. We evaluated the RMLStreamer-SISO's capability to join two data streams with a constant throughput of around 17000 messages per second. CPU and memory usage of both modes of RMLStreamer-SISO are similar throughout the evaluation. However, despite the similar performance in terms of CPU and memory usage, *parallelized* mode fared significantly better in terms of the latency metric than *unparallelized* mode. Unparallelized mode has a median latency of around 50000 ms whereas *parallelized* mode has a median latency of around 57ms. This is around 1000x lower in terms of the median latency. Moreover, the minimum latency of *parallelized*

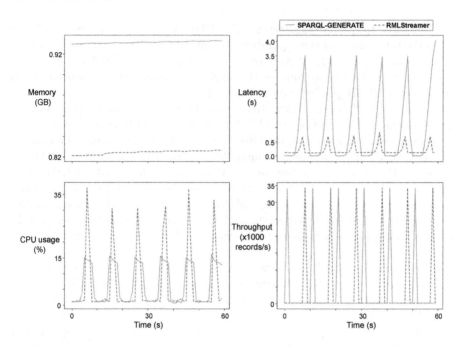

Fig. 5. Performance of SUTs in the last one minute of the periodic burst workload evaluation. A part of the *throughput* graph is blurred to give more clarity to the relationship between the trends in *latency* and *throughput* of the engines.

RMLStreamer-SISO at 8 ms is 10,000x lower than the minimum latency of *unparallelized* RMLStreamer-SISO at 13653 ms. The latency is kept low with high parallelization due to the effective distribution of the workload amongst the different parallelized tasks by the underlying DSP engine (Apache Flink). We conclude that RMLStreamer scales extremely well with significantly better performance in terms of latency if configured to be executed in a distributed mode.

6   Use Cases

RMLStreamer-SISO has seen uptake in multiple projects – covering different use cases in different architectures – to process streaming data and generate RDF streams. Largest validation was in research and development (R&D) projects between imec and Flemish companies such as DyVerSIFy on streaming data analysis and visualisation [20,24], together with Televic Rail on IoT data, DAIQUIRI[13] together with VRT on sport sensor data, and ESSENCE and H2020 project MOS2S[14] on media data. Other projects include DiSSeCt[15] on health data and transport data [4]. The variety of use cases shows that the resource is

---

[13] https://www.imec-int.com/en/what-we-offer/research-portfolio/daiquiri.

[14] https://innovatie.vrt.be/project/essence, https://itea4.org/project/mos2s.html.

[15] https://smit.vub.ac.be/project/dissect.

suitable for solving the task at hand and also applicable to a multitude of use cases for society in general. Applications – within the knowledge graph construction problem domain – are varied, i.e., processing a large amount of low-frequency sensor data, a small amount of high-frequency sensor data, and large data sets combined with streaming data, processing Kafka streams, MQTT, Socket.io, and TCP streams. Beyond Belgium, RMLStreamer has received attention by the Institute of Data Science, proposed as part of RDF graph generation tutorials such as those by STIInnsbruck in Austria, and services such as Data2Services[16] by the Institute of Data Science in Maastricht in the Netherlands.

7 Conclusion and Future Work

In this paper, we present RMLStreamer-SISO, a highly scalable solution to seamlessly generate RDF streams thanks to its dynamic window algorithm which adapts its window size to handle the dynamic characteristics of the data stream. This way, RMLStreamer-SISO enables low latency and high throughput mapping of heterogeneous data to RDF data. We showed that our solution scales better than the state-of-the-art in terms of latency, memory, and throughput. It is the only RDF stream generator which joins unbounded data streams and scale horizontally and vertically, enabling RDF streams generation from heterogeneous data streams which was not possible so far. Given it is open source and already widely used in different use cases involving not only academia but also industry, as shown in our use cases, it is expected that the community that grew around it will further grow and contribute at its maintenance, while its extensive documentation and tutorials allow for easy reuse[17]. The RML extensions will be further discussed with the W3C community group on knowledge graph construction and eventually will be incorporated to the revised RML specification.

RMLStreamer-SISO increases the availability of RDF streams following the high availability of data streams. Using a low-latency tool like RMLStreamer-SISO, legacy streaming systems could exploit the unique characteristics of real-life streaming data, while enabling analysts to exploit the semantic reasoning using knowledge graphs in real-time. This way, we enabled access to more data which should impact the further improvements of RSP engines and other semantic web technologies on top of RDF streams which were not possible so far.

Resource Availability Statement: Source code for RMLStreamer-SISO is available at https://github.com/RMLio/RMLStreamer. The source code for the benchmark is available at https://github.com/s-minoo/rmlstreamer-benchmark-rust. The dataset used for the benchmark is available at https://github.com/Klarrio/open-stream-processing-benchmark/tree/master/data-stream-generator.

---

[16] https://maastrichtu-ids.github.io/best-practices/blog/2021/03/18/build-a-kg/, https://stiinnsbruck.github.io/lkgt/, https://d2s.semanticscience.org/docs/d2s-rml/.

[17] Example of tutorial for use with docker technology, https://github.com/RMLio/RMLStreamer/tree/development/docker.

References

1. Barbieri, D.F., Braga, D., Ceri, S., Della Valle, E., Grossniklaus, M.: C-SPARQL: SPARQL for continuous querying. In: Proceedings of the 18th International Conference on World Wide Web. WWW 2009, pp. 1061–1062. Association for Computing Machinery, New York (2009). https://doi.org/10.1145/1526709.1526856

2. Belcao, M., Falzone, E., Bionda, E., Valle, E.D.: Chimera: a bridge between big data analytics and semantic technologies. In: Hotho, A., et al. (eds.) ISWC 2021. LNCS, vol. 12922, pp. 463–479. Springer, Cham (2021). https://doi.org/10.1007/978-3-030-88361-4_27

3. Botan, I., Derakhshan, R., Dindar, N., Haas, L., Miller, R.J., Tatbul, N.: Secret: a model for analysis of the execution semantics of stream processing systems. Proc. VLDB Endow. **3**(1–2), 232–243 (2010). https://doi.org/10.14778/1920841.1920874

4. Brouwer, M.D., et al.: Distributed continuous home care provisioning through personalized monitoring & treatment planning. In: Companion Proceedings of the Web Conference 2020. ACM, April 2020. https://doi.org/10.1145/3366424.3383528

5. Calbimonte, J.-P., Corcho, O., Gray, A.J.G.: Enabling ontology-based access to streaming data sources. In: Patel-Schneider, P.F., et al. (eds.) ISWC 2010. LNCS, vol. 6496, pp. 96–111. Springer, Heidelberg (2010). https://doi.org/10.1007/978-3-642-17746-0_7

6. Carbone, P., Katsifodimos, A., Ewen, S., Markl, V., Haridi, S., Tzoumas, K.: Apache flink^{TM}: stream and batch processing in a single engine. IEEE Data Eng. Bull. **38**, 28–38 (2015)

7. Chiu, D.M., Jain, R.: Analysis of the increase and decrease algorithms for congestion avoidance in computer networks. Comput. Netw. ISDN Syst. **17**(1), 1–14 (1989)

8. De Meester, B., Dimou, A., Verborgh, R., Mannens, E.: An ontology to semantically declare and describe functions. In: Sack, H., Rizzo, G., Steinmetz, N., Mladenić, D., Auer, S., Lange, C. (eds.) ESWC 2016. LNCS, vol. 9989, pp. 46–49. Springer, Cham (2016). https://doi.org/10.1007/978-3-319-47602-5_10

9. Dias de Assunção, M., da Silva Veith, A., Buyya, R.: Distributed data stream processing and edge computing: a survey on resource elasticity and future directions. J. Netw. Comput. Appl. **103**, 1–17 (2018). https://doi.org/10.1016/j.jnca.2017.12.001, https://www.sciencedirect.com/science/article/pii/S1084804517303971

10. Dimou, A., Vander Sande, M., Colpaert, P., Verborgh, R., Mannens, E., Van de Walle, R.: RML: a generic language for integrated RDF mappings of heterogeneous data, vol. 1184 (2014)

11. van Dongen, G., Van den Poel, D.: Evaluation of stream processing frameworks. IEEE Trans. Parallel Distrib. Syst. **31**(8), 1845–1858 (2020). https://doi.org/10.1109/TPDS.2020.2978480

12. Gedik, B.: Generic windowing support for extensible stream processing systems. Softw. Pract. Exper. **44**(9), 1105–1128 (2014). https://doi.org/10.1002/spe.2194

13. Haesendonck, G., Maroy, W., Heyvaert, P., Verborgh, R., Dimou, A.: Parallel RDF generation from heterogeneous big data. In: Proceedings of the International Workshop on Semantic Big Data. SBD 2019. Association for Computing Machinery, New York (2019). https://doi.org/10.1145/3323878.3325802

14. Iglesias, E., Jozashoori, S., Chaves-Fraga, D., Collarana, D., Vidal, M.E.: SDM-RDFIZER. In: Proceedings of the 29th ACM International Conference on Information and Knowledge Management, October 2020. https://doi.org/10.1145/3340531.3412881

15. Karimov, J., Rabl, T., Katsifodimos, A., Samarev, R., Heiskanen, H., Markl, V.: Benchmarking distributed stream data processing systems. In: 2018 IEEE 34th International Conference on Data Engineering (ICDE), April 2018. https://doi.org/10.1109/icde.2018.00169

16. Le Phuoc, D., Dao-Tran, M., Le Tuan, A., Duc, M.N., Hauswirth, M.: RDF stream processing with CQELS framework for real-time analysis. In: Proceedings of the 9th ACM International Conference on Distributed Event-Based Systems. DEBS 2015, pp. 285–292. Association for Computing Machinery, New York (2015). https://doi.org/10.1145/2675743.2772586

17. Lefrançois, M., Zimmermann, A., Bakerally, N.: A SPARQL extension for generating RDF from heterogeneous formats. In: Blomqvist, E., Maynard, D., Gangemi, A., Hoekstra, R., Hitzler, P., Hartig, O. (eds.) ESWC 2017. LNCS, vol. 10249, pp. 35–50. Springer, Cham (2017). https://doi.org/10.1007/978-3-319-58068-5_3

18. Mauri, A., et al.: TripleWave: spreading RDF streams on the web. In: Groth, P., et al. (eds.) ISWC 2016. LNCS, vol. 9982, pp. 140–149. Springer, Cham (2016). https://doi.org/10.1007/978-3-319-46547-0_15

19. N.A: Apache storm. https://storm.apache.org/

20. Paepe, D.D., et al.: A complete software stack for IoT time-series analysis that combines semantics and machine learning—lessons learned from the dyversify project. Appl. Sci. **11**(24), 11932 (2021). https://doi.org/10.3390/app112411932

21. Santipantakis, G.M., Kotis, K.I., Vouros, G.A., Doulkeridis, C.: RDF-GEN: generating RDF from streaming and archival data. In: Proceedings of the 8th International Conference on Web Intelligence, Mining and Semantics. WIMS 2018. Association for Computing Machinery, New York (2018). https://doi.org/10.1145/3227609.3227658

22. Scrocca, M., Comerio, M., Carenini, A., Celino, I.: Turning transport data to comply with EU standards while enabling a multimodal transport knowledge graph. Semant. Web - ISWC **2020**, 411–429 (2020). https://doi.org/10.1007/978-3-030-62466-8_26

23. Simsek, U., Kärle, E., Fensel, D.A.: RocketRML - a NodeJS implementation of a use case specific RML mapper. arXiv abs/1903.04969 (2019). https://doi.org/10.48550/ARXIV.1903.04969

24. Steenwinckel, B., et al.: FLAGS: a methodology for adaptive anomaly detection and root cause analysis on sensor data streams by fusing expert knowledge with machine learning. Futur. Gener. Comput. Syst. **116**, 30–48 (2021). https://doi.org/10.1016/j.future.2020.10.015

25. Tommasini, R., Della Valle, E., Mauri, A., Brambilla, M.: RSPLab: RDF stream processing benchmarking made easy. In: d'Amato, C., et al. (eds.) ISWC 2017. LNCS, vol. 10588, pp. 202–209. Springer, Cham (2017). https://doi.org/10.1007/978-3-319-68204-4_21

26. Zaharia, M., et al.: Apache spark: a unified engine for big data processing. Commun. ACM **59**(11), 56–65 (2016). https://doi.org/10.1145/2934664

27. Zhang, Q., Song, Y., Routray, R.R., Shi, W.: Adaptive block and batch sizing for batched stream processing system. In: 2016 IEEE International Conference on Autonomic Computing (ICAC), pp. 35–44 (2016). https://doi.org/10.1109/ICAC.2016.27

WDBench: A Wikidata Graph Query Benchmark

Renzo Angles[1,2], Carlos Buil Aranda[1,3], Aidan Hogan[1,4], Carlos Rojas[1], and Domagoj Vrgoč[1,5(✉)]

[1] IMFD Chile, Santiago, Chile
[2] DCC, Universidad de Talca, Talca, Chile
[3] Universidad Técnica Federico Santa María, Valparaíso, Chile
[4] DCC, Universidad de Chile, Santiago, Chile
[5] PUC Chile, Santiago, Chile
dvrgoc@ing.puc.cl

Abstract. We propose WDBench: a query benchmark for knowledge graphs based on Wikidata, featuring real-world queries extracted from the public query logs of the Wikidata SPARQL endpoint. While a number of benchmarks for graph databases (including SPARQL engines) have been proposed in recent years, few are based on real-world data, even fewer use real-world queries, and fewer still allow for comparing SPARQL engines with (non-SPARQL) graph databases. The raw Wikidata query log contains millions of diverse queries, where it would be prohibitively costly to run all such queries, and difficult to draw conclusions given the mix of features that these queries use. WDBench thus focuses on three main query features that are common to SPARQL and graph databases: (i) basic graph patterns, (ii) optional graph patterns, (iii) path patterns, and (iv) navigational graph patterns. We extract queries from the Wikidata logs specifically to test these patterns, clean them of non-standard features, remove duplicates, classify them into different structural subsets, and present them in two different syntaxes. Using this benchmark, we present and compare performance results for evaluating queries using Blazegraph, Jena/Fuseki, Virtuoso and Neo4j.

1 Introduction

Recent years have seen renewed interest in querying graphs, driven in particular by the growing popularity of knowledge graphs [25]. There are two related options for querying knowledge graphs. On the one hand, SPARQL [22] is the standard query language for RDF graphs/datasets [16], and has enjoyed significant developments down through the years, including the publication of hundreds of public query services [43], the development of hundreds of SPARQL query engines and prototypes [1], the release of dozens of benchmarks [1], an extended version of the original standard [22], etc. SPARQL is the query language of choice for prominent open knowledge graphs – such as DBpedia [29], Wikidata [44], etc. – which provide public query services that can receive in the order of hundreds of thousand

© The Author(s), under exclusive license to Springer Nature Switzerland AG 2022
U. Sattler et al. (Eds.): ISWC 2022, LNCS 13489, pp. 714–731, 2022.
https://doi.org/10.1007/978-3-031-19433-7_41

or even millions of queries per day [30,35]. On the other hand, a variety of graph query languages, databases, etc., have been proposed and developed within the NoSQL/Database community [13], and have become widely used, particularly for enterprise knowledge graphs, with Neo4j [46] and its query language Cypher [20] leading the way in terms of popularity.[1]

With may options available, it can be difficult to choose a suitable engine to support queries over a given knowledge graph, which calls for graph query benchmarks that reflect real-world workloads. For example, the Wikidata community is currently seeking an alternative to replace Blazegraph [42], whose development team has moved on to work on other projects.[2]

While dozens of query benchmarks have been proposed down through the years for RDF/SPARQL [2,9,12,17,19,21,26,31,36,39,40,48] and graph databases [7,19], most rely on synthetic data generated according to a fixed schema [2,7,12,17,19,21,39,40]. While benchmarks based on synthetic data are useful for scalability testing, since most allow for generating graphs of arbitrary size, the schemas used for such benchmarks are hand-crafted and thus often much simpler than the organic, collaboratively-generated schemas that emerge within knowledge graphs such as DBpedia [29] and Wikidata [44].

A smaller number of benchmarks have been proposed based on real-world knowledge graphs [9,26,31,36,48], but either rely on synthetic queries [26], a small number of hand-selected queries [9,48], or instances of a small number of templates induced through log analysis [31,36]. One of the challenges of using query logs [30,35] for benchmarks is the sheer number and diversity of queries available, with, for example, millions of queries available in the Wikidata query logs [30]. Running all such queries over multiple engines on a large knowledge graph would not only be prohibitively costly, but would also generate results that are difficult to interpret, given that real-world queries will often mix features. Approaches to deal with this have focused on generating templates [31,36].

In this paper, we rather follow a *feature-based approach*: we generate a real-world benchmark by extracting a large and diverse set of queries from the query log of an open knowledge graph, but only for selected core features that are common to both SPARQL engines and graph databases [5]. Within these features, we define high-level subclasses in order to gain more detailed insights into the performance of different engines. The specific benchmark we propose here, which we call *WDBench*, is based on the Wikidata knowledge graph [44] and query logs [30]. The features we currently focus on are basic graph patterns, optional graph patterns, path patterns, and navigational graph patterns, which can be translated to SPARQL and Cypher. We use WDBench to compare the query performance of Blazegraph [42], Jena TDB [27], Virtuoso [18] and Neo4j [46].

Paper Structure. Section 2 discusses related work, Sect. 3 describes the design of WDBench, Sect. 4 describes the experimental design, Sect. 5 describes the results of these experiments, while Sect. 6 concludes.

---

[1] See https://db-engines.com/en/ranking/graph+dbms; retr. 2022-05-06.
[2] See https://phabricator.wikimedia.org/T206560; retr. 2022-05-06.

2   Related Work

As highlighted previously, dozens of benchmarks have been proposed for RDF and other graph databases over the years. They can be classified in two general classes: benchmarks based on synthetic and real-world graphs. Some benchmarks target RDF/SPARQL engines, while others target other graph databases; to the best of our knowledge, the latter exclusively use synthetic datasets.

Synthetic SPARQL-Oriented Benchmarks. The Lehigh University Benchmark (LUBM) [21] was one of the first benchmarks proposed for RDF/SPARQL, generating synthetic data about universities. Berlin [12] generates data following an e-commerce use-case, with comparable SPARQL and SQL queries provided. SP^2Bench [39] generates an arbitrarily-large graph following the schema of DBLP database, with queries provided in a variety of shapes. BowlognaBench [17] generates synthetic RDF graphs about universities, providing queries inspired by the Bologna reform of European universities. WatDiv [2] presents an approach that focuses on generating diverse graph data and basic graph patterns in order to address the "structuredness" problem of other benchmarks [37]; queries follow star, path and snowflake query shapes. TrainBench [40] is another synthetic benchmark, this time inspired by a railway network, defining six queries encoding network validation constraints.

Synthetic Graph Database-Oriented Benchmarks. gMark [7] provides a domain- and query language-independent driver, generating query workloads for a user-defined schema. The user can define the scenario from which the data is generated (i.e. social network, biological database, etc.) and from that data the driver generates the queries and translates them to the desired engine (i.e. Neo4J, SPARQL, etc.). The Linked Data Benchmark Council's Social Network Benchmark LDBC-SNB [19] is a benchmark that provides a common synthetic dataset for two different query workloads. The dataset represents a social network and the two workloads differ in the use case they evaluate the engine for: one focuses on transactional graph processing queries that target neighbouring nodes and update operations that continuously insert new data in the graph. The second workload focuses on aggregate queries accessing large parts of the graph.

Real-World RDF-Oriented Benchmarks. DBpedia SPARQL Benchmark (DBSBM) [31] generates queries for a specific version of DBpedia based on real-world query logs. The queries in the log files are cleaned and clustered according to the SPARQL features, generating 25 query templates from the most prominent clusters with placeholder variables that can be instantiated from the data in order to generate multiple instances per template. FEASIBLE [36] builds upon this idea of generating benchmarks from query logs. The query generation takes into account several query characteristics such as number of triple patterns or number of join vertices, generates vectors that represent queries according to the features, and generates queries based on the patterns from the vectors. BioBenchmark [48] defines a benchmark over five biomedical datasets (Cell, Allie, PDBJ,

DDBJ, and UniProt), providing 48 queries extracted from real-world applications. The Wikidata Graph Pattern Benchmark [26] is based on Wikidata, but rather uses synthetic queries following structural graph pattern templates.

Comparison and Novelty. We refer to Saleem et al. [37] for a detailed comparison of the benchmarks discussed here. In terms of the novelty of WDBench, it uses real-world data and queries; to the best of our knowledge, only DBSBM [31] and FEASIBLE [36] share this characteristic. Unlike these two benchmarks, WDBench (1) is based on Wikidata rather than DBpedia; (2) uses a larger graph (1.257 billion triples/edges vs. 232 million triples/edges); (3) contains path patterns that can match arbitrary length paths, which are a key feature of graph queries; (4) is offered in both SPARQL and Cypher variants; (5) does not apply templates or clustering, but rather contains a larger and more diverse query set that includes thousands of queries. It is important to note that the goal of WDBench is to complement existing benchmarks rather than to replace them. We see WDBench as being a useful resource to test query performance for core features of graph queries over a real-world knowledge graph using realistic workloads. However, other benchmarks may have other benefits, and could be run alongside WDBench. For example, synthetic benchmarks have the benefit of being able to generate graphs of arbitrary size, where one could be run alongside WDBench in order to stress-test scalability. Other benchmarks could be used to test SPARQL-specific or relational features not included in WDBench.

3 WDBench: Graph and Queries

We now discuss the design of WDBench. We start by explaining the rationale behind the subset of Wikidata used for benchmarking, and then specify the process for selecting a representative query set out of the millions of queries available in the Wikidata public endpoint log [13,30]. We then discuss conversion of the benchmark into a property graph with Cypher queries for running Neo4j.

3.1 WDBench Graph

In order to define the graph used in WDBench, we were guided by three criteria: (i) that it is representative of a diverse, large-scale, real-world knowledge graph; (ii) that it covers a wide range of queries from the public query log of Wikidata; and (iii) that it is succinct, i.e., that it does not contain massive amounts of data irrelevant for the queries that would increase load times for different engines. To balance these criteria, we base WDBench on the Wikidata truthy dump [41] for three reasons: (1) it is more concise and thus faster to load: some engines can take over a week to load the complete version of Wikidata; (2) it is sufficient to address the majority of queries in the log chosen: 86.8% of the queries in this log use only truthy properties; (3) it avoids issues relating to how Wikidata-specific qualifiers should be reified in different databases: this topic diverges from our goal of a general query benchmark for knowledge graphs and is addressed elsewhere [23,24]. To further prune the dataset, we only kept triples in which (a) the subject position is a Wikidata entity, and (b) the predicate is a truthy (direct) property. This allows us to focus on structural properties of the queries and the graph, while increasing succinctness. The particular Wikidata truthy dump we used is `20210623-truthy-BETA`, which contains 18,579,709,438 triples. After pruning based on the described criteria, the final dataset contains 1,257,169,959 triples. Many of the triples pruned are labels and descriptions in multiple languages, which we deem as inessential for testing the performance of graph pattern evaluation (rarely are joins or paths expressed via labels or descriptions). The dataset is available for download online at [3], and the scripts used to prune a truthy dump can be found online at [4].

3.2   WDBench Queries

WDBench is based on real-world queries posted by Wikidata users, as found in Wikidata's query logs [30,47]. Given that the log files contain millions of queries, where it would be prohibitively costly to run them all, and where the results would be difficult to interpret given the mix of features that they use, we reduce the queries in several phases and classify them by their features.

The first choice we made was to concentrate exclusively on queries that timed out on the Wikidata endpoint (code 500 queries in the log files [30,47]). While endpoint timeouts can be caused by many factors (including temporary server load), we wish to focus on challenging queries, where this subset of queries largely filters out the multitude of trivial queries in the log. Additionally, focusing on the code 500 queries reduces the set to 122,980 queries. If the query uses vocabulary not present in our graph, we discard it (note that queries generating empty results are kept so long as they only use relevant vocabulary terms).

The next reduction was based on the operators used by the queries. Considering that we aim to compare note only RDF/SPARQL engines, but also other graph databases, we decided to focus on four types of graph patterns at the core of popular graph query languages [5]: (i) basic graph patterns; (ii) optional graph patterns; (iii) path patterns; and (iv) navigational graph patterns (using paths). Other features – including relational-style operators such as projection, difference, selection (filter), union, aggregation, solution modifiers, etc. – could be added in future using a similar methodology; however, adding more features would complicate generating comparable queries in distinct graph query languages. We thus pruned queries that use any operator different from basic graph patterns, optionals and property paths. However, we keep queries with `SERVICE`, since this operator is used in the majority of Wikidata queries in order to specify language preferences for labels; and `DISTINCT`, `GROUP BY`, `ORDER BY`, `LIMIT`, since these solution modifiers are generally applied after processing the base query pattern. In these exceptional cases, we remove the service and solution modifier clauses and keep the resulting query. Given that the labelling service can produce new variables that can be referenced in projected results, we use `SELECT *` such that our queries are of the form `SELECT * WHERE {graph_pattern}`. From there, we profiled the following four groups of graph pattern queries.

Basic Graph Patterns. These were the queries that consisted exclusively of joins between triple patterns. In order to eliminate duplicate queries, we sort the triple patterns, and rename the variables they use, allowing us to detect the queries which differ only in variable names, or the order of triples. The result is a set of 1,335 BGP queries. We further partition BGPs into two disjoint subsets:

- SINGLE. This set contains BGPs with a single triple pattern. While relatively simple to evaluate, these queries test the engines' data retrieval and result enumeration capabilities, which are key to evaluating any query efficiently. We ended up with 280 queries in this set.
- MULTIPLE. These are queries consisting exclusively of BGPs, which have at least two triple patterns, and thus require a join to be performed. Again, being able to evaluate joins within basic graph patterns efficiently is crucial for query performance. This set contains a total of 681 queries.

Optional Graph Patterns. We choose optional graph patterns as a focus of WDBench since they are frequently used to query incomplete knowledge graphs [13], and they have been widely studied in the literature as a characteristic feature of graph queries that can increase the computational complexity of query evaluation [33,34]. Queries in this set include (only) basic graph patterns and one or more (potentially nested) OPTIONAL patterns. We further remove queries that artificially create a cross product via OPTIONAL whereby the right-hand side of an OPTIONAL contains only variables that are not mentioned elsewhere; such queries might skew the benchmark results. This OPTIONALS set contains 498 distinct queries. We partition OPTIONALS into two disjoint sets:

- WELL-DESIGNED (WD). An OPTIONAL query Q is *well-designed* if and only if, for every optional clause $O = \{P_1\}$ OPTIONAL $\{P_2\}$ it contains, each variable in P_2 either appears in P_1 or appears nowhere else in Q besides P_2 [33]. Such queries avoid leaps in complexity associated with optional graph patterns [10, 33,34]. This subset contains 390 queries.
- NOT-WELL-DESIGNED (NWD). These are OPTIONAL queries that are not well-designed, and are thus associated with leaps in computational complexity for key decision problems [33]. This subset contains 108 queries.

Path Patterns. We further test the performance of executing a single property path query (excluding simple predicates). These queries test the engines' ability to detect whether there is a path connecting two nodes that conforms to a regular expression. In the research literature this class of queries is known as two-way regular path queries (2RPQs) [6], and in SPARQL standard they are called property paths [22,28].[3] Given that property paths almost exclusively form part of a larger query in our log, we extracted path patterns from queries in order to achieve a larger query set. Thus, if a query contains two property paths, this will result in two new queries being added to PATHS. After eliminating duplicates PATHS contains 660 queries. We partition PATHS into two disjoint subsets:

---

[3] Property paths include negated property sets that fall outside 2RPQs [28], but these are rarely used [13], and can be partially emulated through disjunction (|) [28].

- RECURSIVE (R). We call a PATH query *recursive* if and only if it uses Kleene star (*) or Kleene plus (+), i.e., if and only if it can match paths of arbitrary length. There were 594 queries in this subset.
- NON-RECURSIVE (NR). We call a PATH query non-recursive if and only if it does not use Kleene star (*) nor Kleene plus (+), i.e., if and only if it can match paths of fixed length. There were 66 queries in this subset.

Navigational Graph Patterns. The final set of queries considers navigational graph patterns, which incorporate property paths [22], triple patterns, and joins; i.e., they are BGPs with property paths. To be more precise, we keep queries which use either joins, or property paths, thus having a set of queries akin to conjunctive two-way regular path queries (C2RPQs) [15]. We call this query set NAVIGATIONAL [5]. In order to not have an overlap with the PATHS query set, all queries in C2RPQs must perform at least one join. These are more advanced queries, and SPARQL engines are known to run into issues when evaluating them [8]. The set C2RPQs contains a total of 539 queries. We further partition NAVIGATIONAL into two disjoint subsets:

- RECURSIVE (R). We call a NAVIGATIONAL query *recursive* if and only if it contains a recursive path pattern. There are 515 such queries.
- NON-RECURSIVE (NR). We call a PATH query non-recursive if and only if it does not contain a recursive path pattern. There were 24 such queries.

3.3   Conversion to Cypher

The Wikidata dump and query logs are natively expressed as RDF/SPARQL. However, we aim for WDBench to also be usable for comparing graph databases. A complication here is that graph databases often define their own declarative query language. For now we thus focus on creating a version of the benchmark for testing with Neo4j. This requires mapping the Wikidata graph to a property graph, which is straightforwardly achieved given that we only include binary (truthy) relations: each triple is simply represented as an edge in the property graph. The more complex part involves converting the queries to Cypher [20]: Neo4j's query language. Graph patterns are expressed using a MATCH clause, while optional graph patterns use the OPTIONAL MATCH clause. Within a MATCH clause, Neo4j applies an edge-isomorphism semantics, while SPARQL uses a homomorphism semantics [5]; thus Cypher's query results can differ, but we found such differences to be marginal in practice. Regarding path patterns, Neo4j only supports Kleene star (i.e., zero or more, which it denotes by "*"). Where possible, we rewrite path expressions into other available Neo4j operators, with concatenations rewritten to basic graph patterns, inverses rewritten by swapping source and target nodes, etc.; however, not all property paths (2RPQs) can be supported. Neo4j allows for returning string representations of paths; to be comparable with SPARQL, we project only the endpoints of paths.

4   Running WDBench

We now turn to using WDBench in order to test the performance of four query engines. This section specifies the operational parameters for these experiments.

The Machine. All experiments were run on a single commodity server with an Intel®Xeon®Silver 4110 CPU, and 128 GB of DDR4/2666 MHz RAM, running Linux Debian 10 with the kernel version 5.10. The hard disk used to store the data was a SEAGATE ST14000NM001G with 14 TB of storage.

How we Ran the Queries. To simulate a realistic database load, we do not split queries into cold/hot run segments. Rather we run them in succession, one after another, after a cold start of each system (and after cleaning the OS cache[4]). This simulates the fact that query performance can vary significantly based on the state of the system buffer, or even on the state of the hard drive, or the state of OS's virtual memory. For each system, queries were run in the same order. We record the execution time of each individual query, which includes iterating over all results. We set a limit of 100,000 distinct results for each query, again in order to enable comparability as some engines showed instability when returning larger results (also Virtuoso is hard-limited to $2^{20} = 1,048,576$ results). We replicated this setup for each query set described above. This allows us to gauge the systems' performance on each particular type of query.

Handling Timeouts. We defined a timeout of 1 min per query for each system. This is a common limit available of SPARQL endpoints, so we replicated it in the benchmark. Apart from that, we note that most systems had to be restarted upon a timeout as they often showed instability, particularly while evaluating path queries. This was done without cleaning the OS cache in order to preserve some of the virtual memory mapping that the OS built up to that point.

Tested Engines. We use four persistent graph query engines that are popular in practice. First, we include three RDF/SPARQL engines: Jena TDB version 4.1.0 [27], Blazegraph (BlazeG for short) version 2.1.6 [42], and Virtuoso version 7.2.6 [18]. We further include a property graph engine: Neo4J community edition 4.3.5 [46]. Jena and Blazegraph were assigned 64GB of RAM, and Virtuoso was set up with 64GB or more of RAM as is recommended. Neo4J was run with default settings. The size of the WDBench dataset when loaded into each of the engines can be found in Table 1.

5   Experimental Results

In this section we present results for the tested engines on each query set specified in WDBench. We divide the discussion by the different query features described

---

[4] This is done by the command "`# sync; echo 3 > /proc/sys/vm/drop_caches`".

Table 1. WDBench dataset sizes when loaded into each engine.

BlazeG	Jena	Virtuoso	Neo4J
70 GB	110 GB	70 GB	112 GB

in Sect. 3.2 – namely basic graph patterns, optional graph patterns, path patterns, navigational graph patterns and their sub-variants – and discuss explanations for the behaviour we observe. All experimental results, including runtimes for individual queries on each engine tested, can be found online [4].

5.1   Basic Graph Patterns

We begin by examining the performance of each query engine for basic graph patterns (BGPs), considering both SINGLE and MULTIPLE subsets. A summary of the results can be observed in Table 2 and Fig. 1. The box plots are generated in the standard manner, showing the range between the first and the third quartile, with the midline representing the median, and the whiskers represented by thin lines. Table 2 additionally indicates how many queries are supported by the engine, the number of errors and timeouts, the average, and the median.

We can observe that as far as SINGLE is concerned, Virtuoso is the most stable engine, returning no timeouts, nor errors, closely followed by Blazegraph. In terms of performance, Blazegraph is the clear winner in the SINGLE query set, followed thereafter by Virtuoso. Both Jena and Neo4j are lagging in terms of performance, with averages 4–5 times higher than the other two engines. Neo4j's median is also above the third quartile for both Blazegraph and Virtuoso. Queries from the SINGLE set have precisely the same structure. However, depending on the exact constants they use, the results can vary from timeouts to fast runs, depending on the data distribution, number of results, etc. For this reason we believe that it is beneficial to have a large number of queries that might be structurally similar, but that access different parts of the dataset.

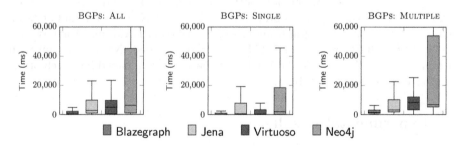

Fig. 1. Performance for all BGPs (left), SINGLE (middle), and MULTIPLE (right)

Table 2. Summary of runtimes (in seconds) for BGPs

Engine	Supported	Timeouts	Error	Average	Median
BGPs (961 QUERIES)					
Blazegraph	961	55	0	6.51	1.05
Jena	961	79	0	10.73	2.71
Virtuoso	961	8	3	6.79	4.90
Neo4j	961	206	1	20.16	6.17
BGPs SINGLE (280 QUERIES)					
Blazegraph	280	3	0	1.73	0.07
Jena	280	25	0	9.92	0.46
Virtuoso	280	1	0	2.12	0.28
Neo4j	280	47	0	15.28	2.03
BGPs MULTIPLE (681 QUERIES)					
Blazegraph	681	52	0	8.47	1.34
Jena	681	54	0	11.06	3.16
Virtuoso	681	7	3	8.71	8.34
Neo4j	681	159	1	22.17	6.75

When considering join queries in MULTIPLE, we observe a rather similar pattern. Virtuoso is again the most stable engine, but it falls behind Blazegraph slightly in the average case. Medians and boxplots tell another story here, showing that both Jena and Blazegraph outperform Virtuoso on the majority of the queries, where even Neo4j's median, and first to third quartiles, are lower than that of Virtuoso's. Thus it would seem that Blazegraph and Jena, in particular, can evaluate the majority of these queries faster than Virtuoso, but Virtuoso performs relatively better for higher percentiles (more costly queries).

5.2 Optional Graph Patterns

The results for OPTIONALS is given in Table 3, and in Fig. 2. Blazegraph is the clear winner here, both in stability, with only 28 timeouts, and in speed, with its median being below the first quartile of the next best competitor, Jena. Jena also outperforms Virtuoso by a wide margin, and Neo4j trails further behind.

Considering only well-designed OPTIONAL patterns, the performance of Virtuoso improves drastically. Blazegraph wins in terms of runtimes, but Virtuoso surpasses other engines in stability, timing out on only 5 of 390 queries. Non well-designed optionals seems to be a major issue for Virtuoso, where it times out in

64 of 108 cases, and its performance drops significantly. Other engines actually perform significantly better on OPTIONALS NWD. Looking a bit deeper into this performance gain, we speculate that this is mostly due to the non well-designed optionals simulating a cross-product, which generates 100,000 results, our query limit, quite fast, at least when the engine is optimised for such cases, per the results for Blazegraph and Jena (but not Virtuoso nor Neo4j).

Table 3. Summary of runtimes (in seconds) for optional graph patterns

Engine	Supported	Timeouts	Error	Average	Median
OPTIONALS (498 QUERIES)					
Blazegraph	498	37	0	8.55	2.16
Jena	498	59	0	13.56	4.34
Virtuoso	498	69	2	17.29	9.45
Neo4j	498	146	1	27.09	17.87
OPTIONALS WELL-DESIGNED (390 QUERIES)					
Blazegraph	390	36	0	9.99	2.32
Jena	390	56	0	14.91	4.66
Virtuoso	390	5	1	10.37	7.70
Neo4j	390	113	1	28.21	18.89
OPTIONALS NOT WELL-DESIGNED (108 QUERIES)					
Blazegraph	108	1	0	3.37	1.89
Jena	108	3	0	8.68	3.46
Virtuoso	108	64	1	42.26	60.00
Neo4j	108	33	0	23.08	5.89

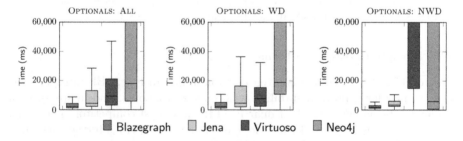

Fig. 2. Performance for OPTIONALS (left), OPTIONALS WD (middle), and OPTIONALS NWD (right)

Table 4. Summary of runtimes (in seconds) for path patterns

Engine	Supported	Timeouts	Error	Average	Median
PATHS (660 QUERIES)					
Blazegraph	660	87	0	11.00	0.82
Jena	660	96	0	11.74	0.81
Virtuoso	660	24	27	4.71	0.70
Neo4j	639	134	6	20.89	9.74
PATHS RECURSIVE (594 QUERIES)					
Blazegraph	594	79	0	11.13	0.78
Jena	594	75	0	10.52	0.62
Virtuoso	594	24	25	4.65	0.43
Neo4j	575	104	5	19.48	9.36
PATHS NON-RECURSIVE (66 QUERIES)					
Blazegraph	66	8	0	9.89	1.19
Jena	66	21	0	22.71	3.04
Virtuoso	66	0	2	5.23	3.72
Neo4j	64	30	1	33.56	42.95

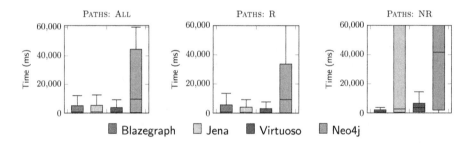

Fig. 3. Performance for PATHS (left), PATHS R (middle), and PATHS NR (right)

5.3 Path Patterns

Considering that property paths are known to give trouble to graph query engines [8], it is interesting to consider their performance in the context of this benchmark. We summarise our findings in Table 4, and in Fig. 3.

Considering all property paths in the PATHS query set, we can see that Virtuoso is the clear winner, both in stability and performance. Both Jena and Blazegraph trail some distance behind, and Neo4j is an order of magnitude slower in the median case. Similarly as in SINGLE, we can observe that the form of the query (almost identical for all the queries in the set) does not matter much, but that the distribution of the data dictates query performance. We even managed to identify paths which use the exact same regular expression to specify the query, but have a different starting point for the search, where one finishes almost instantaneously, and the other one times out.

When we analyse queries that use recursion, versus the path queries that use no recursion, we can see that all engines except Jena perform similarly in the average case, with Virtuoso being again the most stable and the fastest in terms of the median case. Blazegraph performs better than the other engines in the median case for non-recursive paths. Interestingly, Jena seems to perform better on recursive patterns. Likewise, all systems perform better in the median case for recursive patterns as compared to non-recursive ones. This is a surprising result since one should expect recursive queries to be more costly. In the case of the RDF/SPARQL engines, the SPARQL standard indicates that (most) non-recursive path patterns should be rewritten to BGPs and unions of BGPs, rather than evaluating them directly as paths, meaning that implementations following this strategy will follow very different query evaluation plans when comparing recursive and non-recursive cases.

5.4   Navigational Graph Patterns

The results for NAVIGATIONAL are given in Table 5 and Fig. 4. As before, we provide the results for all the queries in this set, and then analyse the recursive and the non-recursive cases within the set.

When we consider all navigational graph patterns, this set is clearly the most challenging thus far, where we observe the highest average and median runtimes for all engines across all patterns, except in the case of Neo4j, which was slower in the average case for OPTIONALS. Virtuoso is a clear winner in this category, particularly in the average case, although both Blazegraph and Jena come close in terms of median runtimes. Neo4j is again the slowest of all the engines.

When comparing recursive and non-recursive navigational graph patterns, we see different effects on different systems. Blazegraph is slightly slower for non-recursive queries, Jena is notably faster for non-recursive queries, Virtuoso is notably slower for non-recursive queries, and finally Neo4j is considerably slower for non-recursive queries. This is similar to what we observed for PATHS, except in the case of Jena, where the trend is reversed. Many queries in NAVIGATIONAL that timed out contain a query in PATHS that also times out. This would suggest that an important factor in timeouts is the performance of property paths.

Table 5. Summary of runtimes (in seconds) for navigational graph patterns

Engine	Supported	Timeouts	Error	Average	Median
NAVIGATIONAL (539 QUERIES)					
Blazegraph	539	180	0	22.32	2.58
Jena	539	245	0	30.98	29.83
Virtuoso	539	37	2	10.42	4.36
Neo4j	531	211	0	31.07	24.83
NAVIGATIONAL RECURSIVE (515 QUERIES)					
Blazegraph	515	172	0	22.29	2.58
Jena	515	238	0	31.31	35.47
Virtuoso	515	36	2	10.15	4.03
Neo4j	509	199	0	30.69	24.09
NAVIGATIONAL NON-RECURSIVE (24 QUERIES)					
Blazegraph	24	8	0	22.96	2.94
Jena	24	7	0	23.97	10.07
Virtuoso	24	1	0	16.24	6.48
Neo4j	22	12	0	40.01	60.00

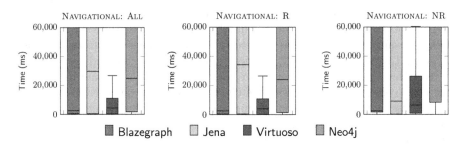

Fig. 4. Performance for NAVIGATIONAL (left), NAVIGATIONAL R (middle), and NAVIGATIONAL NR (right)

6 Conclusions

We conclude with a recap of our contributions, a summary of our results, and a discussion on limitations and future directions.

Contributions: We have developed WDBench: a query benchmark for knowledge graphs based on real-world data (Wikidata) and queries (from Wikidata logs). The benchmark allows for measuring the performance of RDF/SPARQL and graph query engines. In this first release, we have focused on analysing four classes of queries corresponding to core features of graph queries: basic graph patterns, optional graph patterns, path patterns, and navigational graph patterns. We have further partitioned these sets into finer subsets: single vs. multiple, well-designed vs. not well-designed, and recursive vs. non-recursive. We have published two versions of the benchmark: an RDF/SPARQL version, and a property graph/Cypher version. We have further presented empirical results for the performance of Blazegraph, Jena, Virtuoso and Neo4j using this benchmark.

Results: We observed that Blazegraph and Virtuoso were the best-performing query engines for WDBench, followed by Jena, with Neo4j generally offering the slowest runtimes. Comparing Blazegraph and Virtuoso, the former is slightly faster than the latter for basic graph patterns, considerably faster for optional graph patterns (particularly for not well-designed patterns), considerably slower for path patterns (except the median case of non-recursive queries), and faster in the median case but slower in the average case for navigational graph patterns. In terms of cases where engines could be better optimised, we see that Virtuoso underperforms for not well-designed patterns, while Jena underperforms for non-recursive path queries. Neo4j does not appear to offer competitive performance in the Wikidata setting: while there is the caveat that the query semantics of Cypher varies slightly in some cases from SPARQL, the differences in performance would seem to go beyond such variations; indeed, our results are consistent with previous results for querying Wikidata with Neo4j [24].

Limitations and Future Directions: WDBench currently focuses on core features of graph queries, where languages such as SPARQL and Cypher include a wide range of other features that are frequently used in practice. As part of future work, the same methodology as presented here could be straightforwardly used for generating sets of SPARQL queries using other features and combinations thereof. However, as new features are introduced, it will become increasingly complex to offer analogous versions in Cypher (and other query languages), particularly for features using built-in expressions, such as filters, aggregations, and variable binding. We currently compare the performance of four query engines, but there are other systems that would be interesting to compare in future, including QLever [11], RDF-3x [32] (for SPARQL 1.0), RDF4j [14], etc.[5] Unlike synthetic benchmarks, the scale of WDBench is limited by the size of Wikidata. While it would be possible to test, for example, on the complete version of Wikidata, query results would not change. We view WDBench as a real-world benchmark that can complement other benchmarks, where synthetic benchmarks can be used for stress-testing scalability. Finally, WDBench is a read-only benchmark. An interesting direction for an extended version of the benchmark could include a workload of real-world updates mined from Wikidata [38].

Supplemental Material. The Wikidata graph is available on Figshare [3]. Scripts for data preparation, queries, and detailed results are available on Github [4].

---

[5] We also have results for MillenniumDB [45], which we do not include here since the system has been developed by the authors. We keep our results third-party.

References

1. Ali, W., Saleem, M., Yao, B., Hogan, A., Ngomo, A.-C.N.: A survey of RDF stores & SPARQL engines for querying knowledge graphs. VLDB J. 1–26 (2021). https://doi.org/10.1007/s00778-021-00711-3

2. Aluç, G., Hartig, O., Özsu, M.T., Daudjee, K.: Diversified stress testing of RDF data management systems. In: Mika, P., et al. (eds.) ISWC 2014. LNCS, vol. 8796, pp. 197–212. Springer, Cham (2014). https://doi.org/10.1007/978-3-319-11964-9_13

3. Angles, R., Aranda, C.B., Hogan, A., Rojas, C., Vrgoč, D.: WDBench: a Wikidata graph query benchmark (2022). https://figshare.com/s/50b7544ad6b1f51de060

4. Angles, R., Aranda, C.B., Hogan, A., Rojas, C., Vrgoč, D.: WDBench: a Wikidata graph query benchmark (2022). https://github.com/MillenniumDB/WDBench

5. Angles, R., Arenas, M., Barceló, P., Hogan, A., Reutter, J.L., Vrgoc, D.: Foundations of modern query languages for graph databases. ACM Comput. Surv. **50**(5), 68:1–68:40 (2017)

6. Baeza, P.B., Querying graph databases. In: Proceedings of the 32nd ACM SIGMOD-SIGACT-SIGART Symposium on Principles of Database Systems, PODS 2013, New York, NY, USA, 22–27 June 2013, pp. 175–188 (2013)

7. Bagan, G., Bonifati, A., Ciucanu, R., Fletcher, G.H.L., Lemay, A., Advokaat, N.: gMark: Schema-driven generation of graphs and queries. IEEE Trans. Knowl. Data Eng. **29**(4), 856–869 (2017)

8. Baier, J.A., Daroch, D., Reutter, J.L., Vrgoc, D.: Evaluating navigational RDF queries over the web. In: Proceedings of the 28th ACM Conference on Hypertext and Social Media, HT 2017, Prague, Czech Republic, 4–7 July 2017, pp. 165–174 (2017)

9. Bail, S., et al.: FishMark: a linked data application benchmark. In: Fokoue, A., Liebig, T., Goodman, E.L., Weaver, J., Urbani, J., Mizell, D. (eds.) Proceedings of the Joint Workshop on Scalable and High-Performance Semantic Web Systems. CEUR Workshop Proceedings, Boston, 11 November 2012, vol. 943, pp. 1–15. CEUR-WS.org (2012)

10. Barceló, P., Kröll, M., Pichler, R., Skritek, S.: Efficient evaluation and static analysis for well-designed pattern trees with projection. ACM Trans. Database Syst. **43**(2), 8:1–8:44 (2018)

11. Bast, H., Buchhold, B.: QLever: a query engine for efficient SPARQL+Text search. In: Lim, E., et al. (eds.) Proceedings of the 2017 ACM on Conference on Information and Knowledge Management, CIKM 2017, Singapore, 06–10 November 2017, pp. 647–656. ACM (2017)

12. Bizer, C., Schultz, A.: The berlin SPARQL benchmark. Int. J. Semant. Web Inf. Syst. **5**(2), 1–24 (2009)

13. Bonifati, A., Martens, W., Timm, T.: An analytical study of large SPARQL query logs. VLDB J. 655–679 (2019). https://doi.org/10.1007/s00778-019-00558-9

14. Broekstra, J., Kampman, A., van Harmelen, F.: Sesame: an architecture for storing and querying RDF data and schema information. In: Fensel, D., Hendler, J.A., Lieberman, H., Wahlster, W. (eds.) Spinning the Semantic Web: Bringing the World Wide Web to Its Full Potential [Outcome of a Dagstuhl Seminar], pp. 197–222. MIT Press (2003)

15. Calvanese, D., Giacomo, G.D., Lenzerini, M., Vardi, M.Y.: Reasoning on regular path queries. SIGMOD Rec. **32**(4), 83–92 (2003)

16. Cyganiak, R., Wood, D., Lanthaler, M.: RDF 1.1 Concepts and Abstract Syntax. W3C Recommendation (2014)

17. Demartini, G., Enchev, I., Wylot, M., Gapany, J., Cudré-Mauroux, P.: BowlognaBench—benchmarking RDF analytics. In: Aberer, K., Damiani, E., Dillon, T. (eds.) SIMPDA 2011. LNBIP, vol. 116, pp. 82–102. Springer, Heidelberg (2012). https://doi.org/10.1007/978-3-642-34044-4_5

18. Erling, O.: Virtuoso, a hybrid RDBMS/graph column store. IEEE Data Eng. Bull. **35**(1), 3–8 (2012)

19. Erling, O., et al.: The LDBC social network benchmark: interactive workload. In: Sellis, T.K., Davidson, S.B., Ives, Z.G. (eds.) Proceedings of the 2015 ACM SIGMOD International Conference on Management of Data, Melbourne, Victoria, Australia, 31 May–4 June 2015, pp. 619–630. ACM (2015)

20. Francis, N., et al.: Cypher: an evolving query language for property graphs. In: Das, G., Jermaine, C.M., Bernstein, P.A. (eds.) Proceedings of the 2018 International Conference on Management of Data, SIGMOD Conference 2018, Houston, TX, USA, 10–15 June 2018, pp. 1433–1445. ACM (2018)

21. Guo, Y., Pan, Z., Heflin, J.: LUBM: a benchmark for OWL knowledge base systems. J. Web Semant. **3**(2–3), 158–182 (2005)

22. Harris, S., Seaborne, A., Prud'hommeaux, E.: SPARQL 1.1 Query Language. W3C Recommendation (2013)

23. Hernández, D., Hogan, A., Krötzsch, M.: Reifying RDF: what works well with Wikidata? In: Liebig, T., Fokoue, A. (eds.) Proceedings of the 11th International Workshop on Scalable Semantic Web Knowledge Base Systems Co-located with 14th International Semantic Web Conference (ISWC 2015), Bethlehem, PA, USA, 11 October 2015, vol. 1457. CEUR Workshop Proceedings, pp. 32–47. CEUR-WS.org (2015)

24. Hernández, D., Hogan, A., Riveros, C., Rojas, C., Zerega, E.: Querying Wikidata: comparing SPARQL, relational and graph databases. In: Groth, P., et al. (eds.) ISWC 2016. LNCS, vol. 9982, pp. 88–103. Springer, Cham (2016). https://doi.org/10.1007/978-3-319-46547-0_10

25. Hogan, A., et al.: Knowledge graphs. ACM Comput. Surv. **54**(4), 71:1–71:37 (2021)

26. Hogan, A., Riveros, C., Rojas, C., Soto, A.: A worst-case optimal join algorithm for SPARQL. In: Ghidini, C., et al. (eds.) ISWC 2019. LNCS, vol. 11778, pp. 258–275. Springer, Cham (2019). https://doi.org/10.1007/978-3-030-30793-6_15

27. Jena Team: TDB Documentation (2021)

28. Kostylev, E.V., Reutter, J.L., Romero, M., Vrgoč, D.: SPARQL with property paths. In: Arenas, M., et al. (eds.) ISWC 2015. LNCS, vol. 9366, pp. 3–18. Springer, Cham (2015). https://doi.org/10.1007/978-3-319-25007-6_1

29. Lehmann, J., et al.: DBpedia - a large-scale, multilingual knowledge base extracted from Wikipedia. Semant. Web **6**(2), 167–195 (2015)

30. Malyshev, S., Krötzsch, M., González, L., Gonsior, J., Bielefeldt, A.: Getting the most out of Wikidata: semantic technology usage in Wikipedia's knowledge graph. In: Vrandečić, D., et al. (eds.) ISWC 2018. LNCS, vol. 11137, pp. 376–394. Springer, Cham (2018). https://doi.org/10.1007/978-3-030-00668-6_23

31. Morsey, M., Lehmann, J., Auer, S., Ngonga Ngomo, A.-C.: DBpedia SPARQL benchmark – performance assessment with real queries on real data. In: Aroyo, L., et al. (eds.) ISWC 2011. LNCS, vol. 7031, pp. 454–469. Springer, Heidelberg (2011). https://doi.org/10.1007/978-3-642-25073-6_29

32. Neumann, T., Weikum, G.: The RDF-3X engine for scalable management of RDF data. VLDB J. **19**(1), 91–113 (2010)

33. Pérez, J., Arenas, M., Gutiérrez, C.: Semantics and complexity of SPARQL. ACM Trans. Database Syst. **34**(3), 16:1–16:45 (2009)
34. Romero, M.: The tractability frontier of well-designed SPARQL queries. In: den Bussche, Arenas, M. (eds.) Proceedings of the 37th ACM SIGMOD-SIGACT-SIGAI Symposium on Principles of Database Systems, Houston, TX, USA, 10–15 June 2018, pp. 295–306. ACM (2018)
35. Saleem, M., Ali, M.I., Hogan, A., Mehmood, Q., Ngomo, A.-C.N.: LSQ: the linked SPARQL queries dataset. In: Arenas, M., et al. (eds.) ISWC 2015. LNCS, vol. 9367, pp. 261–269. Springer, Cham (2015). https://doi.org/10.1007/978-3-319-25010-6_15
36. Saleem, M., Mehmood, Q., Ngonga Ngomo, A.-C.: FEASIBLE: a feature-based SPARQL benchmark generation framework. In: Arenas, M., et al. (eds.) ISWC 2015. LNCS, vol. 9366, pp. 52–69. Springer, Cham (2015). https://doi.org/10.1007/978-3-319-25007-6_4
37. Saleem, M., Szárnyas, G., Conrads, F., Bukhari, S.A.C., Mehmood, Q., Ngomo, A.N.: How representative is a SPARQL benchmark? An analysis of RDF triplestore benchmarks. In: The World Wide Web Conference, pp. 1623–1633. ACM (2019)
38. Schmelzeisen, L., Dima, C., Staab, S.: Wikidated 1.0: an evolving knowledge graph dataset of Wikidata's revision history. In: Kaffee, L., Razniewski, S., Hogan, A. (eds.) Proceedings of the 2nd Wikidata Workshop (Wikidata 2021) Co-located with the 20th International Semantic Web Conference (ISWC 2021), Virtual Conference, 24 October 2021, vol. 2982. CEUR Workshop Proceedings. CEUR-WS.org (2021)
39. Schmidt, M., Hornung, T., Lausen, G., Pinkel, C.: SP^2Bench: a SPARQL performance benchmark. In: Ioannidis, Y.E., Lee, D.L., Ng, R.T. (eds.) Proceedings of the 25th International Conference on Data Engineering, ICDE 2009, 29 March 2009–2 April 2009, Shanghai, China, pp. 222–233. IEEE Computer Society (2009)
40. Szárnyas, G., Izsó, B., Ráth, I., Varró, D.: The train benchmark: cross-technology performance evaluation of continuous model queries. Softw. Syst. Model. **17**(4), 1365–1393 (2017). https://doi.org/10.1007/s10270-016-0571-8
41. The Wikimedia Foundation. Wikidata: Database download (2021)
42. Thompson, B.B., Personick, M., Cutcher, M.: The Bigdata® RDF graph database. In: Harth, A., Hose, K., Schenkel, R. (eds.) Linked Data Management, pp. 193–237. Chapman and Hall/CRC, Boca Raton (2014)
43. Vandenbussche, P., Umbrich, J., Matteis, L., Hogan, A., Aranda, C.B.: SPARQLES: monitoring public SPARQL endpoints. Semant. Web **8**(6), 1049–1065 (2017)
44. Vrandecic, D., Krötzsch, M.: Wikidata: a free collaborative knowledgebase. Commun. ACM **57**(10), 78–85 (2014)
45. Vrgoc, D., et al.: MillenniumDB: a persistent, open-source, graph database. CoRR, abs/2111.01540 (2021)
46. Webber, J.: A programmatic introduction to Neo4j. In: Leavens, G.T. (ed.) Conference on Systems, Programming, and Applications: Software for Humanity, SPLASH 2012, Tucson, AZ, USA, 21–25 October 2012, pp. 217–218. ACM (2012)
47. Wikimedia Foundation: Wikidata SPARQL Logs (2022). https://iccl.inf.tu-dresden.de/web/Wikidata_SPARQL_Logs/en
48. Wu, H., Fujiwara, T., Yamamoto, Y., Bolleman, J.T., Yamaguchi, A.: BioBenchmark Toyama 2012: an evaluation of the performance of triple stores on biological data. J. Biomed. Semant. **5**, 32 (2014)

In-Use Track

Leveraging Knowledge Graph Technologies to Assess Journals and Conferences at Springer Nature

Simone Angioni[1]([✉]), Angelo Salatino[2], Francesco Osborne[2,3], Aliaksandr Birukou[4], Diego Reforgiato Recupero[1], and Enrico Motta[2]

[1] Department of Mathematics and Computer Science, University of Cagliari, Cagliari, Italy
{simone.angioni,diego.reforgiato}@unica.it
[2] Knowledge Media Institute, The Open University, Milton Keynes, UK
{angelo.salatino,francesco.osborne,enrico.motta}@open.ac.uk
[3] Department of Business and Law, University of Milano Bicocca, Milan, Italy
[4] Springer-Verlag GmbH, Tiergartenstrasse 17, 69121 Heidelberg, Germany
aliaksandr.birukou@springer.com

Abstract. Research publishing companies need to constantly monitor and compare scientific journals and conferences in order to inform critical business and editorial decisions. Semantic Web and Knowledge Graph technologies are natural solutions since they allow these companies to integrate, represent, and analyse a large quantity of information from heterogeneous sources. In this paper, we present the AIDA Dashboard 2.0, an innovative system developed in collaboration with Springer Nature to analyse and compare scientific venues, now also available to the public. This tool builds on a knowledge graph which includes over 1.5B RDF triples and was produced by integrating information about 25M research articles from Microsoft Academic Graph, Dimensions, DBpedia, GRID, CSO, and INDUSO. It can produce sophisticated analytics and rankings that are not available in alternative systems. We discuss the advantages of this solution for the Springer Nature editorial process and present a user study involving 5 editors and 5 researchers, which yielded excellent results in terms of quality of the analytics and usability.

Keywords: Scholarly data · Knowledge graphs · Scholarly ontologies · Science of science · Scholarly analytics · Scholarly knowledge

1 Introduction

Springer Nature (SN) is one of the main publishers of research in Computer Science and manages a vast catalogue of about 162 journals in this field and several series of proceedings books (e.g., LNCS, LNAI, IFIP-AICT, CCIS, LNBIP) for a total of about 800 volumes per year. Their data analysts have to regularly integrate and analyse a large quantity of information regarding these venues[1] for

---

[1] In this paper, we use the term 'venue' to denote both journals and conferences.

U. Sattler et al. (Eds.): ISWC 2022, LNCS 13489, pp. 735–752, 2022.
https://doi.org/10.1007/978-3-031-19433-7_42

supporting crucial business and editorial decisions. In particular, SN editorial team needs to compare all journals and conferences in a field according to several metrics, be aware of which venues are rising and attracting more attention in the community, monitor how they change over time in terms of researchers and topics distribution, and assess the involvement of commercial organisations. However, bibliometric systems and academic search engines provide a limited support for analysing scientific venues. This led to the creation of the AIDA Dashboard, an innovative tool for supporting editors in performing advanced analysis of these dynamics.

In this paper, we present the AIDA Dashboard 2.0, the last version of the system developed in collaboration with SN to analyse and compare journals and conferences, which we are now releasing to the wider scientific community. This tool builds on the *Academia/Industry DynAmics Knowledge Graph* (AIDA KG) [3], a knowledge graph which includes over 1.5B RDF triples and was produced by integrating information about 25M papers from Microsoft Academic Graph, Dimensions, DBpedia, and the Global Research Identifier Database (GRID). Journals and conferences are categorised according to the *Focus Areas Taxonomy*[2], a new ontology detailing the 124 most prominent research fields within Computer Science venues. The specific research topics in these venues are instead represented according to 14K research topics from the *Computer Science Ontology*[3] (CSO) [24], whereas the industrial sectors of the organisations (e.g., education, energy, financial, technology) are represented with the *Industrial Sectors Ontology*[4] (INDUSO). The last version of the AIDA knowledge graph (ver. 3.0) is publicly available via a dump and a SPARQL endpoint at https://w3id.org/aida.

The main novelties with respect to the earlier version of AIDA Dashboard reported in previous work [4] and presented as a demo at ISWC 2020 [5] include: 1) the ability to analyse journals in addition to conferences, 2) a new expert search functionality that allows users to browse, compare, and order journals and conferences according to several metrics and ranking systems, 3) a new taxonomy of high-level research areas, representing the main research fields used to classify the venues, and 4) the full integration of the dashboard with the SN Data Cloud Infrastructure.

The AIDA Dashboard was evaluated by performing a user study involving five SN editors and five researchers, which yielded excellent results in terms of usability and quality of the analytics.

In order to support the scientific community, we recently released a publicly available version of the system, that can be accessed at https://w3id.org/aida/dashboard. We hope that it could become a standard tool used by researchers, institutions, and funding agencies for analysing venues in Computer Science. We plan to keep updating it in the following years and also add more entities to analyse (e.g., researchers, organizations, countries, topics).

---

[2] Focus Areas Taxonomy - https://w3id.org/aida/fat.

[3] CSO - https://cso.kmi.open.ac.uk/.

[4] INDUSO - https://w3id.org/aida/downloads/induso.ttl.

We also release the *AIDA Venue dataset*[5], a machine readable version of all the analytics produced by the AIDA Dashboard on journals and conferences that can support bibliometric analysis and be used to train machine learning systems.

In summary, the novel contributions of this paper include:

- the AIDA Dashboard 2.0, a new version of the AIDA Dashboard which offers several new functionalities;
- a user study involving five SN editors and five researchers;
- a discussion of the impact and uptake of this tool within SN;
- the AIDA KG 3.0, the last version of the AIDA KG including 25M publications;
- the AIDA Venues dataset 2.0, a new resource describing 3,263 journals and 2,003 conferences in Computer Science[6] according to all the data produced by the AIDA Dashboard back-end.

The remainder of the paper is structured as follows. In Sect. 2, we describe the AIDA Dashboard back-end and the sustainability plan. Section 3 details the AIDA Dashboard GUI. Section 4 presents the evaluation study and Sect. 5 describes the uptake and impact of the AIDA Dashboard within SN. Section 6 presents the related work. Finally, Sect. 7 concludes the paper and discusses future work.

2   The AIDA Engine

The AIDA Dashboard is powered by a complex pipeline for data integration and analysis. Figure 1 summarises its architecture, which is composed by three main components (grey dashed boxes): i) the pipeline for the generation of AIDA KG, ii) the module for pre-computing the analytics, and iii) the AIDA Dashboard GUI. The main data about research articles and relevant metadata are stored in the SN Data Cloud Infrastructure (purple dashed box), which is based on a Google BigQuery instance. This infrastructure regularly downloads four datasets from external data sources, i.e., MAG, Dimensions, DBLP, and OpenAlex. These data are then integrated with several other knowledge bases (upper part of the figure) for generating the AIDA Knowledge Graph. We then compute several analytics that will be reported by the AIDA Dashboard GUI. The following subsections will describe more in detail the generation of AIDA KG and the analytics. The interface of the AIDA Dashboard will be instead described in Sect. 3.

2.1   The AIDA Knowledge Graph

The AIDA Knowledge Graph is automatically generated by integrating several knowledge bases, including MAG, Dimensions, CSO, DBpedia, GRID, and

---

[5] AIDA Downloads - https://w3id.org/aida/downloads.
[6] These numbers are the results of a selection process that identifies only venues active in the last 5 years.

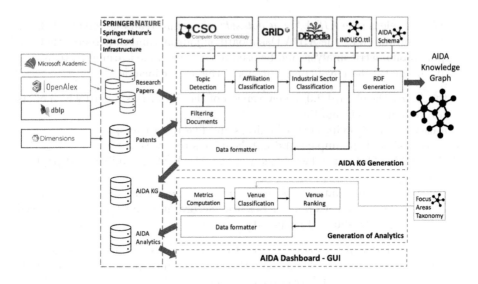

Fig. 1. The AIDA engine architecture

INDUSO. The knowledge graph describes 25M research papers and 8M patents in the field of Computer Science. All these documents are classified with the Computer Science Ontology topics [25]. 6.7M papers and 5.6M patents are also classified based on the type of authors' affiliations (i.e., academia, industry, collaborative), and the industrial sectors from INDUSO. Patents are used by SN analysts for supporting analysis on research impact, but they are not employed yet by the AIDA Dashboard. Since Microsoft recently decommissioned MAG, we are now switching to a combination of OpenAlex and DBLP, as detailed by Sect. 2.3 (Sustainability Plan).

The integration pipeline first selects all research papers and patents respectively from MAG and Dimensions. It applies filters to select the documents within the Computer Science field. It then uses the CSO Classifier [20] to annotate all documents with their relevant research topics. Next, it leverages the GRID IDs associated with the original data to determine whether the documents are authored by either academic or industrial institutions, or through a collaborative effort. For all papers authored by industrial affiliations, it uses DBpedia to classify their industrial sectors according to INDUSO. The reader can refer to [2] for additional details about the AIDA KG generation.

The data model of the resulting knowledge graph builds on the AIDA Schema[7] (aida:), Schema.org (schema:), FOAF, OWL, CSO schema[8] (cso:), Microsoft Academic KG schema[9] (mag:), GRID schema[10] (grid:) and others. Specifi-

---

[7] The AIDA Schema - https://w3id.org/aida/ontology.

[8] The CSO Schema - https://w3id.org/cso/schema/cso.

[9] The MAKG Schema - https://makg.org/ontology.owl.

[10] The GRID ontology - http://www.grid.ac/ontology/.

cally, in the context of the AIDA Dashboard, we leverage five main entities defined in the AIDA Schema (`aida:paper`, `aida:author`, `aida:affiliation`, `aida:industrialSector`, and `aida:DBpediaCategory`) as well as seven additional entities reused from external ontologies (`mag:paper`, `mag:author`, `grid:affiliation`, `mag:Journal`, `mag:ConferenceSeries`, `mag:ConferenceInstance`, and `cso:Topic`). These entities are interconnected through 23 semantic relations, 10 defined in the AIDA schema and 13 reused from external ontologies (e.g., `cito:cites`, `datacite:doi`, `dc:title`, `prism:publicationDate`, `schema:memberOf`). In particular, the following 4 relations (out of the 10 defined in the schema) characterise articles according to the relevant information from DBpedia, GRID, INDUSO, and CSO:

- `aida:hasDBpediaCategory`, indicating the industrial sectors (DBpediaCategory) obtained from several DBpedia fields, such as `About:Property` and `About:Industry`;
- `aida:hasGridType` showing the type of an affiliation according to the GRID classification (e.g., education, company, government, non-profit);
- `aida:hasIndustrialSector`, indicating the INDUSO industrials sector of an affiliation;
- `aida:hasTopic`, indicating the CSO topics identified in a paper.

A more comprehensive description of the AIDA Schema is available at http://w3id.org/aida/#aidaschema. The AIDA knowledge graph is serialised in RDF and can be downloaded from https://w3id.org/aida/downloads. It can also be queried via a SPARQL endpoint at https://w3id.org/aida/sparql.

2.2   Generation of Analytics

The second component of the AIDA Engine takes in input the AIDA KG and produces the analytics related to journals and conferences. We pre-computed all analytics to improve scalability and response time. The analytics are computed in three phases: i) we retrieve all information about venues and produce a very comprehensive set of metrics about them and related entities (e.g., topics, authors, organisations); ii) we classify venues according to their main research fields, using the Focus Areas Taxonomy; iii) we produce the venue rankings in different fields according to both our metrics and a set of external ratings, such as SJR and CORE.

Metrics Computation. We first get from AIDA KG the journals and conferences which counted at least 50 publications in the last 5 years. The current version includes 3,263 journals and 2,003 conferences. We then compute a set of performance metrics based on citations, such as h-index, h5-index, and impact factor (on the previous 2 years). Next, we use the `schema:creator`, `aida:hasAffiliation`, `grid:countryName`, and `aida:hasTopic` relationships to select the top 100 authors, organisations, countries, and main topics in terms of publications and citations. These are computed both as totals (e.g., all years, last 5 years, last 10 years) and as distributions over time. For authors and organisations, we also compute their h-index and h5-index considering all their publications in the knowledge graph. In addition to the main topics, we also identify the top 100 *fingerprint topics*, which are ranked according to the difference between the fraction of relevant publications in the venue and the average distribution in the whole Computer Science. This metric usually identifies the topics that are most significant for the underlying venue, also according to the user assessment [4]. Finally, we compute the number of publications and citations received from the research papers written by academia, industry, and collaborations, and the distribution of the industrial sectors at the venue.

Venue Classification. It is crucial to categorise journals and conferences with their research fields, in order to contextualise performance metrics and comparisons with other venues. Indeed, comparing the h-index or impact factor of a journal in the area of *Neural Networks* with one in *Formal Logic* would neither be fair nor informative. To this end, we created the *Focus Areas Taxonomy*[11] containing 124 broad areas organised into 4 levels. In contrast, the taxonomy used by Google Scholar Metrics for characterising venues includes only 26 categories relevant to Computer Science.

The Focus Areas Taxonomy has been created following both bottom-up and top-down strategies. We first selected 200 research areas from CSO that appeared as sub-string in a venue name and were also in the top 10 fingerprint topics for at least 10 venues. We then included all the super-topics of the first set (which are 392), resulting in a total of 592 candidate topics. We then associated them with various metrics linked with their prevalence in the 5.2K venues in our system. These included the frequency of appearance in journal or conference titles and the number of journals and conferences in which it appears among the top 10 topics. Finally, we arranged all the topics within a taxonomy following the same structure of CSO. We then asked three senior researchers in Computer Science to revise the taxonomy by 1) selecting the most significant topics on the basis of the metrics and their expertise, and 2) rearranging their position in the taxonomy if needed. We plan to keep updating this knowledge base according to feedback from the editors and the community.

In order to classify venues with the fields of the Focus Areas Taxonomy, we first check if the venue mentions a focus area in the name and in that case we directly assign to this area. For instance, the *International Conference on Robotics and Automation (ICRA)* is automatically assigned to "Robotics". Otherwise, we identify the focus area with the highest coverage in the distribution of fingerprint topics and, among its descendants, we select the most specific area with at least 20% of publications in the venue.

Venue Ranking. The last step consists of pre-computing the rankings of the venues across specific fields. For each focus area, we generate a list of all relevant venues along with a set of metrics, such as h5-index, average h5-index of the

---

[11] Focus Areas Taxonomy is browsable here: https://w3id.org/aida/fat.

relevant organizations, and average number of papers in the last 5 years. We also include well-known external journal and conference ratings made available by various associations. For journals, we use the SCIMAGO Journal Rank (SJR), and the SCIMAGO Quartile[12]. For conferences, we use the ranks provided by liveSHINE[13], CORE[14], and GII-GRIN-SCIE (GGS)[15].

2.3   Sustainability Plan

We plan to keep maintaining and updating the dashboard in the following years. For this reason, we set up an automatic pipeline that will update the data every 6 months. In addition, we will keep developing the main functionalities, following the feedback of the community and the editors (see Sect. 4).

At the end of 2021 Microsoft decommissioned the MAG project[16]. We thus decided to introduce two additional datasets within our integration pipeline: OpenAlex[17] and DBLP[18], as shown in Fig. 1. We included OpenAlex because it shares the same schema with MAG and it has a low cost of integration. However, since OpenAlex does not disambiguate conferences yet, we leveraged the conference representation of DBLP, by mapping papers across the two datasets. To achieve this, we designed a two-stage pipeline. We firstly mapped papers with the same DOI. Then, for the conferences that do not assign DOIs to articles (e.g., AAAI, NeurIPS), we mapped the papers across the two datasets by computing the string similarity of their titles. We worked in close collaboration with the SN Data Science team and we now have stable version with over 95% conference papers matched between DBLP and OpenAlex. Future versions of AIDA KG and the generated analytics will be based on these newly integrated datasets.

3   The AIDA Dashboard

The AIDA Dashboard is a web application that allows users to analyse and compare journals and conferences. In May 2022, we released a public version, independent from Springer Nature internal workflow, that is available at https:// w3id.org/aida/dashboard.

In the starting page, the users can search either for a venue or a research topic. If the user selects a conference or a journal, the system will retrieve the pre-computed analytics (as JSON file) and display them in the *venue panel*. If the user selects a research field (e.g., *Artificial Intelligence*) the application will

---

[12] SCIMAGO - https://www.scimagojr.com.

[13] liveSHINE - http://web.archive.org/web/20180728060959/http://liveshine.icomp.ufam.edu.l

[14] CORE - https://www.core.edu.au/team.

[15] GGS - https://scie.lcc.uma.es:8443/conferenceRating.jsf.

[16] Next Steps for Microsoft Academic - Expanding into New Horizons - https://www. microsoft.com/en-us/research/project/academic/articles/microsoft-academic-to-expand-horizons-with-community-driven-approach/.

[17] OpenAlex - https://openalex.org.

[18] DBLP - https://dblp.org.

return the *advanced search panel* that ranks all venues in the field according to a variety of metrics and allows the user to navigate and compare them. In the following, we describe these two interfaces in details.

Fig. 2. Overview page of Scientometrics (journal).

3.1   Venue Panel

The venue panel is structured in eight tabs: i) *Overview*, ii) *Citation Analysis*, iii) *Organizations*, iv) *Countries*, v) *Authors*, vi) *Topics*, vii) *Related Conferences/Journals*, and viii) *Industry*.

The users first lands on the **Overview** tab, shown in Fig. 2, which displays the most important metrics and a selection of charts, including: a) publications and citations across time, b) the top fingerprint topics in terms of publications and citations in the last 10 years, and c) the top 10 authors and organisations in the last 10 years.

The **Citation Analysis** tab reports how the venue is performing in terms of citation-based metrics, such as impact factor and average citations over time. Notably, it also shows the evolution of the venue's rank and percentile within its focus areas. This is a very intuitive measure of the prominence of the conference in the field over time, which is not available in alternative tools.

The **Organizations, Authors, Countries**, and **Topics** tabs allows users to rank and inspect these entities in terms of publications, citations, and average citations. All metrics can be displayed either as totals (all years, last 5 years, or last 10 years) or as time-based distributions.

The **Related Conferences/Journals** tab allows users to compare the venue of interest with other venues in the same fields according to their number of publications, citations, and average citations across time. This diachronic view is very useful for identifying emerging conferences or journals that may not be dominant yet, but exhibit a strong positive trend.

The **Industry** tab presents the distribution of publications and citations of academic institutions, industrial organisations, and collaborative efforts. This tab displays also the distribution of publications and citations of the different industrial sectors that published at the venue. For instance, the *NeurIPS* conference attracts publications prevalently from companies in the sectors: *"Technology"*, *"Computing and IT"*, *"Marketing"*, and *"Electronics"*.

3.2 Advanced Search

Figure 3 displays the Advanced Search panel, which allows users to browse and compare venues according to their fields. The user can browse the different fields using the selection menus and switch between journals and conferences with the button in the upper right. For instance, a user checking all the conferences in the field *"The Web"* can decide to focus further the analysis and only show the subset of venues within the sub-area *"Semantic Web"*. Clicking on a specific venue will bring the user to the relevant venue panel.

Fig. 3. The Advanced Search Panel displaying conferences in Artificial Intelligence ranked by h5-index.

Journals and conferences can be ranked according several metrics, including: a) average citations received in the last five years, b) average articles published in the last 5 years, c) h5-index, d) the average h5-index of the relevant organisations, and e) the average h5-index of the relevant authors. The last two metrics are not typically offered by alternative systems, but are very useful to identify emergent conferences that are attracting strong research groups but may not have yet received a good number of citations. Venues can be also ranked according to the set of external ratings discussed in Sect. 2.2.

4   User Study

We performed a user study on the AIDA Dashboard to assess the quality and usefulness of the analytics as well as the usability of the user interface. To this end, we organised individual sessions with 5 SN editors and 5 researchers in Computer Science. In each session, we first presented the AIDA Dashboard 2.0 for about 20 min. We then assigned to the users the task of analysing two venues and a focus area of their expertise in order to assess the quality of the resulting analytics. After the hands-on session the users filled a five-parts survey about their experience. The first part covered the users background and expertise. The second part was a standard System Usability Scale[19] (SUS) [7] questionnaire to gauge the usability of the AIDA dashboard. The third section asked the users to rate the quality of the analytics for the two venues and the focus area on a Likert scale in the [1–5] range. The fourth part included four open questions about strengths and weaknesses of the dashboard asked to all users and two further questions that were asked only to the editors. Finally, the fifth part asked to list at least three of the most useful functionalities.

The data produced during the user study are available online[20].

4.1   User Background

The five researchers in the user study are all senior researchers, with an average of 13.4 years of experience, and come from different institutions: i) University of Cagliari (IT), ii) Institute for Applied Informatics (DE), iii) FIZ Karlsruhe - Leibniz (DE), iv) University of Paris 13 (FR), and v) National Council of Research (IT). The five editors are at various career stages (1, 5, 13, 21, and 25 years of experience) and come from different departments within SN.

The areas of expertise of the 10 users include Artificial Intelligence, Natural Language Processing, Semantic Web, Robotics, Machine Learning, Multimedia Systems, and Theoretical Computer Science.

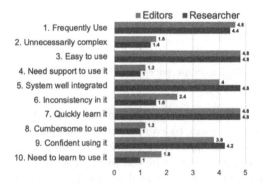
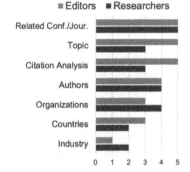

Fig. 4. The SUS Questionnaire results. (Color figure online)

Fig. 5. Number of votes received by each Section/Functionality.

---

[19] System Usability Scale (SUS) - https://www.usability.gov/how-to-and-tools/methods/system-usability-scale.html.

[20] AIDA Evaluations - https://w3id.org/aida/downloads#evaluation.

4.2 SUS Questionnaire

The SUS questionnaire provided excellent results obtaining a score of 88.5/100 considering all users. This corresponds to the 97% percentile rank in terms of usability (A+ grade) according to the SUS guidelines[21]. In general, editors were more severe than researchers, mostly because they consider the dashboard an important working tool and they where very motivated in suggesting further improvements. Indeed, editors scored an average 84.5 SUS score (96% percentile rank), while researchers yielded 92.5 (98%). This version of the dashboard (2.0) showed a better usability than the previous one, which achieved a SUS score of 87.5 in a user study involving 10 researchers [4].

Figure 4 reports the average score given by researchers (red bars) and editors (blue bars) to specific questions in the SUS questionnaire. Odd questions are positive (a higher score is better) while even ones are negative (a lower score is better). Overall, all the users found the system very easy to use (high values in question 3), they could easily learn the system (question 7), and they do not need support to use the system (question 4). The editors found some inconsistency in the integration of the functionalities (question 5). Finally, all users would like to frequently use the dashboard (question 1).

4.3 Quality Assessment

We asked the users to evaluate the quality of the analytics produced by the AIDA Dashboard for the two venues and the focus area according to a Likert scale. On average, editors scored 3.8 for venues and 4 for focus areas, whereas researchers 4.2 for both venues and focus areas. The range of fields and venues analysed by the users included Artificial Intelligence (AAAI, ICML, EANN, NC&L, Machine Learning), Natural Language Processing (EMNLP, ACL, EACL), Multimedia Systems (ACM Multimedia, Multimedia Tools & Applications), Robotics (ICRA, IROS), The Web (The Web Conference), Information Retrieval (SIGIR), Digital Library (TPDL), Semantic Web (ISWC), and Theoretical Computer Science (Information & Computation, iConference).

4.4 Open Questions

We summarise here the main feedback emerged from questions Q1–Q4 (all users) and questions Q5–Q6 (only editors).

Q1. What are the main strengths of AIDA Dashboard? Users were positively impressed by the easy and intuitive interface and the large amount of analytics. Other positive feedback regarded the granularity of the topic classification and the fact that the system addressed a real need in the community, i.e. analysing and comparing venues.

Q2. What are the main weaknesses of AIDA Dashboard? Users listed a range of issues that we plan to address in the future. One researcher suggested

---

[21] Interpreting a SUS score - https://measuringu.com/interpret-sus-score/.

that the major limitation is that the coverage is constrained to the Computer Science domain. Another one reported some disambiguation issues, in particular regarding authors with similar names. One more suggested that certain functionalities were hard to locate because the second level tabs were not particularly discernible. One editor mentioned the need of analysing venues in time ranges smaller than 5 years. Another one criticised the current interface for navigating the taxonomy based on selection menu. Finally, one editor did not find smooth the integration of journals and conferences and asked to be able to compare both of them in the same panel.

Q3. Can you think of any additional features to be included in AIDA Dashboard? Researchers mentioned: 1) adding more type of scholarly entities to analyse (e.g., organisations, researchers), 2) the ability to compare specific charts from different venues, 3) some additional metrics (e.g., number of papers that contributed to the citation count), 4) various minor GUI improvements, and 5) the ability to rank topics alphabetically. Editors mentioned: 1) the ability to directly compare conferences to journals; 2) a better integration with the CSO taxonomy; 3) adding information about the publishers of the venues, and 4) considering also books series.

Q4. How comprehensive/accurate do you consider the list of focus areas associated with the venues in AIDA Dashboard? All the researchers found the list of focus areas accurate and comprehensive. However, two of them suggest that they were sometimes too broad and would have liked the ability to browse venues also according to arbitrary research topics. Four editors found the list very accurate and comprehensive, while one of them identified some missing areas in their field of expertise and suggest edits for the Machine Learning branch (already implemented in the current version).

Q5. In which way the AIDA Dashboard support your work? Two editors reported that the system was very useful for supporting junior or new editors in analysing specific research fields. Two found it very helpful in identifying notable trends in venues topics and performing country-centric analysis. One found it very useful in identifying and comparing venues. Some editors also highlighted how the dashboard supports the detection of conferences and workshops that could produce special issues about specific emerging topics.

Q6. What competitive advantages would you say the AIDA Dashboard provides with respect to Scopus/Google Scholar (if any)? One editor pointed out that the AIDA Dashboard provides better visualisations as well as more granular analytics compared to Scopus and Google Scholar. One considered the auto-suggested search more helpful and simpler than the one in Scopus search. Finally, an editor found the AIDA Dashboard more powerful in analysing conferences and journals, preferring instead Google Scholar for analysing individual researchers or articles.

4.5   Best Functionalities

We asked the ten users to list at least three of the most useful sections of the AIDA Dashboard. Figure 5 reports the user preferences. The *Related Conferences/Journals* tab was the most appreciated section for both editors and researchers. This highlights how comparing venues is a critical task that was not well supported by previous solutions. Interestingly, researchers preferred the analytics about topics and citation analysis, while editors the analysis on authors and organisations.

5   Uptake and Impact

The partnership between The Open University and SN has produced a wide range of intelligent tools and services for automatically classifying articles [23] and proceeding books [21], recommending publications [26], evolving domain ontologies [18], and predicting the emergence of research topics [22]. The very first prototype of the AIDA Dashboard was introduced at SN in 2020 and has since been used by their editors and analysts to assess venues in Computer Science. The aim was to inform editorial and marketing decisions regarding the 162 journals and the about 800 proceedings books produced each year. In particular, editors need to monitor the performance across time of journals and conferences within specific fields and take action for improving the coverage and quality of SN catalogue. They also need to scan the horizon to detect the emergence of new scientific communities and relevant venues. It is typically ideal to establish a solid presence in new fields as early as possible by starting relevant journals and publishing the proceedings of new conferences. The editors need also to gain an understanding of the key persons within specific communities that may be invited to editorial boards or to organise special issues. Finally, it is important to assess what industrial sectors are interested in specific community in order to support targeted marketing campaign and specific editorial products. These are very complex and time-consuming analyses that were performed by senior editors on the basis of their personal knowledge and standard metrics offered by commercial datasets, resulting into bottlenecks, delays, and high costs. A task such as comparing all the journals and conferences within a specific research areas (e.g., Cloud Computing), considering also the potential for growth, used to take days of work by editors and assistant editors.

The adoption of AIDA has drastically improved the situation and brought three major benefits. First, it halved the time needed for analysing venues and prepare relevant analytics. Second, it reduced the complexity of the task, allowing less experienced junior editors and editorial assistants to also perform these analysis, improving the distribution of the workload and freeing up the time of the senior editors and analysts. Overall, this resulted in an estimated 60% cost reduction. Finally, the dashboard had a positive effect on both the velocity and the quality of the decision making process, that can be now continuously supported by advanced large-scale analytics.

In preparation to the public release of the AIDA Dashboard, we also made it available to selected members of the research community. During this pilot, the AIDA Dashboard informed the decisions of members of the organiser committees of conferences (SEMANTICS, EKAW) and workshops (DL4KG, Text2KG, Sci-K). For instance, one of the chairs of SEMANTICS 2023 used the dashboard for gaining a deeper understanding of the conference trends in terms of topics, countries, and organisations, with the aim of supporting strategic decisions for the next edition.

6   Related Work

Within the scholarly domain, many knowledge graphs offer a good representation of research papers and their metadata, such as authors, affiliations, topics, and so on. Among them, we find AMiner [30], Microsoft Academic Graph (MAG) [28], PID Graph [8], the Research Graph [6], ScholarlyData [17], the OpenAIRE Research Graph [15], SciGraph[22] [11], OpenCitations [19], the Open Research Knowledge Graph (ORKG) [12], Nanopublications [9,29], and the AIDA Knowledge Graph [2].

Several bibliometric tools and search engines can be used to query information about journals and conferences. For instance, Microsoft Academic Search, now dismissed, offered several metrics relevant to scientific venues, including their citations, topics, related venues, authors, and institutions. However, it did not let users compare venues or examine how research topics evolved across time. AMiner[23] and Semantic Scholar [1] support users in exploring journals and conferences, but they report only the most prominent authors and papers. Scholia[24] [16] consists of a Web service that builds scholarly profiles for topics, people, organisations, and venues on top of the information available in Wikidata[25]. If a journal or conference are selected, Scholia reports some relevant information, such as the main articles ranked by their citations, the main topics, related authors, and organisations. One drawback of this tool is that the topics are associated to venues as a whole and cannot be used to evaluate their temporal evolution. The Scopus[26] web application is a widely used online platform that offers several analytics regarding both researchers and scientific papers. However, it does not aggregate information on conference series. Lens.org [13] is another web application that integrates data from MAG, Crossref[27], CORE [14], and PubMed[28]. It enables the analysis of several entities (e.g., authors, institutions, countries, journals, conferences, topics), but it is built on top of MAG and therefore shares the same limitations of Microsoft Academic Search. RelPath [10]

---

[22] SciGraph datasets - https://sn-scigraph.figshare.com.
[23] AMiner - https://www.aminer.org/.
[24] Scholia - https://scholia.toolforge.org.
[25] Wikidata - https://www.wikidata.org.
[26] Scopus.com - https://www.scopus.com/.
[27] Crossref - https://www.crossref.org/.
[28] PubMed - https://pubmed.ncbi.nlm.nih.gov/.

leverages the citation network to identify experts in a certain domain that can act as reviewers of a target paper. The rationale behind the approach is that if a given paper shares similar scientific elements with some of its references, then the authors of such references can be considered experts. The approach may be extended at journal and conference level to suggest who can act as a programme committee member or co-editor of a journal special issues. SciKGraph is another approach that leverages semantic technologies and natural language processing techniques to identify research fields from research papers [27]. Given a dataset of papers, it finds their main concepts and creates a knowledge graph based on their co-occurrence in papers. Concepts are then clustered to show how a scientific area is organised. Likewise, it is straightforward to apply the same approach to journals and conferences for identifying similar papers through their topical characterisation.

All the mentioned systems allow only a coarse-grained analysis of the involved actors (e.g., conferences, journals, authors, organisations, countries, topics). Furthermore, they do not take into account how much a venue attracts commercial organizations or specific industrial sectors. Therefore, the original idea when building the AIDA Dashboard was to integrate different knowledge graphs with the goal of enhancing the set of available analytics and performing more fine-grained analyses.

7   Conclusions

We have illustrated the second version of the AIDA Dashboard, a system developed within SN to support the analysis and comparison of journals and conferences according to several metrics. The AIDA Dashboard is built on top of the Academia/Industry Dynamics Knowledge Graph, a large knowledge graph containing over 1.5B triples obtained by merging data of 25M papers conferences from Microsoft Academic Graph, Dimensions, DBpedia and GRID. This version greatly improves the first prototype [4] by offering i) journals in addition to conferences, ii) an advanced search functionality to browse, compare, and rank journals and conferences, iii) the Focus Areas Taxonomy, a new taxonomy of research areas that we have produced to classify research venues, and iv) the integration of the dashboard with the SN Data Cloud Infrastructure. We have carried out a user evaluation involving 10 users of which 5 SN editors and 5 researchers, obtaining excellent results.

The AIDA Dashboard is now freely available online and the underneath data can be downloaded as well.

In future work, we plan to further enhance the AIDA Dashboard according to the feedback from editors and researchers. In particular, we are working in collaboration with the SN Data Science team on improving the intuitiveness of the interface and widening the coverage by expanding to other research fields, starting with Engineering. We also plan to include new types of entities for the user to inspect and compare, such as countries, researchers, organisations, and scientific communities.

Supplemental Material Availability: The AIDA KG 3.0, the AIDA Schema, the AIDA Venues dataset 2.0, INDUSO, the Focus Areas Taxonomy, and the evaluation data are available at https://w3id.org/aida.

References

1. Ammar, W., et al.: Construction of the literature graph in semantic scholar. In: Proceedings of the 2018 Conference of the North American Chapter of the Association for Computational Linguistics: Human Language Technologies, pp. 84–91. Association for Computational Linguistics (2018)
2. Angioni, S., Salatino, A., Osborne, F., Recupero, D.R., Motta, E.: AIDA: a knowledge graph about research dynamics in academia and industry. Quant. Sci. Stud. **2**(4), 1356–1398 (2022). https://doi.org/10.1162/qss_a_00162, https://doi.org/10.1162/qss_a_00162
3. Angioni, S., Salatino, A.A., Osborne, F., Recupero, D.R., Motta, E.: Integrating knowledge graphs for analysing academia and industry dynamics. In: Bellatreche, L., et al. (eds.) TPDL/ADBIS -2020. CCIS, vol. 1260, pp. 219–225. Springer, Cham (2020). https://doi.org/10.1007/978-3-030-55814-7_18
4. Angioni, S., Salatino, A.A., Osborne, F., Recupero, D.R., Motta, E.: The AIDA dashboard: a web application for assessing and comparing scientific conferences. IEEE Access **10**, 39471–39486 (2022). https://doi.org/10.1109/ACCESS.2022.3166256
5. Angioni, S., Salatino, A.A., Osborne, F., Recupero, D.R., Motta, E.: The AIDA dashboard: analysing conferences with semantic technologies. In: Taylor, K.L., Gonçalves, R.S., Lécué, F., Yan, J. (eds.) Proceedings of the ISWC 2020 Demos and Industry Tracks: From Novel Ideas to Industrial Practice Co-located with 19th International Semantic Web Conference (ISWC 2020), Globally Online, 1–6 November 2020 (UTC). CEUR Workshop Proceedings, vol. 2721, pp. 271–276. CEUR-WS.org (2020). https://ceur-ws.org/Vol-2721/paper570.pdf
6. Aryani, A., et al.: A research graph dataset for connecting research data repositories using RD-switchboard. Sci. Data **5**(1), 180099 (2018). https://doi.org/10.1038/sdata.2018.99
7. Brooke, J.: Sus: a 'quick and dirty' usability scale. Usabil. Eval. Ind. **189** (1996)
8. Fenner, M., Aryani, A.: Introducing the pID graph (2019). https://doi.org/10.5438/jwvf-8a66
9. Groth, P., Gibson, A., Velterop, J.: The anatomy of a nanopublication. Inf. Serv. Use **30**(1–2), 51–56 (2010)
10. Guilarte, O.F., Barbosa, S.D.J., Pesco, S.: RelPath: an interactive tool to visualize branches of studies and quantify the expertise of authors by citation paths. Scientometrics **126**(6), 4871–4897 (2021). https://doi.org/10.1007/s11192-021-03959-2
11. Iana, A., Jung, S., Naeser, P., Birukou, A., Hertling, S., Paulheim, H.: Building a conference recommender system based on SciGraph and WikiCFP. In: Acosta, M., Cudré-Mauroux, P., Maleshkova, M., Pellegrini, T., Sack, H., Sure-Vetter, Y. (eds.) SEMANTiCS 2019. LNCS, vol. 11702, pp. 117–123. Springer, Cham (2019). https://doi.org/10.1007/978-3-030-33220-4_9
12. Jaradeh, M.Y., et al.: Open research knowledge graph: next generation infrastructure for semantic scholarly knowledge. In: Proceedings of the 10th International Conference on Knowledge Capture, pp. 243–246 (2019)

13. Jefferson, O.A., Koellhofer, D., Warren, B., Jefferson, R.: The lens metarecord and lensid: an open identifier system for aggregated metadata and versioning of knowledge artefacts, November 2019. https://osf.io/preprints/lissa/t56yh

14. Knoth, P., Zdrahal, Z.: Core: three access levels to underpin open access. D-Lib Mag. **18**(11/12), 1–13 (2012)

15. Manghi, P., et al.: Openaire research graph dump (2020). https://doi.org/10.5281/zenodo.4279381

16. Nielsen, F.Å., Mietchen, D., Willighagen, E.: Scholia, Scientometrics and Wikidata. In: Blomqvist, E., Hose, K., Paulheim, H., Ławrynowicz, A., Ciravegna, F., Hartig, O. (eds.) ESWC 2017. LNCS, vol. 10577, pp. 237–259. Springer, Cham (2017). https://doi.org/10.1007/978-3-319-70407-4_36

17. Nuzzolese, A.G., Gentile, A.L., Presutti, V., Gangemi, A.: Conference linked data: the ScholarlyData project. In: Groth, P., et al. (eds.) ISWC 2016. LNCS, vol. 9982, pp. 150–158. Springer, Cham (2016). https://doi.org/10.1007/978-3-319-46547-0_16

18. Osborne, F., Motta, E.: Pragmatic ontology evolution: reconciling user requirements and application performance. In: Vrandečić, D., et al. (eds.) ISWC 2018. LNCS, vol. 11136, pp. 495–512. Springer, Cham (2018). https://doi.org/10.1007/978-3-030-00671-6_29

19. Peroni, S., Shotton, D.: OpenCitations, an infrastructure organization for open scholarship. Quant. Sci. Stud. **1**(1), 428–444 (2020). https://doi.org/10.1162/qss_a_00023

20. Salatino, A., Osborne, F., Motta, E.: CSO classifier 3.0: a scalable unsupervised method for classifying documents in terms of research topics. Int. J. Digit. Libr. **23**(1), 91–110 (2022)

21. Salatino, A.A., Osborne, F., Birukou, A., Motta, E.: Improving editorial workflow and metadata quality at Springer Nature. In: Ghidini, C., et al. (eds.) ISWC 2019. LNCS, vol. 11779, pp. 507–525. Springer, Cham (2019). https://doi.org/10.1007/978-3-030-30796-7_31

22. Salatino, A.A., Osborne, F., Motta, E.: Augur: forecasting the emergence of new research topics. In: Proceedings of the 18th ACM/IEEE on Joint Conference on Digital Libraries. JCDL 2018. ACM, New York (2018). https://doi.org/10.1145/3197026.3197052

23. Salatino, A.A., Osborne, F., Thanapalasingam, T., Motta, E.: The CSO classifier: ontology-driven detection of research topics in scholarly articles. In: Doucet, A., Isaac, A., Golub, K., Aalberg, T., Jatowt, A. (eds.) TPDL 2019. LNCS, vol. 11799, pp. 296–311. Springer, Cham (2019). https://doi.org/10.1007/978-3-030-30760-8_26

24. Salatino, A.A., Thanapalasingam, T., Mannocci, A., Birukou, A., Osborne, F., Motta, E.: The computer science ontology: a comprehensive automatically-generated taxonomy of research areas. Data Intell. 1–38 (2020). https://doi.org/10.1162/dint_a_00055

25. Salatino, A.A., Thanapalasingam, T., Mannocci, A., Osborne, F., Motta, E.: The computer science ontology: a large-scale taxonomy of research areas. In: Vrandečić, D., et al. (eds.) ISWC 2018. LNCS, vol. 11137, pp. 187–205. Springer, Cham (2018). https://doi.org/10.1007/978-3-030-00668-6_12

26. Thanapalasingam, T., Osborne, F., Birukou, A., Motta, E.: Ontology-based recommendation of editorial products. In: Vrandečić, D., et al. (eds.) ISWC 2018. LNCS, vol. 11137, pp. 341–358. Springer, Cham (2018). https://doi.org/10.1007/978-3-030-00668-6_21

27. Tosi, M.D.L., dos Reis, J.C.: Scikgraph: a knowledge graph approach to structure a scientific field. J. Informetrics **15**(1), 101109 (2021). https://doi.org/10.1016/j.joi.2020.101109,   https://www.sciencedirect.com/science/article/pii/S175115772030626X
28. Wang, K., Shen, Z., Huang, C., Wu, C.H., Dong, Y., Kanakia, A.: Microsoft academic graph: when experts are not enough. Quant. Sci. Stud. **1**(1), 396–413 (2020)
29. Wijkstra, M., Lek, T., Kuhn, T., Welbers, K., Steijaert, M.: Living literature reviews. arXiv preprint arXiv:2111.00824 (2021)
30. Zhang, Y., Zhang, F., Yao, P., Tang, J.: Name disambiguation in AMiner: clustering, maintenance, and human in the loop. In: Proceedings of the 24th ACM SIGKDD International Conference on Knowledge Discovery and Data Mining, pp. 1002–1011 (2018)

Semantic Knowledge Graphs for Distributed Data Spaces: The Public Procurement Pilot Experience

Cecile Guasch[1]📍, Giorgia Lodi[2(✉)]📍, and Sander Van Dooren[1]📍

[1] European Commission, DG DIGIT, Brussels, Belgium
{cecile.guasch,Sander.VAN-DOOREN}@ext.ec.europa.eu
[2] Institute of Cognitive Sciences and Technologies of the Italian National Research
Council (ISTC-CNR), Rome, Italy
giorgia.lodi@cnr.it

Abstract. This paper presents the experience gained in the context of a European pilot project funded by the ISA2 programme. It aims at constructing a semantic knowledge graph that establishes a distributed data space for public procurement. We describe the results obtained, the follow up actions and the main lessons learnt from the construction of the knowledge graph. This latter requires to support different data governance scenarios: some partners control, with their own tools, the building process of their portion of the knowledge graph. Other partners participate in the pilot by providing only their open CSV/XML/JSON datasets, in which case transformations are required. These are performed on the infrastructure made available by the European Big Data Test Infrastructure (BDTI). The paper introduces the design and implementation of the knowledge graph construction process within such a BDTI infrastructure. By instantiating an OWL ontology created for this purpose, we are able to provide a declarative description of the whole workflow required to transform input data into RDF output data, which form the knowledge graph. The declarative description is therefore used to provide instructions to a workflow engine we use (Apache Airflow) for knowledge graph construction purposes.

Keywords: Knowledge graph · Data space · Linked (Open) data · Data transformation

1 Introduction

The importance of Public Procurement in the economy of the EU is well documented. Over 250.000 public authorities in the EU spend around 14% of GDP,

Supported by (formerly) ISA2 programme. We thank all the European partners that contributed to this work: AGID, ANAC, Consip, IMPIC, DFO and DG DIGIT.

U. Sattler et al. (Eds.): ISWC 2022, LNCS 13489, pp. 753–769, 2022.
https://doi.org/10.1007/978-3-031-19433-7_43

around 2 trillion euros per year[1]. Therefore, it is important to make the best use of the data it generates. Traditionally, public procurement has been mainly document-based. However, with the increasing use of digital technologies and digital negotiation instruments, public procurement has faced a variety of new interoperability challenges. These are related to insufficient sharing and re-use of data, overall lack of quality for the available data, inability to match related data from numerous and heterogeneous databases and systems. To start facing some of these challenges, the Publications Office published an OWL ontology named ePO - eProcurement Ontology[2], aligned with the latest related EU directives and regulations. ePO describes the main objects of public procurement and their relationships.

In order to test and exploit this ontology, the European Commission has implemented a pilot project whose aim is to lay the foundations for the creation of a European public procurement data space. In this data space, a semantic knowledge graph, i.e., a knowledge graph constructed using semantic web standards such as RDF and OWL (henceforth referred to as 'KG'), is exploited for the integration of data between different public procurement actors. The KG consists of public procurement data modelled through the aforementioned ePO ontology.

In the light of this scenario, the main contributions of this paper are:

- a distributed architecture that exploits semantic web technologies for the EU public procurement data space, where different governance scenarios are possible;
- a novel declarative approach for creating and managing KGs. This approach consists of defining an OWL ontology we present, whose instances are declarative descriptions used by a workflow engine. The workflow engine orchestrates tasks based on these declarative descriptions, aiming at transforming input datasets into the desired representation. Overall, this contributes to the creation of the KG of the data space, reducing possible manual interventions and making it maintainable and sustainable over time;
- a workflow process that, using this OWL ontology, is able to orchestrate the tasks to be performed to produce RDF datasets, compliant with a reference domain ontology;
- an open data based approach for ETL - Extract Transform and Load, by which the catalogue of transformed federated datasets is built in, thus reducing the maintenance efforts and increasing overall consistency;
- a number of lesson learnt for future developments of the EU Public Procurement data space.

The rest of this paper is structured as follows. Section 2 presents an overview of related work. Section 3 describes the pilot experience and its configuration. Section 4 introduces the solution we designed and implemented for the realisation of the pilot. Section 5 discusses the main lesson learnt and Sect. 6 the uptake. Finally, Sect. 7 concludes the paper with future work.

---

[1] https://ec.europa.eu/growth/single-market/public-procurement_en.
[2] https://github.com/OP-TED/ePO.

2   Related Work

We present different works that we have analysed because they are similar to the overall work we propose. These are divided into: i) similar approaches in the use of semantic standards in the procurement domain; ii) similar works on the use of ontologies as declarative descriptions to govern workflow systems.

In the procurement domain, semantic technologies have been used in different projects. A recent one is The Buy for You Platform [24] that applies an approach that is similar to the one used in our pilot. It exploits KGs based on ontologies, proposing an infrastructure with rest APIs for easy access to data. The ontologies form a network and deal with two types of data: procurement-related data (e.g., contract, award, plan, tender) on one hand [25] and company data on the other hand (e.g., registered organisation, address, site). For the procurement-related data, it uses a data specification that is emerging in the contract management context named OCDS - Open Contracting Data Specification, entirely based on JSON and JSON-based rest APIs.

Other past attempts to model public procurement have been done with the LOTED2 [13], PPROC [21] and PublicContract[3] OWL ontologies; however, they seem focused on some specific elements of the procurement, only: LOTED2 on legal notices, PPROC and PublicContract on public contracts.

As for the use of ontologies for guiding the KG production, in [11], the authors pose a set of research challenges, also mentioning the use of *"declarative descriptions of workflows"* as a possible technique that is appearing, as we proposed in our pilot.

In [5], the authors introduce TITAN, a system that uses the BIGOWL ontology for describing workflows and entities that contain software components of the system. TITAN proposes a similar approach to ours, but more general. In contrast, we focus on describing specific activities on the creation of KGs in specific contexts, and for this we extend ontologies used in the public sector to document datasets in catalogues.

In [15] and [16], the LinkedPipes ETL tool is introduced and described. Its aim is to support the whole process of data publication, especially the lifting of internal data in relational databases or Excel, CSV, XML or JSON files to Linked Open Data, with a successive cataloguing activity. The data transformation pipelines are stored in the system as RDF but no specific OWL ontology is used to govern the pipeline, as in our case.

In [23], the authors provide a holistic approach and architecture to populate a commercial KG based on heterogeneous data sources. Although the approach is similar to ours, and enables the automation of the creation of the KG, the use of an OWL ontology that describes the workflow in a declarative way is not treated as in our case. The authors use the PROV-O ontology to keep track of the source information, but do not exploit it to provide the necessary instructions for a workflow system as we propose.

---

[3] https://w3id.org/italia/onto/PublicContract.

3 The Public Procurement Pilot

An attempt to get public procurement data at EU level has been done by establishing an European system named TED (Tender Electronic Daily) that mandates Member States to publish all the notices of their national tenders above the regulatory thresholds. While the latest reform of the regulation intends to get more and better public procurement data, it does not address some problems that were detected with the system [2]: i) fragmentation and complexity of procurement systems in Member States; ii) lack of compatibility between TED and Member State systems; iii) publication of mainly documents (notices) rather than data. This prevents the adoption of an effective data-driven approach to public procurement depriving the stakeholders of the possible savings and improvements that such a paradigm can bring, even in terms of transparency, corruption fight and governance of public procurement.

In 2020, Italy requested the ISA2 programme to develop, maintain and promote an infrastructure to gather, process, analyse and publish public procurement data based on the earlier cited ePO ontology. One key requirement is to work on reusable open source tools that can be implemented in the national (or regional) eProcurement infrastructures to carry out successive data analysis. In essence, the idea is to lay the foundations for creating a data ecosystem. Within it, public procurement data and data products can be seamlessly exchanged among stakeholders, allowing for their reuse to build advanced applications and services.

The pilot was launched after gathering strategic input from the Analytics subgroup of the expert group on eProcurement, who expressed the following guiding principles: i) to allow all data sources to be included in a reusable way, once they become relevant for supporting the policy objectives; ii) to make data timely accessible, traceable and comparable; iii) to reuse as much as possible data, data products and tools.

In the light of these considerations, the objectives of the pilot are: i) to explore the harmonisation of the public procurement data landscape thanks to the use of the ePO ontology built for such purpose; ii) to pilot a federated solution, paving the way towards a data space instead of a centralized data warehouse; iii) to explore the construction of quality processes and use of tools that involve the data owners and data providers at various levels: EU, national and local. To simulate the heterogeneity of the European public procurement landscape, the pilot selected several national data providers: ANAC the Italian National Anti-Corruption Authority collecting all Italian procurement data, IMPIC, the Portuguese public authority collecting all Portuguese procurement data, DFO the Norwegian Public and Financial Management Agency collecting all the Norwegian procurement data. In the Public Procurement data provisioning landscape, CONSIP, the Italian Central Purchasing Body, a primary data owner, is also involved to explore how the existing organisation of data provisioning mandated by law may be complemented by voluntary adhesion of data owners to the federated data space. The pilot also involves the Publications Office, owner of the earlier cited TED system and EU data provider. The Institute of

Cognitive Science and Technologies (ISTC) of the Italian National Council of Research (CNR) contributes in the pilot from a technological transfer perspective, supporting in the technical work related to the use of semantic technologies. Directorate General DIGIT of the EU Commission coordinates the pilot.

The heterogeneity and complexity to be dealt with in the construction of the resulting KG led the participants to automate the transformation processes, from the very beginning, in such a way as to reduce as much as possible any manual interventions.

The pilot aims at analysing the number of received tenders since 2017 until the latest available data, using contract award notice information. Therefore, in the KG, we did not instantiate all the ePO ontology (version 2.0.1) elements; rather, we mainly used the following classes: `Procedure`, `Lot`, `Technique`, `Purpose`, `StatisticalInformation`, `AwardDecision`, `ContractAwardNotice`, `Organisation`, `Role`.

4   Proposed Solution for the Pilot Implementation

As shown in Fig. 1, we designed a distributed architecture coherent with the pilot objectives and guiding principles. Multiple data sources are used, with different source data models, reflecting the diversity of the landscape. Two partners, Consip and Publications Office contribute with linked open datasets already in compliance with the ePO ontology, produced through their internal processes and infrastructures. The ISTC-CNR partner supported Consip in their KG construction processes, providing the required mapping rules from the original data to the ePO-based RDF target datasets. The rest of the partners from Italy, Portugal and Norway contribute with many open datasets available in a variety of data formats and structures (see Fig. 1). This requires data transformations that have been carried out using the European Big Data Test Infrastructure (BDTI) (see Sect. 4.1).

Within the BDTI, a transformation process is managed by a workflow management system whose tasks are governed by the instances of the OWL transformation ontology we developed for such a purpose (Fig. 1).

4.1   The Big Data Test Infrastructure

The Big Data Test Infrastructure (BDTI[4]) is a technical building block of the Digital Europe Programme of the European Commission that can be used, on a per-request basis, to support public administrations in their prototype analytic and Big Data solutions. Instead of setting up a testing environment for these solutions, the use of such an infrastructure allows public administrations to concentrate on the core business, insights and value they can obtain from their data.

---

[4] https://ec-europa.github.io/bdti-infrastructure/.

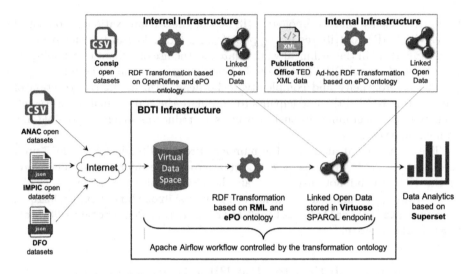

Fig. 1. Pilot architectural scenario

The infrastructure was assessed as particularly useful to support all those public sector partners in the pilot that do not participate with their own internal tools but only by providing open datasets already available in their data catalogues in different formats (e.g., JSON, CSV).

In particular, the BDTI was used to: (i) manually save datasets from ANAC, IMPIC and DFO in the BDTI cloud storage space; (ii) transform the content of the datasets into a KG according to the RDF standard and the ePO ontology earlier mentioned; (iii) publish the data in the SPARQL Virtuoso endpoint instance of the BDTI; and (iv) publish the metadata of transformed data in the SPARQL Virtuoso endpoint instance of the BDTI, thus forming a catalogue of federated transformed data sources.

4.2   Data Transformation Process in the BDTI

To carry out all these activities, we designed and implemented a process that, starting from datasets located in the cloud storage space of the BDTI, is capable of transforming the data into a KG by leveraging the RDF Mapping Language (RML) [12], using a set of its functions for data manipulation purposes (e.g., `array-join` for defining URIs[5], `controls_if` for verifying specific values). In the RML mapping rules, we also managed the creation of links (i.e., `owl:sameAs`) to other linked open datasets available in the Web of Data such as controlled

---

[5] We used the same URI schema for all those partners using the BDTI. The schema followed the '10 persistent rules for URIs' - https://joinup.ec.europa.eu/collection/semantic-interoperability-community-semic/document/10-rules-persistent-uris, where the domain part depends on the specific EU country.

vocabularies[6] published by the Publications Office and recommended in the ePO ontology. The RML mapping rules[7], expressed in R2RML [9] syntax, were saved in the cloud storage space of the BDTI and executed using the RML mapper[8] through instructions configured in a workflow management system.

In order to make this process manageable and sustainable over time, thus minimising any possible manual interventions, we designed an OWL ontology that describes all the activities and resources required by a workflow engine, used successively to orchestrate the stages of the building process. In essence, the RDF triples, instances of the OWL ontology we introduce in this paper, can be thought of as *declarative descriptions for a workflow system.* In the implementation of our pilot, we adopted Apache Airflow (see below) as workflow engine. We argue that one of the strengths of this approach is that the update of transformed datasets can be done reducing any manual interventions by querying the specific metadata of the input datasets (e.g., last modification date), while the monitoring of the construction of the KG is ensured by querying the transformation metadata. Finally, a further unforeseen result is that the declaration of transformations contributes to the creation of a catalogue of federated transformed data sources, ensuring by design their findability.

Transformation Ontology. The OWL ontology that controls the transformation process is illustrated in Fig. 2.

Ontology Modelling Approach. It is grounded on two foundational ontologies for metadata description; namely, DCAT-AP - European Application Profile for Data Catalogue Vocabulary [10], which extends the DCAT Web Recommendation [4] in order to describe datasets available in data catalogues, and PROV-O - Provenance Ontology [17], another Web Recommendation which allows one to represent all provenance information related to activities and entities. Our ontology imports PROV-O and extends it with a minimum set of classes and properties (the bottom level in Fig. 2) that represent the specific transformation activities and resources to be done and used in the KG construction process. Moreover, we extend DCAT-AP, based on DCAT version 2, by defining a data distribution concept used to support the core elements of the ontology (see below). In general, we favoured the approach of maintaining the control on our semantics and extend existing ontologies according to our requirements. In essence, we applied an indirect re-use of existing ontologies [22].

The resulting ontology is simple, with elements that can be clearly understood in contexts such as the public sector, as the use of DCAT-AP is becoming increasingly popular due to European and national requirements for federated data catalogues.

Competency Questions. The ontology has been developed using the methodology available in the literature called eXtreme Design [6,7] (e.g., definition of CQs,

---

[6] https://op.europa.eu/en/web/eu-vocabularies/authority-tables.

[7] https://git.fpfis.eu/public-datateam/eprocurement/-/tree/develop/rml-mappings.

[8] https://github.com/RMLio/rmlmapper-java.

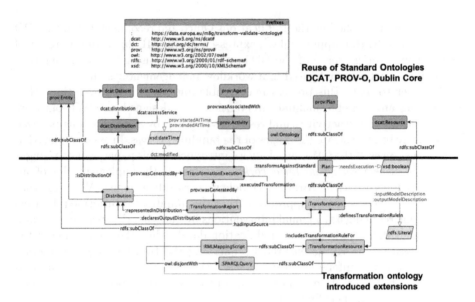

Fig. 2. Graffoo diagram of the transformation ontology

reuse of ontology design patterns). Therefore, we started from the elicitation of specific requirements translating them into so-called Competency Questions (CQs) that represent the de-facto ontological commitments. A non exhaustive list of CQs for the transformation process modelled in the ontology is provided in Table 1.

Ontology Description. A transformation (the class :Transformation) is a specific type of PROV-O plan (thus represented as subclass of prov:Plan), and it is defined as a planned set of operations to be executed by one or more agents; it aims at transforming a given input dataset distribution into an output dataset distribution.

To identify a dataset distribution, which is a representation of a dataset used to distribute it according to different serializations or formats, we extend the same concept as the one defined in DCAT so as to link it to the core elements of the proposed ontology. For instance, we added an inverse property from our :Distribution concept to the dcat:Dataset class and an OWL restriction that represents the connection of the distribution of a dataset to the execution of a transformation plan. This extension is represented by the class :Distribution (bottom part of Fig. 2); it inherits all the properties of the main dcat:Distribution (e.g., dct:modified, dcat:accessURL, etc.), including the relationship with the class dcat:DataService.

Table 1. Competency questions of the OWL ontology.

ID	Competency question
CQ1	Which is the input distribution to be used for the transformation?
CQ2	Which are the standards used in the transformation?
CQ3	Which is the transformation resource to be used in a transformation plan?
CQ4	What is the output dataset distribution generated by a transformation?
CQ5	Who executed the transformation activity?
CQ6	When the transformation resource of the transformation plan has been updated?
CQ7	Which are the output distributions generated by the execution of a transformation plan?

A transformation plan defines transformation rules within specific types of transformation resources (the class `:TransformationResource` intended as a subclass of `dcat:Resource`).

During our pilot, we identified two types of transformation resources; namely RML mapping rules files (the class `:RMLMappingScript` which is currently the de-facto standard for the construction of KGs, and SPARQL query. This latter class `:SPARQLQuery` allows us to represent alternative approaches with respect to the use of mapping languages like RML. Tools such as SPARQL Generate [18] or SPARQL Anything [8] can be captured using the `:SPARQLQuery` class where a SPARQL query is used to specify mapping rules. We believe that these transformation resources are sufficient to model well-established mechanisms for transforming different dataset formats (e.g., XML, JSON, CSV) into RDF, thus making the ontology applicable in domains other than our own, where RML mapping rules only are used.

A `:TransformationExecution` activity (a subclass of `prov:Activity`), executed by some Agent (`prov:Agent`), is defined. It generates a dataset distribution (`:Distribution`), executes (the `:executeTransformation` property) a transformation plan and produces a report (the class `:TransformationReport`). This activity is started and ended at some time (since `:TransformationExecution` is a subclass of `prov:Activity`, it inherits the properties `prov:startedAtTime` and `prov:endedAtTime` both typed literals `xsd:dateTime`). The produced report is a `prov:Entity` representing any return message that gives information on the success or otherwise of the transformation operation.

Transformation System. In order to execute the data transformation process at scheduled times and based on the activities and resources identified by the instances of the transformation OWL ontology, it was necessary to select a workflow/task runner engine. Apache Airflow [1] was selected as it is the most suitable solution for the purpose that meets the following criteria: i) Open source, as to lower the barriers for adoption of the paradigm; ii) scalable; iii) tasks can be defined in code, so that the instance data of the ontology can be used to define the tasks. Apache Airflow fits these criteria as it is Open source software that allows for the scheduled execution of workflow tasks on a cluster of workers. Airflow provides the framework for workflow definition and scheduling, but the actual task execution is delegated to a Celery cluster. The Celery cluster is a distributed job queue: jobs get added to the queue, and are executed asynchronously on the worker nodes. This allows one to scale the process, as additional worker nodes can be added.

Inside Airflow, workflows consist of tasks which can depend on one another. Each task can be executed by a cluster node, once all its dependencies have successfully been fulfilled; the upstream tasks have been executed successfully. This model allows tasks to be performed in parallel as much as possible, limited only by the tasks dependencies and the availability of cluster capacity to execute the task. Since tasks can be scheduled on any node in the Celery cluster, data cannot be stored on disk at the node. Instead, an external system should be used, such as a database, object store or network file system, which must be moved to and from the node when needed. Moreover, although not implemented in the pilot, the model allows transformations to depend on multiple input distributions, which in turn could be the result of another transformation. As transformations are executed once one of their input distributions has changed (this is detected by the date of last update, i.e., the `dct:modified` property of the class `:Distribution`), a more complex logic should be considered to determine the order of scheduling if several input distributions of the transformation have a high update frequency.

Workflow Definition. In our pilot, the (extended) catalogue is the only place where the state of the workflow process is persisted. This guarantees a clear separation between the business processes whose output is recorded in the catalogue and the operational side, in the form of code executed by the engine. The workflow representation in Apache Airflow (tasks and their dependencies) is created through the execution of a Python program, that takes the instance data of the ontology as its input. The following instance data in Listing 1.1 is an example of how a ETL transformation can be defined.

Listing 1.1. Turtle instance data for transformation

```
@prefix dcat: <http://www.w3.org/ns/dcat#> .
@prefix etl: <https://data.europa.eu/a4g/transform-validate-
    ontology#> .
@prefix eproc: <http://eprocurement-placeholder/> .
@prefix rdfs: <http://www.w3.org/2000/01/rdf-schema#> .

# Datasets
eproc:example_input_dataset a dcat:Dataset;
    dcat:distribution eproc:example_input_distribution .

eproc:example_transformed_dataset a dcat:Dataset;
    dcat:distribution eproc:example_output_dist .
```

```
# Distributions
eproc:example_input_distribution a etl:Distribution ;
    dcat:accessURL eproc:input.csv .

eproc:example_output_distribution a etl:Distribution .
    dcat:accessURL eproc:output.ttl .

# Transformation
eproc:example_transformation a etl:Transformation ;
    rdfs:label "Example data transformation" ;
    etl:hadInputSource eproc:example_input_distribution ;
    etl:declaresOutputDistribution eproc:
        example_output_distribution ;

    etl:definesTransformationRuleIn eproc:
        example_rml_transformation_script .

# Transformation Resource
eproc:example_rml_transformation_script a etl:RMLMappingScript ;
    rdfs:label "RML mapping rules used to transform the input
        distribution into the output distribution." ;
    etl:accessURL eproc:rml-transformation-rules.ttl ;
```

By using the instance data, it is possible to automatically generate the workflow in Apache Airflow. The basis of the process is that each instance of the :Transformation class in the catalogue (eproc:example_transformation in Listing 1.1) is turned into a workflow object.

Listing 1.2. Apache Airflow code for transformation data

```
g = Graph()
# Parse turtle file into in-memory graph
g.parse("catalogue.ttl", format='text/turtle')
# Use catalogue graph to create entity model
catalogue = EntityRepository(g)
transformations = catalogue.getTransformations()
workflow_creator = DagTransform()
for transformation in transformations:
    # Create workflow object from the transformation instance.
    workflow = workflow_creator.transformationToDag(
        transformation)
```

In its most basic setup, each workflow contains a single Transformation task, which performs the execution of the transformation script. Additional tasks can be defined, e.g. to load the transformed data into a target database. To access the data catalogue in a developer friendly way, and separate the ontology/data concerns from workflow's business logic, a rudimentary Object RDF Mapper (ORM)[9] is developed and used.

---

[9] ORM code on GitLab.

Workflow Execution. The tasks are planned by the Airflow scheduler, and executed by the Celery cluster. When the transformation task is executed, the :TransformationExecution class is instantiated. In Airflow, the equivalent of a :TransformationExecution is an Airflow DAG run. The main steps then can be summarised as follows.

– **Extract.** The file referenced by the dcat:accessUrl property of the input distribution, referenced through the :hadInputSource property of the ontology defined for the :Transformation class instance, gets downloaded to the Celery worker node. This file is the input data to the transformation process. Also, the :RMLMappingScript (in case of a RML transformation), also referenced from the :Transformation class instance, is downloaded to the node. In our pilot, both are stored in the AWS S3 objectstore. In the future, the system can be extended to support a wider variety of transformation systems. A plugin would subclass the :TransformationResource of the ontology and the Airflow code to support the transformation engine.
– **Transform.** After moving the downloaded :Distribution into the working directory of the Airflow runner, the transformations must be executed. In our pilot, this is done via the external executable process RMLMapper, passing it the file name of the input :Distribution and the RML mapping rules file(s) as parameters. The result of the transformation is stored in a temporary file on the Celery node.
– **Load.** The transformation result is written back to the dcat:accessUrl of the output distribution. In our pilot, this is the S3 object store. It is worth noting that this approach differs from a traditional ETL process, where the Load stage loads the data into the target database. In our case, the data merely gets stored as a file. If further representation of the data (for instance in a triplestore) is needed, an instance of the dcat:DataService class (see Fig. 2) must be added, linked to the output distribution. This will result in an additional workflow task to be added to the workflow to materialise the data into the database.

5   Lesson Learnt

From the pilot project experience we can draw a number of lessons learnt, useful for anyone, in different domains, when leveraging semantic technologies and KGs as means for the definition of a data space. These, related with each other, are summarised as follows.

RDF Declarative Approach to Data Transformation. The instantiation of our transformation ontology, as a declarative description of jobs to be executed by a workflow engine, allows us to make the process of building the KG sustainable and maintainable over time, as manual human interventions are greatly reduced. We argue that this approach is particularly effective in the scenarios we faced, where large numbers of data distributions consisting of even more than 100 data files for 4 years of procurement data for Italy, only, must be managed and transformed.

Lightweight Transformation Ontology. The benefits of extending DCAT-AP and PROV-O, well-known standards of the Semantic Web, to manage the transformation operations on the data are: i) helping in monitoring which data sources have been analysed and then transformed; ii) guaranteeing the discoverability of the transformed data sources results as the metadata of the output datasets is added to the output data catalogue at the time of the declaration of the transformation; iii) allowing for monitoring the transformation operations, thus understanding the status of the overall construction process; iv) allowing for traceability of the operations performed between the input data source and the output data source, discoverable through the data catalogue; v) allowing for automating the refresh of output datasets when input datasets have changed or when the transformation code has been revised.

Use of EU Commodities. Most of the pilot participants did not own infrastructures for managing KG. The use of commodities like the BDTI becomes crucial when supporting the data space establishment.

Fostering DCAT-AP in Europe. The use of DCAT-AP for datasets findability is increasing in Europe. However, this is not yet common practice in all EU countries. Due to the role of DCAT we described in this paper, promoting its adoption is crucial. In addition, adopting the solution we propose naturally contributes to increasing the reach of DCAT-AP.

Define a Common Language in the Data Space. In a data space, one key point is that actors 'speak the same language'. Data transformation towards a shared semantic layer, like the ePO ontology, has to happen as soon as possible in the data management process so as to build additional artefacts on a standardised and high quality set of datasets.

Define Streamlined ETL Processes. In a data space, another key point is that data is of good quality. Our generic approach ensures that the risks of degrading data quality through transformation are minimized. This is guaranteed thanks to the separation of concerns between the transformation scripts and automation of the process.

Issues When Working with Current Available Open Data. While working with existing open datasets seems desirable as a set of available resources that can be easily re-used, the pilot identified a drawback in this scenario: open data is often treated as a process apart from the main internal data management processes (processes on data that is not publicly available). This practice inevitably introduces delays between data changes in internal systems (e.g. a data warehouse) and the publication of data under the open data paradigm. In addition, it reduces the potential richness of the data as not all that available is publicly published. In essence, the mere use of these open sources may hinder easier and more timely data management than would be possible with a direct access to the data stored in internal systems. In our experience, some input open datasets required a first data manipulation for allowing RML processes to run smoothly. This was particularly the case with Portuguese JSON files: the lot identifiers were simply incremental numbers without including the relevant procedure context. Due to some limitations in navigating JSON files in RML, this scenario prevented us from constructing persistent URIs for the lots. Therefore, a manipulation of the data to include the identifiers of the parent procedure in the lot identifier was done in Python. Finally, when linking some datasets from Italy to TED open datasets, we discovered entity duplication issues in TED. This happened when the same entity was used in different phases of the procurement (at contract notice and contract award notice times). The Publications Office is carrying out a work to ensure entity deduplication. These issues did not occur for the datasets we produced within the BDTI.

6   Uptake

The pilot experience led to follow-up actions described below. Firstly, Consip decided to publish online for anyone its produced portion of KG. Therefore, they enriched their open data catalogue[10] with a specific section named "Linked Open Data"[11] where the results of the work carried out in the pilot can be queried and re-used.

Secondly, the proposed RDF declarative approach to data transformation is used in a European funded project named WHOW - Water Health Open Knowledge[12]. In WHOW, open datasets located in data catalogues and documented using DCAT-AP are to be transformed in linked open data and the use of such an approach allows the project to meet its objectives in a sustainable and maintainable manner [19].

Finally, the future Public Procurement Data Space (PPDS) that the European Commission is currently designing and implementing will leverage the main results and digital artefacts presented in this paper. In particular, the PPDS is considering the transformation ontology as a key asset to support the transformation process through the use of a workflow engine. The plan also foresees to extend this approach for automating data extraction from data catalogues in Europe, validating the data according to specific business rules. The plan is not yet publicly available for anyone; however, from a high level overview of the public procurement data strategy[13], the main principles here described can be found.

---

[10] https://dati.consip.it/.

[11] https://dati.consip.it/linked_opendata.

[12] https://whowproject.eu/.

[13] https://vkazprodwordpressstacc01.blob.core.windows.net/wordpress/2021/07/PP-Data-strategy.pdf.

7   Conclusions and Future Work

This paper shows that the construction of a European public procurement data space based on semantic web standards and technologies and reusable open software solutions is feasible and effective in ensuring interoperability. It focuses on a distributed architecture capable of dealing with different data governance scenarios, where RDF transformations are performed and orchestrated via instances of an OWL ontology that describes the tasks of a workflow system.

Future Work. There is currently an on-going work for officially assigning to the presented ontology an URI under the European Core Vocabularies namespace, according to the URI policies adopted by the EU institutions and bodies[14]. This will also enable content negotiation mechanisms for the proposed ontology. We are planning to implement the workflow that allows us to validate the transformation against specific procurement business rules. In this sense, we have already considered the use of the ontology to control the execution of different types of validation, through existing validation engines (e.g., the SHACL validator already provided in the BDTI[15]).

Moreover, we are planning to extend the transformation ontology in order to represent data quality metrics. These can be used for example to create a transformation and validation monitoring dashboard that developers can leverage in assessing the overall effectiveness of the KG construction process. The Data Quality Vocabulary [3] can be taken into account as an additional modelling part of the proposed transformation ontology.

Finally, further investigation can be required to understand how the workflow engine can be made more flexible through ontology-code plugins, following the approach of the function ontology [20]. A plugin would consist of a function definition and an implementation in code. For example an 'FTP Distribution' plugin would allow for transparent access of distributions accessible over FTP. A micro-kernel architecture would allow one to add plugins to the workflow engine in a modular way.

Supplemental Material Availability: The source code and RML mapping rules that have been produced for the knowledge graph production process in the BDTI can be found in the following GitLab space: https://git.fpfis.eu/public-datateam/eprocurement

The transformation ontology is open for the re-use by anyone and it is available for the download on the gitlab repository of the European pilot project[16]. Moreover, we setup a github repository[17] to let users navigate it via HTML[18] by means of tools such as Widoco [14].

---

[14] https://data.europa.eu/URI.html.

[15] https://www.itb.ec.europa.eu/shacl/any/upload.

[16] https://git.fpfis.eu/public-datateam/eprocurement/-/blob/develop/transform-validate-ontology.ttl.

[17] https://github.com/transformationvalidation/transformationontology.

[18] https://transformationvalidation.github.io/transformationontology/.

References

1. Apache Airflow (2022). https://airflow.apache.org/
2. Ackermann, R., Sanz, M., Sanz, A., Milicevic, V.: Gaps and errors in the ted database (2019). https://www.europarl.europa.eu/cmsdata/161426/CONT_Gaps
3. Alberton, R., Isaac, A.: Data on the Web Best Practices: Data Quality Vocabulary - W3C Working Group Note, December 2016. https://www.w3.org/TR/vocab-dqv/
4. Albertoni, R., Browning, D., Cox, S., Beltran, A.G., Perego, A., Winstanley, P.: Data Catalog Vocabulary (DCAT) - Version 2–W3C Recommendation https://www.w3.org/TR/vocab-dcat-2/ (February 2020)
5. Benítez-Hidalgo, A., et al.: TITAN: a knowledge-based platform for big data workflow management. Knowl.-Based Syst. **232**, 107489 (2021). https://doi.org/10.1016/j.knosys.2021.107489
6. Blomqvist, E., Hammar, K., Presutti, V.: Engineering ontologies with patterns - the eXtreme design methodology. In: Hitzler, P., Gangemi, A., Janowicz, K., Krisnadhi, A., Presutti, V. (eds.) Ontology Engineering with Ontology Design Patterns - Foundations and Applications, Studies on the Semantic Web, vol. 25. IOS Press (2016). https://doi.org/10.3233/978-1-61499-676-7-23
7. Blomqvist, E., Presutti, V., Daga, E., Gangemi, A.: Experimenting with eXtreme design. In: Cimiano, P., Pinto, H.S. (eds.) EKAW 2010. LNCS (LNAI), vol. 6317, pp. 120–134. Springer, Heidelberg (2010). https://doi.org/10.1007/978-3-642-16438-5_9
8. Daga, E., Asprino, L., Mulholland, P., Gangemi, A.: Facade-x: an opinionated approach to SPARQL anything. In: Alam, M., Groth, P., de Boer, V., Pellegrini, T., Pandit, H.J. (eds.) Volume 53: Further with Knowledge Graphs, vol. 53, pp. 58–73. IOS Press (2021). http://oro.open.ac.uk/78973/
9. Das, S., Sundara, S., Cyganiak, R.: R2RML: RDB to RDF Mapping Language - W3C Recommendation, September 2012. https://www.w3.org/TR/r2rml/
10. DIGIT: European Commission: Discover the new DCAT-AP release 2.0.1 - Joinup, June 2020. https://joinup.ec.europa.eu/collection/semantic-interoperability-community-semic/news/dcat-ap-release-201
11. Dimou, A., Chaves-Fraga, D.: Declarative description of knowledge graphs construction automation: status and challenges. In: To appear in Proceedings of Third International Workshop on Knowledge Graph Construction, KGCW 2022, Greece, May 2022
12. Dimou, A., Vander Sande, M., Colpaert, P., Verborgh, R., Mannens, E., Van de Walle, R.: RML: a generic language for integrated RDF mappings of heterogeneous data. In: Proceedings of the 7th Workshop on Linked Data on the Web, April 2014. http://events.linkeddata.org/ldow2014/papers/ldow2014_paper_01.pdf
13. Distinto, I., d'Aquin, M., Motta, E.: LOTED2: an ontology of European public procurement notices. Semant. Web **7**(3), 267–293 (2016)
14. Garijo, D.: WIDOCO: a wizard for documenting ontologies. In: d'Amato, C., et al. (eds.) ISWC 2017. LNCS, vol. 10588, pp. 94–102. Springer, Cham (2017). https://doi.org/10.1007/978-3-319-68204-4_9, http://dgarijo.com/papers/widoco-iswc2017.pdf
15. Klímek, J., Škoda, P.: Linkedpipes ETL in use: practical publication and consumption of linked data. In: Proceedings of the 19th International Conference on Information Integration and Web-based Applications and Services, pp. 441–445 (2017)

16. Klímek, J., Skoda, P.: Linkedpipes DCAT-AP viewer: a native DCAT-AP data catalog. In: International Semantic Web Conference (P&D/Industry/BlueSky) (2018)
17. Lebo, T., Sahoo, S., McGuinness, D.: PROV-O: The PROV Ontology - W3C Recommendation, April 2013. https://www.w3.org/TR/prov-o/
18. Lefrançois, M., Zimmermann, A., Bakerally, N.: A SPARQL extension for generating RDF from heterogeneous formats. In: Proceedings of Extended Semantic Web Conference (ESWC 2017), Portoroz, Slovenia, May 2017. http://www.maxime-lefrancois.info/docs/LefrancoisZimmermannBakerally-ESWC2017-Generate.pdf
19. Lippolis, A.S., et al.: Linked open data process design is finalised, June 2022. https://doi.org/10.5281/zenodo.6685819, https://doi.org/10.5281/zenodo.6685819, Deliverable n. 3.2 Activity title: Knowledge Graph Definition - Task 3.3 Linked Open Data production process design
20. Meester, B.D., Dimou, A., Verborgh, R., Mannens, E.: An ontology to semantically declare and describe functions. In: ESWC (2016)
21. Muñoz-Soro, J.F., Esteban, G., Corcho, O., Serón, F.: PPROC, an ontology for transparency in public procurement. Semant. Web **7**(3), 295–309 (2016)
22. Presutti, V., Lodi, G., Nuzzolese, A., Gangemi, A., Peroni, S., Asprino, L.: The role of ontology design patterns in linked data projects. In: Comyn-Wattiau, I., Tanaka, K., Song, I.-Y., Yamamoto, S., Saeki, M. (eds.) ER 2016. LNCS, vol. 9974, pp. 113–121. Springer, Cham (2016). https://doi.org/10.1007/978-3-319-46397-1_9
23. Simsek, U., Umbrich, J., Fensel, D.: Towards a knowledge graph lifecycle: a pipeline for the population of a commercial knowledge graph. In: Proceedings of Conference on Digital Curation Technologies (Qurator). CEUR-WS, Berlin (2020). http://ceur-ws.org/Vol-2535/paper10.pdf
24. Soylu, A., et al.: Theybuyforyou platform and knowledge graph: expanding horizons in public procurement with open linked data. Semant. Web **13** (2021). https://doi.org/10.3233/SW-210442
25. Soylu, A., et al.: Towards an ontology for public procurement based on the open contracting data standard. In: Pappas, I.O., Mikalef, P., Dwivedi, Y.K., Jaccheri, L., Krogstie, J., Mäntymäki, M. (eds.) I3E 2019. LNCS, vol. 11701, pp. 230–237. Springer, Cham (2019). https://doi.org/10.1007/978-3-030-29374-1_19

Ontology Reshaping for Knowledge Graph Construction: Applied on Bosch Welding Case

Dongzhuoran Zhou[1,2], Baifan Zhou[2(✉)], Zhuoxun Zheng[1,3], Ahmet Soylu[3],
Gong Cheng[4], Ernesto Jimenez-Ruiz[2,5], Egor V. Kostylev[2], and Evgeny Kharlamov[1,2]

[1] Bosch Center for Artificial Intelligence, Renningen, Germany
dongzhuoran.zhou@de.bosch.com
[2] Department of Informatics, Univeristy of Oslo, Oslo, Norway
baifanz@ifi.uio.no
[3] Department of Computer Science, Oslo Metropolitan University, Oslo, Norway
[4] State Key Laboratory for Novel Software Technology, Nanjing University,
Nanjing, China
[5] Department of Computer Science, City University of London, London, UK

Abstract. Automatic knowledge graph (KG) construction is widely used in
industry for data integration and access, and there are several approaches to
enable (semi-)automatic construction of knowledge graphs. One important approach is to map the raw data to a given knowledge graph schema, often a
domain ontology, and construct the entities and properties according to the ontology. However, the existing approaches to construct knowledge graphs are not
always efficient enough and the resulting knowledge graphs are not sufficiently
application-oriented and user-friendly. The challenge arises from the trade-off:
the domain ontology should be knowledge-oriented, to reflect the general domain
knowledge rather than data particularities; while a knowledge graph schema
should be data-oriented, to cover all data features. If the former is directly used as
the knowledge graph schema, this can cause issues like blank nodes created due
to classes unmapped to data and deep knowledge graph structures. To this end,
we propose a system for ontology reshaping, which generates knowledge graph
schemata that fully cover the data while also covers domain knowledge well. We
evaluated our approach extensively with a user study and three real manufacturing
datasets from Bosch against four baselines, showing promising results.

Keywords: Semantic data integration · Knowledge graph · Ontology
reshaping · Graph algorithm · Automatic knowledge graph construction

1 Introduction

Knowledge graphs (KG) allow to structure information in terms of nodes and
edges [17]. The nodes represent entities of interests. The edges that connect entities
represent relationships between them. The edges that connect entities to their data values, represent the data properties of the entities. In the context of Industry 4.0 [26] and

---

D. Zhou and B. Zhou—Contributed equally to this work as first authors.

U. Sattler et al. (Eds.): ISWC 2022, LNCS 13489, pp. 770–790, 2022.
https://doi.org/10.1007/978-3-031-19433-7_44

Internet of Things [20], knowledge graphs have been successfully used in a wide range of applications and industrial sectors [18,37,38,41,52,59].

Due to the complexity and variety of industrial data (the typical example is relational tables [54]), it is very desired to facilitate automation of knowledge graph construction [39]. A common approach on knowledge graph construction is to construct entities and properties by relying on a given knowledge graph schema, often a domain ontology (Fig. 1a). This approach matches the attributes names in raw data to entities and properties in knowledge graph, then organise them in the same pattern as the schema [9,22,28]. However, the existing approaches to construct knowledge graphs are not always efficient enough and the resulting knowledge graphs are not sufficiently application-oriented and user-friendly. The challenge arises from the trade-off between the knowledge-orientation and data-orientation: A classical domain ontology is a formal specification of shared conceptualisation of knowledge [14,40]. It should be *knowledge-oriented*, to reflect the experts knowledge on upper level concepts, specific domains, or applications, rather than data particularities of arbitrary datasets [27]; while a knowledge graph schema should be *data-oriented*, to cover all the features (columns in tables) and have limited number of blank nodes. If a knowledge-oriented domain ontology is directly used as the knowledge graph schema, this can cause a series of issues, e.g., the data integrated with the help of domain ontologies suffers from a high load of blank nodes in knowledge graphs that result from data integration, e.g., up to 90% of information in the knowledge graph are blank nodes [16].

Indeed, sparse knowledge graphs are hard to digest for end-users: browsing them is a bad experience, users will have to go through hordes of blank nodes. Then, blank nodes affect application development. The applications should adapt to the structure of the knowledge graph, e.g., by reflecting this structure in SPARQL queries, thus the queries will have to handle and skip many bank nodes. Then, the bigger a knowledge graph gets the mode difficult is to process or search in it. Thus, it is desired to reduce the number of spurious blank nodes and to make knowledge graphs more compact.

Considering an example in Fig. 1c-d, where classes and data properties in the domain ontology ($\mathcal{G}^{do}$) are mapped to tables and attributes in the relational schema (R). There exist many discrepancies between $\mathcal{G}^{do}$ and R. If $\mathcal{G}^{do}$ is directly used as the schema to construct knowledge graphs, a number of issues will arise: many classes in $\mathcal{G}^{do}$ that are not mapped to any tables or attributes in R will lead to blank nodes (or dummy nodes); the attribute DP2 will be connected to a dummy class C6, instead of C1, which it should be connected to, etc.

Past works like ontology modularisation, summarisation did not address the challenge, because they still use the domain ontology to construct knowledge graph. Our previous work [60] could convert the domain ontology to data-oriented ontologies as knowledge graph schemata, but did not provide interoperability between these knowledge graphs and also did not fully exploit the knowledge in the domain ontology. A better solution is to have data-oriented knowledge graph schemata while still preserve knowledge in the domain ontology.

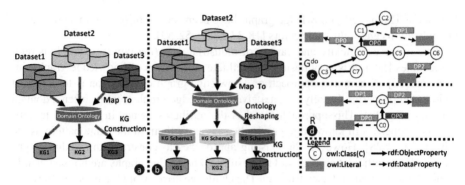

Fig. 1. (a) Ontology-based knowledge graph construction without ontology reshaping generates sparse knowledge graphs with many dummy nodes, which are generated based on classes in the knowledge graph schema that do not have correspondence in the raw data; (b) knowledge graph-construction with ontology reshaping that converts the general domain ontology to data-specific knowledge graph schemata, which makes the knowledge graph more user-friendly. (c) Domain ontology reflects the domain knowledge; (d) The knowledge graph schema needs to reflect raw relational data schema specificities and usability. orange and red circles: classes that can be mapped to attributes in the relational data schema; blue circles: classes that cannot be found in the relational data schema. (Color figure online)

To this end, we propose our knowledge graph construction system that relies on the OntoReshape⁺ algorithm to "reshape" a given domain ontology to data-oriented knowledge graph schemata (Fig. 1b), better incorporates knowledge in the domain ontology, and provide interoperability between the knowledge graphs based on the reshaped knowledge graph schemata. Our contributions are as follows:

- We introduce a use case of knowledge graph generation for welding quality monitoring which shows the challenge of sparse knowledge graphs constructed from raw data based on the domain ontology as the schema.
- We derive the four requirements: data coverage, knowledge coverage, user-friendliness and efficiency, from the use case perspective, and mathematically abstract them.
- We propose an algorithm, OntoReshape⁺, which can fully satisfy data coverage while better incorporates knowledge from the domain ontology, compared to the baselines.
- We implemented the algorithms in system of knowledge graph construction enhanced by ontology reshaping, which can automatically reshape the domain ontology to data-oriented ontologies that serve as knowledge graph schemata, and construct the knowledge graph without dummy nodes.
- We evaluated our approach extensively with a user study and three real manufacturing dataset from Bosch against four benchmarks, showing promising results.

This paper is organised as follows. Section 2 introduces Bosch manufacturing welding use case. Section 3 introduces some preliminary knowledge. Section 4 presents our method. Section 5 evaluates the method. Section 6 discusses related work. Section 7 concludes the paper.

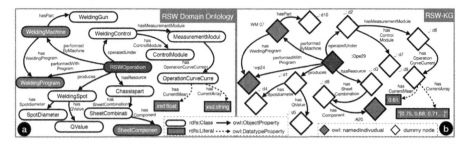

Fig. 2. Schematic illustration of the (a) domain ontology (partial) and (b) an excerpt of knowledge graph constructed by directly using the domain ontology as the knowledge graph schema, which has many dummy nodes due to classes in (a) that are unmapped to the data.

2   The Bosch Welding Use Case

Resistance Spot Welding and Quality Monitoring. Resistance spot welding is a type of automated welding process that accounts for millions of car production globally. During the welding, the electrode presses the worksheets (car bodies) and passes a high current through the electrodes and the worksheets [53,55]. The material in the small area between the electrodes will melt due to the heat generated by electricity and then congeal after cooling down, forming a welding spot that connects the worksheets by controlling robot arm positioning [3,34]. Multiple quality indicators, e.g. the spot diameter, are monitored to ensure the welding quality. The quality monitoring of resistance spot welding is essential and involves large amounts of data collected from welding process.

Bosch Welding Data with High Variety. Bosch welding data come from multiple sources [44,57], e.g. welding production plants, welding laboratories, analytical or numerical simulation models in Bosch's research centres. Just taking the production data as example, whose sources are hundreds of Bosch plants worldwide and many Bosch's renowned customers [47]. These data are highly diversified because they are collected with various sensors settings, formats, databases, software versions, etc. that are tailored to individual customer needs and factory specifications [51,58,61].

Data Integration, Domain Ontology and Knowledge Graph. Due to the many discrepancies of data semantics and formats, data integration is essential for building user-friendly, sustainable and efficient industrial solutions [45,56]. Bosch adopts semantic data integration that relies on domain ontologies to transform various data into uniform data formats, one typical example of which is knowledge graph for it provides an efficient foundation for many applications. The welding domain ontology is usually generated by semantic experts or domain experts, and should reflect the general resistance welding knowledge across different scenarios of production, laboratory and simulation (Fig. 2). It is modelled in OWL 2 language and has a large number of axioms. One of such example has 1181 axioms that describe 210 classes, 203 object properties, and 191 datatype properties. In contrast, the various welding datasets may have a much smaller scope. For example, one production dataset only contains data generated by the welding control of a particular welding setting or a specific software version, and miss large data that are measured in other settings, software versions, or in laboratory or simulation. On the other hand, laboratory and simulation data enjoy the flexibility of sensor installation that would be otherwise extremely costly to realise in the real production. Traditional approaches that use a common domain ontology as the knowledge graph schema for integrating various data will cause a series of issues, discussed in next section.

```
SELECT ?ca                                    SELECT ?ca
WHERE {                                       WHERE {
    ?op rdf:type rsw:RSWOperation                 ?op rdf:type  rsw:RSWOperation
    ?op rsw_kg:operatedUnder ?wc .                ?op rsw_kg:CurrentArray ?ca .
    ?wc rsw_kg:hasMeasurementModule ?mm .     }
    ?mm rsw_kg:hasOperationCurveCurent ?occ
    ?occ rsw_kg:CurrentArray ?ca .
}  a                                          b
```

Fig. 3. (a) An example query to retrieve the current sensor measurement array, over knowledge graph constructed based on the domain ontology. (b) The query that retrieves the same results over knowledge graph constructed based on the reshaped ontology, which is much user-friendly than that in (a).

Cumbersome KGs and Long Queries due to KG Schema. The knowledge graphs integrated from various data sources with the same domain ontology as the knowledge graph schema enjoys the data interoperability, namely uniform data access across all datasets. However, it also has serious drawbacks. Considering the example knowledge graph (Fig. 5b) generated with the schema in Fig. 5a, where the black blocks with white background are dummy nodes, generated because classes in the domain ontology is not mapped to anything in the data. The number of such dummy nodes are very high, up to 63.6%. The dummy nodes cause the knowledge graph to be unnecessarily cumbersome, consuming much computational power in generation and storage resource in the database. In addition, they also lead to superfluously long queries (Fig. 3a) that need to traverse many dummy nodes during data accessing, which is neither technologically-friendly nor user-friendly. Moreover, our users also complain that some knowledge graphs based on domain ontologies have disconnected sub-graphs that cannot be reached with queries starting from the welding operation, which is the most important node in the knowledge graphs that they usually start in the queries. They prefer connected knowledge graphs schemata.

Requirements for the Ontology Reshaping System. Both from the system and user view, it is highly desired to simplify the knowledge graph schemata to avoid the dummy nodes while still cover all the data and reflect the domain knowledge, so that the knowledge graphs become much more efficient and queries become simpler (Fig. 3b). We thus derive the following requirements for the new knowledge graph schemata and for the algorithm and system that generates the knowledge graph schemata and facilitates knowledge graph construction:

- *R1 Data Coverage.* The knowledge graph schemata generated by system should still cover all the data, e.g. including table names and attribute names for relational tables.

- *R2 Knowledge Coverage.* The knowledge graph schemata should still possibly preserve the knowledge encoded in the domain ontology. It should be similar to the domain ontology, either judged by the users or with some metrics.
- *R3 User-friendliness.* The user-friendliness involves at least 3 aspects: R3.1, the knowledge graphs constructed based on the new knowledge graph schemata should possible have very few dummy nodes, ideally zero (we call this the *succinctness* of the knowledge graph schemata or the knowledge graph); R3.2, the knowledge graphs schemata should be connected, namely no disconnected sub-graphs, so that the users can reach all nodes relevant to when they write queries (connectivity); R3.3, users prefer simpler and shorter queries than long queries when they can retrieve the same information. Thus, the constructed knowledge graphs should possibly have shallower structure (simplicity). Apart from that, the system for generating knowledge graph schemata and constructing knowledge graphs should also be user-friendly. This is commonly known as system usability [19] in terms of human machine interaction. It is evaluated by effectiveness, user efficiency (note this is the efficiency of users using the system, different from the R4 system efficiency), and user satisfaction of the system.
- *R4 System Efficiency.* The system efficiency measures two aspects: time efficiency, namely the overall time for generating the knowledge graph schemata and constructing the knowledge graphs, and the space efficiency, the storage space needed for the knowledge graphs to store the same information.

3   Preliminaries

Concepts and Problem Formulation. We formulate the problem of *Ontology Reshaping* as problem of computing from a given ontology and some context, a new ontology that *fully* satisfies the requirement R1 (Sect. 2) and achieves possibly good performance in terms of R2-R4. In particular, in this work we focus on specific type of contexts that can be formulated as follows:

$$\text{Ontology Reshaping} : (\mathcal{G}^{do}, R, M^{do}, U) \rightarrow \mathcal{G}^{ro}, M^{ro} \tag{1}$$

where $\mathcal{G}^{do}$ is a given domain ontology, R is a relational schema of relational tables, M^{do} is a mapping between R and $\mathcal{G}^{do}$, U is optional user information, and $\mathcal{G}^{ro}$ is the "reshaped" ontology, M^{ro} is a mapping between $\mathcal{G}^{ro}$ and $R-$ defined as follows:

An *Ontology* in the context of our work is a directed labelled multigraph $\mathcal{G}(\mathcal{N}, \mathcal{E})$, e.g., projected[1] from a set of OWL 2 axioms (e.g., the domain ontology $\mathcal{G}^{do}$ and reshaped ontology $\mathcal{G}^{ro}$) as follows: The classes are projected to class nodes $\mathcal{N}^{C}$, the datatypes to datatype nodes $\mathcal{N}^{D}$, the object properties to object property edges $\mathcal{E}^{O}$, and the datatype properties to datatype property edges $\mathcal{E}^{D}$.

A *Relational Schema* (R) is a finite set relational tables $R = \{\text{T}_1(\text{A}), ..., \text{T}_n(\text{A})\}$, where T_i is a table name while A is a finite set of attributes $\text{A} = \{a_1, ..., a_k\}$ represented by

---

[1] Ontology projections typically do not preserve all information captured by ontologies, but they are sufficient for our purpose of ontology reshaping.

their attribute names a_j. Among the attributes, there exist attributes called the primary key A_p (each table only one) that uniquely identifies the rows, (optionally) foreign key attributes A^f refer to the primary keys of other tables, and normal attributes A^n that contain normal data.

A *Mapping* (M) is a bidirectional function that maps the elements in R to elements in $\mathcal{G}$. The Raw-to-DO Mapping (raw data to domain ontology mapping) M^{do} maps the table names T in R to class nodes $\mathcal{N}^C$ in $\mathcal{G}^{do}$, normal attributes A^n to datatype property edges $\mathcal{E}^D$, and foreign keys A^f to object property edges $\mathcal{E}^O$, and vice versa. Similarly, the generated Raw-to-RO Mapping (raw data to reshaped ontology mapping) M^{ro} maps the T, A^n, A^f to $\mathcal{N}^C$, $\mathcal{E}^D$, $\mathcal{E}^O$ in $\mathcal{G}^{ro}$. In this work, we assume the mapping M^{do} is one-to-one mapping that maps all elements in R to elements in $\mathcal{G}^{do}$.[2] Similarly, the generated M^{ro} is also one-to-one mapping.

$$M : \{T \leftrightarrow \mathcal{N}^C, A^n \leftrightarrow \mathcal{E}^D, A^f \leftrightarrow \mathcal{E}^O \mid T, A^n, A^f \in R,\ \mathcal{N}^C, \mathcal{E}^D, \mathcal{E}^O \in \mathcal{G}\}.$$

The *User Information* (U) can be understood as (1) a mandatory label that labels a node in $\mathcal{G}^{do}$ as the most important node for the users, named as the *main node*, n_m; (2) an extra set of mappings that map some normal attributes A^n in R to class nodes $\mathcal{N}^C$ in $\mathcal{G}^{do}$: $U : \{A^n \leftrightarrow \mathcal{N}^C \mid A^n \in R, \mathcal{N}^C \in \mathcal{G}^{do}\}$.

The *Dummy Nodes* $\mathcal{N}^{dummy}$ are the nodes in the knowledge graph schema $\mathcal{G}$ (and the knowledge graph constructed based on $\mathcal{G}$) that cannot be mapped to any elements in R.

Mathematical Abstraction of Requirements. Following the requirements for the system in Sect. 2, we derive their mathematical abstraction. The R1-R3 are designed in a way that they range from 0 to 1. The closer to 1 they are, the better performance the ontology reshaping algorithm has

- *R1 Data Coverage*, this is measured by the number of elements in R mapped to $\mathcal{G}^{ro}$:
- *R2 Knowledge Coverage*, $\mathcal{G}^{ro}$ should preserve possible many nodes and edges in $\mathcal{G}^{do}$, measured by the number of elements in $\mathcal{G}^{do}$ kept in $\mathcal{G}^{ro}$. We use the formula to transform this metric to a range between$(0,1]$: $(\,|\{n\}| + |\{e\}|\,) / (\,|\mathcal{N}^{do}| + |\mathcal{E}^{do}|\,)$, where $\exists\, n^{do} \in \mathcal{N}^{do}, n \leftrightarrow n^{do}, \exists\, e^{do} \in \mathcal{E}^{do}, e \leftrightarrow e^{do}$, n,e$\in \mathcal{G}^{ro}$.
- *R3 User-friendliness*, calculated in 3 aspects:
  - *R3.1 Succinctness*, measured by the percentage of non-dummy nodes divided by the total number of nodes: $|\mathcal{N}^{dummy}|/|\mathcal{N}^{ro}|, \mathcal{N}^{dummy} \subset \mathcal{N}^{ro}$.
  - *R3.2 Connectivity*, determined by the number of required extra edges e needed to connect $\mathcal{G}^{do}$. We use the formula to transform this metric to a range between $(0,1]$: $1/(1 + \#e)$.
  - *R3.3 Simplicity*, determined by the graph diameter d of $\mathcal{G}^{ro}$. We use the formula to transform this metric to a range between $(0,1]$: $1/d$.
- *R4 Efficiency*. The time efficiency is measured by the total time of ontology reshaping and knowledge graph construction based on knowledge graph schema. The space efficiency is measured by the storage space needed for the constructed knowledge graph.

---

[2] Note it is not the same case for the other way around: there normally exist many nodes or edges in $\mathcal{G}^{do}$ that cannot be mapped to any elements in R.

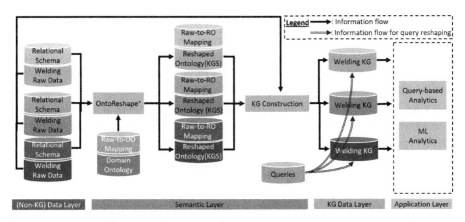

Fig. 4. An architectural overview of our KG solution. KG: knowledge graph. KGS: KG schema.

4   Our Approach

4.1   Architectural Overview

We now walk through the readers through our ontology reshaping system (Fig. 4) The system consists of four layers: *(Non-KG) Data Layer*, *Semantic Layer*, *KG Data Layer*, and *Application Layer*. From the very left, the *(Non-KG) Data Layer* contains the *Welding Raw Data*. The *Welding Raw Data* are in the form of relational tables and also have their corresponding *Relational Schemata*. The *Semantic Layer* contains several semantic artefacts and semantic modules. The *OntoReshape$^+$* module takes the *Domain Ontology* $\mathcal{G}^{do}$, the *Raw-to-DO Mapping* M^{do} (raw data to domain ontology), and the *Relational Schemata* R (in addition, the user information U) as inputs, and generates a series of *Reshaped Ontology* $\mathcal{G}^{ro}$ (*KG Schemata* at the same time) and their corresponding *Raw-to-RO Mappings* M^{ro}. These *KG Schemata* and *Raw-to-RO Mappings* are then used by the *KG Construction* module to construct the *Welding KGs* from the *Welding Raw Data*. And common *Queries* are selected by the users for welding quality monitoring. The *Welding KGs* in the *KG Data Layer* then can be used for applications like *Query-Based Analytics* and *ML Analytics* [59] in *Application Layer*.

4.2   Semantic Artefacts

Ontologies. The three different type of ontologies are domain ontology, relational schema graph and KG schema.

Domain Ontology $\mathcal{G}^{do}$. The domain ontology models the general knowledge of resistance welding spot manufacturing process (Fig. 2) and should cover all attributes in the common Bosch datasets in our consideration. The domain ontology has the RSWOperation as the most important class, where the RSWOperation is a welding operation that produces an atomic product. The RSWOperation takes sheet components with specified combination in, choose the specific welding machine and outputs the welding sheet combination with welding spots.

Reshaped Ontology $\mathcal{G}^{ro}$. The reshaped ontology is similar to domain ontologies. Our reshaped ontology are reshaped from the Domain Ontology $\mathcal{G}^{do}$ by Algorithm 1. An example is given by Fig. 5d. The reshaped ontologies are the simplified knowledge graph schemata, and keep the necessary parts to cover the specified datasets, which are then used as the schema of Welding knowledge graph.

Mapping. The system has two types of mappings: Raw-to-DO Mapping M^{do} (raw data to domain ontology) and the Raw-to-RO Mapping M^{ro} (raw data to reshaped ontology).

Raw-to-DO Mapping M^{do} is generated manually by users (welding experts). It should map all tables and attributes in the data to the nodes or edges in the domain ontology. Thus, each dataset has its own M^{do}.

Raw-to-RO Mapping M^{ro} is automatically generated by the ontology reshaping algorithm, accompanying the reshaped ontology $\mathcal{G}^{ro}$. It is needed for every $\mathcal{G}^{ro}$ since every $\mathcal{G}^{ro}$ will be used for data integration. M^{ro} reuses most of the M^{do} and should map all tables and attributes in the raw data to the nodes and edges in $\mathcal{G}^{ro}$.

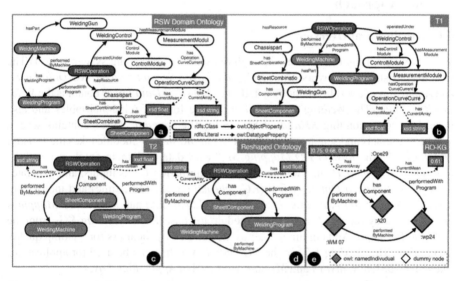

Fig. 5. (a) Schematic illustration of a small excerpt of the domain ontology $\mathcal{G}^{do}$. (b) Intermediate results in OntoReshape$^+$: Tree 1 $\mathcal{T}_1$ and (c) Tree 2 $\mathcal{T}_2$. (d) Reshaped ontology $\mathcal{G}^{ro}$. (e) knowledge graph constructed based on (d).

Queries. The queries in our system are SPARQL queries with the backbone as Basic Graph Pattern (BGP) query.

4.3   The Algorithm OntoReshape$^+$

Intuition. The intuition behind our algorithm OntoReshape$^+$ is to select subsets of nodes and edges from a given domain ontology $\mathcal{G}^{do}$, which can be mapped to a relational schema R or included in the user information U, and then connect the selected

---

Algorithm 1: Schema Reshaping

Input: $\mathcal{G}^{do}$, R, M^{ro}, U
Output: $\mathcal{G}^{ro}$

1   $\mathcal{T}_1$, $\mathcal{E}_1^{deleted}$ ← Graph2Tree($\mathcal{G}^{do}$, U)
2   $\mathcal{T}_2$, $\mathcal{E}_2^{deleted}$, M^{ro} ← TreeCollapse($\mathcal{T}_1$, R, M^{do}, U)
3   $\mathcal{G}^{ro}$ ← $\mathcal{T}_2 \cup \{e(n_t, n_h) \mid e(n_t, n_h) \in \mathcal{E}_1^{deleted} \cup \mathcal{E}_2^{deleted}, n_t \in \mathcal{T}_2, n_h \in \mathcal{T}_2\}$

---

subsets with possibly more edges in $\mathcal{G}^{do}$, thus generating the reshaped ontology $\mathcal{G}^{ro}$. More specifically, OntoReshape$^+$ does so in three steps:

- *Step 1*, it transforms $\mathcal{G}^{do}$ (Fig. 5.a) to a tree $\mathcal{T}_1$ (Fig. 5 b) by removing some edges, where the tree has the *main node* n_m given in U as the root;
- *Step 2*, it selects the subsets of nodes and edges of $\mathcal{T}_1$ that are mapped in R by M^{do} or pointed by the users, creating a $\mathcal{T}_2$ (Fig. 5 c);
- *Step 3*, some deleted edges in Step1 and Step 2 are added back to $\mathcal{T}_2$, where these edges have both their head and tail in $\mathcal{T}_2$, resulting $\mathcal{G}^{ro}$ (Fig. 5 d).

Step 1. Graph2Tree. With n_m as the root node, Step 1 (Algorithm 2) expands the tree $\mathcal{T}_1$ with nodes and edges selected from $\mathcal{G}^{do}$ layer by layer, in a way that there exists only one path between any node and n_m. We first clarify several concepts used in the step: $\mathcal{N}^{leaf}$ refer to the set of leaf nodes of $\mathcal{T}_1$, $\mathcal{N}^{ring}$ refers to the set of "ring nodes" (nodes in a outer layer of the leaf nodes) that are potential to be added to $\mathcal{T}_1$, $\mathcal{N}^{visited}$ is the set of visited nodes, and $\mathcal{E}_1^{deleted}$ is a set of the deleted edges. Then we introduce the procedure. First, Algorithm 2 reads the user information to mark the main node n_m, and initialise $\mathcal{T}_1$, $\mathcal{N}^{leaf}$, $\mathcal{N}^{visited}$ with n_m, and the set $\mathcal{E}_1^{deleted}$ with the empty set (Line 1). Next, if $\mathcal{N}^{leaf}$ is not empty, Algorithm 2 does the following steps: it initialises an empty set $\mathcal{N}^{ring}$ (Line3), then it enumerates each node n_i in the current $\mathcal{N}^{leaf}$ (Line 4) and create an empty set of ring nodes $\mathcal{N}_i^{ring}$ that belong to n_i. For each leaf node n_i, it enumerates the edges incident to the node n_i in $\mathcal{G}^{do}$, $e^u(n_i, n_j)^3$, but not in $\mathcal{E}_1^{deleted}$, and exams the other node n_j that this edge is connected to. If n_j is not visited (not in $\mathcal{N}^{visited}$), then the node n_j and the edge $e^u(n_i, n_j)$ are added to $\mathcal{T}_1$ (Line 8), n_j is added to $\mathcal{N}^{visited}$ and a new ring set $\mathcal{N}_i^{ring}$ that belongs to n_i (Line 9–10), and . If n_j is already visited, the edge $e^u(n_i, n_j)$ is added to $\mathcal{E}_1^{deleted}$ (Line 12). After all $e^u(n_i, n_j)$ are enumerated, all elements in $\mathcal{N}_i^{ring}$ are added to $\mathcal{N}^{ring}$ (Line 13). After all n_i are numerated, the $\mathcal{N}^{ring}$ becomes the new $\mathcal{N}^{leaf}$ (Line 14).

Step 3. Tree collapse. Step 3 (in Algorithm 3) selects nodes in $\mathcal{G}^{rs}$, by user or rule, and save them in $\mathcal{N}^{selected}$, then deletes the nodes not in $\mathcal{N}^{selected}$ from $\mathcal{T}_2$ which is copied by $\mathcal{T}_1$, at the same time keeps the connectivity of $\mathcal{T}_2$. It takes 4 inputs: the tree $\mathcal{T}_1$, the relational schema R, raw data to domain ontology mapping M^{do}, and user information U. The algorithm firstly inisialised the ring node set $\mathcal{N}^{ring}$ with main node n_m, $\mathcal{T}_2$ with $\mathcal{T}_1$, and deleted edge set $\mathcal{E}_2^{deleted}$ for$\mathcal{T}_2$ with empty set (Line 1). Then the algorithm selects the nodes in relational schema graph $\mathcal{G}^{rs}$, or with datatype property

---

[3] Here we use $e^u(n_i, n_j)$ to represent both the edge $e(n_i, n_j)$ and $e(n_i, n_j)$.

Algorithm 2: Graph2Tree

Input: $\mathcal{G}^{do}, U$

Output: $\mathcal{T}_1, \mathcal{E}_1^{deleted}$

1 **Initialisation:** $n_m \leftarrow ReadUserInfo(U)$; $\mathcal{T}_1, \mathcal{N}^{leaf}, \mathcal{N}^{visited} \leftarrow \{n_m\}$; $\mathcal{E}_1^{deleted} \leftarrow \{\}$

2 **while** $\mathcal{N}^{leaf} \neq \varnothing$ **do**

3      $\mathcal{N}^{ring} \leftarrow \{\}$

4   **foreach** $n_i \in \mathcal{N}^{leaf}$ **do**

5          $\mathcal{N}_i^{ring} \leftarrow \{\}$

6   **foreach** $e^u(n_i, n_j) \in \mathcal{G}^{do} \setminus \mathcal{E}_1^{deleted}, n_j \in \mathcal{G}^{do}$ **do**

7   **if** $n_j \notin \mathcal{N}^{visited}$ **then**

8                  $\mathcal{T}_1 := \mathcal{T}_1 \cup \{n_j, e^u(n_i, n_j)\}$

9                  $\mathcal{N}^{visited} := \mathcal{N}^{visited} \cup \{n_j\}$

10                  $\mathcal{N}_i^{ring} := \mathcal{N}_i^{ring} \cup \{n_j\}$

11   **else**

12                  $\mathcal{E}_1^{deleted} := \mathcal{E}_1^{deleted} \cup \{e^u(n_i, n_j)\}$

13          $\mathcal{N}^{ring} := \mathcal{N}^{ring} \cup \mathcal{N}_i^{ring}$

14      $\mathcal{N}^{leaf} \leftarrow \mathcal{N}^{ring}$

---

having"ID" or "Name", or by user choices. These nodes are added into $\mathcal{N}^{selected}$ (Line 2). If $\mathcal{N}^{ring}$ is not empty, the Algorithm 3 does the following steps: it inisialise an empty set $\mathcal{N}_{next}^{ring}$, then it enumerate each node n_i in the current $\mathcal{N}^{leaf}$ (Line 4). For each leaf node n_i, it enumerates the edges incident to the node n_i in $\mathcal{T}_1$, $e^u(n_i, n_j)$. If n_j is not selected (not in $\mathcal{N}^{selected}$), then the node n_j and edge $e^u(n_i, n_j)$ are deleted from $\mathcal{T}_2$ and $e^u(n_i, n_j)$ is added to $\mathcal{E}_2^{deleted}$. If the edge $e^u(n_j, n_k)$ is in $\mathcal{T}_1$, then $e^u(n_j, n_k)$ is deleted from $\mathcal{T}_2$, and a new edge $e^u(n_i, n_j)$ with same label of $e^u(n_j, n_k)$ is added to $\mathcal{T}_2$. The $e^u(n_j, n_k)$ is added to $\mathcal{N}^{selected}$ and the n_i is added to $\mathcal{N}_{next}^{ring}$. If n_j is in $\mathcal{N}^{selected}$, n_j is added to $\mathcal{N}_{next}^{ring}$. After all n_i are enumerated, The $\mathcal{N}^{ring}$ is added to $\mathcal{N}_{visited}$, the $\mathcal{N}_{next}^{ring}$ becomes the new $\mathcal{N}^{ring}$. After $\mathcal{N}^{ring}$ is empty, items in M^{do}, of which exist in $\mathcal{T}_2$, are added in M^{ro}.

Step 4. Add edges back. The algorithm adds the edge back into $\mathcal{T}_2$, which is in $\mathcal{E}_1^{deleted}$ or $\mathcal{E}_2^{deleted}$, and the endpoints are both in $\mathcal{T}_2$. The final tree is the reshaped ontology $\mathcal{G}^{ro}$.

4.4   Knowledge Graph Construction

The *KG Construction* module takes the reshaped ontology $\mathcal{G}^{ro}$, the *Raw-to-RO Mapping* M^{ro} and the *Welding Raw Data* as inputs, and generates a series corresponding *Welding KG*. We enumerate all class nodes in $\mathcal{G}^{ro}$. For each node and its datatype property edges, we find the primary keys for node and attributes for the edge respectively in the mapped tables and attributes in *Welding Raw Data* via M^{ro}, and create an entity for each key, and create datatype properties for each such edge. Next, we enumerate all object property edges in $\mathcal{G}^{ro}$, find the mapped foreign keys in the *Welding Raw Data* via M^{ro}, and create links (object properties) between the entity represented by the primary key and the entity represented by the foreign key. An small excerpt is shown in Fig. 5e, which shows the knowledge graphs constructed based on $\mathcal{G}^{ro}$ as the schema has zero dummy nodes.

5   Evaluation

This section includes a preliminary user study and a system evaluation that evaluate our system from the user view and system view, respectively.

5.1   Preliminary User Study

Participants. We deployed our system with tasks and questionnaires on a Bosch environment and received a number of results. The participants (Table 1) include Bosch welding experts, engineers, welding, and production, and additionally software engineers and data scientists. They need to input their age, occupation, education and skills for semantic web, query, and welding, ranging from 0 (no knowledge), to 5 (experts).

Algorithm 3: TreeCollapse

Input: $\mathcal{T}_1$, R, M^{do}, U
Output: $\mathcal{T}_2$, $\mathcal{E}_2^{deleted}$, M^{ro}

1 **Initialisation:** $\mathcal{N}^{ring} \leftarrow \{n_m\}$, $\mathcal{T}_2 \leftarrow \mathcal{T}_1$, $\mathcal{E}_2^{deleted} \leftarrow \{\}$
2 $\mathcal{N}^{selected} \leftarrow \text{GetNodes}(R, M^{do}) \cup \text{ReadUserInfo}(U) \cup \text{IdentifyID}(\mathcal{G}^{rs})$
3 **while** $\mathcal{N}^{ring} \neq \varnothing$ **do**
4      $\mathcal{N}_{next}^{ring} \leftarrow \{\}$
5   **foreach** $n_i \in \mathcal{N}^{ring}$ **do**
6   **foreach** $e^u(n_i, n_j) \in \mathcal{T}_1$ **do**
7   **if** $n_j \notin \mathcal{N}^{selected}$ **then**
8               $\mathcal{T}_2 := \mathcal{T}_2 \setminus \{n_j, e^u(n_i, n_j)\}$
9               $\mathcal{E}_2^{deleted} := \mathcal{E}_2^{deleted} \cup \{e^u(n_i, n_j)\}$
10   **if** $e^u(n_j, n_k) \in \mathcal{T}_1$ **then**
11                 $\mathcal{T}_2 := \mathcal{T}_2 \setminus \{e^u(n_j, n_k)\}$
12                 $\mathcal{T}_2 := \mathcal{T}_2 \cup \{e^u(n_i, n_k)\}$, where $e^u(n_i, n_k)$ adopts the label of $e^u(n_j, n_k)$
13                 $\mathcal{E}^{deleted} := \mathcal{E}^{deleted} \cup \{e^u(n_j, n_k)\}$
14                 $\mathcal{N}_{next}^{ring} := \mathcal{N}_{next}^{ring} \cup \{n_i\}$
15   **else**
16              $\mathcal{N}_{next}^{ring} := \mathcal{N}_{next}^{ring} \cup \{n_j\}$
17     $\mathcal{N}^{ring} \leftarrow \mathcal{N}_{next}^{ring}$
18 $M^{ro} \leftarrow MappingGeneration(T2, M^{do})$

Tasks. We selected 7 tasks (Table 2) that should reach a balance between testing the system and maintaining a controllable scope. The tasks include two types: Type 1, to input user information for ontology reshaping and Type 2, to select one query from four options (only one option is correct) to perform data inspection or diagnostics in

Table 1. User profiles in the user study

#	Age	Occupation	Education	Sem. Web	Query	Welding skills
P1	28	R&D Engineer	MSc	2	2	3
P2	29	R&D Engineer	MSc	2	1	3
P3	29	Welding Engineer	MSc	1	0	3
P4	41	Senior Welding Expert	MSc	0	0	5
P5	45	Welding Engineer	MSc	0	0	4
P6	25	Welding Engineer	BSc	0	0	4
P7	42	Software Engineer	BSc	3	2	2
P8	39	Production Engineer	BSc	0	0	3
P9	23	Data Scientist	MSc	2	2	2
P10	44	Data Scientist	PhD	2	1	2

Table 2. Tasks and type in the user study

#	Tasks	Type
T1	Select "RSWOperation" as the main node	Type 1
T2	Mark "SheetComponent1" as a table node	Type 1
T3	Create a new table node "SheetCombination"	Type 1
T4	Inspect operation curves on KG^{ro}	Type 2
T5	Inspect operation curves on KG^{do}	Type 2
T6	Detect abnormal welding operations KG^{ro}	Type 2
T7	Detect abnormal welding operations KG^{do}	Type 2

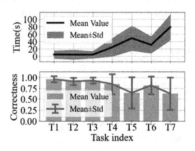

Fig. 6. Time/correctness for tasks

the knowledge graph (KG^{ro}) with the reshaped knowledge graph schema and in the knowledge graph (KG^{do}) with the domain ontology as the schema. Type 1 measure the usability of using our ontology reshaping system, and Type 2 compares users' perception of querying knowledge graphs with and without the ontology reshaping. Specifically, Type 1 has three tasks: T1, select the main node; T2, mark an attribute to table node in R; T3, create a new table node in R. Type 2 has four tasks: T4, select a query to inspect operation curves in KG^{ro}; T5, do the same on T4 in the KG^{do}; T6, select a query to detect abnormal welding operations (exceeding tolerance limit) in the KG^{ro}; T7, do the same on T6 in the KG^{do}.

Workflow of the User Study. For the user study, we first give the participants a short introduction with background knowledge, including basics of semantic technology like ontology, knowledge graph construction, and SPARQL query. Then, we explain them some relevant concepts of welding and the welding data (some users are not welding experts), present them visualisation of resistance welding domain ontology (Fig. 5). Then, we introduce them our tasks and how to use our GUI system. This introduction text is shown later constantly during the tasks. After that, the participants use the GUI system to perform the tasks. We record the time they use for each task, and the results of their actions stored in json. At the end, they answer a questionnaire (Table 3) with 12 questions that represent dimensions of their satisfaction about the system.

Results and Discussion. The results reflect the system usability (R3) [19] in efficiency (time used for tasks), effectiveness (correctness of user actions), and satisfaction. The recorded time (Fig. 6) show that the users need very limited time (average 28.0s) to perform the tasks, and thus the system is efficient. We compared the user results with a list of recommended results (we designed the tasks in a way so that the comparison is possible) and calculate the correctness. The results show (Fig. 6) that the correctness is always very high (average 82.1%) for the ontology reshaping tasks (Type 1) and for the query on the KG^{ro} (Type 2). The results also show that the correctness of selecting queries on KG^{ro} is higher than that on KG^{do} (T4>T5, T6>T7), which demonstrates the benefit of our ontology reshaping system.

The questionnaires (Table 3) subjectively evaluate the users' satisfaction about our system in four requirements (Sect. 2). From the aggregated scores, it can be seen that the users unanimously agree that our ontology reshaping system has good data coverage (R1); The knowledge coverage (R2) is scored 3.8, relatively good but has improvement room; The user-friendliness (R3) that covers connectivity, succinctness, simplicity and usability is also evaluated relatively high; The users are also quite satisfied with the system efficiency in terms of saving time and space (R4).

5.2 System Evaluation with Bosch Welding Dataset

We evaluated our system with OntoReshape$^+$ on 3 industrial datasets. In addition to baseline of using $\mathcal{G}^{do}$ as knowledge graph schema, we also compare with other 3 baselines.

Data Description. We now describe the datasets, including 3 industrial datasets D for knowledge graph construction and four inputs for ontology reshaping: 1 domain ontology $\mathcal{G}^{do}$, 3 relational schema R, 3 data to domain mappings M, and user information U.

Table 3. Questionnaires and scores for subjective evaluation. The scores range from 1 (disagree), 2 (fairly disagree), 3 (neutral), 4 (fairly agree), to 5 (agree). The column *Score* is aggregated by reversing the scores of negative questions (Q2, 4, 6, 8, 10, 12) and then computing the average (avg.) and standard deviation (std.) (`avg.±std.`)

#	Questions	Dimension	Score
Q1	I'm in general satisfied that KG^{ro} cover the data that I need.	Data coverage	4.31 ± 0.87
Q2	I found KG^{ro} miss some welding parameters that I need.		
Q3	I felt the knowledge represented by KG^{ro} is reasonable.	Knowledge coverage	4.63 ± 0.32
Q4	I thought KG^{ro} differs much from my understanding of welding.		
Q5	I like that in KG^{ro} all data can be reached from the main node.	User-friendliness	4.23 ± 0.71
Q6	I do not think that the queries over KG^{ro} become simpler.		
Q7	I found that it is great that KG^{ro} contains no dummy nodes.		
Q8	I hardly found KG^{ro} became simpler compared to KG^{do}.		
Q9	I found very confident using the system		
Q10	I needed to learn many things before I could use the system.		
Q11	I like that KG^{ro} saves storage space.	System efficiency	4.46 ± 0.33
Q12	I find it unnecessary the small amount of time saved by KG^{ro}.		

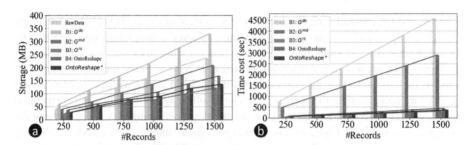

Fig. 7. Evaluation of space efficiency with storage taken by the constructed knowledge graph (a) and consumed time (b). The figure exemplifies the results obtained on D_1 since the results obtained on D_2 and D_3 are very similar.

Industrial Datasets D. Two production datasets D_1 and D_2 are collected from production lines in a factory of resistance spot welding in Germany. The third dataset D_3 is collected from a laboratory for welding research in Germany. After some processing they are transformed into relational tables. D_1 and D_2 contain 4 types of tables: they are the welding operation table, welding setting table, operation curve tables and reference curve tables. D_1 has 121 attributes and D_2 has 147 attributes. D_3 contains 5 types of tables: similar 4 types of tables as in D_1 and D_2 and an extra table of control parameter setting. D_3 has 160 attributes. For the evaluation purpose and a fair comparison, we select 1000 welding operations from each dataset.

Domain Ontology $\mathcal{G}^{rsw}$. The domain ontology models general knowledge of resistance spot welding. It is projected to a graph $\mathcal{G}^{rsw}$ with 210 class nodes and 191 datatype nodes, and 203 edges for object properties and 191 edges for datatype properties.

Relational Schema Rand Mappings M. The 3 relational schemata are information of table names and attribute names stored in csv. They are extracted from the three datasets D_1, D_2, and D_3. The 3 mappings map the table names and attribute names in the relational schemata to the domain ontology $\mathcal{G}^{rsw}$. These two help to generate the relational graphs $\mathcal{G}^{rs}$.

Table 4. The data coverage of all methods is 100%, and thus not displayed in the table. B: baseline.

Dataset	Evaluation metrics		Baseline methods/Ontology reshape methods				
			B1: $\mathcal{G}^{do}$	B2: $\mathcal{G}^{md}$	B3: $\mathcal{G}^{rs}$	B4: OntoRe-shape	OntoReshape$^+$
Production1 (D_1)	Knowledge coverage		1.00	0.36	0.21	0.42	0.74
	User-friendliness	Succinctness	0.38	0.46	1.00	1.00	1.00
		Connectivity	1.00	0.50	1.00	1.00	1.00
		Simplicity	0.13	0.17	0.33	0.33	0.33
Production2 (D_2)	Knowledge coverage		1.00	0.42	0.25	0.42	0.61
	User-friendliness	Succinctness	0.45	0.57	1.00	1.00	1.00
		Connectivity	1.00	0.50	1.00	1.00	1.00
		Simplicity	0.13	0.14	0.33	0.33	0.33
Lab data (D_3)	Knowledge coverage		1.00	0.45	0.27	0.42	0.81
	User-friendliness	Succinctness	0.51	0.59	1.00	1.00	1.00
		Connectivity	1.00	0.50	0.60	1.00	1.00
		Simplicity	0.13	0.17	0.33	0.33	0.33

Baselines. We compare the OntoReshape$^+$ algorithm with the traditional approach (Baseline 1, B1) that directly uses the domain ontology $\mathcal{G}^{do}$ as the schema for knowledge graph construction, in terms of the four requirements and 7 performance metrics (Sect. 3). In addition, we also compare with three other state-of-the-art baselines: Baseline 2 (B2) adopts an established ontology modularisation method [13,23] and uses the graph $\mathcal{G}^{md}$ projected from the modular ontology as the knowledge graph schema, which is computed with a signature of all table and attribute names in R; Baseline 3 (B3) uses the relational graph $\mathcal{G}^{rs}$ as the knowledge graph schema, which is trivially transformed from the relational schema R and the mapping M^{do}; Baseline 4 (B4) is a previous work of ontology reshaping [60].

Results and Discussion. We now discuss the performance of OntoReshape$^+$ in terms of the 4 requirements. We show the results evaluated in Table 4 and Fig. 7. We first look at D_1. It can be seen from Fig. 7a that our OntoReshape$^+$ outperforms the RawData, B1, B2 significantly in terms of the storage space (system efficiency R4), fairly better than B4, and slightly worse but comparable to B3. In terms of time efficiency (Fig. 7b), OntoReshape$^+$ significantly outperforms B1 and B2, while achieving comparable performance with respect to B3, B4.

All approaches have 100% data coverage (R1). Thus it is not displayed in the table. In terms of knowledge coverage (R2), it can be seem that OntoReshape$^+$ outperforms B2-B4 significantly, which means OntoReshape$^+$ keep the most knowledge of the domain ontology. It of course cannot beat B1 because B1 directly uses $\mathcal{G}^{do}$ as the knowledge graph schema, but B1 suffers substantially in terms of the later two metrics. The user-friendliness (R3) is decomposed to three metrics. OntoReshape$^+$ outperforms B1 and B2, and is equally good as B3 and B4 concerning succinctness. In respect to connectivity B3 is the worst and the others are equally good. As to simplicity, OntoReshape$^+$ outperforms B1, B2 and B4 and is equally good as B3. Thus, OntoReshape$^+$ either beats the baselines or is equally good as some. Regarding efficiency (R4), OntoReshape$^+$

saves time and space for knowledge graph generation when compared to B1, B2, and is comparable to B3 and B4. When looking at D_2 and D_3, it can be seem that the results are quite consistent across the datasets.

In summary, baselines B1, B2, B3 all are too focused either on knowledge coverage or data coverage. B4 and OntoReshape$^+$ are a balance between them, but OntoReshape$^+$ outperforms B4 in knowledge coverage and is comparable in other requirements.

6   Related Work

Knowledge graphs provide semantically structured information that can be interpreted by computing machines [49,62] and are widely used in industries [11,18,37,50]. The methods for knowledge graph construction have also been studied in many works [12,21,33], with focus on the rule-based approach [15], the combination of rule-based and similarity-based approach [29], the connection of data silos methods [18]. RDF lifting and lowering [2]. Commercial tools like OpenRefine [46] and OntoRefine [10] can transfer XML or tabular data to knowledge graphs or generate RML [1] and SPARQL [32]. Yet, they do not provide docking interface to our ML Mapping Reasoner/Annotator that reasons over domain ontologies, mappings and ML ontology.

The problem of transforming a bigger ontology to a smaller ontology of the same domain is often referred to as ontology modularisation [4–7,31] and ontology summarisation [35,36,48]. Most of them focus on the problem of selecting a subset of the ontology that is interesting for the users [30], but they still cannot avoid dummy entities. Works on ontology reengineering [42,43] also talked about reuse/adjustment of ontologies, they do not focus on the challenge of creating an ontology that reflect data specificities.

Previous work on ontology evolution [13] did not focus on the data coverage requirement. Our previous work on ontology reshaping [60] insufficiently address the knowledge coverage. Works on ontology bootstrapping [8,24,25] attempt to align ontologies with relational data schemata by automatically computing mappings between the ontologies and the data schemata, but the ontologies in these work only serve as a vocabulary for computing the mapping and new ontologies. Not much information from the original ontologies are retained.

In summary, past works insufficiently addressed the requirements R1-R4. Thus, we propose our work that can better address them overall.

7   Conclusion and Outlook

This work addresses the challenge of sparse knowledge graphs with many dummy nodes when domain ontologies that reflect general knowledge are directly used as the knowledge graph schemata. To this end, we proposed the ontology reshaping system and the algorithm OntoReshape$^+$. We evaluated the approach with a user study and a system evaluation in terms of four requirements, which shows promising results.

Our system is currently deployed in our Bosch evaluation environment, and we are considering to push it further into a more advanced and strict evaluation phase of production that runs in real-time. To show the benefits, we also plan to demonstrate our knowledge graph solution with more users and more use cases. In the future, we plan to study the compatibility between domain ontologies and knowledge graph schemata, i.e. to ensure that the semantics of the domain is respected in the smaller ontology.

Acknowledgements. The work was partially supported by the H2020 projects Dome 4.0 (Grant Agreement No. 953163), OntoCommons (Grant Agreement No. 958371), and DataCloud (Grant Agreement No. 101016835) and the SIRIUS Centre, Norwegian Research Council project number 237898.

References

1. Arenas-Guerrero, J., et al.: Knowledge graph construction with R2RML and RML: an ETL system-based overview (2021)
2. Bischof, S., Decker, S., Krennwallner, T., Lopes, N., Polleres, A.: Mapping between RDF and XML with XSPARQL. J. Data Semant. **1**(3), 147–185 (2012)
3. Celik, O., Zhou, D., Li, G., Becker, P., Neumann, G.: Specializing versatile skill libraries using local mixture of experts. In: Conference on Robot Learning, pp. 1423–1433. PMLR (2022)
4. Chen, J., Ludwig, M., Ma, Y., Walther, D.: Zooming in on ontologies: minimal modules and best excerpts. In: d'Amato, C., et al. (eds.) ISWC 2017. LNCS, vol. 10587, pp. 173–189. Springer, Cham (2017). https://doi.org/10.1007/978-3-319-68288-4_11
5. Chen, J., Ludwig, M., Ma, Y., Walther, D.: Computing minimal projection modules for $\mathcal{ELH}^r$-terminologies. In: Calimeri, F., Leone, N., Manna, M. (eds.) JELIA 2019. LNCS (LNAI), vol. 11468, pp. 355–370. Springer, Cham (2019). https://doi.org/10.1007/978-3-030-19570-0_23
6. Chen, J., Ludwig, M., Walther, D.: On computing minimal $\mathcal{EL}$-subsumption modules. In: Proceedings of WOMoCoE 2016. CEUR-WS.org (2016)
7. Chen, J., Ludwig, M., Walther, D.: Computing minimal subsumption modules of ontologies. In: Proceedings of GCAI 2018, pp. 41–53. EasyChair (2018)
8. Ehrig, M., Staab, S., Sure, Y.: Bootstrapping ontology alignment methods with APFEL. In: Gil, Y., Motta, E., Benjamins, V.R., Musen, M.A. (eds.) ISWC 2005. LNCS, vol. 3729, pp. 186–200. Springer, Heidelberg (2005). https://doi.org/10.1007/11574620_16
9. Fan, M., Zhou, Q., Chang, E., Zheng, F.: Transition-based knowledge graph embedding with relational mapping properties. In: Proceedings of the 28th Pacific Asia Conference on Language, Information And Computing, pp. 328–337 (2014)
10. Fiorelli, M., Stellato, A.: Lifting tabular data to RDF: a survey. Metadata Semant. Res. **1355**, 85 (2021)
11. Garofalo, M., Pellegrino, M.A., Altabba, A., Cochez, M.: Leveraging knowledge graph embedding techniques for industry 4.0 use cases. In: Cyber Defence in Industry 4.0 Systems and Related Logistics and IT Infrastructures, pp. 10–26. IOS Press (2018)
12. Goodwin, T., Harabagiu, S.M.: Automatic generation of a qualified medical knowledge graph and its usage for retrieving patient cohorts from electronic medical records. In: 2013 IEEE Seventh International Conference on Semantic Computing, pp. 363–370. IEEE (2013)
13. Grau, B.C., Horrocks, I., Kazakov, Y., Sattler, U.: Modular reuse of ontologies: theory and practice. J. Artif. Intell. Res. **31**, 273–318 (2008)
14. Guarino, N., Oberle, D., Staab, S.: What is an ontology? In: Staab, S., Studer, R. (eds.) Handbook on Ontologies. IHIS, pp. 1–17. Springer, Heidelberg (2009). https://doi.org/10.1007/978-3-540-92673-3_0

15. Heyvaert, P., De Meester, B., Dimou, A., Verborgh, R.: Rule-driven inconsistency resolution for knowledge graph generation rules. Semant. Web **10**(6), 1071–1086 (2019)
16. Hogan, A., Arenas, M., Mallea, A., Polleres, A.: Everything you always wanted to know about blank nodes. J. Web Semant. **27**, 42–69 (2014)
17. Hogan, A., et al.: Knowledge graphs. ACM Comput. Surv. (CSUR) **54**(4), 1–37 (2021)
18. Hubauer, T., Lamparter, S., Haase, P., Herzig, D.M.: Use cases of the industrial knowledge graph at siemens. In: International Semantic Web Conference (P&D/Industry/BlueSky) (2018)
19. ISO, C.: 9241–11.3. Part II: Guidance on specifying and measuring usability. ISO 9241 Ergonomic Requirements for Office Work With Visual Display Terminals (VDTs) (1993)
20. ITU: Recommendation ITU - T Y.2060: Overview of the Internet of Things. Technical report, International Telecommunication Union
21. Jain, N.: Domain-specific knowledge graph construction for semantic analysis. In: Harth, A., Presutti, V., Troncy, R., Acosta, M., Polleres, A., Fernández, J.D., Xavier Parreira, J., Hartig, O., Hose, K., Cochez, M. (eds.) ESWC 2020. LNCS, vol. 12124, pp. 250–260. Springer, Cham (2020). https://doi.org/10.1007/978-3-030-62327-2_40
22. Ji, G., He, S., Xu, L., Liu, K., Zhao, J.: Knowledge graph embedding via dynamic mapping matrix. In: Proceedings of the 53rd Annual Meeting of the Association for Computational Linguistics and the 7th International Joint Conference on Natural Language Processing (Volume 1: Long Papers), pp. 687–696 (2015)
23. Jiménez-Ruiz, E., Grau, B.C., Sattler, U., Schneider, T., Berlanga, R.: Safe and economic reuse of ontologies: a logic-based methodology and tool support. In: Bechhofer, S., Hauswirth, M., Hoffmann, J., Koubarakis, M. (eds.) ESWC 2008. LNCS, vol. 5021, pp. 185–199. Springer, Heidelberg (2008). https://doi.org/10.1007/978-3-540-68234-9_16
24. Jiménez-Ruiz, E., et al.: BootOX: bootstrapping OWL 2 ontologies and R2RML mappings from relational databases. In: International Semantic Web Conference (Posters & Demos) (2015)
25. Jiménez-Ruiz, E., et al.: BootOX: practical mapping of RDBs to OWL 2. In: Arenas, M., et al. (eds.) ISWC 2015. LNCS, vol. 9367, pp. 113–132. Springer, Cham (2015). https://doi.org/10.1007/978-3-319-25010-6_7
26. Kagermann, H.: Change through digitization—value creation in the age of industry 4.0. In: Albach, H., Meffert, H., Pinkwart, A., Reichwald, R. (eds.) Management of Permanent Change, pp. 23–45. Springer, Wiesbaden (2015). https://doi.org/10.1007/978-3-658-05014-6_2
27. Kaiya, H., Saeki, M.: Using domain ontology as domain knowledge for requirements elicitation. In: 14th IEEE International Requirements Engineering Conference (RE 2006), pp. 189–198. IEEE (2006)
28. Kartsaklis, D., Pilehvar, M.T., Collier, N.: Mapping text to knowledge graph entities using multi-sense LSTMs. arXiv preprint arXiv:1808.07724 (2018)
29. Kertkeidkachorn, N., Ichise, R.: An automatic knowledge graph creation framework from natural language text. IEICE Trans. Inf. Syst. **101**(1), 90–98 (2018)
30. Konev, B., Lutz, C., Walther, D., Wolter, F.: Model-theoretic inseparability and modularity of description logic ontologies. Artif. Intell. **203**, 66–103 (2013)
31. Koopmann, P., Chen, J.: Deductive module extraction for expressive description logics. In: Bessiere, C. (ed.) Proceedings of the Twenty-Ninth International Joint Conference on Artificial Intelligence, IJCAI-2020, pp. 1636–1643. International Joint Conferences on Artificial Intelligence Organization, July 2020
32. Lefrançois, M., Zimmermann, A., Bakerally, N.: A SPARQL extension for generating RDF from heterogeneous formats. In: Blomqvist, E., Maynard, D., Gangemi, A., Hoekstra, R., Hitzler, P., Hartig, O. (eds.) ESWC 2017. LNCS, vol. 10249, pp. 35–50. Springer, Cham (2017). https://doi.org/10.1007/978-3-319-58068-5_3

33. Liebig, T., Maisenbacher, A., Opitz, M., Seyler, J.R., Sudra, G., Wissmann, J.: Building a Knowledge Graph for Products and Solutions in the Automation Industry (2019)
34. Naab, C., Zheng, Z.: Application of the unscented Kalman filter in position estimation a case study on a robot for precise positioning. Robot. Auton. Syst. **147**, 103904 (2022)
35. Ozacar, T., Ozturk, O.: Karyon: a scalable and easy to integrate ontology summarisation framework. J. Inf. Sci. **47**(2), 255–268 (2021)
36. Pouriyeh, S., et al.: Ontology summarization: graph-based methods and beyond. Int. J. Semant. Comput. **13**(2), 259–283 (2019). https://doi.org/10.1142/S1793351X19300012
37. Ringsquandl, M., et al.: On event-driven knowledge graph completion in digital factories. In: 2017 IEEE International Conference on Big Data (Big Data), pp. 1676–1681. IEEE (2017)
38. Roman, D.: The euBusiness graph ontology: a lightweight ontology for harmonizing basic company information. Semant. Web **13**(1), 41–68 (2022)
39. Ryen, V., Soylu, A., Roman, D.: Building semantic knowledge graphs from (semi-)structured data: a review. Future Internet **14**(5), 129 (2022)
40. Smith, B.: Ontology. In: The furniture of the world, pp. 47–68. Brill (2012)
41. Soylu, A., et al.: TheyBuyForYou platform and knowledge graph: expanding horizons in public procurement with open linked data. Semant. Web **13**(2), 265–291 (2022)
42. Suárez-Figueroa, M.C., Gómez-Pérez, A., Fernández-López, M.: The NeOn methodology for ontology engineering. In: Suárez-Figueroa, M.C., Gómez-Pérez, A., Motta, E., Gangemi, A. (eds.) Ontology Engineering in a Networked World, pp. 9–34. Springer, Heidelberg (2012). https://doi.org/10.1007/978-3-642-24794-1_2
43. Suárez-Figueroa, M.C., Gómez-Pérez, A., Motta, E., Gangemi, A.: Introduction: ontology engineering in a networked world. In: Suárez-Figueroa, M.C., Gómez-Pérez, A., Motta, E., Gangemi, A. (eds.) Ontology Engineering in a Networked World, pp. 1–6. Springer, Heidelberg (2012). https://doi.org/10.1007/978-3-642-24794-1_1
44. Svetashova, Y., et al.: Ontology-enhanced machine learning: a Bosch use case of welding quality monitoring. In: ISWC (2020)
45. Svetashova, Y., Zhou, B., Schmid, S., Pychynski, T., Kharlamov, E.: SemML: reusable ML for condition monitoring in discrete manufacturing. In: ISWC (Demos/Industry), vol. 2721, pp. 213–218 (2020)
46. Verborgh, R., De Wilde, M.: Using OpenRefine. Packt Publishing Ltd. (2013)
47. Yahya, M., et al.: Towards generalized welding ontology in line with ISO and knowledge graph construction. In: Paul, G., et al. (eds.) The Semantic Web: ESWC 2022 Satellite Events. ESWC 2022. LNCS, vol. 13384, pp. 83–88. Springer, Cham (2022). https://doi.org/10.1007/978-3-031-11609-4_16
48. Zhang, X., Cheng, G., Qu, Y.: Ontology summarization based on RDF sentence graph. In: WWW, pp. 707–716. ACM (2007)
49. Zhao, Z., Han, S.K., So, I.M.: Architecture of knowledge graph construction techniques. Int. J. Pure Appl. Math. **118**(19), 1869–1883 (2018)
50. Zheng, P., Xia, L., Li, C., Li, X., Liu, B.: Towards self-x cognitive manufacturing network: an industrial knowledge graph-based multi-agent reinforcement learning approach. J. Manuf. Syst. **61**, 16–26 (2021)
51. Zheng, Z., et al.: Query-based industrial analytics over knowledge graphs with ontology reshaping. In: Paul, G. et al. (eds.) The Semantic Web: ESWC 2022 Satellite Events. ESWC 2022. LNCS, vol. 13384, pp. 123–128. Springer, Cham (2022). https://doi.org/10.1007/978-3-031-11609-4_23
52. Zheng, Z., et al.: Executable knowledge graph for machine learning: a Bosch case for welding monitoring. In: ISWC (2022)
53. Zhou, B.: Machine Learning Methods for Product Quality Monitoring in Electric Resistance Welding. Ph.D. thesis, Karlsruhe Institute of Technology, Germany (2021)

54. Zhou, B., Pychynski, T., Reischl, M., Kharlamov, E., Mikut, R.: Machine learning with domain knowledge for predictive quality monitoring in resistance spot welding. J. Intell. Manuf. **33**(4), 1139–1163 (2022)
55. Zhou, B., Svetashova, Y., Byeon, S., Pychynski, T., Mikut, R., Kharlamov, E.: Predicting quality of automated welding with machine learning and semantics: a Bosch case study. In: CIKM (2020)
56. Zhou, B., et al.: SemML: facilitating development of ML models for condition monitoring with semantics. J. Web Semant. **71**, 100664 (2021)
57. Zhou, B., Svetashova, Y., Pychynski, T., Kharlamov, E.: Semantic ML for manufacturing monitoring at Bosch. In: ISWC (Demos/Industry), vol. 2721, p. 398 (2020)
58. Zhou, B., et al.: The data value quest: a holistic semantic approach at Bosch. In: Paul, et al. (eds.) The Semantic Web: ESWC 2022 Satellite Events. ESWC 2022. LNCS, vol. 13384, pp. 287–290. Springer, Cham (2022). https://doi.org/10.1007/978-3-031-11609-4_42
59. Zhou, B., Zhou, D., Chen, J., Svetashova, Y., Cheng, G., Kharlamov, E.: Scaling usability of ML analytics with knowledge graphs: exemplified with a Bosch welding case. In: IJCKG (2021)
60. Zhou, D., Zhou, B., Chen, J., Cheng, G., Kostylev, E.V., Kharlamov, E.: Towards ontology reshaping for kg generation with user-in-the-loop: applied to Bosch welding. In: IJCKG (2021)
61. Zhou, D., et al.: Enhancing knowledge graph generation with ontology reshaping-Bosch case. In: Paul, et al. (eds.) The Semantic Web: ESWC 2022 Satellite Events. ESWC 2022. LNCS, vol. 13384, pp. 299–302. Springer, Cham (2022). https://doi.org/10.1007/978-3-031-11609-4_42
62. Zou, X.: A survey on application of knowledge graph. In: Journal of Physics: Conference Series, vol. 1487, p. 012016. IOP Publishing (2020)

Executable Knowledge Graphs for Machine Learning: A Bosch Case of Welding Monitoring

Zhuoxun Zheng[1,2], Baifan Zhou[3(✉)], Dongzhuoran Zhou[1,3], Xianda Zheng[4],
Gong Cheng[5], Ahmet Soylu[2], and Evgeny Kharlamov[1,3]

[1] Bosch Center for Artificial Intelligence, Renningen, Germany
zhuoxun.zheng@de.bosch.com
[2] Department of Computer Science, Oslo Metropolitan University, Oslo, Norway
[3] SIRIUS Centre, University of Oslo, Oslo, Norway
baifanz@ifi.uio.no
[4] State Key Laboratory for Novel Software Technology, Nanjing University,
Nanjing, China
[5] School of Computer Science and Engineering, Southeast University, Nanjing, China

Abstract. Data analysis including ML are essential to extract insights from production data in modern industries. However, industrial ML is affected by: the low transparency of ML towards non-ML experts; poor and non-unified descriptions of ML practices for reviewing or comprehension; ad hoc fashion of ML solutions tailored to specific applications, which affects their re-usability. To address these challenges, we propose the concept and a system of executable Knowledge Graph (KG). It relies on semantic technologies to formally encode ML knowledge and solutions in KGs, which can be translated to executable scripts in a reusable and modularised fashion. In addition, the executable KGs also serve as common language between ML experts and non-ML experts, and facilitate their communication. We evaluated our system extensively with an impactful industrial use case at Bosch, including a user study, workshops and scalability evaluation. The evaluation demonstrates the system offers a user-friendly way for even non-ML experts to discuss, customise, and reuse ML methods.

Keywords: Knowledge graph · Machine learning · Data analytics · Industrial application · Welding monitoring

1 Introduction

Data analysis technologies play an important role in modern manufacturing industries. Examples include production monitoring, fault detection, root cause analysis, as well as robot positioning [1–3]. Among these technologies, machine learning attracts substantial yet increasing attention, for its strong modelling capability without the need of explicit programming [4] and the voluminous data that become available due to the introduction of internet of things into manufacturing [5]. Take the welding monitoring at Bosch as an example (Fig. 1a), which is an impactful automated manufacturing process that accounts for the global production of millions of cars every year. In welding monitoring, massive heterogeneous data from many sources need to be analysed for

---

Z. Zheng and B. Zhou—Contributed equally to this work as first authors.

ⓒ The Author(s), under exclusive license to Springer Nature Switzerland AG 2022
U. Sattler et al. (Eds.): ISWC 2022, LNCS 13489, pp. 791–809, 2022.
https://doi.org/10.1007/978-3-031-19433-7_45

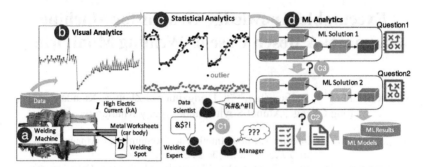

Fig. 1. Three of the activities of machine learning practice for (a) welding quality monitoring: visual analytics (b), statistical analytics (c), machine learning analytics (d). It faces three challenges: (C1) transparency of machine learning; (C2) standardised description; (C3) reusability.

various applications to solve different questions, e.g., to estimate or predict numerical quality indicators that are essential for ensuring high quality car production. Traditional quality monitoring approaches often require tearing the welded car bodies apart in random samples and measuring the diameter of the welded parts connection point, which is extremely costly. In contrast, data-driven methods like machine learning will help reduce the waste and contribute to more economical manufacturing industry [6]. Three important activities of machine learning practice at Bosch (Fig. 1b–d) include visual, statistical analytics (these two are often known as exploratory data analysis and seen as important preceding steps for machine learning analytics [7]), and machine learning analytics based on algorithms such as neural networks.

However, there exist still challenges of machine learning practice (Fig. 1) in modern industry, which often involve an interdisciplinary team of experts with distinct background. The transparency of machine learning (C1) to non-machine learning experts is usually challenging, since the latter often specialise in their domain knowledge and did not receive excessive training of machine learning that is often required to understand the sophisticated machine learning methods and interpret the machine learning results. The non-machine learning experts need to understand machine learning and trust that machine learning applied in manufacturing robots operating with high electricity can ensure product quality and personnel safety [8]. In addition, in traditional machine learning projects, the machine learning procedures, methods, scripts, and decisions are described in the technical language of machine learning, which is highly dependent on the person who writes the document. Machine learning knowledge and solutions are hardly described or documented in a standardised way (C2), causing difficulties for later review and retrospective comprehension of the projects in big companies like Bosch, which have strict regulations in reporting the details for later audit and analysis. Moreover, ML solutions are often developed in an ad hoc fashion and tailored to specific applications, which complicates its reusability (C3) for new data or questions.

To address these challenges, we propose to combine semantic technologies and machine learning, to encode machine learning solutions in knowledge graphs in a smart way, so that the knowledge graphs help in describing machine learning knowledge and solutions in a standardised and transparent way via GUI-based system and knowledge graphs visualisation. We name our approach as executable knowledge graphs, because our knowledge graphs can be translated to modularised executable machine learning scripts that can be modified and reused for new questions. In particular, our contributions are as follows:

- We introduce the concept and a basic framework of executable knowledge graph, that represents the machine learning solutions for solving machine learning questions. The executable knowledge graphs can be translated into modularised executable scripts and are highly reusable.
- We present a use case of Bosch welding monitoring with machine learning, and derive the requirements for executable knowledge graph system.
- We propose a system of executable knowledge graphs. The system has five layers, including the layer of semantic artefacts that serve as the schemata of the knowledge graphs, the of layer semantic modules which construct the knowledge graphs in a semi-automatic fashion based on GUI, knowledge graph data layer that stores the knowledge graphs, application layer that covers visual analytics, statistical analytics and ML analytics, and the (non-knowledge graph) data layer.
- We evaluate our system of executable knowledge graphs extensively: in an user study that verifies whether our system really help in improve the transparency, reusability, etc.; and a system evaluation that verifies the scalability of our approach.

The paper is organised as follows: Sect. 2 explains the use case of Bosch Welding Monitoring, Sect. 4 introduces our framework for executable knowledge graphs, Sect. 5 describes the executable knowledge graph system, Sect. 6 demonstrates the evaluation, Sect. 3 discusses some related work, Sect. 7 presents the conclusion.

2   Use Case: Bosch Welding Monitoring

Resistance Spot Welding and Quality Monitoring. Resistance Spot Welding is a type of fully automated and impactful manufacturing process widely applied in automotive industry [9], accounting for the production of millions of cars globally every year. We illustrate RSW with Fig. 1a, in which the two electrode caps of the welding gun press two or three metal worksheets between the electrodes with force, and pass a high electric current flow through the worksheets. A huge amount of heat is generated due to resistance. The material in a small area between the electrodes will melt, and form a welding nugget connecting the worksheets, known as the welding spot. The quality of welding operations is typically quantified by quality indicators like spot diameters, as prescribed in international and German standards [10, 11]. To obtain the spot diameters precisely, the common practice is to tear the welded car body apart and measure them [11], which destroys the welded cars and is extremely expensive. Now Bosch is developing machine learning-based methods to reduce the need of destroyed car bodies and thus reducing waste, aiming at more economical and sustainable manufacturing [12].

Machine Learning Development: Interdisciplinary, Documented, Reusable. Machine learning projects at Bosch involve experts of distinct backgrounds [13, 14]: e.g., welding experts know the domain knowledge of the process and the questions that need to be solved, measurement experts know the data particularities like sensor setting, data scientists (typically machine learning experts) know the machine learning technology to solve the question, managers need to prioritise the activities according to available resource the strategic interest of the companies. They work together for machine learning development yet speak different language. Their communication requires the transparency of machine learning practice (knowledge, solution, options, etc.), so that the non-machine learning experts can understand machine learning and trust that machine learning applied in heavy robots that operate with high electricity can ensure product quality and personnel safety [15, 16]. In addition, Bosch has strict regulations on documenting and reporting machine learning projects for later review or audit. Thus, the process of machine learning development, and the developed machine learning solutions, knowledge, and insights need to be documented properly by the experts. Moreover, Bosch has many data sources, similar manufacturing processes. Alone the resistance spot welding has data sources of at least 4 locations and 3 customers, while Bosch has other similar welding processes like hot-staking, ultrasonic welding, etc. Thus the reusability of machine learning solutions is highly desired so that they can be transferred to similar data or machine learning questions.

Visual Analytics, Statistical Analytics, and ML Analytics. Here we discuss three important ML activities at Bosch. We refer *visual analytics* to the visualisation of data in various plots [17], e.g., line plot, scatter plot, bar plot, heat map. It helps the experts to gain an intuitive understanding of the data, detect potential interest data subset, and visualise machine learning results. We discuss *statistical analytics* as using a broad range of statistical methods for generating insights from data [18], such as calculation of mean, median, standard deviation, sliding window filter, outlier detection, etc. *machine learning analytics* is understood [19] as relying on two schools of machine learning approaches, feature engineering and deep learning, to train machine learning models and make machine learning inference, e.g., classification, regression.

Requirements for Executable Knowledge Graph System. We derive the requirements for the proposed system and the executable knowledge graphs in the system as follows:

- *R1 Transparency.* Our system should provide standardised description of machine learning knowledge and solutions and make them easier to understand for the non-machine learning experts. It is essential for big manufacturing companies like Bosch since machine learning can only be trusted when they are understood for manufacturing industries with high standards of quality and safety regulations.
- *R2 Usability.* The system should be easy to use, in three aspects [20]: effectiveness – users can use the system correctly; efficiency – users can use the system fast; satisfaction – users are satisifed with the system.
- *R3 Executability.* The executable knowledge graphs in the system should be able to be translated to scripts that are executable, namely not having bugs.
- *R4 Coverage.* The executable knowledge graphs should be able to represent most solutions of visual analytics, statistical analytics, and ML analytics.
- *R5 Reusability and Modularity.* The system and the executable knowledge graphs should support users to reuse developed solutions for similar data or questions by e.g., slightly modifying existing solutions or reusing modules of the solutions.
- *R6 Scalability.* The scripts translated from the executable knowledge graphs should not consume excessive time and thus be scalable for large-scale deployment.

3   Related Work

In recent years, researchers have begun to use graph structures and knowledge graphs to represent codes and the relationships between them in programming languages. They both treat code artefacts, which containing classes, methods, variables, as nodes, use their predefined relationships as edges [21, 22], and use them to complete downstream tasks like defect prediction [23] and query-based analytics [24]. However, these approaches only consider the connections and semantic relationships between codes and insufficiently discuss the more complex graph form, knowledge graphs, which provide more expressivity, e.g., treat the information flow of data between codes as edges and define semantic constraints. Many knowledge graphs were discussed in the literature, e.g., Freebase [25], DBpedia [26]. Specialised knowledge graphs have been used in areas, e.g., e-commerce [27], procurement [28, 29], and healthcare [30]. KGs are gaining popularity in the industries [31–33], but few works were dedicated into describing machine learning practice in industries.

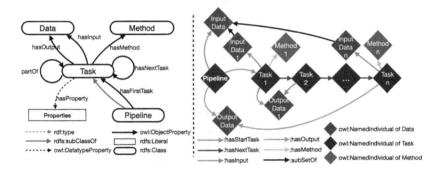

Fig. 2. Framework of executable knowledge graph

4   Executable Knowledge Graphs Framework

In this section we introduce the framework for executable knowledge graph that represents the ML solutions (pipelines) for solving machine learning questions. The framework supports the executable knowledge graph to be translated to executable scripts and modularised, thus the system based on executable knowledge graph can fulfil the requirements of *Executability* and *Reusability and Modularity*.

We first define data, methods and tasks in this framework. *Data $\mathcal{D}$* is a set of items of information, it can be in forms such as numerals, diagrams or strings organised in different structures such as tables. A *Method $\mathcal{F}$* is a function in form of language-dependent script. A method takes some data which fulfils certain constraints as input and can output specific data. Formally, $\mathcal{D}_{out} = \mathcal{F}(\mathcal{D}_{in})$. A *Task $\mathcal{T}$* is the process of invoking a method by feeding it with some data that meets certain constraints, and obtaining some other data. Formally, $\mathcal{T}\langle \mathcal{D}_{in}, \mathcal{F} \rangle = \mathcal{F}(\mathcal{D}_{in}) = \mathcal{D}_{out}$.

Some tasks have methods which are unified, while other more complex tasks can not solved by invoking a single integrated method while can be unfolded into a sequence of tasks where each task is a part of the complex one. We refer the complex tasks as data pipelines $\mathcal{T}_p$. Formally, a pipeline $\mathcal{T}_p$ with input data $\mathcal{D}_{in}$ to get $\mathcal{D}_{out}$, expressed as $\mathcal{T}_p\langle\mathcal{D}_{in}, \mathcal{F}\rangle = \mathcal{D}_{out}$ can be unfolded in the sequence $\{\mathcal{T}_1, \mathcal{T}_2, ..., \mathcal{T}_n\}$. Formally:

$$\mathcal{T}_1\langle\mathcal{D}_{in_1}, \mathcal{F}_1\rangle = \mathcal{D}_{out_1}, \mathcal{D}_{in_1} \in \mathcal{D}_{in}, ...\mathcal{T}_n\langle\mathcal{D}_{in_n}, \mathcal{F}_n\rangle = \mathcal{D}_{out_n},$$

$$\mathcal{D}_{in_n} \in \bigcup_{i\in\{1,2...n-1\}} \mathcal{D}_{out_i} \cup \mathcal{D}_{in}, \longrightarrow \mathcal{D}_{out} \in \bigcup_{i\in\{1,2,...,n\}} \mathcal{D}_{out_i}.$$

Based on the above definitions, we determine the framework for the executable knowledge graphs as the left part of Fig. 2, such executable knowledge graph should take the form as the right part of Fig. 2. Here we split the properties from the data $\mathcal{D}$, which strictly speaking also belong to $\mathcal{D}$, but correspond to the properties rather than objects of a $Task$. Except those $Tasks$ with their $Methods$ already been integrated in script, all other $Tasks$ can be modularised in a $Pipeline$ and be unfolded into a sequence of $Tasks$. The objectProperty $:hasFirstTask$ connects the $Pipeline$ with the first task in its unfolded sequence, while $:hasNextTask$ connects the task in the sequence with its following task. In this framework, as long as the $Data$ and $Properties$ of every $Task$ fulfil the constraints of the $Method$ in the $Task$, the $Task$ is executable. If every $Task$ in a $Pipeline$ is executable, the $Pipeline$ is executable. In addition, as a $Task$, the $Pipeline$ can also be a part of another $Task$, which represents the modularity of the executable knowledge graph.

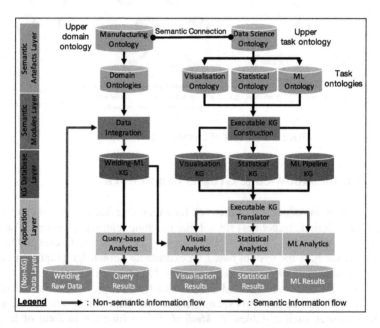

Fig. 3. An architectural overview of our knowledge graph solution

5   Our Executable Knowledge Graph Based ML System

5.1   Architectural Overview

We now give an architectural overview of our system. Our system consists of five layers (Fig. 3). These layers are (from bottom to top): (non-knowledge graph) data layer, application layer, knowledge graph database layer, semantic modules layer, and semantic artefacts layer. From the bottom left, we start with the welding raw data collected from production lines. These data are transformed by the Data Integration module (with the help of domain ontologies) to Welding-machine learning knowledge graphs, which is a type of welding data knowledge graph with some machine learning annotation [34]. These knowledge graphs are used by four types of analytics applications in the application layer.

The domain ontologies include various welding ontologies, e.g., resistance spot welding ontology, hot-staking ontology. These ontologies are created based on the upper domain ontology [2], the manufacturing ontology. The manufacturing ontology is semantically connected with an upper task ontology, the data science ontology (O^{ds}), in a way that the datatype properties in the former one are annotated by some classes in the latter one. A series of task ontologies (Fig. 4), including the visualisation ontology (O^{visu}), the statistical ontology (O^{stats}), and ML ontology (O^{ml}), are created based on the O^{ds}. These task ontologies serve as the schemata for the Executable knowledge graph Construction module, which encodes the executable data pipelines in the executable knowledge graphs, including the visualisation knowledge graph, statistical knowledge graph, and ML pipeline knowledge graph. These executable knowledge graphs then can be translated by the Executable knowledge graph Translator module to executable scripts for three analytics applications: Visual Analytics, Statistic Analytics, and ML Analytics, which generate the corresponding results.

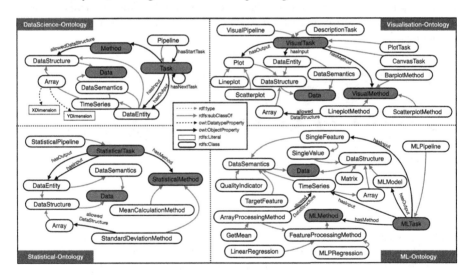

Fig. 4. Task Ontologies for the executable KG

5.2 Semantic Artefacts

We now introduce our ontologies some of which are in Fig. 4.

Upper Domain Ontology and Domain Ontologies. The upper domain ontology, the manufacturing ontology, consists of 1170 axioms containing 95 classes, 70 object properties and 122 datatype properties [9]. It is an OWL 2 ontology modelling the general knowledge of discrete manufacturing process, which refers to a broad range of manu-facturing processes whose products are easily identifiable and countable, e.g., welding spots, and differ greatly from continuous process manufacturing where the products are undifferentiated, e.g. petrol. The ontology has the manufacturing *operation* as the most important class, and has other classes to describe other concepts related to the *operation*, e.g., the operations process *resource*, produce *products* and are performed by *machines*. The domain ontologies describe several manufacturing domains at Bosch, e.g., resis-tance spot welding ontology, hot-staking ontology [35]. These ontologies are created by domain experts in such a way that all classes (properties) in the domain ontologies are sub-classes (sub-properties) of that in upper domain ontologies.

Data Science Ontology. The upper task ontology is the data science ontology O^{ds} (OWL 2) created by Bosch data scientists, which formalise the general knowledge of data science activities. It contains three most important classes (Fig. 4a): *Data* that is the class of all data concepts (the existential being in data science), *Method* is the class of all algorithms and functions (the way that data move), whose allowed input, output and parameters are defined, and *Task* is the class of the scripts that invoke the functions, which has an important sub-class, *Pipeline* that consists of a series of ordered tasks (the way that the data movement is organised). The *Data* can have *DataSemantics* that describe the meaning of data and *DataStructure* that prescribes the format (in the form of datatype properties) of the data, e.g., a *TimeSeries* has the format *Array*. A *DataEntity* is the class for a concrete dataset or a feature. In addition, there exist some constraints, e.g., an *Array* must have *XDimension* greater than 1 and *YDimension* smaller than 2.

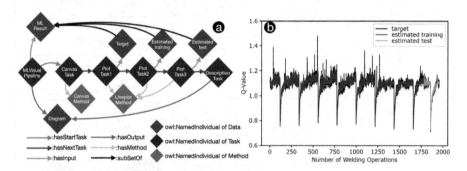

Fig. 5. The executable KG for visualisation (a) and its results (b). It needs to be created in *Visu-Task1* in the user study (Sect. 6), which aims to visualise the ML learning results by plotting the q-value arrays of target (ground-truth), and estimated q-value training and test.

Visualisation, Statistical, and Machine Learning Ontologies are the three task ontologies created based on O^{ds} in such as way that all classes in the task ontologies are sub-classes of that in O^{ds}, and all properties in the task ontologies are sub-properties of that in O^{ds}. The visualisation ontology O^{visu} describes most common visual analytics methods, such as *Lineplot*, *Scatterplot*, etc., and the *DataStructure* that is allowed for the methods, e.g., *Lineplot* allows *Array*s as input. In addition, O^{visu} also prescribes the construction of a visualisation *Pipeline*, which should has the *CanvasTask* as the first task, several *PlotTask* after that, and has *DescriptionTask* as the last task. Similarly, the statistic ontology O^{stats} (and the machine learning ontology O^{ml}, resp.) describes the most common statistical analytics (machine learning analytics, resp.) methods, their allowed *DataStructure*, and the organisation of the tasks in *Pipeline*. In addition, some rules determine explicitly the constraints between the input data of *Task*, e.g., the input *DataEntity*s of the *Concatenation* task should have the same concatenation dimension.

Executable Knowledge Graphs. Based on the task ontologies, executable knowledge graphs are constructed for visual, statistical and machine learning analytics, including *visualisation*, *statistical* and *Machine Learning Knowledge Graph*s. All such knowledge graphs are in the form of pipelines, which consist of a series of tasks. We illustrate this with example knowledge graphs in Fig. 5, Fig. 6, and Fig. 7.

5.3   Executable KG Construction

In our system the executable KGs are constructed semi-automatically in three ways: KG creation, KG modification and KG integration.

Executable Knowledge Graph Creation via GUI is common for relative easy ones such as visualisation and statistical knowledge graphs. For ML pipeline knowledge graphs, advanced users can also create knowledge graphs from the scratch, but most users would prefer to modify or integrate existing ML pipeline knowledge graphs.

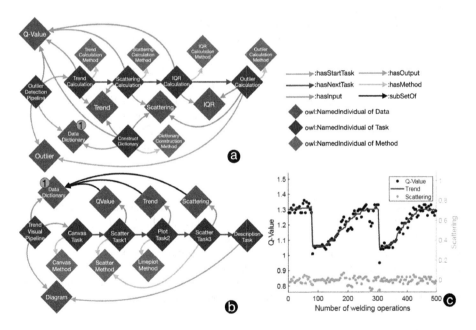

Fig. 6. The knowledge graph for (a) computing the outliers of the *Q-Value* array and (b) visualising the Q-Value array and its the trend, scattering statistical analysis. (c) The visualisation diagram of (b). (a) and (b) are used in *VisuT2* and *StatsT3* in Table 2, respectively.

Visualisation Knowledge Graph (Fig. 5a). Once the user chooses to create a visualisation knowledge graph, by default the GUI will show a *owl:NamedIndividual* with the label *VisualPipeline* (the user can change it), the *CanvasTask* and *DescriptionTask*. Next the users will need to select the input data (commonly a csv file), and several *PlotTask*s from available tasks based on O^{visu}, between the *CanvasTask* and the *DescriptionTask*. For each *PlotTask*, the input data, the method and some parameters will mandatorily be given based on O^{visu}. After that, the visualisation knowledge graph creation is finished.

Statistical Knowledge Graph (Fig. 6a). Once the user chooses to create a statistical knowledge graph, by default the GUI will show a *owl:NamedIndividual* with the label *StatisticalPipeline*, and the *DictionaryTask*, which wraps the output into a dictionary (user can opt to delete it). Next the users will need to select the input data (commonly a csv file), and *StatisticalTask*s from available tasks based on O^{stats}. For each *StatisticalTask*, the users need to select the input data, the method and some mandatory parameters, based on O^{stats}. After the user configuration, constraints verification and resolution, the statistical knowledge graph creation is finished.

Executable Knowledge Graph Modification. Another way to create an executable knowledge graph is to modify existing knowledge graphs, which is common for all three types of knowledge graphs, especially ML pipeline knowledge graphs.

Statistical Knowledge Graph (Fig. 7a–b). Once the user chooses to modify an existing knowledge graph, first the user needs to load a knowledge graph from our knowledge graph database. Now we load the statistical knowledge graph in Fig. 7a, which calculates *mean*, *standard deviation* (std.), *minimum* (min.), and *maximum* (max.) from an array. We want to modify this knowledge graph to another knowledge graph that can do *z-score normalisation*, which subtracts the mean from the array and then divides by std., $(arr - mean)/std.$. To achieve this, the user only need to delete the two statistical tasks, namely *MinimumCalculation* (Fig. 7 3) and *MaximumCalculation* (Fig. 7 4), then add another task *NormalisationCalculation* (Fig. 7 6) (which has *NormalisationMethod*, and select its input as the *MeanValue* and *StandardDeviation*. After that, the system will suggest *NormalisedData* as the output of the task *NormalisationCalculation*. The user then select *NormalisedData* as the final output of the pipeline and change the label of the pipeline. Knowledge graph modification is done.

Machine Learning Knowledge Graph. (Fig. 7c) takes *TimeSeries* and *SingleFeatures* as input data, and does *LRRegression* to predict the *Q-Value*. The users can simply change the input data, output data, and method of the pipeline, by changing the named individuals, e.g., the users can delete *TimeSeries* if they do not have the sensor curves in their data, because the sensor curves are costly to collect. The users can also change the machine learning method (from *LRRegression* to *MLP*), the output data (from *Q-Value* to *spot diameter*) and some hyper-parameters (MLT2 in Table 2).

Executable Knowledge Graph Integration. (Fig. 6), where a statistical pipeline that does outlier detection can be integrated with a visualisation pipeline to visualise the detection results. To do so, the users only need to select one output of Fig. 6a, the

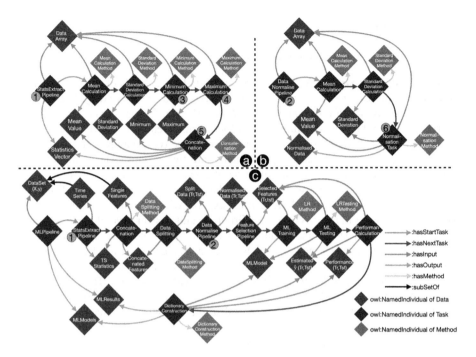

Fig. 7. (a) *StatsExtractPipeline* that extracts four statistics for a data array: mean, std., min., max. (b) *DataNormalisePipeline* that performs z-score normalisation for a data array. (c) *MLPipeline* that takes time series and single features as inputs and relies on linear regression (LRMethod). (a)(b)(c) are used in *StatsT1*, *StatsT2*, *MLT1* in Table 2, respectively.

DataDictionary, *Trend*, and *Scattering*) as the inputs of the *TrendVisualPipeline* in Fig. 6b. Another example is Fig. 7c, which is the result of reusing/integrating the *StatsExtractPipeine* (Fig. 7I) in Fig. 7a and *DataNormalisationPipeline* in Fig. 7b.

5.4 Executable Knowledge Graph Translation

The translation of executable knowledge graphs is language-dependent. Here we use Python as the language for discussion. Each individual of *Method* is a Python function script, whose mandatory inputs/outputs and parameters are clearly defined. Each executable knowledge graph is in the form of a *Pipeline*, which consists of a series of *Tasks* of sequential or parallel structures connected with *hasNextTask*. Thus, the translation of an executable knowledge graph invokes the Python function scripts with the inputs/outputs and parameters given by *DataEntity* and datatype properties of knowledge graphs, according to the order defined by *hasNextTask*.

6 Evaluation

6.1 User Study: Transparency and Usability

Design of the User Study. We invited 28 experts in backgrounds of machine learning experts, welding experts, sensor engineers, etc. to attend the user study. For the user study, we first give a short *introduction* of our system, then the participants will perform a series of *tasks* related to visual, statistical and machine learning analytics, and finally they will answer *questionnaires* to record their subjective evaluation. For the tasks, to avoid user bias, we divided the participants into two groups, who will follow the schedule in Table 1. To contrast the situation of doing analytic tasks without and with our system, we designed the workflow as follows: Each group, including 2 machine learning experts and 12 non-machine learning experts, will first perform an analytic task without our system (T1), e.g. VisuT1 for Group A, and answer several single selection questions (SSQ) to test the understanding of the non-machine learning experts about the task (T2). We have designed 5–7 SSQs for each task, and there are 18 SSQs in total (Table 3). Then, they will do a similar task with our system (T3) and answer the SSQs (T4). Finally, they will revisit the previous task (T1) with our system. The same process repeat for the StatsT (T6–T10) and MLT (T12–T16). In addition, we design T11, T17 and T18 to test whether our system can realise the modularised reuse of executable knowledge graphs.

Tasks and Metrics. We list the tasks, their content and their knowledge graph visualisation in Table 2. For each task, the machine learning experts will explain the non-machine learning experts the tasks. In the case of "without our system" (T1, 6, 12), the experts communicate with technical language, and the non-machine learning experts will need to perform the tasks. Due to time limit, it is infeasible to do coding during the user study. The non-machine learning experts will answer whether they can finish the tasks with their programming an machine learning knowledge, and estimate the needed time for that. Thus, we will have two metrics: *complete percentage* and *time*. In addition, we compare the answers of SSQs with the correct answers and record the *correctness* (T2, 7, 13). In case of "with our system" (T3, 5, 8, 10, 11, 14, 16–18), the experts communicate using our system and the non-machine learning experts will need to perform the tasks. They do so by creating, modifying or merging knowledge graphs via a GUI. We record their actions and needed *time* for each task, and compare their action with a ground truth (we designed the task and GUI to make such comparison possible) to measure the *correctness*. Some users cannot finish the task, and thus we also recorded the *complete percentage*. In addition, we compare the answers of SSQs with the correct answers and record the *correctness* (T4, 9, 15).

Results and Discussion. We first look at results of using our system (Fig. 8a–c). It can be seen that most users have a high *complete percentage* (above 90%) using the system. When they complete the tasks, their correctness is also very high, about 80% (effectiveness, R2), even for the complex tasks T17 and T18. In addition, they usually do not need much time for each task, in average only 227.3 s, about 4 min (user efficiency, R2). Then we compare the correctness of SSQs without and with our system (Fig. 8d), which also show that the non-experts can gain better understanding of the three machine learning

Table 1. Workflow of the tasks in the user study.

#	Group A	Group B	Method
T1	VisuT1	VisuT2	Without our system
T2	VisuT1 SSQ	VisuT2 SSQ	–
T3	VisuT2	VisuT1	With our system: create KG
T4	VisuT2 SSQ	VisuT1 SSQ	–
T5	VisuT1	VisuT2	With our system: modify KG
T6	StatsT1	StatsT2	Without our system
T7	StatsT1 SSQ	StatsT2 SSQ	–
T8	StatsT2	StatsT1	With our system: create KG
T9	StatsT2 SSQ	StatsT1 SSQ	–
T10	StatsT1	StatsT2	With our system: modify KG
T11	StatsT3	StatsT3	With our system: modify KG
T12	MLT1	MLT2	Without our system
T13	MLT1 SSQ	MLT2 SSQ	–
T14	MLT2	MLT1	With our system: modify KG
T15	MLT2 SSQ	MLT1 SSQ	–
T16	MLT1	MLT2	With our system: modify KG
T17	ComplexTask1	ComplexTask1	With our system: merge KG
T18	ComplexTask2	ComplexTask2	With our system: merge KG

Table 2. Tasks and their content

Tasks	Content	KG
VisuT1	Visualise machine learning results with three line plots: target, estimated training, estimated test	Fig. 5
VisuT2	Visualise a quality indicator, its trend and scattering with scatter plots and line plots	Fig. 6b
StatsT1	Extract four statistics from a sequence: mean, std., min. and max	Fig. 7a
StatsT2	Z-score normalise a vector by substracting the mean and dividing by the standard deviation	Fig. 7b
StatsT3	Compute the trend, scattering and outliers of a sequence with median filter, etc.	Fig. 6a
MLT1	Reuse a ML pipeline for q-value estimation with linear regression	Fig. 7c
MLT2	Reuse a ML pipeline for diameter estimation with multilayer perceptron	Fig. 7c
ComplexT1	Visualise the results of StatsT1: merging/reusing the pipelines of StatsT1 and VisuT2	Fig. 7c
ComplexT2	Visualise the results of MLT1: merging/reusing the pipelines of StatsT1, StatsT2, MLT1 and VisuT1	Fig. 7c

Table 3. Examples of single selection questions (SSQ) for machine learning tasks.

Questions (Q) and Answers (A)
Q1: What are the input data we use for machine learning training? I: single features, II: sensor curves, III: quality indicator
A1: (A) I + II + III (B) I + II (C) II (D) II + III
Q2: What is the output feature we try to estimate?
A2: (A) Diameter (B) Q-value (C) Current mean (D) Process stability factor
Q3: What features will be the input of StatsExtractPipeline? I: single features, II: sensor curves, III: quality indicator
A3: (A) I + II + III (B) I + II (C) II (D) II + III

Table 4. Questionnaires (partial) and scores for subjective evaluation. The scores range from 1 (disagree), 2 (fairly disagree), 3 (neutral), 4 (fairly agree), to 5 (agree). The column *Score* is aggregated by reversing the scores of negative questions (such as Q2, 4, 6, 8, 9) and then computing the average (avg.) and standard deviation (std.) (`avg.±std.`)

#	Questions	Dimensions	Score
Q1	(For ML experts) I am confident to help non-expert to develop ML approaches based on the system	R1 Transparency	4.28 ± 0.47
	(For non-ML experts) I found it's easy to get basic understanding for ML approaches based on the system		
Q2	I felt the system hampers the communication on ML approaches		
Q3	I felt very confident using the system	R2 Usability	4.73 ± 0.39
Q4	I thought there was too much inconsistency in this system		
Q5	(For ML experts) I have confidence in the system to perform ML tasks	R3 Executability	4.60 ± 0.72
	(For non-ML experts) I am happy about the executability of this system		
Q6	I need the support of technical persons to be able to use this system		
Q7	I think the system can in general cover my need	R4 Coverage	4.24 ± 0.83
Q8	(For ML experts) I found the system didn't cover some basic ML functions that are commonly used in industry		
	(For non-ML experts) I think the system has very limited application in production		
Q9	(For ML experts) I think the ML pipelines developed in the system can only be reused in a limited range of applications	R5 Reusability	4.87 ± 0.36
	(For non-ML experts) I don't think I would try to reuse a developed pipeline when facing a new task		
Q10	I am happy that the system reduce time for reusing developed pipelines.		

activities (transparency, R1), as their SSQ correctness systematically increases when they use our system for communication. The comparison of time and task correctness without (w/o) and with (w) our system (Fig. 8e–f) shows that when users doing tasks with our systems they can save substantial time and increase the complete percentage (user efficiency, R2), and make analytics tasks that cannot be done by the non-machine learning experts now doable (usability, R2). The users also save much time when they reuse and modify (contrasting bars with m and w) existing knowledge graphs to solve the tasks.

It can be seen from the scores of questionnaires (Table 4) that the users indeed think our system improves the transparency (R1), and has good usability (R2), as these scores are all above 4. In addition, the users also satisfied with the coverage of the tasks (R4), and the reusability and modularity of the analytics pipelines (R5) brought by our system. The later two will be further discussed in the next section.

6.2 Evaluation of Executability, Coverage, and Reusability

Executability (R3). Beside the 9 executable knowledge graphs in the user study, we also programmatically generate 1372 executable knowledge graphs covering most of the tasks (Table 5) encountered by automated modification of a set of executable knowledge graph templates. As expected, all these knowledge graphs can be translated into scripts that are executable (Fig. 9). Thus, the executable knowledge graphs that follow the our framework in Sect. 4 are also evaluated as executable.

Coverage (R4). We organised extensive workshops with the machine learning and non-machine learning experts. After discussion, we categorised most tasks of visual, statistical and machine learning analytics encountered in our project in groups (see Table 5), and give the coverage percentage according to our empirical cases. Observe, for the 3 groups of visual analytics, and 5 groups of statistical, most of them can be covered (above 80%). While for the feature engineering school of machine learning analytics, we cover 80%. The feature learning school is currently not our focus of the work.

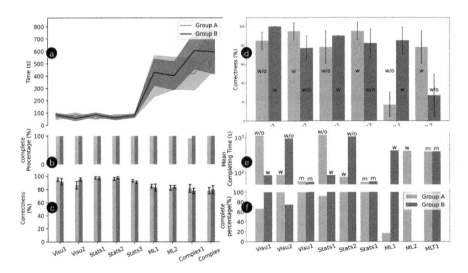

Fig. 8. The user study results in time (a), complete percentage (b) and correctness (c); comparing the SSQ correctness between without and with our system (d); comparing users doing tasks without (w/o) and with (w) our system or only modify knowledge graph (m) in time (e) and complete percentage (f)

Reusability (R5). In user study, multiple tasks demonstrate the high reusability and modularity supported by our system. In T5, 10, 14, 16 (Fig. 5a, Fig. 6a, Fig. 7a and c), users modify existing knowledge graphs by adding named individuals and changing task parameters, and thus reuse the knowledge graphs for new tasks, which is a strong evidence of reusability. In T17 and 18 (Fig. 7c), they simply merge existing knowledge graphs and form more complicated ones, this demonstrates the modularity (and thus also reusability).

Table 5. Tasks categories and coverage

Category	Sub-category	Coverage
Visual	Line plot, scatter plot, bar chart	100%
	Pie chart	85%
	Heatmap	85%
Statistic	Statistics calculation	95%
	Basic mathematical operation	100%
	Sliding window filtering	90%
	Sub-sampling	80%
	Interpolation & extrapolation	80%
ML	Feature engineering	80%
	Feature learning	0%

6.3   System Evaluation of Scalability

Apart from the aforementioned requirements, we evaluate the scalability (R6) of our system for large deployment. We tested the running time of different types of analytics pipelines for welding quality monitoring (Fig. 9). The tasks include 1372 programmatically generated analytics pipelines and thus 1372 executable knowledge graphs, including 242 knowledge graphs for visual analytics, 253 knowledge graphs for statistical analytics, 291 merged knowledge graphs that combine visual and statistical analytics, 272 merge knowledge graphs the combine statistical and ML analytics, and 314 merge knowledge graphs that combine three of them. We conducted experiments on an Mac-Book Pro with Apple M1 Processor, 16 GB of RAM. To have controllable scope, we tested these executable knowledge graphs on a sample welding production dataset collected from a factory in Germany. The dataset is in the form of relational tables after integration, and contains 4585 welding operation records.

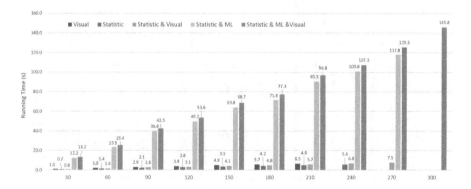

Fig. 9. System evaluation results for the Bosch welding use cases. x-Axis: number of tasks.

Results and Discussion. The running time (including knowledge graph translation and execution time) in Fig. 9 demonstrate that our system scales well since it takes limited time to translate the executable knowledge graphs to scripts and execute the scripts. Specifically, the running time grows sublinearly with respect to the number of tasks. On the most right hand side, 300 of the most challenging tasks, namely the hybrid tasks that combine statistic, machine learning modelling and visual analysis only takes less than 3 min on the given data, which is considered to have good scalability by our experts.

7   Conclusion, Lessons Learned, And Outlook

In this work we present our concept and system of executable knowledge graphs, which address the challenges of transparency, formal description, and reusability of machine learning practice, including visual, statistical, and machine learning analytics tasks. The system helps users to do the machine learning-related analytics tasks by providing a GUI and executable knowledge graphs that can be translated to executable scripts. We evaluated our approach with a user study, discussion, workshops, and system evaluation and obtained promising results. The lessons learned for us that as follows: many users are very interested in machine learning-related knowledge and solutions. They are eager to spend time to learn such knowledge and practice machine learning, but did not have a good starting point. They highly value our system and proposed many comments for improvement, especially for the GUI, and for covering the hyper-parameter tuning and feature learning. In the future, we plan to further improve our system, to host the system regularly on the Bosch environment and constantly collect more user feed-backs. We also plan to develop more theory to improve the generality of the approach.

Acknowledgements. The work was partially supported by the H2020 projects Dome 4.0 (Grant Agreement No. 953163), OntoCommons (Grant Agreement No. 958371), and DataCloud (Grant Agreement No. 101016835) and the SIRIUS Centre, Norwegian Research Council project number 237898.

References

1. Naab, C., Zheng, Z.: Application of the unscented Kalman filter in position estimation a case study on a robot for precise positioning. Robot. Auton. Syst. **147**, 103904 (2022)
2. Svetashova, Y., et al.: Ontology-enhanced machine learning: a bosch use case of welding quality monitoring. In: ISWC (2020)
3. Celik, O., Zhou, D., Li, G., Becker, P., Neumann, G.: Specializing versatile skill libraries using local mixture of experts. In: Conference on Robot Learning, PMLR, pp. 1423–1433 (2022)
4. Mahesh, B.: Machine learning algorithms-a review. Int. J. Sci. Res. (IJSR) (Internet) **9**, 381–386 (2020)
5. Kagermann, H.: Change through digitization - value creation in the age of industry 4.0. In: Management of Permanent Change (2015)
6. Zhou, B., et al.: The data value quest: a holistic semantic approach at Bosch. In: European Semantic Web Conference, pp. 287–290. Springer, Cham (2022). https://doi.org/10.1007/978-3-031-11609-4_42
7. Perer, A., Shneiderman, B.: Integrating statistics and visualization: case studies of gaining clarity during exploratory data analysis. In: Proceedings of the SIGCHI Conference on Human Factors in Computing Systems, pp. 265–274 (2008)

8. Zhou, B., et al.: SemML: facilitating development of ML models for condition monitoring with semantics. J. Web Semant. **71**, 100664 (2021)
9. Zhou, B., Pychynski, T., Reischl, M., Kharlamov, E., Mikut, R.: Machine learning with domain knowledge for predictive quality monitoring in resistance spot welding. J. Intell. Manuf. **33**(4), 1139–1163 (2022)
10. ISO, Resistance Welding - Procedures for Determining the Weldability Lobe for Resistance Spot, Projection and Seam Welding, Standard, International Organization for Standardization, Geneva, CH (2004)
11. DVS, Widerstandspunktschweißen von Stählen bis 3 mm Einzeldicke - Konstruktion und Berechnung, Standard, Deutscher Verband für Schweißen und verwandte Verfahren e. V., Düsseldorf, DE (2016)
12. Zhou, B., Svetashova, Y., Byeon, S., Pychynski, T., Mikut, R., Kharlamov, E.: Predicting quality of automated welding with machine learning and semantics: a Bosch case study. In: CIKM (2020)
13. Zhou, B., Svetashova, Y., Pychynski, T., Kharlamov, E.: Semantic ML for manufacturing monitoring at Bosch. In: ISWC (Demos/Industry), vol. 2721, p. 398 (2020)
14. Svetashova, Y., Zhou, B., Schmid, S., Pychynski, T., Kharlamov, E.: SemML: reusable ML for condition monitoring in discrete manufacturing. In: ISWC (Demos/Industry), vol. 2721, pp. 213–218 (2020)
15. Zhou, B.: Machine learning methods for product quality monitoring in electric resistance welding, Ph.D. thesis, Karlsruhe Institute of Technology, Germany (2021)
16. Zhou, B., Zhou, D., Chen, J., Svetashova, Y., Cheng, G., Kharlamov, E.: Scaling usability of ML analytics with knowledge graphs: exemplified with a Bosch welding case. In: The 10th International Joint Conference on Knowledge Graphs, pp. 54–63 (2021)
17. Keim, D., Andrienko, G., Fekete, J.-D., Görg, C., Kohlhammer, J., Melançon, G.: Visual analytics: definition, process, and challenges. In: Kerren, A., Stasko, J.T., Fekete, J.-D., North, C. (eds.) Information Visualization. LNCS, vol. 4950, pp. 154–175. Springer, Heidelberg (2008). https://doi.org/10.1007/978-3-540-70956-5_7
18. Endert, A., Han, C., Maiti, D., House, L., North, C.: Observation-level interaction with statistical models for visual analytics. In: IEEE Conference on Visual Analytics Science and Technology (VAST), pp. 121–130. IEEE (2011)
19. LaCasse, P.M., Otieno, W., Maturana, F.P.: A survey of feature set reduction approaches for predictive analytics models in the connected manufacturing enterprise. Appl. Sci. **9**(5), 843 (2019)
20. C. ISO, 9241-11.3. Part II: Guidance on Specifying and Measuring Usability, ISO 9241 Ergonomic Requirements for Office Work With Visual Display Terminals (VDTs) (1993)
21. Kartchner, D., Christensen, T., Humpherys, J., Wade, S.: Code2Vec: embedding and clustering medical diagnosis data. In: 2017 IEEE International Conference on Healthcare Informatics, ICHI 2017, Park City, UT, USA, 23–26 August 2017, pp. 386–390. IEEE Computer Society (2017)
22. Atzeni, M., Atzori, M.: CodeOntology: RDF-ization of source code. In: d'Amato, C., et al. (eds.) ISWC 2017. LNCS, vol. 10588, pp. 20–28. Springer, Cham (2017). https://doi.org/10.1007/978-3-319-68204-4_2
23. Qu, Y., et al.: node2defect: using network embedding to improve software defect prediction. In: 2018 33rd IEEE/ACM International Conference on Automated Software Engineering (ASE), pp. 844–849. IEEE (2018)
24. Zheng, Z., et al.: Query-based industrial analytics over knowledge graphs with ontology reshaping. In: ESWC (Posters & Demos). Springer, Cham (2022). https://doi.org/10.1007/978-3-031-11609-4_23
25. Bollacker, K., Evans, C., Paritosh, P., Sturge, T., Taylor, J.: Freebase: a collaboratively created graph database for structuring human knowledge, in: Proceedings of the 2008 ACM SIGMOD International Conference on Management of Data, pp. 1247–1250 (2008)

26. Auer, S., Bizer, C., Kobilarov, G., Lehmann, J., Cyganiak, R., Ives, Z.: DBpedia: a nucleus for a web of open data. In: Aberer, K., et al. (eds.) ASWC/ISWC -2007. LNCS, vol. 4825, pp. 722–735. Springer, Heidelberg (2007). https://doi.org/10.1007/978-3-540-76298-0_52

27. Li, F.-L., et al.: AliMeKG: domain knowledge graph construction and application in e-commerce. In: Proceedings of the 29th ACM International Conference on Information & Knowledge Management, pp. 2581–2588 (2020)

28. Soylu, A., et al.: TheyBuyForYou platform and knowledge graph: expanding horizons in public procurement with open linked data. Semant. Web **13**(2), 265–291 (2022)

29. Roman, D., et al.: The euBusinessGraph ontology: a lightweight ontology for harmonizing basic company information. Semant. Web **13**(1), 41–68 (2022). https://doi.org/10.3233/SW-210424

30. Li, L., et al.: Real-world data medical knowledge graph: construction and applications. Artif. Intell. Med. **103**, 101817 (2020)

31. Ryen, V., Soylu, A., Roman, D.: Building semantic knowledge graphs from (semi-)structured data: a review. Future Internet **14**(5), 129 (2022). https://doi.org/10.3390/fi14050129

32. Zhou, D., et al.: Ontology reshaping for knowledge graph construction: applied on Bosch welding case. In: ISWC. Springer, Cham (2022)

33. Zhou, D., Zhou, B., Chen, J., Cheng, G., Kostylev, E.V., Kharlamov, E.: Towards ontology reshaping for KG generation with user-in-the-loop: applied to Bosch welding. In: IJCKG (2021)

34. Zhou, D., et al.: Enhancing knowledge graph generation with ontology reshaping-Bosch case. In: ESWC (Demos/Industry). Springer, Cham (2022). https://doi.org/10.1007/978-3-031-11609-4_45

35. Yahya, M., et al.: Towards generalized welding ontology in line with ISO and knowledge graph construction. In: ESWC (Posters & Demos). Springer, Cham (2022). https://doi.org/10.1007/978-3-031-11609-4_16

Scaling Knowledge Graphs
for Automating AI of Digital Twins

Joern Ploennigs$^{(\boxtimes)}$ ⓘ, Konstantinos Semertzidis ⓘ, Fabio Lorenzi,
and Nandana Mihindukulasooriya ⓘ

IBM Research Europe, Dublin, Ireland
`Joern.Ploennigs@ie.ibm.com`,
{`konstantinos.semertzidis1,fabio.lorenzi1,nandana`}`@ibm.com`

Abstract. Digital Twins are digital representations of systems in the
Internet of Things (IoT) that are often based on AI models that are trained
on data from those systems. Semantic models are used increasingly to link
these datasets from different stages of the IoT systems life-cycle together
and to automatically configure the AI modelling pipelines. This combination of semantic models with AI pipelines running on external datasets
raises unique challenges particular if rolled out at scale. Within this paper
we will discuss the unique requirements of applying semantic graphs to
automate Digital Twins in different practical use cases. We will introduce the benchmark dataset DTBM that reflects these characteristics and
look into the scaling challenges of different knowledge graph technologies.
Based on these insights we will propose a reference architecture that is
in-use in multiple products in IBM and derive lessons learned for scaling
knowledge graphs for configuring AI models for Digital Twins.

Keywords: Knowledge graphs · Semantic models · Scalability ·
Internet of Things · Machine learning · Digital twins

1 Introduction

Semantic models are establishing across industries in the Internet of Things
(IoT) to model and manage domain knowledge. They range from driving the
next generation of manufacturing in Industry 4.0 [3,17,19], to explainable transport [29], energy savings in buildings for a sustainable future [5,11]. Their application cumulates in the use of semantic integration of various IoT sensors [28]
to automate analytics of the created data [11,37].

Digital Twins are one area of applying semantic models. A *Digital Twin* is a
digital representation of an IoT system that is able to continuously learn across
the systems life cycle and predict the behaviour of the IoT system [26]. They have
multiple uses across the life cycle from providing recommendations in the design
of the system, to automating its manufacturing and optimizing its operation
by diagnosing anomalies or improving controls with prediction [36]. The core
of a Digital Twin is formed by two tightly interacting concepts. First, an AI
model, such as a Machine Learning (ML) or simulation model, that is capable

U. Sattler et al. (Eds.): ISWC 2022, LNCS 13489, pp. 810–826, 2022.
https://doi.org/10.1007/978-3-031-19433-7_46

of continuous learning from data and explaining and predicting its behaviour. Second, a *Digital Thread* that is linking these underlying data sources across the systems life cycle [34]. Both approaches interact tightly as the Thread needs to be used to automate the configuration of the AI models to allow to scale their application while results from the AI model should be injected back into the Thread to learn and explain knowledge.

Semantic Knowledge Graph technologies are very well suited for implementing this Digital Thread [1]. They promise to solve several common challenges from normalizing labelling of the various data sources to being flexible enough to be extended over the life cycle when new applications arise [8]. However, scaling knowledge graphs is challenging in its own terms [24] and in our practice we experience multiple issues in scaling Digital Threads. Within this paper we will deep dive into this use case and discuss some of the practical issues. We will follow the typical industry workflow for designing and selecting a solution from collecting requirements and defining a test example, to deriving a reference architecture and evaluating final realization options for some large scale examples. The contributions of the paper are:

- *Requirements for Digital Twins*: We collect the requirements for semantic representation of Digital Twins in Sect. 3.
- *In-Use Experience for Scaling*: We discuss our in-use experience in scaling Digital Twins and propose a reference architecture.
- *Benchmark model for Digital Twins*: We define a benchmark model for semantic Digital Twins for an manufacturing example that tests some of the identified requirements in Sect. 5.
- *Comparison of KG Technologies*: We compare different knowledge graph technologies for managing the semantic models for Digital Twins in Sect. 6 including our own semantic property graph.

2   State of the Art

Knowledge Graphs for Digital Twins: There are several examples of applying semantic models for representing Digital Twins [1,18,20]. Kharlamov et al. [18] argues for the benefits of using semantic models for digital twins e.g. to simplify analytics in Industry 4.0 settings. Similarly, Kalayci et al. [17] shows how to manage industry data with semantic models. Lietaert et al. [21] presents a Digital Twin architecture for Industry 4.0. Chevallier et al. [10] proposes one for Smart Buildings. Akroyd et al. [1] reviews multiple approaches for geospatial knowledge graph for a Digital Twin of the UK. Their work demonstrates the challenges in incorporating data from different domains into one knowledge graph like the heterogenity of data sources. These example represent the use of semantic models for building Digital Twins in different industries that we also see in practise.

Semantic Data Management: A common goal of using knowledge graphs for Digital Twins is to integrate data from various systems. Established solutions exist for doing this with semantic knowledge graphs that also may integrate external data. Pan et al. [25] presents a survey of semantic data management systems and benchmarks. The authors classify the systems using a taxonomy that includes native RDF stores, RDBMS-based and NoSql-based data management systems. Besta et al. [6] provide a classification based on the database technology. Their analysis shows that the different design have various pros and cons. Some of the widely-used generic triple-stores such as OpenLink Virtuoso [13], Apache Jena, Blazegraph, GraphDB excel on managing RDF data, but, do not scale well in integrating non RDF data. General purpose property graphs like Neo4J or Janus-Graph lack intrinsic understanding of semantic models. Multi-modal databases like ArgangoDB or Redis combine a no-sql database with a graph database that allows to manage documents alongside the graph. But, they also suffer from a good understanding of semantic [30]. Entris [12] and Schmidt [31] extend this idea and use semantic models to manage additional data in a data lake. In Sect. 3 we will discuss some unique requirements that create challenges in scaling such knowledge graphs. We derive a reference architecture that separation the semantic graph layer from the data layer to scale better to large volumes of data and have federated access to address the Semantic Digital Threads requirements. As shown by our experiments, such design seems to provide better scalability for our use case compared to the other semantic data management approaches.

Benchmarks for Semantic Data: To validate that the requirements in modelling Digital Twins are unique and evaluate different knowledge graph technologies, we created a new Digital Twin Benchmark Model (DTBM). We compare it against some established benchmarks. The *Berlin SPARQL Benchmark (BSBM)* [7] and *Lehigh University Benchmark (LUBM)* [14] are generic RDF Benchmarks that run a variant of queries on generated datasets. *SP²Bench* [33] is based on DBLP library dataset and reflects the social network characteristics of semantic web data. *DBpedia SPARQL benchmark* [23] uses real queries that were performed by humans and applications against on DBpedia. Additional work reflects the requirements and characteristics of certain domains. *PODiGG* [35] and *GTFS-Madrid-Bench* [9] are examples of benchmarks for public transport domain focused on use cases and requirements on route planning on gespatial and temporal transport data. *LSLOD* [15] contains datasets from the life sciences domain and the Linked Data cloud and 10 simple and 10 complex queries that need query federation. *Fedbench suite* [32] evaluates efficiency and effectiveness of federated SPARQL queries over three different datasets: cross-domain, life science, and SPBenc. We will use BSBM and LUBM in the evaluation in Sect. 6 as they are very well established and tested for many knowledge graphs technologies and address themselves different RDF characteristics. In addition, we will propose a new benchmark focused on our use case.

3 Requirements for Semantic Digital Threads

A Digital Thread is linking data from different life cycle stages of a Digital Twin. This starts from design documents such as textual requirements, test specifications, to CAD-files and handbooks that may exist in different formats. During production additional properties may be attached to a Digital Twin such as sensor data from machines, materials used, material providers, and test results. During operation the data collected from the final system is also added. It is often related to asset management data such as fault reports, maintenance work-orders, and replacement histories as well as timeseries data collected from IoT sensors embedded in the systems such as temperature measurements, operational states or alarms. The different datasets that are collected across the life cycle are linked together in the Digital Thread and often analyzed by Machine Learning algorithms to discover and explain anomalies, predict the behaviour of the system and advise people in improved manufacturing and operation of the system.

From this description we can synthesize some *characteristics* to a semantic knowledge graph that can be used to implement such a Digital Thread.

- *C1 - Heterogenous Semantic Types:* The connected data is very heterogenous, representing domainspecific semantic types. A domain ontology can contain thousands of types. For example, the BRICK ontology [5] contains ca. 3.000 classes for modelling smart buildings datasets.
- *C2 - Multi-modal Representation:* The data is multi-modal and represented in different formats from timeseries, to binary files, and text documents.
- *C3 - Federated Data:* The data is stored and managed in various systems such as complex Continuous Engineering Systems, Asset Management Systems, or IoT platforms.
- *C4 - Flexible Hierarchies:* Data is often structured in hierarchical models such as location hierarchies (`Country` > `City` > `Factory` > `Production_Line`) and asset hierarchies (`Robot` > `Arm` > `Joint`) that are of flexible depth.
- *C5 - Large size:* We see graph sizes often in the range of 100.000 datasets for a mid-size Digital Twin.
- *C6 - Composability:* Digital Twins often contain other Digital Twins. For example, a factory twin may contain a robot twin.
- *C7 - Lack of semantic knowledge:* We often experience that domain experts do not have deep semantic knowledge. Though, they often understand software engineering concepts like classes and inheritance.
- *C8 - Dynamic:* Digital Twins change over their lifetime and so does the Digital Thread. In consequence, the knowledge graph does change regularly bringing in the need to represent time, states and versioning.

The *goals* for building the Digital Thread are:

- *G1 - Data Linking:* The first goal of the Digital Thread is to link data from various life cycle stages and backend systems together to create an integrated view of the data.
- *G2 - Data Contextualization:* The second goal of building Digital Threads is to contextualize the data and understand spatial and functional context to summarize and explain the data.

- *G3 - Data Model Normalization:* The third goal is to reduce the heterogeneity of the underlying data and normalize it on: common semantics (C1), a common data modality (C2), and common hierarchical model (C4).
- *G4 - Data Access Abstraction:* The next goal is to abstract the access to the underlying data in the federated systems (C3) to allow users to query data by its semantics rather then storage specific IDs like asset or sensor IDs.
- *G5 - AI Automation:* The final goal is to automate lifecycle processes like analytics. This is needed as manual configuration of these analytic processes is not possible due to the data size (C5) and regular changes (C8).

From these characteristics and goals we can derive a set of requirements:

- *R1 - Domain Taxonomies:* From G3 and C1 we can derive the requirement to model both normalized upper ontologies (e.g. `Sensor`) with generic types on the top and more specific types on lower level of the taxonomy (e.g. `Temperature_Sensor` $\sqsubseteq$ `Sensor`).
- *R2 - Subsumption:* From C1 and R1 we can derive the requirement to use subsumption in the taxonomies. Taxonomies may have multiple levels, e.g. most sensor tags in BRICK have about 3–5 levels of parents.
- *R3 - Inheritance:* From C1, C6, C7 we can derive the requirement to support inheritance of properties from concepts to instances. In practise, we use this heavily to propagate for example units of measurement or ML model configurations.
- *R4 - Semantic Data Access:* The solution needs to provide semantic data access according to G4 to the underlying federated data (C3).
- *R5 - Backend agnostic:* The system needs to support various data representation (C2) and federated storage solutions (C3) in a hybrid cloud.
- *R6 - Flexible Depth Queries:* The hierarchies from C4 provide some means of structuring and querying data. However, the lack of defined structures with fixed query depth requires the use of transitive property chains in queries.
- *R7 - Event-based Reasoning:* Reasoning approaches are a good way of automating processes in the knowledge graph for G5 to replicate knowledge for sub-components (C6). The high dynamic of the graph (C8) asks for ways to automate these reasoning steps on graph events, when for example sub-components are added.
- *R8 - Guaranteed Consistency:* C1 and C8 mean also that users regularly change the domain taxonomies and there need to be ways to propagate changes in the subsumption taxonomies or the deletion of concepts that keep the graph consistent and not end up with orphaned elements.
- *R9 - Element-level Access Control:* The Digital Twin is integrating data from various systems (C3, C6) and needs to support different use cases and user roles (C8). In consequence, a fine grained access control on graph element level is needed [4].

Some of these requirements are of common nature for semantic knowledge graphs like R1, R2, R5 and therefore support the applicability of this technology. We consider the requirements R3, R4, R5, R7, R8, R9 more specific for Digital Twins and do not see them in other applications [22, 24].

4   Architecture for Semantic Digital Twins

Based on the goals and requirements defined in the last section, we derive a reference architecture for a Semantic Digital Twin in Fig. 1. We keep the reference architecture on purpose generic as we need to support different backends (C3) and want to give readers implementation options. We realized the reference architecture in our own implementation KITT, which is used in different products like IBM Maximo®or IBM TRIRIGA®to integrating data from multiple different solutions in a Digital Threads. The system is deployed and in-use for various customers since multiple years.

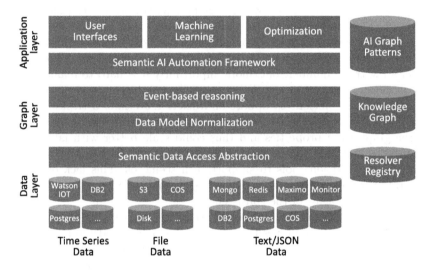

Fig. 1. Reference architecture for semantic Digital Twin

The core design of the architecture is a separation of the data layer from the graph layer. The *data layer* links to data from various federated backend systems. They are integrated by a *Semantic Data Access Abstraction Layer*. This is a microservice environment that is implementing for each backend a resolver microservice that maps the backends onto a key/value interface to query the respective data in a normalized way according to G4. We differentiate three types of data representations to address the multi-modality (C2): (i) Timeseries Data (DB2®, PostgreSQL, Watson IoT®, ...); (ii) Binary File Data (Disk, RocksDB, COS®, ...); (iii) Textual/JSON Data (MongoDB, Redis, Maximo®, ...). A registry allows to dynamically add new resolvers. The mapping to a key/value interface provides a simple interface for implementation of the resolvers and allows us to store the keys as properties in the graph.

The *graph layer* contains the knowledge graph that is linking the meta-data from the various backends (G1). The semantic graph represents the normalized data model (G3) annotated with the associated keys from the data layer.

By storing only the data keys in the graph we get a separation of the metadata graph from the data layer that serves two purposes. First, it keeps the graph manageable in size as the underlying large volume of raw data that often reaches multiple terabytes are kept out of the graph. Second, it helps to solve the federated data problem as clients do not want to move the data out of the master data systems.

We developed our own in-house knowledge graph technology based on our learnings from using over the years different off-the-shelf triple stores and property graphs as backend. Due to the unique requirements, none of them could scale to achieve the desired performance (see Sect. 6) and manageability targets. Based on our experience with triple stores they present two challenges. First, the graph sizes quickly explode when large numbers of properties (like keys) are added, which are secondary for traversals. Although they provide good support for basic RDF semantics most triple stores do not support subsumption inference out-of-the-box (R2) and rely on rule-based materialization. This not only increases the triple number, but, more importantly it is hard to manage consistency in our production context. When users change the structure of taxonomies it is not easy and efficient to update and delete materialized triples such that a consistent state of the graph can be maintained (R8). Property graphs separate the graph from properties and thus could scale better with large number of properties but they do not necessarily are targeting RDF natively resorting to arbitrary conversion tools to support such scenarios. This lack of semantic understanding inflicts subsumption query performance (Sect. 6) and has similar manageability problems of the consistency.

Our knowledge graph is an in-memory semantic property graph called KITT (Keep IoT Trivial). It combines the benefits of semantic understanding of RDF stores and the compact representation of property graphs. It uses an in-memory multigraph representation [2,16] of nodes and edges decorated with properties. Subsumption relationships are directly represented in-memory and allow for guaranteed consistency (R8) such that subconcepts, instances, or relationships cannot exist without the respective parent concepts or property types. The subsumption relationships can also be directly walked by the reasoner. The reasoner is a traversal-based RDFS+ reasoner that supports transitive queries (R6) alongside event-based reasoning (R7) so that whenever new data instances for a concept are added the reasoner will automatically execute relevant update queries. We use this to automatically instantiate e.g. analytic functions as discussed in the next section. Another unique aspect of the graph is its support for property inheritance (R3) that is used to propagate properties, like AI function configurations from concepts. It also supports element-level access control (R9) to homogenize access control across the applications. The graph does not provide a SPARQL interface as user often lack the required semantic knowledge (C7) and provides an easier to use structured YAML/JSON based query format.

The *application layer* contains the various solutions that utilize the Digital Twin. They consist of AI tools for machine learning and optimization that are automatically configured from the knowledge graph and of frontend user interfaces. To simplify usage of the platform for domain experts (C7) we provide development frameworks in Java and Python that simplify querying and automation of tasks such as AI pipelines.

Through this architecture we support semantic retrieval of data streams which returns with a single call of the in-built reasoner the data alongside it's semantic context in the knowledge graph. For example, the user can ask for all `Power` data attached to a `Robot`, with its `Workorder` history and the last `Image` of a camera monitoring the robot. This query will pull the power consumption data from the IoT platform (Watson IoT®), the maintenance history from an asset management system (Maximo®) and images from an object store (COS®).

5 Digital Twin Benchmark Model

The requirement analysis in Sect. 3 identified the main requirements for designing a knowledge graph for Digital Twins. To test and compare different technologies for scaling knowledge graphs we created the Digital Twin Benchmark Model (DTBM) that shares the identified characteristics. Figure 2 shows the main elements of the model structure.

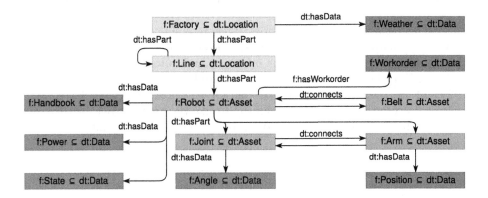

Fig. 2. Digital Twin benchmark model structure

The DTBM benchmark is representing an Industry 4.0 example and creates the knowledge graph for the Digital Twin of a production line. The RDF model is split in a core model (`dt:*`) and a domain taxonomy (`f:*`) according to requirement R1. The core model defines the trinity of `Locations`, `Asset`, and `Data` that is common with other IoT ontologies like BRICK [5]. To keep the benchmark self-contained we refrained from using any upper ontologies. The domain model represents of a location hierarchy in a `Factory` ⊑ `Location` with multiple production lines. The production `Lines` ⊑ `Location` may have a random depth of 1 to 3 levels to represent flexible hierarchies (C4).

Each production line has multiple `Robots` ⊑ `Asset` of different types as example for subsumption (R3) with different machine types. Each robot is composed off two to four `Joint` ⊑ `Asset` and `Arm` ⊑ `Asset` segments determining the degree of freedom to demonstrate composability (C6).

The robots are connected by `Belts` ⊑ `Asset` as example for a logistic transport system. It is to note, that the logistic system is introducing a horizontal element cutting across the hierarchical factory structure. These horizontal structures are very common and allow different views on the represented data.

For simplicity we stick to robots and belts in this example, but, they may be any machine and logistic element in a typical production process where a product passes trough a sequence of production steps.

Each robot has different data types attached (C2): a handbook (`Data_File` ⊑ `Data`), workorder data (`Json` ⊑ `Data`), a power meter (`Data_Series_Numeric` ⊑ `Data_Series` ⊑ `Data`), and on/off state (`Data_Series_Categoric` ⊑ `Data_Series` ⊑ `Data`) coming from different datastorage systems (C3). Each robot joint has angle measurements and each robot arm has a position measurement to illustrate heterogenity (C1). The belt has power meter and state as well to illustrate that data type may repeat across assets. The factory has weather data as example for a dataset at root level. All elements contain additional data properties to store meta-data such as asset ids or data keys linking to the data in the various backend systems.

The benchmark contains 12 queries. They resemble common type of queries that we see in applications run on the knowledge graph from querying information on specific assets to drive user interfaces and automatically configure and execute ML tasks on the data. The queries are heavily relying on subsumption (R2) and are using primarily generic concepts (`Locations`, `Asset`, `Data`). The queries also use transitive relationships (R6) like the `hasPart` relationship that is used to link the factory to lines, down to the robot, and its joints.

```
INSERT {
    ?newfunc rdf:type dt:Function .
    ?newfunc dt:hasInputData ?weather .
    ?newfunc dt:hasInputData ?input .
    ?newfunc dt:hasOutputData ?newout .
    ?newout rdf:type f:Data_Power_Pred .
    ?newout dt:hasDataKeySeries "TBD" .
} WHERE {
    ?loc rdf:type dt:Location .
    ?loc dt:hasSeries ?weather .
    ?weather rdf:type f:Data_Weather .
    ?loc dt:hasPart+ ?asset .
    ?asset rdf:type f:Asset .
    ?asset dt:hasSeries ?input .
    ?input rdf:type f:Data_Power .
    BIND(IRI(CONCAT(STR(?asset),"_Pred")) AS ?newout).
    BIND(IRI(CONCAT(STR(?asset),"_Func")) AS ?newfunc).
}
```

(a) Query 10 to configure an AI function

```
CONSTRUCT {
    ?func rdf:type ?functype .
    ?func dt:hasInputData ?input .
    ?input dt:hasDataKey ?input_key .
    ?func dt:hasOutputData ?output .
    ?output dt:hasDataKey ?output_key .
} WHERE {
    BIND (f:factory1_line_1_robot_1_Func AS ?func) .
    ?func rdf:type dt:Function .
    ?func rdf:type ?functype .
    ?func dt:hasInputData ?input .
    ?input dt:hasDataKey ?input_key .
    ?func dt:hasOutputData ?output .
    ?output dt:hasDataKey ?output_key .
}
```

(b) Query 12 to retrieve the sub-graph of an AI function configuration

Fig. 3. Query example from the Digital Twin benchmark model

Figure 3 shows two example queries from the benchmark. Query 10 in Fig. 3a uses SPARQL update to configures a new analytic AI function for each asset (Robot or Belt) that has an associated power timeseries. It uses this power data as input for the analytic function and also adds the weather data as additional input feature from the closes parent owning one (factory). It then assigns an "TBD" data key to the also newly created output timeseries that later will be replaced with a pointer to the newly computed data. The benchmark contains also other examples for configuring AI functions like: Q9 - to aggregate across a location hierarchy or Q11 - to aggregate all instances by asset type. All queries follow the same template of utilizing a graph pattern (WHERE) to identify deployment locations for the AI functions with relevant inputs and a creation (INSERT) part to materialize the respective AI function. Their configurations could be added to the (INSERT) section [27] or are in our case inherited from their type (R3).

Query 12 in Fig. 3b retrieves the sub-graph for one of these created configurations that contains the inputs and outputs for computing the prediction in an ML job including the data keys. In the given example, this would be a new AI function to compute the prediction of the power meter at robot 1 on line 1 that uses as input the power meter history and the weather data and the newly created output.

6 Experiments

The goal of our experimental evaluation is threefold. First, we want to illustrate the unique challenges that scaling knowledge graphs for digital twins create across various knowledge graph technologies. Second, we want to prove that the proposed Digital Twin Benchmark Model has different behaviour than other benchmarks to verify the need for another model and explore the different characteristics these benchmarks expect of the knowledge graph. Last, we want to validate the benefits of semantic knowledge graphs at the example of our implementation in comparison to established triple stores and property graphs across different benchmarks.

Knowledge Graphs: The first three knowledge graph technologies we evaluate are Blazegraph, GraphDB, and Virtuoso all of which are triple stores that expose SPARQL endpoints. The fourth system is Neo4j as most common property graph. The last one is KITT which is our semantic property graph. The selection is based purely on the availability of information on how to run BSBM and LUBM for these backends.

We used the same workflow to set the systems up, load the data into them, and evaluate their performance. Specifically, we used a containerization version for each graph without following any optimization strategy. The purpose is to replicate a cloud environment where a user will not have access to optimize the backend systems nor the knowledge (C7).

Benchmarks and Datasets: We present the results of two well known RDF benchmarks namely BSBM [7] and LUBM [14] as well as our proposed Digital Twin Benchmark Model (DTBM). Each of them generates RDF datasets which can easily be loaded into the triple stores. For Neo4J we use the neosemantics plugin to import RDF and had to write custom Cypher queries to support all subsumption alternatives. For KITT we use our own RDF loader hat converts RDF in a class and instance model. More details about the benchmarks:

1. The Berlin SPAQRL Benchmark (BSBM) [7] is built around an e-commerce use case and it is scaled via the number of the products. It creates a set of products offered by different vendors and reviewed by consumers. In general, the generated datasets are property heavy and consist of subsumption hierarchies and their depth depends on the chosen scale factor. For evaluating the different systems, BSBM uses a query generator which generates queries that emulate the search and navigation pattern of a consumer looking for a product.
2. The Lehigh University Benchmark (LUBM) [14] was developed to evaluate the performance of the semantic web knowledge base systems with respect to use in large OWL applications. It generates a dataset for the university domain and its query evaluation uses subsumptions and recursive queries such as transitive closure.
3. The Digital Twin Benchmark (DTBM) was introduced in the last section. It is subsumption heavy with transitive queries of flexible depth to query information and configure AI functions.

The characteristics of the datasets generated by the different benchmarks are summarized in Table 1. For the BSBM dataset the real "Dataset scale" factor is the value the reported value multiplied by 1,000. For example, S2 in BSBM refers to 2,000 products. BSBM is evaluated with 16 queries in parallel in Java, while LUBM and DTBM are evaluated with single-threaded sequential queries in Python. We do not run parallel tests to not skew results with Pythons bad parallelization behaviour.

Table 1. Dataset characteristics with their number of elements

Dataset	BSBM				LUBM				DTBM			
scale	triplets	nodes	edges	props	triplets	nodes	edges	props	triplets	nodes	edges	props
S2	377,241	36,871	102,315	37,022	288,894	38,349	113,463	36,834	114,177	35,702	41,698	35,601
S5	1,711,567	152,965	454,334	153,294	781,694	102,383	309,393	100,018	283,785	88,895	103,874	88,713
S10	3,738,188	315,148	982,502	315,477	1,591,643	207,441	630,753	203,625	570,232	178,118	208,224	177,801
S20	7,749,994	632,447	2,018,821	632,776	3,360,686	437,570	1,332,029	430,559	1,136,634	356,087	416,285	355,500
S50	17,571,059	1,593,382	5,132,438	1,594,113	8,317,905	1,082,833	3,298,813	1,067,023	2,844,499	890,624	1,041,300	889,227
S100	35,159,904	3,196,023	10,104,195	3,198,020	16,753,468	2,179,781	6,645,928	2,148,846	5,693,601	1,781,866	2,083,488	1,779,119

Query Configuration: In BSBM, we use the default BSBM test driver [7] which executes sequences of SPARQL queries over the SPARQL protocol against the system under test. In order to emulate a realistic workload, the test driver can simulate multiple clients that concurrently execute query mixes against the test system. The queries are parameterized with random values from the benchmark dataset, in order to make it more difficult for the test system to apply caching techniques. The test driver executes a series of warm-up query mixes before the actual performance is measured in order to benchmark systems under normal working conditions. To make a fair comparison, we implemented our own test driver that follows a similar design to evaluate Neo4j and KITT. Note, BSBM test driver measures the response time excluding the time needed to deserialize the response and it puts a constraint to the result size.

In LUBM and DTBM, we use our own query executor in Python to evaluate the performance of the various systems. We execute each query 500 times and we report the average response time including the deserialization of the response. We also place a constraint to the result size limiting the result to 1,000 records to put the focus on the query execution time and not the serialization time.

Overall, all benchmarks use SPARQL queries; corresponding Cypher queries for Neo4j or YAML queries for KITT. We optimize the representation for each graph and e.g. directly represent properties in Neo4j and optimize queries accordingly to e.g. activate subsumption support (RDFS+) for all RDF stores. All benchmarks have been executed on a Linux machine with a AMD Ryzen 3959X processor and 64 GB memory and SSDs with the backends running on Docker.

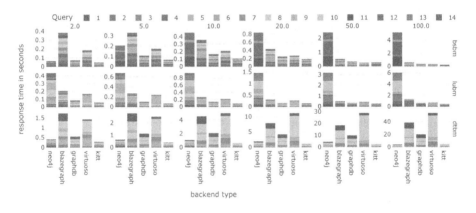

Fig. 4. Query response times for different sizes (columns) and benchmarks (rows)

6.1 BSBM Evaluation

Figure 4 summarizes the average response time for all benchmarks in seconds. We will first discuss the BSBM results in the first row. For this one all queries run in less than a second even for the big graphs. We observe that Neo4j performs well only for small graphs and worse for larger. It seems that it cannot understand the semantics hidden in the dataset and it does not perform well when queries use subsumption. Comparing the triple stores, we find that GraphDB has the lowest response times while Blazegraph has the worst performance. It seems that the queries using filtering by multiple properties such as Query 5 are costly for the

RDF triple stores. KITT outperforms the other knowledge graphs in all datasets slightly. This shows its ability as a semantic property graph to understand the model and the semantics contained in the dataset.

6.2   LUBM Evaluation

The results for LUBM on the second row in Fig. 4 show about the same characteristics as BSBM. However, we observe that Neo4j is not able to perform well for any size. This is due to the fact that LUBM uses many subsumptions and recursive queries and Neo4j seems unable to process them efficiently. Furthermore, we observe for the different graphs that the ratio some queries have in the stacked bars change with the experiment sizes. This hints that the knowledge graphs struggle with different queries characteristics when a graph grows. For example, Query 9 is the most expensive for triple stores up to dataset size S20, and then we see an increase in response time for Query 2. This can be explained by the fact that Query 2 fetches for each department of a university, all the graduate students and searches for those who have obtained their undergraduate degree from the given university. This breadth exploration becomes very costly in larger graphs because the number of students becomes huge and many invalid pathes need to be evaluated before they are dropped from the result set. In addition, Query 9 returns students who have taken a course of their faculty advisor which also leads to multiple traversals of the hierarchy that links advisors to students through a course. Although the query is of a similar structure to Query 2, it is less costly in large graphs due to the smaller search space. Finally, we observe that KITT again surpasses all knowledge graphs and it can produce the result in a few milliseconds. This again shows the benefits of an in-memory semantic property graph that can directly walk the subsumption taxonomy from high-level concepts to instances and their transitive relationships.

6.3   DTBM Evaluation

The results for our proposed benchmark illustrate first the bad scaling behaviour of traditional knowledge graphs in a Digital Twin scenario as discussed in the beginning. While common execution times for BSBM and LUBM were usually under one second for the triple stores they grow to multiple seconds for some queries for larger graphs, which is not acceptable for driving user interfaces. This magnitude differences in response times for DTBM is particularly notable as that the size in triples of the dataset size S100 is only 1/3 of LUBM and 1/6 of BSBM (Table 1).

The second notable aspect is that the performance characteristics between the triple stores change. While Blazegraph was performing worst for BSBM and LUBM it is now Virtuoso that has the largest response times. It is particularly struggling with Query 10 (Fig. 3a) and actually failed out-the-box for S100 due to too large implication space.

Along the same line it is now Neo4J that overtakes the triple stores in the benchmark. It probably benefits from the lower number of nodes and the property representation. It is notable that across all benchmarks it scales constantly along to the number of nodes. However, we have to note that we had to write custom Cypher queries for Neo4J to support all subsumption alternatives for all use cases. In production this is not feasible because taxonomies are domain specific (R1) and change (C8).

KITT outperforms the other graph stores also for this scenario. This demonstrates the generalizable benefit of a semantic property graph across multiple use case from RDF specific benchmarks like BSBM or LUBM to the digital twin use case addressed in DTBM.

7 Summary

In this paper we share our experience in scaling semantic knowledge graphs for automating AI of Digital Twins in the IoT domain. We analyze the unique characteristics, goals and requirements of the use case that uniquely links semantic models to multi-modal data management across different federated data systems.

We derive from this a reference architecture for a Digital Twin knowledge graph solution that we use in multiple products. It separates the knowledge graph from the underlying data in a micro-service environment that is easy to scale and extend.

To enable the community to evaluate different knowledge graph technologies for this architecture we open source a new Digital Twin Benchmark Model (DTBM) that represent the specific requirements of the domain. The DTBM generator creates an Industry 4.0 production line and contains multiple queries that we use in production. We demonstrate in some query examples how AI functions can be automatically configured from the semantic graph. We execute the benchmark for different knowledge graph technologies and compare it to the well established BSBM and LUBM. The result highlight the different behaviour of DTBM in comparison to BSBM and LUBM and substantiate the need of the new benchmark. They also illustrate the challenges in scaling knowledge graphs for Digital Twins that already show by a magnitude larger response times for even smaller graphs. It may be possible to optimize the parameters, indexes and queries for the different knowledge graph technologies, but, given the domain specificity (R1) and dynamic nature (C8) of these models and queries this is not feasible in production for a general purpose cloud service where users have neither access to these configurations nor the expertise (C7).

That our own knowledge graph KITT shows the best performance across all benchmarks demonstrates the advantage of semantic property graphs that combine benefits of RDF and property graphs and support subsumption and transitivity out of the box. We would like to see more graphs that address this need and not specialize on one or the other. For that purpose we open sourced the script for creating the Digital Twin Benchmark Model as well as the used benchmark configuration such that other can replicate and extend our results.

Supplemental Material Availability: The source code and queries for DTBM as well as the used configurations for the benchmark are available at https://github.com/IBM/digital-twin-benchmark-model.

References

1. Akroyd, J., Mosbach, S., Bhave, A., Kraft, M.: Universal digital twin-a dynamic knowledge graph. Data-Centric Engineering, vol. 2 (2021)
2. Ali, W., Saleem, M., Yao, B., Hogan, A., Ngomo, A.C.N.: A survey of RDF stores & SPARQL engines for querying knowledge graphs. VLDB J. **31**, 1–26 (2021)
3. Bader, S.R., Grangel-Gonzalez, I., Nanjappa, P., Vidal, M.E., Maleshkova, M.: A knowledge graph for industry 4.0. In: Extended Semantic Web Conference (ESWC), pp. 465–480 (2020)
4. Bader, S.R., Maleshkova, M., García-Castro, R., Davies, J., Antoniou, G., Fortuna, C.: Towards integrated data control for digital twins in industry 4.0. In: International Workshop on Semantic Digital Twins (SeDiT) at Extended Semantic Web Conference (ESWC) (2020)
5. Balaji, B., et al.: Brick: metadata schema for portable smart building applications. Appl. Energy **226**, 1273–1292 (2018)
6. Besta, M., et al.: Demystifying graph databases: analysis and taxonomy of data organization, system designs, and graph queries. arXiv preprint arXiv:1910.09017 (2019)
7. Bizer, C., Schultz, A.: The Berlin SPARQL benchmark. Int. J. Semant. Web Inf. Syst. (IJSWIS) **5**(2), 1–24 (2009)
8. Bone, M., Blackburn, M., Kruse, B., Dzielski, J., Hagedorn, T., Grosse, I.: Toward an interoperability and integration framework to enable digital thread. Systems **6**(4), 46 (2018)
9. Chaves-Fraga, D., Priyatna, F., Cimmino, A., Toledo, J., Ruckhaus, E., Corcho, O.: GTFS-Madrid-Bench: a benchmark for virtual knowledge graph access in the transport domain. J. Web Semantics **65**, 100596 (2020)
10. Chevallier, Z., Finance, B., Boulakia, B.C.: A reference architecture for smart building digital twin. In: International Workshop on Semantic Digital Twins (SeDiT) at Extended Semantic Web Conference (ESWC) (2020)
11. Dibowski, H., Massa Gray, F.: Applying knowledge graphs as integrated semantic information model for the computerized engineering of building automation systems. In: Extended Semantic Web Conference (ESWC), pp. 616–631 (2020)
12. Endris, K.M., Rohde, P.D., Vidal, M.-E., Auer, S.: Ontario: federated query processing against a semantic data lake. In: Hartmann, S., Küng, J., Chakravarthy, S., Anderst-Kotsis, G., Tjoa, A.M., Khalil, I. (eds.) DEXA 2019. LNCS, vol. 11706, pp. 379–395. Springer, Cham (2019). https://doi.org/10.1007/978-3-030-27615-7_29
13. Erling, O.: Virtuoso, a hybrid RDBMS/graph column store. IEEE Data Eng. Bull. **35**(1), 3–8 (2012)
14. Guo, Y., Pan, Z., Heflin, J.: LUBM: a benchmark for OWL knowledge base systems. J. Web Semant. **3**(2–3), 158–182 (2005)
15. Hasnain, A., et al.: BioFed: federated query processing over life sciences linked open data. J. Biomed. Semant. **8**(1), 1–19 (2017)
16. Ingalalli, V., Ienco, D., Poncelet, P., Villata, S.: Querying RDF data using a multigraph-based approach. In: Extending Database Technology (EDBT), pp. 245–256 (2016)

17. Kalaycı, E.G., Grangel González, I., Lösch, F., Xiao, G., Kharlamov, E., Calvanese, D., et al.: Semantic integration of Bosch manufacturing data using virtual knowledge graphs. In: International Semantic Web Conference (ISWC), pp. 464–481 (2020)
18. Kharlamov, E., Martin-Recuerda, F., Perry, B., Cameron, D., Fjellheim, R., Waaler, A.: Towards semantically enhanced digital twins. In: IEEE International Conference on Big Data, pp. 4189–4193 (2018)
19. Kumar, V.R.S., et al.: Ontologies for industry 4.0. Knowl. Eng. Rev. **34**, e17 (2019)
20. Li, X., Wang, L., Zhu, C., Liu, Z.: Framework for manufacturing-tasks semantic modelling and manufacturing-resource recommendation for digital twin shop-floor. J. Manuf. Syst. **58**, 281–292 (2021)
21. Lietaert, P., Meyers, B., Van Noten, J., Sips, J., Gadeyne, K.: Knowledge graphs in digital twins for AI in production. In: Advances in Production Management Systems (APMS), pp. 249–257 (08 2021)
22. Mihindukulasooriya, N., et al.: Knowledge graph induction enabling recommending and trend analysis: a corporate research community use case. In: International Semantic Web Conference (ISWC) (2022)
23. Morsey, M., Lehmann, J., Auer, S., Ngonga Ngomo, A.C.: DBpedia SPARQL benchmark-performance assessment with real queries on real data. In: International Semantic Web Conference (ISWC), pp. 454–469 (2011)
24. Noy, N., Gao, Y., Jain, A., Narayanan, A., Patterson, A., Taylor, J.: Industry-scale knowledge graphs: lessons and challenges. Commun. ACM **62**(8), 36–43 (2019)
25. Pan, Z., Zhu, T., Liu, H., Ning, H.: A survey of RDF management technologies and benchmark datasets. J. Ambient Intell. Humanized Comput. **9**(5), 1693–1704 (2018)
26. Ploennigs, J., Cohn, J., Stanford-Clark, A.: The future of IoT. IEEE Internet Things Mag. **1**(1), 28–33 (2018)
27. Ploennigs, J., Schumann, A., Lécué, F.: Adapting semantic sensor networks for smart building diagnosis. In: Mika, P., et al. (eds.) ISWC 2014. LNCS, vol. 8797, pp. 308–323. Springer, Cham (2014). https://doi.org/10.1007/978-3-319-11915-1_20
28. Rahman, H., Hussain, M.I.: A comprehensive survey on semantic interoperability for internet of things: state-of-the-art and research challenges. Trans. Emerg. Telecom. Tech. **31**(12), e3902 (2020)
29. Rojas, J.A., et al.: Leveraging semantic technologies for digital interoperability in the European railway domain. In: International Semantic Web Conference (ISWC), pp. 648–664 (2021)
30. Samuelsen, S.D., Nikolov, N., Soylu, A., Roman, D.: An approach for representing and storing RDF data in multi-model databases. In: Research Conference on Metadata and Semantics Research, pp. 47–52 (2020)
31. Schmid, S., Henson, C., Tran, T.: Using knowledge graphs to search an enterprise data lake. In: Extended Semantic Web Conference (ESWC), pp. 262–266 (2019)
32. Schmidt, M., Görlitz, O., Haase, P., Ladwig, G., Schwarte, A., Tran, T.: FedBench: a benchmark suite for federated semantic data query processing. In: Aroyo, L., et al. (eds.) ISWC 2011. LNCS, vol. 7031, pp. 585–600. Springer, Heidelberg (2011). https://doi.org/10.1007/978-3-642-25073-6_37
33. Schmidt, M., Hornung, T., Lausen, G., Pinkel, C.: SP²Bench: a SPARQL performance benchmark. In: IEEE International Conference on Data Engineering, pp. 222–233 (2009)
34. Singh, V., Willcox, K.E.: Engineering design with digital thread. AIAA J. **56**(11), 4515–4528 (2018)

35. Taelman, R., Colpaert, P., Mannens, E., Verborgh, R.: Generating public transport data based on population distributions for RDF benchmarking. Semant. Web **10**(2), 305–328 (2019)
36. Zheng, X., Lu, J., Kiritsis, D.: The emergence of cognitive digital twin: vision, challenges and opportunities. Int. J. Prod. Res. 1–23 (2021)
37. Zhou, B., Pychynski, T., Reischl, M., Kharlamov, E., Mikut, R.: Machine learning with domain knowledge for predictive quality monitoring in resistance spot welding. J. Intell. Manuf. **33**(4), 1139–1163 (2022). https://doi.org/10.1007/s10845-021-01892-y

Knowledge Graph Induction Enabling Recommending and Trend Analysis: A Corporate Research Community Use Case

Nandana Mihindukulasooriya[(✉)], Mike Sava, Gaetano Rossiello,
Md. Faisal Mahbub Chowdhury, Irene Yachbes, Aditya Gidh,
Jillian Duckwitz, Kovit Nisar, Michael Santos, and Alfio Gliozzo

IBM Research AI, Yorktown Heights, NY, USA
nandana@ibm.com

Abstract. A research division plays an important role of driving innovation in an organization. Drawing insights, following trends, keeping abreast of new research, and formulating strategies are increasingly becoming more challenging for both researchers and executives as the amount of information grows in both velocity and volume. In this paper we present a use case of how a corporate research community, IBM Research, utilizes Semantic Web technologies to induce a unified Knowledge Graph from both structured and textual data obtained by integrating various applications used by the community related to research projects, academic papers, datasets, achievements and recognition. In order to make the Knowledge Graph more accessible to application developers, we identified a set of common patterns for exploiting the induced knowledge and exposed them as APIs. Those patterns were born out of user research which identified the most valuable use cases or user pain points to be alleviated. We outline two distinct scenarios: recommendation and analytics for business use. We will discuss these scenarios in detail and provide an empirical evaluation on entity recommendation specifically. The methodology used and the lessons learned from this work can be applied to other organizations facing similar challenges.

Keywords: Knowledge graph · Knowledge induction ·
Recommending · Trend analysis

1 Introduction

Research and innovation is the heart of any organization that is focused on advancing technologies to meet the challenges of solving real world problems by bridging the business needs with scientific discoveries. In fast moving research areas such as artificial intelligence or quantum computing, there is a tremendous growth of research activities in both velocity and volume happening within and

N. Mihindukulasooriya, M. Sava, G. Rossiello and Md. F. M. Chowdhury—Equal contributions.

outside the organization [5,37]. It is challenging to understand the trends and draw insights, and doing so manually is becoming unfeasible. Nevertheless, such insights are of utmost important for the executives who make strategy decisions on the impact of current investments and decide on future directions [36] and for the researchers who are looking for effective collaborations to optimize the reuse of research assets. In addition, in large organizations involving thousands of people and various scientific disciplines, it is difficult to keep abreast of individual projects. Weekly updates are often overwhelming but essential to make sure that people are informed of progress, to prevent redundant work, enhance re-usability, and cross fertilize ideas and assets. However, those has to be personalized to each person's user's interests to keep the information overload minimal.

One major challenge in generating insights is that generally data is scattered across different applications in their own siloed spaces. If integrated manually, this requires a lot of effort and hinders their full potential use for downstream applications. Thus, it is useful for an organization to have a unified integrated view of the data. Furthermore, these applications capture both structured metadata and also a lot of unstructured textual data. It's challenging to analyze the useful insights hidden in large volumes of text and uncover the insights.

For example, in the IBM research community, there are different applications for managing research projects, academic papers, datasets, internal achievements and external recognition. Researchers are both the content providers who contribute to these applications as well as end users that gets the recomendations and insights. From the adoption point of view, it is important that they have to spend only a minimum amount of valuable time without duplication of effort in multiple apps for the same information and get high value and useful insights in order to increase the engagement.

Before jumping to the solutions, we have first conducted a user study to understand the most valuable user pain points to be alleviated. Through a set of in-depth interviews from a set of selected users in different stages of their career, recommendations and trend analytics were identified as two main use cases that most requested by the community, as discussed in Sect. 2.

The aforementioned scenario provided us an excellent use case to test the boundaries of Knowledge Graph Induction (KGI) framework which is presented in this paper. Specifically, we apply our technology to mitigate some of the challenges in a corporate research community: IBM Research. While we restrict our focus to a research community in this paper, KGI framework can be applied to any organization that has a large volume of structured and unstructured data to be integrated and analyzed.

We will discuss how we address the common challenges of extraction of knowledge from both structured and unstructured data, how to enrich the KG from information available in the vast amounts of unstructured text and how to use the enriched KG to power Knowledge Exploitation Patterns (KEP) for entity recommendation and trend analytics. We will also discuss how the external encyclopedic knowledge such as Wikidata [38] can be seamlessly integrated to internal knowledge enabling traversal following the Linked Data principles to get more context or provide more structure to the data using the taxonomic knowledge.

The main contributions of this paper are as follows:

- We introduce an end-to-end framework for Knowledge Graph Induction from both structured, semi-structured, and unstructured data. KGI is easily portable across domains and enables the reuse of high level abstractions, i.e. KEP, for recommending and trend analysis.
- We introduce the Wikidata Parser, a Knowledge Generation and Linking approach based on transformer based generative models, which achieves the state of the art performances on information extraction benchmarks.
- We demonstrate the effectiveness of the KGI framework in two different scenarios: IBM research internal community and ISWC 2002–2021 proceedings.
- We discuss how a research organization can benefit from building a KG from both structured and unstructured data motivated by the pain points identified in a user study.

The rest of this paper is structured as follows. Section 2 discusses the use cases identified after an extensive user study. Section 3 introduces the KGI framework including knowledge integration, Wikidata parser and evaluate the knowledge generation using an academic benchmark. Section 4 introduces KEP for Entity Recommendation, Trend Analysis, and Infobox Generation, providing and empirical evaluation of the recommending capabilities based on user evaluation. Section 5 presents a review of related work, while Sect. 6 concludes the paper highlighting directions for future work.

2   Application Use Cases

The Apps@Research team, an application design and development team inside IBM Research, designs, develops, and supports a portfolio of cloud-based web applications providing rich, intuitive, integrated experiences that serve the unique needs of the IBM Research community. These include collaborative tools for:

- proposing and reporting progress on research projects including tracking staff effort, milestones, and impact (Research Project Portal)
- tracking the status of papers submitted to conferences and journal throughout the cycle from submission to decision (Academic Paper Portal)
- cataloging datasets approved for use by the legal team and datasets published by our teams (Dataset catalog)
- nominating, reviewing and selecting projects to receive yearly internal accomplishment awards (Achievements Portal)
- tracking external recognition and awards won by IBM researchers (Recognition Portal)

The Apps@Research team engaged the IBM Research AI team to partner on ways to incorporate IBM Research's own artificial intelligence technologies to augment the user experience in these applications. The key motivations were to:

- Unlock the content potential of the Apps@Research applications, which reflects the work and expertise across each division and teams.

– Improve user experience by creating exceptional, well-curated, concise and personalized information.
– Leverage and offer a testbed for IBM Research's own AI technology

In order to inform prioritization for the product roadmap for one of the most pervasive applications, we undertook a foundational user research study in 2020 to better understand user needs. The study included over 100 interviews and 220 survey responses from users of our applications. From this study, one key pain point was identified: because the content in our tools describe detailed research project proposals and plans of thousands of research projects, the content is too dense to be easily digestible. Users struggle in discovering relevant content and are under the perception that other users will find their content either. In turn, many users could become frustrated and stop using the tools for their key intended purposes - collaboration, innovation, and sharing updates.

Our hypothesis was that if we were to find a way to help the content become more discoverable, personalized, and digestible, that users would be motivated to keep their content up-to-date and visit the tool more frequently to find synergies and sparking innovation across research projects.

After doing some preliminary technical discovery and feasibility study with the AI Research team, we performed a more detailed user study. We recruited 12 participants from a representative sample of researcher and strategists at different stages in their career. They had varying experience with AI technology concepts. We conducted 60 min structured interview sessions with users in which we asked open-ended questions and then engaged them in an interactive exercise in a mural application.

The purpose of the interactive exercise was to identify various possible use cases and to prioritize them. We gave the users a hypothetical "$100" and asked them how they would "spend" the money, dividing among the use case ideas (Hundred dollar prioritization [20]). The purpose of the exercise was to understand the quantitative value that participants would ascribe to various use cases.

Upon completion of the interviews, we then performed a design thinking exercise called affinity mapping, to group ideas and identify common themes and patterns. We also analyzed the "$100 prioritization" to help quantify the value of use cases to all the participants.

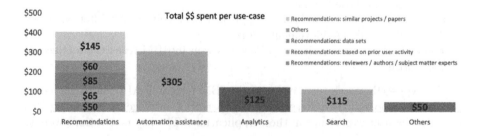

Fig. 1. User Interview $100 "spending" results

Figure 1 shows that most users identified "recommendations" as the most valuable use case. Recommendations would be automatically generated with information of which the user might otherwise not be aware. Recommendations would be personalized, based on users' previous activities such as papers/patents published, expertise, current projects, etc. - all of which could be derived from data in our KG. Figure 1 also shows that users wanted several types of recommendations such as related research projects, relevant papers, collaborators, experts to review their papers, etc.

The second most valuable use case would be "automation assistance". This would include help to pre-fill forms in the various tools in a smart way, saving the user time and anticipating their needs. This was a technical requirements and having an integrated view in KG would allow us to pre-fill a lot of information in different applications based on the context.

Next, users were interested in "analytics" - smart reports and dashboards that could be generated to provide business insights. The users have found that the data in our portals are dense and overwhelming and wanted to have high-level overview summaries so that can understand the common trends and dig more into the details.

Users were interested in improved Search and Filtering. Currently most of our applications' search is based on keywords and users were interested in more advanced semantic search capabilities. A KG would allow us to perform more complex structured searches.

Knowing that recommendations ranked highest as the most important use case, we analyzed further which types of content would be of greatest interest, so that we could prioritize developing those features first. We found that users ascribed the most value to being recommended projects and papers.

The insights gained from the user study led us to focus on the following two use case scenarios:

- **Recommending**: For researchers keeping abreast of colleagues' work (project status and publications) is very difficult in a large organization focusing on many technology areas. This is a hindrance to effective collaborations and reuse of research assets. There is a need for technologies and tools to make this process more seamless.
- **Trend Analysis**: For executives it is difficult to understand the breadth of the research portfolio, gain useful insights, and formulate a future strategy. There is a need to process large volumes of unstructured data and provide useful insights.

In the following sections, we will discuss our NLP and Semantic Web-driven approach for addressing these two main use case scenarios.

3   Knowledge Graph Induction

The overview of our KGI framework is illustrated in Fig. 2. It consists on three main conceptual blocks: data integration, whose main goal is to integrate heterogeneous semi-structured data from siloed applications using a domain ontology;

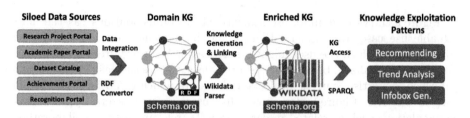

Fig. 2. The knowledge graph induction framework

knowledge extraction and linking, implemented by the *Wikidata Parser*, a component capable of generating RDF compliant knowledge by processing all textual content attached to entities in the domain KG; and *Knowledge Exploitation Patterns*, a set of abstractions over the induced KG that are domain-agnostic and generalized to use cases such as *recommending* and *analytics*.

3.1 Data Integration

Data related to IBM Research is scattered across multiple siloed applications. We used a knowledge representation approach based on Semantic Web standards and unified them into a single KG with links to both internal entities as well as relevant information extracted from background knowledge sources such as Wikidata.

Internal data pertains to items that are of particular interest to a research organization: research projects (science, strategy), people (eminence), academic publications and datasets (eminence), achievements and recognition (impact).

Each of the applications provides an API to extract data, which is then processed through a RDF conversion pipeline following a process similar to RML-based tools [10]. For this purpose, a Research KG ontology was built by reusing and extending the Schema.org with classes and relations that were more specific to our use case. The data schema of each of the five applications were aligned to the ontology by a knowledge engineer and the mappings were created.

The Schema.org ontology was selected as the base because it covered most of the concepts in our applications and is used by some of our collaborators. In addition, entities and relations from Wikidata are also reused. This enables us to easily integrate with third parties. The conversion process consists of (a) data extraction and (b) cleaning to normalize certain values, (c) mapping and RDF generation. Entity resolution is carried out to convert mentions to people, projects, and other entities to their canonical identifiers through a deterministic process. To this aim, we used unique identifiers such as emails and other internal conventions.

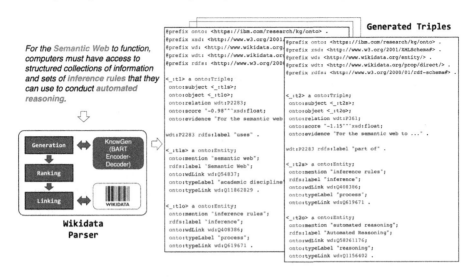

Fig. 3. The Wikidata Parser architecture and an example output.

3.2 Knowledge Generation and Linking: Wikidata Parser

A large part of our data is unstructured text. In order to incorporate them in the KG, we extract the textual values attached to each entity such as article content or a project description, chunk them into sentences and parse them using *Wikidata Parser*, a novel tool integrated in our KGI framework [9,13].

Wikidata Parser allows converting unstructured text into structured data represented as a set of ABox assertions compliant with the TBox of Wikidata. We address this problem as a sequence generation task, similar to machine translation or text summarization, where the input is an English sentence and the output is a set of facts. To this aim we leveraged large pre-trained sequence-to-sequence language models, such as BART [23] and train them from large dataset derived using distant supervision, by exploiting the alignments between Wikidata facts with the abstracts of Wikipedia pages.

Specifically, given a sentence, we fine-tune the language model to detect pairs of entity mentions and jointly generate a set of facts (i.e. <SUBJECT (SUBJECT TYPE), RELATION, OBJECT (OBJECT TYPE)>) representing entity labels, entity types and their relationships. The output of the system is then deterministically converted in RDF statements, as shown in Fig. 3.

Our experiments and analysis show that Wikidata Parser produces more accurate triples improving in both precision and recall if compared with the state-of-the-art generative information extraction methods [6,19,32].

Table 1 reports the F1 results of Wikidata Parser for each type of semantic annotations part of the triples generated from the abstracts, in terms of correct predictions of entity mentions, entity labels, entity types and their joint relations. For training and evaluation purposes, we extended a distantly supervised dataset for relation extraction [6] with the full set of Wikidata-based annotations for each matched triple found in the abstracts of Wikipedia.

Table 1. Information extraction results. **MD** = Mention Detection. **TYPE** = Type Prediction. **EL** = Entity Label. **RN** = Relation Name. **REL** = Relation Prediction with Label Match. **P** = Precision. **R** = Recall. **F1** = Micro F1-score.

	MD-F1	TYPE-F1	EL-F1	RN-F1	REL-P	REL-R	REL-F1
Approach							
SOTA IE pipeline [19]	–	–	–	–	43.30	41.73	42.50
GenIE [19]	-	-	79.69	78.21	68.02	**69.87**	68.93
Wikidata Parser	84.27	79.65	**82.73**	**80.84**	**73.88**	67.85	**70.74**

For both subject and object, we generate the surface form mention, canonical label, type label, relation label. Whenever applicable, we link the entities and types to Wikidata entities. Relations are also linked to Wikidata. This information is then converted in RDF and represented using a reified statement meta model. In addition, the facts are associated to an evidence attribute, which contains the provenance (i.e. the sentence) from which the triple has been generated together with its confidence score. An example output is shown in Fig. 3. In addition, each triple is linked to the corresponding entity where the text was extracted.

3.3   Implementation Details

The KG implementation consists of several components. First and foremost is the actual deployment and hosting of the knowledge graph. Our knowledge graph is hosted on a Blazegraph triplestore inside a RedHat OpenShift Container platform which gives us all the advantages of a cloud deployment (scaling, flexibility, storage). We have a second component, a reverse proxy for Single Sign-On (SSO) authentication and authorization to the graph. Some of the data in our graph is confidential and therefore requires a need to know access to prevent traversing and querying the graph by unintended parties. The final set of components relate to the ETL (Extraction, Transform, and Load) process. Currently we build and load the graph on weekly basis. Our ETL process consists of extracting the data from all of the application APIs (both GraphQL and REST) as JSON documents, keeping an in-memory representation of the documents, and then converting these documents to RDF in Turtle format. The textual raw data of each entity is enriched with Wikidata parser as described in Sect. 3.2 with automated OpenShift cronjobs. Finally, RDF data coming from both structured and textual sources is integrated and loaded into the triple store on a scheduled basis.

The current ETL process will be vastly be improved in the future to address the evolution of data by limiting text processing only to detected changes in the KG. Some of this future work will require including a text fingerprinting service to decide if the data has indeed changed (*i.e.* for computational cost, we only care about the free text changes and not usually the meta data).

4   Knowledge Exploitation Patterns

To make the KG easy to use and adapt across different domains, we identified a set of common usage patterns, *Knowledge Exploitation Patterns (KEP)*, and expose them as parameterized client API library to minimize the learning curve for the technology. These APIs generate the corresponding SPARQL queries and handle other cross-cutting concerns such as security or caching. Nevertheless, developers also can run queries directly in the SPARQL endpoint if needed. Currently, we provide APIs required for induced ontology exploration (type hierarchies, infoboxes), entity recommendation, and trend analysis. The idea behind the use of KEP is that certain functionalities can be abstracted out of the specific application domain by performing queries against the KG metamodel that is then used differently in downstream applications for the specific domain.

4.1   Entity Recommendations

Based on our use cases study described in Sect. 2, the automatic recommendations of items, such as publications, projects or collaborators, is one of the main desiderata for the members of our enterprise research community. Collaborative filtering [22] is arguably the most common approach for recommendation systems, especially in environments with a large user base where the state-of-the-art methods are based on advanced deep learning techniques. However, an enterprise research community might not have enough users to train large parametric models due to the sparsity of user log activities. For this reason, we adopt a hybrid content-based recommendation system method [12,24] by exploiting jointly the textual content, structured data and induced semantic annotations generated from our Wikidata Parser (see Sect. 3.2).

The idea is to convert our KG in an entity-feature Vector Space Model (VSM) model, where the rows are represented by the different type of entities in the KG, such as people, publications, projects and accomplishments, and the columns represent the feature space. In detail, let us consider $VSM^{n,m}$ a matrix using the standard tf-idf weighting schema, where each row $e_{i,*}$ is an entity vector created by concatenating different groups of features, described as follow:

Bag of Words. The textual content of entities, such as publications or projects, are tokenized and each token is considered as a single (sparse) feature. For entities representing people, where the textual context is not available, we exploit our KG to collect the textual content, e.g., from the publications or projects linked to the specific user by a multi-hop navigation in the graph.

Structured Data. This feature set represents relations derived from knowledge integration from our original data sources. For instance, the research division and topic of a project, the upper-line management for a person, and so on.

Entities. This feature set represent the entities extracted from Wikidata parser, grouped by their Wikidata type. For example, given the triples in Fig. 3, we create entity features such as SEMANTIC WEB:ACADEMIC DISCIPLINE, INFERENCE:PROCESS, and so on.

Frames. We also leverage the semantic relational information from the extracted triples. In order to alleviate the sparsity problem, we only concatenate the semantic annotations w.r.t. the domain, relation and range of each triple. For instance, <ACADEMIC DISCIPLINE, USES, PROCESS> for one of the generated triple in Fig. 3.

It is important to note that our feature set does not depend on the specific entity and relation set. Instead, this pattern is totally domain-agnostic and reusable and can be applied to any KG and entity type generated from our KG induction pipeline and integration process.

After the VSM is built, the recommendation inference for a user is implemented in a non-parametric manner by exploiting the cosine similarity between the user and the target item vectors, such as publications, projects or other users. In other words, the recommended items for a user are the nearest neighbor entities in the vector space ranked by their cosine similarity scores.

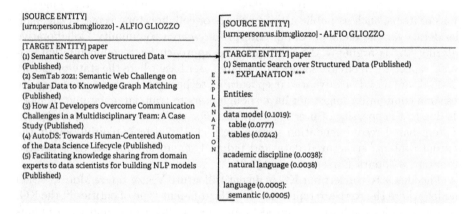

Fig. 4. An example of paper recommendations for a researcher. The figure on the left reports the list of recommended publications. The explanation for the top ranked item is shown in the figure on the right as a list of relevant entities grouped by their semantic types.

Figure 4 shows an example of a list of recommended publications for an researcher using the aforementioned KG-based VSM. The KG induced from text allows us to provide meaningful explanations for the user that justify the recommendation. The explanation is obtained by measuring and selecting the most relevant entities (i.e. those that contributed most to the similarity score), ranked by their combined tf-idf weights.

Table 2. User evaluation for scholary article, project and achievement recommendations for 30 users.

Criteria	Papers		Projects		Achievements	
	MAP	P @ 10	MAP	P @ 10	MAP	P @ 5
LOW	0.89	0.76	0.92	0.81	0.87	0.82
MEDIUM	0.51	0.34	0.65	0.45	0.51	0.36
HIGH	0.21	0.08	0.50	0.14	0.41	0.17

To evaluate the quality of the recommendations, we recruited 30 volunteer researchers from various disciplines. For each participant, we recommended 10 projects, 10 papers and 5 achievements. Each participant was asked to rate the recommendations on the following scale:

- NONE: No value to me
- LOW: Good to know but I am not going to read anytime soon
- MEDIUM: Relevant for my specific area of interest (must read)
- HIGH: Relevant to my current project(s) and work

We performed a quantitative analysis by evaluating Mean Average Precision (MAP) and Precision@K (P@K) metrics, which are popular choices to evaluate recommendation systems. Both MAP and P@K take in consideration only binary assessments, i.e. if the recommended item is relevant or non-relevant. In order to convert our graded rating into a binary assessment, we adopt three different criteria, namely HIGH (i.e. only HIGH category is regarded as positive), MEDIUM (i.e. HIGH and MED categories are positive), LOW (i.e. HIGH, MED and LOW are positive). As shown in Table 2, the performance of our recommendation system is consistent across the different type of recommended items. Moreover, the MAP is consistently higher than P@K, showing that the system tends to provide higher scores to those items considered relevant for the users.

We also performed an analysis focusing on irrelevant recommendations. One repeating pattern was the users who have recently moved to a different research area tends to have less accurate recommendation. This is can be explained by observing that their historical publication profile did not reflect their current information needs. Another commonly reported problem is that in many cases the researchers were aware of the recommended items already, in spite of the fact that we filtered out those items were they were explicitly listed as authors or contributors. The explanation for that is that there could be multiple relations between a person and an information object, besides being `authorOf`. For example, one researcher might have been the mentor of one of those authors, might have been part of a review committee and so on. In future work, we planned to address the above issues by applying more sophisticated machine learning-based recommendation techniques able to learn how to traverse the graph structure from the user provided feedback.

4.2   Trend Analysis

The KG induced from the unstructured text is used to implement KEPs for trend analysis. Once a corpus is completely processed by Wikidata parser, trend analytics provide an overview of the concepts found in the corpus simply by performing aggregation queries the induced KG.

Since we can not show examples of analytic from the IBM internal data due to privacy of strategic information, we have created a KG by processing ISWC papers from year 2002–2021 using DBLP RDF data[1]. For each paper, we collected the title and the abstract of the paper and parsed them using the Wikidata Parser to create an Induced KG. Examples in this section uses that KG. This also provides evidence that the approach that we have proposed can be easily adapted to other communities.

Figure 5 shows the most frequent types found in the ISWC 2002–2021 corpus with the number of unique entities found in the corpus and number of associated triples. Any type can be selected and expanded to see its subtypes in the corpus ordered by their cumulative frequency (direct children and all descendants). Figure 5 (right) illustrates the expansion of type `algorithm` which has 473 direct entities and 746 transitive entities. The subclass relations are both induced from text and extracted from Wikidata. Users can select any of 4739 types generated in the case of the ISWC corpus and generate a trend analysis for the given type.

Induced Types in the KG (Top 15 out of 4739)

	Type	# of Entities	# of Triples	Wikidata Link
1	software	1127	3920	http://www.wikidata.org/entity/Q7397
2	academic discipline	936	20313	http://www.wikidata.org/entity/Q11862829
3	free software	879	3941	http://www.wikidata.org/entity/Q341
4	concept	707	2702	http://www.wikidata.org/entity/Q151885
5	data structure	547	1929	http://www.wikidata.org/entity/Q175263
6	ontology	502	1448	http://www.wikidata.org/entity/Q44325
7	algorithm	473	1516	http://www.wikidata.org/entity/Q8366
8	software feature	472	1625	http://www.wikidata.org/entity/Q4485156
9	process	462	2025	http://www.wikidata.org/entity/Q619671
10	programming language	438	2572	http://www.wikidata.org/entity/Q9143
11	file format	432	5417	http://www.wikidata.org/entity/Q235557
12	computer science term	429	1447	http://www.wikidata.org/entity/Q66747126
13	website	423	1868	http://www.wikidata.org/entity/Q35127
14	data set	370	1857	http://www.wikidata.org/entity/Q1172284
15	database	311	1896	http://www.wikidata.org/entity/Q8513

Type hierarchy for algorithm

```
algorithm[Q8366] (746)
+- artificial intelligence[Q11660] (253)
|  +- machine learning[Q2539] (212)
|  |  +- artificial neural network[Q192776] (26)
|  |  |  +- feedforward neural network[Q5441227] (7)
|  |  |  |  +- convolutional neural network[Q17084460] (2)
|  |  |  +- recurrent neural network[Q1457734] (1)
|  |  +- statistical classification[Q1744628] (20)
|  |  +- supervised learning[Q334384] (5)
|  |  +- deep learning[Q197536] (3)
|  |  +- multi-task learning[Q6934509] (1)
|  |  +- unsupervised learning[Q1152135] (1)
|  +- natural language processing[Q30642] (22)
|  |  +- speech recognition[Q189436] (2)
|  |  +- natural language generation[Q1513879] (1)
|  +- heuristic[Q1981968] (4)
|  +- sentiment analysis[Q2271421] (4)
|  +- knowledge engineering[Q1540472] (1)
|  +- cognitive science[Q147638] (1)
+- search algorithm[Q755673] (102)
+- combinatorial algorithm[Q41883552] (32)
|  +- graph algorithm[Q30503704] (9)
|  +- sorting algorithm[Q181593] (5)
+- optimization algorithm[Q2835765] (20)
|  +- evolutionary algorithm[Q14489129] (1)
+- cipher[Q4681865] (14)
|  +- block cipher[Q543151] (10)
+- parallel algorithm[Q18879871] (13)
```

Fig. 5. A snippet from induced types from the ISWC corpus.

Figure 6 shows the trend analysis for entities belonging to the type `academic discipline`. The last column shows the total number of occurrences of each entity in all ISWC papers from 2002–2021. Individual cells show the distribution of the papers in different years as a percentage. Such trend analysis can highlight

---

[1] https://blog.dblp.org/2022/03/02/dblp-in-rdf/.

some interesting facts. For instance, it shows that there was a high interest in *"Ontology"* and "Semantic Web" throughout from the beginning but the interest diversify more in later years. Similarly, we can see that there is a high interest in *"Linked Data"* from year 2009 which is at highest during the 2013–2017 period. In contrast, *"Semantic Web Services"* are of high interest during 2003–2009 period but the interest completely vanishes on later years. It is important to notice that the list of entities belonging to the type `academic discipline` or any other type is automatically generated. The analyst is just supposed to point to the right concept in the taxonomy to get her job done.

Trend analysis for type **'academic discipline'** in from KG

Entity	2002	2003	2004	2005	2006	2007	2008	2009	2010	2011	2012	2013	2014	2015	2016	2017	2018	2019	2020	2021	Total
1 Ontology	0.02	0.05	0.06	0.07	0.08	0.08	0.07	0.06	0.07	0.07	0.05	0.06	0.05	0.04	0.04	0.04	0.03	0.03	0.03	0.02	6708
2 Semantic Web	0.07	0.10	0.08	0.11	0.11	0.09	0.05	0.06	0.06	0.06	0.04	0.03	0.02	0.02	0.04	0.02	0.01	0.01	0.02	0.02	6455
3 Linked data	0.00	0.00	0.00	0.00	0.00	0.01	0.00	0.04	0.11	0.10	0.08	0.08	0.15	0.10	0.07	0.08	0.02	0.06	0.02	0.07	979
4 Machine learning	0.00	0.04	0.07	0.04	0.00	0.04	0.02	0.04	0.07	0.03	0.04	0.03	0.09	0.02	0.05	0.09	0.08	0.08	0.10	0.07	690
5 Metadata	0.03	0.05	0.06	0.04	0.02	0.11	0.10	0.03	0.04	0.09	0.04	0.04	0.04	0.04	0.02	0.12	0.06	0.03	0.01	0.01	671
6 Natural language processing	0.00	0.00	0.00	0.01	0.07	0.07	0.01	0.03	0.05	0.00	0.13	0.07	0.00	0.02	0.01	0.03	0.19	0.09	0.14	0.05	467
7 Statistics	0.00	0.01	0.02	0.04	0.06	0.02	0.03	0.02	0.13	0.11	0.07	0.07	0.03	0.07	0.01	0.05	0.10	0.08	0.03	0.03	348
8 Semantic intelligence	0.00	0.03	0.01	0.03	0.07	0.07	0.02	0.07	0.01	0.07	0.05	0.03	0.09	0.00	0.04	0.09	0.02	0.15	0.06	0.10	255
9 Logic	0.04	0.04	0.08	0.09	0.06	0.07	0.03	0.10	0.06	0.03	0.04	0.06	0.02	0.03	0.00	0.10	0.00	0.06	0.09	0.00	231
10 Semantic Web Services	0.00	0.04	0.27	0.16	0.39	0.03	0.08	0.04	0.00	0.00	0.00	0.00	0.00	0.00	0.00	0.00	0.00	0.00	0.00	0.00	226

(Only top 10 out of 936 entities shown here)   Heatmap Legend   Low ▇▇▇▇▇▇ High

Fig. 6. An example of trends analytics for entities of type academic discipline

4.3 Infobox Generation

Once an entity of interest is selected, for example, *"Linked Data"*, the users can automatically generate an infobox, as shown in Fig. 7. We first induce a schema for each type, by counting the most frequent relations extracted by the parser for entities of that type. For example, for the type `academic discipline` the important relations are `part of`, `facet of`, `based on`, `studies` and so on. Then we collect the object filling those relations for a specific target entity (*Linked Data*, in the example). Those relations might come from induced triples or from Wikidata itself. Each of the relations in the infobox is also associated to its provenance (might be a textual occurrence or a pre-existing triple in Wikidata) as illustrated by Fig. 8.

5 Related Work

KGs are a common way to organize data from multiple sources providing a unified view and represent them in a semantically rich manner empowering a wide range of downstream applications [15,18,29]. More specifically, Scholarly KGs such as ORKG [16], MAG [39], OpenAIRE [25] are becoming popular way to represent research data. Such KGs are used for search [4,14], question answering [17], recommendation [26,27], analysis of research trends [36], performing

Infobox for **Linked Data** (academic discipline) - **Q515701**

WIKIDATA RELATION	VALUES INDUCED FROM TEXT	EXTRACTED FROM WIKIDATA
part of	Open Data, Semantic Web, Semantic metadata, Web of data, World Wide Web, +7 more	
facet of	metadata, Semantic technology, Ontology	
based on	Resource Description Framework, XML	
studies	Ontology, Graph, Information, Artificial intelligence	
has quality	Accessibility, Data integration, Context-aware web	
used by	E-commerce, Federal government	Semantic Web
designed by		World Wide Web Consortium
official website		http://linkeddata.org/
described at URL		https://www.w3.org/wiki/Link edData

Fig. 7. An example of infobox for *"Linked Data"* an entity including both induced facts and integrated Wikidata facts.

Evidences for the fact: <Linked Data, part of, Open Data>

paper	sentence	score
https://doi.org/10.1007/978-3-030-30796-7_27	"An Assessment of Adoption and Quality of Linked Data in European Open Government Data."	1.0
https://doi.org/10.1007/978-3-319-25010-6_4	"Collecting, Integrating, Enriching and Republishing Open City Data as Linked Data."	0.1

Fig. 8. Evidences for the induced fact (Linked Data, part of, Open Data)

surveys [30], and understanding the dynamics between academia and industry [3].

The Semantic Web community has developed several methods and tools for building KGs. There are comprehensive survey articles on building KGs from relational databases [35], semi-structued data [33], and unstructured text [1,8, 11,28,34]. Rezayi et al. [31] propose an approach to augment a KG with key phrases generated from textual content of entities. In our work, we augment our KG with semantically rich triples generated from textual content of each entity. Furthermore, we integrate the induced knowledge with the relevant portion of background knowledge from Wikidata.

Trend analysis on KGs has been used for analysing research topics [21,36,41], patents [40], market trends [2]. Wikidata parser presented in our approach allows automatically create an induced knowledge graphs from text with a large number of Wikidata types (50K in 2022) enabling fine-grain analysis and seamless integration of background knowledge from Wikidata that can be used in the analysis.

Cai et al. [7] proposes an explainable recommender by generating the candidates using a KG and using an evolutionary algorithm. We use a simpler vector space model to produce recommendations between different types of entities.

6   Conclusions and Future Work

In this work, we presented an application of the Knowledge Graph Induction (KGI) technology to fulfill the requirements identified by a user study to enhancing cooperation in a research community. We have shown how the induced knowledge enables several downstream applications, such as recommending and trend analytics, providing evaluation for most of the component based on both quantitative and qualitative approaches. This year, we intend to deploy the recommending technology to all the member of the IBM research community, in the order of 6,000 people. We envision both in-app and "meet users where they are" experiences outside the apps. In all cases, we will provide feedback mechanisms (e.g. thumbs up/down, free text explanations) for users to share their view on the quality of the recommendations. The intention is to feed this back into a deep learning based recommender to learn how to better exploit the graph traversals.

In addition to trend analysis, we believe that KGI technology could also be leveraged for flexible and on-demand business analytics, providing powerful insights to accelerate business, for example:

Predicting Success. What are the characteristics of research projects that result in recognition and awards. How do we invest in new projects that exhibit these characteristics to better steer the IBM research agenda? Which papers should we support to have the best chance of publication at key conferences?

Business Development. Quickly identifying relevant research activity of interest to current or prospective clients or partners

Operations and Efficiency. Who is working on what projects and is time being used effectively? Is there duplicate activity? Where are the gaps? What are best opportunities for cross-collaboration?

Talent. Who are the rising stars? How do we find the right projects for them, or nominate them for external awards?

Portfolio. Tracing research projects and outcomes to Objects and Key Results.

We plan to develop KEP for the use cases above that can be generalized beyond the research community use case. We believe that the KEPs can be designed to cover variety of different use cases in many different organizations.

Moreover, we are planning to acquire KGs from different research communities (e.g. Semantic Web, NLP, Deep Learning communities) and make them available to the community. The goal is to act as a catalyzer for future research work in the research community beyond IBM.

References

1. Al-Aswadi, F.N., Chan, H.Y., Gan, K.H.: Automatic ontology construction from text: a review from shallow to deep learning trend. Artif. Intell. Rev. **53**(6), 3901–3928 (2019). https://doi.org/10.1007/s10462-019-09782-9
2. Albrecht, J., Belger, A., Blum, R., Zimmermann, R.: Business analytics on knowledge graphs for market trend analysis. In: LWDA, pp. 371–376 (2019)
3. Angioni, S., Salatino, A.A., Osborne, F., Recupero, D.R., Motta, E.: Integrating knowledge graphs for analysing academia and industry dynamics. In: Bellatreche, L., et al. (eds.) TPDL/ADBIS -2020. CCIS, vol. 1260, pp. 219–225. Springer, Cham (2020). https://doi.org/10.1007/978-3-030-55814-7_18
4. Heidari, G., Ramadan, A., Stocker, M., Auer, S.: Leveraging a federation of knowledge graphs to improve faceted search in digital libraries. In: Berget, G., Hall, M.M., Brenn, D., Kumpulainen, S. (eds.) TPDL 2021. LNCS, vol. 12866, pp. 141–152. Springer, Cham (2021). https://doi.org/10.1007/978-3-030-86324-1_18
5. Bornmann, L., Mutz, R.: Growth rates of modern science: a bibliometric analysis based on the number of publications and cited references. J. Am. Soc. Inf. Sci. **66**(11), 2215–2222 (2015)
6. Cabot, P.H., Navigli, R.: REBEL: relation extraction by end-to-end language generation. In: EMNLP (Findings), pp. 2370–2381. Association for Computational Linguistics (2021)
7. Cai, X., Xie, L., Tian, R., Cui, Z.: Explicable recommendation based on knowledge graph. Expert Syst. Appl. **15**, 117035 (2022)
8. Carlson, A., Betteridge, J., Kisiel, B., Settles, B., Hruschka Jr., E.R., Mitchell, T.M.: Toward an architecture for never-ending language learning. In: AAAI. AAAI Press (2010)
9. Chowdhury, M.F.M., Glass, M.R., Rossiello, G., Gliozzo, A., Mihindukulasooriya, N.: KGI: an integrated framework for knowledge intensive language tasks. CoRR abs/2204.03985 (2022)
10. Dimou, A., Vander Sande, M., Colpaert, P., Verborgh, R., Mannens, E., Van de Walle, R.: RML: a generic language for integrated RDF mappings of heterogeneous data. In: LDOW (2014)
11. Dong, X., et al.: Knowledge vault: a web-scale approach to probabilistic knowledge fusion. In: KDD, pp. 601–610. ACM (2014)
12. de Gemmis, M., Lops, P., Musto, C., Narducci, F., Semeraro, G.: Semantics-Aware content-based recommender systems. In: Ricci, F., Rokach, L., Shapira, B. (eds.) Recommender Systems Handbook, pp. 119–159. Springer, Boston, MA (2015). https://doi.org/10.1007/978-1-4899-7637-6_4
13. Glass, M.R., Rossiello, G., Chowdhury, M.F.M., Gliozzo, A.: Robust retrieval augmented generation for zero-shot slot filling. In: EMNLP (1), pp. 1939–1949. Association for Computational Linguistics (2021)
14. Heidari, G., Ramadan, A., Stocker, M., Auer, S.: Demonstration of faceted search on scholarly knowledge graphs. In: Companion Proceedings of the Web Conference 2021, pp. 685–686 (2021)
15. Hogan, A., et al.: Knowledge graphs. Synth. Lect. Data Semant. Knowl. **12**(2), 1–257 (2021)
16. Jaradeh, M.Y., et al.: Open research knowledge graph: next generation infrastructure for semantic scholarly knowledge. In: Proceedings of the 10th International Conference on Knowledge Capture, pp. 243–246 (2019)

17. Jaradeh, M.Y., Stocker, M., Auer, S.: Question answering on scholarly knowledge graphs. In: Hall, M., Merčun, T., Risse, T., Duchateau, F. (eds.) TPDL 2020. LNCS, vol. 12246, pp. 19–32. Springer, Cham (2020). https://doi.org/10.1007/978-3-030-54956-5_2

18. Ji, S., Pan, S., Cambria, E., Marttinen, P., Philip, S.Y.: A survey on knowledge graphs: representation, acquisition, and applications. IEEE Trans. Neural Netw. Learn. Syst. **33**(2), 494–514 (2021)

19. Josifoski, M., Cao, N.D., Peyrard, M., West, R.: Genie: generative information extraction. CoRR abs/2112.08340 (2021)

20. Khan, J.A., Rehman, I.U., Khan, Y.H., Khan, I.J., Rashid, S.: Comparison of requirement prioritization techniques to find best prioritization technique. Int. J. Mod. Educ. Comput. Sci. **7**(11), 53–59 (2015)

21. Kim, Y., Ju, Y., Hong, S., Jeong, S.R.: Practical text mining for trend analysis: ontology to visualization in aerospace technology. KSII Trans. Internet Inf. Syst. (TIIS) **11**(8), 4133–4145 (2017)

22. Koren, Y., Bell, R.: Advances in collaborative filtering. In: Ricci, F., Rokach, L., Shapira, B. (eds.) Recommender Systems Handbook, pp. 77–118. Springer, Boston (2015). https://doi.org/10.1007/978-1-4899-7637-6_3

23. Lewis, M., et al.: BART: denoising sequence-to-sequence pre-training for natural language generation, translation, and comprehension. In: ACL, pp. 7871–7880. Association for Computational Linguistics (2020)

24. Liu, J., Duan, L.: A survey on knowledge graph-based recommender systems. In: 2021 IEEE 5th Advanced Information Technology, Electronic and Automation Control Conference (IAEAC), vol. 5, pp. 2450–2453. IEEE (2021)

25. Manghi, P., Houssos, N., Mikulicic, M., Jörg, B.: The data model of the OpenAIRE scientific communication e-Infrastructure. In: Dodero, J.M., Palomo-Duarte, M., Karampiperis, P. (eds.) MTSR 2012. CCIS, vol. 343, pp. 168–180. Springer, Heidelberg (2012). https://doi.org/10.1007/978-3-642-35233-1_18

26. Manrique, R., Marino, O.: Knowledge graph-based weighting strategies for a scholarly paper recommendation scenario. In: KaRS@ RecSys, pp. 5–8 (2018)

27. Nayyeri, M., Vahdati, S., Zhou, X., Shariat Yazdi, H., Lehmann, J.: Embedding-based recommendations on scholarly knowledge graphs. In: Harth, A., et al. (eds.) ESWC 2020. LNCS, vol. 12123, pp. 255–270. Springer, Cham (2020). https://doi.org/10.1007/978-3-030-49461-2_15

28. Niu, F., Zhang, C., Ré, C., Shavlik, J.W.: DeepDive: web-scale knowledge-base construction using statistical learning and inference. In: VLDS. CEUR Workshop Proceedings, vol. 884, pp. 25–28. CEUR-WS.org (2012)

29. Noy, N., Gao, Y., Jain, A., Narayanan, A., Patterson, A., Taylor, J.: Industry-scale knowledge graphs: lessons and challenges. Commun. ACM **62**(8), 36–43 (2019)

30. Oelen, A., Jaradeh, M.Y., Stocker, M., Auer, S.: Generate fair literature surveys with scholarly knowledge graphs. In: Proceedings of the ACM/IEEE Joint Conference on Digital Libraries in 2020, pp. 97–106 (2020)

31. Rezayi, S., Zhao, H., Kim, S., Rossi, R., Lipka, N., Li, S.: Edge: enriching knowledge graph embeddings with external text. In: Proceedings of the 2021 Conference of the North American Chapter of the Association for Computational Linguistics: Human Language Technologies (NAACL), pp. 2767–2776 (2021)

32. Rossiello, G., et al.: Generative relation linking for question answering over knowledge bases. In: Hotho, A., et al. (eds.) ISWC 2021. LNCS, vol. 12922, pp. 321–337. Springer, Cham (2021). https://doi.org/10.1007/978-3-030-88361-4_19

33. Ryen, V., Soylu, A., Roman, D.: Building semantic knowledge graphs from (semi-) structured data: a review. Future Internet **14**(5), 129 (2022)

34. de Sá Mesquita, F., Cannaviccio, M., Schmidek, J., Mirza, P., Barbosa, D.: KnowledgeNet: a benchmark dataset for knowledge base population. In: EMNLP/IJCNLP (1), pp. 749–758. Association for Computational Linguistics (2019)
35. Sahoo, S.S., et al.: A survey of current approaches for mapping of relational databases to RDF. W3C RDB2RDF Incubator Group Rep. 1, 113–130 (2009)
36. Salatino, A.A., Mannocci, A., Osborne, F.: Detection, analysis, and prediction of research topics with scientific knowledge graphs. In: Predicting the Dynamics of Research Impact, pp. 225–252. Springer, Cham (2021). https://doi.org/10.1007/978-3-030-86668-6_11
37. Savage, N.: The race to the top among the world's leaders in artificial intelligence. Nature 588(7837), S102–S102 (2020)
38. Vrandečić, D., Krötzsch, M.: WikiData: a free collaborative knowledgebase. Commun. ACM 57(10), 78–85 (2014)
39. Wang, K., Shen, Z., Huang, C., Wu, C.H., Dong, Y., Kanakia, A.: Microsoft academic graph: when experts are not enough. Quant. Sci. Stud. 1(1), 396–413 (2020)
40. Weber, L., Böhme, T., Irmer, M.: Ontology-based content analysis of US patent applications from 2001–2010. Pharm. Patent Analyst 2(1), 39–54 (2013)
41. Wohlgenannt, G., Belk, S., Karacsonyi, M., Schett, M.: Using an ontology learning system for trend analysis and detection. In: International Semantic Web Conference (Posters & Demos), pp. 37–40. Citeseer (2014)

SeLoC-ML: Semantic Low-Code Engineering for Machine Learning Applications in Industrial IoT

Haoyu Ren[1,3], Kirill Dorofeev[1]([✉]), Darko Anicic[1], Youssef Hammad[1,3], Roland Eckl[2], and Thomas A. Runkler[1,3]

[1] Siemens AG, Otto-Hahn-Ring 6, 81739 Munich, Germany
{haoyu.ren,kirill.dorofeev,darko.anicic,youssef.hammad,
thomas.runkler}@siemens.com
[2] Siemens AG, Siemenspromenade 1, 91058 Erlangen, Germany
eckl.roland@siemens.com
[3] Technical University of Munich, Arcisstr. 21, 80333 Munich, Germany

Abstract. Internet of Things (IoT) is transforming the industry by bridging the gap between Information Technology (IT) and Operational Technology (OT). Machines are being integrated with connected sensors and managed by intelligent analytics applications, accelerating digital transformation and business operations. Bringing Machine Learning (ML) to industrial devices is an advancement aiming to promote the convergence of IT and OT. However, developing an ML application in Industrial IoT (IIoT) presents various challenges, including hardware heterogeneity, non-standardized representations of ML models, device and ML model compatibility issues, and slow application development. Successful deployment in this area requires a deep understanding of hardware, algorithms, software tools, and applications. Therefore, this paper presents a framework called **S**emantic **L**ow-**C**ode Engineering for **ML** Applications (SeLoC-ML), built on a low-code platform to support the rapid development of ML applications in IIoT by leveraging Semantic Web technologies. SeLoC-ML enables non-experts to easily model, discover, reuse, and matchmake ML models and devices at scale. The project code can be automatically generated for deployment on hardware based on the matching results. Developers can benefit from semantic application templates, called *recipes*, to fast prototype end-user applications. The evaluations confirm an engineering effort reduction by a factor of at least three compared to traditional approaches on an industrial ML classification case study, showing the efficiency and usefulness of SeLoC-ML. We share the code and welcome any contributions (https://github.com/Haoyu-R/SeLoC-ML).

Keywords: Machine learning · Neural network · Industrial internet of things · Semantic web · Knowledge graph · Low-code engineering

© The Author(s), under exclusive license to Springer Nature Switzerland AG 2022
U. Sattler et al. (Eds.): ISWC 2022, LNCS 13489, pp. 845–862, 2022.
https://doi.org/10.1007/978-3-031-19433-7_48

1 Introduction

One of the biggest challenges in industrial digitization is to bridge the gap between Operational Technology (OT) and Information Technology (IT). OT is centered on a physical world composed of machines, manufacturing equipment, and other hardware, where a massive amount of data is generated. However, IT is focused on the contemporary digital world, using data centers, servers, and smart applications to consume the data. These two domains have traditionally functioned in isolation [6]. The rise of Industry 4.0, along with increasing connectivity between humans, machines, and sensors, is driving the convergence of IT and OT, shifting data-supported decision-making from the individual to the system level and enhancing factory efficiency. However, IT/OT convergence is difficult to achieve. One example is the deployment of ML on industrial devices, where ML presents the IT world and industrial devices present the OT world.

ML is one of the fast-growing technical advancements. Applying ML, specifically Neural Network (NN), in the industry by leveraging sensor and system data can provide reliable insights into the factory and accelerate smart manufacturing. Standard ML applications transfer massive field data to the cloud and centrally process the data against NN models. Concerns have been raised because this data transfer causes numerous issues, such as high energy consumption and latency, privacy leaks, bandwidth congestion.

With the Internet of Things (IoT) growth, factories will be equipped with increasingly powerful, connected, and intelligent devices. This plays a key role in the continuing industrial evolution. Offloading ML intelligence from the cloud to the Industrial IoT (IIoT) devices enables performing ML tasks near data sources and reducing reliance on data transfer, which addresses the latency and security concerns. However, applying on-device ML in the industry where mass deployment happens is still challenging.

IIoT devices are specialized to fulfill different tasks. They come in all shapes and sizes, differ in terms of onboard sensors, available memory and storage capacities, and have various runtime platforms. In the context of on-device ML, they rely on NN models to interpret sensor data, make predictions about their environments, and take intelligent actions locally. NN models are developed with various structures, e.g., different combinations of layers and individualized pre- and postprocessing blocks. Additionally, most trained NN models are distributed as binary files without a clear and standardized description of their usages. The diversification and proliferation of hardware (IIoT devices) and software (NN models) widen the gap between each other.

Many compatibility issues must be carefully investigated to run ML properly on the devices, such as sensor input format, memory constraints, and sensor availability. Specifically, we want to answer two sets of questions:

1. How do we achieve the co-management of IIoT devices and NN models?
   (a) How do we determine which devices may execute a specific NN?
   (b) Given a device, how do we determine which trained NN model is compatible with it? Does the model meet requirements for accuracy, memory, and latency?

2. How do we accelerate the engineering and deployment of ML applications in IIoT? How might cross-domain collaborations be facilitated and the solution be made accessible to all?

We present a framework called Semantic Low-Code Engineering for ML Applications (SeLoC-ML), a system for managing and deploying ML on devices in IIoT at scale. Here, we propose to use formalized semantic models to describe heterogeneous IIoT devices and NN models, respectively. With ontology schemas, we can model the knowledge about devices and NN models semantically in a unified language and centrally store it in a Knowledge Graph (KG), making the knowledge searchable like Web resources. As a result, many features are enabled, such as vendor-agnostic knowledge discovery and matchmaking model requirements with device capabilities.

Another aspect of our work is deploying NN models on the devices and integrating ML applications into end-user IIoT applications. More crucially, we aim to make the approach accessible and understandable to non-experts. We propose integrating SeLoC-ML into a low-code platform, allowing developers without necessary expertise to use semantic services and deploy ML models declaratively, advancing IT/OT convergence. In the background, user inputs are parsed, and corresponding SPARQL queries[1] are formulated to retrieve the information from the central graph database automatically. Additionally, different deployment options will become available depending on matching results, allowing developers to generate projects and deploy ML on the devices with minimal effort. Last but not least, we leverage semantic application templates, so-called *recipes* [24], to assist developers in integrating ML applications into greater pipelines and creating end-user applications rapidly. We support application development by matching the data types used in *recipes* with the data points provided by the devices, which are defined by common semantic models.

As an example of this approach, we present the solution on a Siemens Programmable Logic Controller (PLC) SIMATIC S7-1500[2] using the Siemens low-code platform Mendix[3] [12]. We demonstrate in Mendix how to search and matchmake an NN model with a SIMATIC S7-1500 Technology Module Neural Processing Unit (TM NPU)[4] connected with an Intel RealSense camera[5]. The goal is to find an trained NN model compatible with the TM NPU for classifying different types of objects on a conveyor belt. Following a successful match, an engineering project for Totally Integrated Automation (TIA) Portal[6] - a Siemens

---

[1] https://www.w3.org/TR/rdf-sparql-query.

[2] https://new.siemens.com/global/en/products/automation/systems/industrial/plc/simatic-s7-1500.html.

[3] https://www.mendix.com.

[4] https://new.siemens.com/global/en/products/automation/systems/industrial/plc/simatic-s7-1500/simatic-s7-1500-tm-npu.html.

[5] https://www.intel.com/content/www/us/en/architecture-and-technology/realsense-overview.html.

[6] https://new.siemens.com/global/en/products/automation/industry-software/automation-software/tia-portal.html.

Integrated Development Environment (IDE) for industrial automation - can be automatically created and ready for deployment. Later, we present how to use a semantic *recipe* to orchestrate the ML application and easily build an end-user application in Mendix to monitor the classification results. The evaluation results show that SeLoC-ML can reduce engineering effort by a factor of at least three compared to conventional approaches.

The remainder of this paper first presents related work on ML in IoT, Semantic Web technologies, ML management, and low-code programming in Sect. 2. Section 3 describes SeLoC-ML from the semantic system to low-code platform integration. Section 4 demonstrates SeLoC-ML on an industrial classification problem using Siemens products as an example. In Sect. 5, we evaluate the approach, compare it with the traditional workflow and provide the benefits of SeLoC-ML. Finally, Sect. 6 concludes the paper and discusses future work.

2   Related Work

Advancements of On-Device ML. On-device ML is more than just an algorithm. It is about the proliferation of hardware, progress on algorithms, emerging ecosystem, and transformative applications. Ultra-low-power devices have been designed for always-on applications [7,11]. Various algorithms have been proposed to fully exploit ML models on the devices without compromising performance [17,22]. Collaborative ecosystems can further squeeze the potential from the synergism of hardware and software [5,16]. Last but not least, many applications have been brought from a proof-of-concept to products [1,8].

Semantic Web Technologies. Semantic Web technology provides means for building, storing, and handling diverse data sources of different structures, making it an ideal candidate for information modeling and integration in IoT. Evidence has shown the benefits of semantics in industrial domains [13,19]. In the context of IoT, ontologies like Sensor, Observation, Sample, and Actuator Ontology (SOSA) [10], Semantic Sensor Network Ontology (SSN) [3], and Semantic Smart Sensor Network Ontology (S3N) [20] are few prominent semantic models for describing intelligent IoT devices, their properties, and interactions. The Thing Description (TD) [2] ontology developed by the World Wide Web Consortium (W3C) Web of Things (WoT)[7] working group specifies the metadata and interfaces of IoT devices. *iotschema.org*[8] is yet another semantic model in the IoT domain, which is used to enrich the data among connected things. This study is interested in combining these semantic schemas with our proposed NN model ontology [18] for modeling the heterogeneous knowledge about devices and NN models in IIoT.

---

[7] https://www.w3.org/WoT.
[8] http://iotschema.org/.

Management of On-Device ML. There are hundreds of billions of IoT devices today, and new ML models are developed and distributed daily. To manage these resources at scale, it is necessary to increase the interoperability and transparency of the ecosystem. Open Neural Network Exchange (ONNX)[9] aims to provide a shared exchange format that allows developers to use ML models across different deep learning frameworks. However, it fails to provide descriptions of models in a formal way. To overcome this limitation, TensorFlow Lite Metadata[10] and Model Card [14] are introduced to formally document ML models. Few databases [15,26] are introduced for tracking ML models. Nevertheless, they do not scale well since many manual works are required, and their information models do not express the relationships between ML models and hardware. ML models need to be studied together with the specifications of hardware to achieve joint management.

Low-Code Engineering. Despite remarkable IT/OT integration achievements, the current state of developing complex IIoT applications is still far from satisfactory [25]. The concept of low-code engineering and corresponding platforms, such as Mendix [12], are introduced to support fast application development without a prerequisite of having enhanced coding skills [9]. Low-code concepts find their applications in the manufacturing domain [21,27], allowing to quickly build industrial applications based on the services provided by the machines on the shop floor. To match the business requirements with the existing functionalities of the machines and compose them meaningfully, we use the notion of *recipes* [24] as an easy way to model such compositions. *Recipes* can be seen as application templates [23] developed to solve a class of problems and can be later easily configured for a specific use case.

3   Approach

We present SeLoC-ML considering the interoperability and deployment obstacles in ML applications in IIoT. This section starts by introducing the framework setup. The proposed architecture relies on a semantic system designed to cover but not be limited to the use case addressed in this study. We illustrate the semantic system, from the ontology to the semantic services. Next, a simplified KG and two SPARQL queries are presented to exemplify the system's advantages. We then propose integrating SeLoC-ML into the Siemens Mendix low-code platform allowing developers to easily identify and matchmake components, deploy NN models to the devices upon matching, and quickly prototype IIoT user applications.

3.1   Framework Architecture

Figure 1 presents the SeLoC-ML framework. The figure on the left illustrates that developers are faced with a gap between software (NN models) and hardware

---

[9] https://onnx.ai.
[10] https://www.tensorflow.org/lite/convert/metadata.

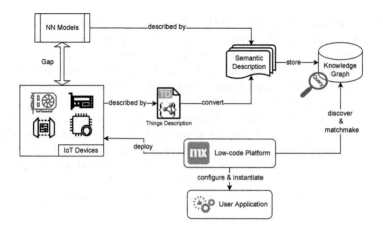

Fig. 1. Framework architecture of SeLoC-ML.

(IIoT devices). We first propose to utilize two semantic models to describe IIoT devices and NN models, respectively. Here, any formalized semantic models can be applied, but for demonstrating the technology in the industrial environment, we choose the standardized W3C TD [2] to describe devices. Aligning with the TD, we design a semantic ontology [18] with a conversion tool for describing NN models in terms of their metadata, structures, and hardware requirements. Thus, knowledge about heterogeneous IIoT devices and NN models can be translated into unified semantic descriptions against their ontologies and be hosted together in a KG, as shown on the right side of the figure. The bottom of the figure shows that even non-experts can easily scrape the KG with Mendix. Mendix will automatically formulate queries based on user inputs and retrieve desired answers from the graph. Upon matchmaking, different deployment options are made available. A ready-to-be-deployed engineering project can be generated based on user configurations and the retrieved semantic information. This is known as ML-as-a-service [4]. Finally, developers can leverage semantic application templates *recipes* to accelerate user application development.

3.2 Semantic System

Ontology. We presented an ontology[11] [17] to describe NN models in the context of IoT, as shown in Fig. 2. By reusing existing schemas, such as S3N and SOSA, we aligned the ontology with other Web standards and avoided reinventing the wheel. For research and demonstration purposes, the ontology has been designed to guarantee its interoperability and compatibility with TD, which we

---

[11] https://tinyml-schema-collab.github.io.

applied to describe IIoT devices. The ontology can render three different forms of information about a NN: 1) metadata, such as the date of creation, category, and literal description; 2) structure, such as the input and output layers; 3) hardware requirements, such as memory and sensors.

As references, we provide interested readers with examples of semantic descriptions of IoT devices and NN models in our repository. Additionally, scripts are available, which can generate a semantic representation of a given NN model along with some user inputs since not all information can be obtained by parsing the NN model, such as dataset and author information.

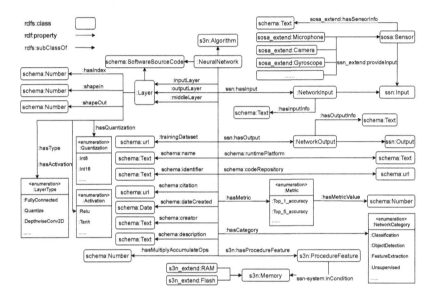

Fig. 2. Ontology of NN model in IoT.

Knowledge Graph. We can design a central KG that stores information from NN models and IoT devices using the semantic schemas introduced above. For an example, we used GraphDB[12] to demonstrate a simplified KG composed of nine IoT devices and 22 NN models. As depicted in Fig. 3, the NN model and device nodes are drawn on the left and right sides of the figure, respectively. An NN model called *Move* is expanded in the center, displaying its properties. We collect NN models trained using TensorFlow, one of the most prominent deep learning frameworks. However, our approach can be easily scaled to cover different devices, NN models, and frameworks. As previously mentioned, we provide the code and examples for creating KG and interacting with it.

---

[12] https://www.ontotext.com/products/graphdb.

Discovery and Matchmaking. Many specific uses and services can be enabled once the KG has been created. We use two simple queries to answer two questions against the KG example introduced above for a demonstration. More queries can be found in our repository. The used namespaces and corresponding prefixes are given as follows:

```
# Our NN ontology
nnet: <http://tinyml-schema.org/
      networkschema/>
# Schema.org Vocabulary
schema: <https://schema.org> .
# Units of Measure Vocabulary
om: <http://www.ontology-of-units-of
      -measure.org/resource/om-2/> .
# SSN Ontology
ssn: <http://www.w3.org/ns/ssn/> .
```

```
# S3N Ontology
s3n: <http://w3id.org/s3n/> .
# Extension of the SOSA ontology
sosa_extend:  <http://tinyml-schema.org/
                sosa_extend#> .
# Extension of the SSN ontology
ssn_extend:  <http://tinyml-schema.org/
              ssn_extend#> .
# Extension of the S3N ontology
s3n_extend:  <http://tinyml-schema.org/
              s3n_extend#> .
```

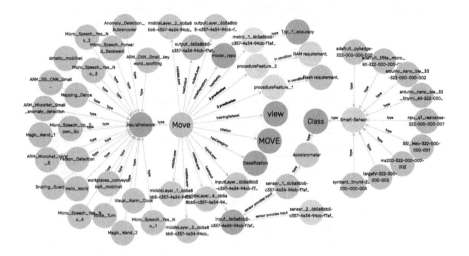

Fig. 3. A simplified KG containing 22 ML models and nine devices.

1. We have an IoT device on which we want to deploy an NN model. The device is equipped with a camera, and it has 144 and 621 Kb of available RAM and Flash, respectively. We want to determine all possible NN models that can be executed on this device.
2. We trained an NN model for motion classification using gyroscope and accelerometer data. Given that the minimum RAM and Flash requirements for running this model are 121 and 610 Kb, respectively, we want to know which available devices can run this model.

Query 1:

```
SELECT ?uuid ?MACs ?RAM ?Flash ?Description
WHERE {
    ?nn a nnet:NeuralNetwork ;
        schema:identifier ?uuid ;
        schema:description ?Description ;
        ssn:hasInput ?input;
        nnet:hasMultiplyAccumulateOps ?MACs ;
        s3n:hasProcedureFeature ?x_1 ;
        s3n:hasProcedureFeature ?x_2 .
    ?x_1 ssn-system:inCondition ?cond_1 .
    ?x_2 ssn-system:inCondition ?cond_2 .
    ?cond_1 a s3n_extend:RAM ;
        schema:minValue ?RAM ;
        schema:unitCode om:kilobyte .
    ?cond_2 a s3n_extend:Flash ;
        schema:minValue ?Flash ;
        schema:unitCode om:kilobyte .
    ?sensor ssn_extend:provideInput ?input;
        a sosa_extend:Camera .
    FILTER (?RAM <= 144)
    FILTER (?Flash <= 621)
}
```

Result:
uuid: 2c... ; MACs: 7158144; RAM: 94 Kb; ...
uuid: 49... ; MACs: 7387976; RAM: 116 Kb; ...

Query 2:

```
SELECT ?Device ?RAM ?Flash
WHERE {
    ?Device a s3n:SmartSensor ;
        ssn:hasSubSystem ?system_1 ;
        ssn:hasSubSystem ?system_2 ;
        ssn:hasSubSystem ?system_3 .
    ?system_1 a sosa_extend:Accelerometer .
    ?system_2 a sosa_extend:Gyroscope .
    ?system_3 a s3n:MicroController ;
        s3n:hasSystemCapability ?x .
    ?x ssn-system:hasSystemProperty ?cond_1 .
    ?x ssn-system:hasSystemProperty ?cond_2 .
    ?cond_1 a s3n_extend:RAM ;
        schema:value ?RAM ;
        schema:unitCode om:kilobyte .
    ?cond_2 a s3n_extend:Flash ;
        schema:value ?Flash ;
        schema:unitCode om:kilobyte .
    FILTER (?RAM >= 121)
    FILTER (?Flash >= 610)
}
ORDER BY ?RAM
```

Result:
Device: 002; RAM: 172 Kb; Flash: 628 Kb.
Device: 003; RAM: 187 Kb; Flash: 785 Kb.

Fig. 4. Semantic similarity search.

3.3   Low-Code Platform Integration

Semantic Web techniques are not easy to learn and use. Likewise, on-device ML is another entirely different field that is challenging to understand. To motivate cross-domain collaborations and simplify IT/OT convergence, we encourage integrating SeLoC-ML into a low-code platform - Mendix. Mendix allows developers to design, build, deploy, and operate IoT applications rapidly.

Semantic Management of On-Device ML. We created a Mendix application with a user-friendly Graphical User Interface (GUI) connected with a KG in the background. The application package is published in our repository. Three main semantic services are provided in the application:

1. **Discovery**: Developers can browse through all available NN models and IIoT devices in the graph database and inspect their details.
2. **Matchmaking**: Once the developer selects an IIoT device/NN model in the application, SPARQL queries are automatically formulated to retrieve all compatible NN models/devices.
3. **Semantic Similarity Search**: Imagine if hundreds of thousands of IIoT devices and NN models were hosted in the KG, it would be tedious to examine them one after another manually. Semantic similarity search[13] enables users to explore relevant objects in the KG by typing a search text, similar to Google Search. In our example, users can search the stored components by filling in the provided form with their requirements, as shown in Fig. 4.

ML-As-a-Service. Moreover, depending on the matched devices, different deployment options become available, and corresponding project code can be generated by parsing the retrieved information. Of course, specific user configurations will be asked to complete the project creation. We aim to provide a high-level abstraction for deployment, which is as hardware-agnostic as possible.

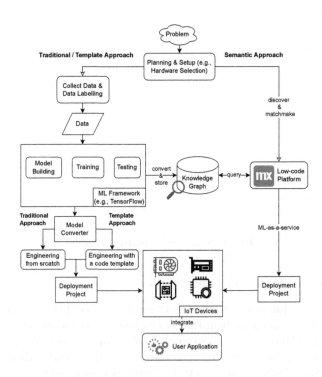

Fig. 5. Comparison between the traditional, template, and semantic approach.

---

[13] https://graphdb.ontotext.com/documentation/standard/semantic-similarity-searches.html.

Rapid User Applications Development. Further, we use Mendix to rapidly prototype an IIoT application using the concept of *recipes*. *Recipes* provide platform-agnostic application templates that can be easily deployed and configured for common automation tasks. They specify the application logic and the information about input and output required by the tasks [23]. Device data is described using standardized semantic models, such as OPC UA companion specifications[14]. Such a semantic model is stored in the knowledge graph and, at the same time, it is used for developing the *recipes* logic in Mendix. End-user applications can be instantiated by matching the data points provided by system components with the data types required by the *recipe*. As a result, developers quickly orchestrate an end-user application, ready to be delivered.

4   Workflow Comparison and Case Study

This section first outlines SeLoC-ML by comparing it with the State-of-the-Art approaches. Figure 5 presents three different workflows for constructing ML applications in IIoT. Traditionally, after the project planning, ML developers are engaged to engineer an ML model systematically, from data collection and labeling to model building and training. Afterward, embedded engineers take over the work, where the trained model is optimized and converted for the target runtime platform through Model Optimizer. An embedded project is then engineered with the ML model and uploaded to the device. Later, software engineers design a user application to integrate the ML application and report the results to end-users. As can be seen, it is difficult to feature an IIoT ML application that requires cross-domain expertise and a significant amount of engineering work.

SeLoC-ML offers an all-in-one solution based on Mendix low-code platform to alleviate the situation. SeLoC-ML is generic enough, but for easily quantifying the evaluation and demonstrating its benefits, we illustrate it on an industrial ML classification use case where a NN model is to be discovered and applied on a Siemens TM NPU. Of course, the SeLoC-ML framework can be quickly scaled and applied to other domains and/or use cases.

In-Use: Building an ML Application on Siemens SIMATIC

The case study is conducted on a Festo Didactic workstation[15] controlled by a Siemens SIMATIC S7-1500 PLC, as shown in Fig. 6. In the running example, the vacuum gripper on the left side puts workpieces on the conveyor belt, transporting them to the following process. Different workpieces need to be classified for different downstream handlings, and unidentified objects should be sorted out before the next step. A TM NPU connected with an Intel RealSense camera

---

[14] https://opcfoundation.org/about/opc-technologies/opc-ua/ua-companion-specifications/.

[15] https://www.festo-didactic.com/int-en/learning-systems/process-automation-control-theory.

Fig. 6. Festo Didactic working station controlled by a SIMATIC S7-1500 PLC with a connected TM NPU.

is installed on the workstation, controlled by the SIMATIC S7-1500 PLC. TM NPU enables the execution of ML models directly on Siemens PLCs. Our goal is to leverage Mendix to discover, configure, and deploy an NN model on the TM NPU for classifying workpieces on the conveyor belt using images captured by the camera.

Discovery and Matchmaking. We explore all the reusable ML models in the KG that can run on the SIMATIC TM NPU without spending much time going through the traditional approach and generating a new model from scratch. This can be done in Mendix with a simple click, and all compatible ML models will show up in a pop-up window, as depicted in Fig. 7. After reviewing the results, we select the model *workpieces_conveyorbelt_mobilnet* for our use case.

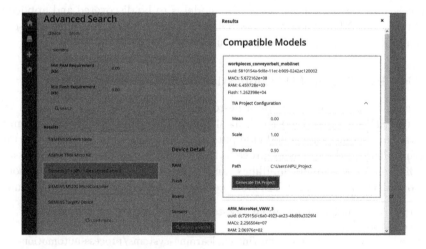

Fig. 7. Discovery and matchmaking results.

Deploying ML on Hardware. After matchmaking, different deployment options become available depending on the selected devices and their runtime platforms. In our case, Mendix creates relevant files for the TM NPU and PLC project. As shown in Fig. 7, specific configurations still need to be given by users, but most of the information in the project is filled automatically by parsing the retrieved semantic descriptions. With all project files loaded to the hardware, the ML application is now ready for execution.

Creating a User Application Using Recipe. The classification results from the TM NPU are made available via an OPC UA server. We created a *recipe* that provides a template for visualizing object classification results based on their color for our running example. To instantiate the *recipe*, Mendix matches the data supplied by the PLC with the data types defined in the *recipe*, based on the definitions given in the OPC UA companion specification. The application developer must acknowledge the match before the application can run. Then, Mendix runtime gets the results of the NN processing, available in the address space of the respective OPC UA server, and represents them in the dashboard, enabling real-time monitoring, as illustrated in Fig. 8.

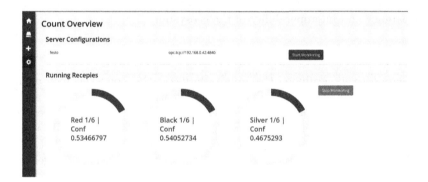

Fig. 8. End-user application that monitors the classification results.

5   Evaluation

This section first compares SeLoC-ML with the traditional approach qualitatively. Further, a quantitative analysis is conducted. For that, the example from the last section is chosen based on our available products to quickly generate results.

5.1   Qualitative Analysis

Reliability and Flexibility. Reliability is one of the essential factors in the industry since a single failure can cause significant losses. Unfortunately, it is not easy to achieve successful ML applications in IIoT using the conventional workflow since many processes are involved, each of which requires extensive domain knowledge and labor. This can potentially raise the failure probability. SeLoC-ML provides consistent services within one tool that can automate the engineering work by complying with semantic standards, reducing error, and guaranteeing reliability. Moreover, it is important to provide flexible solutions to keep pace with the fast-evolving IIoT world. SeLoC-ML is generic enough to be applied in other scenarios, avoiding examination on a per-instance basis.

Scalability and Interoperability. It is more beneficial to reuse existing ML models than to invent a new one every time since reusability means less cost and better scalability. However, one of the major concerns in IIoT is heterogeneity. Numerous trained NNs could be used for various industrial applications, but it is unclear how to apply them in a concrete use case or on specific hardware. As the IIoT network expands, millions of devices from different vendors emerge, making manual management of a massive amount of hardware and software almost impossible. The proposed approach presents information in a unified language. This ensures that both humans and machines can consistently interpret the stored data and enable automatic development at scale. Besides, our semantic framework is vendor-independent and platform-neutral, enhancing the transparency and interoperability of the ecosystem.

5.2   Quantitative Analysis

We quantitatively evaluate the approach using the conveyor belt example, described in Sect. 4, since this industrial application is representative and similar results have been achieved on other use cases and platforms. We present the experimental results in the following steps: 1) we describe the file structure in the deployment project; 2) we compare the semantic approach (SeLoC-ML) against the other two methods regarding the engineering effort for generating the project, scalability, error rate, and tools required.

A minimum of five engineering artifacts should be engineered and created in the project: a configuration of the ML model used, and a user logic for processing, as well as the corresponding logic in the PLC for exchanging the data with TM NPU and consuming its results, as shown in Table 1.

Table 1. Project files

	Function
npu_app.conf	Configure the ML model on TM NPU
main.py	Configure on-device ML model execution
DataTypes.udt	Define data type(s) for PLC/TM NPU interaction
fbLogic.scl	Define function block to interact with TM NPU
ControlData.db	Define data block to store the data internally in PLC memory

We compare the implementation effort for programming our running example project for three different implementations: 1) traditional approach: programming the whole application from scratch; 2) template approach: providing a user with the pre-developed ready code template that need to be additionally configured for a specific application; 3) semantic approach: SeLoC-ML. We count the number of LOC needed to be manually programmed to implement the running example for every solution. Here, we define LOC to include the number of lines developers need to program and other configuration input that they must provide, for example, the user input in Mendix, as shown in Fig. 7. Table 2 presents the results of measuring the engineering effort.

Table 2. Engineering effort in LOC based on the running example

	npu.conf	main.py	datatypes.udt	fbLogic.scl	dataBlock.db	Total
Traditional approach	20	284	40	408	14	766
Template approach	10	19	3	3	3	38
Semantic approach	4	6	1	1	1	13

Moreover, we studied the flexibility of the approaches in terms of their scalability, i.e., the ability to add new data to the interaction between the PLC and TM NPU. This is especially important when switching between different use cases and/or NNs. Compared to the traditional approach, both template and semantic approaches showed a significant reduction of the LOC. It is worth noting that the semantic approach scales better than the template approach, as we managed to reduce the engineering effort by a factor of three with SeLoC-ML.

Another aspect to consider is the error rate. Getting the most of the code generated will decrease the number of errors made during programming. Once the code generation process is validated, the produced code will be errorless.

Additionally, we consider the number of tools needed to create the entire project for PLC and TM NPU. Using our approach, we generate the entire solution in one place using our Mendix application. Both traditional and template approaches require an engineer to have competencies in at least three different tools: a model converter tool is needed for creating the NN configuration (npu.conf), some IDE for python programming to edit the user logic for NN processing (main.py), and TIA Portal for PLC programming. Table 3 provides an overview of the tools required for each solution.

Table 3. Engineering tools used for programming the running example

	npu.conf	main.py	*.udt, *.scl, *.db	Total
Traditional approach	Model converter	Python IDE	TIA Portal	3
Template approach	Model converter	Python IDE	TIA Portal	3
Semantic approach	Mendix			1

6   Conclusion and Future Work

We have experienced various challenges in implementing ML in IIoT due to the heterogeneity of the ecosystem. This study presents SeLoC-ML for managing and deploying ML on the IIoT devices at scale by leveraging Semantic Web technology. Many out-of-the-box features were enabled using KG, such as knowledge discovery, similarity search, and matchmaking software (NN models) and hardware (devices). By integrating SeLoC-ML in the low-code platform, Mendix, we open new possibilities even for non-experts to easily access these semantic functionalities, use ML-as-a-service for deploying ML models to hardware across the platforms, and prototype end-user applications. The ontology and code examples are available online and can be freely used and further extended.

The next steps, which are already underway, include further improvement and integration of our approach to the production processes. As illustrated in our repository, we have developed SeLoC-ML to support other platforms than in our running example presented in the paper, such as, Arduino[16]. We intend to conduct additional analysis on other scenarios and platforms and collect feedback to further advance the robustness and scalability of our system. We hope to foster the collaboration between the ML and the Semantic Web communities. Therefore, provisioning the framework and making the toolchain available for everyone is also one of our next steps.

References

1. Bejarano-Carbo, A., et al.: Millimeter-scale ultra-low-power imaging system for intelligent edge monitoring (2022). https://doi.org/10.48550/ARXIV.2203.04496, https://arxiv.org/abs/2203.04496
2. Charpenay, V., Käbisch, S., Kosch, H.: Introducing thing descriptions and interactions: an ontology for the web of things. In: 2016 International Semantic Web Conference, pp. 55–66. Springer, Kobe (2016)
3. Compton, M., et al.: The SSN ontology of the W3C semantic sensor network incubator group. J. Web Semant. **17**, 25–32 (2012). https://doi.org/10.2139/ssrn.3198991
4. Doyu, H., Morabito, R., Brachmann, M.: A TinyMLaaS ecosystem for machine learning in IoT: overview and research challenges. In: 2021 International Symposium on VLSI Design, Automation and Test (VLSI-DAT), pp. 1–5. IEEE, Hsinchu, Taiwan (2021). https://doi.org/10.1109/vlsi-dat52063.2021.9427352
5. Duan, S., Xu, X., Ren, S.: A brain-inspired low-dimensional computing classifier for inference on tiny devices (2022). https://doi.org/10.48550/ARXIV.2203.04894, https://arxiv.org/abs/2203.04894
6. Garimella, P.K.: IT-OT integration challenges in utilities. In: 2018 IEEE 3rd International Conference on Computing, Communication and Security (ICCCS), pp. 199–204. IEEE (2018). https://doi.org/10.1109/cccs.2018.8586807
7. Giordano, M., et al.: CHIMERA: A 0.92 TOPS, 2.2 TOPS/W edge AI accelerator with 2 MByte on-chip foundry resistive RAM for efficient training and inference. In: 2021 Symposium on VLSI Circuits, pp. 1–2. IEEE, Kyoto, Japan (2021). https://doi.org/10.23919/VLSICircuits52068.2021.9492347

---

[16] https://www.arduino.cc/.

8. Gomez, J., et al.: Distributed on-sensor compute system for AR/VR devices: a semi-analytical simulation framework for power estimation (2022). https://doi.org/10.48550/ARXIV.2203.07474, https://arxiv.org/abs/2203.07474

9. Ihirwe, F., Di Ruscio, D., Mazzini, S., Pierini, P., Pierantonio, A.: Low-code engineering for internet of things: a state of research. In: Proceedings of the 23rd ACM/IEEE International Conference on Model Driven Engineering Languages and Systems: Companion Proceedings, pp. 1–8 (2020). https://doi.org/10.1145/3417990.3420208

10. Janowicz, K., Haller, A., Cox, S.J., Le Phuoc, D., Lefrançois, M.: SOSA: a lightweight ontology for sensors, observations, samples, and actuators. J. Web Semant. **56**, 1–10 (2019). https://doi.org/10.1016/j.websem.2018.06.003

11. Jiao, B., et al.: A 0.57-GOPS/DSP object detection PIM accelerator on FPGA. In: Proceedings of the 26th Asia and South Pacific Design Automation Conference, ASPDAC 2021, pp. 13–14. ACM, New York, USA (2021). https://doi.org/10.1145/3394885.3431659

12. Litman, M., Field, D.: Mendix as a solution for present gaps in computer programming in higher educationD. AMCIS **1**(1), 1 (2018)

13. Mehdi, G., et al.: Semantic rule-based equipment diagnostics. In: d'Amato, C., et al. (eds.) ISWC 2017. LNCS, vol. 10588, pp. 314–333. Springer, Cham (2017). https://doi.org/10.1007/978-3-319-68204-4_29

14. Mitchell, M., et al.: Model cards for model reporting. In: Proceedings of the Conference on Fairness, Accountability, and Transparency, FAT* 2019, pp. 220–229. ACM, New York, USA (2019). https://doi.org/10.1145/3287560.3287596, https://doi.org/10.1145/3287560.3287596

15. Nguyen, A., Weller, T., Färber, M., Sure-Vetter, Y.: Making neural networks FAIR. In: Villazón-Terrazas, B., Ortiz-Rodríguez, F., Tiwari, S.M., Shandilya, S.K. (eds.) KGSWC 2020. CCIS, vol. 1232, pp. 29–44. Springer, Cham (2020). https://doi.org/10.1007/978-3-030-65384-2_3

16. Rashid, H.A., Ovi, P.R., Busart, C., Gangopadhyay, A., Mohsenin, T.: TinyM^{2}Net: a flexible system algorithm co-designed multimodal learning framework for tiny devices (2022). https://doi.org/10.48550/ARXIV.2202.04303, https://arxiv.org/abs/2202.04303

17. Ren, H., Anicic, D., Runkler, T.A.: TinyOL: TinyML with online-learning on microcontrollers. In: 2021 International Joint Conference on Neural Networks (IJCNN), pp. 1–8. IEEE, Shenzhen, China (2021). https://doi.org/10.1109/ijcnn52387.2021.9533927

18. Ren, H., Anicic, D., Runkler, T.A.: How to manage tiny machine learning at scale: an industrial perspective (2022). https://doi.org/10.48550/ARXIV.2202.09113, https://arxiv.org/abs/2202.09113

19. Rojas, J.A., et al.: Leveraging semantic technologies for digital interoperability in the European railway domain. In: Hotho, A., et al. (eds.) ISWC 2021. LNCS, vol. 12922, pp. 648–664. Springer, Cham (2021). https://doi.org/10.1007/978-3-030-88361-4_38

20. Sagar, S., et al.: Modeling smart sensors on top of SOSA/SSN and WoT TD with the Semantic Smart Sensor Network (S3N) modular ontology. In: ISWC 2018: 17th Internal Semantic Web Conference, pp. 163–177 (2018)

21. Sanchis, R., García-Perales, O., Fraile, F., Poler, R.: Low-code as enabler of digital transformation in manufacturing industry. Appl. Sci. **10**(1), 12 (2020). https://doi.org/10.3390/app10010012, https://www.mdpi.com/2076-3417/10/1/12

22. Song, J., Lin, F.: PocketNN: integer-only training and inference of neural networks without quantization via direct feedback alignment and pocket activations in pure C++ (2022). https://doi.org/10.48550/ARXIV.2201.02863, https://arxiv.org/abs/2201.02863

23. Thuluva, A.S., Anicic, D., Rudolph, S., Adikari, M.: Semantic node-RED for rapid development of interoperable industrial IoT applications. Semant. Web **11**(6), 949–975 (2020). https://doi.org/10.3233/sw-200405

24. Thuluva, A.S., Bröring, A., Medagoda, G.P., Don, H., Anicic, D., Seeger, J.: Recipes for IoT applications. In: Proceedings of the Seventh International Conference on the Internet of Things, IoT 2017. Association for Computing Machinery, New York, NY, USA (2017). https://doi.org/10.1145/3131542.3131553

25. Udoh, I.S., Kotonya, G.: Developing IoT applications: challenges and frameworks. IET Cyber-Phys. Syst. Theory Appl. **3**(2), 65–72 (2018). https://doi.org/10.1049/iet-cps.2017.0068

26. Vartak, M., et al.: ModelDB: a system for machine learning model management. In: Proceedings of the Workshop on Human-In-the-Loop Data Analytics, HILDA 2016. ACM, New York, USA (2016). https://doi.org/10.1145/2939502.2939516

27. Waszkowski, R.: Low-code platform for automating business processes in manufacturing. IFAC-PapersOnLine **52**(10), 376–381 (2019). https://doi.org/10.1016/j.ifacol.2019.10.060

Author Index